Copyright©2015 All Rights Reserved

ISBN:978-0692512630

Publication rights Sefer Press Publishing House
Questions Comments; BenShlomo@Israelmail.com

Publisher grants permission to reference short quotations (less than 400 words) in reviews, magazines, newspapers, Websites, or other publications in accordance with the citation standards at Sefer Press. Request permission to reproduce more than 400 words to SeferPress@Israelmail.com

Cover by Sefer Press 2015

Book Format by Sefer Press 2015

Hebrew:Modern Hebrew Text Form
Greek:Majority Text (Byzantine) Text Form

Commentary Editing by Al Garza PhD

For Questions Contact A.G. Ben Shlomo At
BenShlomo@Israelmail.com

Printed in the United States of America© 2015

MATTHEW

A RABBINIC JEWISH SOURCE

COMMENTARY

AND LANGUAGE STUDY BIBLE

Volume 1

KJV-GREEK-HEBREW

WITH TRANSLITERATION

PUBLISHED BY SEFER PRESS PUBLISHING HOUSE©2015

TABLE OF CONTENTS

Chapter 1..pg.5
Chapter 2..pg.21
Chapter 3..pg.42
Chapter 4..pg.56
Chapter 5..pg.69
Chapter 6..pg.104
Chapter 7..pg.126
Chapter 8..pg.141
Chapter 9..pg.160
Chapter 10..pg.187
Chapter 11..pg.215
Chapter 12..pg.231
Chapter 13..pg.258
Chapter 14..pg.287
Chapter 15..pg.304
Chapter 16..pg.323
Chapter 17..pg.337
Chapter 18..pg.351
Chapter 19..pg.369
Chapter 20..pg.385
Chapter 21..pg.402
Chapter 22..pg.428
Chapter 23..pg.450
Chapter 24..pg.475
Chapter 25..pg.507
Chapter 26..pg.527
Chapter 27..pg.567
Chapter 28..pg.601

TITLE: Gospel of Matthew

AUTHOR: Mattinyahu (Matthew) According to Early Sources

DATE: 35AD TO 60AD

LANGUAGE: Hebrew According to Early Sources

WRITTEN TO: 1ST Century Hebrew Reading Jews

THEME: Demonstrate Yeshua/Jesus As Messiah

PaRDeS: D'rash-Also known as Midrash, "inquire" or to "seek". To draw out the meaning of a text. Jewish writers may take two or more unrelated verses and combine them to create a verse(s) with a third meaning.

There are three rules to consider when utilizing the d'rash interpretation of a text:

1. A drash understanding can not be used to strip a passage of its p'shat meaning, nor may any such understanding contradict the p'shat meaning of any other scripture passage. As the Talmud states, *"No passage loses its p'shat."* (Simple, plain, intended meaning)

2. Let scripture interpret scripture. Look for the scriptures themselves to define the components of an allegory.

3. The primary components of an allegory represent specific realities. We should limit ourselves to these primary components when understanding the text.

THE GOSPEL ACCORDING TO ST MATTHEW
Matthew, Chapter 1

1. The book of the generation of Jesus Christ, the son of David, the son of Abraham.

Greek/Transliteration

1. Βίβλος γενέσεως Ἰησοῦ χριστοῦ, υἱοῦ Δαυίδ, υἱοῦ Ἀβραάμ.

1. Biblos geneseos Yeisou christou, 'wiou Dauid, 'wiou Abra'am.

Hebrew/Transliteration

א. זֶה סֵפֶר תּוֹלְדֹת הַמָּשִׁיחַ יֵשׁוּעַ בֶּן-דָּוִד בֶּן-אַבְרָהָם:

1. Ze se•fer tol•dot ha•Ma•shi•ach Yeshua ben - David ben - Avraham.

TaNaKh/Old Testament/Rabbinic Jewish Commentary

This genealogy recalls the pattern of those in the *Tanakh* (Genesis 5, 10; 1 Chronicles 1-9, etc.).

The New Testament begins with the genealogy of Yeshua in order to show that he meets the requirements set by the *Tanakh* for who the Messiah must be-a descendant of Avraham (Gen_22:18), Ya'akov (Num_24:17), Y'hudah (Gen_49:10), Yishai (Isa_11:1), David (2Sa_7:13)

"R. Jochanan says, in the generation in which בן דוד "the son of David" comes, the disciples of the wise men shall be lessened, and the rest, their eyes shall fail with grief and sorrow, and many calamities and severe decrees shall be renewed; when the first visitation is gone, a second will hasten to come. It is a tradition of the Rabbi's (about) the week (of years) in which בן דוד "the son of David" comes.

The tradition of R. Nehorai says, In the generation in which בן דוד "the son of David" comes, young men shall make ashamed the faces of old men, and old men shall stand before young men, the daughter shall rise up against her mother, and the daughter-in-law against her mother-in-law; nor will a son reverence his father. The tradition of R. Nehemiah says, In the generation in which בן דוד "the son of David" comes, impudence will increase, and the honourable will deal wickedly, and the whole kingdom will return to the opinion of the Sadducees, and there will be no reproof. --It is a tradition of the Rabbi's, that בן דוד "the son of David" will not come, until traitorous practices are increased, or the disciples are lessened or until the smallest piece of money fails from the purse, or until redemption is despaired of."

(p) T. Bab. Sanhedrim, fol. 97. 1. Shir Hashirim Rabba, fol. 11. 4.

2. Abraham begat Isaac; and Isaac begat Jacob; and Jacob begat Judas and his brethren;

Greek/Transliteration
2. Ἀβραὰμ ἐγέννησεν τὸν Ἰσαάκ· Ἰσαὰκ δὲ ἐγέννησεν τὸν Ἰακώβ· Ἰακὼβ δὲ ἐγέννησεν τὸν Ἰούδαν καὶ τοὺς ἀδελφοὺς αὐτοῦ·

2. Abra'am egenneisen ton Ysa'ak. Ysa'ak de egenneisen ton Yakob. Yakob de egenneisen ton Youdan kai tous adelphous autou.

Hebrew/Transliteration
ב. אַבְרָהָם הוֹלִיד אֶת-יִצְחָק וְיִצְחָק הוֹלִיד אֶת-יַעֲקֹב וְיַעֲקֹב הוֹלִיד אֶת-יְהוּדָה וְאֶת-אֶחָיו:
2. Av•ra•ham ho•lid et - Yitzchak ve•Yitzchak ho•lid et - Yaakov ve•Yaakov ho•lid et - Yehooda ve•et - echav.

---

3. And Judas begat Phares and Zara of Thamar; and Phares begat Esrom; and Esrom begat Aram;

Greek/Transliteration
3. Ἰούδας δὲ ἐγέννησεν τὸν Φαρὲς καὶ τὸν Ζαρὰ ἐκ τῆς Θάμαρ· Φαρὲς δὲ ἐγέννησεν τὸν Ἐσρώμ· Ἐσρὼμ δὲ ἐγέννησεν τὸν Ἀράμ·

3. Youdas de egenneisen ton Phares kai ton Zara ek teis Thamar. Phares de egenneisen ton 'Esrom. 'Esrom de egenneisen ton Aram.

Hebrew/Transliteration
ג. וִיהוּדָה הוֹלִיד אֶת-פֶּרֶץ וְאֶת-זֶרַח מִתָּמָר וּפֶרֶץ הוֹלִיד אֶת-חֶצְרוֹן וְחֶצְרוֹן הוֹלִיד אֶת-רָם:
3. Vi•Y`hoo•da ho•lid et - Pe•retz ve•et - Ze•rach mi•Tamar oo•Fe•retz ho•lid et - Chetz•ron ve•Chetz•ron ho•lid et - Ram.

TaNaKh/Old Testament
Tamar... Rachav ... Rut ... the wife of Uriyah (Bat-sheva)... Miryam. Women, especially those born Gentiles, were rarely included in biblical genealogies. The first four were Gentile women whom God honored by including them among the recorded ancestors of Yeshua the Jewish Messiah-through whom Gentiles, women and slaves are saved equally with Jews, men and free (Gal_3:28). On whether these women became Jews or continued to be Gentiles see Act_16:1.

they say, (r). "there are two women from whom come David the king, and Solomon, and the king Messiah; and these two are Thamar and Ruth."

Jonathan Ben Uzziel on Gen_38:6 says, that Thamar was the daughter of Shem the great.
(r) Shemot Rabba, sect. 30. fol. 131. 4. Caphtor, fol. 122. 1.

4. And Aram begat Aminadab; and Aminadab begat Naasson; and Naasson begat Salmon;

Greek/Transliteration
4. Ἀράμ δὲ ἐγέννησεν τὸν Ἀμιναδάβ· Ἀμιναδὰβ δὲ ἐγέννησεν τὸν Ναασσών· Ναασσὼν δὲ ἐγέννησεν τὸν Σαλμών·

4. Aram de egenneisen ton Aminadab. Aminadab de egenneisen ton Na'asson. Na'asson de egenneisen ton Salmon.

Hebrew/Transliteration
ד: וְרָם הוֹלִיד אֶת-עַמִּינָדָב וְעַמִּינָדָב הוֹלִיד אֶת-נַחְשׁוֹן וְנַחְשׁוֹן הוֹלִיד אֶת-שַׂלְמוֹן

4. Ve•Ram ho•lid et - Ami•na•dav ve•Ami•na•dav ho•lid et - Nach•shon ve•Nach•shon ho•lid et - Salmon.

5. And Salmon begat Booz of Rachab; and Booz begat Obed of Ruth; and Obed begat Jesse;

Greek/Transliteration
5. Σαλμὼν δὲ ἐγέννησεν τὸν Βοὸζ ἐκ τῆς Ῥαχάβ· Βοὸζ δὲ ἐγέννησεν τὸν Ὠβὴδ ἐκ τῆς Ῥούθ· Ὠβὴδ δὲ ἐγέννησεν τὸν Ἰεσσαί·

5. Salmon de egenneisen ton Bo'oz ek teis 'Rachab. Bo'oz de egenneisen ton Obeid ek teis 'Routh. Obeid de egenneisen ton Yessai.

Hebrew/Transliteration
ה: וְשַׂלְמוֹן הוֹלִיד אֶת-בֹּעַז מֵרָחָב וּבֹעַז הוֹלִיד אֶת-עוֹבֵד מֵרוּת וְעוֹבֵד הוֹלִיד אֶת-יִשָׁי

5. Ve•Salmon ho•lid et - Boaz me•Ra•chav oo•Voaz ho•lid et - O•ved me•Root ve•O•ved ho•lid et - Yi•shai.

6. And Jesse begat David the king; and David the king begat Solomon of her that had been the wife of Urias;

Greek/Transliteration
6. Ἰεσσαὶ δὲ ἐγέννησεν τὸν Δαυὶδ τὸν βασιλέα. Δαυὶδ δὲ ὁ βασιλεὺς ἐγέννησεν τὸν Σολομῶνα ἐκ τῆς τοῦ Οὐρίου·

6. Yessai de egenneisen ton Dauid ton basilea. Dauid de 'o basileus egenneisen ton Solomona ek teis tou Ouriou.

Hebrew/Transliteration

ו׃ וְיִשַׁי הוֹלִיד אֶת־הַמֶּלֶךְ דָּוִד וְדָוִד הוֹלִיד אֶת־שְׁלֹמֹה מֵהָאִשָּׁה אֲשֶׁר לָקַח מֵאוּרִיָּה:

6. Ve•Yi•shai ho•lid et - ha•me•lech David ve•David ho•lid et - Sh`lo•mo me•ha•ee•sha asher la•kach me•Oo•riya.

---

7. And Solomon begat Roboam; and Roboam begat Abia; and Abia begat Asa;

Greek/Transliteration

7. Σολομὼν δὲ ἐγέννησεν τὸν Ῥοβοάμ· Ῥοβοὰμ δὲ ἐγέννησεν τὸν Ἀβιά· Ἀβιὰ δὲ ἐγέννησεν τὸν Ἀσά·

7. Solomon de egenneisen ton 'Roboam. 'Roboam de egenneisen ton Abya. Abya de egenneisen ton Asa.

Hebrew/Transliteration

ז׃ וּשְׁלֹמֹה הוֹלִיד אֶת־רְחַבְעָם וּרְחַבְעָם הוֹלִיד אֶת־אֲבִיָּה וַאֲבִיָּה הוֹלִיד אֶת־אָסָא:

7. Oo•Sh`lo•mo ho•lid et - R`chav•am oo`R`chav`am ho•lid et - Avi•ya va•Avi•ya ho•lid et - Asa.

---

8. And Asa begat Josaphat; and Josaphat begat Joram; and Joram begat Ozias;

Greek/Transliteration

8. Ἀσὰ δὲ ἐγέννησεν τὸν Ἰωσαφάτ· Ἰωσαφὰτ δὲ ἐγέννησεν τὸν Ἰωράμ· Ἰωρὰμ δὲ ἐγέννησεν τὸν Ὀζίαν·

8. Asa de egenneisen ton Yosaphat. Yosaphat de egenneisen ton Yoram. Yoram de egenneisen ton Ozian.

Hebrew/Transliteration

ח׃ וְאָסָא הוֹלִיד אֶת־יְהוֹשָׁפָט וִיהוֹשָׁפָט הוֹלִיד אֶת־יְהוֹרָם וִיהוֹרָם הוֹלִיד אֶת־עֻזִּיָּהוּ:

8. Ve•Asa ho•lid et - Ye•ho•sha•fat vi•Yeho•sha•fat ho•lid et - Ye•ho•ram vi•Ye•ho•ram ho•lid et - Oo•zi•yahoo.

---

9. And Ozias begat Joatham; and Joatham begat Achaz; and Achaz begat Ezekias;

Greek/Transliteration

9. Ὀζίας δὲ ἐγέννησεν τὸν Ἰωάθαμ· Ἰωάθαμ δὲ ἐγέννησεν τὸν Ἄχαζ· Ἄχαζ δὲ ἐγέννησεν τὸν Ἐζεκίαν·

9. Ozias de egenneisen ton Yoatham. Yoatham de egenneisen ton Achaz. Achaz de egenneisen ton 'Ezekian.

Hebrew/Transliteration

ט. וְעֻזִּיָּהוּ הוֹלִיד אֶת-יוֹתָם וְיוֹתָם הוֹלִיד אֶת-אָחָז וְאָחָז הוֹלִיד אֶת-חִזְקִיָּהוּ:

9. Ve•Oozi•yahoo ho•lid et - Yotam ve•Yotam ho•lid et - A•chaz ve•A•chaz ho•lid et - Chiz•ki•yahoo.

---

10. And Ezekias begat Manasses; and Manasses begat Amon; and Amon begat Josias;

Greek/Transliteration

10. Ἐζεκίας δὲ ἐγέννησεν τὸν Μανασσῆ· Μανασσῆς δὲ ἐγέννησεν τὸν Ἀμών· Ἀμὼν δὲ ἐγέννησεν τὸν Ἰωσίαν·

10. 'Ezekias de egenneisen ton Manassei. Manasseis de egenneisen ton Amon. Amon de egenneisen ton Yosian.

Hebrew/Transliteration

י. וְחִזְקִיָּהוּ הוֹלִיד אֶת-מְנַשֶּׁה וּמְנַשֶּׁה הוֹלִיד אֶת-אָמוֹן וְאָמוֹן הוֹלִיד אֶת-יֹאשִׁיָּהוּ:

10. Ve•Chiz•ki•yahoo ho•lid et - Me•na•she oo•Me•na•she ho•lid et - Amon ve•Amon ho•lid et - Yo•shi•yahoo.

---

11. And Josias begat Jechonias and his brethren, about the time they were carried away to Babylon:

Greek/Transliteration

11. Ἰωσίας δὲ ἐγέννησεν τὸν Ἰεχονίαν καὶ τοὺς ἀδελφοὺς αὐτοῦ, ἐπὶ τῆς μετοικεσίας Βαβυλῶνος.

11. Yosias de egenneisen ton Yechonian kai tous adelphous autou, epi teis metoikesias Babulonos.

Hebrew/Transliteration

יא. וְיֹאשִׁיָּהוּ הוֹלִיד אֶת-יְכָנְיָהוּ וְאֶת-אֶחָיו בִּימֵי גְלוֹתָם בָּבֶלָה:

11. Ve•Yo•shi•yahoo ho•lid et - Ye•chon•ya•hoo ve•et - echav bi•mey g`lo•tam Ba•vela.

---

12. And after they were brought to Babylon, Jechonias begat Salathiel; and Salathiel begat Zorobabel;

Greek/Transliteration
12. Μετὰ δὲ τὴν μετοικεσίαν Βαβυλῶνος, Ἰεχονίας ἐγέννησεν τὸν Σαλαθιήλ· Σαλαθιὴλ δὲ ἐγέννησεν τὸν Ζοροβάβελ·

12. Meta de tein metoikesian Babulonos, Yechonias egenneisen ton Salathieil. Salathieil de egenneisen ton Zorobabel.

Hebrew/Transliteration
יב. וְאַחֲרֵי הָגְלָם לְבָבֶל יְכָנְיָהוּ הוֹלִיד אֶת-שְׁאַלְתִּיאֵל וּשְׁאַלְתִּיאֵל הוֹלִיד אֶת-זְרֻבָּבֶל:

12. Ve•a•cha•rey hog•lam le•Vavel Ye•chan•ya•hoo ho•lid et - Sh`al•ti•el oo•She•al•ti•el ho•lid et - Z`roo•ba•vel.

Rabbinic Commentary
The Talmud says,
"R. Johanan said: Exile atones for everything, for it is written, Thus saith the L-rd, write ye this man childless, a man that shall not prosper in his days, for no man of his seed shall prosper sitting upon the throne of David and ruling any more in Judah. (Jer. XXII, 30). Whereas after he [the king] was exiled, it is written, And the sons of Jechoniah, — the same is Assir — Shealtiel his son etc. (1 Chr. III, 17)33. [He was called] Assir, (imprisoned) because his mother conceived him in prison. Shealtiel, because God did not plant him in the way that others are planted. We know by tradition that a woman cannot conceive in a standing position. [yet she did conceive standing. Another interpretation: Shealtiel, because God obtained [of the Heavenly court] absolution from His oath.4 Zerubbabel [was so called] because he was sown in Babylon. But [his real name was] Nehemiah the son of Hachaliah." Sanhedrin 37b – 38a, Soncino Press Edition

Midrash Rabbah comments
". . . they made the Calf and deserved to be exterminated, and I would have thought that He would curse and destroy them, yet, no sooner had they repented, than the danger was averted, And the L-rd repented of the evil (ib. XXXII, 14).And so in many places. For example, He said about Jeconiah: For no man of his seed shall prosper (Jer. XXII, 30) and it says, I will overthrow the throne of kingdoms, and I will destroy the strength of the kingdoms of the nations... In that day, saith the L-rd of hosts, will I take thee, O Zerubbabel, My servant, the son of Shealtiel, saith the L-rd, and will make thee as a signet (Hag. II, 22 f.). Thus was annulled that which He had said to his forefather, viz. As I live, saith the L-rd, though Coniah the son of Jehoiakim King of Judah were the signet upon My right hand, yet I would pluck thee thence (Jer. XXII, 24)."
Numbers Rabbah 20:20, Soncino Press Edition

Pesikta Rabbati continues
"R. Joshua ben Levi, however, argued as follows: Repentance sets aside the entire decree, and prayer half the decree. You find that it was so with Jeconiah, king of Judah. For the Holy One, blessed be He, swore in His anger, As I live, saith the L-rd, though Coniah the son of Jehoiakhim king of Judah were the signet on a hand, yet by My right – note, as R. Meir said, that is was by His right hand that God

swore – I would pluck thee hence (Jer. 22:24). And what was decreed against Jeconiah? That he die childless. As is said Write ye this man childless (Jer. 22:40). But as soon as he avowed penitence, the Holy One, blessed be He, set aside the decree, as is shown by Scripture's reference to The sons of Jeconiah – the same is Assir – Shealtiel his son, etc. (1 Chron 3:17). And Scripture says further: In that day . . . will I take thee, O Zerubbabel . . . the son of Shealtiel . . . and will make thee as a signet (Haggai 2:23). Behold, then, how penitence can set aside the entire decree! Pesikta Rabbati, Piska 47, translated by William G. Braude, Yale University Press, pg. 797-798

Regarding Zerubavel, Zechariah says
In the book of Zechariah it says, "Who are you, great mountain? Before Zerubbabel you are a plain; and he will bring out the capstone with shouts of Grace, grace, to it! Zechariah 4:7

Midrash Tanchuma, as the Jewish Encyclopedia cites above, says the following on this passage, "What does it mean, Who art thou O great mountain? This is King Messiah. And why does he call him great mountain? Because he is greater than the Fathers…loftier than Abraham…more elevated than Moses…and higher than the ministering angels…and from whom will he issue? From Zerubbabel…" Midrash Tanchuma, Toledot 14, ed. Buber 1:139, cited in the Messiah Texts by Raphael Patai, pg. 41 [2]

---

13. And Zorobabel begat Abiud; and Abiud begat Eliakim; and Eliakim begat Azor;

Greek/Transliteration
13. Ζοροβάβελ δὲ ἐγέννησεν τὸν Ἀβιούδ· Ἀβιοὺδ δὲ ἐγέννησεν τὸν Ἐλιακείμ· Ἐλιακεὶμ δὲ ἐγέννησεν τὸν Ἀζώρ·

13. Zorobabel de egenneisen ton Abioud. Abioud de egenneisen ton Elyakeim. Elyakeim de egenneisen ton Azor.

Hebrew/Transliteration
יג. וּזְרֻבָּבֶל הוֹלִיד אֶת-אֲבִיהוּד וַאֲבִיהוּד הוֹלִיד אֶת-אֶלְיָקִים וְאֶלְיָקִים הוֹלִיד אֶת-עַזּוּר:

13. Oo•Z`roo•ba•vel ho•lid et - Avi•hood va•Avi•hood ho•lid et - El•ya•kim ve•El•ya•kim ho•lid et - A•zoor.

Rabbinic Jewish Commentary
It is very remarkable that the Jewish Targum (o) traces the descent of the Messiah from the family of David in the line of Zorobabel, as Matthew does; and reckons the same number of generations, wanting one, from Zorobabel to the Messiah, as the Evangelist does, from Zorobabel to Yeshua; according to Matthew, the genealogy stands thus, Zorobabel, Abiud, Eliakim, Azor, Sadoc, Achim, Eliud, Eleazar, Matthan, Jacob, Joseph, Jesus; and according to the Targum the order is this, "Zorobabel, Hananiah, Jesaiah, Rephaiah, Arnon, Obadiah, Shecaniah,

Shemnigh, Neariah, Elioenai, Anani; this is the king Messiah, who is to be revealed."

The difference of names may be accounted for by their having two names, as before observed. This is a full proof, that, according to the Jews own account, and expectation, the Messiah must be come many years and ages ago.

(o) In 1 Chron. iii. 24. Vid. Beckii Not. in ib. p. 56, 57.

---

14. And Azor begat Sadoc; and Sadoc begat Achim; and Achim begat Eliud;

Greek/Transliteration
14. Ἀζὼρ δὲ ἐγέννησεν τὸν Σαδώκ· Σαδὼκ δὲ ἐγέννησεν τὸν Ἀχείμ· Ἀχεὶμ δὲ ἐγέννησεν τὸν Ἐλιούδ·

14. Azor de egenneisen ton Sadok. Sadok de egenneisen ton Acheim. Acheim de egenneisen ton Elioud.

Hebrew/Transliteration
יד. וְעַזּוּר הוֹלִיד אֶת-צָדוֹק וְצָדוֹק הוֹלִיד אֶת-יָכִין וְיָכִין הוֹלִיד אֶת-אֱלִיהוּד:

14. Ve•Azoor ho•lid et - Tza•dok ve•Tza•dok ho•lid et - Ya•chin ve•Ya•chin ho•lid et - Eli•hood.

---

15. And Eliud begat Eleazar; and Eleazar begat Matthan; and Matthan begat Jacob;

Greek/Transliteration
15. Ἐλιοὺδ δὲ ἐγέννησεν τὸν Ἐλεάζαρ· Ἐλεάζαρ δὲ ἐγέννησεν τὸν Ματθάν· Ματθὰν δὲ ἐγέννησεν τὸν Ἰακώβ·

15. Elioud de egenneisen ton Eleazar. Eleazar de egenneisen ton Matthan. Matthan de egenneisen ton Yakob.

Hebrew/Transliteration
טו. וֶאֱלִיהוּד הוֹלִיד אֶת-אֶלְעָזָר וְאֶלְעָזָר הוֹלִיד אֶת-מַתָּן וּמַתָּן הוֹלִיד אֶת-יַעֲקֹב:

15. Ve•Eli•hood ho•lid et - El•a•zar ve•El•a•zar ho•lid et - Ma•tan oo•Ma•tan ho•lid et - Yaakov.

---

16. And Jacob begat Joseph the husband of Mary, of whom was born Jesus, who is called Christ.

Greek/Transliteration
16. Ἰακὼβ δὲ ἐγέννησεν τὸν Ἰωσὴφ τὸν ἄνδρα Μαρίας, ἐξ ἧς ἐγεννήθη Ἰησοῦς, ὁ λεγόμενος χριστός.

16. Yakob de egenneisen ton Yoseiph ton andra Marias, ex 'eis egenneithei Yeisous, 'o legomenos christos.

Hebrew/Transliteration
טז: וְיַעֲקֹב הוֹלִיד אֶת-יוֹסֵף אִישׁ מִרְיָם אֲשֶׁר נוֹלַד מִמֶּנָּה יֵשׁוּעַ הַנִּקְרָא מָשִׁיחַ

16. Ve•Yaakov ho•lid et - Yo•sef eesh Mir•yam asher no•lad mi•me•na Yeshua ha•nik•ra Ma•shi•ach.

Rabbinic/Jewish New Testament Commentary
The change in language from the litany, "X was the father of Y," signals that Yeshua was not conceived in the usual way; other passages state that the Holy Spirit of God overshadowed Miryam, causing her to become pregnant without sexual union

The Talmudic Jews own that Yeshua, or Yeshu, as they call him, was put to death because he (s), קרוב למלכות היה "was nigh to the kingdom", or nearly related to it. Yea, even in that malicious book (t) they have written of his life, they represent him as akin to queen Helena, who they say, on that account, would have saved his life. (s) T. Bab. Sanhed. fol. 43. 1. (t) Toldos Jesu, p. 10.

---

17. So all the generations from Abraham to David are fourteen generations; and from David until the carrying away into Babylon are fourteen generations; and from the carrying away into Babylon unto Christ are fourteen generations.

Greek/Transliteration
17. Πᾶσαι οὖν αἱ γενεαὶ ἀπὸ Ἀβραὰμ ἕως Δαυὶδ γενεαὶ δεκατέσσαρες· καὶ ἀπὸ Δαυὶδ ἕως τῆς μετοικεσίας Βαβυλῶνος, γενεαὶ δεκατέσσαρες· καὶ ἀπὸ τῆς μετοικεσίας Βαβυλῶνος ἕως τοῦ χριστοῦ, γενεαὶ δεκατέσσαρες.

17. Pasai oun 'ai geneai apo Abra'am 'eos Dauid geneai dekatessares. kai apo Dauid 'eos teis metoikesias Babulonos, geneai dekatessares. kai apo teis metoikesias Babulonos 'eos tou christou, geneai dekatessares.

Hebrew/Transliteration
יז. וְהִנֵּה כָּל-הַדֹּרוֹת מֵאַבְרָהָם עַד-דָּוִד אַרְבָּעָה עָשָׂר דֹּרוֹת וּמִדָּוִד עַד-גָּלוּת בָּבֶל אַרְבָּעָה עָשָׂר דֹּרוֹת וּמִגָּלוּת-בָּבֶל עַד-הַמָּשִׁיחַ אַרְבָּעָה עָשָׂר דֹּרוֹת

17. Ve•hee•ne kol - ha•do•rot me•Av•ra•ham ad - David ar•ba•ah asar do•rot oo•mi•David ad - ga•loot Bavel ar•ba•ah asar do•rot oo•mi•ga•loot Bavel ad ha•Ma•shi•ach ar•ba•ah asar do•rot.

18. Now the birth of Jesus Christ was on this wise: When as his mother Mary was espoused to Joseph, before they came together, she was found with child of the Holy Ghost.

Greek/Transliteration
18. Τοῦ δὲ Ἰησοῦ χριστοῦ ἡ γέννησις οὕτως ἦν. Μνηστευθείσης γὰρ τῆς μητρὸς αὐτοῦ Μαρίας τῷ Ἰωσήφ, πρὶν ἢ συνελθεῖν αὐτούς, εὑρέθη ἐν γαστρὶ ἔχουσα ἐκ πνεύματος ἁγίου.

18. Tou de Yeisou christou 'ei genneisis 'outos ein. Mneisteutheiseis gar teis meitros autou Marias to Yoseiph, prin ei sunelthein autous, 'eurethei en gastri echousa ek pneumatos 'agiou.

Hebrew/Transliteration
יח. וְזֹאת הָיְתָה לֵדַת יֵשׁוּעַ הַמָּשִׁיחַ כַּאֲשֶׁר מִרְיָם אִמּוֹ מְאֹרָשָׂה הָיְתָה לְיוֹסֵף טֶרֶם יָבוֹא אֵלֶיהָ וַתִּמָּצֵא כִּי הָרָה:הִיא כִּי מֵרוּחַ הַקֹּדֶשׁ הָרָתָה.

18. Ve•zot hai•ta le•dat Yeshua ha•Ma•shi•ach ka•a•sher Mir•yam ee•mo me•o•ra•sa hai•ta le•Yosef te•rem ya•vo e•le•ha va•ti•ma•tze ki ha•ra hee ki me•Roo•ach ha•Ko•desh ha•ra•ta.

Jewish New Testament Commentary/Rabbinic Commentary
The Hebrew/Aramaic word for betrothal is "*kiddushin*," which signifies "sanctification, separation," i.e., the setting aside and separating of a particular woman for a particular man. According to the Mishna, adultery during the betrothal period is a more serious sin than adultery after marriage.

The Mishna specifies four kinds of death penalty in descending order of gravity: stoning, burning, beheading and strangling (Sanhedrin 7:1). A man who has intercourse with a betrothed girl is subject to the same penalty as one who has intercourse with his mother, namely, stoning (Sanhedrin 7: 4). Someone who has intercourse with another man's wife is liable to death by strangling (Sanhedrin 11:1). Today, partly in order to eliminate the possibility of committing this grave sin, formal Jewish betrothal (*kiddushin* or *'erusin*) and marriage (*nisu'in*) are generally combined in a single ceremony.

Mattityahu informs his readers of Yeshua's supernatural conception in order to counter the obvious and natural inference that Miryam had misbehaved. The early Rabbis developed a tradition that Yeshua was the illegitimate son of Miryam and a Roman soldier named Pantera (in the second-century Tosefta, a collection similar to the Mishna, see Chullin 2:23; in the fifth-century Babylonian Talmud see Sanhedrin 43a, 67a). This calumny, invented, of course, to counter the claims of the Gospel, was worked up further in the sixth-century anti-gospel, *Toledot-Yeshu*.

---

19. Then Joseph her husband, being a just man, and not willing to make her a publick example, was minded to put her away privily.

Greek/Transliteration
19. Ἰωσὴφ δὲ ὁ ἀνὴρ αὐτῆς, δίκαιος ὤν, καὶ μὴ θέλων αὐτὴν παραδειγματίσαι, ἐβουλήθη λάθρᾳ ἀπολῦσαι αὐτήν.

19. Yoseiph de 'o aneir auteis, dikaios on, kai mei thelon autein paradeigmatisai, ebouleithei lathra apolusai autein.

Hebrew/Transliteration
יט. וְיוֹסֵף אִישׁ צַדִּיק הָיָה וְלֹא אָבָה לְתִתָּהּ לְדִבַּת־עָם וַיֹּאמֶר לְשַׁלְחָהּ בַּסָּתֶר:

19. Ve•Yo•sef eesh tza•dik ha•ya ve•lo ava le•ti•ta le•di•bat - am va•yo•mer le•shal•cha ba•sa•ter.

TaNaKh/Old Testament/Rabbinic Commentary
As the Torah states,

"... if this thing be true, that the tokens of virginity were not found in the young lady, then they shall bring out the young lady to the door of her father's house, and the men of her city shall stone her to death with stones, because she has done folly in Israel, to play the prostitute in her father's house. So you shall put away the evil from the midst of you. Deuteronomy 22:20-21

An ancient Aramaic interpretive translation, called a *Targum*, on Deuteronomy adds a small detail not found in the original Hebrew, shedding light upon Joseph's decision to divorce her:

"... if a man find a damsel (who is betrothed to a man) in the wilderness, and do violence to her and lie with her, the man only shall die who lay with her, for the damsel is not guilty of death, *but her husband may put her away from him by a bill of divorcement*; for as when a man lies in wait for his neighbor and takes his life, so is this matter: he found her upon the face of the field, the betrothed damsel cried out for help, but there was no one to deliver her."
Targum Pseudo-Jonathan, Translated by J.W. Etheridge, 1892

Yet, "Joseph, her husband, being a righteous man, and not willing to make her a public example, intended *to put her away* privately," (Matthew 1:19). The Greek word απολυσαι, in this context, means to formally divorce, as it is in Yeshua's discussion of divorce in the Gospels, where he interprets the Torah's prescription for divorce in Deuteronomy 24:1-2,

"When a man takes a wife, and marries her, then it shall be, if she find no favor in his eyes, because he has found some unseemly thing in her, that he shall write her a bill of divorce, and give it in her hand, and send her out of his house. When she is departed out of his house, she may go and be another man's wife."

20. But while he thought on these things, behold, the angel of the Lord appeared unto him in a dream, saying, Joseph, thou son of David, fear not to take unto thee Mary thy wife: for that which is conceived in her is of the Holy Ghost.

Greek/Transliteration
20. Ταῦτα δὲ αὐτοῦ ἐνθυμηθέντος, ἰδού, ἄγγελος κυρίου κατ᾽ ὄναρ ἐφάνη αὐτῷ, λέγων, Ἰωσήφ, υἱὸς Δαυίδ, μὴ φοβηθῇς παραλαβεῖν Μαριὰμ τὴν γυναῖκά σου· τὸ γὰρ ἐν αὐτῇ γεννηθὲν ἐκ πνεύματός ἐστιν ἁγίου.

20. Tauta de autou enthumeithentos, idou, angelos kuriou kat onar ephanei auto, legon, Yoseiph, 'wios Dauid, mei phobeitheis paralabein Maryam tein gunaika sou. to gar en autei genneithen ek pneumatos estin 'agiou.

Hebrew/Transliteration
כ. עוֹדֶנּוּ מְדַבֵּר אֶל-לִבּוֹ כָּזֹאת וְהִנֵּה מַלְאַךְ יְהֹוָה נִרְאָה אֵלָיו בַּחֲלוֹם לֵאמֹר יוֹסֵף בֶּן-דָּוִד אַל-תִּירָא מִקַּחַת:אֵלֶיךָ אֶת-מִרְיָם אִשְׁתֶּךָ כִּי הַיֶּלֶד בְּקִרְבָּהּ נוֹצַר מֵרוּחַ הַקֹּדֶשׁ

20. O•de•noo me•da•ber el - li•bo ka•zot ve•hi•ne mal•ach Adonai nir•ah elav ba•cha•lom le•mor Yo•sef ben - David al - ti•ra mi•ka•chat e•le•cha et - Mir•yam eesh•te•cha ki ha•ye•led be•kir•ba no•tzar me•Roo•ach ha•Ko•desh.

TaNaKh-Old Testament/Rabbinic Commentary
The identity of the Messenger of the LORD is clear in the Torah of Moses. Moses tells the Hebrew people that the Messenger of the Lord is YHWH himself, see Genesis 16:7-13. The Messenger of YHWH appears to Hagar and gives her the news of her son as He has just given to Joseph, see also Luke 1:26-31

"Behold you are with child, and you will bear a son; and you shall call his name Ismael…"

If we will believe the Jews, this Messenger must be Gabriel, since he is the Messenger who they say (d) דממנא על חלמא "is appointed over dreams" (d) Zohar in Gen. fol. 103. 3.

---

21. And she shall bring forth a son, and thou shalt call his name JESUS [Yeshua]: for he shall save [yashu] his people from their sins.

Greek/Transliteration
21. Τέξεται δὲ υἱόν, καὶ καλέσεις τὸ ὄνομα αὐτοῦ Ἰησοῦν· αὐτὸς γὰρ σώσει τὸν λαὸν αὐτοῦ ἀπὸ τῶν ἁμαρτιῶν αὐτῶν.

21. Texetai de 'wion, kai kaleseis to onoma autou Yeisoun. autos gar sosei ton laon autou apo ton 'amartion auton.

Hebrew/Transliteration
כא. וְהִיא יֹלֶדֶת בֵּן וְקָרָאתָ אֶת-שְׁמוֹ יֵשׁוּעַ כִּי הוּא יוֹשִׁיעַ אֶת-עַמּוֹ מֵחַטֹּאתֵיהֶם:

21. Ve•hee yo•le•det ben ve•ka•ra•ta et - sh`mo Yeshua ki hoo yo•shi•a et – amo me•cha•to•tey•hem.

Jewish New Testament Commentary/Rabbinic Commentary
According to the Shem Tov Hebrew Matthew text the second part should read, "…for he shall save MY people from their sins." This rendering helps to confirm the identity of the Messenger of the Lord as YHWH from verse 20 above.

This verse is an example of a "semitism" (an allusion to Hebrew or Aramaic) brought over literally into the Greek text. It provides strong evidence in favor of the theory that there was a Hebrew or Aramaic oral or written tradition behind the extant Greek manuscripts, for only in Hebrew or Aramaic does the explanation here of Yeshua's name make any sense; in Greek (or English) it explains nothing. The Hebrew word for "**he will save**" is "*yoshia'*," which has the same Hebrew root (*yud-shin-'ayin*) as the name **Yeshua** (*yud-shin-vav-'ayin*). Thus the Messiah's name is explained on the basis of what he will do. Etymologically the name *Yeshua'* is a contraction of the Hebrew name *Y'hoshua'* (English "Joshua"), which means "*YHVH* saves." It is also the masculine form of the Hebrew word "*yeshu'ah*," which means "salvation."

According to Professors David Flusser and Shmuel Safrai, Orthodox Jews, "*Yeshu*" was how the name "*Yeshua'* " was pronounced by Galilean Jews in the first century. We know from Mat_26:73 below that Jews of the Galil had a different dialect than those of Judea. According to Flusser (*Jewish Sources in Early Christianity*, p. 15) Galileans did not pronounce the Hebrew letter *'ayin* at the end of a word, much as Cockneys drop "h" at the beginning. That is, instead of saying "Ye-**shoo**-ah" they said "**Yeh**-shoo." Undoubtedly some people began spelling the name according to this pronunciation.

In Jewish anti-Christian polemic it became customary not to use Yeshua's correct name but intentionally and consciously to use the distortion "*Yeshu*," because at some point someone realized that "*Yeshu*" is also an acronym consisting of the first letters of the Hebrew insult, "*Yimach sh'mo v'zikhro*" ("May his name and memory be blotted out"; the words adapt and expand the last phrase of Psa_109:13). Thus "*Yeshu*" was a kind of coded incantation against Christian evangelism. Moreover, since Yeshua came to be regarded in non-Messianic Judaism as a false prophet, blasphemer and idolater wrongly being worshipped as God, and since the *Torah* says, "You shall not even pronounce the names of their gods" (Exo_3:13), the Messiah's name was purposely *mis*pronounced. Today most Israelis saying "*Yeshu*" suppose this is the man's correct name and intend no disparagement. The *JNT* avoids "*Yeshu*" because of its history and also because in Hebrew it, like "Jesus" in English, carries the valence of "the god the Gentiles worship."

But Yosef Vaktor reinterprets the acronym to praise Yeshua, "*Yitgadal sh'mo umalkhuto*!" ("May his name and kingdom be magnified!")

22. Now all this was done, that it might be fulfilled which was spoken of the Lord by the prophet, saying,

Greek/Transliteration
22. Τοῦτο δὲ ὅλον γέγονεν, ἵνα πληρωθῇ τὸ ῥηθὲν ὑπὸ τοῦ κυρίου διὰ τοῦ προφήτου, λέγοντος,

22. Touto de 'olon gegonen, 'ina pleirothei to 'reithen 'upo tou kuriou dya tou propheitou, legontos,

Hebrew/Transliteration
‏:כב. וְכָל-זֹאת הָיְתָה לְמַלֹּאת אֵת אֲשֶׁר-דִּבֶּר יְהֹוָה בְּיַד-הַנָּבִיא לֵאמֹר
22. Ve•chol - zot hai•ta le•ma•lot et asher - di•ber Adonai be•yad - ha•na•vee le•mor.

Jewish New Testament Commentary
There have been more than fifty messianic pretenders in the last two thousand years of Jewish history, starting with Todah (Theudas) and Judah HaG'lili (Act_5:36-37), continuing with Shim'on Bar-Kosiba (died 135 C.E.), whom Rabbi Akiva recognized as the Messiah by changing his name to "Bar-Kochva" ("son of a star"; see 2Pe_1:19 on "the Morning Star"), and culminating in Shabtai Tzvi (1626-1676), who became a Moslem, and Jacob Frank (1726-1791), who became a Roman Catholic. But none of them met the criteria laid down in the *Tanakh* concerning the identity of the Messiah; whereas Yeshua met all of them that are applicable to his first coming (these fulfilled prophecies are listed in Mat_26:24. Of the four gospel writers Mattityahu especially concerns himself with pointing out these fulfillments (see Mat_2:5, Mat_2:15, Mat_2:17; Mat_3:3; Mat_4:14; Mat_8:17; Mat_11:10; Mat_12:17; Mat_13:14, Mat_13:35; Mat_21:4; Mat_22:43; Mat_26:31, Mat_27:9). His object is to demonstrate that Yeshua should be recognized as the Messiah because he fulfilled what *Adonai* said about the Messiah through the prophets of the *Tanakh*.

---

23. Behold, a virgin shall be with child, and shall bring forth a son, and they shall call his name Emmanuel, which being interpreted is, God with us.

Greek/Transliteration
23. Ἰδού, ἡ παρθένος ἐν γαστρὶ ἕξει καὶ τέξεται υἱόν, καὶ καλέσουσιν τὸ ὄνομα αὐτοῦ Ἐμμανουήλ, ὅ ἐστιν μεθερμηνευόμενον, Μεθ᾽ ἡμῶν ὁ θεός.

23. Ydou, 'ei parthenos en gastri 'exei kai texetai 'wion, kai kalesousin to onoma autou Emmanoueil, 'o estin methermeineuomenon, Meth 'eimon 'o theos.

Hebrew/Transliteration
‏:כג. הִנֵּה הָעַלְמָה הָרָה וְיֹלֶדֶת בֵּן וְקָרְאוּ שְׁמוֹ עִמָּנוּאֵל אֲשֶׁר יֵאָמֵר אֵל עִמָּנוּ

23. Hee•ne ha•al•ma ha•ra ve•yo•le•det ben ve•kar•oo sh`mo Eema•noo•el asher ye•a•mer El ee•ma•noo.

TaNaKh/Old Testament/Jewish New Testament Commentary
Usually objection to a virgin birth as impossible follows as a logical consequence of objecting to any and all supernaturalism. But the God of the Bible is literally "supernatural," above nature, since he created nature and its laws. Therefore, if it suits his purpose he can suspend those laws. The Bible in both the *Tanakh* and the New Testament teaches repeatedly that God does intervene in human history and does sometimes overrule the natural course of events for his own reasons.

Frequently his reason, as in this instance, is to give humanity a sign of his sovereignty, presence and concern. In fact, Isa_7:14, immediately preceding the portion quoted, reads, "Therefore the Lord himself will give you a sign." The Hebrew word for sign (" *'ot*") means an extraordinary event that demonstrates and calls attention to God's direct involvement in human affairs. The "God" of Deism, pictured as starting the universe like a man winding a watch and leaving it to run by itself, is not the God of the Bible.

" *'Almah*" is used seven times in the Hebrew Bible, and in each instance it either explicitly means a virgin or implies it, because in the Bible " *'almah*" always refers to an unmarried woman of good reputation. In Gen_24:43 it applies to Rebecca, Isaac's future bride, already spoken of in Gen_24:16 as a *b'tulah*. In Exo_2:8 it describes the infant Moshe's older sister Miryam, a nine-year-old girl and surely a virgin. (Thus the name of Yeshua's mother recalls this earlier virgin.) The other references are to young maidens playing on timbrels (Psa_68:25), maidens being courted (Pro_30:19) and virgins of the royal court (Son_1:3, Son_6:8). In each case the context requires a young unmarried woman of good reputation, i.e., a virgin.

The prophecy is introduced here as in Isaiah with a "behold!" not only to raise and fix the attention, but to denote that it was something wonderful and extraordinary which was about to be related; and is therefore called אות a "sign", wonder, or miracle; which lay not, as some Jewish writers (g) affirm, in this, that the person spoken of was unfit for conception at the time of the prophecy, since no such thing is intimated. (g) Jarchi. in Isa. vii. 14.

In another Jewish source we read the following, "God said to Israel: 'You have said to me, "We have become orphans without a father"; therefore the redeemer I will bring from amoung you has no father, for it is said…"Today I have begotten you"'" (Psalm 2:7) The convert "concluded from this that their Messiah …has no human father." (Sefer Yeshu'ot Meshicho, part 2,3:3)

---

24. Then Joseph being raised from sleep did as the angel of the Lord had bidden him, and took unto him his wife:

Greek/Transliteration
24. Διεγερθεὶς δὲ ὁ Ἰωσὴφ ἀπὸ τοῦ ὕπνου, ἐποίησεν ὡς προσέταξεν αὐτῷ ὁ ἄγγελος κυρίου· καὶ παρέλαβεν τὴν γυναῖκα αὐτοῦ,

24. Diegertheis de 'o Yoseiph apo tou 'upnou, epoieisen 'os prosetaxen auto 'o angelos kuriou. kai parelaben tein gunaika autou,

Hebrew/Transliteration
:כד. וַיִּיקַץ יוֹסֵף מִשְּׁנָתוֹ וַיַּעַשׂ כַּאֲשֶׁר צִוָּה אֹתוֹ מַלְאַךְ יְהוָה וַיִּקַּח אֶת-אִשְׁתּוֹ

24. Va•yi•katz Yo•sef mish•na•to va•ya•as ka•a•sher tzi•va o•to mal•ach Adonai va•yi•kach et - eesh•to.

Jewish New Testament Commentary
Yosef's behavior shows that he accepted Yeshua as his son. According to the Mishna, "If one say, 'This is my son,' he is to be believed" (Bava Batra 8:6). The Gemara explains that he is believed "as regards the right of inheritance" (Bava Batra 134a). Thus Yeshua, as a legally acknowledged son, is entitled to inherit the throne of King David from Yosef, a descendant of David (Mat_1:8). (This point is made in Phillip Goble, *How to Point to Yeshua in Your Rabbi's Bible*, New York: Artists for Israel, 1986.)

---

25. And knew her not till she had brought forth her firstborn son: and he called his name JESUS [Yeshua].

Greek/Transliteration
25. καὶ οὐκ ἐγίνωσκεν αὐτὴν ἕως οὗ ἔτεκεν τὸν υἱὸν αὐτῆς τὸν πρωτότοκον· καὶ ἐκάλεσεν τὸ ὄνομα αὐτοῦ Ἰησοῦν.

25. kai ouk eginosken autein 'eos 'ou eteken ton 'wion auteis ton prototokon. kai ekalesen to onoma autou Yeisoun.

Hebrew/Transliteration
:כה. וְלֹא יָדַע אֹתָהּ עַד כִּי-יָלְדָה בֵן אֶת-בְּכוֹרָהּ וַיִּקְרָא אֶת-שְׁמוֹ יֵשׁוּעַ

25. Ve•lo ya•da o•ta ad ki - yal•da ben et - be•cho•ra va•yik•ra et - sh`mo Yeshua.

Jewish New Testament Commentary
Protestants generally affirm that Miryam was a virgin when Yeshua was born, but that "his sisters" (plural: at least two) and four brothers (Mat_13:55-56, Mar_6:3) were Miryam and Yosef's natural children. The Roman Catholic Church teaches that Miryam remained a virgin all her life, and that the terms "brothers" and "sisters" are used loosely to refer to more distant relatives (compare Gen_14:12-16, Gen_31:32, Lev_10:4). The Greek phrase "*eôs ou*" ("until") is inconclusive because it does not necessarily imply a change; that is, the Greek could mean either that they did not have relations during the period before she gave birth but did afterwards, or that they remained celibate afterwards as well. But celibacy in

particular and asceticism in general, though regarded by pagans as spiritually meritorious, were and are the exception in Judaism and in New Covenant faith, as both Yeshua and Sha'ul teach (see Mat_19:10-12, 1Co_7:1-40, Col_2:18-23, 1Ti_4:3).

Matthew, Chapter 2

1. Now when Jesus was born in Bethlehem of Judaea in the days of Herod the king, behold, there came wise men from the east to Jerusalem,

Greek/Translitration
1. Τοῦ δὲ Ἰησοῦ γεννηθέντος ἐν Βηθλεὲμ τῆς Ἰουδαίας, ἐν ἡμέραις Ἡρῴδου τοῦ βασιλέως, ἰδού, μάγοι ἀπὸ ἀνατολῶν παρεγένοντο εἰς Ἱεροσόλυμα,

1. Tou de Yeisou genneithentos en Beithle'em teis Youdaias, en 'eimerais 'Eirodou tou basileos, idou, magoi apo anatolon paregenonto eis 'Yerosoluma,

Hebrew/Transliteration
א. וַיְהִי כַּאֲשֶׁר נוֹלַד יֵשׁוּעַ בְּבֵית-לֶחֶם יְהוּדָה בִּימֵי הַמֶּלֶךְ הוֹרְדוֹס וְהִנֵּה חֹזֵי כוֹכָבִים בָּאוּ מֵאֶרֶץ קֶדֶם יְרוּשָׁלַיְמָה:לֵאמֹר

1. Vay•hi ka•a•sher no•lad Yeshua be•Veit - Le•chem Yehooda bi•mey ha•me•lech Hordos ve•hee•ne cho•zey cho•cha•vim ba•oo me•e•retz ke•dem Ye•roo•sha•lai•ma le•mor.

Rabbinic Jewish Commentary/Jewish New Testament Commentary
The first century Jewish mystic Philo comments,
"And in the land of the barbarians. . . there are very numerous companies of virtuous and honorable men celebrated. Among the Persians there exists a group, the Magi, who investigating the works of nature for the purpose of becoming acquainted with the truth. . . initiate others in the divine virtues, by very clear explanations." (Philo, Every Good Man is Free, *74*)

Herod the Great (c. 73-4 B.C.E.) founded the Herodian dynasty (see Luk_3:1), which ruled the Land of Israel and its surroundings from 37 B.C.E. until the war with Rome in 66-70 C.E. Herod himself was a man of great physical energy and ambition. His career comes to the notice of historians in 47 B.C.E. in Syria and the Galil; a combination of military successes, political machinations and bribery of Roman superiors enabled him to replace the last of the Hasmonean rulers, Antigonus, when the latter died in 37 B.C.E. (possibly in consequence of one of Herod's bribes). He did, however, reconstruct and enlarge the Second Temple, which had been built under Z'rubavel (see the book of Haggai) in 520-516 B.C.E. The Talmudic rabbis said, "One who has not seen Herod's temple has never seen a beautiful building" (Bava Batra 4a), but also, "It was built by a sinful king, and the building was intended by him as an atonement for having slain Israel's sages" (Numbers Rabbah 4:14).

Even the ancient Jews have owned that the Messiah is already born, and that he was born at Bethlehem; as appears from their Talmud (p), where we meet with such a passage. "It happened to a certain Jew, that as he was ploughing, one of his oxen bellowed; a certain Arabian passed by and heard it, who said, O Jew, Jew, loose thy oxen, and loose thy ploughshare, for lo, the house of the sanctuary is destroyed: it bellowed a second time; he said unto him, O Jew, Jew, bind thy oxen, and bind thy ploughshare, for lo יליד מלכא משיחא "the king Messiah is born". He said to him, what is his name? Menachem (the comforter); he asked again, what is his father's name? Hezekiah; once more he says, from whence is he? He replies מן בירת מלכא ביתלחם יהודה "from the palace of the king of Bethlehem Judah"; he went and sold his oxen and his ploughshares, and became a seller of swaddling clothes for infants; and he went from city to city till he came to that city, (Bethlehem,) and all the women bought of him, but the mother of Menachem bought nothing."

(p) Hieros. Beracot. fol. 5. 1.

---

2. Saying, Where is he that is born King of the Jews? for we have seen his star in the east, and are come to worship him.

Greek/Transliteration
2. λέγοντες, Ποῦ ἐστιν ὁ τεχθεὶς βασιλεὺς τῶν Ἰουδαίων; Εἴδομεν γὰρ αὐτοῦ τὸν ἀστέρα ἐν τῇ ἀνατολῇ, καὶ ἤλθομεν προσκυνῆσαι αὐτῷ.

2. legontes, Pou estin 'o techtheis basileus ton Youdaion? Eidomen gar autou ton astera en tei anatolei, kai eilthomen proskuneisai auto.

Hebrew/Transliteration
ב. אַיֵּה הַמֶּלֶךְ הַנּוֹלָד לַיְּהוּדִים כִּי רָאִנוּ כוֹכָבוֹ בַּקֶּדֶם וַנָּבֹא לְהִשְׁתַּחֲוֹת לוֹ:

2. A•ye ha•Me•lech ha•no•lad la•Ye•hoo•dim ki ra•ee•noo cho•cha•vo ba•ke•dem va•na•vo le•hish•ta•cha•vot lo.

Rabbinic Jewish Commentary
To this it maybe replied, that there is a prophecy of Balaam's which is thus expressed, "there shall come a star out of Jacob, and a sceptre shall rise out of Israel", Num_24:17 which is owned by some Jewish writers (k) to be a prophecy of the Messiah; though the star there mentioned is considered by them as one of the Messiah's titles; hence one who set up himself, and for a while was by some received as the Messiah, was called by them בר כוכבא "the son of a star"; but when he was discovered to be an impostor, they called him בר כוזיבא "the son of a lie": but I rather take it to be a sign of the Messiah's coming, and the meaning is, when a star shall דרך "walk" or steer its course from Jacob, or above, or over the land of Israel, then a sceptre, or sceptre bearer, that is, a king, shall rise out of Israel.

That the Jews have expected that a star should appear at the time of the Messiah's coming, is certain, from some passages in a book of theirs of great value and esteem among them, in which are the following things: in one place it is said (o).

"The king Messiah shall be revealed in the land of Galilee, and lo a star in the east shall swallow up seven stars in the north, and a flame of red fire shall be in the firmament six days;"

And in another place, (p). "When the Messiah shall be revealed, there shall rise up in the east a certain Star, flaming with all sorts of colours--and all men shall see it:"

once more it is affirmed as a tradition (q) that "The holy blessed God hath determined to build Jerusalem, and to make a certain (fixed) star appear sparkling with seven blazing tails shining from it in the midst of the firmament--and then shall the king Messiah be revealed in all the world."

Pliny (t) makes mention "of a bright comet with a silver beard, which was so refulgent that it could scarce be looked upon, showing in itself the effigies of God in human form."

(k) Targum Onk. Jon. & Aben Ezra in loc. Zohar. in Exod. fol. 4. 1. Abarbinel Mashmia Jeshua, fol. 4. 3. Tzeror Hamor, fol. 126. 3. (o) Zohar. in Gen. fol. 74. 3. (p) Zohar. in Exod. fol. 3. 3, 4. (q) Ib. in Numb. fol 85. 4. and 86. 1. (t) Nat. Hist. l. 2. c. 25. (u) Vid. Fabricii Bibliothec. Latin. p. 142-146.

---

3. When Herod the king had heard these things, he was troubled, and all Jerusalem with him.

Greek/Transliteration
3. Ἀκούσας δὲ Ἡρῴδης ὁ βασιλεὺς ἐταράχθη, καὶ πᾶσα Ἱεροσόλυμα μετ' αὐτοῦ·

3. Akousas de 'Eirodeis 'o basileus etarachthei, kai pasa 'Yerosoluma met autou.

Hebrew/Transliteration
ג: וַיִּשְׁמַע הַמֶּלֶךְ הוֹרְדוֹס וַיָּנַע לְבָבוֹ וּלְבַב כָּל-יְרוּשָׁלַיִם עִמּוֹ

3. Va•yish•ma ha•me•lech Hordos va•ya•na le•va•vo ool•vav kol - Ye•roo•sha•la•yim ee•mo.

Historical Commentary
Sights like the star above were believed by the ancients to portend the fall of rulers. When a comet appeared, the crazed emperor Nero later acted in a very similar fashion to Herod, "It chanced that a comet had begun to appear on several successive nights, a thing which is commonly believed to portend the death of great rulers. Worried by this, and learning from the astrologer Balbillus that kings usually averted such omens by the death of some distinguished man, thus turning them from themselves upon the heads of the nobles, he resolved on the death of all the eminent men of the State..." Suetonius, (The Lives of the Caesars, Book 6, Nero, pg. 188)

The Targumists on it, who paraphrases it after this manner; "Kings and governors shall not cease from the house of Judah, nor scribes, who teach the law, from his seed, until the time that the king Messiah, the least of his sons, comes, "and because of him", יתימסון עממיא, "the people shall melt." (w) Jonathan ben Uzziel in loc.

---

4. And when he had gathered all the chief priests and scribes of the people together, he demanded of them where Christ should be born.

Greek/Transliteration
4. καὶ συναγαγὼν πάντας τοὺς ἀρχιερεῖς καὶ γραμματεῖς τοῦ λαοῦ, ἐπυνθάνετο παρ' αὐτῶν ποῦ ὁ χριστὸς γεννᾶται.

4. kai sunagagon pantas tous archiereis kai grammateis tou laou, epunthaneto par auton pou 'o christos gennatai.

Hebrew/Transliteration
:ד. וַיַּקְהֵל אֶת-כָּל-רָאשֵׁי הַכֹּהֲנִים וְהַסּוֹפְרִים בָּעָם וַיִּשְׁאַל אֶת-פִּיהֶם לֵאמֹר אַיֵּה יִוָּלֵד הַמָּשִׁיחַ

4. Va•yak•hel et - kol - ra•shey ha•ko•ha•nim ve•ha•sof•rim ba•am va•yish•al et - pi•hem le•mor a•ye yi•va•led ha•Ma•shi•ach.

Jewish New Testament Commentary
Cohanim (plural; singular *cohen*), "priests," a word which today evokes the image of clerics in formal Christian denominations or functionaries in eastern or primitive religions. This is because the Jewish priesthood has been dormant since the destruction of the Second Temple in 70 C.E. But in Yeshua's day, when the Temple still stood, Judaism without a priesthood was unimaginable.

The *cohanim* serving in the Temple were descendents of Moshe's brother Aharon, great-grandson of L'vi, Ya'akov's third son. In terms of practical job-description their primary duty was to offer sacrificial animals on the altar. The ever-bloody altar in the Temple of God was a continual witness to Israel that God's penalty for sin is death (see Heb_10:3).

---

5. And they said unto him, In Bethlehem of Judaea: for thus it is written by the prophet,

Greek/Transliteration
5. Οἱ δὲ εἶπον αὐτῷ, Ἐν Βηθλεὲμ τῆς Ἰουδαίας· οὕτως γὰρ γέγραπται διὰ τοῦ προφήτου,

5. 'Oi de eipon auto, En Beithle'em teis Youdaias. 'outos gar gegraptai dya tou propheitou,

Hebrew/Transliteration
:ה. וַיֹּאמְרוּ אֵלָיו בְּבֵית-לֶחֶם יְהוּדָה כִּי כֹה-כָּתוּב בְּיַד-הַנָּבִיא

5. Va•yom•roo elav be•Veit - Le•chem Yehooda ki cho - ka•toov be•yad - ha•na•vee.

---

6. And thou Bethlehem, in the land of Juda, art not the least among the princes of Juda: for out of thee shall come a Governor, that shall rule my people Israel.

Greek/Transliteration
6. Καὶ σὺ Βηθλεέμ, γῆ Ἰούδα, οὐδαμῶς ἐλαχίστη εἶ ἐν τοῖς ἡγεμόσιν Ἰούδα· ἐκ σοῦ γὰρ ἐξελεύσεται ἡγούμενος, ὅστις ποιμανεῖ τὸν λαόν μου τὸν Ἰσραήλ.

6. Kai su Beithle'em, gei Youda, oudamos elachistei ei en tois 'eigemosin Youda. ek sou gar exeleusetai 'eigoumenos, 'ostis poimanei ton laon mou ton Ysraeil.

Hebrew/Transliteration
ו. וְאַתָּה בֵּית-לֶחֶם אֶפְרָתָה יְהוּדָה אֵינְךָ צָעִיר בְּאַלְפֵי יְהוּדָה כִּי מִמְּךָ יֵצֵא מוֹשֵׁל אֲשֶׁר יִרְעֶה אֶת-עַמִּי יִשְׂרָאֵל:

6. Ve•a•ta Beit - Le•chem e•retz Yehooda eyn•cha tza•eer be•a•loo•fey Yehooda ki mim•cha ye•tze mo•shel asher yir•eh et - ami Israel.

Rabbinic Jewish Commentary
"But you, Bethlehem Ephratah, being small among the clans of Judah, out of you one will come forth to me that is to be ruler in Israel; whose goings forth are from of old (mi'Kedem), from the days of old. Micah 5:2

The phrase 'from days of old' refers to the Six Days of Creation. The Talmud says, "Seven things were created before the world was created, and these are they: The Torah, repentance, the Garden of Eden, Gehenna, the Throne of Glory, the Temple, and the name of the Messiah. The Torah, for it is written, "The Lord made me [the Torah] as the beginning of his way." Repentance, for it is written, "Before the mountains were brought forth," and it is written, "You turn man to contrition, and say, Repent, ye children of men." The Garden of Eden, as it is written, 'And the Lord planted a garden in Eden from aforetime (mi'Kedem)." The Gehenna, for it is written, "For Tophet [Gehenna] is ordered of old." The Throne of Glory and the Temple, for it is written, "You throne of glory, on high from the beginning, You place of our sanctuary." The name of the Messiah, as it is written, "His [the Messiah's] name shall endure for ever, and has existed before the sun!" (Pesachim 54a, Soncino Press Edition)

Rashi, commenting on Micah 5 states,
"and his origin is from of old: "Before the sun his name is Yinnon" (Ps. 72:17).
(Rashi on Micah 5, cited at Chabad.org)

Lamentations says,
"For these things I weep; my eye, my eye runs down with water; Because the Comforter who should refresh my soul is far from me: My children are desolate, because the enemy has prevailed." (Lamentations 1:16)

Commenting on this passage, the Midrash identifies the name of the Messiah as Menachem, the Comforter, and speaks of his birth in Bethlehem, "BECAUSE THE COMFORTER IS FAR FROM ME, EVEN HE THAT SHOULD REFRESH MY SOUL. What is the name of King Messiah? R. Abba b. Kahana said: His name is 'YHWH'; as it is stated, 'And this is the name whereby he shall be called, YHWH is our righteousness (Jer 23:6).' For R. Levi said: It is good for a province when its name is identical with that of its king, and the name of its king identical with that of its God. 'It is good for a province when its name is identical with that of its king,' as it is written, 'And the name of the city from that day shall be YHWH is there' (Ezek. XLVIII, 35). 'And the name of its king identical with that of its God,' as it is stated, ''And this is the name whereby he shall be called, YHWH is Our Rightieousness.

R. Joshua b. Levi said: His name is ' Shoot; as it is stated, "Behold, a man whose name is Shoot, and who shall shoot up out of his place, and build the temple of the Lord (Zech 4:12)". R. Judan said in the name of R. Aibu: His name is Comforte; as it is said," THE COMFORTER IS FAR FROM ME." R. Hanina said: They do not really differ, because the numerical value of the names is the same, so that 'Comforter' (Menachem) is identical with Shoot (Tzemach).

The following supports the saying of R. Aibu: "It happened that a man was plowing, when one of his oxen lowed. An Arab passed by and asked, "What are you?" He answered, "I am a Jew." He said to him, "Unharness your ox and untie your plough [as a mark of mourning].' Why? ' he asked. 'Because the Temple of the Jews is destroyed." He inquired, "From where do you know this?" He answered,"I know it from the lowing of your ox." While he was conversing with him, the ox lowed again. The Arab said to him,"Harness your ox and tie up your plough, because the deliverer of the Jews is born." "What is his name?" he asked, and he answered, "His name is (Menachem) "Comforter".What is his father's name? He answered, 'Hezekiah.' Where do they live? ' He answered, "In Birath Arba, in Bethlehem of Judah." Lamentations Rabbah 1:51, Soncino Press Edition

The Jerusalem Talmud, in Berachot 25b, echoes this tradition closely, but says, "From Biryat Malka in Beit Lechem of Yehudah" Talmud Yerushalmi, Berachot 25b

---

7. Then Herod, when he had privily called the wise men, inquired of them diligently what time the star appeared.

Greek/Transliteration

7. Τότε Ἡρῴδης, λάθρᾳ καλέσας τοὺς μάγους, ἠκρίβωσεν παρ᾽ αὐτῶν τὸν χρόνον τοῦ φαινομένου ἀστέρος.

7. Tote 'Eirodeis, lathra kalesas tous magous, eikribosen par auton ton chronon tou phainomenou asteros.

Hebrew/Transliteration

ז. וַיִּקְרָא הוֹרְדוֹס אֶל-חֹזֵי הַכּוֹכָבִים בַּסֵּתֶר וַיַּחְקֹר אֹתָם לָדַעַת אֶת-הָעֵת אֲשֶׁר נִרְאָה הַכּוֹכָב

7. Va•yik•ra Hordos el - cho•zey ha•ko•cha•vim ba•se•ter va•yach•kor o•tam la•da•at et - ha•et asher nir•ah ha•ko•chav.

---

8. And he sent them to Bethlehem, and said, Go and search diligently for the young child; and when ye have found him, bring me word again, that I may come and worship him also.

Greek/Transliteration

8. Καὶ πέμψας αὐτοὺς εἰς Βηθλεὲμ εἶπεν, Πορευθέντες ἀκριβῶς ἐξετάσατε περὶ τοῦ παιδίου· ἐπὰν δὲ εὕρητε, ἀπαγγείλατέ μοι, ὅπως κἀγὼ ἐλθὼν προσκυνήσω αὐτῷ.

8. Kai pempsas autous eis Beithle'em eipen, Poreuthentes akribos exetasate peri tou paidiou. epan de 'eureite, apangeilate moi, 'opos kago elthon proskuneiso auto.

Hebrew/Transliteration

ח. וַיִּשְׁלַח אֹתָם בֵּית-לֶחֶם וַיֹּאמֶר לְכוּ וְדִרְשׁוּ הֵיטֵב עַל-הַיֶּלֶד וְכַאֲשֶׁר תִּמְצָאוּן אֹתוֹ שׁוּבוּ וְהַגִּידוּ לִי וְאָבֹאָה לְהִשְׁתַּחֲוֹת-לוֹ גַם-אָנִי

8. Va•yish•lach o•tam Beit - Le•chem va•yo•mar le•choo ve•dir•shoo hei•tev al - ha•ye•led ve•cha•a•sher tim•tze•oon o•to shoo•voo ve•ha•gi•doo li ve•a•vo•ah le•hish•ta•cha•vot - lo gam - ani.

---

9. When they had heard the king, they departed; and, lo, the star, which they saw in the east, went before them, till it came and stood over where the young child was.

Greek/Transliteration

9. Οἱ δὲ ἀκούσαντες τοῦ βασιλέως ἐπορεύθησαν· καὶ ἰδού, ὁ ἀστήρ, ὃν εἶδον ἐν τῇ ἀνατολῇ, προῆγεν αὐτούς, ἕως ἐλθὼν ἔστη ἐπάνω οὗ ἦν τὸ παιδίον.

9. 'Oi de akousantes tou basileos eporeutheisan. kai idou, 'o aster, 'on eidon en tei anatolei, proeigen autous, 'eos elthon estei epano 'ou ein to paidion.

Hebrew/Transliteration

ט. וַיִּשְׁמְעוּ אֶל־הַמֶּלֶךְ וַיֵּלְכוּ וְהִנֵּה הַכּוֹכָב אֲשֶׁר־רָאוּ בַקֶּדֶם עָלָה לִפְנֵיהֶם עַד אֲשֶׁר־בָּא וַיַּעֲמֹד מִמַּעַל לַאֲשֶׁר־הָיָה שָׁם הַיָּלֶד׃

9. Va•yish•me•oo el - ha•me•lech va•ye•le•choo ve•hee•ne ha•ko•chav asher - ra•oo va•ke•dem ala lif•ney•hem ad asher - ba va•ya•a•mod mi•ma•al la•a•sher ha•ya sham ha•ya•led.

Historical/Rabbinic Jewish Commentary

"I see him, but not now. I see him, but not near. A star will come out of Jacob. A scepter will rise out of Israel, and shall strike through the corners of Moab, and break down all the sons of Sheth." Numbers 24:17

Regarding the birth of Abraham, the Midrash says,
"When our father Abraham was born, a star rose in the east and swallowed four stars in the four corners of heaven. Nimrod's wizards said to him: To Terah, at this hour, a son has been born, out of whom will issue a people destined to inherit this world and the world-to-come. With your permission, let his father be given a house full of silver and gold, on condition that his newly born son be slain."
Beit haMidrash 2:118-196 cited in Sefer HaAggadah, Schocken Books

Like Abraham birth, the revelation of the Messiah is connected to the Star in the East, 'A star steps forth from Jacob' (Num 24:17). It is taught in the name of our Sages: the septennial cycle wherein the Son of David comes (will transpire as follows): (in) the first (year), there will not be food for all who need it; (in) the second (year), the 'arrows of famine' (cf. Ezek 5:16) will be unleashed; (in) the third (year), a severe famine; in the fourth (year), neither famine nor plenty; in the fifth (year), great plenty, and a star will emerge in the east. This is the star of the Messiah, and it will be visible in the east for fifteen days. Should it linger, it will be to Israel's benefit. (In) the sixth (year), noises and sounds. (In) the seventh (year), battles. And at the end of the seventh (year), one will behold the Messiah. (Aggadat HaMashiach, Trajectories in Near Eastern Apocalyptic, Translated by *John C. Reeves*)

The concept of the star linking to the Messiah is an ancient thread in Jewish tradition. R' Akiba gave Shimon bar Kozeba the name "Bar Kochva" (Son of the Star), proclaiming him the Messiah, linking him to the prophecy in Numbers 24:17. During this time, after the destruction of the Temple, Israel was battling the Roman Empire in a last stand for freedom.

The text named 'The Prayer of Rabbi Shimon bar Yochai' states,
"And during the sixth (year) a star shall appear from the east and on top of it a rod of fire like a spear. The Gentile nations will claim 'this star is ours,' but it is not so; rather, it pertains to Israel, as Scripture forecasts: 'a star shall step forth from Jacob, etc.' (Num 24:17). The time of its shining will be during the first watch of the night for two hours. It will set (for) fifteen days in the east, and then revolve to the west and act (similarly?) for fifteen days. If it should be more (its period of shining), this is good for Israel." (Tefilat Shimon Bar Yochai, Trajectories in Near

Eastern Apocalyptic, Translated by *John C. Reeves*)

All of these traditions are linked together and show a consistent theme connecting the Star in the East with the coming of the King Messiah,
"And this will be the sign for you—when you see that at the beginning of one week there is rain, and in the second (week) the loosing of the 'arrows of hunger,' and in the third a severe famine, and in the fourth no hunger but (also) no satisfaction, and in the fifth there is great satiety. A star shall appear from the east with a rod on top of it—this is the star of Israel, as Scripture says: 'a star shall step forth from Jacob etc.' (Num 24:17). If it shines, it is for the benefit of Israel. Then the Messiah of the lineage of David shall emerge."
(Nistarot Shimon Bar Yochai, Trajectories in Near Eastern Apocalyptic, Translated by *John C. Reeves*)

The Zohar amazingly links this revelation of the Messiah to the land of Galilee, "The glory of his majesty" refers to the Messiah when he shall reveal himself in the land of Galilee; for in this part of the Holy Land the desolation first began, and therefore he will manifest himself there first . . . and when the Messiah shall have manifested himself, a star shall come forth from the East variegated in hue and shining brilliantly, and seven other stars shall surround it, and make war on it from all sides, three times a day for seventy days, before the eyes of the whole world. The one star shall fight against the seven with rays of fire flashing on every side, and it shall smite them until they are extinguished, evening after evening. . . .
After the seventy days the one star shall vanish."
(Zohar, Volume II, Shemot 7b, Soncino Press Edition, pg. 21)

---

10. When they saw the star, they rejoiced with exceeding great joy.

Greek/Transliteration
10. Ἰδόντες δὲ τὸν ἀστέρα, ἐχάρησαν χαρὰν μεγάλην σφόδρα.

10. Idontes de ton astera, echareisan charan megalein sphodra.

Hebrew/Transliteration
י. וְהֵם חָזוּ בַכּוֹכָב וַיִּשְׂמְחוּ שִׂמְחָה גְדֹלָה עַד-מְאֹד:

10. Ve•hem cha•zoo va•ko•chav va•yis•me•choo sim•cha ge•do•la ad - me•od.

Rabbinic Jewish Commentary
The Midrash notes that Gentile astrologers will recognize the star,
"And there shall be a ruler amidst Jacob [Numb. 24.19] At first a star arose in the east, at the head of which there was a sword. Israel saw it, and said to one another, "What is that?" The other nations asked their astrologers, "What is the character of this star?" They [the astrologers] said to them, "This is the star of Israel. This is the king who shall yet arise for them.: As soon as Israel heard that, they

approached the prophet Samuel and said to him, *Give us a king to judge us, just like all the nations*[I Sam. 8.5] – just as the nations said. in this context it says, *a star shall arise from Jacob.* [Num. 24.17] And so also at the end [of days], a star shall arise in the east, and it is the star of the Messiah; as it says, and there shall be a ruler (yerd) amidst Jacob. Rabbi Yose said: In the language of the Arameans, the east is called *yerd.* And it spends fifteen days in the east. If it tarries even longer, it is only for the good of Israel; and then you may expect the footsteps of the Messiah." (Midrash ha-Gadol, Numbers, Yemenite Midrash, translated by Yitzchak Tzvi Langerman, HarperCollins, pg. 175-176)

The process of the stars coming out, and finally the dawn breaking upon the world, is a pattern of what the Final Geulah, Redemption will look like,
"At night, though it be night, one has the light of the moon, the stars, and the planets. Then when is it really dark? Just before dawn! After the moon sets and the stars set and the planets vanish, there is no darkness deeper than the hour before dawn. And in that hour the Holy One answers the world and all that are in it: out of the darkness He brings forth the dawn and gives light to the world. The hind of the dawn [the morning star]–its light rays out as it rises. At the beginning, light comes little by little; then it spreads wider and wider, grows and increases; and at last it bursts into shining glory." (Sefer HaAggadah, Translated by Schocken Books, citing MTeh 22:4 and 22:13; Aggadat Esther 7:10 (ed. Buber, p. 68); B. Yoma 29a)

Ancient Jews interpreted the Star of Numbers 24 as the Messiah,
"The star is the Interpreter of the Law who comes to Damascus as it is written, "A star has left Jacob, a staff has risen from Israel" (Numbers 24:17).
(Dead Sea Scrolls, Damascus Document 7:19-21, Translated by Abegg, Wise and Cook, pg. 58)

The Ramban states,
"THERE SHALL STEP FORTH A STAR OUT OF JACOB. Because the Messiah will gather together the dispersed of Israel from all corners of the earth, Balaam compares him [metaphorically] to a star that passes through the firmament from the ends of heaven, just as it is said about [the Messiah]: and behold, there came with the clouds of heaven, one like unto a son of man etc."
(Ramban, Balak, Translated by Rabbi C. Chavel, Shilo Publishing House, Pg 283)

The Zohar says,
"Moreover the light of the moon shall be as the light of the sun (Isa. xxx, 26), and then will this cause the seventh window to open to the whole world, whose star is the Star of Jacob, concerning which Balaam said: There shall come a star out of Jacob (Num. XXIV, 17). This star will shine for forty days and forty nights, and when the Messiah shall be revealed and all the nations of the world shall gather around him, then will the verse of Scripture be fulfilled which says: And in that day the root of Jesse which stands for an ensign of the peoples, to it shall the Gentiles seek: and his rest shall be glorious (Isa. XI, 10)."
(Zohar II:172b, Soncino Press Edition)

Yeshua, in the Book of Revelation, reveals himself as the Star awaited by the world, "I am the Root and the Offspring of David, the Bright and Morning Star." Revelation 22:16

---

11. And when they were come into the house, they saw the young child with Mary his mother, and fell down, and worshipped him: and when they had opened their treasures, they presented unto him gifts; gold, and frankincense, and myrrh.

Greek/Transliteration
11. καὶ ἐλθόντες εἰς τὴν οἰκίαν, εἶδον τὸ παιδίον μετὰ Μαρίας τῆς μητρὸς αὐτοῦ, καὶ πεσόντες προσεκύνησαν αὐτῷ, καὶ ἀνοίξαντες τοὺς θησαυροὺς αὐτῶν προσήνεγκαν αὐτῷ δῶρα, χρυσὸν καὶ λίβανον καὶ σμύρναν.

11. kai elthontes eis tein oikian, eidon to paidion meta Marias teis meitros autou, kai pesontes prosekuneisan auto, kai anoixantes tous theisaurous auton proseinegkan auto dora, chruson kai libanon kai smurnan.

Hebrew/Transliteration
יא. וַיָּבֹאוּ הַבַּיְתָה וַיִּרְאוּ אֶת-הַיֶּלֶד עִם-מִרְיָם אִמּוֹ וַיִּפְּלוּ וַיִּשְׁתַּחֲווּ-לוֹ וַיִּפְתְּחוּ אֶת-אֹצְרֹתֵיהֶם וַיַּקְרִיבוּ לוֹ מִנְחָה:זָהָב וּלְבוֹנָה וָמֹר

11. Va•ya•vo•oo ha•bai•ta va•yir•oo et - ha•ye•led eem - Mir•yam ee•mo va•yip•loo va•yish•ta•cha•voo - lo va•yif•te•choo et - otz•ro•tey•hem va•yak•ri•voo lo min•cha za•hav ool•vo•na va•mor.

Rabbinic Jewish Commentary
The gifts of the Magi have special significance, as illustrated by the Zohar, "Sin is red, as it says, "Though your sins be as scarlet"; man puts the sacrificial animal on the fire, which is also red; the priest sprinkles the red blood round the altar, but the smoke ascending to heaven is white. Thus the red is turned to white. The attribute of Justice is turned into the attribute of Mercy. . . R. Issac said: 'Red (blood) and white (fat) are offered for sacrifice, and the odour ascends from both. The spices of incense are in part red and in part white – frankincense is white, pure myrrh is red – and the odour ascends from red to white. (Zohar, Volume III, Shemoth 20b. Soncino Press Edition, pg. 6)

Rashi cites Onkelos explaining the link between "myrrh" and Moriah, the site of Yitzchak's sacrifice, "Onkelos rendered it ["the land of service"] as alluding to the service of the incense, which contained myrrh ["mor" is phonetically similar to Moriah], spikenard, and other spices." Rashi on Genesis 22, cited at Chabad.org

The gifts that are brought to the Messiah are a foreshadow of the Messianic era, in which all of the non-Jews of the world will bring gifts to the King Messiah, "R. Judah bar Simon taught: The nations of the earth will bring gifts to the King

Messiah the son of David, and to Messiah the son of Ephraim. . . the nations will bring gifts to the King Messiah. And as soon as the nations of the earth come to the King Messiah, he will ask: "Are there children of Israel among you? Bring them as gifts to me...." (Midrash Tehilim 87.6, translated by William G. Braude, Yale University Press, pg. 77)

---

12. And being warned of God in a dream that they should not return to Herod, they departed into their own country another way.

Greek/Transliteration
12. Καὶ χρηματισθέντες κατ' ὄναρ μὴ ἀνακάμψαι πρὸς Ἡρῴδην, δι' ἄλλης ὁδοῦ ἀνεχώρησαν εἰς τὴν χώραν αὐτῶν.

12. Kai chreimatisthentes kat onar mei anakampsai pros 'Eirodein, di alleis 'odou anechoreisan eis tein choran auton.

Hebrew/Transliteration
יב. וְהֵם צֻוּוּ בַחֲלוֹם לְבִלְתִּי שׁוּב אֶל-הוֹרְדוֹס וַיִּפְנוּ וַיֵּלְכוּ בְּדֶרֶךְ אַחֵר לְאַרְצָם:

12. Ve•hem tzoo•voo va•cha•lom le•vil•ti shoov el - Hordoos va•yif•noo va•yel•choo be•de•rech a•cher le•ar•tzam.

---

13. And when they were departed, behold, the angel of the Lord appeareth to Joseph in a dream, saying, Arise, and take the young child and his mother, and flee into Egypt, and be thou there until I bring thee word: for Herod will seek the young child to destroy him.

Greek/Transliteration
13. Ἀναχωρησάντων δὲ αὐτῶν, ἰδού, ἄγγελος κυρίου φαίνεται κατ' ὄναρ τῷ Ἰωσήφ, λέγων, Ἐγερθεὶς παράλαβε τὸ παιδίον καὶ τὴν μητέρα αὐτοῦ, καὶ φεῦγε εἰς Αἴγυπτον, καὶ ἴσθι ἐκεῖ ἕως ἂν εἴπω σοί· μέλλει γὰρ Ἡρῴδης ζητεῖν τὸ παιδίον, τοῦ ἀπολέσαι αὐτό.

13. Anachoreisanton de auton, idou, angelos kuriou phainetai kat onar to Yoseiph, legon, Egertheis paralabe to paidion kai tein meitera autou, kai pheuge eis Aigupton, kai isthi ekei 'eos an eipo soi. mellei gar 'Eirodeis zeitein to paidion, tou apolesai auto.

Hebrew/Transliteration
יג. וַיְהִי בְּלֶכְתָּם וַיֵּרָא מַלְאַךְ יְהוָֹה אֶל-יוֹסֵף בַּחֲלוֹם לֵאמֹר קוּם קַח אֶת-הַיֶּלֶד וְאֶת-אִמּוֹ וּבְרַח-לְךָ מִצְרַיְמָה:וְשֵׁב-שָׁם עַד-אֲשֶׁר אֹמַר אֵלֶיךָ כִּי הוֹרְדוֹס מְבַקֵּשׁ אֶת-נֶפֶשׁ הַיֶּלֶד לְקַחְתָּהּ

13. Vay•hi be•lech•tam va•ye•ra mal•ach Adonai el - Yo•sef ba•cha•lom le•mor koom kach et - ha•ye•led ve•et - ee•mo oov•rach - le•cha Mitz•rai•ma ve•shev - sham ad – asher o•mar e•le•cha ki Hordos me•va•kesh et - ne•fesh ha•ye•led le•kach•ta.

---

14. When he arose, he took the young child and his mother by night, and departed into Egypt:

Greek/Transliteration
14. Ὁ δὲ ἐγερθεὶς παρέλαβεν τὸ παιδίον καὶ τὴν μητέρα αὐτοῦ νυκτός, καὶ ἀνεχώρησεν εἰς Αἴγυπτον,

14. 'O de egertheis parelaben to paidion kai tein meitera autou nuktos, kai anechoreisen eis Aigupton,

Hebrew/Transliteration
יד. וַיָּקָם וַיִּקַּח אֶת-הַיֶּלֶד וְאֶת-אִמּוֹ לַיְלָה וַיֵּלֶךְ מִצְרָיְמָה:

14. Va•ya•kom va•yi•kach et - ha•ye•led ve•et - ee•mo lai•la va•ye•lech Mitz•rai•ma.

Rabbinic Jewish Commentary
The Jews say that Jesus went to Alexandria in Egypt, and which is probable enough; since this was a place greatly resorted to at this time by Jews, and where provision was made for their sustenance; though they greatly mistake the person with whom he went; for they say (f) that R. Joshua ben Perachiah, whom they pretend was his master, went to Alexandria in Egypt, and Jesus with him. However, this is an acknowledgment of the truth of this part of Christ's history, that he was in Egypt; as also when they blasphemously and maliciously say (g), did not Ben Stada, by whom they mean Jesus, bring enchantments or magic, כשפים ממצרים, "out of Egypt", in a cutting in the flesh? To which wicked accusation Arnobius seems to refer (h), when he says,

"perhaps we may meet with many other of these reproachful and childish sayings; as that he was a magician, that he performed all these things by secret arts, and that he stole strange sciences, and the names of mighty angels, out of the temples of the Egyptians."

(f) T. Bab. Sanhedrim, fol. 107. 2. Cabala R. Abraham. Juchasin, fol. 16. 2. (g) T. Hieros. Sabbat. fol. 13. 1. Bab. Sabbat. fol. 104. 2. (h) Adv. Gentes, l. 1. p. 36.

---

15. And was there until the death of Herod: that it might be fulfilled which was spoken of the Lord by the prophet, saying, Out of Egypt have I called my son.

Greek/Transliteration
15. καὶ ἦν ἐκεῖ ἕως τῆς τελευτῆς Ἡρῴδου· ἵνα πληρωθῇ τὸ ῥηθὲν ὑπὸ τοῦ κυρίου διὰ τοῦ προφήτου, λέγοντος, Ἐξ Αἰγύπτου ἐκάλεσα τὸν υἱόν μου.

15. kai ein ekei 'eos teis teleuteis 'Eirodou. 'ina pleirothei to 'reithen 'upo tou kuriou dya tou propheitou, legontos, Ex Aiguptou ekalesa ton 'wion mou.

Hebrew/Transliteration
טו. וַיֵּשֶׁב שָׁם עַד-מוֹת הוֹרְדוֹס לְמַלֹּאת אֶת אֲשֶׁר דִּבֶּר יְהֹוָה בְּיַד-הַנָּבִיא לֵאמֹר מִמִּצְרַיִם קָרָאתִי לִבְנִי:

15. Va•ye•shev sham ad - mot Hordos le•ma•lot et asher di•ber Adonai be•yad - ha•na•vee le•mor mi•Mitz•ra•yim ka•ra•ti liv•ni.

Rabbinic Jewish Commentary/Jewish New Testament Commentary
The idea that the Messiah personifies or is identified intimately with Israel is a Jewish one. First of all, we see it in the *Tanakh* itself. Compare Isa_49:3 ("You are my servant Israel, in whom I will be glorified.") with Isa_49:6 ("Is it too slight a thing that you should be my servant... to restore the preserved (of Israel?"). The servant is at once Israel and he who restores Israel, that is, the Messiah. In chapter 12 of Raphael Patai's *The Messiah Texts* he quotes Pesikta Rabbati 161-162, where the Messiah is called Efrayim (a name symbolizing Israel) and is at the same time presented as bearing Israel's sufferings. Likewise the thirteenth-century work which is at the core of the Jewish mystical approach called *kabbalah*, the Zohar (2:212a), links the Messiah's suffering with that of Israel. Patai also retells the eighteenth-century Rabbi Nachman of Bratslav's story of the viceroy and the king's daughter, adding that most interpreters understand the viceroy to represent both Israel and the suffering Messiah.

---

16. Then Herod, when he saw that he was mocked of the wise men, was exceeding wroth, and sent forth, and slew all the children that were in Bethlehem, and in all the coasts thereof, from two years old and under, according to the time which he had diligently inquired of the wise men.

Greek/Transliteration
16. Τότε Ἡρῴδης, ἰδὼν ὅτι ἐνεπαίχθη ὑπὸ τῶν μάγων, ἐθυμώθη λίαν, καὶ ἀποστείλας ἀνεῖλεν πάντας τοὺς παῖδας τοὺς ἐν Βηθλεὲμ καὶ ἐν πᾶσιν τοῖς ὁρίοις αὐτῆς, ἀπὸ διετοῦς καὶ κατωτέρω, κατὰ τὸν χρόνον ὃν ἠκρίβωσεν παρὰ τῶν μάγων.

16. Tote 'Eirodeis, idon 'oti enepaichthei 'upo ton magon, ethumothei lian, kai aposteilas aneilen pantas tous paidas tous en Beithle'em kai en pasin tois 'oriois auteis, apo dietous kai katotero, kata ton chronon 'on eikribosen para ton magon.

Hebrew/Transliteration
טז. וַיְהִי כִּרְאוֹת הוֹרְדוֹס כִּי הֵתֵלוּ בּוֹ הַחֹזִים וַיִּקְצֹף עַד-מְאֹד וַיִּשְׁלַח וַיַּךְ אֶת-כָּל-הַיְלָדִים אֲשֶׁר בְּבֵית-לֶחֶם:וּבְכָל-גְּבוּלֶיהָ מִבֶּן-שְׁנָתַיִם וּלְמָטָּה לְפִי הָעֵת אֲשֶׁר חָקַר מִפִּי הַחֹזִים

16. Vay•hi kir•ot Hordos ki he•te•loo vo ha•cho•zim va•yik•tzof ad - me•od va•yish•lach va•yach et - kol - ha•y`la•dim asher be•Veit - Le•chem oov•chol - g`voo•le•ha mi•ben - sh`na•ta•yim ool•ma•ta le•fi ha•et asher cha•kar mi•pi ha•cho•zim.

Historical/Rabbinic Jewish Commentary
The ancient Roman writer Macrobius (395 CE- 423 CE) [1], who lived in the 4th and 5th centuries, wrote the following words,

"Cum audisset inter pueros quos in Syria Herodes rex Iudaeorum intra bimatum iussit interfici filium quoque eius occisum, ait: Melius est Herodis porcum esse quam filium."

"When he [emperor Augustus] heard that among the boys in Syria under two years old whom Herod, king of the Jews, had ordered to kill, his own son was also killed, he said: 'It is better to be Herod's pig, than his son." Ambrosius Theodosius Macrobius, Saturnalia, Book II, Chapter IV:11

This cruel murder of the infants seems to be hinted at by Josephus (o), where he says, that "many slaughters followed the prediction of a new king"; and is more manifestly referred to by Macrobins, a Heathen author, though the story is mixed and confounded with other things; who reports (p), that

"when Augustus heard, that among the children under two years of age, whom Herod king of the Jews ordered to be slain in Syria, that his son was also killed, said, it was better to be Herod's hog than his son."

Killing of infants as soon as born, or while in their cradles, is by the Jews ascribed to one Lilith, which, R. Elias (q) says, is the name of a devil, which kills children; and indeed such an action is truly a diabolical one.

(o) Antiq. l. 17. c. 3. (p) Saturnal. l. 2. c. 4. (q) Methurgemau in voce **לילית**. Vid. Buxtorf. Lexicon Rab. in cadem voce & Synagog. Jud. c. 4. p. 80.

---

17. Then was fulfilled that which was spoken by Jeremy the prophet, saying,

Greek/Transliteration
17. Τότε ἐπληρώθη τὸ ῥηθὲν ὑπὸ Ἰερεμίου τοῦ προφήτου, λέγοντος,

17. Tote epleirothei to 'reithen 'upo Yeremiou tou propheitou, legontos,

Hebrew/Transliteration
יז. אָז הוּקַם אֲשֶׁר נֶאֱמַר בְּיַד-יִרְמְיָהוּ הַנָּבִיא לֵאמֹר

17. Az hoo•kam asher ne•e•mar be•yad - Yir•me•ya•hoo ha•na•vee le•mor.

Rabbinic Jewish Commentary

Another criticism is that Jeremiah 31:15-17 is not a Messianic prophecy and does not predict the death of the children in Bethlehem. As stated above, Jeremiah's words were written at the beginning of the Galut Bavel (Babylonian Exile) and in the midst of the ashes of Solomon's Temple. Exiles would pass by the grave of Rachel on the road to servitude, and Jeremiah poetically drew upon the history of Israel and its geography to inspire repentance and even hope. While all of this is true, the position that this passage is not Messianic and has no connection to what Matthew is writing misunderstands the profound nature of Matthew's *midrash*. Not only has its significance eluded skeptics, but even Christian commentators as well.

Was Matthew wrong, or was he pointing to something deeper than the surface understanding? The passage absolutely refers to the exile and beyond. Yet, the Babylonian exile is a part of a much larger exile process, which is exile from the Garden of Eden. The voice of Rachel's cry shakes the very foundations of Creation. Ramban writes,

"I have seen that Yonasan ben Uzziel . . . says, "A voice is heard in the heights of the universe…," and he translates the whole verse as talking about the Jewish nation. (Ramban on Genesis, Mesorah Publishers, pg. 245)

---

18. In Rama was there a voice heard, lamentation, and weeping, and great mourning, Rachel weeping for her children, and would not be comforted, because they are not.

Greek/Transliteration
18. Φωνὴ ἐν ʹΡαμᾶ ἠκούσθη, θρῆνος καὶ κλαυθμὸς καὶ ὀδυρμὸς πολύς, ʹΡαχὴλ κλαίουσα τὰ τέκνα αὐτῆς, καὶ οὐκ ἤθελεν παρακληθῆναι, ὅτι οὐκ εἰσίν.

18. Phonei en 'Rama eikousthei, threinos kai klauthmos kai odurmos polus, 'Racheil klaiousa ta tekna auteis, kai ouk eithelen parakleitheinai, 'oti ouk eisin.

Hebrew/Transliteration
יח. קוֹל בְּרָמָה נִשְׁמָע נְהִי בְּכִי תַמְרוּרִים רָחֵל מְבַכָּה עַל־בָּנֶיהָ מֵאֲנָה לְהִנָּחֵם כִּי אֵינֶנּוּ:

18. Kol be•Rama nish•ma n`hi be•chi tam•roo•rim Ra•chel me•va•ka al - ba•ne•ha me•a•na le•hi•na•chem ki ey•ne•noo.

Rabbinic Jewish Commentary/TaNaKh Old Testament

Midrash Rabbah says,"AND RACHEL DIED, AND WAS BURIED IN THE WAY TO EPHRATH" (35:19). What was Jacob's reason for burying Rachel in the way to Ephrath? Jacob foresaw that the exiles would pass on from thence,

therefore he buried her there so that she might pray for mercy for them. Thus it is written, 'A voice is heard in Ramah… Rachel weeping for her children…"
(Genesis Rabbah 82:10, Soncino Press Edition)

Jeremiah's passage, though difficult and painful, contains a distant glimmer of hope, "Thus says YHWH, 'A voice is heard in Ramah, lamentation, and bitter weeping, Rachel weeping for her children; she refuses to be comforted for her children, because they are no more. Thus says YHWH: "Refrain your voice from weeping, and your eyes from tears; for your work shall be rewarded," says YHWH, "and they shall come again from the land of the enemy. 'There is hope for your latter end,' says YHWH 'and your children shall come again to their own border." (Jeremiah 31:15-17)

It is well known within Judaism, that there is one person who can end the exile: The Mashiach. The Zohar illuminates the relationship of Rachel's weeping and the coming of Mashiach, "The Messiah…lifts up his eyes and beholds the Fathers (Patriarchs) visiting the ruins of God's Sanctuary. He perceives mother Rachel, with tears upon her face; the Holy One, blessed be He, tries to comfort her, but she refuses to be comforted (Jer. 31:14). Then the Messiah lifts up his voice and weeps, and the whole Garden of Eden quakes, and all the righteous and saints who are there break out in crying and lamentation with him…All through the seven days the Messiah shall be crowned on earth. Where shall this be? "By the way", to wit, Rachel's grave, which is on the cross-road. To mother Rachel he will give glad tidings and comfort her, and now she will let herself be comforted, and will rise and kiss him." (Soncino Zohar, Shemoth, Section 2, Page 8a-b.)

---

19. But when Herod was dead, behold, an angel of the Lord appeareth in a dream to Joseph in Egypt,

Greek/Transliteration
19. Τελευτήσαντος δὲ τοῦ Ἡρῴδου, ἰδού, ἄγγελος κυρίου κατ' ὄναρ φαίνεται τῷ Ἰωσὴφ ἐν Αἰγύπτῳ,

19. Teleuteisantos de tou 'Eirodou, idou, angelos kuriou kat onar phainetai to Yoseiph en Aigupto,

Hebrew/Transliteration
יט. וַיְהִי אַחֲרֵי מוֹת הוֹרְדוֹס וַיֵּרָא מַלְאַךְ יְהֹוָה בַּחֲלוֹם אֶל-יוֹסֵף בְּמִצְרַיִם לֵאמֹר:

19. Vay•hi a•cha•rey mot Hordos va•ye•ra mal•ach Adonai ba•cha•lom el - Yo•sef be•Mitz•ra•yim le•mor.

---

20. Saying, Arise, and take the young child and his mother, and go into the land of Israel: for they are dead which sought the young child's life.

Greek/Transliteration

20. λέγων, Ἐγερθεὶς παράλαβε τὸ παιδίον καὶ τὴν μητέρα αὐτοῦ, καὶ πορεύου εἰς γῆν Ἰσραήλ· τεθνήκασιν γὰρ οἱ ζητοῦντες τὴν ψυχὴν τοῦ παιδίου.

20. legon, Egertheis paralabe to paidion kai tein meitera autou, kai poreuou eis gein Ysraeil. tethneikasin gar 'oi zeitountes tein psuchein tou paidiou.

Hebrew/Transliteration

כ. קוּם קַח אֶת-הַיֶּלֶד וְאֶת-אִמּוֹ וְלֵךְ שׁוּב אַרְצָה יִשְׂרָאֵל כִּי-מֵתוּ הַמְבַקְשִׁים אֶת-נֶפֶשׁ הַיָּלֶד:

20. Koom kach et - ha•ye•led ve•et - ee•mo ve•lech shoov ar•tza Israel ki - me•too ha•m`vak•shim et - ne•fesh ha•ya•led.

---

21. And he arose, and took the young child and his mother, and came into the land of Israel.

Greek/Transliteration

21. Ὁ δὲ ἐγερθεὶς παρέλαβεν τὸ παιδίον καὶ τὴν μητέρα αὐτοῦ, καὶ ἦλθεν εἰς γῆν Ἰσραήλ.

21. 'O de egertheis parelaben to paidion kai tein meitera autou, kai eilthen eis gein Ysraeil.

Hebrew/Transliteration

כא. וַיָּקָם וַיִּקַּח אֶת-הַיֶּלֶד וְאֶת-אִמּוֹ וַיָּבֹא אַרְצָה יִשְׂרָאֵל:

21. Va•ya•kom va•yi•kach et - ha•ye•led ve•et - ee•mo va•ya•vo ar•tza Israel.

---

22. But when he heard that Archelaus did reign in Judaea in the room of his father Herod, he was afraid to go thither: notwithstanding, being warned of God in a dream, he turned aside into the parts of Galilee:

Greek/Transliteration

22. Ἀκούσας δὲ ὅτι Ἀρχέλαος βασιλεύει ἐπὶ τῆς Ἰουδαίας ἀντὶ Ἡρῴδου τοῦ πατρὸς αὐτοῦ, ἐφοβήθη ἐκεῖ ἀπελθεῖν· χρηματισθεὶς δὲ κατ' ὄναρ, ἀνεχώρησεν εἰς τὰ μέρη τῆς Γαλιλαίας,

22. Akousas de 'oti Archelaos basileuei epi teis Youdaias anti 'Eirodou tou patros autou, ephobeithei ekei apelthein. chreimatistheis de kat onar, anechoreisen eis ta merei teis Galilaias,

Hebrew/Transliteration

כב. וּבְשָׁמְעוֹ כִּי אַרְקְלוֹס מָלַךְ בִּיהוּדָה תַּחַת הוֹרְדוֹס אָבִיו וַיִּירָא לָלֶכֶת שָׁמָּה וַיֻּגַּד-לוֹ דָבָר בַּחֲלוֹם - וַיִּסֹּב אֶל:גְּלִילוֹת הַגָּלִיל

22. Oov•shom•oh ki Ar•kelos ma•lach bi•Y`hoo•da ta•chat Hordos aviv va•yi•ra la•le•chet sha•ma va•yoo•gad - lo da•var ba•cha•lom va•yi•sov el - g`li•lot ha•Galil.

Historical Commentary
"And now Herod altered his testament upon the alteration of his mind, for he appointed Antipas, to whom he had before left the kingdom, to be tetrarch of Galilee and Perea, and granted the kingdom to Archelaus."
(Josephus, Antiquities 17.8.1)

---

23. And he came and dwelt in a city called Nazareth: that it might be fulfilled which was spoken by the prophets, He shall be called a Nazarene.

Greek/Transliteration
23. καὶ ἐλθὼν κατῴκησεν εἰς πόλιν λεγομένην Ναζαρέτ· ὅπως πληρωθῇ τὸ ῥηθὲν διὰ τῶν προφητῶν, ὅτι Ναζωραῖος κληθήσεται.

23. kai elthon katokeisen eis polin legomenein Nazaret. 'opos pleirothei to 'reithen dya ton propheiton, 'oti Nazoraios kleitheisetai.

Hebrew/Transliteration
כג: וַיָּבֹא וַיֵּשֶׁב בָּעִיר הַנִּקְרֵאת נְצֶרֶת לְמַלֹּאת אֶת־דִּבְרֵי הַנְּבִיאִים כִּי נָצְרִי יִקָּרֵא לוֹ.

23. Va•ya•vo va•ye•shev ba•eer ha•nik•ret N`tza•ret le•ma•lot et - div•rey ha•n`vi•eem ki Notz•ri yi•ka•re lo.

Rabbinic/Jewish New Testament Commentary
Mattityahu is speaking of the prediction that the Messiah will be a *netzer* ("branch") from the stock of Yishai, King David's father (Isa_11:1); but compare Jer_23:5, Jer_33:15; Zec_3:8, Zec_6:12, where the word is "*tzemach*," ("sprout"). Thus several prophets use the idea, though not the word "*netzer*." (For more on "the prophets" see Mat_5:17.)

What I consider most probable is that Mattityahu is combining the second and third alternatives by means of wordplay, a technique very common in Jewish writing, including the Bible. Yeshua is both *netzer* and *Natzrati*.

Finally, although one of the earliest names for the Jewish believers was "*Notzrim*" ("Nazareth-ites," that is, "followers of the man from Nazareth," Act_24:5), it would be odd for Mattityahu to use the same term for the one they followed. The Talmud refers to him as *Yeshu HaNotzri* (B'rakhot 17b, Sotah 47a). In modern Hebrew "*Notzri*" remains the everyday word for "Christian"; but it is wrong and confusing to speak of "Yeshua the Christian," i.e., the follower of Christ-he could not follow himself! The Talmud's expression should be understood as meaning "Yeshua the *Natzrati*, Yeshua from Natzeret." I use the term "*Natzrati*" instead of "*Notzri*" (both are acceptable modern Hebrew) in order to get away from the modern connotations of "*Notzri*" in Hebrew.

(h). They also design him by בן נצר, "Ben Netzer" (i), of whom they say a great many evil things. (h) Ganz. par. 1. fol. 24. 2.

Matthew, Chapter 3

1. In those days came John the Baptist, preaching in the wilderness of Judaea,

Greek/Transliteration
1. Ἐν δὲ ταῖς ἡμέραις ἐκείναις παραγίνεται Ἰωάννης ὁ βαπτιστής, κηρύσσων ἐν τῇ ἐρήμῳ τῆς Ἰουδαίας,

1. En de tais 'eimerais ekeinais paraginetai Yoanneis 'o baptisteis, keirusson en tei ereimo teis Youdaias,

Hebrew/Transliteration
א. וַיְהִי בַּיָּמִים הָהֵם וַיָּבֹא יוֹחָנָן הַמַּטְבִּיל וַיִּקְרָא בְּמִדְבַּר יְהוּדָה וַיֹּאמַר:

1. Vay•hi ba•ya•mim ha•hem va•ya•vo Yo•cha•nan ha•Mat•bil va•yik•ra ve•mid•bar Yehooda va•yo•mar.

TaNaKh-Old Testament/Jewish New Testament Commentary
According to the *Torah* one had to be ritually pure before entering the Tabernacle or Temple. Ritual purity could be lost in many ways; the preeminent means of restoring it was through washing. A quick review of Leviticus shows how frequently the matter is mentioned, and one of the six major divisions of the Talmud (*Taharot*, "Cleansings") is devoted to it. Even though there is no longer a Temple, observant Jewish women immerse themselves in a *mikveh* (ritual bath) after each menstrual period, in obedience to Leviticus 15.

---

2. And saying, Repent ye: for the kingdom of heaven is at hand.

Greek/Transliteration
2. καὶ λέγων, Μετανοεῖτε· ἤγγικεν γὰρ ἡ βασιλεία τῶν οὐρανῶν.

2. kai legon, Metanoeite. eingiken gar 'ei basileia ton ouranon.

Hebrew/Transliteration
ב. שׁוּבוּ כִּי-מַלְכוּת הַשָּׁמַיִם קָרְבָה לָבֹא:

2. Shoo•voo ki - mal•choot ha•sha•ma•yim kar•va la•vo.

TaNaKh-Old Testament/Jewish New Testament Commentary
The Greek word "*metanoiete*," related to "*nous*" ("mind"), means "change your mind, have a complete change of heart." The underlying Hebrew concept is expressed in the word "*t'shuvah*" ("turning, returning"), which in the context of religious behavior means "turning" from one's sins and "returning" to God. Note that there is not only a "from" but a "to," for turning from one's sins is impossible unless at the same time one turns to God-otherwise one only turns from one set of sins to another! The Jewish understanding of repentance, correct on this point, is that each individual must do it, yet it requires God's grace (Lam_5:21)

The concept of the Kingdom of God is crucial to understanding the Bible. It refers neither to a place nor to a time, but to a condition in which the rulership of God is acknowledged by humankind, a condition in which God's promises of a restored universe free from sin and death are, or begin to be, fulfilled. It also refers to the accountability of mans sin that comes from the Kingdom of God through Yeshua.

Nor ought the Jews above all people to object to John's method of preaching; since they make repentance absolutely necessary to the revelation of the Messiah and his kingdom, and redemption by him; for they say (x) in so many words, that

"if Israel do not repent, they will never be redeemed; but as soon as they repent, they will be redeemed; yea, if they repent but one day, immediately the son of David will come."

(x) T. Hieros. Taanith, fol. 63. 4. & 64. 1. & Bab. Sanhed. fol. 97. 2.

---

3. For this is he that was spoken of by the prophet Esaias, saying, The voice of one crying in the wilderness, Prepare ye the way of the Lord, make his paths straight.

Greek/Transliteration

3. Οὗτος γάρ ἐστιν ὁ ῥηθεὶς ὑπὸ Ἡσαΐου τοῦ προφήτου, λέγοντος, Φωνὴ βοῶντος ἐν τῇ ἐρήμῳ, Ἑτοιμάσατε τὴν ὁδὸν κυρίου· εὐθείας ποιεῖτε τὰς τρίβους αὐτοῦ.

3. 'Outos gar estin 'o 'reitheis 'upo Eisaiou tou propheitou, legontos, Phonei boontos en tei ereimo, 'Etoimasate tein 'odon kuriou. eutheias poieite tas tribous autou.

Hebrew/Transliteration

ג׃ הוּא אֲשֶׁר נִבָּא עָלָיו יְשַׁעְיָהוּ הַנָּבִיא לֵאמֹר קוֹל קוֹרֵא בַּמִּדְבָּר פַּנּוּ דֶרֶךְ יְהֹוָה יַשְּׁרוּ מְסִלּוֹתָיו

3. Hoo asher ni•ba alav Ye•sha•a•ya•hoo ha•na•vee le•mor kol ko•re ba•mid•bar pa•noo de•rech Adonai yash•roo me•si•lo•tav.

Jewish New Testament Commentary

This quotation initiates the second part of the book of Isaiah (chapters 40-66), which offers comfort to Israel and contains many references to the Messiah. The one who cries is Yochanan, identified in spirit with the prophet Elijah;

KJV has, "The voice of one crying in the wilderness, Prepare ye the way of the Lord"; and most versions say that the crier is in the desert. But this is wrong; one learns it by examining the punctuation/cantillation marks in the Masoretic Hebrew text of Isaiah. These show that "in the desert" goes with "prepare the way," not with "someone crying." Although these markings are not God-inspired, they indicate how the text was read and understood at the time they were added (not later than the 8th century C.E.); and without a positive reason for understanding the text differently, it is best to assume these markings are correct.

---

4. And the same John had his raiment of camel's hair, and a leathern girdle about his loins; and his meat was locusts and wild honey.

Greek/Transliteration
4. Αὐτὸς δὲ ὁ Ἰωάννης εἶχεν τὸ ἔνδυμα αὐτοῦ ἀπὸ τριχῶν καμήλου, καὶ ζώνην δερματίνην περὶ τὴν ὀσφὺν αὐτοῦ· ἡ δὲ τροφὴ αὐτοῦ ἦν ἀκρίδες καὶ μέλι ἄγριον.

4. Autos de 'o Yoanneis eichen to enduma autou apo trichon kameilou, kai zonein dermatinein peri tein osphun autou. 'ei de trophei autou ein akrides kai meli agrion.

Hebrew/Transliteration
ד: וְיוֹחָנָן הָיָה לָבוּשׁ שְׂעַר גְּמַלִּים וְאֵזוֹר עוֹר אָזוּר בְּמָתְנָיו וּמַאֲכָלוֹ חֲגָבִים וּדְבַשׁ מִיַּעַר

4. Ve•Yo•cha•nan ha•ya la•voosh s`ar g`ma•lim ve•e•zor or A•zoor be•mot•nav oo•ma•a•cha•lo cha•ga•vim ood•vash mi•yaar.

TaNaKh O.T./Jewish New Testement Commentary
2 Kings describes Elijah the Prophet,
"They answered him, 'He was a hairy man, and wearing a leather belt around his waist.' He said, 'It is Elijah the Tishbite.' 2 Kings 1:8

Lev_11:21-22 mentions four species of locusts that may be eaten. Mishna Chullin 3:7 defines the characteristics of *kosher* locusts and in the Gemara, Chullin 65a-66a analyzes these rules at length. Locusts were food for the poor in Yeshua's day; Bedouins cook and eat them to this day, as did the Jews of Yemen before that community was removed to Israel by Operation Flying Carpet in 1950.

---

5. Then went out to him Jerusalem, and all Judaea, and all the region round about Jordan,

Greek/Transliteration
5. Τότε ἐξεπορεύετο πρὸς αὐτὸν Ἱεροσόλυμα καὶ πᾶσα ἡ Ἰουδαία καὶ πᾶσα ἡ περίχωρος τοῦ Ἰορδάνου·

5. Tote exeporeueto pros auton 'Yerosoluma kai pasa 'ei Youdaia kai pasa 'ei perichoros tou Yordanou.

Hebrew/Transliteration
ה: וַיֵּצְאוּ אֵלָיו יְרוּשָׁלַיִם וְכָל־יְהוּדָה וְכָל־כִּכַּר הַיַּרְדֵּן

5. Va•yetz•oo elav Ye•roo•sha•la•yim ve•chol - Yehooda ve•chol - ki•kar ha•Yarden.

---

6. And were baptized of him in Jordan, confessing their sins.

Greek/Transliteration
6. καὶ ἐβαπτίζοντο ἐν τῷ Ἰορδάνῃ ὑπ᾽ αὐτοῦ, ἐξομολογούμενοι τὰς ἁμαρτίας αὐτῶν.

6. kai ebaptizonto en to Yordanei 'up autou, exomologoumenoi tas 'amartias auton.

Hebrew/Transliteration
ו. וַיִּטָּבְלוּ עַל־יָדוֹ בַּיַּרְדֵּן בְּהִתְוַדֹּתָם אֶת־חַטֹּאתֵיהֶם:

6. Va•yi•tav•loo al - ya•do ba•Yarden be•hit•va•do•tam et - cha•to•tey•hem.

Jewish New Testament Commentary
Greek *exomologe*, "agree, admit, acknowledge, declare publicly, confess," literally, "say the same thing." In the case of confessing one's sins, one is saying the same thing about them that God says, acknowledging the deeds to be wrong, willing to declare publicly one's sorrow, guilt and resolution to change. On *Yom-Kippur* (the Day of Atonement) and other fast days, *s'lichot* (penitential prayers) are recited which can help people who say them with *kavvanah* (intention, devotion) to become more willing to admit their sins and agree with God's opinion of them. We live in an age when many people do not know what sin is. Sin is violation of *Torah* (1Jn_3:4), transgression of the law God gave his people in order to help them live a life which would be in their own best interests as well as holy and pleasing to God.

---

7. But when he saw many of the Pharisees and Sadducees come to his baptism, he said unto them, O generation of vipers, who hath warned you to flee from the wrath to come?

Greek/Transliteration
7. Ἰδὼν δὲ πολλοὺς τῶν Φαρισαίων καὶ Σαδδουκαίων ἐρχομένους ἐπὶ τὸ βάπτισμα αὐτοῦ, εἶπεν αὐτοῖς, Γεννήματα ἐχιδνῶν, τίς ὑπέδειξεν ὑμῖν φυγεῖν ἀπὸ τῆς μελλούσης ὀργῆς;

7. Idon de pollous ton Pharisaion kai Saddoukaion erchomenous epi to baptisma autou, eipen autois, Genneimata echidnon, tis 'upedeixen 'umin phugein apo teis mellouseis orgeis?

Hebrew/Transliteration
ז. אַךְ כַּאֲשֶׁר רָאָה רַבִּים מִן־הַפְּרוּשִׁים וּמִן־הַצַּדּוּקִים בָּאִים אֵלָיו לְהִטָּבֵל וַיֹּאמֶר לָהֶם יַלְדֵי צִפְעֹנִים מִי הוֹרָה־אֶתְכֶם לְהִמָּלֵט עַל־נַפְשְׁכֶם מִפְּנֵי חֲרוֹן אַף הַבָּא

7. Ach ka•a•sher ra•ah ra•bim min - ha•P`roo•shim oo•min - ha•Tza•doo•kim ba•eem elav le•hi•ta•vel va•yo•mer la•hem yal•dey tzif•o•nim mee ho•ra et•chem le•hi•ma•let al - naf•she•chem mip•ney cha•ron af ha•ba.

Rabbinic/Jewish New Testament Commentary

"Pharisees and Sadducees.", *P'rushim* and *Tz'dukim* (plural; singular *Parush*, *Tzadok*), These were the two main factions of the religious establishment in Yeshua's time. In 586 B.C.E. Babylon conquered Judea and Jerusalem, laid waste the First Temple, which King Solomon had built, and deported the ruling classes to Babylon. With the Temple, the sacrifices and the *cohanim* no longer functioning, the Jews in exile and after their return seventy years later sought another organizing principle on which to center their communal life. They found it in the *Torah* (the "Law"; see Mat_5:17), as can be seen already in the report of the reading of the *Torah* by Ezra (Nehemiah 8). The earliest students, developers and upholders of the *Torah* seem to have been of the hereditary priestly caste-Ezra himself was both a *cohen* and a *sofer* ("scribe"). But later, as the *cohanim* were drawn back into caring for the sacrificial system as it developed during the Second Temple period, a lay movement which supported the *Torah* and favored its adaptation to the needs of the people arose and began to challenge the authority of the *cohanim*. The *cohanim* and their backers in the first century C.E. were known as *Tz'dukim*, after the *cohen gadol* appointed by King Solomon, Tzadok (his name means "righteous"; compare Mat_6:1-4 Mat_13:17).

In Yeshua's day the *Tz'dukim* tended to be richer, more skeptical, more worldly, and more willing to cooperate with the Roman rulers than the *P'rushim*. However, the destruction of the Second Temple in 70 C.E. ended the viability of the *Tz'dukim* by destroying the venue of their chief responsibility; and whatever tradition they may have developed has for the most part been lost.

The Talmudic writers (z) say, there were "seven" sorts of them, and if it would not be too tedious to the reader, I would give the names of them; and the rather, because some of them seem to tally with the complexion and conduct of the Pharisees mentioned in the scriptures. There were then,

1. פרוש שיכמי the "Shechemite Pharisee", who does as Shechem did; is circumcised, not on God's account, or for his glory, or because circumcision is a command of his, but for his own profit and advantage, and that he may get honour from men.

2. פרוש ניקפי "the dashing Pharisee"; who walks gently, the heel of one foot touching the great toe of the other; and scarce lifts up his feet from the earth, so that he dashes them against the stones, and would be thought hereby to be in deep meditation.

3. פרוש קיזאי the "Pharisee letting blood"; who makes as if he shut his eyes, that he may not look upon women, and so runs and dashes his head against the wall, till the blood gushes out, as though a vein was opened.

4. **פרוש מדוכיא** the "depressed Pharisee"; who went double, or bowed down, or as others render the phrase, "the mortar Pharisee"; either because he wore a garment like a mortar, with the mouth turned downwards; or a hat resembling such a vessel; so that he could not look upward, nor on either side, only downward, or right forward.

5. **פרוש מה חובתי ואעשנה** the Pharisee, that said, what is my duty and I will do it? the gloss upon it is, teach me what is my duty, and I will do it: Lo! this is his excellency, if he is not expert in the prohibitions and niceties of the commands, and comes to learn; or thus, what is more to be done and I have not done it? so that he shows himself, or would appear as if he had performed all.

6. **פרוש יראה** "the Pharisee of fear"; who does what he does from fear of punishment.

7. **פרוש אהבה** "the Pharisee of love"; who does what he does from love; which the gloss explains thus: for the love of the reward of the commandment, and not for the love of the commandment of his Creator; though they say of all these there is none to be beloved, but the Pharisee of love.

The Jews say (a), that when the temple was destroyed the second time, the Pharisees increased in Israel.

(z) T. Hieros. Beracot, fol. 14. 2. & Sota fol. 20. 3. Bab. Sota, fol. 22. 2. eight sorts are reckoned in Abot R. Nathan, c. 37. fol. 8. 4. (a) T. Bab. Bava Bathra, fol. 60. 2.

---

8. Bring forth therefore fruits meet for repentance:

Greek/Translitration
8. Ποιήσατε οὖν καρπὸν ἄξιον τῆς μετανοίας·

8. Poieisate oun karpon axion teis metanoias.

Hebrew/Transliteration
ח. לָכֵן עֲשׂוּ פְּרִי טוֹב לִתְשׁוּבָה:

8. La•chen a•soo f ri tov lit•shoo•va.

---

9. And think not to say within yourselves, We have Abraham to our father: for I say unto you, that God is able of these stones to raise up children unto Abraham.

Greek/Transliteration
9. καὶ μὴ δόξητε λέγειν ἐν ἑαυτοῖς, Πατέρα ἔχομεν τὸν Ἀβραάμ· λέγω γὰρ ὑμῖν, ὅτι δύναται ὁ θεὸς ἐκ τῶν λίθων τούτων ἐγεῖραι τέκνα τῷ Ἀβραάμ.

9. kai mei doxeite legein en 'eautois, Patera echomen ton Abra'am. lego gar 'umin, 'oti dunatai 'o theos ek ton lithon touton egeirai tekna to Abra'am.

Hebrew/Transliteration
ט. וְאַל-תֶּהְגּוּ בִלְבַבְכֶם לֵאמֹר אַבְרָהָם לָנוּ לְאָב כִּי אֲנִי אֹמֵר לָכֶם גַּם מִן-אֲבָנִים אֵלֶּה תַּשִּׂיג יַד-אֱלֹהִים לְהָקִים־בָּנִים:לְאַבְרָהָם

9. Ve•al - te•he•goo vil•vav•chem le•mor Avraham la•noo le•av ki ani o•mer la•chem gam min - ava•nim ele ta•sig yad - Elohim le•ha•kim ba•nim le•Avraham.

Jewish New Testament Commentary
The Messianic Jewish scholar Alfred Edersheim wrote,
"[D]id they imagine that, according to the common notion of the time, the vials of wrath were to be poured out only on the Gentiles, while they, as Abraham's children, were sure of escape-in the words of the Talmud, that 'the night' (Isa_21:12) was 'only to the nations of the world, but the morning to Israel' (Jer. Ta'anit 64a)?

"For, no principle was more fully established in the popular conviction than that all Israel had part in the world to come (Sanhedrin 10:1 [quoted in Rom_11:26]), and this specifically because of their connection with Abraham." (*The Life and Times of Jesus the Messiah*, New York: Anson D. F. Randolph and Company, 2nd edition [1884], Volume I, p. 271)

The English phrase, "sons from these stones" is an attempt to preserve by alliteration the Hebrew wordplay which the Greek text ignores. "Sons" in Hebrew is *banim*, "stones" is written *abanim* (pronounced *avanim*). A less likely possibility is that "from these *stones*" means "from these clods, these *'am-ha'aretz*" (see Joh_7:49, Act_4:13). Wordplay has been common in Jewish speech from ancient times to the present, with many examples in the *Tanakh* itself; see Mat_2:23.

---

10. And now also the axe is laid unto the root of the trees: therefore every tree which bringeth not forth good fruit is hewn down, and cast into the fire.

Greek/Transliteration
10. Ἤδη δὲ καὶ ἡ ἀξίνη πρὸς τὴν ῥίζαν τῶν δένδρων κεῖται· πᾶν οὖν δένδρον μὴ ποιοῦν καρπὸν καλὸν ἐκκόπτεται καὶ εἰς πῦρ βάλλεται.

10. Eidei de kai 'ei axinei pros tein 'rizan ton dendron keitai. pan oun dendron mei poioun karpon kalon ekkoptetai kai eis pur balletai.

Hebrew/Transliteration
י. וְגַם-כְּבָר נָטוּי הַגַּרְזֶן עַל-שֹׁרֶשׁ הָעֵצִים וְלָכֵן כָּל-עֵץ אֲשֶׁר לֹא יַעֲשֶׂה פְּרִי טוֹב יִגָּדַע וְהָשְׁלַךְ בְּמוֹ-אֵשׁ:

10. Ve•gam - k`var na•tooy ha•gar•zen al - sho•resh ha•e•tzim ve•la•chen kol - etz asher lo ya•a•se f'ri tov yi•ga•da ve•hosh•lach be•mo - esh.

Rabbinic/Jewish New Testament Commentary

Some commentators see this as a purifying fire that will eliminate the wicked from the Jewish people along lines set forth in Mal_3:19-21 (Mal_4:1-3) and Psa_1:6 ("The way of the wicked will perish"); see Rev_20:15. The same psalm also compares the ungodly with straw (Psa_1:4). Others take it as enthusiasm for holiness, being on fire for God.

There is an opinion that the fig was the fruit of the tree of knowledge and good and evil, "R' Meir holds that the tree of which Adam ate was the vine, since the thing that most causes wailing to a man is wine, as it says, And he drank of the wine and was drunken. R' Nehemiah says it was the fig tree, so that they repaired their misdeed with the instrument of it, as it says, 'And they sewed fig leaves together." (Berakhot 40a, Soncino Press Edition)

Therefore they shall fall among those who fall, in the time of their visitation they shall be cast down,' says YHWH. 'I will utterly consume them,' says YHWH,'there shall be no grapes on the vine, nor figs on the fig tree, and the leaf shall fade, and the things that I have given them, those who pass over them."
(Jeremiah 8:10-13)

---

11. I indeed baptize you with water unto repentance: but he that cometh after me is mightier than I, whose shoes I am not worthy to bear: he shall baptize you with the Holy Ghost, and with fire:

Greek/Transliteration

11. Ἐγὼ μὲν βαπτίζω ὑμᾶς ἐν ὕδατι εἰς μετάνοιαν· ὁ δὲ ὀπίσω μου ἐρχόμενος ἰσχυρότερός μου ἐστίν, οὗ οὐκ εἰμὶ ἱκανὸς τὰ ὑποδήματα βαστάσαι· αὐτὸς ὑμᾶς βαπτίσει ἐν πνεύματι ἁγίῳ.

11. Ego men baptizo 'umas en 'udati eis metanoyan. 'o de opiso mou erchomenos ischuroteros mou estin, 'ou ouk eimi 'ikanos ta 'upodeimata bastasai. autos 'umas baptisei en pneumati 'agio.

Hebrew/Transliteration

יא. וַאֲנִי הִנְנִי מְטַבֵּל אֶתְכֶם בַּמַּיִם לִתְשׁוּבָה אַךְ הַבָּא אַחֲרַי חָסֹן הוּא מִמֶּנִּי אֲשֶׁר קָטֹנְתִּי מִשֵּׂאת אֶת־נְעָלָיו הוּא: יְטַבֵּל אֶתְכֶם בְּרוּחַ הַקֹּדֶשׁ וּבָאֵשׁ

11. Va•a•ni hi•ne•ni me•ta•bel et•chem ba•ma•yim lit•shoo•va ach ha•ba a•cha•rai cha•son hoo mi•me•ni asher ka•ton•ti mi•s•et et - n`a•lav hoo ye•ta•bel et•chem be•Roo•ach ha•Ko•desh oo•va•esh.

Rabbinic/Jewish Commentary

In the Talmud (e) it is asked, "What is the manner of possessing of servants? or what is their service? He buckles his (master's) shoes; he "unlooses his shoes", and "carries them before him to the bath.""

Or, as is elsewhere (f) said, "he unlooses his shoes, or carries after him his vessels (whatever he wants) to the bath; he unclothes him, he washes him, he anoints him, he rubs him, he clothes him, he buckles his shoes, and lifts him up."

This was such a servile work, that it was thought too mean for a scholar or a disciple to do; for it is (g) said,

"all services which a servant does for his master, a disciple does for his master, חוץ מהתרת לו מנעל, "except unloosing his shoes"."

The gloss on it says, "he that sees it, will say, he is a "Canaanitish servant":"

for only a Canaanitish, not an Hebrew servant (h), might be employed in, or obliged to such work; for it was reckoned not only, mean and servile, but even base and reproachful. It is one of their (i) canons;

"if thy brother is become poor, and is sold unto thee, thou shalt not make him do the work of a servant; that is, עבורת של נגאי, any reproachful work; such as to buckle his shoes, or unloose them, or carry his instruments (or necessaries) after him to the bath."

In the Talmud (k) one puts the question, In what does he (God,) dip? You will say in water, as it is written, "who hath measured the waters in the hollow of his hand?" Another replies, בנורא טביל, "he dips in fire"; as it is written, "for behold the Lord will come with fire". What is the meaning of טבילותא בנורא, "baptism in fire?" He answers, according to the mind of Rabbah, the root of "dipping in the fire", is what is written; "all that abideth not the fire, ye shall make go" through the water. Dipping in the fire of the law, is a phrase used by the Jews (l). The phrases of "dipping, and washing in fire", are also used by Greek (m) authors.

(e) T. Hieros. Kiddushin, fol. 59. 4. Maimon. & T. Bartenora in Misu. Kiddushin, c. 1. sect. 3. (f) T. Bab. Kiddushin, fol. 22. 2. Maimon. Hilch. Mechirah, c. 2. sect. 2. (g) T. Bab. Cetubot, fol. 96. 1. Maimon. Talmud Torn, c. 5. sect. 8. (h) Maimon. Hilch. Abadim, c. 1. sect. 7. (i) Moses Kotzensis Mitzvot Torah, precept. neg. 176. (k) T. Bab. Sanhedrim, fol. 39. 1. (l) Tzeror Hammor. fol. 104. 4. & 142. 3. & 170. 1. (m) Moschi Idyll. 1. Philostrat, Vit. Apollon, l. 3. c. 5.

---

12. Whose fan is in his hand, and he will throughly purge his floor, and gather his wheat into the garner; but he will burn up the chaff with unquenchable fire.

Greek/Transliteration
12. Οὗ τὸ πτύον ἐν τῇ χειρὶ αὐτοῦ, καὶ διακαθαριεῖ τὴν ἅλωνα αὐτοῦ, καὶ συνάξει τὸν σῖτον αὐτοῦ εἰς τὴν ἀποθήκην, τὸ δὲ ἄχυρον κατακαύσει πυρὶ ἀσβέστῳ.

12. 'Ou to ptuon en tei cheiri autou, kai dyakathariei tein 'alona autou, kai sunaxei ton siton autou eis tein apotheikein, to de achuron katakausei puri asbesto.

Hebrew/Transliteration
יב. אֲשֶׁר מִזְרֵהוּ בְיָדוֹ לִזְרוֹת וּלְהָבֵר אֶת-גָּרְנוֹ וְאָסַף אֶת-הַחִטִּים אֶל-תּוֹךְ אֲסָמָיו וְאֶת-הַמֹּץ יִשְׂרֹף בָּאֵשׁ אֲשֶׁר לֹא:תִכְבֶּה

12. Asher miz•re•hoo ve•ya•do liz•rot ool•ha•ver et - gor•no ve•a•saf et - ha•chi•tim el - toch asa•mav ve•et - ha•motz yis•rof ba•esh asher lo tich•be.

Rabbinic Jewish Commentary
John the Immerser prophesied from the beginning of his mission that Yeshua would cleanse the Temple. The term "threshing floor" refers to the Temple, as David purchased the plot of land for the altar,

"Gad came that day to David, and said to him, 'Go up, build an altar to YHWH on the threshing floor of Araunah the Jebusite."
(2 Samuel 24:18)

To understand the deeper meaning behind the Temple cleansing, we must note that it is bracketed by the cursing of the fig tree. The Fig Tree is a key to understand the cleansing of the Temple and the spiritual status of First Century Israel. Why did Yeshua curse the Fig Tree? Anti-missionaries and skeptics have attacked Yeshua's action as an unnecessary, petty tantrum. On the other side of the coin, some Christian interpretations attempt to use the text for theological proof that Yeshua was canceling God's covenant with Israel, cursing the nation or the Temple. This idea explicitly contradicts the teachings of Yeshua and even his instruction to leper to offer the gift that Moshe commanded (Matthew 8:4).

That this is the meaning of the "Baptist", seems evident, since "fanning" is always, when figuratively taken, used for judgments, Isa_41:16. By "his floor", is meant the land of Israel, where he was born, brought up, and lived; of which the Lord says, "O my threshing, and the corn of my floor!" Isa_21:10. This, he says, "he will thoroughly purge" of all his refuse and chaff, that is, by fanning: so fanning and cleansing, or purging, are joined together, Jer_4:11 so ברר is used for purging by fanning, in the Misnic writings (o). By "his wheat", are meant his elect among the Jews, the chosen of God and precious; so called because of their excellency, purity, usefulness, solidity, and constancy: these he "will gather into his garner"; meaning either some place of protection, where he would direct his people to for safety from that wrath, ruin, and destruction; which should fall upon the Jewish nation; or else the kingdom of heaven, into which he would bring them, by taking them out of the world from the evil to come. By "the chaff", are meant wicked and ungodly persons, such as are destitute of the grace of God, whether professors, or profane; being empty, barren, and unfruitful; and so good for nothing but the fire, which therefore "he will burn with unquenchable fire", of divine wrath and vengeance: an allusion to a custom among the Jews, who, when they purified the increase of their unclean fields, gathered it together in an "area" or floor, in the midst of them, and then sifted it with sieves; one sort with two sieves, another with three, that they might thoroughly purge it, and burnt the chaff and stalks (p); see Isa_5:24. (o) Misn. Sabbat. c. 7. sect. 2. & Gittin, c. 5. sect. 9. (p) Misn. Oholot. c. 18. sect. 2.

---

13. Then cometh Jesus from Galilee to Jordan unto John, to be baptized of him.

Greek/Transliteration
13. Τότε παραγίνεται ὁ Ἰησοῦς ἀπὸ τῆς Γαλιλαίας ἐπὶ τὸν Ἰορδάνην πρὸς τὸν Ἰωάννην, τοῦ βαπτισθῆναι ὑπ᾽ αὐτοῦ.

13. Tote paraginetai 'o Yeisous apo teis Galilaias epi ton Yordanein pros ton Yoannein, tou baptistheinai 'up autou.

Hebrew/Transliteration
:יג. אָז יָבֹא יֵשׁוּעַ מִן-הַגָּלִיל אֶל-הַיַּרְדֵּן לִפְנֵי יוֹחָנָן לְהִטָּבֵל עַל-יָדוֹ

13. Az ya•vo Yeshua min - ha•Galil el - ha•Yarden lif•ney Yo•cha•nan le•hi•ta•vel al - ya•do.

---

14. But John forbad him, saying, I have need to be baptized of thee, and comest thou to me?

Greek/Transliteration
14. Ὁ δὲ Ἰωάννης διεκώλυεν αὐτόν, λέγων, Ἐγὼ χρείαν ἔχω ὑπὸ σοῦ βαπτισθῆναι, καὶ σὺ ἔρχῃ πρός με;

14. 'O de Yoanneis diekoluen auton, legon, Ego chreian echo 'upo sou baptistheinai, kai su erchei pros me?

Hebrew/Transliteration
:יד. וַיַּעֲצָר-בּוֹ יוֹחָנָן לֵאמֹר הֲלֹא נָכוֹן לִי לְהִטָּבֵל עַל-יָדְךָ וְאַתָּה בָּאתָ אֵלָי

14. Va•ya•a•tzor - bo Yo•cha•nan le•mor ha•lo na•chon li le•hi•ta•vel al - yad•cha ve•a•ta ba•ta e•lai.

---

15. And Jesus answering said unto him, Suffer it to be so now: for thus it becometh us to fulfill all righteousness. Then he suffered him.

Greek/Transliteration
15. Ἀποκριθεὶς δὲ ὁ Ἰησοῦς εἶπεν πρὸς αὐτόν, Ἄφες ἄρτι· οὕτως γὰρ πρέπον ἐστὶν ἡμῖν πληρῶσαι πᾶσαν δικαιοσύνην. Τότε ἀφίησιν αὐτόν.

15. Apokritheis de 'o Yeisous eipen pros auton, Aphes arti. 'outos gar prepon estin 'eimin pleirosai pasan dikaiosunein. Tote aphieisin auton.

Hebrew/Transliteration
:טו. וַיַּעַן יֵשׁוּעַ וַיֹּאמֶר אֵלָיו הֶרֶף כַּיּוֹם כִּי-כֹה יָאֲתָה לָנוּ לְמַלֵּא כָל-צְדָקָה וַיֶּרֶף מִמֶּנּוּ

15. Va•ya•an Yeshua va•yo•mer elav he•ref ka•yom ki - cho ya•a•ta la•noo le•ma•le chol - tze•da•ka va•yi•ref mi•me•noo.

Jewish New Testament Commentary
Yeshua himself did not have to be immersed for his sins because he committed none (Heb_4:15). Some have suggested he was fully identifying with sinful humanity, who did need purification (see Mat_2:15, Rom_8:3, Php_2:6-8). On what it is that God's righteousness requires, see Rom_3:24-26.

---

16. And Jesus, when he was baptized, went up straightway out of the water: and, lo, the heavens were opened unto him, and he saw the Spirit of God descending like a dove, and lighting upon him:

Greek/Transliteration
16. Καὶ βαπτισθεὶς ὁ Ἰησοῦς ἀνέβη εὐθὺς ἀπὸ τοῦ ὕδατος· καὶ ἰδού, ἀνεῴχθησαν αὐτῷ οἱ οὐρανοί, καὶ εἶδεν τὸ πνεῦμα τοῦ θεοῦ καταβαῖνον ὡσεὶ περιστερὰν καὶ ἐρχόμενον ἐπ᾽ αὐτόν.

16. Kai baptistheis 'o Yeisous anebei euthus apo tou 'udatos. kai idou, aneochtheisan auto 'oi ouranoi, kai eiden to pneuma tou theou katabainon 'osei peristeran kai erchomenon ep auton.

Hebrew/Transliteration
טז. וַיִּטָּבֵל יֵשׁוּעַ וַיְמַהֵר וַיַּעַל מִן-הַמַּיִם וְהִנֵּה נִפְתְּחוּ-לוֹ הַשָּׁמַיִם וַיַּרְא אֶת-רוּחַ אֱלֹהִים יֹרֶדֶת בִּדְמוּת-יוֹנָה:וַתָּנַח עָלָיו

16. Va•yi•ta•vel Yeshua vay•ma•her va•ya•al min - ha•ma•yim ve•hee•ne nif•te•choo – lo ha•sha•ma•yim va•yar et - Roo•ach Elohim yo•re•det bid•moot - yo•na va•ta•nach alav.

Rabbinic Jewish Commentary
As Yeshua was in the waters, and the dove was hovering over him, one of the meanings is that he is the Beginning of the New Creation, as Genesis says, "The Spirit of G-d was hovering over the surface of the waters."
(Genesis 1:2)

The Targum interprets,
"...and the Spirit of mercies from before the Lord breathed upon the face of the waters. Targum Pseudo-Jonathan on Gen 1:2

Rebbe Nachman says,
"...[Mashiach's] "breathing" will have a very positive effect upon mankind. . . The breath that Mashiach will breathe will emanate from the Torah and its 613 mitzvot. This is "The spirit of God [that] hovered over the waters." The spirit is Mashiach and the waters are the Torah. Mashiach's spirit is embedded in the Torah and he will draw his breath, the awe of God, from it. With this spirit, he will be able to "breathe into others" filing them with an awe and respect for God."
(Mashiach, Who, What, Why, How, Where, When, Chaim Kramer, Breslov Research Institute, pg.63)

A curious tale is told of Ben zoma in the Talmud,
"Our Rabbis taught: Once R. Joshua b. Hanania was standing on a step on the Temple Mount, and Ben Zoma saw him and did not stand up before him. So [R. Joshua] said to him: Whence and whither, Ben Zoma?5 He replied: I was gazing between the upper and the lower waters, and there is only a bare three fingers [breadth] between them, for it is said: And the spirit of God hovered over the face of the waters like a dove which hovers over her young without touching [them].8 Thereupon R. Joshua said to his disciples: Ben Zoma is still outside. See now, when was it that the spirit of God hovered over the face of the water? On the first day [of Creation]; but the division took place on the second day, for it is written: And let it divide the waters from the waters! And how big [is the interval]? R. Aha b. Jacob said, As a hair's breadth; and the Rabbis said: As [between] the boards of a landing bridge. Mar Zutra, or according to others R. Assi, said: As [between] two cloaks spread one over the other; and others say, as [between] two cups tilted one over the other." (Chagigah 15a, Soncino Press Edition)

Rashi comments,
"The Throne of Glory was suspended in the air and hovered over the face of the water with the breath of the mouth of the Holy One, blessed be He and with His word, *like a dove*, which hovers over the nest . . . " (Rashi, Chabad.org)

Genesis Rabbah says,
"AND THE SPIRIT OF GOD HOVERED: this alludes to the spirit of Messiah, as you read, *And the spirit of the Lord shall rest upon him* (Isaiah 11:2). In the merit of what will [this spirit] eventually come? [For the sake of that which] HOVERED OVER THE FACE OF THE WATERS, i.e. in the merit of repentance which is likened to water, as it is written, *Pour out thy heart like water* (Lamentations 2:19)." (Genesis Rabbah 2:4, Soncino Press Edition)

The Spirit of God, here said to descend and light on Christ, is the same, which in the first creation moved upon the face of the waters; and now comes down on Christ, just as he was coming up out of the waters of Jordan, where he had been baptized; and which the Jews (r) so often call של מלך המשיח רוח, "the Spirit of the king Messiah, and the spirit of the Messiah". The descent of him was in a "bodily shape", as Luke says in Luk_3:22.

Zohar (s); "a door shall be opened, and out of it shall come forth the dove which Noah sent out in the days of the flood, as it is written, "and he sent forth the dove", that famous dove; but the ancients speak not of it, for they knew not what it was, only from whence it came, and did its message; as it is written, "it returned not again unto him any more": no man knows whither it went, but it returned to its place, and was hid within this door; and it shall take a crown in its mouth, and put it upon the head of the king Messiah."

(r) Bereshit Rabba, fol. 2. 4. & 6. 3. Vajikra Rabba, fol. 156. 4. Zohar in Gen. fol. 107. 3. & 128. 3. Baal Hatturim in Gen. i. 2. Caphtor Uperah, fol. 113. 2. (s) In Num. fol. 68. 3, 4.

---

17. And lo a voice from heaven, saying, This is my beloved Son, in whom I am well pleased.

Greek/Transliteration
17. Καὶ ἰδού, φωνὴ ἐκ τῶν οὐρανῶν, λέγουσα, Οὗτός ἐστιν ὁ υἱός μου ὁ ἀγαπητός, ἐν ᾧ εὐδόκησα.

17. Kai idou, phonei ek ton ouranon, legousa, 'Outos estin 'o 'wios mou 'o agapeitos, en 'o eudokeisa.

Hebrew/Transliteration
יז. וְהִנֵּה קוֹל קֹרֵא מִשָּׁמַיִם זֶה הוּא בְנִי יְדִידִי בּוֹ רָצְתָה נַפְשִׁי:

17. Ve•hee•ne kol ko•re mi•sha•ma•yim ze hoo V`ni ye•di•di bo ratz•ta naf•shi.

Jewish New Testament Commentary
While it is true that everyone is in a sense God's son, Yeshua is so in a unique way-his "only" (or "only-begotten") son (Joh_1:18). Two other passages come to mind: one in which Adam is referred to as God's son (Luk_3:23), and Psa_2:7, "*Adonai* said to me, 'You are my son; today I have become your father.' "Combined with 1Co_15:45, in which Yeshua is called "the last Adam," and Rom_5:12-21, where Yeshua and Adam are further compared, these texts show us that in thinking about Yeshua's person and ministry one must keep Adam in mind. This is especially important in the verses immediately following, in which Yeshua, like Adam, is tempted by the Adversary, Satan. See also Mat_3:15.

The language is reminiscent of Isa_42:1, one of the "Servant" passages; Isa_42:1-4 is quoted below (Mat_12:18-21); see also Mat_17:5. The "Servant" passages sometimes refer to the people of Israel and sometimes to the Messiah, a fact which strengthens the point made in Mat_2:15 that Yeshua the Messiah represents and stands for the whole Jewish people.

Matthew, Chapter 4

1. Then was Jesus led up of the Spirit into the wilderness to be tempted of the devil.

Greek/Transliteration
1. Τότε ὁ Ἰησοῦς ἀνήχθη εἰς τὴν ἔρημον ὑπὸ τοῦ πνεύματος, πειρασθῆναι ὑπὸ τοῦ διαβόλου.

1. Tote 'o Yeisous aneichthei eis tein ereimon 'upo tou pneumatos, peirastheinai 'upo tou dyabolou.

Hebrew/Transliteration
א: אָז הוּבַל יֵשׁוּעַ בָּרוּחַ הַמִּדְבָּרָה לְבַעֲבוּר יְנַסֵּהוּ שָׁם הַשָּׂטָן.

1. Az hoo•val Yeshua ba•Roo•ach ha•mid•ba•ra le•va•a•voor ye•na•se•hoo sham ha•Satan.

Jewish New Testament Commentary
Greek *diabolos* (usually transliterated "devil") translates Hebrew *satan*, "adversary, opponent, rebel." In Isa_14:11-15, between the lines of a taunt against the king of Babylon, can be read the downfall of a creature who was once both powerful and beautiful but who in pride rebelled against God and came to oppose him; Eze_28:11-19 is similar.

---

2. And when he had fasted forty days and forty nights, he was afterward an hungred.

Greek/Transliteration
2. Καὶ νηστεύσας ἡμέρας τεσσαράκοντα καὶ νύκτας τεσσαράκοντα, ὕστερον ἐπείνασεν.

2. Kai neisteusas 'eimeras tessarakonta kai nuktas tessarakonta, 'usteron epeinasen.

Hebrew/Transliteration
ב: וַיָּצָם אַרְבָּעִים יוֹם וְאַרְבָּעִים לַיְלָה וַיִּרְעָב.

2. Va•ya•tzom ar•ba•eem yom ve•ar•ba•eem lai•la va•yir•av.

Rabbinic/Old Testament Commentary
Matthew includes the detail that Yeshua not only fasts for forty days, but also for "forty nights". This links to Exodus 34:28,

"He was there with the HaShem forty days and forty nights; he neither ate bread, nor drank water. He wrote on the tablets the words of the covenant, the Ten Commandments." (Exodus 34:28)

The Midrash says,
"AND HE WAS THERE WITH THE LORD FORTY DAYS AND FORTY NIGHTS (XXXIV, 28). Is it then possible for any man to be forty days without food or drink? ...When Moses ascended on high, where there is no eating or drinking, he emulated the heavenly example...For whereas the entire world and the fullness thereof were created in six days, the Torah was given at the end of forty days.' HE DID NEITHER EAT BREAD, eating only the bread of the Torah: NOR DRINK WATER. drinking only of the water of the Torah. He learnt [fresh] Torah by day and revised it by himself at night. Why did he do thus? In order to teach ...Another explanation of AND HE WAS THERE WITH THE LORD. HE DID NEITHER EAT BREAD, NOR DRINK WATER, that is, in this world; but in the World to Come he will eat of the bread of the Torah and drink of its waters. For this reason HE DID NEITHER EAT BREAD, etc. Whence did he derive his nourishment?- From the lustre of God's presence. Lest this seem surprising, then remember that the Chayyot who bear the Divine Throne are also nourished from the splendor of the Shechinah." (Exodus Rabbah 47:5, Soncino Press Edition)

---

3. And when the tempter came to him, he said, If thou be the Son of God, command that these stones be made bread.

Greek/Transliteration
3. Καὶ προσελθὼν αὐτῷ ὁ πειράζων εἶπεν, Εἰ υἱὸς εἶ τοῦ θεοῦ, εἰπὲ ἵνα οἱ λίθοι οὗτοι ἄρτοι γένωνται.

3. Kai proselthon auto 'o peirazon eipen, Ei 'wios ei tou theou, eipe 'ina 'oi lithoi 'outoi artoi genontai.

Hebrew/Transliteration
‎:ג. וַיִּגַּשׁ הַמְנַסֶּה וַיֹּאמֶר אֵלָיו אִם בֶּן-הָאֱלֹהִים אַתָּה אֱמֹר וַאֲבָנִים אֵלֶּה תִּהְיֶינָה לְלָחֶם

3. Va•yi•gash ham•na•se va•yo•mer elav eem Ben - ha•Elohim ata emor va•a•va•nim ele ti•hi•ye•na le•la•chem.

Jewish New Testament/Rabbinic Commentary
The *Tanakh* says little explicitly about Son of God, yet it does offer strong *r'mazim* ("hints"; see Mat_2:15) at Isa_9:5-6 (Isa_9:6-7), Mic_5:1 (Mic_5:2), Psa_2:7, Pro_30:4 and Dan_7:13. In ancient Jewish literature Enoch 105:2 and , 4 Ezra 7:28-29, 13:32-52, 14:9 refer to the Messiah as the Son of God. Compare Mat_8:20 on "son of man."

The ancient mystical Zohar explaniation of "You Are My Son", from Psalm 2:7, says that in order for the Messiah to accomplish his task He must be clothed with divine attributes (binah). The Zohar also states that this Son of God must have two sides: Son of David and Son of Joseph.

4. But he answered and said, It is written, Man shall not live by bread alone, but by every word that proceedeth out of the mouth of God.

Greek/Transliteration
4. Ὁ δὲ ἀποκριθεὶς εἶπεν, Γέγραπται, Οὐκ ἐπ' ἄρτῳ μόνῳ ζήσεται ἄνθρωπος, ἀλλ' ἐπὶ παντὶ ῥήματι ἐκπορευομένῳ διὰ στόματος θεοῦ.

4. 'O de apokritheis eipen, Gegraptai, Ouk ep arto mono zeisetai anthropos, all epi panti 'reimati ekporeuomeno dya stomatos theou.

Hebrew/Transliteration
:ד. וַיַּעַן וַיֹּאמֶר כָּתוּב כִּי לֹא עַל-הַלֶּחֶם לְבַדּוֹ יִחְיֶה הָאָדָם כִּי עַל-כָּל-מוֹצָא פִי-יְהֹוָה

4. Va•ya•an va•yo•mar ka•toov ki lo al - ha•le•chem le•va•do yich•ye ha•a•dam ki al - kol - mo•tza fi - Adonai.

Old Testament/Jewish New Testament Commentary
"And He has humbled you, and caused you to hunger, and caused you to eat the manna, which you had not known, and your fathers had not known, in order to cause you to know that man shall not live by bread alone, but man shall live by every Word that proceeds from the mouth of YAHWEH." (Deuteronomy 8:4)

The Old Testament-rendered "Scripture" or "it is written" in most translations. The Hebrew word "*Tanakh*" is an acronym formed from the first letters of the three parts of the Hebrew Bible:

(1) *Torah* ("Teaching")-the Five Books of Moses or Pentateuch (Genesis, Exodus, Leviticus, Numbers, Deuteronomy).
(2) *N'vi'im* ("Prophets")-the historical books (Joshua, Judges, Samuel and Kings), the three Major Prophets (Isaiah, Jeremiah, Ezekiel), and the twelve Minor Prophets.
(3) *K'tuvim* ("Writings")-Psalms, Proverbs, Job, the "five scrolls" (Song of Songs, Ruth, Lamentations, Ecclesiastes, Esther), Daniel, Ezra-Nehemiah and Chronicles.

---

5. Then the devil taketh him up into the holy city, and setteth him on a pinnacle of the temple,

Greek/Transliteration
5. Τότε παραλαμβάνει αὐτὸν ὁ διάβολος εἰς τὴν ἁγίαν πόλιν, καὶ ἵστησιν αὐτὸν ἐπὶ τὸ πτερύγιον τοῦ ἱεροῦ,

5. Tote paralambanei auton 'o dyabolos eis tein 'agian polin, kai 'isteisin auton epi to pterugion tou 'ierou,

Hebrew/Transliteration
:ה. וַיִּקָּחֵהוּ הַשָּׂטָן אֶל-עִיר הַקֹּדֶשׁ וַיַּעֲמִדֵהוּ עַל-פִּנַּת גַּג בֵּית-הַמִּקְדָּשׁ

5. Va•yi•ka•che•hoo ha•Satan el - eer ha•ko•desh va•ya•a•mi•de•hoo al - pi•nat gag beit - ha•mik•dash.

---

6. And saith unto him, If thou be the Son of God, cast thyself down: for it is written, He shall give his angels charge concerning thee: and in their hands they shall bear thee up, lest at any time thou dash thy foot against a stone.

Greek/Transliteration

6. καὶ λέγει αὐτῷ, Εἰ υἱὸς εἶ τοῦ θεοῦ, βάλε σεαυτὸν κάτω· γέγραπται γὰρ ὅτι Τοῖς ἀγγέλοις αὐτοῦ ἐντελεῖται περὶ σοῦ, καὶ ἐπὶ χειρῶν ἀροῦσίν σε, μήποτε προσκόψῃς πρὸς λίθον τὸν πόδα σοῦ.

6. kai legei auto, Ei 'wios ei tou theou, bale seauton kato. gegraptai gar 'oti Tois angelois autou enteleitai peri sou, kai epi cheiron arousin se, meipote proskopseis pros lithon ton poda sou.

Hebrew/Transliteration

ו. וַיֹּאמֶר אֵלָיו אִם בֶּן־הָאֱלֹהִים אַתָּה הִתְנַפֵּל אָרְצָה כִּי כָתוּב כִּי מַלְאָכָיו יְצַוֶּה־לָּךְ עַל־כַּפַּיִם יִשָּׂאוּנְךָ פֶּן־תִּגֹּף בָּאֶבֶן רַגְלֶךָ׃

6. Va•yo•mer elav eem Ben - ha•Elohim ata hit•na•pel ar•tza ki cha•toov ki mal•a•chav ye•tza•ve - lach al - ka•pa•yim yi•sa•oon•cha pen - ti•gof ba•e•ven rag•le•cha.

---

7. Jesus said unto him, It is written again, Thou shalt not tempt the Lord thy God.

Greek/Transliteration

7. Ἔφη αὐτῷ ὁ Ἰησοῦς, Πάλιν γέγραπται, Οὐκ ἐκπειράσεις κύριον τὸν θεόν σου.

7. Ephei auto 'o Yeisous, Palin gegraptai, Ouk ekpeiraseis kurion ton theon sou.

Hebrew/Transliteration

ז. וַיֹּאמֶר אֵלָיו יֵשׁוּעַ וְעוֹד כָּתוּב לֹא תְנַסֶּה אֶת־יְהוָֹה אֱלֹהֶיךָ׃

7. Va•yo•mer elav Yeshua ve•od ka•toov lo te•na•se et - Adonai Elohe•cha.

Rabbinic Jewish Commentary

The Hebrew word תנסו "tempt", as Manasseh ben (f) Israel observes, is always taken in an ill part, and is to be understood of such who would try the power, goodness, or will of God. (f) Conciliat. in Deut. Quaest. 3. p. 223.

8. Again, the devil taketh him up into an exceeding high mountain, and sheweth him all the kingdoms of the world, and the glory of them;

Greek/Transliteration
8. Πάλιν παραλαμβάνει αὐτὸν ὁ διάβολος εἰς ὄρος ὑψηλὸν λίαν, καὶ δείκνυσιν αὐτῷ πάσας τὰς βασιλείας τοῦ κόσμου καὶ τὴν δόξαν αὐτῶν,

8. Palin paralambanei auton 'o dyabolos eis oros 'upseilon lian, kai deiknusin auto pasas tas basileias tou kosmou kai tein doxan auton,

Hebrew/Transliteration
ח. וַיּוֹסֶף הַשָּׂטָן וַיִּקָּחֵהוּ אֶל-הַר גָּבֹהַּ מְאֹד וַיַּרְאֵהוּ אֶת-כָּל-מַמְלְכוֹת הָאָרֶץ וּכְבוֹדָן:

8. Va•yo•sef ha•Satan va•yi•ka•che•hoo el - har ga•vo•ha me•od va•yar•e•hoo et - kol - mam•le•chot ha•a•retz ooch•vo•dan.

---

9. And saith unto him, All these things will I give thee, if thou wilt fall down and worship me.

Greek/Transliteration
9. καὶ λέγει αὐτῷ, Ταῦτα πάντα σοι δώσω, ἐὰν πεσὼν προσκυνήσῃς μοι.

9. kai legei auto, Tauta panta soi doso, ean peson proskuneiseis moi.

Hebrew/Transliteration
ט. וַיֹּאמֶר אֵלָיו אֶת-כָּל-אֵלֶּה אֶתֶּן-לָךְ אִם-תִּפֹּל וְתִשְׁתַּחֲוֶה לִי:

9. Va•yo•mer elav et - kol - ele e•ten - le•cha eem - ti•pol ve•tish•ta•cha•ve li.

---

10. Then saith Jesus unto him, Get thee hence, Satan: for it is written, Thou shalt worship the Lord thy God, and him only shalt thou serve.

Greek/Transliteration
10. Τότε λέγει αὐτῷ ὁ Ἰησοῦς, Ὕπαγε ὀπίσω μου, Σατανᾶ· γέγραπται γάρ, Κύριον τὸν θεόν σου προσκυνήσεις, καὶ αὐτῷ μόνῳ λατρεύσεις.

10. Tote legei auto 'o Yeisous, 'Upage opiso mou, Satana. gegraptai gar, Kurion ton theon sou proskuneiseis, kai auto mono latreuseis.

Hebrew/Transliteration
י. אָז אָמַר אֵלָיו יֵשׁוּעַ גֶּשׁ-הָלְאָה הַשָּׂטָן כִּי כָתוּב לַיהֹוָה אֱלֹהֶיךָ תִשְׁתַּחֲוֶה וְאֹתוֹ לְבַדּוֹ תַעֲבֹד:

10. Az amar elav Yeshua gesh - hal•ah ha•Satan ki cha•toov la`Adonai Elohe•cha tish•ta•cha•ve ve•o•to le•va•do ta•a•vod.

Jewish New Testament Commentary

Satan was already using the same three kinds of temptations in the Garden of Eden: "When the woman saw that the tree was good for food" (desires of the flesh), "and that it was a delight to the eyes" (desires of the eyes), "and a tree to be desired to make one wise" (pretensions of life), "she took of the fruit and ate" (Gen_3:6). Yeshua, showing the power of the Word of God in resisting the Adversary (Jas_4:7), quotes the *Torah* in answer to all three temptations-Deu_8:3 at Mat_4:4, Deu_6:16 at Mat_4:7, and Deu_6:13 at Mat_4:10. But Satan, "the inventor of the lie" (Joh_8:44), can misuse Scripture to deceive-Psa_91:11-12 at Mat_4:6

---

11. Then the devil leaveth him, and, behold, angels came and ministered unto him.

Greek/Transliteration
11. Τότε ἀφίησιν αὐτὸν ὁ διάβολος· καὶ ἰδού, ἄγγελοι προσῆλθον καὶ διηκόνουν αὐτῷ.

11. Tote aphieisin auton 'o dyabolos. kai idou, angeloi proseilthon kai dieikonoun auto.

Hebrew/Transliteration
יא. וַיִּרֶף מִמֶּנּוּ הַשָּׂטָן וַיִּגְּשׁוּ אֵלָיו מַלְאָכִים וַיְשָׁרְתֵהוּ:

11. Va•yi•ref mi•me•noo ha•Satan va•yig•shoo elav mal•a•chim vay•shar•too•hoo.

---

12. Now when Jesus had heard that John was cast into prison, he departed into Galilee;

Greek/Transliteration
12. Ἀκούσας δὲ ὁ Ἰησοῦς ὅτι Ἰωάννης παρεδόθη, ἀνεχώρησεν εἰς τὴν Γαλιλαίαν·

12. Akousas de 'o Yeisous 'oti Yoanneis paredothei, anechoreisen eis tein Galilaian.

Hebrew/Transliteration
יב. וַיְהִי כְּשָׁמְעוֹ יֵשׁוּעַ כִּי נִסְגַּר יוֹחָנָן וַיָּשָׁב הַגָּלִילָה:

12. Vay•hi che•shom•oh Yeshua ki nis•gar Yo•cha•nan va•ya•shov ha•Ga•li•la.

13. And leaving Nazareth, he came and dwelt in Capernaum, which is upon the sea coast, in the borders of Zabulon and Nephthalim:

Greek/Transliteration
13. καὶ καταλιπὼν τὴν Ναζαρέτ, ἐλθὼν κατῴκησεν εἰς Καπερναοὺμ τὴν παραθαλασσίαν, ἐν ὁρίοις Ζαβουλὼν καὶ Νεφθαλείμ·

13. kai katalipon tein Nazaret, elthon katokeisen eis Kapernaoum tein parathalassian, en 'oriois Zaboulon kai Nephthaleim.

Hebrew/Transliteration
יג. וַיַּעֲזֹב אֶת-נְצָרֶת וַיָּבֹא וַיֵּשֶׁב בִּכְפַר-נַחוּם עַל-שְׂפַת הַיָּם בִּגְבוּלֵי זְבֻלוּן וְנַפְתָּלִי:

13. Va•ya•a•zov et - N`tza•ret va•ya•vo va•ye•shev bi•Ch`far - Na•choom al - s`fat ha•yam big•voo•ley Ze•voo•loon ve•Naf•tali.

Jewish New Testament Commentary
K'far-Nachum (Capernaum; the Hebrew name means "village of Nahum") was located on the northwest shore of Lake Kinneret (the Sea of Galilee; see Mat_4:18) and site of much of Yeshua's activity as described in the New Testament. Now an archeological park supervised by the Roman Catholic Church, it is a standard stop on Christian tours of Israel. An octagonal 5th-century Byzantine structure amidst earlier ruins is said to mark where Kefa lived (Mat_8:14); if so, the older remains may be part of the first Messianic Jewish congregation building. The walls of a fourth-century synagogue still stand.

---

14. That it might be fulfilled which was spoken by Esaias the prophet, saying,

Greek/Transliteration
14. ἵνα πληρωθῇ τὸ ῥηθὲν διὰ Ἡσαΐου τοῦ προφήτου, λέγοντος,

14. 'ina pleirothei to 'reithen dya Eisaiou tou propheitou, legontos,

Hebrew/Transliteration
יד. לְמַלֹּאת אֵת אֲשֶׁר-נֶאֱמַר בְּיַד-יְשַׁעְיָהוּ הַנָּבִיא לֵאמֹר:

14. Le•ma•lot et asher - ne•e•mar be•yad - Ye•sha•a•ya•hoo ha•na•vee le•mor.

---

15. The land of Zabulon, and the land of Nephthalim, by the way of the sea, beyond Jordan, Galilee of the Gentiles;

Greek/Transliteration
15. Γῆ Ζαβουλὼν καὶ γῆ Νεφθαλείμ, ὁδὸν θαλάσσης, πέραν τοῦ Ἰορδάνου, Γαλιλαία τῶν ἐθνῶν,

15. Gei Zaboulon kai gei Nephthaleim, 'odon thalasseis, peran tou Yordanou, Galilaia ton ethnon,

Hebrew/Transliteration
טו. אַרְצָה זְבֻלוּן וְאַרְצָה נַפְתָּלִי דֶּרֶךְ הַיָּם עֵבֶר הַיַּרְדֵּן גְּלִיל הַגּוֹיִם:

15. Ar•tza Ze•voo•loon ve•ar•tza Naf•tali de•rech ha•yam ever ha•Yarden G`lil ha•go•yim.

Rabbinic Jewish Commentary
The ancient Jews expected the Messiah to make his first appearance in Galilee; which expectation must be grounded on this prophecy; for so they say (y) expressly, "the king Messiah shall be revealed בארעא דגליל, "in the land of Galilee.""

And in another place (z) explaining Isa_2:19 they paraphrase it thus, "for fear of the Lord"; this is the indignation of the whole world: and for the "glory of his majesty"; this is the Messiah; when he ariseth to shake terribly the earth, when he shall arise and be revealed בארעא דגליל, "in the land of Galilee": because that this is the first place to be destroyed in the holy land; therefore he shall be revealed there the first of all places." (y) Zohar in Gen. fol. 74. 3. (z) Ib. in Exod. fol. 3. 3. & 88. 3.

---

16. The people which sat in darkness saw great light; and to them which sat in the region and shadow of death light is sprung up.

Greek/Transliteration
16. ὁ λαὸς ὁ καθήμενος ἐν σκότει εἶδεν φῶς μέγα, καὶ τοῖς καθημένοις ἐν χώρᾳ καὶ σκιᾷ θανάτου, φῶς ἀνέτειλεν αὐτοῖς.

16. 'o laos 'o katheimenos en skotei eiden phos mega, kai tois katheimenois en chora kai skya thanatou, phos aneteilen autois.

Hebrew/Transliteration
טז. הָעָם הַהֹלְכִים בַּחֹשֶׁךְ רָאוּ אוֹר גָּדוֹל יֹשְׁבֵי בְּאֶרֶץ צַלְמָוֶת אוֹר נָגַהּ עֲלֵיהֶם:

16. Ha•am ha•hol•chim ba•cho•shech ra•oo or ga•dol yosh•vey be•e•retz tzal•ma•vet or na•ga aley•hem.

Rabbinic Jewish Commentary
R, Aba (a) Serungia, "and the light dwelleth with him"; this is the king Messiah. The note of R. Sol. Jarchi on these words, "send forth thy light", is, the king Messiah; who is compared to light, according to Psa_132:17 the days of the Messiah are by them said to (b) be ימי אורה "days of light"; and so these Galilaeans found them to be; as all do, to whom the Gospel of Christ comes with power and demonstration of the Spirit. And these days of light first begun in the land of Zabulon which, according to Philo the Jew (c), was "a symbol of light"; since

(adds he) its name signifies the nature of night; but, the night removing, and departing, light necessarily arises." (a) Bereshith Rabba, fol. 1. 3. & Echa Rabbati, fol. 50. 2. (b) Baal Hatturim in Gen. fol. 2. 2. (c) De Somniis, p. 1113.

---

17. From that time Jesus began to preach, and to say, Repent: for the kingdom of heaven is at hand.

Greek/Transliteration
17. Ἀπὸ τότε ἤρξατο ὁ Ἰησοῦς κηρύσσειν καὶ λέγειν, Μετανοεῖτε· ἤγγικεν γὰρ ἡ βασιλεία τῶν οὐρανῶν.

17. Apo tote eirxato 'o Yeisous keirussein kai legein, Metanoeite. eingiken gar 'ei basileia ton ouranon.

Hebrew/Transliteration
יז. מֵהָעֵת הַהִיא הֵחֵל יֵשׁוּעַ לִקְרֹא וְלֵאמֹר שׁוּבוּ מִדַּרְכֵיכֶם כִּי מַלְכוּת הַשָּׁמַיִם קָרְבָה לָבֹא:

17. Me•ha•et ha•hee he`chel Yeshua lik•ro ve•le•mor shoo•voo mi•dar•chey•chem ki mal•choot ha•sha•ma•yim kar•va la•vo.

---

18. And Jesus, walking by the sea of Galilee, saw two brethren, Simon called Peter, and Andrew his brother, casting a net into the sea: for they were fishers.

Greek/Transliteration
18. Περιπατῶν δὲ παρὰ τὴν θάλασσαν τῆς Γαλιλαίας εἶδεν δύο ἀδελφούς, Σίμωνα τὸν λεγόμενον Πέτρον, καὶ Ἀνδρέαν τὸν ἀδελφὸν αὐτοῦ, βάλλοντας ἀμφίβληστρον εἰς τὴν θάλασσαν· ἦσαν γὰρ ἁλιεῖς.

18. Peripaton de para tein thalassan teis Galilaias eiden duo adelphous, Simona ton legomenon Petron, kai Andrean ton adelphon autou, ballontas amphibleistron eis tein thalassan. eisan gar 'alieis.

Hebrew/Transliteration
יח. וַיִּתְהַלֵּךְ יֵשׁוּעַ עַל-יַד יַם-הַגָּלִיל וַיַּרְא שְׁנֵי אַחִים שִׁמְעוֹן הַנִּקְרָא פֶּטְרוֹס וְאַנְדְּרַי אָחִיו פֹּרְשִׂים מִכְמֹרֶת עַל-פְּנֵי-הַיָּם כִּי דַיָּגִים הָיוּ -

18. Va•yit•ha•lech Yeshua al - yad yam - ha•Galil va•yar sh`ney a•chim Shimon ha•nik•ra Petros ve•Ande•rai a•chiv por•sim mich•mo•ret al - p`ney - ha•yam ki da•ya•gim ha•yoo.

Jewish New Testament Commentary
Lake Kinneret is the name used in Israel for the body of fresh water formed by the River Yarden (Jordan) in the Galil (Galilee); it is so called because it is shaped like a harp (*kinnor* in ancient Hebrew). English versions of the Bible identify it as the

Sea of Galilee; at Joh_6:1, Joh_6:23 andJoh_21:1 the Greek text calls it "the Sea of Tiberias."

Kefa is the name Yeshua gave Shim'on Bar-Yochanan (Joh_1:42); it means "rock" in Aramaic. The Greek word for "rock" is "*petros*," which is usually brought into English as "Peter." Occasionally, instead of translating "*Kefa*" as "*Petros*," the Greek text transliterates "*Kefa*" as "*Kephas*"; this appears in English versions as "Cephas."

---

19. And he saith unto them, Follow me, and I will make you fishers of men.

Greek/Transliteration
19. Καὶ λέγει αὐτοῖς, Δεῦτε ὀπίσω μου, καὶ ποιήσω ὑμᾶς ἁλιεῖς ἀνθρώπων

19. Kai legei autois, Deute opiso mou, kai poieiso 'umas 'alieis anthropon.

Hebrew/Transliteration
יט. וַיֹּאמֶר אֲלֵיהֶם לְכוּ אַחֲרַי וְאֶעֱשֶׂה אֶתְכֶם לְדַיָּגֵי אָדָם:

19. Va•yo•mer aley•hem le•choo a•cha•rai ve•e•e•se et•chem le•day•gey adam.

Rabbinic Jewish Commentary
The net they were to spread and cast was the Gospel, see Mat_13:47 for Yeshua made them not דייגי תורה, "fishers of the law", to use the words of Maimonides (g), but fishers of the Gospel.

(g) Hilcot. Talmud. Torah, c. 1. sect. 12. so Dr. Lightfoot cites the phrase, but in Ed. Amsterd. it is דיני תורה, "the judgments of the law".

---

20. And they straightway left their nets, and followed him.

Greek/Transliteration
20. Οἱ δὲ εὐθέως ἀφέντες τὰ δίκτυα ἠκολούθησαν αὐτῷ.

20. 'Oi de eutheos aphentes ta diktua eikoloutheisan auto.

Hebrew/Transliteration
כ. וַיַּעַזְבוּ אֶת-מִכְמֹרוֹתָם כְּרֶגַע וַיֵּלְכוּ אַחֲרָיו:

20. Va•ya•az•voo et - mich•mo•ro•tam ke•ra•ga va•yel•choo a•cha•rav.

---

21. And going on from thence, he saw other two brethren, James the son of Zebedee, and John his brother, in a ship with Zebedee their father, mending their nets; and he called them.

Greek/Transliteration
21. Καὶ προβὰς ἐκεῖθεν, εἶδεν ἄλλους δύο ἀδελφούς, Ἰάκωβον τὸν τοῦ Ζεβεδαίου καὶ Ἰωάννην τὸν ἀδελφὸν αὐτοῦ, ἐν τῷ πλοίῳ μετὰ Ζεβεδαίου τοῦ πατρὸς αὐτῶν, καταρτίζοντας τὰ δίκτυα αὐτῶν· καὶ ἐκάλεσεν αὐτούς.

21. Kai probas ekeithen, eiden allous duo adelphous, Yakobon ton tou Zebedaiou kai Yoannein ton adelphon autou, en to ploio meta Zebedaiou tou patros auton, katartizontas ta diktua auton. kai ekalesen autous.

Hebrew/Transliteration
כא. וַיַּעֲבֹר מִשָּׁם וַיַּרְא שְׁנֵי אַחִים אֲחֵרִים יַעֲקֹב בֶּן-זַבְדִּי וְיוֹחָנָן אָחִיו בָּאֳנִיָּה עִם-זַבְדִּי אֲבִיהֶם מְתַקְּנִים:מִכְמֹרוֹתָם וַיִּקְרָא אֲלֵיהֶם

21. Va•ya•a•vor mi•sham va•yar sh`ney a•chim a•che•rim Yaakov ben - Zav•di ve•Yo•cha•nan a•chiv ba•o•ni•ya eem - Zav•di avi•hem me•tak•nim mich•mo•ro•tam va•yik•ra aley•hem.

---

22. And they immediately left the ship and their father, and followed him.

Greek/Transliteration
22. Οἱ δὲ εὐθέως ἀφέντες τὸ πλοῖον καὶ τὸν πατέρα αὐτῶν ἠκολούθησαν αὐτῷ.

22. 'Oi de eutheos aphentes to ploion kai ton patera auton eikoloutheisan auto.

Hebrew/Transliteration
כב. וְגַם-הֵמָּה כְּרֶגַע עָזְבוּ אֶת-הָאֳנִיָּה וְאֶת-אֲבִיהֶם וַיֵּלְכוּ אַחֲרָיו:

22. Ve•gam - he•ma ke•re•ga az•voo et - ha•o•ni•ya ve•et - avi•hem va•yel•choo a•cha•rav.

---

23. And Jesus went about all Galilee, teaching in their synagogues, and preaching the gospel of the kingdom, and healing all manner of sickness and all manner of disease among the people.

Greek/Transliteration
23. Καὶ περιῆγεν ὅλην τὴν Γαλιλαίαν ὁ Ἰησοῦς, διδάσκων ἐν ταῖς συναγωγαῖς αὐτῶν, καὶ κηρύσσων τὸ εὐαγγέλιον τῆς βασιλείας, καὶ θεραπεύων πᾶσαν νόσον καὶ πᾶσαν μαλακίαν ἐν τῷ λαῷ.

23. Kai perieigen 'olein tein Galilaian 'o Yeisous, didaskon en tais sunagogais auton, kai keirusson to euangelion teis basileias, kai therapeuon pasan noson kai pasan malakian en to lao.

Hebrew/Transliteration
כג. וַיָּסָב יֵשׁוּעַ בְּכָל-הַגָּלִיל וַיְלַמֵּד-שָׁם בְּבָתֵּי הַכְּנֶסֶת קָרֹא בְשׂוֹרַת הַמַּלְכוּת וְרָפֹא כָּל-מַחֲלָה וְכָל-מַדְוֶה בָּעָם:

23. Va•ya•sav Yeshua be•chol - ha•Galil vay•la•med - sham be•va•tey ha•k`ne•set ka•ro b`so•rat ha•mal•choot ve•ra•fo kol - ma•cha•la ve•chol - mad•ve ba•am.

---

24. And his fame went throughout all Syria: and they brought unto him all sick people that were taken with divers diseases and torments, and those which were possessed with devils, and those which were lunatick, and those that had the palsy; and he healed them.

Greek/Transliteration
24. Καὶ ἀπῆλθεν ἡ ἀκοὴ αὐτοῦ εἰς ὅλην τὴν Συρίαν· καὶ προσήνεγκαν αὐτῷ πάντας τοὺς κακῶς ἔχοντας, ποικίλαις νόσοις καὶ βασάνοις συνεχομένους, καὶ δαιμονιζομένους, καὶ σεληνιαζομένους, καὶ παραλυτικούς· καὶ ἐθεράπευσεν αὐτούς.

24. Kai apeilthen 'ei akoei autou eis 'olein tein Surian. kai proseinegkan auto pantas tous kakos echontas, poikilais nosois kai basanois sunechomenous, kai daimonizomenous, kai seleinyazomenous, kai paralutikous. kai etherapeusen autous.

Hebrew/Transliteration
כד. וַיֵּצֵא שָׁמְעוֹ בְּכָל-אֶרֶץ סוּרְיָא וַיָּבִיאוּ אֵלָיו אֵת כָּל-הַחוֹלִים אֲשֶׁר דָּבְקוּ בָם תַּחֲלֻאִים שׁוֹנִים וָחֳלָיִם רָעִים:אֲחֻזֵי רוּחוֹת רָעוֹת מֻכֵּי יָרֵחַ וּנְכֵי עֲצָמוֹת וַיִּרְפָּאֵם

24. Va•ye•tze shim•oh be•chol - eretz Soor•ya va•ya•vi•oo elav et kol - ha•cho•lim asher dav•koo vam ta•cha•loo•eem sho•nim va•cho•la•yim ra•eem achoo•zey roo•chot ra•ot moo•key ya•re•ach oon•chey a•tza•mot va•yir•pa•em.

Jewish New Testament Commentary
According to the New Testament, demons-also called unclean or evil spirits, lying spirits, and messengers of the devil-can affect people by causing physical illness, mental aberrations, emotional malaise and moral temptation. "Demonized" means "affected by demons" in one or more of these ways. Actual "possession" or "ownership" of a human being by a demon is not taught in the Bible.

---

25. And there followed him great multitudes of people from Galilee, and from Decapolis, and from Jerusalem, and from Judaea, and from beyond Jordan.

Greek/Transliteration

25. Καὶ ἠκολούθησαν αὐτῷ ὄχλοι πολλοὶ ἀπὸ τῆς Γαλιλαίας καὶ Δεκαπόλεως καὶ Ἱεροσολύμων καὶ Ἰουδαίας καὶ πέραν τοῦ Ἰορδάνου.

25. Kai eikoloutheisan auto ochloi polloi apo teis Galilaias kai Dekapoleos kai 'Yerosolumon kai Youdaias kai peran tou Yordanou.

Hebrew/Trnsliteration

כה. וַיֵּלְכוּ אַחֲרָיו קָהָל רָב מִן־הַגָּלִיל וּמִן־דְּכַפֹּלִיס וּמִן־יְרוּשָׁלַיִם וִיהוּדָה וְעֵבֶר הַיַּרְדֵּן:

25. Va•yel•choo a•cha•rav ka•hal rav min - ha•Galil oo•min - Deka•polis oo•min - Ye•roo•sha•la•yim vi•Y`hoo•da ve•e•ver ha•Yarden.

Matthew, Chapter 5

1. And seeing the multitudes, he went up into a mountain: and when he was set, his disciples came unto him:

Greek/Transliteration

1. Ἰδὼν δὲ τοὺς ὄχλους, ἀνέβη εἰς τὸ ὄρος· καὶ καθίσαντος αὐτοῦ, προσῆλθον αὐτῷ οἱ μαθηταὶ αὐτοῦ·

1. Idon de tous ochlous, anebei eis to oros. kai kathisantos autou, proseilthon auto 'oi matheitai autou.

Hebrew/Transliteration

א: וַיְהִי כַּאֲשֶׁר רָאָה אֶת-הֲמוֹן הָעָם וַיַּעַל אֶל-הָהָר וַיֵּשֶׁב שָׁם וַיִּגְּשׁוּ אֵלָיו תַּלְמִידָיו

1. Vay•hi ka•a•sher ra•ah et - ha•mon ha•am va•ya•al el - ha•har va•ye•shev sham va•yig•shoo elav tal•mi•dav.

Old Testament/Jewish New Testament Commentary

"Moses went up on the mountain, and the cloud covered the mountain."
Exodus 24:15

Talmidim (plural; singular *talmid*), "disciples." The English word "disciple" fails to convey the richness of the relationship between a rabbi and his *talmidim* in the first century C.E. Teachers, both itinerant like Yeshua and settled ones, attracted followers who wholeheartedly gave themselves over to their teachers (though not in a mindless way, as happens today in some cults). The essence of the relationship was one of trust in every area of living, and its goal was to make the *talmid* like his rabbi in knowledge, wisdom and ethical behavior.

(z). "The master sits at the head, or in the chief place, and the disciples before him in a circuit, like a crown; so that they all see the master, and hear his words; and the master may not sit upon a seat, and the scholars upon the ground; but either all upon the earth, or upon seats: indeed from the beginning, or formerly, היה הרב יושב "the master used to sit", and the disciples stand; but before the destruction of the second temple, all used to teach their disciples as they were sitting."

Talmudists say (a), that "from the days of Moses, to Rabban Gamaliel (the master of the Apostle Paul), they did not learn the law, unless standing; after Rabban Gamaliel died, sickness came into the world, and they learnt the law sitting: hence it is a tradition, that after Rabban Gamaliel died, the glory of the law ceased."

(z) Hilch. Talmud Torah, c. 4. sect. 2. (a) T. Bab. Megilla, fol. 21. 1. Vid. Misn. Sota, c. 9. sect. 15. & Jarchi, Maimon, & Bartenora in ib.

2. And he opened his mouth, and taught them, saying,

Greek/Transliteration
2. καὶ ἀνοίξας τὸ στόμα αὐτοῦ, ἐδίδασκεν αὐτούς, λέγων,

2. kai anoixas to stoma autou, edidasken autous, legon,

Hebrew/Transliteration
:ב. וַיִּפְתַּח אֶת-פִּיהוּ וַיּוֹרֶה לָהֶם לֵאמֹר

2. Va•yif•tach et - pi•hoo va•yo•re la•hem le•mor.

---

3. Blessed are the poor in spirit: for theirs is the kingdom of heaven.

Greek/Transliteration
3. Μακάριοι οἱ πτωχοὶ τῷ πνεύματι· ὅτι αὐτῶν ἐστιν ἡ βασιλεία τῶν οὐρανῶν.

3. Makarioi 'oi ptochoi to pneumati. 'oti auton estin 'ei basileia ton ouranon.

Hebrew/Transliteration
:ג. אַשְׁרֵי עֲנִיֵּי הָרוּחַ כִּי לָהֶם מַלְכוּת הַשָּׁמָיִם

3. Ash•rey ani•yey ha•roo•ach ki la•hem mal•choot ha•sha•ma•yim.

Jewish New Testament Commentary
Hebrew *asher* and means "blessed," "happy," and "fortunate" all at once, so that no one English word is adequate. For a Hebrew example, compare Psa_144:15 : "How blessed/happy/fortunate the people whose God is *Adonai*!" Mat_5:3-12 are known as the Beatitudes because the word "*beatus*" was used in the best-known Latin version, Jerome's "Vulgate" (c. 410 C.E.), to translate "*makarios*."

Beatitudes are actually *Tanakh* phrases in the form of blessings representing the messianic age. At the end of them, Yeshua says, "How blessed *you* are when people insult *you* and persecute *you* and tell all kinds of vicious lies about *you* because *you* follow *me*" (Mat_5:11; italics added). By pronouncing this blessing in the context of messianic blessings, he is saying, in code, that he is the Messiah- which must have surprised and shocked his hearers.

---

4. Blessed are they that mourn: for they shall be comforted.

Greek/Transliteration
4. Μακάριοι οἱ πενθοῦντες· ὅτι αὐτοὶ παρακληθήσονται.

4. Makarioi 'oi penthountes. 'oti autoi parakleitheisontai.

Hebrew/Transliteration
:ד. אַשְׁרֵי הַמִּתְאַבְּלִים כִּי-הֵם יְנֻחָמוּ

4. Ash•rey ha•mit•ab•lim ki - hem ye•noo•cha•moo.

---

5. Blessed are the meek: for they shall inherit the earth.

Greek/Transliteration
5. Μακάριοι οἱ πραεῖς· ὅτι αὐτοὶ κληρονομήσουσιν τὴν γῆν.

5. Makarioi 'oi praeis. 'oti autoi kleironomeisousin tein gein.

Hebrew/Transliteration
:ה. אַשְׁרֵי הָעֲנָוִים כִּי-הֵם יִירְשׁוּ-אָרֶץ

5. Ash•rey ha•a•na•vim ki - hem yir•shoo - a•retz.

Rabbinic/Old Testament/Jewish New Testament Commentary

The word for "earth" in Hebrew is "eretz". It can mean "land" or "earth." This phrase is found threaded throughout the Psalms and Tanakh. Psalms says, "But the humble shall inherit the land, and shall delight themselves in the abundance of peace." Psalms 37:11, Psalm 37 continues, "The righteous shall inherit the land, and live in it forever." Psalms 37:29

Although Greek *gê* can mean either "earth" or "land," in Psalm 37 the Hebrew word "*eretz*" means "Land" (and not "earth") not less than six times: those of Israel who trust in *Adonai* will "dwell in the Land" (Mat_5:3); and those of Israel who wait upon *Adonai* (Mat_5:9), are meek (Mat_5:11, cited here), are blessed by *Adonai* (Mat_5:22), are righteous (Mat_5:29) and keep his way (Mat_5:34) will "inherit the Land." The term "inherit" in the *Tanakh* refers to the Jewish people's inheritance from God, which includes, in addition to spiritual elements, not the whole earth but a specific small territory on the east shore of the Mediterranean Sea.

The Jews, though a proud, haughty, and wrathful people, cannot but speak in its praise: "Wisdom, fear, and meekness, say (b) they, are of high esteem; but ענוה, "meekness", is greater than them all."

They had two very considerable Rabbi's in the time of Yeshua, Hillell and Shammai; the one was of a meek, the other of an angry disposition: hence, say they (c), "Let a man be always meek as Hillell, and let him not be angry as Shammai."

(b) Piske Tosaphot Yebamot, art. 196. (c) T. Bab. Sabbat. fol. 30. 2.

6. Blessed are they which do hunger and thirst after righteousness: for they shall be filled.

Greek/Transliteration
6. Μακάριοι οἱ πεινῶντες καὶ διψῶντες τὴν δικαιοσύνην· ὅτι αὐτοὶ χορτασθήσονται.

6. Makarioi 'oi peinontes kai dipsontes tein dikaiosunein. 'oti autoi chortastheisontai.

Hebrew/Transliteration
:ו. אַשְׁרֵי הָרְעֵבִים וְהַצְמֵאִים לִצְדָקָה כִּי-הֵם יִרְוָיֻן

6. Ash•rey har•e•vim ve•hatz•me•eem litz•da•ka ki - hem yir•va•yoon.

---

7. Blessed are the merciful: for they shall obtain mercy.

Greek/Transliteration
7. Μακάριοι οἱ ἐλεήμονες· ὅτι αὐτοὶ ἐλεηθήσονται.

7. Makarioi 'oi eleeimones. 'oti autoi eleeitheisontai.

Hebrew/Transliteration
:ז. אַשְׁרֵי בַּעֲלֵי-רַחֲמִים כִּי-הֵם יְרֻחָמוּ

7. Ash•rey ba•a•ley - ra•cha•mim ki - hem ye•roo•cha•moo.

Rabbinic Commentary
"It was taught R. Gamaliel Beribbi said: And he shall give you mercy, and have compassion upon you, and multiply you: he who is merciful to others, mercy is shown to him by Heaven, while he who is not merciful to others, mercy is not shown to him by Heaven." Shabbat 151b, Soncino Press Edition

---

8. Blessed are the pure in heart: for they shall see God.

Greek/Transliteration
8. Μακάριοι οἱ καθαροὶ τῇ καρδίᾳ· ὅτι αὐτοὶ τὸν θεὸν ὄψονται.

8. Makarioi 'oi katharoi tei kardia. 'oti autoi ton theon opsontai.

Hebrew/Transliteration
:ח. אַשְׁרֵי בָּרֵי לֵבָב כִּי-הֵם יֶחֱזוּ אֶת-אֱלֹהִים

8. Ash•rey ba•rey le•vav ki - hem ye•che•zoo et - Elohim.

9. Blessed are the peacemakers: for they shall be called the children of God.

Greek/Transliteration
9. Μακάριοι οἱ εἰρηνοποιοί· ὅτι αὐτοὶ υἱοὶ θεοῦ κληθήσονται.

9. Makarioi 'oi eireinopoioi. 'oti autoi 'wioi theou kleitheisontai.

Hebrew/Transliteration
ט. אַשְׁרֵי עֹשֵׂי שָׁלוֹם כִּי-הֵם יִקָּרְאוּ בְּנֵי-אֱלֹהִים:

9. Ash•rey o•sey sha•lom ki - hem yi•kar•oo b`ney - Elohim.

Rabbinic Commentary
"Hillel said, "Be of the disciples of Aaron, loving peace, and pursuing peace, loving mankind, and bringing them near to the Torah." Pirkei Avot 1:12

The Jews speak very highly, and much, in the commendation of peace making; they reckon this among the things which shall be of use to a man, both in this, and the other world.

"These are the things, (say they (e),) the fruit of which a man enjoys in this world, and his lot or portion remains for him in the world to come; honouring father and mother, liberality, והבאת שלום בין אדם לחבירו, "and making peace between a man and his neighhour.""

This, they say (f), Aaron was much disposed to. "Moses used to say, let justice break through the mountain; but Aaron loved peace, and pursued it, and made peace between a man and his neighhour, as is said, Mal_2:6"

(e) Misn. Peah. c. 1. sect. 1. T. Bab. Sabbat. fol. 127. 1. & Kiddushin. fol. 40. 1. (f) T. Bab. Sanhedrim, fol. 6. 2. Vid. Abot. R. Nathan, c. 12. fol. 4. 2.

---

10. Blessed are they which are persecuted for righteousness' sake: for theirs is the kingdom of heaven.

Greek/Transliteration
10. Μακάριοι οἱ δεδιωγμένοι ἕνεκεν δικαιοσύνης· ὅτι αὐτῶν ἐστιν ἡ βασιλεία τῶν οὐρανῶν.

10. Makarioi 'oi dediogmenoi 'eneken dikaiosuneis. 'oti auton estin 'ei basileia ton ouranon.

Hebrew/Transliteration
י. אַשְׁרֵי הַנִּרְדָּפִים עֵקֶב צִדְקָתָם כִּי לָהֶם מַלְכוּת הַשָּׁמָיִם:

10. Ash•rey ha•nir•da•fim e•kev tzid•ka•tam ki la•hem mal•choot ha•sha•ma•yim.

Rabbinic Commentary

"R. Abbahu said: A man should always strive to be rather of the persecuted than of the persecutors as there is none among the birds more persecuted than doves and pigeons, and yet Scripture made them [alone] eligible for the altar."
Baba Kama 93a, Soncino Press Edition

---

11. Blessed are ye, when men shall revile you, and persecute you, and shall say all manner of evil against you falsely, for my sake.

Greek/Transliteration

11. Μακάριοί ἐστε, ὅταν ὀνειδίσωσιν ὑμᾶς καὶ διώξωσιν, καὶ εἴπωσιν πᾶν πονηρὸν ῥῆμα καθ᾽ ὑμῶν ψευδόμενοι, ἕνεκεν ἐμοῦ.

11. Makarioi este, 'otan oneidisosin 'umas kai dioxosin, kai eiposin pan poneiron 'reima kath 'umon pseudomenoi, 'eneken emou.

Hebrew/Transliteration

יא. אַשְׁרֵיכֶם אִם-יְחָרְפוּ אִם-יִרְדְּפוּ אֶתְכֶם וּבְשֶׁקֶר יָבִיאוּ דִבַּתְכֶם רָעָה בַּעֲבוּר שְׁמִי:

11. Ash•rey•chem eem - ye•char•foo eem - yir•de•foo et•chem oo•va•she•ker ya•vi•oo di•bat•chem ra•ah ba•a•voor sh`mi.

Rabbinic Jewish Commentary

The Jews have some sayings not unlike these, and which may serve to illustrate them: "be thou cursed", or bearing curses, but do not curse (g). The gloss upon it is, it is better to be one of them that are cursed, than to be of them that curse; for, at the end, the curse causeless returns to him that curseth."

Again (h), "for ever let a man be of them that are persecuted, and not of them that persecute; of them that suffer injury, and not of them that do it."

Once more (i), "they that suffer injury, and do it not; who hear reproach, and do not return it; who act from love, and rejoice in chastisements, of them the Scripture says, "let them that love him", Jdg_5:31."

(g) T. Bab. Sanhedrim, fol. 49. 1. (h) T. Bab. Bava Kama, fol. 93. 1. Maimon. Hilch. Deyot. c. 5. sect. 13. (i) T. Bab. Sabbat. fol. 88. 2. Yoma, fol. 23. 1. & Gittin, fol. 36. 2.

---

12. Rejoice, and be exceeding glad: for great is your reward in heaven: for so persecuted they the prophets which were before you.

Greek/Transliteration

12. Χαίρετε καὶ ἀγαλλιᾶσθε, ὅτι ὁ μισθὸς ὑμῶν πολὺς ἐν τοῖς οὐρανοῖς· οὕτως γὰρ ἐδίωξαν τοὺς προφήτας τοὺς πρὸ ὑμῶν.

12. Chairete kai agallyasthe, 'oti 'o misthos 'umon polus en tois ouranois. 'outos gar edioxan tous propheitas tous pro 'umon.

Hebrew/Transliteration
יב. שִׂישׂוּ וְגִילוּ כִּי שְׂכַרְכֶם הַרְבֵּה מְאֹד בַּשָּׁמָיִם כִּי-כֵן רָדְפוּ אֶת-הַנְּבִיאִים אֲשֶׁר הָיוּ לִפְנֵיכֶם:

12. Si•soo ve•gi•loo ki s`char•chem har•be me•od ba•sha•ma•yim ki - chen rad•foo et - ha•n`vi•eem asher ha•yoo lif•ney•chem.

---

13. Ye are the salt of the earth: but if the salt have lost his savour, wherewith shall it be salted? It is thenceforth good for nothing, but to be cast out, and to be trodden under foot of men.

Greek/Transliteration
13. Ὑμεῖς ἐστε τὸ ἅλας τῆς γῆς· ἐὰν δὲ τὸ ἅλας μωρανθῇ, ἐν τίνι ἁλισθήσεται; Εἰς οὐδὲν ἰσχύει ἔτι, εἰ μὴ βληθῆναι ἔξω καὶ καταπατεῖσθαι ὑπὸ τῶν ἀνθρώπων.

13. 'Umeis este to 'alas teis geis. ean de to 'alas moranthei, en tini 'alistheisetai? Eis ouden ischuei eti, ei mei bleitheinai exo kai katapateisthai 'upo ton anthropon.

Hebrew/Transliteration
יג. אַתֶּם מֶלַח הָאָרֶץ וְאִם-הַמֶּלַח יָפוּג טַעְמוֹ בַּמֶּה יָמְלָח תָּפֵל לֹא-יִצְלַח לַכֹּל כִּי אִם-יְזֹרֶה הַחוּצָה וְהָיָה:לְמִרְמַס רָגֶל

13. Atem me•lach ha•a•retz ve•eem - ha•me•lach ya•foog ta•a•mo ba•me yom•lach ta•fel lo - yitz•lach la•kol ki eem - ye•zo•re ha•choo•tza ve•ha•ya le•mir•mas ra•gel.

Jewish New Testament Commentary
Jewish believers are salt, a seasoning and a preservative, for the Land of Israel (see Mat_5:5), that is, for the Jewish people, and light for the world, for the Gentiles, as taught in Isa_49:6. God established a "covenant of salt" (Num_18:19), which is applied to King David and his descendants-that is, to the Messiah-in 2Ch_13:5.

---

14. Ye are the light of the world. A city that is set on an hill cannot be hid.

Greek/Transliteration
14. Ὑμεῖς ἐστε τὸ φῶς τοῦ κόσμου· οὐ δύναται πόλις κρυβῆναι ἐπάνω ὄρους κειμένη·

14. 'Umeis este to phos tou kosmou. ou dunatai polis krubeinai epano orous keimenei.

Hebrew/Transliteration
יד. אַתֶּם אוֹר הָעוֹלָם עִיר יֹשֶׁבֶת עַל-הָהָר לֹא תוּכַל לְהִסָּתֵר.

14. Atem or ha•o•lam eer yo•she•vet al - ha•har lo too•chal le•hi•sa•ter.

Rabbinic Jewish Commentary
(l), Rabbi's teach "on the fourth day it was said, "let there be light": which was done with respect to the Israelites, because they are they מאירים לעולם, "which give light to the world", as it is written, Dan_12:3'

And in another place (m), say they, "how beautiful are the great ones of the congregation, and the wise men, who sit in the sanhedrim! for they are they מנהרין לעלמא, "that enlighten the world", the people of the house of Israel."

So. R. Meir, R. Akiba his disciple, and R. Judah the prince, are each of them called (n) אור העולם, "the light of the world"; as R. Jochanan ben Zaccai is by his disciples, נר עולם, "the lamp of the world" (o): and it was usual for the head of a school, or of an university to be styled (p) נהורא דעלמא, "the light of the world"; but this title much better agrees and suits with the persons Yeshua gives it to, who, no question, had a view to those exalted characters the Jews gave to their celebrated Rabbi's.

(l) Tzeror Hammor, fol. 1. 3. (m) Targum in Cant. iv. 1. (n) Juchasin, fol. 63. 2. (o) Abot R. Nathan, c. 25. fol. 6. 3. (p) Juchasin. fol. 121. 1.

---

15. Neither do men light a candle, and put it under a bushel, but on a candlestick; and it giveth light unto all that are in the house.

Greek/Transliteration
15. οὐδὲ καίουσιν λύχνον καὶ τιθέασιν αὐτὸν ὑπὸ τὸν μόδιον, ἀλλ᾽ ἐπὶ τὴν λυχνίαν, καὶ λάμπει πᾶσιν τοῖς ἐν τῇ οἰκίᾳ.

15. oude kaiousin luchnon kai titheasin auton 'upo ton modion, all epi tein luchnian, kai lampei pasin tois en tei oikia.

Hebrew/Transliteration
טו. וְאֵין מַדְלִיקִים נֵר לְתִתּוֹ תַּחַת הָאֵיפָה כִּי אִם-אֶל-הַמְּנֹרָה לְהָאִיר לְכֹל אֲשֶׁר בַּבָּיִת:

15. Ve•eyn mad•li•kim ner le•ti•to ta•chat ha•ey•fa ki eem - el - ha•m`no•ra le•ha•eer le•chol asher ba•ba•yit.

Rabbinic Jewish Commentary
Much such a proverbial saying is used by the Jews (r): "do not leave a vessel of balsam in a dunghill, but move it from its place, that its smell may spread, and men may receive profit from it."

(r) Vid. Joh. Isaac. Praefat. ad Eliae Levit. Methurgeman.

16. Let your light so shine before men, that they may see your good works, and glorify your Father which is in heaven.

Greek/Transliteration
16. Οὕτως λαμψάτω τὸ φῶς ὑμῶν ἔμπροσθεν τῶν ἀνθρώπων, ὅπως ἴδωσιν ὑμῶν τὰ καλὰ ἔργα, καὶ δοξάσωσιν τὸν πατέρα ὑμῶν τὸν ἐν τοῖς οὐρανοῖς.

16. 'Outos lampsato to phos 'umon emprosthen ton anthropon, 'opos idosin 'umon ta kala erga, kai doxasosin ton patera 'umon ton en tois ouranois.

Hebrew/Transliteration
טז. כֹּה יָאֵר אוֹרְכֶם לְעֵינֵי בְנֵי-הָאָדָם וְרָאוּ מַעֲשֵׂיכֶם הַטּוֹבִים וְאֶת-אֲבִיכֶם בַּשָּׁמַיִם יְכַבֵּדוּ:

16. Ko ya•er or•chem le•ey•ney v`ney - ha•a•dam ve•ra•oo ma•a•sey•chem ha•to•vim ve•et - Avi•chem ba•sha•ma•yim ye•cha•be•doo.

Rabbinic Jewish Commentary
אבינו שבשמים, "Our and your Father which is in heaven", is a name, appellation, or periphrasis of God, frequently used by Jewish writers (s); and is often expressed by Yeshua in these his sermons on the mount.

(s) Vid. Misn. Sota, c. 9. sect. 15. & Yoma, c. 8. sect. 9.

---

17. Think not that I am come to destroy the law, or the prophets: I am not come to destroy, but to fulfill.

Greek/Transliteration
17. Μὴ νομίσητε ὅτι ἦλθον καταλῦσαι τὸν νόμον ἢ τοὺς προφήτας· οὐκ ἦλθον καταλῦσαι ἀλλὰ πληρῶσαι.

17. Mei nomiseite 'oti eilthon katalusai ton nomon ei tous propheitas. ouk eilthon katalusai alla pleirosai.

Hebrew/Transliteration
יז. אַל תַּחְשְׁבוּ כִּי בָאתִי לְהָפֵר הַתּוֹרָה אוֹ הַנְּבִיאִים לֹא לְהָפֵר בָּאתִי כִּי אִם-לְמַלֹּאת:

17. Al tach•she•voo ki va•ti le•ha•fer ha•Torah oh ha•n`vi•eem lo le•ha•fer ba•ti ki eem - le•mal•ot.

Rabbinic/Jewish New Testament Commentary
Yeshua did not come to abolish but "to make full" *(plêroôsai)* the meaning of what the *Torah* and the ethical demands of the Prophets require. Thus he came to complete our understanding of the *Torah* and the Prophets, so that we can try more effectively to be and do what they say to be and do. Mat_5:18-20 enunciate three ways in which the *Torah* and the Prophets remain necessary, applicable and in force. The remainder of chapter 5 gives six specific cases in which Yeshua explains the fuller spiritual meaning of points in the Jewish Law. In fact, this verse

states the theme and agenda of the entire Sermon on the Mount, in which Yeshua completes, makes fuller, the understanding of his *talmidim* concerning the *Torah* and the Prophets, so that they can more fully express what being God's people is all about.

" '... I came not to destroy, but to fulfil.' And surely 'to fulfil' means to complete, in the sense of bringing to perfection, not, as Christians have all too often interpreted it, to render obsolete; to fulfil in such a way as to perfect a foundation on which to build further." (*Christianity's Jewish Heritage*, West Sussex:Angel Press,1988,p.8)

This passage of Yeshua is cited in the Talmud (u), after this manner:

"it is written in it, i.e. in the Gospel, "I Aven", neither to diminish from the law of Moses am I come, "but", or "nor" (for in the Amsterdam edition they have inserted ולא between two hooks), to add to the law of Moses am I come."

Which, with their last correction, though not a just citation, yet tolerably well expresses the sense; but a most blasphemous character is affixed to Yeshua, when they call him "Aven"; which signifies "iniquity" itself, and seems to be a wilful corruption of the word "Amen", which begins the next "verse".

(t) R. Isaac Chizuk Emuna, par. 2. c. 10. p. 401. (u) T. Bab. Sabbat. fol. 116. 2.

---

18. For verily I say unto you, Till heaven and earth pass, one jot or one tittle shall in no wise pass from the law, till all be fulfilled.

Greek/Transliteration
18. Ἀμὴν γὰρ λέγω ὑμῖν, ἕως ἂν παρέλθῃ ὁ οὐρανὸς καὶ ἡ γῆ, ἰῶτα ἓν ἢ μία κεραία οὐ μὴ παρέλθῃ ἀπὸ τοῦ νόμου, ἕως ἂν πάντα γένηται.

18. Amein gar lego 'umin, 'eos an parelthei 'o ouranos kai 'ei gei, iota 'en ei mia keraia ou mei parelthei apo tou nomou, 'eos an panta geneitai.

Hebrew/Transliteration
יח. כִּי הֵן אָמֵן אָנֹכִי מַגִּיד לָכֶם עַד אֲשֶׁר הַשָּׁמַיִם וְהָאָרֶץ יַעֲברוּן לֹא תַעֲבֹר יוּד אַחַת מִן-הַתּוֹרָה אַף לֹא קוֹץ:אֶחָד עַד כִּי-כֻלָּם יָקוּמוּ

18. Ki hen amen ano•chi ma•gid la•chem ad asher ha•sha•ma•yim ve•ha•a•retz ya•a•vo•roon lo ta•a•vor yood a•chat min - ha•Torah af lo kotz e•chad ad ki - choo•lam ya•koo•moo.

Rabbinic/Jewish New Testament Commentary
The word is used by the Jews (w) for an oath; they swore by it; and it is a rule with them, that whoever answers "Amen" after an oath, it is all one as if he had pronounced the oath itself.

"When God gave the Torah to Israel, He inserted therein positive and negative commands and gave some commandments for a king, as it says: 'Only he shall not multiply horses to himself... Neither shall he multiply wives to himself, that his heart turn not away; neither silver and gold' (Deut 17:16-17). But Solomon arose and studied the reason of God's decree, saying: 'Why did God command, "He shall not multiply wives to himself?' Is it not " That his heart turn not away "? Well, I will multiply and still my heart will not turn away. Our Sages said: 'that time, the yud of the word *yarbeh* went up on high and prostrated itself before God and said: 'Master of the Universe! Have You not said that no letter shall ever be abolished from the Torah? Behold, Solomon has now arisen and abolished one. Who knows? Today he has abolished one letter, tomorrow he will abolish another until the whole Torah will be nullified? ' God replied: ' Solomon and a thousand like him will pass away, but the smallest tittle will not be erased from you."
Shemot Rabbah 6:1, Soncino Press Edition.

Yud is the smallest letter of the Hebrew alphabet. Only a small **stroke** distinguishes one Hebrew letter from another-for example *dalet* (d) from *resh* (r) or *beit* (b) from *kaf* (k). KJV transliterates "*yud*" as "jot" and renders "stroke" as "tittle" (the corresponding Hebrew term is "*kotz*," literally, "thorn").

So says R. Meir (b), "in the time of the prophets there were such who very diligently searched every letter in the law, and explained every letter by itself; and do not wonder at this that they should expound every letter by itself, for they commented על כל קוץ וקוץ של כל אות ואות, upon everyone of the tops of each letter."

Akiba ben Joseph (c) "If, (say they (d),) all the nations of the world were gathered together, "to root one word out of the law", they could not do it; which you may learn from Solomon, who sought to root "one letter out of the law", the letter "jod", in Deu_17:16 but the holy blessed God said, Solomon shall cease, and an hundred such as he (in the Talmud (e) it is a thousand such as he) ויוד ממך אינה בטילה לעולם, "but, jod shall not cease from thee (the law) for ever"."

And elsewhere the same expression is used (f), and it is added, "but a tittle from thee shall not perish.""

It is a saying of one of the Jewish Rabbi's (g), that "the whole world is not equal even to one word out of the law," in which it is said, there is not one letter deficient or superfluous.

(w) T. Hieros. Kiddushin, fol. 60. 4. Misn. Bava Kama, c. 9. sect. 7, 8. T. Bab. Shebuot, fol. 36. 1. Debarim Rabba, fol. 242. 2. Maimon Hilch. Shebuot, c. 2. sect. 1. (x) T. Bab. Taanith, fol. 21. 2. & Gloss. in ib. (y) T. Bab. Taanith, fol. 22. 2. (z) Fol. 93. 2. (a) T. Bab. Menachot, fol. 29. 2. (b) In Semitis fidei, fol. 104. 4. & 105. 1. apud Capell. in loc. (c) T. Bab. Menachot, fol. 29. 2. (d) Vajikra Rabba, fol. 160. 3. Shirhashirim Rabba, fol 20. 2. (e) T. Hieros. Sanhedrim, fol. 20. 3. (f) Shemot Rabba, fol. 96. 1. (g) T. Hieros. Peah, fol. 15. 4.

19. Whosoever therefore shall break one of these least commandments, and shall teach men so, he shall be called the least in the kingdom of heaven: but whosoever shall do and teach them, the same shall be called great in the kingdom of heaven.

Greek/Transliteration
19. Ὃς ἐὰν οὖν λύσῃ μίαν τῶν ἐντολῶν τούτων τῶν ἐλαχίστων, καὶ διδάξῃ οὕτως τοὺς ἀνθρώπους, ἐλάχιστος κληθήσεται ἐν τῇ βασιλείᾳ τῶν οὐρανῶν· ὃς δ᾽ ἂν ποιήσῃ καὶ διδάξῃ, οὗτος μέγας κληθήσεται ἐν τῇ βασιλείᾳ τῶν οὐρανῶν.

19. 'Os ean oun lusei mian ton entolon touton ton elachiston, kai didaxei 'outos tous anthropous, elachistos kleitheisetai en tei basileia ton ouranon. 'os d an poieisei kai didaxei, 'outos megas kleitheisetai en tei basileia ton ouranon.

Hebrew/Transliteration
יט. לָכֵן כָּל-הַמֵּפֵר אַחַת מִמִּצְוֹת קְטַנּוֹת אֵלֶּה וְהוֹרָה כָזֹאת לַאֲנָשִׁים נִקְלֶה יִקָּרֵא בְּמַלְכוּת הַשָּׁמַיִם וְהָעֹשֶׂה:אֹתָן וּמְלַמֵּד לַעֲשׂוֹתָן נִכְבָּד יִקָּרֵא בְּמַלְכוּת הַשָּׁמָיִם

19. La•chen kol - ha•me•fer a•chat mi•mitz•vot ke•ta•not ele ve•ho•ra cha•zot la•a•na•shim nik•le yi•ka•re be•mal•choot ha•sha•ma•yim ve•ha•o•se o•tan oom•la•med la•a•so•tan nich•bad yi•ka•re be•mal•choot ha•sha•ma•yim.

Rabbinic/Jewish New Testament Commentary
Mitzvot (singular *mitzvah*). A *mitzvah* is a commandment; traditionally in the *Torah* (the Pentateuch) there are 613 *mitzvot* for the Jewish people to obey. In casual Jewish English, "doing a *mitzvah*" means "doing a good deed, something nice, something helpful to someone, a favor"; but these meanings derive from the original sense, "a commandment" from God. Elsewhere I have discussed at length whether, and/or in what sense, Messianic Jews are expected to observe the *Torah* and obey the *mitzvot*; see my *Messianic Jewish Manifesto* (Jewish New Testament Publications, 2nd edition, 1991), especially Chapter V.

(k) "if a prophet, whom we know to be a prophet, should order us לעבור על אחת מכל מצות, "to transgress anyone of the commands", which are mentioned in the law, or many commands, whether light or heavy, for a time, we are ordered to hearken to him; and so we learn from the former wise men, by tradition, that in everything a prophet shall say to thee עבור על דברי תורה, "transgress the words of the law", as Elias on Mount Carmel, hear him, except in the case of idolatry."

And another of their writers says (l), "it is lawful sometimes to make void the law, and to do that which appears to be forbidden."

They even (m) say, that if a Gentile should bid an Israelite transgress anyone of the commands mentioned in the law, excepting idolatry, adultery, and murder, he may transgress with impunity, provided it is done privately. You see what reason Yeshua had to express himself in the manner he does, and that with resentment.

The Jews have a saying somewhat like this; "he that lessens himself for the words of the law in this world, נעשה גדול, "he shall become great" in the world to come (n)," or days of the Messiah.

(k) Hilch. Yesode Hattorah, c. 9. sect. 3. (l) Bartenora in, Misn. Beracot, c. 9. sect. 5. (m) T. Hicros. Sheviith, fol. 35. 1. (n) T. Bab. Bava Metzia, fol. 85. 2.

---

20. For I say unto you, That except your righteousness shall exceed the righteousness of the scribes and Pharisees, ye shall in no case enter into the kingdom of heaven.

Greek/Transliteration
20. Λέγω γὰρ ὑμῖν ὅτι ἐὰν μὴ περισσεύσῃ ἡ δικαιοσύνη ὑμῶν πλεῖον τῶν γραμματέων καὶ Φαρισαίων, οὐ μὴ εἰσέλθητε εἰς τὴν βασιλείαν τῶν οὐρανῶν.

20. Lego gar 'umin 'oti ean mei perisseusei 'ei dikaiosunei 'umon pleion ton grammateon kai Pharisaion, ou mei eiseltheite eis tein basileian ton ouranon.

Hebrew/Transliteration
:כ. וַאֲנִי אֹמֵר לָכֶם אִם לֹא-תִגְדַּל צִדְקַתְכֶם מִצִּדְקַת הַסּוֹפְרִים וְהַפְּרוּשִׁים לֹא תָבֹאוּ לְמַלְכוּת הַשָּׁמַיִם

20. Va•a•ni o•mer la•chem eem lo - tig•dal tzid•kat•chem mi•tzid•kat ha•sof•rim ve•haP`roo•shim lo ta•vo•oo le•mal•choot ha•sha•ma•yim.

---

21. Ye have heard that it was said by them of old time, Thou shalt not kill; and whosoever shall kill shall be in danger of the judgment:

Greek/Transliteration
21. Ἠκούσατε ὅτι ἐρρέθη τοῖς ἀρχαίοις, Οὐ φονεύσεις· ὃς δ᾽ ἂν φονεύσῃ, ἔνοχος ἔσται τῇ κρίσει·

21. Eikousate 'oti errethei tois archaiois, Ou phoneuseis. 'os d an phoneusei, enochos estai tei krisei.

Hebrew/Transliteration
:כא. שְׁמַעְתֶּם אֵת אֲשֶׁר נֶאֱמַר לַקַּדְמֹנִים לֹא תִרְצָח וְהָאִישׁ אֲשֶׁר יִרְצַח יִנָּתֵן לַמִּשְׁפָּט בִּפְלִילִים

21. Sh`ma•a•tem et asher ne•e•mar la•kad•mo•nim lo tir•tzach ve•ha•eesh asher yir•tzach yi•na•ten la•mish•pat bif•li•lim.

Rabbinic/Jewish New Testament Commentary
Sixth of the Ten Commandments (Exo_20:13, Deu_5:17). In this commentary I use the Jewish enumeration of the Ten Commandments, in which the first Commandment is, "I am *Adonai*, who brought you out of the land of Egypt, out of the house of bondage." Since this is in fact not a commandment but a declaration, Christian enumerations do not include it. But the Hebrew phrase for "the Ten

Commandments" is " *'aseret-hadibrot*," literally, "the ten sayings." This first "saying" is actually the basis for the other nine *dibrot* as well as for all the *mitzvot* (see Mat_5:19). It is because of who God is ("I am *Adonai*") and because of his benevolent involvement in the ongoing life and history of his people ("who brought you out of the land of Egypt") and his concern for their welfare ("out of the house of bondage") that, in faith, hope, love and gratitude, his people should obey him. Yeshua begins his detailed "filling" of the *Torah* (Mat_5:17) with one of the Ten Commandments, implicitly alluding to this underlying ground for all obedience to God. "In Judaism the citation of a Scripture text implies the whole context," all Ten Commandments, "not merely the quoted words" (Mat_2:6).

Ye have heard,.... That is, from the Scriptures being read to them, and the explanations of the ancients, which were called שמעתא, "hearing", being read in the schools, and heard by the scholars (o); so that to "hear", was along with the recital of the text, to receive by tradition, the sense the elders had given of it: of this kind is the instance produced by Yeshua. Thus Onkelos, and Jonathan ben Uzziel, render the phrase, "him shall ye hear", in Deu_18:15 by מניה תקבלין, "from him shall ye receive"; so those phrases (p), למדו מפי השמועה, "they learn from hearing", or by report from others; and אמרו מפי השמועה "they speak from hearing", or from what they have heard, are often used for receiving and reporting things as they have them by tradition. That "it was said", or "it hath been said"; this is also a Talmudic form of expression; often is this phrase to be met with in the Talmud, איתאמר, "it has been said" (q); that is, by the ancient doctors, as here, "by them of old time", or "to the ancients", לקדמונים.

"everyone that kills his neighbour with his hand; as if he strikes him with a sword, or with a stone that kills him; or strangles him till he die; or burns him in fire; seeing he kills him in any manner, in his own person, lo! such an one must be put to death בבית דין, "by the house of judgment", or the sanhedrim (s)."

"if a man hires a murderer to kill his neighbour, or sends his servants, and they kill him, or binds him, and leaves him before a lion, or the like, and the beast kills him, everyone of these is a shedder of blood; and the sin of slaughter is in his hand; and he is guilty of death by the hand of heaven, i.e. God; but he is not to be put to death by the house of judgment, or the sanhedrim (t)."

(o) Vid. Buxtorf. Lex. Rabbin, fol. 2453. (p) Maimon. Hilch. Issure Mizbeach, c. 1. sect. 2, 4, 5, 7, 10. & passim, & T. Bab. Sanhedrim, fol. 88. 1. (q) Vid. Edzardi Not. in Avoda Zara, c. 2. p. 284. (r) Vid. R. Aben Ezra in Exod. xxi. 17. & in Isa. lii. 13. & lxvi. 24. (s) Maimon. Hilch. Rotseach, c. 2. sect. 1. (t) Maimon. Hilch. Rotseach, c. 2. sect. 2.

---

22. But I say unto you, That whosoever is angry with his brother without a cause shall be in danger of the judgment: and whosoever shall say to his brother, Raca, shall be in danger of the council: but whosoever shall say, Thou fool, shall be in danger of hell fire.

Greek Transliteration
22. ἐγὼ δὲ λέγω ὑμῖν ὅτι πᾶς ὁ ὀργιζόμενος τῷ ἀδελφῷ αὐτοῦ εἰκῇ ἔνοχος ἔσται τῇ κρίσει· ὃς δ' ἂν εἴπῃ τῷ ἀδελφῷ αὐτοῦ, ῾Ρακά, ἔνοχος ἔσται τῷ συνεδρίῳ· ὃς δ' ἂν εἴπῃ, Μωρέ, ἔνοχος ἔσται εἰς τὴν γέενναν τοῦ πυρός.

22. ego de lego 'umin 'oti pas 'o orgizomenos to adelpho autou eikei enochos estai tei krisei. 'os d an eipei to adelpho autou, 'Raka, enochos estai to sunedrio. 'os d an eipei, More, enochos estai eis tein geennan tou puros.

Hebrew/Transliteration
כב. וַאֲנִי אֹמֵר לָכֶם הַמִּתְעַבֵּר בְּאָחִיו חִנָּם יִנָּתֵן לַמִּשְׁפָּט בִּפְלִילִים וְהַקּוֹרֵא לְאָחִיו רֵיקָא יִנָּתֵן בִּידֵי הַסַּנְהֶדְרִין וְאִם:נָבָל יִקְרָא-לוֹ יִפֹּל לְאֵשׁ גֵּיהִנֹּם

22. Va•a•ni o•mer la•chem ha•mit•a•ber be•a•chiv chi•nam yi•na•ten la•mish•pat bif•li•lim ve•ha•ko•re le•a•chiv Rey•ka yi•na•ten biy•dey ha•San•hed•rin ve•eem na•val yik•ra - lo yi•pol le•esh Gey•hi•nom.

Rabbinic/Jewish New Testament Commentary
Yeshua is not here abrogating the Law (Mat_5:17); so his "but" does not introduce something that contradicts or contrasts with the ideas of the prior "You have heard" (Mat_5:21, Mat_5:27, Mat_5:33, Mat_5:38, Mat_5:43) or "It was said" (Mat_5:31). Yeshua is not telling his audience that they have heard something which is wrong that he is now about to correct. Rather, his "but" completes and "fills" (Mat_5:17) the full sense of the *Torah* which they have already heard. At Mat_5:22, Mat_5:28 andMat_5:34 "*de*" can successfully be rendered "and" or "moreover," to bring out how Yeshua's remark carries forward and completes the thought of the previous verse. However, in Mat_5:32, Mat_5:39 andMat_5:44 "but" does the job better while also remaining satisfactory in the other three verses.

Gey-Hinnom, brought over into Greek and English as "Gehenna" and usually translated "hell." Literally, "valley of Hinnom" (a personal name); located both then and now just south of the Old City of Jerusalem. Rubbish fires were always burning there; Hebrew Bible at Isa_66:24.

But I say unto you,.... This is a Rabbinical way of speaking, used when a question is determined, and a false notion is refuted; it is a magisterial form of expression, and well suits with Christ, the great teacher and master in Israel; who spake as one having authority, opposing himself, not to the law of "Moses, thou shalt not kill"; but to the false gloss the ancient doctors had put upon it, with which their later ones agreed.

"Thou fool", is, thou wicked man, thou ungodly wretch, thou graceless creature, whose portion will be eternal damnation. Calling a man by such names was not allowed of by the Jews themselves, whose rules are:

"he that calls his neighbour a servant, let him be excommunicated; a bastard, let him be beaten with forty stripes; רשע, "a wicked man", let him descend with him into his life or livelihood (z)."

The gloss upon it is, "as if he should say, to this the sanhedrim is not obliged, but it is lawful to hate him, yea to lessen his sustenance, and exercise his trade,"

Again, they say, "it is forbidden a man to call his neighbour by a name of reproach (a) everyone that calls his neighbour רשע, "a wicked man", shall be brought down to Gehenna;"

The Hebrew גיא הנם, "Ge-Hinnom", the valley of Hinnom, where the children were caused to pass through the fire to Mo. This place, the Jewish writers (b) say,

"Was a place well known, near to Jerusalem, a valley, whose fire was never quenched; and in which they burned the bones of anything that was unclean, and dead carcasses, and other pollutions."

(w) T. Bab. Sanhedrim, fol. 100. 1. T. Bava Bathra, fol. 75. 1. (x) Massechet Derach Eretz, c. 4. fol. 18. 1. (y) Vid. T. Bab. Beracot, fol. 32. 2. Zohar in Exod. fol. 50. 2. (z) T. Bab. Kiddushin, fol. 28. 1. Bava Metzia, fol. 71. 1. (a) Zohar in Exod. fol. 50. 3. (b) Sepher Cosri, fol. 57. 2. Vid. Kimchi in Psal. xxvii. 13.

---

23. Therefore if thou bring thy gift to the altar, and there rememberest that thy brother hath ought against thee;

Greek/Transliteration
23. Ἐὰν οὖν προσφέρῃς τὸ δῶρόν σου ἐπὶ τὸ θυσιαστήριον, καὶ ἐκεῖ μνησθῇς ὅτι ὁ ἀδελφός σου ἔχει τι κατὰ σοῦ,

23. Ean oun prosphereis to doron sou epi to thusyasteirion, kai ekei mneistheis 'oti 'o adelphos sou echei ti kata sou,

Hebrew/Transliteration
:כג. עַל-כֵּן אֵפוֹא כִּי-תַקְרִיב קָרְבָּן עַל-הַמִּזְבֵּחַ וְלִבְּךָ יַגֶּד-לְךָ שָׁם כִּי-דְבַר רִיב לְאָחִיךָ עִמָּךְ

23. Al - ken e•fo ki - tak•riv kor•ban al - ha•miz•be•ach ve•lib•cha ya•ged - le•cha sham ki - de•var riv le•a•chi•cha ee•mach.

Rabbinic Commentary
Traditional Judaism expresses this idea in the Mishna:
"*Yom-Kippur* [the Day of Atonement] atones for a person's transgressions against God, but it does not atone for his transgressions against his fellow-man until he appeases him." (Yoma 8:9)

The Jews obliged such who had done any damage to their neighbours, by stealing from them, to make satisfaction before they brought their offering; concerning which they say (c), "he that brings what he has stolen, before he brings his trespass offering, is right; he that brings his trespass offering, before he brings that which he has stolen, is not right."

Again (d), "they do not bring the trespass offering before the sum of what is stolen is returned, either to the owners, or to the priests."

(c) Misn. Bava Kama, c. 9. sect. 12. (d) Maimon. Hilch. Gezela, c. 8. sect. 13.

---

24. Leave there thy gift before the altar, and go thy way; first be reconciled to thy brother, and then come and offer thy gift.

Greek/Transliteration
24. ἄφες ἐκεῖ τὸ δῶρόν σου ἔμπροσθεν τοῦ θυσιαστηρίου, καὶ ὕπαγε, πρῶτον διαλλάγηθι τῷ ἀδελφῷ σου, καὶ τότε ἐλθὼν πρόσφερε τὸ δῶρόν σου.

24. aphes ekei to doron sou emprosthen tou thusyasteiriou, kai 'upage, proton dyallageithi to adelpho sou, kai tote elthon prosphere to doron sou.

Hebrew/Transliteration
כד: הַנַּח שָׁם קָרְבָּנְךָ לִפְנֵי הַמִּזְבֵּחַ וְלֵךְ הִתְרַפֵּס וּרְהַב אָחִיךָ וְאָז בֹּא וְהַקְרֵב קָרְבָּנֶךָ

24. Ha•nach sham kor•ban•cha lif•ney ha•miz•be•ach ve•lech hit•ra•pes oor•hav a•chi•cha ve•az bo ve•hak•rev kor•ba•ne•cha.

Rabbinic Jewish Commentary
(e): "that transgressions, which are between a man and God, the day of atonement expiates; the transgressions which are between a man and his neighbour, the day of atonement does not expiate, עד שירצה את חבירו, "until he hath reconciled his neighbour." (e) Misn. Yoma, c. 8. sect. 9.

---

25. Agree with thine adversary quickly, whiles thou art in the way with him; lest at any time the adversary deliver thee to the judge, and the judge deliver thee to the officer, and thou be cast into prison.

Greek/Transliteration
25. Ἴσθι εὐνοῶν τῷ ἀντιδίκῳ σου ταχύ, ἕως ὅτου εἶ ἐν τῇ ὁδῷ μετ᾽ αὐτοῦ, μήποτέ σε παραδῷ ὁ ἀντίδικος τῷ κριτῇ, καὶ ὁ κριτής σε παραδῷ τῷ ὑπηρέτῃ, καὶ εἰς φυλακὴν βληθήσῃ.

25. Ysthi eunoon to antidiko sou tachu, 'eos 'otou ei en tei 'odo met autou, meipote se parado 'o antidikos to kritei, kai 'o kriteis se parado to 'upeiretei, kai eis phulakein bleitheisei.

Hebrew/Transliteration
כה. מַהֵר הַשְׁלֵם עִם-אִישׁ רִיבְךָ בְּעוֹדְךָ עִמּוֹ בַדָּרֶךְ פֶּן-יַסְגִּיר אֹתְךָ אִישׁ רִיבְךָ בִּידֵי הַשֹּׁפֵט וְהַשֹּׁפֵט יַסְגִּירְךָ בְּיַד-הַשּׁוֹטֵר וְהוּא יִתֶּנְךָ לְבֵית הַסֹּהַר

25. Ma•her hash•lem eem - eesh riv•cha be•od•cha ee•mo va•da•rech pen - yas•gir ot•cha eesh riv•cha biy•dey ha•sho•fet ve•ha•sho•fet yas•gir•cha be•yad ha•sho•ter ve•hoo yi•ten•cha le•veit ha•so•har.

Rabbinic Jewish Commentary

The Talmud (h), as here, where it seems to be a common proverb; for it is said, "there are men that say, or men usually say, אגב אורחך לבעל דבבך אישתמע, "whilst thou art in the way with thine adversary, be obedient".

The Jewish (i); canons: "if the creditor says we will go to the great sanhedrim, they compel the debtor, and he goes up with them, as it is said, "the borrower is servant to the lender" "It was an affirmative command in the law, says Maimonides, to appoint "judges" and "officers" in every country and province, as it is said, Deu_16:18. שופטים, "judges" they are the judges that are fixed in the sanhedrim, and such that engage in law suits come before them: שוטרים, "officers"; these are the masters of the rod and scourge, i.e. who beat and scourge delinquents; and these stand before the judges--and all they do, is by the order of the judges."

(g) Misn. Sanhedrim, c. 1. sect. 1. (h) T. Bab. Sanhedrim, fol. 95. 2. (i) Maimof. Hilch. Sanhedrim, c. 6. sect. 7.

---

26. Verily I say unto thee, Thou shalt by no means come out thence, till thou hast paid the uttermost farthing.

Greek/Transliteration
26. Ἀμὴν λέγω σοι, οὐ μὴ ἐξέλθῃς ἐκεῖθεν, ἕως ἂν ἀποδῷς τὸν ἔσχατον κοδράντην.

26. Amein lego soi, ou mei exeltheis ekeithen, 'eos an apodos ton eschaton kodrantein.

Hebrew/Transliteration
כו. וַאֲנִי אָמֵן אֹמֵר לְךָ כִּי לֹא תַעֲלֶה מִשָּׁם עַד אֲשֶׁר תְּשַׁלֵּם אֶת-הַפְּרוּטָה הָאַחֲרֹנָה:

26. Va•a•ni amen o•mer le•cha ki lo ta•a•le mi•sham ad asher te•sha•lem et - hap•roo•ta ha•a•cha•ro•na.

---

27. Ye have heard that it was said by them of old time, Thou shalt not commit adultery:

Greek/Transliteration
27. Ἠκούσατε ὅτι ἐρρέθη, Οὐ μοιχεύσεις·

27. Eikousate 'oti errethei, Ou moicheuseis.

Hebrew/Trasnsliteration
כז. שְׁמַעְתֶּם אֶת אֲשֶׁר נֶאֱמַר לַקַּדְמֹנִים לֹא תִנְאָף:

27. Sh`ma•a•tem et asher ne•e•mar la•kad•mo•nim lo tin•af.

---

28. But I say unto you, That whosoever looketh on a woman to lust after her hath committed adultery with her already in his heart.

Greek/Transliteration
28. ἐγὼ δὲ λέγω ὑμῖν, ὅτι πᾶς ὁ βλέπων γυναῖκα πρὸς τὸ ἐπιθυμῆσαι αὐτὴν ἤδη ἐμοίχευσεν αὐτὴν ἐν τῇ καρδίᾳ αὐτοῦ.

28. ego de lego 'umin, 'oti pas 'o blepon gunaika pros to epithumeisai autein eidei emoicheusen autein en tei kardia autou.

Hebrew/Transliteration
כח. וַאֲנִי אֹמֵר לָכֶם כָּל-הַנֹּתֵן עֵינוֹ בְּאִשָּׁה לַחֲשָׁק-בָּהּ בְּרוּחַ-זְנוּנִים נָאַף אֹתָהּ בְּלִבּוֹ:

28. Va•a•ni o•mer la•chem kol - ha•no•ten ey•no ve•ee•sha la•cha•shok - ba be•roo•ach - ze•noo•nim na•af o•ta be•li•bo.

Rabbinic Commentary

"R. Aha of the school of R. Josiah said: He who gazes at a woman eventually comes to sin, and he who looks even at a woman's heel will beget degenerate children." Nedarim 20a, Babylonian Talmud, Soncino Press Edition

But these men, who forbad external looking upon a woman, generally speaking, had no notion of heart sins; and which was the prevailing opinion of the Pharisees.

"A good thought, they (r) allow, is reckoned as if done; as it is said, Mal_3:16. Upon which it is asked, what is the meaning of that, and "that thought" upon "his name?" Says R. Ase, if a man thinks to do a good work, and is hindered, and does it not, the Scripture reckons it to him, as if he did it; but an evil thought, the holy blessed God does not account of it as if done, as is said, Psa_66:18."

(s) "Though I regard iniquity in my heart to do it, even in thought, yea, against God himself, as if I had expressed it with my lips, he does not hear it; that is, לֹא חָשַׁב לִי עָוֹן, "he does not reckon it to me for sin"; because the holy blessed God does not account an evil thought for an action, to them that are in the faith of God, or of the true religion."

For it seems, this is only true of the Israelites; it is just the reverse with the Gentiles, in whom God does not reckon of a good thought, as if it was done, but does of an evil one, as if it was in act (t).

Though some affirmed what Yeshua was teaching; "everyone that looks upon a woman בכוונה, with intention, it is all one as if he lay with her."

And that נואף בעיניו נקרא נואף, "he that committeth adultery with his eyes, is called an adulterer" (x). Yea, they also observe (y), that a woman may commit adultery in her heart, as well as a man; but the Pharisees of Christ's time were of another mind.

(r) T. Bab. Kiddushin, fol. 40. 1. (s) R. David Kimchi, in Psal. lxvi. 18. (t) T. Hieros. Peah, fol. 16. 2. (x) Vajikra Rabba, sect. 23. fol. 265. 1. (y) Bemidbar Rabba, sect. 9. fol. 196. 1.

---

29. And if thy right eye offend thee, pluck it out, and cast it from thee: for it is profitable for thee that one of thy members should perish, and not that thy whole body should be cast into hell.

Greek/Transliteration
29. Εἰ δὲ ὁ ὀφθαλμός σου ὁ δεξιὸς σκανδαλίζει σε, ἔξελε αὐτὸν καὶ βάλε ἀπὸ σοῦ· συμφέρει γάρ σοι ἵνα ἀπόληται ἓν τῶν μελῶν σου, καὶ μὴ ὅλον τὸ σῶμά σου βληθῇ εἰς γέενναν.

29. Ei de 'o ophthalmos sou 'o dexios skandalizei se, exele auton kai bale apo sou. Sumpherei gar soi 'ina apoleitai 'en ton melon sou, kai mei 'olon to soma sou bleithei eis geennan.

Hebrew/Transliteration
כט. וְאִם עֵינְךָ הַיְמָנִית תַּכְשִׁילְךָ נַקְּרֶהָ וְהַשְׁלִיכָהּ מִמֶּךָ טוֹב לְךָ בַּאֲבֹד אֵבֶר אֶחָד מֵהָשְׁלַח כָּל-בְּשָׂרְךָ לְגֵיהִנֹּם:

29. Ve•eem eyn•cha hay`ma•nit tach•shi•le•cha nak•re•ha ve•hash•li•che•ha mi•me•cha tov le•cha ba•a•vod ever e•chad me•hash•lach kol - be•sar•cha le•gey•hi•nom.

Rabbinic Jewish Commentary
The eye is often the instrument of ensnaring the heart this way: hence the Jews have a (z) saying, "whoever looks upon women, at the end comes into the hands of transgression." (z) T. Bab. Nedarim, fol. 20. 1.

Mention is only made of the right eye; not but that the left may be an occasion of sinning, as well as the right; but that being most dear and valuable, is instanced in, and ordered to be parted with.

---

30. And if thy right hand offend thee, cut if off, and cast it from thee: for it is profitable for thee that one of thy members should perish, and not that thy whole body should be cast into hell.

Greek/Transliteration
30. Καὶ εἰ ἡ δεξιά σου χεὶρ σκανδαλίζει σε, ἔκκοψον αὐτὴν καὶ βάλε ἀπὸ σοῦ· συμφέρει γάρ σοι ἵνα ἀπόληται ἓν τῶν μελῶν σου, καὶ μὴ ὅλον τὸ σῶμά σου βληθῇ εἰς γέενναν.

30. Kai ei 'ei dexya sou cheir skandalizei se, ekkopson autein kai bale apo sou. sumpherei gar soi 'ina apoleitai 'en ton melon sou, kai mei 'olon to soma sou bleithei eis geennan.

Hebrew/Transliteration
ל. וְאִם-יָדְךָ הַיְמָנִית תַּכְשִׁילֶךָ קַצְּצָהּ וְהַשְׁלִיכֶהָ מִמֶּךָּ טוֹב לְךָ בַּאֲבֹד אֵבֶר אֶחָד מֵהָשְׁלַךְ כָּל-בְּשָׂרְךָ לְגֵיהִנֹּם:

30. Ve•eem - yad•cha hay`ma•nit tach•shi•le•cha ka•tze•tze•ha ve•hash•li•che•ha mi•me•cha tov le•cha ba•a•vod ever e•chad me•hash•lach kol - be•sar•cha le•gey•hi•nom.

Rabbinic Jewish Commentary
As adultery may be committed in the heart, and by the eye, so with the hand:

"says R. Eliezer (a) what is the meaning of that Scripture, "your hands are full of blood", Isa_1:15? It is replied, אלו המנאפים ביד, "these are they, that commit adultery with the hand". It is a tradition of the house of R. Ishmael, that the sense of that command, "thou shalt not commit adultery", is, there shall be none that commits adultery in thee, whether "with the hand", or "with the foot".

The Jews enjoined cutting off of the hand, on several accounts; if in a morning, before a man had washed his hands, he put his hand to his eye, nose, mouth, ear.. תיקצץ, it was to be "cut off" (b); particularly, the handling of the "membrum virile", was punishable with cutting off of the hand.

"Says R. (c) Tarphon, if the hand is moved to the privy parts, תקצץ ידו, "let his hand be cut off to his navel".

(a) T. Bab. Nidda, fol. 13. 2. Vid. Maimon. Issure Bia, c. 21. sect. 18. (b) T. Bab. Sabbat. fol. 108. 2. Massechet Callah, fol. 17. 1. (c) T. Bab. Nidda, fol. 13. 2

---

31. It hath been said, Whosoever shall put away his wife, let him give her a writing of divorcement:

Greek/Transliteration
31. Ἐρρέθη δὲ ὅτι Ὃς ἂν ἀπολύσῃ τὴν γυναῖκα αὐτοῦ, δότω αὐτῇ ἀποστάσιον·

31. Errethei de 'oti 'Os an apolusei tein gunaika autou, doto autei apostasion.

Hebrew/Transliteration
לֹא. וְנֶאֱמַר כִּי־יְשַׁלַּח אִישׁ אִשְׁתּוֹ וְנָתַן בְּיָדָהּ סֵפֶר כְּרִיתֻת:

31. Ve•ne•e•mar ki - yee•sha•lach eesh eesh•to ve•na•tan be•ya•da se•fer k`ri•toot.

Jewish New Testament Commentary

Deu_24:1 mentions a "writing of divorcement" (Hebrew *sefer-k'ritut*) but does not specify its contents or the conditions under which divorce was permitted. The rabbis call such a document a *get* and discuss divorce in the Talmud (for more, see Mat_19:6).

For though a wife was obtained by several ways, there was but one way of dismissing her, as the Jews observe (f), and that was, by giving her a bill. The form of a writing of divorcement, as given by Maimonides (g), is as follows:

"On such a day of the week, in such a month, of such a year, either from the creation, or the epocha of contracts, according to the usual way of computation, which we observe in such a place; I such an one, the son of such an one, of such a place; or if I have any other name, or surname, or my parents, or my place, or the place of my parents; by my own will, without any force, I put away, dismiss, and divorce thee. Thee, I say, who art such an one, the daughter of such an one, of such a place; or if thou hast any other name, or surname, or thy parents, or thy place, or the place of thy parents; who wast my wife heretofore, but now I put thee away, dismiss and divorce thee; so that thou art in thine own hand, and hast power over thyself, to go, and marry any other man, whom thou pleasest; and let no man hinder thee in my name, from this day forward and for ever; and lo! thou art free to any man: and let this be unto thee, from me, a bill of divorce, an instrument of dismission, and a letter of forsaking, according to the law of Moses and Israel."

(f) Baal Hatturim in Deut. xxiv. 1. Maimon. Hilchot Ishot, c. 1. sect. 2, 3. (g) Hilchot Gerushin, c. 4. sect. 12.

---

32. But I say unto you, That whosoever shall put away his wife, saving for the cause of fornication, causeth her to commit adultery: and whosoever shall marry her that is divorced committeth adultery.

Greek/Transliteration
32. ἐγὼ δὲ λέγω ὑμῖν, ὅτι ὃς ἂν ἀπολύσῃ τὴν γυναῖκα αὐτοῦ, παρεκτὸς λόγου πορνείας, ποιεῖ αὐτὴν μοιχᾶσθαι· καὶ ὃς ἐὰν ἀπολελυμένην γαμήσῃ μοιχᾶται.
32. ego de lego 'umin, 'oti 'os an apolusei tein gunaika autou, parektos logou porneias, poiei autein moichasthai. kai 'os ean apolelumenein gameisei moichatai.

Hebrew/Transliteration
לב. וַאֲנִי אֹמֵר לָכֶם אִם יְשַׁלַּח אִישׁ אִשְׁתּוֹ אִם לֹא עַל־דְּבַר זְנוּת מֵשִׂים אֹתָהּ לְנֹאָפֶת וְהַלֹּקֵחַ גְּרוּשָׁה לוֹ לְאִשָּׁה:נֹאֵף הוּא

32. Va•a•ni o•mer la•chem eem ye•sha•lach eesh eesh•to eem lo al - de•var z`not me•sim o•ta le•no•a•fet ve•ha•lo•ke•ach g`roo•sha lo le•ee•sha no•ef hoo.

Rabbinic/Jewish New Testament Commentary

The principle does not prevent believers divorced before coming to Messianic faith from remarrying, since all sins prior to salvation are forgiven when repentance has taken place. Anyone unmarried at the time of his salvation is free to marry (but apparently only to another believer-see 1Co_7:39).

For so it is written (i), "The house of Shammai say, a man may not put away his wife, unless he finds some uncleanness in her, according to Deu_24:1 The house of Hillell say, if she should spoil his food, (that is, as Jarchi and Bartenora explain it, burns it either at the fire, or with salt, i.e. over roasts or over salts it,) who appeal also to Deu_24:1. R. Akiba says, if he finds another more beautiful than her, as it is said, Deu_24:1 "and it come to pass that she find no favour in his eyes."

The commentators (k) on this passage say that the determination of the matter is, according to the school of Millell; so that, according to them, a woman might be put away for a very trivial thing: some difference is made by some of the Jewish doctors, between a first and second wife; the first wife, they say (l), might not be put away, but for adultery; but the second might be put away, if her husband hated her; or she was of ill behaviour, and impudent, and not modest, as the daughters of Israel. Now our Lord says, without any exception, that a man ought not to put away his wife, whether first or second, for any other reason than uncleanness; and that whoever does, upon any other account, causeth her to commit adultery.

(i) Misn. Gittin, c. 9. sect. 10. Vid. T. Hieros. Gittin, fol. 49. 4. & Sota, fol. 16. 2. & Bemidbar Rabba, sect. 9. fol. 195. 2. (k) Maimon. & Bartenora in Gittin, c. 9. sect. 10. (l) T. Bab. Gittin, fol. 90. 2. Maimon. Hilch. Gerushin, c. 10. sect. 21, 22.

---

33. Again, ye have heard that it hath been said by them of old time, Thou shalt not forswear thyself, but shalt perform unto the Lord thine oaths:

Greek/Transliteration
33. Πάλιν ἠκούσατε ὅτι ἐρρέθη τοῖς ἀρχαίοις, Οὐκ ἐπιορκήσεις, ἀποδώσεις δὲ τῷ κυρίῳ τοὺς ὅρκους σου·

33. Palin eikousate 'oti errethei tois archaiois, Ouk epiorkeiseis, apodoseis de to kurio tous 'orkous sou.

Hebrew/Transliteration
לג. וְעוֹד שְׁמַעְתֶּם אֶת אֲשֶׁר נֶאֱמַר לַקַּדְמֹנִים לֹא תִשָּׁבַע לַשֶּׁקֶר וְאֶת-נְדָרֶיךָ תְּשַׁלֵּם לַיהוָֹה:

33. Ve•od sh`ma•a•tem et asher ne•e•mar la•kad•mo•nim lo ti•sha•va la•she•ker ve•et - n`da•re•cha te•sha•lem la`Adonai.

Jewish New Testament Commentary

Do not break your oath (or: "Do not swear falsely," or: "Do not perjure yourself"). **Keep your vows to** *Adonai*. The distinction between vows and oaths is hazy not only to us, but also within Judaism; and the issue doesn't seem important today. The early believers understood Yeshua not as prohibiting all vows (see Act_18:5 Act_21:23), but as prohibiting vain oaths-the rabbis of the time did the same. In the Apocrypha compare Sir_23:9, "Do not accustom your mouth to swearing oaths, and do not habitually use the name of the Holy One." Philo of Alexandria recommended avoiding oaths entirely (Decalogue 84). The Talmud has this parallel to v. 37: "Let your 'no' and 'yes' both be righteous [i.e., straightforward]." (Bava Metzia 49a)

---

34. But I say unto you, Swear not at all; neither by heaven; for it is God's throne:

Greek/Transliteration
34. ἐγὼ δὲ λέγω ὑμῖν μὴ ὀμόσαι ὅλως· μήτε ἐν τῷ οὐρανῷ, ὅτι θρόνος ἐστὶν τοῦ θεοῦ·

34. ego de lego 'umin mei omosai 'olos. meite en to ourano, 'oti thronos estin tou theou.

Hebrew/Transliteration
:לד. וַאֲנִי אֹמֵר לָכֶם לֹא תִשָּׁבַע כָּל-שְׁבוּעָה לֹא תִשָּׁבַע בַּשָּׁמַיִם כִּי-כִסֵּא אֱלֹהִים הֵמָּה

34. Va•a•ni o•mer la•chem lo ti•sha•va kol - sh`voo•ah lo ti•sha•va ba•sha•ma•yim ki - chi•se Elohim he•ma.

Rabbinic Jewish Commentary

But I say unto you, swear not at all [falsely],.... Which must not be understood in the strictest sense, as though it was not lawful to take an oath upon any occasion, in an affair of moment, in a solemn serious manner, and in the name of God; which may be safely done: but of rash swearing, about trivial matters, and by the creatures or falsely in His name, Lev_19:12; as appears by what follows,

neither by heaven; which is directly contrary to the Jewish canons (m), which say, "they that swear בשמים, "by heaven", and by earth, are free."

Upon the words in Son_2:7, "I adjure you", it is asked (n), "by what does she adjure them? R. Eliezer says, by the heavens, and by the earth; by the hosts, the host above, and the host below."

So Philo the Jew says (o) that the most high and ancient cause need not to be immediately mentioned in swearing; but the "earth", the sun, the stars, ουρανον, "heaven", and the whole world. So R. Aben Ezra, and R. David Kimchi, explain Amo_4:2. "The Lord God hath sworn by his holiness"; that is, say they, בשמים, "by heaven": which may be thought to justify them, in this form of swearing;

though they did not look upon it as a binding oath, and therefore if broken they were not criminal (p). "He that swears בשמים by heaven, and by the earth, and by the sun, and the like; though his intention is nothing less than to him that created them, this is no oath."

(m) Misn. Shebuot, c. 4. sect. 13. (n) Shirhashirim Rabba, fol. 10. 4. (o) De Special. leg. p 770. (p) Maimon. Hilch. Shebuot, c. 12. sect. 3.

---

35. Nor by the earth; for it is his footstool: neither by Jerusalem; for it is the city of the great King.

Greek/Transliteration
35. μήτε ἐν τῇ γῇ, ὅτι ὑποπόδιόν ἐστιν τῶν ποδῶν αὐτοῦ· μήτε εἰς Ἱεροσόλυμα, ὅτι πόλις ἐστὶν τοῦ μεγάλου βασιλέως·

35. meite en tei gei, 'oti 'upopodion estin ton podon autou. meite eis 'Yerosoluma, 'oti polis estin tou megalou basileos.

Hebrew/Transliteration
לה. וְלֹא בָאָרֶץ כִּי-הֲדֹם רַגְלָיו הִיא וְלֹא בִירוּשָׁלַיִם כִּי-הִיא קִרְיַת מֶלֶךְ רָב:

35. Ve•lo va•a•retz ki - ha•dom rag•lav hee ve•lo vi•Ye•roo•sha•la•yim ki - hee kir•yat Me•lech rav.

Rabbinic Jewish Commentary
Neither by Jerusalem, which the Jews used to swear by: such forms of vows as these are to be met with in their writings (q); "as the altar, as the temple, כירושלם, "as Jerusalem";" that is, by Jerusalem, I vow I will do this, or the other thing.

"R. Judah says, he that says Jerusalem (i.e. as Bartenora observes (r), without the note of comparison, as) says nothing."

In the Gemara (s) it is, "he that says as Jerusalem, does not say anything, till he has made his vow concerning a thing, which is offered up in Jerusalem."

(q) Misn. Nedarim, c. 1. sect. 3. (r) In. ib. (s) T. Bab. Nedarim, fol. 11. 1.

---

36. Neither shalt thou swear by thy head, because thou canst not make one hair white or black.

Greek/Tranliteration
36. μήτε ἐν τῇ κεφαλῇ σου ὀμόσῃς, ὅτι οὐ δύνασαι μίαν τρίχα λευκὴν ἢ μέλαιναν ποιῆσαι.

36. meite en tei kephalei sou omoseis, 'oti ou dunasai mian tricha leukein ei melainan poieisai.

Hebrew/Transliteration
:לו. וְלֹא תִשָּׁבַע בְּרֹאשְׁךָ כִּי-לֹא תוּכַל לַהֲפֹךְ שֵׂעָר אֶחָד לָבָן אוֹ שָׁחֹר

36. Ve•lo ti•sha•va be•ro•she•cha ki - lo too•chal la•ha•foch se•ar e•chad la•van oh sha•chor.

Rabbinic Jewish Commentary
This also was a common form of swearing among the Jews: take a few instances.

"If anyone is bound to his friend by an oath, and says to him, vow unto me בחיי ראשך, "by the life of thy head"; R. Meir says (u), he may retract it; but the wise men say, he cannot."

Again (w), a certain Rabbi said to Elijah, "I heard "Bath Kol" (or the voice from heaven) mourning like a dove, and saying, woe to my children; for, because of their sins, I have destroyed my house, and have burnt my temple, and have carried them captive among the nations: and he (Elijah) said unto him חייך וחיי ראשך, "by thy life, and by the life of thy head", not this time only it says so, but it says so three times every day."

Once more (x), says R. Simeon ben Antipatras, to R. Joshua, "I have heard from the mouth of the wise men, that he that vows in the law, and transgresses, is to be beaten with forty stripes: he replies, blessed art thou of God, that thou hast so done, חייך וחיי ראשך, "by thy life, and by the life of thy head", he that is used to do so is to be beaten."

(u) Misn. Sanhedrim, c. 3. sect 2. (w) T. Bab. Beracot, fol. 3. 1. (x) Derech. Eretz, c. 6. fol. 18. 2.

---

37. But let your communication be, Yea, yea; Nay, nay: for whatsoever is more than these cometh of evil.

Greek/Transliteration
37. Ἔστω δὲ ὁ λόγος ὑμῶν, ναὶ ναί, οὒ οὔ· τὸ δὲ περισσὸν τούτων ἐκ τοῦ πονηροῦ ἐστιν.

37. Esto de 'o logos 'umon, nai nai, ou ou. to de perisson touton ek tou poneirou estin.

Hebrew/Transliteration
:לז. אַךְ זֶה זֶה יְהִי דְבַרְכֶם הֵן הֵן לֹא לֹא וְיֹתֵר מִזֶּה מִמְּקוֹר הָרָע הוּא

37. Ach ze ye•hee d`var•chem hen hen lo lo ve•yo•ter mi•ze mim•kor ha•ra hoo.

Rabbinic Commentary
"…your 'yes' should be just and your 'no' should be just! Abaye said: That means that one must not speak one thing with the mouth and another with the heart."
Baba Metzia 49a, Soncino Press Edition

"Says R. Eliezer (a), לאו שבועה הן שבועה, "nay is an oath; yea is an oath", absolutely; "nay" is an oath, as it is written, Gen_9:11 and Isa_54:9. But that "yea" is an oath, how does it appear? It is concluded from hence, that "nay" is an oath; saith Rabba, there are that say "nay, nay", twice; and there are that say "yea, yea", twice; as it is written, Gen_9:11 and from hence, that "nay" is twice, "yea" is also twice said."

The gloss upon it is, "he that says either "nay, nay", twice, or "yea, yea", twice; lo! it is כשבועה מאחר "as an after oath", which confirms his words."

(a) T. Bab. Shebuot, fol. 36. 1. Vid. Maimon. Hilch. Shebuot, c. 2. sect. 1.

---

38. Ye have heard that it hath been said, An eye for an eye, and a tooth for a tooth:

Greek/Transliteration
38. Ἠκούσατε ὅτι ἐρρέθη, Ὀφθαλμὸν ἀντὶ ὀφθαλμοῦ, καὶ ὀδόντα ἀντὶ ὀδόντος·

38. Eikousate 'oti errethei, Ophthalmon anti ophthalmou, kai odonta anti odontos.

Hebrew/Transliteration
לח. שְׁמַעְתֶּם כִּי נֶאֱמַר עַיִן תַּחַת עַיִן וְשֵׁן תַּחַת שֵׁן:

38. Sh`ma•a•tem ki ne•e•mar a•yin ta•chat a•yin ve•shen ta•chat shen.

Rabbinic Commentary
The following citation of the Mishna is given at length in order to show that rabbinic thinking on the matter of legal damages goes far beyond the simple *lex talionis* (Latin, "law of retaliation," i.e., eye for eye): "If someone wounds his fellow, he becomes liable to compensate the injured party for five different aspects of the injury: damage, pain, healing, loss of time from work, and insult.
"In the case of damage, here is an example of how restitution is determined.

Suppose someone blinded someone else's eye, cut off his hand or broke his leg. They value the injured person as if he were a slave for sale in the market, and they appraise his value before the injury and now.

"Here is an example of determining the compensation for pain. Suppose someone burns another with a skewer or nail, even if only on his fingernail, where it doesn't actually produce a wound. They determine how much a man of his position would be willing to be paid to suffer that amount of pain.

"For healing the indemnity is determined in this way. If someone hit another person, he must pay all the expenses of healing him. If he develops ulcers, then if they come about in consequence of the blow, he is liable; but if not, he is not liable. If the wound heals, reopens, heals and reopens again, he is liable for all the expenses. But once it has healed thoroughly, he does not remain liable to pay the expenses of healing him.

"The value of time lost is estimated in this way. They consider what he would earn if he were a watchman over a cucumber field [a job requiring no special skills], for he has already been paid for the loss of his hand or foot. [In practice, this means they determine what kind of work he will be fit for when he fully recovers and evaluate the time lost by this standard.]

"For insult the compensation is determined entirely in accordance with the social status of both the one who caused the indignity and the one who suffered it. If someone insults a person who is naked, blind or asleep, he is liable. But if a sleeping person causes an insult, he is not liable. Someone who falls from a roof and causes injury and insult at the same time is liable for the injury but not for the insult,... because one should not be held responsible for an indignity one did not intend to cause." (Bava Kama 8:1)

R. Sol. Jarchi (c) explains the law thus: "He that puts out his neighbour's eye, must give him דמי עינו, "the price of his eye", according to the price of a servant sold in the market; and so the same of them all; for, not taking away of the member is strictly meant." (c) In Exod_21:24.

Now Yeshua here, does not find fault with the law of retaliation, as delivered by Moses, but with the false gloss of the Scribes and Pharisees; who, as they interpreted it of pecuniary mulcts, as a compensation for the loss of a member, which sometimes exceeded all just and due bounds; so they applied it to private revenge, and in favour of it: whereas this law did not allow of a retaliation to be made, by private persons, at their pleasure, but by the civil magistrate only.

---

39. But I say unto you, That ye resist not evil: but whosoever shall smite thee on thy right cheek, turn to him the other also.

Greek/Transliteration

39. ἐγὼ δὲ λέγω ὑμῖν μὴ ἀντιστῆναι τῷ πονηρῷ· ἀλλ᾽ ὅστις σε ῥαπίσει ἐπὶ τὴν δεξιὰν σιαγόνα, στρέψον αὐτῷ καὶ τὴν ἄλλην·

39. ego de lego 'umin mei antisteinai to poneiro. all 'ostis se 'rapisei epi tein dexyan syagona, strepson auto kai tein allein.

Hebrew/Transliteration

לט: וַאֲנִי אֹמֵר לָכֶם לֹא תִתְיַצֵּב בִּפְנֵי הַבָּא לְהָרַע לָךְ אִם יַכְּךָ עַל-הַלְּחִי הַיְמָנִית תֶּן-לוֹ גַּם-הַשְּׂמָאלִית

39. Va•a•ni o•mer la•chem lo tit•ya•tzev bif•ney ha•ba le•ha•ra lach eem yak•cha al - hal•chi hay`ma•nit ten - lo gam - has•ma•lit.

Old Testament
Proverbs says, "Do not say, "I will do to him as he has done to me…Do not say, "I will pay back evil. Wait for HaShem, and He will save you. Proverbs 24:29, 20:22

Proverbs continues, "If your enemy is hungry, give him food to eat. If he is thirsty, give him water to drink: for you will heap coals of fire on his head, and YHWH will reward you. Proverbs 25:21-22

(g). "He that strikes his neighbour (which Maimonides explains, he that strikes his neighbour with his hand shut, about the neck) he shall give him a "sela", or "shekel": R. Judah says, in the name of R. Jose the Galilean, one pound: if he smite him (i.e. as Maimonides says, if he smite him with his double fist upon the face; or, as Bartenora, with the palm of his hand, לחיי, "on the cheek", which is a greater reproach) he shall give him two hundred "zuzim"; and if he does it with the back of his hand, four hundred "zuzim".

(g) Misn. Bava Kama, c. 8. sect. 6. Vid. Maimon. & Bartenora in ib.

---

40. And if any man will sue thee at the law, and take away thy coat, let him have thy cloke also.

Greek/Transliteration
40. καὶ τῷ θέλοντί σοι κριθῆναι καὶ τὸν χιτῶνά σου λαβεῖν, ἄφες αὐτῷ καὶ τὸ ἱμάτιον·

40. kai to thelonti soi kritheinai kai ton chitona sou labein, aphes auto kai to 'imation.

Hebrew/Transliteration
:מ. וְכָל-הֶחָפֵץ לָרִיב עִמְּךָ לָקַחַת הַכְּתֹנֶת מֵעָלֶיךָ הַנַּח לוֹ גַם-מְעִילֶךָ

40. Ve•chol - he•cha•fetz la•riv eem•cha la•ka•chat ha•k`to•net me•a•le•cha ha•nach lo gam - me•ee•lecha.

Rabbinic Jewish Commentary
This also is contrary to the above canon of the Jews (i), which says;

"If a man should pull another by his ear, or pluck off his hair, or spit, and his spittle should come to him, העביר טליתו ממנו or "should take his coat from him", or uncover a woman's head in the street, he shall pay four hundred "zuzim", and all this is according to his dignity; says R. Akiba; even the poor in Israel, they consider them as if they were noblemen, who are fallen from their estates, for they are the children of Abraham, Isaac, and Jacob." (i) Misn. Bava Kama, c. 8. sect. 6.

41. And whosoever shall compel thee to go a mile, go with him twain.

Greek/Transliteration
41. καὶ ὅστις σε ἀγγαρεύσει μίλιον ἕν, ὕπαγε μετ' αὐτοῦ δύο.

41. kai 'ostis se angareusei milion 'en, 'upage met autou duo.

Hebrew/Transliteration
מא. וְהַנֹּגֵשׂ בְּךָ לָלֶכֶת עִמּוֹ כִּבְרַת אֶרֶץ אֶחָת לֵךְ עִמּוֹ שְׁתָּיִם:

41. Ve•ha•no•ges be•cha la•le•chet ee•mo kiv•rat e•retz e•chat lech ee•mo sh`ta•yim.

Jewish New Testament Commentary
The context is the Roman conquest; soldiers could make subjects do their work for them. Yeshua's advice is a specific application of Mat_5:16.

---

42. Give to him that asketh thee, and from him that would borrow of thee turn not thou away.

Greek/Transliteration
42. Τῷ αἰτοῦντί σε δίδου· καὶ τὸν θέλοντα ἀπὸ σοῦ δανείσασθαι μὴ ἀποστραφῇς.

42. To aitounti se didou. kai ton thelonta apo sou daneisasthai mei apostrapheis.

Hebrew/Transliteration
מב. תֵּן לַמְבַקֵּשׁ מִמֶּךָ וּמֵאֵת הֶחָפֵץ לִלְוֹת מִיָּדְךָ אַל-תַּסְתֵּר פָּנֶיךָ:

42. Ten lam•va•kesh mi•me•cha oo•me•et he•cha•fetz lil•vot mi•yad•cha al -tas•ter pa•ne•cha.

---

43. Ye have heard that it hath been said, Thou shalt love thy neighbour, and hate thine enemy.

Greek/Transliteration
43. Ἠκούσατε ὅτι ἐρρέθη, Ἀγαπήσεις τὸν πλησίον σου, καὶ μισήσεις τὸν ἐχθρόν σου·

43. Eikousate 'oti errethei, Agapeiseis ton pleision sou, kai miseiseis ton echthron sou.

Hebrew/Transliteration
מג. שְׁמַעְתֶּם כִּי נֶאֱמַר וְאָהַבְתָּ אֶת-רֵעֲךָ וְאָיַבְתָּ אֶת-אֹיְבֶךָ:

43. Sh`ma•a•tem ki ne•e•mar ve•a•hav•ta et - re•a•cha ve•a•yav•ta et - oy•ve•cha.

Rabbinic/Jewish New Testament

Lev_19:18 told our fathers to "love your neighbor as yourself." While in Psa_139:21-22 the writer commends himself for hating *God's* enemies, nowhere does the *Tanakh* teach that you should hate *your* enemy. Such a teaching must have come from the misinterpretations of those who "teach man-made rules as if they were doctrines" of God (Isa_29:13, cited by Yeshua below at 15:9). On "Jacob I loved but Esau I hated" (Mal_1:2-3) see Rom_9:10-13.

(p) "When one man sins against another, he may not hate him in his heart, and be silent, as is said of the wicked; Absalom spoke not with Amnon: but it is commanded to make it known to him, and to say to him, why hast thou done to me so and so? As it is said, "rebuking, thou shalt rebuke thy neighbour"; and if he returns, and desires him to pardon him, he shall not be implacable and cruel; but if he reproves him many times, and he does not receive his reproof, nor turn from his sin, then מותר לשנאותו, "it is lawful to hate him"."

Again, they say (q), "Every disciple of a wise man, שאינו נוקם ונוטר כנחש, "who does not revenge, and keep as a serpent"; that is, as the gloss explains it, "enmity in his heart", as a serpent, is no disciple of a wise man."

And so Maimonides (r), one of their better sort of writers, says; "A disciple of a wise man, or a scholar, whom a man despises and reproaches publicly, it is forbidden him to forgive him, because of his honour; and if he forgives him, he is to be punished, for this is a contempt of the law; but "he must revenge, and keep the thing as a serpent", until the other asks pardon of him, and then he may forgive him."

Thus they bred their scholars in hatred and malice against their enemies. This arises from a mistaken sense of the word "neighbour", which they understood only of a friend; and concluded, that if a friend was to be loved, an enemy was to be hated; not the Gentiles only, but anyone, among themselves, which could come under that name.

(o) R. Isaac Chizuk Emunah, par. 2. c. 11. p. 402. (p) Moses Kotsensis Mitzvot Tora precept. neg. 5. Vid. Maimon. Hilchot Rotseach, c. 13. sect. 14. (q) T. Bab. Yoma, fol. 22. 2. & 23. 1. (r) Maimon. Hilch. Talmud Tora, c. 7. sect. 13.

---

44. But I say unto you, Love your enemies, bless them that curse you, do good to them thathate you, and pray for them which despitefully use you, and persecute you;

Greek/Transliteration
44. ἐγὼ δὲ λέγω ὑμῖν, Ἀγαπᾶτε τοὺς ἐχθροὺς ὑμῶν, εὐλογεῖτε τοὺς καταρωμένους ὑμᾶς, καλῶς ποιεῖτε τοῖς μισοῦσιν ὑμᾶς, καὶ προσεύχεσθε ὑπὲρ τῶν ἐπηρεαζόντων ὑμᾶς, καὶ διωκόντων ὑμᾶς·

44. ego de lego 'umin, Agapate tous echthrous 'umon, eulogeite tous kataromenous 'umas, kalos poieite tois misousin 'umas, kai proseuchesthe 'uper ton epeireazonton 'umas, kai diokonton 'umas.

Hebrew/Transliteration
מד. וַאֲנִי אֹמֵר לָכֶם אֶהֱבוּ אֶת-אֹיְבֵיכֶם בָּרְכוּ אֶת-מְקַלְלֵיכֶם הֵיטִיבוּ לְשֹׂנְאֵיכֶם וְהַעְתִּירוּ בְעַד מַכְאִיבֵיכֶם וְרֹדְפֵיכֶם:

44. Va•a•ni o•mer la•chem e•he•voo et - oy•vey•chem bar•choo et - me•ka•le•ley•chem hey•ti•voo le•son•ey•chem ve•ha•a•ti•roo be•ad mach•ee•vey•chem ve•rod•fey•chem.

Rabbinic/Jewish New Testament Commentary
Isaiah speaks of Messiah,
"I gave my back to the strikers, and my cheeks to those who plucked off the hair. I didnt hide my face from shame and spitting. For the Lord HaShem will help me; therefore I have not been confounded: therefore have I set my face like a flint, and I know that I shall not be disappointed. Isaiah 50:6-7

Love your enemies! Some contrast the "realistic" ethics of Judaism with "Christian romanticism" and cite this as an example. However, the command is not to have good feelings about your enemies, but to want and do good for them, and, more specifically, to pray for those who persecute you. It is realistic enough to have been flattered by imitation in a well-known medieval Jewish work: "Pray for your enemy that he serve God." (*Orchot Tzaddikim* 15c)

The whole of this is directly opposite to the tenets of the Jews, particularly the Scribes and Pharisees; who allowed of revenge, and keeping anger against any person that had done them an injury, as has been observed: and which were also the sentiments of the Karaites, or Scripturarians, another sect among them who kept to the letter of the Scriptures, and rejected the traditions of the elders, which the Pharisees held: but in this they agreed with them,

"that it was right to do good to their friends, and to forgive them that asked pardon of them; but to such men who rendered evil, and did not return to do well, that they might receive forgiveness, אינו אסור לנקום ולנטור מהם, "it is not forbidden to revenge, and to keep anger against them" (s)."

It is indeed said (t) of their former holy men, חסידים, "Hasideans", which some have thought to be the same with the "Essenes", and a sort of Christians; however, were a better sort of Jews; that these

"heard their reproach, but did not return it; and not only so, but they pardoned him that reproached them, and forgave him."

And it is reported of these men, that they used to pray to God to pardon and forgive all that disturbed them. But the Pharisees, whom Yeshua had to do with, and against whom he inveighs, were men of another complexion.

(s) R. Eliahu in Adderet, c. 3. apud Trigland. de Sect. Karaeorum, c. 10. p. 166, 167. (t) Maimon. Hilch. Talmud Tora. c. 7. sect. 13.

---

45. That ye may be the children of your Father which is in heaven: for he maketh his sun to rise on the evil and on the good, and sendeth rain on the just and on the unjust.

Greek/Transliteration
45. ὅπως γένησθε υἱοὶ τοῦ πατρὸς ὑμῶν τοῦ ἐν τοῖς οὐρανοῖς, ὅτι τὸν ἥλιον αὐτοῦ ἀνατέλλει ἐπὶ πονηροὺς καὶ ἀγαθούς, καὶ βρέχει ἐπὶ δικαίους καὶ ἀδίκους.

45. 'opos geneisthe 'wioi tou patros 'umon tou en tois ouranois, 'oti ton 'eilion autou anatellei epi poneirous kai agathous, kai brechei epi dikaious kai adikous.

Hebrew/Transliteration
מה. לְמַעַן תִּהְיוּ בָנִים אֶל-אֲבִיכֶם בַּשָּׁמַיִם הַמֵּאִיר שִׁמְשׁוֹ לָרָעִים וְלַטּוֹבִים וּמַמְטִיר לַצַּדִּיקִים וְלָרְשָׁעִים:

45. Le•ma•an ti•hi•yoo va•nim el - Avi•chem ba•sha•ma•yim ha•me•eer shim•sho la•ra•eem ve•la•to•vim oo•mam•tir la•tza•di•kim ve•lar•sha•eem.

Rabbinic Commentary
"R. Abbahu said: The day when rain fails is greater than [the day of] the Revival of the Dead, for the Revival of the Dead is for the righteous only whereas rain is both for the righteous and for the wicked." Ta'anit 7a, Soncino Press Edition

They also used to praise God for rain, on this consideration, because it was given to unworthy persons. "(y) R. Jose Bar Jacob went to visit R. Joden of Magdala; whilst he was there, rain descended, and he heard his voice, saying, thousands of thousands, and millions of millions are bound to praise thy name, O our king, for every drop thou causest to descend upon us, שאת גומל טובה לחייבים, "because thou renderest good to the wicked".

(y) T. Hieros. Beracot, fol. 14. 1. & Taanith, fol. 64. 2.

---

46. For if ye love them which love you, what reward have ye? do not even the publicans the same?

Greek/Transliteration
46. Ἐὰν γὰρ ἀγαπήσητε τοὺς ἀγαπῶντας ὑμᾶς, τίνα μισθὸν ἔχετε; Οὐχὶ καὶ οἱ τελῶναι τὸ αὐτὸ ποιοῦσιν;

46. Ean gar agapeiseite tous agapontas 'umas, tina misthon echete? Ouchi kai 'oi telonai to auto poiousin?

Hebrew/Transliteration
:מו. כִּי אִם-תֶּאֱהֲבוּן אֶת-אֹהֲבֵיכֶם מַה-שָּׂכָר לָכֶם הֲלֹא גַּם-הַמּוֹכְסִים יַעֲשׂוּן כְּמוֹ-כֵן

46. Ki eem - te•e•ha•voon et - o•ha•vey•chem ma - sa•char la•chem ha•lo gam - ha•moch•sim ya•a•soon k`mo - chen.

Jewish New Testament Commentary
Jews who undertook to collect taxes for the Roman rulers were the most despised people in the Jewish community. Not only were they serving the oppressors, but they found it easy to abuse the system so as to line their own pockets by exploiting their fellow Jews.

---

47. And if ye salute your brethren only, what do ye more than others? do not even the publicans so?

Greek/Transliteration
47. Καὶ ἐὰν ἀσπάσησθε τοὺς φίλους ὑμῶν μόνον, τί περισσὸν ποιεῖτε; Οὐχὶ καὶ οἱ τελῶναι οὕτως ποιοῦσιν;

47. Kai ean aspaseisthe tous philous 'umon monon, ti perisson poieite? Ouchi kai 'oi telonai 'outos poiousin?

Hebrew/Transliteration
:מז. וְאִם-תִּפְקְדוּ לְשָׁלוֹם רַק אֶת-אֲחֵיכֶם מַה-יִּתְרוֹן לָכֶם כֵּן יַעֲשׂוּן גַּם-הַמֹּכְסִים

47. Ve•eem - tif•ke•doo le•sha•lom rak et - a•chey•chem ma - yit•ron la•chem ken ya•a•soon gam - ha•moch•sim.

Jewish New Testament
Goyim. The Greek word "*ethnê*" (singular "*ethnos*") corresponds to Hebrew *goyim* (singular *goy*), "Gentiles," "nations," "pagans" or "non-Jews"; KJV sometimes renders it "heathen." Jews who speak English often use the Hebrew (and Yiddish) word "*goyim*" to refer to non-Jews. Although today "*Goyim*" sometimes carries a mildly pejorative tone linked to the idea that a *goy* is not "one of us" (see Gal_2:15), Yeshua here is referring to the fact that the *Goyim* had not received God's revelation as had the Jews, and therefore less was to be expected of them; since this was God's doing, there is no defamatory connotation. See also Mat_10:5 Mat_24:7.

"A man, (says Maimonides (f),) might not salute his master, nor return a salutation to him in the manner they gave a salutation לרעים, to "friends": and they return it to one another."

They were not very free in saluting any persons, as strangers and Gentiles: such advice as this is indeed given הוי מקדים בשלום כל אדם (g), "prevent every man with a salutation", or be first in saluting every man; upon which passage their commentators (h) say, even a Gentile in the streets.

(f) Hilch. Talmud Tora, c. 5. sect. 5. (g) Pirke Abot, c. 4. sect. 15. (h) Jarchi & Bartenora in ib.

---

48. Be ye therefore perfect, even as your Father which is in heaven is perfect.

Greek/Transliteration
48. Ἔσεσθε οὖν ὑμεῖς τέλειοι, ὥσπερ ὁ πατὴρ ὑμῶν ὁ ἐν τοῖς οὐρανοῖς τέλειός ἐστιν.

48. Esesthe oun 'umeis teleioi, 'osper 'o pateir 'umon 'o en tois ouranois teleios estin.

Hebrew/Transliteration
:מח. לָכֵן הֱיוּ תְמִימִם כַּאֲשֶׁר אֲבִיכֶם בַּשָּׁמַיִם תָּמִים הוּא

48. La•chen he•yoo t`mi•mim ka•a•sher Avi•chem ba•sha•ma•yim ta•mim hoo.

Matthew, Chapter 6

1. Take heed that ye do not your alms before men, to be seen of them: otherwise ye have no reward of your Father which is in heaven.

Greek/Transliteration
1. Προσέχετε τὴν ἐλεημοσύνην ὑμῶν μὴ ποιεῖν ἔμπροσθεν τῶν ἀνθρώπων, πρὸς τὸ θεαθῆναι αὐτοῖς· εἰ δὲ μήγε, μισθὸν οὐκ ἔχετε παρὰ τῷ πατρὶ ὑμῶν τῷ ἐν τοῖς οὐρανοῖς.

1. Prosechete tein eleeimosunein 'umon mei poiein emprosthen ton anthropon, pros to theatheinai autois. ei de meige, misthon ouk echete para to patri 'umon to en tois ouranois.

Hebrew/Transliteration
א. הִשָּׁמְרוּ לָכֶם מֵעֲשׂוֹת צְדָקָה לְמַרְאֵה עֵינֵי הָאָדָם פֶּן שָׂכָר לֹא תַשִּׂיגוּ מֵאֵת אֲבִיכֶם שֶׁבַּשָּׁמָיִם:

1. Hi•sham•roo la•chem me•a•sot tze•da•ka le•mar•eh ey•ney ha•a•dam pen sa•char lo ta•si•goo me•et Avi•chem she•ba•sha•ma•yim.

Rabbinic/Jewish New Testament Commentary
Tzedakah, Hebrew for "righteousness," but in a Jewish context "doing *tzedakah*" means "giving to charity, doing acts of mercy." This is reflected in the Greek text: in Mat_6:1 the Greek word used means "righteousness," but in Mat_6:2-4 a different Greek word is used which means "kind deeds, alms, charitable giving."

Now this work, or duty, they magnify at a very great rate: not content to say (g), that "he that does alms, does that which is more excellent than all offerings;"

they further affirm (h), that "giving of alms and beneficence כנגד התורה כולה, "are equal to the whole law";"

or, it is all one as if a man performed the whole law. Moreover, they give (i) out, "that whoever takes of his goods, and does alms with them, he shall be delivered from the "damnation of hell"."

Yea, they reckon that this gives a right and title to eternal life (k). "He that says, let this "sela", or "shekel", be for alms, that his children may live, and that he may be worthy of the life of the world to come, lo! this is צדיק גמור, "a perfect righteous man"."

Or, as elsewhere (l) expressed, "let this sela be for alms, that my son may live, and that he may be a son of the world to come; lo! this is a perfect righteous man."

(g) T. Bab. Succa, fol. 49. 2. (h) T. Hieros. Peah, fol. 15. 2, 3. (i) T. Bab. Gittin, fol. 7. 1, 2. (k) T. Bab. Roshhashanah, fol. 4. 1. Bava Bathra, fol. 10. 2. (l) T. Bab. Pesachim, fol. 8. 1, 2.

2. Therefore when thou doest thine alms, do not sound a trumpet before thee, as the hypocrites do in the synagogues and in the streets, that they may have glory of men. Verily I say unto you, They have their reward.

Greek/Transliteration
2. Ὅταν οὖν ποιῇς ἐλεημοσύνην, μὴ σαλπίσῃς ἔμπροσθέν σου, ὥσπερ οἱ ὑποκριταὶ ποιοῦσιν ἐν ταῖς συναγωγαῖς καὶ ἐν ταῖς ῥύμαις, ὅπως δοξασθῶσιν ὑπὸ τῶν ἀνθρώπων· ἀμὴν λέγω ὑμῖν, ἀπέχουσιν τὸν μισθὸν αὐτῶν.

2. 'Otan oun poieis eleeimosunein, mei salpiseis emprosthen sou, 'osper 'oi 'upokritai poiousin en tais sunagogais kai en tais 'rumais, 'opos doxasthosin 'upo ton anthropon. amein lego 'umin, apechousin ton misthon auton.

Hebrew/Transliteration
ב. לָכֵן בַּעֲשׂוֹתְךָ צְדָקָה לֹא תַשְׁמִיעַ קוֹל תְּרוּעָה לְפָנֶיךָ כַּאֲשֶׁר יַעֲשׂוּ הַחֲנֵפִים בְּבָתֵּי הַכְּנֶסֶת וּבָרְחֹבוֹת לְמַעַן יַשִּׂיגוּ כָבוֹד לְעֵינֵי בְּנֵי-הָאָדָם אָמֵן אֲנִי אֹמֵר לָכֶם הִנֵּה שְׂכָרָם לִפְנֵיהֶם.

2. La•chen ba•a•sot•cha tze•da•ka lo tash•mi•a kol t`roo•ah le•fa•ne•cha ka•a•sher ya•a•soo ha•cha•ne•fim be•va•tey ha•k`ne•set oo•var•cho•vot le•ma•an ya•si•goo cha•vod le•ei•ney v`ney - ha•a•dam amen ani o•mer la•chem hee•ne s`cha•ram lif•ney•hem.

Rabbinic Jewish Commentary
R. Aben Ezra (n) says, that "a man that gives alms to the poor, must not give it because of the glory of the collector, i.e. that he may have glory of him; nor that the children of men may praise him."

"He that glories in anything done by himself, הוא נוטל את שכרו, "he takes", or receives "his reward" (o); for as for any reward from God, they will have none;"

(n) In Exod. xx. 3. (o) R. Jona apud Capell. Spicileg. in loc.

---

3. But when thou doest alms, let not thy left hand know what thy right hand doeth:

Greek/Transliteration
3. Σοῦ δὲ ποιοῦντος ἐλεημοσύνην, μὴ γνώτω ἡ ἀριστερά σου τί ποιεῖ ἡ δεξιά σου,

3. Sou de poiountos eleeimosunein, mei gnoto 'ei aristera sou ti poiei 'ei dexya sou,

Hebrew/Transliteration
ג. וְאַתָּה בַּעֲשׂוֹתְךָ צְדָקָה אַל-תֵּדַע שְׂמֹאלְךָ אֵת אֲשֶׁר עֹשָׂה יְמִינֶךָ:

3. Ve•a•ta ba•a•sot•cha tze•da•ka al - te•da s`mol•cha et asher o•sa ye•mi•ne•cha.

Rabbinic Jewish Commentary

It is a Jewish canon (p), that "he that gives a gift to his friend out of love, may make it known, אבל לא בצדקה, "but not if it be by way of alms"."

(p) Piske Tosephot in Sabbat. c. 1. art. 134.

---

4. That thine alms may be in secret: and thy Father which seeth in secret himself shall reward thee openly.

Greek/Transliteration

4. ὅπως ᾖ σου ἡ ἐλεημοσύνη ἐν τῷ κρυπτῷ· καὶ ὁ πατήρ σου ὁ βλέπων ἐν τῷ κρυπτῷ αὐτὸς ἀποδώσει σοι ἐν τῷ φανερῷ.

4. 'opos ei sou 'ei eleeimosunei en to krupto. kai 'o pateir sou 'o blepon en to krupto autos apodosei soi en to phanero.

Hebrew/Transliteration

ד: לְמַעַן תִּהְיֶה צִדְקָתְךָ בַּסָּתֶר וְאָבִיךָ הָרֹאֶה בַסֵּתֶר גְּמוּלְךָ בַּגָּלוּי יְשַׁלֶּם-לָךְ

4. Le•ma•an ti•hi•ye tzid•kat•cha ba•sa•ter ve•Avi•cha ha•ro•eh va•se•ter g'mool•cha ba•ga•looy ye•sha•lem - lach.

Rabbinic Jewish Commentary

"What kind of charity is that which delivers a man from an unnatural death? When a man gives without knowing to whom he gives. and the beggar receives without knowing from whom he receives. Baba Batra 10a-b, Soncino Press Edition

The allusion seems to be to the secret chamber, where money was brought privately for the relief of the poor.

"There were two chambers in the sanctuary, the one was לשכת חשאים, "the chamber of secrets", and the other the chamber of vessels: the chamber of secrets was that into which pious persons put בחשאי, "in secret", and the poor children of good men were maintained out of it privately (q)."

The Jews say many things in favour of doing alms privately. "Greater, (say they (r),) is he that gives alms בסתר, in secret, than Moses our master."

They tell us (s), that "R. Jannai seeing a certain man give Zuz (a piece of money) to a poor man publicly, said unto him, it would have been better, if thou hadst not have given him anything, than to have given him in this manner."

(q) Misn. Shekalim, c. 5. sect. 6. Mainnon. Hilch. Eracin, c. 2. sect. 12. (r) T. Bab. Bava Bathra, fol. 9. 2. (s) T. Bab. Chagiga, fol. 5. 1.

5. And when thou prayest, thou shalt not be as the hypocrites are: for they love to pray standing in the synagogues and in the corners of the streets, that they may be seen of men. Verily I say unto you, They have their reward.

Greek/Transliteration
5. Καὶ ὅταν προσεύχῃ, οὐκ ἔσῃ ὥσπερ οἱ ὑποκριταί, ὅτι φιλοῦσιν ἐν ταῖς συναγωγαῖς καὶ ἐν ταῖς γωνίαις τῶν πλατειῶν ἑστῶτες προσεύχεσθαι, ὅπως ἂν φανῶσιν τοῖς ἀνθρώποις· ἀμὴν λέγω ὑμῖν ὅτι ἀπέχουσιν τὸν μισθὸν αὐτῶν.

5. Kai 'otan proseuchei, ouk esei 'osper 'oi 'upokritai, 'oti philousin en tais sunagogais kai en tais goniais ton plateion 'estotes proseuchesthai, 'opos an phanosin tois anthropois. amein lego 'umin 'oti apechousin ton misthon auton.

Hebrew/Transliteration
ה. וְכִי תָבֹאוּ לְהִתְפַּלֵּל אַל-תִּהְיוּ כְּאַנְשֵׁי חֹנֶף הָאֹהֲבִים לַעֲמֹד לְהִתְפַּלֵּל בְּבָתֵּי הַכְּנֶסֶת וּפִנּוֹת הַשְּׁוָקִים לְמַעַן:תִּירְאֶינָה אֹתָם עֵינֵי בְנֵי-הָאָדָם אָמֵן אֲנִי אֹמֵר לָכֶם הִנֵּה שְׂכָרָם לִפְנֵיהֶם

5. Ve•chi ta•vo•oo le•hit•pa•lel al - ti•hi•yoo ke•an•shey cho•nef ha•o•ha•vim la•a•mod le•hit•pa•lel be•va•tey ha•k`ne•set oo•fi•not hash•va•kim le•ma•an tir•ei•na o•tam ey•ney v`ney - ha•a•dam amen ani o•mer la•chem hee•ne s`cha•ram lif•ney•hem.

Rabbinic Jewish Commentary
It was their usual custom to pray "standing"; nay, it is established by their canons.

"There are eight things, (says Maimonides (u),) that a man that prays ought to take heed to do; and the first he mentions is "standing"; for, says he, no man may pray אלא מעימד, "but standing"; if he is sitting in a ship, or in a cart, if he can stand, he must stand; if not, he may sit in his place and pray."

Several hints of this custom there are in the Misna (w).

"On their fast days they used to bring out the ark into the streets-- עמדו בתפלה, "and they stood in prayer", or praying; and caused an old man to go down before the ark, who was used to recite prayers, and he said them."

Again (x), "whoever עומד בתפלה, "stood praying", and remembered that any uncleanness attended him, he might not break off, but he might shorten."

Yea, standing itself is interpreted of praying; for it is said (y), "and Abraham rose up early in the morning to the place, where he stood, ואין תפלה אלא בעמידה, "and there is no prayer but standing"

(u) Hilch. Tephilla. c. 5. sect. 1, 2. (w) Misn. Taanith, c. 2. sect. 1, 2. (x) Misn. Beracot, c. 3. sect. 5. (y) Zohar in Lev. fol. 47. 1. T. Bab. Beracot, fol. 26. 2.

6. But thou, when thou prayest, enter into thy closet, and when thou hast shut thy door, pray to thy Father which is in secret; and thy Father which seeth in secret shall reward thee openly.

Greek/Transliteration
6. Σὺ δέ, ὅταν προσεύχῃ, εἴσελθε εἰς τὸ ταμιεῖόν σου, καὶ κλείσας τὴν θύραν σου, πρόσευξαι τῷ πατρί σου τῷ ἐν τῷ κρυπτῷ· καὶ ὁ πατήρ σου ὁ βλέπων ἐν τῷ κρυπτῷ ἀποδώσει σοι ἐν τῷ φανερῷ.

6. Su de, 'otan proseuchei, eiselthe eis to tamieion sou, kai kleisas tein thuran sou, proseuxai to patri sou to en to krupto. kai 'o pateir sou 'o blepon en to krupto apodosei soi en to phanero.

Hebrew/Transliteration
ו. וְאַתָּה בִּתְפִלָּתְךָ בֹּא בַחֲדָרֶיךָ וּסְגֹר דְּלָתְךָ בַּעֲדֶךָ וְהִתְפַּלֵּל אֶל-אָבִיךָ אֲשֶׁר סֵתֶר סְבִיבָיו וְאָבִיךָ הָרֹאֶה בַּסֵּתֶר: גְּמוּלְךָ בַּגָּלוּי יְשַׁלֶּם-לָךְ

6. Ve•a•ta bit•fi•lat•cha bo va•cha•da•re•cha oos•gor de•lat•cha ba•a•de•cha ve•hit•pa•lel el - Avi•cha asher se•ter se•vi•vav ve•Avi•cha ha•ro•eh va•se•ter g`mool•cha ba•ga•looy ye•sha•lem - lach.

Rabbinic/Jewish New Testament Commentary
Mishna:
"Rabbi Shim'on said, '... When you pray, do not make your prayer fixed [repetitive, mechanical], but [appeal for] mercy and supplication before the Omnipresent, blessed be he.' " (Avot 2:13) Likewise the Gemara: "When you address the Holy One, blessed be he, let your words be few." (B'rakhot 61a)

his is agreeable to what the Jews sometimes say, "that a man ought not to cause his voice to be heard in prayer; but should pray בלחש, "silently", with a voice that is not heard; and this is the prayer which is daily accepted (g)." (g) Zohar in Gen. fol. 114. 4.

Jacob Neusner, a well-known Jewish scholar who deals with New Testament materials as pertinent to establishing the course of Jewish history, stresses the importance of dating any rabbinic or New Testament reference, together with its antecedents, before drawing conclusions about who influenced whom. Since the same first-century Jewish society was the crucible out of which came both Messianic and rabbinic Judaism, often the most reasonable conclusion is that both the rabbis and the New Testament figures and writers drew on a common pool of ideas.

As for giving credit, one can make the case that in fact the New Testament does acknowledge positive contributions made by "tradition" (i.e., the rabbis; see Mar_7:5-13) and by the *P'rushim* (Mat_23:2).

7. But when ye pray, use not vain repetitions, as the heathen do: for they think that they shall be heard for their much speaking.

Greek/Transliteration
7. Προσευχόμενοι δὲ μὴ βαττολογήσητε, ὥσπερ οἱ ἐθνικοί· δοκοῦσιν γὰρ ὅτι ἐν τῇ πολυλογίᾳ αὐτῶν εἰσακουσθήσονται.

7. Proseuchomenoi de mei battologeiseite, 'osper 'oi ethnikoi. dokousin gar 'oti en tei polulogia auton eisakoustheisontai.

Hebrew/Transliteration
ז: וְכַאֲשֶׁר אַתֶּם מִתְפַּלְלִים אַל-תְּבַטְאוּ בִשְׂפָתַיִם כַּגּוֹיִם אֲשֶׁר יַחְשֹׁב לִבָּם כִּי-יִשָּׁמְעוּ בַּעֲטֶרֶת דְּבָרִים

7. Ve•cha•a•sher atem mit•pa•le•lim al - te•vat•oo vis•fa•ta•yim ka•go•yim asher yach•shov li•bam ki - yi•sham•oo ba•a•te•ret d`va•rim.

---

8. Be not ye therefore like unto them: for your Father knoweth what things ye have need of, before ye ask him.

Greek/Transliteration
8. Μὴ οὖν ὁμοιωθῆτε αὐτοῖς· οἶδεν γὰρ ὁ πατὴρ ὑμῶν ὧν χρείαν ἔχετε, πρὸ τοῦ ὑμᾶς αἰτῆσαι αὐτόν.

8. Mei oun 'omoiotheite autois. oiden gar 'o pateir 'umon 'on chreian echete, pro tou 'umas aiteisai auton.

Hebrew/Transliteration
ח: לָכֵן אַל-תִּשְׁווּ לָמוֹ כִּי יֹדֵעַ אֲבִיכֶם מַה-מַּחְסוֹרְכֶם טֶרֶם תִּשְׁאָלוּ מִיָּדוֹ

8. La•chen al - tish•voo la•mo ki yo•de•a Avi•chem ma - mach•sor•chem te•rem tish•a•loo mi•ya•do.

TaNaKh/Old Testament
"And it shall be that before they call, I answer. And while they are still speaking, I hear." Isaiah 65:24

---

9. After this manner therefore pray ye: Our Father which art in heaven, Hallowed be thy name.

Greek/Transliteration
9. Οὕτως οὖν προσεύχεσθε ὑμεῖς· Πάτερ ἡμῶν ὁ ἐν τοῖς οὐρανοῖς, ἁγιασθήτω τὸ ὄνομά σου.

9. 'Outos oun proseuchesthe 'umeis. Pater 'eimon 'o en tois ouranois, 'agyastheito to onoma sou.

Hebrew/Transliteration
ט. וְאַתֶּם כֹּה תִתְפַּלָּלוּ אָבִינוּ שֶׁבַּשָּׁמַיִם יִתְקַדַּשׁ שְׁמֶךָ:

9. Ve•a•tem ko tit•pa•la•loo Avi•noo she•ba•sha•ma•yim yit•ka•dash sh`me•cha.

Rabbinic/Jewish New Testament Commentary

These verses include what is widely known as the Lord's Prayer, since it was taught by the Lord Yeshua. All of its elements may be found in the Judaism of Yeshua's day, so in this sense it is not original with him; but it is properly revered for its beauty and economy. Its first words, Our Father in heaven (*Avinu sh'baShammayim*), open many Hebrew prayers. The next two lines recall the first portion of the synagogue prayer known as the *Kaddish*, which says, "Magnified and sanctified (*Yitgadal v'yitkadash*) be his great name throughout the world which he has created according to his will, and may he establish his Kingdom in your lifetime...." The plural phrasing-"Give us ... forgive... lead us"-is characteristically Jewish, focussing on the group rather than the isolated individual.

In Jewish writings we have read; (k)"our Father which art in heaven", show mercy "to us, because thy great name is called upon us." Or (m) "do not consider the glory of the law; and how, say they, "our Father which art in heaven", hear our voice, have mercy on us, and receive our prayer?"

So the Jews (p) in their prayers, "let thy name be hallowed", or "sanctified by us", O Lord our God, before the eyes of all living."

And very often (q), "let his great name be magnified and sanctified in the world, which he hath created according to his will."

And again (r), "let us sanctify thy name in the world, as they sanctify it in the highest heavens."

(k) Seder Tephillot, fol. 4. 2. Ed. Basil. (m) Raya Mehimna in Zohar in Lev. fol. 34. 1. (p) Seder Tephillot, fol. 78. 1. Ed. Amstelod. Zohar in Exod. fol. 43. 4. (q) Seder Tephillot, fol. 17. 2, Ed. Basil. & passim. (r) Seder Tephillot, fol. 22. 1. & passim.

---

10. Thy kingdom come. Thy will be done in earth, as it is in heaven.

Greek/Transliteration
10. Ἐλθέτω ἡ βασιλεία σου. Γενηθήτω τὸ θέλημά σου, ὡς ἐν οὐρανῷ, καὶ ἐπὶ τῆς γῆς.

10. Eltheto 'ei basileia sou. Geneitheito to theleima sou, 'os en ourano, kai epi teis geis.

Hebrew/Transliteration
י. תָּבֹא מַלְכוּתֶךָ יֵעָשֶׂה רְצוֹנְךָ בָּאָרֶץ כַּאֲשֶׁר נַעֲשָׂה בַשָּׁמָיִם:

10. Ta•vo mal•choo•te•cha ye•a•se r`tzon•cha ba•a•retz ka•a•sher na•a•sa va•sha•ma•yim.

Rabbinic Jewish Commentary
(s) "every blessing, or prayer, in which there is no **זברת השם**, "mention made of the name", i.e. of God, is no prayer; and that every prayer, in which there is not **מלכות**, "the kingdom", is no prayer."

(t) Jews call the short prayer: "what is the short prayer? R. Eliezer says, **עשה רצונך בשמים**, "do thy will in heaven"; and give quietness of spirit, or acquiescence of spirit in thy will, to them that fear thee below."

(r) Seder Tephillot, fol. 128. 2. Ed. Basil. (s) T. Bab. Beracot, fol. 40. 2. (t) Ib. fol. 29. 2.

---

11. Give us this day our daily bread.

Greek/Transliteration
11. Τὸν ἄρτον ἡμῶν τὸν ἐπιούσιον δὸς ἡμῖν σήμερον.

11. Ton arton 'eimon ton epiousion dos 'eimin seimeron.

Hebrew/Transliteration
יא. תֶּן-לָנוּ הַיּוֹם לֶחֶם חֻקֵּנוּ:

11. Ten - la•noo ha•yom le•chem choo•ke•noo.

Rabbinic Jewish Commentary
(u) Jews: "The necessities of thy people are great, and their knowledge short; let it be thy good will and pleasure, O Lord, our God, that thou wouldst give to everyone **כדי פרנסתו**, "what is sufficient for his sustenance", and to every one's body what it wants."

"Says R. Jose (w), all the children of faith seek "every day" **לשאלא מזונייהו**, "to ask their food" of the Lord, and to pray a prayer for it."

(u) T. Bab. Beracot, fol. 29. 2. (w) Zohar in Exod. fol. 26. 2.

---

12. And forgive us our debts, as we forgive our debtors.

Greek/Transliteration
12. Καὶ ἄφες ἡμῖν τὰ ὀφειλήματα ἡμῶν, ὡς καὶ ἡμεῖς ἀφίεμεν τοῖς ὀφειλέταις ἡμῶν.

12. Kai aphes 'eimin ta opheileimata 'eimon, 'os kai 'eimeis aphiemen tois opheiletais 'eimon.

Hebrew/Transliteration
יב. וּסְלַח-לָנוּ אֶת-אַשְׁמָתֵנוּ כַּאֲשֶׁר סֹלְחִים אֲנַחְנוּ לַאֲשֶׁר אָשְׁמוּ לָנוּ:

12. Oos•lach - la•noo et - ash•ma•te•noo ka•a•sher sol•chim a•nach•noo la•a•sher ash•moo la•noo.

Rabbinic Jewish Commentary
Thus the prayer of Solomon is paraphrased (y) by the Targumist: "and hear thou the petition of thy servant, and of thy people Israel, which they shall make before this place; and do thou receive it from the place of the house of thy Shekinah, from heaven; and do thou accept their prayer ותשבק לחוביהון, "and forgive their debts"."

"forgive, I pray thee now, the trespass of thy brethren, and their sin"; which is rendered by the Chaldee paraphrasts (z) שבוק לחובי, "forgive the debts" of thy brethren, and their sins.

(y) Targum in 2 Chron. vi. 21. (z) Targum Onkelos & Jon. ben Uzziel in Gen. l. 17. Vid. Targum in 1 Chron. iv. 18. & in Cant. i. 1. & in Gen. iv. 13. & passim.

---

13. And lead us not into temptation, but deliver us from evil: For thine is the kingdom, and the power, and the glory, for ever. Amen.

Greek/Transliteratin
13. Καὶ μὴ εἰσενέγκῃς ἡμᾶς εἰς πειρασμόν, ἀλλὰ ῥῦσαι ἡμᾶς ἀπὸ τοῦ πονηροῦ. Ὅτι σοῦ ἐστιν ἡ βασιλεία καὶ ἡ δύναμις καὶ ἡ δόξα εἰς τοὺς αἰῶνας. Ἀμήν.

13. Kai mei eisenegkeis 'eimas eis peirasmon, alla 'rusai 'eimas apo tou poneirou. 'Oti sou estin 'ei basileia kai 'ei dunamis kai 'ei doxa eis tous aionas. Amein.

Hebrew/Transliteration
יג. וְאַל-תְּבִיאֵנוּ לִידֵי מַסָּה כִּי אִם-הַצִּילֵנוּ מִן-הָרָע כִּי לְךָ הַמַּמְלָכָה וְהַגְּבוּרָה וְהַתִּפְאֶרֶת לְעוֹלְמֵי עוֹלָמִים אָמֵן:

13. Ve•al - te•vi•e•noo li•dey ma•sa ki eem - ha•tzi•le•noo min - ha•ra ki le•cha ha•mam•la•cha ve•hag•voo•ra ve•ha•tif•eret le•ol•mey o•la•mim Amen.

Rabbinic/Jewish New Testament Commentary
Such a petition as this is often to be observed in the prayers of the Jews (a),

אל תביאני, "do not lead me" neither into sin, nor into transgression and iniquity, ולא לידי נסיון, "nor into temptation", or "into the hands of temptation";"

The Evil One. The Greek may also be translated simply, "evil," in the sense of "bad things that happen." The Talmud (Kiddushin 81a) reports that "Whenever Rabbi Chiyya ben-Abba fell on his face [in prayer] he used to say, 'May the Merciful One save us from the Tempter.' "

[For kingship, power and glory are yours forever. *Amen.*] This doxology echoes 1Ch_29:11. The oldest New Testament manuscripts lack it, hence the brackets. Roman Catholics do not include it when reciting the Lord's Prayer; Protestants do. On "*Amen*" see Mat_5:18; here it signals an expected congregational response.

This petition, with the Jews, is in this (b) form: "but deliver me from an evil accident", and diseases; and do not trouble me with evil dreams, and evil imaginations."

It stands thus in the Jewish prayers (d),
כי המלכות שלך היא, "for the kingdom is thine", and thou shalt reign in glory for ever and ever."

The usual response at the close of prayers, and reading the Shema, instead of "Amen", was (e) this: "Blessed be the name of the glory of his kingdom, for ever and ever."

(a) Seder Tephillot, fol. 3. 1. Ed. Basil. fol. 4. 2. Ed. Amstelod. Shaare Zion, fol. 73. 1. T. Bab. Beracot, fol. 60. 2. (b) T. Bab. Beracot, fol. 60. 2. (d) Seder Tephillot, fol. 280. 1. Ed. Basil. (e) Misn. Yoma, c. 4. sect. 1. & 6. 2. T. Bab. Pesachim, fol. 56. 1. & Taanith, fol. 16. 2. Seder Tephillot, fol. 70. 2. Ed. Basil.

---

14. For if ye forgive men their trespasses, your heavenly Father will also forgive you:

Greek/Transliteration
14. Ἐὰν γὰρ ἀφῆτε τοῖς ἀνθρώποις τὰ παραπτώματα αὐτῶν, ἀφήσει καὶ ὑμῖν ὁ πατὴρ ὑμῶν ὁ οὐράνιος·

14. Ean gar apheite tois anthropois ta paraptomata auton, apheisei kai 'umin 'o pateir 'umon 'o ouranios.

Hebrew/Transliteration
יד. כִּי אִם-תִּסְלְחוּ לִבְנֵי-אָדָם אֶת-אַשְׁמָתָם גַּם-אֲבִיכֶם בַּשָּׁמַיִם יִסְלַח לָכֶם:

14. Ki eem - tis•le•choo liv•ney - adam et - ash•ma•tam gam - Avi•chem ba•sha•ma•yim yis•lach la•chem.

15. But if ye forgive not men their trespasses, neither will your Father forgive your trespasses.

Greek/Transliteration
15. ἐὰν δὲ μὴ ἀφῆτε τοῖς ἀνθρώποις τὰ παραπτώματα αὐτῶν, οὐδὲ ὁ πατὴρ ὑμῶν ἀφήσει τὰ παραπτώματα ὑμῶν.

15. ean de mei apheite tois anthropois ta paraptomata auton, oude 'o pateir 'umon apheisei ta paraptomata 'umon.

Hebrew/Transliteration
טו: וְאִם-לֹא תִסְלְחוּ לִבְנֵי-אָדָם אֶת-אַשְׁמָתָם גַּם-אֲבִיכֶם לֹא-יִסְלַח לָכֶם אַשְׁמַתְכֶם

15. Ve•eem - lo tis•le•choo liv•ney - adam et - ash•ma•tam gam - Avi•chem lo - yis•lach la•chem ash•mat•chem.

---

16. Moreover when ye fast, be not, as the hypocrites, of a sad countenance: for they disfigure their faces, that they may appear unto men to fast. Verily I say unto you, They have their reward.

Greek/Transliteration
16. Ὅταν δὲ νηστεύητε, μὴ γίνεσθε ὥσπερ οἱ ὑποκριταὶ σκυθρωποί· ἀφανίζουσιν γὰρ τὰ πρόσωπα αὐτῶν, ὅπως φανῶσιν τοῖς ἀνθρώποις νηστεύοντες· ἀμὴν λέγω ὑμῖν ὅτι ἀπέχουσιν τὸν μισθὸν αὐτῶν.

16. 'Otan de neisteueite, mei ginesthe 'osper 'oi 'upokritai skuthropoi. aphanizousin gar ta prosopa auton, 'opos phanosin tois anthropois neisteuontes. amein lego 'umin 'oti apechousin ton misthon auton.

Hebrew/Transliteration
טז. וְכִי תָצוּמוּ אַל-תִּהְיוּ כְחַנְפֵי-לֵב מַקְדִּירֵי פָנִים אֲשֶׁר יַפִּילוּ פְנֵיהֶם לְהִוָּדַע לִבְנֵי-אָדָם בְּתַעֲנִיתָם אָמֵן אֲנִי אֹמֵר לָכֶם הִנֵּה שְׂכָרָם לִפְנֵיהֶם

16. Ve•chi ta•tzoo•moo al - ti•hi•yoo che•chan•fey - lev mak•di•rey fa•nim asher ya•pi•loo fe•ney•hem le•hi•va•da liv•ney - adam be•ta•a•ni•tam amen ani o•mer la•chem hee•ne s`cha•ram lif•ney•hem.

Rabbinic Jewish Commentary
It is said (f), in commendation of R. Joshua ben Chanamah, that all his days הושחרו פניו, "his face was black", through fastings; and this is said (g) to be the reason of Ashur's name, in 1Ch_4:5 because "his face was black" with fasting: yea, they looked upon such a disfiguring of the face to be meritorious, and what would be rewarded hereafter.

"Whoever (say they (h)) המשחיר פניו, "makes his face black", on account of the law in this world, God will make his brightness to shine in the world to come."

(f) Juchasin, fol. 59. 1. (g) T. Bab. Sota, fol. 12. 1. (h) T. Bab. Sanhedrim, fol. 100. 1.

---

17. But thou, when thou fastest, anoint thine head, and wash thy face;

Greek/Transliteration
17. Σὺ δὲ νηστεύων ἄλειψαί σου τὴν κεφαλήν, καὶ τὸ πρόσωπόν σου νίψαι,

17. Su de neisteuon aleipsai sou tein kephalein, kai to prosopon sou nipsai,

Hebrew/Transliteration
יז. וְאַתָּה כִּי תָצוּם תָּסוּךְ רֹאשְׁךָ וְתִרְחַץ פָּנֶיךָ:

17. Ve•a•ta ki ta•tzoom ta•sooch rosh•cha ve•tir•chatz pa•ne•cha.

Rabbinic Jewish Commentary
Anoint thine head, and wash thy face; directly contrary to the Jewish canons, which forbid these things, with others, on fast days:

"On the day of atonement, (say (i) they,) a man is forbidden eating and drinking, וברחיצהובסיכה "and washing and anointing", and putting on of shoes, and the use of the bed."

And the same were forbidden on other fasts: in anointings, the head was anointed first, and this rule and reason are given for it:

"he that would anoint his whole body, סך ראשו תחילה, "let him anoint his head first", because it is king over all its members (k)."

Anointing and washing were signs of cheerfulness and joy; see Rth_3:3.

(i) Misn. Yoma, c. 8. sect. 1. & Taanith, c. 1. sect. 4, 5, 6. T. Bab. Yoma, fol. 77. 2. Taanith, fol. 12. 2. Moses Kotsensis Mitzvot Tora, pr. affirm. 32. (k) T. Bab. Sabbat, fol. 61. 1.

---

18. That thou appear not unto men to fast, but unto thy Father which is in secret: and thy Father, which seeth in secret, shall reward thee openly.

Greek/Transliteration
18. ὅπως μὴ φανῇς τοῖς ἀνθρώποις νηστεύων, ἀλλὰ τῷ πατρί σου τῷ ἐν τῷ κρυπτῷ· καὶ ὁ πατήρ σου ὁ βλέπων ἐν τῷ κρυπτῷ ἀποδώσει σοι.

18. 'opos mei phaneis tois anthropois neisteuon, alla to patri sou to en to krupto. kai 'o pateir sou 'o blepon en to krupto apodosei soi.

Hebrew/Transliteration
יח. וְלֹא תִוָּדַע לְאָדָם בְּתַעֲנִיתְךָ כִּי אִם-לְאָבִיךָ בַּסֵּתֶר וְאָבִיךָ הָרֹאֶה בַסֵּתֶר גְּמוּלְךָ בַּגָּלוּי יְשַׁלֶּם-לָךְ:

18. Ve•lo ti•va•da le•a•dam be•ta•a•nit•cha ki eem - le•Avi•cha ba•sa•ter ve•Avi•cha ha•ro•eh va•se•ter g`mool•cha ba•ga•looy ye•sha•lem - lach.

Rabbinic Jewish Commentary
Which is just the reverse of the hypocrites, the Scribes and Pharisees; and quite contrary to the customs of the Jews, who when they fasted, particularly on their noted fasts (l),

"brought out the ark into the street of the city, and put burnt ashes upon it, and upon the head of the prince, and upon the head of the president of the sanhedrim, and every man upon his own head."

(l) Misn. Taanith, c. 2. sect. 1.

---

19. Lay not up for yourselves treasures upon earth, where moth and rust doth corrupt, and where thieves break through and steal:

Greek/Transliteration
19. Μὴ θησαυρίζετε ὑμῖν θησαυροὺς ἐπὶ τῆς γῆς, ὅπου σὴς καὶ βρῶσις ἀφανίζει, καὶ ὅπου κλέπται διορύσσουσιν καὶ κλέπτουσιν·

19. Mei theisaurizete 'umin theisaurous epi teis geis, 'opou seis kai brosis aphanizei, kai 'opou kleptai diorussousin kai kleptousin.

Hebrew/Transliteration
יט. לֹא תַאַצְרוּ לָכֶם אוֹצָרוֹת בְּקֶרֶב הָאָרֶץ שֶׁשָּׁם יֹאכַל עָשׁ וְרָקָב וְגַנָּבִים יַחְתְּרוּ וְיִגְנֹבוּ:

19. Lo ta•atz•roo la•chem o•tza•rot be•ke•rev ha•a•retz she•sham yo•chal ash ve•ra•kav ve•ga•na•vim yach•te•roo ve•yig•no•voo.

---

20. But lay up for yourselves treasures in heaven, where neither moth nor rust doth corrupt, and where thieves do not break through nor steal:

Greek/Transliteration
20. Θησαυρίζετε δὲ ὑμῖν θησαυροὺς ἐν οὐρανῷ, ὅπου οὔτε σὴς οὔτε βρῶσις ἀφανίζει, καὶ ὅπου κλέπται οὐ διορύσσουσιν οὐδὲ κλέπτουσιν.

20. theisaurizete de 'umin theisaurous en ourano, 'opou oute seis oute brosis aphanizei, kai 'opou kleptai ou diorussousin oude kleptousin.

Hebrew/Transliteration
כ. אֶפֶס אִצְרוּ לָכֶם אוֹצָרוֹת בַּשָּׁמַיִם שָׁם לֹא יֹאכַל עָשׁ וְרָקָב וְגַנָּבִים לֹא יַחְתְּרוּ וְלֹא יִגְנֹבוּ:

20. E•fes eetz•roo la•chem o•tza•rot ba•sha•ma•yim sham lo yo•chal ash ve•ra•kav ve•ga•na•vim lo yach•te•roo ve•lo yig•no•voo.

Rabbinic Jewish Commentary
Heaven is often represented by the Jewish writers as a treasury; and the treasures which are in it are said (n) to be

"treasures of life", and treasures of peace, and treasures of blessing; and the souls of the righteous, and the spirits and souls that shall be created, and the dew with which God will quicken the dead."

Those words in Deu_31:16. "And the Lord said unto Moses, thou shalt sleep with thy fathers", are thus (o) paraphrased.

"And the Lord said unto Moses, lo! thou shalt sleep in the dust with thy fathers, and thy soul shall be treasured up בגנזי חיי עלמא, "in the treasury of eternal life", with thy fathers."

One of their commentators (q) on the phrase, "my fathers laid up treasures below", as it is in the Babylonish Talmud (r), has this remark:

"for lo! all that they treasured up was for the necessaries of this world; which is מקום עפר רמה תולעה, "a place of dust and vermin", which corrupt and destroy everything; "but I have laid up treasures above", a place secure and firm, and which preserves everything that is put into it."

(n) T. Bab. Chagiga, fol. 12. 2. (o) Targum Jon. ben Uzziel, in Deut. xxxi. 16. (q) Caphtor, fol. 97. 1. (r) T. Bab. Bava Bathra, fol. 11.

---

21. For where your treasure is, there will your heart be also.

Greek/Transliteration
21. Ὅπου γάρ ἐστιν ὁ θησαυρὸς ὑμῶν, ἐκεῖ ἔσται καὶ ἡ καρδία ὑμῶν.

21. 'Opou gar estin 'o theisauros 'umon, ekei estai kai 'ei kardia 'umon.

Hebrew/Transliteration
:כא. כִּי בִמְקוֹם אוֹצָרְךָ שָׁם יִהְיֶה גַם-לִבֶּךָ

21. Ki vim•kom o•tza•re•cha sham yi•hee•ye gam - li•be•cha.

Jewish New Testament Commentary
Pharaoh understood very well that where your wealth is, there will your heart be also. This is why he refused to let the Israelites take their property (Exo_10:8-11, Exo_10:24-27).

22. The light of the body is the eye: if therefore thine eye be single, thy whole body shall be full of light.

Greek/Transliteration
22. Ὁ λύχνος τοῦ σώματός ἐστιν ὁ ὀφθαλμός· ἐὰν οὖν ὁ ὀφθαλμός σου ἁπλοῦς ᾖ, ὅλον τὸ σῶμά σου φωτεινὸν ἔσται·

22. 'O luchnos tou somatos estin 'o ophthalmos. ean oun 'o ophthalmos sou 'aplous ei, 'olon to soma sou photeinon estai.

Hebrew/Transliteration
:כב. נֵר הַגּוּף הוּא הָעַיִן לָכֵן אִם-עֵינְךָ תְּמִימָה בְּכָל-חַדְרֵי בִטְנְךָ יִהְיֶה אוֹר

22. Ner ha•goof hoo ha•a•yin la•chen eem - eyn•cha t`mi•ma be•chol - chad•rey vit•ne•cha yi•hee•ye or.

Jewish New Testament Commentary
"Apparently Yeshua quotes a common proverb and comments on it. If you have a "good eye." This is in the Greek text, but the explanation, that is, if you are generous, is added by me the translator because in Judaism "having a good eye," an *'ayin tovah*, means "being generous," and "having a bad eye," an *'ayin ra'ah*, means "being stingy." That this is the correct interpretation is confirmed by the context, greed and anxiety about money being the topic in both the preceding and following verses. This passage is another link in the chain of evidence that New Testament events took place in Hebrew.

(s)Upon which the commentators say (t), a "good eye" means one that is liberal, and an "evil eye" the contrary: hence you often read (u) of "trading, dedicating", and "giving with a good" or "an evil eye"; that is, either generously, liberally, or in a niggardly and grudging manner; which may help us to the sense of our Lord in these words; whose meaning is, that if a man is not covetous, but his mind is disposed to generosity and liberality.

(s) Misn. Trumot, c. 4. sect. 3. (t) Maimon. Bartenora & Ez. Chayim in ib. (u) T. Bab. Bava Bathra, fol. 37. 2. & 71. 1. & 72. 1.

---

23. But if thine eye be evil, thy whole body shall be full of darkness. If therefore the light that is in thee be darkness, how great is that darkness!

Greek/Transliteration
23. ἐὰν δὲ ὁ ὀφθαλμός σου πονηρὸς ᾖ, ὅλον τὸ σῶμά σου σκοτεινὸν ἔσται. Εἰ οὖν τὸ φῶς τὸ ἐν σοὶ σκότος ἐστίν, τὸ σκότος πόσον;

23. ean de 'o ophthalmos sou poneiros ei, 'olon to soma sou skoteinon estai. Ei oun to phos to en soi skotos estin, to skotos poson?

Hebrew/Transliteration
:כג. וְאִם-עֵינְךָ רָעָה בְּכָל-חַדְרֵי בִטְנֶךָ וְאִם-הָאוֹר בְּךָ חֹשֶׁךְ מַה-גָּדוֹל חָשְׁכֶּךָ

23. Ve•eem - eyn•cha ra•ah cho•shech be•chol - chad•rey vit•ne•cha ve•eem - ha•or be•cha cho•shech ma - ga•dol chosh•ke•cha.

---

24. No man can serve two masters: for either he will hate the one, and love the other; or else he will hold to the one, and despise the other. Ye cannot serve God and mammon.

Greek/Transliteration
24. Οὐδεὶς δύναται δυσὶν κυρίοις δουλεύειν· ἢ γὰρ τὸν ἕνα μισήσει, καὶ τὸν ἕτερον ἀγαπήσει· ἢ ἑνὸς ἀνθέξεται, καὶ τοῦ ἑτέρου καταφρονήσει. Οὐ δύνασθε Θεῷ δουλεύειν καὶ μαμωνᾷ.

24. Oudeis dunatai dusin kuriois douleuein. ei gar ton 'ena miseisei, kai ton 'eteron agapeisei. Ei 'enos anthexetai, kai tou 'eterou kataphroneisei. Ou dunasthe theo douleuein kai mamona.

Hebrew/Transliteration
כד. לֹא-יוּכַל אִישׁ לַעֲבֹד אֲדֹנִים שְׁנַיִם כִּי אִם-יִשְׂנָא אֶת-הָאֶחָד וְאֶת-הָאַחֵר יֶאֱהַב אוֹ יִדְבַּק בָּאֶחָד וְהַשֵּׁנִי יִנְמָאַס בְּעֵינָיו לֹא תוּכְלוּ לַעֲבֹד אֶת-הָאֱלֹהִים וְאֶת-הַמָּמוֹן:

24. Lo - yoo•chal eesh la•a•vod ado•nim sh`na•yim ki eem - yis•na et - ha•e•chad ve•et - ha•a•cher ye•e•hav oh yid•bak ba•e•chad ve•ha•she•ni nim•as be•ey•nav lo tooch•loo la•a•vod et - ha•Elohim ve•et - ha•ma•mon.

Rabbinic Jewish Commentary

The Jews have sayings pretty much like it, and of the same sense as when they say (w), "we have not found that כל אדם זוכה לשתי שולחנות, "any man is fit for two tables.""

And again (x), "that it is not proper for one man to have two governments:"

The Jews, in Yeshua's time, were notorious for the love of "mammon"; and they themselves own, that this was the cause of the destruction of the second temple: the character they give of those, who lived under the second temple, is this:

"we know that they laboured in the law, and took care of the commandments, and of the tithes, and that their whole conversation was good; only that they אוהבין את הממון, "loved the mammon", and hated one another without a cause (b)."

(w) Praefat. Celi Jaker, fol. 3. 1. (x) Piske Tosephot Cetubot, art. 359. (y) Vid. Targum Onkelos & Jon. in Gen. xiii. 13. & in Jud. v. 19. & in Prov. iii. 9. & in Isa. xlv. 13. & passim. (z) Misn. Sanhed. c. 1. sect. 1. & c. 4. sect. 1. (a) Adv. Haeres. l. 3. c. 8. p. 249. (b) T. Hieros. Yoma, fol. 38. 3.

25. Therefore I say unto you, Take no thought for your life, what ye shall eat, or what ye shall drink; nor yet for your body, what ye shall put on. Is not the life more than meat, and the body than raiment?

Greek/Transliteration
25. Διὰ τοῦτο λέγω ὑμῖν, μὴ μεριμνᾶτε τῇ ψυχῇ ὑμῶν, τί φάγητε καὶ τί πίητε· μηδὲ τῷ σώματι ὑμῶν, τί ἐνδύσησθε. Οὐχὶ ἡ ψυχὴ πλεῖόν ἐστιν τῆς τροφῆς, καὶ τὸ σῶμα τοῦ ἐνδύματος;

25. Dya touto lego 'umin, mei merimnate tei psuchei 'umon, ti phageite kai ti pieite. meide to somati 'umon, ti enduseisthe. Ouchi 'ei psuchei pleion estin teis tropheis, kai to soma tou endumatos?

Hebrew/Transliteration
כה. לָכֵן הִנְנִי אֹמֵר לָכֶם לֹא תִדְאֲגוּ לְנַפְשְׁכֶם מַה-תֹּאכְלוּ מַה-תִּשְׁתּוּ וּמַה-כְּסוּת לִכְסוֹת בְּשַׂרְכֶם הֲלֹא הַנֶּפֶשׁ יְקָרָה מֵאֹכֶל וּבָשָׂר אִישׁ מִכְּסוּתוֹ:

25. La•chen hi•ne•ni o•mer la•chem lo tid•a•goo le•naf•she•chem ma - toch•loo ma - tish•too oo•ma - k`soot le•cha•sot be•sar•chem ha•lo ha•ne•fesh ye•ka•ra me•o•chel oov•sar eesh mik•soo•to.

---

26. Behold the fowls of the air: for they sow not, neither do they reap, nor gather into barns; yet your heavenly Father feedeth them. Are ye not much better than they?

Greek/Transliteration
26. Ἐμβλέψατε εἰς τὰ πετεινὰ τοῦ οὐρανοῦ, ὅτι οὐ σπείρουσιν, οὐδὲ θερίζουσιν, οὐδὲ συνάγουσιν εἰς ἀποθήκας, καὶ ὁ πατὴρ ὑμῶν ὁ οὐράνιος τρέφει αὐτά· οὐχ ὑμεῖς μᾶλλον διαφέρετε αὐτῶν;

26. Emblepsate eis ta peteina tou ouranou, 'oti ou speirousin, oude therizousin, oude sunagousin eis apotheikas, kai 'o pateir 'umon 'o ouranios trephei auta. ouch 'umeis mallon dyapherete auton?

Hebrew/Transliteration
כו. הַבִּיטוּ אֶל-עוֹף הַשָּׁמַיִם לֹא יִזְרְעוּ לֹא יִקְצְרוּ וְלֹא יַאַסְפוּ לִמְגוּרוֹת וַאֲבִיכֶם בַּשָּׁמַיִם מְכַלְכֵּל אֹתָם וְאַתֶּם הֲלֹא:נַעֲלֵיתֶם יֶתֶר הַרְבֵּה עֲלֵיהֶם

26. Ha•bi•too el - of ha•sha•ma•yim lo yiz•re•oo lo yik•tze•roo ve•lo ya•as•foo lim•goo•rot va•Avi•chem ba•sha•ma•yim me•chal•kel o•tam ve•a•tem ha•lo na•a•ley•tem ye•ter har•be aley•hem.

Rabbinic Jewish Commentary
The Jews acknowledge this, that the least and meanest of creatures are fed by God.

"Mar says (c), the holy blessed God sits וזן, "and feeds", i.e. all creatures, and takes care of them."

In the Mishna (d) it is said, that R. Simeon ben Eleazer should say, "Did you ever see a beast, or a fowl, that had a trade? but they are fed without trouble."

In the Gemara (e) is added, "Did you ever see a lion bearing burdens, an hart gathering summer fruits, a fox a money changer, or a wolf selling pots? And yet מתפרנסין בלא צער, "they are nourished without labour", and wherefore are they created? To serve me, and I am created to serve my Maker: and lo! these things have in them an argument, "from the less to the greater"; for if these, which are created to serve me after this manner, are supported without trouble; I, who am created to serve my Maker, is it not fit that I should be supplied without trouble? And what is the reason that I am sustained with trouble? My sins."

(c) T. Bab. Sabbat, fol. 107. 2. Avoda Zara, fol. 3. 2. (d) Kiddushin, c. 4. sect. 14.
(e) T. Hieros. Kiddushin, fol. 66. 2. Vid. T. Bab. Kiddushin, fol. 82. 1, 2.

---

27. Which of you by taking thought can add one cubit unto his stature?

Greek/Transliteration
27. Τίς δὲ ἐξ ὑμῶν μεριμνῶν δύναται προσθεῖναι ἐπὶ τὴν ἡλικίαν αὐτοῦ πῆχυν ἕνα;

27. Tis de ex 'umon merimnon dunatai prostheinai epi tein 'eilikian autou peichun 'ena?

Hebrew/Tranliteration
כז. וּמִי הוּא הֶחָרֵד מִכֶּם יוּכַל לְהוֹסִיף עַל-קוֹמָתוֹ גֹּמֶד אֶחָד:

27. Oo•mi hoo he•cha•red mi•kem yoo•chal le•ho•sif al - ko•ma•to go•med e•chad.

Rabbinic Jewish Commentary
add one cubit unto his stature, or "to his age" "the stature of a middling man (says (f) Bartenora) is three cubits."

(f) In Misn. Erubim, c. 4. sect. 5. & Negaim, c. 13. sect. 11.

---

28. And why take ye thought for raiment? Consider the lilies of the field, how they grow; they toil not, neither do they spin:

Greek/Transliteration
28. Καὶ περὶ ἐνδύματος τί μεριμνᾶτε; Καταμάθετε τὰ κρίνα τοῦ ἀγροῦ, πῶς αὐξάνει· οὐ κοπιᾷ, οὐδὲ νήθει·

28. Kai peri endumatos ti merimnate? Katamathete ta krina tou agrou, pos auxanei. ou kopya, oude neithei.

Hebrew/Transliteration
:כח. וְלָמָּה תִדְאֲגוּ לִכְסוּת הִתְבּוֹנְנוּ אֶל-שׁוֹשַׁנֵּי הַשָּׂדֶה אֵיכָה יַעֲלוּ יָצִיצוּ וְלֹא יִיגְעוּן וְלֹא יִטְווּן

28. Ve•la•ma tid•a•goo lich•soot hit•bo•ne•noo el - sho•sha•ney ha•sa•de ey•cha ya•a•loo ya•tzi•tzoo ve•lo yig•oon ve•lo yit•voon.

---

29. And yet I say unto you, That even Solomon in all his glory was not arrayed like one of these.

Greek/Transliteration
29. λέγω δὲ ὑμῖν ὅτι οὐδὲ Σολομὼν ἐν πάσῃ τῇ δόξῃ αὐτοῦ περιεβάλετο ὡς ἓν τούτων.

29. lego de 'umin 'oti oude Solomon en pasei tei doxei autou periebaleto 'os 'en touton.

Hebrew/Transliteration
:כט. וַאֲנִי אֹמֵר לָכֶם גַּם-שְׁלֹמֹה בְּכָל-הֲדָרוֹ לֹא-הָיָה לָבוּשׁ כְּאַחַת מֵהֶן

29. Va•a•ni o•mer la•chem gam - Sh`lo•mo be•chol - ha•da•ro lo - ha•ya la•voosh ke•a•chat me•hen.

Rabbinic Jewish Commentary
This phrase, "Solomon in all his glory", is the same which the Jewish Rabbi's, in their writings, express by שלמה בשעתו, "Solomon in his hour" (g): that is as their commentators explain it (h), בעת מלכותו, "in the time of his reign"; for they say he was first a king, and then a private person. Now, not whilst he was a private person, but when a king, in the height of his grandeur and magnificence, and when dressed out in the most splendid manner, he was exceeded in array by a single lily: or the sense is, in his royal apparel. For as the same Rabbi's say,

"what is a man's "glory?" It is his clothing that is his outward glory; and again, garments are the glory of a man (i)."

(g) Misn. Bava Metzia, c. 7. sect. 1. T. Bab. ib. fol. 49. 1. & 83. 1. & 86. 2. (h) Jarchi & Bartenora in ib. (i) Tzeror Hammor, fol. 95. 1. & 99. 4. & 110. 4.

---

30. Wherefore, if God so clothe the grass of the field, which to day is, and to morrow is cast into the oven, shall he not much more clothe you, O ye of little faith?

Greek/Transliteration
30. Εἰ δὲ τὸν χόρτον τοῦ ἀγροῦ, σήμερον ὄντα, καὶ αὔριον εἰς κλίβανον βαλλόμενον, ὁ θεὸς οὕτως ἀμφιέννυσιν, οὐ πολλῷ μᾶλλον ὑμᾶς, ὀλιγόπιστοι;

30. Ei de ton chorton tou agrou, seimeron onta, kai aurion eis klibanon ballomenon, 'o theos 'outos amphiennusin, ou pollo mallon 'umas, oligopistoi?

Hebrew/Transliteration
ל. וְאִם-כָּכָה יַעֲשֶׂה אֱלֹהִים אֶת-עֵשֶׂב הַשָּׂדֶה אֲשֶׁר יָצִיץ הַיּוֹם וּלְמָחֳרָתוֹ יֻתַּן בַּתַּנּוּר אַף כִּי-אֶתְכֶם קְטַנֵּי אֲמָנָה:

30. Ve•eem - ka•cha ya•a•te Elohim et - esev ha•sa•de asher ya•tzitz ha•yom ool•mo•cho•ra•to yoo•tan be•ta•noor af ki - et•chem k`ta•ney e•moo•na.

Rabbinic/Jewish New Testament Commentary
How much more. This phrase signals a form of argument known in rabbinic literature as *kal v'chomer* ("light and heavy"), corresponding to what philosophers call *a fortiori* reasoning: If A is true, then, *a fortiori* (Latin, "with [even] greater strength"), B must also be true. The English phrase, "how much more," equivalent to Hebrew *kol sh'khen*, expresses this sense and force. Explicit *kal v'chomer* arguments appear in the New Testament twenty-one times, the others being at 7:11, 10:25, 12:12.

In the Misna (k), that pots and furnaces were heated;

"a pot which they heat "with straw and stubble", they put into it that which is to be boiled--a furnace which they heat "with straw and stubble", they put nothing into it, nor upon it (i.e. till they have removed the coals or ashes): a little furnace, which they heat בקש ובגבבא, "with straw and stubble", is as the pots."

The phrase, קטני אמנה, "men of little faith", is often to be met with in the Rabbinical writings:

(q) passage; "Says R. Eliezer the Great, whoever has a morsel in his basket, and says, what shall I eat tomorrow? is no other than מקמני אמנה, "one of those of little faith"."

(k) Sabbat, c. 3. sect. 1, 2. (q) T. Bab. Sota, fol. 48. 2.

---

31. Therefore take no thought, saying, What shall we eat? or, What shall we drink? or, Wherewithal shall we be clothed?

Greek/Transliteration
31. Μὴ οὖν μεριμνήσητε, λέγοντες, Τί φάγωμεν, ἢ τί πίωμεν, ἢ τί περιβαλώμεθα;

31. Mei oun merimneiseite, legontes, Ti phagomen, ei ti piomen, ei ti peribalometha?

Hebrew/Transliteration
לא. לָכֵן אַל-תֶּחֶרְדוּ לֵאמֹר מַה-נֹּאכַל וּמַה-נִּשְׁתֶּה אוֹ מַה-נִּלְבָּשׁ:

31. La•chen al - te•cher•doo le•mor ma - no•chal oo•ma - nish•te oh ma - nil•bash.

---

32. (For after all these things do the Gentiles seek:) for your heavenly Father knoweth that ye have need of all these things.

Greek/Transliteration
32. Πάντα γὰρ ταῦτα τὰ ἔθνη ἐπιζητεῖ· οἶδεν γὰρ ὁ πατὴρ ὑμῶν ὁ οὐράνιος ὅτι χρῄζετε τούτων ἁπάντων.

32. Panta gar tauta ta ethnei epizeitei. oiden gar 'o pateir 'umon 'o ouranios 'oti chreizete touton 'apanton.

Hebrew/Transliteration
לב. כִּי כָל-אֵלֶּה מְבַקְשִׁים הַגּוֹיִם וַאֲבִיכֶם בַּשָּׁמַיִם יֹדֵעַ כִּי אֵלֶּה מַחְסֹרֵיכֶם הֵמָּה:

32. Ki chol - ele me•vak•shim ha•go•yim va•Avi•chem ba•sha•ma•yim yo•de•a ki ele mach•so•rey•chem he•ma.

---

33. But seek ye first the kingdom of God, and his righteousness; and all these things shall be added unto you.

Greek/Transliteration
33. Ζητεῖτε δὲ πρῶτον τὴν βασιλείαν τοῦ θεοῦ καὶ τὴν δικαιοσύνην αὐτοῦ, καὶ ταῦτα πάντα προστεθήσεται ὑμῖν.

33. Zeiteite de proton tein basileian tou theou kai tein dikaiosunein autou, kai tauta panta prostetheisetai 'umin.

Hebrew/Transliteration
לג. אַךְ בַּקְּשׁוּ רִאשֹׁנָה מַלְכוּת אֱלֹהִים וְצִדְקָתוֹ וְכָל-הַחֲפָצִים הָהֵם יִנָּתְנוּ לָכֶם מַתָּנוֹת נוֹסָפוֹת:

33. Ach bak•shoo ri•sho•na mal•choot Elohim ve•tzid•ka•to ve•chol - ha•cha•fa•tzim ha•hem yi•nat•noo la•chem ma•ta•not no•sa•fot.

Rabbinic Jewish Commentary
The Hebrews (r) say, "that no good sign will be shown to Israel, until they return and "seek" three things: "afterwards the children of Israel shall return and seek the Lord"; זו מלכות שמים, "this is the kingdom of heaven"; and "David their king", according to its literal sense; "and shall fear the Lord and his goodness"; this is the house of the sanctuary, as it is said, "this goodly mountain", and Lebanon."

(r) Jarchi & Kimchi, in Hos. iii. 5.

34. Take therefore no thought for the morrow: for the morrow shall take thought for the things of itself. Sufficient unto the day is the evil thereof.

Greek/Transliteration
34. Μὴ οὖν μεριμνήσητε εἰς τὴν αὔριον· ἡ γὰρ αὔριον μεριμνήσει τὰ ἑαυτῆς. Ἀρκετὸν τῇ ἡμέρᾳ ἡ κακία αὐτῆς.

34. Mei oun merimneiseite eis tein aurion. 'ei gar aurion merimneisei ta 'eauteis. Arketon tei 'eimera 'ei kakia auteis.

Hebrew/Transliteration
לד. לָכֵן אַל-תִּדְאֲגוּ לְיוֹם מָחָר יוֹם מָחָר יִדְאַג לְעַצְמוֹ דַּי לַיּוֹם בְּצָרָתוֹ:

34. La•chen al - tid•a•goo le•yom ma•char yom ma•char yid•ag le•atz•mo dai la•yom be•tza•ra•to.

Jewish New Testament Commentary
Tsuris, Yiddish adaptation of Hebrew *tzarot*, "troubles." Leo Rosten's informal lexicon, *The Joys Of Yiddish*, lists under "*tsuris*" what he calls a "folk saying": "Don't worry about tomorrow; who knows what will befall you today?" This could be an instance of New Testament material, purged of its origin, resurfacing in a Jewish context (see Mat_5:21); or, alternatively, Yeshua may in this verse be quoting a proverb already current in the Jewish culture of his own time.

This is expressed in the Talmud (s), nearer the sense of Yeshua's words, after this manner: אל תצר צרת מחר, "do not distress thyself with tomorrow's affliction, for thou knowest not what a day may bring forth"; perhaps tomorrow may not be, and thou wilt be found distressing thyself, for the time which is nothing to thee."

This proverb is thus expressed in the Talmud (t), דיה לצרה בשעתה, "sufficient for distress", or "vexation, is the present time"; which the gloss explains thus,

"sufficient for the vexation it is, that men should grieve for it, at the time that it comes upon them."

(s) T. Bab. Sanhedrim, fol. 100. 2. (t) T. Bab. Beracot, fol. 9. 2.

Matthew, Chapter 7

1. Judge not, that ye be not judged.

Greek/Transliteration
1. Μὴ κρίνετε, ἵνα μὴ κριθῆτε·

1. Mei krinete, 'ina mei kritheite.

Hebrew/Transliteration
א: לֹא תִשְׁפְּטוּ וְלֹא תִשָׁפֵטוּ

1. Lo tish•pe•too ve•lo ti•sha•fe•too.

Rabbinic Jewish Commentary
Good is the advice given by the famous Hillell (u), who lived a little before Yeshua's time; "Do not judge thy neighbour, (says he,) until thou comest into his place." (u) Pirke Abot, c. 2. sect. 4.

---

2. For with what judgment ye judge, ye shall be judged: and with what measure ye mete, it shall be measured to you again.

Greek/Transliteration
2. ἐν ᾧ γὰρ κρίματι κρίνετε, κριθήσεσθε· καὶ ἐν ᾧ μέτρῳ μετρεῖτε, μετρηθήσεται ὑμῖν.

2. en 'o gar krimati krinete, kritheisesthe. kai en 'o metro metreite, metreitheisetai 'umin.

Hebrew/Transliteration
ב: כִּי בַמִשְׁפָּט אֲשֶׁר תִּשְׁפֹּטוּ תִּשָׁפְטוּ גַם-אַתֶּם וּבַמִדָּה אֲשֶׁר תָּמֹדּוּ יִמַּד לָכֶם גַּם-אַתֶּם

2. Ki va•mish•pat asher tish•po•too ti•shaf•too gam - atem oo•va•mi•da asher ta•mo•doo yim•ad la•chem gam - atem.

Rabbinic Commentary
"It is even given an almost mathematical exactitude with the often reiterated belief in "measure for measure" (middah keneged middah): "all the measures [of punishment and reward] taken by the Holy One, blessed be He, are in accordance with the principle of measure for measure" (Sanh. 90a; cf. Sot. 8b); and "from the very creation of the world the Holy One, blessed be He, arranged that by the measure with which a man measures is he measured" (Gen. R. 9:11)."
JewishVirtualLibrary.org, Reward and Punishment.

"He that judgeth his neighbour according to the balance of righteousness, or innocence, they judge him according to righteousness."

(w) And a little after, "As ye have judged me according to the balance of righteousness, God will judge you according to the balance of righteousness."

Hence that advice of Joshua ben Perachiah (x), who, by the Jewish writers, is said to be the master of Yeshua; "Judge every man according to the balance of righteousness."

(w) T. Bab. Sabbat, fol. 127. 2. (x) Pirke Abot, c. 1. sect. 6.

---

3. And why beholdest thou the mote that is in thy brother's eye, but considerest not the beam that is in thine own eye?

Greek/Transliteration
3. Τί δὲ βλέπεις τὸ κάρφος τὸ ἐν τῷ ὀφθαλμῷ τοῦ ἀδελφοῦ σου, τὴν δὲ ἐν τῷ σῷ ὀφθαλμῷ δοκὸν οὐ κατανοεῖς;

3. Ti de blepeis to karphos to en to ophthalmo tou adelphou sou, tein de en to so ophthalmo dokon ou katanoeis?

Hebrew/Transliteration
ג. וְלָמָּה תַבִּיט אֶל-שְׁבָבִים אֲשֶׁר בְּעֵין אָחִיךָ וְלֹא תָשֵׁת-לֵב אֶל-הַקּוֹרָה אֲשֶׁר בְּעֵינֶךָ:

3. Ve•la•ma ta•bit el - sh`va•vim asher be•eyn a•chi•cha ve•lo ta•shet - lev el - ha•ko•ra asher be•ey•ne•cha.

---

4. Or how wilt thou say to thy brother, Let me pull out the mote out of thine eye; and, behold, a beam is in thine own eye?

Greek/Transliteration
4. Ἢ πῶς ἐρεῖς τῷ ἀδελφῷ σου, Ἄφες ἐκβάλω τὸ κάρφος ἀπὸ τοῦ ὀφθαλμοῦ σου· καὶ ἰδού, ἡ δοκὸς ἐν τῷ ὀφθαλμῷ σου;

4. Ei pos ereis to adelpho sou, Aphes ekbalo to karphos apo tou ophthalmou sou. kai idou, 'ei dokos en to ophthalmo sou?

Hebrew/Transliteration
ד. אוֹ אֵיךְ תֹּאמַר לְאָחִיךָ הֶרֶף וְאָסִירָה שְׁבָבִים מֵעֵינֶךָ וְהִנֵּה קוֹרָה בְּעֵינֶךָ:

4. Oh eych to•mar le•a•chi•cha he•ref ve•a•si•ra sh`va•vim me•ey•ne•cha ve•hee•ne ko•ra be•ey•ne•cha.

---

5. Thou hypocrite, first cast out the beam out of thine own eye; and then shalt thou see clearly to cast out the mote out of thy brother's eye.

Greek/Transliteration
5. Ὑποκριτά, ἔκβαλε πρῶτον τὴν δοκὸν ἐκ τοῦ ὀφθαλμοῦ σου, καὶ τότε διαβλέψεις ἐκβαλεῖν τὸ κάρφος ἐκ τοῦ ὀφθαλμοῦ τοῦ ἀδελφοῦ σου.

5. 'Upokrita, ekbale proton tein dokon ek tou ophthalmou sou, kai tote dyablepseis ekbalein to karphos ek tou ophthalmou tou adelphou sou.

Hebrew/Transliteration
ה. הָסֵר חָנֵף רִאשׁנָה אֶת-הַקּוֹרָה מֵעֵינֶךָ וְאַחֲרֵי כֵן רָאֹה תִרְאֶה לְהָסִיר שְׁבָבִים מֵעֵין אָחִיךָ:

5. Ha•ser cha•nef ri•sho•na et - ha•ko•ra me•ey•ne•cha ve•a•cha•rey chen ra•oh tir•eh le•ha•sir sh`va•vim me•eyn a•chi•cha.

Rabbinic Jewish Commentary
Our Lord here speaks in the language of the Jewish nation, with whom such like expressions were common, and of long standing (c).

"In the generation that judged the judges, one said to another, טול קיסם מבין עיניך, "cast out the mote out of thine eye"; to whom it was replied, טול קורה מבין עיניך, "cast out the beam from thine eye": one said to another, "thy silver is become dross": the other replies, "thy wine is mixed with water"."

Again (d), "R. Taphon said, I wonder whether there is any in this generation, that will receive reproof; if one should say to him, "cast out the mote out of thine eye", will he say to him, "cast out the beam out of thine eye?" Says R. Eleazer ben Azariah, I wonder whether there is any in this generation, that knows how to reprove."

(c) T. Bab. Bava Bathra, fol. 15. 2. (d) T. Bab. Erachin, fol. 16. 2.

---

6. Give not that which is holy unto the dogs, neither cast ye your pearls before swine, lest they trample them under their feet, and turn again and rend you.

Greek/Trasnliteration
6. Μὴ δῶτε τὸ ἅγιον τοῖς κυσίν· μηδὲ βάλητε τοὺς μαργαρίτας ὑμῶν ἔμπροσθεν τῶν χοίρων, μήποτε καταπατήσωσιν αὐτοὺς ἐν τοῖς ποσὶν αὐτῶν, καὶ στραφέντες ῥήξωσιν ὑμᾶς.

6. Mei dote to 'agion tois kusin. meide baleite tous margaritas 'umon emprosthen ton choiron, meipote katapateisosin autous en tois posin auton, kai straphentes 'reixosin 'umas.

Hebrew/Transliteration
ו. לֹא תִתְּנוּ הַקֹּדֶשׁ לַכְּלָבִים וְאֶת-פְּנִינֵיכֶם לַחֲזִירִים פֶּן-יִרְמְסוּם בְּרַגְלֵיהֶם וְשָׁבוּ וְטָרְפוּ אֶתְכֶם:

6. Lo tit•noo ha•ko•desh lak•la•vim ve•et - p`ni•ney•chem la•cha•zi•rim pen - yir•me•soom be•rag•ley•hem ve•sha•voo ve•tar•foo et•chem.

Rabbinic Jewish Commentary

Dogs were unclean creatures by the law; the price of one might not be brought into the house of the Lord, for a vow, Deu_23:18 yea, these creatures were not admitted into several temples of the Heathens (h). Things profane and unclean, as flesh torn by beasts, were ordered to be given to them, Exo_22:31 but nothing that was holy was to be given them, as holy flesh, or the holy oblations, or anything that was consecrated to holy uses; to which is the allusion here. It is a common maxim (i) with the Jews,

שאין פודין את הקדשים להאכילן לכלבים, "that they do not redeem holy things, to give to the dogs to eat"."

The Jews have some sayings much like these, and will serve to illustrate them (k);

אל תשליכו הפנינים לפני החזירים, "do not cast pearls before swine", nor deliver wisdom to him, who knows not the excellency of it; for wisdom is better than pearls, and he that does not seek after it, is worse than a swine."

(h) Vid. Alex. ab. Alex. Gaeial. Dier. l. 2. c. 14. (i) T. Bab. Temura, fol. 17. 1. & 31. 1. & 33. 2. Becorot, fol. 15. 1. Hieros. Pesachim, fol. 27. 4. & Maaser Sheni, fol. 53. 3. (k) Mischar Happeninim apud Buxtorf. Florileg. Heb. p. 306.

---

7. Ask, and it shall be given you; seek, and ye shall find; knock, and it shall be opened unto you:

Greek/Translitertion
7. Αἰτεῖτε, καὶ δοθήσεται ὑμῖν· ζητεῖτε, καὶ εὑρήσετε· κρούετε, καὶ ἀνοιγήσεται ὑμῖν.

7. Aiteite, kai dotheisetai 'umin. zeiteite, kai 'eureisete. krouete, kai anoigeisetai 'umin.

Hebrew/Transliteration
ז. שַׁאֲלוּ וְיִנָּתֵן לָכֶם דִּרְשׁוּ וְתִמְצָאוּ דִּפְקוּ וְיִפָּתַח לָכֶם:

7. Sha•a•loo ve•yi•na•ten la•chem dir•shoo ve•tim•tza•oo dif•koo ve•yi•pa•tach la•chem.

---

8. For every one that asketh receiveth; and he that seeketh findeth; and to him that knocketh it shall be opened.

Greek/Transliteration
8. Πᾶς γὰρ ὁ αἰτῶν λαμβάνει, καὶ ὁ ζητῶν εὑρίσκει, καὶ τῷ κρούοντι ἀνοιγήσεται.

8. Pas gar 'o aiton lambanei, kai 'o zeiton 'euriskei, kai to krouonti anoigeisetai.

Hebrew/Transliteration

ח: כִּי כָל־הַשֹּׁאֵל יִקָּח וְהַדֹּרֵשׁ יִמְצָא וְהַדֹּפֵק יִפָּתַח לוֹ.

8. Ki kol - ha•sho•el yi•kach ve•ha•do•resh yim•tza ve•ha•do•fek yi•pa•tach lo.

---

9. Or what man is there of you, whom if his son ask bread, will he give him a stone?

Greek/Transliteration

9. Ἢ τίς ἐστιν ἐξ ὑμῶν ἄνθρωπος, ὃν ἐὰν αἰτήσῃ ὁ υἱὸς αὐτοῦ ἄρτον, μὴ λίθον ἐπιδώσει αὐτῷ;

9. Ei tis estin ex 'umon anthropos, 'on ean aiteisei 'o 'wios autou arton, mei lithon epidosei auto?

Hebrew/Transliteration

ט: כִּי מִי אִישׁ מִכֶּם אֲשֶׁר בְּנוֹ שָׁאַל מִמֶּנּוּ לָחֶם וַיִּתֶּן־לוֹ אָבֶן

9. Ki mee eesh mi•kem asher b`no sha•al mi•me•noo la•chem va•yi•ten - lo aven.

---

10. Or if he ask a fish, will he give him a serpent?

Greek/Translitertion

10. Καὶ ἐὰν ἰχθὺν αἰτήσῃ, μὴ ὄφιν ἐπιδώσει αὐτῷ;

10. Kai ean ichthun aiteisei, mei ophin epidosei auto?

Hebrew/Transliteration

י: אוֹ אִם־בִּקֵּשׁ דָּג וַיִּתֶּן־לוֹ נָחָשׁ

10. Oh eem - bi•kesh dag va•yi•ten - lo na•chash.

---

11. If ye then, being evil, know how to give good gifts unto your children, how much more shall your Father which is in heaven give good things to them that ask him?

Greek/Transliteration

11. Εἰ οὖν ὑμεῖς, πονηροὶ ὄντες, οἴδατε δόματα ἀγαθὰ διδόναι τοῖς τέκνοις ὑμῶν, πόσῳ μᾶλλον ὁ πατὴρ ὑμῶν ὁ ἐν τοῖς οὐρανοῖς δώσει ἀγαθὰ τοῖς αἰτοῦσιν αὐτόν;

11. Ei oun 'umeis, poneiroi ontes, oidate domata agatha didonai tois teknois 'umon, poso mallon 'o pateir 'umon 'o en tois ouranois dosei agatha tois aitousin auton?

Hebrew/Transliteration
יא. וְאַף כִּי רָעִים אַתֶּם תֵּדְעוּן לָתֵת מַתָּנוֹת טֹבוֹת לִבְנֵיכֶם אַף כִּי-אֲבִיכֶם שֶׁבַּשָּׁמַיִם יִתֶּן-טוֹב לְדֹרְשָׁיו:

11. Ve•af ki ra•eem atem ted•oon la•tet ma•ta•not to•vot liv•ney•chem af ki - Avi•chem she•ba•sha•ma•yim yi•ten - tov le•dor•shav.

---

12. Therefore all things whatsoever ye would that men should do to you, do ye even so to them: for this is the law and the prophets.

Greek/Transliteration
12. Πάντα οὖν ὅσα ἂν θέλητε ἵνα ποιῶσιν ὑμῖν οἱ ἄνθρωποι, οὕτως καὶ ὑμεῖς ποιεῖτε αὐτοῖς· οὗτος γάρ ἐστιν ὁ νόμος καὶ οἱ προφῆται.

12. Panta oun 'osa an theleite 'ina poiosin 'umin 'oi anthropoi, 'outos kai 'umeis poieite autois. 'outos gar estin 'o nomos kai 'oi propheitai.

Hebrew/Transliteration
יב. לָכֵן כֹּל אֲשֶׁר תַּחְפְּצוּ שֶׁיַּעֲשׂוּן לָכֶם אֲנָשִׁים עֲשׂוּ לָהֶם כְּמוֹ-כֵן גַּם-אַתֶּם כִּי זֹאת הַתּוֹרָה וְהַנְּבִיאִים:

12. La•chen kol asher tach•pe•tzoo she•ya•a•soon la•chem a•na•shim a•soo la•hem k`mo - chen gam - atem ki zot ha•Torah ve•ha•n`vi•eem.

Rabbinic/Jewsh New Testament Commentary
The Golden Rule can be found in Jewish writings as early as the Apocryphal book of Tobit (third century B.C.E.), "What you hate, do to no one" (Tob_4:15); similar sayings are attributed to Isocrates, Aristotle and Confucius. Rabbi Hillel expressed it in the generation before Yeshua; a famous passage in the Talmud comparing Hillel with his contemporary, Shammai, tells the story:

"A pagan came came before Shammai and said to him, 'Make me a proselyte, but on condition that you teach me the entire *Torah* while I am standing on one foot!' Shammai drove him off with the builder's measuring rod which he had in his hand. When he appeared before Hillel, the latter told him, 'What is hateful to you, do not do to your neighbor. That is the whole *Torah*. The rest is commentary. Go and learn it!' " (Shabbat 31a)

---

13. Enter ye in at the strait gate: for wide is the gate, and broad is the way, that leadeth to destruction, and many there be which go in thereat:

Greek/Transliteration
13. Εἰσέλθετε διὰ τῆς στενῆς πύλης· ὅτι πλατεῖα ἡ πύλη, καὶ εὐρύχωρος ἡ ὁδὸς ἡ ἀπάγουσα εἰς τὴν ἀπώλειαν, καὶ πολλοί εἰσιν οἱ εἰσερχόμενοι δι᾽ αὐτῆς·

13. Eiselthete dya teis steneis puleis. 'oti plateia 'ei pulei, kai euruchoros 'ei 'odos 'ei apagousa eis tein apoleyan, kai polloi eisin 'oi eiserchomenoi di auteis.

Hebrew/Transliteration
יג. בֹּאוּ בַשַּׁעַר הַצַּר כִּי רָחָב הַשַּׁעַר וְהַדֶּרֶךְ רְחָבָה הַמּוֹלִיכָה אֶל-הָאֲבַדּוֹן וְרַבִּים הֵם הַבָּאִים שָׁמָּה:

13. Bo•oo va•sha•ar ha•tzar ki ra•chav ha•sha•ar ve•ha•de•rech r`cha•va ha•mo•li•cha el - ha•a•va•don ve•ra•bim hem ha•ba•eem sha•ma.

Rabbinic Jewish Commentary
Yeshua seems to allude to the private and public roads, whose measures are fixed by the Jewish canons; which say (p), that

"a private way was four cubits broad, a way from city to city eight cubits, a public way sixteen cubits, and the way to the cities of refuge thirty two cubits."

(p) T. Bab. Bava Bathra, fol. 100. 1, 2. Vid. Maimon. & R. Sampson in Misn. Peah, c. 2. sect. 1. & Maimon in Sabbat. c. 1. sect. 1.

---

14. Because strait is the gate, and narrow is the way, which leadeth unto life, and few there be that find it.

Greek/Transliteration
14. τί στενὴ ἡ πύλη, καὶ τεθλιμμένη ἡ ὁδὸς ἡ ἀπάγουσα εἰς τὴν ζωήν, καὶ ὀλίγοι εἰσὶν οἱ εὑρίσκοντες αὐτήν.

14. ti stenei 'ei pulei, kai tethlimmenei 'ei 'odos 'ei apagousa eis tein zoein, kai oligoi eisin 'oi 'euriskontes autein.

Hebrew/Transliteration
יד. וּמַה-צַּר הַשַּׁעַר וְהַדֶּרֶךְ מַה-צָּרָה הַמּוֹלִיכָה אֶל-הַחַיִּים וּמֹצְאֶיהָ מְתֵי מִסְפָּר הֵם:

14. Oo•ma - tzar ha•sha•ar ve•ha•de•rech ma - tza•ra ha•mo•li•cha el - ha•cha•yim oo•motz•e•ha me•tey mis•par hem.

Rabbinic Jewish Commentary
It is asked in the Talmud (q), "why is the world to come created with "jod?" (the least of the letters in the "Hebrew alphabet") the answer is, because צדיקים שבו מועטים, "the righteous which are in it are few"."

(q) T. Bab. Menachot, fol. 29. 2.

15. Beware of false prophets, which come to you in sheep's clothing, but inwardly they are ravening wolves.

Greek/Transliteration
15. Προσέχετε δὲ ἀπὸ τῶν ψευδοπροφητῶν, οἵτινες ἔρχονται πρὸς ὑμᾶς ἐν ἐνδύμασιν προβάτων, ἔσωθεν δέ εἰσιν λύκοι ἅρπαγες.

15. Prosechete de apo ton pseudopropheiton, 'oitines erchontai pros 'umas en endumasin probaton, esothen de eisin lukoi 'arpages.

Hebrew/Transliteration
טו. הִשָּׁמְרוּ לָכֶם מִנְּבִיאֵי שֶׁקֶר הַבָּאִים לִפְנֵיכֶם בְּעוֹר כְּבָשִׂים וְהֵם זְאֵבֵי טָרֶף:

15. Hi•sham•roo la•chem min•vi•ey sha•ker ha•ba•eem lif•ney•chem be•or ke•va•sim ve•hem ze•e•vey ta•ref.

Rabbinic Jewish Commentary
Jarchi (s) says, that "it was the way of deceivers, and profane men, to cover themselves, בטליתאם, "with their talith", or long garment, "as if they were righteous men", that persons might receive their lies."

The Jews speak of a "wolfish humility"; like that of the wolf in the fable, which put on a sheep skin.

"There are some men, (says one of their (t) writers,) who appear to be humble, and fear God in a deceitful and hypocritical way, but inwardly lay wait: this humility our wise men call ענוה זאבית, "wolfish humility"."

Such is this Yeshua inveighs against, and bids his followers beware of.

(r) T. Bab. Sanhedrim, fol. 41. 1. (s) In Zech. xiii. 4. (t) Abarbinel Nachalath Abot, fol. 192. 1.

---

16. Ye shall know them by their fruits. Do men gather grapes of thorns, or figs of thistles?

Greek/Transliteration
16. Ἀπὸ τῶν καρπῶν αὐτῶν ἐπιγνώσεσθε αὐτούς· μήτι συλλέγουσιν ἀπὸ ἀκανθῶν σταφυλήν, ἢ ἀπὸ τριβόλων σῦκα;

16. Apo ton karpon auton epignosesthe autous. meiti sullegousin apo akanthon staphulein, ei apo tribolon suka?

Hebrew/Transliteration
טז. בְּפִרְיָם תַּכִּירוּ אֹתָם הֲיִבְצְרוּ עֲנָבִים מֵעַקְרַבִּים אוֹ תְאֵנִים מִצְּנִינִם:

16. Be•fir•yam ta•ki•roo o•tam ha•yiv•tze•roo ana•vim me•ak•ra•bim oh te•e•nim mitz•ni•nim.

Rabbinic Jewish Commentray

The Jews have a proverb pretty much like this (u), בוצין מקטפיה ידיע, "a gourd is known by its branches". The gloss upon it is,

"it is, as if it was said, from the time it buds forth, and goes out of the branch, it is known whether it is good or not;" (u) T. Bab. Beracot, fol. 48. 1.

---

17. Even so every good tree bringeth forth good fruit; but a corrupt tree bringeth forth evil fruit.

Greek/Transliteration

17. Οὕτως πᾶν δένδρον ἀγαθὸν καρποὺς καλοὺς ποιεῖ· τὸ δὲ σαπρὸν δένδρον καρποὺς πονηροὺς ποιεῖ.

17. 'Outos pan dendron agathon karpous kalous poiei. to de sapron dendron karpous poneirous poiei.

Hebrew/Transliteration

יז. כֵּן כָּל-עֵץ טוֹב יַעֲשֶׂה פְּרִי טוֹב וְעֵץ נִשְׁחָת פְּרִי מָשְׁחָת:

17. Ken kol - etz tov ya•a•se f`ri tov ve•etz nish•chat p`ri mosh•chat.

---

18. A good tree cannot bring forth evil fruit, neither can a corrupt tree bring forth good fruit.

Greek/Transliteration

18. Οὐ δύναται δένδρον ἀγαθὸν καρποὺς πονηροὺς ποιεῖν, οὐδὲ δένδρον σαπρὸν καρποὺς καλοὺς ποιεῖν.

18. Ou dunatai dendron agathon karpous poneirous poiein, oude dendron sapron karpous kalous poiein.

Hebrew/Transliteration

יח. עֵץ טוֹב לֹא-יוּכַל לַעֲשׂוֹת פְּרִי מָשְׁחָת וְעֵץ נִשְׁחָת לֹא-יוּכַל לַעֲשׂוֹת פְּרִי טוֹב:

18. Etz tov lo - yoo•chal la•a•sot p`ri mosh•chat ve•etz nish•chat lo - yoo•chal la•a•sot p`ri tov.

---

19. Every tree that bringeth not forth good fruit is hewn down, and cast into the fire.

Greek/Transliteration
19. Πᾶν δένδρον μὴ ποιοῦν καρπὸν καλὸν ἐκκόπτεται καὶ εἰς πῦρ βάλλεται.
19. Pan dendron mei poioun karpon kalon ekkoptetai kai eis pur balletai.

Hebrew/Transliteration
יט. וְכָל-עֵץ בִּלְתִּי עֹשֶׂה פְרִי טוֹב יִגָּדַע וְיֻתַּן לְמַאֲכֹלֶת אֵשׁ:

19. Ve•chol - etz bil•tee o•se f'ri tov yi•ga•da ve•yoo•tan le•ma•a•cho•let esh.

Rabbinic Jewish Commentary
(x)"he that marries his daughter to a scholar, it is like to grapes of the vine, with grapes of the vine, a thing beautiful and acceptable; but he that marries his daughter to a Roman, it is like to grapes of the vine, בענבי הסנה, "with grapes of the thorn", a thing ugly, and unacceptable."

(x) T. Bab. Pesachim, fol. 49. 1.

---

20. Wherefore by their fruits ye shall know them.

Greek/Transliteration
20. Ἄρα γε ἀπὸ τῶν καρπῶν αὐτῶν ἐπιγνώσεσθε αὐτούς.

20. Ara ge apo ton karpon auton epignosesthe autous.

Hebrew/Transliteration
כ. עַל-כֵּן בְּפִרְיָם תַּכִּירוּ אֹתָם:

20. Al - ken be•fir•yam ta•ki•roo o•tam.

Rabbinic Commentary/TaNaKh-Old Testament
"Micah compares the small number of righteous people of his generation to the spare number of summer fruit (Metsudos) or to the unripe figs of inferior quality that remain on the trees after the harvest (Rashi)... Alternatively, he is lamenting over Israel who refused to hearken to his rebuke. He grieves over the extent of their wickedness and the retribution that God has prepared for them (Radak)." Artscroll Commentary on Micah, Chapter 7, Trei Asar, The Twelve Prophets, Volume II, Mesorah Publications, pg 52

"I found Israel like grapes in the wilderness. I saw your fathers as the first ripe in the fig tree at its first season . . . Hosea 9:10

---

21. Not every one that saith unto me, Lord, Lord, shall enter into the kingdom of heaven; but he that doeth the will of my Father which is in heaven.

Greek/Transliteration
21. Οὐ πᾶς ὁ λέγων μοι, Κύριε, κύριε, εἰσελεύσεται εἰς τὴν βασιλείαν τῶν οὐρανῶν· ἀλλ᾽ ὁ ποιῶν τὸ θέλημα τοῦ πατρός μου τοῦ ἐν οὐρανοῖς.

21. Ou pas 'o legon moi, Kurie, kurie, eiseleusetai eis tein basileian ton ouranon. all 'o poion to theleima tou patros mou tou en ouranois.

Hebrew/Transliteration
כא: לֹא כָל-הַקֹּרֵא לִי אָדוֹן אָדוֹן יָבֹא לְמַלְכוּת הַשָּׁמַיִם כִּי אִם-הָעֹשֶׂה רְצוֹן אָבִי אֲשֶׁר בַּשָּׁמָיִם.

21. Lo chol - ha•ko•re li Adon Adon ya•vo le•mal•choot ha•sha•ma•yim ki eem - ha•o•se r`tzon Avi asher ba•sha•ma•yim.

Jewish New Testament Commentary
In the present verse, Yeshua seems to say that a day will come when people will address him as the divine Lord-more than human but not necessarily *YHVH*; however, see Php_2:9-11. In the Septuagint "*kurios*" is the most common rendering of "*YHVH*." In Paul's writings and in the General Letters "*kurios*" sometimes refers to Yeshua.

---

22. Many will say to me in that day, Lord, Lord, have we not prophesied in thy name? and in thy name have cast out devils? and in thy name done many wonderful works?

Greek/Transliteration
22. Πολλοὶ ἐροῦσίν μοι ἐν ἐκείνῃ τῇ ἡμέρᾳ, Κύριε, κύριε, οὐ τῷ σῷ ὀνόματι προεφητεύσαμεν, καὶ τῷ σῷ ὀνόματι δαιμόνια ἐξεβάλομεν, καὶ τῷ σῷ ὀνόματι δυνάμεις πολλὰς ἐποιήσαμεν;

22. Polloi erousin moi en ekeinei tei 'eimera, Kurie, kurie, ou to so onomati proepheiteusamen, kai to so onomati daimonya exebalomen, kai to so onomati dunameis pollas epoieisamen?

Hebrew/Transliteration
כב. וְהָיָה בַּיּוֹם הַהוּא יֹאמְרוּ אֵלַי רַבִּים אֲדֹנִי אֲדֹנִי הֲלֹא בְשִׁמְךָ נִבֵּאנוּ בְשִׁמְךָ גֵרַשְׁנוּ שֵׁדִים וּבְשִׁמְךָ עָשִׂינוּ נִפְלָאוֹת רַבּוֹת:

22. Ve•ha•ya ba•yom ha•hoo yom•roo e•lai ra•bim Adoni Adoni ha•lo ve•shim•cha ni•be•noo be•shim•cha ge•rash•noo she•dim oov•shim•cha asi•noo nif•la•ot ra•bot.

Jewish New Testament Commentary
That Day is the Day of Judgment (Hebrew *Yom-haDin*)

23. And then will I profess unto them, I never knew you: depart from me, ye that work iniquity.

Greek/Transliteration
23. Καὶ τότε ὁμολογήσω αὐτοῖς ὅτι Οὐδέποτε ἔγνων ὑμᾶς· ἀποχωρεῖτε ἀπ' ἐμοῦ οἱ ἐργαζόμενοι τὴν ἀνομίαν.

23. Kai tote 'omologeiso autois 'oti Oudepote egnon 'umas. apochoreite ap emou 'oi ergazomenoi tein anomian.

Hebrew/Transliteration
:כג. אָז כֹּה אַגִּיד לָהֶם לֹא יָדַעְתִּי אֶתְכֶם מֵעוֹדִי סוּרוּ מִמֶּנִּי פֹּעֲלֵי אָוֶן

23. Az ko agid la•hem lo ya•da•a•ti et•chem me•o•di soo•roo mi•me•ni po•a•ley aven.

Rabbinic/Jewish New Testament Commentary
Lawlessness, Greek *anomia*, "absence of law, absence of *Torah*." Hence you workers of lawlessness means "you who act as if there were no *Torah*"; it confirms Yeshua's teaching on the permanence of the *Torah* (Mat_5:17-20). The Greek word "*anomia*" can be rendered "wickedness," but doing so here skirts the Jewish context.

In this sense the phrase is used in the Talmud (y):

"Bar Kaphra went to visit R. Juda; he says to him, Bar Kaphra, איני מכירך מעולם, "I never knew thee"."

The gloss upon it is, "he intimates, that he would not see him."

(y) T. Bab. Moed Katon, fol. 16. 1.

---

24. Therefore whosoever heareth these sayings of mine, and doeth them, I will liken him unto a wise man, which built his house upon a rock:

Greek/Transliteration
24. Πᾶς οὖν ὅστις ἀκούει μου τοὺς λόγους τούτους καὶ ποιεῖ αὐτούς, ὁμοιώσω αὐτὸν ἀνδρὶ φρονίμῳ, ὅστις ᾠκοδόμησεν τὴν οἰκίαν αὐτοῦ ἐπὶ τὴν πέτραν·

24. Pas oun 'ostis akouei mou tous logous toutous kai poiei autous, 'omoioso auton andri phronimo, 'ostis okodomeisen tein oikian autou epi tein petran.

Hebrew/Transliteration
:כד. לָכֵן כָּל-הַשֹּׁמֵעַ לִדְבָרַי אֵלֶּה וְעֹשֶׂה אֹתָם אֲעֶרְכֶנּוּ לַחֲכַם-לֵב אֲשֶׁר בָּנָה בֵיתוֹ עַל-הַסָּלַע

24. La•chen kol - ha•sho•me•a lid•va•rai ele ve•o•se o•tam e•er•che•noo la•cha•cham – lev asher ba•na vey•to al - ha•sa•la.

25. And the rain descended, and the floods came, and the winds blew, and beat upon that house; and it fell not: for it was founded upon a rock.

Greek/Transliteration

25. καὶ κατέβη ἡ βροχὴ καὶ ἦλθον οἱ ποταμοὶ καὶ ἔπνευσαν οἱ ἄνεμοι, καὶ προσέπεσον τῇ οἰκίᾳ ἐκείνῃ, καὶ οὐκ ἔπεσεν· τεθεμελίωτο γὰρ ἐπὶ τὴν πέτραν.

25. kai katebei 'ei brochei kai eilthon 'oi potamoi kai epneusan 'oi anemoi, kai prosepeson tei oikia ekeinei, kai ouk epesen. tethemelioto gar epi tein petran.

Hebrew/Transliteration

כה. הַגֶּשֶׁם נִתַּךְ אַרְצָה נַחֲלֵי מַיִם יִשְׁטֹפוּ וְרוּחַ גְּדוֹלָה בָּאָה וַיִּפְגְּעוּ בַּבַּיִת הַהוּא וְלֹא נָפַל כִּי יֻסַּד בַּסֶּלַע:

25. Ha•ge•shem ni•tach ar•tza na•cha•ley ma•yim yish•to•foo ve•roo•ach ge•do•la ba•ah va•yif•ge•oo va•ba•yit ha•hoo ve•lo na•fal ki yoo•sad ba•sa•la.

---

26. And every one that heareth these sayings of mine, and doeth them not, shall be likened unto a foolish man, which built his house upon the sand:

Greek/Transliteration

26. Καὶ πᾶς ὁ ἀκούων μου τοὺς λόγους τούτους καὶ μὴ ποιῶν αὐτούς, ὁμοιωθήσεται ἀνδρὶ μωρῷ, ὅστις ᾠκοδόμησεν τὴν οἰκίαν αὐτοῦ ἐπὶ τὴν ἄμμον·

26. Kai pas 'o akouon mou tous logous toutous kai mei poion autous, 'omoiotheisetai andri moro, 'ostis okodomeisen tein oikian autou epi tein ammon.

Hebrew/Transliteration

כו. וְכָל-הַשֹּׁמֵעַ לִדְבָרַי אֵלֶּה וְלֹא יַעֲשֶׂה אֹתָם נִמְשַׁל לַחֲסַר-לֵב אֲשֶׁר בָּנָה בֵיתוֹ עַל-הַחוֹל:

26. Ve•chol - ha•sho•me•a lid•va•rai ele ve•lo ya•a•se o•tam nim•shal la•cha•sar – lev asher ba•na vey•to al - ha•chol.

---

27. And the rain descended, and the floods came, and the winds blew, and beat upon that house; and it fell: and great was the fall of it.

Greek/Transliteration

27. καὶ κατέβη ἡ βροχὴ καὶ ἦλθον οἱ ποταμοὶ καὶ ἔπνευσαν οἱ ἄνεμοι, καὶ προσέκοψαν τῇ οἰκίᾳ ἐκείνῃ, καὶ ἔπεσεν· καὶ ἦν ἡ πτῶσις αὐτῆς μεγάλη.

27. kai katebei 'ei brochei kai eilthon 'oi potamoi kai epneusan 'oi anemoi, kai prosekopsan tei oikia ekeinei, kai epesen. kai ein 'ei ptosis auteis megalei.

Hebrew/Transliteration
כז. הַגֶּשֶׁם נִתַּךְ אַרְצָה נַחֲלֵי מַיִם יִשְׁטֹפוּ וְרוּחַ גְדוֹלָה בָּאָה וַיִּפְגְעוּ בַּבַּיִת הַהוּא וַיִּפֹּל וַיְהִי לְמַפֵּלָה גְדוֹלָה:

27. Ha•ge•shem ni•tach ar•tza na•cha•ley ma•yim yish•to•foo ve•roo•ach ge•do•la ba•ah va•yif•ge•oo va•ba•yit ha•hoo va•yi•pol vay•hi le•ma•pe•la ge•do•la.

Rabbinic Jewish Commentary
The Jews make use of some similes, which are pretty much like these of Yeshua's.

"R. Eliezer ben Azariah used to say (z), he whose wisdom is greater than his works, to what is he like? to a tree, whose branches are many, and its roots few, "and the wind comes", and roots it up, and overturns it; as it is said, Jer_17:6 but he whose works are greater than his wisdom, to what is he like? to a tree, whose branches are few, and its roots many, "against which, if all the winds in the world were to come and blow", they could not move it out of its place: as it is said, Jer_17:8."

Again (a), "Elisha ben Abuijah used to say, a man who hath good works, and learns the law much, to what is he like? to a man that "builds with stones below", and afterwards with bricks; and though באים מים הרבה, "many waters come", and stand at their side, they cannot remove them out of their place; but a man who hath no good works, and learns the law, to what is he like? to a man that "builds with bricks first", and afterwards with stones; and though few waters come, they immediately overturn them."

The same used to say, "a man who hath good works, and learns the law much, to what is he like? to mortar spread upon bricks; and though יורדין עליו גשמים, "the rains descend upon it", they cannot remove it out of its place: a man that hath no good works, and learns the law much, to what is he like? to mortar thrown upon bricks; and though but a small rain descends upon it, it is immediately dissolved, and "falls"."

(z) Pirke Abot, c. 3. sect. 17. & Abot R. Nathan, c. 22. fol. 6. 1, 2. (a) Abot R. Nathan, c. 24. fol. 6. 2.

---

28. And it came to pass, when Jesus had ended these sayings, the people were astonished at his doctrine:

Greek/Transliteration
28. Καὶ ἐγένετο ὅτε συνετέλεσεν ὁ Ἰησοῦς τοὺς λόγους τούτους, ἐξεπλήσσοντο οἱ ὄχλοι ἐπὶ τῇ διδαχῇ αὐτοῦ·

28. Kai egeneto 'ote sunetelesen 'o Yeisous tous logous toutous, expleissonto 'oi ochloi epi tei didachei autou.

Hebrew/Transliteration
:כח. וַיְהִי כְּכַלּוֹת יֵשׁוּעַ אֶת-הַדְּבָרִים הָאֵלֶּה וַיִּתְמְהוּ הֲמוֹן הָעָם עַל-תּוֹרָתוֹ

28. Vay•hi ke•cha•lot Yeshua et - ha•d`va•rim ha•e•le va•yit•me•hoo ha•mon ha•am al - to•ra•to.

---

29. For he taught them as one having authority, and not as the scribes.

Greek/Transliteration
29. ἦν γὰρ διδάσκων αὐτοὺς ὡς ἐξουσίαν ἔχων, καὶ οὐχ ὡς οἱ γραμματεῖς.

29. ein gar didaskon autous 'os exousian echon, kai ouch 'os 'oi grammateis.

Hebrew/Transliteration
:כט. כִּי הָיָה מוֹרֶה אֹתָם כְּהוֹרֹת אִישׁ-שִׁלְטוֹן וְלֹא כַסּוֹפְרִים

29. Ki ha•ya mo•re o•tam ke•ho•rot eesh - shil•ton ve•lo cha•sof•rim.

Matthew, Chapter 8

1. When he was come down from the mountain, great multitudes followed him.

Greek/Transliteration
1. Καταβάντι δὲ αὐτῷ ἀπὸ τοῦ ὄρους, ἠκολούθησαν αὐτῷ ὄχλοι πολλοί·

1. Katabanti de auto apo tou orous, eikoloutheisan auto ochloi polloi.

Hebrew/Transliteration
א. וַיֵּרֶד מִן־הָהָר וַהֲמוֹן עַם רַב הֹלְכִים אַחֲרָיו:

1. Va•ye•red min - ha•har va•ha•mon am rav hol•chim a•cha•rav.

---

2. And, behold, there came a leper and worshipped him, saying, Lord, if thou wilt, thou canst make me clean.

Greek/Transliteration
2. καὶ ἰδού, λεπρὸς ἐλθὼν προσεκύνει αὐτῷ, λέγων, Κύριε, ἐὰν θέλῃς, δύνασαί με καθαρίσαι.

2. kai idou, lepros elthon prosekunei auto, legon, Kurie, ean theleis, dunasai me katharisai.

Hebrew/Transliteration
ב. וְהִנֵּה אִישׁ מְצֹרָע בָּא וַיִּשְׁתַּחוּ־לוֹ לֵאמֹר אֲדֹנִי אִם־חָפֵץ אַתָּה הֲלֹא תוּכַל לְטַהֲרֵנִי:

2. Ve•hee•ne eesh me•tzo•ra ba va•yish•ta•choo - lo le•mor Adoni eem - cha•fetz ata ha•lo too•chal le•ta•ha•re•ni.

Rabbinic/Jewish New Testament Commentary
The Ben Ish Chai, R' Yosef Chayyim, says,
"The Sages say that the Messiah is called "the leper of the house of Rabbi". . . The Josephian Messiah suffers illnesses and afflictions to atone for the people of Israel and for the destruction of Jerusalem and of the Temple. He is called "the leper of the house of Rabbi" meaning, the one who suffers for Israel and Jerusalem. The Josephian Messiah sites near the Garden of Eden, suffering for the people of Israel..." Ben Ish Chai, Ben Yehoyada, Days of Peace, Days of Peace,Yeshivat Ahavat Shalom Publications, pg. 130

Make me clean, not only free of the repulsive skin disease called "leprosy" in many translations (but probably not Hansen's Disease, which is what "leprosy" means today); but also ritually clean (Hebrew *tahor*), so that I will not have to be separated from the community. The rules applicable to "lepers" are specified in Talmud tractate N'ga'im, based on Leviticus 13-14.

3. And Jesus put forth his hand, and touched him, saying, I will; be thou clean. And immediately his leprosy was cleansed.

Greek/Transliteration
3. Καὶ ἐκτείνας τὴν χεῖρα, ἥψατο αὐτοῦ ὁ Ἰησοῦς, λέγων, Θέλω, καθαρίσθητι. Καὶ εὐθέως ἐκαθαρίσθη αὐτοῦ ἡ λέπρα.

3. Kai ekteinas tein cheira, 'eipsato autou 'o Yeisous, legon, Thelo, katharistheiti. Kai eutheos ekatharisthei autou 'ei lepra.

Hebrew/Transliteration
:ג. וַיּוֹשֶׁט אֶת-יָדוֹ וַיִּגַּע-בּוֹ יֵשׁוּעַ וַיֹּאמֶר חָפֵץ אֲנִי וּטְהָר וַיִּטְהַר מִצָּרַעְתּוֹ כְּרָגַע

3. Va•yo•shet et - ya•do va•yi•ga - bo Yeshua va•yo•mar cha•fetz ani oot•har va•yit•har mi•tza•ra•a•to ke•ra•ga.

Rabbinic/Jewish New Testament
The Talmud says, "What is his [the Messiah's] name? . . . The Rabbis said: His name is Chivra (the Leper), as it is written, "Surely he hath borne our griefs, and carried our sorrows: yet we did esteem him a leper, smitten of God, and afflicted." (Isaiah 53:4)" Talmud, Sanhedrin 98b, Soncino Press Edition.

Go and let the *cohen* examine you, and offer the sacrifice that Moshe commanded in Lev_14:1-32. In other words, do what the *Torah* commands after recovery from such a skin disease. This sends a message to the religious establishment that the Messiah has come and is at work, doing what only the Messiah can do (Mat_8:1-4). The testimony to the people is to go "through channels"-initially to the leadership.

The Jews, themselves acknowledge this fact; for so they tell us in their wicked and blasphemous book (e), that Yeshua should say, "bring me a leper, and I will heal him; and they brought him a leper, and he healed him also by Shemhamphorash,"

(e) Toldos Jesu, p. 8.

---

4. And Jesus saith unto him, See thou tell no man; but go thy way, shew thyself to the priest, and offer the gift that Moses commanded, for a testimony unto them.

Greek/Transliteration
4. Καὶ λέγει αὐτῷ ὁ Ἰησοῦς, Ὅρα μηδενὶ εἴπῃς· ἀλλὰ ὕπαγε, σεαυτὸν δεῖξον τῷ ἱερεῖ, καὶ προσένεγκε τὸ δῶρον ὃ προσέταξεν Μωσῆς, εἰς μαρτύριον αὐτοῖς.

4. Kai legei auto 'o Yeisous, 'Ora meideni eipeis. alla 'upage, seauton deixon to 'ierei, kai prosenegke to doron 'o prosetaxen Moseis, eis marturion autois.

Hebrew/Transliteration
ד. וַיֹּאמֶר אֵלָיו יֵשׁוּעַ רְאֵה אַל-תַּגֵּד לְאִישׁ רַק לֵךְ וְהֵרָאֵה לְעֵינֵי הַכֹּהֵן וְהַקְרֵב אֶת-הַקָּרְבָּן אֲשֶׁר צִוָּה מֹשֶׁה:לְעֵדוּת לָהֶם

4. Va•yo•mer elav Yeshua r`•eh al - ta•ged le•eesh rak lech ve•he•ra•eh le•ei•ney ha•ko•hen ve•hak•rev et - ha•kor•ban asher tzi•va Moshe le•e•doot la•hem.

TaNaKh-Old Testament
"YHWH spoke to Moshe, saying, 'This shall be the law of the leper in the day of his cleansing. He shall be brought to the priest, and the priest shall go forth out of the camp. The priest shall examine him, and behold, if the plague of leprosy is healed in the leper, then the priest shall command them to take for him who is to be cleansed two living clean birds, and cedar wood, and scarlet, and hyssop. The priest shall command them to kill one of the birds in an earthen vessel over running water. As for the living bird, he shall take it, and the cedar wood, and the scarlet, and the hyssop, and shall dip them and the living bird in the blood of the bird that was killed over the running water. He shall sprinkle on him who is to be cleansed from the leprosy seven times, and shall pronounce him clean, and shall let the living bird go into the open field." Leviticus 14:1-7

---

5. And when Jesus was entered into Capernaum, there came unto him a centurion, beseeching him,

Greek/Transliteration
5. Εἰσελθόντι δὲ αὐτῷ εἰς Καπερναούμ, προσῆλθεν αὐτῷ ἑκατόνταρχος παρακαλῶν αὐτόν,

5. Eiselthonti de auto eis Kapernaoum, proseilthen auto 'ekatontarchos parakalon auton,

Hebrew/Transliteration
ה: וְכַאֲשֶׁר בָּא יֵשׁוּעַ אֶל-כְּפַר-נַחוּם וַיִּגַּשׁ אֵלָיו שַׂר-מֵאָה אֶחָד וַיִּתְחַנֶּן-לוֹ לֵאמֹר

5. Ve•cha•a•sher ba Yeshua el - K`far - Na•choom va•yi•gash elav sar - me•ah e•chad va•yit•cha•nen - lo le•mor.

Rabbinic Jewish Commentary
beseeching him, not in person, but by his messengers; see Luk_7:3 and the Jews (h) say, ששלוחו של אדם כמותו, "that a man's messenger is as himself".

(h) T. Bab. Beracot, fol. 34. 2.

6. And saying, Lord, my servant lieth at home sick of the palsy, grievously tormented.

Greek/Transliteration
6. καὶ λέγων, Κύριε, ὁ παῖς μου βέβληται ἐν τῇ οἰκίᾳ παραλυτικός, δεινῶς βασανιζόμενος.

6. kai legon, Kurie, 'o pais mou bebleitai en tei oikia paralutikos, deinos basanizomenos.

Hebrew/Transliteration
:ו. אֲדֹנִי הִנֵּה נַעֲרִי נָפַל לְמִשְׁכָּב בְּבֵיתִי נְכֵה-עֲצָמוֹת וּמְעֻנֶּה מְאֹד

6. A•do•ni hee•ne na•a•ri na•fal le•mish•kav be•vey•ti n`che - a•tza•mot oom•oo•ne me•od.

---

7. And Jesus saith unto him, I will come and heal him.

Greek/Transliteration
7. Καὶ λέγει αὐτῷ ὁ Ἰησοῦς, Ἐγὼ ἐλθὼν θεραπεύσω αὐτόν.

7. Kai legei auto 'o Yeisous, Ego elthon therapeuso auton.

Hebrew/Transliteration
:ז. וַיֹּאמֶר אֵלָיו יֵשׁוּעַ הִנְנִי בָא וּרְפָאתִיו

7. Va•yo•mer elav Yeshua hi•ne•ni va oor•fa•tiv.

---

8. The centurion answered and said, Lord, I am not worthy that thou shouldest come under my roof: but speak the word only, and my servant shall be healed.

Greek/Transliteration
8. Καὶ ἀποκριθεὶς ὁ ἑκατόνταρχος ἔφη, Κύριε, οὐκ εἰμὶ ἱκανὸς ἵνα μου ὑπὸ τὴν στέγην εἰσέλθῃς· ἀλλὰ μόνον εἰπὲ λόγῳ, καὶ ἰαθήσεται ὁ παῖς μου.

8. Kai apokritheis 'o 'ekatontarchos ephei, Kurie, ouk eimi 'ikanos 'ina mou 'upo tein stegein eiseltheis. alla monon eipe logo, kai iatheisetai 'o pais mou.

Hebrew/Transliteration
ח. וַיַּעַן שַׂר-הַמֵּאָה וַיֹּאמֶר אֲדֹנִי נְקַלֹּתִי מִזֹּאת כִּי אַתָּה תָבֹא בְּצֵל קֹרָתִי אַךְ רַק דַּבְּרָה דָבָר וְהַנַּעַר יֶחִי:

8. Va•ya•an sar - ha•me•ah va•yo•mar Adoni n`ka•lo•ti mi•zot ki ata ta•vo ve•tzel ko•ra•ti ach rak dab•ra da•var ve•ha•na•ar ye•chi.

9. For I am a man under authority, having soldiers under me: and I say to this man, Go, and he goeth; and to another, Come, and he cometh; and to my servant, Do this, and he doeth it.

Greek/Transliteration
9. Καὶ γὰρ ἐγὼ ἄνθρωπός εἰμι ὑπὸ ἐξουσίαν, ἔχων ὑπ᾽ ἐμαυτὸν στρατιώτας· καὶ λέγω τούτῳ, Πορεύθητι, καὶ πορεύεται· καὶ ἄλλῳ, Ἔρχου, καὶ ἔρχεται· καὶ τῷ δούλῳ μου, Ποίησον τοῦτο, καὶ ποιεῖ.

9. Kai gar ego anthropos eimi 'upo exousian, echon 'up emauton stratiotas. kai lego touto, Poreutheiti, kai poreuetai. kai allo, Erchou, kai erchetai. kai to doulo mou, Poieison touto, kai poiei.

Hebrew/Transliteration
ט. כִּי גַם-אֲנִי שַׂר לְמִשְׁמַעַת מִמְּעָלָה וַאֲנָשֵׁי שָׂרִים לְמִשְׁמַעְתִּי וְכִי אֹמַר לְאֶחָד מֵהֶם לֵךְ וְיֵלֵךְ וּלְאַחֵר בֹּא וְיָבֹא:וּלְעַבְדִּי עֲשֵׂה-זֹאת וְיַעֲשֶׂה

9. Ki gam - ani sar le•mish•ma•at mem•sha•la va•a•na•shai sa•rim le•mish•ma•a•ti ve•chi o•mar le•e•chad me•hem lech ve•ye•lech ool•a•cher bo ve•ya•vo ool•av•di ase - zot ve•ya•a•se.

Rabbinic Jewish Commentary
The Jews (l) have a saying, that "a servant over whom his master אין רשות, hath no power", is not called a servant."

(l) T. Bab. Kiddushin, fol. 72. 2.

---

10. When Jesus heard it, he marvelled, and said to them that followed, Verily I say unto you, I have not found so great faith, no, not in Israel.

Greek/Transliteration
10. Ἀκούσας δὲ ὁ Ἰησοῦς ἐθαύμασεν, καὶ εἶπεν τοῖς ἀκολουθοῦσιν, Ἀμὴν λέγω ὑμῖν, οὐδὲ ἐν τῷ Ἰσραὴλ τοσαύτην πίστιν εὗρον.

10. Akousas de 'o Yeisous ethaumasen, kai eipen tois akolouthousin, Amein lego 'umin, oude en to Ysraeil tosautein pistin 'euron.

Hebrew/Transliteration
י. וַיִּשְׁמַע יֵשׁוּעַ וַיִּשְׁתָּאֶה וַיֹּאמֶר אֶל-הַהֹלְכִים אַחֲרָיו אָמֵן אֲנִי מַגִּיד לָכֶם אֱמוּנָה גְדוֹלָה כָּמוֹהָ גַם-בְּיִשְׂרָאֵל לֹא:מָצָאתִי

10. Va•yish•ma Yeshua va•yish•ta•eh va•yo•mer el - ha•hol•chim a•cha•rav amen ani ma•gid la•chem e•moo•na ge•do•la cha•mo•ha gam - be•Israel lo ma•tza•ti.

Rabbinic Jewish Commentary

There is a phrase in the Talmud (m) somewhat like this, only used of a person of a different character; where a certain Jew, observing another called by some of his neighbours Rabbi, thus expressed himself;

"If this be a Rabbi, אל ירבו כמותו בישראל, "let there not be many such as he in Israel"."

And it is said (n) of Nadab and Abihu, "that two such were not found כוותייהו בישראל, "as they in Israel"."

(m) T. Bab. Taanith, fol. 20. 2. Derech Eretz. fol. 18. 1 (n) Zohar in Lev. fol. 24. 1. & 25. 4.

---

11. And I say unto you, That many shall come from the east and west, and shall sit down with Abraham, and Isaac, and Jacob, in the kingdom of heaven.

Greek/Transliteration
11. Λέγω δὲ ὑμῖν, ὅτι πολλοὶ ἀπὸ ἀνατολῶν καὶ δυσμῶν ἥξουσιν, καὶ ἀνακλιθήσονται μετὰ Ἀβραὰμ καὶ Ἰσαὰκ καὶ Ἰακὼβ ἐν τῇ βασιλείᾳ τῶν οὐρανῶν·

11. Lego de 'umin, 'oti polloi apo anatolon kai dusmon 'eixousin, kai anaklitheisontai meta Abra'am kai Ysa'ak kai Yakob en tei basileia ton ouranon.

Hebrew/Transliteration
יא. וְהִנְנִי אֹמֵר לָכֶם כִּי רַבִּים יָבֹאוּ מִמִּזְרָח וּמִמַּעֲרָב וְיֵשְׁבוּ בִּמְסִבָּה עִם-אַבְרָהָם יִצְחָק וְיַעֲקֹב בְּמַלְכוּת הַשָּׁמָיִם:

11. Ve•hi•ne•ni o•mer la•chem ki ra•bim ya•vo•oo mi•miz•rach oo•mi•ma•a•rav ve•yesh•voo bim•si•ba eem - Avraham Yitzchak ve•Yaakov be•mal•choot ha•sha•ma•yim.

---

12. But the children of the kingdom shall be cast out into outer darkness: there shall be weeping and gnashing of teeth.

Greek/Transliteration
12. οἱ δὲ υἱοὶ τῆς βασιλείας ἐκβληθήσονται εἰς τὸ σκότος τὸ ἐξώτερον· ἐκεῖ ἔσται ὁ κλαυθμὸς καὶ ὁ βρυγμὸς τῶν ὀδόντων.

12. 'oi de 'wioi teis basileias ekbleitheisontai eis to skotos to exoteron. ekei estai 'o klauthmos kai 'o brugmos ton odonton.

Hebrew/Transliteration
:יב. וּבְנֵי הַמַּלְכוּת יְדֻחוּ אֶל-הַחשֶׁךְ הַחוּצָה שָׁם יִהְיֶה בְכִי וַחֲרֹק שִׁנָּיִם

12. Oov•ney ha•mal•choot yi•da•choo el - ha•cho•shech ha•choo•tza sham yi•hee•ye ve•chi va•cha•rok shi•na•yim.

Rabbinic Jewish Commentary

These phrases, בן העולם הבא, "a son of the world to come", and בני עלמא דאתי, "children of the world to come" (o), are frequent in their writings: these,

The Jews say (p), "he that studies not in the law in this world, but is defiled with the pollutions of the world, he is taken וישליכו אותו הברה, "and cast without": this is Sheol itself, to which such are condemned, who do not study the law."

(q) "for the flattery with which they flattered Korah, in the business of rioting, "the prince of Gehenna חרק שניו, gnashed his teeth at them"."

The whole of this may be what they call רוגז גהנם, "the indignation", or "tumult of Gehenna" (r).

(o) T. Bab. Beracot, fol. 4. 2. Taanith, fol. 22. 1. Megilla, fol. 28. 2. Yoma, fol. 88. 1. & Sanhedrim, fol. 88. 2. Raziel, fol. 37. 1. & 38. 1. Caphtor, fol. 15. 1. & 18. 2. & 60. 1. & 84. 2. Raya Mehimna, in Zohar in Lev. fol. 34. 2. (p) Zohar in Gen. fol. 104. 3. (q) T. Bab. Sanhedrim, fol. 52. 1. (r) Targum in Job, iii 17.

---

13. And Jesus said unto the centurion, Go thy way; and as thou hast believed, so be it done unto thee. And his servant was healed in the selfsame hour.

Greek/Transliteration
13. Καὶ εἶπεν ὁ Ἰησοῦς τῷ ἑκατοντάρχῃ, Ὕπαγε, καὶ ὡς ἐπίστευσας γενηθήτω σοι. Καὶ ἰάθη ὁ παῖς αὐτοῦ ἐν τῇ ὥρᾳ ἐκείνῃ.

13. Kai eipen 'o Yeisous to 'ekatontarchei, 'Upage, kai 'os episteusas geneitheito soi. Kai iathei 'o pais autou en tei 'ora ekeinei.

Hebrew/Transliteration
:יג. וְאֶל-שַׂר-הַמֵּאָה אָמַר יֵשׁוּעַ לֵךְ כַּאֲשֶׁר הֶאֱמַנְתָּ כֵּן יָקוּם לָךְ וַיְחִי הַנַּעַר מֵחָלְיוֹ בַּשָּׁעָה הַהִיא

13. Ve•el - sar - ha•me•ah amar Yeshua lech ka•a•sher he•e•man•ta ken ya•koom lach vay•chi ha•na•ar me•chol•yo ba•sha•ah ha•hee.

---

14. And when Jesus was come into Peter's house, he saw his wife's mother laid, and sick of a fever.

Greek/Transliteration
14. Καὶ ἐλθὼν ὁ Ἰησοῦς εἰς τὴν οἰκίαν Πέτρου, εἶδεν τὴν πενθερὰν αὐτοῦ βεβλημένην καὶ πυρέσσουσαν,

14. Kai elthon 'o Yeisous eis tein oikian Petrou, eiden tein pentheran autou bebleimenein kai puressousan,

Hebrew/Transliteration
יד. וַיָּבֹא יֵשׁוּעַ בֵּית-פֶּטְרוֹס וַיַּרְא אֶת-חֹתַנְתּוֹ שֹׁכֶבֶת חוֹלַת קַדָּחַת:

14. Va•ya•vo Yeshua beit - Petros va•yar et - cho•tan•to sho•che•vet cho•lat ka•da•chat.

---

15. And he touched her hand, and the fever left her: and she arose, and ministered unto them.

Greek/Transliteration
15. καὶ ἥψατο τῆς χειρὸς αὐτῆς, καὶ ἀφῆκεν αὐτὴν ὁ πυρετός· καὶ ἠγέρθη, καὶ διηκόνει αὐτῷ.

15. kai 'eipsato teis cheiros auteis, kai apheiken autein 'o puretos. kai eigerthei, kai dieikonei auto.

Hebrew/Transliteration
טו. וַיִּגַּע בְּיָדָהּ וַתִּרֶף הַקַּדַּחַת מִמֶּנָּה וַתָּקָם וַתְּשָׁרֶת לִפְנֵיהֶם:

15. Va•yi•ga be•ya•da va•ti•ref ha•ka•da•chat mi•me•na va•ta•kom vat•sha•ret lif•ney•hem.

---

16. When the even was come, they brought unto him many that were possessed with devils: and he cast out the spirits with his word, and healed all that were sick:

Greek/Transliteration
16. Ὀψίας δὲ γενομένης προσήνεγκαν αὐτῷ δαιμονιζομένους πολλούς· καὶ ἐξέβαλεν τὰ πνεύματα λόγῳ, καὶ πάντας τοὺς κακῶς ἔχοντας ἐθεράπευσεν·

16. Opsias de genomeneis proseinegkan auto daimonizomenous pollous. kai exebalen ta pneumata logo, kai pantas tous kakos echontas etherapeusen.

Hebrew/Transliteration
טז. וַיְהִי בָעֶרֶב וַיָּבִיאוּ אֵלָיו רַבִּים אֲשֶׁר דָּבְקוּ בָם רוּחוֹת רָעוֹת וַיְגָרֶשׁ אֶת-הָרוּחוֹת בִּדְבַר-פִּיו וְאֵת כָּל-הַחוֹלִים:הֶחֱיָה מֵחָלְיָם.

16. Vay•hi ba•e•rev va•ya•vi•oo elav ra•bim asher dav•koo bam roo•chot ra•ot va•y`ga•resh et - ha•roo•chot bid•var - piv ve•et kol - ha•cho•lim he•che•ya me•chol•yam.

---

17. That it might be fulfilled which was spoken by Esaias the prophet, saying, Himself took our infirmities, and bare our sicknesses.

Greek/Transliteration
17. ὅπως πληρωθῇ τὸ ῥηθὲν διὰ Ἡσαΐου τοῦ προφήτου, λέγοντος, Αὐτὸς τὰς ἀσθενείας ἡμῶν ἔλαβεν, καὶ τὰς νόσους ἐβάστασεν.

17. 'opos pleirothei to 'reithen dya Eisaiou tou propheitou, legontos, Autos tas astheneias 'eimon elaben, kai tas nosous ebastasen.

Hebrew/Transliteration
:יז. לְמַלֹּאת אֶת אֲשֶׁר נֶאֱמַר בְּיַד-יְשַׁעְיָהוּ הַנָּבִיא לֵאמֹר חֳלָיֵנוּ הוּא נָשָׂא וּמַכְאֹבֵינוּ סְבָלָם

17. Le•ma•lot et asher ne•e•mar be•yad - Ye•sha•a•ya•hoo ha•na•vee le•mor cho•la•ye•noo hoo na•sa oo•mach•o•vey•noo se•va•lam.

Rabbinic/Jewish New Testament Commentary
This is the first citation in the New Testament from Isa. 52:13-Isa. 53:12, the *Tanakh* passage that most clearly portrays the Messiah as a servant of *Adonai* who suffers for the sins of the people. For more on this passage, see Act_8:34.

Midrash Tehillim tells us of the great suffering the Messiah takes upon himself, "R. Levi taught in the name of R. Idi: Suffering is divided into three portions: One, the Patriarchs and all the generations of men took; the generation that lived in the time of [Hadrian's] persecution took; and one, the lord Messiah will take." Midrash Tehillilm, Psalm 16.5, Yale University Press, pg. 198

The Ben Ish Chai comments on Sanhedrin 93b,
"...through afflictions, the Messiah rises to great spiritual heights. In addition, his afflictions atone for Israel so that they can continue to live and perform mitzvot. Since without the Messiah, these mitzvot would not have been done, he is a partner in Israel's mitzvot. Thus because He loaded him up with afflictions like millstones, He loaded him up with mitzvot as well." Ben Ish Chai, Benayahu, Days of Peace, Days of Peace,Yeshivat Ahavat Shalom Publications, pgs. 117

He continues,
"...the Messiah is Israel's guarantor; he has undertaken suffering to atone for Israel's sins in order to shorten the exile (Yalkut Shimoni 499)."
Ben Ish Chai, Aderet Eliyahu, Haftarat Yitro, Days of Peace,Yeshivat Ahavat Shalom Publications, pgs. 127

Commenting on Isaiah 53, the Zohar makes the remarkable statement: "When the Messiah hears of the great suffering of Israel in their dispersion, and of the wicked amongst them who seek not to know their Master, he weeps aloud on account of those wicked ones amongst them, as it is written: But he was wounded because of our transgression, he was crushed because of our iniquities (Isaiah 53:5). The souls then return to their place. The Messiah, on his part, enters a certain Hall in the Garden of Eden, called the Hall of the Afflicted. There he calls for all the diseases and pains and sufferings of Israel, bidding them settle on himself, which they do. And were it not that he thus eases the burden from Israel, taking it on himself, no one could endure the sufferings meted out to Israel in expiation on account of their neglect of the Torah. So Scripture says, "Surely our diseases he did bear, etc. (Isaiah 53:4). A similar function was performed by R. Eleazar here on earth. For, indeed, beyond number are the chastisements awaiting every man daily for the neglect of the Torah, all of which descended into the world at the time when the Torah was given. As long as Israel were in the Holy Land, by means of the Temple service and sacrifices they averted all evil diseases and afflictions from the world. Now it is the Messiah who is the means of averting them from mankind until the time when a man quits this world and receives his punishment, as already said. Zohar, Shemoth, Section 2, Page 212a, Soncino Press Edition

"The Rabbi's say, "a leper" of the house of Rabbi is his name; as it is said, "surely he hath borne our griefs, and carried our sorrows, yet we did esteem him stricken, smitten of God and afflicted". Says R. Nachman, if he is of the living, he is as I am, as it is said, Jer_30:21 Says Rab, if of the living, he is as our Rabbi, the holy."

Upon which last clause the gloss is,

"If the Messiah is of them that are alive, our Rabbi the holy is he, "because דסובל תחלואים he bears infirmities"."

Elsewhere (w) they say, "There is one temple that is called the temple of the sons of afflictions; and when the Messiah comes into that temple, and reads all the afflictions, all the griefs, and all the chastisements of Israel, which come upon them, then all of them shall come upon him: and if there was any that would lighten them off of Israel, and take them upon himself, there is no son of man that can bear the chastisements of Israel, because of the punishments of the law; as it is said, "surely he hath borne our griefs"

And in another ancient book (x) of their's, God is represented saying to the Messiah,

תסבול יסורין, "wilt thou bear chastisements", in order to remove their iniquities? (the iniquities of the children of God,) as it is written, "surely he hath borne our griefs": he replied, "I will bear them with joy"."

(u) T. Bab. Sanhedrim, fol. 98. 2. (w) Zohar in Exod. fol. 85. 2. (x) Pesikta in Abkath Rochel, l. 1. par. 2. p. 309. Ed. Huls.

18. Now when Jesus saw great multitudes about him, he gave commandment to depart unto the other side.

Greek/Transliteration
18. Ἰδὼν δὲ ὁ Ἰησοῦς πολλοὺς ὄχλους περὶ αὐτόν, ἐκέλευσεν ἀπελθεῖν εἰς τὸ πέραν.

18. Idon de 'o Yeisous pollous ochlous peri auton, ekeleusen apelthein eis to peran.

Hebrew/Transliteration
:יח. וַיְהִי כִרְאוֹת יֵשׁוּעַ הֲמוֹן עַם רָב סָבִיב-לוֹ וַיְצַו לַעֲבֹר מִשָּׁם אֶל-עֵבֶר הַיָּם

18. Vay•hi kir•ot Yeshua ha•mon am rav sa•viv - lo vay•tzav la•a•vor mi•sham el – ever ha•yam.

---

19. And a certain scribe came, and said unto him, Master [Rabbi] , I will follow thee whithersoever thou goest.

Greek/Transliteration
19. Καὶ προσελθὼν εἷς γραμματεὺς εἶπεν αὐτῷ, Διδάσκαλε, ἀκολουθήσω σοι ὅπου ἐὰν ἀπέρχῃ.

19. Kai proselthon 'eis grammateus eipen auto, Didaskale, akoloutheiso soi 'opou ean aperchei.

Hebrew/Transliteration
:יט. וַיִּגַּשׁ אֵלָיו אֶחָד הַסּוֹפְרִים וַיֹּאמֶר לוֹ רַבִּי אֵלֵךְ אַחֲרֶיךָ אֶל-כָּל-אֲשֶׁר תֵּלֵךְ

19. Va•yi•gash elav achad ha•sof•rim va•yo•mer lo Rabbi e•lech a•cha•re•cha el - kol - asher te•lech.

Jewish New Testament Commentary
Rabbi (Hebrew, literally, "my great one") here renders Greek *didaskalos*, "teacher. Teaching *talmidim* was, and sometimes still is, the chief task of a rabbi.

---

20. And Jesus saith unto him, The foxes have holes, and the birds of the air have nests; but the Son of man hath not where to lay his head.

Greek/Transliteration
20. Καὶ λέγει αὐτῷ ὁ Ἰησοῦς, Αἱ ἀλώπεκες φωλεοὺς ἔχουσιν, καὶ τὰ πετεινὰ τοῦ οὐρανοῦ κατασκηνώσεις· ὁ δὲ υἱὸς τοῦ ἀνθρώπου οὐκ ἔχει ποῦ τὴν κεφαλὴν κλίνῃ.

20. Kai legei auto 'o Yeisous, 'Ai alopekes pholeous echousin, kai ta peteina tou ouranou kataskeinoseis. 'o de 'wios tou anthropou ouk echei pou tein kephalein klinei.

Hebrew/Transliteration
כ. וַיֹּאמֶר אֵלָיו יֵשׁוּעַ הַשּׁוּעָלִים חוֹרִים לָהֶם וְצִפּוֹר הַשָּׁמַיִם קֵן לָהּ וּבֶן-הָאָדָם אֵין לוֹ מָקוֹם לְהָנִיחַ אֶת-רֹאשׁוֹ:

20. Va•yo•mer elav Yeshua ha•shoo•a•lim cho•rim la•hem ve•tzi•por ha•sha•ma•yim ken la oo•Ven - ha•adam eyn lo ma•kom le•ha•ni•ach et - ro•sho.

TaNaKh-Old Testament/Jewish New Testament Commentary
"Jacob went out from Beersheba, and went toward Haran. He came to a certain place, and stayed there all night, because the sun had set. He took one of the stones of the place, and put it under his head, and lay down in that place to sleep."
Genesis 28:10-11

Son of Man. One of the titles of the Messiah, based on Dan_7:13-14, where the text has "*bar-enosh*" (Aramaic). "*Bar-enosh*," like Hebrew *ben-adam*, can also mean "son of man," "typical man," "one schooled to be a man," or simply "man" (see Mat_1:1 on "son of"). Yeshua is all of these: the Messiah, a typical (ideal) man, and one schooled both in heaven and on earth to be a man. Yeshua refers to himself by this title frequently, stressing his full identification with the human condition, as taught in Rom_5:12-21, Rom_8:3-39; 1Co_15:21-49; Php_2:5-11; Heb_2:5-18, Heb_4:15. Compare Mat_4:3 on "son of God."

If he (the Messiah) should come, לי דוכתא דיתיבנא ביה, "there's no place in which he can sit down" (c). (c) T. Bab. Sanhedrim, fol. 96. 2.

---

21. And another of his disciples said unto him, Lord, suffer me first to go and bury my father.

21. Ἕτερος δὲ τῶν μαθητῶν αὐτοῦ εἶπεν αὐτῷ, Κύριε, ἐπίτρεψόν μοι πρῶτον ἀπελθεῖν καὶ θάψαι τὸν πατέρα μου.

21. 'Eteros de ton matheiton autou eipen auto, Kurie, epitrepson moi proton apelthein kai thapsai ton patera mou.

Hebrew/Transliteration
כא. וְאִישׁ אַחֵר מִקֶּרֶב תַּלְמִידָיו אָמַר אֵלָיו אֲדֹנִי תְּנָה-לִּי לָלֶכֶת וְלִקְבֹּר אֶת-אָבִי רִאשֹׁנָה:

21. Ve•eesh a•cher mi•ke•rev tal•mi•dav amar elav Ado•ni te•na - li la•le•chet ve•lik•bor et - avi ri•sho•na.

Jewish New Testament Commentary

First let me go and bury my father. Don't suppose this would-be *talmid* is traveling around with Yeshua while his father's corpse is waiting at home, stinking in the sun. The father is not dead yet! If he had been, the son would have been at home, sitting *shiv'ah* (see Joh_11:19-20). The son wishes to go home, live in comfort with his father till his death perhaps years hence, collect his inheritance and then, at his leisure, become a disciple. On this and other excuses see Luk_9:57-62.

Let the physically who are already dying, those concerned with the benefits of this world, including inheritances, remain with each other in life and eventually bury their own physically dead. The true *talmid* must get his priorities straight. Note the consequences of not doing so at 13:7, 22; 19:16-26; Luk_14:15-24.

---

22. But Jesus said unto him, Follow me; and let the dead bury their dead.

Greek/Transliteration

22. Ὁ δὲ Ἰησοῦς εἶπεν αὐτῷ, Ἀκολούθει μοι, καὶ ἄφες τοὺς νεκροὺς θάψαι τοὺς ἑαυτῶν νεκρούς.

22. 'O de Yeisous eipen auto, Akolouthei moi, kai aphes tous nekrous thapsai tous 'eauton nekrous.

Hebrew/Transliteration

כב. וַיֹּאמֶר אֵלָיו יֵשׁוּעַ לֵךְ אַחֲרַי וְהַנַּח לַמֵּתִים לִקְבֹּר אֶת-מֵתֵיהֶם:

22. Va•yo•mer elav Yeshua lech a•cha•rai ve•ha•nach la•me•tim lik•bor et - me•tey•hem.

Rabbinic Jewish Commentary

And however strange and odd such a phrase may sound in the ears of some, of one dead man's burying another, it was easily understood by a Jew; with whom it is common to say, החוטא חשוב כמת, "that a sinner is counted as (g) dead, and that ungodly persons, even while they are alive", קרויין מתים, are "called dead" (h).

(g) Tzeror Hammor, fol. 6. 2. (h) T. Bab. Beracot, fol. 18. 2. Jarchi in Gen. 11. 32. Baal Hatturim, in Deut. xvii. 6. Tzeror Hammor, fol. 58. 3. Midrash Kohelet. fol. 78. 2. Caphtor, fol. 79. 1, 2. & 84. 1.

---

23. And when he was entered into a ship, his disciples followed him.

Greek/Transliteration

23. Καὶ ἐμβάντι αὐτῷ εἰς τὸ πλοῖον, ἠκολούθησαν αὐτῷ οἱ μαθηταὶ αὐτοῦ.

23. Kai embanti auto eis to ploion, eikoloutheisan auto 'oi matheitai autou.

Hebrew/Transliteration
:כג. וַיֵּרֶד בָּאֳנִיָּה וְתַלְמִידָיו יָרְדוּ עִמּוֹ

23. Va•ye•red ba•o•ni•ya ve•tal•mi•dav yar•doo ee•mo.

---

24. And, behold, there arose a great tempest in the sea, insomuch that the ship was covered with the waves: but he was asleep.

Greek/Transliteration
24. Καὶ ἰδού, σεισμὸς μέγας ἐγένετο ἐν τῇ θαλάσσῃ, ὥστε τὸ πλοῖον καλύπτεσθαι ὑπὸ τῶν κυμάτων· αὐτὸς δὲ ἐκάθευδεν.

24. Kai idou, seismos megas egeneto en tei thalassei, 'oste to ploion kaluptesthai 'upo ton kumaton. autos de ekatheuden.

Hebrew/Transliteration
:כד. וְהִנֵּה סַעַר גָּדוֹל נֵעוֹר בַּיָּם עַד-כַּסּוֹת הַגַּלִּים אֶת-הָאֳנִיָּה וְהוּא נִרְדָּם

24. Ve•hee•ne sa•ar ga•dol ne•or ba•yam ad - ka•sot ha•ga•lim et - ha•o•ni•ya ve•hoo nir•dam.

TaNaKh-Old Testament/Rabbinic Commentary
This passage links Yeshua to Yonah HaNavi,
"But HaShem sent out a great wind on the sea, and there was a mighty storm on the sea, so that the ship was likely to break up. Then the mariners were afraid, and every man cried to his god. They threw the cargo that was in the ship into the sea to lighten the ship. But Jonah had gone down into the innermost parts of the ship, and he was laying down, and was fast asleep Jonah 1:4-5

Kol HaTor, written by R' Hillel Shklover, links Yonah HaNavi to Mashiach ben Yosef, "The commandment to expand the borders is the mission of Mashiach ben Yosef as God had told the prophet Jonah, who was on the level of Mashiach ben Yosef, to restore the border of Israel (II Kings 14:25)."
Kol HaTor 2.36

The Kol HaTor continues,
"*Admonish to repent* – not only Israel, but also the other nations, in the line of the prophet Jonah, who was the Mashiach ben Yosef in his generation, as is written: (Isa. 2:4) "He will admonish many peoples. Kol HaTor 2.75

---

25. And his disciples came to him, and awoke him, saying, Lord, save us: we perish.

Greek/Transliteration
25. Καὶ προσελθόντες οἱ μαθηταὶ ἤγειραν αὐτόν, λέγοντες, Κύριε, σῶσον ἡμᾶς, ἀπολλύμεθα.

25. Kai proselthontes 'oi matheitai eigeiran auton, legontes, Kurie, soson 'eimas, apollumetha.

Hebrew/Transliteration
:כה. וַיִּגְּשׁוּ אֵלָיו וַיְעִירֻהוּ וַיִּקְרָאוּ הוֹשִׁיעָה אֲדֹנֵינוּ כִּי אָבָדְנוּ

25. Va•yig•shoo elav vay•ee•roo•hoo va•yik•ra•oo ho•shi•ah Ado•ney•noo ki avad•noo.

---

26. And he saith unto them, Why are ye fearful, O ye of little faith? Then he arose, and rebuked the winds and the sea; and there was a great calm.

Greek/Transliteration
26. Καὶ λέγει αὐτοῖς, Τί δειλοί ἐστε, ὀλιγόπιστοι; Τότε ἐγερθεὶς ἐπετίμησεν τοῖς ἀνέμοις καὶ τῇ θαλάσσῃ, καὶ ἐγένετο γαλήνη μεγάλη.

26. Kai legei autois, Ti deiloi este, oligopistoi? Tote egertheis epetimeisen tois anemois kai tei thalassei, kai egeneto galeinei megalei.

Hebrew/Transliteration
:כו. וַיֹּאמֶר אֲלֵיהֶם לָמָּה אַתֶּם חֲרֵדִים קְטַנֵּי אֱמוּנָה וַיָּקָם וַיִּגְעַר בָּרוּחוֹת וּבַיָּם וַתְּהִי דְּמָמָה גְדוֹלָה

26. Va•yo•mer aley•hem la•ma atem cha•re•dim k`ta•ney e•moo•na va•ya•kom va•yig•ar ba•roo•chot oo•va•yam va•t`hi d`ma•ma ge•do•la.

TaNaKh-Old Testament/Jewish New Testament Commentary
"Then they cry to YHWH in their trouble, and he brings them out of their distress. He makes the storm a calm, so that its waves are still. Then they are glad because it is calm, so he brings them to their desired haven." Psalms 107:28-30, cf. Psalm 89:9

Calming wind and waves recalls Psa_107:28-29, "Then they cried out to *Adonai* in their trouble, and he brought them out of their distress. He stilled the storm to a whisper, and the waves of the sea were hushed. They were glad when it grew calm, and he guided them to their desired haven." Seeing that Yeshua's miracle reflects this psalm shows how the New Testament sets about establishing Yeshua's divinity.

---

27. But the men marvelled, saying, What manner of man is this, that even the winds and the sea obey him!

Greek/Transliteration
27. Οἱ δὲ ἄνθρωποι ἐθαύμασαν, λέγοντες, Ποταπός ἐστιν οὗτος, ὅτι καὶ οἱ ἄνεμοι καὶ ἡ θάλασσα ὑπακούουσιν αὐτῷ;

27. 'Oi de anthropoi ethaumasan, legontes, Potapos estin 'outos, 'oti kai 'oi anemoi kai 'ei thalassa 'upakouousin auto?

Hebrew/Transliteration
כז: וַיִּתְמְהוּ הָאֲנָשִׁים לֵאמֹר מִי הוּא זֶה אֲשֶׁר גַּם-הָרוּחוֹת וְהַיָּם מַקְשִׁיבִים לְקֹלוֹ

27. Va•yit•me•hoo ha•a•na•shim le•mor mee hoo ze asher gam - ha•roo•chot ve•ha•yam mak•shi•vim le•ko•lo.

---

28. And when he was come to the other side into the country of the Gergesenes, there met him two possessed with devils, coming out of the tombs, exceeding fierce, so that no man might pass by that way.

Greek/Transliteration
28. Καὶ ἐλθόντι αὐτῷ εἰς τὸ πέραν εἰς τὴν χώραν τῶν Γεργεσηνῶν, ὑπήντησαν αὐτῷ δύο δαιμονιζόμενοι ἐκ τῶν μνημείων ἐξερχόμενοι, χαλεποὶ λίαν, ὥστε μὴ ἰσχύειν τινὰ παρελθεῖν διὰ τῆς ὁδοῦ ἐκείνης·

28. Kai elthonti auto eis to peran eis tein choran ton Gergeseinon, 'upeinteisan auto duo daimonizomenoi ek ton mneimeion exerchomenoi, chalepoi lian, 'oste mei ischuein tina parelthein dya teis 'odou ekeineis.

Hebrew/Transliteration
כח. וַיְהִי כְּבֹאוֹ אֶל-עֵבֶר הַיָּם אֶל-אֶרֶץ הַגַּדְרִיִּים וַיִּפְגְּשֻׁהוּ שְׁנֵי אֲנָשִׁים אֲשֶׁר דָּבְקוּ בָּם רוּחוֹת רָעוֹת יֹצְאִים מִבָּתֵּי הַקְּבָרוֹת וּפְנֵיהֶם זֹעֲפִים עַד-מְאֹד עַד-אֲשֶׁר לֹא יָכֹל אִישׁ לַעֲבֹר בַּדֶּרֶךְ הַהוּא מִפָּחַד

28. Vay•hi ke•vo•o el - ever ha•yam el - e•retz ha•gad•ri•yim va•yif•ge•shoo•hoo sh`ney a•na•shim asher dav•koo bam roo•chot ra•ot yotz•eem mi•ba•tey hak•va•rot oof•ney•hem zo•a•fim ad - me•od ad - asher lo ya•chol eesh la•a•vor ba•de•rech ha•hoo mi•pa•chad.

Rabbinic Jewish Commentary
It is a notion that obtains among the Jews (p), that the spirit for twelve months after its separation from the body, is more or less with it, hovering about it; and hence, some have been induced to go and dwell among the tombs, and inquire of spirits: they tell us (q),

"it happened to a certain holy man, that he gave a penny to a poor man, on the "eve" of the new year; and his wife provoked him, and he went וילן בבית הקברות, "and lodged among the tombs", and heard two spirits talking with one another."

(p) Nishmat Chayim, par. 2. c. 22. p. 81. 2. c. 24. p. 85. 1. & c. 29. p. 93. 1. p. 94. 1, 2. (q) T. Bab. Beracot, fol. 18. 2.

29. And, behold, they cried out, saying, What have we to do with thee, Jesus, thou Son of God? art thou come hither to torment us before the time?

Greek/Transliteration
29. καὶ ἰδού, ἔκραξαν λέγοντες, Τί ἡμῖν καὶ σοί, Ἰησοῦ υἱὲ τοῦ θεοῦ; Ἦλθες ὧδε πρὸ καιροῦ βασανίσαι ἡμᾶς;

29. kai idou, ekraxan legontes, Ti 'eimin kai soi, Yeisou 'wie tou theou? Eilthes 'ode pro kairou basanisai 'eimas?

Hebrew/Transliteration
:כט. וְהִנֵּה הֵם צֹעֲקִים לֵאמֹר מַה-לָּנוּ וָלָךְ יֵשׁוּעַ בֶּן-הָאֱלֹהִים הַאִם בָּאתָ לְעַנּוֹתֵנוּ טֶרֶם בָּאָה הָעֵת

29. Ve•hee•ne hem tzo•a•kim le•mor ma - la•noo va•lach Yeshua Ben - ha•Elohim ha•eem ba•ta le•a•no•te•noo te•rem ba•ah ha•et.

Rabbinic Commentary
"What is meant by 'in Thy light do we see light'? What light is it that the congregation of Israel looks for as from a watchtower? It is the light of Messiah, of which it is said, 'And God saw the light that it was good' (Gen 1:4). This verse proves that the Holy One, blessed be He, contemplated the Messiah and his works before the world was created, and then under His throne of glory put away His Messiah until the time of the generation in which he will appear. Satan asked the Holy One, blessed be He, for whom is the light which is put away under Thy throne of glory? God replied: For him who will turn thee back and put thee to utter shame. Satan said: Master of the universe, show him to me. God replied: Come and see him. And when he saw him, Satan was shaken, and he fell upon his face and said: Surely this is the Messiah who will cause me and all the counterparts in heaven of the princes of the earth's nations to be swallowed up in Gehenna…in that hour all the princely counterparts of the nations, in agitation, will say to Him: Master of the universe, who is this through whose power we are to be swallowed up? What is his name? What kind of being is he?" Pesikta Rabbati 36.1, translated by William Braude, Yale University Press, pg. 677-678

---

30. And there was a good way off from them an herd of many swine feeding.

Greek/Transliteration
30. Ἦν δὲ μακρὰν ἀπ᾽ αὐτῶν ἀγέλη χοίρων πολλῶν βοσκομένη.

30. Ein de makran ap auton agelei choiron pollon boskomenei.

Hebrew/Transliteration
:ל. וְעֵדֶר חֲזִירִים רַבִּים הָיָה רֹעֶה שָׁם מֵרָחוֹק לָהֶם

30. Ve•e•der cha•zi•rim ra•bim ha•ya ro•eh sham me•ra•chok la•hem.

Jewish New Testament Commentary

Pigs. The Gadarenes were presumably not Jewish and had no compunctions about raising pigs. See Mar_5:11-17, Luk_15:1.

(t) "the wise men say, cursed is he that brings up dogs and hogs, מפני שהזיקן מרובה, "because they do much hurt"." (w) "It is forbidden to bring up a hog, in order to get any profit by his skin, or by his lard, or fat, to anoint with, or to light (lamps) with; yea, though it may fall to him by inheritance."
But after all, it was only an Israelite that was forbid this; a stranger might bring them up, for this is one of their canons (z).

"A man may sell fetches to give to a stranger that breeds hogs, but to an Israelite it is forbidden to breed them."

Yea, they say (a), "If others breed them to anoint skins with their lard, or to sell them to an Israelite to anoint with them, it was lawful: all fat may be sold, which is not for eating."

(t) Maimon. Nezike Mammon, c. 5. sect. 9. (w) Tosaphot in Pesach, art. 62. (z) Piske Tosaphot in Sabbat, art. 317. (a) Yom. Tob. & Ez. Chayim, in Misn. Bava Kama, c. 7. sect. 7.

---

31. So the devils besought him, saying, If thou cast us out, suffer us to go away into the herd of swine.

Greek/Transliteration
31. Οἱ δὲ δαίμονες παρεκάλουν αὐτόν, λέγοντες, Εἰ ἐκβάλλεις ἡμᾶς, ἐπίτρεψον ἡμῖν ἀπελθεῖν εἰς τὴν ἀγέλην τῶν χοίρων.

31. 'Oi de daimones parekaloun auton, legontes, Ei ekballeis 'eimas, epitrepson 'eimin apelthein eis tein agelein ton choiron.

Hebrew/Transliteration
לא. וַיִּתְחַנְנוּ־לוֹ הָרוּחוֹת לֵאמֹר אִם לְגָרְשֵׁנוּ אַתָּה אֹמֵר תְּנָה־לָנוּ לָבוֹא בְּעֵדֶר הַחֲזִירִים:

31. Va•yit•cha•ne•noo - lo ha•roo•chot le•mor eem le•gar•she•noo ata o•mer ti•na - la•noo la•vo be•e•der ha•cha•zi•rim.

---

32. And he said unto them, Go. And when they were come out, they went into the herd of swine: and, behold, the whole herd of swine ran violently down a steep place into the sea, and perished in the waters.

Greek/Transliteration
32. Καὶ εἶπεν αὐτοῖς, Ὑπάγετε. Οἱ δὲ ἐξελθόντες ἀπῆλθον εἰς τὴν ἀγέλην τῶν χοίρων· καὶ ἰδού, ὥρμησεν πᾶσα ἡ ἀγέλη τῶν χοίρων κατὰ τοῦ κρημνοῦ εἰς τὴν θάλασσαν, καὶ ἀπέθανον ἐν τοῖς ὕδασιν.

32. Kai eipen autois, 'Upagete. 'Oi de exelthontes apeilthon eis tein agelein ton choiron. kai idou, 'ormeisen pasa 'ei agelei ton choiron kata tou kreimnou eis tein thalassan, kai apethanon en tois 'udasin.

Hebrew/Transliteration
לב. וַיֹּאמֶר לָהֶם לְכוּ וַיֵּצְאוּ וַיָּבֹאוּ בְּעֵדֶר הַחֲזִירִים וְהִנֵּה כָל-הָעֵדֶר שָׁטְפוּ בַמּוֹרָד אֶל-תּוֹךְ הַיָּם וַיֹּאבְדוּ בַמָּיִם:

32. Va•yo•mer la•hem le•choo va•yetz•oo va•ya•vo•oo be•e•der ha•cha•zi•rim ve•hee•ne kol - ha•e•der shat•foo va•mo•rad el - toch ha•yam va•yov•doo ba•ma•yim.

---

33. And they that kept them fled, and went their ways into the city, and told every thing, and what was befallen to the possessed of the devils.

Greek/Transliteration
33. Οἱ δὲ βόσκοντες ἔφυγον, καὶ ἀπελθόντες εἰς τὴν πόλιν ἀπήγγειλαν πάντα, καὶ τὰ τῶν δαιμονιζομένων.

33. 'Oi de boskontes ephugon, kai apelthontes eis tein polin apeingeilan panta, kai ta ton daimonizomenon.

Hebrew/Transliteration
לג. וְהָרֹעִים נָסוּ וַיָּבֹאוּ הָעִירָה וַיַּגִּידוּ אֶת-כָּל אֲשֶׁר נִהְיָתָה וְאֵת אֲשֶׁר קָרָה לַאֲשֶׁר דָּבְקוּ בָם הָרוּחוֹת הָרָעוֹת:

33. Ve•ha•ro•eem na•soo va•ya•vo•oo ha•ee•ra va•ya•gi•doo et - kol asher ni•hi•yata ve•et asher ka•ra la•a•sher dav•koo bam ha•roo•chot ha•ra•ot.

---

34. And, behold, the whole city came out to meet Jesus: and when they saw him, they besought him that he would depart out of their coasts.

Greek/Transliteration
34. Καὶ ἰδού, πᾶσα ἡ πόλις ἐξῆλθεν εἰς συνάντησιν τῷ Ἰησοῦ· καὶ ἰδόντες αὐτόν, παρεκάλεσαν ὅπως μεταβῇ ἀπὸ τῶν ὁρίων αὐτῶν.

34. Kai idou, pasa 'ei polis exeilthen eis sunanteisin to Yeisou. kai idontes auton, parekalesan 'opos metabei apo ton 'orion auton.

Hebrew/Transliteration
לד. וְהִנֵּה כָל-הָעִיר יָצְאָה לִקְרַאת יֵשׁוּעַ וַיִּרְאֵהוּ וַיִּפְצְרוּ-בוֹ לַעֲבֹר מִגְּבוּלָם:

34. Ve•hee•ne kol - ha•eer yatz•ah lik•rat Yeshua va•yir•oo•hoo va•yif•tze•roo – vo la•a•vor mig•voo•lam.

Matthew, Chapter 9

1. And he entered into a ship, and passed over, and came into his own city.

Greek/Transliteration
1. Καὶ ἐμβὰς εἰς τὸ πλοῖον διεπέρασεν καὶ ἦλθεν εἰς τὴν ἰδίαν πόλιν.

1. Kai embas eis to ploion dieperasen kai eilthen eis tein idian polin.

Hebrew/Transliteration
א: וַיֵּרֶד בָּאֳנִיָּה וַיַּעֲבֹר וַיָּבֹא אֶל-עִירוֹ

1. Va•ye•red ba•o•ni•ya va•ya•a•vor va•ya•vo el - ee•ro.

---

2. And, behold, they brought to him a man sick of the palsy, lying on a bed: and Jesus seeing their faith said unto the sick of the palsy; Son, be of good cheer; thy sins be forgiven thee.

Greek/Transliteration
2. Καὶ ἰδού, προσέφερον αὐτῷ παραλυτικὸν ἐπὶ κλίνης βεβλημένον· καὶ ἰδὼν ὁ Ἰησοῦς τὴν πίστιν αὐτῶν εἶπεν τῷ παραλυτικῷ, Θάρσει, τέκνον· ἀφέωνταί σοι αἱ ἁμαρτίαι σου.

2. Kai idou, prosepheron auto paralutikon epi kleineis bebleimenon. kai idon 'o Yeisous tein pistin auton eipen to paralutiko, Tharsei, teknon. apheontai soi 'ai 'amartiai sou.

Hebrew/Transliteration
ב. וְהִנֵּה הֵבִיאוּ אֵלָיו אִישׁ נְכֵה עֲצָמוֹת שֹׁכֵב עַל-הַמִּטָּה וּבִרְאוֹת יֵשׁוּעַ אֶת-אֱמוּנָתָם אָמַר אֶל-נְכֵה הָעֲצָמוֹת:חֲזַק בְּנִי נִסְלְחוּ-לְךָ חַטֹּאתֶיךָ

2. Ve•hee•ne he•vi•oo elav eesh n`che a•tza•mot sho•chev al - ha•mi•ta oo•vir•ot Yeshua et - emoo•na•tam amar el - n`che ha•a•tza•mot cha•zak b`ni nis•le•choo - le•cha cha•to•te•cha.

Rabbinic Jewish Commentary
The Jews regarded disease as the effect of sin, Joh_9:2; Jam_5:14-15. There is a "real" connection between sin and suffering, as in the case of gluttony, intemperate drinking, lewdness, debauchery. Jesus might be willing to direct the minds of the spectators "to this fact;" and, by pointing them to a manifest instance of the effect of sin, to lead them to hate and forsake it. Diseases are sometimes the direct judgment of God for sin, 1Co_5:3-5; 1Co_11:30; 2Sa_24:10-14. This truth, also, Messiah might have been desirous of impressing on the people.

He calls him son, either meaning by it no more than "man"; see Luk_5:20 or using it as a kind, tender, and endearing appellation; or as considering him in the grace of adoption, as one that God had put among the children, had given to him as such, and whom he should bring to glory. He bids him "be of good cheer", whose animal spirits were fainting through the disease that was upon him, and the fatigue he had underwent in being brought to him; and his soul more distressed and dejected, under a sense of his sins and transgressions; which Jesus knowing, very pertinently says, "thy sins be forgiven thee"; than which, nothing could be more cheering and reviving to him: or Christ says this to show, that sin was the cause of the disease and affliction that were upon him, for אין יסורין בלא עון, "there are no chastisements without sin", as the Jews say (f); and that the cause being removed, the effects would cease; of both which he might be assured, and therefore had good reason to cheer up, and be of good heart. This was a wonderful instance of the grace of Messiah, to bestow a blessing unasked, and that of the greatest moment and importance.

(f) T. Bab. Sabbat, fol. 55. 1. Midrash Hohelet, fol. 70. 4. Tzeror. Hammor, fol. 99. 1.

3. And, behold, certain of the scribes said within themselves, This man blasphemeth.

Greek/Transliteration
3. Καὶ ἰδού, τινὲς τῶν γραμματέων εἶπον ἐν ἑαυτοῖς, Οὗτος βλασφημεῖ.

3. Kai idou, tines ton grammateon eipon en 'eautois, 'Outos blaspheimei.

Hebrew/Transliteration
ג. וְשָׁם אֲנָשִׁים סוֹפְרִים אָמְרוּ בְלִבָּם הָאִישׁ הַזֶּה מְגַדֵּף הוּא׃

3. Ve•sham a•na•shim sof•rim am•roo ve•li•bam ha•eesh ha•ze me•ga•def hoo.

Rabbinic Jewish Commentary
The word "blaspheme" originally means to speak evil of anyone; to injure by words; to blame unjustly. When applied to God, it means to speak of him unjustly; to ascribe to him acts and attributes which he does not possess; or to speak impiously or profanely. It also means to say or do anything by which his name or honor is insulted, or which conveys an "impression" unfavourable to God. It means. also, to attempt to do, or say a thing, which belongs to him alone, or which he only can do. This is its meaning here. Yeshua was charged "with saying a thing in his own name, or attempting to do a thing, which properly belonged to God;" thus assuming the place of God, and doing him injury, as the scribes supposed, by an invasion of his prerogatives. "None," said they (see Mark and Luke), "can forgive sins but God only." In this they reasoned correctly. See Isa_43:25; Isa_44:22. None of the prophets had this power; and by saying that "he forgave sins," Jesus was understood to affirm that he was divine; and as he proved this by working a miracle expressly to confirm the claim, it follows that he is divine, or equal with the Father.

4. And Jesus knowing their thoughts said, Wherefore think ye evil in your hearts?

Greek/Transliteration
4. Καὶ ἰδὼν ὁ Ἰησοῦς τὰς ἐνθυμήσεις αὐτῶν εἶπεν, Ἵνα τί ὑμεῖς ἐνθυμεῖσθε πονηρὰ ἐν ταῖς καρδίαις ὑμῶν;

4. Kai idon 'o Yeisous tas enthumeiseis auton eipen, 'Yna ti 'umeis enthumeisthe poneira en tais kardiais 'umon?

Hebrew/Transliteration
ד. וַיֵּדַע יֵשׁוּעַ אֶת-מַחְשְׁבֹתָם וַיֹּאמֶר מַדּוּעַ תֶּהְגּוּ רָעוֹת בִּלְבַבְכֶם:

4. Va•ye•da Yeshua et - mach•she•vo•tam va•yo•mar ma•doo•a te•he•goo ra•ot bil•vav•chem.

Rabbinic Jewish Commentary
And Yeshua knowing their thoughts,.... Which was a clear evidence, and full demonstration of his deity; for none knows the thoughts of the heart but God; and since he knew the thoughts of men's hearts, it could be no blasphemy in him to take that to himself which belonged to God, even to forgive sins. And this, one would think, would have been sufficient to have approved himself to them as the true Messiah; since this is one of the ways of knowing the Messiah, according to the Jews, and which they made use of to discover a false one.

"Bar Coziba, (they say (g)), reigned two years and a half: he said to the Rabbi's, I am the Messiah; they replied to him, it is written of the Messiah, that he is "of quick understanding, and judges", (referring to Isa_11:3) let us see whether this man is of quick understanding, and can make judgment, i.e. whether a man is wicked, or not, without any external proof; and when they saw he was not of quick understanding, and could not judge in this manner, they slew him."

But now Yeshua needed not any testimony of men; he knew what was in the hearts of men, of which this instance is a glaring proof: hence he said, wherefore think ye evil in your hearts? it was no evil in them to think that God only could forgive sin; but the evil was, that they thought Yeshua was a mere man, and ought not to have took so much upon him; and that, for so doing, he was a wicked man, and a blasphemer. (g) T. Bab. Sanhedrim, fol. 93. 2.

---

5. For whether is easier, to say, Thy sins be forgiven thee; or to say, Arise, and walk?

Greek/Transliteration
5. Τί γάρ ἐστιν εὐκοπώτερον, εἰπεῖν, Ἀφέωνταί σου αἱ ἁμαρτίαι· ἢ εἰπεῖν, Ἔγειραι καὶ περιπάτει;

5. Ti gar estin eukopoteron, eipein, Apheontai sou 'ai 'amartiai. ei eipein, Egeirai kai peripatei?

Hebrew/Transliteration
ה. כִּי מָה נָקֵל אִם לֵאמֹר נִסְלְחוּ-לְךָ חַטֹּאתֶיךָ אוֹ לֵאמֹר קוּם וְהִתְהַלָּךְ:

5. Ki ma na•kel eem le•mor nis•le•choo - le•cha cha•to•te•cha oh le•mor koom ve•hit•ha•lach.

Rabbinic Jewish Commentary
Yeshua proceeds to clear himself of the charge of blasphemy, and to prove his power to forgive sins, by putting a case to them, of which he makes themselves Judges, and is this: which is easiest to be said, thy sins are forgiven thee? or to say, arise and walk? Neither of them were easy to a mere creature, but both of them easy to God; and he that could say the one with power and efficacy going along with his word, could say the other as effectually.

---

6. But that ye may know that the Son of man hath power on earth to forgive sins, (then saith he to the sick of the palsy,) Arise, take up thy bed, and go unto thine house.

Greek/Transliteration
6. Ἵνα δὲ εἰδῆτε, ὅτι ἐξουσίαν ἔχει ὁ υἱὸς τοῦ ἀνθρώπου ἐπὶ τῆς γῆς ἀφιέναι ἁμαρτίας- τότε λέγει τῷ παραλυτικῷ- Ἐγερθεὶς ἆρόν σου τὴν κλίνην, καὶ ὕπαγε εἰς τὸν οἶκόν σου.

6. 'Yna de eideite, 'oti exousian echei 'o 'wios tou anthropou epi teis geis aphienai 'amartias- tote legei to paralutiko- Egertheis aron sou tein klinein, kai 'upage eis ton oikon sou.

Hebrew/Transliteration
ו. אַךְ לְמַעַן תֵּדְעוּן כִּי יֵשׁ רִשְׁיוֹן לְבֶן-הָאָדָם בָּאָרֶץ לִסְלֹחַ חַטָּאִים אָז אָמַר אֶל-נְכֵה הָעֲצָמוֹת קוּם שָׂא אֶת-מִטָּתְךָ וְלֶךְ-לְךָ אֶל-בֵּיתֶךָ -:

6. Ach le•ma•an ted•oon ki yesh rish•yon le•Ven - ha•adam ba•a•retz lis•loach cha•ta•eem az amar el - n`che ha•a•tza•mot koom sa et - mi•tat•cha ve•lech - le•cha el - bey•te•cha.

Rabbinic Jewish Commentary
That they might have a visible proof, an ocular demonstration, that though he was the son of man, truly and really man, yet not a mere man; but also as truly and properly God, God and man in one person.

7. And he arose, and departed to his house.

Greek/Transliteration
7. Καὶ ἐγερθεὶς ἀπῆλθεν εἰς τὸν οἶκον αὐτοῦ.

7. Kai egertheis apeilthen eis ton oikon autou.

Hebrew/Transliteration
ז. וַיָּקָם וַיֵּלֶךְ אֶל־בֵּיתוֹ:

7. Va•ya•kom va•ye•lech el - bei•to.

---

8. But when the multitudes saw it, they marvelled, and glorified God, which had given such power unto men.

Greek/Transliteration
8. Ἰδόντες δὲ οἱ ὄχλοι ἐθαύμασαν, καὶ ἐδόξασαν τὸν θεόν, τὸν δόντα ἐξουσίαν τοιαύτην τοῖς ἀνθρώποις.

8. Idontes de 'oi ochloi ethaumasan, kai edoxasan ton theon, ton donta exousian toyautein tois anthropois.

Hebrew/Transliteration
ח. וַיִּרְאוּ הֲמוֹן הָעָם וַיִּשְׁתּוֹמֲמוּ וַיִּתְּנוּ כָבוֹד לֵאלֹהִים אֲשֶׁר נָתַן שִׁלְטוֹן כָּזֶה לִבְנֵי־אָדָם:

8. Va•yir•oo ha•mon ha•am va•yish•to•ma•moo va•yit•noo cha•vod le•Elohim asher na•tan shil•ton ka•ze liv•ney - adam.

Jewish New Testament Commentary
A *b'rakhah* ("blessing"; plural *b'rakhot*) in Judaism is a sentence or paragraph of praise to God; usually commencing with the formula, *Barukh attah, Adonai* ("Praised be you, *Adonai*," quoting Psa_119:12); and continuing with a description of the specific reason for praising God at that moment. Thus here God is praised as the Giver of such authority to human beings. A similar *b'rakhah* is said by observant Jews upon seeing a person of profound secular learning: "Praised be you, *Adonai* our God, king of the universe, who has given of his wisdom to flesh and blood," i.e., to human beings. Likewise, on seeing an exalted ruler: "Praised be you, *Adonai* our God, king of the universe, who has given of his glory to flesh and blood." For more on *b'rakhot* see Mat_14:19 Mat_26:27-29, Luk_5:26, 2Ti_4:6-8, 1Pe_1:3-4.

---

9. And as Jesus passed forth from thence, he saw a man, named Matthew, sitting at the receipt of custom: and he saith unto him, Follow me. And he arose, and followed him.

Greek/Transliteration

9. Καὶ παράγων ὁ Ἰησοῦς ἐκεῖθεν εἶδεν ἄνθρωπον καθήμενον ἐπὶ τὸ τελώνιον, Ματθαῖον λεγόμενον, καὶ λέγει αὐτῷ, Ἀκολούθει μοι. Καὶ ἀναστὰς ἠκολούθησεν αὐτῷ.

9. Kai paragon 'o Yeisous ekeithen eiden anthropon katheimenon epi to telonion, Matthaion legomenon, kai legei auto, Akolouthei moi. Kai anastas eikoloutheisen auto.

Hebrew/Transliteration

ט. וַיַּעֲבֹר יֵשׁוּעַ מִשָּׁם וַיַּרְא אִישׁ אֶחָד יֹשֵׁב בְּבֵית-הַמֶּכֶס וּשְׁמוֹ מַתִּתְיָהוּ וַיֹּאמֶר אֵלָיו לֵךְ אַחֲרַי וַיָּקָם וַיֵּלֶךְ אַחֲרָיו:

9. Va•ya•a•vor Yeshua mi•sham va•yar eesh e•chad yo•shev be•veit - ha•me•ches oo•sh`mo Ma•tit•ya•hoo va•yo•mer elav lech a•cha•rai va•ya•kom va•ye•lech a•cha•rav.

Rabbinic Jewish Commentary

The Jews say (h), that one of Yeshua's disciples was called מתאי, Matthew, which, as Levi, is an Hebrew name; for though he was a publican, yet a Jew; for it was common with the Jews either to be employed by the Roman officers in collecting the toll or tribute, or to farm it of them.

Sitting at the receipt of custom, or "at the custom house", or "toll booth"; which both the Syriac version, and Munster's Hebrew Gospel, call מכס, or בית מוכסא, the "publican's house". In the (i) Talmud mention is made of it, in the following parable, upon citing Isa 61:8

"it is like, (say the Rabbi's,) to a king of flesh and blood, who passing by בית המכס, "the toll booth", or "publican's house", says to his servants, give "toll to the publicans": they reply to him, is not all the toll thine? he says to them, all that pass by the ways will learn of me, and will not avoid the toll; so says the holy blessed God."

The publicans had houses, or booths built for them, at the foot of bridges, at the mouth of rivers, and by the sea shore, where they took toll of passengers that went to and fro: hence we read (k) of bridges being made to take toll at, and of publicans being at the water side (l), and of קישרי מוכס (m), "the tickets", or "seals of the publicans"; which, when a man had paid toll on one side of a river, were given him by the publican, to show to him that sat on the other side, that it might appear he had paid: in which were written two great letters, bigger than those in common use (n). Thus Matthew was sitting in a toll booth, near the seashore, to receive the toll of passengers that came, or went in ships or boats.

(h) T. Bab. Sanhedrim, fol. 43. 1. (i) T. Bab. Succa, fol. 30. 1. (k) T. Bab. Sabbat, fol. 33. 2. (l) Jarchi in Jud. v. 10. (m) Misn. Sabbat, c. 8. sect. 2. T. Hieros. Sabbat, fol. 11. 2. T. Bab. Sabbat, fol. 78. 2. & Bechorot, fol. 30. 2. & Avoda Zara, fol. 39. 1. (n) Jarchi, Maimonides, & Bartenora in Misn. Sabbat, c. 8. sect. 2. & Gloss. in T. Bab. Bechorot, fol. 30. 2.

10. And it came to pass, as Jesus sat at meat in the house, behold, many publicans and sinners came and sat down with him and his disciples.

Greek/Transliteration
10. Καὶ ἐγένετο αὐτοῦ ἀνακειμένου ἐν τῇ οἰκίᾳ, καὶ ἰδού, πολλοὶ τελῶναι καὶ ἁμαρτωλοὶ ἐλθόντες συνανέκειντο τῷ Ἰησοῦ καὶ τοῖς μαθηταῖς αὐτοῦ.

10. Kai egeneto autou anakeimenou en tei oikia, kai idou, polloi telonai kai 'amartoloi elthontes sunanekeinto to Yeisou kai tois matheitais autou.

Hebrew/Transliteration
י. וַיְהִי בְּשִׁבְתּוֹ עַל-הַלֶּחֶם בְּבֵיתוֹ וְהִנֵּה מוֹכְסִים וְחַטָּאִים רַבִּים בָּאוּ וַיֵּשְׁבוּ לֶאֱכֹל עִם-יֵשׁוּעַ וְתַלְמִידָיו:

10. Vay•hi be•shiv•to al - ha•le•chem be•vey•to ve•hee•ne moch•sim ve•cha•ta•eem ra•bim ba•oo va•yesh•voo le•e•chol eem - Yeshua ve•tal•mi•dav.

Jewish New Testament Commentary
Sinners. This term came to be used by the *P'rushim* to refer to prostitutes, thieves and others of low reputation whose sins were blatant and obvious, not the kind the establishment winked at. Yeshua taught that those who considered themselves not sinners but "righteous" (Mat_9:13) were in fact worse, because they made themselves unteachable (see also Joh_9:38-41).

---

11. And when the Pharisees saw it, they said unto his disciples, Why eateth your Master with publicans and sinners?

Greek/Transliteration
11. Καὶ ἰδόντες οἱ Φαρισαῖοι εἶπον τοῖς μαθηταῖς αὐτοῦ, Διὰ τί μετὰ τῶν τελωνῶν καὶ ἁμαρτωλῶν ἐσθίει ὁ διδάσκαλος ὑμῶν;

11. Kai idontes 'oi Pharisaioi eipon tois matheitais autou, Dya ti meta ton telonon kai 'amartolon esthiei 'o didaskalos 'umon?

Hebrew/Transliteration
יא. וַיִּרְאוּ הַפְּרוּשִׁים וַיֹּאמְרוּ אֶל-תַּלְמִידָיו מַדּוּעַ יֹאכַל רַבְּכֶם עִם-הַמּוֹכְסִים וְהַחַטָּאִים:

11. Va•yir•oo ha•P`roo•shim va•yom•roo el - tal•mi•dav ma•doo•a yo•chal Rab•chem eem - ha•moch•sim ve•ha•cha•ta•eem.

Rabbinic Jewish Commentary
why eateth your master with publicans and sinners? The "publicans", or gatherers of the Roman tax, toll, or tribute of any sort, whether Jews or Gentiles, were persons of a very infamous character; and, as here, so often, in Jewish writings, are ranked with "sinners", and those of the worst sort: so false swearing was allowed to be made להורגים ולחרמין ולמוכסין, "to murderers, and to robbers, and to

publicans" (o); and so "publicans and thieves" are joined together by Maimonides (p), and a publican is said by him to be as a thief. And indeed this was not only the sense of the Jews, but also of other people, according to those words of Zeno the poet, παντες τελωναι παντες εισιν αρπαγες (q), "all publicans are all of them robbers": though this was not originally their character; for formerly the best of the Roman gentry were employed in this office, till by malpractices it became scandalous, when the meaner sort of people, yea, even vassals, were put into it (r). Now, with such sort of men as these the Pharisees held it unlawful to have any sort of conversation; they expelled such their society, would not dwell with them in the same house, nor eat or drink with them; concerning which, their rules and methods are these;

"a companion, or friend, who becomes the king's collector, or a "publican", or the like, they drive him from society with them: if he abstains from his evil works, then he is as any other man (s)."

Again, "when the king's collectors enter into a house to dwell, all that are in the house are defiled (t)."

Moreover, it is (u) said, that "the former saints ate their common food with purity, i.e. with their hands washed, and took care of all defilements every day; and these were called Pharisees; and this sect was exceedingly holy, and was the way of piety; for such a man was separated, and he abstained from the rest of the people, and he did not touch them, ולא יאכל וישתה עמהם, "nor did he eat and drink with them"."

It was a general rule with them, that a clean person ought not to eat with an unclean, as they judged the common people to be; nay, that a Pharisee, who was unclean himself, might not eat with another person that was so, and which they boast of, as a great degree of holiness.

"Come and see, (say they (w),) to what a pitch purity has arrived in Israel; for they not only teach, that a pure person may not eat with one that is defiled, but that one that has a "gonorrhoea" may not eat with another that has one, lest he should be used to transgress this way; and a Pharisee that has a "gonorrhoea" may not eat with a common person that has one, lest he should be used to do so."

Hence they looked upon Yeshua and his disciples as such, and would insinuate that they were evil men, who had no regard to purity of life and conversation.

(o) Mis. Nedarim, c. 3. sect. 4. (p) Hilch. Gezela, c. 5. sect. 9. 11. (q) Apud Fabricii Graec. Biblioth. l. 2. c. 22. p. 755. (r) Alex. ab Alex. Genial. Dier. l. 2. c. 29. (s) Maimon. Mishcab & Moshab, c. 10. sect. 8. (t) Ib. c. 12. sect. 12. (u) Ib. Hilchoth Tumaot Okelim. c. 16. sect. 12. (w) T. Bab. Sabbat, fol. 13. 1.

12. But when Jesus heard that, he said unto them, They that be whole need not a physician, but they that are sick.

Greek/Transliteration

12. Ὁ δὲ Ἰησοῦς ἀκούσας εἶπεν αὐτοῖς, Οὐ χρείαν ἔχουσιν οἱ ἰσχύοντες ἰατροῦ, ἀλλ᾽ οἱ κακῶς ἔχοντες.

12. 'O de Yeisous akousas eipen autois, Ou chreian echousin 'oi ischuontes iatrou, all 'oi kakos echontes.

Hebrew/Transliteration

יב. וַיִּשְׁמַע יֵשׁוּעַ וַיֹּאמֶר אֲלֵיהֶם הַחֲזָקִים אֵין לָהֶם דָּבָר עִם-הָרֹפֵא כִּי אִם-הַחוֹלִים:

12. Va•yish•ma Yeshua va•yo•mer aley•hem ha•cha•za•kim eyn la•hem da•var eem - ha•ro•fe ki eem - ha•cho•lim.

Rabbinic Jewish Commentary

they that be whole need not a physician; by which he would signify that he was a "physician": and so he is in a spiritual sense, and that a very skilful one: he knows the nature of all the diseases of the soul, without being told them by the patient; what are the true causes of them; what is proper to apply; when is the best time, and what the best manner: he is an universal one, with regard both to diseases and to persons, that apply to him; he heals all sorts of persons, and all sorts of diseases; such as are blind from their birth, are as deaf as the deaf adder, the halt, and the lame, such as have broken hearts, yea the plague in their hearts, and have stony ones, and all the relapses of his people; which he does by his stripes and wounds, by the application of his blood, by his word and Gospel, through sinners looking to him, and touching him: he is an infallible one, none ever went from him without a cure; none ever perished under his hands; the disease he heals never returns more to prevail, so as to bring on death and destruction; and he does all freely, without money, and without price. So Philo the Jew calls the Logos, or word, ιατρον κακων, "an healer of diseases" (x), and God our legislator, των της ψυχης παθων αριστος ιατρος, "the best physician of the diseases of the soul" (y). Now Yeshua argues from this his character, in vindication of himself; as that he was with these persons, not as a companion of their's, but as a physician to them; and as it is not unlawful, but highly proper and commendable, that a physician should be with the sick; so it was very lawful, fit, and proper, yea praiseworthy in him, to be among these publicans and sinners, for their spiritual good. He suggests indeed, that "they that be whole", in perfect health and strength, as the Pharisees thought themselves to be, even free from all the maladies and diseases of sin, were strong, robust, and able to do anything, and everything of themselves; these truly stood in no "need of" him, as a physician, in their own apprehension; they saw no need of him; in principle they had no need of him, and in practice did not make use of him; and therefore it was to no purpose to attend them, but converse with others, who had need of him:

but they that are sick; who are not only diseased and disordered in all the powers and faculties of their souls, as all Adam's posterity are, whether sensible of it or not; but who know themselves to be so, these see their need of Christ as a physician, apply to him as such, and to them he is exceeding precious, a physician of value; and such were these "publicans" and sinners. These words seem to be a proverbial expression, and there is something like it in the (z) Talmud, דכאיב ליה כאיבא אזיל לבי אסיא, "he that is afflicted with any pain goes", or "let him go to the physician's house"; that is, he that is attended with any sickness, or disease, does, or he ought to, consult a physician.

(x) Allegor. l. 2. p. 93. (y) Quod Deus sit immutab. p. 303. (z) T. Bab. Bava Kama, fol. 46. 2.

---

13. But go ye and learn what that meaneth, I will have mercy, and not sacrifice: for I am not come to call the righteous, but sinners to repentance.

Greek/Transliteration
13. Πορευθέντες δὲ μάθετε τί ἐστιν, Ἔλεον θέλω, καὶ οὐ θυσίαν· οὐ γὰρ ἦλθον καλέσαι δικαίους, ἀλλὰ ἁμαρτωλοὺς εἰς μετάνοιαν.

13. Poreuthentes de mathete ti estin, Eleon thelo, kai ou thusian. ou gar eilthon kalesai dikaious, alla 'amartolous eis metanoyan.

Hebrew/Transliteration
יג. וְאַתֶּם לְכוּ לִמְדוּ לָדַעַת מַה-זֶה חֶסֶד חָפַצְתִּי וְלֹא זָבַח כִּי לֹא-בָאתִי לִקְרֹא לַצַּדִּיקִים לָבֹא כִּי אִם-לַחַטָּאִים לִתְשׁוּבָה:

13. Ve•a•tem le•choo lim•doo la•da•at ma - ze che•sed cha•fatz•ti ve•lo za•vach ki lo - va•ti lik•ro la•tza•di•kim la•vo ki eem - la•cha•ta•eem lit•shoo•va.

Rabbinic Jewish Commentary
But go ye and learn what that meaneth,..... צא ולמד, "go and learn", is a phrase used by the Jews (a), when they are about to explain a passage of Scripture, and fetch an argument from the connection of the text. So the phrase τι εστιν, "what that is", or "what that meaneth", is Talmudic, as, מהי, "what is it?" מאי דכתיב, "what is that which is written?" מאי קרא, "what is the Scripture?" that is, what is the meaning of it? Our Lord speaks in their own dialect, and tacitly reproves their ignorance of the Scriptures; and instead of finding fault with him, and his conduct, he intimates, it would better become them to endeavour to find out the meaning of that passage in Hos_6:6 "I will have mercy, and not sacrifice"; which, if rightly understood, was sufficient to silence all their cavils and objections: and which words are to be taken, not in an absolute and unlimited sense; for sacrifices even of slain beasts, which were offered up in the faith of Yeshua's sacrifice, and were attended with other acts of religion and piety, were acceptable to God, being his own institutions and appointments; but in a comparative sense, as the following clause in the prophet shows; "and the knowledge of God more than burnt offerings"; and so the sense is given in the "Chaldee paraphrase", after this manner: "for in those that

exercise mercy is my good will and pleasure", or "delight", ממדבח, "more than in sacrifice": and the meaning is, that God takes more delight and pleasure, either in showing mercy himself to poor miserable sinners; or in acts of mercy, compassion, and beneficence done by men, to fallen creatures in distress, whether for the good of their bodies, or more especially for the welfare of their souls, than he does even in sacrifices, and in any of the rituals of the ceremonial law, though of his own appointing: and therefore must be supposed to have a less regard to sacrifices, which were offered, neither in a right manner, nor from a right principle, nor to a right end; and still less to human traditions, and customs, which were put upon a level, and even preferred to his institutions; such as these the Pharisees were so zealous of. The force of our Lord's reasoning is, that since his conversation, with publicans and sinners, was an act of mercy and compassion to their souls, and designed for their spiritual good; it must be much more pleasing to God, than had he attended to the traditions of the elders, they charge him with the breach of: besides, what he was now doing was the end of his coming into this world, and which was answered hereby;

The phrase, "to repentance", is not in the Vulgate Latin, nor in Munster's Hebrew Gospel, nor in the Syriac, Ethiopic, and Persic versions; but is in the Arabic, and in the ancient Greek copies, and is very justly retained. The "repentance" here designed, is not a legal, but an evangelical one: which is attended with faith in Yeshua, with views, at least hopes of pardon through his blood, and springs from a discovery and sense of his love: it lies in a true sense of sin, and the exceeding sinfulness of it, by the light of the Spirit of God; in a godly sorrow for it, and hearty loathing of it; in real shame and blushing for it, ingenuous confession of it, and departing from it; all which is brought on, influenced, heightened, and increased, by displays of the love of God through Yeshua. The persons called to this are not the "righteous"; meaning either such who are really so, because these are already called to it, though, whilst in a state of imperfection, daily need the exercise of this grace; or rather such who are so in their own opinion, and in the sight of men only, not in the sight of God, which was the case of the Scribes and Pharisees, and very few of these were called and brought to repentance; but "sinners", even the worst, and chief of sinners, who, as they stand in need of this grace, and when thoroughly convinced, see they do; so Messiah came into this world as prophet and minister of the word to "call" them to it: which call of his does not suppose that they had a power to repent of themselves; for this man has not, he is naturally blind, and do not see his sin; his heart is hard and obdurate, and till his eyes are opened, and his stony heart taken away by a superior power to his own, he will never repent; though he may have space, yet if he has not grace given him, he will remain impenitent. No means will bring him to it of themselves, neither the most severe judgments, nor the greatest kindnesses, nor the most powerful ministry; repentance is entirely a free grace gift: nor does the call of Yeshua imply the contrary; which may be considered either as external, as a preacher of the word, and as such was not always attended to, and effectual, but often slighted and rejected: or as internal, being by the power of his grace effectual; for he who called to repentance, as a minister of the word, as a prince and a saviour, was able to give it, and which none but a divine person is able to do.

The Jews have a saying (b) of "shepherds, collectors of taxes and "publicans", תשובתן קשה, "that their repentance is difficult"."

Now, since this was the end of his coming into the world, his conduct in conversing with publicans and sinners was in all respects highly to be justified.

(a) T. Bab. Succa, fol. 5. 1. & Sanhedrim, fol. 86. 1. Moses Kotsensis Mitzvot Tora pr. neg. 116. Vid. Maimon. Hilchot Melachim, c. 5. sect. 11. (b) T. Bab. Bava Kama, fol. 94. 3.

---

14. Then came to him the disciples of John, saying, Why do we and the Pharisees fast oft, but thy disciples fast not?

Greek/Transliteration
14. Τότε προσέρχονται αὐτῷ οἱ μαθηταὶ Ἰωάννου, λέγοντες, Διὰ τί ἡμεῖς καὶ οἱ Φαρισαῖοι νηστεύομεν πολλά, οἱ δὲ μαθηταί σου οὐ νηστεύουσιν;

14. Tote proserchontai auto 'oi matheitai Yoannou, legontes, Dya ti 'eimeis kai 'oi Pharisaioi neisteuomen polla, 'oi de matheitai sou ou neisteuousin?

Hebrew/Transliteration
יד. וַיִּגְּשׁוּ אֵלָיו תַּלְמִידֵי יוֹחָנָן וַיֹּאמְרוּ מַדּוּעַ אֲנַחְנוּ עִם-הַפְּרוּשִׁים מַרְבִּים לָצוּם וְתַלְמִידֶיךָ לֹא יָצֻמוּ:

14. Va•yig•shoo elav tal•mi•dey Yo•cha•nan va•yom•roo ma•doo•a a•nach•noo eem - ha•P`roo•shim mar•bim la•tzoom ve•tal•mi•de•cha lo ya•tzoo•moo.

Rabbinic Jewish Commentary
The fastings here referred to are not the public fasts enjoined by the law of Moses, or in any writings of the Old Testament; but private fasts, which were enjoined by John to his disciples, and by the Pharisees to their's; or which were, according to the traditions of the elders, or of their own appointing, and which were very "often" indeed: for besides their fasting twice a week, on Monday and Thursday, Luk_18:12 they had a multitude of fasts upon divers occasions, particularly for rain (c). If the 17th of Marchesvan, or October, came, and there was no rain, private persons kept three days of fasting, viz. Monday, Thursday, and Monday again: and if the month of Cisleu, or November, came, and there was no rain, then the sanhedrim appointed three fast days, which were on the same days as before, for the congregation; and if still there was no rain came, they added three more; and if yet there were none, they enjoined seven more, in all thirteen, which R. Acha and R. Barachiah kept themselves (d). Fasts were kept also on account of many other evils, as pestilence, famine, war, sieges, inundations, or any other calamity; sometimes for trifling things, as for dreams (e), that they might have good ones, or know how to interpret them, or avoid any ill omen by them; and it is almost incredible what frequent fastings some of the Rabbi's exercised themselves with, on very insignificant occasions.

They (f) say, "R. Jose צָם תְּמָנֵיי צוֹמִין, "fasted fourscore fasts" to see R. Chiyah Rubba; at last he saw, and his hands trembled, and his eyes grew dim: --R. Simeon Ben Lakish צָם תְּלַת מְאָוָן צוֹמִין, "fasted three hundred fastings" to see R. Chiyah Rubba, and did not see him."

Elsewhere it is said, that R. Ase fasted "thirty days" to see the same person, and saw him not (g). Again (h),

"R. Jonathan fasted every eve of the new year, R. Abin fasted every eve of the feast of tabernacles, R. Zeura fasted "three hundred fasts", and there are that say "nine hundred fasts"."

This may serve to illustrate and prove the frequency of the Jewish fastings. Luke represents this question as put by the Pharisees, which is here put by the disciples of John: it was doubtless put by both agreeing in this matter; and which shows that John's disciples were instigated to it by the Pharisees, who sought to sow discord between them, and to bring Yeshua and his disciples into contempt with them.

(c) Misn. Taanith, c. 1. sect. 4. 5, 6. & c. 3. sect. 4, 5, 6, 7, 8. Maimon. & Bartenora in ib. (d) T. Hieros. Taanlot, fol. 65. 2. & 66. 4. (e) T. Bab. Sabbat. fol. 10. 1. Maimon Taaniot, c. 1. sect. 12-14. (f) T. Hieros. Cilaim, fol. 32. 2. & Cetubot, fol. 35. 1. (g) Midrash Kohelet, fol. 79. 1. (h) Ib. Nedarim, fol. 40. 4. & Taanioth, fol. 66. 1.

---

15. And Jesus said unto them, Can the children of the bridechamber mourn, as long as the bridegroom is with them? but the days will come, when the bridegroom shall be taken from them, and then shall they fast.

Greek/Transliteration
15. Καὶ εἶπεν αὐτοῖς ὁ Ἰησοῦς, Μὴ δύνανται οἱ υἱοὶ τοῦ νυμφῶνος πενθεῖν, ἐφ᾽ ὅσον μετ᾽ αὐτῶν ἐστιν ὁ νυμφίος; Ἐλεύσονται δὲ ἡμέραι ὅταν ἀπαρθῇ ἀπ᾽ αὐτῶν ὁ νυμφίος, καὶ τότε νηστεύσουσιν.

15. Kai eipen autois 'o Yeisous, Mei dunantai 'oi 'wioi tou numphonos penthein, eph 'oson met auton estin 'o numphios? Eleusontai de 'eimerai 'otan aparthei ap auton 'o numphios, kai tote neisteusousin.

Hebrew/Transliteration
טו. וַיֹּאמֶר אֲלֵיהֶם יֵשׁוּעַ הֲיִתְאַבְּלוּ קְרֻאֵי הַחֲתֻנָּה בְּעוֹד הֶחָתָן עִמָּהֶם וְהִנֵּה יָמִים יָבֹאוּ וְלֻקַּח מֵהֶם הֶחָתָן וְאָז יָצֻמוּ:

15. Va•yo•mer aley•hem Yeshua ha•yit•ab•loo ke•roo•ey ha•cha•too•na be•od he•cha•tan ee•ma•hem ve•hee•ne ya•mim ya•vo•oo ve•loo•kach me•hem he•cha•tan ve•az ya•tzoo•moo.

Rabbinic Jewish Commentary

When both bride and bridegroom have their friends attending them, who used to be called בני החופה, "the children of the bride chamber". The bride had her maidens waiting on her; and it is said (i),

"she did not go into the bridechamber but with them; and these are called, בני חופתא, "the children of the bride chamber"."

So the young men that were the friends of the bridegroom, which attended him, were called by the same name; and, according to the Jewish canons, were free from many things they were otherwise obliged to: thus it is said (k):

"the bridegroom, his friends, and all בני החופה, "the children of the bride chamber", are free from the booth all the seven days;"

that is, from dwelling in booths at the feast of tabernacles, which was too strait a place for such festival solemnities. And again,

"the bridegroom, his friends, and all בני החופה, "the children of the bride chamber", are free from prayer and the phylacteries;"

that is, from observing the stated times of attending to these things, and much more then were they excused from fasting and mourning; so that the Pharisees had an answer sufficient to silence them, agreeably to their own traditions. Give me leave to transcribe one passage more, for the illustration of this text (l).

"When R. Lazar ben Arach opened, in the business of Mercava, (the visions in the beginning of Ezekiel,) Rabban Jochanan ben Zaccai alighted from his ass; for he said it is not fit I should hear the glory of my Creator, and ride upon an ass: they went, and sat under a certain tree, and fire came down from heaven and surrounded them; and the ministering angels leaped before them, כבני חופה, "as the children of the bride chamber" rejoice before the bridegroom."

"all fasts shall cease in the days of the Messiah; and there shall be no more but good days, and days of joy and rejoicing, as it is said, Zec_8:19."

(i) Zohar in Gen. fol. 6. 4. (k) T. Bab. Succa, fol. 25. 2. & Hieros. Succa, fol. 53. 1. Maimon. Succa, c. 6. sect. 3. (l) T. Hieros. Chagiga, fol. 77. 1. (m) Maimon. Hilchot Taaniot, c. 5. sect. 19.

---

16. No man putteth a piece of new cloth unto an old garment, for that which is put in to fill it up taketh from the garment, and the rent is made worse.

Greek/Transliteration
16. Οὐδεὶς δὲ ἐπιβάλλει ἐπίβλημα ῥάκους ἀγνάφου ἐπὶ ἱματίῳ παλαιῷ· αἴρει γὰρ τὸ πλήρωμα αὐτοῦ ἀπὸ τοῦ ἱματίου, καὶ χεῖρον σχίσμα γίνεται.

16. Oudeis de epiballei epibleima 'rakous agnaphou epi 'imatio palaio. airei gar to pleiroma autou apo tou 'imatiou, kai cheiron schisma ginetai.

Hebrew/Transliteration

טז. וְאֵין תֹּפְרִים טְלָאָה חֲדָשָׁה עַל-שִׂמְלָה בָלָה פֶּן-הַטְּלָאָה בִּמְלֵאָתָהּ תִּגְרַע מִן-הַשִּׂמְלָה וְתוֹסִיף עַל-קְרָעֶיהָ:

16. Ve•eyn tof•rim te•la•ah cha•da•sha al - sim•la va•la pen - hat•la•ah be•mi•loo•a•ta tig•ra min - ha•sim•la ve•to•sif al - ke•ra•e•ha.

Jewish New Testament Commentary

This verse and the next speak to the issue of whether faith in Yeshua the Messiah can be combined with Judaism. Here the old coat is Judaism. The unshrunk cloth is Messianic faith which has not been adapted ("shrunk") to the framework of Judaism as currently practiced. ("Shrinking" here is simply an aspect of Yeshua's "patch" metaphor. It does not imply that Messianic faith must be diminished in order to fit into Judaism.) Combining unadapted Messianic faith with traditional Judaism doesn't work-the patch tears away from the coat; that is, faith in Yeshua apart from Judaism-and, later on in the case of Gentiles, faith in Yeshua apart from the foundational truths about God taught in the *Tanakh*-is useless and worthless.

Not only that, but it leaves a worse hole-attempting to combine unadapted Messianic faith with traditional Judaism leaves Judaism worse off than before.

The implication is that one must shrink the new cloth-adapt Messianic faith to Judaism-for Yeshua does not imply that there is anything wrong with patching an old coat! The early Messianic Jews did adapt Messianic faith to Judaism, but the later Gentile Church did not. Instead, some forms of Gentile Christianity became paganized precisely because the *Tanakh* was forgotten or underemphasized. Messianic Jews today are once again trying to bring New Testament faith back to its Jewish roots.

---

17. Neither do men put new wine into old bottles: else the bottles break, and the wine runneth out, and the bottles perish: but they put new wine into new bottles, and both are preserved.

Greek/Transliteration

17. Οὐδὲ βάλλουσιν οἶνον νέον εἰς ἀσκοὺς παλαιούς· εἰ δὲ μήγε, ῥήγνυνται οἱ ἀσκοί, καὶ ὁ οἶνος ἐκχεῖται, καὶ οἱ ἀσκοὶ ἀπολοῦνται· ἀλλὰ βάλλουσιν οἶνον νέον εἰς ἀσκοὺς καινούς, καὶ ἀμφότεροι συντηροῦνται.

17. Oude ballousin oinon neon eis askous palaious. ei de meige, 'reignuntai 'oi askoi, kai 'o oinos ekcheitai, kai 'oi askoi apolountai. alla ballousin oinon neon eis askous kainous, kai amphoteroi sunteirountai.

Hebrew/Transliteration

יז. וְתִירוֹשׁ לֹא יִתֵּן בְּנֹאדוֹת בָּלִים פֶּן-יְבַקְּעוּ הַנֹּאדוֹת וְנִשְׁפַּךְ הַיַּיִן וְהַנֹּאדוֹת יִכָּלְיוּן אֲבָל תִּירוֹשׁ יִתֵּן בְּנֹאדוֹת חֲדָשִׁים וּשְׁמֻרִים יִהְיוּ שְׁנֵיהֶם:

17. Ve•ti•rosh lo yoo•tan be•no•dot ba•lim pen - yi•bak•oo ha•no•dot ve•nish•pach ha•ya•yin ve•ha•no•dot yich•la•yoon aval ti•rosh yoo•tan be•no•dot cha•da•shim oosh•moo•rim yi•hee•yoo sh`ney•hem.

Rabbinic/Jewish New Testament Commentary

Whereas in Mat_9:16 Messianic faith has to be adapted to Judaism, here it is Judaism which must be adjusted to Messianic faith. If one tries to put new wine, Messianic faith, into old wineskins, traditional Judaism, the faith is lost and Judaism ruined. But if Judaism is freshly prepared, reconditioned so that it can accommodate trust in Yeshua the Messiah, both the faith and the renewed Judaism, Messianic Judaism, are preserved.

The allusion is to bottles, made of the skins of beasts, which in time decayed, waxed old, and became unfit for use: such were the wine bottles, old and rent, the Gibeonites brought with them, and showed to Joshua, Jos_9:4 and to which the Psalmist compares himself, Psa_119:83 and which the Misnic doctors call חמתות, and their commentators (o) say, were נודת של עור, "bottles made of skin", or "leather", and so might be rent. Of the use of new and old bottles, take the following hint out of the "Talmud" (p).

"The bottles of the Gentiles, if scraped and חדשים, "new", they are free for use; if ישנים, "old", they are forbidden."

(o) Jarchi & Bartenora in Misn. Celim, c. 24. sect. 11. & Negaim, c. 11. sect. 11.
(p) T. Bab. Avoda Zara, fol. 33. 1.

---

18. While he spake these things unto them, behold, there came a certain ruler, and worshipped him, saying, My daughter is even now dead: but come and lay thy hand upon her, and she shall live.

Greek/Transliteration

18. Ταῦτα αὐτοῦ λαλοῦντος αὐτοῖς, ἰδού, ἄρχων εἷς ἐλθὼν προσεκύνει αὐτῷ, λέγων ὅτι Ἡ θυγάτηρ μου ἄρτι ἐτελεύτησεν· ἀλλὰ ἐλθὼν ἐπίθες τὴν χεῖρά σου ἐπ᾽ αὐτήν, καὶ ζήσεται.

18. Tauta autou lalountos autois, idou, archon 'eis elthon prosekunei auto, legon 'oti 'Ei thugateir mou arti eteleuteisen. alla elthon epithes tein cheira sou ep autein, kai zeisetai.

Hebrew/Transliteration

יח. עוֹדֶנּוּ מְדַבֵּר אֲלֵיהֶם כַּדְּבָרִים הָאֵלֶּה וְהִנֵּה אַחַד הָרָאשִׁים בָּא וַיִּשְׁתַּחוּ-לוֹ לֵאמֹר בִּתִּי מֵתָה עָלַי בָּזֶה אֲבָל:בֹּא וְשִׂים-נָא יָדְךָ עָלֶיהָ וְחָיֹה תִחְיֶה

18. O•de•noo me•da•ber aley•hem ka•d`va•rim ha•e•le ve•hee•ne achad ha•ra•shim ba va•yish•ta•choo - lo le•mor bi•ti me•ta a•lai ba•ze aval bo ve•sim - na yad•cha a•le•ha ve•cha•yo tich•ye.

Rabbinic Jewish Commentary

This man, as both Mark and Luke say, was named Jairus; and was a ruler, not of the sanhedrim, or lesser consistory, but of the synagogue that was at Capernaum; and whom the Jews call, ראש הכנסת, "the head of the synagogue". Mark says, he was "one of the rulers": not that there were more rulers than one, in one synagogue (q): but as in great cities, so it is likely in Capernaum there were more synagogues than one, of which he was one of the rulers: so we read of ראשי כנסיות (r), "heads", or "rulers of synagogues". As this is one mistake, so it is another to say, that Dr. Lightfoot speaks of this ruler, as the same with the "minister" of the congregation; when both here, and in the place referred to, he manifestly distinguishes them; as do the Jews: for, by this ruler, as their commentators (s) say,

"the necessary affairs of the synagogue were determined, as who should dismiss with a prophet, who should divide the "shema", and who should go before the ark."

Whereas the business of חזן הכנסת, "the minister of the synagogue", was to bring in and out the ark, or chest, in which was the book of the law; and particularly, when the high priest read, or pronounced the blessings, "he" took the book, and gave it to "the ruler of the synagogue"; and the ruler of the synagogue gave it to the "sagan", and the "sagan" to the high priest (t). The doctor makes indeed שליח הצבור, "the messenger of the congregation", to be the same with "the minister of the synagogue", and which is his mistake; for these were two different officers (u): the former was the lecturer, or preacher; and the latter, a sort of a sexton to keep the synagogue clean, open and shut the doors, and do other things before mentioned. This Jairus was a man of great power and significance; who in such a very humble manner prostrated himself at the feet of Jesus, and expressed such strong faith in him:

Luke says, she was "his only daughter": and Mark calls her his "little daughter": though both he and Luke say, she was about "twelve" years of age, and that with strict propriety, according to the Jewish canons, which (w) say; that

"a daughter, from the day of her birth until she is twelve years complete, is called קטנה, "a little one" and when she is twelve years of age, and one day and upwards, she is called נערה, "a young woman"."

(q) Vid. Rhenfurd. de decem otiosis dissert. 2. c. 7. (r) T. Bab. Gittin, fol. 60. 1. (s) Jarchi & Bartenora in Misn. Yoma, c. 7. sect. 1. & Sota, c. 7. sect. 7. (t) Misn. Sota, c. 7. sect. 7. & Bartenora in ib. (u) Vid. Rhenfurd, dissert. 1. p. 81, etc. (w) Maimon. Hilchot Ishot, c. 2. sect. 1. & Bartenora in Misn. Nidda, c. 5. sect. 6.

---

19. And Jesus arose, and followed him, and so did his disciples.

Greek/Transliteration
19. Καὶ ἐγερθεὶς ὁ Ἰησοῦς ἠκολούθησεν αὐτῷ καὶ οἱ μαθηταὶ αὐτοῦ.

19. Kai egertheis 'o Yeisous eikolautheisen auto kai 'oi matheitai autou.

Hebrew/Transliteration
:יט. וַיָּקָם יֵשׁוּעַ וַיֵּלֶךְ עִמּוֹ הוּא וְתַלְמִידָיו

19. Va•ya•kom Yeshua va•ye•lech ee•mo hoo ve•tal•mi•dav.

---

20. And, behold, a woman, which was diseased with an issue of blood twelve years, came behind him, and touched the hem of his garment:

Greek/Transliteration
20. Καὶ ἰδού, γυνὴ αἱμορροοῦσα δώδεκα ἔτη, προσελθοῦσα ὄπισθεν, ἥψατο τοῦ κρασπέδου τοῦ ἱματίου αὐτοῦ.

20. Kai idou, gunei 'aimorroousa dodeka etei, proselthousa opisthen, 'eipsato tou kraspedou tou 'imatiou autou.

Hebrew/Transliteration
:כ. וְהִנֵּה אִשָּׁה זָבַת-דָּם אֲשֶׁר יְמֵי זוֹבָהּ נִמְשְׁכוּ שְׁתֵּים עֶשְׂרֵה שָׁנָה קָרְבָה וַתִּגַּע בִּכְנַף בִּגְדוֹ מֵאַחֲרָיו

20. Ve•hee•ne ee•sha za•vat - dam asher ye•mey zo•va nim•she•choo sh`teim es•re sha•na kar•va va•ti•ga bich•naf big•do me•a•cha•rav.

Rabbinic/Jewish New Testament Commentary
Observant Jewish men in Yeshua's time and today have worn fringes on the corners of their garments, in obedience to Num_15:37-41, the third of the three *Torah* passages recited in the *Sh'ma* portion of the synagogue service. These fringes are made in a special way and have a unique appearance. Their purpose is to remind God's people to obey his commandments. Since they are not merely decorations, the usual renderings of Greek *kraspedon*-"hem," "fringe," "border," "tassel"-are replaced here by "*tzitzit*." Today Jewish men wear *tzitziyot* on a *tallit gadol* ("large *tallit*"), which is not an article of clothing but a ritual cloth donned primarily for synagogue worship, or on a *tallit katan* ("little *tallit*"), which is an undergarment especially designed with corners for the *tzitziyot*. But Yeshua wore his on his robe, a heavy blanket-like over-garment similar to that worn by Bedouins today.

---

21. For she said within herself, If I may but touch his garment, I shall be whole.

Greek/Transliteration
21. Ἔλεγεν γὰρ ἐν ἑαυτῇ, Ἐὰν μόνον ἅψωμαι τοῦ ἱματίου αὐτοῦ, σωθήσομαι.

21. Elegen gar en 'eautei, Ean monon 'apsomai tou 'imatiou autou, sotheisomai.

Hebrew/Transliteration

:כא. כִּי אָמְרָה בְּלִבָּהּ אִם אַךְ־אֶגַּע בְּבִגְדוֹ וְאִוָּשֵׁעָה

21. Ki am•ra be•li•ba eem ach - ega be•vig•do ve•ee•va•she•ah.

Rabbinic Jewish Commentary

Which was the ציצת, or "fringes", the Jews were obliged to wear upon the borders of their garments, and on it a ribband of blue; see Num_15:38 in both which places Onkelos uses the word כרוספדין, the same with κράσπεδον, used here, and in Mar_6:56 and rendered "hem". The Jews placed much sanctity in the wear and use of these fringes; and the Pharisees, who pretended to more holiness than others, enlarged them beyond their common size; but it was not on account of any peculiar holiness in this part of Christ's garment, that induced this poor woman to touch it; but this being behind him, and more easy to be come at, she therefore laid hold on it; for it was his garment, any part of it she concluded, if she could but touch, she should have a cure. However, we learn from hence, that Yeshua complied with the rites of the ceremonial law in apparel, as well as in other things.

(x) Ib. Issure Bia, c. 6. sect. 7, 8. & in Misn. Nidda, c. 4. sect. 7.

---

22. But Jesus turned him about, and when he saw her, he said, Daughter, be of good comfort; thy faith hath made thee whole. And the woman was made whole from that hour.

Greek/Transliteration

22. Ὁ δὲ Ἰησοῦς ἐπιστραφεὶς καὶ ἰδὼν αὐτὴν εἶπεν, Θάρσει, θύγατερ· ἡ πίστις σου σέσωκέν σε. Καὶ ἐσώθη ἡ γυνὴ ἀπὸ τῆς ὥρας ἐκείνης.

22. 'O de Yeisous epistrapheis kai idon autein eipen, Tharsei, thugater. 'ei pistis sou sesoken se. Kai esothei 'ei gunei apo teis 'oras ekeineis.

Hebrew/Transliteration

:כב. וַיִּפֶן יֵשׁוּעַ וַיַּרְא אֹתָהּ וַיֹּאמַר חִזְקִי בִּתִּי אֱמוּנָתֵךְ הוֹשִׁיעָה לָּךְ וּבָעֵת הַהִיא עָלְתָה אֲרֻכָה לָהּ

22. Va•yi•fen Yeshua va•yar o•ta va•yo•mar chiz•ki vi•ti emoo•na•tech ho•shi•ah lach oo•va•et ha•hee al•ta aroo•cha la.

---

23. And when Jesus came into the ruler's house, and saw the minstrels and the people making a noise,

Greek/Transliteration

23. Καὶ ἐλθὼν ὁ Ἰησοῦς εἰς τὴν οἰκίαν τοῦ ἄρχοντος, καὶ ἰδὼν τοὺς αὐλητὰς καὶ τὸν ὄχλον θορυβούμενον,

23. Kai elthon 'o Yeisous eis tein oikian tou archontos, kai idon tous auleitas kai ton ochlon thoruboumenon,

Hebrew/Transliteration
כג. וַיָּבֹא יֵשׁוּעַ אֶל-בֵּית-הָרֹאשׁ וַיַּרְא אֶת-הַמְחַלְלִים בַּחֲלִלִים וְאֶת-הָעָם הֹמֶה:

23. Va•ya•vo Yeshua el - beit - ha•rosh va•yar et - ham•cha•le•lim ba•cha•li•lim ve•et - ha•am ho•me.

Rabbinic Jewish Commentary
saw the minstrels, or "pipers"; how many there were, is not known: it is certain there were more than one; and it was a rule with the (z) Jews that

"the poorest man in Israel (when his wife died) had not less משני חלילים, "than two pipes", and one mourning woman."

These instruments were made use of, not to remove the melancholy of surviving friends, or allay the grief of the afflicted family; but, on the contrary, to excite it: for the Jewish writers say (a), these pipes were hollow instruments, with which they made a known sound, לעורר הבכיה והאבל, "to stir up lamentation and mourning"

z) Misn. Cetubot. c. 4. sect. 4. Maimon Ishot, c. 14. sect. 23. (a) Maimon & Bartenora in Misn. Sabbat, c. 23. sect. 4.

---

24. He said unto them, Give place: for the maid is not dead, but sleepeth. And they laughed him to scorn.

Greek/Transliteration
24. λέγει αὐτοῖς, Ἀναχωρεῖτε· οὐ γὰρ ἀπέθανεν τὸ κοράσιον, ἀλλὰ καθεύδει. Καὶ κατεγέλων αὐτοῦ.

24. legei autois, Anachoreite. ou gar apethanen to korasion, alla katheudei. Kai kategelon autou.

Hebrew/Transliteration
כד. וַיֹּאמֶר צְאוּ מִזֶּה הַיַּלְדָּה לֹא מֵתָה כִּי רַק יְשֵׁנָה הִיא וַיִּלְעֲגוּ לוֹ:

24. Va•yo•mar tze•oo mi•ze ha•yal•da lo me•ta ki rak ye•she•na hee va•yil•a•goo lo.

Rabbinic Jewish Commentary
For the maid is not dead, but sleepeth: not but that she was really dead; and Yeshua signifies as much, when he says, she "sleepeth"; a phrase that is often used in (e) Talmudic writings, for one that is dead: but Yeshua's meaning is, that she was not so dead as the company thought; as always to remain in the state of the dead, and not to be restored to life again: whereas our Lord signifies, it would be

seen in a very little time, that she should be raised again, just as a person is awaked out of sleep; so that there was no occasion to make such funeral preparations as they did. The Jews say (f) of some of their dead, that they are asleep, and not dead: it is said, Isa_26:19 "Awake and sing, ye that dwell in the dust".

"These, say they, are they that sleep and die not; and such are they that sleep in Hebron, for they לאו מתין אלא דמיכין, "do not die, but sleep", --the four couples in Hebron (Adam and Eve, &c.) they "sleep, but are not dead"."

(e) T. Hieros. Beracot, fol. 6. 1. Avoda Zara, fol. 42. 3. Bereshit Rabba Parash. 91. fol. 79. 3. (f) Zohar in Exod. fol. 62. 4.

---

25. But when the people were put forth, he went in, and took her by the hand, and the maid arose.

Greek/Transliteration
25. Ὅτε δὲ ἐξεβλήθη ὁ ὄχλος, εἰσελθὼν ἐκράτησεν τῆς χειρὸς αὐτῆς, καὶ ἠγέρθη τὸ κοράσιον.

25. 'Ote de exebleithei 'o ochlos, eiselthon ekrateisen teis cheiros auteis, kai eigerthei to korasion.

Hebrew/Transliteration
כה. וְכַאֲשֶׁר הוֹצִיאוּ אֶת-הָעָם מִשָּׁם וַיָּבֹא הַבַּיְתָה וַיַּחֲזֶק בְּיָדָהּ וַתָּקָם הַנַּעֲרָה עַל-רַגְלֶיהָ:

25. Ve•cha•a•sher ho•tzi•oo et - ha•am mi•sham va•ya•vo ha•bai•ta va•ya•cha•zek be•ya•da va•ta•kom ha•na•a•ra al - rag•le•ha.

---

26. And the fame hereof went abroad into all that land.

Greek/Transliteration
26. Καὶ ἐξῆλθεν ἡ φήμη αὕτη εἰς ὅλην τὴν γῆν ἐκείνην.

26. Kai exeilthen 'ei pheimei 'autei eis 'olein tein gein ekeinein.

Hebrew/Transliteration
כו. וְהַשְּׁמֻעָה הַזֹּאת יָצְאָה בְּכָל-הָאָרֶץ הַהִיא:

26. Ve•hash•moo•ah ha•zot yatz•ah be•chol - ha•a•retz ha•hee.

---

27. And when Jesus departed thence, two blind men followed him, crying, and saying, Thou Son of David, have mercy on us.

Greek/Transliteration
27. Καὶ παράγοντι ἐκεῖθεν τῷ Ἰησοῦ, ἠκολούθησαν αὐτῷ δύο τυφλοί, κράζοντες καὶ λέγοντες, Ἐλέησον ἡμᾶς, υἱὲ Δαυίδ.

27. Kai paragonti ekeithen to Yeisou, eikoloutheisan auto duo tuphloi, krazontes kai legontes, Eleeison 'eimas, 'wie Dauid.

Hebrew/Transliteration
כז. וַיַּעֲבֹר יֵשׁוּעַ מִשָּׁם וּשְׁנֵי אֲנָשִׁים עִוְרִים הָלְכוּ אַחֲרָיו צֹעֲקִים וְקֹרְאִים חָנֵּנוּ בֶּן-דָּוִד:

27. Va•ya•a•vor Yeshua mi•sham oosh•ney a•na•shim eev•rim hal•choo a•cha•rav tzo•a•kim ve•kor•eem cha•ne•noo Ben - David.

Jewish New Testament Commentary
By shouting, "Son of David!" the blind men were publicly acclaiming Yeshua as the Messiah.

---

28. And when he was come into the house, the blind men came to him: and Jesus saith unto them, Believe ye that I am able to do this? They said unto him, Yea, Lord.

Greek/Transliteratioin
28. Ἐλθόντι δὲ εἰς τὴν οἰκίαν, προσῆλθον αὐτῷ οἱ τυφλοί, καὶ λέγει αὐτοῖς ὁ Ἰησοῦς, Πιστεύετε ὅτι δύναμαι τοῦτο ποιῆσαι; Λέγουσιν αὐτῷ, Ναί, κύριε.

28. Elthonti de eis tein oikian, proseilthon auto 'oi tuphloi, kai legei autois 'o Yeisous, Pisteuete 'oti dunamai touto poieisai? Legousin auto, Nai, kurie.

Hebrew/Transliteration
כח. וּכְבֹאוֹ אֶל-הַבַּיִת וַיִּגְּשׁוּ לְפָנָיו הָעִוְרִים וַיֹּאמֶר יֵשׁוּעַ אֲלֵיהֶם הֲתַאֲמִינוּ כִּי יֶשׁ-לְאֵל יָדִי לַעֲשׂוֹת כָּזֹאת וַיַּעֲנוּ:אֹתוֹ הֵן אֲדֹנֵינוּ

28. Ooch•vo•o el - ha•ba•yit va•yig•shoo le•fa•nav ha•eev•rim va•yo•mer Yeshua aley•hem ha•ta•a•mi•noo ki yesh - le•el ya•di la•a•sot ka•zot va•ya•a•noo o•to hen Ado•ney•noo.

---

29. Then touched he their eyes, saying, According to your faith be it unto you.

Greek/Transliteration
29. Τότε ἥψατο τῶν ὀφθαλμῶν αὐτῶν, λέγων, Κατὰ τὴν πίστιν ὑμῶν γενηθήτω ὑμῖν.

29. Tote 'eipsato ton ophthalmon auton, legon, Kata tein pistin 'umon geneitheito 'umin.

Hebrew/Transliteration
כט. וַיִּגַּע בְּעֵינֵיהֶם וַיֹּאמַר כֶּאֱמוּנַתְכֶם כֵּן יָקוּם לָכֶם:

29. Va•yi•ga be•ey•ne•hem va•yo•mar ke•e•moo•nat•chem ken ya•koom la•chem.

---

30. And their eyes were opened; and Jesus straitly charged them, saying, See that no man know it.

Greek/Transliteration
30. Καὶ ἀνεῴχθησαν αὐτῶν οἱ ὀφθαλμοί· καὶ ἐνεβριμήσατο αὐτοῖς ὁ Ἰησοῦς, λέγων, Ὁρᾶτε μηδεὶς γινωσκέτω.

30. Kai aneochtheisan auton 'oi ophthalmoi. kai enebrimeisato autois 'o Yeisous, legon, 'Orate meideis ginosketo.

Hebrew/Transliteration
ל. וַתִּפָּקַחְנָה עֵינֵיהֶם וַיָּעַד בָּם יֵשׁוּעַ לֵאמֹר רְאוּ לְבִלְתִּי יִוָּדַע הַדָּבָר לְאִישׁ:

30. Va•ti•pa•kach•na ey•ne•hem va•ya•ad bam Yeshua le•mor r`oo le•vil•ti yi•va•da ha•da•var le•eesh.

---

31. But they, when they were departed, spread abroad his fame in all that country.

Greek/Transliteration
31. Οἱ δὲ ἐξελθόντες διεφήμισαν αὐτὸν ἐν ὅλῃ τῇ γῇ ἐκείνῃ.

31. 'Oi de exelthontes diepheimisan auton en 'olei tei gei ekeinei.

Hebrew/Transliteration
לא. וְהֵם יָצְאוּ וַיֹּצִיאוּ אֶת-שָׁמְעוֹ בְּכָל-הָאָרֶץ הַהִיא:

31. Ve•hem yatz•oo va•yo•tzi•oo et - shim•oh be•chol - ha•a•retz ha•hee.

---

32. As they went out, behold, they brought to him a dumb man possessed with a devil.

Greek/Transliteration
32. Αὐτῶν δὲ ἐξερχομένων, ἰδού, προσήνεγκαν αὐτῷ ἄνθρωπον κωφὸν δαιμονιζόμενον.

32. Auton de exerchomenon, idou, proseinegkan auto anthropon kophon daimonizomenon.

Hebrew/Transliteration
לב. אַךְ הֵם יֹצְאִים וְאִישׁ אִלֵּם הוּבָא לְפָנָיו אֲשֶׁר רוּחַ רָע דָּבַק בּוֹ:

32. Ach hem yotz•eem ve••eesh ee•lem hoo•va le•fa•nav asher roo•ach ra da•vak bo.

Rabbinic Jewish Commentary
Behold, they brought to him a dumb man possessed with a devil. The word signifies one that is deaf, as well as dumb; as does the Hebrew word חרש, often used by the Jewish writers for a deaf and dumb man; one, they say (g), that can neither hear nor speak, and is unfit for sacrifice, and excused many things: and indeed these two, deafness and dumbness, always go together in persons, who are deaf from their birth; for as they cannot hear, they cannot learn to speak: but this man seems to be dumb, not by nature, but through the possession of Satan, who had taken away, or restrained the use of his speech, out of pure malice and ill will, that he might not have the benefit of conversation with men, nor be able to say anything to the glory of God.

(g) Maimon. & Bartenora in Misn. Trumot, c. 1. sect. 2. T. Bab. Chagiga, fol. 2. 2.

---

33. And when the devil was cast out, the dumb spake: and the multitudes marvelled, saying, It was never so seen in Israel.

Greek/Transliteration
33. Καὶ ἐκβληθέντος τοῦ δαιμονίου, ἐλάλησεν ὁ κωφός· καὶ ἐθαύμασαν οἱ ὄχλοι, λέγοντες, Οὐδέποτε ἐφάνη οὕτως ἐν τῷ Ἰσραήλ.

33. Kai ekbleithentos tou daimoniou, elaleisen 'o kophos. kai ethaumasan 'oi ochloi, legontes, Oudepote ephanei 'outos en to Ysraeil.

Hebrew/Transliteration
לג. וַיְגָרֶשׁ אֶת־הָרוּחַ הָרָע מִמֶּנּוּ וְהָאִלֵּם הֵחֵל לְדַבֵּר וַיִּתְמְהוּ הֲמוֹן הָעָם וַיֹּאמְרוּ מֵעוֹלָם לֹא־נִרְאֲתָה כָּזֹאת בְּיִשְׂרָאֵל:

33. Va•y`ga•resh et - ha•roo•ach ha•ra mi•me•noo ve•ha•ee•lem he`chel le•da•ber va•yit•me•hoo ha•mon ha•am va•yom•roo me•o•lam lo - nir•a•ta cha•zot be•Israel.

Rabbinic Jewish Commentary
In Beza's most ancient manuscript, and in some others, this whole verse is not present; and were it not, for the general consent of copies, one should be tempted to think these words were not said at this time, because Christ returns no answer to them; and what is observed by Luk_11:15 as following this miracle, is the selfsame as was spoken by Christ in Mat_12:24 and where this passage is more thoroughly considered.

34. But the Pharisees said, He casteth out devils through the prince of the devils.

Greek/Transliteration
34. Οἱ δὲ Φαρισαῖοι ἔλεγον, Ἐν τῷ ἄρχοντι τῶν δαιμονίων ἐκβάλλει τὰ δαιμόνια.

34. 'Oi de Pharisaioi elegon, En to archonti ton daimonion ekballei ta daimonya.

Hebrew/Transliteration
לד. אֶפֶס הַפְּרוּשִׁים אָמְרוּ עַל-יְדֵי שַׂר-הַשֵּׁדִים הוּא מְגָרֵשׁ אֶת-הַשֵּׁדִים:

34. E•fes ha•P`roo•shim am•roo al - ye•dey sar - ha•she•dim hoo me•ga•resh et - ha•she•dim.

---

35. And Jesus went about all the cities and villages, teaching in their synagogues, and preaching the gospel of the kingdom, and healing every sickness and every disease among the people.

Greek/Transliteration
35. Καὶ περιῆγεν ὁ Ἰησοῦς τὰς πόλεις πάσας καὶ τὰς κώμας, διδάσκων ἐν ταῖς συναγωγαῖς αὐτῶν, καὶ κηρύσσων τὸ εὐαγγέλιον τῆς βασιλείας, καὶ θεραπεύων πᾶσαν νόσον καὶ πᾶσαν μαλακίαν ἐν τῷ λαῷ.

35. Kai perieigen 'o Yeisous tas poleis pasas kai tas komas, didaskon en tais sunagogais auton, kai keirusson to euangelion teis basileias, kai therapeuon pasan noson kai pasan malakian en to lao.

Hebrew/Transliteration
לה. וַיָּסָב יֵשׁוּעַ בְּכָל-הֶעָרִים וְהַכְּפָרִים וַיּוֹרֶה לָהֶם בְּבָתֵּי הַכְּנֶסֶת מְבַשֵּׂר בְּשׂוֹרַת הַמַּלְכוּת וְרֹפֵא כָל-מַחֲלָה וְכָל-מַדְוֶה בָּעָם:

35. Va•ya•sav Yeshua be•chol - he•a•rim ve•hak•fa•rim va•yo•re la•hem be•va•tey ha•k`ne•set me•va•ser be•so•rat ha•mal•choot ve•ro•fe chol - ma•cha•la ve•chol - mad•ve ba•am.

Rabbinic Jewish Commentary
Teaching in their synagogues; which were places of public worship, where prayer was made, the law and the prophets were read, and a word of exhortation given to the people; and which, it seems, were in villages, as well as in cities and towns: and indeed it is a rule with the Jews (h), that

"in what place soever there are ten Israelites, they ought to build a house, to which they may go to prayer, at all times of prayer; and such a place is called בית הכנסת, "a synagogue"."

And hence we often read of (i) בית הכנסת של כפרים, "the synagogue of villages", as distinct from the synagogues of cities and walled towns; which confutes a notion of the learned Dr. Lightfoot (k), who thought there were no synagogues in villages. Now, wherever Yeshua found any of these, he entered into them, and taught the people publicly,

(h) Maimon Hilchot Tephilla, c. 11. sect. 1. (i) T. Bab. Megilla. fol. 26. 1. & Gloss. in ib. Maimon. & Bartenora in Misn. Megilla, c. 3. sect. 1. & Maimon. Hilch. Tephilla, c. 11. sect. 16. (k) In Mark i. 38. & Chorograph. ad Matt. c. 98

---

36. But when he saw the multitudes, he was moved with compassion on them, because they fainted, and were scattered abroad, as sheep having no shepherd.

Greek/Transliteration
36. Ἰδὼν δὲ τοὺς ὄχλους, ἐσπλαγχνίσθη περὶ αὐτῶν, ὅτι ἦσαν ἐσκυλμένοι καὶ ἐρριμμένοι ὡσεὶ πρόβατα μὴ ἔχοντα ποιμένα.

36. Idon de tous ochlous, esplagchnisthei peri auton, 'oti eisan eskulmenoi kai errimmenoi 'osei probata mei echonta poimena.

Hebrew/Transliteration
לו. וְכַאֲשֶׁר רָאָה אֶת-הַהֲמֹנִים נִכְמְרוּ רַחֲמָיו עֲלֵיהֶם כִּי הֵם מִתְעַלְּפִים וּנְפֹצִים כַּצֹּאן אֲשֶׁר אֵין-לָהֶם רֹעֶה:

36. Ve•cha•a•sher ra•ah et - ha•ha•mo•nim nich•me•roo ra•cha•mav aley•hem ki hem mit•al•fim oon•fo•tzim ka•tzon asher eyn - la•hem ro•eh.

---

37. Then saith he unto his disciples, The harvest truly is plenteous, but the labourers are few;

Greek/Transliteration
37. Τότε λέγει τοῖς μαθηταῖς αὐτοῦ, Ὁ μὲν θερισμὸς πολύς, οἱ δὲ ἐργάται ὀλίγοι·

37. Tote legei tois matheitais autou, 'O men therismos polus, 'oi de ergatai oligoi.

Hebrew/Transliteraiton
לז. וַיֹּאמֶר אֶל-תַּלְמִידָיו אוּלָם הַקָּצִיר רַב וְהַפֹּעֲלִים מְעַטִּים:

37. Va•yo•mer el - tal•mi•dav oo•lam ha•ka•tzir rav ve•ha•po•a•lim me•a•tim.

38. Pray ye therefore the Lord of the harvest, that he will send forth labourers into his harvest.

Greek/Transliteration
38. δεήθητε οὖν τοῦ κυρίου τοῦ θερισμοῦ, ὅπως ἐκβάλῃ ἐργάτας εἰς τὸν θερισμὸν αὐτοῦ.

38. deeitheite oun tou kuriou tou therismou, 'opos ekbalei ergatas eis ton therismon autou.

Hebrew/Transliteration
לח. עַל-כֵּן הַעְתִּירוּ אֶל-אֲדוֹן הַקָּצִיר לִשְׁלֹחַ פֹּעֲלִים לִקְצִירוֹ:

38. Al - ken ha•a•ti•roo el - Adon ha•ka•tzir lish•lo•ach po•a•lim lik•tzi•ro.

Matthew, Chapter 10

1. And when he had called unto him his twelve disciples, he gave them power against unclean spirits, to cast them out, and to heal all manner of sickness and all manner of disease.

Greek/Transliteration
1. Καὶ προσκαλεσάμενος τοὺς δώδεκα μαθητὰς αὐτοῦ, ἔδωκεν αὐτοῖς ἐξουσίαν πνευμάτων ἀκαθάρτων, ὥστε ἐκβάλλειν αὐτά, καὶ θεραπεύειν πᾶσαν νόσον καὶ πᾶσαν μαλακίαν.

1. Kai proskalesamenos tous dodeka matheitas autou, edoken autois exousian pneumaton akatharton, 'oste ekballein auta, kai therapeuein pasan noson kai pasan malakian.

Hebrew/Transliteration
א. וַיִּקְרָא אֵלָיו שְׁנֵים עָשָׂר תַּלְמִידָיו וַיִּתֵּן בְּיָדָם כֹּחַ עַל-רוּחוֹת הַטֻּמְאָה לְגָרְשָׁן וְלִרְפֹּא כָּל-מַחֲלָה וְכָל-מַדְוֶה:

1. Va•yik•ra elav sh`neym asar tal•mi•dav va•yi•ten be•ya•dam ko•ach al - roo•chot ha•toom•ah le•gar•shan ve•lir•po kol - ma•cha•la ve•chol - mad•ve.

Rabbinic Jewish Commentary
he gave them power against unclean spirits, to cast them out; or "over all devils", as Luk_9:1. It was usual with the Jews to call a demon or devil רוח טומאה, "an unclean spirit"; especially such as frequented burying places: so in one place (l), an unclean spirit is interpreted, רוח שדים, "the spirit of the demons", or devils; and in another (m) place, שד בית הקברות, "the demon of the graves"

(l) T. Bab. Chagiga, fol. 3. 2. (m) T. Bab. Sanhedrim, fol. 65. 2.

---

2. Now the names of the twelve apostles are these; The first, Simon, who is called Peter, and Andrew his brother; James the son of Zebedee, and John his brother;

Greek/Transliteration
2. Τῶν δὲ δώδεκα ἀποστόλων τὰ ὀνόματά ἐστιν ταῦτα· πρῶτος Σίμων ὁ λεγόμενος Πέτρος, καὶ Ἀνδρέας ὁ ἀδελφὸς αὐτοῦ· Ἰάκωβος ὁ τοῦ Ζεβεδαίου, καὶ Ἰωάννης ὁ ἀδελφὸς αὐτοῦ·

2. Ton de dodeka apostolon ta onomata estin tauta. protos Simon 'o legomenos Petros, kai Andreas 'o adelphos autou. Yakobos 'o tou Zebedaiou, kai Yoanneis 'o adelphos autou.

Hebrew/Transliteration
ב. וְאֵלֶּה שְׁמוֹת שְׁנֵים עָשָׂר הַשְּׁלִיחִים הָרִאשׁוֹן שִׁמְעוֹן הַמְכֻנֶּה פֶּטְרוֹס וְאַנְדְּרַי אָחִיו יַעֲקֹב בֶּן-זַבְדִּי וִיוֹחָנָן אָחִיו:

2. Ve•e•le sh`mot sh`neym asar ha•sh`li•chim ha•ri•shon Shimon ham•choo•ne Fetros ve•Ande•rai a•chiv Yaakov ben - Zav•di ve•Yo•cha•nan a•chiv.

Rabbinic Jewish Commentary

This is the first time these disciples are called "apostles", they were learners before; now being instructed, they are sent forth to preach publicly, and therefore are called apostles, or messengers, persons that were sent: so the elders of the priesthood are called שלוחי בית דין, "the apostles", or sent out ones "of the sanhedrim" (n), to whom the high priest were delivered, before the day of atonement. So six months in the year, שלוחים, "apostles", or sent out ones, were sent by the (o) sanhedrim, throughout all the land of Israel, and to the captive Jews in other parts, to give notice of the new moon; in allusion to which, the disciples might be so called. It was proper to give the names of them, for the truth of the history, and confirmation of it; for the sake of the persons themselves, and the honour done them; and for the exclusion and detection of false apostles.

The first, Simon, who is called Peter; his pure Hebrew name was שמעון, Simeon, as he is called, Act_15:14 but in the then Jerusalem dialect, and in Rabbinical language, this name is frequently read and pronounced סימון, "Simon", as here: we often read of R. Simon, and of R. Juda bar Simon, in both Talmuds (p).

(n) Misn. Yoma, c. 1. sect. 5. (o) Misn. Roshhashana, c. 1. sect. 3. & Maimon. & Bartenora in ib. (p) T. Hieros. Shekalim, fol. 46. 4. Bab. Sabbath, fol. 55. 1. & Bava Kama, fol. 47. 2.

---

3. Philip, and Bartholomew; Thomas, and Matthew the publican; James the son of Alphaeus, and Lebbaeus, whose surname was Thaddaeus;

Greek/Transliteration
3. Φίλιππος, καὶ Βαρθολομαῖος· Θωμᾶς, καὶ Ματθαῖος ὁ τελώνης· Ἰάκωβος ὁ τοῦ Ἀλφαίου, καὶ Λεββαῖος ὁ ἐπικληθεὶς Θαδδαῖος·

3. Philippos, kai Bartholomaios. Thomas, kai Matthaios 'o teloneis. Yakobos 'o tou Alphaiou, kai Lebbaios 'o epikleitheis Thaddaios.

Hebrew/Transliteration
:ג. פִּילִפּוֹס וּבַר-תַּלְמַי תּוֹמָא וּמַתִּתְיָהוּ הַמּוֹכֵס יַעֲקֹב בֶּן-חַלְפַּי וְלַבַּי הַמְכֻנֶּה תַדָּי

3. Pi•li•pos oo•Var - Talmai Toma oo•Ma•tit•ya•hoo ha•mo•ches Yaakov ben – Chalpai ve•Labai ham•choo•ne Tadai.

Rabbinic Jewish Commentary

Philip and Bartholomew,.... The first of these was called next; his name is a Greek one, which his parents, though Jews, might take from the Greeks that dwelt among them, see Joh_12:20 mention is made of one R. Phelipi, and Phulipa, in the Jewish writings (q). The latter of these, Bartholomew, is conjectured, by Dr. Lightfoot, to be the same with Nathanael, he being called next in order after Philip; and that his name was Nathanael, בר תלמי, "Bar Talmai", or "the son of Talmai", or "Ptolomy": a name once common to the kings of Egypt: so Talmai, king of Geshur, is by the Septuagint, in 2Sa_3:3 2Sa_13:37 called Tholmi, and in 1Ch_3:2 Tholmai: hence it appears, that Bartholomew is no other than Bartholmi, or the son of Tholmi. We read of one R. Jonathan, בן אבטולמוס, "ben Abtolemus", in the Talmud (r), whether the same name with this, may be considered.

Thomas, and Matthew the publican: by the other evangelists Matthew is mentioned first; but he being the writer of this Gospel, puts Thomas first, which is an instance of his modesty; and also calls himself the "publican", which the other do not: this he mentions, to magnify the grace of God in his vocation. The Jews (s) speak of מתאי, "Matthai", or "Matthew", as a disciple of Yeshua. Thomas was sometimes called Didymus; the one was his Hebrew, the other his Greek name, and both signify a "twin", as it is very likely he was: mention is made of R. Thoma, or Thomas bar Papias, in a Jewish writer (t). Next follow,

James the son of Alphaeus, and Lebbaeus, whose surname was Thaddaeus: the former of these is so called, to distinguish him from James, the son of Zebedee. This is the James, who was the brother of Yeshua, Gal_1:19 and is called "James the less", Mar_15:40. Alphaeus his father, is the same with Cleopas, Luk_24:18 or Cleophas, Joh_19:25. The Hebrew name, חלפי, which often occurs among the Jews (u), may be pronounced either Chlophi, or Alphi, or with the Greek termination Cleopas, or Alphaeus. The latter of this pair of apostles is the same person with Jude, the writer of the epistle, which bears that name, and was the brother of James, with whom he is coupled: he was called Lebbaeus, either from the town of Lebba, a sea coast town of Galilee, as Dr. Lightfoot thinks; or from the Hebrew word לבי, "my heart", as others, either for his prudence, or through the affections of his parents to him; as the Latins call one they love, "meum corculum", "my little heart"; or from לביא, "a lion", that being the motto of the tribe of Judah. His surname Thaddaeus, is thought by some to be a deflexion of Jude; or Judas, and as coming from the same root, ידה, which signifies "to praise", or "give thanks"; or from the Syriac word, תד, "a breast", and may be so called for the same reason as he was Lebbaeus. Frequent mention is made of this name, תדיא, "Thaddai", or "Thaddaeus", among the Talmudic (w) Rabbi's. The Jews themselves speak (x) of one תודה, "Thodah", as a disciple of Yeshua, by whom no doubt they mean this same disciple. Eusebius (y) mentions one Thaddaeus, as one of the seventy disciples, who was sent to Agbarus, king of Edessa, who was healed and converted by him. This Agbarus is reported to have wrote a letter to Yeshua Messiah, desiring him to come and cure him of his disease; to which Yeshua is said to return an answer, promising to send one of his disciples, who should do it; and that accordingly, after Yeshua's death, Thomas sent this Thaddaeus to him.

(q) Massechet Sopherim, c. 21. sect. 7. Bereshit Rabba, sect. 71. fol. 63. 4. (r) T. Bab. Nidda, fol. 19. 1. (s) T. Bab. Sanhedrim, fol. 43. 1. (t) Juchasin, fol. 105. 2. (u) Echa Rabbati, fol. 58. 4. Midrash Kohelet, fol. 60. 4. Juchasin, fol. 92. 1. (w) T. Hieros. Celaim, fol. 27. 2. Sabbat, fol. 6. 1. Erubim, fol. 23. 3. Bab. Sabbat, fol. 123. 1. & Erubim, fol. 71. 2. Juchasin, fol. 81. 1. & 105. 2. & 108. 1. (x) T. Bab. Sanhedrim, fol. 43. l. (y) Eccl. Hist. l. 1. c. 12, 13.

4. Simon the Canaanite, and Judas Iscariot, who also betrayed him.

Greek/Transliteration
4. Σίμων ὁ Κανανίτης, καὶ Ἰούδας Ἰσκαριώτης ὁ καὶ παραδοὺς αὐτόν.

4. Simon 'o Kananiteis, kai Youdas Yskarioteis 'o kai paradous auton.

Hebrew/Transliteration
ד. שִׁמְעוֹן הַכְּנַעֲנִי וִיהוּדָה אִישׁ-קְרִיּוֹת הוּא הַמַּסְגִּיר אֹתוֹ:

4. Shimon haK`na•a•ni vi•Y`hoo•da Eesh - K`ri•yot hoo ha•mas•gir o•to.

Rabbinic Jewish Commentary
Simon the Canaanite, and Judas Iscariot,.... This is the last couple, for they are all mentioned by pairs, because they were sent forth "by two and two", as the Evangelist Mark says, Mar_6:7. The former of these is called Simon the Canaanite, to distinguish him from Simon Peter, before mentioned; not that he was a Canaanite, that is, an inhabitant of the land of Canaan, a man of Canaan, as a certain woman is called a woman of Canaan, Mat_15:22 for all the disciples of Christ were Jews; though in Munster's Hebrew Gospel he is called שמעון הכנעני, "Simeon the Canaanite", or of Canaan, as if he belonged to that country; nor is he so called from Cana of Galilee, as Jerorm and others have thought; but he was one of the קנאים, "Kanaim", or "Zealots"; and therefore Luke styles him, "Simon called Zelotes", Luk_6:15. The Kanaites, or Zelotes, were a set of men, who, in imitation of Phinehas, who slew Zimri and Cozbi in the very act of uncleanness, when they found any persons in the act of adultery, idolatry, blasphemy, or theft, would immediately kill them without any more ado: this they did, from a pretended zeal for the honour and glory of God: nor were they accountable to any court of judicature for it; yea, such an action was highly applauded, as a very laudable one (z): under this specious name of Zealots, innumerable murders, and most horrible wickedness were committed, both before, and during the siege of Jerusalem, as Josephus (a) relates. Now Simon was one of this sect before his conversion, and still retained the name afterwards. Judas, the last of the twelve, is called Iscariot; concerning which name, the notation of it, and the reason of his being so called, many are the conjectures of learned men: some think that he belonged to the tribe of Issachar, and that he is called from thence, איש יששכר, "a man of Issachar", as a certain man is, in Jdg_10:1 others, that he takes his name from the place he belonged to, and that he was called איש קריות, "a man of Kerioth". A place of this name is mentioned, Jos_15:25 and some manuscripts and copies in some places read Judas απο Καρυωτου, of "Caryot". Caryota is said (b) to be a plain of the city of Jericho, about eighteen miles from Jerusalem, which abounded in palm trees, called קורייטי, "Caryotae", of which mention is made in the (c) Talmud, and other writers (d). Others think he is so called, from the Syriac word, סכריוטא, "secariota", which signifies a "purse", or bag, because he carried the bag. Some copies read it, σκαριωτες, "scariotes": others are of opinion, that he is so called, from the manner of death he died, which was strangling: for אסכרא, "ascara", a word often used in the (e) Talmudic writings, signifies "strangling"; and is accounted by the Jews the hardest of deaths, and an evil one; and which seems to bid fair for the true reason

of his name: however, it is mentioned here, as elsewhere, to distinguish him from Jude, or Judas, the true and faithful follower of Yeshua.

(z) Misn. Sanhedrim, c. 9. sect. 6. & Bartenora, in ib. T. Avoda Zara, fol. 36. 2. Maimon. Issure Bia, c. 12. sect. 4, 5, 6. 14. & Sanhedrim, c. 18. sect. 6. & Obede Cochabim, c. 2. sect. 9. Philo de Monarchia, l. 1. p. 818. (a) De Bello Jud. l. 5. c. 1, 2. & 6. 1. Vid. Abot R. Nathan, c. 6. fol. 3. 2. (b) Vid. Wolfi Heb. Bibl. p. 410. (c) T. Bab. Beracot, fol. 50. 2. & Avoda Zara, fol. 14. 2. (d) Plin. Nat. Hist. l. 13. c. 4. (e) T. Bab. Beracot, fol. 8. 1. & Sabbat, fol. 33. 1. Sota, fol. 35. 1. Pesachim, fol. 105. 1. Taanith, fol. 19. 2. & 27. 2. Yebamot, fol. 62. 2.

---

5. These twelve Jesus sent forth, and commanded them, saying, Go not into the way of the Gentiles, and into any city of the Samaritans enter ye not:

Greek/Transliteration
5. Τούτους τοὺς δώδεκα ἀπέστειλεν ὁ Ἰησοῦς, παραγγείλας αὐτοῖς, λέγων, Εἰς ὁδὸν ἐθνῶν μὴ ἀπέλθητε, καὶ εἰς πόλιν Σαμαρειτῶν μὴ εἰσέλθητε·

5. Toutous tous dodeka apesteilen 'o Yeisous, parangeilas autois, legon, Eis 'odon ethnon mei apeltheite, kai eis polin Samareiton mei eiseltheite.

Hebrew/Transliteration
ה. אֶת-שְׁנֵים עָשָׂר הָאֵלֶּה שָׁלַח יֵשׁוּעַ וַיְצַו עֲלֵיהֶם לֵאמֹר אַל-תָּשִׂימוּ לְדֶרֶךְ הַגּוֹיִם פַּעֲמֵיכֶם וְאֶל-עָרֵי הַשֹּׁמְרֹנִים:אַל-תָּבֹאוּ

5. Et - sh`neym asar ha•e•le sha•lach Yeshua vay•tzav aley•hem le•mor al - ta•si•moo le•de•rech ha•go•yim pa•a•mey•chem ve•el - arey ha•Shom•ro•nim al - ta•vo•oo.

Rabbinic/Jewish New Testament Commentary
Goyim, "Gentiles" (see Mat_5:47). In some Jewish circles today "Gentile" and "Christian" are regarded as interchangeable terms, but this is a mistake, confusing one's people with one's religion. The word "Gentile" means only "non-Jew"; it does not mean "Christian." A member of the Jewish people, a Jew, can opt for a form of non-Messianic Judaism (e.g., Orthodox, Conservative, Reform), or for Messianic Judaism, or for some other religion or none. Likewise a Gentile can decide to follow a form of non-Messianic Judaism and become a proselyte; or he can become a Christian in the same way a Jew becomes Messianic, namely, by putting his trust in God and in his son Yeshua the Messiah; or he can follow another religion or none. Because the religion of Judaism implies membership in the Jewish people, a Gentile who becomes a Jew by religion also becomes a member of the Jewish people, and his children will be Jews. Because Messianic faith-Gentile Christianity and Messianic Judaism-is transcultural and can be held by members of any people, a Jew who becomes a follower of Yeshua remains a member of the Jewish people and does not become a Gentile.

There was a very great hatred subsisting between the Jews, and the Samaritans, insomuch that they had no conversation with each other in things civil or religious. The Samaritans, though they boasted of their descent from Jacob, were a mongrel sort of people, partly Jews, and partly Gentiles, a mixture of both; and therefore are distinguished from both and though they had, and held the law, and five books of Moses, yet corrupted them in many places, to serve their purpose, and countenance their religion, particularly their worshipping at Mount Gerizim; on which account they were looked upon by the Jews as apostates, idolaters, and even as Heathens (f), and are therefore here joined with them; and to shun giving offence to the Jews, seems to be the reason of this prohibition; see Gill on Joh_4:20.

(f) T. Hieros. Shekelim, fol. 46. 2. Bartenora in Misn. Taharot, c. 5. sect. 8.

---

6. But go rather to the lost sheep of the house of Israel.

Greek/Transliteration
6. πορεύεσθε δὲ μᾶλλον πρὸς τὰ πρόβατα τὰ ἀπολωλότα οἴκου Ἰσραήλ.

6. poreuesthe de mallon pros ta probata ta apololota oikou Ysraeil.

Hebrew/Transliteration
‏:ו. כִּי אִם-לְצֹאן אֹבְדוֹת מִבֵּית יִשְׂרָאֵל תֵּלֵכוּ

6. Ki eem - le•tzon ov•dot mi•beit Israel te•le•choo.

Rabbinic Jewish Commentary
By "the house of Israel" is meant the whole Jewish nation; for though this phrase, when distinguished from the house of Judah, designs only the ten tribes; yet here it intends all the Jews, then living in the land of Judea, among whom there were some of all the tribes: and by "the lost sheep" of this house, are meant either all the people of the Jews in general, who were wandering, and were lost in error and sin, and to whom the external ministry of the Gospel came; or rather the elect of God among them, for whose sake particularly the apostles were sent unto them. These are called "sheep", because they were chosen of God, and given to Christ to be redeemed, looked up, sought out, and saved by him; and "lost" ones, not only because lost in Adam, and by their own transgressions, so that neither they themselves, nor any mere creature, could save them from eternal ruin and destruction; but also, because they were made to go astray, and were lost through the negligence and errors of their pastors, the Scribes and Pharisees: and this character is the rather given of them, partly to reflect upon the characters of the shepherds of Israel: and partly to magnify the grace of God, in having regard to such ruined and miserable creatures; and also to excite the compassion and diligence of the apostles, to preach the Gospel to them: respect seems to be had to Jer_1:16.

7. And as ye go, preach, saying, The kingdom of heaven is at hand.

Greek/Transliteration
7. Πορευόμενοι δὲ κηρύσσετε, λέγοντες ὅτι Ἤγγικεν ἡ βασιλεία τῶν οὐρανῶν.

7. Poreuomenoi de keirussete, legontes 'oti Eingiken 'ei basileia ton ouranon.

Hebrew/Transliteration
ז. וְכַאֲשֶׁר תֵּלְכוּן קִרְאוּ לֵאמֹר מַלְכוּת הַשָּׁמַיִם קְרוֹבָה לָבֹא:

7. Ve•cha•a•sher tel•choon kir•oo le•mor mal•choot ha•sha•ma•yim ke•ro•va la•vo.

Rabbinic Jewish Commentary
Preach, saying, the kingdom of heaven is at hand. This was to be the subject matter of their ministry, which they were to proclaim aloud in every place; and which is expressed in the same words with which John the Baptist, and Yeshua himself, began their ministry. The Kingdom represents the accountability and repentance of man or face the judgment of the King who has come.

Mat_3:2 which shows the entire harmony, and strict agreement, there were between them: for the meaning of the phrase.

---

8. Heal the sick, cleanse the lepers, raise the dead, cast out devils: freely ye have received, freely give.

Greek/Transliteration
8. Ἀσθενοῦντας θεραπεύετε, λεπροὺς καθαρίζετε, δαιμόνια ἐκβάλλετε· δωρεὰν ἐλάβετε, δωρεὰν δότε.

8. Asthenountas therapeuete, leprous katharizete, daimonya ekballete. dorean elabete, dorean dote.

Hebrew/Transliteration
ח. רִפְאוּ אֶת-הַחוֹלִים הָקִימוּ אֶת-הַמֵּתִים טַהֲרוּ אֶת-הַמְצֹרָעִים וְגָרְשׁוּ אֶת-הָרוּחוֹת הָרָעוֹת חִנָּם לְקַחְתֶּם:וְחִנָּם תִּתֵּנוּ

8. Rif•oo et - ha•cho•lim ha•ki•moo et - ha•me•tim ta•ha•roo et - ham•tzo•ra•eem ve•gar•shoo et - ha•roo•chot ha•ra•ot chi•nam le•kach•tem ve•chi•nam ti•te•noo.

Rabbinic/Jewish New Testament Commentary
You have received without paying, so give without asking payment. The Talmud gives the same advice:

"Rav Y'hudah said in the name of Rav: Scripture says, 'Behold, I have taught you [statutes and judgments]... ' (Deu_4:5). Just as I teach for free, so you should teach for free. Similarly it has been taught: The next words of this verse are, ' ... as *Adonai* my God commanded me.' This too implies: Just as I teach for free, so you should teach for free.

"Whence do we deduce that if it isn't possible to find someone who will teach gratuitously, one must pay to learn? A verse says, 'Buy the truth... ' (Pro_23:23). And whence do we deduce that one who has to pay in order to learn should not say, 'Since I had to pay to learn *Torah*, I will charge to teach it'? From the same text, which adds, '... and do not sell it.' " (Bekorot 29a)

Yeshua seems to have respect to a rule frequently learned by the Jews concerning teaching their oral law (g); which is this;

"in the place where they teach the written law for a reward, it is lawful to teach it for a reward; but it is forbidden to teach the oral law for a reward, as it is said, "behold, I have taught you statutes and judgments, even as the Lord my God commanded me". Deu_4:5. As I have בחנם, "freely" learned, and ye have also בחנם, "freely" learnt of me; so when ye learn posterity, למדו בחנם כמו שלמד־תאם ממני, "teach them freely, as ye have learnt of me".

(g) Maimon. Talmud Tora, c. 1. sect. 7. T. Bab. Nedarim, fol. 36. 2. & 37. 1. & Becorat, fol. 29. 1. Maimon. & Bartenora in Misn. Nedarim, c. 4. sect. 3. & in Pirke Abot. c. 4. sect. 5.

---

9. Provide neither gold, nor silver, nor brass in your purses,

Greek/Transliteration
9. Μὴ κτήσησθε χρυσόν, μηδὲ ἄργυρον, μηδὲ χαλκὸν εἰς τὰς ζώνας ὑμῶν,

9. Mei kteiseisthe chruson, meide arguron, meide chalkon eis tas zonas 'umon,

Hebrew/Transliteration
ט. אַל-תִּקְחוּ לָכֶם זָהָב אוֹ כֶסֶף אוֹ נְחֹשֶׁת בַּכִּיס:

9. Al - tik•choo la•chem za•hav oh che•sef oh n`cho•shet ba•kis.

Rabbinic Jewish Commentary
in your purses: or, as it may be rendered, "in", or "within your girdles"; in which travellers, among the Jews, used to carry their money; and who, in their travelling dress, might not go into the temple, and are thus described (h);

"a man may not go into the mountain of the house with his staff, or with his shoes on, nor בפונדתו, "with his girdle"."

The פונדא "phunda", Maimonides says (i), is an inner garment, wore to keep off sweat from other garments, to which were sewed hollow things like purses, in which a man put what he pleased; though other (k) interpreters say it is אזור חלול

שנותנין בו מעות, "a hollow girdle, in which they put their money": and so the Romans (l) had used to do; and so do the Turks (m) to this day; to which practice the allusion is here.

(h) Misn. Beracot, c. 9. sect. 5. (i) In ib. & Celim. c. 29. 1. & Sabbat, c. 10. 3. (k) Bartenora & Yom Tob in ib. Gloss in T. Bab. Beracot, fol. 62. 2. & in Sabbat. fol. 92. 1. & 113. 1. & 120. 1. & Nedarim, fol. 55. 2. (l) Gracchus apud A. Gell. Noct. Attic. 1. 15. c. 12. Sueton. in Vita Vitellii, c. 16. (m) Bobovius de Peregr. Meccan. p. 14.

---

10. Nor scrip for your journey, neither two coats, neither shoes, nor yet staves: for the workman is worthy of his meat.

Greek/Transliteration
10. μὴ πήραν εἰς ὁδόν, μηδὲ δύο χιτῶνας, μηδὲ ὑποδήματα, μηδὲ ῥάβδους· ἄξιος γὰρ ὁ ἐργάτης τῆς τροφῆς αὐτοῦ ἐστιν.

10. mei peiran eis 'odon, meide duo chitonas, meide 'upodeimata, meide 'rabdous. axios gar 'o ergateis teis tropheis autou estin.

Hebrew/Transliteration
י. וְלֹא יַלְקוּט לַדֶּרֶךְ וְלֹא חֲלִיפוֹת בְּגָדִים וְלֹא נַעֲלַיִם וְלֹא מַטֶּה כִּי-נָכוֹן לַפֹּעֵל דֵּי מִחְיָתוֹ:

10. Ve•lo yal•koot la•de•rech ve•lo cha•li•fot be•ga•dim ve•lo na•a•la•yim ve•lo ma•te ki - na•chon la•po•el dey mich•ya•to.

Rabbinic Jewish Commentary
This the Jews call תרמיל, "tarmil": and which their commentators (n) say, is a large leathern bag, in which shepherds and travellers put their food, and other things, and carried with them, hanging it about their necks; so that the disciples were neither to carry money with them, nor any provisions for their journey:

nor shoes, only sandals, as Mark says; for there was a difference between shoes and sandals, as appears from the case of the plucking off the shoe, when a man refused his brother's wife (o): if the "shoe" was plucked off it was regarded; but if the "sandal", it was not minded: this was the old tradition, though custom went against it. Sandals were made of harder leather than shoes (p), and sometimes of wood covered with leather, and stuck with nails, to make them more durable (q); though sometimes of bulrushes, and bark of palm trees, and of cork (r), which were light to walk with.

"Says R. Bar bar Chanah (s), I saw R. Eleazar of Nineveh go out on a fast day of the congregation, בסנדל שעם, "with a sandal of cork"."

(n) Maimon. & Bartenora in Misn. Sheviith, c. 2. sect. 8. & in Celim. c. 16. 4. & 24. 11. & Negaim. c. 11. sect. 11. (o) T. Hieros. Yebamot, fol. 12. 3. T. Bab. Yebamot, fol. 102. 1. & Menachot, fol. 32. 1. (p) Gloss. in T. Bab. Yebamot, fol.

101. 1. & Bartenora in Misn. Yebamot, c. 12. sect. 1. (q) Misn. Yebamot, c. 12. sect. 2. Maimon. Bartenora in Sabbat, c. 6. sect. 2. & Edayot, c. 2. sect. 8. (r) T. Bab. Yoma, fol. 78. 2. Gloss. in ib. Maimon. Hilch. Shebitat. Ashur, c. 3. sect. 7. (s) T. Bab. Yoma, fol. 78. 2. Juchasin, fol. 81. 1.

---

11. And into whatsoever city or town ye shall enter, inquire who in it is worthy; and there abide till ye go thence.

Greek/Transliteration

11. Εἰς ἣν δ᾽ ἂν πόλιν ἢ κώμην εἰσέλθητε, ἐξετάσατε τίς ἐν αὐτῇ ἄξιός ἐστιν· κἀκεῖ μείνατε, ἕως ἂν ἐξέλθητε.

11. Eis 'ein d an polin ei komein eiseltheite, exetasate tis en autei axios estin. kakei meinate, 'eos an exeltheite.

Hebrew/Transliteration

יא. וּבְכָל-עִיר אוֹ כְפָר אֲשֶׁר תָּבֹאוּ דִּרְשׁוּ מִי הוּא שָׁמָּה הַנִּכְבָּד וִישַׁבְתֶּם עִמּוֹ עַד כִּי-תַעֲבֹרוּן:

11. Oov•chol - eer oh che•far asher ta•vo•oo dir•shoo mee hoo sha•ma ha•nich•bad viy•shav•tem ee•mo ad ki - ta•a•vo•roon.

Rabbinic Jewish Commentary

Yeshua here speaks in the language of the masters of Israel; take an instance or two:

"saith R. Jona, blessed is the man that giveth to the poor; it is not written so, but "blessed is he that considereth the poor": he looks upon him, how he may לזכות עמו, "give alms to him"."

And a little after, ""God hath set one against the other", that when evil comes to thy friend, thou mayest see how לזכות בו, "to do thine alms to him", and nourish him, so that thou mayest receive the gift of its reward."

Again, so a man says to his neighbour, זכי בי, "give alms unto me": and afterwards, in the same place, it is said, זכי בההיא איתתא, "give alms unto that woman" (t). Now, it was such a worthy generous man, that was beneficent to the poor, and kind to strangers, that the apostles were to inquire out, wherever they came; and having found such a person, they were to continue with him:

(t) Vajikra Rabba, sect. 34. fol. 173. 3, 4. & 174. 4. Midrash Kohelet c. 11. 1. fol. 82. 2.

12. And when ye come into an house, salute it.

Greek/Transliteration
12. Εἰσερχόμενοι δὲ εἰς τὴν οἰκίαν, ἀσπάσασθε αὐτήν.

12. Eiserchomenoi de eis tein oikian, aspasasthe autein.

Hebrew/Transliteration
:יב. וּבְבֹאֲכֶם הַבַּיְתָה תִּפְקְדוּ לִשְׁלוֹם הַבָּיִת

12. Oo•ve•vo•a•chem ha•bai•ta tif•ke•doo lish•lom ha•ba•yit.

Jewish New Testament Commentary
The word "*shalom*" means not only "peace" but also tranquillity, safety, well-being, welfare, health, contentment, success, comfort, wholeness and integrity. "*Shalom aleikhem*" means "Peace be upon you" and is a common greeting, as is simply "*Shalom!*" Thus there is a deeper meaning to Yeshua's instruction in Mat_10:13 on when to give or withhold *shalom*, for he refers not only to the greeting but to the whole complex of peace/wholeness/well-being that the Messiah offers through his *talmidim*-and similarly at many places in the New Testament.

---

13. And if the house be worthy, let your peace come upon it: but if it be not worthy, let your peace return to you.

Greek/Transliteration
13. Καὶ ἐὰν μὲν ᾖ ἡ οἰκία ἀξία, ἐλθέτω ἡ εἰρήνη ὑμῶν ἐπ' αὐτήν· ἐὰν δὲ μὴ ᾖ ἀξία, ἡ εἰρήνη ὑμῶν πρὸς ὑμᾶς ἐπιστραφήτω.

13. Kai ean men ei 'ei oikia axia, eltheto 'ei eireinei 'umon ep autein. ean de mei ei axia, 'ei eireinei 'umon pros 'umas epistrapheito.

Hebrew/Transliteration
יג. אִם-נֶחְשָׁב הַבַּיִת מְאוּמָה יָחוֹל שְׁלוֹמְכֶם עָלָיו וְאִם לֹא-נֶחְשָׁב הַבַּיִת מְאוּמָה שְׁלוֹמְכֶם אֲלֵיכֶם יָשׁוּב:

13. Eem - nech•shav ha•ba•yit me•oo•ma ya•chool sh`lom•chem alav ve•eem lo - nech•shav ha•ba•yit me•oo•ma sh`lom•chem aley•chem ya•shoov.

---

14. And whosoever shall not receive you, nor hear your words, when ye depart out of that house or city, shake off the dust of your feet.

Greek/Transliteration
14. Καὶ ὃς ἐὰν μὴ δέξηται ὑμᾶς μηδὲ ἀκούσῃ τοὺς λόγους ὑμῶν, ἐξερχόμενοι τῆς οἰκίας ἢ τῆς πόλεως ἐκείνης, ἐκτινάξατε τὸν κονιορτὸν τῶν ποδῶν ὑμῶν.

14. Kai 'os ean mei dexeitai 'umas meide akousei tous logous 'umon, exerchomenoi teis oikias ei teis poleos ekeineis, ektinaxate ton koniorton ton podon 'umon.

Hebrew/Transliteration
יד. וְכָל-אִישׁ אֲשֶׁר לֹא-יֶאֱסֹף אֶתְכֶם וְלֹא יַקְשִׁיב לְדִבְרֵיכֶם צְאוּ לָכֶם מִן-הַבַּיִת הַהוּא אוֹ מִן-הָעִיר הַהִיא:וּנְעַרְתֶּם אֶת-הָאָבָק מֵעַל רַגְלֵיכֶם

14. Ve•chol - eesh asher lo - ye•e•sof et•chem ve•lo yak•shiv le•div•rey•chem tze•oo la•chem min - ha•ba•yit ha•hoo oh min - ha•eer ha•hee oon•ar•tem et - ha•a•vak me•al rag•ley•chem.

Rabbinic Jewish Commentary

There seems to be an allusion to some maxims and customs of the Jews, with respect to the dust of Heathen countries.

"On account of six doubts, they say (u), they burn the first offering, for a doubt of a field in which a grave might be, and for a doubt עפר הבא מארץ העמים, "of the dust which comes from the land of the Gentiles", &c."

On which Bartenora has this note; "all dust which comes from the land of the Gentiles, is reckoned by us as the rottenness of a dead carcass; and of these two, "the land of the Gentiles", and a field in which is a grave, it is decreed that they "defile" by touching, and by carrying."

Again (w), "the dust of a field in which is a grave, and the dust without the land (of Israel) which comes along with an herb, are unclean."

Upon which Maimonides makes this remark, "that the dust of a field that has a grave in it, and the dust which is without the land of Israel, defile by touching and carrying; or if, when it hangs at the end of an herb, when they root it out of the dust of such a field, it is unclean."

Hence they would not suffer herbs to be brought out of an Heathen country into the land of Israel, lest dust should be brought along with them.

"A Mishnic doctor teaches (x), that they do not bring herbs from without the land (of Israel into it), but our Rabbins permit it; what difference is there between them? Says R. Jeremiah, they take care of their dust; that is the difference between them."

On that clause, "they take care of their dust", the gloss is, "lest there should be brought with it מגוש ארץ העמים, "any of the dust of the land of the Gentiles", which defiles in the tent, and pollutes the purity of the land of Israel."

(u) Misn. Taharot, c. 4. sect. 5. Vid. c. 5. 1. & Maimon & Bartenora in ib. (w) Misn. Oholot. c. 17. sect. 5. (x) T. Bab. Sanhedrim, fol. 12. 1.

15. Verily I say unto you, It shall be more tolerable for the land of Sodom and Gomorrha in the day of judgment, than for that city.

Greek/Transliteration
15. Ἀμὴν λέγω ὑμῖν, ἀνεκτότερον ἔσται γῇ Σοδόμων καὶ Γομόρρων ἐν ἡμέρᾳ κρίσεως, ἢ τῇ πόλει ἐκείνῃ.

15. Amein lego 'umin, anektoteron estai gei Sodomon kai Gomorron en 'eimera kriseos, ei tei polei ekeinei.

Hebrew/Transliteration
טו. אָמֵן אֲנִי מַגִּיד לָכֶם נָקֵל יִהְיֶה יוֹם הַמִּשְׁפָּט לְאֶרֶץ סְדוֹם וַעֲמֹרָה מֵאֲשֶׁר לָעִיר הַזֹּאת:

15. Amen ani ma•gid la•chem na•kel yi•hee•ye yom ha•mish•pat le•e•retz S`dom va•A•mo•ra me•a•sher la•eer ha•zot.

Rabbinic Jewish Commentary
Jews made no doubt; for they say (y),
"the men of Sodom have no part in the world to come; as it is said, Gen_13:13 "the men of Sodom were wicked, and sinners, before the Lord exceedingly": they were "wicked" in this world, and "sinners" in the world to come;"

The time referred to, signified by "the day of judgment", respects not the destruction of Jerusalem, which was a very severe judgment on that people, but the general judgment, at the end of the world, which is appointed and fixed by God, though unknown to messengers and men. The phrase is Jewish, and often to be met with in their writings, who use it in the same sense; particularly in the book of Zohar (z), mention is made of יומא דדינא, "the day of judgment", when there will be no pollution in the sanctuary.

(y) Misn. Sanhedrim, c. 11. sect. 3. Hieros. Sanhedrim, fol. 29. 3. (z) In Gen. fol 13. 3. & 16. 1.

---

16. Behold, I send you forth as sheep in the midst of wolves: be ye therefore wise as serpents, and harmless as doves.

Greek/Transliteration
16. Ἰδού, ἐγὼ ἀποστέλλω ὑμᾶς ὡς πρόβατα ἐν μέσῳ λύκων· γίνεσθε οὖν φρόνιμοι ὡς οἱ ὄφεις, καὶ ἀκέραιοι ὡς αἱ περιστεραί.

16. Ydou, ego apostello 'umas 'os probata en meso lukon. ginesthe oun phronimoi 'os 'oi opheis, kai akeraioi 'os 'ai peristerai.

Hebrew/Transliteration
טז. הִנֵּה אָנֹכִי שֹׁלֵחַ אֶתְכֶם כְּצֹאן בְּקֶרֶב זְאֵבִים עַל-כֵּן הֱיוּ עֲרוּמִים כַּנְּחָשִׁים וּתְמִימִים כַּיּוֹנִים:

16. Hee•ne ano•chi sho•le•ach et•chem ke•tzon be•ke•rev ze•e•vim al - ken he•yoo a•roo•mim kan•cha•shim oot•mi•mim ka•yo•nim.

Rabbinic Jewish Commentary
be ye therefore wise as serpents, and harmless as doves. Much such an expression as this God is represented as saying of Israel (a):

"Says R. Judah, in the name of R. Simon, the holy blessed God said, concerning Israel, with me they are תמימים כיונים, "harmless as doves"; but among the nations of the world, they are ערומים כנחשים, "subtle as serpents"."

(a) Shirhashirim Rabba, c. 2. 14. fol. 12. 1.

---

17. But beware of men: for they will deliver you up to the councils, and they will scourge you in their synagogues;

Greek/Transliteration
17. Προσέχετε δὲ ἀπὸ τῶν ἀνθρώπων· παραδώσουσιν γὰρ ὑμᾶς εἰς συνέδρια, καὶ ἐν ταῖς συναγωγαῖς αὐτῶν μαστιγώσουσιν ὑμᾶς·

17. Prosechete de apo ton anthropon. paradosousin gar 'umas eis sunedrya, kai en tais sunagogais auton mastigosousin 'umas.

Hebrew/Transliteration
יז. רַק הִשָּׁמְרוּ לָכֶם מִפְּנֵי בְנֵי-אָדָם כִּי הֵם יַסְגִּירוּ אֶתְכֶם לִידֵי-הַסַּנְהֶדְרִין וְהִכִּיתֶם בַּשּׁוֹטִים בְּבָתֵּי הַכְּנֶסֶת:

17. Rak hi•sham•roo la•chem mip•ney v`ney - adam ki hem yas•gi•roo et•chem li•dey - ha•San•hed•rin ve•hoo•key•tem ba•sho•tim be•va•tey ha•k`ne•set.

Rabbinic Jewish Commentary
And they will scourge you in their synagogues; where the bench of three Judges kept their court; under whose cognizance were pecuniary judgments, and such as related to thefts, damages, restitutions, ravishing, and enticing of virgins, and defamation; also to plucking off of the shoe, and refusing a brother's wife, to the plant of the fourth year, second tithes whose price is unknown, holy things, and the estimations of goods; to these belonged also laying on of hands, the beheading of the heifer, among the rest, מכות בשלשה, "scourging was by the bench of three" (c)

(c) Misn. Sanhedrim, c. 1. sect. 1, 2, 3.

---

18. And ye shall be brought before governors and kings for my sake, for a testimony against them and the Gentiles.

Greek/Transliteration
18. καὶ ἐπὶ ἡγεμόνας δὲ καὶ βασιλεῖς ἀχθήσεσθε ἕνεκεν ἐμοῦ, εἰς μαρτύριον αὐτοῖς καὶ τοῖς ἔθνεσιν.

18. kai epi 'eigemonas de kai basileis achtheisesthe 'eneken emou, eis marturion autois kai tois ethnesin.

Hebrew/Transliteration
יח. וְלִפְנֵי מֹשְׁלִים וּמְלָכִים תּוּבָלוּ לְמַעֲנִי לִהְיוֹת לְעֵדוּת לָהֶם וְלַגּוֹיִם:

18. Ve•lif•ney mosh•lim oo•m`la•chim too•va•loo le•ma•a•ni li•hee•yot le•e•doot la•hem ve•la•go•yim.

TaNaKh-Old Testament
Psa_119:46, "I will also speak of your testimonies before kings, and I will not be put to shame."

Meaning Roman governors; so Paul was had before Gallio, Felix, and Festas; for judgments relating to life and death were to be taken away, and were taken away from the Jewish sanhedrim; and as they themselves say (f), forty years before the destruction of the second temple, which was much about the time of Yeshua's death.

(f) Hieros. Sanhedrim, fol. 18. 1. & 24. 2. Juchasin, fol. 26. 2. & 51. 1. Maimon. Hilch. Sanhedrim. c. 14. sect. 13.

---

19. But when they deliver you up, take no thought how or what ye shall speak: for it shall be given you in that same hour what ye shall speak.

Greek/Transliteration
19. Ὅταν δὲ παραδιδῶσιν ὑμᾶς, μὴ μεριμνήσητε πῶς ἢ τί λαλήσητε· δοθήσεται γὰρ ὑμῖν ἐν ἐκείνῃ τῇ ὥρᾳ τί λαλήσετε·

19. 'Otan de paradidosin 'umas, mei merimneiseite pos ei ti laleiseite. dotheisetai gar 'umin en ekeinei tei 'ora ti laleisete.

Hebrew/Transliteration
יט. וְכַאֲשֶׁר יַסְגִּירוּ אֶתְכֶם אַל-תֶּחֶרְדוּ לֵאמֹר אֵיכָה נְדַבֵּר אוֹ מַה-נְּדַבֵּר כִּי בְּעֶצֶם הָעֵת הַהִיא יוּשַׂם בְּפִיכֶם אֵת:אֲשֶׁר-תְּדַבֵּרוּן

19. Ve•cha•a•sher yas•gi•roo et•chem al - te•cher•doo le•mor ey•cha n`da•ber oh ma - n`da•ber ki be•e•tzem ha•et ha•hee yoo•sam be•fi•chem et asher - te•da•be•roon.

---

20. For it is not ye that speak, but the Spirit of your Father which speaketh in you.

Greek/Transliteration
20. οὐ γὰρ ὑμεῖς ἐστὲ οἱ λαλοῦντες, ἀλλὰ τὸ πνεῦμα τοῦ πατρὸς ὑμῶν τὸ λαλοῦν ἐν ὑμῖν.

20. ou gar 'umeis este 'oi laluntes, alla to pneuma tou patros 'umon to laloun en 'umin.

Hebrew/Transliteration
כ. כִּי לֹא אַתֶּם הֵם הַמְדַבְּרִים כִּי אִם רוּחַ-אֲבִיכֶם הַדֹּבֵר בָּכֶם:

20. Ki lo atem hem ha•m`dab•rim ki eem Roo•ach - Avi•chem ha•do•ver ba•chem.

---

21. And the brother shall deliver up the brother to death, and the father the child: and the children shall rise up against their parents, and cause them to be put to death.

Greek/Transliteration
21. Παραδώσει δὲ ἀδελφὸς ἀδελφὸν εἰς θάνατον, καὶ πατὴρ τέκνον· καὶ ἐπαναστήσονται τέκνα ἐπὶ γονεῖς, καὶ θανατώσουσιν αὐτούς.

21. Paradosei de adelphos adelphon eis thanaton, kai pateir teknon. kai epanasteisontai tekna epi goneis, kai thanatosousin autous.

Hebrew/Transliteration
כא. וְאָח יַסְגִּיר אֶת-אָחִיו לַמָּוֶת וְאָב אֶת-בְּנוֹ וְיָקוּמוּ בָנִים עַל-אֲבוֹתָם וְהֵמִיתוּם:

21. Ve•ach yas•gir et - a•chiv la•ma•vet ve•av et - b`no ve•ya•koo•moo va•nim al - avo•tam ve•he•mi•toom.

Rabbinic Jewish Commentary
Something like this is said by the Jews themselves, as what shall be in the times of the Messiah; for a little before his coming, or in the age in which the son of David comes, they say, "the son shall deal basely by his father, the daughter shall rise up against her mother--a man's enemies shall be of his own household; the face of that generation shall be as the face of a dog; and the son shall not reverence his father (g)." (g) Misn. Sota, c. 9. sect. 15.

---

22. And ye shall be hated of all men for my name's sake: but he that endureth to the end shall be saved.

Greek/Transliteration
22. Καὶ ἔσεσθε μισούμενοι ὑπὸ πάντων διὰ τὸ ὄνομά μου· ὁ δὲ ὑπομείνας εἰς τέλος, οὗτος σωθήσεται.

22. Kai esesthe misoumenoi 'upo panton dya to onoma mou. 'o de 'upomeinas eis telos, 'outos sotheisetai.

Hebrew/Transliteration
כב. וְאַתֶּם שְׂנֵאִים תִּהְיוּ לְכָל-אָדָם בַּעֲבוּר שְׁמִי אַךְ הַמְחַכֶּה עַד-הַקֵּץ יִוָּשֵׁעַ:

22. Ve•a•tem s`noo•eem ti•hi•yoo le•chol - adam ba•a•voor sh`mi ach ham•cha•ke ad - ha•ketz yi•va•she•a.

---

23. But when they persecute you in this city, flee ye into another: for verily I say unto you, Ye shall not have gone over the cities of Israel, till the Son of man be come.

Greek/Transliteration
23. Ὅταν δὲ διώκωσιν ὑμᾶς ἐν τῇ πόλει ταύτῃ, φεύγετε εἰς τὴν ἄλλην· ἀμὴν γὰρ λέγω ὑμῖν, οὐ μὴ τελέσητε τὰς πόλεις τοῦ Ἰσραήλ, ἕως ἂν ἔλθῃ ὁ υἱὸς τοῦ ἀνθρώπου.

23. 'Otan de diokosin 'umas en tei polei tautei, pheugete eis tein allein. amein gar lego 'umin, ou mei teleseite tas poleis tou Ysrael, 'eos an elthei 'o 'wios tou anthropou.

Hebrew/Transliteration
כג. וְכִי-יִרְדְּפוּ אֶתְכֶם בְּעִיר אַחַת נוּסוּ לָכֶם אֶל-עִיר אַחֶרֶת אָמֵן אֲנִי אֹמֵר לָכֶם לֹא תְכַלּוּ לַעֲבֹר עָרֵי יִשְׂרָאֵל עַד:כִּי-יָבֹא בֶּן-הָאָדָם.

23. Ve•chi - yir•de•foo et•chem be•eer a•chat noo•soo la•chem el - eer a•che•ret amen ani o•mer la•chem lo te•cha•loo la•a•vor arey Israel ad ki - ya•vo Ben - ha•a•dam.

Rabbinic Jewish Commentary
till the son of man be come; which is not to be understood of his second coming to judgment, but of his coming to take vengeance on his enemies, that would not have him to rule over them, and the persecutors of his ministers, at the destruction of Jerusalem in 70AD.

---

24. The disciple is not above his master, nor the servant above his lord.

Greek/Transliteration
24. Οὐκ ἔστιν μαθητὴς ὑπὲρ τὸν διδάσκαλον, οὐδὲ δοῦλος ὑπὲρ τὸν κύριον αὐτοῦ.

24. Ouk estin matheiteis 'uper ton didaskalon, oude doulos 'uper ton kurion autou.

Hebrew/Transliteration
:כד. הַתַּלְמִיד אֵינֶנּוּ רַב מֵרַבּוֹ וְעֶבֶד מֵאֲדֹנָיו

24. Ha•tal•mid ey•ne•noo rav mi•ra•bo ve•e•ved me•a•do•nav.

Rabbinic Jewish Commentary
nor the servant above his Lord; and both seem to be proverbial expressions. The Jews have a saying (h) much like unto them, אין העבד זכה מרבו, "no servant is worthier than his master"; and Yeshua might make use of such common, well known expressions, that he might be the more easily understood, and in the most familiar manner convey what he intended, into the minds of his disciples; as, that since he was their Lord, and they were his servants, if his superior character and dignity did not secure him from the obloquy and insults of men, it could not be thought by them, who were inferior to him, that they should escape them.

(h) T. Hieros. Maaser Sheni, fol. 55. 1.

---

25. It is enough for the disciple that he be as his master, and the servant as his lord. If they have called the master of the house Beelzebub, how much more shall they call them of his household?

Greek/Transliteration
25. Ἀρκετὸν τῷ μαθητῇ ἵνα γένηται ὡς ὁ διδάσκαλος αὐτοῦ, καὶ ὁ δοῦλος ὡς ὁ κύριος αὐτοῦ. Εἰ τὸν οἰκοδεσπότην Βεελζεβοὺλ ἐκάλεσαν, πόσῳ μᾶλλον τοὺς οἰκειακοὺς αὐτοῦ;

25. Arketon to matheitei 'ina geneitai 'os 'o didaskalos autou, kai 'o doulos 'os 'o kurios autou. Ei ton oikodespotein Beelzeboul ekalesan, poso mallon tous oikeyakous autou?

Hebrew/Transliteration
:כה. דַּי לַתַּלְמִיד לִהְיוֹת כְּרַבּוֹ וְלָעֶבֶד כַּאדֹנָיו אִם בַּעַל-זְבוּב קָרְאוּ לְבַעַל הַבַּיִת אַף כִּי-לְאַנְשֵׁי בֵיתוֹ

25. Dai la•tal•mid li•hee•yot ke•ra•bo ve•la•e•ved ka•do•nav eem Ba•al - Z`voov kar•oo le•va•al ha•ba•yit af ki - le•an•shey vey•to.

Rabbinic/Jewish New Testament Commentary
Ba'al-Zibbul or Ba'al-z'vuv (the manuscripts differ); usually seen in English as "Beelzebul" and "Beelzebub": derogatory names for the Adversary (see Mat_4:1). The latter is the name of a Philistine god (2Ki_1:2) and in Hebrew means "lord of a fly." The Ugaritic root *z-b-l* means "prince," making the former name imply that the Adversary has a measure of status and power; but in post-biblical Hebrew the root *z-b-l* means "dung," with "Ba'al-zibbul" meaning "defecator." Other interpretations are possible.

This was the god of the Ekronites, 2Ki_1:2. The word signifies "a masterfly" or the "lord of a fly": and so the Septuagint there call him βααλ μυιαν, "Baal the fly", the god of the Ekronites. And this idol was so called, either because it was in the form of a fly: or else from the abundance of flies about it, by reason of the sacrifices, which it was not able to drive away; and therefore the Jews contemptuously gave it this name. They observe (k), that in the temple, notwithstanding the multitude of sacrifices offered up there, there never was seen a fly in the slaughter house: or else this deity was so called from its being invoked to drive away flies, and the same with Myiodes, the god of flies, mentioned by Pliny (l), or Myagros, which the same author (m) speaks of; so Jupiter was called απομυιος, a driver away of flies; as was also Hercules (n); and were worshipped by some nations on this account. In most copies, and so in the Arabic version, it is read Beelzebul; that is, as it is commonly rendered, the "lord of dung", or a dunghill god; and it is generally thought the Jews called the god of the Ekronites so, by way of contempt; as it was usual with them to call an idol's temple זבול, "zebul", "dung", and worshipping of idols מזבל, "dunging" (o): but I must own, that I should rather think, that as Beelsamin, the god of the Phoenicians, is the same with Beelzebul, the god of the Ekronites, so it signifies the same thing: now בעל שמין, "Beelsamin", is "the lord of the heavens", and so is Beelzebul; for זבול, "Zebul", signifies "heaven"; so the word is used in Hab_3:11 "the sun and the moon stood still", זבלה, "in their habitation"; by which, as a Jewish (p) writer observes, הרצון בו השמים, "is meant the heavens"; for they are the habitation of the sun and moon: see also Isa_63:15 and so among the seven names of the heavens, reckoned up by them, this is accounted one (q)

(k) Pirke Abot, c. 5. sect. 5. (l) Nat. Hist. 1. 29. sect. 6. (m) Ib. 1. 10. c. 28. (n) Pausanias, 1. 5. p. 313. & 1. 8. p. 497. Clement. Alex. ad Gentes, p. 24. (o) T. Hieros. Beracot, fol. 13. 2. (p) R. Sol. Urbinas in Ohel Moed, fol. 100. 1. (q) T. Bab. Chagiga, fol. 12. 2.

---

26. Fear them not therefore: for there is nothing covered, that shall not be revealed; and hid, that shall not be known.

Greek/Transliteration
26. Μὴ οὖν φοβηθῆτε αὐτούς· οὐδὲν γάρ ἐστιν κεκαλυμμένον ὃ οὐκ ἀποκαλυφθήσεται· καὶ κρυπτὸν ὃ οὐ γνωσθήσεται.

26. Mei oun phobeitheite autous. ouden gar estin kekalummenon 'o ouk apokaluphtheisetai. Kai krupton 'o ou gnostheisetai.

Hebrew/Transliteration
כו. עַל-כֵּן אַל-תִּירְאוּ מִפְּנֵיהֶם כִּי אֵין-דָּבָר נִסְתָּר אֲשֶׁר לֹא יִגָּלֶה וְאֵין נֶעְלָם אֲשֶׁר לֹא יִוָּדֵעַ:

26. Al - ken al - tir•oo mip•ney•hem ki eyn - da•var nis•tar asher lo yi•ga•le ve•eyn ne•e•lam asher lo yi•va•dea.

27. What I tell you in darkness, that speak ye in light: and what ye hear in the ear, that preach ye upon the housetops.

Greek/Transliteration
27. Ὅ λέγω ὑμῖν ἐν τῇ σκοτίᾳ, εἴπατε ἐν τῷ φωτί· καὶ ὃ εἰς τὸ οὖς ἀκούετε, κηρύξατε ἐπὶ τῶν δωμάτων.

27. 'O lego 'umin en tei skotia, eipate en to photi. kai 'o eis to ous akouete, keiruxate epi ton domaton.

Hebrew/Transliteration
כז. אֶת אֲשֶׁר אַגֵּדְכֶם בְּחֹשֶׁךְ הַגִּידוּ לְעֵין הַשֶּׁמֶשׁ וְאֶת אֲשֶׁר תִּשְׁמַע אָזְנְכֶם בְּלַחַשׁ הַשְׁמִיעוּ עַל־הַגַּגּוֹת:

27. Et asher aged•chem be•cho•shech ha•gi•doo le•ein ha•sha•mesh ve•et asher tish•ma oz•ne•chem be•la•chash hash•mi•oo al - ha•ga•got.

Rabbinic Jewish Commentary
And what ye hear in the ear, or is whispered to you by me, as your master. Christ alludes to the custom of the Jewish Rabbi's, who had each an interpreter, into whose ear he used to whisper his doctrine, and then the interpreter delivered it to the people: so it is said (s), "Rab came to the place of R. Shilla, and he had no speaker to stand by him; wherefore Rab stood by him, and explained."

"an interpreter stands before a Rabbi whilst he is preaching, and the Rabbi לוחש לו, "whispers to him" in the Hebrew tongue, and he interprets it to the multitude in a tongue they understand."

Again (t), "they said to Judah bar Nachmani, the interpreter of Resh Lekish, stand for a speaker for him." "to cause his exposition to be heard by the congregation, שילחוש לך, "which he shall whisper to thee".

Now it was absolutely requisite, that the speaker, or interpreter, should faithfully relate what the doctor said; sometimes, it seems, he did not: it is said (u) in commendation of the meekness of R. Aba, "that he delivered one sense, and his speaker said another, and he was not angry."

(s) T. Bab. Yoma, fol. 20. 2. (t) T. Bab. Sanhed. fol. 7. 2. (u) T. Bab. Sota, fol. 40. 1.

---

28. And fear not them which kill the body, but are not able to kill the soul: but rather fear him which is able to destroy both soul and body in hell.

Greek/Transliteration
28. Καὶ μὴ φοβεῖσθε ἀπὸ τῶν ἀποκτενόντων τὸ σῶμα, τὴν δὲ ψυχὴν μὴ δυναμένων ἀποκτεῖναι· φοβήθητε δὲ μᾶλλον τὸν δυνάμενον καὶ τὴν ψυχὴν καὶ τὸ σῶμα ἀπολέσαι ἐν γεέννῃ.

28. Kai mei phobeisthe apo ton apoktenonton to soma, tein de psuchein mei dunamenon apokteinai. phobeitheite de mallon ton dunamenon kai tein psuchein kai to soma apolesai en ge'ennei.

Hebrew/Transliteration
כח. וְאַל-תִּירְאוּ מִפְּנֵי הֹרְגֵי הַבָּשָׂר וְלַהֲרֹג אֶת-הַנֶּפֶשׁ לֹא תַשִּׂיג יָדָם כִּי אִם-יִרְאוּ מִפָּנָיו אֲשֶׁר יָדָיו רַב לוֹ לַהֲרֹג:גַּם אֶת-הַנֶּפֶשׁ וְגַם אֶת-הַבָּשָׂר בְּגֵיהִנֹּם

28. Ve•al - tir•oo mip•ney hor•gey ha•ba•sar ve•la•ha•rog et - ha•ne•fesh lo ta•sig ya•dam ki eem - yir•oo mi•pa•nav asher ya•dav rav lo la•ha•rog gam et - ha•ne•fesh ve•gam et - ha•ba•sar be•gey•hi•nom.

Rabbinic Jewish Commentary
In Hebrew the body and soul are sometimes interchangible. The body here is *basar* while the soul is *nefesh*. The body is the meat of the person while the soul is the inner most parts of the body. Both will be destroyed in the fire of Gehenna when Jerusalem is destroyed by fire.

---

29. Are not two sparrows sold for a farthing? and one of them shall not fall on the ground without your Father.

Greek/Transliteration
29. Οὐχὶ δύο στρουθία ἀσσαρίου πωλεῖται; Καὶ ἓν ἐξ αὐτῶν οὐ πεσεῖται ἐπὶ τὴν γῆν ἄνευ τοῦ πατρὸς ὑμῶν·

29. Ouchi duo strouthia assariou poleitai? Kai 'en ex auton ou peseitai epi tein gein aneu tou patros 'umon.

Hebrew/Transliteration
כט. הֲלֹא שְׁתֵּי צִפֳּרִים נִמְכָּרוֹת בְּאִסָּר אֶחָד וְאַחַת מֵהֶן לֹא תִפֹּל אַרְצָה בִּבְלִי רְצוֹן אֲבִיכֶם:

29. Ha•lo sh`tey tzi•po•rim nim•ka•rot be•ee•sar e•chad ve•a•chat me•hen lo ti•pol ar•tza biv•li r`tzon Avi•chem.

Rabbinic Jewish Commentary
A farthing, with the Jews, was a very small coin; according to them it contained four grains of silver (b); was the ninety sixth part of a "sela", or shilling (c); and sometimes they make it to be of the same value with an Italian farthing: for they say (d), it is of the value of eight "prutahs": and a "prutah" is the eighth part of an Italian farthing: it is used proverbially to signify a very little thing in the Misna (e);

"if of a command, which is light כאיסר "as a farthing", which Bartenora explains a "very little thing", the law says, "that it may be well with thee", much more of the weighty commands in the law."

Hence, in Munster's Hebrew Gospel, it is rendered by טבע קטון, "a little piece of money"; and this was the common price of two sparrows.

Much such a way of arguing is used by the Jews, who (f) say, צפור מבלעדי שמיא לא יבדא כל שכן בר נשא, "a bird without God does not perish, much less a man"; or, as it is elsewhere (g) expressed,

"a bird "without God" is not hunted, or taken, how much less does the soul of a man go out of him?"

(b) Maimon. in Misn. Peah, c. 8. sect. 1. (c) Maimon. & Bartenora in Misn. Maaser Sheni, c. 4. sect. 3. (d) Ib. in Misn. Eracin, c. 8. sect. 1. (e) Cholin, c. 12. sect. 5. (f) T. Hieros. Sheviith, fol. 38. 4. (g) Bereshit Rabba, fol. 69. 3.

---

30. But the very hairs of your head are all numbered.

Greek/Transliteration
30. ὑμῶν δὲ καὶ αἱ τρίχες τῆς κεφαλῆς πᾶσαι ἠριθμημέναι εἰσίν.

30. 'umon de kai 'ai triches teis kephaleis pasai eirithmeimenai eisin.

Hebrew/Transliteration
ל. וְאַתֶּם גַּם-שַׂעֲרוֹת רֹאשְׁכֶם נִמְנוּ לְמִסְפָּרָם:

30. Ve•a•tem gam - sa•a•rot rosh•chem nim•noo le•mis•pa•ram.

Rabbinic Jewish Commentary
(i); "do not I number all the hairs of every creature?"
(i) Pesikta, fol. 18. 4. apud Drusium in loc.

---

31. Fear ye not therefore, ye are of more value than many sparrows.

Greek/Transliteration
31. Μὴ οὖν φοβηθῆτε· πολλῶν στρουθίων διαφέρετε ὑμεῖς.

31. Mei oun phobeitheite. pollon strouthion dyapherete 'umeis.

Hebrew/Transliteration
לא. עַל-כֵּן אַל-תִּירָאוּ עֶרְכְּכֶם רַב מִצִּפֳּרִים רַבּוֹת:

31. Al - ken al - ti•ra•oo er•ke•chem rav mi•tzi•po•rim ra•bot.

---

32. Whosoever therefore shall confess me before men, him will I confess also before my Father which is in heaven.

Greek/Transliteration
32. Πᾶς οὖν ὅστις ὁμολογήσει ἐν ἐμοὶ ἔμπροσθεν τῶν ἀνθρώπων, ὁμολογήσω κἀγὼ ἐν αὐτῷ ἔμπροσθεν τοῦ πατρός μου τοῦ ἐν οὐρανοῖς.

32. Pas oun 'ostis 'omologeisei en emoi emprosthen ton anthropon, 'omologeiso kago en auto emprosthen tou patros mou tou en ouranois.

Hebrew/Transliteration
לב: לָכֵן כָּל-אִישׁ אֲשֶׁר יַאֲמִירֵנִי לִפְנֵי בְנֵי-הָאָדָם אַאֲמִירֶנּוּ לִפְנֵי אָבִי בַשָּׁמַיִם גַּם-אָנֹכִי.

32. La•chen kol - eesh asher ya•a•mi•re•ni lif•ney v`ney - ha•a•dam a•a•mi•re•noo lif•ney Avi va•sha•ma•yim gam - ano•chi.

---

33. But whosoever shall deny me before men, him will I also deny before my Father which is in heaven.

Greek/Transliteration
33. Ὅστις δ᾽ ἂν ἀρνήσηταί με ἔμπροσθεν τῶν ἀνθρώπων, ἀρνήσομαι αὐτὸν κἀγὼ ἔμπροσθεν τοῦ πατρός μου τοῦ ἐν οὐρανοῖς.

33. 'Ostis d an arneiseitai me emprosthen ton anthropon, arneisomai auton kago emprosthen tou patros mou tou en ouranois.

Hebrew/Transliteration
לג: וְכָל-אִישׁ אֲשֶׁר יְכַחֶשׁ-בִּי לִפְנֵי בְנֵי-הָאָדָם אֲכַחֶשׁ-בּוֹ לִפְנֵי אָבִי בַשָּׁמַיִם גַּם-אָנִי.

33. Ve•chol - eesh asher ye•cha•chesh - bi lif•ney v`ney - ha•a•dam a•cha•chesh - bo lif•ney Avi va•sha•ma•yim gam - ani.

Rabbinic Jewsh Commentary
Deny that he is a disciple of Yeshua, and that Yeshua is his Lord and master, act contrary to him, deliver things repugnant to his mind and will; which for a disciple to do to his master was a very heinous crime with the Jews:

"if (say they (n)) Rabbi Jochanan, **יכפור**, "deny" Rabbi Eleazar, his disciple, he will not "deny" Rabbi Jannai, his "master"." (n) Juchasin, fol. 80. 2.

---

34. Think not that I am come to send peace on earth: I came not to send peace, but a sword.

Greek/Transliteration
34. Μὴ νομίσητε ὅτι ἦλθον βαλεῖν εἰρήνην ἐπὶ τὴν γῆν· οὐκ ἦλθον βαλεῖν εἰρήνην, ἀλλὰ μάχαιραν.

34. Mei nomiseite 'oti eilthon balein eireinein epi tein gein. ouk eilthon balein eireinein, alla machairan.

Hebrew/Transliteration
לד: אַל-תַּחְשְׁבוּ כִּי בָאתִי לְהָבִיא שָׁלוֹם בָּאָרֶץ לֹא בָאתִי לְהָבִיא שָׁלוֹם כִּי אִם-חָרֶב.

34. Al - tach•she•voo ki va•ti le•ha•vee sha•lom ba•a•retz lo va•ti le•ha•vee sha•lom ki eem - cha•rev.

---

35. For I am come to set a man at variance against his father, and the daughter against her mother, and the daughter in law against her mother in law.

Greek/Transliteration
35. Ἦλθον γὰρ διχάσαι ἄνθρωπον κατὰ τοῦ πατρὸς αὐτοῦ, καὶ θυγατέρα κατὰ τῆς μητρὸς αὐτῆς, καὶ νύμφην κατὰ τῆς πενθερᾶς αὐτῆς·

35. Eilthon gar dichasai anthropon kata tou patros autou, kai thugatera kata teis meitros auteis, kai numphein kata teis pentheras auteis.

Hebrew/Transliteration
לה: כִּי בָאתִי לְהַפְרִיד בֵּין אִישׁ לְאָבִיו בֵּין בַּת לְאִמָּהּ וּבֵין כַּלָּה לַחֲמוֹתָהּ

35. Ki va•ti le•haf•rid bein eesh le•a•viv bein bat le•ee•ma oo•vein ka•la la•cha•mo•ta.

---

36. And a man's foes shall be they of his own household.

Greek/Transliteration
36. καὶ ἐχθροὶ τοῦ ἀνθρώπου οἱ οἰκειακοὶ αὐτοῦ.

36. kai echthroi tou anthropou 'oi oikeyakoi autou.

Hebrew/Transliteration
לו: וְאֹיְבֵי אִישׁ אַנְשֵׁי בֵיתוֹ

36. Ve•oy•vey eesh an•shey vey•to.

Rabbinic Jewish Commentary
"The government shall be turned to heresy (Sadducism), and there will be no reproof; the synagogue shall become a brothel house, Galilee shall be destroyed, and Gablan shall be laid waste, and the men of the border shall wander from city to city, and shall obtain no mercy; the wisdom of the Scribes shall stink, and they that fear to sin shall be despised, and truth shall fail; young men shall turn pale, or put to shame, the faces of old men, and old men shall stand before young men; the "son" shall deal basely "with his father, the daughter shall rise up against her mother, and the daughter-in-law against her mother-in-law, and the enemies of a man shall be they of his own house": the face of that generation shall be as the face of a dog, and the son shall not reverence his father (o)."

All which characters, how exactly they agree with the generation in which Yeshua lived, is easy to observe.

(o) Misn. Sota, c. 9. sect. 15. T. Bab. Sanhedrim, fol. 97. 1. Zohar in Num. fol. 102. 3. & Raya Mehimna in ib. in Lev. fol. 28. 2. Shirhashirim Rabba, fol. 11. 4. Derech Eretz Zuta, fol. 19. 4.

---

37. He that loveth father or mother more than me is not worthy of me: and he that loveth son or daughter more than me is not worthy of me.

Greek/Transliteration
37. Ὁ φιλῶν πατέρα ἢ μητέρα ὑπὲρ ἐμέ, οὐκ ἔστιν μου ἄξιος· καὶ ὁ φιλῶν υἱὸν ἢ θυγατέρα ὑπὲρ ἐμέ, οὐκ ἔστιν μου ἄξιος·

37. 'O philon patera ei meitera 'uper eme, ouk estin mou axios. kai 'o philon 'wion ei thugatera 'uper eme, ouk estin mou axios.

Hebrew/Transliteration
לז. הָאֹהֵב אֶת-אָבִיו אוֹ אֶת-אִמּוֹ יוֹתֵר מִמֶּנִּי אֵינֶנּוּ שׁוֶֹה לִי וְהָאֹהֵב אֶת-בְּנוֹ אוֹ אֶת-בִּתּוֹ יוֹתֵר מִמֶּנִּי אֵינֶנּוּ שׁוֶֹה:לִי

37. Ha•o•hev et - aviv oh et - ee•mo yo•ter mi•me•ni ey•ne•noo sho•ve li ve•ha•o•hev et - b`no oh et - bi•to yo•ter mi•me•ni ey•ne•noo sho•ve li.

---

38. And he that taketh not his cross, and followeth after me, is not worthy of me.

Greek/Transliteration
38. καὶ ὃς οὐ λαμβάνει τὸν σταυρὸν αὐτοῦ καὶ ἀκολουθεῖ ὀπίσω μου, οὐκ ἔστιν μου ἄξιος.

38. kai 'os ou lambanei ton stauron autou kai akolouthei opiso mou, ouk estin mou axios.

Hebrew/Transliteration
:לח. וּמִי אֲשֶׁר לֹא-יִקַּח אֶת-צְלָבוֹ וְיֵלֵךְ אַחֲרַי אֵינֶנּוּ שׁוֶֹה לִי

38. Oo•mi asher lo - yi•kach et - tze•la•vo ve•ye•lech a•cha•rai ey•ne•noo sho•ve li.

Jewish New Testament Commentary
Greek *stavros*, usually translated "cross." Actually it was a vertical wooden stake with a crossbar, usually shaped more like a "T" than the Christian symbol, used by the Romans to execute criminals who were not Roman citizens (Roman citizens sentenced to death were given a less painful way to die). It was not a normal

Jewish means of execution. *Halakhah* specified four methods of execution-stoning, burning, beheading and strangling (Mishna Sanhedrin 7:1)-but not hanging or being suspended from a cross (see Gal_3:13, 1Pe_2:24).

---

39. He that findeth his life shall lose it: and he that loseth his life for my sake shall find it.

Greek/Transliteration

39. Ὁ εὑρὼν τὴν ψυχὴν αὐτοῦ ἀπολέσει αὐτήν· καὶ ὁ ἀπολέσας τὴν ψυχὴν αὐτοῦ ἕνεκεν ἐμοῦ εὑρήσει αὐτήν.

39. 'O 'euron tein psuchein autou apolesei autein. kai 'o apolesas tein psuchein autou 'eneken emou 'eureisei autein.

Hebrew/Transliteration

לט. הַמֹּצֵא אֶת-נַפְשׁוֹ תֹּאבַד לוֹ וְהַמַּשְׁלִיךְ אֶת-נַפְשׁוֹ בִּגְלָלִי יִמְצָאֶנָּה:

39. Ha•mo•tze et - naf•sho to•vad lo ve•ha•mash•lich et - naf•sho big•la•li yim•tza•e•na.

---

40. He that receiveth you receiveth me, and he that receiveth me receiveth him that sent me.

Greek/Transliteration

40. Ὁ δεχόμενος ὑμᾶς ἐμὲ δέχεται· καὶ ὁ ἐμὲ δεχόμενος δέχεται τὸν ἀποστείλαντά με.

40. 'O dechomenos 'umas eme dechetai. kai 'o eme dechomenos dechetai ton aposteilanta me.

Hebrew/Transliteration

מ. הַמְקַבֵּל פְּנֵיכֶם מְקַבֵּל פָּנָי וְהַמְקַבֵּל פָּנַי הוּא מְקַבֵּל פְּנֵי שֹׁלְחִי:

40. Ha•m`ka•bel p`ney•chem me•ka•bel pa•nai ve•ha•m`ka•bel pa•nai hoo me•ka•bel p`ney shol•chi.

Rabbinic Jewish Commentary

and he that receiveth me, receiveth him that sent me. To which agrees, what the Jews say (p) of the messenger, in Exo_23:22 "If thou shalt indeed obey his voice, and do all that I shall speak": who observe, that it is not written, "that he shall speak", but "that I shall speak"; intimating, that אם מקבלין א־תאם הימנו כאלו לי א־תאם מקבלים, "if ye receive him, it is all one as if you received me": and the whole of this accords with a common saying among (q) them, ששלוחו של אדם כמותו, "that a man's messenger is as himself". The Jew (r), therefore, has no reason to reproach Yeshua and his followers as he does, as if it was the sense of these words of Yeshua, and which the believers give of them, that Yeshua and his twelve apostles were but one person.

(p) Shemot Rabba Parash. 32. fol. 135. 3. (q) T. Bab. Baracot, fol. 34. 2. Kiddushin, fol. 41. 2. 42. 1. & 43. 1. Bava Metzia, fol. 96. 1. (r) R. Isaac Chizzuk Emuna, par 2. sect. 14. p. 404.

---

41. He that receiveth a prophet in the name of a prophet shall receive a prophet's reward; and he that receiveth a righteous man in the name of a righteous man shall receive a righteous man's reward.

Greek/Transliteration
41. Ὁ δεχόμενος προφήτην εἰς ὄνομα προφήτου μισθὸν προφήτου λήψεται· καὶ ὁ δεχόμενος δίκαιον εἰς ὄνομα δικαίου μισθὸν δικαίου λήψεται.

41. 'O dechomenos propheitein eis onoma propheitou misthon propheitou leipsetai. kai 'o dechomenos dikaion eis onoma dikaiou misthon dikaiou leipsetai.

Hebrew/Transliteratioin
מא. הַמְקַבֵּל פְּנֵי נָבִיא בְּשֵׁם נָבִיא יַשִּׂיג שְׂכַר נָבִיא וְהַמְקַבֵּל פְּנֵי צַדִּיק בְּשֵׁם צַדִּיק יַשִּׂיג שְׂכַר צַדִּיק:

41. Ha•m`ka•bel p`ney na•vi be•shem na•vi ya•sig s`char na•vi ve•ha•m`ka•bel p`ney tza•dik be•shem tza•dik ya•sig s`char tza•dik.

Rabbinic Jewish Commentary
The phrase, לשם, "in the name", or on the account of anything, is often used in the Mishnic writings (s) "authority" or "character of"

(s) Misn. Zebachim, c. 1. sect. 1. 2, 3, 4. &. 4. 6. &. 6. 7. & 7. 1, 2, 3, 4.

---

42. And whosoever shall give to drink unto one of these little ones a cup of cold water only in the name of a disciple, verily I say unto you, he shall in no wise lose his reward.

Greek/Transliteration
42. Καὶ ὃς ἐὰν ποτίσῃ ἕνα τῶν μικρῶν τούτων ποτήριον ψυχροῦ μόνον εἰς ὄνομα μαθητοῦ, ἀμὴν λέγω ὑμῖν, οὐ μὴ ἀπολέσῃ τὸν μισθὸν αὐτοῦ.

42. Kai 'os ean potisei 'ena ton mikron touton poteirion psuchrou monon eis onoma matheitou, amein lego 'umin, ou mei apolesei ton misthon autou.

Hebrew/Transliteration
מב. וּמִי אֲשֶׁר יַשְׁקֶה אֶת-אַחַד הַקְּטַנִּים הָאֵלֶּה רַק כּוֹס מַיִם קָרִים בְּשֵׁם תַּלְמִיד אָמֵן אֲנִי מַגִּיד לָכֶם כִּי לֹא:יֹאבַד שְׂכָרוֹ -

42. Oo•mi asher yash•ke et - achad ha•ke•ta•nim ha•e•le rak kos ma•yim ka•rim be•shem tal•mid amen ani ma•gid la•chem ki lo - yo•vad s`cha•ro.

Rabbinic Jewish Commentary

"So says (t) Maimonides, one that calls to his friend to dine with him, and he refuses, and swears, or vows, that he shall not enter into his house, nor will he give him to drink, טפת צונן "a drop of cold water".

The Jews say many things in praise of hospitality, to תלמיד חכם, "a disciple of a wise man"; and observe (u), that he that hospitably entertains such an one in his house, and causes him to eat and drink, and partake of the goods of his house, there is reason to believe, he shall be much more blessed than the house of Obed Edom was for the ark's sake, which neither ate nor drank with him; and which may be compared with this passage.

(t) Hilchot Nedarim, c. 8. sect. 10. (u) T. Bab, Beracot, fol. 63. 2. & 64. 1.

Matthew, Chapter 11

1. And it came to pass, when Jesus had made an end of commanding his twelve disciples, he departed thence to teach and to preach in their cities.

Greek/Transliteration
1. Καὶ ἐγένετο ὅτε ἐτέλεσεν ὁ Ἰησοῦς διατάσσων τοῖς δώδεκα μαθηταῖς αὐτοῦ, μετέβη ἐκεῖθεν τοῦ διδάσκειν καὶ κηρύσσειν ἐν ταῖς πόλεσιν αὐτῶν.

1. Kai egeneto 'ote etelesen 'o Yeisous dyatasson tois dodeka matheitais autou, metebei ekeithen tou didaskein kai keirussein en tais polesin auton.

Hebrew/Transliteration
א. וַיְהִי כְּכַלּוֹת יֵשׁוּעַ לְצַוּוֹת אֶת-שְׁנֵים עָשָׂר תַּלְמִידָיו וַיַּעֲבֹר מִשָּׁם לְלַמֵּד וּלְהַשְׁמִיעַ יְשׁוּעָתוֹ בְּעָרֵיהֶם:

1. Vay•hi ke•cha•lot Yeshua le•tza•vot et - sh`neym asar tal•mi•dav va•ya•a•vor mi•sham le•la•med ool•hash•mia ye•shoo•a•to be•a•rey•hem.

Rabbinic Jewish Commentary
Literally, "in their towns." Whose towns? Some say, "the Jews' towns," as if Mattityahu or his redactor were writing specifically for non-Jews or trying to distance himself from the Jews. I prefer to think what is meant is simply the towns of the people with whom Yeshua was then spending his time, the people of the Galil, or possibly the home-towns of his *talmidim*. (Robertson's *A Grammar of the Greek New Testament*, p. 683, takes the Greek word "*avtôn*" ("their") in this verse as being according to the sense of the surrounding words, with the narrative itself being compressed.

---

2. Now when John had heard in the prison the works of Christ, he sent two of his disciples,

Greek/Transliteration
2. Ὁ δὲ Ἰωάννης ἀκούσας ἐν τῷ δεσμωτηρίῳ τὰ ἔργα τοῦ χριστοῦ, πέμψας δύο τῶν μαθητῶν αὐτοῦ,

2. 'O de Yoanneis akousas en to desmoteirio ta erga tou christou, pempsas duo ton matheiton autou,

Hebrew/Transliteration
ב. וְיוֹחָנָן בְּבֵית הָאֲסוּרִים שָׁמַע אֶת-עֲלִלוֹת הַמָּשִׁיחַ וַיִּשְׁלַח אֵלָיו שְׁנַיִם מִתַּלְמִידָיו:

2. Ve•Yo•cha•nan be•veit ha•a•soo•rim sha•ma et - ali•lot ha•Ma•shi•ach va•yish•lach elav sh`na•yim mi•tal•mi•dav.

Rabbinic Jewish Commentary
A "periphrasis" of the Messiah, well known to the Jews; for he had been spoken of frequently in the prophecies of the Old Testament, as the Shiloh, the Redeemer, the Prophet, and King that should come; particularly, by this circumlocution, reference seems to be had to Hab_2:3. "It shall surely come", כי בא יבא, which may be rendered, "for he that cometh", or "is to come, shall come".

---

3. And said unto him, Art thou he that should come, or do we look for another?

Greek/Transliteration
3. εἶπεν αὐτῷ, Σὺ εἶ ὁ ἐρχόμενος, ἢ ἕτερον προσδοκῶμεν;

3. eipen auto, Su ei 'o erchomenos, ei 'eteron prosdokomen?

Hebrew/Transliteration
ג: וַיֹּאמֶר הָאַתָּה הוּא הַבָּא אוֹ אִם-נְחַכֶּה לְאַחֵר

3. Va•yo•mar ha•a•ta hoo ha•ba oh eem - n`cha•ke le•a•cher.

---

4. Jesus answered and said unto them, Go and shew John again those things which ye do hear and see:

Greek/Transliteration
4. Καὶ ἀποκριθεὶς ὁ Ἰησοῦς εἶπεν αὐτοῖς, Πορευθέντες ἀπαγγείλατε Ἰωάννῃ ἃ ἀκούετε καὶ βλέπετε·

4. Kai apokritheis 'o Yeisous eipen autois, Poreuthentes apangeilate Yoannei 'a akouete kai blepete.

Hebrew/Transliteration
ד: וַיַּעַן יֵשׁוּעַ וַיֹּאמֶר אֲלֵיהֶם לְכוּ וְהַגִּידוּ לְיוֹחָנָן אֵת אֲשֶׁר-שְׁמַעְתֶּם וְאֵת אֲשֶׁר-רְאִיתֶם

4. Va•ya•an Yeshua va•yo•mer aley•hem le•choo ve•ha•gi•doo le•Yo•cha•nan et asher - sh`ma•a•tem ve•et asher - r`ee•tem.

Jewish New Testament Commentary
He refers to prophecies in the book of Isaiah of six signs which the Messiah will give when he comes: he will make the blind see (Isa_29:18, Isa_35:5), make the lame walk (Isa_35:6, Isa_61:1), cleanse lepers (Isa_61:1), make the deaf hear (Isa_29:18, Isa_35:5), raise the dead (implied in Isa_11:1-2 but not made specific), and evangelize the poor (Isa_61:1-2 in the light of Mat_4:23 above). Since he has done all these things (chapters 8-9), the message should be clear: Yeshua is the one; Yochanan need not look for another.

5. The blind receive their sight, and the lame walk, the lepers are cleansed, and the deaf hear, the dead are raised up, and the poor have the gospel preached to them.

Greek/Transliteration
5. τυφλοὶ ἀναβλέπουσιν, καὶ χωλοὶ περιπατοῦσιν, λεπροὶ καθαρίζονται, καὶ κωφοὶ ἀκούουσιν, νεκροὶ ἐγείρονται, καὶ πτωχοὶ εὐαγγελίζονται·

5. tuphloi anablepousin, kai choloi peripatousin, leproi katharizontai, kai kophoi akouousin, nekroi egeirontai, kai ptochoi euangelizontai.

Hebrew/Transliteration
ה. עִוְרִים רֹאִים וּפִסְחִים הֹלְכִים מְצֹרָעִים נִרְפָּאִים וְחֵרְשִׁים שֹׁמְעִים מֵתִים קָמִים וַעֲנִיִּים מִתְבַּשְׂרִים יְשׁוּעָה:

5. Eev•rim ro•eem oo•fis•chim hol•chim me•tzo•ra•eem nir•pa•eem ve•cher•shim shom•eem me•tim ka•mim va•a•ni•yim mit•bas•rim ye•shoo•ah.

---

6. And blessed is he, whosoever shall not be offended in me.

Greek/Transliteration
6. καὶ μακάριός ἐστιν, ὃς ἐὰν μὴ σκανδαλισθῇ ἐν ἐμοί.

6. kai makarios estin, 'os ean mei skandalisthei en emoi.

Hebrew/Transliteration
ו. וְאַשְׁרֵי הָאִישׁ אֲשֶׁר לֹא-יִכָּשֶׁל בִּי:

6. Ve•ash•rey ha•eesh asher lo - yi•ka•shel bi.

Jewish New Testament Commentary
But his answer avoids mentioning the Messianic sign of "proclaiming liberty to the captives" (Isa_61:1). Added to his remark, "How blessed is anyone not offended by me," Yeshua seems to be saying delicately that even though he is the Messiah, Yochanan will not be set free-as proves to be the case (below, Mat_14:1-12).

---

7. And as they departed, Jesus began to say unto the multitudes concerning John, What went ye out into the wilderness to see? A reed shaken with the wind?

Greek/Transliteration
7. Τούτων δὲ πορευομένων, ἤρξατο ὁ Ἰησοῦς λέγειν τοῖς ὄχλοις περὶ Ἰωάννου, Τί ἐξήλθετε εἰς τὴν ἔρημον θεάσασθαι; Κάλαμον ὑπὸ ἀνέμου σαλευόμενον;

7. Touton de poreuomenon, eirxato 'o Yeisous legein tois ochlois peri Yoannou, Ti exeilthete eis tein ereimon theasasthai? Kalamon 'upo anemou saleuomenon?

Hebrew/Transliteration

ז. וּבְלֶכְתָּם הֵחֵל יֵשׁוּעַ לְדַבֵּר אֶל-הֲמוֹן הָעָם עַל-יוֹחָנָן מַה-זֶּה יְצָאתֶם הַמִּדְבָּרָה לִרְאוֹת הָאִם קָנֶה אֲשֶׁר יִנּוֹעַ:מִפְּנֵי-רוּחַ

7. Oov•lech•tam he`chel Yeshua le•da•ber el - ha•mon ha•am al - Yo•cha•nan ma – ze ye•tza•tem ha•mid•ba•ra lir•ot ha•eem ka•ne asher yi•noa mip•ney - roo•ach.

Rabbinic Jewish Commentary

The Jews use this comparison of a man to a reed, in a sense just the reverse, and make it to signify constancy, and not inconstancy, as well as tenderness, in opposition to roughness, severity, and stubbornness.

"Let a man (say they (w)) be always רך בקנה, "tender as a reed", and let him not be hard and stubborn as a cedar: when the four winds of the world go out, the reed goes and comes with them; and when the winds are still, the reed stands in its place."

So they observe (x), that it is said, that "the Lord shall smite Israel, as a reed shaken in the water", 1Ki_14:15 which they interpret by way of blessing.

"As a reed (say they) stands in a place of water, its body waves about, and its roots are many; and though all the winds in the world come and blow upon it, they cannot move it out of its place, but it goes and comes with them; and when the winds are still, the reed stands in its place."

(w) Derech Eretz, fol. 18. 1. (x) T. Bab. Taanith, fol. 20. 1.

---

8. But what went ye out for to see? A man clothed in soft raiment? behold, they that wear soft clothing are in kings' houses.

Greek/Transliteration

8. Ἀλλὰ τί ἐξήλθετε ἰδεῖν; Ἄνθρωπον ἐν μαλακοῖς ἱματίοις ἠμφιεσμένον; Ἰδού, οἱ τὰ μαλακὰ φοροῦντες ἐν τοῖς οἴκοις τῶν βασιλείων εἰσίν.

8. Alla ti exeilthete idein? Anthropon en malakois 'imatiois eimphiesmenon? Ydou, 'oi ta malaka phorountes en tois oikois ton basileion eisin.

Hebrew/Transliteration

ח. אַךְ מַה-זֶּה יְצָאתֶם לִרְאוֹת הָאִם אִישׁ לָבוּשׁ בִּגְדֵי חֲמֻדוֹת הִנֵּה לֹבְשֵׁי חֲמֻדוֹת בְּבָתֵּי מְלָכִים הֵמָּה:

8. Ach ma - ze ye•tza•tem lir•ot ha•eem eesh la•voosh big•dey cha•moo•dot hee•ne lov•shey cha•moo•dot be•va•tey m`la•chim he•ma.

9. But what went ye out for to see? A prophet? yea, I say unto you, and more than a prophet.

Greek/Transliteration
9. Ἀλλὰ τί ἐξήλθετε ἰδεῖν; Προφήτην; Ναί, λέγω ὑμῖν, καὶ περισσότερον προφήτου·

9. Alla ti exeilthete idein? Propheitein? Nai, lego 'umin, kai perissoteron propheitou.

Hebrew/Transliteration
:ט. אַךְ מַה - זֶה יְצָאתֶם הַאִם לִרְאוֹת אִישׁ נָבִיא הֵן אֲנִי אֹמֵר לָכֶם כִּי גַם - גָּדוֹל הוּא מִנָּבִיא

9. Ach ma - ze ye•tza•tem ha•eem lir•ot eesh na•vi hen ani o•mer la•chem ki gam - ga•dol hoo mi•na•vi.

---

10. For this is he, of whom it is written, Behold, I send my messenger before thy face, which shall prepare thy way before thee.

Greek/Transliteration
10. οὗτος γάρ ἐστιν περὶ οὗ γέγραπται, Ἰδού, ἐγὼ ἀποστέλλω τὸν ἄγγελόν μου πρὸ προσώπου σου, ὃς κατασκευάσει τὴν ὁδόν σου ἔμπροσθέν σου.

10. 'outos gar estin peri 'ou gegraptai, Ydou, ego apostello ton angelon mou pro prosopou sou, 'os kataskeuasei tein 'odon sou emprosthen sou.

Hebrew/Transliteration
:י. זֶה הוּא אֲשֶׁר כָּתוּב עָלָיו הִנְנִי שֹׁלֵחַ מַלְאָכִי לְפָנֶיךָ וּפִנָּה דַרְכְּךָ לְפָנֶיךָ

10. Ze hoo asher ka•toov alav hi•ne•ni sho•le•ach mal•a•chi le•fa•ne•cha oo•fi•na dar•ke•cha le•fa•ne•cha.

Rabbinic Jewish Commentary
Behold I send my messenger before thy face, which shall prepare thy way before thee. That these words belong לעולם הבא, to the world to come, or the times of the Messiah, that is, the Gospel dispensation, the Jews (z) themselves own; but as to the particular person meant by the "messenger", or "angel", because they are not willing to acknowledge the right person, are at the utmost loss. Jarchi makes him to be the angel of death, who is to destroy the wicked; Aben Ezra conjectures it may be Messiah the son of Joseph, who they fancy will come before Messiah the son of David. Kimchi thinks an angel from heaven is designed; and Abarbinel Malachi himself: but the more ancient sense of the synagogue was, that the same person is meant, as in Mar_9:5 under the name of Elijah the prophet;

(z) Bemidbar Rabba, sect. 15. fol. 219. 4.

11. Verily I say unto you, Among them that are born of women there hath not risen a greater than John the Baptist: notwithstanding he that is least in the kingdom of heaven is greater than he.

Greek/Transliteration
11. Ἀμὴν λέγω ὑμῖν, οὐκ ἐγήγερται ἐν γεννητοῖς γυναικῶν μείζων Ἰωάννου τοῦ βαπτιστοῦ. Ὁ δὲ μικρότερος ἐν τῇ βασιλείᾳ τῶν οὐρανῶν μείζων αὐτοῦ ἐστιν.

11. Amein lego 'umin, ouk egeigertai en genneitois gunaikon meizon Yoannou tou baptistou. 'O de mikroteros en tei basileia ton ouranon meizon autou estin.

Hebrew/Transliteration
יא. אָמֵן אֲנִי אֹמֵר לָכֶם לֹא קָם בֵּין יְלִידֵי אִשָּׁה גָּדוֹל מִיּוֹחָנָן הַמַּטְבִּיל וְהַקָּטֹן בְּמַלְכוּת הַשָּׁמַיִם יִגְדַּל מִמֶּנּוּ:

11. Amen ani o•mer la•chem lo kam bein ye•li•dey ee•sha ga•dol mi•Yocha•nan ha•Mat•bil ve•ha•ka•ton be•mal•choot ha•sha•ma•yim yig•dal mi•me•noo.

---

12. And from the days of John the Baptist until now the kingdom of heaven suffereth violence, and the violent take it by force.

Greek/Transliteration
12. Ἀπὸ δὲ τῶν ἡμερῶν Ἰωάννου τοῦ βαπτιστοῦ ἕως ἄρτι ἡ βασιλεία τῶν οὐρανῶν βιάζεται, καὶ βιασταὶ ἁρπάζουσιν αὐτήν.

12. Apo de ton 'eimeron Yoannou tou baptistou 'eos arti 'ei basileia ton ouranon byazetai, kai byastai 'arpazousin autein.

Hebrew/Transliteration
יב. וּמִימֵי יוֹחָנָן הַמַּטְבִּיל עַד-הֵנָּה מַלְכוּת הַשָּׁמַיִם נִתְפְּשָׂה בְחָזְקָה וּזְרֹעֵי-כֹּחַ יַחֲזִיקוּ בָהּ:

12. Oo•mi•mey Yo•cha•nan ha•Mat•bil ad - he•na mal•choot ha•sha•ma•yim nit•pe•sa ve•choz•ka ooz•ro•ey - cho•ach ya•cha•zi•koo va.

Jewish New Testament Commentary
The Greek is difficult. As rendered, it means that violent ones (demons and their human vehicles) are trying to keep God from carrying out his plan through Yeshua, e.g., through Herod's having put Yochanan in prison (Mat_11:2).

---

13. For all the prophets and the law prophesied until John.

Greek/Transliteration
13. Πάντες γὰρ οἱ προφῆται καὶ ὁ νόμος ἕως Ἰωάννου προεφήτευσαν·

13. Pantes gar 'oi propheitai kai 'o nomos 'eos Yoannou proepheiteusan.

Hebrew/Transliteration
יג. כִּי כָל-הַנְּבִיאִים וְהַתּוֹרָה עַד-יוֹחָנָן נִבָּאוּ:

13. Ki chol - ha•n`vi•eem ve•ha•To•rah ad - Yo•cha•nan ni•ba•oo.

Rabbinic Jewish Commentary
John spake of him as already come, and in plain terms, and directed to his very person; and since his time, there have been no prophecies concerning the Messiah and his kingdom; vision and prophecy are now sealed up; all which are acknowledged by the Jews themselves, who (b) say, כל הנביאים כולן לא נתנבאו אלא לימות המשיח, "all the prophets did not prophesy but to, or of the days of the Messiah". This was the subject, and these the limits of their prophecies; for they own (c), that,

"from the day that the temple was destroyed, בטילה נבואה מן הנביאי, "prophecy was taken away from the prophets"."

Since that time, they confess they have had no prophet (d), and that they are not able to observe their signs.

(b) T. Bab. Beracot, fol. 34. 2. Sabbat, fol. 63. 1. Sanhedrim, fol. 99. 1. (c) T. Bava Bathra, fol. 12. 1. (d) Abarbinel in Dan. fol. 63. 4.

---

14. And if ye will receive it, this is Elias, which was for to come.

Greek/Transliteration
14. καὶ εἰ θέλετε δέξασθαι, αὐτός ἐστιν Ἠλίας ὁ μέλλων ἔρχεσθαι.

14. kai ei thelete dexasthai, autos estin Eilias 'o mellon erchesthai.

Hebrew/Transliteration
יד. וְאִם-תֹּאבוּ לִשְׁמֹעַ זֶה הוּא אֵלִיָּהוּ הֶעָתִיד לָבֹא:

14. Ve•eem - to•voo lish•mo•a ze hoo Eli•ya•hoo he•a•tid la•vo.

Rabbinic Jewish Commentary
is Elias, which was for to come; who was appointed by God to come, and was prophesied of Mal_4:5 that he should come; and even according to the doctrine of the Scribes and Rabbi's, he was expected to come before the Messiah; only they in general thought that Elijah the Tishbite, in person, was meant; though some, as before observed (e), were of opinion, that some great prophet equal to Elijah, and endued with the same spirit, is intended; and which is true of John the Baptist, who came "in the Spirit" and "power" of Elias, Luk_1:17. And, as it was usual with the Jews (f), to call Phinehas by the name of Elias, and Elias Phinehas, because of his

zeal for the Lord of hosts; for the same reason may John be called by the same name, there being a great resemblance between Elias and him;

John understood them, and very honestly and sincerely replies, he was not: but he does not deny that he was intended by this Elias, that was prophesied should come; yea, he says such things as might induce them to believe he was that person; hence, Christ, and he, say nothing contrary to, and irreconcilable, as the Jew (g) suggests, with each other.

(e) Vid. Pocock. not. in porta Mosis, p. 219. (f) Baal Hatturim in Num. xxv. 12. Kimchi in 1 Chron. ix. 20. Targum Jon. in Exod. vi. 18. (g) R. Isaac Chizzuk Emuna, par. 1. c. 39. & par. 2. c. 15.

---

15. He that hath ears to hear, let him hear.

Greek/Transliteration
15. Ὁ ἔχων ὦτα ἀκούειν ἀκουέτω.

15. 'O echon ota akouein akoueto.

Hebrew/Transliteration
טו. מִי אֲשֶׁר אָזְנַיִם לוֹ לִשְׁמֹעַ יִשְׁמָע:

15. Mee asher oz•na•yim lo lish•mo•a yish•ma.

Rabbinic Jewish Commentary
The phrase is to be met with in Jewish writings, where it is thus expressed (h); ""He that hears let him hear, and he that understandeth let him understand";"
(h) Zohar in Num. fol. 60. 3.

---

16. But whereunto shall I liken this generation? It is like unto children sitting in the markets, and calling unto their fellows,

Greek/Transliteration
16. Τίνι δὲ ὁμοιώσω τὴν γενεὰν ταύτην; Ὁμοία ἐστὶν παιδίοις ἐν ἀγοραῖς καθημένοις, καὶ προσφωνοῦσιν τοῖς ἑταίροις αὐτῶν,

16. Tini de 'omoioso tein genean tautein? 'Omoia estin paidiois en agorais katheimenois, kai prosphonousin tois 'etairois auton,

Hebrew/Transliteration
טז. וְאֶל-מִי אֲדַמֶּה אֶת-הַדּוֹר הַזֶּה נִדְמֶה הוּא לַיְלָדִים יֹשְׁבִים בִּשְׁוָקִים וְקֹרְאִים לְרֵעֵיהֶם לֵאמֹר:

16. Ve•el - mee a•da•me et - ha•dor ha•ze nid•me hoo lay•la•dim yosh•vim bish•va•kim ve•kor•eem le•re•ey•hem le•mor.

17. And saying, We have piped unto you, and ye have not danced; we have mourned unto you, and ye have not lamented.

Greek/Transliteration
17. καὶ λέγουσιν, Ηὐλήσαμεν ὑμῖν, καὶ οὐκ ὠρχήσασθε· ἐθρηνήσαμεν ὑμῖν, καὶ οὐκ ἐκόψασθε.

17. kai legousin, Eiuleisamen 'umin, kai ouk orcheisasthe. ethreineisamen 'umin, kai ouk ekopsasthe.

Hebrew/Transliteration
:יז. מְזַמְּרִים הָיִינוּ לָכֶם וְלֹא רְקַדְתֶּם מְקוֹנְנִים וְלֹא סְפַדְתֶּם

17. Me•zam•rim ha•yi•noo la•chem ve•lo r`ka•de•tem me•ko•ne•nim ve•lo se•fa•de•tem.

Rabbinic Jewish Commentary
Solomon says, "If a wise man contendeth with a foolish man, whether he rage or laugh, there is no rest", Pro_29:9. Upon which the Talmudists (i) comment, and illustrate it in this manner, and produce a proverbial saying, much like this in the text.

"Says God, I was angry with Ahaz, and I delivered him into the hands of the kings of Damascus; he sacrificed and burnt incense to their gods, 2Ch_28:22. I played with Amaziah, and I gave the king of Edom into his hands; he brought their gods and worshipped them, 2Ch_25:14. Says R. Papa, this is what men say, or it is a common proverb, בכיי ליה למר דלא ידע חייכי ליה למר דלא ידע, "they weep to a man who takes no notice of it, they laugh to a man who does not observe it"; woe to that man, who knows not the difference between good and evil."
(i) T. Bab. Sanhedrim, fol. 103. 1.

---

18. For John came neither eating nor drinking, and they say, He hath a devil.

Greek/Transliteration
18. Ἦλθεν γὰρ Ἰωάννης μήτε ἐσθίων μήτε πίνων, καὶ λέγουσιν, Δαιμόνιον ἔχει.

18. Eilthen gar Yoanneis meite esthion meite pinon, kai legousin, Daimonion echei.

Hebrew/Transliteration
:יח. כִּי-בָא יוֹחָנָן לֹא אֹכֵל וְלֹא שֹׁתֶה וְאָמְרוּ שֵׁד בּוֹ

18. Ki - va Yo•cha•nan lo o•chel ve•lo sho•te ve•am•roo shed bo.

19. The Son of man came eating and drinking, and they say, Behold a man gluttonous, and a winebibber, a friend of publicans and sinners. But wisdom is justified of her children.

Greek/Transliteration
19. Ἦλθεν ὁ υἱὸς τοῦ ἀνθρώπου ἐσθίων καὶ πίνων, καὶ λέγουσιν, Ἰδού, ἄνθρωπος φάγος καὶ οἰνοπότης, τελωνῶν φίλος καὶ ἁμαρτωλῶν. Καὶ ἐδικαιώθη ἡ σοφία ἀπὸ τῶν τέκνων αὐτῆς.

19. Eilthen 'o 'wios tou anthropou esthion kai pinon, kai legousin, Ydou, anthropos phagos kai oinopoteis, telonon philos kai 'amartolon. Kai edikaiothei 'ei sophia apo ton teknon auteis.

Hebrew/Transliteration
יט. וּבֶן-הָאָדָם בָּא אֹכֵל וְשֹׁתֶה וְהֵם אֹמְרִים הִנֵּה אִישׁ זוֹלֵל וְסֹבֵא וְאֹהֵב לַמּוֹכְסִים וְחַטָּאִים אַךְ הַחָכְמָה תִּצְטַדֵּק:בְּבָנֶיהָ

19. Oo•Ven - ha•adam ba o•chel ve•sho•te ve•hem om•rim hee•ne eesh zo•lel ve•so•ve ve•o•hev la•moch•sim ve•cha•ta•eem ach ha•choch•ma titz•ta•dek be•va•ne•ha.

Rabbinic Jewish Commentary
A winebibber, a common tippler, one that drinks to excess; whom the Rabbi's call (k), גרגרן, who is one, they say, that drinks up his cup at one draught; one that is given to wine and is greedy of it: (k) T. Bab. Pesachim, fol. 86. 2. Betza, fol. 25. 2.

---

20. Then began he to upbraid the cities wherein most of his mighty works were done, because they repented not:

Greek/Transliteration
20. Τότε ἤρξατο ὀνειδίζειν τὰς πόλεις ἐν αἷς ἐγένοντο αἱ πλεῖσται δυνάμεις αὐτοῦ, ὅτι οὐ μετενόησαν.

20. Tote eirxato oneidizein tas poleis en 'ais egenonto 'ai pleistai dunameis autou, 'oti ou metenoeisan.

Hebrew/Transliteration
כ. אָז הֵחֵל לָגֹל חֶרְפָּה עַל-הֶעָרִים אֲשֶׁר נַעֲשׂוּ בְתוֹכָן רֹב נִפְלְאוֹתָיו וְלֹא שָׁבוּ:

20. Az he`chel la•gol cher•pa al - he•a•rim asher na•a•soo ve•to•chan rov nif•le•o•tav ve•lo sha•voo.

---

21. Woe unto thee, Chorazin! woe unto thee, Bethsaida! for if the mighty works, which were done in you, had been done in Tyre and Sidon, they would have repented long ago in sackcloth and ashes.

Greek/Transliteration
21. Οὐαί σοι, Χοραζίν, οὐαί σοι, Βηθσαϊδά, ὅτι εἰ ἐν Τύρῳ καὶ Σιδῶνι ἐγένοντο αἱ δυνάμεις αἱ γενόμεναι ἐν ὑμῖν, πάλαι ἂν ἐν σάκκῳ καὶ σποδῷ μετενόησαν.

21. Ouai soi, Chorazin, ouai soi, Beithsaida, 'oti ei en Turo kai Sidoni egenonto 'ai dunameis 'ai genomenai en 'umin, palai an en sakko kai spodo metenoeisan.

Hebrew/Transliteration
כא. אוֹי לָךְ כּוֹרָזִין אוֹי לָךְ בֵּית-צָיְדָה כִּי לוּ נַעֲשׂוּ בְצוֹר וּבְצִידוֹן הַנִּפְלָאוֹת אֲשֶׁר נַעֲשׂוּ בְּתוֹכְכֶן כְּבָר שָׁבוּ בְשַׂק:וָאֵפֶר

21. Oy lach Korazin oy lach Beit - Tzai•da ki loo na•a•soo ve•Tzor oov•Tzi•don ha•nif•la•ot asher na•a•soo be•to•che•chen k`var sha•voo be•sak va•e•fer.

TaNaKh-Old Testament
Tzor and Tzidon. The wickedness of Tyre and Sidon and the predictions of judgment against them are detailed in Isa_23:1-8, Ezekiel 26-28, Joe_3:4-8, Amo_1:9-10 and Zec_9:2-4.

---

22. But I say unto you, It shall be more tolerable for Tyre and Sidon at the day of judgment, than for you.

Greek/Transliteration
22. Πλὴν λέγω ὑμῖν, Τύρῳ καὶ Σιδῶνι ἀνεκτότερον ἔσται ἐν ἡμέρᾳ κρίσεως, ἢ ὑμῖν.

22. Plein lego 'umin, Turo kai Sidoni anektoteron estai en 'eimera kriseos, ei 'umin.

Hebrew/Transliteration
כב. אֶפֶס אֲנִי אֹמֵר לָכֶן נָקֵל יִהְיֶה יוֹם הַמִּשְׁפָּט לְצוֹר וּלְצִידוֹן מֵאֲשֶׁר לָכֶן:

22. E•fes ani o•mer la•chen na•kel yi•hee•ye yom ha•mish•pat le•Tzor ool•Tzidon me•a•sher la•chen.

---

23. And thou, Capernaum, which art exalted unto heaven, shalt be brought down to hell: for if the mighty works, which have been done in thee, had been done in Sodom, it would have remained until this day.

Greek/Transliteration
23. Καὶ σύ, Καπερναούμ, ἡ ἕως τοῦ οὐρανοῦ ὑψωθεῖσα, ἕως ᾅδου καταβιβασθήσῃ· ὅτι εἰ ἐν Σοδόμοις ἐγένοντο αἱ δυνάμεις αἱ γενόμεναι ἐν σοί, ἔμειναν ἂν μέχρι τῆς σήμερον.

23. Kai su, Kapernaoum, 'ei 'eos tou ouranou 'upsotheisa, 'eos 'dou katabibastheisei. 'oti ei en Sodomois egenonto 'ai dunameis 'ai genomenai en soi, emeinan an mechri teis seimeron.

Hebrew/Transliteration

כג. וְאַתְּ כְּפַר-נַחוּם אֲשֶׁר רוֹמַמְתְּ עַד-הַשָּׁמַיִם אֶל-שְׁאוֹל תּוּרָדִי כִּי לוּ נַעֲשׂוּ בִסְדֹם הַנִּפְלָאוֹת אֲשֶׁר נַעֲשׂוּ בְתוֹכֵכִי וְעָמְדָה עַל-תִּלָּהּ עַד-הַיּוֹם הַזֶּה

23. Ve•at K`far - Na•choom asher ro•mamt ad - ha•sha•ma•yim el - sh`ol too•ra•di ki loo na•a•soo vi•S`dom ha•nif•la•ot asher na•a•soo be•to•che•chi ve•am•da al - ti•la ad - ha•yom ha•ze.

Rabbinic/Jewish New Testament Commentary

The phrase remained is Jewish, and is used of Sodom by the Rabbi's, who say (o), that "Abraham was "ninety nine" years of age when he was circumcised, and then was the overthrow of Sodom; which was "fifty one" years, after the generation of the division (of the people and languages), and near "fifty two" years; but "Zoar remained" one year, אחר ישוב סדום, "after Sodom remained"."

According to the Jews, it stood but fifty two years at most (p): and they have a notion, that Sodom and Gomorrha will be built again in the future state (q), or world to come, the times of the Messiah.

(n) Itinerarium, p. 37. (o) Juchasin, fol. 8. 1. (p) T. Bab. Sabbat, fol. 11. 2. & Gloss. in ib. Jarchi in Gen. xix. 20. (q) Shemot Rabba, sect. 15. fol. 101. 3.

Sh'ol. Usually brought into English as "Sheol"; Greek *adês* ("Hades"), the place of the dead. In the *Tanakh* Sh'ol is the grave where dead wait. Sometimes English versions use "Hell" to translate "*adês*"; this can be confusing, because "Hell" also translates "*gehenna*," a place of fire for the dead bodies. But see Luk_16:23, where *adês* is also described as a place of fire.

---

24. But I say unto you, That it shall be more tolerable for the land of Sodom in the day of judgment, than for thee.

Greek/Transliteration

24. Πλὴν λέγω ὑμῖν, ὅτι γῇ Σοδόμων ἀνεκτότερον ἔσται ἐν ἡμέρᾳ κρίσεως, ἢ σοί.

24. Plein lego 'umin, 'oti gei Sodomon anektoteron estai en 'eimera kriseos, ei soi.

Hebrew/Transliteration

כד. אֶפֶס אֲנִי אֹמֵר לָכֶן נָקֵל יִהְיֶה יוֹם הַמִּשְׁפָּט לְאַדְמַת סְדֹם מֵאֲשֶׁר לָכֶן:

24. E•fes ani o•mer la•chen na•kel yi•hee•ye yom ha•mish•pat le•ad•mat S`dom me•a•sher la•chen.

Rabbinic Commentary

Such a way of expressing and setting forth the severer punishment of others, by that of Sodom, is not unusual in the Old Testament; see Lam_4:6 nor in Jewish writers, who say (r), that "the Israelites were fit for, or deserved, חמור מעונש סדום לעונש יותר, "a far more heavy punishment than the punishment of Sodom": because they abounded with prophets, rising early, and sending them, but they did not hearken; whereas Sodom had no hands stayed on her, or prophets to warn them." (r) Tzeror Hammor, fol. 82. 1.

---

25. At that time Jesus answered and said, I thank thee, O Father, Lord of heaven and earth, because thou hast hid these things from the wise and prudent, and hast revealed them unto babes.

Greek/Transliteration

25. Ἐν ἐκείνῳ τῷ καιρῷ ἀποκριθεὶς ὁ Ἰησοῦς εἶπεν, Ἐξομολογοῦμαί σοι, πάτερ, κύριε τοῦ οὐρανοῦ καὶ τῆς γῆς, ὅτι ἀπέκρυψας ταῦτα ἀπὸ σοφῶν καὶ συνετῶν, καὶ ἀπεκάλυψας αὐτὰ νηπίοις.

25. En ekeino to kairo apokritheis 'o Yeisous eipen, Exomologoumai soi, pater, kurie tou ouranou kai teis geis, 'oti apekrupsas tauta apo sophon kai suneton, kai apekalupsas auta neipiois.

Hebrew/Transliteration

כה. בָּעֵת הַהִיא עָנָה יֵשׁוּעַ וַיֹּאמַר אוֹדְךָ אָבִי אֲדוֹן הַשָּׁמַיִם וְהָאָרֶץ כִּי הִסְתַּרְתָּ אֶת-אֵלֶּה מֵעֵינֵי חֲכָמִים וּנְבוֹנִים:וְגִלִּיתָ אֹתָם לְעוֹלָלִים

25. Ba•et ha•hee ana Yeshua va•yo•mar od•cha Avi Adon ha•sha•ma•yim ve•ha•a•retz ki his•tar•ta et - ele me•ey•ney cha•cha•mim oon•vo•nim ve•gi•li•ta o•tam le•o•la•lim.

Rabbinic Jewish Commentary

The persons from whom these things were hid, are "the wise and prudent"; in things worldly, natural, and civil; men of great parts and learning, of a large compass of knowledge, having a considerable share of sagacity, penetration, and wisdom; or, at least, who were wise and prudent in their own conceits, as were the Scribes and Pharisees, and the schools of Hillell and Shammai, the two famous doctors of that day: and indeed the people of the Jews in common were so; who thus applaud themselves at the eating of the passover every year, and say, כלנו חכמים כלנו נבונים כלנו יודעים את התורה, "we are all wise, we are all prudent, we all understand the law" (s); the same is elsewhere (t) said of all Israel; in their opinion they were so, yet the things of the Gospel are hidden from them.
The Jews themselves have a notion, that in the days of the Messiah, children and babes shall have knowledge of divine things.

"Says Simeon ben Jochai (u), it is not the pleasure of God that wisdom should be so revealed to the world; but when it is near the days of the Messiah, even רביי דעלמא, "little children", or the "babes that are in the world", shall find out the hidden things of wisdom, and know thereby the ends, and the computations of times; and at that time it shall be revealed to all:" and there is more truth in what they own elsewhere (w), than they themselves are aware of, when they say, that

"from the day that the temple was destroyed, prophecy has been taken away from the prophets, and given לשוטים ולתינוקות, "to fools and babes"."

(s) Haggada Shel Pesach, p. 5. Ed. Ritangel. (t) Tzeror Hammor, fol. 135. 1. (u) Zohar in Gen. fol. 74. 1. (w) T. Bab. Bava Bathra, fol. 12. 2.

---

26. Even so, Father: for so it seemed good in thy sight.

Greek/Transliteration
26. Ναί, ὁ πατήρ, ὅτι οὕτως ἐγένετο εὐδοκία ἔμπροσθέν σου.

26. Nai, 'o pateir, 'oti 'outos egeneto eudokia emprosthen sou.

Hebrew/Transliteration
:כו. אָכֵן אָבִי כֵּן הָיָה הָרָצוֹן לְפָנֶיךָ

26. A•chen Avi ken ha•ya ha•ra•tzon le•fa•ne•cha.

Rabbinic Jewish Commentary
Or, "so is the good will", or "pleasure before thee": thus, יהי רצון מלפניך, "let it be the good will before thee", or "in thy sight, O Lord", is a phrase often to be met with in the Jews' forms of prayer (x). (x) Seder Tephillot, fol. 4. 2. & 5. 1. & passim. Ed. Amsterdam.

---

27. All things are delivered unto me of my Father: and no man knoweth the Son, but the Father; neither knoweth any man the Father, save the Son, and he to whomsoever the Son will reveal him.

Greek/Transliteration
27. Πάντα μοι παρεδόθη ὑπὸ τοῦ πατρός μου· καὶ οὐδεὶς ἐπιγινώσκει τὸν υἱόν, εἰ μὴ ὁ πατήρ· οὐδὲ τὸν πατέρα τις ἐπιγινώσκει, εἰ μὴ ὁ υἱός, καὶ ᾧ ἐὰν βούληται ὁ υἱὸς ἀποκαλύψαι.

27. Panta moi paredothei 'upo tou patros mou. kai oudeis epiginoskei ton 'wion, ei mei 'o pateir. oude ton patera tis epiginoskei, ei mei 'o 'wios, kai 'o ean bouleitai 'o 'wios apokalupsai.

Hebrew/Transliteration
כז. הַכֹּל נִמְסַר בְּיָדִי מֵאֵת אָבִי וְאֵין אִישׁ יֹדֵעַ אֶת-הַבֵּן זוּלָתִי הָאָב וְאֶת-הָאָב אֵין אִישׁ יֹדֵעַ זוּלָתִי הַבֵּן וְהַהוּא:אֲשֶׁר חָפֵץ בּוֹ הַבֵּן לְגַלּוֹתוֹ לוֹ

27. Ha•kol nim•sar be•ya•di me•et Avi ve•eyn eesh yo•de•a et - ha•Ben zoo•la•tee ha•Av ve•et - ha•Av eyn eesh yo•de•a zoo•la•tee ha•Ben ve•ha•hoo asher cha•fetz bo ha•Ben le•ga•lo•to lo.

---

28. Come unto me, all ye that labour and are heavy laden, and I will give you rest.

Greek/Transliteration
28. Δεῦτε πρός με πάντες οἱ κοπιῶντες καὶ πεφορτισμένοι, κἀγὼ ἀναπαύσω ὑμᾶς.

28. Deute pros me pantes 'oi kopiontes kai pephortismenoi, kago anapauso 'umas.

Hebrew/Transliteration
כח. פְּנוּ-אֵלַי כָּל-עָמֵל וּמְסֻבָּל וַאֲנִי אֶתֵּן לָכֶם מַרְגּוֹעַ:

28. P`noo - e•lai kol - amel oom•soo•bal va•a•ni e•ten la•chem mar•go•a.

Rabbinic Jewish Commentary
The Jews say (y), that מנוחת תורה, "the law is rest"; and so explain Gen_49:15 of it: but a truly sensible sinner enjoys no rest, but in Yeshua; it is like Noah's dove, which could find no rest for the soles of its feet, until it returned to the ark; and they themselves expect perfect rest in the days of the Messiah, and call his world מנוחה, rest (z). (y) Tzeror Hammor, fol. 39. 3. (z) Tzeror Hammor, fol. 150. 2.

---

29. Take my yoke upon you, and learn of me; for I am meek and lowly in heart: and ye shall find rest unto your souls.

Greek/Transliteration
29. Ἄρατε τὸν ζυγόν μου ἐφ᾽ ὑμᾶς καὶ μάθετε ἀπ᾽ ἐμοῦ, ὅτι πρᾷός εἰμι καὶ ταπεινὸς τῇ καρδίᾳ· καὶ εὑρήσετε ἀνάπαυσιν ταῖς ψυχαῖς ὑμῶν.

29. Arate ton zugon mou eph 'umas kai mathete ap emou, 'oti praos eimi kai tapeinos tei kardia. kai 'eureisete anapausin tais psuchais 'umon.

Hebrew/Transliteration
כט. שְׂאוּ אֶת-עֻלִּי עֲלֵיכֶם וְלִמְדוּ מִמֶּנִּי כִּי-עָנָיו אָנֹכִי וְשַׁח לֵבָב וְתִמְצְאוּ מְנוּחָה לְנַפְשֹׁתֵיכֶם:

29. S`oo et - oo•li aley•chem ve•lim•doo mi•me•ni ki - anav ano•chi ve•shach le•vav ve•tim•tze•oo me•noo•cha le•naf•sho•tey•chem.

Rabbinic Jewish Commentary
R' Menachem Schneerson writes, "The unique quality of Mashiach is that he will be humble. Though he will be the ultimate in greatness, for he will teach Torah to the Patriarchs and to Moshe Rabeinu (alav hashalom), still he will be the ultimate

in humility and self-nullification, for he will also teach simple folk"
Hayom Yom: Menachem Av 1, Rosh Chodesh, Compiled by the Lubavitcher Rebbe, free translation by Yitschak Meir Kagan, Kehot Publication Society

The phrase is Rabbinical. The Jewish Rabbi's often speak (a) of עול מלכות שמים, "the yoke of the kingdom of heaven", and of persons taking it upon them; and which they exhort to, and express in much such language as here (b); קבילו קדישא עלייכו עול מלכותא, "take upon you the yoke of the holy kingdom", every day. They distinguish this from the yoke of the law, and say (c).

"a man must first take upon him the yoke of the kingdom of heaven, and after that take upon him the "yoke" of the commandment."

The Jews have a saying (d),

"for ever let a man ענוותן כהילל, "be meek as Hillell", and let him not be wrathful as "Shammai":" which two men were presidents of their universities about the times of Yeshua. But Yeshua says, "learn of me", not of "Hillell", or any of your Rabbi's.

(a) T. Hieros. Beracot, fol. 4. 1. Bab. Beracot, fol. 61. 2. Zohar in Lev. fol. 46. 4. Caphtor, fol. 44. 2. Tzeror Hammor, fol. 2. 2. (b) Zohar in Num. fol. 51. 2. Caphtor, fol. 48. 2. (c) Misn. Beracot, c. 2. sect. 2. T. Hieros. Beracot, fol. 4. 2. (d) T. Bab. Sabbat, fol. 30. 2.

---

30. For my yoke is easy, and my burden is light.

Greek/Transliteration
30. Ὁ γὰρ ζυγός μου χρηστός, καὶ τὸ φορτίον μου ἐλαφρόν ἐστιν.

30. 'O gar zugos mou chreistos, kai to phortion mou elaphron estin.

Hebrew/Transliteration
ל. כִּי עֻלִּי רַךְ וּמַשָּׂאִי קָל:

30. Ki oo•li rach oo•ma•sa•ee kal.

Matthew, Chapter 12

1. At that time Jesus went on the sabbath day through the corn; and his disciples were an hungred, and began to pluck the ears of corn, and to eat.

Greek/Transliteration
1. Ἐν ἐκείνῳ τῷ καιρῷ ἐπορεύθη ὁ Ἰησοῦς τοῖς σάββασιν διὰ τῶν σπορίμων· οἱ δὲ μαθηταὶ αὐτοῦ ἐπείνασαν, καὶ ἤρξαντο τίλλειν στάχυας καὶ ἐσθίειν.

1. En ekeino to kairo eporeuthei 'o Yeisous tois sabbasin dya ton sporimon. 'oi de matheitai autou epeinasan, kai eirxanto tillein stachuas kai esthiein.

Hebrew/Transliteration
א. בָּעֵת הַהִיא הָלַךְ יֵשׁוּעַ בְּשָׂדֵה קָמָה בְּיוֹם הַשַׁבָּת וַיִּרְעָבוּ תַלְמִידָיו וַיָּחֵלּוּ לִקְטוֹף מְלִילֹת בְּיָדָם וַיֹּאכֵלוּ:

1. Ba•et ha•hee ha•lach Yeshua bis•de ka•ma be•yom ha•Sha•bat va•yir•a•voo tal•mi•dav va•ya•che•loo lik•tof me•li•lot be•ya•dam va•yo•che•loo.

Rabbinic/Jewish New Testament Commentary
Shabbat. The Hebrew word has entered English as "Sabbath." The biblical concept of a weekly day for resting from workaday purposes has no close parallel in the ancient world. The fourth commandment (Exo_20:8-11, Deu_5:12-14) connects *Shabbat* with the fact that God rested after the six days of creation (Gen_2:1-3); makes it a day of equality in which all, high and low alike, are entitled to rest; and sets it aside as a day which is holy, on which God is to be honored.

Luke adds, "rubbing them in their hands"; and so here in the Syriac, Arabic, and Persic versions, it is rendered, "they began to rub": as they passed along, they plucked off the ears of corn, either barley or wheat, and rubbed them in their hands, to get the grain clear of the husk, or beard, and eat them; contenting themselves with such mean and unprepared food, when the Jews on that day fed on the best of foods (e). (e) *Vid. Maimon. Hilch. Sabbat, c. 30. sect. 7, 8, 9, 10.*

---

2. But when the Pharisees saw it, they said unto him, Behold, thy disciples do that which is not lawful to do upon the sabbath day.

Greek/Transliteration
2. Οἱ δὲ Φαρισαῖοι ἰδόντες εἶπον αὐτῷ, Ἰδού, οἱ μαθηταί σου ποιοῦσιν ὃ οὐκ ἔξεστιν ποιεῖν ἐν σαββάτῳ.

2. 'Oi de Pharisaioi idontes eipon auto, Ydou, 'oi matheitai sou poiousin 'o ouk exestin poiein en sabbato.

Hebrew/Transliteration
ב: וַיִּרְאוּ הַפְּרוּשִׁים וַיֹּאמְרוּ אֵלָיו הִנֵּה תַלְמִידֶיךָ עֹשִׂים אֵת אֲשֶׁר לֹא-יֵעָשֶׂה בְּשַׁבָּת

2. Va•yir•oo ha•P`roo•shim va•yom•roo elav hee•ne tal•mi•de•cha o•sim et asher lo - ye•a•se va•Sha•bat.

Rabbinic/Jewish New Testament Commentary

The Greek text says, literally, "doing what is unlawful on *Shabbat*," that is, doing something the *P'rushim* considered to be against the *Torah*. The argument was not over whether it was permitted to pick grain by hand from someone else's field, for that is expressly allowed by Deu_23:26 (Deu_23:25), but whether it could be done on *Shabbat*. At issue behind this seemingly minor matter is whether the Pharisaic tradition-which evolved into what rabbinic Judaism calls the Oral *Torah*, later committed to writing in the Mishna, Gemara and other works-is God's revelation to man and binding on all Jews.

According to them (g), "it was not lawful for a man to visit his gardens, ושדותיו, "or his fields", on the sabbath day, to see what they want, or how the fruits grow; for such walking is to do his own pleasure." Their rule is (h).

"he that reaps (on the sabbath day) ever so little, is guilty (of stoning), ותולש תולדה קוצר הוא, and "plucking of ears of corn is a derivative of reaping";"

(f) Ib. c. 27. sect. 1. (g) R. Moses Kotzensis Mitzvot Tora prec. neg. 65. (h) Maimon. Hilch. Sabbat, c. 8. sect. 3. & 7. 1

---

3. But he said unto them, Have ye not read what David did, when he was an hungred, and they that were with him;

Greek/Transliteration

3. Ὁ δὲ εἶπεν αὐτοῖς, Οὐκ ἀνέγνωτε τί ἐποίησεν Δαυίδ, ὅτε ἐπείνασεν αὐτὸς καὶ οἱ μετ᾽ αὐτοῦ·

3. 'O de eipen autois, Ouk anegnote ti epoieisen Dauid, 'ote epeinasen autos kai 'oi met autou.

Hebrew/Transliteration

ג. וַיֹּאמֶר אֲלֵיהֶם הֲלֹא קְרָאתֶם מֶה עָשָׂה דָוִד כַּאֲשֶׁר רָעֵב הוּא וְאֵלֶּה אֲשֶׁר אִתּוֹ:

3. Va•yo•mer aley•hem ha•lo ke•ra•tem me asa David ka•a•sher ra•ev hoo ve•e•le asher ee•to.

Rabbinic/Jewish New Testament Commentary

Though Lev_24:5-9 allows only *cohanim* to eat the bread of the Presence set aside for display before the ark in the house of God (Tabernacle), 1Sa_21:1-6 (1Sa_21:2-7) recounts how King David and the priest Achimelekh violated this *mitzvah* of the Written *Torah*-which the *P'rushim* would accept as more authoritative than a rule in the Oral *Torah*. A *kal v'chomer* argument (Mat_6:30) is implied.

4. How he entered into the house of God, and did eat the shewbread, which was not lawful for him to eat, neither for them which were with him, but only for the priests?

Greek/Transliteration
4. πῶς εἰσῆλθεν εἰς τὸν οἶκον τοῦ θεοῦ, καὶ τοὺς ἄρτους τῆς προθέσεως ἔφαγεν, οὓς οὐκ ἐξὸν ἦν αὐτῷ φαγεῖν, οὐδὲ τοῖς μετ᾽ αὐτοῦ, εἰ μὴ τοῖς ἱερεῦσιν μόνοις;

4. pos eiseilthen eis ton oikon tou theou, kai tous artous teis protheseos ephagen, 'ous ouk exon ein auto phagein, oude tois met autou, ei mei tois 'iereusin monois?

Hebrew/Transliteration
ד. אֲשֶׁר בָּא אֶל-בֵּית הָאֱלֹהִים וַיֹּאכַל אֶת-לֶחֶם הַפָּנִים אֲשֶׁר עַל-פִּי הַתּוֹרָה לֹא יֹאכַל הוּא וּנְעָרָיו - בִּלְתִּי אִם:הַכֹּהֲנִים לְבַדָּם

4. Asher ba el - beit ha•Elohim va•yo•chal et - le•chem ha•pa•nim asher al - pi ha•Torah lo yo•chal hoo oon•a•rav bil•tee eem - ha•ko•ha•nim le•va•dam.

Rabbinic Jewish Commentary
and did eat the shewbread; for that this is meant by the hallowed bread, in 1Sa_21:6 is certain; though R. Joseph Kimchi (n) thinks it was the bread of the thank offering; to which R. Levi ben Getsom (o) seems to incline: but the general sense of the Jewish Rabbi's (p) is, that it was the showbread; and which is very clear from that text, and is rightly affirmed by Yeshua;

(n) Apud R. David Kimchi in 1 Sam. xxi. 6. (o) In ib. (p) T. Bab. Menachot, fol. 95. 2. R. David Kimchi, Abarbinel & Laniado in 1 Sam. xxi. 6.

---

5. Or have ye not read in the law, how that on the sabbath days the priests in the temple profane the sabbath, and are blameless?

Greek/Transliteration
5. Ἢ οὐκ ἀνέγνωτε ἐν τῷ νόμῳ, ὅτι τοῖς σάββασιν οἱ ἱερεῖς ἐν τῷ ἱερῷ τὸ σάββατον βεβηλοῦσιν, καὶ ἀναίτιοί εἰσιν;

5. Ei ouk anegnote en to nomo, 'oti tois sabbasin 'oi 'iereis en to 'iero to sabbaton bebeilousin, kai anaitioi eisin?

Hebrew/Transliteration
ה. וְגַם הֲלֹא קְרָאתֶם בַּתּוֹרָה כִּי הַכֹּהֲנִים בַּמִּקְדָּשׁ יְחַלְּלוּ אֶת-יוֹם הַשַּׁבָּת וְאֵין בָּהֶם עָוֹן:

5. Ve•gam ha•lo ke•ra•tem ba•To•rah ki ha•ko•ha•nim ba•mik•dash ye•cha•le•loo et - yom ha•Sha•bat ve••eyn ba•hem a•von.

Rabbinic/Jewish New Testament Commentary

The *Torah* itself specifies that some *mitzvot* are more important than others (see Joh_5:22-23, Gal_2:12). Keeping *Shabbat* is important, but the animal sacrifices required by Num_28:1-10 are more so, so that the *cohanim* work on *Shabbat* in order to offer them. ("Temple service takes precedence over *Shabbat*," Shabbat 132b.) What exculpated these men was, that what they did was done in the temple, and for the service of it, upon which an emphasis is put; and agrees with their canons, which say, that there is no prohibition in the sanctuary; איסור שבות במקדש התר הוא, "that which is forbidden to be done on the sabbath, is lawful to be done in the sanctuary" (y): and whereas, it might be objected to the disciples of Yeshua, that they were not priests; and what they did was not in the temple, but in the fields; to this it is replied, in the following words.

(y) Hilchot Sabbat, c. 21. sect. 27.

---

6. But I say unto you, That in this place is one greater than the temple.

Greek/Transliteration
6. Λέγω δὲ ὑμῖν ὅτι τοῦ ἱεροῦ μεῖζόν ἐστιν ὧδε.

6. Lego de 'umin 'oti tou 'ierou meizon estin 'ode.

Hebrew/Transliteration
:ו. וַאֲנִי אֹמֵר לָכֶם כִּי יֵשׁ בָּזֶה גָּדוֹל מִן-הַמִּקְדָּשׁ

6. Va•a•ni o•mer la•chem ki yesh ba•ze ga•dol min - ha•mik•dash.

Rabbinic Jewish Commentary
"Mashiach must be able to transcend anything and everything in the world-even and especially all evil that was ever perpetrated-to rectify and perfect all mankind. Thus, Mashiach must be someone extremely unique and very awesome."
Machiach:Who, What, Why, How, Where, When; Chaim Kramer, pg.18

---

7. But if ye had known what this meaneth, I will have mercy, and not sacrifice, ye would not have condemned the guiltless.

Greek/Transliteration
7. Εἰ δὲ ἐγνώκειτε τί ἐστιν, Ἔλεον θέλω καὶ οὐ θυσίαν, οὐκ ἂν κατεδικάσατε τοὺς ἀναιτίους.

7. Ei de egnokeite ti estin, Eleon thelo kai ou thusian, ouk an katedikasate tous anaitious.

Hebrew/Tranliteration
:ז. וְלוּ יְדַעְתֶּם מַה-זֶּה חֶסֶד חָפַצְתִּי וְלֹא זָבַח לֹא הִרְשַׁעְתֶּם אֶת-הַנְּקִיִּם

7. Ve•loo ye•da•a•tem ma - ze che•sed cha•fatz•ti ve•lo za•vach lo hir•sha•a•tem et - ha•ne•ki•yim.

---

8. For the Son of man is Lord even of the sabbath day.

Greek/Transliteration
8. κύριος γάρ ἐστιν τοῦ σαββάτου ὁ υἱὸς τοῦ ἀνθρώπου.

8. kurios gar estin tou sabbatou 'o 'wios tou anthropou.

Hebrew/Transliteration
ח: כִּי בֶן-הָאָדָם גַּם-אֲדוֹן הַשַּׁבָּת הוּא.

8. Ki Ben - ha•a•dam gam - Adon ha•Sha•bat hoo.

Rabbinic Jewish Commentary
Jews so far agree to this, that he that commanded the law of the sabbath, could dispense with it; they say (z), that "the day on which Jericho was taken was the sabbath day; and that though they slew and burnt on the sabbath day, מי שצוה על השבת צוה לחלל שבת, "he that commanded the observation of the sabbath, commanded the profanation of it". (z) R. David Kimchi in Josh. vi. 11.

---

9. And when he was departed thence, he went into their synagogue:

Greek/Transliteration
9. Καὶ μεταβὰς ἐκεῖθεν ἦλθεν εἰς τὴν συναγωγὴν αὐτῶν.

9. Kai metabas ekeithen eilthen eis tein sunagogein auton.

Hebrew/Transliteration
ט: וַיַּעֲבֹר מִשָּׁם וַיָּבֹא אֶל-בֵּית-הַכְּנֶסֶת אֲשֶׁר לָהֶם.

9. Va•ya•a•vor mi•sham va•ya•vo el - beit - ha•k`ne•set asher la•hem.

---

10. And, behold, there was a man which had his hand withered. And they asked him, saying, Is it lawful to heal on the sabbath days? that they might accuse him.

Greek/Transliteration
10. Καὶ ἰδού, ἄνθρωπος ἦν τὴν χεῖρα ἔχων ξηράν· καὶ ἐπηρώτησαν αὐτόν, λέγοντες, Εἰ ἔξεστιν τοῖς σάββασιν θεραπεύειν; ἵνα κατηγορήσωσιν αὐτοῦ.

10. Kai idou, anthropos ein tein cheira echon xeiran. kai epeiroteisan auton, legontes, Ei exestin tois sabbasin therapeuein? 'ina kateigoreisosin autou.

Hebrew/Transliteration
י. וְהִנֵּה-שָׁם אִישׁ אֲשֶׁר יָדוֹ יְבֵשָׁה וַיִּשְׁאָלֻהוּ לֵאמֹר הַאִם כַּתּוֹרָה לְרַפֵּא בְשַׁבָּת לְמַעַן תִּמְצְאוּ יָדָם לְשִׂטְנוֹ:

10. Ve•hee•ne - sham eesh asher ya•do ye•ve•sha va•yish•a•loo•hoo le•mor ha•eem ka•To•rah le•ra•pe va•Sha•bat le•ma•an tim•tza ya•dam le•sit•no.

Rabbinic Jewish Commentary

Such a case is mentioned in the Talmud (a), "it happened to one, "wewrz hvbyv, that his arm was dry, or withered. Jerom says (b), in the Gospel which the Nazarenes and Hebionites used, this man is said to be a plasterer, and so might possibly come by his misfortune through his business; and being a man that got his bread by his hand labour, the case was the more affecting... for their determinations were, that healing was not lawful on such a day; nor were any means to be made use of for that purpose: if a man received a cure accidentally, it was very well; but no methods were to be taken with intention: as for instance (c);

"if a man had an ailment in his throat, he might not gargle it with oil, but he might swallow a large quantity of oil, ואם נתרפא נתרפא "and "if he was healed, he was healed" (i.e. it was very well, it was no breach of the sabbath); they may not chew mastic, nor rub the teeth with spice, on the sabbath day, בזמן שמתכוין לרפואה, "when it is intended "for healing"; but if it is intended for the savour of his mouth, it is free."

There are several things they allowed might be done on the sabbath; but then they did not reckon them to come under the notion of healing.

"Three (d) things R. Ishmael bar Jose said he had heard from R. Matthia ben Charash; they might let blood for the stranguary on the sabbath day; one that was bit by a mad dog, they might give him hog's liver to eat; and he that had an ailment in his mouth, they might put spice to it on the sabbath day: but the wise men say of these, that there is not in them משום רפואה, anything of medicine."

Indeed, in case of extreme danger of life they did admit of the use of medicine, by the prescription of a physician (e).

(a) T. Hieros. Yoma, fol. 40. 1. (b) In loc. (c) Maimon. Hilchot Sabbat, c. 21. sect. 24. (d) T. Bab. Yoma, fol. 84. 1. Vid. Misn. Yoma, e. 8. sect. 7. (e) Kotsensis Mitzvot Tora pr. neg. 65. Maimon. in Misn. Sabbat, c. 18. sect. 3.

---

11. And he said unto them, What man shall there be among you, that shall have one sheep, and if it fall into a pit on the sabbath day, will he not lay hold on it, and lift it out?

Greek/Transliteration
11. Ὁ δὲ εἶπεν αὐτοῖς, Τίς ἔσται ἐξ ὑμῶν ἄνθρωπος, ὃς ἕξει πρόβατον ἕν, καὶ ἐὰν ἐμπέσῃ τοῦτο τοῖς σάββασιν εἰς βόθυνον, οὐχὶ κρατήσει αὐτὸ καὶ ἐγερεῖ;

11. 'O de eipen autois, Tis estai ex 'umon anthropos, 'os 'exei probaton 'en, kai ean empesei touto tois sabbasin eis bothunon, ouchi krateisei auto kai egerei?

Hebrew/Transliteration

יא. וַיֹּאמֶר אֲלֵיהֶם מִי אִישׁ מִכֶּם אֲשֶׁר-לוֹ כִּבְשָׂה וְהִיא כִי תִפּוֹל אֶל-הַבּוֹר בַּשַׁבָּת לֹא יַחֲזִיק בָּהּ וְיַעֲלֶנָּה:

11. Va•yo•mer aley•hem mee eesh mi•kem asher - lo kiv•sa ve•hee chi ti•pol el - ha•bor ba•Sha•bat lo ya•cha•zik ba ve•ya•a•le•na.

Rabbinic Jewish Commentary

(f): "if a beast fall into a ditch, or a pool of water, if food can be given it, where it is, they feed it till the going out of the sabbath; but if not, bolsters and pillows may be brought, and put under it, and if it can come out: it may come out:" and which is elsewhere (g) a little differently expressed; "if a beast fall into a ditch, or pool of water, it is forbidden a man to bring it out with his hand; but if he can give it food where it is, it may be fed till the going out of the sabbath:" which seems to have been made since the times of Yeshua, and in opposition to this observation of his. (f) Maimon. Hilchot Sabbat, c. 25. sect. 26. (g) Kotsensis Mitzvot Tora pr. neg. 65.

---

12. How much then is a man better than a sheep? Wherefore it is lawful to do well on the sabbath days.

Greek/Transliteration

12. Πόσῳ οὖν διαφέρει ἄνθρωπος προβάτου. Ὥστε ἔξεστιν τοῖς σάββασιν καλῶς ποιεῖν.

12. Poso oun dyapherei anthropos probatou. 'Oste exestin tois sabbasin kalos poiein.

Hebrew/Transliteration

יב. וּמַה-יָּקָר עֵרֶךְ אָדָם מִן-הַכֶּבֶשׂ עַל-כֵּן כַּתּוֹרָה הוּא לַעֲשׂוֹת טוֹב בַּשַׁבָּת:

12. Oo•ma - ya•kar e•rech adam min - ha•ke•ves al - ken ka•To•rah hoo la•a•sot tov ba•Sha•bat.

Rabbinic Jewish Commentary

It is said of Hillell (i), that, "he sat by a window to hear the words of the living God, from the mouth of Shemaia and Abtalion; and they say that that day was the evening of the sabbath, and the winter solstice, and the snow descended from heaven; and when the pillar of the morning ascended, (when it was daylight,) Shemaia said to Abtalion, brother Abtalion, all other days the house is light, but today it is dark, perhaps it is a cloudy day: they lift up their eyes, and saw the form of a man at the window; they went up, and found upon him snow the height of three cubits; they broke through and delivered him; and they washed him, and anointed him, and set him over against his dwelling, and said, very worthy is this man להלל עליו את שבת, "to profane the sabbath for him". (i) T. Bab. Yoma, fol. 35. 2.

---

13. Then saith he to the man, Stretch forth thine hand. And he stretched it forth; and it was restored whole, like as the other.

Greek/Transliteration

13. Τότε λέγει τῷ ἀνθρώπῳ, Ἔκτεινον τὴν χεῖρά σου. Καὶ ἐξέτεινεν, καὶ ἀποκατεστάθη ὑγιὴς ὡς ἡ ἄλλη.

13. Tote legei to anthropo, Ekteinon tein cheira sou. Kai exeteinen, kai apokatestathei 'ugieis 'os 'ei allei.

Hebrew/Transliteration

:יג. אָז אָמַר אֶל-הָאִישׁ הוֹשֵׁט אֶת-יָדֶךָ וַיּוֹשֶׁט אֹתָהּ וַתָּשָׁב לְאֵיתָנָהּ כָּאַחֶרֶת

13. Az amar el - ha•eesh ho•shet et - ya•de•cha va•yo•shet o•ta va•ta•shov le•ey•ta•na ka•a•che•ret.

---

14. Then the Pharisees went out, and held a council against him, how they might destroy him.

Greek/Transliteration

14. Οἱ δὲ Φαρισαῖοι συμβούλιον ἔλαβον κατ' αὐτοῦ ἐξελθόντες, ὅπως αὐτὸν ἀπολέσωσιν.

14. 'Oi de Pharisaioi sumboulion elabon kat autou exelthontes, 'opos auton apolesosin.

Hebrew/Transliteration

:יד. וְהַפְּרוּשִׁים יָצְאוּ וַיָּשִׂיתוּ עֵצוֹת עָלָיו בַּמֶּה לְהַשְׁחִיתוֹ

14. Ve•haP`roo•shim yatz•oo va•ya•shee•too e•tzot alav ba•me le•hash•chi•to.

---

15. But when Jesus knew it, he withdrew himself from thence: and great multitudes followed him, and he healed them all;

Greek/Transliteration

15. Ὁ δὲ Ἰησοῦς γνοὺς ἀνεχώρησεν ἐκεῖθεν· καὶ ἠκολούθησαν αὐτῷ ὄχλοι πολλοί, καὶ ἐθεράπευσεν αὐτοὺς πάντας,

15. 'O de Yeisous gnous anechoreisen ekeithen. kai eikoloutheisan auto ochloi polloi, kai etherapeusen autous pantas,

Hebrew/Transliteration

טו. וַיֵּדַע יֵשׁוּעַ וַיִּפֶן וַיֵּלֶךְ מִשָּׁם וַיֵּלֶךְ אַחֲרָיו הָמוֹן עַם רָב וַיִרְפָּא אֶת־כֻּלָּם:

15. Va•ye•da Yeshua va•yi•fen va•ye•lech mi•sham va•ye•lech a•cha•rav ha•mon am rav vay•ra•pe et - koo•lam.

---

16. And charged them that they should not make him known:

Greek/Transliteration

16. καὶ ἐπετίμησεν αὐτοῖς, ἵνα μὴ φανερὸν αὐτὸν ποιήσωσιν·

16. kai epetimeisen autois, 'ina mei phaneron auton poieisosin.

Hebrew/Transliteration

טז. וַיָּעַד בָּם לְבִלְתִּי יְגַלּוּ אֹתוֹ:

16. Va•ya•ad bam le•vil•ti ye•ga•loo o•to.

---

17. That it might be fulfilled which was spoken by Esaias the prophet, saying,

Greek/Transliteration

17. ὅπως πληρωθῇ τὸ ῥηθὲν διὰ Ἡσαΐου τοῦ προφήτου, λέγοντος,

17. 'opos pleirothei to 'reithen dya Eisaiou tou propheitou, legontos,

Hebrew/Transliteration

יז. לְמַלֹּאת אֶת אֲשֶׁר־דִּבֶּר יְשַׁעְיָהוּ הַנָּבִיא לֵאמֹר:

17. Le•ma•lot et asher - di•ber Ye•sha•a•ya•hoo ha•na•vee le•mor.

---

18. Behold my servant, whom I have chosen; my beloved, in whom my soul is well pleased: I will put my spirit upon him, and he shall shew judgment to the Gentiles.

Greek/Transliteration

18. Ἰδού, ὁ παῖς μου ὃν ᾑρέτισα· ὁ ἀγαπητός μου εἰς ὃν εὐδόκησεν ἡ ψυχή μου· θήσω τὸ πνεῦμά μου ἐπ' αὐτόν, καὶ κρίσιν τοῖς ἔθνεσιν ἀπαγγελεῖ.

18. Ydou, 'o pais mou 'on 'eiretisa. 'o agapeitos mou eis 'on eudokeisen 'ei psuchei mou. Theiso to pneuma mou ep auton, kai krisin tois ethnesin apangelei.

Hebrew/Transliteration

יח. הֵן עַבְדִּי בָּחַרְתִּי בּוֹ יְדִידִי רָצְתָה נַפְשִׁי נָתַתִּי רוּחִי עָלָיו מִשְׁפָּט לַגּוֹיִם יוֹצִיא:

18. Hen av•di ba•char•ti vo ye•di•di ratz•ta naf•shi na•ta•ti roo•chi alav mish•pat la•go•yim yo•tzi.

Rabbinic/Jewish New Testament Commentary
Isa_42:1-4 is the first of several "suffering servant" passages in Isaiah 42-53. Some parts of these passages seem to refer primarily to the people Israel, others to the Messiah yet in Isaiah's future. This fact emphasizes the close identification of the Messiah Yeshua with the Jewish people, as pointed out above, Mat_2:15.

For that this prophecy belongs to the Messiah in Isaiah 42:1, is owned by the Jews themselves (k).

(k) Targum & Kimchi in loc. Abarbinel Mashmia Jeshua, fol. 9. 1, 2. & 10. 1, 2. & 21. 2. & in Is. fol 64. 3, 4. R. Isaac Chizzuk Emuna, p. 299.

---

19. He shall not strive, nor cry; neither shall any man hear his voice in the streets.

Greek/Transliteration
19. Οὐκ ἐρίσει, οὐδὲ κραυγάσει· οὐδὲ ἀκούσει τις ἐν ταῖς πλατείαις τὴν φωνὴν αὐτοῦ.

19. Ouk erisei, oude kraugasei. oude akousei tis en tais plateiais tein phonein autou.

Hebrew/Transliteration
:יט. לֹא יִצְעַק וְלֹא יִשָּׂא וְלֹא-יַשְׁמִיעַ בַּחוּץ קוֹלוֹ

19. Lo yitz•ak ve•lo yi•sa ve•lo - yi•sha•ma ba•chootz ko•lo.

---

20. A bruised reed shall he not break, and smoking flax shall he not quench, till he send forth judgment unto victory.

Greek/Transliteration
20. Κάλαμον συντετριμμένον οὐ κατεάξει, καὶ λίνον τυφόμενον οὐ σβέσει· ἕως ἂν ἐκβάλῃ εἰς νῖκος τὴν κρίσιν.

20. Kalamon suntetrimmenon ou kateaxei, kai linon tuphomenon ou sbesei. 'eos an ekbalei eis nikos tein krisin.

Hebrew/Transliteration
:כ. קָנֶה רָצוּץ לֹא יִשְׁבּוֹר וּפִשְׁתָּה כֵהָה לֹא יְכַבֶּנָּה

20. Ka•ne ra•tzootz lo yish•bor oo•fish•ta che•ha lo ye•cha•be•na.

21. And in his name shall the Gentiles trust.

Greek/Transliteration
21. Καὶ τῷ ὀνόματι αὐτοῦ ἔθνη ἐλπιοῦσιν.

21. Kai to onomati autou ethnei elpiousin.

Hebrew/Transliteration
כא. עַד־יוֹצִיא לָנֶצַח מִשְׁפָּט וְלִשְׁמוֹ גּוֹיִם יְיַחֵלוּ׃

21. Ad - yo•tzi la•ne•tzach mish•pat ve•lish•mo go•yim ye•ya•che•loo.

---

22. Then was brought unto him one possessed with a devil, blind, and dumb: and he healed him, insomuch that the blind and dumb both spake and saw.

Greek/Transliteration
22. Τότε προσηνέχθη αὐτῷ δαιμονιζόμενος, τυφλὸς καὶ κωφός· καὶ ἐθεράπευσεν αὐτόν, ὥστε τὸν τυφλὸν καὶ κωφὸν καὶ λαλεῖν καὶ βλέπειν.

22. Tote proseinechthei auto daimonizomenos, tuphlos kai kophos. kai etherapeusen auton, 'oste ton tuphlon kai kophon kai lalein kai blepein.

Hebrew/Transliteration
כב. אָז הוּבָא לְפָנָיו אִישׁ עִוֵּר וְאִלֵּם אֲשֶׁר רוּחַ רָע דָּבַק בּוֹ וַיִּרְפָּאֵהוּ וְהָעִוֵּר הָאִלֵּם דִּבֶּר וְרָאָה׃

22. Az hoo•va le•fa•nav eesh ee•ver ve•ee•lem asher roo•ach ra da•vak bo va•yir•pa•e•hoo ve•ha•ee•ver ha•ee•lem di•ber ve•ra•ah.

Rabbinic Jewish Commentary
The word rendered "dumb", signifies both deaf and dumb, and answers to the Hebrew word חרש, which sometimes (m) is used of a deaf man only, who can speak, but not hear; and often of one that can neither speak, nor hear; which is the case of such as are born deaf: it seems as if this man could hear, though he could not speak. (m) Maimon. & Bartenora in Misn. Trumot, c. 1. sect. 2.

---

23. And all the people were amazed, and said, Is not this the son of David?

Greek/Transliteration
23. Καὶ ἐξίσταντο πάντες οἱ ὄχλοι καὶ ἔλεγον, Μήτι οὗτός ἐστιν ὁ υἱὸς Δαυίδ;

23. Kai existanto pantes 'oi ochloi kai elegon, Meiti 'outos estin 'o 'wios Dauid?

Hebrew/Transliteration
כג. וַיִּשְׁתָּאוּ כָּל־הֲמוֹן הָעָם וַיֹּאמְרוּ הֲכִי זֶה בֶּן־דָּוִד׃

23. Va•yish•ta•oo kol - ha•mon ha•am va•yom•roo ha•chi ze ben - David.

Rabbinic Jewish Commentary
Or the Messiah; for בן דוד, "the son of David", is a character of the Messiah, well known among the Jews because he was promised to David, was to be raised up of his seed, and to spring from his loins. This question they put, not as doubting of it, but as inclining, at least, to believe it, if not as expressing their certainty of it: and is, as if they had said, who can this person be but the true Messiah, that has brought such a miracle as this? for from his miracles they rightly concluded who he was; though the Jews since, in order to deprive Yeshua of this true characteristic of the Messiah, deny that miracles are to be performed by him (n).
(n) Maimon. Hilch. Melacim, c. 11. sect. 3.

---

24. But when the Pharisees heard it, they said, This fellow doth not cast out devils, but by Beelzebub the prince of the devils.

Greek/Transliteration
24. Οἱ δὲ Φαρισαῖοι ἀκούσαντες εἶπον, Οὗτος οὐκ ἐκβάλλει τὰ δαιμόνια, εἰ μὴ ἐν τῷ Βεελζεβοὺλ ἄρχοντι τῶν δαιμονίων.

24. 'Oi de Pharisaioi akousantes eipon, 'Outos ouk ekballei ta daimonya, ei mei en to Beelzeboul archonti ton daimonion.

Hebrew/Transliteration
כד. וְהַפְּרוּשִׁים שָׁמְעוּ וְאָמְרוּ אֵין זֶה מְגָרֵשׁ אֶת-הַשֵּׁדִים כִּי אִם בְּבַעַל-זְבוּב שַׂר הַשֵּׁדִים:

24. Ve•haP`roo•shim sham•oo ve•am•roo eyn ze me•ga•resh et - ha•she•dim ki eem be•Va•al - Z`voov sar ha•she•dim.

Rabbinic Jewish Commentary
the Jews have learnt to fix this vile imputation, and blasphemous piece of slander upon Yeshua; who, they say (o), brought enchantments, or witchcrafts, out of Egypt, in the cuttings of his flesh, whereby he performed the things he did. Concerning Beelzebub; "the prince of devils"; it being a prevailing notion among the Jews, that there is one devil who is the head of all the rest, and who is by them sometimes called Asmodeus: they say (p), when Solomon sinned against the Lord, he sent to him אשמדאי מלכא דשידי, "Asmodeus the king of the devils", and drove him from his throne, and so elsewhere (q): and sometimes Samael, who is styled (r) Samael the prince, מלכא דשדים, "the king of devils"; and the angel Samael, the wicked, ראש כל השטנים, "the head of all the Satans", or devils (s): and we often read (t) of שר הגיהנם, "the prince of hell"; by whom the same is meant, as here, by Beelzebub; for if anyone devil is more wicked, odious, and execrable than the rest, the chief of them may be thought to be so; for which reason he is here mentioned.

(o) T. Hieros. Sabbat, fol. 13. 4. T. Bab. Sabbat, fol. 104. 2. (p) Targum in Eccl. i. 12. (q) T. Bab. Pesach, fol. 110. 1. Gittin, fol. 68. 1. & Raziel, fol. 41. 2. (r) Zohar in Deut. fol. 120. 3. (s) Debarim Rabba, fol. 245. 3. (t) T. Bab. Sanhedrim, fol. 52. 1. Imre Binah in Zohar in Gen. fol. 22. 3.

---

25. And Jesus knew their thoughts, and said unto them, Every kingdom divided against itself is brought to desolation; and every city or house divided against itself shall not stand:

Greek/Transliteration
25. Εἰδὼς δὲ ὁ Ἰησοῦς τὰς ἐνθυμήσεις αὐτῶν εἶπεν αὐτοῖς, Πᾶσα βασιλεία μερισθεῖσα καθ᾽ ἑαυτῆς ἐρημοῦται· καὶ πᾶσα πόλις ἢ οἰκία μερισθεῖσα καθ᾽ ἑαυτῆς οὐ σταθήσεται.

25. Eidos de 'o Yeisous tas enthumeiseis auton eipen autois, Pasa basileia meristheisa kath 'eauteis ereimoutai. kai pasa polis ei oikia meristheisa kath 'eauteis ou statheisetai.

Hebrew/Transliteration
כה. וַיֵּדַע יֵשׁוּעַ אֶת-מַחְשְׁבֹתָם וַיֹּאמֶר אֲלֵיהֶם כָּל-מַמְלָכָה הַנִּפְלְגָה עַל-נַפְשָׁהּ תֶּחֱרָב וְכָל-עִיר וּבַיִת הַנִּפְלָגִים עַל-נַפְשָׁם לֹא יָקוּמוּ

25. Va•ye•da Yeshua et - mach•she•vo•tam va•yo•mer aley•hem kol - mam•la•cha ha•nif•le•ga al - naf•sha te•che•rav ve•chol - eer oo•va•yit ha•nif•le•gim al - naf•sham lo ya•koo•moo.

Rabbinic Jewish Commentary
These, it is very likely, were common sayings among the Jews, and they might be very easily understood by them; and are very appropriately produced by Christ to illustrate the present case, and confute the vile and blasphemous suggestions of the Pharisees: a proverbial expression, much like to these, is to be read in the writings of the Jews, כל בית שיש בו מחלוקת סופו ליחרב, "every house, in which there is a division, at the end shall come to desolation" (u). (u) Derech Eretz, c. 5.

---

26. And if Satan cast out Satan, he is divided against himself; how shall then his kingdom stand?

Greek/Transliteration
26. Καὶ εἰ ὁ Σατανᾶς τὸν Σατανᾶν ἐκβάλλει, ἐφ᾽ ἑαυτὸν ἐμερίσθη· πῶς οὖν σταθήσεται ἡ βασιλεία αὐτοῦ;

26. Kai ei 'o Satanas ton Satanan ekballei, eph 'eauton emeristhei. pos oun statheisetai 'ei basileia autou?

Hebrew/Transliteration
כו. וְאִם-הַשָּׂטָן מְגָרֵשׁ אֶת-הַשָּׂטָן נִפְלָג הוּא עַל-נַפְשׁוֹ וְאֵיךְ תָּקוּם מַלְכוּתוֹ:

26. Ve•eem - ha•Satan me•ga•resh et - ha•Satan nif•lag hoo al - naf•sho ve•eych ta•koom mal•choo•to.

---

27. And if I by Beelzebub cast out devils, by whom do your children cast them out? Therefore they shall be your judges.

Greek/Transliteration
27. Καὶ εἰ ἐγὼ ἐν Βεελζεβοὺλ ἐκβάλλω τὰ δαιμόνια, οἱ υἱοὶ ὑμῶν ἐν τίνι ἐκβάλλουσιν; Διὰ τοῦτο αὐτοὶ ὑμῶν ἔσονται κριταί.

27. Kai ei ego en Beelzeboul ekballo ta daimonya, 'oi 'wioi 'umon en tini ekballousin? Dya touto autoi 'umon esontai kritai.

Hebrew/Transliteration
:כז. וְאִם-אֲנִי גֵרֵשׁ אֶת-הַשֵּׁדִים בְּבַעַל-זְבוּב בְּנֵיכֶם בְּמִי יְגָרְשׁוּ אֹתָם עַל-כֵּן הֵם יִהְיוּ שֹׁפְטֵיכֶם

27. Ve•eem - ani go•resh et - ha•she•dim be•Va•al - Z`voov b`ney•chem be•mi ye•gar•shoo o•tam al - ken hem yi•hee•yoo shof•tey•chem.

Rabbinic Jewish Commentary
A story is reported (x), "concerning Ben Talmion, that a miracle was done by R. Eleazar bar Jose, who healed a king's daughter at Rome, in whose body the devil entered, whose name was Ben Talmion; and they brought him (the Jew) to the king's treasury, to take what he would, but he would take nothing from thence, but letters, in which were written the decrees they had decreed against Israel; and when he found them, he tore them to pieces, and there he saw the vessels of the house of the sanctuary, in the treasury." (x) In Gloss. in T. Bab. Yoma, fol. 57. 1. Meilah, fol. 17. 2.

---

28. But if I cast out devils by the Spirit of God, then the kingdom of God is come unto you.

Greek/Transliteration
28. Εἰ δὲ ἐν πνεύματι θεοῦ ἐγὼ ἐκβάλλω τὰ δαιμόνια, ἄρα ἔφθασεν ἐφ᾽ ὑμᾶς ἡ βασιλεία τοῦ θεοῦ.

28. Ei de en pneumati theou ego ekballo ta daimonya, ara ephthasen eph 'umas 'ei basileia tou theou.

Hebrew/Transliteration
:כח. אֶפֶס אִם בְּרוּחַ אֱלֹהִים אֲנִי גֵרֵשׁ אֶת-הַשֵּׁדִים מַלְכוּת אֱלֹהִים בָּאָה אֲלֵיכֶם אֶל-נָכוֹן

28. E•fes eem be•Roo•ach Elohim ani go•resh et - ha•she•dim mal•choot Elohim ba•ah aley•chem el - na•chon.

29. Or else how can one enter into a strong man's house, and spoil his goods, except he first bind the strong man? and then he will spoil his house.

Greek/Transliteration
29. Ἡ πῶς δύναταί τις εἰσελθεῖν εἰς τὴν οἰκίαν τοῦ ἰσχυροῦ καὶ τὰ σκεύη αὐτοῦ διαρπάσαι, ἐὰν μὴ πρῶτον δήσῃ τὸν ἰσχυρόν; Καὶ τότε τὴν οἰκίαν αὐτοῦ διαρπάσει.

29. Ei pos dunatai tis eiselthein eis tein oikian tou ischurou kai ta skeuei autou dyarpasai, ean mei proton deisei ton ischuron? Kai tote tein oikian autou dyarpasei.

Hebrew/Transliteration
כט. או איך יוכל איש לבא בית הגבור ולשלל את-כליו אם-לא יאסר את-הגבור ראשנה ואחר ישלל את:אשר בביתו

29. Oh eych yoo•chal eesh la•vo beit ha•gi•bor ve•lish•lol et - ke•lav eem - lo ye•e•sor et - ha•gi•bor ri•sho•na ve•a•char yish•lol et asher be•vey•to.

---

30. He that is not with me is against me; and he that gathereth not with me scattereth abroad.

Greek/Transliteration
30. Ὁ μὴ ὢν μετ᾽ ἐμοῦ, κατ᾽ ἐμοῦ ἐστιν, καὶ ὁ μὴ συνάγων μετ᾽ ἐμοῦ, σκορπίζει.

30. 'O mei on met emou, kat emou estin, kai 'o mei sunagon met emou, skorpizei.

Hebrew/Transliteration
ל. מי אשר איננו לי לצרי הוא ומי אשר איננו מאסף אתי מפזר הוא:

30. Mee asher ey•ne•noo li le•tza•rai hoo oo•mi asher ey•ne•noo me•a•sef ee•ti me•fa•zer hoo.

Jewish New Testament Commentary
Here and in the next seven verses the *P'rushim* are presented with a last chance to stand with Yeshua. More generally, a standard is set by which a *talmid* can test himself: if he is not actively on Yeshua's side, he is on the side of the Adversary.

---

31. Wherefore I say unto you, All manner of sin and blasphemy shall be forgiven unto men: but the blasphemy against the Holy Ghost shall not be forgiven unto men.

Greek/Transliteration

31. Διὰ τοῦτο λέγω ὑμῖν, Πᾶσα ἁμαρτία καὶ βλασφημία ἀφεθήσεται τοῖς ἀνθρώποις· ἡ δὲ τοῦ πνεύματος βλασφημία οὐκ ἀφεθήσεται τοῖς ἀνθρώποις.

31. Dya touto lego 'umin, Pasa 'amartia kai blaspheimia aphetheisetai tois anthropois. 'ei de tou pneumatos blaspheimia ouk aphetheisetai tois anthropois.

Hebrew/Transliteration

לֹא. עַל-כֵּן אֲנִי אֹמֵר לָכֶם כָּל-חֵטְא וְגִדּוּפָה יְכֻפְּרוּ לָאָדָם אֶפֶס הַמְגַדֵּף אֶת-הָרוּחַ לֹא יְכֻפַּר-לוֹ:

31. Al - ken ani o•mer la•chem kol - chet ve•gi•doo•fa ye•choop•roo la•a•dam e•fes ham•ga•def et - ha•Roo•ach lo ye•choo•par - lo.

Rabbinic/Jewish New Testament Commentary

Blaspheming (that is, insulting) the *Ruach HaKodesh* consists in either (1) wilfully continuing to deny the Gospel when the Holy Spirit has made clear to you that it is true, or (2) attributing the works of the Holy Spirit to the Adversary (Satan); in the present context these amount to about the same thing (other interpretations have been offered). The Jews have a saying (z), that God pardons all sins,

חוץ מן הזמה, "except lasciviousness"." But this is not excepted by Yeshua.
(z) Tanchuma apud Buxtorf. Heb. Florileg. p. 126.

---

32. And whosoever speaketh a word against the Son of man, it shall be forgiven him: but whosoever speaketh against the Holy Ghost, it shall not be forgiven him, neither in this world, neither in the world to come.

Greek/Transliteration

32. Καὶ ὃς ἐὰν εἴπῃ λόγον κατὰ τοῦ υἱοῦ τοῦ ἀνθρώπου, ἀφεθήσεται αὐτῷ· ὃς δ᾽ ἂν εἴπῃ κατὰ τοῦ πνεύματος τοῦ ἁγίου, οὐκ ἀφεθήσεται αὐτῷ, οὔτε ἐν τῷ νῦν αἰῶνι οὔτε ἐν τῷ μέλλοντι.

32. Kai 'os ean eipei logon kata tou 'wiou tou anthropou, aphetheisetai auto. 'os d an eipei kata tou pneumatos tou 'agiou, ouk aphetheisetai auto, oute en to nun aioni oute en to mellonti.

Hebrew/Transliteration

לב. וּמִי אֲשֶׁר יְדַבֵּר דָּבָר בְּבֶן-הָאָדָם יְכֻפַּר-לוֹ וּמִי אֲשֶׁר יְדַבֵּר בָּרוּחַ הַקֹּדֶשׁ לֹא יְכֻפַּר-לוֹ לֹא-בָעוֹלָם הַזֶּה וְלֹא:בָעוֹלָם הַבָּא -

32. Oo•mi asher ye•da•ber da•var be•Ven - ha•adam ye•choo•par - lo oo•mi asher ye•da•ber be•Roo•ach ha•Ko•desh lo ye•choo•par - lo lo - va•o•lam ha•ze ve•lo - va•o•lam ha•ba.

Rabbinic/Jewish New Testament Commentary

'olam hazeh... 'olam haba, "this world... the world to come." These concepts are part of rabbinic Judaism. The distinction here used, does not refer to a common one among the Jews, of the Jewish state and the times of the Messiah; but to the present state of life, and that which will be after, or upon death: and it does not suppose there may be forgiveness of other sins, though not of this, in the other world; (a). The form of confession used by sick persons is the following (b);

"I confess before thee, O Lord our God, and the God of our fathers, that my cure is in thy hands, and my death is in thy hands; if it be thy good pleasure, heal me with a perfect healing: but if I die, תהא מיתתי סליחה, "let my death be for the pardon", forgiveness, and atonement of all the sins, iniquities, and transgressions, which I have sinned, acted perversely in, and transgressed before thee; and give me my portion in paradise, and justify me "in the world to come", which is hidden for the righteous." The Jews use the phrase in the same sense (c); a certain sick man said to his son, "give me water, and such certain food; but if not, I will not "forgive thee, neither in this world, nor in the world to come"." That is, I will never forgive thee. (a) T. Bab. Yoma, fol. 86. 1. (b) Seder Tephillot, fol. 333. 2. Ed. Basil. Vid. T. Bab. Beracot, fol. 60. 1. (c) Sepher Chasidim: num. 234.

---

33. Either make the tree good, and his fruit good; or else make the tree corrupt, and his fruit corrupt: for the tree is known by his fruit.

Greek/Transliteration

33. Ἢ ποιήσατε τὸ δένδρον καλόν, καὶ τὸν καρπὸν αὐτοῦ καλόν, ἢ ποιήσατε τὸ δένδρον σαπρόν, καὶ τὸν καρπὸν αὐτοῦ σαπρόν· ἐκ γὰρ τοῦ καρποῦ τὸ δένδρον γινώσκεται.

33. Ei poieisate to dendron kalon, kai ton karpon autou kalon, ei poieisate to dendron sapron, kai ton karpon autou sapron. ek gar tou karpou to dendron ginosketai.

Hebrew/Transliteration

לג. אוֹ עֲשׂוּ אֶת-הָעֵץ טוֹב וּפִרְיוֹ טוֹב אוֹ עֲשׂוּ אֶת-הָעֵץ רָע וּפִרְיוֹ רָע כִּי בְּפִרְיוֹ נִכָּר הָעֵץ:

33. Oh a•soo et - ha•etz tov oo•fir•yo tov oh a•soo et - ha•etz ra oo•fir•yo ra ki be•fir•yo ni•kar ha•etz.

---

34. O generation of vipers, how can ye, being evil, speak good things? for out of the abundance of the heart the mouth speaketh.

Greek/Transliteration

34. Γεννήματα ἐχιδνῶν, πῶς δύνασθε ἀγαθὰ λαλεῖν, πονηροὶ ὄντες; Ἐκ γὰρ τοῦ περισσεύματος τῆς καρδίας τὸ στόμα λαλεῖ.

34. Genneimata echidnon, pos dunasthe agatha lalein, poneiroi ontes? Ek gar tou perisseumatos teis kardias to stoma lalei.

Hebrew/Transliteration
:לד. יַלְדֵי צִפְעֹנִים אֵיךְ תּוּכְלוּ לְדַבֵּר טֹבוֹת בְּרָעַתְכֶם כִּי-מִמְּלֹא הַלֵּב יַבִּיעַ הַפֶּה

34. Yal•dey tzif•o•nim eych tooch•loo le•da•ber to•vot be•ra•at•chem ki - mim•lo ha•lev ya•bi•a ha•pe.

TaNaKh-Old Testament Commentary
A phrase much like this is used by the Septuagint, in Ecc_2:15. "I spoke abundance", or "much in my heart"; διοτο ο αφρων εκ περισσευματος λαλει, "for the fool out of his abundance speaketh": as there is abundance of folly in him, there is much delivered out by him; and where there is abundance of wickedness in the heart, if the grace of God is wanting to restrain it, much of it will come out by the lips; as is a man's heart, ordinarily is his language.

---

35. A good man out of the good treasure of the heart bringeth forth good things: and an evil man out of the evil treasure bringeth forth evil things.

Greek/Transliteration
35. Ὁ ἀγαθὸς ἄνθρωπος ἐκ τοῦ ἀγαθοῦ θησαυροῦ ἐκβάλλει ἀγαθά· καὶ ὁ πονηρὸς ἄνθρωπος ἐκ τοῦ πονηροῦ θησαυροῦ ἐκβάλλει πονηρά.

35. 'O agathos anthropos ek tou agathou theisaurou ekballei agatha. kai 'o poneiros Anthropos ek tou poneirou theisaurou ekballei poneira.

Hebrew/Transliteration
:לה. אִישׁ-טוֹב מֵאוֹצָרוֹ לִבּוֹ הַטּוֹב יוֹצִיא טֹבוֹת וְאִישׁ-רָע מֵאוֹצָרוֹ הָרָע יוֹצִיא רָעוֹת

35. Eesh - tov me•o•tza•ro li•bo ha•tov yo•tzi to•vot ve•eesh - ra me•o•tza•ro ha•ra yo•tzi ra•ot.

---

36. But I say unto you, That every idle word that men shall speak, they shall give account thereof in the day of judgment.

Greek/Transliteration
36. Λέγω δὲ ὑμῖν, ὅτι πᾶν ῥῆμα ἀργόν, ὃ ἐὰν λαλήσωσιν οἱ ἄνθρωποι, ἀποδώσουσιν περὶ αὐτοῦ λόγον ἐν ἡμέρᾳ κρίσεως.

36. Lego de 'umin, 'oti pan 'reima argon, 'o ean laleisosin 'oi anthropoi, apodosousin peri autou logon en 'eimera kriseos.

Hebrew/Transliteration
:לו. וַאֲנִי אֹמֵר לָכֶם כִּי עַל כָּל-שִׂיחַ תָּפֵל אֲשֶׁר יְבַטְּאוּ בְּנֵי הָאָדָם יִתְּנוּ חֶשְׁבּוֹן בְּיוֹם הַמִּשְׁפָּט

36. Va•a•ni o•mer la•chem ki al kol - si•ach ta•fel asher ye•vat•oo v`ney ha•a•dam yit•noo chesh•bon be•yom ha•mish•pat.

Rabbinic Jewish Commentary
By an "idle word" is meant, what the Jews call, שיחה קלה, "light conversation", and דבר בטל, "vain discourse", as the Hebrew Gospel of Munster reads it here; frothy language, unprofitable talk, which, though it does not directly hurt God or man, yet is of no use to speaker or hearer; and yet even this, in the last general and awful judgment, if not forgiven, and repented of, must be accounted for; and much more such horrid blasphemies the Pharisees had vented against Yeshua, and the Spirit of Messiah. The Jews (d) have a saying pretty much like this,

"That even על שיחה קלה, "for any light conversation", which passes between a man and his wife, he shall "be brought to judgment"." (d) R. Jonah apud L. Capell. in loc.

---

37. For by thy words thou shalt be justified, and by thy words thou shalt be condemned.

Greek/Transliteration
37. Ἐκ γὰρ τῶν λόγων σου δικαιωθήσῃ, καὶ ἐκ τῶν λόγων σου καταδικασθήσῃ.

37. Ek gar ton logon sou dikaiotheisei, kai ek ton logon sou katadikastheisei.

Hebrew/Transliteration
לז. כִּי בִדְבָרֶיךָ תִּצָּדֵק וּבִדְבָרֶיךָ תֵּאָשֵׁם:

37. Ki bid•va•re•cha ti•tza•dek oo•vid•va•re•cha te•e•sham.

Rabbinic Jewish Commentary
"Says Resh Lakish (e), such an one and such an one, they justify; and such an one and such an one, they condemn. R. Eliezer replies, מדבריהן גזדכה פלוני, "by their words such an one and such an one are justified"." "upon hearing the difference there is between them, and between their words, they are justified."

That it is the opinion of Jewish writers, that words, as well as actions, will be accounted for hereafter: they say (f), "When a man dies, he lifts up his eyes and sees two come to him, and write before him all that he has done in this world, וכל מה דאפיק מן פומיה, "and all that has proceeded out of his mouth", ויהיב דינא על כלא, "and he gives an account for all"; and a little after, כל אינון מלין, "all the words" of a man in this world, are prepared before him, and not one of them lost; and in the hour he goes to his grave, they are all set before him."

(e) T. Bab. Sanhedrim, fol. 30. 1. (f) Zohar in Num. fol. 53. 2.

38. Then certain of the scribes and of the Pharisees answered, saying, Master, we would see a sign from thee.

Greek/Transliteration
38. Τότε ἀπεκρίθησάν τινες τῶν γραμματέων καὶ Φαρισαίων, λέγοντες, Διδάσκαλε, θέλομεν ἀπὸ σοῦ σημεῖον ἰδεῖν.

38. Tote apekritheisan tines ton grammateon kai Pharisaion, legontes, Didaskale, thelomen apo sou seimeion idein.

Hebrew/Transliteration
לח. וַיַּעֲנוּ אֲנָשִׁים מִן-הַסּוֹפְרִים וְהַפְּרוּשִׁים לֵאמֹר רַבִּי חָפַצְנוּ לִרְאוֹת אוֹת מֵאוֹתֹתֶיךָ:

38. Va•ya•a•noo a•na•shim min - ha•sof•rim ve•haP`roo•shim le•mor Rabbi cha•fatz•noo lir•ot ot me•o•to•te•cha.

---

39. But he answered and said unto them, An evil and adulterous generation seeketh after a sign; and there shall no sign be given to it, but the sign of the prophet Jonas:

Greek/Transliteration
39. Ὁ δὲ ἀποκριθεὶς εἶπεν αὐτοῖς, Γενεὰ πονηρὰ καὶ μοιχαλὶς σημεῖον ἐπιζητεῖ· καὶ σημεῖον οὐ δοθήσεται αὐτῇ, εἰ μὴ τὸ σημεῖον Ἰωνᾶ τοῦ προφήτου.

39. 'O de apokritheis eipen autois, Genea poneira kai moichalis seimeion epizeitei. kai seimeion ou dotheisetai autei, ei mei to seimeion Yona tou propheitou.

Hebrew/Transliteration
לט. וַיַּעַן וַיֹּאמֶר אֲלֵיהֶם דּוֹר רָע וּמְנָאֵף מְבַקֵּשׁ אוֹת וְאוֹת לֹא יִנָּתֶן-לוֹ זוּלָתִי אוֹת יוֹנָה הַנָּבִיא:

39. Va•ya•an va•yo•mer aley•hem dor ra oom•na•ef me•va•kesh ot ve•ot lo yi•na•ten - lo zoo•la•tee ot Yona ha•na•vee.

Rabbinic Jewish Commentary
With the Jews themselves, is a character of the generation in which the Messiah comes: for they say (h), "that just when the Messiah comes, or in the age the son of David comes, "impudence shall be increased", corn and wine shall be dear, the government shall be heretics, בית וועד יהיה לזנות, "and the synagogue shall become a brothel house"." Their writings (i) frequently speak of the increase and abounding of adulteries, under the second temple, and about this time; which obliged Jochanan ben Zaccai and the sanhedrim, to leave off the use of the bitter waters.

Seeketh after a sign; this is perfectly Talmudic language, the language of the Jews (k)."The disciples of R. Jose ben Kismai, asked him, when did the Son of David come? He replied, I am afraid, lest תבקשו ממני אות, "ye should seek of me a sign"; they say unto him, we will not "seek of thee a sign"."

(h) Misn. Sota c. 9. sect. 15. T. Bab. Sanhed. fol. 97. 1. (i) Misn. Sota, c. 9. sect. 9. & Maimon. Hilch. Sota, c. 3. sect. 19. (k) T. Bab. Sanhedrim, fol. 98. 1. so מבקש סימן, "seeketh a sign", Shemot Rabba, Parash. 9. fol. 97. 2.

---

40. For as Jonas was three days and three nights in the whale's belly; so shall the Son of man be three days and three nights in the heart of the earth.

Greek/Transliteration
40. Ὥσπερ γὰρ ἦν Ἰωνᾶς ἐν τῇ κοιλίᾳ τοῦ κήτους τρεῖς ἡμέρας καὶ τρεῖς νύκτας, οὕτως ἔσται ὁ υἱὸς τοῦ ἀνθρώπου ἐν τῇ καρδίᾳ τῆς γῆς τρεῖς ἡμέρας καὶ τρεῖς νύκτας.

40. 'Osper gar ein Yonas en tei koilia tou keitous treis 'eimeras kai treis nuktas, 'outos estai 'o 'wios tou anthropou en tei kardia teis geis treis 'eimeras kai treis nuktas.

Hebrew/Transliteration
מ. כִּי כַּאֲשֶׁר הָיָה יוֹנָה בִּמְעֵי הַדָג שְׁלֹשָׁה יָמִים וּשְׁלֹשָׁה לֵילוֹת כֵּן יִהְיֶה בֶן-הָאָדָם בְּלֵב הָאָרֶץ שְׁלֹשָׁה יָמִים:וּשְׁלֹשָׁה לֵילוֹת

40. Ki ka•a•sher ha•ya Yona bim•ey ha•dag sh`lo•sha ya•mim oosh•lo•sha ley•lot ken yi•hee•ye Ven - ha•adam be•lev ha•a•retz sh`lo•sha ya•mim oosh•lo•sha ley•lot.

Rabbinic Jewish Commentary
To solve this difficulty, and set the matter in a clear light, let it be observed, that the three days and three nights, mean three natural days, consisting of day and night, or twenty four hours, and are what the Greeks call νυχθημερα, "night days"; but the Jews have no other way of expressing them, but as here; and with them it is a well known rule, and used on all occasions, as in the computation of their feasts and times of mourning, in the observance of the passover, circumcision, and divers purifications, that מקצת היום ככולו, "a part of a day is as the whole" (n):

Among other things these words occur; "R. Ismael saith, *Sometimes it contains four Onoth* sometimes five, sometimes six. But how much is the space of *an Onah*? R. Jochanan saith either a day or a night." And so also the Jerusalem Talmud; "R. Akiba fixed a day for an Onah; and a night for an Onah; but the tradition is, that R. Eliezar Ben Azariah said, *A day and a night make an Onah, and a part of an Onah is as the whole*." And a little after, *R. Ismael computeth a part of the Onah for the whole*. Compare the latter sense with the words of our Saviour, which are now before us: "A day and a night (saith the tradition) make an Onah; and a part of an Onah is as the whole." Therefore Yeshua may truly be said to have been in his grave three Onoth; or *three natural days* (when yet the greatest part of the first day was wanting, and the night altogether, and the greatest part by far of the third day also), the consent of the schools and dialect of the nation agreeing thereunto. For, "the least part of the Onah concluded the whole." (n) T. Hieros. Pesach. fol. 31. 2. T. Bab. Moed. Katon, fol. 16. 2. 17. 2. 19. 2. & 20. 2. Bechorot, fol. 20. 2. & 21. 1, Nidda, fol. 33. 1. Maimon. Hilch. Ebel, c. 7. sect. 1, 2, 3. Aben Ezra in Lev. xii. 3.

---

41. The men of Nineveh shall rise in judgment with this generation, and shall condemn it: because they repented at the preaching of Jonas; and, behold, a greater than Jonas is here.

Greek/Transliteration
41. Ἄνδρες Νινευῖται ἀναστήσονται ἐν τῇ κρίσει μετὰ τῆς γενεᾶς ταύτης καὶ κατακρινοῦσιν αὐτήν· ὅτι μετενόησαν εἰς τὸ κήρυγμα Ἰωνᾶ· καὶ ἰδού, πλεῖον Ἰωνᾶ ὧδε.

41. Andres Nineuitai anasteisontai en tei krisei meta teis geneas tauteis kai katakrinousin autein. 'oti metenoeisan eis to keirugma Yona. kai idou, pleion Yona 'ode.

Hebrew/Transliteration
מא. אַנְשֵׁי נִינְוֵה יָקוּמוּ בַמִּשְׁפָּט עִם-הַדּוֹר הַזֶּה וְיַרְשִׁיעוּ אתוֹ כִּי שָׁבוּ בִּקְרִיאַת יוֹנָה וְהִנֵּה יֶשְׁנוֹ בָזֶה גָּדוֹל מִיּוֹנָה:

41. An•shey Nin•ve ya•koo•moo va•mish•pat eem - ha•dor ha•ze ve•yar•shi•oo o•to ki sha•voo bik•ri•at Yona ve•hee•ne yesh•no va•ze ga•dol mi•Yona.

Rabbinic Jewish Commentary
and shall condemn them; not as judges of them, but by their example and practices, which will be brought above board, and observed as an aggravation of the guilt and condemnation of the Jews: so the lives and conversations of the saints condemn the wicked now, and will do hereafter: in this sense the word is used in the Talmud (o); where having related how Hillell, though a poor man, and R. Eleazar, though a rich man, studied in the law, and Joseph, though youthful, gay, and beautiful, withstood the importunities of his mistress, it is observed, that Hillell מחייב, "condemned" the poor; and R. Eleazar ben Harsum condemned the rich; and Joseph condemned the wicked: in like manner, the Ninevites will condemn the Jews. (o) T. Bab. Yoma, fol. 35. 2.

---

42. The queen of the south shall rise up in the judgment with this generation, and shall condemn it: for she came from the uttermost parts of the earth to hear the wisdom of Solomon; and, behold, a greater than Solomon is here.

Greek/Transliteration
42. Βασίλισσα νότου ἐγερθήσεται ἐν τῇ κρίσει μετὰ τῆς γενεᾶς ταύτης καὶ κατακρινεῖ αὐτήν· ὅτι ἦλθεν ἐκ τῶν περάτων τῆς γῆς ἀκοῦσαι τὴν σοφίαν Σολομῶνος· καὶ ἰδού, πλεῖον Σολομῶνος ὧδε.

42. Basilissa notou egertheisetai en tei krisei meta teis geneas tauteis kai katakrinei autein. 'oti eilthen ek ton peraton teis geis akousai tein sophian Solomonos. kai idou, pleion Solomonos 'ode.

Hebrew/Transliteration
מב. מַלְכַּת תֵּימָן תָּקוּם בַּמִּשְׁפָּט עִם-הַדּוֹר הַזֶּה וְתַרְשִׁיעַ אֹתוֹ כִּי בָאָה מִקְצוֹת הָאָרֶץ לִשְׁמֹעַ חָכְמַת שְׁלֹמֹה:וְהִנֵּה יֶשְׁנוֹ בָזֶה גָּדוֹל מִשְּׁלֹמֹה

42. Mal•kat Tey•man ta•koom ba•mish•pat eem - ha•dor ha•ze ve•tar•shi•a o•to ki va•ah mik•tzot ha•a•retz lish•mo•a choch•mat Sh`lo•mo ve•hee•ne yesh•no va•ze ga•dol mi•Sh`lo•mo.

Rabbinic Jewish Commentary
Called the queen of Sheba, 1Ki_10:1. Sheba was one of the sons of Joktan, a grandchild of Arphaxad, who settled in the southern parts of Arabia: hence this queen is called the queen of the south. Sheba is by the Targumist (p) called Zemargad: and this queen the queen of Zemargad: she goes by different names. According to some, her name was Maqueda (q), and, as others say, Balkis (r): a Jewish chronologer (s) tells us, that the queen of Sheba, who is called Nicolaa, of the kingdom of Jaman, or the south, came to Solomon, to hear his wisdom, and gave him much riches: and Josephus (t) calls her Nicaulis, queen of Egypt and Ethiopia;

or she came from the uttermost parts of the earth; an hyperbolical expression, meaning a great way off from a far country, a very distant part of the world from Jerusalem, לשמוע חכמת שלמה, "to hear the wisdom of Solomon"; the very phrase used by the above Jewish (u) writer. The Jews themselves (w) own, that the king, meaning the Messiah, that shall be raised up of the seed of David, בעל חכמה יהיה יתר משלמה, "shall be a greater master of wisdom", or "wiser than Solomon".

(p) In 1 Chron. i. 9. & 2 Chron. ix. 1. (q) Ludolph. Hist. Aethiop. 1. 2. c. 3. & not. in Claud. Confess. sect. 1. (r) Pocock. Specimen Hist. Arab. p. 59. (s) Juchasin, fol. 136. 1. (t) Antiqu. 1. 8. c. 2. (u) Juchasin, fol. 136. 1. (w) Maimon. Hilchot. Teshuba, c. 9. sect. 2.

---

43. When the unclean spirit is gone out of a man, he walketh through dry places, seeking rest, and findeth none.

Greek/Transliteration
43. Ὅταν δὲ τὸ ἀκάθαρτον πνεῦμα ἐξέλθῃ ἀπὸ τοῦ ἀνθρώπου, διέρχεται δι᾽ ἀνύδρων τόπων, ζητοῦν ἀνάπαυσιν, καὶ οὐχ εὑρίσκει.

43. 'Otan de to akatharton pneuma exelthei apo tou anthropou, dierchetai di anudron topon, zeitoun anapausin, kai ouch 'euriskei.

Hebrew/Transliteration
מג. וְרוּחַ הַטֻּמְאָה בְּצֵאתָהּ מִן־הָאָדָם תְּשׁוֹטֵט בְּאֶרֶץ תַּלְאוּבֹת תְּבַקֵּשׁ וְלֹא־תִמְצָא מַרְגֵּעָה:

43. Ve•roo•ach ha•toom•ah be•tze•ta min - ha•a•dam te•sho•tet be•e•retz tal•oo•vot te•va•kesh ve•lo - tim•tza mar•ge•ah.

Rabbinic Jewish Commentary
By "the unclean" spirit, is meant Satan, the old serpent, the devil; who by the Jews, is to be called as here, רוח מסאבא, "the unclean spirit" Zohar in Gen. fol. 77. 2.

---

44. Then he saith, I will return into my house from whence I came out; and when he is come, he findeth it empty, swept, and garnished.

Greek/Transliteration
44. Τότε λέγει, Ἐπιστρέψω εἰς τὸν οἶκόν μου ὅθεν ἐξῆλθον· καὶ ἐλθὸν εὑρίσκει σχολάζοντα, σεσαρωμένον, καὶ κεκοσμημένον.

44. Tote legei, Epistrepso eis ton oikon mou 'othen exeilthon. kai elthon 'euriskei scholazonta, sesaromenon, kai kekosmeimenon.

Hebrew/Transliteration
מד. אָז תֹּאמַר אָשׁוּבָה אֶל־מִשְׁכָּנִי אֲשֶׁר יָצָאתִי מִשָּׁם וּבְשׁוּבָהּ תִּמְצָאֶנּוּ רֵק מִבְּלִי יֹשֵׁב וּמְנֻקֶּה וּמְפֹאָר:

44. Az to•mar ashoo•va el - mish•ka•ni asher ya•tza•ti mi•sham oov•shoo•va tim•tza•e•noo rek mi•b`li yo•shev oom•noo•ke oom•fo•ar.

Rabbinic Jewish Commentary
And when he is come, he findeth it empty: not empty of sin: this puts me in mind of a passage in the Misna (y), where it is said, that on a fast day, "when they stand in prayer, they cause to descend, or go before the ark, an old man, who is used (to prayer,) whose children, וביתו ריקם, "and his house, are empty", so that his heart is perfect in prayer," (y) Taanith, c. 2. sect. 2. Maimon. & Bartenora in ib.

---

45. Then goeth he, and taketh with himself seven other spirits more wicked than himself, and they enter in and dwell there: and the last state of that man is worse than the first. Even so shall it be also unto this wicked generation.

Greek/Transliteration
45. Τότε πορεύεται καὶ παραλαμβάνει μεθ᾽ ἑαυτοῦ ἑπτὰ ἕτερα πνεύματα πονηρότερα ἑαυτοῦ, καὶ εἰσελθόντα κατοικεῖ ἐκεῖ· καὶ γίνεται τὰ ἔσχατα τοῦ ἀνθρώπου ἐκείνου χείρονα τῶν πρώτων. Οὕτως ἔσται καὶ τῇ γενεᾷ ταύτῃ τῇ πονηρᾷ.

45. Tote poreuetai kai paralambanei meth 'eautou 'epta 'etera pneumata poneirotera 'eautou, kai eiselthonta katoikei ekei. kai ginetai ta eschata tou anthropou ekeinou cheirona ton proton. 'Outos estai kai tei genea tautei tei poneira.

Hebrew/Transliteration
מה. אָז תֵּלֵךְ וְלָקְחָה לָּהּ שֶׁבַע רוּחוֹת אֲחֵרוֹת רָעוֹת מִמֶּנָּה וּבָאוּ וְשָׁכְנוּ שָׁם וְהָיְתָה אַחֲרִית הָאִישׁ הַהוּא רָעָה מֵרֵאשִׁיתוֹ וְכֵן יִהְיֶה לַדּוֹר הָרָע הַזֶּה:

45. Az te•lech ve•lak•cha la she•va roo•chot a•che•rot ra•ot mi•me•na oo•va•oo ve•shach•noo sham ve•hai•ta acha•rit ha•eesh ha•hoo ra•ah me•re•shi•to ve•chen yi•hee•ye la•dor ha•ra ha•ze.

---

46. While he yet talked to the people, behold, his mother and his brethren stood without, desiring to speak with him.

Greek/Transliteration
46. Ἔτι δὲ αὐτοῦ λαλοῦντος τοῖς ὄχλοις, ἰδού, ἡ μήτηρ καὶ οἱ ἀδελφοὶ αὐτοῦ εἱστήκεισαν ἔξω, ζητοῦντες αὐτῷ λαλῆσαι.

46. Eti de autou lalountos tois ochlois, idou, 'ei meiteir kai 'oi adelphoi autou 'eisteikeisan exo, zeitountes auto laleisai.

Hebrew/Transliteration
מו. עוֹדֶנּוּ מְדַבֵּר אֶל-הֲמוֹן הָעָם וְהִנֵּה אִמּוֹ וְאֶחָיו עָמְדוּ בַחוּץ וּמְבַקְשִׁים לְדַבֵּר אִתּוֹ:

46. O•de•noo me•da•ber el - ha•mon ha•am ve•hee•ne ee•mo ve•e•chav am•doo va•choo•tz oom•vak•shim le•da•ber ee•to.

---

47. Then one said unto him, Behold, thy mother and thy brethren stand without, desiring to speak with thee.

Greek/Transliteration
47. Εἶπεν δέ τις αὐτῷ, Ἰδού, ἡ μήτηρ σου καὶ οἱ ἀδελφοί σου ἔξω ἑστήκασιν, ζητοῦντές σοι λαλῆσαι.

47. Eipen de tis auto, Ydou, 'ei meiteir sou kai 'oi adelphoi sou exo 'esteikasin, zeitountes soi laleisai.

Hebrew/Transliteration
מז. וַיֻּגַּד לוֹ הִנֵּה אִמְּךָ וְאַחֶיךָ עֹמְדִים בַּחוּץ וּמְבַקְשִׁים לְדַבֵּר אִתָּךְ:

47. Va•yoo•gad lo hee•ne eem•cha ve•a•che•cha om•dim ba•chootz oom•vak•shim le•da•ber ee•tach.

---

48. But he answered and said unto him that told him, Who is my mother? and who are my brethren?

Greek/Transliteration
48. Ὁ δὲ ἀποκριθεὶς εἶπεν τῷ εἰπόντι αὐτῷ, Τίς ἐστιν ἡ μήτηρ μου; Καὶ τίνες εἰσὶν οἱ ἀδελφοί μου;

48. 'O de apokritheis eipen to eiponti auto, Tis estin 'ei meiteir mou? Kai tines eisin 'oi adelphoi mou?

Hebrew/Transliteration
מח. וַיַּעַן וַיֹּאמֶר אֶל-הַמַּגִּיד לוֹ מִי אִמִּי וּמִי אֶחָי:

48. Va•ya•an va•yo•mer el - ha•ma•gid lo mee ee•mi oo•mi e•chai.

---

49. And he stretched forth his hand toward his disciples, and said, Behold my mother and my brethren!

Greek/Tranliteration
49. Καὶ ἐκτείνας τὴν χεῖρα αὐτοῦ ἐπὶ τοὺς μαθητὰς αὐτοῦ εἶπεν, Ἰδού, ἡ μήτηρ μου καὶ οἱ ἀδελφοί μου.

49. Kai ekteinas tein cheira autou epi tous matheitas autou eipen, Ydou, 'ei meiteir mou kai 'oi adelphoi mou.

Hebrew/Transliteration
מט. וַיֵּט אֶת-יָדוֹ עַל-תַּלְמִידָיו וַיֹּאמַר הִנֵּה אִמִּי וְאֶחָי:

49. Va•yet et - ya•do al - tal•mi•dav va•yo•mar hee•ne ee•mi ve•e•chai.

---

50. For whosoever shall do the will of my Father which is in heaven, the same is my brother, and sister, and mother.

Greek/Transliteration
50. Ὅστις γὰρ ἂν ποιήσῃ τὸ θέλημα τοῦ πατρός μου τοῦ ἐν οὐρανοῖς, αὐτός μου ἀδελφὸς καὶ ἀδελφὴ καὶ μήτηρ ἐστίν.

50. 'Ostis gar an poieisei to theleima tou patros mou tou en ouranois, autos mou adelphos kai adelphei kai meiteir estin.

Hebrew/Transliteration
נ: כִּי אִישׁ אִישׁ אֲשֶׁר יַעֲשֶׂה רְצוֹן אָבִי בַּשָּׁמַיִם הוּא אָחִי וַאֲחֹתִי וְאִמִּי

50. Ki eesh eesh asher ya•a•se r`tzon Avi ba•sha•ma•yim hoo achi va•a•cho•ti ve•ee•mi.

Rabbinic Jewish Commentary
All these relative characters may be observed in the book of Solomon's Song, to which Yeshua may be reasonably thought to have respect; see Son_3:11.

Matthew, Chapter 13

1. The same day went Jesus out of the house, and sat by the sea side.

Greek/Transliteration
1. Ἐν δὲ τῇ ἡμέρᾳ ἐκείνῃ ἐξελθὼν ὁ Ἰησοῦς ἀπὸ τῆς οἰκίας ἐκάθητο παρὰ τὴν θάλασσαν.

1. En de tei 'eimera ekeinei exelthon 'o Yeisous apo teis oikias ekatheito para tein thalassan.

Hebrew/Transliteration
א. בַּיּוֹם הַהוּא יָצָא יֵשׁוּעַ מִן-הַבַּיִת וַיֵּשֶׁב עַל-שְׂפַת הַיָּם:

1. Ba•yom ha•hoo ya•tza Yeshua min - ha•ba•yit va•ye•shev al - s`fat ha•yam.

---

2. And great multitudes were gathered together unto him, so that he went into a ship, and sat; and the whole multitude stood on the shore.

Greek/Transliteration
2. Καὶ συνήχθησαν πρὸς αὐτὸν ὄχλοι πολλοί, ὥστε αὐτὸν εἰς τὸ πλοῖον ἐμβάντα καθῆσθαι· καὶ πᾶς ὁ ὄχλος ἐπὶ τὸν αἰγιαλὸν εἱστήκει.

2. Kai suneichtheisan pros auton ochloi polloi, 'oste auton eis to ploion embanta katheisthai. Kai pas 'o ochlos epi ton aigyalon 'eisteikei.

Hebrew/Transliteration
ב. וַהֲמוֹן עַם רָב נִקְהֲלוּ אֵלָיו וַיֵּרֶד וַיֵּשֶׁב בָּאֳנִיָּה וְכָל-הָעָם עֹמְדִים עַל-הַחוֹף:

2. Va•ha•mon am rav nik•ha•loo elav va•ye•red va•ye•shev ba•o•ni•ya ve•chol - ha•am om•dim al - ha•chof.

Jewish New Testament Commentary
There are five collections of Yeshua's teachings in Mattityahu, corresponding to the Five Books of Moses. The first, the Sermon on the Mount (chapters 5-7), was for the multitude; the second, the commissioning (chapter 10), was for the *talmidim*; this, the third, is for both but is presented at two levels through the medium of the parable (Greek *parabôleê*, Hebrew *mashal*). chapter 18 is the fourth, and the Olivet Discourse (chapters 24-25) is the last.

---

3. And he spake many things unto them in parables, saying, Behold, a sower went forth to sow;

Greek/Transliteration
3. Καὶ ἐλάλησεν αὐτοῖς πολλὰ ἐν παραβολαῖς, λέγων, Ἰδού, ἐξῆλθεν ὁ σπείρων τοῦ σπείρειν.

3. Kai elaleisen autois polla en parabolais, legon, Ydou, exeilthen 'o speiron tou speirein.

Hebrew/Transliteration
ג. וַיְשָׂא דְבָרָיו בִּמְשָׁלִים רַבִּים וַיֹּאמַר הִנֵּה הַזּוֹרֵעַ יָצָא לִזְרֹעַ:

3. Va•yi•sa d`va•rav bim•sha•lim ra•bim va•yo•mar hee•ne ha•zo•re•a ya•tza liz•roa.

Rabbinic Jewish Commentary
This way of speaking by parables was much in use among the eastern nations, and particularly the Jews who only spoke parables in Hebrew. R. Meir was very famous among them for this way of teaching: they say (a), "that when R. Meir died, בטלו מושלי משלים, "they that were skilled in, and used parables, ceased"." The commentators (b) on this passage say, "that he preached a third part tradition, and a third part mystical discourse, ותילתא מתלי, "and a third part parables":"

(a) Misn. Sota, c. 9. sect. 15. (b) Jarchi & Bartenora in ib. e Talmud. Bab. Sanhedrim, fol. 38. 2.

---

4. And when he sowed, some seeds fell by the way side, and the fowls came and devoured them up:

Greek/Transliteration
4. Καὶ ἐν τῷ σπείρειν αὐτόν, ἃ μὲν ἔπεσεν παρὰ τὴν ὁδόν· καὶ ἦλθεν τὰ πετεινὰ καὶ κατέφαγεν αὐτά.

4. Kai en to speirein auton, 'a men epesen para tein 'odon. kai eilthen ta peteina kai katephagen auta.

Hebrew/Transliteration
ד. וּבְזָרְעוֹ פִּזַּר מִן-הַזֶּרַע עַל-יַד הַדֶּרֶךְ וַיָּבֹא עוֹף הַשָּׁמַיִם וַיֹּאכְלֻנּוּ:

4. Oov•zar•oh pi•zar min - ha•ze•ra al - yad ha•da•rech va•ya•vo of ha•sha•ma•yim va•yoch•le•noo.

Rabbinic Jewish Commentary
some seeds fell; either out of his hand, or out of the cart drawn by oxen; hence the (c) Talmudists distinguish between מפולת יד, "the falling of the hand", or what falls out of the hand; and מפולת שוורים, "the falling of the oxen", or what falls from them; where the gloss is, "in some places they sow the grain with the hand; and in other places they put the seed on a cart full of holes, and oxen draw the cart on the ploughed land, and it falls upon it." (c) T. Bab. Bava Metzia, fol. 105. 2.

5. Some fell upon stony places, where they had not much earth: and forthwith they sprung up, because they had no deepness of earth:

Greek/Transliteration
5. Ἄλλα δὲ ἔπεσεν ἐπὶ τὰ πετρώδη, ὅπου οὐκ εἶχεν γῆν πολλήν· καὶ εὐθέως ἐξανέτειλεν, διὰ τὸ μὴ ἔχειν βάθος γῆς·

5. Alla de epesen epi ta petrodei, 'opou ouk eichen gein pollein. kai eutheos exaneteilen, dya to mei echein bathos geis.

Hebrew/Transliteration
ה. וְיֵשׁ מִן-הַזֶּרַע אֲשֶׁר נָפַל עַל-אַדְמַת סֶלַע וְלֹא הָיָה שָׁם דֵּי אֲדָמָה וַיְמַהֵר לִצְמֹחַ מִבְּלִי אֲשֶׁר הָיָה לוֹ עֹמֶק אֲדָמָה:

5. Ve•yesh min - ha•ze•ra asher na•fal al - ad•mat s•ela ve•lo ha•ya sham dey ada•ma vay•ma•her litz•mo•ach mi•b`li asher ha•ya lo o•mek ada•ma.

Rabbinic Jewish Commentary
Such a place as the Jews call חולסית, a barren, stony place, a place from whence, they say, they take stones, and בית סלע, and which אינו ראוי לזריעה, "is not fit for sowing" (d); and such were those places and spots of ground, that some of these seeds fell upon; and design such hearers, in whom the natural hardness of their hearts continues, and who remain unbroken by the word, and are without any true sense of sin, and repentance for it. (d) T. Bab. Erachin, fol. 32. 1. & Gloss. in ib. & Bava Bathra, fol. 156. 2. & Gloss. in ib.

---

6. And when the sun was up, they were scorched; and because they had no root, they withered away.

Greek/Transliteration
6. ἡλίου δὲ ἀνατείλαντος ἐκαυματίσθη, καὶ διὰ τὸ μὴ ἔχειν ῥίζαν, ἐξηράνθη.

6. 'eiliou de anateilantos ekaumatisthei, kai dya to mei echein 'rizan, exeiranthei.

Hebrew/Transliteration
ו. וַיְהִי כִּזְרֹחַ הַשֶּׁמֶשׁ וַיִּצָרֵב וַיִּיבָשׁ כִּי לֹא הָיָה-לוֹ שֹׁרֶשׁ לְמָטָה:

6. Vay•hi kiz•ro•ach ha•she•mesh va•yi•tza•rev va•yi•vash ki lo ha•ya - lo sho•resh le•ma•ta.

---

7. And some fell among thorns; and the thorns sprung up, and choked them:

Greek/Transliteration
7. Ἄλλα δὲ ἔπεσεν ἐπὶ τὰς ἀκάνθας, καὶ ἀνέβησαν αἱ ἄκανθαι καὶ ἀπέπνιξαν αὐτά.

7. Alla de epesen epi tas akanthas, kai anebeisan 'ai akanthai kai apepnixan auta.

Hebrew/Transliteration
:ז. וְיֵשׁ אֲשֶׁר נָפַל אֶל-הַקֹּצִים וַיַּעֲלוּ הַקֹּצִים וַיְבַלְעוּ אֹתוֹ

7. Ve•yesh asher na•fal el - ha•ko•tzim va•ya•a•loo ha•ko•tzim vay•val•oo o•to.

Rabbinic Jewish Commentary
On a spot of ground which was full of the roots of thorns, and briars, which was not cleared of them as it should be. We often read (e) of שדה שנתקוצה, "a field cleared of thorns"; but such was not this piece of ground, it was overrun with them, not on the surface of the earth, but within it: for it follows,

So that they came to nothing; hence the advice, "sow not among thorns", Jer_4:3 and a lost kindness, or what is bestowed in vain, is expressed in this proverbial manner (f), שקולה טיבותיך ושדיא אחיזרי, "thy beneficence is taken away, and cast among thorns"

(e) Misn. Sheviith, c. 4. sect. 2. T. Hieros. Sheviith, fol. 34. 3. & 35. 1. T. Bab. Bechorot, fol. 34. 2. (f) T. Bab. Sabbat, fol. 63. 2. Bava Kama, fol. 83. 1. Cetubot, fol. 53. 2. & Betza, fol. 29. 2.

---

8. But other fell into good ground, and brought forth fruit, some an hundredfold, some sixtyfold, some thirtyfold.

Greek/Transliteration
8. Ἄλλα δὲ ἔπεσεν ἐπὶ τὴν γῆν τὴν καλήν, καὶ ἐδίδου καρπόν, ὃ μὲν ἑκατόν, ὃ δὲ ἑξήκοντα, ὃ δὲ τριάκοντα.

8. Alla de epesen epi tein gein tein kalein, kai edidou karpon, 'o men 'ekaton, 'o de 'exeikonta, 'o de tryakonta.

Hebrew/Transliteration
ח. וְיֵשׁ אֲשֶׁר נָפַל עַל-חֶלְקָה טוֹבָה וַיַּעַשׂ תְּבוּאָה זֶה מֵאָה שְׁעָרִים וְזֶה שִׁשִּׁים שְׁעָרִים וְזֶה שְׁלֹשִׁים שְׁעָרִים:

8. Ve•yesh asher na•fal al - chel•ka to•va va•ya•as te•voo•ah ze me•ah sh`a•rim ve•ze shi•shim sh`a•rim ve•ze sh`lo•shim sh`a•rim.

Rabbinic Jewish Commentary
Jewish Rabbi's say some things incredible: they tell us a story (h) of "one that sowed a measure of vetches, or pease, ועשה שלש מאות סאין, "and it produced three hundred measures"; they say unto him, the Lord hath begun to bless thee, &c." (h) T. Hieros. Peah, fol. 20. 2.

9. Who hath ears to hear, let him hear.

Greek/Transliteration
9. Ὁ ἔχων ὦτα ἀκούειν ἀκουέτω.

9. 'O echon ota akouein akoueto.

Hebrew/Transliteration
ט. מִי אֲשֶׁר אָזְנַיִם לוֹ לִשְׁמֹעַ יִשְׁמָע:

9. Mee asher oz•na•yim lo lish•mo•a yish•ma.

---

10. And the disciples came, and said unto him, Why speakest thou unto them in parables?

Greek/Transliteration
10. Καὶ προσελθόντες οἱ μαθηταὶ εἶπον αὐτῷ, Διὰ τί ἐν παραβολαῖς λαλεῖς αὐτοῖς;

10. Kai proselthontes 'oi matheitai eipon auto, Dya ti en parabolais laleis autois?

Hebrew/Transliteration
י. וַיִּגְּשׁוּ תַלְמִידָיו וַיֹּאמְרוּ אֵלָיו מַדּוּעַ תְּמַשֵּׁל לָהֶם מְשָׁלִים:

10. Va•yig•shoo tal•mi•dav va•yom•roo elav ma•doo•a te•ma•shel la•hem me•sha•lim.

---

11. He answered and said unto them, Because it is given unto you to know the mysteries of the kingdom of heaven, but to them it is not given.

Greek/Transliteration
11. Ὁ δὲ ἀποκριθεὶς εἶπεν αὐτοῖς ὅτι Ὑμῖν δέδοται γνῶναι τὰ μυστήρια τῆς βασιλείας τῶν οὐρανῶν, ἐκείνοις δὲ οὐ δέδοται.

11. 'O de apokritheis eipen autois 'oti 'Umin dedotai gnonai ta musteirya teis basileias ton ouranon, ekeinois de ou dedotai.

Hebrew/Transliteration
יא. וַיַּעַן וַיֹּאמֶר אֲלֵיהֶם כִּי לָכֶם נִתַּן לָדַעַת רָזֵי מַלְכוּת הַשָּׁמַיִם וְלָהֶם לֹא נִתָּן:

11. Va•ya•an va•yo•mer aley•hem ki la•chem ni•tan la•da•at ra•zey mal•choot ha•sha•ma•yim ve•la•hem lo ni•tan.

Jewish New Testament Commentary
It has been given to you to know the secrets... but ... not ... to them. By itself this is a harsh statement, seemingly out of keeping with the Talmudic epigram of Rabbi Chanina, "Everything is in the hands of Heaven except the fear of Heaven" (B'rakhot 33b), which implies that anyone can turn to God, so that there is not one group to whom "it has been given" and another to whom it has not.

---

12. For whosoever hath, to him shall be given, and he shall have more abundance: but whosoever hath not, from him shall be taken away even that he hath.

Greek/Transliteration
12. Ὅστις γὰρ ἔχει, δοθήσεται αὐτῷ καὶ περισσευθήσεται· ὅστις δὲ οὐκ ἔχει, καὶ ὃ ἔχει ἀρθήσεται ἀπ᾽ αὐτοῦ.

12. 'Ostis gar echei, dotheisetai auto kai perisseutheisetai. 'ostis de ouk echei, kai 'o echei artheisetai ap autou.

Hebrew/Transliteration
:יב. כִּי מִי אֲשֶׁר יֶשׁ-לוֹ יֻתַּן לוֹ וְיַעְדִּיף וּמִי אֲשֶׁר אֵין-לוֹ יֻקַּח מִמֶּנּוּ גַּם אֶת-אֲשֶׁר לוֹ

12. Ki mee asher yesh - lo yoo•tan lo ve•ya•a•dif oo•mi asher eyn - lo yoo•kach mi•me•noo gam et - asher lo.

---

13. Therefore speak I to them in parables: because they seeing see not; and hearing they hear not, neither do they understand.

Greek/Transliteration
13. Διὰ τοῦτο ἐν παραβολαῖς αὐτοῖς λαλῶ, ὅτι βλέποντες οὐ βλέπουσιν, καὶ ἀκούοντες οὐκ ἀκούουσιν, οὐδὲ συνιοῦσιν.

13. Dya touto en parabolais autois lalo, 'oti blepontes ou blepousin, kai akouontes ouk akouousin, oude suniousin.

Hebrew/Transliteration
:יג. עַל-כֵּן מְשָׁלִים אֶמְשֹׁל לָהֶם כִּי בִרְאֹתָם לֹא יִרְאוּ וּבְשָׁמְעָם לֹא יִשְׁמְעוּ וְלֹא יָבִינוּ

13. Al - ken me•sha•lim em•shol la•hem ki vir•o•tam lo yir•oo oov•shom•am lo yish•me•oo ve•lo ya•vi•noo.

Rabbinic Jewish Commentary
Wherefore he spoke to them in this abstruse and parabolical way, that they might be what they really were, seers and not seers, hearers and not hearers, at least not understanding ones; and that what he said might remain sealed and hidden to them, as the things contained in the sealed book were to the Jews of old; the reason of which was, as a writer of their's (k) says, and which agrees with Yeshua's

reason and conduct here, שהיו במשל וחידה, "because they were in parable and riddle". (k) Abarbinel in Isa. 29. 11.

---

14. And in them is fulfilled the prophecy of Esaias, which saith, By hearing ye shall hear, and shall not understand; and seeing ye shall see, and shall not perceive:

Greek/Transliteration
14. Καὶ ἀναπληροῦται αὐτοῖς ἡ προφητεία Ἡσαΐου, ἡ λέγουσα, Ἀκοῇ ἀκούσετε, καὶ οὐ μὴ συνῆτε· καὶ βλέποντες βλέψετε, καὶ οὐ μὴ ἴδητε.

14. Kai anapleiroutai autois 'ei propheiteia Eisaiou, 'ei legousa, Akoei akousete, kai ou mei suneite. kai blepontes blepsete, kai ou mei ideite.

Hebrew/Transliteration
:יד. וְהוּקַם בָּם דְּבַר הַנְּבוּאָה מִפִּי יְשַׁעְיָהוּ לֵאמֹר שִׁמְעוּ שָׁמוֹעַ וְאַל-תָּבִינוּ וּרְאוּ רָאוֹ וְאַל-תֵּדָעוּ

14. Ve•hoo•kam bam de•var ha•n`voo•ah mi•pi Ye•sha•a•ya•hoo le•mor shim•oo sha•mo•a ve•al - ta•vi•noo oor•oo ra•o ve•al - te•da•oo.

Rabbinic Jewish Commentary
The sense of the prophecy is, with respect to the times of the Messiah, that the Jews, whilst hearing the sermons preached by him, whether with, or without parables, should hear his voice, and the sound of it, but not understand his words internally, spiritually, and experimentally; and whilst they saw, with the eyes of their bodies, the miracles he did, they should see the facts done, which could not be denied and gainsayed by them, but should not take in the clear evidence, full proof, and certain demonstration given thereby, of his Messiahship. In the prophecy of Isaiah, the words run in the imperative, "hear ye, see ye", &c. but are here rendered in the future, "shall hear, shall see". which rendering of the words is supported and established by the version of the Septuagint, by the Chaldee paraphrase, and by many Jewish commentators (l); who allow, that the words in Isaiah may be so understood, which is sufficient to vindicate the citation of them, by the evangelist, in this form of them.(l) *In R. David Kimchi in Isa. vi. 9.*

---

15. For this people's heart is waxed gross, and their ears are dull of hearing, and their eyes they have closed; lest at any time they should see with their eyes, and hear with their ears, and should understand with their heart, and should be converted, and I should heal them.

Greek/Transliteration
15. Ἐπαχύνθη γὰρ ἡ καρδία τοῦ λαοῦ τούτου, καὶ τοῖς ὠσὶν βαρέως ἤκουσαν, καὶ τοὺς ὀφθαλμοὺς αὐτῶν ἐκάμμυσαν· μήποτε ἴδωσιν τοῖς ὀφθαλμοῖς, καὶ τοῖς ὠσὶν ἀκούσωσιν, καὶ τῇ καρδίᾳ συνῶσιν, καὶ ἐπιστρέψωσιν, καὶ ἰάσομαι αὐτούς.

15. Epachunthei gar 'ei kardia tou laou toutou, kai tois osin bareos eikousan, kai tous ophthalmous auton ekammusan. meipote idosin tois ophthalmois, kai tois osin akousosin, kai tei kardia sunosin, kai epistrepsosin, kai iasomai autous.

Hebrew/Transliteration

טו. הַשְׁמֵן לֵב-הָעָם הַזֶּה וְאָזְנָיו הַכְבֵּד וְעֵינָיו הָשַׁע פֶּן-יִרְאֶה בְעֵינָיו וּבְאָזְנָיו יִשְׁמָע וּלְבָבוֹ יָבִין וָשָׁב וְרָפָא לוֹ:

15. Hash•men lev - ha•am ha•ze ve•oz•nav hach•bed ve•ey•nav ha•sha pen - yir•eh ve•ey•nav oov•oz•nav yish•ma ool•va•vo ya•vin va•shav ve•ra•fa lo.

Rabbinic Jewish Commentary

and I should heal them; or, as in Mark, "and their sins should be forgiven them"; for healing of diseases, and forgiveness of sins, are, in Scripture language, one and the same thing; and this sense of the phrase here, is justified by the Chaldee paraphrase, which renders it, וישתבק להון, "and they be forgiven", or "it be forgiven them", and by a Jewish commentator on the place; who interprets healing, of the healing of the soul, and adds והיא הסליחה, "and this is pardon" (m).

(m) R. David Kimchi in loc.

---

16. But blessed are your eyes, for they see: and your ears, for they hear.

Greek/Transliteration

16. Ὑμῶν δὲ μακάριοι οἱ ὀφθαλμοί, ὅτι βλέπουσιν· καὶ τὰ ὦτα ὑμῶν, ὅτι ἀκούει.

16. 'Umon de makarioi 'oi ophthalmoi, 'oti blepousin. kai ta ota 'umon, 'oti akouei.

Hebrew/Transliteration

טז. וְאַתֶּם אַשְׁרֵי עֵינֵיכֶם כִּי רָאוּ וְאָזְנֵיכֶם כִּי שָׁמֵעוּ:

16. Ve•a•tem ash•rey ey•ne•chem ki ra•oo ve•oz•ney•chem ki sha•me•oo.

Rabbinic Jewish Commentary

They heard the Gospel preached by him, not only so as to be affected with it, and give their assent to it, but also to understand it spiritually, and experimentally, and to bring forth the fruit of it; and so were that sort of hearers, signified by the good ground in the parable Christ had just delivered. The forms of speech, in which the happiness of the disciples is here expressed, seem to be in common use with the Jews, when they would extol the peculiar attainments of a man, especially in matters of wisdom, knowledge, and understanding. Thus, it being told R. Jochanan ben Zaccai of some persons that had expounded the work of Mercavah, that is, the beginning of Ezekiel's prophecy, and the mysterious passages in it, and what befell them, expressed himself thus concerning them (n); "blessed are you, and blessed are your children, אשרי עיני שכך ראו, "and blessed are the eyes that so see"."

And elsewhere (o) mention being made of a book of secrets delivered to Solomon, and which he had understanding of, it is said,

אשרי עין שראה ואוזן ששמע, "blessed is the eye that sees, and the ear that hears", and the heart that understands, and causes to understand, the wisdom of it."

(n) T. Bab. Chagiga, fol. 14. 2. (o) Sepher Raziel, fol. 34. 1.

---

17. For verily I say unto you, That many prophets and righteous men have desired to see those things which ye see, and have not seen them; and to hear those things which ye hear, and have not heard them.

Greek/Transliteration
17. Ἀμὴν γὰρ λέγω ὑμῖν ὅτι πολλοὶ προφῆται καὶ δίκαιοι ἐπεθύμησαν ἰδεῖν ἃ βλέπετε, καὶ οὐκ εἶδον· καὶ ἀκοῦσαι ἃ ἀκούετε, καὶ οὐκ ἤκουσαν.

17. Amein gar lego 'umin 'oti polloi propheitai kai dikaioi epethumeisan idein 'a blepete, kai ouk eidon. kai akousai 'a akouete, kai ouk eikousan.

Hebrew/Transliteration
יז. כִּי-אָמֵן אֲנִי אֹמֵר לָכֶם נְבִיאִים וְצַדִּיקִים רַבִּים נִכְסְפוּ לִרְאוֹת אֶת אֲשֶׁר אַתֶּם רֹאִים וְלֹא רָאוּ וְלִשְׁמֹעַ אֵת אֲשֶׁר:אַתֶּם שֹׁמְעִים וְלֹא שָׁמֵעוּ

17. Ki - amen ani o•mer la•chem n`vi•eem ve•tza•di•kim ra•bim nich•se•foo lir•ot et asher atem ro•eem ve•lo ra•oo ve•lish•moa et asher atem shom•eem ve•lo sha•me•oo.

Rabbinic/Jewish New Testament Commentary
Tzaddik, "righteous one." In Jewish tradition generally, a godly, holy, righteous man. In Hasidic tradition such people, thought to have had supernatural powers, attracted followers and taught their disciples how to live. The implication of Mat_13:16-17 is that nothing inherent in the *talmidim* earned them the privilege of seeing the things you are seeing; the prophets and *tzaddikim* may well have been more meritorious; but God reveals himself not on the basis of human merit but by his own sovereign will (Mat_11:25-30, Rom_9:6-18, 1Co_1:17-31). In this sense, since Yeshua had to be born at a particular time and place (Gal_4:4-5), there necessarily had to be some to whom "it was given" (Mat_13:11) and others to whom it was not. A way of speaking, somewhat like this, stands in the Talmud (p);

"Many have watched to expound in Mercavah (the beginning of Ezekiel's prophecy), ולא ראו אותה מימיהם, "and have not seen it all their days"."
(p) T. Bab. Megilla, fol. 24. 2.

18. Hear ye therefore the parable of the sower.

Greek/Transliteration
18. Ὑμεῖς οὖν ἀκούσατε τὴν παραβολὴν τοῦ σπείροντος.

18. 'Umeis oun akousate tein parabolein tou speirontos.

Hebrew/Transliteration
יח. עַל-כֵּן שִׁמְעוּ-נָא אַתֶּם אֶת מְשַׁל הַזּוֹרֵעַ:

18. Al - ken shim•oo - na atem et me•shal ha•zo•re•a.

---

19. When any one heareth the word of the kingdom, and understandeth it not, then cometh the wicked one, and catcheth away that which was sown in his heart. This is he which received seed by the way side.

Greek/Transliteration
19. Παντὸς ἀκούοντος τὸν λόγον τῆς βασιλείας καὶ μὴ συνιέντος, ἔρχεται ὁ πονηρός, καὶ ἁρπάζει τὸ ἐσπαρμένον ἐν τῇ καρδίᾳ αὐτοῦ· οὗτός ἐστιν ὁ παρὰ τὴν ὁδὸν σπαρείς.

19. Pantos akouontos ton logon teis basileias kai mei sunientos, erchetai 'o poneiros, kai 'arpazei to esparmenon en tei kardia autou. 'outos estin 'o para tein 'odon spareis.

Hebrew/Transliteration
יט. כָּל-הַשֹּׁמֵעַ דְּבַר הַמַּלְכוּת וְלֹא יִתְבּוֹנֶן-בּוֹ וּבָא הָרָע וְחָטַף אֶת אֲשֶׁר נִזְרַע בִּלְבָבוֹ זֶה הוּא הַזָּרוּעַ עַל-יַד:הַדָּרֶךְ

19. Kol - ha•sho•me•a de•var ha•mal•choot ve•lo yit•bo•nen - bo oo•va ha•ra ve•cha•taf et asher niz•ra bil•va•vo ze hoo ha•za•roo•a al - yad ha•da•rech.

Rabbinic Jewish Commentary
The Jews frequently call (q) Samael, by whom they mean the devil, Samael, הדשע, "the wicked". This evil spirit, as soon as ever he observes one hearing the word, especially that has not been used to attend, comes immediately and as he is hearing.
(q) Sepher Bahir apud Zohar in Gen. fol. 27. 2. Debarim Rabba, fol. 145. 3.

---

20. But he that received the seed into stony places, the same is he that heareth the word, and anon with joy receiveth it;

Greek/Transliteration
20. Ὁ δὲ ἐπὶ τὰ πετρώδη σπαρείς, οὗτός ἐστιν ὁ τὸν λόγον ἀκούων, καὶ εὐθὺς μετὰ χαρᾶς λαμβάνων αὐτόν·

20. 'O de epi ta petrodei spareis, 'outos estin 'o ton logon akouon, kai euthus meta charas lambanon auton.

Hebrew/Transliteration

כ. וְהַנִּזְרָע עַל־אַדְמַת סֶלַע זֶה הוּא הַשֹּׁמֵעַ אֶת־הַדָּבָר וְעַד־מְהֵרָה יְקַבְּלֶנּוּ בְּשִׂמְחָה:

20. Ve•ha•niz•ra al - ad•mat sa•la ze hoo ha•sho•me•a et - ha•da•var ve•ad - me•he•ra ye•kab•le•noo be•sim•cha.

---

21. Yet hath he not root in himself, but dureth for a while: for when tribulation or persecution ariseth because of the word, by and by he is offended.

Greek/Transliteation

21. οὐκ ἔχει δὲ ῥίζαν ἐν ἑαυτῷ, ἀλλὰ πρόσκαιρός ἐστιν· γενομένης δὲ θλίψεως ἢ διωγμοῦ διὰ τὸν λόγον, εὐθὺς σκανδαλίζεται.

21. ouk echei de 'rizan en 'eauto, alla proskairos estin. genomeneis de thlipseos ei diogmou dya ton logon, euthus skandalizetai.

Hebrew/Transliteration

כא. אֶפֶס כִּי אֵין־לוֹ שֹׁרֶשׁ בְּנַפְשׁוֹ וּבֶן רֶגַע הוּא וְכִי תִקְרֶה כָּל־צָרָה וְרָדְפוּ אֹתוֹ עַל־דְּבַר אֱמוּנָתוֹ יִכָּשֵׁל כְּרָגַע:

21. E•fes ki eyn - lo sho•resh be•naf•sho oo•vin re•ga hoo ve•chi tik•re chol - tza•ra ve•rad•foo o•to al - de•var emoo•na•to yi•ka•shel ke•ra•ga.

---

22. He also that received seed among the thorns is he that heareth the word; and the care of this world, and the deceitfulness of riches, choke the word, and he becometh unfruitful.

Greek/Transliteration

22. Ὁ δὲ εἰς τὰς ἀκάνθας σπαρείς, οὗτός ἐστιν ὁ τὸν λόγον ἀκούων, καὶ ἡ μέριμνα τοῦ αἰῶνος τούτου καὶ ἡ ἀπάτη τοῦ πλούτου συμπνίγει τὸν λόγον, καὶ ἄκαρπος γίνεται.

22. 'O de eis tas akanthas spareis, 'outos estin 'o ton logon akouon, kai 'ei merimna tou aionos toutou kai 'ei apatei tou ploutou sumpnigei ton logon, kai akarpos ginetai.

Hebrew/Transliteration

כב. וְהַנִּזְרָע אֶל־הַקֹּצִים זֶה הַשֹּׁמֵעַ אֶת־הַדָּבָר וְדַאֲגַת הָעוֹלָם הַזֶּה וְנִכְלֵי הָעשֶׁר מְבַלְּעִים אֶת־הַדָּבָר וְלֹא־יַעֲשֶׂה־פֶּרִי:

22. Ve•ha•niz•ra el - ha•ko•tzim ze ha•sho•me•a et - ha•da•var ve•da•a•gat ha•o•lam ha•ze ve•nich•ley ha•o•sher me•val•eem et - ha•da•var ve•lo ya•a•se - tze•mach.

Rabbinic Jewish Commentary
And the deceitfulness of riches, the phrase is Jewish (r);
"says R. Judah, the prince, whoever takes upon him, תענוגי העולם הזה, "the pleasures of this world", to him are denied the pleasures of the world to come: and whoever does not take upon him "the pleasures of this world", to him are given the pleasures of the world to come." (r) Abot R. Nathan, c. 28. Vid. Kimchi & Ben Melech in Psal. xvi 5. & Eben Ezra in Psal. xix. 10.

---

23. But he that received seed into the good ground is he that heareth the word, and understandeth it; which also beareth fruit, and bringeth forth, some an hundredfold, some sixty, some thirty.

Greek/Transliteration
23. Ὁ δὲ ἐπὶ τὴν γῆν τὴν καλὴν σπαρείς, οὗτός ἐστιν ὁ τὸν λόγον ἀκούων καὶ συνιών· ὃς δὴ καρποφορεῖ, καὶ ποιεῖ ὁ μὲν ἑκατόν, ὁ δὲ ἑξήκοντα, ὁ δὲ τριάκοντα.

23. 'O de epi tein gein tein kalein spareis, 'outos estin 'o ton logon akouon kai sunion. 'os dei karpophorei, kai poiei 'o men 'ekaton, 'o de 'exeikonta, 'o de tryakonta.

Hebrew/Transliteration
כג. וְהַנִּזְרָע עַל-הַחֶלְקָה הַטּוֹבָה הוּא הַשּׁמֵעַ אֶת-הַדָּבָר וּמִתְבּוֹנֵן-בּוֹ וְעֹשֶׂה פְּרִי תְּבוּאָה וְנֹתֵן זֶה מֵאָה שְׁעָרִים:וְזֶה שִׁשִּׁים שְׁעָרִים וְזֶה שְׁלֹשִׁים שְׁעָרִים

23. Ve•ha•niz•ra al - ha•chel•ka ha•to•va hoo ha•sho•me•a et - ha•da•var oo•mit•bo•nen - bo ve•o•se f`ri te•voo•ah ve•no•ten ze me•ah sh`a•rim ve•ze shi•shim sh`a•rim ve•ze sh`lo•shim sh`a•rim.

---

24. Another parable put he forth unto them, saying, The kingdom of heaven is likened unto a man which sowed good seed in his field:

Greek/Transliteration
24. Ἄλλην παραβολὴν παρέθηκεν αὐτοῖς, λέγων, Ὡμοιώθη ἡ βασιλεία τῶν οὐρανῶν ἀνθρώπῳ σπείροντι καλὸν σπέρμα ἐν τῷ ἀγρῷ αὐτοῦ·

24. Allein parabolein paretheiken autois, legon, 'Omoiothei 'ei basileia ton ouranon anthropo speironti kalon sperma en to agro autou.

Hebrew/Transliteration
כד. וַיִּשָּׂא לִפְנֵיהֶם מָשָׁל אַחֵר וַיֹּאמַר דָּמְתָה מַלְכוּת הַשָּׁמַיִם לְאִישׁ הַזּוֹרֵעַ זֶרַע טוֹב בְּשָׂדֵהוּ:

24. Va•yi•sa lif•ney•hem ma•shal a•cher va•yo•mar dam•ta mal•choot ha•sha•ma•yim le•eesh ha•zo•re•a ze•ra tov be•sa•de•hoo.

---

25. But while men slept, his enemy came and sowed tares among the wheat, and went his way.

Greek/Transliteration
25. ἐν δὲ τῷ καθεύδειν τοὺς ἀνθρώπους, ἦλθεν αὐτοῦ ὁ ἐχθρὸς καὶ ἔσπειρεν ζιζάνια ἀνὰ μέσον τοῦ σίτου, καὶ ἀπῆλθεν.

25. en de to katheudein tous anthropous, eilthen autou 'o echthros kai espeiren zizanya ana meson tou sitou, kai apeilthen.

Hebrew/Transliteration
:כה. וּבְהְיוֹת אֲנָשָׁיו יְשֵׁנִים בָּא אֹיְבוֹ וַיִּזְרַע זוֹנִין בְּתוֹךְ הַחִטִּים וַיֵּלֶךְ

25. Oo•vi•hi•yot ana•shav ye•she•nim ba oy•vo va•yiz•ra zo•nin be•toch ha•chi•tim va•ye•lech.

Rabbinic Jewish Commentary
and went his way; somewhere else, to do more mischief; and having done all he could at present here, undiscovered, not taken notice of by ministers and churches; they being all asleep, and having lost, in a great measure, the spirit of discerning. The word ζιζάνια, we render "tares", and the Ethiopic version "thistles", probably means the same the Jewish doctors call זונין, Zunin (s); and which, they say, is a sort of wheat, and not of a different kind from it; that when it is sown it looks like wheat, and is sown for it, but is changed in the earth, both as to its nature and form, and brings forth this kind. In the generation in which the flood was, they say (t), they sowed wheat, and the earth brought forth זונין, ζιζάνια, what we render "tares", and bids fair to be what is here meant; and fitly expresses false professors, nominal Christians, men of degenerate principles and practices: for not what we call tares, or vetches, can be meant, which may be removed from the wheat without danger, but rather this degenerate wheat; or that wheat which is blasted, and which may be observed sometimes to grow upon the same root, and therefore cannot be taken away, without rooting up the wheat also.

(s) Misn. Kilaim, c. 1. sect. 1. & Trumot, c. 2. sect, 6. & Maimon. in ib. T. Hieros. Kilaim, fol. 26. 4. Maimon. Hilch. Kilaim, c. 3. sect. 3. (t) Bereshit Rabba, sect. 28. fol. 23. 4.

---

26. But when the blade was sprung up, and brought forth fruit, then appeared the tares also.

Greek/Transliteration
26. Ὅτε δὲ ἐβλάστησεν ὁ χόρτος καὶ καρπὸν ἐποίησεν, τότε ἐφάνη καὶ τὰ ζιζάνια.

26. 'Ote de eblasteisen 'o chortos kai karpon epoieisen, tote ephanei kai ta zizanya.

Hebrew/Transliteration
כו. וְכַאֲשֶׁר צָץ הַקָּנֶה וְהַחִטָּה אָבִיב נִרְאוּ אָז גַּם-הַזּוּנִין:

26. Ve•cha•a•sher tzatz ha•ka•ne ve•ha•chi•ta aviv nir•oo az gam - ha•zo•nin.

---

27. So the servants of the householder came and said unto him, Sir, didst not thou sow good seed in thy field? from whence then hath it tares?

Greek/Transliteration
27. Προσελθόντες δὲ οἱ δοῦλοι τοῦ οἰκοδεσπότου εἶπον αὐτῷ, Κύριε, οὐχὶ καλὸν σπέρμα ἔσπειρας ἐν τῷ σῷ ἀγρῷ; Πόθεν οὖν ἔχει ζιζάνια;

27. Proselthontes de 'oi douloi tou oikodespotou eipon auto, Kurie, ouchi kalon sperma espeiras en to so agro? Pothen oun echei zizanya?

Hebrew/Transliteration
כז. וַיִּגְּשׁוּ הָעֲבָדִים אֶל-אֲדֹנֵיהֶם וַיֹּאמְרוּ אֲדֹנֵינוּ הֲלֹא-זֶרַע טוֹב זָרַעְתָּ בְשָׂדֶךָ וּמֵאַיִן שָׁם הַזּוּנִין:

27. Va•yig•shoo ha•a•va•dim el - ado•ney•hem va•yom•roo ado•ney•noo ha•lo - ze•ra tov za•ra•ata ve•sa•de•cha oo•me•ayin sham ha•zo•nin.

---

28. He said unto them, An enemy hath done this. The servants said unto him, Wilt thou then that we go and gather them up?

Greek/Transliteration
28. Ὁ δὲ ἔφη αὐτοῖς, Ἐχθρὸς ἄνθρωπος τοῦτο ἐποίησεν. Οἱ δὲ δοῦλοι εἶπον αὐτῷ, Θέλεις οὖν ἀπελθόντες συλλέξομεν αὐτά;

28. 'O de ephei autois, Echthros anthropos touto epoieisen. 'Oi de douloi eipon auto, Theleis oun apelthontes sullexomen auta?

Hebrew/Transliteration
כח. וַיֹּאמֶר אֲלֵיהֶם אִישׁ אֹיֵב עָשָׂה זֹאת וַיֹּאמְרוּ אֵלָיו הָעֲבָדִים הֲתַחְפֹּץ כִּי-נֵלֵךְ לַעֲקוֹר אֹתָם:

28. Va•yo•mer aley•hem eesh o•yev asa zot va•yom•roo elav ha•a•va•dim ha•tach•potz ki - ne•lech la•a•kor o•tam.

Rabbinic Jewish Commentary
He said unto them, an enemy has done this,.... This is the answer of the householder to the question of his servants. In the Greek text it is, "an enemy man"; and is so rendered in the several versions; meaning, not that the enemy was a man; for he was the devil, as in Mat_13:39 but it is an Hebraism; such as in Est_7:6, איש צר ואויב, "the man adversary and enemy".

29. But he said, Nay; lest while ye gather up the tares, ye root up also the wheat with them.

Greek/Transliteration

29. Ὁ δὲ ἔφη, Οὔ· μήποτε, συλλέγοντες τὰ ζιζάνια, ἐκριζώσητε ἅμα αὐτοῖς τὸν σῖτον.

29. 'O de ephei, Ou. meipote, sullegontes ta zizanya, ekrizoseite 'ama autois ton siton.

Hebrew/Transliteration

כט. וַיֹּאמֶר לֹא כִּי-בְעוֹד תְּעַקְּרוּ אֶת-הַזּוּנִין פֶּן-תְּשָׁרְשׁוּ גַּם-הַחִטִּים עִמָּהֶם:

29. Va•yo•mer lo ki - ve•od te•ak•roo et - ha•zo•nin pen - te•shar•shoo gam - ha•chi•tim ee•ma•hem.

---

30. Let both grow together until the harvest: and in the time of harvest I will say to the reapers, Gather ye together first the tares, and bind them in bundles to burn them: but gather the wheat into my barn.

Greek/Transliteration

30. Ἄφετε συναυξάνεσθαι ἀμφότερα μέχρι τοῦ θερισμοῦ· καὶ ἐν καιρῷ τοῦ θερισμοῦ ἐρῶ τοῖς θερισταῖς, Συλλέξατε πρῶτον τὰ ζιζάνια, καὶ δήσατε αὐτὰ εἰς δέσμας πρὸς τὸ κατακαῦσαι αὐτά· τὸν δὲ σῖτον συναγάγετε εἰς τὴν ἀποθήκην μου.

30. Aphete sunauxanesthai amphotera mechri tou therismou. kai en kairo tou therismou ero tois theristais, Sullexate proton ta zizanya, kai deisate auta eis desmas pros to katakausai auta. Ton de siton sunagagete eis tein apotheikein mou.

Hebrew/Transliteration

ל. הַנִּיחוּ לָהֶם וְגָדְלוּ שְׁנֵיהֶם יַחְדָּו עַד-הַקָּצִיר וּלְעֵת הַקָּצִיר אֹמַר לַקּוֹצְרִים לִקְטוּ אֶת-הַזּוּנִין רִאשׁנָה וְאִלְּמוּ:אֹתָם לַאֲלֻמִּים לְשָׂרְפָם וְאֶת-הַחִטִּים אִסְפוּ אֶל-גָּרְנִי

30. Ha•ni•choo la•hem ve•gad•loo sh`ney•hem yach•dav ad - ha•ka•tzir ool•et ha•ka•tzir o•mar la•kotz•rim lik•too et - ha•zo•nin ri•sho•na ve•al•moo o•tam la•a•loo•mim le•sor•fam ve•et - ha•chi•tim ees•foo el - gor•ni.

---

31. Another parable put he forth unto them, saying, The kingdom of heaven is like to a grain of mustard seed, which a man took, and sowed in his field:

Greek/Transliteration

31. Ἄλλην παραβολὴν παρέθηκεν αὐτοῖς, λέγων, Ὁμοία ἐστὶν ἡ βασιλεία τῶν οὐρανῶν κόκκῳ σινάπεως, ὃν λαβὼν ἄνθρωπος ἔσπειρεν ἐν τῷ ἀγρῷ αὐτοῦ·

31. Allein parabolein paretheiken autois, legon, 'Omoia estin 'ei basileia ton ouranon kokko sinapeos, 'on labon anthropos espeiren en to agro autou.

Hebrew/Transliteration
לא. וַיִּשָּׂא לִפְנֵיהֶם מָשָׁל אַחֵר וַיֹּאמַר דָּמְתָה מַלְכוּת הַשָּׁמַיִם לְגַרְגֵּר חַרְדָּל אֲשֶׁר לָקַח אִישׁ וַיִּזְרַע בְּשָׂדֵהוּ:

31. Va•yi•sa lif•ney•hem ma•shal a•cher va•yo•mar dam•ta mal•choot ha•sha•ma•yim le•gar•ger char•dal asher la•kach eesh va•yiz•ra be•sa•de•hoo.

---

32. Which indeed is the least of all seeds: but when it is grown, it is the greatest among herbs, and becometh a tree, so that the birds of the air come and lodge in the branches thereof.

Greek/Transliteration
32. ὃ μικρότερον μέν ἐστιν πάντων τῶν σπερμάτων· ὅταν δὲ αὐξηθῇ, μεῖζον τῶν λαχάνων ἐστίν, καὶ γίνεται δένδρον, ὥστε ἐλθεῖν τὰ πετεινὰ τοῦ οὐρανοῦ καὶ κατασκηνοῦν ἐν τοῖς κλάδοις αὐτοῦ.

32. 'o mikroteron men estin panton ton spermaton. 'otan de auxeithei, meizon ton lachanon estin, kai ginetai dendron, 'oste elthein ta peteina tou ouranou kai kataskeinoun en tois kladois autou.

Hebrew/Transliteration
לב. הֲלֹא קָטֹן הוּא מִכָּל-זֶרַע אַךְ כַּאֲשֶׁר יִצְמַח יִגְדַּל מִכָּל-יָרָק וְהָיָה לְעֵץ עַד-אֲשֶׁר יָבֹא עוֹף הַשָּׁמַיִם וְקִנְּנוּ בַּעֲנָפָיו:

32. Ha•lo ka•ton hoo mi•kol - ze•ra ach ka•a•sher yitz•mach yig•dal mi•kol - ye•rek ve•ha•ya le•etz ad - asher ya•vo of ha•sha•ma•yim ve•ki•ne•noo ba•a•na•fav.

Rabbinic/Jewish New Testament Commentary
Mustard is a very small seed, but not the world's smallest. Scripture, to be inspired by God, does not require that every fact of nature be woodenly reported. For Yeshua's hearers, mustard might well have been the smallest seed frequently encountered. God used the culture of the age to convey spiritual truth. Apposite is the Talmudic epigram, "The *Torah* speaks in the language of men" (or: "The *Torah* uses everyday human expressions," B'rakhot 31b). The rabbis too used the mustard seed in figures of speech for smallness; see B'rakhot 31a and Leviticus Rabbah 31:9 (on Lev_24:2). So mustard with the Jews (u), is called מין זרעים, "a kind of seeds"; and being very small, hence כחרדל, "as a grain of mustard", is often used, proverbially (w), for the least thing, as it is by Yeshua

But when it is grown, it is the greatest among herbs, and becometh a tree. Luke says, "a great tree", Luk_13:19 for to such a size did the mustard tree grow in the land of Judea, of which take the following instances (x), "At Shichin there was a mustard stalk, which had three branches, and one of them was cut down, and they covered a potter's booth with it; and found in it שלשת קבין של חרדל, "three kabs of mustard seed" (elsewhere (y) it is said, nine kabs).

Says R. Simeon ben Chelphetha, I have one stalk of mustard seed in my field, and I go up to it, בראש התאנה.

כעולה, "as one goes up to the top of a fig tree". And though the mustard tree grew to this height and size, it was reckoned among herbs, as here by Yeshua; for they say (z), "they do not put mustard in a field of fruits, but in a field of herbs.

(u) Misn. Kilaim, c. 3. sect. 2. (w) T. Bab. Beracot, fol. 31. 1. Megilla, fol. 23. 2. Nidda, fol. 66. 1. (x) T. Hieros. Peah, fol. 20. 2. (y) T. Bab, Cetubot, fol. 111. 2. (z) Misn. Kilaim, c. 2. sect. 8.

---

33. Another parable spake he unto them; The kingdom of heaven is like unto leaven, which a woman took, and hid in three measures of meal, till the whole was leavened.

Greek/Transliteration
33. Ἄλλην παραβολὴν ἐλάλησεν αὐτοῖς, Ὁμοία ἐστὶν ἡ βασιλεία τῶν οὐρανῶν ζύμῃ, ἣν λαβοῦσα γυνὴ ἔκρυψεν εἰς ἀλεύρου σάτα τρία, ἕως οὗ ἐζυμώθη ὅλον.

33. Allein parabolein elaleisen autois, 'Omoia estin 'ei basileia ton ouranon zumei, 'ein labousa gunei ekrupsen eis aleurou sata tria, 'eos 'ou ezumothei 'olon.

Hebrew/Transliteration
לג. וַיְמַשֵּׁל לָהֶם מָשָׁל אַחֵר לֵאמֹר דָּמְתָה מַלְכוּת הַשָּׁמַיִם לִשְׂאֹר אֲשֶׁר לָקְחָה אִשָּׁה וַתַּלָּשׁ בִּשְׁלֹשׁ סְאִים קֶמַח:עַד-אֲשֶׁר חָמְצָה כָּל-הָעֲרִיסָה.

33. Vay•ma•shel la•hem ma•shal a•cher le•mor dam•ta mal•choot ha•sha•ma•yim lis•or asher lak•cha ee•sha va•ta•lash bish•losh se•eem ke•mach ad - asher cham•tza kol - ha•a•ri•sa.

Rabbinic Jewish Commentary
The measure here designed, is the Hebrew seah, which held a gallon and an half, and three of these made an ephah; and which is often rendered by the (a) Targumists, תלת סאין, "three seahs", or "measures", the very phrase here used; and the reason why three are particularly mentioned is, because such a quantity used to be fermented and kneaded by women at one time; see Gen_18:6 and for the further illustration of this, take the following passage out of the Talmud (b),

"The wise men say, that three women may be employed in one lump of dough; one may knead it, another may make it into loaves, and another may bake it--and it is a tradition, בחיטין שלשת קבין "that in wheat they use three kabs", or "measures", and in barley four "kabs".

(a) Targum Onketos & Jarchi, in Exod. xvi. 36. & Targum Jon. in Ruth ii. 17. (b) T. Hieros. Pesachim, fol. 30. 2. (c) Vid. Teelman. Specimen Explic. Parabolarum, p. 64, 65, 66, 67, 68.

---

34. All these things spake Jesus unto the multitude in parables; and without a parable spake he not unto them:

Greek/Transliteration
34. Ταῦτα πάντα ἐλάλησεν ὁ Ἰησοῦς ἐν παραβολαῖς τοῖς ὄχλοις, καὶ χωρὶς παραβολῆς οὐκ ἐλάλει αὐτοῖς·

34. Tauta panta elaleisen 'o Yeisous en parabolais tois ochlois, kai choris paraboleis ouk elalei autois.

Hebrew/Transliteration
לד: כָּל-אֵלֶּה דִּבֶּר יֵשׁוּעַ אֶל-הֲמוֹן הָעָם בִּמְשָׁלִים וּבִבְלִי מָשָׁל לֹא דִבֶּר אֲלֵיהֶם דָּבָר.

34. Kol - ele di•ber Yeshua el - ha•mon ha•am bim•sha•lim oo•viv•li ma•shal lo di•ber aley•hem da•var.

---

35. That it might be fulfilled which was spoken by the prophet, saying, I will open my mouth in parables; I will utter things which have been kept secret from the foundation of the world.

Greek/Transliteration
35. ὅπως πληρωθῇ τὸ ῥηθὲν διὰ τοῦ προφήτου, λέγοντος, Ἀνοίξω ἐν παραβολαῖς τὸ στόμα μου, ἐρεύξομαι κεκρυμμένα ἀπὸ καταβολῆς κόσμου.

35. 'opos pleirothei to 'reithen dya tou propheitou, legontos, Anoixo en parabolais to stoma mou, ereuxomai kekrummena apo kataboleis kosmou.

Hebrew/Transliteration
לה: לְמַלֹּאת אֶת אֲשֶׁר דִּבֶּר הַנָּבִיא לֵאמֹר אֶפְתְּחָה בְמָשָׁל פִּי אַבִּיעָה חִידוֹת מִנִּי-קֶדֶם.

35. Le•ma•lot et asher di•ber ha•na•vee le•mor ef•te•cha ve•ma•shal pi abi•ah chi•dot mi•ni - ke•dem.

Rabbinic Jewish Commentary
Not Isaiah, as some copies in the times of Jerom read, but Asaph, who is called Asaph the seer, 2Ch_29:30 which is all one as a prophet; vision is one sort of prophecy (d) (d) R. David Kimchi, Shorash. rad. חזה.

36. Then Jesus sent the multitude away, and went into the house: and his disciples came unto him, saying, Declare unto us the parable of the tares of the field.

Greek/Transliteration

36. Τότε ἀφεὶς τοὺς ὄχλους ἦλθεν εἰς τὴν οἰκίαν ὁ Ἰησοῦς· καὶ προσῆλθον αὐτῷ οἱ μαθηταὶ αὐτοῦ, λέγοντες, Φράσον ἡμῖν τὴν παραβολὴν τῶν ζιζανίων τοῦ ἀγροῦ.

36. Tote apheis tous ochlous eilthen eis tein oikian 'o Yeisous. kai proseilthon auto 'oi matheitai autou, legontes, Phrason 'eimin tein parabolein ton zizanion tou agrou.

Hebrew/Transliteration

לו. אָז שִׁלַּח יֵשׁוּעַ אֶת-הֲמוֹן הָעָם וַיָּבֹא הַבַּיְתָה וַיִּגְּשׁוּ אֵלָיו תַּלְמִידָיו וַיֹּאמְרוּ בָּאֶר-נָא לָנוּ אֶת-מְשַׁל הַזּוֹנִין בַּשָּׂדֶה:

36. Az shi•lach Yeshua et - ha•mon ha•am va•ya•vo ha•bai•ta va•yig•shoo elav tal•mi•dav va•yom•roo ba•er - na la•noo et - me•shal ha•zo•nin ba•sa•de.

---

37. He answered and said unto them, He that soweth the good seed is the Son of man;

Greek/Transliteration

37. Ὁ δὲ ἀποκριθεὶς εἶπεν αὐτοῖς, Ὁ σπείρων τὸ καλὸν σπέρμα ἐστὶν ὁ υἱὸς τοῦ ἀνθρώπου·

37. 'O de apokritheis eipen autois, 'O speiron to kalon sperma estin 'o 'wios tou anthropou.

Hebrew/Transliteration

לז. וַיַּעַן וַיֹּאמֶר אֲלֵיהֶם הַזּוֹרֵעַ הַזֶּרַע הַטּוֹב הוּא בֶּן-הָאָדָם:

37. Va•ya•an va•yo•mer aley•hem ha•zo•re•a ha•ze•ra ha•tov hoo Ben - ha•a•dam.

---

38. The field is the world; the good seed are the children of the kingdom; but the tares are the children of the wicked one;

Greek/Transliteration

38. ὁ δὲ ἀγρός ἐστιν ὁ κόσμος· τὸ δὲ καλὸν σπέρμα, οὗτοί εἰσιν οἱ υἱοὶ τῆς βασιλείας· τὰ δὲ ζιζάνιά εἰσιν οἱ υἱοὶ τοῦ πονηροῦ·

38. 'o de agros estin 'o kosmos. to de kalon sperma, 'outoi eisin 'oi 'wioi teis basileias. ta de zizanya eisin 'oi 'wioi tou poneirou.

Hebrew/Transliteration
לח. וְהַשָּׂדֶה הוּא הָעוֹלָם וְהַזֶּרַע הַטוֹב בְּנֵי הַמַּלְכוּת וְהַזּוֹנִין בְּנֵי הָרַע הֵמָּה:

38. Ve•ha•sa•de hoo ha•o•lam ve•ha•ze•ra ha•tov b`ney ha•mal•choot ve•ha•zo•nin b`ney ha•ra he•ma.

---

39. The enemy that sowed them is the devil; the harvest is the end of the world; and the reapers are the angels.

Greek/Transliteration
39. ὁ δὲ ἐχθρὸς ὁ σπείρας αὐτά ἐστιν ὁ διάβολος· ὁ δὲ θερισμὸς συντέλεια τοῦ αἰῶνός ἐστιν· οἱ δὲ θερισταὶ ἄγγελοί εἰσιν.

39. 'o de echthros 'o speiras auta estin 'o dyabolos. 'o de therismos sunteleya tou aionos estin. 'oi de theristai angeloi eisin.

Hebrew/Transliteration
לט. הָאֹיֵב הַזּוֹרֵעַ אֹתָם הוּא הַשָּׂטָן הַקָּצִיר קֵץ הָעוֹלָם וְהַקּוֹצְרִים הֵם הַמַּלְאָכִים:

39. Ha•o•yev ha•zo•re•a o•tam hoo ha•Satan ha•ka•tzir ketz ha•o•lam ve•ha•kotz•rim hem ha•mal•a•chim.

---

40. As therefore the tares are gathered and burned in the fire; so shall it be in the end of this world [Gk.*aion-age*]

Greek/Transliteration
40. Ὥσπερ οὖν συλλέγεται τὰ ζιζάνια καὶ πυρὶ καίεται, οὕτως ἔσται ἐν τῇ συντελείᾳ τοῦ αἰῶνος τούτου.

40. 'Osper oun sullegetai ta zizanya kai puri kaietai, 'outos estai en tei sunteleia tou aionos toutou.

Hebrew/Transliteration
מ. וְכַאֲשֶׁר הַזּוֹנִין יְלֻקְטוּ וְהָיוּ לְמַאֲכֹלֶת אֵשׁ כֵּן יִהְיֶה בְּקֵץ הָעוֹלָם הַזֶּה:

40. Ve•cha•a•sher ha•zo•nin ye•look•too ve•ha•yoo le•ma•a•cho•let esh ken yi•hee•ye be•ketz ha•o•lam ha•ze.

---

41. The Son of man shall send forth his angels, and they shall gather out of his kingdom all things that offend, and them which do iniquity;

Greek/Transliteration
41. Ἀποστελεῖ ὁ υἱὸς τοῦ ἀνθρώπου τοὺς ἀγγέλους αὐτοῦ, καὶ συλλέξουσιν ἐκ τῆς βασιλείας αὐτοῦ πάντα τὰ σκάνδαλα καὶ τοὺς ποιοῦντας τὴν ἀνομίαν,

41. Apostelei 'o 'wios tou anthropou tous angelous autou, kai sullexousin ek teis basileias autou panta ta skandala kai tous poiountas tein anomian,

Hebrew/Transliteration
מא. בֶּן־הָאָדָם יִשְׁלַח אֶת־מַלְאָכָיו וְהֵסִירוּ מִתּוֹךְ מַלְכוּתוֹ כָּל־מַכְשֵׁלָה וְכָל־עֹשֵׂה עַוְלָה:

41. Ben - ha•a•dam yish•lach et - mal•a•chav ve•he•si•roo mi•toch mal•choo•to kol - mach•she•la ve•chol - o•se av•la.

---

42. And shall cast them into a furnace of fire: there shall be wailing and gnashing of teeth.

Greek/Transliteration
42. καὶ βαλοῦσιν αὐτοὺς εἰς τὴν κάμινον τοῦ πυρός· ἐκεῖ ἔσται ὁ κλαυθμὸς καὶ ὁ βρυγμὸς τῶν ὀδόντων.

42. kai balousin autous eis tein kaminon tou puros. ekei estai 'o klauthmos kai 'o brugmos ton odonton.

Hebrew/Transliteration
מב. וְהִשְׁלִיכוּ אֹתָם אֶל־כִּבְשַׁן אֵשׁ שָׁם יִהְיֶה בְכִי וַחֲרֹק שִׁנָּיִם:

42. Ve•hish•li•choo o•tam el - kiv•shan esh sham yi•hee•ye ve•chi va•cha•rok shi•na•yim.

Rabbinic Jewish Commentary
Not a material, but a metaphorical one; denoting the wrath of God, which shall fall upon wicked men: which is sometimes called Gehenna fire, sometimes a lake which burns with fire and brimstone; and here a furnace of fire, expressing the vehemency and intenseness of divine wrath, which will be intolerable; in allusion either to Nebuchadnezzar's fiery furnace, or as some think, to the custom of burning persons alive in some countries; or rather, to the burning of chaff and stubble, and the stalks of any unprofitable things that grew in the field (f), for the heating of furnaces, and is the very language of the Jews, who used to compare hell to a furnace; so Gen_15:17 is paraphrased by them (g),

"And behold the sun set, and there was darkness; and lo! Abraham saw until the seats were set, and the thrones cast down; and lo! "gehenna", which is prepared for the wicked in the world to come, כתנורא, "as a furnace", which sparks and flames of fire surrounded; דבגוה, "in the midst of which", the wicked fell, because they rebelled against the law, in their lifetime. (f) Misn. Sabbat. c. 3. sect. 1. & Maimon, & Bartenora in ib. (g) Hieros. Targum in Gen. xv. 17.

43. Then shall the righteous shine forth as the sun in the kingdom of their Father. Who hath ears to hear, let him hear.

Greek/Transliteration
43. Τότε οἱ δίκαιοι ἐκλάμψουσιν ὡς ὁ ἥλιος ἐν τῇ βασιλείᾳ τοῦ πατρὸς αὐτῶν. Ὁ ἔχων ὦτα ἀκούειν ἀκουέτω.

43. Tote 'oi dikaioi eklampsousin 'os 'o 'eilios en tei basileia tou patros auton. 'O echon ota akouein akoueto.

Hebrew/Transliteration
מג: וְהַצַּדִּיקִים יַזְהִירוּ אָז כַּשֶּׁמֶשׁ בְּמַלְכוּת אֲבִיהֶם מִי אֲשֶׁר אָזְנַיִם לוֹ לִשְׁמֹעַ יִשְׁמָע

43. Ve•ha•tza•di•kim yaz•hi•roo az ka•she•mesh be•mal•choot Avi•hem mee asher oz•na•yim lo lish•mo•a yish•ma.

---

44. Again, the kingdom of heaven is like unto treasure hid in a field; the which when a man hath found, he hideth, and for joy thereof goeth and selleth all that he hath, and buyeth that field.

Greek/Transliteration
44. Πάλιν ὁμοία ἐστὶν ἡ βασιλεία τῶν οὐρανῶν θησαυρῷ κεκρυμμένῳ ἐν τῷ ἀγρῷ, ὃν εὑρὼν ἄνθρωπος ἔκρυψεν· καὶ ἀπὸ τῆς χαρᾶς αὐτοῦ ὑπάγει, καὶ πάντα ὅσα ἔχει πωλεῖ, καὶ ἀγοράζει τὸν ἀγρὸν ἐκεῖνον.

44. Palin 'omoia estin 'ei basileia ton ouranon theisauro kekrummeno en to agro, 'on 'euron anthropos ekrupsen. kai apo teis charas autou 'upagei, kai panta 'osa echei polei, kai agorazei ton agron ekeinon.

Hebrew/Transliteration
מד. עוֹד דָּמְתָה מַלְכוּת הַשָּׁמַיִם לְאוֹצָר טָמוּן בַּשָּׂדֶה אֲשֶׁר יִמְצָאֵהוּ אִישׁ וְיַצְפִּנֵהוּ וּבְשִׂמְחָתוֹ יֵלֵךְ וְיִמְכֹּר אֶת-כָּל-אֲשֶׁר-לוֹ וְקָנָה לוֹ אֶת-הַשָּׂדֶה הַהוּא

44. Od dam•ta mal•choot ha•sha•ma•yim le•o•tzar ta•moon ba•sa•de asher yim•tza•e•hoo eesh ve•yatz•pi•ne•hoo oov•sim•cha•to ye•lech ve•yim•kor et - kol - asher – lo ve•ka•na lo et - ha•sa•de ha•hoo.

---

45. Again, the kingdom of heaven is like unto a merchant man, seeking goodly pearls:

Greek/Transliteration
45. Πάλιν ὁμοία ἐστὶν ἡ βασιλεία τῶν οὐρανῶν ἀνθρώπῳ ἐμπόρῳ ζητοῦντι καλοὺς μαργαρίτας·

45. Palin 'omoia estin 'ei basileia ton ouranon anthropo emporo zeitounti kalous margaritas.

Hebrew/Transliteration
מה. עוֹד דָּמְתָה מַלְכוּת הַשָּׁמַיִם לְאִישׁ סוֹחֵר הַמְבַקֵּשׁ פְּנִינִים יְקָרוֹת:

45. Od dam•ta mal•choot ha•sha•ma•yim le•eesh so•cher ham•va•kesh pe•ni•nim ye•ka•rot.

---

46. Who, when he had found one pearl of great price, went and sold all that he had, and bought it.

Greek/Transliteration
46. ὃς εὑρὼν ἕνα πολύτιμον μαργαρίτην, ἀπελθὼν πέπρακεν πάντα ὅσα εἶχεν, καὶ ἠγόρασεν αὐτόν.

46. 'os 'euron 'ena polutimon margaritein, apelthon pepraken panta 'osa eichen, kai eigorasen auton.

Hebrew/Transliteration
מו. וּבְמָצְאוֹ פְּנִינָה אַחַת יִקְרַת-עֵרֶךְ עַד-מְאֹד יֵלֵךְ וְיִמְכֹּר אֶת-כָּל-אֲשֶׁר-לוֹ וְיִקְנֶהָ:

46. Oov•motz•oh p`ni•na a•chat yik•rat - e•rech ad - me•od ye•lech ve•yim•kor et - kol - asher - lo ve•yik•ne•ha.

Jewish New Testament Commentary
The Hidden Treasure and The Pearl of Great Price.
The subject of this last pair, as of the two former, is the same, but also under a slight diversity of aspect: namely - The priceless value of the blessings of the kingdom. And while the one parable represents the Kingdom as "found without seeking," the other holds forth the Kingdom as "sought and found."

---

47. Again, the kingdom of heaven is like unto a net, that was cast into the sea, and gathered of every kind:

Greek/Transliteration
47. Πάλιν ὁμοία ἐστὶν ἡ βασιλεία τῶν οὐρανῶν σαγήνῃ βληθείσῃ εἰς τὴν θάλασσαν, καὶ ἐκ παντὸς γένους συναγαγούσῃ·

47. Palin 'omoia estin 'ei basileia ton ouranon sageinei bleitheisei eis tein thalassan, kai ek pantos genous sunagagousei.

Hebrew/Transliteration
מז. עוֹד דָּמְתָה מַלְכוּת הַשָּׁמַיִם לְמִכְמֹרֶת פְּרוּשָׂה עַל-פְּנֵי הַיָּם אֲשֶׁר יֵאָסְפוּ בָהּ מִמִּינִים שׁוֹנִים:

47. Od dam•ta mal•choot ha•sha•ma•yim le•mich•mo•ret p`roo•sa al - p`ney ha•yam asher ye•as•foo va mi•mi•nim sho•nim.

48. Which, when it was full, they drew to shore, and sat down, and gathered the good into vessels, but cast the bad away.

Greek/Transliteration

48. ἥν, ὅτε ἐπληρώθη, ἀναβιβάσαντες ἐπὶ τὸν αἰγιαλόν, καὶ καθίσαντες, συνέλεξαν τὰ καλὰ εἰς ἀγγεῖα, τὰ δὲ σαπρὰ ἔξω ἔβαλον.

48. 'ein, 'ote epleirothei, anabibasantes epi ton aigyalon, kai kathisantes, sunelexan ta kala eis angeia, ta de sapra exo ebalon.

Hebrew/Transliteration

מח. וּבְהִמָּלְאָהּ יִמְשְׁכוּ אֹתָהּ אֶל-הַחוֹף וְיֵשְׁבוּ וְיִבְחֲרוּ אֶת-הַטּוֹבִים לְשׂוּמָם אֶל-הַכֵּלִים וְאֶת-הָרָעִים יַשְׁלִיכוּ: חוּצָה

48. Oov•hi•mal•ah yim•she•choo o•ta el - ha•chof ve•yesh•voo ve•yiv•cha•roo et - ha•to•vim le•soo•mam el - ha•ke•lim ve•et - ha•ra•eem yash•li•choo choo•tza.

---

49. So shall it be at the end of the world [age]: the angels shall come forth, and sever the wicked from among the just,

Greek/Translitertion

49. Οὕτως ἔσται ἐν τῇ συντελείᾳ τοῦ αἰῶνος· ἐξελεύσονται οἱ ἄγγελοι, καὶ ἀφοριοῦσιν τοὺς πονηροὺς ἐκ μέσου τῶν δικαίων,

49. 'Outos estai en tei sunteleia tou aionos. exeleusontai 'oi angeloi, kai aphoriousin tous poneirous ek mesou ton dikaion,

Hebrew/Transliteration

מט. כָּכָה יִהְיֶה בְּקֵץ הָעוֹלָם כִּי הַמַּלְאָכִים יָבֹאוּ וְהִבְדִּילוּ אֶת-הָרְשָׁעִים מִתּוֹךְ הַצַּדִּיקִים:

49. Ka•cha yi•hee•ye be•ketz ha•o•lam ki ha•mal•a•chim ya•vo•oo ve•hiv•di•loo et - har•sha•eem mi•toch ha•tza•di•kim.

---

50. And shall cast them into the furnace of fire: there shall be wailing and gnashing of teeth.

Greek/Translitertion

50. καὶ βαλοῦσιν αὐτοὺς εἰς τὴν κάμινον τοῦ πυρός· ἐκεῖ ἔσται ὁ κλαυθμὸς καὶ ὁ βρυγμὸς τῶν ὀδόντων.

50. kai balousin autous eis tein kaminon tou puros. ekei estai 'o klauthmos ka 'o brugmos ton odonton.

Hebrew/Transliteration

נ. וְהִשְׁלִיכוּ אֹתָם אֶל-כִּבְשַׁן אֵשׁ שָׁם יִהְיֶה בְכִי וַחֲרֹק שִׁנָּיִם:

50. Ve•hish•li•choo o•tam el - kiv•shan esh sham yi•hee•ye ve•chi va•cha•rok shi•na•yim.

Rabbinic Jewish Commentary

Not a material, but a metaphorical one; denoting the wrath of God, which shall fall upon wicked men: which is sometimes called Gehenna fire, sometimes a lake which burns with fire and brimstone; and here a furnace of fire, expressing the vehemency and intenseness of divine wrath, which will be intolerable; in allusion either to Nebuchadnezzar's fiery furnace, or as some think, to the custom of burning persons alive in some countries; or rather, to the burning of chaff and stubble, and the stalks of any unprofitable things that grew in the field (f), for the heating of furnaces, and is the very language of the Jews, who used to compare Gehenna to a furnace; so Gen_15:17 is paraphrased by them (g),

"And behold the sun set, and there was darkness; and lo! Abraham saw until the seats were set, and the thrones cast down; and lo! "gehenna", which is prepared for the wicked in the world to come, כתנורא, "as a furnace", which sparks and flames of fire surrounded; דבגוה, "in the midst of which", the wicked fell, because they rebelled against the law, in their lifetime.

(f) Misn. Sabbat. c. 3. sect. 1. & Maimon, & Bartenora in ib. (g) Hieros. Targum in Gen. xv. 17.

---

51. Jesus saith unto them, Have ye understood all these things? They say unto him, Yea, Lord.

Greek/Transliteration

51. Λέγει αὐτοῖς ὁ Ἰησοῦς, Συνήκατε ταῦτα πάντα; Λέγουσιν αὐτῷ, Ναί, κύριε.

51. Legei autois 'o Yeisous, Suneikate tauta panta? Legousin auto, Nai, kurie.

Hebrew/Transliteration

נא. וַיֹּאמֶר אֲלֵיהֶם יֵשׁוּעַ הֲכִי בַנְתֶּם כָּל-אֵלֶּה וַיֹּאמְרוּ הֵן אֲדֹנֵנוּ:

51. Va•yo•mer aley•hem Yeshua ha•chi van•tem kol - ele va•yom•roo hen Ado•ne•noo.

---

52. Then said he unto them, Therefore every scribe which is instructed unto the kingdom of heaven is like unto a man that is an householder, which bringeth forth out of his treasure things new and old.

Greek/Transliteration

52. Ὁ δὲ εἶπεν αὐτοῖς, Διὰ τοῦτο πᾶς γραμματεὺς μαθητευθεὶς εἰς τὴν βασιλείαν τῶν οὐρανῶν ὅμοιός ἐστιν ἀνθρώπῳ οἰκοδεσπότῃ, ὅστις ἐκβάλλει ἐκ τοῦ θησαυροῦ αὐτοῦ καινὰ καὶ παλαιά.

52. 'O de eipen autois, Dya touto pas grammateus matheiteutheis eis tein basileian ton ouranon 'omoios estin anthropo oikodespotei, 'ostis ekballei ek tou theisaurou autou kaina kai palaya.

Hebrew/Transliteration
נב. וַיֹּאמֶר אֲלֵיהֶם לָכֵן כָּל-סוֹפֵר מַשְׂכִּיל לְמַלְכוּת הַשָּׁמַיִם נִדְמֶה לְאִישׁ בַּעַל-הַבַּיִת הַמּוֹצִיא מֵאוֹצָרוֹ חֲדָשׁוֹת:וְגַם-יְשָׁנוֹת

52. Va•yo•mer aley•hem la•chen kol - so•fer mas•kil le•mal•choot ha•sha•ma•yim nid•me le•eesh ba•al - ha•ba•yit ha•mo•tzi me•o•tza•ro cha•da•shot ve•gam - ye•sha•not.

Rabbinic Jewish Commentary
The allusion is either to a good provider for his family, who lays up stores for them of all sorts, and upon proper occasions brings them forth for their relief; or to the people under the law, bringing their offerings out of the fruits, both of the old and new year; concerning which, take the following rule (m), "All offerings, both of the congregation and of a private person, came from the land (of Israel), and without the land, מן החדש ומן הישן, "from the new and from the old" (i.e. from the new and old stock, the increase of the new and old year), except the sheaf of the first fruits, and the two wave loaves; for they come only from the new, and from the land of Israel.

The place where fruits of any kind were laid up, was called a treasure; hence it is said (n), the palm tree has its fallen fruits, which they do not bring לאוצר, "into the treasure"; and it produces dates, which they put into the treasure: perhaps some reference is had to Son_7:13 where mention is made of fruits new and old, and which the Jewish writers (o) interpret of the words of the Scribes, and of the words of the law; the fruits "new", are the words and sayings of the Scribes, their doctrines and decisions; and the "old", are the words of the law; and one that was well versed in both these; was with them a well instructed Scribe.

(m) Misn. Parah, c. 2. sect. 1. (n) Bemidbar Rabba, sect. 3. fol. 180. 3. (o) Targum in Cant. vii. 13. T. Bab. Erubim, fol. 21. 2. & Gloss. in ib.

---

53. And it came to pass, that when Jesus had finished these parables, he departed thence.

Greek/Transliteration
53. Καὶ ἐγένετο ὅτε ἐτέλεσεν ὁ Ἰησοῦς τὰς παραβολὰς ταύτας, μετῆρεν ἐκεῖθεν·

53. Kai egeneto 'ote etelesen 'o Yeisous tas parabolas tautas, meteiren ekeithen.

Hebrew/Transliteration
נג: וַיְהִי כְּכַלּוֹת יֵשׁוּעַ אֶת־הַמְּשָׁלִים הָאֵלֶּה וַיַּעֲבֹר מִשָּׁם׃

53. Vay•hi ke•cha•lot Yeshua et - ha•m`sha•lim ha•e•le va•ya•a•vor mi•sham.

---

54. And when he was come into his own country, he taught them in their synagogue, insomuch that they were astonished, and said, Whence hath this man this wisdom, and these mighty works?

Greek/Transliteration
54. καὶ ἐλθὼν εἰς τὴν πατρίδα αὐτοῦ ἐδίδασκεν αὐτοὺς ἐν τῇ συναγωγῇ αὐτῶν, ὥστε ἐκπλήττεσθαι αὐτοὺς καὶ λέγειν, Πόθεν τούτῳ ἡ σοφία αὕτη καὶ αἱ δυνάμεις;

54. kai elthon eis tein patrida autou edidasken autous en tei sunagogei auton, 'oste ekpleittesthai autous kai legein, Pothen touto 'ei sophia 'autei kai 'ai dunameis?

Hebrew/Transliteration
נד: וַיָּבֹא אֶל־אַרְצוֹ וַיּוֹרֶה לָהֶם בְּבֵית הַכְּנֶסֶת וְהֵמָּה כֵּן תָּמְהוּ לֵאמֹר מֵאַיִן לָזֶה הַחָכְמָה וְהַנִּפְלָאוֹת׃

54. Va•ya•vo el - ar•tzo va•yo•re la•hem be•veit ha•k`ne•set ve•he•ma ken tam•hoo le•mor me•a•yin la•ze ha•choch•ma ve•ha•nif•la•ot.

Rabbinic Jewish Commentary
he taught them in their synagogue, it being the sabbath day; see Mar_6:1. The Vulgate Latin, and all the Eastern versions, the Syriac, Arabic, Persic, and Ethiopic, and Munster's Hebrew Gospel read, "in their synagogues"; but as Nazareth was so mean and obscure a place, it is not likely that there should be in it more synagogues than one; and of no more do we read in Luk_4:16 where an account is given of Yeshua's preaching in this place before this time.

---

55. Is not this the carpenter's son? is not his mother called Mary? and his brethren, James, and Joses, and Simon, and Judas?

Greek/Transliteration
55. Οὐχ οὗτός ἐστιν ὁ τοῦ τέκτονος υἱός; Οὐχὶ ἡ μήτηρ αὐτοῦ λέγεται Μαριάμ, καὶ οἱ ἀδελφοὶ αὐτοῦ Ἰάκωβος καὶ Ἰωσῆς καὶ Σίμων καὶ Ἰούδας;
55. Ouch 'outos estin 'o tou tektonos 'wios? Ouchi 'ei meiteir autou legetai Maryam, kai 'oi adelphoi autou Yakobos kai Yoseis kai Simon kai Youdas?

Hebrew/Transliteration
נה: הַאֵין זֶה בֶּן־הֶחָרָשׁ הֲכִי לֹא נִקְרֵאת אִמּוֹ מִרְיָם וְאֶחָיו יַעֲקֹב וְיוֹסֵף שִׁמְעוֹן וִיהוּדָה׃

55. Ha•ein ze ben - he•cha•rash ha•chi lo nik•ret ee•mo Mir•yam ve•e•chav Yaakov ve•Yo•sef Shimon vi•Y`hoo•da.

Rabbinic Jewish Commentary

The Jews make mention of one Abba Joseph, הבנאי, "the builder", or carpenter (s); but whether the same, is not certain. What they here say, was no doubt by way of derision and contempt; and yet the same phrase is used by them of a person of great note and fame, for his wisdom and knowledge: thus speaking of a difficult point, they (t) say,

"לית נגר ולא בר נגר". "no carpenter", or smith, or a carpenter's son, can solve this: says R. Shesheth, I am neither a carpenter, nor a carpenter's son, and I can solve it.

Is not his mother called Mary? Plain Mary, without any other title, or civil respect; a poor spinstress, that got her bread by her hand labour: the Jews say (u), she was a plaiter of women's hair, and treat her with the utmost scorn.

s) Shemoth Rabba, sect. 13. fol. 99. 2. (t) T. Bab. Avoda Zara, fol. 50. 2. (u) T. Bab. Sabbat. fol. 104. 2. Chagiga, fol. 4. 2. Sanhedrim, fol. 67. 1.

---

56. And his sisters, are they not all with us? Whence then hath this man all these things?

Greek/Transliteration
56. Καὶ αἱ ἀδελφαὶ αὐτοῦ οὐχὶ πᾶσαι πρὸς ἡμᾶς εἰσίν; Πόθεν οὖν τούτῳ ταῦτα πάντα;

56. Kai 'ai adelphai autou ouchi pasai pros 'eimas eisin? Pothen oun touto tauta panta?

Hebrew/Transliteration
‏:נו. וְאַחְיוֹתָיו הֲלֹא הֵנָּה כֻּלָּן אִתָּנוּ וּמֵאַיִן לוֹ כָּל-אֵלֶּה

56. Ve•ach•yo•tav ha•lo he•na koo•lan ee•ta•noo oo•me•ayin lo kol - ele.

---

57. And they were offended in him. But Jesus said unto them, A prophet is not without honour, save in his own country, and in his own house.

Greek/Transliteration
57. Καὶ ἐσκανδαλίζοντο ἐν αὐτῷ. Ὁ δὲ Ἰησοῦς εἶπεν αὐτοῖς, Οὐκ ἔστιν προφήτης ἄτιμος, εἰ μὴ ἐν τῇ πατρίδι αὐτοῦ καὶ ἐν τῇ οἰκίᾳ αὐτοῦ.

57. Kai eskandalizonto en auto. 'O de Yeisous eipen autois, Ouk estin propheiteis atimos, ei mei en tei patridi autou kai en tei oikia autou.

Hebrew/Transliteration
‏:נז. וַיְהִי לָהֶם לְאֶבֶן נָגֶף וְיֵשׁוּעַ אָמַר אֲלֵיהֶם אֵין נָבִיא בִּבְלִי כָבוֹד זוּלָתִי בְּאֶרֶץ מוֹלַדְתּוֹ וּבְתוֹךְ בֵּיתוֹ

57. Vay•hi la•hem le•e•ven na•gef ve•Yeshua amar aley•hem eyn na•vi biv•li cha•vod zoo•la•tee be•e•retz mo•la•d`to oov•toch bei•to.

Rabbinic Jewish Commentary
Not without honour (ouk estin atimos). This is a proverb found in Jewish, Greek, and Roman writers. Seen also in the *Logia of Jesus* (*Oxyr. Papyri* i. 3).

---

58. And he did not many mighty works there because of their unbelief.

Greek/Transliteration
58. Καὶ οὐκ ἐποίησεν ἐκεῖ δυνάμεις πολλάς, διὰ τὴν ἀπιστίαν αὐτῶν.

58. Kai ouk epoieisen ekei dunameis pollas, dya tein apistian auton.

Hebrew/Transliteration
נח. וְלֹא-פָעַל שָׁם נִפְלָאוֹת רַבּוֹת מִפְּנֵי חֹסֶר אֱמוּנָתָם:

58. Ve•lo - fa•al sham nif•la•ot ra•bot mip•ney cho•ser emoo•na•tam.

Matthew, Chapter 14

1. At that time Herod the tetrarch heard of the fame of Jesus,

Greek/Transliteration
1. Ἐν ἐκείνῳ τῷ καιρῷ ἤκουσεν Ἡρῴδης ὁ τετράρχης τὴν ἀκοὴν Ἰησοῦ,

1. En ekeino to kairo eikousen 'Eirodeis 'o tetrarcheis tein akoein Yeisou,

Hebrew/Transliteration
א: בָּעֵת הַהִיא שָׁמַע הוֹרְדוֹס שַׂר-רֹבַע הַמְּדִינָה אֶת-שֵׁמַע יֵשׁוּעַ

1. Ba•et ha•hee sha•ma Hordos sar - ro•va ham•di•na et - she•ma Yeshua.

Rabbinic Jewish Commentary
Not Herod the Great, in whose reign Yeshua was born, and who slew the infants of Bethlehem, but his son; this was, as the Jewish chronologer (c) rightly observes, "Herod Antipater, whom they call טיתרקי, "the tetrarch"; the son of Herod the First, and brother of Archelaus, and the third king of the family of Herod."

(c) David Ganz. Tzemach David, par. 1. fol. 25. 2. and so in Juchasin, fol. 142. 2.

---

2. And said unto his servants, This is John the Baptist; he is risen from the dead; and therefore mighty works do shew forth themselves in him.

Greek/Transliteration
2. καὶ εἶπεν τοῖς παισὶν αὐτοῦ, Οὗτός ἐστιν Ἰωάννης ὁ βαπτιστής· αὐτὸς ἠγέρθη ἀπὸ τῶν νεκρῶν, καὶ διὰ τοῦτο αἱ δυνάμεις ἐνεργοῦσιν ἐν αὐτῷ.

2. kai eipen tois paisin autou, 'Outos estin Yoanneis 'o baptisteis. autos eigerthei apo ton nekron, kai dya touto 'ai dunameis energousin en auto.

Hebrew/Transliteration
ב: וַיֹּאמֶר אֶל-עֲבָדָיו הֲלֹא הוּא יוֹחָנָן הַמַּטְבִּיל הוּא קָם מִן-הַמֵּתִים עַל-כֵּן גַּבְרָה יָדוֹ לַעֲשׂוֹת נִפְלָאוֹת

2. Va•yo•mer el - ava•dav ha•lo hoo Yo•cha•nan ha•Mat•bil hoo kam min - ha•me•tim al - ken gav•ra ya•do la•a•sot nif•la•ot.

---

3. For Herod had laid hold on John, and bound him, and put him in prison for Herodias' sake, his brother Philip's wife.

Greek/Transliteration
3. Ὁ γὰρ Ἡρῴδης κρατήσας τὸν Ἰωάννην ἔδησεν αὐτὸν καὶ ἔθετο ἐν φυλακῇ, διὰ Ἡρῳδιάδα τὴν γυναῖκα Φιλίππου τοῦ ἀδελφοῦ αὐτοῦ.

3. 'O gar 'Eirodeis krateisas ton Yoannein edeisen auton kai etheto en phulakei, dya 'Eirodyada tein gunaika Philippou tou adelphou autou.

Hebrew/Transliteration
ג: כִּי הוֹרְדוֹס תָּפַשׂ אֶת-יוֹחָנָן וַיַּאַסְרֵהוּ וְנָתוֹן אֹתוֹ בַּמִּשְׁמָר עַל-דְּבַר הוֹרוֹדְיָה אֵשֶׁת פִּילִפּוֹס אָחִיו.

3. Ki Hordos ta•fas et - Yo•cha•nan va•ya•as•re•hoo ve•na•ton o•to ba•mish•mar al - de•var Horodya eshet Pilipos a•chiv.

---

4. For John said unto him, It is not lawful for thee to have her.

Greek/Transliteration
4. Ἔλεγεν γὰρ αὐτῷ ὁ Ἰωάννης, Οὐκ ἔξεστίν σοι ἔχειν αὐτήν.

4. Elegen gar auto 'o Yoanneis, Ouk exestin soi echein autein.

Hebrew/Transliteration
ד: כִּי הוֹכִיחוֹ יוֹחָנָן בְּאָמְרוֹ לֹא כַתּוֹרָה לָקַחַת אֹתָהּ לְךָ לְאִשָּׁה.

4. Ki ho•chi•cho Yo•cha•nan be•om•ro lo cha•Torah la•ka•chat o•ta le•cha le•ee•sha.

Rabbinic Jewish Commentary

According to the Jewish (h) canons, Herod deserved cutting off, or death by the hand of God. Josephus (i) gives another reason of the imprisonment and death of John, that Herod feared that the people of the Jews, through his means, would be moved to sedition, and revolt from his government; which might be what Herodias suggested to him, or what he gave out himself, to cover the true cause of his proceedings: but the true reason is, what is here given, and is to be confirmed by the testimony of Jewish writers. One of their chronologers (k) delivers the account in these express words:

"Herod Antipater was a very wicked and pernicious man, many of the wise men of Israel he slew with the sword; and he took to wife, his brother Philip's wife, whilst he was living; and because John the high priest (for so through mistake they call him) הוכיחו על זה "reproved him for this"; (see Luk_3:19) he slew him with the sword, with many of the wise men of Israel."

And, says their historian (l),

"also he, Herod, slew John, because he said unto him, it is forbidden thee to take the wife of Philip, and he slew him; this is that John that practised baptism."

(h) Misn. Ceritot, c. 1. sect. 1. (i) Antiqu. lsss. 18. c. 6. (k) Ganz. Tzemach David, par. 1. fol. 25. 2. (l) Joseph. Gorionides, 1. 5. c. 45.

5. And when he would have put him to death, he feared the multitude, because they counted him as a prophet.

Greek/Transliteration
5. Καὶ θέλων αὐτὸν ἀποκτεῖναι, ἐφοβήθη τὸν ὄχλον, ὅτι ὡς προφήτην αὐτὸν εἶχον.

5. Kai thelon auton apokteinai, ephobeithei ton ochlon, 'oti 'os propheitein auton eichon.

Hebrew/Transliteration
‏ה. וַיְבַקֵּשׁ הֲמִיתוֹ אֶפֶס כִּי יָרֵא אֶת-הָעָם אֲשֶׁר חִשְּׁבוּ אֹתוֹ לְנָבִיא:

5. Vay•va•kesh ha•mi•to e•fes ki ya•re et - ha•am asher chish•voo o•to le•na•vi.

Rabbinic Jewish Commentary
John was with the people of the Jews in general, may be learned from the character Josephus gives of him, as a good man; who stirred up the Jews to the practice of virtue, especially piety and justice; which made the common people fond of him and his doctrine; and who were of opinion, that the defeat of Herod's army, which followed the death of John, was a just judgment of God upon him for it (m). (m) Antiqu. 1. 18. c. 6.

---

6. But when Herod's birthday was kept, the daughter of Herodias danced before them, and pleased Herod.

Greek/Translitration
6. Γενεσίων δὲ ἀγομένων τοῦ Ἡρῴδου, ὠρχήσατο ἡ θυγάτηρ τῆς Ἡρῳδιάδος ἐν τῷ μέσῳ, καὶ ἤρεσεν τῷ Ἡρῴδῃ·

6. Genesion de agomenon tou 'Eirodou, orcheisato 'ei thugateir teis 'Eirodyados en to meso, kai eiresen to 'Eirodei.

Hebrew/Transliteration
‏ו. וַיְהִי בְּיוֹם הֻלֶּדֶת אֶת-הוֹרְדוֹס וַתִּרְקֹד בַּת-הוֹרוֹדְיָה בְּמָחוֹל לִפְנֵיהֶם וַתִּיטַב בְּעֵינֵי הוֹרְדוֹס:

6. Vay•hi be•yom hoo•le•det et - Hordos va•tir•kod bat - Horodya be•ma•chol lif•ney•hem va•ti•tav be•ei•ney Hordos.

---

7. Whereupon he promised with an oath to give her whatsoever she would ask.

Greek/Transliteration
7. ὅθεν μεθ᾽ ὅρκου ὡμολόγησεν αὐτῇ δοῦναι ὃ ἐὰν αἰτήσηται.

7. 'othen meth 'orkou 'omologeisen autei dounai 'o ean aiteiseitai.

Hebrew/Transliteration
ז: וּבִגְלַל הַדָּבָר הַזֶּה נִשְׁבַּע לָתֶת-לָהּ כָּל-אֲשֶׁר תִּשְׁאַל מִמֶּנּוּ

7. Oo•vig•lal ha•da•var ha•ze nish•ba la•tet - la kol - asher tish•al mi•me•noo.

Rabbinic Jewish Commentary
to give her whatsoever she would ask; and then repeating it, he confirmed it with an oath; adding, as Mark says, that he would give it her, even "to the half of his kingdom": a way of speaking used by princes, when they give full power to persons to ask what they will of them; and to express their great munificence and liberality; signifying, let it be ever so great, or cost what it will, though as much as half a kingdom comes to, it shall be granted, Est_5:3.

---

8. And she, being before instructed of her mother, said, Give me here John Baptist's head in a charger.

Greek/Transliteration
8. Ἡ δέ, προβιβασθεῖσα ὑπὸ τῆς μητρὸς αὐτῆς, Δός μοι, φησίν, ὧδε ἐπὶ πίνακι τὴν κεφαλὴν Ἰωάννου τοῦ βαπτιστοῦ.

8. 'Ei de, probibastheisa 'upo teis meitros auteis, Dos moi, pheisin, 'ode epi pinaki tein kephalein Yoannou tou baptistou.

Hebrew/Transliteration
ח: וְהִיא כַּאֲשֶׁר שׂוּמָה בְּפִיהָ מֵאִמָּהּ אָמְרָה אֵלָיו תְּנָה-לִי בָזֶה בַּסֵּפֶל אֶת-רֹאשׁ יוֹחָנָן הַמַּטְבִּיל

8. Ve•hee ka•a•sher soo•ma be•fi•ha me•ee•ma am•ra elav te•na - li ba•ze ba•se•fel et - rosh Yo•cha•nan ha•Mat•bil.

---

9. And the king was sorry: nevertheless for the oath's sake, and them which sat with him at meat, he commanded it to be given her.

Greek/Transliteration
9. Καὶ ἐλυπήθη ὁ βασιλεύς, διὰ δὲ τοὺς ὅρκους καὶ τοὺς συνανακειμένους ἐκέλευσεν δοθῆναι·

9. Kai elupeithei 'o basileus, dya de tous 'orkous kai tous sunanakeimenous ekeleusen dotheinai.

Hebrew/Transliteration
ט: וַיֵּצֶר לַמֶּלֶךְ מְאֹד וְאַךְ בַּעֲבוּר שְׁבוּעָתוֹ וְהַיֹּשְׁבִים בִּמְסִבּוֹ צִוָּה לְתִתּוֹ לָהּ

9. Va•ye•tzer la•me•lech me•od ve•ach ba•a•voor sh`voo•a•to ve•ha•yosh•vim bim•si•bo tzi•va le•ti•to la.

10. And he sent, and beheaded John in the prison.

Greek/Transliteration
10. καὶ πέμψας ἀπεκεφάλισεν τὸν Ἰωάννην ἐν τῇ φυλακῇ.

10. kai pempsas apekephalisen ton Yoannein en tei phulakei.

Hebrew/Transliteration
י: וַיִּשְׁלַח וַיִּשָּׂא אֶת-רֹאשׁ יוֹחָנָן מֵעָלָיו בַּמִּשְׁמָר.

10. Va•yish•lach va•yi•sa et - rosh Yo•cha•nan me•a•lav ba•mish•mar.

Rabbinic Jewish Commentary
The word is also used by the Jewish Rabbi's, and in the same sense: take the following instance among many (z). "R. Ishmael said to R. Simeon ben Gamaliel (when they were both apprehended, in order to be executed), brother, there was a man ready to receive his blow, and they entreated לאספקלטור, "the speculator": one said, I am a priest, the son of an high priest, slay me first, that I may not see the death of my companion; and the other said to him, I am a prince, the son of a prince, slay me first, that I may not see the death of my companion: he replied unto them, cast lots; and they cast lots, and the lot fell on R. Simeon ben Gamaliel; immediately he took a sword, "and cut off his head"." (z) Abot R. Nathan, c. 38. fol. 9. 1.

---

11. And his head was brought in a charger, and given to the damsel: and she brought it to her mother.

Greek/Transliteration
11. Καὶ ἠνέχθη ἡ κεφαλὴ αὐτοῦ ἐπὶ πίνακι, καὶ ἐδόθη τῷ κορασίῳ· καὶ ἤνεγκεν τῇ μητρὶ αὐτῆς.

11. Kai einechthei 'ei kephalei autou epi pinaki, kai edothei to korasio. kai einegken tei meitri auteis.

Hebrew/Transliteration
יא: וַיּוּבָא אֶת-רֹאשׁוֹ בַּסֵּפֶל וַיִּנָּתֵן לִידֵי הַנַּעֲרָה וְהִיא הֱבִיאַתְהוּ אֶל-אִמָּהּ.

11. Va•yoo•va et - ro•sho ba•se•fel va•yi•na•ten li•dey ha•na•a•ra ve•hee he•vi•at•hoo el - ee•ma.

---

12. And his disciples came, and took up the body, and buried it, and went and told Jesus.

Greek/Transliteration
12. Καὶ προσελθόντες οἱ μαθηταὶ αὐτοῦ ἦραν τὸ σῶμα, καὶ ἔθαψαν αὐτό· καὶ ἐλθόντες ἀπήγγειλαν τῷ Ἰησοῦ.

12. Kai proselthontes 'oi matheitai autou eiran to soma, kai ethapsan auto. kai elthontes apeingeilan to Yeisou.

Hebrew/Transliteration
יב. וַיָּבֹאוּ תַלְמִידָיו וַיִּשְׂאוּ אֶת-הֶחָלָל וַיִּקְבְּרֻהוּ וַיָּבֹאוּ וַיַּגִּידוּ לְיֵשׁוּעַ:

12. Va•ya•vo•oo tal•mi•dav va•yis•oo et - he•cha•lal va•yik•be•roo•hoo va•ya•vo•oo va•ya•gi•doo le•Yeshua.

---

13. When Jesus heard of it, he departed thence by ship into a desert place apart: and when the people had heard thereof, they followed him on foot out of the cities.

Greek/Transliteration
13. Καὶ ἀκούσας ὁ Ἰησοῦς ἀνεχώρησεν ἐκεῖθεν ἐν πλοίῳ εἰς ἔρημον τόπον κατ᾽ ἰδίαν· καὶ ἀκούσαντες οἱ ὄχλοι ἠκολούθησαν αὐτῷ πεζῇ ἀπὸ τῶν πόλεων.

13. Kai akousas 'o Yeisous anechoreisen ekeithen en ploio eis ereimon topon kat idian. Kai akousantes 'oi ochloi eikoloutheisan auto pezei apo ton poleon.

Hebrew/Transliteration
יג. כִּשְׁמֹעַ יֵשׁוּעַ אֶת-הַדָּבָר הַזֶּה וַיַּעֲבֹר מִשָּׁם בָּאֳנִיָּה וַיָּבֹא אֶל-מָקוֹם שָׁמֵם לְבַדּוֹ וַיִּשְׁמְעוּ הֲמוֹן הָעָם וַיֵּלְכוּ אַחֲרָיו מִן-הֶעָרִים דֶּרֶךְ הַיַּבָּשָׁה.

13. Ki•sh`mo•a Yeshua et - ha•da•var ha•ze va•ya•a•vor mi•sham ba•o•ni•ya va•ya•vo el - ma•kom sha•mem le•va•do va•yish•me•oo ha•mon ha•am va•yel•choo a•cha•rav min - he•a•rim de•rech ha•ya•ba•sha.

---

14. And Jesus went forth, and saw a great multitude, and was moved with compassion toward them, and he healed their sick.

Greek/Transliteration
14. Καὶ ἐξελθὼν ὁ Ἰησοῦς εἶδεν πολὺν ὄχλον, καὶ ἐσπλαγχνίσθη ἐπ᾽ αὐτοῖς, καὶ ἐθεράπευσεν τοὺς ἀρρώστους αὐτῶν.

14. Kai exelthon 'o Yeisous eiden polun ochlon, kai esplagchnisthei ep autois, kai etherapeusen tous arrostous auton.

Hebrew/Transliteration
יד. וַיֵּצֵא יֵשׁוּעַ וַיַּרְא הֲמוֹן עַם-רָב וְרַחֲמָיו נִכְמְרוּ עֲלֵיהֶם וַיִּרְפָּא אֶת-חוֹלֵיהֶם:

14. Va•ye•tze Yeshua va•yar ha•mon am - rav ve•ra•cha•mav nich•me•roo aley•hem va•yir•pa et - cho•ley•hem.

---

15. And when it was evening, his disciples came to him, saying, This is a desert place, and the time is now past; send the multitude away, that they may go into the villages, and buy themselves victuals.

Greek/Transliteration
15. Ὀψίας δὲ γενομένης, προσῆλθον αὐτῷ οἱ μαθηταὶ αὐτοῦ, λέγοντες, Ἔρημός ἐστιν ὁ τόπος, καὶ ἡ ὥρα ἤδη παρῆλθεν· ἀπόλυσον τοὺς ὄχλους, ἵνα ἀπελθόντες εἰς τὰς κώμας ἀγοράσωσιν ἑαυτοῖς βρώματα.

15. Opsias de genomeneis, proseilthon auto 'oi matheitai autou, legontes, Ereimos estin 'o topos, kai 'ei 'ora eidei pareilthen. apoluson tous ochlous, 'ina apelthontes eis tas komas agorasosin 'eautois bromata.

Hebrew/Transliteration
טו. וַיְהִי לִפְנוֹת-עֶרֶב וַיִּגְּשׁוּ אֵלָיו תַּלְמִידָיו וַיֹּאמְרוּ הַמָּקוֹם שָׁמֵם וְהַיּוֹם רַד מְאֹד שַׁלַּח אֶת-הֲמוֹן הָעָם וְיֵלְכוּ אֶל-הַכְּפָרִים לִקְנוֹת לָהֶם אֹכֶל:

15. Vay•hi lif•not - erev va•yig•shoo elav tal•mi•dav va•yom•roo ha•ma•kom sha•mem ve•ha•yom rad me•od sha•lach et - ha•mon ha•am ve•yel•choo el - hak•fa•rim lik•not la•hem o•chel.

Rabbinic Jewish Commentary
"the first hour is the time of eating for Lydians; the second, for thieves; the third, for heirs; the fourth, for workmen; the fifth, for scholars; and the sixth, for every man: but does not R. Papa say,...." T. Bab. Pesachim, fol. 12. 2.

---

16. But Jesus said unto them, They need not depart; give ye them to eat.

Greek/Transliteration
16. Ὁ δὲ Ἰησοῦς εἶπεν αὐτοῖς, Οὐ χρείαν ἔχουσιν ἀπελθεῖν· δότε αὐτοῖς ὑμεῖς φαγεῖν.

16. 'O de Yeisous eipen autois, Ou chreian echousin apelthein. dote autois 'umeis phagein.

Hebrew/Transliteration
טז. וַיֹּאמֶר אֲלֵיהֶם יֵשׁוּעַ לֹא הֻטַּל עֲלֵיהֶם לָלֶכֶת לִקְנוֹת תְּנוּ לָהֶם אַתֶּם לֶאֱכֹל:

16. Va•yo•mer aley•hem Yeshua lo hoo•tal aley•hem la•le•chet lik•not t`noo la•hem atem le•e•chol.

17. And they say unto him, We have here but five loaves, and two fishes.

Greek/Transliteration
17. Οἱ δὲ λέγουσιν αὐτῷ, Οὐκ ἔχομεν ὧδε εἰ μὴ πέντε ἄρτους καὶ δύο ἰχθύας.

17. 'Oi de legousin auto, Ouk echomen 'ode ei mei pente artous kai duo ichthuas.

Hebrew/Transliteration
יז. וַיֹּאמְרוּ אֵלָיו לֹא-נִמְצָא אִתָּנוּ פֹּה כִּי אִם-חָמֵשׁ כִּכְּרוֹת-לֶחֶם וְדָגִים שְׁנָיִם:

17. Va•yom•roo elav lo - nim•tza ee•ta•noo po ki eem - cha•mesh kik•rot - le•chem ve•da•gim sh`na•yim.

Rabbinic Jewish Commentary
The five loaves speak of the five books of YHWH's Torah (since the number five alludes to Torah in Hebraic thought and bread or manna is symbolic of the Word of Elohim [Matt 4:4]. This points to Yeshua who, spiritually speaking, is the Bread of Life and Torah-Word of Elohim made flesh [John 1:1, 14; 6:32–58]). The two fish could either refer to the two houses of Israel (the houses of Judah and Ephraim) or to Ephraim and Manasseh (the two dominate tribes of the northern kingdom of Israel) who are likened to fish of the sea in Genesis 48:16 (and who would "proliferate abundantly like fish," according to *The ArtScroll Stone Edition Tanach* translation). The fact that a lad provided the makings for the dinner shows us that the Torah-Word of Elohim is neither too difficult for YHWH's people to understand nor to obey (Deut 30:11–14), for even a child is able to provide this food. Elsewhere Yeshua taught that we must become humble, simple and teachable as little children if we are to enter his spiritual kingdom (Matt 18:2–5).

---

18. He said, Bring them hither to me.

Greek/Transliteration
18. Ὁ δὲ εἶπεν, Φέρετέ μοι αὐτοὺς ὧδε.

18. 'O de eipen, Pherete moi autous 'ode.

Hebrew/Transliteration
יח. וַיֹּאמֶר הֲבִיאוּם אֵלַי הֵנָּה:

18. Va•yo•mar ha•vi•oom e•lai he•na.

---

19. And he commanded the multitude to sit down on the grass, and took the five loaves, and the two fishes, and looking up to heaven, he blessed, and brake, and gave the loaves to his disciples, and the disciples to the multitude.

Greek/Transliteration
19. Καὶ κελεύσας τοὺς ὄχλους ἀνακλιθῆναι ἐπὶ τοὺς χόρτους, λαβὼν τοὺς πέντε ἄρτους καὶ τοὺς δύο ἰχθύας, ἀναβλέψας εἰς τὸν οὐρανόν, εὐλόγησεν, καὶ κλάσας ἔδωκεν τοῖς μαθηταῖς τοὺς ἄρτους, οἱ δὲ μαθηταὶ τοῖς ὄχλοις.

19. Kai keleusas tous ochlous anaklitheinai epi tous chortous, labon tous pente artous kai tous duo ichthuas, anablepsas eis ton ouranon, eulogeisen, kai klasas edoken tois matheitais tous artous, 'oi de matheitai tois ochlois.

Hebrew/Transliteration
יט. וַיְצַו אֶת-הֲמוֹן הָעָם לָשֶׁבֶת שָׁם בִּנְאוֹת דֶּשֶׁא וַיִּקַּח אֶת-חֲמֵשֶׁת הַלֶּחֶם וְאֶת-שְׁנֵי-הַדָּגִים וַיִּשָּׂא עֵינָיו לַמָּרוֹם: וַיְבָרֵךְ וַיִּפְרֹס וַיִּתֵּן אֶת-הַלֶּחֶם אֶל-הַתַּלְמִידִים וְהַתַּלְמִידִים אֶל-הֲמוֹן הָעָם

19. Vay•tzav et - ha•mon ha•am la•she•vet sham bin•ot de•she va•yi•kach et - cha•me•shet ha•le•chem ve•et - sh`ney - ha•da•gim va•yi•sa ey•nav la•ma•rom vay•va•rech va•yif•ros va•yi•ten et - ha•le•chem el - ha•tal•mi•dim ve•ha•tal•mi•dim el - ha•mon ha•am.

Jewish New Testament Commentary
Yeshua is reported in six places to have prayed with his eyes open (here; Mar_6:41, Mar_7:34; Luk_9:16; Joh_11:41, Joh_17:1). Jews generally do so today; Christians often pray with them closed. There is no command on the subject in the Bible. In an age when people are easily distracted, closing one's eyes may help one to concentrate on God. On the other hand, those who choose to keep their eyes open have the Messiah as their model. The phrase, "toward heaven," can also carry the secondary meaning, "toward God" (see Mat_3:2).

The Jewish-English phrase means "said a blessing." The Greek here is *evlogeô*, "bless, speak well of"; elsewhere it is often *evcharistô*, "thank." Although the text does not say so specifically, it is reasonable to suppose that he recited the customary *b'rakhah* ("benediction"; see Mat_9:8) which Jews have said for more than two thousand years before meals that include bread: *Barukh attah, Adonai Eloheynu, Melekh-ha'olam, haMotzi lechem min ha'aretz* ("Praised be you, *Adonai* our God, King of the universe, who brings forth bread from the earth").

---

20. And they did all eat, and were filled: and they took up of the fragments that remained twelve baskets full.

Greek/Transliteration
20. Καὶ ἔφαγον πάντες, καὶ ἐχορτάσθησαν· καὶ ἦραν τὸ περισσεῦον τῶν κλασμάτων, δώδεκα κοφίνους πλήρεις.

20. Kai ephagon pantes, kai echortastheisan. kai eiran to perisseuon ton klasmaton, dodeka kophinous pleireis.

Hebrew/Transliteration
כ. וַיֹּאכְלוּ כֻלָּם וַיִּשְׂבָּעוּ וַיִּשְׂאוּ אֶת-הַפְּתוֹתִים הַנּוֹתָרִים שְׁנֵים עָשָׂר סַלִּים מְלֵאִים:

20. Va•yoch•loo choo•lam va•yis•ba•oo va•yis•oo et - hap•to•tim ha•no•ta•rim sh`neym asar sa•lim me•le•eem.

Rabbinic Jewish Commentary
and were filled; they were satisfied, they had a full meal, they had enough, and to spare; see 2Ch_31:10 which the Targumist paraphrases.

"And Azariah said unto him, who was appointed chief over the house of Zadok, and said, from the time that they began to separate the offering, to bring it into the sanctuary of the Lord, אכלין ושבעין, "we have eat and are filled", and have "left much"; for "the word of the Lord" hath blessed his people, and what is left, lo! it is this plenty of good." It is said of R. Siraeon, that when he went to the school, שקיל צנא, "he carried a basket" on his shoulders (l); the gloss suggests, it was to sit upon; but a basket is not very proper for a seat; very likely it was for the above reason: such a custom will account for it, how such a number of baskets could be come at in the wilderness. (l) T. Bab. Nedarim, fol. 49. 2.

---

21. And they that had eaten were about five thousand men, beside women and children.

Greek/Transliteration
21. Οἱ δὲ ἐσθίοντες ἦσαν ἄνδρες ὡσεὶ πεντακισχίλιοι, χωρὶς γυναικῶν καὶ παιδίων.

21. 'Oi de esthiontes eisan andres 'osei pentakischilioi, choris gunaikon kai paidion.

Hebrew/Translteration
כא. וְהָאֹכְלִים הָיוּ כַּחֲמֵשֶׁת אַלְפֵי אִישׁ מִלְּבַד נָשִׁים וָטָף:

21. Ve•ha•och•lim ha•yoo ka•cha•me•shet al•fey eesh mil•vad na•shim va•taf.

Rabbinic/Jewish New Testament Commentary
The word "about", is omitted in the Vulgate Latin, in Munster's Hebrew Gospel, and in the Syriac, Arabic, and Persic versions, which expressly say there were so many. A large number indeed, to be fed with five loaves and two fishes! Elisha, by a similar miracle of creation, fed one hundred people with twenty loaves of bread (2Ki_4:42-44). Here Yeshua fed perhaps ten thousand with fewer loaves.

---

22. And straightway Jesus constrained his disciples to get into a ship, and to go before him unto the other side, while he sent the multitudes away.

Greek/Transliteration
22. Καὶ εὐθέως ἠνάγκασεν ὁ Ἰησοῦς τοὺς μαθητὰς ἐμβῆναι εἰς τὸ πλοῖον, καὶ προάγειν αὐτὸν εἰς τὸ πέραν, ἕως οὗ ἀπολύσῃ τοὺς ὄχλους.

22. Kai eutheos einagkasen 'o Yeisous tous matheitas embeinai eis to ploion, kai proagein auton eis to peran, 'eos 'ou apolusei tous ochlous.

Hebrew/Transliteration
כב. וַיְחַזֵּק יֵשׁוּעַ עַל-תַּלְמִידָיו לְמַהֵר לָרֶדֶת בָּאֳנִיָּה וְלַעֲבֹר לְפָנָיו אֶל-עֵבֶר הַיָּם עַד כִּי יְשַׁלַּח אֶת-הֲמוֹן הָעָם:

22. Va•ye•che•zak Yeshua al - tal•mi•dav le•ma•her la•re•det ba•o•ni•ya ve•la•a•vor le•fa•nav el - ever ha•yam ad ki ye•sha•lach et - ha•mon ha•am.

---

23. And when he had sent the multitudes away, he went up into a mountain apart to pray: and when the evening was come, he was there alone.

Greek/Transliteration
23. Καὶ ἀπολύσας τοὺς ὄχλους, ἀνέβη εἰς τὸ ὄρος κατ᾽ ἰδίαν προσεύξασθαι· ὀψίας δὲ γενομένης, μόνος ἦν ἐκεῖ.

23. Kai apolusas tous ochlous, anebei eis to oros kat idian proseuxasthai. opsias de genomeneis, monos ein ekei.

Hebrew/Transliteration
כג. וַיְהִי בְּשַׁלְּחוֹ אֶת-הֲמוֹן הָעָם וַיַּעַל אֶל-הָהָר בָּדָד לְהִתְפַּלֵּל וַיְהִי-עֶרֶב וַיִּוָּתֵר שָׁם לְבַדּוֹ:

23. Vay•hi be•shal•cho et - ha•mon ha•am va•ya•al el - ha•har ba•dad le•hit•pa•lel vay•hi - erev va•yi•va•ter sham le•va•do.

Rabbinic Jewish Commentary
His going up into a mountain and praying there, were quite contrary to the canons of the Jews; which forbid praying in places ever so little raised. "Let not a man stand (say they (m)) במקום גבוה, "in an high place", and pray, but in a low place and pray; as it is said, "Out of the depths have I cried unto thee, O Lord", Psa_130:1. It is a tradition, that a man may not stand, neither upon a throne, nor upon a footstool, nor in any high place and pray, because there are no high places before God." This rule is delivered by Maimonides (n), in this form: "A man may not stand in a place that is three hands high, or more, and pray, neither upon a bed, nor upon a seat, nor upon a throne." But Yeshua did not look upon himself obliged, by these traditions of the elders; but chose such places, whether high or low, which were most private and retired.

(m) T. Bab. Beracot, fol. 10. 2. Piske Tosaph. in ib. art. 52, T. Hieros. Beracot, fol. 4. 4. Kotsensis Mitzvot Tora precept. Affirm. 19. Midrash Kohelet, fol. 70. 3. (n) Hilch. Tephillah. c. 5. sect. 7.

24. But the ship was now in the midst of the sea, tossed with waves: for the wind was contrary.

Greek/Transliteration
24. Τὸ δὲ πλοῖον ἤδη μέσον τῆς θαλάσσης ἦν, βασανιζόμενον ὑπὸ τῶν κυμάτων· ἦν γὰρ ἐναντίος ὁ ἄνεμος.

24. To de ploion eidei meson teis thalasseis ein, basanizomenon 'upo ton kumaton. ein gar enantios 'o anemos.

Hebrew/Transliteration
כד. וְהָאֳנִיָּה בָאָה אָז בְּלֵב הַיָּם בְּצָרָה גְדוֹלָה מִפְּנֵי מִשְׁבָּרָיו כִּי נָשַׁף הָרוּחַ לִקְרָאתָם:

24. Ve•ha•oni•ya va•ah az be•lev ha•yam be•tza•ra ge•do•la mip•ney mish•ba•rav ki na•shaf ha•roo•ach lik•ra•tam.

Rabbinic Jewish Commentary
That is, the ship in which the disciples were put into, to go on the other side, had by this time got into the midst of the sea: the Syriac and Persic versions say, it was "many furlongs from land"; and the Arabic expressly says, "about twenty five furlongs": which account seems to be taken from Joh_6:19 but this was not all, it was not only at such a distance from land.

---

25. And in the fourth watch of the night Jesus went unto them, walking on the sea.

Greek/Transliteration
25. Τετάρτῃ δὲ φυλακῇ τῆς νυκτὸς ἀπῆλθεν πρὸς αὐτοὺς ὁ Ἰησοῦς, περιπατῶν ἐπὶ τῆς θαλάσσης.

25. Tetartei de phulakei teis nuktos apeilthen pros autous 'o Yeisous, peripaton epi teis thalasseis.

Hebrew/Transliteration
כה. וַיְהִי בְּאַשְׁמֻרָה הָרְבִיעִית בַּלַּיְלָה וַיָּבֹא אֲלֵיהֶם יֵשׁוּעַ דֶּרֶךְ עַל־פְּנֵי הַיָּם:

25. Vay•hi be•ash•moo•ra har•vi•eet ba•lai•la va•ya•vo aley•hem Yeshua do•rech al - p`ney ha•yam.

Rabbinic/TaNaKh-Old Testament Commentary
walking upon the sea; as on dry land: though it was so stormy and boisterous, that the disciples, though in a ship, were in the utmost danger, yet he upon the waves, was in none at all; by which action he showed himself to be the Lord of the sea, and to be truly and properly God; whose character is, that he "…stretching out the heavens by Himself, and *walking on the waves of the sea*;…" Job 9:8

26. And when the disciples saw him walking on the sea, they were troubled, saying, It is a spirit; and they cried out for fear.

Greek/Transliteration
26. Καὶ ἰδόντες αὐτὸν οἱ μαθηταὶ ἐπὶ τὴν θάλασσαν περιπατοῦντα ἐταράχθησαν, λέγοντες ὅτι Φάντασμά ἐστιν· καὶ ἀπὸ τοῦ φόβου ἔκραξαν.

26. Kai idontes auton 'oi matheitai epi tein thalassan peripatounta etarachtheisan, legontes 'oti Phantasma estin. kai apo tou phobou ekraxan.

Hebrew/Transliteration
:כו. כִּרְאוֹת אֹתוֹ הַתַּלְמִידִים דֹּרֵךְ עַל-פְּנֵי הַיָּם וַיָּחִילוּ וַיֹּאמְרוּ כִּי רוּחַ הוּא בְחָזוֹן וַיִּצְעֲקוּ מִפָּחַד

26. Kir•ot o•to ha•tal•mi•dim do•rech al - p`ney ha•yam va•ya•chi•loo va•yom•roo ki roo•ach hoo ve•cha•zon va•yitz•a•koo mi•pa•chad.

Rabbinic Jewish Commentary
The Jews, especially the sect of the Pharisees, had a notion, from whom the disciples might have their's, of spirits, apparitions, and demons, being to be seen in the night; hence that rule (u), "it is forbidden a man to salute his friend in the night, for we are careful, lest שד הוא, "it should be a demon".

They say a great many things of one לילית, "Lilith", that has its name from לילה, "the night", a she demon, that used to appear in the night, with an human face, and carry off young children, and kill them. Some such frightful notions had possessed the minds of the disciples: demons are, by the Jews, called מזיקין, "hurtful", or "hurting", all their study being to do hurt to men; and the same word is here used in Munster's Hebrew Gospel:

(u) T. Bab. Megilla, fol. 3. 1. Sanhedrim, fol. 44. 1.

---

27. But straightway Jesus spake unto them, saying, Be of good cheer; it is I; be not afraid.

Greek/Transliteration
27. Εὐθέως δὲ ἐλάλησεν αὐτοῖς ὁ Ἰησοῦς, λέγων, Θαρσεῖτε· ἐγώ εἰμι· μὴ φοβεῖσθε.

27. Eutheos de elaleisen autois 'o Yeisous, legon, Tharseite. ego eimi. mei phobeisthe.

Hebrew/Transliteration
:כז. וַיְמַהֵר יֵשׁוּעַ וַיְדַבֵּר עַל-לִבָּם וַיֹּאמַר חִזְקוּ אֲנִי הוּא אַל-תִּירָאוּ

27. Vay•ma•her Yeshua va•y`da•ber al - li•bam va•yo•mar chiz•koo ani hoo al - ti•ra•oo.

28. And Peter answered him and said, Lord, if it be thou, bid me come unto thee on the water.

Greek/Transliteration
28. Ἀποκριθεὶς δὲ αὐτῷ ὁ Πέτρος εἶπεν, Κύριε, εἰ σὺ εἶ, κέλευσόν με πρός σε ἐλθεῖν ἐπὶ τὰ ὕδατα.

28. Apokritheis de auto 'o Petros eipen, Kurie, ei su ei, keleuson me pros se elthein epi ta 'udata.

Hebrew/Transliteration
:כח. וַיַּעַן פֶּטְרוֹס וַיֹּאמֶר אֵלָיו אֲדֹנִי אִם-אַתָּה הוּא צַו וְאָבֹא אֵלֶיךָ עַל-פְּנֵי הַמָּיִם

28. Va•ya•an Petros va•yo•mer elav Adoni eem - ata hoo tzav ve•avo e•le•cha al - p`ney ha•ma•yim.

---

29. And he said, Come. And when Peter was come down out of the ship, he walked on the water, to go to Jesus.

Greek/Transliteration
29. Ὁ δὲ εἶπεν, Ἐλθέ. Καὶ καταβὰς ἀπὸ τοῦ πλοίου ὁ Πέτρος περιεπάτησεν ἐπὶ τὰ ὕδατα, ἐλθεῖν πρὸς τὸν Ἰησοῦν.

29. 'O de eipen, Elthe. Kai katabas apo tou ploiou 'o Petros periepateisen epi ta 'udata, elthein pros ton Yeisoun.

Hebrew/Transliteration
:כט. וַיֹּאמֶר בֹּא וַיֵּרֶד פֶּטְרוֹס מִן-הָאֳנִיָּה וַיֵּלֶךְ עַל-פְּנֵי הַמַּיִם לָבֹא אֶל-יֵשׁוּעַ

29. Va•yomer bo va•ye•red Petros min - ha•oni•ya va•ye•lech al - p`ney ha•ma•yim la•vo el - Yeshua.

Rabbinic Jewish Commentary
The Jews (w) indeed, call swimming השיטה על פני המים, "walking upon the face of the waters": hence we read of a swimmer's vessel, which is explained to be what men make to learn in it, how לשוט על פני המים, "to go or walk upon the face of the waters"(x) which was not Peter's case; he did not, as at another time, cast himself into the sea, and swim to Yeshua. (w) R. David Kimchi, Sepher Shorash. rad. שחה. (x) R. Sol. Urbin. Ohel moed, fol. 78. 1.

---

30. But when he saw the wind boisterous, he was afraid; and beginning to sink, he cried, saying, Lord, save me.

Greek/Transliteration
30. Βλέπων δὲ τὸν ἄνεμον ἰσχυρὸν ἐφοβήθη· καὶ ἀρξάμενος καταποντίζεσθαι ἔκραξεν, λέγων, Κύριε, σῶσόν με.

30. Blepon de ton anemon ischuron ephobeithei. kai arxamenos katapontizesthai ekraxen, legon, Kurie, soson me.

Hebrew/Transliteration
:ל. וּבִרְאֹתוֹ אֶת-הָרוּחַ חֲזָקָה וַיִּירָא וַיָּחֶל לִטְבֹּעַ וַיִּצְעַק לֵאמֹר אֲדֹנִי הוֹשִׁיעָה נָּא

30. Oo•vir•o•to et - ha•roo•ach cha•za•ka va•yi•ra va•ya•chel lit•bo•a va•yitz•ak le•mor Adoni ho•shi•ah na.

---

31. And immediately Jesus stretched forth his hand, and caught him, and said unto him, O thou of little faith, wherefore didst thou doubt?

Greek/Transliteration
31. Εὐθέως δὲ ὁ Ἰησοῦς ἐκτείνας τὴν χεῖρα ἐπελάβετο αὐτοῦ, καὶ λέγει αὐτῷ, Ὀλιγόπιστε, εἰς τί ἐδίστασας;

31. Eutheos de 'o Yeisous ekteinas tein cheira epelabeto autou, kai legei auto, Oligopiste, eis ti edistasas?

Hebrew/Transliteration
:לא. וַיְמַהֵר יֵשׁוּעַ וַיִּשְׁלַח יָדוֹ וַיַּחֲזֶק-בּוֹ וַיֹּאמֶר אֵלָיו קְטֹן אֱמוּנָה לָמָה-זֶּה פָּסַחְתָּ עַל-שְׁתֵּי סְעִפִּים

31. Vay•ma•her Yeshua va•yish•lach ya•do va•ya•cha•zek - bo va•yo•mer elav ke•ton e•moo•na la•ma - ze pa•sach•ta al - sh`tey s`ee•pim.

---

32. And when they were come into the ship, the wind ceased.

Greek/Transliteration
32. Καὶ ἐμβάντων αὐτῶν εἰς τὸ πλοῖον, ἐκόπασεν ὁ ἄνεμος·

32. Kai embanton auton eis to ploion, ekopasen 'o anemos.

Hebrew/Transliteration
:לב. וַיָּבֹאוּ אֶל-הָאֳנִיָּה וַיִּשְׁתֹּק הָרוּחַ מִזַּעְפּוֹ

32. Va•ya•vo•oo el - ha•o•ni•ya va•yish•tok ha•roo•ach mi•za•a•po.

Rabbinic Jewish Commentary
The Arabic and Persic versions, and Munster's Hebrew Gospel read, "when he ascended" or "was come into the ship"

---

33. Then they that were in the ship came and worshipped him, saying, Of a truth thou art the Son of God.

Greek/Transliteration
33. οἱ δὲ ἐν τῷ πλοίῳ ἐλθόντες προσεκύνησαν αὐτῷ, λέγοντες, Ἀληθῶς θεοῦ υἱὸς εἶ.

33. 'oi de en to ploio elthontes prosekuneisan auto, legontes, Aleithos theou 'wios ei.

Hebrew/Transliteration
לג: וְנִגְּשׁוּ וַיִּשְׁתַּחֲווּ-לוֹ הָאֲנָשִׁים אֲשֶׁר בָּאֳנִיָּה לֵאמֹר אָכֵן בֶּן-אֱלֹהִים אָתָּה

33. Ve•nig•shoo va•yish•ta•cha•voo - lo ha•a•na•shim asher ba•o•ni•ya le•mor a•chen Ben - Elohim ata.

Rabbinic Jewish Commentary
Not by creation, as angels and men, nor by office, as magistrates, but by nature; being of the same essence, perfections, and power, with God, his Father: all which being observed by the disciples and mariners, drew out this confession upon full conviction from them, that he was a divine person, and the proper object of worship.

---

34. And when they were gone over, they came into the land of Gennesaret.

Greek/Transliteration
34. Καὶ διαπεράσαντες ἦλθον εἰς τὴν γῆν Γεννησαρέτ.

34. Kai dyaperasantes eilthon eis tein gein Genneisaret.

Hebrew/Transliteration
לד: וַיַּעַבְרוּ וַיָּבֹאוּ אַרְצָה גְּנֵיסָרֶת

34. Va•ya•av•roo va•ya•vo•oo ar•tza Ge•ney•sa•ret.

---

35. And when the men of that place had knowledge of him, they sent out into all that country round about, and brought unto him all that were diseased;

Greek/Transliteration
35. Καὶ ἐπιγνόντες αὐτὸν οἱ ἄνδρες τοῦ τόπου ἐκείνου ἀπέστειλαν εἰς ὅλην τὴν περίχωρον ἐκείνην, καὶ προσήνεγκαν αὐτῷ πάντας τοὺς κακῶς ἔχοντας·

35. Kai epignontes auton 'oi andres tou topou ekeinou apesteilan eis 'olein tein perichoron ekeinein, kai proseinegkan auto pantas tous kakos echontas.

Hebrew/Transliteration
לה: וַיַּכִּירוּ אֹתוֹ אַנְשֵׁי הַמָּקוֹם הַהוּא וַיִּשְׁלְחוּ אֶל-כָּל-הַכִּכָּר מִסָּבִיב וַיָּבִיאוּ אֵלָיו אֵת כָּל-חוֹלֵיהֶם

35. Va•ya•ki•roo o•to an•shey ha•ma•kom ha•hoo va•yish•le•choo el - kol - ha•ki•kar mi•sa•viv va•ya•vi•oo elav et kol - cho•ley•hem.

36. And besought him that they might only touch the hem of his garment: and as many as touched were made perfectly whole.

Greek/Transliteration
36. καὶ παρεκάλουν αὐτόν, ἵνα μόνον ἅψωνται τοῦ κρασπέδου τοῦ ἱματίου αὐτοῦ· καὶ ὅσοι ἥψαντο διεσώθησαν.

36. kai parekaloun auton, 'ina monon 'apsontai tou kraspedou tou 'imatiou autou. kai 'osoi 'eipsanto diesotheisan.

Hebrew/Transliteration
:לוֹ. וַיִּתְחַנְּנוּ אֵלָיו לָתֵת לָהֶם לָגַעַת בִּכְנַף בִּגְדוֹ וַיְהִי כֹּל אֲשֶׁר נָגַע-בּוֹ וָחָי

36. Va•yit•cha•ne•noo elav la•tet la•hem la•ga•at bich•naf big•do vay•hi kol asher na•ga - bo va•chai.

Rabbinic/TaNaKh-Old Testament
Yeshua condescended to this their request, and perfectly cured all such of their diseases, of whatever kind they were, who, in the exercise of faith, touched the hem of his garment, the fringe he wore, in compliance with the ceremonial law,

"Speak to the children of Yisra'ĕl, and you shall say to them to make tzitziyot[1] on the corners of their garments throughout their generations, and to put a blue cord in the tzitzit[1] of the corners. (Numbers 15:38) (1)Fringes, Fringe.

Matthew, Chapter 15

1. Then came to Jesus scribes and Pharisees, which were of Jerusalem, saying,

Greek/Transliteration
1. Τότε προσέρχονται τῷ Ἰησοῦ οἱ ἀπὸ Ἱεροσολύμων γραμματεῖς καὶ Φαρισαῖοι, λέγοντες,

1. Tote proserchontai to Yeisou 'oi apo 'Yerosolumon grammateis kai Pharisaioi, legontes,

Hebrew/Transliteration
א. אָז בָּאוּ לִפְנֵי יֵשׁוּעַ פְּרוּשִׁים וְסוֹפְרִים מִירוּשָׁלַיִם לֵאמֹר:

1. Az ba•oo lif•ney Yeshua P`roo•shim ve•sof•rim mi•Ye•roo•sha•la•yim le•mor.

---

2. Why do thy disciples transgress the tradition of the elders? for they wash not their hands when they eat bread.

Greek/Transliteration
2. Διὰ τί οἱ μαθηταί σου παραβαίνουσιν τὴν παράδοσιν τῶν πρεσβυτέρων; Οὐ γὰρ νίπτονται τὰς χεῖρας αὐτῶν, ὅταν ἄρτον ἐσθίωσιν.

2. Dya ti 'oi matheitai sou parabainousin tein paradosin ton presbuteron? Ou gar niptontai tas cheiras auton, 'otan arton esthiosin.

Hebrew/Transliteration
ב. מַדּוּעַ יַעַזְבוּ תַלְמִידֶיךָ אֶת קַבָּלַת הַזְּקֵנִים כִּי לֹא יִרְחֲצוּ אֶת־יְדֵיהֶם לַאֲכִילַת לָחֶם:

2. Ma•doo•a ya•az•voo tal•mi•de•cha et ka•ba•lat haz`ke•nim ki lo yir•cha•tzoo et - ye•dey•hem la•a•chi•lat la•chem.

Rabbinic Jewish Commentary
(d), "Know then, that "the words of the Scribes" are more lovely than the words of the law: for, says R. Tarphon, if a man does not read, he only transgresses an affirmative; but if he transgresses the words of the school of Hillell, he is guilty of death, because he hath broke down a hedge, and a serpent shall bite him. It is a tradition of R. Ishmael, the words of the law have in them both prohibition and permission; some of them are light, and some heavy, but "the words of the Scribes" are all of them heavy--Mynqz דברי המורים, "weightier are the words of the elders", than the words of the prophets."

And elsewhere (e), this advice is given; "My son, attend to "the words of the Scribes", more than to the words of the law; for in the words of the law, are affirmatives and negatives; but the words of the Scribes כל העובר על דברי סופרים, "everyone that transgresses the words of the Scribes", is guilty of death."

It is said (g), that "Hillell and Shammai decreed על טהרות ידים, "concerning the purification of the hands"; R. Jose ben R. Bon, in the name of R. Levi, says, so was the tradition before, but they forgot it; and these two stood up, and agreed with the minds of the former ones."

"However, it is a certain point, that the washing of the hands, and the dipping of them, are מדברי סופרים, "from the words of the Scribes" (h)."

The breach of this rule was reckoned equal to the most flagitious crimes (i): R. Jose says, "whoever eats bread without washing of hands, is as if he lay with a whore: and, says R. Eleazer, whoever despiseth washing of hands, shall be rooted out of the world."

And elsewhere it is said by them (k), that "he that blesseth (food) with defiled hands, is guilty of death."

And again (l), "whoever does not wash his hands as is fitting, although he is punished above, he shall be punished below."

(d) T. Hieros. Beracot, fol. 3. 2. (e) T. Bab. Erubim, fol. 21. 2. T. Bab. Beracot, fol. 4. 2. (f) Misn. Chagiga, c. 2. sect. 5, 6. Maimon. Praefat. ad Tract. Yadaim, & Hilch. Beracot, c. 6. sect. 3. (g) T. Hieros. Sabbat, fol. 3. 4. (h) Maimon Hilch. Mikvaot, c. 11. sect. 1. (i) T. Bab. Sota, fol. 4. 2. (k) Zohar in Deut. fol. 107. 3. (l) Ib. in Gen. fol. 60. 2.

---

3. But he answered and said unto them, Why do ye also transgress the commandment of God by your tradition?

Greek/Transliteration
3. Ὁ δὲ ἀποκριθεὶς εἶπεν αὐτοῖς, Διὰ τί καὶ ὑμεῖς παραβαίνετε τὴν ἐντολὴν τοῦ θεοῦ διὰ τὴν παράδοσιν ὑμῶν;

3. 'O de apokritheis eipen autois, Dya ti kai 'umeis parabainete tein entolein tou theou dya tein paradosin 'umon?

Hebrew/Transliteration
ג: וַיַּעַן וַיֹּאמֶר אֲלֵיהֶם וּמַדּוּעַ תַּעַבְרוּ גַם-אַתֶּם אֶת-מִצְוַת אֱלֹהִים בַּעֲבוּר קַבָּלַתְכֶם

3. Va•ya•an va•yo•mer aley•hem oo•ma•doo•a ta•az•voo gam - atem et - mitz•vat Elohim ba•a•voor ka•ba•lat•chem.

Rabbinic Jewish Commentary
Taking no notice of the tradition about eating bread without washing the hands, whether it was right or wrong; it being at most but an human tradition, of no moment and importance, whether it was broke or kept; he makes a very just recrimination, by putting another question to them, and while they were observing their own traditions: and which observation carries a full acquittance of the

disciples from blame; for, if by keeping the traditions of the elders, they broke the commands of God, it was a very good reason why they should not observe them.

---

4. For God commanded, saying, Honour thy father and mother: and, He that curseth father or mother, let him die the death.

Greek/Transliteration
4. Ὁ γὰρ θεὸς ἐνετείλατο, λέγων, Τίμα τὸν πατέρα καὶ τὴν μητέρα· καί, Ὁ κακολογῶν πατέρα ἢ μητέρα θανάτῳ τελευτάτω·

4. 'O gar theos eneteilato, legon, Tima ton patera kai tein meitera. kai, 'O kakologon patera ei meitera thanato teleutato.

Hebrew/Transliteration
ד. כִּי אֱלֹהִים צִוָּה לֵאמֹר כַּבֵּד אֶת-אָבִיךָ וְאֶת-אִמֶּךָ וּמְקַלֵּל אָבִיו וְאִמּוֹ מוֹת יוּמָת:

4. Ki Elohim tzi•va le•mor ka•bed et - avi•cha ve•et - ee•me•cha oom•ka•lel aviv ve•ee•mo mot yoo•mat.

Rabbinic Jewish Commentary
They say (p), that this is the weightiest commandment among the weighty ones, even this, the honouring of father and mother; and ask, "What is this honour? To which is replied, he must give him food, drink, and clothing; buckle his shoes, and lead him in, and bring him out." They indeed laid down this as a rule, and it seems a very equitable one (q); that, "when a man's father has any money, or substance, he must be supported out of that; but if he has none, he must support him out of his own." But then, as will be seen hereafter, they made void this command of God, and their own explications of it, by some other tradition. Moreover, Yeshua observes, that it is said, Exo_21:17. (p) T. Hieros. Kiddushin, fol. 61. 2. (q) Piske Toseph. ad T. Bab. Kiddushin, art. 61.

---

5. But ye say, Whosoever shall say to his father or his mother, It is a gift, by whatsoever thou mightest be profited by me;

Greek/Transliteration
5. ὑμεῖς δὲ λέγετε, Ὃς ἂν εἴπῃ τῷ πατρὶ ἢ τῇ μητρί, Δῶρον, ὃ ἐὰν ἐξ ἐμοῦ ὠφεληθῇς, καὶ οὐ μὴ τιμήσῃ τὸν πατέρα αὐτοῦ ἢ τὴν μητέρα αὐτοῦ·

5. 'umeis de legete, 'Os an eipei to patri ei tei meitri, Doron, 'o ean ex emou opheleitheis, kai ou mei timeisei ton patera autou ei tein meitera autou.

Hebrew/Transliteration
ה. וְאַתֶּם אֹמְרִים אִישׁ כִּי-יֹאמַר לְאָבִיו אוֹ לְאִמּוֹ קָרְבָּן כָּל-הַנָאָה אֲשֶׁר תֵּהֶנֶה מִמֶּנִּי הֲרֵי זֶה נֶדֶר:

5. Ve•a•tem om•rim eesh ki - yo•mar le•a•viv oh le•ee•mo kor•ban kol - ha•na•ah asher te•he•ne mi•me•ni ha•rey ze ne•der.

Rabbinic Jewish Commentary

For the honour of parents (y). "R. Eliezer says, they open to a man, (i.e. the door of repentance, and dissolve his vow,) for the honour of his father and his mother, but the wise men forbid "it". Says R. Tzadok, if they open to him for the honour of his father and mother, they will open to him for the honour of God, and if so, there will be no vows: however, the wise men agreed with R. Eliezer in the affair between a man and his parents, that they should open to him for the honour of them." (y) Misn. Nedarim, c. 9. sect. 1.

---

6. And honour not his father or his mother, he shall be free. Thus have ye made the commandment of God of none effect by your tradition.

Greek/Transliteration
6. καὶ ἠκυρώσατε τὴν ἐντολὴν τοῦ Θεοῦ διὰ τὴν παράδοσιν ὑμῶν·

6. kai eikurosate tein entolein tou theou dya tein paradosin 'umon.

Hebrew/Transliteration
:ו. וְאֵין עָלָיו לְכַבֵּד עוֹד אֶת-אָבִיו וְאֶת-אִמּוֹ וְהֲפַרְתֶּם אֶת-מִצְוַת אֱלֹהִים בְּקַבָּלַתְכֶם

6. Ve•eyn alav le•cha•bed od et - aviv ve•et - ee•mo ve•he•far•tem et - mitz•vat Elohim be•ka•ba•lat•chem.

---

7. Ye hypocrites, well did Esaias prophesy of you, saying,

Greek/Transliteration
7. ὑποκριταί, καλῶς προεφήτευσεν περὶ ὑμῶν Ἡσαΐας, λέγων,

7. 'upokritai, kalos proepheiteusen peri 'umon Eisaias, legon,

Hebrew/Transliteration
:ז. חַנְפֵי-לֵב הֵיטֵב נִבָּא עֲלֵיכֶם יְשַׁעְיָהוּ לֵאמֹר

7. Chan•fey - lev hei•tev ni•ba aley•chem Ye•sha•a•ya•hoo le•mor.

Rabbinic Jewish Commentary

Says (a) of the men of Jerusalem, that "if the hypocrites of the world were divided into ten parts, nine of them would belong to Jerusalem, and one to the rest of the world."

Well did Esaias prophesy of you, saying, in Isa_29:13 which prophecy, though it was directed to, and suited with many in that generation in which the prophet lived, yet had a further view to the Jews in after times: their own writers (b) acknowledge, that the whole prophecy is spoken of that nation; for by Ariel they understand the altar at Jerusalem, the city in which David dwelt, (a) R. Nathan in Rabba, sect. 1. (b) Abarbinel, Jarchi, Kimchi, & Aben Ezra.

8. This people draweth nigh unto me with their mouth, and honoureth me with their lips; but their heart is far from me.

Greek/Transliteration
8. Ἐγγίζει μοι ὁ λαὸς οὗτος τῷ στόματι αὐτῶν, καὶ τοῖς χείλεσίν με τιμᾷ· ἡ δὲ καρδία αὐτῶν πόρρω ἀπέχει ἀπ᾽ ἐμοῦ.

8. Engizei moi 'o laos 'outos to stomati auton, kai tois cheilesin me tima. 'ei de kardia auton porro apechei ap emou.

Hebrew/Transliteration
ח. הָעָם הַזֶּה בְּפִיו וּבִשְׂפָתָיו כִּבְּדוּנִי וְלִבּוֹ רִחַק מִמֶּנִּי:

8. Ha•am ha•ze be•piv oo•vis•fa•tav kib•doo•ni ve•li•bo ri•chak mi•me•ni.

---

9. But in vain they do worship me, teaching for doctrines the commandments of men.

Greek/Transliteration
9. Μάτην δὲ σέβονταί με, διδάσκοντες διδασκαλίας ἐντάλματα ἀνθρώπων.

9. Matein de sebontai me, didaskontes didaskalias entalmata anthropon.

Hebrew/Transliteration
ט. וְתֹהוּ יִרְאָתָם אֹתִי מִצְוֹת אֲנָשִׁים מְלֻמָּדָה:

9. Ve•to•hoo yir•a•tam o•ti mitz•vot a•na•shim me•loo•mada.

Rabbinic Jewish Commentary
In the Hebrew text it is, "their fear towards me": which is rightly expressed here by "worship"; for the fear of God often intends the whole worship of God, both external and internal: here it only signifies external worship, which these men only attended to. They prayed in the synagogues, read, and, in their way, expounded the books of Moses, and the prophets, to the people, diligently observed the rituals of the ceremonial law, brought their offerings and sacrifices to the temple, and neglected nothing appertaining to the outward service of it; and yet it was all "in vain", and to no purpose; since the heart was wanting, no grace there, they acted from wrong principles, and with wrong views; their worship was merely outward, formal, and customary; and besides, they added doctrines and traditions of their own inventing and devising. The phrase, "in vain", is not in the text in Isaiah: some have thought that it was not originally in Matthew, but inserted by some other hand, to make the sense more complete.

In the text in Isaiah, are only these words, "taught by the precept of men": and which relate to their fear and worship of God; and which is here interpreted of their teachers teaching them it, and that explained of the commandments of men; as if, instead of מלמדה, "taught", it had been read, מלמדים, "teaching". The Jews have no reason to quarrel with this construction and sense, since their Targum paraphrases it thus; "and their fear before me is, כתפקידת גברין מלפין, according to the commandment of men that teach": and a noted commentator (c) of their's has this remark on the text, "their fear towards me is" not with a perfect heart, but "by the commandment האנשים המלמדים אותאם, of the men that teach them". (c) R. Sol. Jarchi in Isa. xxix. 13.

---

10. And he called the multitude, and said unto them, Hear, and understand:

Greek/Transliteration
10. Καὶ προσκαλεσάμενος τὸν ὄχλον, εἶπεν αὐτοῖς, Ἀκούετε καὶ συνίετε.

10. Kai proskalesamenos ton ochlon, eipen autois, Akouete kai suniete.

Hebrew/Transliteration
י. וַיִּקְרָא אֶל-הָעָם וַיֹּאמֶר אֲלֵיהֶם שִׁמְעוּ וְהַשְׂכִּילוּ:

10. Va•yik•ra el - ha•am va•yo•mer aley•hem shim•oo ve•has•ki•loo.

---

11. Not that which goeth into the mouth defileth a man; but that which cometh out of the mouth, this defileth a man.

Greek/Transliteration
11. Οὐ τὸ εἰσερχόμενον εἰς τὸ στόμα κοινοῖ τὸν ἄνθρωπον· ἀλλὰ τὸ ἐκπορευόμενον ἐκ τοῦ στόματος, τοῦτο κοινοῖ τὸν ἄνθρωπον.

11. Ou to eiserchomenon eis to stoma koinoi ton anthropon. alla to ekporeuomenon ek tou stomatos, touto koinoi ton anthropon.

Hebrew/Transliteration
יא. אֲשֶׁר יָבֹא אֶל-תּוֹךְ הַפֶּה לֹא יְטַמֵּא אֶת-הָאָדָם אֶפֶס אֲשֶׁר יֵצֵא מִתּוֹךְ הַפֶּה הוּא יְטַמֵּא אֶת-הָאָדָם:

11. Asher ya•vo el - toch ha•pe lo ye•ta•me et - ha•a•dam e•fes asher ye•tze mi•toch ha•pe hoo ye•ta•me et - ha•a•dam.

Rabbinic Jewish Commentary
These are now the things men should be concerned about, as of a defiling nature; and not about meats and drinks, and the manner of using them, whether with hands washed, or unwashed. This is directly opposite to the notions of the Jews, who say (d), that "forbidden meats are unclean themselves, ומטמאין הגוף והנפש, "and defile both body and soul"." (d) Tzeror Hammor, fol. 142. 1.

---

12. Then came his disciples, and said unto him, Knowest thou that the Pharisees were offended, after they heard this saying?

Greek/Transliteration
12. Τότε προσελθόντες οἱ μαθηταὶ αὐτοῦ εἶπον αὐτῷ, Οἶδας ὅτι οἱ Φαρισαῖοι ἀκούσαντες τὸν λόγον ἐσκανδαλίσθησαν;

12. Tote proselthontes 'oi matheitai autou eipon auto, Oidas 'oti 'oi Pharisaioi akousantes ton logon eskandalistheisan?

Hebrew/Transliteration
יב. וַיִּגְּשׁוּ אֵלָיו תַּלְמִידָיו וַיֹּאמְרוּ הֲיָדַעְתָּ כִּי נִכְשְׁלוּ הַפְּרוּשִׁים בְּשָׁמְעָם הַדָּבָר הַזֶּה:

12. Va•yig•shoo elav tal•mi•dav va•yom•roo ha•ya•da•ata ki nich•she•loo ha•P`roo•shim be•shom•am ha•da•var ha•ze.

---

13. But he answered and said, Every plant, which my heavenly Father hath not planted, shall be rooted up.

Greek/Transliteration
13. Ὁ δὲ ἀποκριθεὶς εἶπεν, Πᾶσα φυτεία, ἣν οὐκ ἐφύτευσεν ὁ πατήρ μου ὁ οὐράνιος, ἐκριζωθήσεται.

13. 'O de apokritheis eipen, Pasa phuteia, 'ein ouk ephuteusen 'o pateir mou 'o ouranios, ekrizotheisetai.

Hebrew/Transliteration
יג. וַיַּעַן וַיֹּאמַר כָּל-מַטָּע אֲשֶׁר אָבִי בַּשָּׁמַיִם לֹא נְטָעוֹ יְשֹׁרָשׁ:

13. Va•ya•an va•yo•mar kol - ma•ta asher Avi ba•sha•ma•yim lo n`ta•o ye•sho•rash.

Rabbinic Jewish Commentary
So the Jews speak of God, as a planter, and of rooting up what he does not like. "The holy, blessed God (say they (e)), "plants" trees in this world; if they prosper, it is well; if they do not prosper, אעקר לון, "he roots them up", and plants them even many times." And elsewhere it is said (f), "let the master of the vineyard come, and consume its thorns: the gloss on it is, the holy, blessed God; for the vineyard of the Lord of hosts, is the house of Israel, and he will consume, and take away the thorns of the vineyard." (e) Zohar in Gen. fol. 105. 3. (f) T. Bab. Bava Metzia, fol. 83. 2.

---

14. Let them alone: they be blind leaders of the blind. And if the blind lead the blind, both shall fall into the ditch.

Greek/Transliteration
14. Ἄφετε αὐτούς· ὁδηγοί εἰσιν τυφλοὶ τυφλῶν· τυφλὸς δὲ τυφλὸν ἐὰν ὁδηγῇ, ἀμφότεροι εἰς βόθυνον πεσοῦνται.

14. Aphete autous. 'odeigoi eisin tuphloi tuphlon. tuphlos de tuphlon ean 'odeigei, amphoteroi eis bothunon pesountai.

Hebrew/Transliteration
יד. הַנִּיחוּ לָהֶם הֵם עִוְרִים מְנַהֲלִים לְעִוְרִים וְכִי עִוֵּר מְנַהֵל לְעִוֵּר שְׁנֵיהֶם יִפְּלוּ אֶל-הַבּוֹר:

14. Ha•ni•choo la•hem hem eev•rim me•na•ha•lim le•eev•rim ve•chi ee•ver me•na•hel le•ee•ver sh`ney•hem yip•loo el - ha•bor.

Rabbinic Jewish Commentary
It was an old tradition (g) among the Jews, "that there should be "blind teachers" at the time when God should have his tabernacle among them." This was predicted, in Isa_42:19 and all such leaders and teachers are blind, who, notwithstanding their natural abilities, and acquired parts, are in a state of unregeneracy; and have nothing more than what they have from nature, or have attained to at school; and as apparently all such are, who lead men from Yeshua, to mere morality, and to a dependence upon their own righteousness for justification, which was the darling principle of the blind leaders in the text. (g) Midrash Tillim in Psal.cxlvi

---

15. Then answered Peter and said unto him, Declare unto us this parable.

Greek/Transliteration
15. Ἀποκριθεὶς δὲ ὁ Πέτρος εἶπεν αὐτῷ, Φράσον ἡμῖν τὴν παραβολὴν ταύτην.

15. Apokritheis de 'o Petros eipen auto, Phrason 'eimin tein parabolein tautein.

Hebrew/Transliteration
טו. וַיַּעַן פֶּטְרוֹס וַיֹּאמֶר אֵלָיו בָּאֶר-לָנוּ אֶת-הַמָּשָׁל הַזֶּה:

15. Va•ya•an Petros va•yo•mer elav ba•er - la•noo et - ha•ma•shal ha•ze.

---

16. And Jesus said, Are ye also yet without understanding?

Greek/Transliteration
16. Ὁ δὲ Ἰησοῦς εἶπεν, Ἀκμὴν καὶ ὑμεῖς ἀσύνετοί ἐστε;

16. 'O de Yeisous eipen, Akmein kai 'umeis asunetoi este?

Hebrew/Transliteration
טז. וַיֹּאמֶר יֵשׁוּעַ הֲכִי גַם-אַתֶּם עוֹד בִּבְלִי בִינָה:

16. Va•yo•mar Yeshua ha•chi gam - atem od biv•li vi•na.

17. Do not ye yet understand, that whatsoever entereth in at the mouth goeth into the belly, and is cast out into the draught?

Greek/Transliteration
17. Οὔπω νοεῖτε, ὅτι πᾶν τὸ εἰσπορευόμενον εἰς τὸ στόμα εἰς τὴν κοιλίαν χωρεῖ, καὶ εἰς ἀφεδρῶνα ἐκβάλλεται;

17. Oupo noeite, 'oti pan to eisporeuomenon eis to stoma eis tein koilian chorei, kai eis aphedrona ekballetai?

Hebrew/Transliteration
:יז. הֲלֹא תַשְׂכִּילוּ כִּי כָל-אֲשֶׁר יָבֹא אֶל-תּוֹךְ הַפֶּה יֵרֵד אֶל-הַקֶּרֶשׁ וּמִשָּׁם יֵצֵא הַפַּרְשְׁדֹנָה

17. Ha•lo tas•ki•loo ki chol - asher ya•vo el - toch ha•pe ye•red el - ha•ka•res oo•mi•sham ye•tze ha•par•she•do•na.

---

18. But those things which proceed out of the mouth come forth from the heart; and they defile the man.

Greek/Transliteration
18. Τὰ δὲ ἐκπορευόμενα ἐκ τοῦ στόματος ἐκ τῆς καρδίας ἐξέρχεται, κἀκεῖνα κοινοῖ τὸν ἄνθρωπον.

18. Ta de ekporeuomena ek tou stomatos ek teis kardias exerchetai, kakeina koinoi ton anthropon.

Hebrew/Transliteration
:יח. אַךְ הַיֹּצֵא מִתּוֹךְ הַפֶּה יָבֹא מִתּוֹךְ הַלֵּב וְהוּא יְטַמֵּא אֶת-הָאָדָם

18. Ach ha•yo•tze mi•toch ha•pe ya•vo mi•toch ha•lev ve•hoo ye•ta•me et - ha•a•dam.

---

19. For out of the heart proceed evil thoughts, murders, adulteries, fornications, thefts, false witness, blasphemies:

Greek/Transliteration
19. Ἐκ γὰρ τῆς καρδίας ἐξέρχονται διαλογισμοὶ πονηροί, φόνοι, μοιχεῖαι, πορνεῖαι, κλοπαί, ψευδομαρτυρίαι, βλασφημίαι·

19. Ek gar teis kardias exerchontai dyalogismoi poneiroi, phonoi, moicheiai, porneiai, klopai, pseudomarturiai, blaspheimiai.

Hebrew/Transliteration
:יט. כִּי מִתּוֹךְ הַלֵּב יֵצְאוּ יִצְרֵי מַחְשְׁבוֹת רָעוֹת רָצֹחַ נָאֹף וְזָנֹה גָּנֹב עֵדוּת שֶׁקֶר וְגִדּוּפִים

19. Ki mi•toch ha•lev yetz•oo yitz•rey mach•she•vot ra•ot ra•tzo•ach na•of ve•za•no ga•nov e•doot she•ker ve•gi•doo•fim.

Rabbinic Jewish Commentary
All manner of uncleanness, and unnatural lusts: "an evil eye"; of envy and covetousness: the vitiosity, or corruption of nature, is, by the Jews (h), called עין רע, "the evil eye": "pride"; in heart and life, in dress and gesture; and "foolishness"; expressed in talk and conduct. (h) Tzeror Hammor, fol. 141. 3.

---

20. These are the things which defile a man: but to eat with unwashen hands defileth not a man.

Greek/Transliteration
20. ταῦτά ἐστιν τὰ κοινοῦντα τὸν ἄνθρωπον· τὸ δὲ ἀνίπτοις χερσὶν φαγεῖν οὐ κοινοῖ τὸν ἄνθρωπον.

20. tauta estin ta koinounta ton anthropon. to de aniptois chersin phagein ou koinoi ton anthropon.

Hebrew/Transliteration
:כ. אֵלֶּה הֵם אֲשֶׁר יְטַמְּאוּ אֶת-הָאָדָם אַךְ אָכוֹל בְּיָדַיִם אֲשֶׁר לֹא רֻחֲצוּ לֹא יְטַמֵּא אֶת-הָאָדָם

20. Ele hem asher ye•tam•oo et - ha•a•dam ach a•chol be•ya•da•yim asher lo roo•cha•tzoo lo ye•ta•me et - ha•a•dam.

---

21. Then Jesus went thence, and departed into the coasts of Tyre and Sidon.

Greek/Transliteration
21. Καὶ ἐξελθὼν ἐκεῖθεν ὁ Ἰησοῦς ἀνεχώρησεν εἰς τὰ μέρη Τύρου καὶ Σιδῶνος.

21. Kai exelthon ekeithen 'o Yeisous anechoreisen eis ta merei Turou kai Sidonos.

Hebrew/Transliteration
:כא. וַיֵּצֵא יֵשׁוּעַ מִשָּׁם וַיָּבֹא אֶל-גְּלִילוֹת צוֹר וְצִידוֹן

21. Va•ye•tze Yeshua mi•sham va•ya•vo el - g`li•lot Tzor ve•Tzi•don.

---

22. And, behold, a woman of Canaan came out of the same coasts, and cried unto him, saying, Have mercy on me, O Lord, thou Son of David; my daughter is grievously vexed with a devil.

Greek/Transliteration

22. Καὶ ἰδού, γυνὴ Χαναναία ἀπὸ τῶν ὁρίων ἐκείνων ἐξελθοῦσα ἐκραύγασεν αὐτῷ, λέγουσα, Ἐλέησόν με, κύριε, υἱὲ Δαυίδ· ἡ θυγάτηρ μου κακῶς δαιμονίζεται.

22. Kai idou, gunei Chananaia apo ton 'orion ekeinon exelthousa ekraugasen auto, legousa, Eleeison me, kurie, 'wie Dauid. 'ei thugateir mou kakos daimonizetai.

Hebrew/Transliteration

כב. וְהִנֵּה אִשָּׁה כְּנַעֲנִית יֹצֵאת מִגְּבוּלוֹת הָהֵם וַתִּצְעַק אֵלָיו לֵאמֹר חָנֵּנִי אֲדֹנִי בֶּן-דָּוִד בִּתִּי רוּחַ רָעָה בָּהּ וְעֻנְיָהּ:מֹרֶה מְאֹד

22. Ve•hee•ne ee•sha K`na•a•nit yo•tzet mig•voo•lot ha•hem va•titz•ak elav le•mor cha•ne•ni Ado•ni Ben - David bi•ti roo•ach ra•ah ba ve•on•ya mo•re me•od.

Rabbinic Jewish Commentary

That is, of Phoenicia, which was called Canaan; so Shaul, the son of a Canaanitish woman, is, by the Septuagint in Exo_6:15 called the son of a Phoenician; and the kings of Canaan are, by the same interpreters in Jos_5:1 called kings of Phoenicia: hence this woman is by Mark said to be a Greek, that is, a Gentile, as the Jews used to call all of another nation, and a Syrophenician, being a native of Phoenicia, called Syrophenician; because it bordered upon Syria, and had been formerly a part of it, by conquest.

O Lord, thou son of David. The first of these characters expresses her faith in his power, dominion, and government, that all persons and things, and so all diseases were at his command, and control; and that being Lord of all, he could remove them at his pleasure: the other shows her knowledge and belief of him, as the Messiah, that being a name by which he was usually known by the Jews.

---

23. But he answered her not a word. And his disciples came and besought him, saying, Send her away; for she crieth after us.

Greek/Transliteration

23. Ὁ δὲ οὐκ ἀπεκρίθη αὐτῇ λόγον. Καὶ προσελθόντες οἱ μαθηταὶ αὐτοῦ ἠρώτων αὐτόν, λέγοντες, Ἀπόλυσον αὐτήν, ὅτι κράζει ὄπισθεν ἡμῶν.

23. 'O de ouk apekrithei autei logon. Kai proselthontes 'oi matheitai autou eiroton auton, legontes, Apoluson autein, 'oti krazei opisthen 'eimon.

Hebrew/Transliteration

כג. וְלֹא-עָנָה אֹתָהּ דָּבָר וַיִּגְּשׁוּ תַלְמִידָיו וַיְבַקְשׁוּ מִלְּפָנָיו לֵאמֹר שַׁלַּח אֹתָהּ כִּי-צֹעֶקֶת הִיא אַחֲרֵינוּ:

23. Ve•lo - ana o•ta da•var va•yig•shoo tal•mi•dav vay•vak•shoo mil•fa•nav le•mor sha•lach o•ta ki - tzo•e•ket hee a•cha•rey•noo.

24. But he answered and said, I am not sent but unto the lost sheep of the house of Israel.

Greek/Transliteration
24. Ὁ δὲ ἀποκριθεὶς εἶπεν, Οὐκ ἀπεστάλην εἰ μὴ εἰς τὰ πρόβατα τὰ ἀπολωλότα οἴκου Ἰσραήλ.

24. 'O de apokritheis eipen, Ouk apestalein ei mei eis ta probata ta apololota oikou Ysraeil.

Hebrew/Transliteration
:כד. וַיַּעַן וַיֹּאמַר לֹא שֻׁלַחְתִּי כִּי אִם-לְצֹאן אֹבְדוֹת לְבֵית יִשְׂרָאֵל

24. Va•ya•an va•yo•mar lo shoo•lach•ti ki eem - le•tzon ov•dot le•veit Israel.

Rabbinic/Jewish New Testament Commentary
Yeshua puts this piece of information in the context of Ezekiel 34; see Eze_34:24. Thus his answer about coming only to the lost sheep of Israel (Mat_15:24) reflects Eze_34:12, Eze_34:16; in effect he says, "If, as you say, I am the Son of David, the shepherd who was King of Israel, I was sent to find my lost sheep and am not sent to you. So I'm surprised that you recognize me." It's a straightforward Middle-Eastern style friendly joke, not an insult. But his remark also reflects the biblical truth that God cares for his own people first-as Sha'ul put it, "Let us do good unto all, especially unto them who are of the household of faith" (Gal_6:10). However, God does not neglect the others, as we learn from 1Ki_7:7 ff., where the prophet Elijah asks to be fed first, yet the widow of Tzarfat, coming second, gains a miraculous lasting food supply. Yeshua's personal mission prior to his death and resurrection was only to Israelites and the Jews, God's people.

---

25. Then came she and worshipped him, saying, Lord, help me.

Greek/Transliteration
25. Ἡ δὲ ἐλθοῦσα προσεκύνησεν αὐτῷ λέγουσα, Κύριε, βοήθει μοι.

25. 'Ei de elthousa prosekuneisen auto legousa, Kurie, boeithei moi.

Hebrew/Transliteration
:כה. וְהִיא בָאָה וַתִּשְׁתַּחוּ לוֹ לֵאמֹר הוֹשִׁיעָה לִּי אֲדֹנִי

25. Ve•hee va•ah va•tish•ta•choo lo le•mor ho•shi•ah li Adoni.

---

26. But he answered and said, It is not meet to take the children's bread, and to cast it to dogs.

Greek/Transliteration
26. Ὁ δὲ ἀποκριθεὶς εἶπεν, Οὐκ ἔστιν καλὸν λαβεῖν τὸν ἄρτον τῶν τέκνων, καὶ βαλεῖν τοῖς κυναρίοις.

26. 'O de apokritheis eipen, Ouk estin kalon labein ton arton ton teknon, kai balein tois kunariois.

Hebrew/Transliteration
:כו. וַיַּעַן וַיֹּאמֶר לֹא-נָכוֹן לָקַחַת אֶת-לֶחֶם הַבָּנִים וּלְהַשְׁלִיכוֹ לִפְנֵי הַכְּלָבִים

26. Va•ya•an va•yo•mar lo - na•chon la•ka•chat et - le•chem ha•ba•nim ool•hash•li•cho lif•ney ha•k`la•vim.

Rabbinic Jewish Commentary

The Jewish Rabbi's say (k), that the idolatrous Gentiles are not called men, that they are comparable to the beasts or the field (l), to oxen, rams, goats (m), and asses (n): the foetus in the bowels of a Canaanitish servant, they say (o),

"is like the foetus in the bowels of a beast"."

Take the following passage, as an illustration of this, and as a further proof of the Jews calling the Gentiles dogs (p).

"A king provides a dinner for the children of his house; whilst they do his will they eat their meat with the king, and he gives to the dogs the part of bones to gnaw; but when the children of the house do not do the king's pleasure, he gives the dogs the dinner, and the bones to them: even so: while the Israelites do the will of their Lord, they eat at the king's table, and the feast is provided for them, and they of their own will give the bones to the Gentiles; but when they do not do the will of their Lord, lo! the feast is לכלבי, "for the dogs", and the bones are their's."

And a little after, "thou preparest a table before me"; this is the feast of the king; "in the presence of mine enemies"; אינון כלבי, "these are the dogs" that sit before the table, looking for their part of the bones."

In which may be clearly discerned the distinction between children and dogs, and the application of the one to the Jews, and the other to the Gentiles, and the different food that belongs to each: and hence it is easy to see from whom Yeshua borrowed this expression, and with what view he made use of it.

(k) T. Bab. Bava Metzia, fol. 114. 2. Zohar in Exod. fol. 35. 4. Tzeror Hammor, fol. 1. 4. (l) Zohar in Gen. fol. 31. 1. & 34. 1. 2. (m) Jarchi in Gen. 15. 10. (n) T. Bab. Kiddushin, fol. 68. 1. (o) Ib. fol. 69. 1. (p) Zohar in Exod. fol. 63. 1, 2. Vid. Tzeror Hammor, fol. 147. 4.

27. And she said, Truth, Lord: yet the dogs eat of the crumbs which fall from their masters' table.

Greek/Transliteration
27. Ἡ δὲ εἶπεν, Ναί, κύριε· καὶ γὰρ τὰ κυνάρια ἐσθίει ἀπὸ τῶν ψιχίων τῶν πιπτόντων ἀπὸ τῆς τραπέζης τῶν κυρίων αὐτῶν.

27. 'Ei de eipen, Nai, kurie. kai gar ta kunarya esthiei apo ton psichion ton piptonton apo teis trapezeis ton kurion auton.

Hebrew/Transliteration
:כז. וַתֹּאמַר כֵּן אֲדֹנִי אֶפֶס גַּם-הַכְּלָבִים יֹאכְלוּן מִן-הַפְּתוֹתִים הַנֹּפְלִים מֵעַל-שֻׁלְחַן אֲדֹנֵיהֶם

27. Va•to•mar ken Adoni e•fes gam - ha•k`la•vim yoch•loon min - hap•to•tim ha•nof•lim me•al - shool•chan ado•ney•hem.

Rabbinic Jewish Commentary
The Syriac and Persic versions add "and live": thus she wisely lays hold upon and improves in a very beautiful manner, in her own favour, what seemed to be so much against her. It is observed (q) of the Syrophoenicians in general, that they have all, in their common talk, something ηδυ και κεχαρισμενον "pleasant and graceful", as there is indeed in this smart reply of her's, who was one of that people. She suggests that though the Gentiles were but dogs, and she one of them; yet their common Lord and Master had a propriety in them, and they in him; and were to be maintained and fed, and ought to live, though not in such fulness of favours and blessings, as the Jews, the children of God: nor did she desire their affluence, only that a crumb of mercy might be given her, that her poor daughter might be healed; which was but a small favour, in comparison of the numerous ones he heaped upon the children, the Jews. (q) Eunapius in Vita Libanii

---

28. Then Jesus answered and said unto her, O woman, great is thy faith: be it unto thee even as thou wilt. And her daughter was made whole from that very hour.

Greek/Transliteration
28. Τότε ἀποκριθεὶς ὁ Ἰησοῦς εἶπεν αὐτῇ, Ὦ γύναι, μεγάλη σου ἡ πίστις· γενηθήτω σοι ὡς θέλεις. Καὶ ἰάθη ἡ θυγάτηρ αὐτῆς ἀπὸ τῆς ὥρας ἐκείνης.

28. Tote apokritheis 'o Yeisous eipen autei, O gunai, megalei sou 'ei pistis. geneitheito soi 'os theleis. Kai iathei 'ei thugateir auteis apo teis 'oras ekeineis.

Hebrew/Transliteration
כח. וַיַּעַן יֵשׁוּעַ וַיֹּאמֶר אֵלֶיהָ אִשָּׁה גְּדוֹלָה אֱמוּנָתֵךְ יְהִי-לָךְ כַּאֲשֶׁר עִם-לְבָבֵךְ וַתֵּרָפֵא בִתָּהּ בָּעֵת הַהִיא:

28. Va•ya•an Yeshua va•yo•mer e•le•ha ee•sha ge•do•la emoo•na•tech ye•hee – lach ka•a•sher eem - le•va•vech va•te•ra•fe vi•ta ba•et ha•hee.

29. And Jesus departed from thence, and came nigh unto the sea of Galilee; and went up into a mountain, and sat down there.

Greek/Transliteration
29. Καὶ μεταβὰς ἐκεῖθεν ὁ Ἰησοῦς ἦλθεν παρὰ τὴν θάλασσαν τῆς Γαλιλαίας· καὶ ἀναβὰς εἰς τὸ ὄρος ἐκάθητο ἐκεῖ.

29. Kai metabas ekeithen 'o Yeisous eilthen para tein thalassan teis Galilaias. kai anabas eis to oros ekatheito ekei.

Hebrew/Transliteration
כט: וַיַּעֲבֹר יֵשׁוּעַ מִשָּׁם וַיָּבֹא עַל-יַד יַם הַגָּלִיל וַיַּעַל אֶל-הָהָר וַיֵּשֶׁב שָׁם

29. Va•ya•a•vor Yeshua mi•sham va•ya•vo al - yad yam ha•Galil va•ya•al el - ha•har va•ye•shev sham.

---

30. And great multitudes came unto him, having with them those that were lame, blind, dumb, maimed, and many others, and cast them down at Jesus' feet; and he healed them:

Greek/Transliteration
30. Καὶ προσῆλθον αὐτῷ ὄχλοι πολλοί, ἔχοντες μεθ᾽ ἑαυτῶν χωλούς, τυφλούς, κωφούς, κυλλούς, καὶ ἑτέρους πολλούς, καὶ ἔρριψαν αὐτοὺς παρὰ τοὺς πόδας τοῦ Ἰησοῦ καὶ ἐθεράπευσεν αὐτούς·

30. Kai proseilthon auto ochloi polloi, echontes meth 'eauton cholous, tuphlous, kophous, kullous, kai 'eterous pollous, kai erripsan autous para tous podas tou Yeisou kai etherapeusen autous.

Hebrew/Transliteration
ל. וַיָּבֹאוּ לְפָנָיו הֲמוֹן עַם-רָב וְעִמָּהֶם פִּסְחִים עִוְרִים חֵרְשִׁים נִדְכָּאִים וְרַבִּים כְּמוֹהֶם וַיַּצִּיגוּם לְרַגְלֵי יֵשׁוּעַ וְהוּא: רִפָּא אֹתָם

30. Va•ya•vo•oo le•fa•nav ha•mon am - rav ve•ee•ma•hem pis•chim eev•rim cher•shim nid•ka•eem ve•ra•bim ke•mo•hem va•ya•tzi•goom le•rag•ley Yeshua ve•hoo ri•pa o•tam.

---

31. Insomuch that the multitude wondered, when they saw the dumb to speak, the maimed to be whole, the lame to walk, and the blind to see: and they glorified the God of Israel.

Greek/Transliteration
31. ὥστε τοὺς ὄχλους θαυμάσαι, βλέποντας κωφοὺς λαλοῦντας, κυλλοὺς ὑγιεῖς, χωλοὺς περιπατοῦντας, καὶ τυφλοὺς βλέποντας· καὶ ἐδόξασαν τὸν θεὸν Ἰσραήλ.

31. 'oste tous ochlous thaumasai, blepontas kophous lalountas, kullous 'ugieis, cholous peripatountas, kai tuphlous blepontas. kai edoxasan ton theon Ysraeil.

Hebrew/Transliteration

לא. וְהָעָם כֵּן תָּמְהוּ בִּרְאוֹתָם הָאֵלְמִים מְדַבְּרִים הַגִּדְּפָאִים נִרְפָּאִים הַפִּסְחִים הֹלְכִים וְהָעִוְרִים רֹאִים וַיִּתְּנוּ־כָבוֹד לֵאלֹהֵי יִשְׂרָאֵל

31. Ve•ha•am ken tam•hoo bir•o•tam ha•eel•mim me•dab•rim ha•nid•ka•eem nir•pa•eem ha•pis•chim hol•chim ve•ha•eev•rim ro•eem va•yit•noo cha•vod le•Elohey Israel.

---

32. Then Jesus called his disciples unto him, and said, I have compassion on the multitude, because they continue with me now three days, and have nothing to eat: and I will not send them away fasting, lest they faint in the way.

Greek/Transliteration

32. Ὁ δὲ Ἰησοῦς προσκαλεσάμενος τοὺς μαθητὰς αὐτοῦ εἶπεν, Σπλαγχνίζομαι ἐπὶ τὸν ὄχλον, ὅτι ἤδη ἡμέραι τρεῖς προσμένουσίν μοι, καὶ οὐκ ἔχουσιν τί φάγωσιν· καὶ ἀπολῦσαι αὐτοὺς νήστεις οὐ θέλω, μήποτε ἐκλυθῶσιν ἐν τῇ ὁδῷ.

32. 'O de Yeisous proskalesamenos tous matheitas autou eipen, Splagchnizomai epi ton ochlon, 'oti eidei 'eimerai treis prosmenousin moi, kai ouk echousin ti phagosin. kai apolusai autous neisteis ou thelo, meipote ekluthosin en tei 'odo.

Hebrew/Transliteration

לב. וַיִּקְרָא יֵשׁוּעַ אֶל־תַּלְמִידָיו וַיֹּאמֶר מָלֵאתִי רַחֲמִים עַל־הָעָם כִּי עָמְדוּ עִמָּדִי זֶה שְׁלֹשֶׁת יָמִים וְאֵין־לָהֶם מַה־לֶאֱכֹל וְאֵין אֶת־נַפְשִׁי לְשַׁלְּחָם רְעֵבִים פֶּן־יִתְעַלְּפוּ בַּדָּרֶךְ

32. Va•yik•ra Yeshua el - tal•mi•dav va•yo•mar ma•le•ti ra•cha•mim al - ha•am ki am•doo ee•ma•di ze sh`lo•shet ya•mim ve•eyn la•hem ma - le•e•chol ve•eyn et - naf•shi le•shal•cham r`e•vim pen - yit•al•foo ba•da•rech.

---

33. And his disciples say unto him, Whence should we have so much bread in the wilderness, as to fill so great a multitude?

Greek/Transliteration

33. Καὶ λέγουσιν αὐτῷ οἱ μαθηταὶ αὐτοῦ, Πόθεν ἡμῖν ἐν ἐρημίᾳ ἄρτοι τοσοῦτοι, ὥστε χορτάσαι ὄχλον τοσοῦτον;

33. Kai legousin auto 'oi matheitai autou, Pothen 'eimin en ereimia artoi tosoutoi, 'oste chortasai ochlon tosouton?

Hebrew/Transliteration
לג: וַיֹּאמְרוּ אֵלָיו תַּלְמִידָיו מֵאַיִן לָנוּ דֵּי-לֶחֶם בַּמִּדְבָּר לְהַשְׂבִּיעַ הָמוֹן רַב כָּמֹהוּ.

33. Va•yom•roo elav tal•mi•dav me•a•yin la•noo dey - le•chem ba•mid•var le•has•bi•a ha•mon rav ka•mo•hoo.

---

34. And Jesus saith unto them, How many loaves have ye? And they said, Seven, and a few little fishes.

Greek/Transliteration
34. Καὶ λέγει αὐτοῖς ὁ Ἰησοῦς, Πόσους ἄρτους ἔχετε; Οἱ δὲ εἶπον, Ἑπτά, καὶ ὀλίγα ἰχθύδια.

34. Kai legei autois 'o Yeisous, Posous artous echete? 'Oi de eipon, 'Epta, kai oliga ichthudya.

Hebrew/Transliteration
לד: וַיֹּאמֶר יֵשׁוּעַ אֲלֵיהֶם כַּמָּה לָכֶם לָחֶם וַיֹּאמְרוּ שִׁבְעָה וּמְעַט דָּגִים קְטַנִּים.

34. Va•yo•mer Yeshua aley•hem ka•ma la•chem la•chem va•yom•roo shiv•ah oom•at da•gim k`ta•nim.

---

35. And he commanded the multitude to sit down on the ground.

Greek/Transliteration
35. Καὶ ἐκέλευσεν τοῖς ὄχλοις ἀναπεσεῖν ἐπὶ τὴν γῆν·

35. Kai ekeleusen tois ochlois anapesein epi tein gein.

Hebrew/Transliteration
לה: וַיְצַו אֶת-הֲמוֹן הָעָם לָשֶׁבֶת עַל-הָאָרֶץ.

35. Vay•tzav et - ha•mon ha•am la•she•vet al - ha•a•retz.

---

36. And he took the seven loaves and the fishes, and gave thanks, and brake them, and gave to his disciples, and the disciples to the multitude.

Greek/Transliteration
36. καὶ λαβὼν τοὺς ἑπτὰ ἄρτους καὶ τοὺς ἰχθύας, εὐχαριστήσας ἔκλασεν, καὶ ἔδωκεν τοῖς μαθηταῖς αὐτοῦ, οἱ δὲ μαθηταὶ τῷ ὄχλῳ.

36. kai labon tous 'epta artous kai tous ichthuas, eucharisteisas eklasen, kai edoken tois matheitais autou, 'oi de matheitai to ochlo.

Hebrew/Transliteration
לו. וַיִּקַּח אֶת-שִׁבְעַת הַלֶּחֶם וְאֶת-הַדָּגִים וַיְבָרֶךְ וַיִּפְרֹס וַיִּתֵּן אֶל-תַּלְמִידָיו וְהַתַּלְמִידִים אֶל-הֲמוֹן הָעָם:

36. Va•yi•kach et - shiv•at ha•le•chem ve•et - ha•da•gim vay•va•rech va•yif•ros va•yi•ten el - tal•mi•dav ve•ha•tal•mi•dim el - ha•mon ha•am.

Rabbinic Jewish Commentary
and gave thanks; to God for the provision, though it was so small, in the name of the whole company, according to the usage of the Jewish nation; who, if there were ten thousand (r), one for the rest used to say, "let us bless the Lord our God, the God of Israel, the God of hosts, that sitteth between the cherubim.
(r) Misn. Beracot, c. 7. sect. 3.

---

37. And they did all eat, and were filled: and they took up of the broken meat that was left seven baskets full.

Greek/Transliteration
37. Καὶ ἔφαγον πάντες καὶ ἐχορτάσθησαν· καὶ ἦραν τὸ περισσεῦον τῶν κλασμάτων, ἑπτὰ σπυρίδας πλήρεις.

37. Kai ephagon pantes kai echortastheisan. kai eiran to perisseuon ton klasmaton, 'epta spuridas pleireis.

Hebrew/Transliteration
לז. וַיֹּאכְלוּ כֻלָּם וַיִּשְׂבָּעוּ וַיִּשְׂאוּ אֶת-הַפְּתוֹתִים הַנּוֹתָרִים שִׁבְעָה סַלִּים מְלֵאִים:

37. Va•yoch•loo choo•lam va•yis•ba•oo va•yis•oo et - hap•to•tim ha•no•ta•rim shiv•ah sa•lim me•le•eem.

Rabbinic Jewish Commentary
This number of men, as well as of the baskets of fragments, clearly shows this to be a distinct miracle from the former of this kind, recorded in Mat_14:15. There the number of men were five thousand, here four thousand; there the quantity of food was five loaves and two fishes, here seven loaves and a few fishes; there the number of the baskets of fragments was twelve, here seven; though the quantity might be as large; since the word here used for a basket is not the same as there, and designs one of a larger size. Seven in Hebrew is *shevah* and is from the root word *savah* meaning, to be full or satisfied, have enough. Here is another Hebrew idiom or word play showing the Hebrew backround of Matthew.

---

38. And they that did eat were four thousand men, beside women and children.

Greek/Transliteration
38. Οἱ δὲ ἐσθίοντες ἦσαν τετρακισχίλιοι ἄνδρες, χωρὶς γυναικῶν καὶ παιδίων.

38. 'Oi de esthiontes eisan tetrakischilioi andres, choris gunaikon kai paidion.

Hebrew/Transliteration
לח: וְהָאֹכְלִים הָיוּ אַרְבַּעַת אַלְפֵי אִישׁ מִלְּבַד נָשִׁים וָטָף.

38. Ve•ha•och•lim ha•yoo ar•ba•at al•fey eesh mil•vad na•shim va•taf.

---

39. And he sent away the multitude, and took ship, and came into the coasts of Magdala.

Greek/Transliteration
39. Καὶ ἀπολύσας τοὺς ὄχλους ἐνέβη εἰς τὸ πλοῖον, καὶ ἦλθεν εἰς τὰ ὅρια Μαγδαλά.

39. Kai apolusas tous ochlous enebei eis to ploion, kai eilthen eis ta 'orya Magdala.

Hebrew/Transliteration
לט: אָז שִׁלַּח אֶת-הֶהָמוֹן הָעָם וְהוּא יָרַד בָּאֳנִיָּה וַיָּבֹא גְּבוּלֹת מָגְדּוֹן.

39. Az shi•lach et - ha•mon ha•am ve•hoo ya•rad ba•o•ni•ya va•ya•vo g`voo•lot Ma•gadon.

Rabbinic Jewish Commentary

and came into the coasts of Magdala: not far from Tiberias; for often mention is made of Magdala in the Talmud (s), along with Tiberias, and Chammath, another place in the same neighbourhood; and was famous for some Rabbi's, as R. Joden and R. Isaac (t), who are said to be מגדלאה, "of Magdala". Thus the Syriac version reads it Magedo, and the Vulgate Latin Magedan; and Beza says, in one Greek exemplar it is read Magadan; and some have thought it to be the same with Megiddo, where Josiah was slain by Pharaohnecho, and which Herodotus calls Magdolos (u). The Evangelist Mark says, that he came into the parts of Dalmanutha, which was a place within the coasts of Magdala. This was not the place, but another of the same name near Jerusalem, from whence Mary Magdalene may be thought to have her name. The Ethiopic version renders it, "they went into a ship, and departed into the mountains of Magdala"; that is, Yeshua, and his disciples.

(s) T. Hieros. Sheviith, fol. 38. 4. Maaserot, fol. 50. 3. Erubin, fol. 21. 4. (t) T. Hieros. Taanith, fol. 64. 3. T. Bab. Yoma, fol. 81. 2. & Nidda, fol. 33. 1. Bereshit Rabba, fol. 4. 4. (u) I. 2. c. 159.

Matthew, Chapter 16

1. The Pharisees also with the Sadducees came, and tempting desired him that he would shew them a sign from heaven.

Greek/Transliteration
1. Καὶ προσελθόντες οἱ Φαρισαῖοι καὶ Σαδδουκαῖοι πειράζοντες ἐπηρώτησαν αὐτὸν σημεῖον ἐκ τοῦ οὐρανοῦ ἐπιδεῖξαι αὐτοῖς.

1. Kai proselthontes 'oi Pharisaioi kai Saddoukaioi peirazontes epeiroteisan auton seimeion ek tou ouranou epideixai autois.

Hebrew/Transliteration
א: וַיָּבֹאוּ פְרוּשִׁים וְצַדּוּקִים לְפָנָיו לְנַסּוֹתוֹ וַיִּשְׁאָלוּ מִמֶּנּוּ לְהַרְאוֹתָם אוֹת מִן-הַשָּׁמָיִם.

1. Va•ya•vo•oo F`roo•shim ve•Tza•dookim le•fa•nav le•na•so•to va•yish•a•loo mi•me•noo le•har•o•tam ot min - ha•sha•ma•yim.

Rabbinic Jewish Commentary
They wanted some such sign, as the standing still of the sun and moon, in the times of Joshua; and as raining manna, in the times of Moses; or some such appearances of thunder and lightning, as at the giving of the law. The appearance of the rainbow, in a very extraordinary manner, is looked upon by the Jews as a sign of the Messiah's coming (x).

"Says a certain Jew, when my father departed out of the world, he said thus to me; do not look for the Messiah until thou seest the bow in the world, adorned with light colours, and the world enlightened by it; then look for the Messiah, as it is written, Gen_9:16." Some very unusual and uncommon sight in the heavens, was what these men asked of Yeshua in proof of his mission from God. (x) Zohar in Gen. fol. 53. 2.

---

2. He answered and said unto them, When it is evening, ye say, It will be fair weather: for the sky is red.

Greek/Transliteration
2. Ὁ δὲ ἀποκριθεὶς εἶπεν αὐτοῖς, Ὀψίας γενομένης λέγετε, Εὐδία· πυρράζει γὰρ ὁ οὐρανός.

2. 'O de apokritheis eipen autois, Opsias genomeneis legete, Eudia. purrazei gar 'o ouranos.

Hebrew/Transliteration
ב: וַיַּעַן וַיֹּאמֶר אֲלֵיהֶם לְעֵת-עֶרֶב תֹּאמְרוּ הִנֵּה יוֹם-צַח בָּא כִּי אָדְמוּ הַשָּׁמָיִם.

2. Va•ya•an va•yo•mer aley•hem le•et - erev tom•roo hee•ne yom - tzach ba ki ad•moo ha•sha•ma•yim.

3. And in the morning, It will be foul weather to day: for the sky is red and lowring. O ye hypocrites, ye can discern the face of the sky; but can ye not discern the signs of the times?

Greek/Translitration
3. Καὶ πρωΐ, Σήμερον χειμών· πυρράζει γὰρ στυγνάζων ὁ οὐρανός. Ὑποκριταί, τὸ μὲν πρόσωπον τοῦ οὐρανοῦ γινώσκετε διακρίνειν, τὰ δὲ σημεῖα τῶν καιρῶν οὐ δύνασθε;

3. Kai proi, Seimeron cheimon. purrazei gar stugnazon 'o ouranos. 'Upokritai, to men prosopon tou ouranou ginoskete dyakrinein, ta de seimeia ton kairon ou dunasthe?

Hebrew/Transliteration
ג. וּבַבֹּקֶר תֹּאמְרוּ יוֹם-סְעָרָה הַיּוֹם כִּי אָדְמוּ הַשָּׁמַיִם וְקֹדָרוּ חֲנֵפִים יֹדְעִים אַתֶּם לִבְחֹן פְּנֵי הַשָּׁמַיִם וְלִבְחֹן אֹתוֹת:הָעִתִּים לֹא תוּכָלוּ

3. Oo•va•bo•ker tom•roo yom - se•a•ra ha•yom ki ad•moo ha•sha•ma•yim ve•ka•da•roo cha•ne•fim yod•eem atem liv•chon p`ney ha•sha•ma•yim ve•liv•chon o•tot ha•ee•tim lo too•cha•loo.

Rabbinic Jewish Commentary
but can ye not discern the signs of the times? or, as the Syriac reads it, "the time", the present time: if they had not been blind, they might easily have discerned, that the signs of the time of the Messiah's coming were upon them, and that Jesus was the Messiah; as the departure of the sceptre from Judah, the ending of Daniel's weeks, the various miracles wrought by Yeshua, the wickedness of the age in which they lived, the ministry of John the Baptist, and of Yeshua, the great flockings of the people, both to one and to the other, with divers other things which were easy to be observed by them: but they pretend this to be a very great secret.

"The secret of the day of death, they say (y), and the secret of the day when the king Messiah comes, who by his wisdom can find out?" (y)Targum in Eccl. vii. 24.

---

4. A wicked and adulterous generation seeketh after a sign; and there shall no sign be given unto it, but the sign of the prophet Jonas. And he left them, and departed.

Greek/Transliteration
4. Γενεὰ πονηρὰ καὶ μοιχαλὶς σημεῖον ἐπιζητεῖ· καὶ σημεῖον οὐ δοθήσεται αὐτῇ, εἰ μὴ τὸ σημεῖον Ἰωνᾶ τοῦ προφήτου. Καὶ καταλιπὼν αὐτούς, ἀπῆλθεν.

4. Genea poneira kai moichalis seimeion epizeitei. kai seimeion ou dotheisetai autei, ei mei to seimeion Yona tou propheitou. Kai katalipon autous, apeilthen.

Hebrew/Transliteration
:ד. דּוֹר רָע וּמְנָאֵף מְבַקֶּשׁ־לּוֹ אוֹת וְאוֹת לֹא יִנָּתֶן־לוֹ זוּלָתִי אוֹת יוֹנָה הַנָּבִיא וַיַּעַזְבֵם וַיֵּלֶךְ לוֹ

4. Dor ra oom•na•ef me•va•kesh - lo ot ve•ot lo yi•na•ten - lo zoo•la•tee ot Yona ha•na•vee va•ya•az•vem va•ye•lech lo.

---

5. And when his disciples were come to the other side, they had forgotten to take bread.

Greek/Transliteration
5. Καὶ ἐλθόντες οἱ μαθηταὶ αὐτοῦ εἰς τὸ πέραν ἐπελάθοντο ἄρτους λαβεῖν.

5. Kai elthontes 'oi matheitai autou eis to peran epelathonto artous labein.

Hebrew/Transliteration
:ה. וְכַאֲשֶׁר בָּאוּ תַלְמִידָיו אֶל־עֵבֶר הַיָּם שָׁכְחוּ לָקַחַת אִתָּם צֵדָה לַדָּרֶךְ

5. Ve•cha•a•sher ba•oo tal•mi•dav el - ever ha•yam sha•che•choo la•ka•chat ee•tam tzey•da la•da•rech.

---

6. Then Jesus said unto them, Take heed and beware of the leaven of the Pharisees and of the Sadducees.

Greek/Transliteration
6. Ὁ δὲ Ἰησοῦς εἶπεν αὐτοῖς, Ὁρᾶτε καὶ προσέχετε ἀπὸ τῆς ζύμης τῶν Φαρισαίων καὶ Σαδδουκαίων.

6. 'O de Yeisous eipen autois, 'Orate kai prosechete apo teis zumeis ton Pharisaion kai Saddoukaion.

Hebrew/Transliteration
:ו. וְיֵשׁוּעַ אָמַר אֲלֵיהֶם רְאוּ וְהִשָּׁמְרוּ לָכֶם מִשְּׂאֹר הַפְּרוּשִׁים וְהַצַּדּוּקִים

6. Ve•Yeshua amar aley•hem r`oo ve•hi•sham•roo la•chem mis•or ha•P`roo•shim ve•ha•Tza•doo•kim.

Jewish New Testament Commentary
Chametz, "leaven," usually a symbol of sin or evil, as is clear at Mat_16:12.

---

7. And they reasoned among themselves, saying, It is because we have taken no bread.

Greek/Transliteration
7. Οἱ δὲ διελογίζοντο ἐν ἑαυτοῖς, λέγοντες ὅτι Ἄρτους οὐκ ἐλάβομεν.

7. 'Oi de dielogizonto en 'eautois, legontes 'oti Artous ouk elabomen.

Hebrew/Transliteration
ז: וַיְהִי הֵם נְדוֹנִים לֵאמֹר כִּי לֹא-לָקַחְנוּ לָחֶם

7. Vay•hi hem n`do•nim le•mor ki lo - la•kach•noo la•chem.

---

8. Which when Jesus perceived, he said unto them, O ye of little faith, why reason ye among yourselves, because ye have brought no bread?

Greek/Transliteration
8. Γνοὺς δὲ ὁ Ἰησοῦς εἶπεν αὐτοῖς, Τί διαλογίζεσθε ἐν ἑαυτοῖς, ὀλιγόπιστοι, ὅτι ἄρτους οὐκ ἐλάβετε;

8. Gnous de 'o Yeisous eipen autois, Ti dyalogizesthe en 'eautois, oligopistoi, 'oti artous ouk elabete?

Hebrew/Transliteration
ח: וַיֵּדַע יֵשׁוּעַ וַיֹּאמֶר אֲלֵיהֶם קְטַנֵּי אֱמוּנָה לָמָּה-זֶּה אַתֶּם נְדוֹנִים כִּי לֹא-לְקַחְתֶּם לָחֶם

8. Va•ye•da Yeshua va•yo•mer aley•hem k`ta•ney e•moo•na la•ma - ze atem n`do•nim ki lo - le•kach•tem la•chem.

Jewish New Testament Commentary
Alfred Edersheim, a nineteenth-century Hebrew Christian scholar, suggests the disciples thought Yeshua believed they had not brought bread in order to have him do another bread-making miracle. This would have been the same sort of sign-fishing the *P'rushim* and *Tz'dukim* had been doing and would have been an indication of their having little trust.

---

9. Do ye not yet understand, neither remember the five loaves of the five thousand, and how many baskets ye took up?

Greek/Transliteration
9. Οὔπω νοεῖτε, οὐδὲ μνημονεύετε τοὺς πέντε ἄρτους τῶν πεντακισχιλίων, καὶ πόσους κοφίνους ἐλάβετε;

9. Oupo noeite, oude mneimoneuete tous pente artous ton pentakischilion, kai posous kophinous elabete?

Hebrew/Transliteration
ט. הֲכִי עוֹד לֹא תַשְׂכִּילוּ וְלֹא תִזְכְּרוּ אֶת-חֲמֵשֶׁת הַלֶּחֶם אָכְלוּ חֲמֵשֶׁת אֲלָפִים וְכַמָּה סַלִּים אֲשֶׁר נְשָׂאתֶם:

9. Ha•chi od lo tas•ki•loo ve•lo tiz•ke•roo et - cha•me•shet ha•le•chem ach•loo cha•me•shet ala•fim ve•cha•ma sa•lim asher n`sa•tem.

10. Neither the seven loaves of the four thousand, and how many baskets ye took up?

Greek/Translieration
10. Οὐδὲ τοὺς ἑπτὰ ἄρτους τῶν τετρακισχιλίων, καὶ πόσας σπυρίδας ἐλάβετε;

10. Oude tous 'epta artous ton tetrakischilion, kai posas spuridas elabete?

Hebrew/Transliteration
:י. וְגַם-שִׁבְעַת הַלֶּחֶם אָכְלוּ אַרְבַּעַת אֲלָפִים וְכַמָּה סַלִּים אֲשֶׁר נְשָׂאתֶם

10. Ve•gam - shiv•at ha•le•chem ach•loo ar•ba•at ala•fim ve•cha•ma sa•lim asher n`sa•tem.

---

11. How is it that ye do not understand that I spake it not to you concerning bread, that ye should beware of the leaven of the Pharisees and of the Sadducees?

Greek/Transliteration
11. Πῶς οὐ νοεῖτε, ὅτι οὐ περὶ ἄρτου εἶπον ὑμῖν προσέχειν ἀπὸ τῆς ζύμης τῶν Φαρισαίων καὶ Σαδδουκαίων;

11. Pos ou noeite, 'oti ou peri artou eipon 'umin prosechein apo teis zumeis ton Pharisaion kai Saddoukaion?

Hebrew/Transliteration
יא. וְאֵיךְ לֹא תַשְׂכִּילוּ כִּי לֹא עַל-דְּבַר לֶחֶם אָמַרְתִּי לָכֶם כִּי אִם-לְהִשָּׁמֵר מִשְּׂאֹר הַפְּרוּשִׁים וְהַצַּדּוּקִים:

11. Ve•eych lo tas•ki•loo ki lo al - de•var le•chem amar•ti la•chem ki eem - le•hi•sha•mer mis•or ha•P`roo•shim ve•ha•Tza•doo•kim.

---

12. Then understood they how that he bade them not beware of the leaven of bread, but of the doctrine of the Pharisees and of the Sadducees.

Greek/Transliteration
12. Τότε συνῆκαν ὅτι οὐκ εἶπεν προσέχειν ἀπὸ τῆς ζύμης τοῦ ἄρτου, ἀλλὰ ἀπὸ τῆς διδαχῆς τῶν Φαρισαίων καὶ Σαδδουκαίων.

12. Tote suneikan 'oti ouk eipen prosechein apo teis zumeis tou artou, alla apo teis didacheis ton Pharisaion kai Saddoukaion.

Hebrew/Transliteration
:יב. אָז הֵבִינוּ כִּי לֹא אָמַר לָהֶם לְהִשָּׁמֵר מִשְּׂאֹר הַלֶּחֶם כִּי אִם-מִתּוֹרַת הַפְּרוּשִׁים וְהַצַּדּוּקִים

12. Az he•vi•noo ki lo amar la•hem le•hi•sha•mer mis•or ha•la•chem ki eem - mi•to•rat ha•P`roo•shim ve•ha•Tza•doo•kim.

Rabbinic Jewish Commentary
It was very common with the Jews (a) to call the corruption and vitiosity of nature by the name of שאור שבעיסה, "leaven in the lump": therefore Yeshua calls their doctrine so, because it proceeded from thence, and was agreeable to that; and uses the phrase on purpose to expose it, and bring it into neglect and contempt.

(a) T. Hieros. Beracot, fol. 7. 4. T. Bab. Beracot, fol. 17. 1. Bereshit Rabba, fol. 29. 4. Caphtor, fol. 38. 2. Tzeror Hammor, fol. 73. 2.

---

13. When Jesus came into the coasts of Caesarea Philippi, he asked his disciples, saying, Whom do men say that I the Son of man am?

Greek/Transliteration
13. Ἐλθὼν δὲ ὁ Ἰησοῦς εἰς τὰ μέρη Καισαρείας τῆς Φιλίππου ἠρώτα τοὺς μαθητὰς αὐτοῦ, λέγων, Τίνα με λέγουσιν οἱ ἄνθρωποι εἶναι, τὸν υἱὸν τοῦ ἀνθρώπου;

13. Elthon de 'o Yeisous eis ta merei Kaisareias teis Philippou eirota tous matheitas autou, legon, Tina me legousin 'oi anthropoi einai, ton 'wion tou anthropou?

Hebrew/Transliteration
יג. וַיָּבֹא יֵשׁוּעַ אֶל-גְּלִילוֹת קֵיסָרִין אֲשֶׁר לְפִילְפּוֹס וַיִּשְׁאַל אֶת-תַּלְמִידָיו לֵאמֹר מָה-אֹמְרִים הָאֲנָשִׁים עָלַי מִי הוּא:בֶּן-הָאָדָם

13. Va•ya•vo Yeshua el - g`li•lot Kis•rin asher le•Filipos va•yish•al et - tal•mi•dav le•mor ma - om•rim ha•a•na•shim a•lai mee hoo Ben - ha•a•dam.

---

14. And they said, Some say that thou art John the Baptist: some, Elias; and others, Jeremias, or one of the prophets.

Greek/Transliteration
14. Οἱ δὲ εἶπον, Οἱ μὲν Ἰωάννην τὸν βαπτιστήν· ἄλλοι δὲ Ἠλίαν· ἕτεροι δὲ Ἰερεμίαν, ἢ ἕνα τῶν προφητῶν.

14. 'Oi de eipon, 'Oi men Yoannein ton baptistein. alloi de Eilian. 'eteroi de Yeremian, ei 'ena ton propheiton.

Hebrew/Transliteration
יד. וַיַּעֲנוּ יֵשׁ אֹמְרִים יוֹחָנָן הַמַּטְבִּיל וְיֵשׁ אֹמְרִים אֵלִיָּהוּ וַאֲחֵרִים אֹמְרִים יִרְמְיָהוּ אוֹ אֶחָד מִן-הַנְּבִיאִים:

14. Va•ya•a•noo yesh om•rim Yo•cha•nan ha•Mat•bil ve•yesh om•rim Eli•ya•hoo va•a•che•rim om•rim Yir•me•ya•hoo oh e•chad min - ha•n`vi•eem.

Rabbinic Jewish Commentary
and others Jeremias; this is omitted both by Mark and Luke; the reason why he is mentioned, is not because of what is said of him, in Jer_1:5 but because the Jews thought he was that prophet spoken of, in Deu_18:15 that should be raised up from among them, like unto Moses: and this is the sense of some of their writers (g): and in their very ancient writings a parallel is run between Moses and Jeremy (h).

(g) Baal Hatturim in Deut. xviii. 15. R. Abraham Seba; Tzeror Hammor, fol. 127. 4. & 143. 4. (h) Pesikta Rabbati apud R. Abarbinel, Praefat. ad Jer. fol. 96. 2.

---

15. He saith unto them, But whom say ye that I am?

Greek/Transliteration
15. Λέγει αὐτοῖς, Ὑμεῖς δὲ τίνα με λέγετε εἶναι;

15. Legei autois, 'Umeis de tina me legete einai?

Hebrew/Transliteration
טו. וַיֹּאמֶר אֲלֵיהֶם וְאַתֶּם מַה-תֹּאמְרוּ עָלַי מִי אָנִי:

15. Va•yo•mer aley•hem ve•a•tem ma - tom•roo a•lai mee ani.

---

16. And Simon Peter answered and said, Thou art the Christ, the Son of the living God.

Greek/Transliteration
16. Ἀποκριθεὶς δὲ Σίμων Πέτρος εἶπεν, Σὺ εἶ ὁ χριστός, ὁ υἱὸς τοῦ θεοῦ τοῦ ζῶντος.

16. Apokritheis de Simon Petros eipen, Su ei 'o christos, 'o 'wios tou theou tou zontos.

Hebrew/Transliteration
טז. וַיַּעַן שִׁמְעוֹן פֶּטְרוֹס וַיֹּאמַר אַתָּה הוּא הַמָּשִׁיחַ בֶּן-אֱלֹהִים חַיִּים:

16. Va•ya•an Shimon Petros va•yo•mar ata hoo ha•Ma•shi•ach Ben - Elohim cha•yim.

---

17. And Jesus answered and said unto him, Blessed art thou, Simon Barjona: for flesh and blood hath not revealed it unto thee, but my Father which is in heaven.

Greek/Transliteration

17. Καὶ ἀποκριθεὶς ὁ Ἰησοῦς εἶπεν αὐτῷ, Μακάριος εἶ, Σίμων Βαριωνᾶ, ὅτι σὰρξ καὶ αἷμα οὐκ ἀπεκάλυψέν σοι, ἀλλ᾽ ὁ πατήρ μου ὁ ἐν τοῖς οὐρανοῖς.

17. Kai apokritheis 'o Yeisous eipen auto, Makarios ei, Simon Bariona, 'oti sarx kai 'aima ouk apekalupsen soi, all 'o pateir mou 'o en tois ouranois.

Hebrew/Transliteration

יז. וַיַּעַן יֵשׁוּעַ וַיֹּאמֶר אֵלָיו אַשְׁרֶיךָ שִׁמְעוֹן בַּר-יוֹנָה לֹא בָשָׂר וָדָם גִּלָּה-לְךָ זֶה כִּי אִם-אָבִי אֲשֶׁר בַּשָּׁמָיִם:

17. Va•ya•an Yeshua va•yo•mer elav ash•re•cha Shimon Bar - Yona lo va•sar va•dam gila - le•cha ze ki eem - Avi asher ba•sha•ma•yim.

Rabbinic Jewish Commentary

blessed art thou Simon Bar Jona, or son of Jona, or Jonas, as in Joh_1:42. His father's name was Jonah, whence he was so called: so we read (i) of R. Bo bar Jonah, and of a Rabbi of this very name (k), ר שמעון בר יונא, Rabbi Simeon bar Jona; for Simon and Simeon are one, and the same name.

For flesh and blood hath not revealed it unto thee: nothing is more frequent to be met with in Jewish writings, than the phrase of "flesh and blood", as designing men in distinction from God: so the first man is said (l) to be

"the workmanship of the blessed God, and not the workmanship דבשר ודם, "of flesh and blood"."

Again (m), בשר ודם, "flesh and blood", who knows not the times and seasons, &c. but the holy, blessed God, who knows the times and seasons, &c. Instances of this way of speaking are almost without number.

(i) Juchasin, fol. 85. 1. (k) Ib. fol. 105. 1. (l) Zohar in Gen. fol. 43. 3. (m) R. Simeon in Jarchi in Gen. ii. 2.

---

18. And I say also unto thee, That thou art Peter, and upon this rock I will build my church; and the gates of hell shall not prevail against it.

Greek/Transliteration

18. Κἀγὼ δέ σοι λέγω, ὅτι σὺ εἶ Πέτρος, καὶ ἐπὶ ταύτῃ τῇ πέτρᾳ οἰκοδομήσω μου τὴν ἐκκλησίαν, καὶ πύλαι ᾅδου οὐ κατισχύσουσιν αὐτῆς.

18. Kago de soi lego, 'oti su ei Petros, kai epi tautei tei petra oikodomeiso mou tein ekkleisian, kai pulai 'dou ou katischusousin auteis.

Hebrew/Transliteration

יח. וְגַם-אֲנִי אַגִּיד לְךָ כִּי אַתָּה הוּא כֵיפָא וְעַל-הַכֵּף הַזֶּה אֶבְנֶה אֶת-קְהִלָּתִי וְשַׁעֲרֵי שְׁאוֹל לֹא יִגְבְּרוּ עָלֶיהָ:

18. Ve•gam - ani agid le•cha ki ata hoo Keyfa ve•al - ha•kef ha•ze ev•ne et - ke•hi•la•ti ve•sha•a•rey sh`ol lo yig•be•roo a•le•ha.

Rabbinic/Jewish New Testament Commentary

Community, Greek *ekklêsia*, which means "called-out ones," and is used in the Septuagint to translate Hebrew *kahal*, "assembly, congregation, community." The usual English translation of *ekklêsia* is "church"; and from it comes the word "ecclesiastical," meaning, "having to do with the church."

The Jews speak of the gates of gehenna: sometimes of the gate of gehenna, in the singular number (p); and sometimes of the gates of gehenna, in the plural number. They say (q), that "gehenna has three gates", one in the wilderness, one in the sea, and one in Jerusalem." They talk (r) of "an angel that is appointed על תרעי דגיהנם, "over the gates of gehenna", whose name is Samriel; who has three keys in his hands, and opens three doors." And elsewhere (s) they say, that "he that is appointed over sheol his name is Dumah, and many myriads of destroying angels are with him, and he stands על פתחא דגיהנם, "at the gate of gehenna"; and all those that keep the holy covenant in this world, he has no power to bring them in."

Though Yeshua does not speak of gehenna here to Peter he does speak of sheol or the grave. Death and the gates of the grave that lead to gehenna will not prevail, Rev_1:18

(p) T. Bab. Sabbat, fol. 39. 1. Succa, fol. 32. 2. Bava Bathra, fol. 84. 1. (q) T. Bab. Erubin, fol. 19. 1. Menasseh ben Israel, Nishmat Chayim, fol, 33. 1, 2. (r) Zohar in Gen. fol. 47. 4. (s) Ib. fol. 7. 1.

---

19. And I will give unto thee the keys of the kingdom of heaven: and whatsoever thou shalt bind on earth shall be bound in heaven: and whatsoever thou shalt loose on earth shall be loosed in heaven.

Greek/Transliteration

19. Καὶ δώσω σοὶ τὰς κλεῖς τῆς βασιλείας τῶν οὐρανῶν· καὶ ὃ ἐὰν δήσῃς ἐπὶ τῆς γῆς, ἔσται δεδεμένον ἐν τοῖς οὐρανοῖς· καὶ ὃ ἐὰν λύσῃς ἐπὶ τῆς γῆς, ἔσται λελυμένον ἐν τοῖς οὐρανοῖς.

19. Kai doso soi tas kleis teis basileias ton ouranon. kai 'o ean deiseis epi teis geis, estai dedemenon en tois ouranois. kai 'o ean luseis epi teis geis, estai lelumenon en tois ouranois.

Hebrew/Transliteration

יט. וְנָתַתִּי לְךָ אֶת-מַפְתְּחוֹת מַלְכוּת הַשָּׁמַיִם אֶת-אֲשֶׁר תֶּאֱסֹר עַל-הָאָרֶץ אָסוּר יִהְיֶה בַשָּׁמַיִם וְאֶת-אֲשֶׁר תַּתִּיר:עַל-הָאָרֶץ מֻתָּר יִהְיֶה בַשָּׁמָיִם

19. Ve•na•ta•ti le•cha et - maf•te•chot mal•choot ha•sha•ma•yim et - asher te•e•sor al - ha•a•retz a•soor yi•hee•ye ba•sha•ma•yim ve•et - asher ta•tir al - ha•a•retz moo•tar yi•hee•ye va•sha•ma•yim.

Rabbinic Jewish Commentary

Dr. Lightfoot has transcribed a great many, sufficient to satisfy any man, and give him the true sense of these phrases; and after him to mention any other is needless; yet give me leave to produce one, as it is short, and full, and explains these phrases, and points at the persons that had this power, explaining Ecc_12:11 and that clause in it, "masters of the assemblies".

"these (say they (t)) are the disciples of the wise men, who sit in different collections, and study in the law; these pronounce things or persons defiled, and these pronounce things or persons clean, הללו אוסרין והללן מתירין, "these bind, and these loose"; these reject, or pronounce persons or things profane, and these declare them right." And a little after,

"get thyself an heart to hear the words of them that pronounce unclean, and the words of them that pronounce clean; the words of them אוסרין, that "bind", and the words of them מתירין, that "loose"; the words of them that reject, and the words of them that declare it right" (t) T. Bab. Chagiga, fol. 3. 2.

---

20. Then charged he his disciples that they should tell no man that he was Jesus the Christ.

Greek/Transliteration
20. Τότε διεστείλατο τοῖς μαθηταῖς αὐτοῦ ἵνα μηδενὶ εἴπωσιν ὅτι αὐτός ἐστιν Ἰησοῦς ὁ χριστός.

20. Tote diesteilato tois matheitais autou 'ina meideni eiposin 'oti autos estin Yeisous 'o christos.

Hebrew/Transliteration
:כ. אָז צִוָּה עַל-תַּלְמִידָיו לְבִלְתִּי הַגֵּד לְאִישׁ כִּי הוּא יֵשׁוּעַ הַמָּשִׁיחַ

20. Az tzi•va al - tal•mi•dav le•vil•ti ha•ged le•eesh ki hoo Yeshua ha•Ma•shi•ach.

---

21. From that time forth began Jesus to shew unto his disciples, how that he must go unto Jerusalem, and suffer many things of the elders and chief priests and scribes, and be killed, and be raised again the third day.

Greek/Transliteration
21. Ἀπὸ τότε ἤρξατο ὁ Ἰησοῦς δεικνύειν τοῖς μαθηταῖς αὐτοῦ ὅτι δεῖ αὐτὸν ἀπελθεῖν εἰς Ἱεροσόλυμα, καὶ πολλὰ παθεῖν ἀπὸ τῶν πρεσβυτέρων καὶ ἀρχιερέων καὶ γραμματέων, καὶ ἀποκτανθῆναι, καὶ τῇ τρίτῃ ἡμέρᾳ ἐγερθῆναι.

21. Apo tote eirxato 'o Yeisous deiknuein tois matheitais autou 'oti dei auton apelthein eis 'Yerosoluma, kai polla pathein apo ton presbuteron kai archiereon kai grammateon, kai apoktantheinai, kai tei tritei 'eimera egertheinai.

Hebrew/Transliteration
כא. מֵהָעֵת הַהִיא הֵחֵל יֵשׁוּעַ לְהוֹרֹת לְתַלְמִידָיו כִּי עָלָיו לָלֶכֶת יְרוּשָׁלַיְמָה לִהְיוֹת מְעֻנֶּה עַד-מְאֹד עַל-יְדֵי הַזְּקֵנִים וְרָאשֵׁי הַכֹּהֲנִים וְהַסּוֹפְרִים וְגַם מוֹת יוּמָת וּבַיּוֹם הַשְּׁלִישִׁי יָקוּם:

21. Me•ha•et ha•hee he`chel Yeshua le•ho•rot le•tal•mi•dav ki alav la•le•chet Ye•roo•sha•lai•ma li•hee•yot me•oo•ne ad - me•od al - ye•dey haz`ke•nim ve•ra•shey ha•ko•ha•nim ve•ha•sof•rim ve•gam mot yoo•mat oo•va•yom hash•li•shi ya•koom.

---

22. Then Peter took him, and began to rebuke him, saying, Be it far from thee, Lord: this shall not be unto thee.

Greek/Transliteration
22. Καὶ προσλαβόμενος αὐτὸν ὁ Πέτρος ἤρξατο ἐπιτιμᾶν αὐτῷ λέγων, Ἵλεώς σοι, κύριε· οὐ μὴ ἔσται σοι τοῦτο.

22. Kai proslabomenos auton 'o Petros eirxato epitiman auto legon, 'Yleos soi, kurie. ou mei estai soi touto.

Hebrew/Transliteration
כב. וַיִּקָּחֵהוּ פֶטְרוֹס וַיָּחֶל לִגְעָר-בּוֹ לֵאמֹר חָלִילָה לְךָ אֲדֹנִי חָלִילָה לְךָ מִדָּבָר כָּזֶה:

22. Va•yi•ka•che•hoo Fetros va•ya•chel lig•or - bo le•mor cha•li•la le•cha Adoni cha•li•la le•cha mi•da•var ka•ze.

---

23. But he turned, and said unto Peter, Get thee behind me, Satan: thou art an offence unto me: for thou savourest not the things that be of God, but those that be of men.

Greek/Transliteration
23. Ὁ δὲ στραφεὶς εἶπεν τῷ Πέτρῳ, Ὕπαγε ὀπίσω μου, Σατανᾶ, σκάνδαλόν μου εἶ· ὅτι οὐ φρονεῖς τὰ τοῦ θεοῦ, ἀλλὰ τὰ τῶν ἀνθρώπων.

23. 'O de strapheis eipen to Petro, 'Upage opiso mou, Satana, skandalon mou ei. 'oti ou phroneis ta tou theou, alla ta ton anthropon.

Hebrew/Transliteration
כג. וַיִּפֶן וַיֹּאמֶר אֶל-פֶּטְרוֹס סוּר שָׂטָן מֵעַל פָּנַי לְמוֹקֵשׁ אַתָּה לִי כִּי לֹא תַשְׂכִּיל אֵת אֲשֶׁר לֵאלֹהִים כִּי-אִם אֵת אֲשֶׁר לָאָדָם:

23. Va•yi•fen va•yo•mer el - Petros soor Satan me•al pa•nai le•mo•kesh ata li ki lo tas•kil et asher le•Elohim ki - eem et asher la•a•dam.

Rabbinic Jewish Commentary
Yeshua calls Peter by this name, because he was against him, and opposed him in this point; which sense abates the harshness of this expression. But it seems rather to mean the devil, who took the advantage of Peter's weakness and ignorance; and put him upon dissuading Yeshua from suffering, for the salvation of his people: though it should be known that the word Satan is used by the Jews (w), to signify the vitiosity and corruption of nature; of which they say, שטן הוא, this is Satan. (w) T. Bab. Bava Bathra, fol. 16. 1. Tzeror Hammor, fol. 6. 2, 3. & passim.

---

24. Then said Jesus unto his disciples, If any man will come after me, let him deny himself, and take up his cross, and follow me.

Greek/Transliteration
24. Τότε ὁ Ἰησοῦς εἶπεν τοῖς μαθηταῖς αὐτοῦ, Εἴ τις θέλει ὀπίσω μου ἐλθεῖν, ἀπαρνησάσθω ἑαυτόν, καὶ ἀράτω τὸν σταυρὸν αὐτοῦ, καὶ ἀκολουθείτω μοι.

24. Tote 'o Yeisous eipen tois matheitais autou, Ei tis thelei opiso mou elthein, aparneisastho 'eauton, kai arato ton stauron autou, kai akoloutheito moi.

Hebrew/Transliteration
כד. אָז אָמַר יֵשׁוּעַ אֶל-תַּלְמִידָיו מִי הֶחָפֵץ לָלֶכֶת אַחֲרַי יַשְׁלִיךְ אֶת-נַפְשׁוֹ מִנֶּגֶד וְיִשָּׂא אֶת-צְלָבוֹ וְיֵלֵךְ אַחֲרָי:

24. Az amar Yeshua el - tal•mi•dav mee he•cha•fetz la•le•chet a•cha•rai yash•lich et - naf•sho mi•ne•ged ve•yi•sa et - tze•la•vo ve•ye•lech a•cha•rai.

---

25. For whosoever will save his life shall lose it: and whosoever will lose his life for my sake shall find it.

Greek/Transliteration
25. Ὃς γὰρ ἂν θέλῃ τὴν ψυχὴν αὐτοῦ σῶσαι ἀπολέσει αὐτήν· ὃς δ᾽ ἂν ἀπολέσῃ τὴν ψυχὴν αὐτοῦ ἕνεκεν ἐμοῦ εὑρήσει αὐτήν·

25. 'Os gar an thelei tein psuchein autou sosai apolesei autein. 'os d an apolesei tein psuchein autou 'eneken emou 'eureisei autein.

Hebrew/Transliteration
כה. כִּי מִי הֶחָפֵץ לְהַצִּיל אֶת-נַפְשׁוֹ תִּכָּרֶת-לוֹ וּמִי אֲשֶׁר יַכְרִית אֶת-נַפְשׁוֹ לְמַעֲנִי יִמְצָאֶנָּה:

25. Ki mee he•cha•fetz le•ha•tzil et - naf•sho ti•ka•ret - lo oo•mi asher yach•rit et - naf•sho le•ma•a•ni yim•tza•e•na.

26. For what is a man profited, if he shall gain the whole world, and lose his own soul? Or what shall a man give in exchange for his soul?

Greek/Transliteration
26. τί γὰρ ὠφελεῖται ἄνθρωπος ἐὰν τὸν κόσμον ὅλον κερδήσῃ, τὴν δὲ ψυχὴν αὐτοῦ ζημιωθῇ; Ἢ τί δώσει ἄνθρωπος ἀντάλλαγμα τῆς ψυχῆς αὐτοῦ;

26. ti gar opheleitai anthropos ean ton kosmon 'olon kerdeisei, tein de psuchein autou zeimiothei? Ei ti dosei anthropos antallagma teis psucheis autou?

Hebrew/Transliteration
:כו. כִּי מַה-בֶּצַע לָאִישׁ אִם יִקְנֶה-לּוֹ אֶת-כָּל-הָאָרֶץ וְנַפְשׁוֹ תִּכָּרֵת-לוֹ אוֹ מַה-יִּתֵּן אִישׁ פִּדְיוֹן נַפְשׁוֹ

26. Ki ma - be•tza le•eesh eem yik•ne - lo et - kol - ha•a•retz ve•naf•sho ti•ka•ret - lo oh ma - yi•ten eesh pid•yon naf•sho.

Rabbinic Jewish Commentary
This passage is thought to be proverbial; what comes nearest to it, is the following (x). "If a scholar dies, we never find an exchange for him; there are four things which are the ministry or service of the world, אם אבדו יש חליפין, if they are lost, they may be changed; and they are these, gold, silver, iron, and brass, Job 28:1 but if a scholar dies, מי מביא לנו תמורתו, who will bring us his exchange? or an exchange for him: we lost R. Simon, "who will bring us his exchange?"."
(x) Midrash Kohelet, fol. 72. 3, 4. T. Hieros. Beracot, fol. 5. 3.

---

27. For the Son of man shall come in the glory of his Father with his angels; and then he shall reward every man according to his works.

Greek/Transliteration
27. Μέλλει γὰρ ὁ υἱὸς τοῦ ἀνθρώπου ἔρχεσθαι ἐν τῇ δόξῃ τοῦ πατρὸς αὐτοῦ μετὰ τῶν ἀγγέλων αὐτοῦ, καὶ τότε ἀποδώσει ἑκάστῳ κατὰ τὴν πρᾶξιν αὐτοῦ.

27. Mellei gar 'o 'wios tou anthropou erchesthai en tei doxei tou patros autou meta ton angelon autou, kai tote apodosei 'ekasto kata tein praxin autou.

Hebrew/Transliteration
:כז. כִּי עָתִיד בֶּן-הָאָדָם לָבֹא בִּכְבוֹד אָבִיו עִם-מַלְאָכָיו וְאָז יְשַׁלֵּם לְכָל-אִישׁ כְּמַעֲשֵׂהוּ

27. Ki atid Ben - ha•a•dam la•vo bich•vod Aviv eem - mal•a•chav ve•az ye•sha•lem le•chol - eesh ke•ma•a•se•hoo.

---

28. Verily I say unto you, There be some standing here, which shall not taste of death, till they see the Son of man coming in his kingdom.

335

Greek/Transliteration
28. Ἀμὴν λέγω ὑμῖν, εἰσίν τινες ὧδε ἑστῶτες, οἵτινες οὐ μὴ γεύσωνται θανάτου, ἕως ἂν ἴδωσιν τὸν υἱὸν τοῦ ἀνθρώπου ἐρχόμενον ἐν τῇ βασιλείᾳ αὐτοῦ.

28. Amein lego 'umin, eisin tines 'ode 'estotes, 'oitines ou mei geusontai thanatou, 'eos an idosin ton 'wion tou anthropou erchomenon en tei basileia autou.

Hebrew/Transliteration
כח. אָמֵן אֲנִי אֹמֵר לָכֶם יֵשׁ מִן-הַנִּצָּבִים פֹּה אֲשֶׁר לֹא-יִטְעֲמוּ מָוֶת עַד כִּי-יִרְאוּ אֶת-בֶּן-הָאָדָם בָּא בְּמַלְכוּתוֹ:

28. Amen ani o•mer la•chem yesh min - ha•ni•tza•vim po asher lo - yit•a•moo ma•vet ad ki - yir•oo et - Ben - ha•a•dam ba be•mal•choo•to.

Rabbinic Jewish Commentary
Which shall not taste of death: that is, shall not die; a phrase frequently used by the Jewish Rabbi's: they say (y), "All the children of the world, טעמין טעמא דמותא, "taste the taste of death"."

(y) Zohar in Gen. fol. 27. 4. & 37. 1. & in Exod. fol. 19. 2. & in Num. fol. 50. 4. & 51. 2. 4. Vid. Bereshit Rabba, sect. 9. fol. 7. 3, 4. Midrash Kohelet, fol, 83. 2.

Matthew, Chapter 17

1. And after six days Jesus taketh Peter, James, and John his brother, and bringeth them up into an high mountain apart,

Greek/Transliteration
1. Καὶ μεθ᾽ ἡμέρας ἓξ παραλαμβάνει ὁ Ἰησοῦς τὸν Πέτρον καὶ Ἰάκωβον καὶ Ἰωάννην τὸν ἀδελφὸν αὐτοῦ, καὶ ἀναφέρει αὐτοὺς εἰς ὄρος ὑψηλὸν κατ᾽ ἰδίαν.

1. Kai meth 'eimeras 'ex paralambanei 'o Yeisous ton Petron kai Yakobon kai Yoannein ton adelphon autou, kai anapherei autous eis oros 'upseilon kat idian.

Hebrew/Transliteration
א. וְאַחֲרֵי שֵׁשֶׁת יָמִים לָקַח יֵשׁוּעַ אִתּוֹ אֶת-פֶּטְרוֹס וְאֶת-יַעֲקֹב וְאֶת-יוֹחָנָן אָחִיו וַיַּעַל עִמָּהֶם לְבַדָּם אֶל-הַר גָּבֹהַּ:

1. Ve•a•cha•rey she•shet ya•mim la•kach Yeshua ee•to et - Petros ve•et - Yaakov ve•et - Yo•cha•nan a•chiv va•ya•al ee•ma•hem le•va•dam el - har ga•vo•ha.

---

2. And was transfigured before them: and his face did shine as the sun, and his raiment was white as the light.

Greek/Transliteration
2. Καὶ μετεμορφώθη ἔμπροσθεν αὐτῶν, καὶ ἔλαμψεν τὸ πρόσωπον αὐτοῦ ὡς ὁ ἥλιος, τὰ δὲ ἱμάτια αὐτοῦ ἐγένοντο λευκὰ ὡς τὸ φῶς.

2. Kai metemorphothei emprosthen auton, kai elampsen to prosopon autou 'os 'o 'eilios, ta de 'imatya autou egenonto leuka 'os to phos.

Hebrew/Transliteration
ב. וַיִּשְׁתַּנֶּה לְעֵינֵיהֶם פָּנָיו הִזְהִירוּ כַּשֶּׁמֶשׁ וּלְבוּשָׁיו הִלְבִּינוּ כָּאוֹר:

2. Va•yish•ta•ne le•ey•ne•hem pa•nav hiz•hi•roo ka•she•mesh ool•voo•shav hil•bi•noo ka•or.

---

3. And, behold, there appeared unto them Moses and Elias talking with him.

Greek/Transliteration
3. Καὶ ἰδού, ὤφθησαν αὐτοῖς Μωσῆς καὶ Ἠλίας, μετ᾽ αὐτοῦ συλλαλοῦντες.

3. Kai idou, ophtheisan autois Moseis kai Eilias, met autou sullalountes.

Hebrew/Transliteration
ג: וַיֵּרָאוּ אֶת-מֹשֶׁה וְאֶת-אֵלִיָּהוּ וְהִנָּם מְדַבְּרִים אִתּוֹ

3. Va•ye•che•zoo et - Moshe ve•et - Eli•ya•hoo ve•hi•nam me•dab•rim ee•to.

Rabbinic Jewish Commentary
The Jews sometimes speak of these two as together. They say (c), "that the Shekinah never descends below, but משה ואליהו, "Moses and Elias" ascend above."

Yea, they expect that these two will come together in future time; for so they represent (d) a God saying to Moses; "Moses, as thou hast given thy life for them (the Israelites) in this world, so in time to come (the days of the Messiah) when I shall bring Elias the prophet, שניכם באין כאחת, "you two shall come together"."

The Jews often speak of the appearance of Elias to their Rabbi's, and of his conversing with them, and teaching them. "Lo! the pious man, whom Elias used משתעי בהדיה, "to converse with"." And elsewhere it is said (g), "R. Phineas and R. Mari, the sons of R. Chasda, were godly men, ואליהו מדבר עמהם, "and Elias was talking with them", and they were priests."

(c) T. Bab. Succab, fol. 5. 1. (d) Debarim Rabba, sect. 3. fol. 239. 2. (e) T. Bab. Sota, fol. 13. 2. Maimon. praefat. ad Seder Zeraim in Talmud. fol. 86. 4. (f) T. Bab. Bava Bathra, fol. 7. 2. (g) Juchasin, fol. 101. 1. Vid. fol. 79. 1. & 118. 2. & 13. 132. 1. & T. Bab. Cetubot, fol. 106. 1.

---

4. Then answered Peter, and said unto Jesus, Lord, it is good for us to be here: if thou wilt, let us make here three tabernacles; one for thee, and one for Moses, and one for Elias.

Greek/Transliteration
4. Ἀποκριθεὶς δὲ ὁ Πέτρος εἶπεν τῷ Ἰησοῦ, κύριε, καλόν ἐστιν ἡμᾶς ὧδε εἶναι· εἰ θέλεις, ποιήσωμεν ὧδε τρεῖς σκηνάς, σοὶ μίαν, καὶ Μωσῇ μίαν, καὶ μίαν Ἠλίᾳ.

4. Apokritheis de 'o Petros eipen to Yeisou, kurie, kalon estin 'eimas 'ode einai. ei theleis, poieisomen 'ode treis skeinas, soi mian, kai Mosei mian, kai mian Eilia.

Hebrew/Transliteration
ד. וַיַּעַן פֶּטְרוֹס וַיֹּאמֶר אֶל-יֵשׁוּעַ טוֹב לָנוּ אֲדֹנִי לָשֶׁבֶת פֹּה אִם יֵשׁ אֶת-נַפְשְׁךָ נַעֲשֶׂה-פֹּה שָׁלֹשׁ סֻכּוֹת אַחַת לְךָ:אַחַת לְמֹשֶׁה וְאַחַת לְאֵלִיָּהוּ

4. Va•ya•an Petros va•yo•mer el - Yeshua tov la•noo Adoni la•she•vet po eem yesh et - naf•she•cha na•a•se - po sha•losh soo•kot a•chat le•cha a•chat le•Moshe ve•a•chat le•Eli•yahoo.

5. While he yet spake, behold, a bright cloud overshadowed them: and behold a voice out of the cloud, which said, This is my beloved Son, in whom I am well pleased; hear ye him.

Greek/Transliteration
5. Ἔτι αὐτοῦ λαλοῦντος, ἰδού, νεφέλη φωτεινὴ ἐπεσκίασεν αὐτούς· καὶ ἰδού, φωνὴ ἐκ τῆς νεφέλης, λέγουσα, Οὗτός ἐστιν ὁ υἱός μου ὁ ἀγαπητός, ἐν ᾧ εὐδόκησα· αὐτοῦ ἀκούετε.

5. Eti autou lalountos, idou, nephelei photeinei epeskiasen autous. kai idou, phonei ek teis nepheleis, legousa, 'Outos estin 'o 'wios mou 'o agapeitos, en 'o eudokeisa. autou akouete.

Hebrew/Transliteration
ה. עוֹדֶנּוּ מְדַבֵּר וְהִנֵּה עָנָן בָּהִיר סֹכֵךְ עֲלֵיהֶם וְהִנֵּה קוֹל־קוֹרֵא מִן־הֶעָנָן זֶה־בְּנִי יְדִידִי אֲשֶׁר רָצְתָה נַפְשִׁי בוֹ:אֵלָיו תִּשְׁמָעוּן

5. O•de•noo me•da•ber ve•hee•ne anan ba•hir so•chech aley•hem ve•hee•ne kol - ko•re min - he•a•nan ze - B`ni ye•di•di asher ratz•ta naf•shi bo elav tish•ma•oon.

---

6. And when the disciples heard it, they fell on their face, and were sore afraid.

Greek/Transliteration
6. Καὶ ἀκούσαντες οἱ μαθηταὶ ἔπεσον ἐπὶ πρόσωπον αὐτῶν, καὶ ἐφοβήθησαν σφόδρα.

6. Kai akousantes 'oi matheitai epeson epi prosopon auton, kai ephobeitheisan sphodra.

Hebrew/Transliteration
ו. כִּשְׁמֹעַ הַתַּלְמִידִים וַיִּפְּלוּ עַל־פְּנֵיהֶם וַיִּירְאוּ מְאֹד:

6. Ki•sh`mo•a ha•tal•mi•dim va•yip•loo al - p`ney•hem va•yir•oo me•od.

---

7. And Jesus came and touched them, and said, Arise, and be not afraid.

Greek/Transliteration
7. Καὶ προσελθὼν ὁ Ἰησοῦς ἥψατο αὐτῶν καὶ εἶπεν, Ἐγέρθητε καὶ μὴ φοβεῖσθε.

7. Kai proselthon 'o Yeisous 'eipsato auton kai eipen, Egertheite kai mei phobeisthe.

Hebrew/Transliteration
ז. וַיִּגַּשׁ יֵשׁוּעַ וַיִּגַּע-בָּם וַיֹּאמֶר קוּמוּ אַל-תִּירָאוּ:

7. Va•yi•gash Yeshua va•yi•ga - bam va•yo•mar koo•moo al - ti•ra•oo.

---

8. And when they had lifted up their eyes, they saw no man, save Jesus only.

Greek/Transliteration
8. Ἐπάραντες δὲ τοὺς ὀφθαλμοὺς αὐτῶν, οὐδένα εἶδον, εἰ μὴ τὸν Ἰησοῦν μόνον.

8. Eparantes de tous ophthalmous auton, oudena eidon, ei mei ton Yeisoun monon.

Hebrew/Transliteration
ח. וַיִּשְׂאוּ אֶת-עֵינֵיהֶם וַיִּרְאוּ כִּי אֵין אִישׁ זוּלָתִי יֵשׁוּעַ לְבַדּוֹ:

8. Va•yis•oo et - ey•ne•hem va•yir•oo ki eyn eesh zoo•la•tee Yeshua le•va•do.

---

9. And as they came down from the mountain, Jesus charged them, saying, Tell the vision to no man, until the Son of man be risen again from the dead.

Greek/Transliteration
9. Καὶ καταβαινόντων αὐτῶν ἐκ τοῦ ὄρους, ἐνετείλατο αὐτοῖς ὁ Ἰησοῦς, λέγων, Μηδενὶ εἴπητε τὸ ὅραμα, ἕως οὗ ὁ υἱὸς τοῦ ἀνθρώπου ἐκ νεκρῶν ἀναστῇ.

9. Kai katabainonton auton ek tou orous, eneteilato autois 'o Yeisous, legon, Meideni eipeite to 'orama, 'eos 'ou 'o 'wios tou anthropou ek nekron anastei.

Hebrew/Transliteration
ט. וּבְרִדְתָּם מִן-הָהָר צִוָּה עֲלֵיהֶם יֵשׁוּעַ לֵאמֹר אַל-תַּגִּידוּ אֶת-הַמַּרְאֶה לְאִישׁ עַד כִּי-יָקוּם בֶּן-הָאָדָם מִן-הַמֵּתִים:

9. Oov•ri•de•tam min - ha•har tzi•va aley•hem Yeshua le•mor al - ta•gi•doo et - ha•mar•eh le•eesh ad ki - ya•koom Ben - ha•a•dam min - ha•me•tim.

---

10. And his disciples asked him, saying, Why then say the scribes that Elias must first come?

Greek/Transliteration
10. Καὶ ἐπηρώτησαν αὐτὸν οἱ μαθηταὶ αὐτοῦ λέγοντες, Τί οὖν οἱ γραμματεῖς λέγουσιν ὅτι Ἠλίαν δεῖ ἐλθεῖν πρῶτον;

10. Kai epeiroteisan auton 'oi matheitai autou legontes, Ti oun 'oi grammateis legousin 'oti Eilian dei elthein proton?

Hebrew/Transliteration
י. וַיִּשְׁאָלֻהוּ תַלְמִידָיו לֵאמֹר לָמָּה-זֶּה יֹאמְרוּ הַסּוֹפְרִים כִּי אֵלִיָּהוּ בֹּא יָבֹא רִאשׁוֹנָה:

10. Va•yish•a•loo•hoo tal•mi•dav le•mor la•ma - ze yom•roo ha•sof•rim ki Eli•ya•hoo bo ya•vo ri•sho•na.

Rabbinic Jewish Commentary

Why then say the Scribes, that Elias must first come? That is, come before the Messiah comes; for certain it is, that this was the sense of the Scribes, as it was of the ancient Jews, and is still the opinion of the modern ones. They say (h),

"that in the second year of Ahaziah, Elias was hid; nor will he appear, till the Messiah comes; then he will appear, and will be hid a second time; and then will not appear, till Gog and Magog come." And they expressly affirm (i), that

"before the coming of the son of David, יבא אליהו לבשר, "Elias will come to bring the good news" of it."

And this, they say (k), will be one day before the coming of the Messiah. And Maimonides (l) observes,

"that there are of their wise men that say, שקודם ביאת המשיח יבא אליהו, "that before the coming of the Messiah, Elias shall come"."

So Trypho the Jew, the same with R. Tarphon, so often mentioned in Talmudic writings, disputing with Justin Martyr, tells him (m), that the Messiah,

"shall not know himself, nor have any power, μεχρι αν ελθων Ηλιας, "till Elias comes", and anoints him, and makes him known to all."

And hence the Targumist (n) often speaks of Messiah and Elias as together, and of things done by them; and in their prayers, petitions are put for them, as to come together (o): this is founded upon a mistaken sense of Mal_4:5 and which is the general sense of their commentators (p). Now the Scribes made use of this popular sense, to disprove Jesus being the Messiah: they argued, that if he was the Messiah, Elias would be come; but whereas he was not come, therefore he could not be the Messiah.

(h) Seder Olam Rabba, p. 45, 46. (i) Gloss. in T. Bab. Erubin, fol. 43. 2. (k) R. Abraham ben David in Misn. Ediot, c. 8. sect. 7. (l) Hilch. Melacim, c. 12. sect. 2. (m) Dialog. cum Tryph. p. 226. (n) In Exod. xl. 10. Deut. xxx. 4. & Lam. iv. 22. (o) Seder Tephillot, fol. 56. 2. & 128. 2. (p) Aben Ezra, Kimchi, & Abarbinel in loc.

11. And Jesus answered and said unto them, Elias truly shall first come, and restore all things.

Greek/Transliteration
11. Ὁ δὲ Ἰησοῦς ἀποκριθεὶς εἶπεν αὐτοῖς, Ἠλίας μὲν ἔρχεται πρῶτον, καὶ ἀποκαταστήσει πάντα·

11. 'O de Yeisous apokritheis eipen autois, Eilias men erchetai proton, kai apokatasteisei panta.

Hebrew/Transliteration
יא. וַיַּעַן יֵשׁוּעַ וַיֹּאמֶר אֲלֵיהֶם אָכֵן אֵלִיָּהוּ יָבֹא בָרִאשׁוֹנָה לְהָשִׁיב אֶת-הַכֹּל:

11. Va•ya•an Yeshua va•yo•mer aley•hem a•chen Eli•ya•hoo ya•vo va•ri•sho•na le•ha•shiv et - ha•kol.

Rabbinic Jewish Commentary
Jews assign to their Elias, whom they expect, and whom they make to be a restorer of all things, in their way: they often speak of his purifying (q) of things, or pronouncing things pure, that were defiled; and among others, that he will purify bastards, and ישיבם, "restore them" to the congregation of the Lord (r). Though Maimonides (s) denies, that when he comes he will pronounce defiled that which is pure, or pronounce pure, that which is defiled. They pretend (t), that he is now employed, and very busy, in writing everything that is done in every age; so that when he comes, he will be able to give an account of everything: and nothing is more common with them, than to say concerning any matter, that there is any doubt or difficulty about it (u), יהא מונח עד שיבא אליהו, "let it be left till Elias comes".

(q) T. Bab. Chagiga, fol. 25. 1. & Becorot, fol. 33. 2. & 34. 1. (r) Kimchi in Zech. ix. 6. (s) Hilchot Melacim, c. 12. sect. 2. Vid. Misn. Ediot, c. 8. sect. 7. & Maimon & Bartenora in ib. (t) Seder Olam Rabba, p 46. (u) Misn. Bava Metzia, c. 1. sect. 8. T. Bab. Bava Metzia, fol. 3. 1. & 37. 1. & Bava Bathra, fol. 94. 1.

---

12. But I say unto you, That Elias is come already, and they knew him not, but have done unto him whatsoever they listed. Likewise shall also the Son of man suffer of them.

Greek/Transliteration
12. λέγω δὲ ὑμῖν ὅτι Ἠλίας ἤδη ἦλθεν, καὶ οὐκ ἐπέγνωσαν αὐτόν, ἀλλὰ ἐποίησαν ἐν αὐτῷ ὅσα ἠθέλησαν· οὕτως καὶ ὁ υἱὸς τοῦ ἀνθρώπου μέλλει πάσχειν ὑπ᾽ αὐτῶν.

12. lego de 'umin 'oti Eilias eidei eilthen, kai ouk epegnosan auton, alla epoieisan en auto 'osa eitheleisan. 'outos kai 'o 'wios tou anthropou mellei paschein 'up auton.

Hebrew/Transliteration
יב. אֶפֶס אֲנִי אֹמֵר לָכֶם כִּי אֵלִיָּהוּ כְּבָר בָּא וְלֹא הִכִּירֻהוּ וַיַּעֲשׂוּ-בוֹ כִּרְצוֹנָם וְכֵן גַּם-בֶּן-הָאָדָם יְעֻנֶּה תַּחַת יָדָם:

12. E•fes ani o•mer la•chem ki Eli•ya•hoo k`var ba ve•lo hi•ki•roo•hoo va•ya•a•soo – vo kir•tzo•nam ve•chen gam - Ben - ha•a•dam ye•oo•ne ta•chat ya•dam.

---

13. Then the disciples understood that he spake unto them of John the Baptist.

Greek/Transliteration
13. Τότε συνῆκαν οἱ μαθηταὶ ὅτι περὶ Ἰωάννου τοῦ βαπτιστοῦ εἶπεν αὐτοῖς.

13. Tote suneikan 'oi matheitai 'oti peri Yoannou tou baptistou eipen autois.

Hebrew/Transliteration
יג. אָז הִשְׂכִּילוּ הַתַּלְמִידִים כִּי עַל-יוֹחָנָן הַמַּטְבִּיל דִּבֶּר אֲלֵיהֶם:

13. Az his•ki•loo ha•tal•mi•dim ki al - Yo•cha•nan ha•Mat•bil di•ber aley•hem.

---

14. And when they were come to the multitude, there came to him a certain man, kneeling down to him, and saying,

Greek/Transliteration
14. Καὶ ἐλθόντων αὐτῶν πρὸς τὸν ὄχλον, προσῆλθεν αὐτῷ ἄνθρωπος γονυπετῶν αὐτὸν

14. Kai elthonton auton pros ton ochlon, proseilthen auto anthropos gonupeton auton

Hebrew/Transliteration
יד. וַיְהִי בְּבֹאָם אֶל-הֲמוֹן הָעָם וַיִּגַּשׁ אֵלָיו אִישׁ וַיִּכְרַע עַל-בִּרְכָּיו:

14. Vay•hi be•vo•am el - ha•mon ha•am va•yi•gash elav eesh va•yich•ra al - bir•kav.

---

15. Lord, have mercy on my son: for he is lunatick, and sore vexed: for ofttimes he falleth into the fire, and oft into the water.

Greek/Transliteration
15. καὶ λέγων, Κύριε, ἐλέησόν μου τὸν υἱόν, ὅτι σεληνιάζεται καὶ κακῶς πάσχει· πολλάκις γὰρ πίπτει εἰς τὸ πῦρ, καὶ πολλάκις εἰς τὸ ὕδωρ.

15. kai legon, Kurie, eleeison mou ton 'wion, 'oti seleinyazetai kai kakos paschei. pollakis gar piptei eis to pur, kai pollakis eis to 'udor.

Hebrew/Transliteration

טו. וַיֹּאמַר אֲדֹנִי חוּסָה-נָּא עַל-בְּנִי כִּי-מֻכֵּה יָרֵחַ הוּא וּמְעֻנֶּה עַד-מְאֹד כִּי-פְעָמִים רַבּוֹת יִפֹּל אֶל-תּוֹךְ הָאֵשׁ:וּפְעָמִים רַבּוֹת אֶל-תּוֹךְ הַמָּיִם.

15. Va•yo•mar Adoni choo•sa - na al - b`ni ki - moo•ke ya•re•ach hoo oom•oo•ne ad - me•od ki - fe•a•mim ra•bot yi•pol el - toch ha•esh oof•a•mim ra•bot el - toch ha•ma•yim.

---

16. And I brought him to thy disciples, and they could not cure him.

Greek/Transliteration

16. Καὶ προσήνεγκα αὐτὸν τοῖς μαθηταῖς σου, καὶ οὐκ ἠδυνήθησαν αὐτὸν θεραπεῦσαι.

16. Kai proseinegka auton tois matheitais sou, kai ouk eiduneitheisan auton therapeusai.

Hebrew/Transliteration

טז. וַאֲנִי הֲבִיאֹתִיו אֶל-תַּלְמִידֶיךָ וְלֹא מָצְאָה יָדָם לְרַפֵּא אֹתוֹ:

16. Va•a•ni ha•vi•o•tiv el - tal•mi•de•cha ve•lo matz•ah ya•dam le•ra•pe o•to.

---

17. Then Jesus answered and said, O faithless and perverse generation, how long shall I be with you? how long shall I suffer you? bring him hither to me.

Greek/Transliteration

17. Ἀποκριθεὶς δὲ ὁ Ἰησοῦς εἶπεν, Ὦ γενεὰ ἄπιστος καὶ διεστραμμένη, ἕως πότε ἔσομαι μεθ᾽ ὑμῶν; Ἕως πότε ἀνέξομαι ὑμῶν; Φέρετέ μοι αὐτὸν ὧδε.

17. Apokritheis de 'o Yeisous eipen, O genea apistos kai diestrammenei, 'eos pote esomai meth 'umon? 'Eos pote anexomai 'umon? Pherete moi auton 'ode.

Hebrew/Transliteration

יז. וַיַּעַן יֵשׁוּעַ וַיֹּאמַר הוֹי דּוֹר לֹא-אֵמֻן בּוֹ דּוֹר תַּהְפֻּכֹת עַד-מָתַי אֶהְיֶה עִמָּכֶם עַד-מָתַי אֶשָּׂא אֶתְכֶם הֲבִיאֻהוּ אֵלַי:הֵנָּה

17. Va•ya•an Yeshua va•yo•mer hoy dor lo - emoon bo dor ta•ha•poo•chot ad - ma•tai e•he•ye ee•ma•chem ad - ma•tai esa et•chem ha•vi•oo•hoo e•lai he•na.

18. And Jesus rebuked the devil; and he departed out of him: and the child was cured from that very hour.

Greek/Transliteration
18. Καὶ ἐπετίμησεν αὐτῷ ὁ Ἰησοῦς, καὶ ἐξῆλθεν ἀπ᾽ αὐτοῦ τὸ δαιμόνιον, καὶ ἐθεραπεύθη ὁ παῖς ἀπὸ τῆς ὥρας ἐκείνης.

18. Kai epetimeisen auto 'o Yeisous, kai exeilthen ap autou to daimonion, kai etherapeuthei 'o pais apo teis 'oras ekeineis.

Hebrew/Transliteration
יח. וַיִּגְעַר-בּוֹ יֵשׁוּעַ וַיֵּצֵא הָרוּחַ הָרָע מִמֶּנּוּ וַיֵּרָפֵא הַנַּעַר בָּעֵת הַהִיא:

18. Va•yig•ar - bo Yeshua va•ye•tze ha•roo•ach ha•ra mi•me•noo va•ye•ra•fe ha•na•ar ba•et ha•hee.

Rabbinic Jewish Commentary
And it is usual with the Jews, to ascribe diseases to evil spirits; and perhaps this uncommon dispensation in the times of Yeshua, may give rise to such a notion; particularly, they ascribe this very same disease of the "epileptic", or "falling sickness", to the same cause, which they call (x) "Kordicus", or "Cardiacus", the "Cardiac" passion, which one of their commentators (y) explains thus.

"It is a disease which proceeds from the repletion of the vessels of the brain, whereby the understanding is confounded; wherefore it is one of the sorts חולי הנופל, "of the falling sickness"." Says another (z) of them, "It is שם שידה, "the name of a demon", that rules over such, that drink much wine out of the vat."

To which others agree, saying (a), that one attended with this disorder, is one,

"whose understanding is confounded, מחמת שד, "by means of a demon", who rules over such, that drink new wine; and lo! the spirit's name is "Kardiacus"."

From where it is clear, that with them, the disease and the demon go by the same name; and that the former is from the latter.

(x) Misn. Gittin, c. 7. sect. 1. (y) Maimon. in ib. (z) Gloss. in T. Bab. Gittin, fol. 67. 2. (a) Bartenora & Yom Tob. in Misn. Gittin, c. 8. sect. 1.

---

19. Then came the disciples to Jesus apart, and said, Why could not we cast him out?

Greek/Transliteration
19. Τότε προσελθόντες οἱ μαθηταὶ τῷ Ἰησοῦ κατ᾽ ἰδίαν εἶπον, Διὰ τί ἡμεῖς οὐκ ἠδυνήθημεν ἐκβαλεῖν αὐτό;

19. Tote proselthontes 'oi matheitai to Yeisou kat idian eipon, Dya ti 'eimeis ouk eiduneitheimen ekbalein auto?

Hebrew/Transliteration

יט. אָז נִגְּשׁוּ הַתַּלְמִידִים לְבָדָם אֶל־יֵשׁוּעַ וַיֹּאמְרוּ מַדּוּעַ לֹא מָצְאָה יָדֵנוּ אֲנַחְנוּ לְגָרְשׁוֹ:

19. Az nig•shoo ha•tal•mi•dim le•va•dam el - Yeshua va•yom•roo ma•doo•a lo matz•ah ya•de•noo a•nach•noo le•gar•sho.

---

20. And Jesus said unto them, Because of your unbelief: for verily I say unto you, If ye have faith as a grain of mustard seed, ye shall say unto this mountain, Remove hence to yonder place; and it shall remove; and nothing shall be impossible unto you.

Greek/Transliteration

20. Ὁ δὲ Ἰησοῦς εἶπεν αὐτοῖς, Διὰ τὴν ἀπιστίαν ὑμῶν. Ἀμὴν γὰρ λέγω ὑμῖν, ἐὰν ἔχητε πίστιν ὡς κόκκον σινάπεως, ἐρεῖτε τῷ ὄρει τούτῳ, Μετάβηθι ἐντεῦθεν ἐκεῖ, καὶ μεταβήσεται· καὶ οὐδὲν ἀδυνατήσει ὑμῖν.

20. 'O de Yeisous eipen autois, Dya tein apistian 'umon. Amein gar lego 'umin, ean echeite pistin 'os kokkon sinapeos, ereite to orei touto, Metabeithi enteuthen ekei, kai metabeisetai. kai ouden adunateisei 'umin.

Hebrew/Transliteration

כ. וַיֹּאמֶר יֵשׁוּעַ אֲלֵיהֶם מִפְּנֵי חֹסֶר אֱמוּנַתְכֶם כִּי הֵן אֲנִי אֹמֵר לָכֶם אִם־יֵשׁ בָּכֶם אֱמוּנָה כְּגַרְגַּר חַרְדָּל וַאֲמַרְתֶּם לָהָר הַזֶּה הֵעָתֵק מִזֶּה שָׁמָּה וְיֵעָתֵק מִמְּקוֹמוֹ וְלֹא יִפָּלֵא מִכֶּם דָּבָר:

20. Va•yo•mer Yeshua aley•hem mip•ney cho•ser emoo•nat•chem ki hen ani o•mer la•chem eem - yesh ba•chem e•moo•na ke•gar•gar char•dal va•amar•tem la•har ha•ze he•a•tek mi•ze sha•ma ve•ye•a•tek mim•ko•mo ve•lo yi•pa•le mi•kem da•var.

Rabbinic Jewish Commentary

for verily I say unto you, if ye have faith as a grain of mustard seed; which was a very small seed, the least of all seeds, and is used very often proverbially by the Jews, to signify anything of a small quantity or weight (b), and is sometimes used of faith, as here; so speaking of the congregation of Edom, meaning the Christians, they (c) say, "they have not אמונה כמו גרעין של חרדל, "faith as a grain of mustard seed"." And it is used in like sense in other eastern nations; and by Mahomet in his Alcoran (d), who says, "We will appoint just balances in the day of resurrection, neither shall any soul be injured at all, although the merit or guilt of an action be of the weight of "a grain of mustard seed"."

(b) T. Bab. Beracot, fol. 31. 1. Megilla, fol. 28. 2. Nidda, fol. 66. 1. Maimon. Issure Biah, c. 11. sect. 4. Maacolot Asurot, c. 2. sect. 21. &c. 14. sect. 8. Tumaot Okelim, c. 4. sect. 2. & 7. 6. (c) Vet. Nizzachon, p. 148. (d) C. 21. p. 268. & c. 31. p. 336. Ed. Sale.

21. Howbeit this kind goeth not out but by prayer and fasting.

Greek/Transliteration
21. Τοῦτο δὲ τὸ γένος οὐκ ἐκπορεύεται εἰ μὴ ἐν προσευχῇ καὶ νηστείᾳ.

21. Touto de to genos ouk ekporeuetai ei mei en proseuchei kai neisteia.

Hebrew/Transliteration
כא. מִן רוּחַ כָּזֶה לֹא-יְגֹרָשׁ כִּי אִם-בִּתְפִלָּה וּבְצוֹם:

21. Min roo•ach ka•ze lo - ye•go•rash ki eem - bit•fi•la oov•tzom.

Rabbinic Jewish Commentary
but by fasting and prayer; This agrees with the notions of the Jews, who think that, by fasting, a divine soul (f) תשיג את מבוקשה, "may obtain that which is sought for"; and that among other things, for which a private person may afflict himself with fasting, this is one, מפני רוח רעה, "because of an evil spirit" (g); which they think may be got rid of this way.

(f) Jacchiades in Dan. x. 3. (g) T. Bab. Taanith, fol. 22. 2. Maimon. Hilch. Taaniot, c. 1. sect. 6.

---

22. And while they abode in Galilee, Jesus said unto them, The Son of man shall be betrayed into the hands of men:

Greek/Transliteration
22. Ἀναστρεφομένων δὲ αὐτῶν ἐν τῇ Γαλιλαίᾳ, εἶπεν αὐτοῖς ὁ Ἰησοῦς, Μέλλει ὁ υἱὸς τοῦ ἀνθρώπου παραδίδοσθαι εἰς χεῖρας ἀνθρώπων,

22. Anastrephomenon de auton en tei Galilaia, eipen autois 'o Yeisous, Mellei 'o 'wios tou anthropou paradidosthai eis cheiras anthropon,

Hebrew/Transliteration
כב. וַיְהִי בְּעָבְרָם בַּגָּלִיל וַיֹּאמֶר יֵשׁוּעַ אֲלֵיהֶם הִנֵּה בֶן-הָאָדָם יִסָּגֵר בִּידֵי אֲנָשִׁים:

22. Vay•hi be•ov•ram ba•Ga•lil va•yo•mer Yeshua aley•hem hee•ne Ben - ha•adam yi•sa•ger biy•dey a•na•shim.

Rabbinic Jewish Commentary
Now Yeshua intimates, that the son of man, meaning himself, should be betrayed by the Jews, into the hands of the Gentiles; nothing was reckoned a fouler action, or a viler crime; their canons run thus (h): "It is forbidden to betray an Israelite into the hands of the Gentiles, whether in his body or in his substance; and though he may be a wicked man, and a ringleader in sin, and though he may have oppressed and afflicted him; and everyone that betrays an Israelite into the hands of the Gentiles, whether in his body, or in his substance, has no part in the world to come." (h) Maimon. Hilch. Chobel Umazzik, c. 8. sect. 9, 10.

23. And they shall kill him, and the third day he shall be raised again. And they were exceeding sorry.

Greek/Transliteration
23. καὶ ἀποκτενοῦσιν αὐτόν, καὶ τῇ τρίτῃ ἡμέρᾳ ἐγερθήσεται. Καὶ ἐλυπήθησαν σφόδρα.

23. kai apoktenousin auton, kai tei tritei 'eimera egertheisetai. Kai elupeitheisan sphodra.

Hebrew/Transliteration
:כג. וְהֵם יַהַרְגֻהוּ וּבַיּוֹם הַשְּׁלִישִׁי יָקוּם וַיִּתְעַצְּבוּ מְאֹד

23. Ve•hem ya•har•goo•hoo oo•va•yom hash•li•shi ya•koom va•yit•atz•voo me•od.

---

24. And when they were come to Capernaum, they that received tribute money came to Peter, and said, Doth not your master pay tribute?

Greek/Transliteration
24. Ἐλθόντων δὲ αὐτῶν εἰς Καπερναούμ, προσῆλθον οἱ τὰ δίδραχμα λαμβάνοντες τῷ Πέτρῳ καὶ εἶπον, Ὁ διδάσκαλος ὑμῶν οὐ τελεῖ τὰ δίδραχμα;

24. Elthonton de auton eis Kapernaoum, proseilthon 'oi ta didrachma lambanontes to Petro kai eipon, 'O didaskalos 'umon ou telei ta didrachma?

Hebrew/Transliteration
כד. וַיְהִי כְּבֹאָם כְּפַר-נַחוּם וַיִּגְּשׁוּ הַמְמֻנִּים עַל-מַחֲצִית הַשֶּׁקֶל אֶל-פֶּטְרוֹס וַיֹּאמְרוּ הֲלֹא יְשַׁלֵּם רַבְּכֶם אֶת-מַחֲצִית הַשֶּׁקֶל

24. Vay•hi ke•vo•am K`far - Na•choom va•yig•shoo ha•me•moo•nim al - ma•cha•tzit ha•she•kel el - Petros va•yom•roo ha•lo ye•sha•lem rab•chem et - ma•cha•tzit ha•sha•kel.

Rabbinic Jewish Commentary
This was not the Roman tax, nor tribute, on any civil account, but the half shekel for religious service: and it may seem strange that such a question should be asked; and especially since it is a rule with them (t), that "all are bound to give the half shekel, priests, Levites, and Israelites; and the strangers, or proselytes, and servants, that are made free; but not women, nor servants, nor children; though if they gave, they received it of them."

But a following canon (u) explains it, and accounts for it: on the fifteenth "(i.e. of the month Adar,) the collectors sit in every province or city, (that is, in the countries,) ובעין בנחת כל, "and mildly ask everyone": he that gives to them, they receive it of him; and he that does not give, אין כופין אותו ליתן, "they do not oblige

348

him to give": on the five and twentieth they sit in the sanctuary to collect, and from hence and onward, they urge him that will not give, until he gives; and everyone that will not give, they take pawns of him." (s) Maimon Talmud Tora, c. 6. 10. (t) Ib. Hilch. Shekalim, c. 1. sect. 7. (u) Ib. sect. 9.

---

25. He saith, Yes. And when he was come into the house, Jesus prevented him, saying, What thinkest thou, Simon? of whom do the kings of the earth take custom or tribute? of their own children, or of strangers?

Greek/Transliteration

25. Λέγει, Ναί. Καὶ ὅτε εἰσῆλθεν εἰς τὴν οἰκίαν, προέφθασεν αὐτὸν ὁ Ἰησοῦς, λέγων, Τί σοι δοκεῖ, Σίμων; Οἱ βασιλεῖς τῆς γῆς ἀπὸ τίνων λαμβάνουσιν τέλη ἢ κῆνσον; Ἀπὸ τῶν υἱῶν αὐτῶν, ἢ ἀπὸ τῶν ἀλλοτρίων;

25. Legei, Nai. Kai 'ote eiseilthen eis tein oikian, proephthasen auton 'o Yeisous, legon, Ti soi dokei, Simon? 'Oi basileis teis geis apo tinon lambanousin telei ei keinson? Apo ton 'wion auton, ei apo ton allotrion?

Hebrew/Transliteration

כה. וַיֹּאמֶר הֵן וַיָּבֹא הַבַּיְתָה וַיְקַדְּמֵהוּ יֵשׁוּעַ לֵאמֹר מַה-יֶּהְגֶּה לִבְּךָ שִׁמְעוֹן מִמִּי יִקְחוּ מַלְכֵי-הָאָרֶץ מֶכֶס וָמַס:מִבְּנֵיהֶם אוֹ מִן-הַזָּרִים

25. Va•yo•mer hen va•ya•vo ha•bai•ta vay•kad•me•noo Yeshua le•mor ma - ye•he•ge lib•cha Shimon mi•mi yik•choo mal•chey - ha•a•retz me•ches va•mas mib•ney•hem oh min - ha•za•rim.

---

26. Peter saith unto him, Of strangers. Jesus saith unto him, Then are the children free.

Greek/Transliteration

26. Λέγει αὐτῷ ὁ Πέτρος, Ἀπὸ τῶν ἀλλοτρίων. Ἔφη αὐτῷ ὁ Ἰησοῦς, Ἄρα γε ἐλεύθεροί εἰσιν οἱ υἱοί.

26. Legei auto 'o Petros, Apo ton allotrion. Ephei auto 'o Yeisous, Ara ge eleutheroi eisin 'oi 'wioi.

Hebrew/Translieration

:כו. וַיֹּאמֶר אֵלָיו מִן-הַזָּרִים וַיֹּאמֶר אֵלָיו יֵשׁוּעַ לָכֵן חָפְשִׁים הֵם הַבָּנִים

26. Va•yo•mer elav min - ha•za•rim va•yo•mer elav Yeshua la•chen chof•shim hem ha•ba•nim.

27. Notwithstanding, lest we should offend them, go thou to the sea, and cast an hook, and take up the fish that first cometh up; and when thou hast opened his mouth, thou shalt find a piece of money: that take, and give unto them for me and thee.

Greek/Transliteration
27. Ἵνα δὲ μὴ σκανδαλίσωμεν αὐτούς, πορευθεὶς εἰς τὴν θάλασσαν βάλε ἄγκιστρον, καὶ τὸν ἀναβαίνοντα πρῶτον ἰχθὺν ἆρον· καὶ ἀνοίξας τὸ στόμα αὐτοῦ, εὑρήσεις στατῆρα· ἐκεῖνον λαβὼν δὸς αὐτοῖς ἀντὶ ἐμοῦ καὶ σοῦ.

27. 'Yna de mei skandalisomen autous, poreutheis eis tein thalassan bale agkistron, kai ton anabainonta proton ichthun aron. kai anoixas to stoma autou, 'eureiseis stateira. ekeinon labon dos autois anti emou kai sou.

Hebrew/Transliteration
כז. אֶפֶס פֶּן-נִתֵּן מוֹקֵשׁ לִפְנֵיהֶם לֵךְ אֶל-הַיָּם וְהַשְׁלֵךְ חַכָּה וְלָקַחְתָּ אֶת-הַדָּג אֲשֶׁר יַעֲלֶה רִאשֹׁנָה וּפָתַחְתָּ אֶת-פִּיו וּמָצָאתָ בוֹ שֶׁקֶל כֶּסֶף אֹתוֹ קַח וְשַׁלֵּם לָהֶם בַּעֲדִי וּבַעֲדֶךָ -

27. E•fes pen - ni•ten mo•kesh lif•ney•hem lech el - ha•yam ve•hash•lech cha•ka ve•la•kach•ta et - ha•dag asher ya•a•le ri•sho•na oo•fa•tach•ta et - piv oo•ma•tza•ta vo she•kel ke•sef o•to kach ve•sha•lem la•hem ba•a•di oo•va•a•de•cha.

Matthew, Chapter 18

1. At the same time came the disciples unto Jesus, saying, Who is the greatest in the kingdom of heaven?

Greek/Transliteration
1. Ἐν ἐκείνῃ τῇ ὥρᾳ προσῆλθον οἱ μαθηταὶ τῷ Ἰησοῦ, λέγοντες, Τίς ἄρα μείζων ἐστὶν ἐν τῇ βασιλείᾳ τῶν οὐρανῶν;

1. En ekeinei tei 'ora proseilthon 'oi matheitai to Yeisou, legontes, Tis ara meizon estin en tei basileia ton ouranon?

Hebrew/Transliteration
א. בָּעֵת הַהִיא בָּאוּ הַתַּלְמִידִים לִפְנֵי יֵשׁוּעַ וַיֹּאמְרוּ מִי הוּא הַגָּדוֹל בְּמַלְכוּת הַשָּׁמָיִם:

1. Ba•et ha•hee ba•oo ha•tal•mi•dim lif•ney Yeshua va•yom•roo mee hoo ha•ga•dol be•mal•choot ha•sha•ma•yim.

---

2. And Jesus called a little child unto him, and set him in the midst of them,

Greek/Transliteration
2. Καὶ προσκαλεσάμενος ὁ Ἰησοῦς παιδίον ἔστησεν αὐτὸ ἐν μέσῳ αὐτῶν,

2. Kai proskalesamenos 'o Yeisous paidion esteisen auto en meso auton,

Heberw/Transliteration
ב. וַיִּקְרָא יֵשׁוּעַ אֶל-יֶלֶד אֶחָד וַיַּצִּיגֵהוּ בְּתוֹכָם:

2. Va•yik•ra Yeshua el - ye•led e•chad va•ya•tzi•ge•hoo be•to•cham.

---

3. And said, Verily I say unto you, Except ye be converted, and become as little children, ye shall not enter into the kingdom of heaven.

Greek/Transliteration
3. καὶ εἶπεν, Ἀμὴν λέγω ὑμῖν, ἐὰν μὴ στραφῆτε καὶ γένησθε ὡς τὰ παιδία, οὐ μὴ εἰσέλθητε εἰς τὴν βασιλείαν τῶν οὐρανῶν.

3. kai eipen, Amein lego 'umin, ean mei strapheite kai geneisthe 'os ta paidia, ou mei eiseltheite eis tein basileian ton ouranon.

Hebrew/Transliteraton
ג. וַיֹּאמֶר אָמֵן אֲנִי אֹמֵר לָכֶם אִם-לֹא תָשׁוּבוּ לִהְיוֹת כַּיְלָדִים בֹּא לֹא תָבֹאוּ לְמַלְכוּת הַשָּׁמָיִם:

3. Va•yo•mar Amen ani o•mer la•chem eem - lo ta•shoo•voo li•hee•yot ka•ye•la•dim bo lo ta•vo•oo le•mal•choot ha•sha•ma•yim.

Jewish New Testament Commentary

Unless you change. Greek *strephô* ("turn") can mean inward turning, hence "repent" or "change." KJV renders the phrase, "except ye be converted." The "conversion" needed is not from Judaism but from the sin of self-seeking ambition to be "the greatest" (Mat_18:1). The conversion is not to Christianity or to an "-ism," but to God and relating personally with him through Yeshua the Messiah.

---

4. Whosoever therefore shall humble himself as this little child, the same is greatest in the kingdom of heaven.

Greek/Transliteration

4. Ὅστις οὖν ταπεινώσει ἑαυτὸν ὡς τὸ παιδίον τοῦτο, οὗτός ἐστιν ὁ μείζων ἐν τῇ βασιλείᾳ τῶν οὐρανῶν.

4. 'Ostis oun tapeinosei 'eauton 'os to paidion touto, 'outos estin 'o meizon en tei basileia ton ouranon.

Hebrew/Transliteration

ד: לָכֵן מִי אֲשֶׁר יַשְׁפִּיל אֶת-נַפְשׁוֹ כַּיֶּלֶד הַזֶּה הוּא הַגָּדוֹל בְּמַלְכוּת הַשָּׁמָיִם

4. La•chen mee asher yash•pil et - naf•sho ka•ye•led ha•ze hoo ha•ga•dol be•mal•choot ha•sha•ma•yim.

---

5. And whoso shall receive one such little child in my name receiveth me.

Greek/Transliteration

5. Καὶ ὃς ἐὰν δέξηται παιδίον τοιοῦτον ἓν ἐπὶ τῷ ὀνόματί μου, ἐμὲ δέχεται·

5. Kai 'os ean dexeitai paidion toiouton 'en epi to onomati mou, eme dechetai.

Hebrew/Transliteration

ה: וּמִי אֲשֶׁר יְקַבֵּל יֶלֶד כָּזֶה בִּשְׁמִי אֹתִי הוּא מְקַבֵּל

5. Oo•mi asher ye•ka•bel ye•led ka•ze bish•mi o•ti hoo me•ka•bel.

---

6. But whoso shall offend one of these little ones which believe in me, it were better for him that a millstone were hanged about his neck, and that he were drowned in the depth of the sea.

Greek/Transliteration

6. Ὃς δ᾽ ἂν σκανδαλίσῃ ἕνα τῶν μικρῶν τούτων τῶν πιστευόντων εἰς ἐμέ, συμφέρει αὐτῷ ἵνα κρεμασθῇ μύλος ὀνικὸς εἰς τὸν τράχηλον αὐτοῦ, καὶ καταποντισθῇ ἐν τῷ πελάγει τῆς θαλάσσης.

6. 'Os d an skandalisei 'ena ton mikron touton ton pisteuonton eis eme, sumpherei auto 'ina kremasthei mulos onikos eis ton tracheilon autou, kai katapontisthei en to pelagei teis thalasseis.

Hebrew/Transliteration

ו. וּמִי אֲשֶׁר יַכְשִׁיל אֶת אַחַד הַקְּטַנִּים הָאֵלֶה הַמַּאֲמִינִים בִּי טוֹב לוֹ כִּי יִתָּלֶה פֶּלַח-רֶכֶב עַל-צַוָּארוֹ וְיִשְׁקַע:בִּמְצוּלוֹת יָם

6. Oo•mi asher yach•shil et achad ha•ke•ta•nim ha•e•le ha•ma•a•mi•nim bi tov lo ki yit•le pe•lach - re•chev al - tza•va•ro ve•yish•ka bim•tzoo•lot yam.

Rabbinic Jewish Commentary

The word translated "depth", is sometimes used for the Sea itself, Isa_51:10 and signifies the middle, or deeper path, and answers to the Hebrew phrase, "the heart of the sea"; **פילגוס דימא רבא**, used by the Targum, in Psa_46:3 and by Jonathan ben Uzziel, in Exo_15:8.

The phrase of having a mill stone about the neck, I find, is sometimes used to denote anything very troublesome and burdensome (e). "The tradition is, a man that marries a wife, and after that learns the law, R. Jochanan says, **ריחים בצוארו**, "though a mill stone is about his neck", yet he must study in the law: that is, though his worldly circumstances are narrow, and his wife and family are as burdensome as if he had a mill stone about his neck, he must continue his studies." (e) T. Bab. Kiddusbin, fol. 29. 2.

---

7. Woe unto the world because of offences! for it must needs be that offences come; but woe to that man by whom the offence cometh!

Greek/Transliteration

7. Οὐαὶ τῷ κόσμῳ ἀπὸ τῶν σκανδάλων· ἀνάγκη γάρ ἐστιν ἐλθεῖν τὰ σκάνδαλα· πλὴν οὐαὶ τῷ ἀνθρώπῳ ἐκείνῳ, δι᾽ οὗ τὸ σκάνδαλον ἔρχεται.

7. Ouai to kosmo apo ton skandalon. anagkei gar estin elthein ta skandala. plein ouai to anthropo ekeino, di 'ou to skandalon erchetai.

Hebrew/Transliteration

ז. אוֹי לָעוֹלָם מִפְּנֵי מוֹקְשֶׁיהָ כִּי-הַמּוֹקְשִׁים בֹּא יָבֹאוּ אֶל-נָכוֹן אַךְ אוֹי לָאִישׁ הַהוּא אֲשֶׁר הַמּוֹקֵשׁ בָּא עַל-יָדוֹ:

7. Oy la•o•lam mip•ney mok•she•ha ki - ha•mok•shim bo ya•vo•oo el - na•chon ach oy la•eesh ha•hoo asher ha•mo•kesh ba al - ya•do.

---

8. Wherefore if thy hand or thy foot offend thee, cut them off, and cast them from thee: it is better for thee to enter into life halt or maimed, rather than having two hands or two feet to be cast into everlasting fire.

Greek/Transliteration

8. Εἰ δὲ ἡ χείρ σου ἢ ὁ πούς σου σκανδαλίζει σε, ἔκκοψον αὐτὰ καὶ βάλε ἀπὸ σοῦ· καλόν σοι ἐστὶν εἰσελθεῖν εἰς τὴν ζωὴν χωλὸν ἢ κυλλόν, ἢ δύο χεῖρας ἢ δύο πόδας ἔχοντα βληθῆναι εἰς τὸ πῦρ τὸ αἰώνιον.

8. Ei de 'ei cheir sou ei 'o pous sou skandalizei se, ekkopson auta kai bale apo sou. kalon soi estin eiselthein eis tein zoein cholon ei kullon, ei duo cheiras ei duo podas echonta bleitheinai eis to pur to aionion.

Hebrew/Transliteration

ח. וְאִם-יָדְךָ אוֹ רַגְלְךָ תַּכְשִׁילְךָ קַצֵּץ אֹתָהּ וְהַשְׁלִיכָהּ מִמֶּךָּ טוֹב לְךָ לָבֹא אֶל-הַחַיִּים קְטוּעַ-יָד אוֹ רֶגֶל מִהְיוֹת לְךָ שְׁתֵּי יָדַיִם וּשְׁתֵּי רַגְלַיִם וּלְהָשְׁלַךְ לְאֵשׁ עוֹלָם

8. Ve•eem - yad•cha oh rag•le•cha tach•shil•cha ka•tzetz o•ta ve•hash•li•che•ha mi•me•cha tov le•cha la•vo el - ha•cha•yim k`too•a - yad oh re•gel mi•hee•yot le•cha sh`tey ya•da•yim oosh•tey rag•la•yim ool•hosh•lach le•esh o•lam.

---

9. And if thine eye offend thee, pluck it out, and cast it from thee: it is better for thee to enter into life with one eye, rather than having two eyes to be cast into hell fire.

Greek/Transliteration

9. Καὶ εἰ ὁ ὀφθαλμός σου σκανδαλίζει σε, ἔξελε αὐτὸν καὶ βάλε ἀπὸ σοῦ· καλόν σοι ἐστὶν μονόφθαλμον εἰς τὴν ζωὴν εἰσελθεῖν, ἢ δύο ὀφθαλμοὺς ἔχοντα βληθῆναι εἰς τὴν γέενναν τοῦ πυρός.

9. Kai ei 'o ophthalmos sou skandalizei se, exele auton kai bale apo sou. kalon soi estin monophthalmon eis tein zoein eiselthein, ei duo ophthalmous echonta bleitheinai eis tein geennan tou puros.

Hebrew/Transliteration

ט. וְאִם-עֵינְךָ תַּכְשִׁילְךָ נַקֵּר אֹתָהּ וְהַשְׁלִיכָהּ מִמֶּךָּ טוֹב לְךָ לָבֹא אֶל-הַחַיִּים בְּעַיִן אַחַת מִהְיוֹת לְךָ שְׁתֵּי עֵינַיִם וּלְהָשְׁלַךְ לְאֵשׁ גֵּיהִנֹּם

9. Ve•eem - eyn•cha tach•shil•cha na•ker o•ta ve•hash•li•che•ha mi•me•cha tov le•cha la•vo el - ha•cha•yim be•a•yin a•chat mi•hee•yot le•cha sh`tey ey•na•yim ool•hosh•lach le•esh Gey•hi•nom.

---

10. Take heed that ye despise not one of these little ones; for I say unto you, That in heaven their angels do always behold the face of my Father which is in heaven.

Greek/Transliteration

10. Ὁρᾶτε μὴ καταφρονήσητε ἑνὸς τῶν μικρῶν τούτων, λέγω γὰρ ὑμῖν ὅτι οἱ ἄγγελοι αὐτῶν ἐν οὐρανοῖς διὰ παντὸς βλέπουσιν τὸ πρόσωπον τοῦ πατρός μου τοῦ ἐν οὐρανοῖς.

10. 'Orate mei kataphroneiseite 'enos ton mikron touton, lego gar 'umin 'oti 'oi angeloi auton en ouranois dya pantos blepousin to prosopon tou patros mou tou en ouranois.

Hebrew/Transliteration

י. הִשָּׁמְרוּ לָכֶם מִבְּזוֹת אַחַד הַקְּטַנִּים הָאֵלֶּה כִּי הִנְנִי אֹמֵר לָכֶם אֲשֶׁר מַלְאָכֵיהֶם בַּשָּׁמַיִם רֹאִים תָּמִיד אֶת־פְּנֵי־אָבִי אֲשֶׁר בַּשָּׁמָיִם

10. Hi•sham•roo la•chem mib•zot achad ha•ke•ta•nim ha•e•le ki hi•ne•ni o•mer la•chem asher mal•a•chey•hem ba•sha•ma•yim ro•eem ta•mid et - p`ney Avi asher ba•sha•ma•yim.

Rabbinic Jewish Commentary

This seems indeed to have been a notion that prevailed among the Jews, not only that there were messengers which presided over particular nations, but who also had the care of particular persons; so they speak of a messenger that was particularly appointed for Abraham (f). Nor will they allow, that one messenger does two messengers, nor two messengers one (g) messager: but that everyone has his particular place, person, and work. This description of messengers agrees with what the Jews say of them, especially of the chief of them. Michael, they say (h), is the first and principal of the chief princes, רואי פני המלך "that behold the face of the king"; that is, the King of kings, the Lord of hosts. Suriel, which, with them, is another name of a messenger, is called (i), שר הפנים, "the prince of faces", who is always in the presence of God; and, as the gloss says, is "an angel that is counted worthy to come before the king."

(f) T. Bab. Sanhedrim, fol. 96. 1. (g) Bereshit Rabba, sect. 50. fol. 44. 4. (h) Jacchiades in Dan. x. 13. (i) T. Bab. Beracot, fol. 51. 1.

---

11. [For the Son of man is come to save that which was lost.]

Greek/Transliteration

11. Ἦλθεν γὰρ ὁ υἱὸς τοῦ ἀνθρώπου σῶσαι τὸ ἀπολωλός.

11. Eilthen gar 'o 'wios tou anthropou sosai to apololos.

Hebrew/Transliteration

יא. כִּי בָא בֶן־הָאָדָם לְהוֹשִׁיעַ אֶת־הָאֹבֵד:

11. Ki va Ven - ha•adam le•ho•shi•a et - ha•o•ved.

Jewish New Testament Commentary
The manuscripts which add Mat_18:11 probably borrowed from Luk_19:10.

---

12. How think ye? if a man have an hundred sheep, and one of them be gone astray, doth he not leave the ninety and nine, and goeth into the mountains, and seeketh that which is gone astray?

Greek/Transliteration
12. Τί ὑμῖν δοκεῖ; Ἐὰν γένηταί τινι ἀνθρώπῳ ἑκατὸν πρόβατα, καὶ πλανηθῇ ἓν ἐξ αὐτῶν· οὐχὶ ἀφεὶς τὰ ἐνενήκοντα ἐννέα, ἐπὶ τὰ ὄρη πορευθεὶς ζητεῖ τὸ πλανώμενον;

12. Ti 'umin dokei? Ean geneitai tini anthropo 'ekaton probata, kai planeithei 'en ex auton. Ouchi apheis ta eneneikonta ennea, epi ta orei poreutheis zeitei to planomenon?

Hebrew/Transliteration
יב. מַה-תְּחַשְּׁבוּן אַתֶּם כִּי-תִהְיֶינָ לְאִישׁ מֵאָה צֹאן וְאַחַת מֵהֶן תֵּלֵךְ וְתֵתַע הַאִם לֹא יַעֲזֹב אֶת-הַתִּשְׁעִים וְאֶת-הַתֵּשַׁע וְיֵלֵךְ בֶּהָרִים לְבַקֵּשׁ אֶת-הַתֹּעָה -

12. Ma - te•chash•voon atem ki - ti•hi•ye•na le•eesh me•ah tzon ve•a•chat me•hen te•lech ve•te•ta ha•eem lo ya•a•zov et - ha•tish•eem ve•et - ha•te•sha ve•ye•lech be•ha•rim le•va•kesh et - ha•to•ah.

---

13. And if so be that he find it, verily I say unto you, he rejoiceth more of that sheep, than of the ninety and nine which went not astray.

Greek/Transliteration
13. Καὶ ἐὰν γένηται εὑρεῖν αὐτό, ἀμὴν λέγω ὑμῖν ὅτι χαίρει ἐπ᾽ αὐτῷ μᾶλλον, ἢ ἐπὶ τοῖς ἐνενήκοντα ἐννέα τοῖς μὴ πεπλανημένοις.

13. Kai ean geneitai 'eurein auto, amein lego 'umin 'oti chairei ep auto mallon, ei epi tois eneneikonta ennea tois mei peplaneimenois.

Hebrew/Transliteration
יג. וְהָיָה כִּי יִמְצָאֶנָּה הִנְנִי אֹמֵר לָכֶם כִּי-יִרַב לִשְׂמֹחַ עָלֶיהָ מֵעַל הַתִּשְׁעִים וְהַתֵּשַׁע אֲשֶׁר לֹא-תָעוּ:

13. Ve•ha•ya ki yim•tza•e•na hi•ne•ni o•mer la•chem ki - yi•rev lis•mo•ach a•le•ha me•al ha•tish•eem ve•ha•te•sha asher lo - ta•oo.

---

14. Even so it is not the will of your Father which is in heaven, that one of these little ones should perish.

Greek/Transliteration

14. Οὕτως οὐκ ἔστιν θέλημα ἔμπροσθεν τοῦ πατρὸς ὑμῶν τοῦ ἐν οὐρανοῖς, ἵνα ἀπόληται εἰς τῶν μικρῶν τούτων.

14. 'Outos ouk estin theleima emprosthen tou patros 'umon tou en ouranois, 'ina apoleitai 'eis ton mikron touton.

Hebrew/Transliteration

יד. וְכֵן אֵין רָצוֹן לִפְנֵי אֲבִיכֶם בַּשָּׁמַיִם כִּי יֹאבַד אֶחָד מִן-הַקְּטַנִּים הָאֵלֶּה:

14. Ve•chen eyn ra•tzon lif•ney Avi•chem ba•sha•ma•yim ki yo•vad e•chad min - ha•ke•ta•nim ha•e•le.

---

15. Moreover if thy brother shall trespass against thee, go and tell him his fault between thee and him alone: if he shall hear thee, thou hast gained thy brother.

Greek/Transliteration

15. Ἐὰν δὲ ἁμαρτήσῃ εἰς σὲ ὁ ἀδελφός σου, ὕπαγε καὶ ἔλεγξον αὐτὸν μεταξὺ σοῦ καὶ αὐτοῦ μόνου. Ἐάν σου ἀκούσῃ, ἐκέρδησας τὸν ἀδελφόν σου·

15. Ean de 'amarteisei eis se 'o adelphos sou, 'upage kai elegxon auton metaxu sou kai autou monou. Ean sou akousei, ekerdeisas ton adelphon sou.

Hebrew/Transliteration

טו. וְכִי יֶחֱטָא-לְךָ אָחִיךָ לֵךְ וְהוֹכִיחֵהוּ בֵּינְךָ וּבֵינוֹ לְבָד אִם-יַקְשִׁיב אֵלֶיךָ הֲלֹא הִצַּלְתָּ אֶת-אָחִיךָ:

15. Ve•chi yech•ta - le•cha a•chi•cha lech ve•ho•chi•che•hoo bein•cha oo•vey•no le•vad eem - yak•shiv e•le•cha ha•lo hi•tzal•ta et - a•chi•cha.

---

16. But if he will not hear thee, then take with thee one or two more, that in the mouth of two or three witnesses every word may be established.

Greek/Transliteration

16. ἐὰν δὲ μὴ ἀκούσῃ, παράλαβε μετὰ σοῦ ἔτι ἕνα ἢ δύο, ἵνα ἐπὶ στόματος δύο μαρτύρων ἢ τριῶν σταθῇ πᾶν ῥῆμα·

16. ean de mei akousei, paralabe meta sou eti 'ena ei duo, 'ina epi stomatos duo marturon ei trion stathei pan 'reima.

Hebrew/Transliteration

טז. וְאִם-לֹא יַקְשִׁיב לְקוֹלְךָ וְלָקַחְתָּ לְךָ עוֹד אֶחָד אוֹ שְׁנַיִם כִּי עַל-פִּי שְׁנַיִם אוֹ שְׁלֹשָׁה עֵדִים יָקוּם כָּל-דָּבָר:

16. Ve•eem - lo yak•shiv le•kol•cha ve•la•kach•ta le•cha od e•chad oh sh`na•yim ki al - pi sh`na•yim oh sh`lo•sha e•dim ya•koom kol - da•var.

Rabbinic Jewish Commentary

The whole of this is very agreeable to the rules and customs of the Jews, and is founded on the law, in Lev_19:17, upon which they form rules very much like to these. They represent God himself taking such a method as this, with the sons of men (m): "When the holy blessed God reproves a man, he reproves him in love, privately: if he receives it, it is well; if not, he reproves him among his friends: if he receives it, it is well; if not he reproves him openly before the eyes of all; if he receives it is well; if not, he leaves him, and reproves him no more."

And this is an instruction to men, how they should reprove their friends. They say (n), "he that sees anything in his friend that is not becoming, he ought to reprove him." And which is elsewhere more (o) largely expressed: "he that seeth his friend walking in a way that is not good, he is bound to reprove him, even a disciple his master; and this he shall do for his good, and in order to bring him to the life of the world to come, or eternal life; and "if he takes it of him, it is well": but if not, he must reprove again, "a second and a third time"; and so he must reprove him many times, if, or until he hears him." And this they require to be done, in the most private manner: "reproof out of love (they (p) say) is secret from the children of men; whoever reproves his friend in love, seeks to secrete his words from the sons of men, that he may not expose him thereby to shame and reproach."

That is, as the gloss (q) on it observes, "he seeks to reprove him in secret, so that he may not be put to shame before many." If this way does not succeed, they allow of a public reproof, for so it is said (r); "thou mayest not reprove him with hard words, till his countenance changes; for whoever causes the face of his friend to turn pale publicly, has no portion in the world to come; but thou mayest reprove in the words of heaven, or God; and if he does not return privately, thou mayest make him ashamed publicly, and expose his sin before him; and reproach and curse him, until he returns to do well; so did all the prophets to Israel."

They plead also for a second reproof, from the text in Lev_19:17 (s). "From whence does it appear, that he that sees anything in his friend unbecoming, ought to reprove him? As it is said, "thou shalt in any wise rebuke", &c. if he reproves him, ולא קבל, "and he does not receive it", (he does not take it kindly, or, as here, he does not hear him,) from whence is it manifest, that he must return and reprove him (or repeat the reproof)? from what is said, reproving thou shall reprove."

The whole of this is very fully expressed in a few words, by one (t) of their best writers, and in great agreement with these rules of Yeshua: "He that sees his friend sinning, or going in a way not good, he is commanded to cause him to return to that which is good; and to let him know, that he sins against himself by his evil works; as it is said, "thou shalt in any wise rebuke thy neighbour": he that reproveth his friend, whether for things between him and himself, or whether for things between him and God, "ought to reprove him", בינו לבין עצמו, "between him and himself"; and should speak to him mildly, and in tender language; and let him know that he does not speak to, him, but for his good, and to bring him to everlasting life; "and if he receives it of him, it is well, and if not, he must reprove him", פעם שנייה ושלישית, "a second and a third time"; and so a man must continually reprove, until the sinner strikes him and says", I will not hear.""

Buxtorf has produced a passage out of one of their writers (u), in the very language in which Yeshua here delivers himself: "The wise man says, if thy friend does thee an injury, reprove him between him and thee alone: if he hears thee, thou hast already gained; if he does not hear thee, speak to him before one or two, who may hear the matter, and if he will not hear reckon him a "worthless friend"."

One would almost be ready to think, that this writer should mean Yeshua by the wise man, were it not for the implacable enmity they bear unto him. The above author has cited also the following passage out of the same (w) writer, pertinent to the present purpose: "A friend that declares to thee thy faults, "between him and thee", whenever he meets thee, is better to thee than a friend, that whenever he meets thee, gives thee a golden penny."

(m) Raya Mehimna in Zohar, in Lev. fol. 35. 4. (n) T. Bab. Betacot, fol. 31. 1, 2. (o) Moses Kotsensis Mitzvot Tora pr. Affirm. 11. (p) Zohar. in Lev. fol. 19. 3. (q) Imre Binah in ib. (r) Milzvot Tora, pr. neg. 6. (s) T. Bab. Erachin, fol. 16. 2. (t) Maimon. Hilch. Deyot. c. 6. sect. 7. (u) Mischar happeninim apud Buxtorf. Florileg. Heb. p. 297. (w) Ibid.

---

17. And if he shall neglect to hear them, tell it unto the church: but if he neglect to hear the church, let him be unto thee as an heathen man and a publican.

Greek/Transliteration
17. ἐὰν δὲ παρακούσῃ αὐτῶν, εἰπὲ τῇ ἐκκλησίᾳ· ἐὰν δὲ καὶ τῆς ἐκκλησίας παρακούσῃ, ἔστω σοι ὥσπερ ὁ ἐθνικὸς καὶ ὁ τελώνης.

17. ean de parakousei auton, eipe tei ekkleisia. ean de kai teis ekkleisias parakousei, esto soi 'osper 'o ethnikos kai 'o teloneis.

Hebrew/Transliteration
יז. וְאִם יְמָאֵן לְהַקְשִׁיב לָהֶם וְהִגַּדְתָּ אֶל־הָעֵדָה וְאִם גַּם־אֶל־הָעֵדָה מָאֵן יְמָאֵן לִשְׁמֹעַ וְהָיָה לְךָ כְּגוֹי וּכְמוֹכֵס:

17. Ve•eem ye•ma•en le•hak•shiv la•hem ve•hi•ga•de•ta el - ha•e•da ve•eem gam - el - ha•e•da ma•en ye•ma•en lish•mo•a ve•ha•ya le•cha ke•goy ooch•mo•ches.

---

18. Verily I say unto you, Whatsoever ye shall bind on earth shall be bound in heaven: and whatsoever ye shall loose on earth shall be loosed in heaven.

Greek/Transliteration

18. Ἀμὴν λέγω ὑμῖν, ὅσα ἐὰν δήσητε ἐπὶ τῆς γῆς, ἔσται δεδεμένα ἐν τῷ οὐρανῷ· καὶ ὅσα ἐὰν λύσητε ἐπὶ τῆς γῆς, ἔσται λελυμένα ἐν τῷ οὐρανῷ.

18. Amein lego 'umin, 'osa ean deiseite epi teis geis, estai dedemena en to ourano. kai 'osa ean luseite epi teis geis, estai lelumena en to ourano.

Hebrew/Transliteration

יח. אָמֵן אֲנִי אֹמֵר לָכֶם אֵת אֲשֶׁר תַּאַסְרוּ עַל-הָאָרֶץ אָסוּר יִהְיֶה בַּשָּׁמַיִם וְאֵת אֲשֶׁר תַּתִּירוּ עַל-הָאָרֶץ מֻתָּר יִהְיֶה:בַּשָּׁמַיִם

18. Amen ani o•mer la•chem et asher ta•as•roo al - ha•a•retz a•soor yi•hee•ye ba•sha•ma•yim ve•et asher ta•ti•roo al - ha•a•retz moo•tar yi•hee•ye ba•sha•ma•yim.

Jewish New Testamet Commentary

See first Matthew 16:19; The words rendered "prohibit" and "permit" (Mat_18:18) are, literally, "bind" and "loose." These terms were used in first century Judaism to mean "prohibit" and "permit," as is clear from the article, "Binding and Loosing," in the *Jewish Encyclopedia*, 3:215: "BINDING AND LOOSING (Hebrew *asar ve-hittir*)... Rabbinical term for 'forbidding and permitting.' ... "The power of binding and loosing was always claimed by the Pharisees. Under Queen Alexandra the Pharisees, says Josephus (*Wars of the Jews* 1:5:2), 'became the administrators of all public affairs so as to be empowered to banish and readmit whom they pleased, as well as to loose and to bind.'... The various schools had the power 'to bind and to loose'; that is, to forbid and permit (Talmud: Chagigah 3b); and they could bind any day by declaring it a fast-day (... Talmud: Ta'anit 12a ...). This power and authority, vested in the rabbinical body of each age or in the Sanhedrin, received its ratification and final sanction from the celestial court of justice (Sifra, Emor, ix; Talmud: Makkot 23b).

---

19. Again I say unto you, That if two of you shall agree on earth as touching any thing that they shall ask, it shall be done for them of my Father which is in heaven.

Greek/Transliteration

19. Πάλιν ἀμὴν λέγω ὑμῖν, ὅτι ἐὰν δύο ὑμῶν συμφωνήσωσιν ἐπὶ τῆς γῆς περὶ παντὸς πράγματος οὗ ἐὰν αἰτήσωνται, γενήσεται αὐτοῖς παρὰ τοῦ πατρός μου τοῦ ἐν οὐρανοῖς.

19. Palin amein lego 'umin, 'oti ean duo 'umon sumphoneisosin epi teis geis peri pantos pragmatos 'ou ean aiteisontai, geneisetai autois para tou patros mou tou en ouranois.

Hebrew/Transliteration

יט. וְאוֹסִיף אֹמַר לָכֶם אִם שְׁנַיִם מִכֶּם נוֹעֲדוּ יַחְדָּו בָּאָרֶץ עַל-כָּל-דָּבָר אֲשֶׁר יִשְׁאָלוּ וְנָתַן לָהֶם אָבִי בַּשָּׁמַיִם כְּכֹל:מִשְׁאֲלוֹת לִבָּם

19. Ve•o•sif o•mar la•chem eem sh`na•yim mi•kem no•a•doo yach•dav ba•a•retz al – kol - da•var asher yish•a•loo ve•na•tan la•hem Avi ba•sha•ma•yim ke•chol mish•a•lot li•bam.

Jewish New Testament Commentary

The usual Christian view of Mat_18:19-20 is that it defines a "Messianic *minyan*" not as the quorum of ten established by *halakhah* (Talmud, Sanhedrin 2b) for public synagogue prayers, but as two or three assembled in Yeshua's name, plus Yeshua himself, who is there with them (Mat_18:20). The problem with this is that the passage is not about prayer-although it is not wrong to make a *midrash* on it which does apply to prayer (see below and Mat_2:15). Rather, Yeshua, speaking to those who have authority to regulate Messianic communal life (Mat_18:15-17), commissions them to establish New Covenant *halakhah*, that is, to make authoritative decisions where there is a question about how Messianic life ought to be lived. In Mat_18:19 Yeshua is teaching that when an issue is brought formally to a panel of two or three Messianic Community leaders, and they render a halakhic decision here on earth, they can be assured that the authority of God in heaven stands behind them. Compare the Mishna:

"Rabbi Chananyah ben-T'radyon said, 'If two sit together and words of *Torah* pass between them, the *Sh'khinah* abides between them, as it is said, "Those who feared *Adonai* spoke together, and *Adonai* paid heed and listened, and a record was written before him for those who feared *Adonai* and thought on his name" (Mal_3:16).' " (Avot 3:2)

Curiously, the following extract from the Talmud provides a Jewish setting for both my understanding and the traditional Christian one. "How do you know that if ten people pray together the *Sh'khinah* ["manifested divine presence"] is there with them? Because it is said, 'God stands in the congregation of God' (Psa_82:1) [and a "congregation" must have a *minyan* of at least ten]. And how do you know that if three are sitting as a court of judges the *Sh'khinah* is there with them? Because it is said, 'In the midst of judges he renders judgment' (Psa_82:1 [taking *elohim* to mean "judges"; compare Joh_10:34-36])." (B'rakhot 6a)

---

20. For where two or three are gathered together in my name, there am I in the midst of them.

Greek/Transliteration
20. Οὗ γάρ εἰσιν δύο ἢ τρεῖς συνηγμένοι εἰς τὸ ἐμὸν ὄνομα, ἐκεῖ εἰμὶ ἐν μέσῳ αὐτῶν.

20. 'Ou gar eisin duo ei treis suneigmenoi eis to emon onoma, ekei eimi en meso auton.

Hebrew/Transliteration
כ: כִּי בְּכָל-מָקוֹם אֲשֶׁר שְׁנַיִם אוֹ שְׁלֹשָׁה יִקָּהֲלוּ בִשְׁמִי שָׁמָּה אֶהְיֶה אֲנִי בְּתוֹכָם

20. Ki be•chol - ma•kom asher sh`na•yim oh sh`lo•sha yi•ka•ha•loo vish•mi sha•ma e•he•ye ani be•to•cham.

Rabbinic Jewish Commentary

there am I in the midst of them; presiding over them, ruling in their hearts, directing their counsels, assisting them in all they are concerned, confirming what they do, and giving a blessing and success to all they are engaged in. The Jews, though they say there is no congregation less than ten, yet own that the divine presence may be with a lesser number, even as small an one as here mentioned (b).

"Ten that sit and study in the law, the Shechaniah dwells among them, as it is said, Psa_82:1. From whence does this appear, if but five? from Amo_9:6, from whence, if but three? from Psa_82:1, from whence, if but two? from Mal_3:16, from whence, if but one? from Exo_20:24." And again (c),

"two that sit together, and the words of the law are between them, the Shechaniah dwells among them, according to Mal_3:16, from whence does it appear, that if but one sits and studies in the law, the holy blessed God hath fixed a reward for him? from Lam_3:28."

(a) Misn. Sanhedrim, c. 1. sect. 6. T. Bab. Megilia, fol. 23. 2. Gloss. in ib. (b) Pirke Abot, c. 3. sect. 6. (c) Ib. sect. 2.

---

21. Then came Peter to him, and said, Lord, how oft shall my brother sin against me, and I forgive him? till seven times?

Greek/Transliteration

21. Τότε προσελθὼν αὐτῷ ὁ Πέτρος εἶπεν, Κύριε, ποσάκις ἁμαρτήσει εἰς ἐμὲ ὁ ἀδελφός μου, καὶ ἀφήσω αὐτῷ; Ἕως ἑπτάκις;

21. Tote proselthon auto 'o Petros eipen, Kurie, posakis 'amarteisei eis eme 'o adelphos mou, kai apheiso auto? 'Eos 'eptakis?

Hebrew/Transliteration

כא. אָז נִגַּשׁ פֶּטְרוֹס וַיֹּאמֶר לוֹ אֲדֹנִי עַד-כַּמָּה פְעָמִים יֶחֱטָא-לוֹ אָחִי וְאֶסְלַח לוֹ הַאִם עַד-שֶׁבַע פְּעָמִים:

21. Az ni•gash Petros va•yo•mer lo Adoni ad - ka•me fe•a•mim yech•ta - lo achi ve•es•lach lo ha•eem ad - she•va pe•a•mim.

Rabbinic Jewish Commentary

until seven times? Which was, as he might think, a large number; and especially, since it was double the number of times, that the Jewish leaders set for forgiveness: for thus they say (d), "A man that commits a sin, the "first" time they pardon him; the "second" time they pardon him; the "third" time they pardon him: the "fourth" time they do not pardon, according to Amo_2:6." Again, "he that says I have sinned, and I repent, they forgive him "unto three times", and no more (e)."

(d) T. Bab. Yoma, fol. 36. 2. Mainion. Hilch. Teshuba. c. 3. sect. 5. (e) Abot. R. Nathan, c. 40. fol. 9. 3.

22. Jesus saith unto him, I say not unto thee, Until seven times: but, Until seventy times seven.

Greek/Transliteration
22. Λέγει αὐτῷ ὁ Ἰησοῦς, Οὐ λέγω σοι ἕως ἑπτάκις, ἀλλ᾽ ἕως ἑβδομηκοντάκις ἑπτά.

22. Legei auto 'o Yeisous, Ou lego soi 'eos 'eptakis, all 'eos 'ebdomeikontakis 'epta.

Hebrew/Transliteration
כב. וַיֹּאמֶר אֵלָיו יֵשׁוּעַ לֹא-אָמַרְתִּי לְךָ עַד-שֶׁבַע פְּעָמִים כִּי-אִם עַד-שִׁבְעִים וָשֶׁבַע:

22. Va•yo•mer elav Yeshua lo - amar•ti le•cha ad - she•va pe•a•mim ki - eem ad - shiv•eem va•she•va.

23. Therefore is the kingdom of heaven likened unto a certain king, which would take account of his servants.

Greek/Transliteration
23. Διὰ τοῦτο ὡμοιώθη ἡ βασιλεία τῶν οὐρανῶν ἀνθρώπῳ βασιλεῖ, ὃς ἠθέλησεν συνᾶραι λόγον μετὰ τῶν δούλων αὐτοῦ.

23. Dya touto 'omoiothei 'ei basileia ton ouranon anthropo basilei, 'os eitheleisen sunarai logon meta ton doulon autou.

Hebrew/Transliteration
כג. לָכֵן דָּמְתָה מַלְכוּת הַשָּׁמַיִם לְמֶלֶךְ אֲשֶׁר בִּקֵּשׁ חֶשְׁבּוֹן מִן-עֲבָדָיו:

23. La•chen dam•ta mal•choot ha•sha•ma•yim le•me•lech asher bi•kesh chesh•bon min - ava•dav.

24. And when he had begun to reckon, one was brought unto him, which owed him ten thousand talents.

Greek/Transliteration
24. Ἀρξαμένου δὲ αὐτοῦ συναίρειν, προσηνέχθη αὐτῷ εἷς ὀφειλέτης μυρίων ταλάντων.

24. Arxamenou de autou sunairein, proseinechthei auto 'eis opheileteis murion talanton.

Hebrew/Transliteration

כד. וְכַאֲשֶׁר הֵחֵל לְחַשֵּׁב וַיָּבִיאוּ אֵלָיו אִישׁ אֲשֶׁר נָשָׁה בוֹ עֲשֶׂרֶת אֲלָפִים כִּכַּר־כָּסֶף:

24. Ve•cha•a•sher he`chel le•cha•shev va•ya•vi•oo elav eesh asher na•sha vo a•se•ret ala•fim ki•kar - ka•sef.

Jewish New Testament Commentary

Literally, "ten thousand talents." In Roman times one talent equalled 6,000 denarii, a denarius being roughly a day's wages for a common laborer. If a day's wages today is in the neighborhood of $50, 10,000 talents would be $3 billion! In the *Tanakh* a talent weighs 75.6 avoirdupois pounds. This amount of gold, at $350/troy ounce, is worth nearly $4 billion; the same amount of silver, at $4/troy ounce, comes to over $40 million. Haman offered King Achashverosh of Persia 10,000 talents of silver to destroy the Jews (Est_3:9). The museum in Heraklion, Crete, displays 3,500-year-old Minoan talents-metal ingots used to settle debts.

---

25. But forasmuch as he had not to pay, his lord commanded him to be sold, and his wife, and children, and all that he had, and payment to be made.

Greek/Transliteration

25. Μὴ ἔχοντος δὲ αὐτοῦ ἀποδοῦναι ἐκέλευσεν αὐτὸν ὁ κύριος αὐτοῦ πραθῆναι, καὶ τὴν γυναῖκα αὐτοῦ καὶ τὰ τέκνα, καὶ πάντα ὅσα εἶχεν, καὶ ἀποδοθῆναι.

25. Mei echontos de autou apodounai ekeleusen auton 'o kurios autou pratheinai, kai tein gunaika autou kai ta tekna, kai panta 'osa eichen, kai apodotheinai.

Hebrew/Transliteration

כה. וְלֹא הָיָה בְיָדוֹ לְשַׁלֵּם וַיְצַו עָלָיו אֲדֹנָיו כִּי יִמָּכֵר הוּא וְאִשְׁתּוֹ וּבָנָיו וְכָל־אֲשֶׁר־לוֹ וְשַׁלֵּם יְשַׁלֵּם:

25. Ve•lo ha•ya ve•ya•do le•sha•lem vay•tzav alav a•do•nav ki yi•ma•cher hoo ve•eesh•to oo•va•nav ve•chol - asher - lo ve•sha•lem ye•sha•lem.

Rabbinic Jewish Commentary

These children, by the Jewish writers (i), are said to be the children of Obadiah, who contracted the debt to feed the prophets in a cave, when they were persecuted by Jezebel; and the creditor, according to them, was Jehoram, the son of Ahab, who lent him money on usury for this purpose, in his father's time; and now Obadiah being dead, he takes his children for the debt, and makes them bondmen.

(i) Targum Jon. in loc. Tanchuma in Abarbinel in loc. Jarchi, Kimchi & Laniado in ib.

26. The servant therefore fell down, and worshipped him, saying, Lord, have patience with me, and I will pay thee all.

Greek/Transliteration
26. Πεσὼν οὖν ὁ δοῦλος προσεκύνει αὐτῷ, λέγων, Κύριε, Μακροθύμησον ἐπ' ἐμοί, καὶ πάντα σοι ἀποδώσω.

26. Peson oun 'o doulos prosekunei auto, legon, Kurie, Makrothumeison ep emoi, kai panta soi apodoso.

Hebrew/Transliteration
כו. וַיִּפֹּל הָעֶבֶד וַיִּשְׁתַּחוּ לוֹ לֵאמֹר אֲדֹנִי הַאֲרֶךְ-נָא אַפְּךָ וְאֶת-כָּל-נִשְׁיִי אֲשַׁלֵּמָה:

26. Va•yi•pol ha•e•ved va•yish•ta•choo lo le•mor Adoni ha•a•rech - na ap•cha ve•et - kol - nish•yi a•sha•le•ma.

---

27. Then the lord of that servant was moved with compassion, and loosed him, and forgave him the debt.

Greek/Transliteration
27. Σπλαγχνισθεὶς δὲ ὁ κύριος τοῦ δούλου ἐκείνου ἀπέλυσεν αὐτόν, καὶ τὸ δάνειον ἀφῆκεν αὐτῷ.

27. Splagchnistheis de 'o kurios tou doulou ekeinou apelusen auton, kai to daneion apheiken auto.

Hebrew/Transliteration
כז. וַיִּכָּמְרוּ רַחֲמֵי הָאָדוֹן עַל-הָעֶבֶד הַהוּא וַיְשַׁלְּחֵהוּ וְשָׁמוֹט לוֹ חוֹבוֹ:

27. Va•yi•kam•roo ra•cha•mey ha•Adon al - ha•e•ved ha•hoo va•ye•shal•che•hoo ve•sha•mot lo cho•vo.

---

28. But the same servant went out, and found one of his fellowservants, which owed him an hundred pence: and he laid hands on him, and took him by the throat, saying, Pay me that thou owest.

Greek/Transliteration
28. Ἐξελθὼν δὲ ὁ δοῦλος ἐκεῖνος εὗρεν ἕνα τῶν συνδούλων αὐτοῦ, ὃς ὤφειλεν αὐτῷ ἑκατὸν δηνάρια, καὶ κρατήσας αὐτὸν ἔπνιγεν, λέγων, Ἀπόδος μοι εἴ τι ὀφείλεις.

28. Exelthon de 'o doulos ekeinos 'euren 'ena ton sundoulon autou, 'os opheilen auto 'ekaton deinarya, kai krateisas auton epnigen, legon, Apodos moi ei ti opheileis.

Hebrew/Transliteration

כח. וַיֵּצֵא הָעֶבֶד הַהוּא מִלְּפָנָיו וַיִּמְצָא אֶת אַחַד הָעֲבָדִים אִישׁ עֲמִיתוֹ אֲשֶׁר נָשָׁה בוֹ מֵאָה כָסֶף וַיִּתְפָּשׂ-בּוֹ:וַיְחַנְקֵהוּ לֵאמֹר שַׁלֶּם-לִי אֵת אֲשֶׁר נָשִׁיתָ

28. Va•ye•tze ha•e•ved ha•hoo mil•fa•nav va•yim•tza et achad ha•a•va•dim eesh ami•to asher na•sha vo me•ah cha•sef va•yit•pos - bo vay•chan•ke•hoo le•mor sha•lem - li et asher na•shi•ta.

---

29. And his fellowservant fell down at his feet, and besought him, saying, Have patience with me, and I will pay thee all.

Greek/Transliteration

29. Πεσὼν οὖν ὁ σύνδουλος αὐτοῦ εἰς τοὺς πόδας αὐτοῦ παρεκάλει αὐτόν, λέγων, Μακροθύμησον ἐπ᾽ ἐμοί, καὶ ἀποδώσω σοι.

29. Peson oun 'o sundoulos autou eis tous podas autou parekalei auton, legon, Makrothumeison ep emoi, kai apodoso soi.

Hebrew/Transliteration

:כט. וַיִּפֹּל הָעֶבֶד אִישׁ עֲמִיתוֹ לִפְנֵי רַגְלָיו וַיִּתְחַנֶּן-לוֹ לֵאמֹר הַאֲרֶךְ-נָא אַפְּךָ וַאֲשַׁלְּמָה לְךָ הַכֹּל

29. Va•yi•pol ha•e•ved eesh ami•to lif•ney rag•lav va•yit•cha•nen - lo le•mor ha•a•rech - na ap•cha va•a•shal•ma le•cha ha•kol.

---

30. And he would not: but went and cast him into prison, till he should pay the debt.

Greek/Transliteration

30. Ὁ δὲ οὐκ ἤθελεν, ἀλλὰ ἀπελθὼν ἔβαλεν αὐτὸν εἰς φυλακήν, ἕως οὗ ἀποδῷ τὸ ὀφειλόμενον.

30. 'O de ouk eithelen, alla apelthon ebalen auton eis phulakein, 'eos 'ou apodo to opheilomenon.

Hebrew/Transliteration

:ל. וְלֹא אָבָה אַךְ הָלַךְ וַיִּתְּנֵהוּ אֶל-הַמִּשְׁמָר עַד-אֲשֶׁר יְשַׁלֵּם אֶת-נִשְׁיוֹ

30. Ve•lo ava ach ha•lach va•yit•ne•hoo el - ha•mish•mar ad - asher ye•sha•lem et - nish•yo.

---

31. So when his fellowservants saw what was done, they were very sorry, and came and told unto their lord all that was done.

Greek/Transliteration

31. Ἰδόντες δὲ οἱ σύνδουλοι αὐτοῦ τὰ γενόμενα ἐλυπήθησαν σφόδρα· καὶ ἐλθόντες διεσάφησαν τῷ κυρίῳ ἑαυτῶν πάντα τὰ γενόμενα.

31. Idontes de 'oi sundouloi autou ta genomena elupeitheisan sphodra. kai elthontes diesapheisan to kurio 'eauton panta ta genomena.

Hebrew/Transliteration

לא. וְאֶחָיו הָעֲבָדִים בִּרְאוֹתָם אֶת-אֲשֶׁר קָרָה הִתְעַצְּבוּ עַד-מְאֹד וַיָּבֹאוּ וַיְסַפְּרוּ לַאֲדֹנֵיהֶם אֶת-כָּל אֲשֶׁר קָרָה:

31. Ve•e•chav ha•a•va•dim bir•o•tam et - asher ka•ra hit•atz•voo ad - me•od va•ya•vo•oo va•ye•sap•roo la•a•do•ney•hem et - kol asher ka•ra.

---

32. Then his lord, after that he had called him, said unto him, O thou wicked servant, I forgave thee all that debt, because thou desiredst me:

Greek/Transliteration

32. Τότε προσκαλεσάμενος αὐτὸν ὁ κύριος αὐτοῦ λέγει αὐτῷ, Δοῦλε πονηρέ, πᾶσαν τὴν ὀφειλὴν ἐκείνην ἀφῆκά σοι, ἐπεὶ παρεκάλεσάς με·

32. Tote proskalesamenos auton 'o kurios autou legei auto, Doule poneire, pasan tein opheilein ekeinein apheika soi, epei parekalesas me.

Hebrew/Transliteration

לב. אָז קָרָא לוֹ אֲדֹנָיו וַיֹּאמֶר אֵלָיו עֶבֶד בְּלִיַּעַל אֶת-כָּל-הַחוֹב הַהוּא שָׁמַטְתִּי לְךָ כַּאֲשֶׁר הִתְחַנַּנְתָּ לְפָנָי:

32. Az ka•ra lo a•do•nav va•yo•mer elav eved b`li•ya•al et - kol - ha•chov ha•hoo sha•ma•te•ti le•cha ka•a•sher hit•cha•nan•ta le•fa•nai.

---

33. Shouldest not thou also have had compassion on thy fellowservant, even as I had pity on thee?

Greek/Transliteration

33. οὐκ ἔδει καὶ σὲ ἐλεῆσαι τὸν σύνδουλόν σου, ὡς καὶ ἐγώ σε ἠλέησα;

33. ouk edei kai se eleeisai ton sundoulon sou, 'os kai ego se eileeisa?

Hebrew/Transliteration

לג. הֲלֹא הָיָה גַם-עָלֶיךָ לְרַחֵם עַל-הָעֶבֶד אָחִיךָ כַּאֲשֶׁר רִחַמְתִּי עָלֶיךָ אָנִי:

33. Ha•lo ha•ya gam - a•le•cha le•ra•chem al - ha•e•ved a•chi•cha ka•a•sher ri•cham•ti a•le•cha ani.

34. And his lord was wroth, and delivered him to the tormentors, till he should pay all that was due unto him.

Greek/Transliteration
34. Καὶ ὀργισθεὶς ὁ κύριος αὐτοῦ παρέδωκεν αὐτὸν τοῖς βασανισταῖς, ἕως οὗ ἀποδῷ πᾶν τὸ ὀφειλόμενον αὐτῷ.

34. Kai orgistheis 'o kurios autou paredoken auton tois basanistais, 'eos 'ou apodo pan to opheilomenon auto.

Hebrew/Transliteration
:לד. וַיִּחַר אַף אֲדֹנָיו וַיִּתְּנֵהוּ בְּיַד-נֹגְשִׂים עַד-כִּי-יְשַׁלֵּם אֶת-כָּל-אֲשֶׁר נָשָׁה בוֹ

34. Va•yi•char af a•do•nav va•yit•ne•hoo be•yad - nog•shim ad - ki - ye•sha•lem et - kol - asher na•sha vo.

---

35. So likewise shall my heavenly Father do also unto you, if ye from your hearts forgive not every one his brother their trespasses.

Greek/Transliteration
35. Οὕτως καὶ ὁ πατήρ μου ὁ ἐπουράνιος ποιήσει ὑμῖν, ἐὰν μὴ ἀφῆτε ἕκαστος τῷ ἀδελφῷ αὐτοῦ ἀπὸ τῶν καρδιῶν ὑμῶν τὰ παραπτώματα αὐτῶν.

35. 'Outos kai 'o pateir mou 'o epouranios poieisei 'umin, ean mei apheite 'ekastos to adelpho autou apo ton kardion 'umon ta paraptomata auton.

Hebrew/Transliteration
:לה. כָּכָה יַעֲשֶׂה לָכֶם גַּם-אָבִי בַּשָּׁמַיִם אִם-לֹא תִסְלְחוּ בְּכָל-לִבְּכֶם אִישׁ לְאָחִיו עַל-חַטֹּאתָם

35. Ka•cha ya•a•se la•chem gam - Avi ba•sha•ma•yim eem - lo tis•le•choo be•chol - lib•chem eesh eesh le•a•chiv al - cha•to•tam.

Rabbinic Jewish Commentary
he will do also unto you, if ye from your hearts forgive not every one his brother their trespasses. The phrase, "their trespasses", is omitted by the Vulgate Latin, the Arabic, and the Ethiopic versions, but is in all the Greek copies; and designs not pecuniary debts, though these are to be forgiven, and not rigorously exacted in some cases, and circumstances; but all injuries by word or deed, all offences, though ever so justly taken, or unjustly given; these should be forgiven fully, freely, and from the heart, forgetting, as well as forgiving, not upbraiding with them, or with former offences, and aggravating them; and should also pray to God that he would forgive also. It is certainly the will of God, that we should forgive one another all trespasses and offences.

Matthew, Chapter 19

1. And it came to pass, that when Jesus had finished these sayings, he departed from Galilee, and came into the coasts of Judaea beyond Jordan;

Greek/Transliteration
1. Καὶ ἐγένετο ὅτε ἐτέλεσεν ὁ Ἰησοῦς τοὺς λόγους τούτους, μετῆρεν ἀπὸ τῆς Γαλιλαίας, καὶ ἦλθεν εἰς τὰ ὅρια τῆς Ἰουδαίας πέραν τοῦ Ἰορδάνου.

1. Kai egeneto 'ote etelesen 'o Yeisous tous logous toutous, meteiren apo teis Galilaias, kai eilthen eis ta 'orya teis Youdaias peran tou Yordanou.

Hebrew/Transliteration
א. וַיְהִי כַּאֲשֶׁר כִּלָּה יֵשׁוּעַ לְדַבֵּר אֶת הַדְּבָרִים הָאֵלֶּה וַיַּעֲבֹר מִן-הַגָּלִיל וַיָּבֹא גְבוּל יְהוּדָה מֵעֵבֶר לַיַּרְדֵּן:

1. Vay•hi ka•a•sher ki•la Yeshua le•da•ber et ha•d`va•rim ha•e•le va•ya•a•vor min - ha•Galil va•ya•vo g`vool Yehooda me•e•ver la•Yarden.

---

2. And great multitudes followed him; and he healed them there.

Greek/Transliteration
2. Καὶ ἠκολούθησαν αὐτῷ ὄχλοι πολλοί, καὶ ἐθεράπευσεν αὐτοὺς ἐκεῖ.

2. Kai eikoloutheisan auto ochloi polloi, kai etherapeusen autous ekei.

Hebrew/Transliteration
ב. וַהֲמוֹן עַם-רָב הָלְכוּ אַחֲרָיו וַיִּרְפָּאֵם שָׁם מֵחָלְיָם:

2. Va•ha•mon am - rav hal•choo a•cha•rav va•yir•pa•em sham me•chol•yam.

---

3. The Pharisees also came unto him, tempting him, and saying unto him, Is it lawful for a man to put away his wife for every cause?

Greek/Transliteration
3. Καὶ προσῆλθον αὐτῷ οἱ Φαρισαῖοι πειράζοντες αὐτόν, καὶ λέγοντες αὐτῷ, Εἰ ἔξεστιν ἀνθρώπῳ ἀπολῦσαι τὴν γυναῖκα αὐτοῦ κατὰ πᾶσαν αἰτίαν;

3. Kai proseilthon auto 'oi Pharisaioi peirazontes auton, kai legontes auto, Ei exestin anthropo apolusai tein gunaika autou kata pasan aitian?

Hebrew/Transliteration
ג. וַיִּגְּשׁוּ אֵלָיו מִן-הַפְּרוּשִׁים וַיְנַסּוּ אֹתוֹ לֵאמֹר הֲיֵשׁ בְּיַד אִישׁ לְשַׁלַּח אֶת-אִשְׁתּוֹ עַל-כָּל-דָּבָר:

3. Va•yig•shoo elav min - ha•P`roo•shim vay•na•soo o•to le•mor ha•yesh be•yad eesh le•sha•lach et - eesh•to al - kol - da•var.

4. And he answered and said unto them, Have ye not read, that he which made them at the beginning made them male and female,

Greek/Transliteration
4. Ὁ δὲ ἀποκριθεὶς εἶπεν αὐτοῖς, Οὐκ ἀνέγνωτε ὅτι ὁ ποιήσας ἀπ᾽ ἀρχῆς ἄρσεν καὶ θῆλυ ἐποίησεν αὐτούς,

4. 'O de apokritheis eipen autois, Ouk anegnote 'oti 'o poieisas ap archeis arsen kai theilu epoieisen autous,

Hebrew/Transliteration
ד. וַיַּעַן וַיֹּאמֶר הֲלֹא קְרָאתֶם כִּי הָעֹשֶׂה מִקֶּדֶם זָכָר וּנְקֵבָה עָשָׂה אֹתָם:

4. Va•ya•an va•yo•mar ha•lo ke•ra•tem ki ha•o•se mi•ke•dem za•char oon•ke•va asa o•tam.

---

5. And said, For this cause shall a man leave father and mother, and shall cleave to his wife: and they twain shall be one flesh?

Greek/Transliteration
5. καὶ εἶπεν, Ἕνεκεν τούτου καταλείψει ἄνθρωπος τὸν πατέρα καὶ τὴν μητέρα, καὶ προσκολληθήσεται τῇ γυναικὶ αὐτοῦ, καὶ ἔσονται οἱ δύο εἰς σάρκα μίαν;

5. kai eipen, 'Eneken toutou kataleipsei anthropos ton patera kai tein meitera, kai proskolleitheisetai tei gunaiki autou, kai esontai 'oi duo eis sarka mian?

Hebrew/Transliteration
ה. וְאָמַר עַל-כֵּן יַעֲזָב-אִישׁ אֶת-אָבִיו וְאֶת-אִמּוֹ וְדָבַק בְּאִשְׁתּוֹ וְהָיוּ שְׁנֵיהֶם לְבָשָׂר אֶחָד:

5. Ve•a•mar al - ken ya•a•zov - eesh et - aviv ve•et - ee•mo ve•da•vak be•eesh•to ve•ha•yoo sh`ney•hem le•va•sar e•chad.

Rabbinic Jewish Commentary
and they twain shall be one flesh; the word "twain" is: not in the Hebrew text in Genesis, but in the Septuagint version compiled by Jews, in the Samaritan Pentateuch, and version, and in the Targum of Jonathan ben Uzziel, who renders, it as here, ויהון תרוויהון לבישרא חד, "and they two shall be one flesh". This is the true sense, for neither more nor less can possibly be meant; and denotes that near conjunction, and strict union, between a man and his wife, the wife being a part of himself, and both as one flesh, and one body, and therefore not to be parted on every slight occasion; and has a particular respect to the act of carnal copulation, which only ought to be between one man and one woman, lawfully married to each other.

6. Wherefore they are no more twain, but one flesh. What therefore God hath joined together, let not man put asunder.

Greek/Transliteration
6. Ὥστε οὐκέτι εἰσὶν δύο, ἀλλὰ σὰρξ μία· ὃ οὖν ὁ θεὸς συνέζευξεν, ἄνθρωπος μὴ χωριζέτω.

6. 'Oste ouketi eisin duo, alla sarx mia. 'o oun 'o theos sunezeuxen, anthropos mei chorizeto.

Hebrew/Transliteration
ו. וְלָזֹאת אֵפוֹא אֵינָם עוֹד שְׁנַיִם כִּי אִם-בָּשָׂר אֶחָד וְלָכֵן אֵת אֲשֶׁר חִבֵּר אֱלֹהִים אַל-יַפְרֵד אָדָם:

6. Ve•la•zot e•fo ey·nam od sh`na•yim ki eem - ba•sar e•chad ve•la•chen et asher chi•ber Elohim al - yaf•red adam.

Jewish New Testament Commentary
The only text in the Five Books of Moses dealing with divorce is Deu_24:1-4, and its discussion of grounds is perfunctory. Hillel and Shammai, who lived in the generation before Yeshua, took opposing sides in interpreting this passage. "The School of Shammai say a man may not divorce his wife unless he has found unchastity in her, as it is said, '... because he has found in her *indecency* in a matter.' But the School of Hillel say he may divorce her even if she burns his food, as it is said, '... because he has found in her indecency *in a matter*.' " (Mishna: Gittin 9:10)

Yeshua in Mat_19:9 agrees with the strict-constructionist *Beit-Shammai*. But although *Beit-Hillel*'s lenient position became the halakhic norm, Rabbi El'azar, a member of *Beit-Hillel*, commented in the Gemara to this *mishna*, "When a man divorces his first wife, even the altar sheds tears," citing Deu_24:13-14 as evidence (Gittin 90b). There is a Jewish tradition that in Messianic times the stricter rulings of *Beit-Shammai* will become the standard.

Yeshua in adducing Scripture harks back to **the beginning**, in Gan-Eden (Mat_19:4-5), to support his view that a marriage must not be dissolved for anything less than the most direct insult to its one-flesh integrity, **adultery**. Mat_19:9 may imply that divorce without remarriage is allowable for lesser reasons (see Mat_5:31-32). A second ground for divorce is given at 1Co_7:12-16.

---

7. They say unto him, Why did Moses then command to give a writing of divorcement, and to put her away?

Greek/Transliteration
7. Λέγουσιν αὐτῷ, Τί οὖν Μωσῆς ἐνετείλατο δοῦναι βιβλίον ἀποστασίου, καὶ ἀπολῦσαι αὐτήν;

7. Legousin auto, Ti oun Moseis eneteilato dounai biblion apostasiou, kai apolusai autein?

Hebrew/Transliteration
ז. וַיֹּאמְרוּ אֵלָיו וְלָמָה-זֶּה צִוָּה מֹשֶׁה לָתֵת סֵפֶר כְּרִיתֻת וּלְשַׁלְּחָהּ:

7. Va•yom•roo elav ve•la•ma - ze tzi•va Moshe la•tet se•fer k`ri•toot ool•shal•cha.

---

8. He saith unto them, Moses because of the hardness of your hearts suffered you to put away your wives: but from the beginning it was not so.

Greek/Transliteration
8. Λέγει αὐτοῖς ὅτι Μωσῆς πρὸς τὴν σκληροκαρδίαν ὑμῶν ἐπέτρεψεν ὑμῖν ἀπολῦσαι τὰς γυναῖκας ὑμῶν· ἀπ᾽ ἀρχῆς δὲ οὐ γέγονεν οὕτως.

8. Legei autois 'oti Moseis pros tein skleirokardian 'umon epetrepsen 'umin apolusai tas gunaikas 'umon. ap archeis de ou gegonen 'outos.

Hebrew/Transliteration
ח. וַיֹּאמֶר אֲלֵיהֶם בַּעֲבוּר קְשִׁי לְבַבְכֶם נָתַן לָכֶם מֹשֶׁה לְשַׁלַּח אֶת-נְשֵׁיכֶם אֲבָל לֹא הָיָה כֵן מִקֶּדֶם:
8. Va•yo•mer aley•hem ba•a•voor ke•shi le•vav•chem na•tan la•chem Moshe le•sha•lach et - n`shey•chem aval lo ha•ya chen mi•ke•dem.

Rabbinic Jewish Commentary
And so the Jews say (m), that the Gentiles have no divorces: for thus they represent God, saying; "in Israel I have granted divorces, I have not granted divorces among the nations of the world. R. Chananiah, in the name of R. Phineas, observed, that in every other section it is written, the Lord of hosts, but here it is written, the God of Israel; to teach thee, that the holy, blessed God does not join his name to divorces, but in Israel only. R. Chayah Rabbah says, גוים אין להן גירושין, "the Gentiles have no divorces."" (m) T. Hieros. Kiddushin, fol. 58. 3.

---

9. And I say unto you, Whosoever shall put away his wife, except it be for fornication, and shall marry another, committeth adultery: and whoso marrieth her which is put away doth commit adultery.

Greek/Transliteration
9. Λέγω δὲ ὑμῖν ὅτι ὃς ἂν ἀπολύσῃ τὴν γυναῖκα αὐτοῦ, μὴ ἐπὶ πορνείᾳ, καὶ γαμήσῃ ἄλλην, μοιχᾶται· καὶ ὁ ἀπολελυμένην γαμήσας μοιχᾶται.

9. Lego de 'umin 'oti 'os an apolusei tein gunaika autou, mei epi porneia, kai gameisei allein, moichatai. kai 'o apolelumenein gameisas moichatai.

Hebrew/Transliteration
ט. וַאֲנִי אֹמֵר לָכֶם אִישׁ אֲשֶׁר יְשַׁלַּח אֶת-אִשְׁתּוֹ אִם לֹא עַל-דְּבַר זְנוּת וְנָשָׂא לוֹ אַחֶרֶת נֹאֵף הוּא וְהַנֹּשֵׂא:אֶת-הַגְּרוּשָׁה נֹאֵף הוּא

9. Va•a•ni o•mer la•chem eesh eesh asher ye•sha•lach et - eesh•to eem lo al - de•var z`noot ve•no•se lo a•che•ret no•ef hoo ve•ha•no•se et - ha•g•roo•sha no•ef hoo.

---

10. His disciples say unto him, If the case of the man be so with his wife, it is not good to marry.

Greek/Transliteration
10. Λέγουσιν αὐτῷ οἱ μαθηταὶ αὐτοῦ, Εἰ οὕτως ἐστὶν ἡ αἰτία τοῦ ἀνθρώπου μετὰ τῆς γυναικός, οὐ συμφέρει γαμῆσαι.

10. Legousin auto 'oi matheitai autou, Ei 'outos estin 'ei aitia tou anthropou meta teis gunaikos, ou sumpherei gameisai.

Hebrew/Transliteration
:י. וַיֹּאמְרוּ אֵלָיו תַּלְמִידָיו אִם דְּבַר אִישׁ וְאִשָּׁה כָּכָה הוּא לֹא-טוֹב לָקַחַת אִשָּׁה

10. Va•yom•roo elav tal•mi•dav eem de•var eesh ve•ee•sha ka•cha hoo lo - tov la•ka•chat ee•sha.

Jewish New Testament Commentary
Judaism has always considered marriage both normal and desirable-"The unmarried person lives without joy, without blessing and without good.... An unmarried man is not fully a man" (Talmud: Yevamot 62b-63a). On the other hand, some branches of Christianity came to grant abnormally high status to celibacy (on this phenomenon see 1Co_7:1-40). Depending on the calling and preferences of the individual, Yeshua allows that either the married or the single life can be one of service to God and humanity; and he takes care to minimize needless guilt on the part of those making the choice.

---

11. But he said unto them, All men cannot receive this saying, save they to whom it is given.

Greek/Transliteration
11. Ὁ δὲ εἶπεν αὐτοῖς, Οὐ πάντες χωροῦσιν τὸν λόγον τοῦτον, ἀλλ᾽ οἷς δέδοται.

11. 'O de eipen autois, Ou pantes chorousin ton logon touton, all 'ois dedotai.

Hebrew/Translitration
:יא. וַיֹּאמֶר אֲלֵיהֶם לֹא כָל-אִישׁ רַב-כֹּחַ הוּא לִסְבֹּל הַדָּבָר הַזֶּה כִּי-אִם רַק אֵלֶּה אֲשֶׁר נִתַּן לָהֶם

11. Va•yo•mer aley•hem lo chol - eesh rav - ko•ach hoo lis•bol ha•da•var ha•ze ki – eem rak ele asher ni•tan la•hem.

12. For there are some eunuchs, which were so born from their mother's womb: and there are some eunuchs, which were made eunuchs of men: and there be eunuchs, which have made themselves eunuchs for the kingdom of heaven's sake. He that is able to receive it, let him receive it.

Greek/Transliteration

12. Εἰσὶν γὰρ εὐνοῦχοι, οἵτινες ἐκ κοιλίας μητρὸς ἐγεννήθησαν οὕτως· καί εἰσιν εὐνοῦχοι, οἵτινες εὐνουχίσθησαν ὑπὸ τῶν ἀνθρώπων· καί εἰσιν εὐνοῦχοι, οἵτινες εὐνούχισαν ἑαυτοὺς διὰ τὴν βασιλείαν τῶν οὐρανῶν. Ὁ δυνάμενος χωρεῖν χωρείτω.

12. Eisin gar eunouchoi, 'oitines ek koilias meitros egenneitheisan 'outos. kai eisin eunouchoi, 'oitines eunouchistheisan 'upo ton anthropon. kai eisin eunouchoi, 'oitines eunouchisan 'eautous dya tein basileian ton ouranon. 'O dunamenos chorein choreito.

Hebrew/Translitration

יב. כִּי יֵשׁ סָרִיסִים אֲשֶׁר נוֹלְדוּ כֵן מֵרֶחֶם אִמָּם וְיֵשׁ אֲשֶׁר נַעֲשׂוּ סָרִיסִים בִּידֵי אָדָם וְיֵשׁ אֲשֶׁר מִנַּפְשָׁם נִהְיוּ:לְסָרִיסִים לְמַעַן מַלְכוּת הַשָּׁמַיִם מִי אֲשֶׁר כֹּחוֹ רַב לוֹ לִסְבֹּל יִסְבֹּל

12. Ki yesh sa•ri•sim asher nol•doo chen me•re•chem ee•mam ve•yesh asher na•a•soo sa•ri•sim biy•dey adam ve•yesh asher mi•naf•sham ni•hi•yoo le•sa•ri•sim le•ma•an mal•choot ha•sha•ma•yim mee asher ko•cho rav lo lis•bol yis•bol.

Rabbinic Jewish Commentary

The signs of such an eunuch, are given by the Jewish (p) writers, which may be consulted by those, that have ability and leisure. This sort is sometimes (q) called סריס בידי שמים "an eunuch by the hands of heaven", or God, in distinction from those who are so by the hands, or means of men, and are next mentioned.

and there are some eunuchs, which were made eunuchs of men: as among the Romans formerly, and which Domitian the emperor forbid by a law (r); and more especially in the eastern countries, and to this day among the Turks, that they may the more safely be entrusted with the custody of their women; and this sort the Jews call סריס אדם, "an eunuch of men", or בידי אדם, "by the hands of men". The distinction between an "eunuch of the sun", and an "eunuch of men", is so frequent with the Jews (s), and so well known to them, that a question need not be made of our Lord's referring to it:

and there be eunuchs which have made themselves eunuchs; not in a literal sense, in which the words are not to be taken, as they were by Origen; who though otherwise too much pursued the allegorical way of interpreting Scripture, here took it literally, and castrated himself (t); as did also a sort of heretics, called Valesians (u), from one Valens an Arabian; and which practice is recommended by Philo the Jew (w), and by Heathen philosophers (x), for the sake of chastity. But here it means such, who having the gift of continency without mutilating their bodies, or indulging any unnatural lusts, can live chastely without the use of women, and choose celibacy.

(p) Bartenora, ibid. & Maimon. Hilch. Ishot, ut supra. (q) T. Bab. Yebamot, fol. 80. 2. (r) Philostrat. vit. Apollon. l. 6. c. 17. (s) Misn. Yebamot, c. 8. sect. 4. Zabim, c. 2. sect. 1. T. Hieros. Yebamot, fol. 9. 4. Maimon. Hilch. Ishot, c. 2. sect. 26. & 4. 18. Mechosre Caphara, c. 3. sect. 6. Mishcabumoshab, c. l. sect. 5. (t) Euseb. Ecel. Hist. l. 6. c. 8. (u) Augustin de Haeres. c. 37. & Danaeus in ib. (w) Lib. quod deterius, p. 186. (x) Sexti Pythag. Sent. p. 8.

---

13. Then were there brought unto him little children, that he should put his hands on them, and pray: and the disciples rebuked them.

Greek/Transliteration
13. Τότε προσηνέχθη αὐτῷ παιδία, ἵνα τὰς χεῖρας ἐπιθῇ αὐτοῖς, καὶ προσεύξηται· οἱ δὲ μαθηταὶ ἐπετίμησαν αὐτοῖς.

13. Tote proseinechthei auto paidia, 'ina tas cheiras epithei autois, kai proseuxeitai. 'oi de matheitai epetimeisan autois.

Hebrew/Transliteration
יג. אָז הוּבְאוּ יְלָדִים לְפָנָיו לְבַעֲבוּר יָשִׂים אֶת-יָדָיו עֲלֵיהֶם וְיִתְפַּלֵּל בַּעֲדָם וַיִּגְעֲרוּ-בָם הַתַּלְמִידִים:

13. Az hoov•oo ye•la•dim le•fa•nav le•va•a•voor ya•sim et - ya•dav aley•hem ve•yit•pa•lel ba•a•dam va•yig•a•roo - vam ha•tal•mi•dim.

Rabbinic Jewish Commentary
It was indeed a controversy among the Jews, whether the little children of the wicked of Israel, באין לעולם הבא, "go into the world to come": some affirmed, and others denied; but all agreed, that the little children of the wicked of the nations of the world, do not. They dispute about the time of entrance of a child into the world to come; some say, as soon as it is born, according to Psa_22:31 others, as soon as it can speak, or count, according to Psa_22:30 others as soon as it is sown, as the gloss says, as soon as the seed is received in its mother's womb, though it becomes an abortion; according to the same words, "a seed shall serve thee": others, as soon as he is circumcised, according to Psa_88:15 others, as soon as he can say "Amen", according (z) to Isa_26:2 All weak, frivolous, and impertinent.
(z) T. Bab. Sanhedrim, fol. 110. 2.

---

14. But Jesus said, Suffer little children, and forbid them not, to come unto me: for of such is the kingdom of heaven.

Greek/Transliteration
14. Ὁ δὲ Ἰησοῦς εἶπεν, Ἄφετε τὰ παιδία, καὶ μὴ κωλύετε αὐτὰ ἐλθεῖν πρός με· τῶν γὰρ τοιούτων ἐστὶν ἡ βασιλεία τῶν οὐρανῶν.

14. 'O de Yeisous eipen, Aphete ta paidia, kai mei koluete auta elthein pros me. ton gar toiouton estin 'ei basileia ton ouranon.

Hebrew/Transliteration
יד. וַיֹּאמֶר יֵשׁוּעַ אֲלֵיהֶם הַנִּיחוּ לַיְלָדִים וְאַל-תִּכְלְאוּ אֹתָם מִבֹּא אֵלַי כִּי מֵאֵלֶּה מַלְכוּת הַשָּׁמָיִם:

14. Va•yo•mer Yeshua aley•hem ha•ni•choo lay•la•dim ve•al - tich•le•oo o•tam mi•bo e•lai ki me•e•le mal•choot ha•sha•ma•yim.

---

15. And he laid his hands on them, and departed thence.

Greek/Transliteration
15. Καὶ ἐπιθεὶς αὐτοῖς τὰς χεῖρας, ἐπορεύθη ἐκεῖθεν.

15. Kai epitheis autois tas cheiras, eporeuthei ekeithen.

Hebrew/Transliteration
טו. וַיָּשֶׂם אֶת-יָדָיו עֲלֵיהֶם וַיִּפֶן וַיֵּלֶךְ:

15. Va•ya•sem et - ya•dav aley•hem va•yi•fen va•ye•lech.

---

16. And, behold, one came and said unto him, Good Master, what good thing shall I do, that I may have eternal life?

Greek/Transliteration
16. Καὶ ἰδού, εἷς προσελθὼν εἶπεν αὐτῷ, Διδάσκαλε ἀγαθέ, τί ἀγαθὸν ποιήσω, ἵνα ἔχω ζωὴν αἰώνιον;

16. Kai idou, 'eis proselthon eipen auto, Didaskale agathe, ti agathon poieiso, 'ina echo zoein aionion?

Hebrew/Transliteration
טז. וְהִנֵּה-אִישׁ נִגַּשׁ אֵלָיו וַיֹּאמַר רַבִּי הַטּוֹב אֵי-זֶה הַטּוֹב אֶעֱשֶׂה לָרֶשֶׁת חַיֵּי עוֹלָם:

16. Ve•hee•ne - eesh ni•gash elav va•yo•mar Rabbi ha•tov ey - ze ha•tov e•e•se la•re•shet cha•yey o•lam?

Rabbinic Jewish Commentary
what good thing shall I do, that I may have eternal life? Or, as in the other evangelists, "inherit eternal life"; a phrase much in use with the Jewish Rabbi's (a): "Judah confessed, and was not ashamed, and what is his end? נחל חיי העולם הבא, "he inherits the life of the world to come" (i.e. eternal life); Reuben confessed, and was not ashamed, and what is his end? "he inherits the life of the world to come"." (a) T. Bab. Sota, fol. 7. 2.

17. And he said unto him, Why callest thou me good? there is none good but one, that is, God: but if thou wilt enter into life, keep the commandments.

Greek/Transliteration
17. Ὁ δὲ εἶπεν αὐτῷ, Τί με λέγεις ἀγαθόν; Οὐδεὶς ἀγαθός, εἰ μὴ εἷς, ὁ θεός. Εἰ δὲ θέλεις εἰσελθεῖν εἰς τὴν ζωήν, τήρησον τὰς ἐντολάς.

17. 'O de eipen auto, Ti me legeis agathon? Oudeis agathos, ei mei 'eis, 'o theos. Ei de theleis eiselthein eis tein zoein, teireison tas entolas.

Hebrew/Transliteration
יז. וַיֹּאמֶר אֵלָיו לָמָּה-זֶּה קָרָאתָ לִי טוֹב אֵין-טוֹב כִּי אִם-אֶחָד הוּא הָאֱלֹהִים וְאִם-נִכְסַפְתָּ לָבֹא אֶל-הַחַיִּים: שְׁמֹר אֶת הַמִּצְוֹת

17. Va•yo•mer elav la•ma - ze ka•ra•ta li tov eyn - tov ki eem - e•chad hoo ha•Elohim ve•eem - nich•saf•ta la•vo el - ha•cha•yim sh`mor et ha•mitz•vot.

Rabbinic Jewish Commentary
This is to be understood of God considered essentially, and not personally; or it is to be understood, not of the person of the Father, to the exclusion of the Son, or Spirit: who are one God with the Father, and equally good in nature as he. Nor does this contradict and deny that there are good angels, who have continued in that goodness in which they were created; or that there are good men, made so by the grace of God; but that none are absolutely and perfectly good, but God. What Yeshua here says of God, the (b) Jews say of the law of Moses, whose praise they can never enough extol; אין טוב אלא תורה "there is nothing good but the law". The law is good indeed; but the author of it must be allowed to be infinitely more so.

---

18. He saith unto him, Which? Jesus said, Thou shalt do no murder, Thou shalt not commit adultery, Thou shalt not steal, Thou shalt not bear false witness,

Greek/Transliteration
18. Λέγει αὐτῷ, Ποίας; Ὁ δὲ Ἰησοῦς εἶπεν, Τὸ Οὐ φονεύσεις· οὐ μοιχεύσεις· οὐ κλέψεις· οὐ ψευδομαρτυρήσεις·

18. Legei auto, Poias? 'O de Yeisous eipen, To Ou phoneuseis. ou moicheuseis. ou klepseis. Ou pseudomartureiseis.

Hebrew/Transliteration
יח. וַיֹּאמֶר אֵלָיו אֵי-זוֹ הֵנָּה וַיַּעַן יֵשׁוּעַ לֹא תִרְצָח לֹא תִנְאָף לֹא תִגְנֹב לֹא-תַעֲנֶה עֵד שָׁקֶר:

18. Va•yo•mer elav ey - zo he•na va•ya•an Yeshua lo tir•tzach lo tin•af lo tig•nov lo - ta•a•ne ed sha•ker.

19. Honour thy father and thy mother: and, Thou shalt love thy neighbour as thyself.

Greek/Transliteration
19. τίμα τὸν πατέρα καὶ τὴν μητέρα· καί, ἀγαπήσεις τὸν πλησίον σου ὡς σεαυτόν.

19. tima ton patera kai tein meitera. kai, agapeiseis ton pleision sou 'os seauton.

Hebrew/Transliteration
:יט. כַּבֵּד אֶת-אָבִיךָ וְאֶת-אִמֶּךָ וְאָהַבְתָּ לְרֵעֲךָ כָּמוֹךָ

19. Ka•bed et - avi•cha ve•et - ee•me•cha ve•a•hav•ta le•re•a•cha ka•mo•cha.

Rabbinic Jewish Commentary
Honour thy father and thy mother:.... This, as it is the first commandment with promise, so the first of the second table, and yet is here mentioned last; which inversion of order is of no consequence: so the "seventh" command is put before the "sixth", and the "fifth" omitted, in Rom_13:9 and with the Jews it is a common (c) saying, אין מוקדם ומאוחר בתורה, "there is neither first nor last in the law": that is, it is of no consequence which commandment is recited first, or which last. Moreover, it looks as if it was usual to recite these commands in this order, since they are placed exactly in the same method, by a very noted Jewish (d) writer.

(c) T. Bab. Pesach. fol. 6. 2. Zohar in Num. fol. 61. 4. (d) R. Sangari, Sepher Cosri, par. 3. sect. 11, fol. 146. 2.

---

20. The young man saith unto him, All these things have I kept from my youth up: what lack I yet?

Greek/Transliteration
20. Λέγει αὐτῷ ὁ νεανίσκος, Πάντα ταῦτα ἐφυλαξάμην ἐκ νεότητός μου· τί ἔτι ὑστερῶ;

20. Legei auto 'o neaniskos, Panta tauta ephulaxamein ek neoteitos mou. ti eti 'ustero?

Hebrew/Transliteration
:כ. וַיֹּאמֶר הַנַּעַר אֵלָיו כָּל-אֵלֶּה שָׁמַרְתִּי מִנְּעוּרָי וּמַה-יֶּחְסַר לִי עוֹד

20. Va•yo•mer ha•na•ar elav kol - ele sha•mar•ti min•oo•rai oo•ma - yech•sar li od.

21. Jesus said unto him, If thou wilt be perfect, go and sell that thou hast, and give to the poor, and thou shalt have treasure in heaven: and come and follow me.

Greek/Transliteration
21. Ἔφη αὐτῷ ὁ Ἰησοῦς, Εἰ θέλεις τέλειος εἶναι, ὕπαγε, πώλησόν σου τὰ ὑπάρχοντα καὶ δὸς πτωχοῖς, καὶ ἕξεις θησαυρὸν ἐν οὐρανῷ· καὶ δεῦρο, ἀκολούθει μοι.

21. Ephei auto 'o Yeisous, Ei theleis teleios einai, 'upage, poleison sou ta 'uparchonta kai dos ptochois, kai 'exeis theisauron en ourano. kai deuro, akolouthei moi.

Hebrew/Transliteration
כא. וַיֹּאמֶר אֵלָיו יֵשׁוּעַ אִם-חָפַצְתָּ לִהְיוֹת תָּמִים לֵךְ וּמְכֹר אֶת-כָּל-אֲשֶׁר-לְךָ וְתֵן לַעֲנִיִּים וְהָיָה לְךָ אוֹצָר בַּשָּׁמַיִם וּבֹא וְלֵךְ אַחֲרָי:

21. Va•yo•mer elav Yeshua eem - cha•fatz•ta li•hee•yot ta•mim lech oom•chor et - kol - asher - le•cha ve•ten la•a•ni•yim ve•ha•ya le•cha o•tzar ba•sha•ma•yim oo•vo ve•lech a•cha•rai.

Rabbinic Jewish Commentary

it should be observed, that Yeshua is here speaking, not the pure language of the law, or according to the principles of the Gospel, when he seems to place perfection in alms deeds, and as if they were meritorious of eternal life; but according to the doctrine of the Pharisees, and which was of this man; and so upon the plan of his own notions, moves him to seek for perfection, and convicts him of the want of it, in a way he knew would be disagreeable to him; and yet he would not be able to disprove the method, on the foot of his own tenets: for this is their doctrine (e); "It is a tradition, he that says this "sela", or shekel, is for alms, that my son may live, or I may be a son of the world to come, lo! זה צדיק גמור, "this man is a perfect righteous man"."

The gloss adds, "In this thing; and he does not say that he does not do it for the sake of it, but he fulfils the command of his Creator, who has commanded him to do alms; and he also intends profit to himself, that thereby he may be worthy of the world to come, or that his children may live."

And so in answer to a question much like this, the young man put to Yeshua (f); "How shall we come at the life of the world to come?" It is replied, "take thy riches, and give to the fatherless and the poor, and I will give thee a better portion in the law."

(e) T. Bab. Pesach. fol. 8. 1, 2. & Roshhashanah, fol. 4. 1. (f) Zohar in Gen. fol. 60. 4.

22. But when the young man heard that saying, he went away sorrowful: for he had great possessions.

Greek/Transliteration
22. Ἀκούσας δὲ ὁ νεανίσκος τὸν λόγον ἀπῆλθεν λυπούμενος· ἦν γὰρ ἔχων κτήματα πολλά.

22. Akousas de 'o neaniskos ton logon apeilthen lupoumenos. ein gar echon kteimata polla.

Hebrew/Transliteration
כב: וְהַנַּעַר כְּשָׁמְעוֹ הַדָּבָר הַזֶּה הִתְעַצֵּב אֶל-לִבּוֹ וַיֵּלֶךְ-לוֹ כִּי-נְכָסִים רַבִּים הָיוּ לוֹ.

22. Ve•ha•na•ar ke•sham•oh ha•da•var ha•ze hit•a•tzev el - li•bo va•ye•lech - lo ki - n`cha•sim ra•bim ha•yoo lo.

---

23. Then said Jesus unto his disciples, Verily I say unto you, That a rich man shall hardly enter into the kingdom of heaven.

Greek/Transliteration
23. Ὁ δὲ Ἰησοῦς εἶπεν τοῖς μαθηταῖς αὐτοῦ, Ἀμὴν λέγω ὑμῖν ὅτι δυσκόλως πλούσιος εἰσελεύσεται εἰς τὴν βασιλείαν τῶν οὐρανῶν.

23. 'O de Yeisous eipen tois matheitais autou, Amein lego 'umin 'oti duskolos plousios eiseleusetai eis tein basileian ton ouranon.

Hebrew/Transliteration
כג: וַיֹּאמֶר יֵשׁוּעַ אֶל-תַּלְמִידָיו אָמֵן אֲנִי אֹמֵר לָכֶם מַה-קָּשֶׁה לְאִישׁ עָשִׁיר לָבֹא אֶל-מַלְכוּת הַשָּׁמָיִם.

23. Va•yo•mer Yeshua el - tal•mi•dav Amen ani o•mer la•chem ma - ka•she le•eesh ashir la•vo el - mal•choot ha•sha•ma•yim.

---

24. And again I say unto you, It is easier for a camel to go through the eye of a needle, than for a rich man to enter into the kingdom of God.

Greek/Transliteration
24. Πάλιν δὲ λέγω ὑμῖν, εὐκοπώτερόν ἐστιν κάμηλον διὰ τρυπήματος ῥαφίδος διελθεῖν, ἢ πλούσιον εἰς τὴν βασιλείαν τοῦ θεοῦ εἰσελθεῖν.

24. Palin de lego 'umin, eukopoteron estin kameilon dya trupeimatos 'raphidos dielthein, ei plousion eis tein basileian tou theou eiselthein.

Hebrew/Transliteration
כד: וְעוֹד אֲנִי אֹמֵר לָכֶם כִּי-נָקֵל לַגָּמָל לַעֲבֹר דֶּרֶךְ חֹר הַמַּחַט מִבֹּא עָשִׁיר אֶל-מַלְכוּת הָאֱלֹהִים.

24. Ve•od ani o•mer la•chem ki - na•kel la•ga•mal la•a•vor de•rech choor ha•ma•chat mi•bo ashir el - mal•choot ha•Elohim.

Rabbinic Jewish Commentary
it is easier for a camel to go through the eye of a needle, than for a rich man to enter into the kingdom of God: thus, when the Jews would express anything that was rare and unusual, difficult and impossible, they used a like saying with this. So speaking of showing persons the interpretation of their dreams (g);

"Says Rabba, you know they do not show to a man a golden palm tree i.e. the interpretation of a dream about one, which, as the gloss says, is a thing he is not used to see, and of which he never thought, ולא פילא דעייל בקופא דמחטא, "nor an elephant going through the eye of a needle"."

Again, to one that had delivered something as was thought very absurd, it is said (h); "perhaps thou art one of Pombeditha (a school of the Jews in Babylon) דמעיילין פילא בקופא דמחטא, "who make an elephant pass through the eye of a needle"." That is, who teach such things as are equally as monstrous and absurd, and difficult of belief. So the authors of an edition of the book of Zohar, to set forth the difficulty of the work they engaged in, express themselves in this manner (i): "In the name of our God, we have seen fit, להכניס פילא בקופא דמחטא, "to bring an elephant through the eye of a needle"."

And not only among the Jews, but in other eastern nations, this proverbial way of speaking was used, to signify difficulties or impossibilities. Mahomet has it in his Alcoran (k); "Verily, says he, they who shall charge our signs with falsehood, and shall proudly reject them, the gates of heaven shall not be opened to them, neither shall they enter into paradise, "until a camel pass through the eye of a needle".

(g) T. Bab. Beracot fol. 55. 2. (h) T. Bab Bava Metzia, fol. 38. 2. (i) Prefat. ad Zohar, Ed. Sultzbach. (k) Chap. 7. p. 120. Ed. Sale.

---

25. When his disciples heard it, they were exceedingly amazed, saying, Who then can be saved?

Greek/Transliteration
25. Ἀκούσαντες δὲ οἱ μαθηταὶ αὐτοῦ ἐξεπλήσσοντο σφόδρα, λέγοντες, Τίς ἄρα δύναται σωθῆναι;

25. Akousantes de 'oi matheitai autou exepleissonto sphodra, legontes, Tis ara dunatai sotheinai?

Hebrew/Transliteration
כה. וְתַלְמִידָיו שָׁמְעוּ וַיִּשְׁתּוֹמְמוּ עַד-מְאֹד לֵאמֹר מִי אֵפוֹא יוּכַל לְהִוָּשֵׁעַ:

25. Ve•tal•mi•dav sham•oo va•yish•to•me•moo ad - me•od le•mor mee e•fo yoo•chal le•hi•va•she•a.

26. But Jesus beheld them, and said unto them, With men this is impossible; but with God all things are possible.

Greek/Transliteration
26. Ἐμβλέψας δὲ ὁ Ἰησοῦς εἶπεν αὐτοῖς, Παρὰ ἀνθρώποις τοῦτο ἀδύνατόν ἐστιν, παρὰ δὲ θεῷ πάντα δυνατά.

26. Emblepsas de 'o Yeisous eipen autois, Para anthropois touto adunaton estin, para de theo panta dunata.

Hebrew/Transliteration
:כו. וַיַּבֵּט-בָּם יֵשׁוּעַ וַיֹּאמֶר אֲלֵיהֶם מִבְּנֵי-אָדָם יִפָּלֵא הַדָּבָר הַזֶּה אַךְ מֵאֱלֹהִים לֹא יִפָּלֵא כָל-דָּבָר

26. Va•ya•bet - bam Yeshua va•yo•mer aley•hem mi•b`ney - adam yi•pa•le ha•da•var ha•ze ach me•Elohim lo yi•pa•le kol - da•var.

---

27. Then answered Peter and said unto him, Behold, we have forsaken all, and followed thee; what shall we have therefore?

Greek/Transliteration
27. Τότε ἀποκριθεὶς ὁ Πέτρος εἶπεν αὐτῷ, Ἰδού, ἡμεῖς ἀφήκαμεν πάντα καὶ ἠκολουθήσαμέν σοι· τί ἄρα ἔσται ἡμῖν;

27. Tote apokritheis 'o Petros eipen auto, Ydou, 'eimeis apheikamen panta kai eikoloutheisamen soi. ti ara estai 'eimin?

Hebrew/Transliteration
:כז. וַיַּעַן פֶּטְרוֹס וַיֹּאמֶר אֵלָיו הִנֵּה אֲנַחְנוּ עָזַבְנוּ אֶת-כֹּל וַנֵּלֶךְ אַחֲרֶיךָ וּמַה אֵפוֹא יִהְיֶה-לָּנוּ

27. Va•ya•an Petros va•yo•mer elav hee•ne a•nach•noo azav•noo et - kol va•ne•lech a•cha•re•cha oo•ma e•fo yi•hee•ye - la•noo.

---

28. And Jesus said unto them, Verily I say unto you, That ye which have followed me, in the regeneration when the Son of man shall sit in the throne of his glory, ye also shall sit upon twelve thrones, judging the twelve tribes of Israel.

Greek/Transliteration
28. Ὁ δὲ Ἰησοῦς εἶπεν αὐτοῖς, Ἀμὴν λέγω ὑμῖν ὅτι ὑμεῖς οἱ ἀκολουθήσαντές μοι, ἐν τῇ παλιγγενεσίᾳ ὅταν καθίσῃ ὁ υἱὸς τοῦ ἀνθρώπου ἐπὶ θρόνου δόξης αὐτοῦ, καθίσεσθε καὶ ὑμεῖς ἐπὶ δώδεκα θρόνους, κρίνοντες τὰς δώδεκα φυλὰς τοῦ Ἰσραήλ.

28. 'O de Yeisous eipen autois, Amein lego 'umin 'oti 'umeis 'oi akoloutheisantes moi, en tei palingenesia 'otan kathisei 'o 'wios tou anthropou epi thronou doxeis autou, kathisesthe kai 'umeis epi dodeka thronous, krinontes tas dodeka phulas tou Ysraeil.

Hebrew/Transliteration

כח. וַיֹּאמֶר יֵשׁוּעַ אֲלֵיהֶם אָמֵן אֲנִי אֹמֵר לָכֶם כִּי אַתֶּם הַהֹלְכִים אַחֲרַי כַּאֲשֶׁר יֵשֵׁב בֶּן-הָאָדָם עַל-כִּסֵּא כְבוֹדוֹ:בְּהִתְחַדֵּשׁ הַבְּרִיאָה גַּם-אַתֶּם תֵּשְׁבוּ אַף עַל-שְׁנֵים עָשָׂר כִּסְאוֹת לִשְׁפֹּט אֶת-שְׁנֵים עָשָׂר שִׁבְטֵי יִשְׂרָאֵל

28. Va•yo•mer Yeshua aley•hem Amen ani o•mer la•chem ki atem ha•hol•chim a•cha•rai ka•a•sher ye•shev Ben - ha•adam al - ki•se che•vo•do be•hit•cha•desh hab•ri•ah gam - atem tesh•voo az al - sh`neym asar kis•ot lish•pot et - sh`neym asar shiv•tey Israel.

Rabbinic Jewish Commentary

judging the twelve tribes of Israel; doctrinally and practically; by charging them with the sin of crucifying Messiah, condemning them for their unbelief, and rejection of him, denouncing the wrath of God, and the heaviest judgments that should fall upon them, as a nation, for their sin; and by turning from them to the Gentiles, under which judgment they continue to this day. So the leaders among the Jews are represented as sitting and judging others: of "the potters", in 1Ch_4:23 they say (l), "these are the disciples of the law, or the lawyers, for whose sake the world is created, דיתבין על דינא "who sit in judgment", and establish the world; and build, and perfect the ruins of the house of Israel." (l) Targuru in 1 Chron. iv. 23.

---

29. And every one that hath forsaken houses, or brethren, or sisters, or father, or mother, or wife, or children, or lands, for my name's sake, shall receive an hundredfold, and shall inherit everlasting life.

Greek/Transliteration

29. Καὶ πᾶς ὃς ἀφῆκεν οἰκίας, ἢ ἀδελφούς, ἢ ἀδελφάς, ἢ πατέρα, ἢ μητέρα, ἢ γυναῖκα, ἢ τέκνα, ἢ ἀγρούς, ἕνεκεν τοῦ ὀνόματός μου, ἑκατονταπλασίονα λήψεται, καὶ ζωὴν αἰώνιον κληρονομήσει.

29. Kai pas 'os apheiken oikias, ei adelphous, ei adelphas, ei patera, ei meitera, ei gunaika, ei tekna, ei agrous, 'eneken tou onomatos mou, 'ekatontaplasiona leipsetai, kai zoein aionion kleironomeisei.

Hebrew/Transliteration

כט. וְכָל-אִישׁ אֲשֶׁר יַעֲזֹב בָּתִּים אוֹ אַחִים אוֹ אֲחָיוֹת אוֹ אָב אוֹ אֵם אוֹ אִשָּׁה אוֹ בָנִים אוֹ שָׂדוֹת לְמַעַן שְׁמִי יִמְצָא:מֵאָה שְׁעָרִים וְחַיֵּי עוֹלָם יִירָשׁ

29. Ve•chol - eesh asher ya•a•zov ba•tim oh a•chim oh a•cha•yot oh av oh em oh ee•sha oh va•nim oh sa•dot le•ma•an sh`mi yim•tza me•ah sh`a•rim ve•cha•yey o•lam yi•rash.

30. But many that are first shall be last; and the last shall be first.

Greek/Transliteration
30. Πολλοὶ δὲ ἔσονται πρῶτοι ἔσχατοι, καὶ ἔσχατοι πρῶτοι.

30. Polloi de esontai protoi eschatoi, kai eschatoi protoi.

Hebrew/Transliteration
ל. וְרַבִּים הֵם הָרִאשֹׁנִים אֲשֶׁר יִהְיוּ אַחֲרֹנִים וְהָאַחֲרֹנִים רִאשֹׁנִים:

30. Ve•ra•bim hem ha•ri•sho•nim asher yi•hee•yoo acha•ro•nim ve•ha•a•cha•ro•nim ri•sho•nim.

Matthew, Chapter 20

1. For the kingdom of heaven is like unto a man that is an householder, which went out early in the morning to hire labourers into his vineyard.

Greek/Transliteration

1. Ὁμοία γάρ ἐστιν ἡ βασιλεία τῶν οὐρανῶν ἀνθρώπῳ οἰκοδεσπότῃ, ὅστις ἐξῆλθεν ἅμα πρωῒ μισθώσασθαι ἐργάτας εἰς τὸν ἀμπελῶνα αὐτοῦ.

1. 'Omoia gar estin 'ei basileia ton ouranon anthropo oikodespotei, 'ostis exeilthen 'ama proi misthosasthai ergatas eis ton ampelona autou.

Hebrew/Transliteration

א. כִּי דָמְתָה מַלְכוּת הַשָּׁמַיִם לְבַעַל־הַבַּיִת אֲשֶׁר הִשְׁכִּים וַיֵּצֵא בַבֹּקֶר וַיִּשְׂכֹּר פֹּעֲלִים לְכַרְמוֹ:

1. Ki dam•ta mal•choot ha•sha•ma•yim le•va•al - ha•ba•yit asher hish•kim va•ye•tze va•bo•ker va•yis•kor po•a•lim le•char•mo.

Rabbinic Jewish Commentary
Isaiah says,
For the vineyard of YHWH of Hosts is the house of Israel, and the men of Judah his pleasant plant: and he looked for justice, but, behold, oppression; for righteousness, but, behold, a cry of distress, Isaiah 5:7

Midrash Mishle, the Midrash on Proverbs, comments,"R. Simeon ben Yohai said: Why was Israel likened to a vineyard? In the case of a vineyard, in the beginning one must hoe it, then weed it, then erect supports when he sees the clusters [forming]. Then he must return to pluck the grapes and press them in order to extract the wine from them. So also Israel – each and every shepherd who oversees them must tend them [as he would tend a vineyard.] Where in Scripture is Israel called a vineyard? In the verse For the vineyard of the Lord of Hosts is the House of Israel, and the seedlings he lovingly tended are the men of Judah (Isa. 5:7). Midrash on Proverbs, Chapter 19 translated by Burton L. Visotzky, Yal University Press, pg. 89

They have a parable indeed, which, in the several parts of it, greatly resembles this, and begins thus (m); "to what is R. Bon like? to a king that hath a vineyard, ושכר עליו פועלים, "and hires labourers into it", &c."

Out of which some other things will be remarked, in the following parts of this parable: of a son's being sent, and going out to hire labourers into the vineyard, take the following instance (n): "it happened to R. Jochanan ben Matthia, that said to his son, צא ושכר, "go out, and hire labourers" for us: "he went out", and agreed with them for their food."

The time of hiring labourers, here mentioned, exactly agrees with the Jewish accounts (o). "Says R. Juda ben Bethira, when the face of all the east is light unto Hebron, all the people go out, every man to his work; and when it is so light, it is good "to hire labourers we say"."

Upon which the gloss says, "every man goes out to his work, not for labourers, but the "householder", who משכים יותר, "rises earlier to find labourers to hire".

Perhaps it may not be worth while to observe, how large a spot of ground, set with vines, was, by them, called a vineyard: it is frequently said by them (p), "that a vineyard planted by less than four cubits, is no vineyard; but R. Simeon, and the wise men, say it is a vineyard."

(m) Shirhashirim Rabba, fol. 21. 3. Vid. Midrash Kohelet, fol. 72. 4. & Talmud Hicros. Beracot, fol 5. 3. (n) Misua Bava Metzia, c. 7. sect. 1. (o) T. Bab. Yoma, fol. 28. 2. (p) T. Hieros. Sheviith, fol. 33. 2. T. Bab. Bava Bathra, fol. 37. 2. & 33. 1.

---

2. And when he had agreed with the labourers for a penny a day, he sent them into his vineyard.

Greek/Transliteration
2. Καὶ συμφωνήσας μετὰ τῶν ἐργατῶν ἐκ δηναρίου τὴν ἡμέραν, ἀπέστειλεν αὐτοὺς εἰς τὸν ἀμπελῶνα αὐτοῦ.

2. Kai sumphoneisas meta ton ergaton ek deinariou tein 'eimeran, apesteilen autous eis ton ampelona autou.

Hebrew/Transliteration
ב. וּשְׂכַר הַפֹּעֲלִים נָקַב שֶׁקֶל לַיּוֹם וַיִּשְׁלַח אֹתָם אֶל-הַכָּרֶם:

2. Oos•char ha•po•a•lim na•kav she•kel la•yom va•yish•lach o•tam el - ha•ka•rem.

Rabbinic Jewish Commentary
These labourers were of that sort that were called שכיר יום, "hired for a day"; concerning whom is the following rule (q): "he that is hired for a day, may demand it all the night; and he that is hired for a night may demand it all the day: he that is hired for hours, may demand it all the night, and all the day; he that is hired for a week, he that is hired for a month, he that is hired for a year, he that is hired for seven, if he goes out in the day, may demand all the day; and if he goes out in the night, he may demand it all the night, and all the day."

And the wages of a day were usually דינר "a penny"; which, if understood of a Roman penny, was seven pence halfpenny of our money. One of their canons runs thus (r): "he that hires a labourer in the winter, to work with him in the summer, בכל יום, "for a penny every day", and he gives him his hire; and, lo! his hire is alike

386

to that in the winter, a "sela" every day, this is forbidden; because it looks as if he chose that time to lessen his wages; but if he says to him, work with me from this day, to such a time, "for a penny every day", though his hire is the same, a "sela" every day, this is lawful."

(q) Misna Bava Metzia, c. 9. sect. 11. Maimen Hilch. Shericut, c. 11. sect. 2. (r) Maimon. Hilch. Milvah Ulavah, c. 7. sect. 12. Vid. T. Bab. Bava Bathra, fol. 86. 2. & 87. 1. & Gloss. in ib.

---

3. And he went out about the third hour, and saw others standing idle in the marketplace,

Greek/Transliteration

3. Καὶ ἐξελθὼν περὶ τρίτην ὥραν, εἶδεν ἄλλους ἑστῶτας ἐν τῇ ἀγορᾷ ἀργούς·

3. Kai exelthon peri tritein 'oran, eiden allous 'estotas en tei agora argous.

Hebrew/Transliteration

ג. וַיֵּצֵא בַּשָּׁעָה הַשְּׁלִישִׁית וַיַּרְא אֲנָשִׁים אֲחֵרִים עֹמְדִים בִּבְלִי מְלָאכָה בַּשּׁוּק:

3. Va•ye•tze ba•sha•ah hash`li•sheet va•yar a•na•shim a•che•rim om•dim biv•li me•la•cha ba•shook.

---

4. And said unto them; Go ye also into the vineyard, and whatsoever is right I will give you. And they went their way.

Greek/Transliteration

4. καὶ ἐκείνοις εἶπεν, Ὑπάγετε καὶ ὑμεῖς εἰς τὸν ἀμπελῶνα, καὶ ὃ ἐὰν ᾖ δίκαιον δώσω ὑμῖν.

4. kai ekeinois eipen, 'Upagete kai 'umeis eis ton ampelona, kai 'o ean ei dikaion doso 'umin.

Hebrew/Transliteration

ד. וַיֹּאמֶר אֲלֵיהֶם לְכוּ אֶל-כַּרְמִי גַּם-אַתֶּם וִידֵי שְׂכַרְכֶם אֶתֵּן לָכֶם כַּמִּשְׁפָּט וַיֵּלֵכוּ:

4. Va•yo•mer aley•hem le•choo el - kar•mi gam - atem ve•dey s`char•chem e•ten la•chem ka•mish•pat va•yel•choo.

---

5. Again he went out about the sixth and ninth hour, and did likewise.

Greek/Transliteration

5. Οἱ δὲ ἀπῆλθον. Πάλιν ἐξελθὼν περὶ ἕκτην καὶ ἐνάτην ὥραν, ἐποίησεν ὡσαύτως.

5. 'Oi de apeilthon. Palin exelthon peri 'ektein kai enatein 'oran, epoieisen 'osautos.

Hebrew/Transliteration

ה: וַיּוֹסֶף וַיֵּצֵא בַּשָּׁעָה הַשִּׁשִּׁית וְהַתְּשִׁיעִית וַיַּעַשׂ כְּמוֹ-כֵן

5. Va•yo•sef va•ye•tze ba•sha•ah ha•shi•sheet ve•hat•shi•eet va•ya•as k`mo - chen.

---

6. And about the eleventh hour he went out, and found others standing idle, and saith unto them, Why stand ye here all the day idle?

Greek/Transliteration

6. Περὶ δὲ τὴν ἑνδεκάτην ὥραν ἐξελθών, εὗρεν ἄλλους ἑστῶτας ἀργούς, καὶ λέγει αὐτοῖς, Τί ὧδε ἑστήκατε ὅλην τὴν ἡμέραν ἀργοί;

6. Peri de tein 'endekatein 'oran exelthon, 'euren allous 'estotas argous, kai legei autois, Ti 'ode 'esteikate 'olein tein 'eimeran argoi?

Hebrew/Transliteration

ו: וּבַשָּׁעָה הָעַשְׁתֵּי עֶשְׂרֵה יָצָא וַיִּמְצָא אֲחֵרִים עֹמְדִים וַיֹּאמֶר אֲלֵיהֶם מַדּוּעַ תַּעַמְדוּ פֹה כָּל-הַיּוֹם

6. Oo•va•sha•ah ha•ash•tey es•re ya•tza va•yim•tza a•che•rim om•dim va•yo•mer aley•hem ma•doo•a ta•am•doo fo kol - ha•yom.

---

7. They say unto him, Because no man hath hired us. He saith unto them, Go ye also into the vineyard; and whatsoever is right, that shall ye receive.

Greek/Transliteration

7. Λέγουσιν αὐτῷ, Ὅτι οὐδεὶς ἡμᾶς ἐμισθώσατο. Λέγει αὐτοῖς, Ὑπάγετε καὶ ὑμεῖς εἰς τὸν ἀμπελῶνα, καὶ ὃ ἐὰν ᾖ δίκαιον λήψεσθε.

7. Legousin auto, 'Oti oudeis 'eimas emisthosato. Legei autois, 'Upagete kai 'umeis eis ton ampelona, kai 'o ean ei dikaion leipsesthe.

Hebrew/Transliteration

ז. וַיֹּאמְרוּ אֵלָיו כִּי לֹא-שָׂכַר אֹתָנוּ אִישׁ וַיֹּאמֶר אֲלֵיהֶם לְכוּ אֶל-כַּרְמִי גַּם-אַתֶּם וּשְׂכַרְכֶם יִתֵּן לָכֶם כַּמִּשְׁפָּט:

7. Va•yom•roo elav ki lo - sa•char o•ta•noo eesh va•yo•mer aley•hem le•choo el - kar•mi gam - atem oos•char•chem yoo•tan la•chem ka•mish•pat.

Rabbinic Jewish Commentary

This may be fitly applied to the Gentiles, who hundreds of years were neglected by God; he overlooked the times of their ignorance, took no notice of them in their state of stupidity, blindness, and irreligion; but suffered them to walk in their own ways, sent no prophets to instruct them, nor messages, nor messengers to them; till at length the Jews, having rejected and crucified the Messiah, and persecuted his apostles, and contradicted, and blasphemed the Gospel, they were ordered to go to the Gentiles, and preach it to them:

---

8. So when even was come, the lord of the vineyard saith unto his steward, Call the labourers, and give them their hire, beginning from the last unto the first.

Greek/Transliteration
8. Ὀψίας δὲ γενομένης λέγει ὁ κύριος τοῦ ἀμπελῶνος τῷ ἐπιτρόπῳ αὐτοῦ, Κάλεσον τοὺς ἐργάτας, καὶ ἀπόδος αὐτοῖς τὸν μισθόν, ἀρξάμενος ἀπὸ τῶν ἐσχάτων ἕως τῶν πρώτων.

8. Opsias de genomeneis legei 'o kurios tou ampelonos to epitropo autou, Kaleson tous ergatas, kai apodos autois ton misthon, arxamenos apo ton eschaton 'eos ton proton.

Hebrew/Transliteration
ח. וַיְהִי לִפְנוֹת עֶרֶב וַיֹּאמֶר אֲדוֹן הַכֶּרֶם אֶל-פְּקִידוֹ קְרָא אֶת-הַפֹּעֲלִים וְתֶן לָהֶם שְׂכָרָם הָחֵל מִן-הָאַחֲרוֹנִים עַד:הָרִאשֹׁנִים

8. Vay•hi lif•not erev va•yo•mer Adon ha•ke•rem el - p`ki•do k`ra et - ha•po•a•lim ve•ten la•hem s`cha•ram ha•chel min - ha•a•cha•ro•nim ad ha•ri•sho•nim.

Rabbinic Jewish Commentary
At six o'clock, or when the sun was set, which was the time of paying labourers their wages: thus in the parable of the Jews, before referred to, which bears some resemblance to this, it is said, "bre tel, (s) that "at evening time" the labourers came to take their wages." (s) Shirashirim Rabba, fol. 21. 3. Midrash Kohelet, fol. 72. 4. T. Hicros. Beracot, fol. 5. 3.

---

9. And when they came that were hired about the eleventh hour, they received every man a penny.

Greek/Transliteration
9. Καὶ ἐλθόντες οἱ περὶ τὴν ἑνδεκάτην ὥραν ἔλαβον ἀνὰ δηνάριον.

9. Kai elthontes 'oi peri tein 'endekatein 'oran elabon ana deinarion.

Hebrew/Transliteration
ט. וַיָּבֹאוּ הַנִּשְׂכָּרִים בְּשָׁעָה עַשְׁתֵּי עֶשְׂרֵה וַיִּקְחוּ שֶׁקֶל לְאִישׁ אִישׁ:

9. Va•ya•vo•oo ha•nis•ka•rim be•sha•ah ash•tey es•re va•yik•choo she•kel le•eesh eesh.

10. But when the first came, they supposed that they should have received more; and they likewise received every man a penny.

Greek/Transliteration
10. Ἐλθόντες δὲ οἱ πρῶτοι ἐνόμισαν ὅτι πλείονα λήψονται· καὶ ἔλαβον καὶ αὐτοὶ ἀνὰ δηνάριον.

10. Elthontes de 'oi protoi enomisan 'oti pleiona leipsontai. kai elabon kai autoi ana deinarion.

Hebrew/Transliteration
י. וְהָרִאשׁנִים בָּאוּ וַיֹּאמְרוּ בְלִבָּם כִּי יַשִּׂיגוּ יוֹתֵר אַךְ גַּם-הֵמָּה הִשִּׂיגוּ רַק שֶׁקֶל אֶחָד לָאִישׁ:

10. Ve•ha•ri•sho•nim ba•oo va•yom•roo ve•li•bam ki ya•si•goo yo•ter ach gam - he•ma hi•si•goo rak she•kel e•chad la•eesh.

---

11. And when they had received it, they murmured against the goodman of the house,

Greek/Transliteration
11. Λαβόντες δὲ ἐγόγγυζον κατὰ τοῦ οἰκοδεσπότου,

11. Labontes de egonguzon kata tou oikodespotou,

Hebrew/Transliteration
יא. וַיִּקְחוּ וַיִּלֹּנוּ עַל-בַּעַל הַבַּיִת לֵאמֹר:

11. Va•yik•choo va•yi•lo•noo al - ba•al ha•ba•yit le•mor.

---

12. Saying, These last have wrought but one hour, and thou hast made them equal unto us, which have borne the burden and heat of the day.

Greek/Transliteration
12. λέγοντες ὅτι Οὗτοι οἱ ἔσχατοι μίαν ὥραν ἐποίησαν, καὶ ἴσους ἡμῖν αὐτοὺς ἐποίησας, τοῖς βαστάσασιν τὸ βάρος τῆς ἡμέρας καὶ τὸν καύσωνα.

12. legontes 'oti 'Outoi 'oi eschatoi mian 'oran epoieisan, kai isous 'eimin autous epoieisas, tois bastasasin to baros teis 'eimeras kai ton kausona.

Hebrew/Transliteration
יב. הָאַחֲרֹנִים הָאֵלֶּה עָבְדוּ שָׁעָה אַחַת וַתְּשַׁוֶּה אֹתָם כָּמֹנוּ אֲשֶׁר הָיִינוּ כָל-הַיּוֹם לָשֵׂאת סֵבֶל וְהַחֹרֶב אֲכָלָנוּ:

12. Ha•a•cha•ro•nim ha•e•le av•doo sha•ah a•chat vat•shav o•tam ka•mo•noo asher ha•yi•noo kol - ha•yom la•set se•vel ve•ha•cho•rev achola•noo.

Rabbinic Jewish Commentary

His is grudged by the Jews (x); "Bath Kol", a voice from heaven, went out and said, "Ketiah bar Shallum", is prepared for the life of the world to come; Rabbi wept, and said, there is that obtains his world (or the world to come for himself) בשעה אחת, "in one hour"; and there is that obtains it in many years."

The same observation is also made by the same person, on account of R. Eleazar ben Durdia (y). So in the parable of the Jews above mentioned, which is the broken remains of a common proverb among them like (z) this; it is observed, that there being one labourer among those that were hired, who did his work better than all the rest, and who was taken notice of by the king; that when

"at even the labourers came to take their wages, this labourer also came to take his; and the king gave him his wages equal with them, (or, as in another place, a perfect one,) the labourers began to press him with difficulty, (or as elsewhere (a) מתרעמין, "they murmured",) and said, Oh! our Lord, the king, "we have laboured all the day"; but this man has not laboured but two or three hours in the day, and he takes his wages, even as ours, or a perfect reward."

(x) T. Bab. Avoda Zara, fol. 10. 2. (y) Ib. fol. 17. 1. (z) Shirhashirim Rabba, fol 21. 4. Midrash Kohelet, fol. 72. 4. (a) T. Hieros. Beracot, fol. 5. 3.

---

13. But he answered one of them, and said, Friend, I do thee no wrong: didst not thou agree with me for a penny?

Greek/Transliteration
13. Ὁ δὲ ἀποκριθεὶς εἶπεν ἑνὶ αὐτῶν, Ἑταῖρε, οὐκ ἀδικῶ σε· οὐχὶ δηναρίου συνεφώνησάς μοι;

13. 'O de apokritheis eipen 'eni auton, 'Etaire, ouk adiko se. ouchi deinariou sunephoneisas moi?

Hebrew/Transliteration
יג. וַיַּעַן וַיֹּאמֶר לְאֶחָד מֵהֶם רֵעִי לֹא עֲשַׁקְתִּיךָ הֲלֹא שֶׁקֶל נָקַבְתָּ לִי שְׂכָרֶךָ:

13. Va•ya•an va•yo•mer le•e•chad me•hem re•ee lo a•shak•ti•cha ha•lo she•kel na•kav•ta li s`cha•re•cha.

Rabbinic Jewish Commentary
Didst thou not agree with me for a penny? That is, to labour in the vineyard all the day for a penny; yea, this agreement was made personally with him, not with a servant, or messenger of his; though if it had, it ought, according to the Jewish canons, to have been abode by, which run thus (b): "A man says to his messenger, or servant, go and hire workmen for me for three pence; he goes and hires them for four pence: if the messenger says to them, your wages be upon me, he gives them four pence, and takes three pence of the master of the house; he looses one out of his own purse: if he says to them, your hire be upon the master of the house, the

master of the house gives them according to the custom of the province: if there are one in the province that hired for three pence, and others that are hired for four pence, he gives them but three pence, "and the murmuring" is against the messenger; in what things? When the work is not known, but when the work is known, and it is worth four pence, the master of the house gives them four pence; but if his messenger does not say to them four pence, they do not labour and do what deserves four pence. The householder says to him, hire me for four pence, and the messenger goes and hires for three pence, though the work deserves four pence, they have but three pence; because that קִבְּלוּ עַל עַצְמָן, "they took it upon themselves", (i.e. they agreed for so much,) and their murmuring is against the messenger."

Thus the argument in the parable proceeds upon the agreement, which ought to be abode by. (b) Maimon. Hilch, Shecirut, c. 9. sect. 3.

---

14. Take that thine is, and go thy way: I will give unto this last, even as unto thee.

Greek/Transliteration
14. Ἆρον τὸ σὸν καὶ ὕπαγε· θέλω δὲ τούτῳ τῷ ἐσχάτῳ δοῦναι ὡς καὶ σοί.

14. Aron to son kai 'upage. thelo de touto to eschato dounai 'os kai soi.

Hebrew/Transliteration
יד. קַח אֶת אֲשֶׁר-לָךְ וָלֵךְ וַאֲנִי עִם-לִבִּי לָתֵת לָזֶה הָאַחֲרוֹן כָּמוֹךָ:

14. Kach et asher - le•cha va•lech va•a•ni eem - li•bi la•tet la•ze ha•a•cha•ron ka•mo•cha.

---

15. Is it not lawful for me to do what I will with mine own? Is thine eye evil, because I am good?

Greek/Transliteration
15. Ἢ οὐκ ἔξεστίν μοι ποιῆσαι ὃ θέλω ἐν τοῖς ἐμοῖς; Εἰ ὁ ὀφθαλμός σου πονηρός ἐστιν, ὅτι ἐγὼ ἀγαθός εἰμι;

15. Ei ouk exestin moi poieisai 'o thelo en tois emois? Ei 'o ophthalmos sou poneiros estin, 'oti ego agathos eimi?

Hebrew/Transliteration
טו. הַאֵין נָכוֹן לִי לַעֲשׂוֹת בְּשֶׁלִּי כַּאֲשֶׁר עִם-לְבָבִי אוֹ הַאִם רָעָה עֵינְךָ בַּאֲשֶׁר טוֹב אָנֹכִי:

15. Ha•ein na•chon li la•a•sot be•she•li ka•a•sher eem - le•va•vi oh ha•eem ra•ah eyn•cha ba•a•sher tov ano•chi.

Rabbinic Jewish Commentary

An "evil eye", is opposed to a good eye, frequently in Jewish writings, as a "good eye" signifies beneficence and liberality; hence it is said (c). "He that gives a gift, let him give it בְּעַיִן יָפָה "with a good eye"; bountifully and generously; and he that devoteth anything, let him devote it with a "good eye"," cheerfully and freely: so an "evil eye" intends envy and covetousness, as it does here: and the sense is, art thou envious at the good of others, and covetous and greedy to monopolize all to thyself, because I am liberal, kind, and beneficent? Men are apt to complain of God, and charge his procedures in providence and grace, with inequality and injustice; whereas he does, as he may, all things according to his sovereign will, and never contrary to justice, truth, and goodness; though he is not to be brought to man's bar, and men should submit to his sovereignty. (c) T. Bab. Bava Bathra, fol. 65. 1. & 71. 1. & 72. 1.

---

16. So the last shall be first, and the first last: for many be called, but few chosen.

Greek/Transliteration
16. Οὕτως ἔσονται οἱ ἔσχατοι πρῶτοι, καὶ οἱ πρῶτοι ἔσχατοι· πολλοὶ γάρ εἰσιν κλητοί, ὀλίγοι δὲ ἐκλεκτοί.

16. 'Outos esontai 'oi eschatoi protoi, kai 'oi protoi eschatoi. polloi gar eisin kleitoi, oligoi de eklektoi.

Hebrew/Transliteration
טז. כָּכָה יִהְיוּ הָאַחֲרֹנִים רִאשֹׁנִים וְהָרִאשֹׁנִים אַחֲרֹנִים כִּי רַבִּים הֵם הַקְּרוּאִים וּמְעַטִּים הַנִּבְחָרִים:

16. Ka•cha yi•hee•yoo ha•a•cha•ro•nim ri•sho•nim ve•ha•ri•sho•nim acha•ro•nim ki ra•bim hem hak•roo•eem oom•a•tim ha•niv•cha•rim.

Rabbinic Jewish Commentary

It is a saying of R. Simeon ben Jochai (d). "I have seen the children of the world to come (elsewhere (e) it is, of the chamber), וְהֵן מוּעָטִין, "and they are few".

Though he vainly thought, that if those few were but two, they were himself and his son.

(d) T. Hieros. Beracot, fol. 13. 4. (e) T. Bab. Succa, fol. 45. 2. & Sanhedrim, fol. 97. 2.

---

17. And Jesus going up to Jerusalem took the twelve disciples apart in the way, and said unto them,

Greek/Transliteration
17. Καὶ ἀναβαίνων ὁ Ἰησοῦς εἰς Ἱεροσόλυμα παρέλαβεν τοὺς δώδεκα μαθητὰς κατ᾽ ἰδίαν ἐν τῇ ὁδῷ, καὶ εἶπεν αὐτοῖς,

17. Kai anabainon 'o Yeisous eis 'Yerosoluma parelaben tous dodeka matheitas kat idian en tei 'odo, kai eipen autois,

Hebrew/Transliteration
יז. וַיְהִי כַּעֲלוֹת יֵשׁוּעַ יְרוּשָׁלָיְמָה וַיִּקַּח אֶת־שְׁנֵים עָשָׂר הַתַּלְמִידִים לְבַדָּם וַיֹּאמֶר אֲלֵיהֶם בַּדָּרֶךְ:

17. Vay•hi ka•a•lot Yeshua Ye•roo•sha•lai•ma va•yi•kach et - sh`neym asar ha•tal•mi•dim le•va•dam va•yo•mer aley•hem ba•da•rech.

Rabbinic Jewish Commentary
Which was situated (f) in the highest part of the land of Israel: the land of Israel, is said to be higher than any other land whatever; and the temple at Jerusalem, higher than any part of the land of Israel; wherefore Christ's going to Jerusalem, is expressed by going up to it. (f) T. Bab. Sanhedrim, fol. 87. 1.

---

18. Behold, we go up to Jerusalem; and the Son of man shall be betrayed unto the chief priests and unto the scribes, and they shall condemn him to death,

Greek/Transliteration
18. Ἰδού, ἀναβαίνομεν εἰς Ἱεροσόλυμα, καὶ ὁ υἱὸς τοῦ ἀνθρώπου παραδοθήσεται τοῖς ἀρχιερεῦσιν καὶ γραμματεῦσιν· καὶ κατακρινοῦσιν αὐτὸν θανάτῳ,

18. Ydou, anabainomen eis 'Yerosoluma, kai 'o 'wios tou anthropou paradotheisetai tois archiereusin kai grammateusin. kai katakrinousin auton thanato,

Hebrew/Transliteration
יח. הִנֵּה אֲנַחְנוּ עֹלִים יְרוּשָׁלָיְמָה וּבֶן־הָאָדָם יִסָּגֵר בִּידֵי רָאשֵׁי הַכֹּהֲנִים וְהַסֹּפְרִים וְהִרְשִׁיעוּ אֹתוֹ לָמוּת:

18. Hee•ne a•nach•noo o•lim Ye•roo•sha•lai•ma oo•Ven - ha•adam yi•sa•ger biy•dey ra•shey ha•ko•ha•nim ve•ha•sof•rim ve•hir•shi•oo o•to la•moot.

---

19. And shall deliver him to the Gentiles to mock, and to scourge, and to crucify him: and the third day he shall rise again.

Greek/Transliteration
19. καὶ παραδώσουσιν αὐτὸν τοῖς ἔθνεσιν εἰς τὸ ἐμπαῖξαι καὶ μαστιγῶσαι καὶ σταυρῶσαι· καὶ τῇ τρίτῃ ἡμέρᾳ ἀναστήσεται.

19. kai paradosousin auton tois ethnesin eis to empaixai kai mastigosai kai staurosai. kai tei tritei 'eimera anasteisetai.

Hebrew/Transliteration
יט. וְהִסְגִּירוּ אֹתוֹ לַגּוֹיִם לְהִתְעַלֶּל־בּוֹ לְיַסְּרוֹ בַשּׁוֹטִים וְלִצְלֹב אֹתוֹ וּבַיּוֹם הַשְּׁלִישִׁי יָקוּם:

19. Ve•his•gi•roo o•to la•go•yim le•hit•a•lel - bo le•yas•ro va•sho•tim ve•litz•lov o•to oo•va•yom hash•li•shi ya•koom.

---

20. Then came to him the mother of Zebedee's children with her sons, worshipping him, and desiring a certain thing of him.

Greek/Transliteration
20. Τότε προσῆλθεν αὐτῷ ἡ μήτηρ τῶν υἱῶν Ζεβεδαίου μετὰ τῶν υἱῶν αὐτῆς, προσκυνοῦσα καὶ αἰτοῦσά τι παρ᾽ αὐτοῦ.

20. Tote proseilthen auto 'ei meiter ton 'wion Zebedaiou meta ton 'wion auteis, proskunousa kai aitousa ti par autou.

Hebrew/Transliteration
:כ. אָז נִגְּשָׁה אֵלָיו אֵם בְּנֵי זַבְדִּי עִם-בָּנֶיהָ לְהִשְׁתַּחֲוֹת לוֹ וּלְבַקֵּשׁ מִיָּדוֹ דָּבָר

20. Az nig•sha elav em b`ney Zav•di eem - ba•ne•ha le•hish•ta•cha•vot lo ool•va•kesh mi•ya•do da•var.

---

21. And he said unto her, What wilt thou? She saith unto him, Grant that these my two sons may sit, the one on thy right hand, and the other on the left, in thy kingdom.

Greek/Transliteration
21. Ὁ δὲ εἶπεν αὐτῇ, Τί θέλεις; Λέγει αὐτῷ, Εἰπὲ ἵνα καθίσωσιν οὗτοι οἱ δύο υἱοί μου, εἷς ἐκ δεξιῶν σου, καὶ εἷς ἐξ εὐωνύμων σου, ἐν τῇ βασιλείᾳ σου.

21. 'O de eipen autei, Ti theleis? Legei auto, Eipe 'ina kathisosin 'outoi 'oi duo 'wioi mou, 'eis ek dexion sou, kai 'eis ex euonumon sou, en tei basileia sou.

Hebrew/Transliteration
כא. וַיֹּאמֶר אֵלֶיהָ מַה-בַּקָּשָׁתֵךְ וַתֹּאמֶר אֵלָיו צַו-נָא וּשְׁנֵי בָנַי אֵלֶּה יֵשְׁבוּ אֶחָד לִימִינְךָ וְאֶחָד לִשְׂמֹאלְךָ בְּמַלְכוּתֶךָ:

21. Va•yo•mer e•le•ha ma - ba•ka•sha•tech va•to•mer elav tzav - na oosh•ney va•nai ele yesh•voo e•chad liy•min•cha ve•e•chad lis•mol•cha be•mal•choo•te•cha.

---

22. But Jesus answered and said, Ye know not what ye ask. Are ye able to drink of the cup that I shall drink of, and to be baptized with the baptism that I am baptized with? They say unto him, We are able.

Greek/Transliteration

22. Ἀποκριθεὶς δὲ ὁ Ἰησοῦς εἶπεν, Οὐκ οἴδατε τί αἰτεῖσθε. Δύνασθε πιεῖν τὸ ποτήριον ὃ ἐγὼ μέλλω πίνειν, ἢ τὸ βάπτισμα ὃ ἐγὼ βαπτίζομαι βαπτισθῆναι; Λέγουσιν αὐτῷ, Δυνάμεθα.

22. Apokritheis de 'o Yeisous eipen, Ouk oidate ti aiteisthe. Dunasthe piein to poteirion 'o ego mello pinein, ei to baptisma 'o ego baptizomai baptistheinai? Legousin auto, Dunametha.

Hebrew/Transliteration

כב. וַיַּעַן יֵשׁוּעַ וַיֹּאמֶר לֹא יְדַעְתֶּם אֵת אֲשֶׁר תִּשְׁאָלוּן הֲתוּכְלוּ לִשְׁתּוֹת אֶת־הַכּוֹס אֲשֶׁר אֲנִי אֶשְׁתֶּה וּלְהִטָּבֵל טְבִילָה אֲשֶׁר אֲנִי נִטְבָּל וַיֹּאמְרוּ אֵלָיו נוּכָל

22. Va•ya•an Yeshua va•yo•mer lo ye•da•a•tem et asher tish•a•loon ha•tooch•loo lish•tot et - ha•kos asher ani esh•te ool`hi•ta•vel te•vi•la asher ani nit•bal va•yom•roo elav noo•chal.

---

23. And he saith unto them, Ye shall drink indeed of my cup, and be baptized with the baptism that I am baptized with: but to sit on my right hand, and on my left, is not mine to give, but it shall be given to them for whom it is prepared of my Father.

Greek/Transliteration

23. Καὶ λέγει αὐτοῖς, Τὸ μὲν ποτήριόν μου πίεσθε, καὶ τὸ βάπτισμα ὃ ἐγὼ βαπτίζομαι βαπτισθήσεσθε· Τὸ δὲ καθίσαι ἐκ δεξιῶν μου καὶ ἐξ εὐωνύμων μου, οὐκ ἔστιν ἐμὸν δοῦναι, ἀλλ᾽ οἷς ἡτοίμασται ὑπὸ τοῦ πατρός μου.

23. Kai legei autois, To men poteirion mou piesthe, kai to baptisma 'o ego baptizomai baptistheisesthe. To de kathisai ek dexion mou kai ex euonumon mou, ouk estin emon dounai, all 'ois 'eitoimastai 'upo tou patros mou.

Hebrew/Transliteration

כג. וַיֹּאמֶר אֲלֵיהֶם כּוֹסִי שָׁתֹה תִשְׁתּוּ וּטְבִילָה אֲשֶׁר אֲנִי נִטְבָּל תִּטָּבֵלוּ אֲבָל לָשֶׁבֶת לִימִינִי וְלִשְׂמֹאלִי אֵין בְּיָדִי לָתֵת כִּי אִם לָאֵלֶּה אֲשֶׁר יָעַד אֹתָם אָבִי

23. Va•yo•mer aley•hem ko•si sha•to tish•too oot•vi•la asher ani nit•bal ti•ta•ve•loo aval la•she•vet li•y`mi•ni ve•lis•mo•li eyn be•ya•di la•tet ki eem la•e•le asher ya•ad o•tam Avi.

---

24. And when the ten heard it, they were moved with indignation against the two brethren.

Greek/Transliteration

24. Καὶ ἀκούσαντες οἱ δέκα ἠγανάκτησαν περὶ τῶν δύο ἀδελφῶν.

24. Kai akousantes 'oi deka eiganakteisan peri ton duo adelphon.

Hebrew/Transliteration
:כד. וְהָעְשָׂרָה בְּשָׁמְעָם כָּזֹאת חָרָה אַפָּם בִּשְׁנֵי הָאַחִים

24. Ve•ha•a•sa•ra be•shom•am ka•zot cha•ra apam bish•ney ha•a•chim.

---

25. But Jesus called them unto him, and said, Ye know that the princes of the Gentiles exercise dominion over them, and they that are great exercise authority upon them.

Greek/Transliteration
25. Ὁ δὲ Ἰησοῦς προσκαλεσάμενος αὐτοὺς εἶπεν, Οἴδατε ὅτι οἱ ἄρχοντες τῶν ἐθνῶν κατακυριεύουσιν αὐτῶν, καὶ οἱ μεγάλοι κατεξουσιάζουσιν αὐτῶν.

25. 'O de Yeisous proskalesamenos autous eipen, Oidate 'oti 'oi archontes ton ethnon katakurieuousin auton, kai 'oi megaloi katexousyazousin auton.

Hebrew/Transliteration
כה. וַיִּקְרָא יֵשׁוּעַ וַיֹּאמֶר אֲלֵיהֶם הֵן יְדַעְתֶּם כִּי-הַמֹּשְׁלִים בַּגּוֹיִם יִמְשְׁלוּ בָם כָּשָׂרִים בָּעֲבָדִים
:וּגְדוֹלֵיהֶם שֹׁלְטִים עֲלֵיהֶם

25. Va•yik•ra Yeshua va•yo•mer aley•hem hen ye•da•a•tem ki - ha•mosh•lim ba•go•yim yim•she•loo vam ka•sa•rim ba•a•va•dim oog•do•ley•hem shol•tim aley•hem.

Rabbinic Jewish Commentary
"Shemayah and Avtalyon received from them. Shemayah said, "Love work, and hate domination, and make not yourself close to the government."
Pirkei Avot 1:10

---

26. But it shall not be so among you: but whosoever will be great among you, let him be your minister;

Greek/Transliteration
26. Οὐχ οὕτως δὲ ἔσται ἐν ὑμῖν· ἀλλ᾽ ὃς ἐὰν θέλῃ ἐν ὑμῖν μέγας γενέσθαι ἔσται ὑμῶν διάκονος·

26. Ouch 'outos de estai en 'umin. all 'os ean thelei en 'umin megas genesthai estai 'umon dyakonos.

Hebrew/Transliteration
:כו. וְלֹא יִהְיֶה כֵן בְּקִרְבְּכֶם כִּי אִם מִי-הֶחָפֵץ לִהְיוֹת גָּדוֹל בָּכֶם יִהְיֶה לָכֶם לִמְשָׁרֵת

26. Ve•lo yi•hee•ye chen be•kir•be•chem ki eem mee - he•cha•fetz li•hee•yot ga•dol ba•chem yi•hee•ye la•chem lim•sha•ret.

27. And whosoever will be chief among you, let him be your servant:

Greek/Transliteration
27. καὶ ὃς ἐὰν θέλῃ ἐν ὑμῖν εἶναι πρῶτος ἔστω ὑμῶν δοῦλος·

27. kai 'os ean thelei en 'umin einai protos esto 'umon doulos.

Hebrew/Transliteration
כז. וּמִי-מִכֶּם הֶחָפֵץ לִהְיוֹת לְרֹאשׁ יִהְיֶה לָכֶם לְעָבֶד:

27. Oo•mi - mi•kem he•cha•fetz li•hee•yot le•rosh yi•hee•ye la•chem le•a•ved.

Rabbinic Jewish Commentary
The Jews have a saying somewhat like this, that (h). "everyone that makes himself כעבד, as a servant, for the words of the law in this world, shall be made free in the world to come." (h) T. Bab. Bava Metzia, fol. 35. 2.

---

28. Even as the Son of man came not to be ministered unto, but to minister, and to give his life a ransom for many.

Greek/Transliteration
28. ὥσπερ ὁ υἱὸς τοῦ ἀνθρώπου οὐκ ἦλθεν διακονηθῆναι, ἀλλὰ διακονῆσαι, καὶ δοῦναι τὴν ψυχὴν αὐτοῦ λύτρον ἀντὶ πολλῶν.

28. 'osper 'o 'wios tou anthropou ouk eilthen dyakoneitheinai, alla dyakoneisai, kai dounai tein psuchein autou lutron anti pollon.

Hebrew/Transliteration
כח. כַּאֲשֶׁר גַּם בֶּן-הָאָדָם לֹא בָא לְמַעַן יְשָׁרְתֻהוּ אֲחֵרִים כִּי אִם-לְשָׁרֵת הוּא וְלָתֵת אֶת-נַפְשׁוֹ כֹפֶר בְּעַד רַבִּים:

28. Ka•a•sher gam Ben - ha•adam lo va le•ma•an ye•shar•too•hoo a•che•rim ki eem - le•sha•ret hoo ve•la•tet et - naf•sho ko•fer be•ad ra•bim.

---

29. And as they departed from Jericho, a great multitude followed him.

Greek/Transliteration
29. Καὶ ἐκπορευομένων αὐτῶν ἀπὸ Ἰεριχώ, ἠκολούθησεν αὐτῷ ὄχλος πολύς.

29. Kai ekporeuomenon auton apo Yericho, eikolouytheisen auto ochlos polus.

Hebrew/Transliteration
כט. וַיֵּצְאוּ מִירִיחוֹ וַהֲמוֹן עַם-רָב הֹלְכִים אַחֲרָיו:

29. Va•yetz•oo mi•Yeri•cho va•ha•mon am - rav hol•chim a•cha•rav.

Rabbinic Jewish Commentary
Which, was distant about ten parsas, or miles, from Jerusalem (i), through which Yeshua just passed, and had met with Zacchaeus, and called him, and delivered the parable concerning a nobleman's going into a far country. The Syriac and Persic versions render the words, "when Yeshua departed from Jericho"; and the Arabic, "when he went out of Jericho"; not alone, but "with his disciples", as Mark says; and not with them only, for a great multitude followed him out of the city; either to hear him, or be healed by him, or to see him, or behold his miracles, or to accompany him to Jerusalem; whither he was going to keep the feast of the passover, and where they might be in some expectation he would set up his kingdom. The Ethiopic version reads it, "as they went out from Jerusalem", contrary to all copies and versions. (i) Bartenora in Misn. Taraid, c. 3. sect. 8.

---

30. And, behold, two blind men sitting by the way side, when they heard that Jesus passed by, cried out, saying, Have mercy on us, O Lord, thou Son of David.

Greek/Transliteration
30. Καὶ ἰδού, δύο τυφλοὶ καθήμενοι παρὰ τὴν ὁδόν, ἀκούσαντες ὅτι Ἰησοῦς παράγει, ἔκραξαν, λέγοντες, Ἐλέησον ἡμᾶς, κύριε, υἱὸς Δαυίδ.

30. Kai idou, duo tuphloi katheimenoi para tein 'odon, akousantes 'oti Yeisous paragei, ekraxan, legontes, Eleeison 'eimas, kurie, 'wios Dauid.

Hebrew/Transliteration
ל. וְהִנֵּה שְׁנֵי-עִוְרִים יָשְׁבוּ עַל-הַדָּרֶךְ וּבְשָׁמְעָם כִּי יֵשׁוּעַ עֹבֵר שָׁם וַיִּצְעֲקוּ לֵאמֹר הוֹשִׁיעָה-נָּא אֲדֹנֵינוּ בֶּן-דָּוִד:

30. Ve•hee•ne sh`ney - eev•rim yash•voo al - ha•da•rech oov•shom•am ki Yeshua o•ver sham va•yitz•a•koo le•mor ho•shi•ah - na Ado•ney•noo Ben - David.

Rabbinic Jewish Commentary
Mark and Luke make mention but of one; which is no contradiction to Matthew; for they neither of them say that there was but one. A greater difficulty occurs in Luke's account; for whereas Matthew and Mark both agree, that it was when Jesus came out of Jericho, that this cure was wrought, Luke says it was "when he came nigh unto it"; which some reconcile by observing, that that phrase may be rendered, "while he was near Jericho"; and so only signifies his distance from it, and not motion to it; but this will not solve the difficulty, because we after read of his entrance into it, and passing through it. Some therefore have thought, that Yeshua met with, and cured one blind man before he entered the city, and another when he came out of it and that Matthew has put the history of both together: but to me it seems, that there were three blind men cured; one before he went into Jericho, which Luke only relates, and two as he came out of Jericho, which Matthew here speaks of; and one of which, according to Mark, was by name Bartimaeus, the son of Timaeus; for so Bartimaeus signifies. Tima, or Timaeus,

was a name in use among the Jews: we often read of R. Judah בן תימא, Ben Tima (k), the son of Tima, or Timaeus. Origen (l) thinks, he had his name from the Greek word τιμη, which signifies "honour"; and so טימי, "Time", with the Jews, is used for honour and profit (m). This man's father might have been a very honourable and useful man, though the son was fallen into poverty and distress, through blindness; for which reason he may be mentioned, as being a person well known to the Jews.

(k) T. Hieros. Nazir, fol. 52. 1. Erubin, fol. 19. 4. T. Bab. Gittin, fol. 84. 1. Bava Metzig, fol. 94. 1. Massech. Semachot, c. 9. Juchasin, fol. 159. 2. (l) Comment. in Matt. vol. 1. p. 428. Ed. Huet. (m) Targum in Esth. iii. 8. & v. 13. T. Hicros. Peah, fol. 15. 4.

---

31. And the multitude rebuked them, because they should hold their peace: but they cried the more, saying, Have mercy on us, O Lord, thou Son of David.

Greek/Transliteration
31. Ὁ δὲ ὄχλος ἐπετίμησεν αὐτοῖς ἵνα σιωπήσωσιν. Οἱ δὲ μεῖζον ἔκραζον, λέγοντες, Ἐλέησον ἡμᾶς, κύριε, υἱὸς Δαυίδ.

31. 'O de ochlos epetimeisen autois 'ina siopeisosin. 'Oi de meizon ekrazon, legontes, Eleeison 'eimas, kurie, 'wios Dauid.

Hebrew/Transliteration
:לא. וַיִּגְעַר-בָּם הָעָם לְהַחֲשׁוֹתָם וְהֵם הוֹסִיפוּ לִקְרֹא וְלֵאמֹר הוֹשִׁיעָה-נָּא אֲדֹנֵינוּ בֶּן-דָּוִד

31. Va•yig•ar - bam ha•am le•ha•cha•sho•tam ve•hem ho•si•foo lik•ro ve•le•mor ho•shi•ah - na Ado•ney•noo Ben - David.

---

32. And Jesus stood still, and called them, and said, What will ye that I shall do unto you?

Greek/Transliteration
32. Καὶ στὰς ὁ Ἰησοῦς ἐφώνησεν αὐτούς, καὶ εἶπεν, Τί θέλετε ποιήσω ὑμῖν;

32. Kai stas 'o Yeisous ephoneisen autous, kai eipen, Ti thelete poieiso 'umin?

Hebrew/Transliteration
:לב. וַיַּעֲמֹד יֵשׁוּעַ וַיִּקְרָא אֲלֵיהֶם וַיֹּאמַר מַה-תְּבַקְשׁוּן וְאֶעֱשֶׂה לָכֶם

32. Va•ya•a•mod Yeshua va•yik•ra aley•hem va•yo•mar ma - te•vak•shoon ve•e•e•se la•chem.

33. They say unto him, Lord, that our eyes may be opened.

Greek/Transliteration
33. Λέγουσιν αὐτῷ, Κύριε, ἵνα ἀνοιχθῶσιν ἡμῶν οἱ ὀφθαλμοί.

33. Legousin auto, Kurie, 'ina anoichthosin 'eimon 'oi ophthalmoi.

Hebrew/Transliteration
לג. וַיֹּאמְרוּ אֵלָיו אֲדֹנֵינוּ כִּי תִפָּקַחְנָה עֵינֵינוּ:

33. Va•yom•roo elav Ado•ney•noo ki ti•pa•kach•na ey•ney•noo.

---

34. So Jesus had compassion on them, and touched their eyes: and immediately their eyes received sight, and they followed him.

Greek/Transliteration
34. Σπλαγχνισθεὶς δὲ ὁ Ἰησοῦς ἥψατο τῶν ὀφθαλμῶν αὐτῶν· καὶ εὐθέως ἀνέβλεψαν αὐτῶν οἱ ὀφθαλμοί, καὶ ἠκολούθησαν αὐτῷ.

34. Splagchnistheis de 'o Yeisous 'eipsato ton ophthalmon auton. kai eutheos aneblepsan auton 'oi ophthalmoi, kai eikoloutheisan auto.

Hebrew/Transliteration
לד. וַיִּכָּמְרוּ רַחֲמֵי יֵשׁוּעַ עֲלֵיהֶם וַיִּגַּע בְּעֵינֵיהֶם וְעַד-מְהֵרָה הוּשַׁב לָהֶם אוֹר עֵינֵיהֶם וַיֵּלְכוּ אַחֲרָיו:

34. Va•yi•kam•roo ra•cha•mey Yeshua aley•hem va•yi•ga be•ey•ne•hem ve•ad - me•he•ra hoo•shav la•hem or ey•ne•hem va•yel•choo a•cha•rav.

Matthew, Chapter 21

1. And when they drew nigh unto Jerusalem, and were come to Bethphage, unto the mount of Olives, then sent Jesus two disciples,

Greek/Transliteration
1. Καὶ ὅτε ἤγγισαν εἰς Ἱεροσόλυμα, καὶ ἦλθον εἰς Βηθσφαγὴ πρὸς τὸ ὄρος τῶν Ἐλαιῶν, τότε ὁ Ἰησοῦς ἀπέστειλεν δύο μαθητάς,

1. Kai 'ote eingisan eis 'Yerosoluma, kai eilthon eis Beithsphagei pros to oros ton Elaion, tote 'o Yeisous apesteilen duo matheitas,

Hebrew/Transliteration
א. וַיְהִי כַּאֲשֶׁר בָּאוּ מִקָּרוֹב לִירוּשָׁלַיִם אֶל-בֵּית-פַּגֵּי אֶל-הַר הַזֵּיתִים וַיִּשְׁלַח יֵשׁוּעַ שְׁנַיִם מִתַּלְמִידָיו:

1. Vay•hi ka•a•sher ba•oo mi•ka•rov li•Ye•roo•sha•la•yim el - beit - Pa•gai el – Har ha•Zey•tim va•yish•lach Yeshua sh`na•yim mi•tal•mi•dav.

Rabbinic Jewish Commentary
Various are the derivations and etymologies of this place: some say it signifies "the house", or "place of a fountain", from a fountain that was in it; as if it was a compound of "Beth", an house, and πηγη, "pege", a fountain: others, "the house of the mouth of a valley"; as if it was made up of those three words, בית פי גיא, because the outward boundary of it was at the foot of the Mount of Olives, at the entrance of the valley of Jehoshaphat: others say, that the ancient reading was "Bethphage, the house of slaughter"; and Jerom says (q), it was a village of the priests, and he renders it, "the house of jaw bones": here indeed they might bake the showbread, and eat the holy things, as in Jerusalem (r); but the true reading and signification of it is, בית פאגי, "the house of figs"; so called from the fig trees which grew in the outward limits of it, near Bethany, and the Mount of Olives; hence we read of (s) פגי בית היני, "the figs of Bethany"; which place is mentioned along with, Bethphage, both by Mark and Luke, where Christ, and those with him, were now come.

This mount was so called from the abundance of olive trees which grew upon it, and was on the east side of Jerusalem (t); and it was distant from it a sabbath day's journey, Act_1:12 which was two, thousand cubits, or eight furlongs, and which made one mile.

p) Gloss. in T. Bab. Sota, fol. 45. 1. & Bava Metzia fol. 90. 1. (q) In loc. & ad Eustoch, fol. 59. 3. Tom. 1. (r) Misn. Menachot, c. 11. sect. 2. T. Bab. Menachot fol. 63. 1. & 78. 2. Maimon. Hilch. Pesul. Hamukdash, c. 12. sect. 16. Gloss. in Pesach. fol. 63. 2. (s) T. Bab. Pesach. fol. 53. 1. & Erubin, fol. 28. 2. (t) Zech. xiv 4. Targum in Ezek. xi. 23. & Bartenora in Misn. Mid. dot. c. 1. sect. 3.

2. Saying unto them, Go into the village over against you, and straightway ye shall find an ass tied, and a colt with her: loose them, and bring them unto me.

Greek/Transliteration
2. λέγων αὐτοῖς, Πορεύθητε εἰς τὴν κώμην τὴν ἀπέναντι ὑμῶν, καὶ εὐθέως εὑρήσετε ὄνον δεδεμένην, καὶ πῶλον μετ᾽ αὐτῆς· λύσαντες ἀγάγετέ μοι.

2. legon autois, Poreutheite eis tein komein tein apenanti 'umon, kai eutheos 'eureisete onon dedemenein, kai polon met auteis. lusantes agagete moi.

Hebrew/Transliteration
ב. וַיֹּאמֶר אֲלֵיהֶם לְכוּ אֶל-הַכְּפָר אֲשֶׁר מִנֶּגֶד וּמְצָאתֶם שָׁם אָתוֹן אֲסוּרָה וְעַיִר אֶצְלָהּ הַתִּירוּם וַהֲבִיאוּם אֵלָי:

2. Va•yo•mer aley•hem le•choo el - ha•k`far asher mi•ne•ged oom•tza•tem sham aton a•soo•ra ve•a•yir etz•la ha•ti•room va•ha•vi•oom e•lai.

Jewish New Testament Commentary
The Talmud contains an interesting homily based on Zec_9:9, but it obscures the difference between his first and second comings.

"Rabbi Alexandri said, 'Rabbi Y'hoshua set two verses against each other: It is written, "And behold, one like the son of man came with the clouds of heaven" (Dan_7:13), while elsewhere it is written, "See, your king comes unto you,... humbly riding on a donkey" (Zec_9:9). [He resolved the paradox by saying that] if they deserve it [he will come] with the clouds of heaven, but if not, lowly and riding on an ass.' " (Sanhedrin 98a)

---

3. And if any man say ought unto you, ye shall say, The Lord hath need of them; and straightway he will send them.

Greek/Transliteration
3. Καὶ ἐάν τις ὑμῖν εἴπῃ τι, ἐρεῖτε ὅτι Ὁ κύριος αὐτῶν χρείαν ἔχει· εὐθέως δὲ ἀποστέλλει αὐτούς.

3. Kai ean tis 'umin eipei ti, ereite 'oti 'O kurios auton chreian echei. eutheos de apostellei autous.

Hebrew/Transliteration
ג. וְכִי-יֹאמַר אִישׁ אֲלֵיכֶם דָּבָר וַאֲמַרְתֶּם הָאָדוֹן יֶשׁ-לוֹ חֵפֶץ בָּם וְעַד מְהֵרָה יְשַׁלְּחֵם:

3. Ve•chi - yo•mar eesh aley•chem da•var va•amar•tem ha•Adon yesh - lo che•fetz bam ve•ad me•he•ra ye•shal•chem.

4. All this was done, that it might be fulfilled which was spoken by the prophet, saying,

Greek/Transliteration
4. Τοῦτο δὲ ὅλον γέγονεν, ἵνα πληρωθῇ τὸ ῥηθὲν διὰ τοῦ προφήτου, λέγοντος,

4. Touto de 'olon gegonen, 'ina pleirothei to 'reithen dya tou propheitou, legontos,

Hebrew/Transliteration
ד. וְכָל-זֹאת הָיָה לְמַלֹּאת אֵת אֲשֶׁר נֶאֱמַר בְּיַד-הַנָּבִיא לֵאמֹר:

4. Ve•chol - zot ha•ya le•ma•lot et asher ne•e•mar be•yad - ha•na•vee le•mor.

---

5. Tell ye the daughter of Sion, Behold, thy King cometh unto thee, meek, and sitting upon an ass, and a colt the foal of an ass.

Greek/Transliteration
5. Εἴπατε τῇ θυγατρὶ Σιών, Ἰδού, ὁ βασιλεύς σου ἔρχεταί σοι, πραὺς καὶ ἐπιβεβηκὼς ἐπὶ ὄνον καὶ πῶλον υἱὸν ὑποζυγίου.

5. Eipate tei thugatri Sion, Ydou, 'o basileus sou erchetai soi, praus kai epibebeikos epi onon kai polon 'wion 'upozugiou.

Hebrew/Transliteration
ה. אִמְרוּ לְבַת-צִיּוֹן הִנֵּה מַלְכֵּךְ יָבוֹא לָךְ עָנִי וְרֹכֵב עַל-חֲמוֹר וְעַל-עַיִר בֶּן-אֲתֹנוֹת:

5. Eem•roo le•vat - Tzi•yon hee•ne Mal•kech ya•vo lach ani ve•ro•chev al - cha•mor ve•al - a•yir ben - ato•not.

Rabbinic Jewish Commentary
Tell ye the daughter of Zion,.... These words seem to be taken out of Isa_62:11 where it is said, "say ye to the daughter of Zion, behold thy salvation cometh", or "thy Saviour cometh"; meaning, without doubt, the Messiah: by the daughter of Zion is meant, not the city of Jerusalem, but the inhabitants thereof, the Jewish synagogue; or as the Targum renders it, כנישתא דציון, "the congregation of Zion", the people of the Jews; particularly the elect of God among them, those that embraced the true Messiah, and believed in him.

sitting upon an ass, and a colt, the foal of an ass. This is applied to the Messiah by the Jews, both ancient (a) and modern (v), who consider this as an instance and evidence of his humility: they suppose, this ass to be a very uncommon one, having an hundred spots on it; and say, that it was the foal of that which was created on the eve of the sabbath (w); and is the same that Abraham and Moses rode upon: and they own, as before observed, that Jesus of Nazareth rode on one to Jerusalem, as is here related. Their ancient governors, patriarchs, princes, and judges, used to ride on asses, before the introduction and multiplication of horses in Solomon's time, forbidden by the law of God: wherefore, though this might seem mean and despicable at this present time, yet was suitable enough to Yeshua's character as a king, and as the son of David, and king of Israel; strictly observing the law given to the kings of Israel, and riding in such manner as they formerly did.

"Rabbi Alexandri said, 'Rabbi Y'hoshua set two verses against each other: It is written, "And behold, one like the son of man came with the clouds of heaven" (Dan_7:13), while elsewhere it is written, "See, your king comes unto you,... humbly riding on a donkey" (Zec_9:9). [He resolved the paradox by saying that] if they deserve it [he will come] with the clouds of heaven, but if not, lowly and riding on an ass.' " (Sanhedrin 98a)

(a) T. Bab. Sanhedrim, fol. 98. 1. & 99. 1. Bereshit Rabba, fol. 66. 2. & 85. 3. Midrash Kohelet, fol. 63. 2. Zohar in Gen. fol. 127. 3. & in Num. fol. 83. 4. & in Deut. fol. 117. 1. & 118. 3. Raya Mehimna in Zohar. in Lev. fol. 38. 3. & in Num. fol. 97. 2. (v) Jarchi in Isa. xxvi 6. Baal Hatturim in Exod. fol. 88. 2. Abarbimel, Mashmia Jeshua, fol. 15. 4. (w) Pirke Eliezer, c. 31. Caphtor, fol. 81. 2.

---

6. And the disciples went, and did as Jesus commanded them,

Greek/Transliteration

6. Πορευθέντες δὲ οἱ μαθηταί, καὶ ποιήσαντες καθὼς προσέταξεν αὐτοῖς ὁ Ἰησοῦς,

6. Poreuthentes de 'oi matheitai, kai poieisantes kathos prosetaxen autois 'o Yeisous,

Hebrew/Transliteration

ו׃. וַיֵּלְכוּ הַתַּלְמִידִים וַיַּעֲשׂוּ כַּאֲשֶׁר צִוָּה אֹתָם יֵשׁוּעַ

6. Va•yel•choo ha•tal•mi•dim va•ya•a•soo ka•a•sher tzi•va o•tam Yeshua.

---

7. And brought the ass, and the colt, and put on them their clothes, and they set him thereon.

Greek/Translitersation

7. ἤγαγον τὴν ὄνον καὶ τὸν πῶλον, καὶ ἐπέθηκαν ἐπάνω αὐτῶν τὰ ἱμάτια αὐτῶν, καὶ ἐπεκάθισεν ἐπάνω αὐτῶν.

7. eigagon tein onon kai ton polon, kai epetheikan epano auton ta 'imatya auton, kai epekathisen epano auton.

Hebrew/Transliteration

ז׃. וַיָּבִיאוּ אֶת-הָאָתוֹן וְאֶת-הָעַיִר וַיָּשִׂימוּ עַל-גַּבָּם אֶת-בִּגְדֵיהֶם וְהוּא יָשַׁב עֲלֵיהֶם

7. Va•ya•vi•oo et - ha•a•ton ve•et - ha•a•yir va•ya•si•moo al - ga•bam et - big•dey•hem ve•hoo ya•shav aley•hem.

Rabbinic Jewish Commentary
And it should seem, that it was not unusual to put garments on asses to ride on; for the Targumist on Jdg_5:10 represents the princes of Israel as riding upon asses, strewed or saddled with all kind ציורין, of "painted garments". The Persic version, without the least colour of authority from the original text, renders it, "and Jesus put his own garment on the colt, and sat thereon"; which is ridiculous, as well as contrary to truth.

---

8. And a very great multitude spread their garments in the way; others cut down branches from the trees, and strawed them in the way.

Greek/Transliteration
8. Ὁ δὲ πλεῖστος ὄχλος ἔστρωσαν ἑαυτῶν τὰ ἱμάτια ἐν τῇ ὁδῷ· ἄλλοι δὲ ἔκοπτον κλάδους ἀπὸ τῶν δένδρων, καὶ ἐστρώννυον ἐν τῇ ὁδῷ.

8. 'O de pleistos ochlos estrosan 'eauton ta 'imatya en tei 'odo. alloi de ekopton kladous apo ton dendron, kai estronnuon en tei 'odo.

Hebrew/Transliteration
ח. וְרַבִּים מִן-הָעָם פָּרְשׂוּ אֶת-בִּגְדֵיהֶם עַל-פְּנֵי הַדָּרֶךְ וְיֵשׁ מֵהֶם אֲשֶׁר כָּרְתוּ זְמֹרוֹת מִן-הָעֵצִים וַיִּשְׁטְחוּ אֹתָן:שָׁמָּה

8. Ve•ra•bim min - ha•am par•soo et - big•dey•hem al - p`ney ha•da•rech ve•yesh me•hem asher kar•too ze•mo•rot min - ha•e•tzim va•yish•te•choo o•tan sha•ma.

Rabbinic Jewish Commentary
So when Jehu declared to the princes of Israel, that he was anointed king of Israel, they hastened, and took every man his garment, and put it under him, 2Ki_9:13 that is, to tread upon. Jewish writers (x) say, it was done that he might be higher than them all, suitable to the dignity of a king.

Others cut down branches from the trees; It was common with the Jews to signify their joy upon any occasion, by such ways and methods they used at that least: so upon the cleansing of the tower of Jerusalem, by Simon Maccabeus, the Jews entered into it with thanksgiving, and branches of palm trees:

"And entered into it the three and twentieth day of the second month in the hundred seventy and first year, with thanksgiving, and branches of palm trees, and with harps, and cymbals, and with viols, and hymns, and songs: because there was destroyed a great enemy out of Israel." (1 Maccabees 13:51)

Likewise upon purifying the temple, which had been polluted by Antiochus, they kept eight days with gladness as in the feast of tabernacles, and bare branches and fair boughs, and palms also, as in the Apocrypha:

6 And they kept the eight days with gladness, as in the feast of the tabernacles, remembering that not long afore they had held the feast of the tabernacles, when as they wandered in the mountains and dens like beasts. 7 Therefore they bare branches, and fair boughs, and palms also, and sang psalms unto him that had given them good success in cleansing his place. (2 Maccabees 10)

and they strawed them in the way: not in the middle of the road, which would have been an hindrance to riding; but by the way side, upon, the booths, or houses in the road, in honour of him; just as the Jews (c) say,

"the streets were strewed with myrtles, and the courts with purple, when Mordecai went out of the king's gate."

(x) R. Levi ben Gersom, & R. Samuel Laniado in loc. (c) Targum in Esther viii. 15.

---

9. And the multitudes that went before, and that followed, cried, saying, Hosanna to the Son of David: Blessed is he that cometh in the name of the Lord; Hosanna in the highest.

Greek/Transliteration
9. Οἱ δὲ ὄχλοι οἱ προάγοντες καὶ οἱ ἀκολουθοῦντες ἔκραζον, λέγοντες, Ὡσαννὰ τῷ υἱῷ Δαυΐδ· Εὐλογημένος ὁ ἐρχόμενος ἐν ὀνόματι κυρίου· Ὡσαννὰ ἐν τοῖς ὑψίστοις.

9. 'Oi de ochloi 'oi proagontes kai 'oi akolouthountes ekrazon, legontes, 'Osanna to 'wio Dauid. Eulogeimenos 'o erchomenos en onomati kuriou. 'Osanna en tois 'upsistois.

Hebrew/Transliteration
ט. וַהֲמוֹן הָעָם הַהֹלֵךְ מִלְּפָנָיו וּמֵאַחֲרָיו עָנוּ לֵאמֹר הוֹשַׁע-נָא לְבֶן-דָּוִד בָּרוּךְ הַבָּא בְּשֵׁם יְהֹוָה הוֹשַׁע-נָא בִּשְׁמֵי-מָרוֹם

9. Va•ha•mon ha•am ha•ho•lech mil•fa•nav oo•me•a•cha•rav a•noo le•mor Ho•sha – na le•Ven - David ba•rooch ha•ba be•shem Adonai Ho•sha - na bish•mey ma•rom.

Rabbinic/Jewish New Testament Commentary
Shouting, "Please! Deliver us!" to the Son of David. Greek *ôsanna* transliterates Hebrew *hoshia' na* (literally, "Save, please!"). The word, and sometimes the whole phrase, is usually rendered as if it were an acclamation of praise: "shouting, 'Hosanna to the Son of David!' " Actually "*Hoshia' na*" is a prayer addressed to the Messiah, quoted from Psa_118:25-26; Psalm 118 is Messianic throughout (Mattityahu cites another important passage from it at Mat_21:42 below). The implication is that the crowds recognized and honored Yeshua as the Messiah by

shouting, "Please, deliver us, Son of David!"-"Son of David" is a Messianic title (see Mat_1:1), and the crowds wanted their Messiah to deliver them from the Roman overlords.

"Hosana", or "Hosanna", in which form it frequently appears in the Jewish writings; and because of the often use of it at the feast of tabernacles, that feast was called "Hosanna", and the seventh day of it was called הושענא רבה, "the great Hosanna" (d). Moreover, the "Lulabs", or the bundles made of branches of palm trees, and boughs of willow and myrtle, which they carried in their hands at the feast of tabernacles, often go by this name.

Again (f), "it is a tradition of R. Meir, that it was the practice of the honourable men of Jerusalem, to bind their "Lulabs" with golden threads says Rabbah, these are they מגדלי הושענא, "that bind the Hosanna": the gloss on it is, "that bind the Lulabs", of the house of the head of the captivity; for in binding the Hosanna of the house of the head of the captivity, they leave in it an hand's breadth and says the same Rabbah, a man may not hold an Hosanna in a linen cloth."

Now these bundles might be so called, because they were lifted up and shaken, when the above words out of Psa_118:25 were recited: for thus it is said (i),

"when do they shake, that is, their "Lulabs", or "Hosannas?" At those words, "O give thanks unto the Lord", Psa_118:1 the beginning and end; and at those words, "Save now I beseech thee", Psa_118:25. The house of Hillell, and the house of Shammai say also at those words, "O Lord I beseech thee, send now prosperity": says R. Akiba, I have observed Rabban Gamaliel and Rabbi Joshua, that all the people shook their Lulabs, but they did not shake, only at those words, Save now I beseech thee, O Lord."

(d) Seder Tephillot. fol. 298. 2. (f) T. Bab. Succa, fol. 37. 1. (l) Seder Tephillot, fol. 298. 2.

---

10. And when he was come into Jerusalem, all the city was moved, saying, Who is this?

Greek/Transliteration
10. Καὶ εἰσελθόντος αὐτοῦ εἰς Ἱεροσόλυμα, ἐσείσθη πᾶσα ἡ πόλις, λέγουσα, Τίς ἐστιν οὗτος;

10. Kai eiselthontos autou eis 'Yerosoluma, eseisthei pasa 'ei polis, legousa, Tis estin 'outos?

Hebrew/Transliteration
י. וּבְבֹאוֹ יְרוּשָׁלַיִם וַתֵּהוֹם כָּל-הָעִיר לֵאמֹר מִי הוּא זֶה:

10. Oo•ve•voo Ye•roo•sha•la•yim va•te•hom kol - ha•eer le•mor mee hoo ze.

11. And the multitude said, This is Jesus the prophet of Nazareth of Galilee.

Greek/Transliteration
11. Οἱ δὲ ὄχλοι ἔλεγον, Οὗτός ἐστιν Ἰησοῦς ὁ προφήτης, ὁ ἀπὸ Ναζαρὲτ τῆς Γαλιλαίας.

11. 'Oi de ochloi elegon, 'Outos estin Yeisous 'o propheiteis, 'o apo Nazaret teis Galilaias.

Hebrew/Transliteration
יא. וַיֹּאמְרוּ הֲמוֹן הָעָם זֶה הוּא הַנָּבִיא יֵשׁוּעַ מִנְּצֶרֶת אֲשֶׁר בַּגָּלִיל:

11. Va•yom•roo ha•mon ha•am ze hoo ha•na•vee Yeshua mi•N`tze•ret asher ba•Ga•lil.

Jewish New Testament Commentary
This is Jesus the prophet: that prophet Moses spoke of, in Deu_18:15 and the nation of the Jews in general expected.

---

12. And Jesus went into the temple of God, and cast out all them that sold and bought in the temple, and overthrew the tables of the moneychangers, and the seats of them that sold doves,

Greek/Transliteration
12. Καὶ εἰσῆλθεν ὁ Ἰησοῦς εἰς τὸ ἱερὸν τοῦ θεοῦ, καὶ ἐξέβαλεν πάντας τοὺς πωλοῦντας καὶ ἀγοράζοντας ἐν τῷ ἱερῷ, καὶ τὰς τραπέζας τῶν κολλυβιστῶν κατέστρεψεν, καὶ τὰς καθέδρας τῶν πωλούντων τὰς περιστεράς.

12. Kai eiseilthen 'o Yeisous eis to 'ieron tou theou, kai exebalen pantas tous polountas kai agorazontas en to 'iero, kai tas trapezas ton kollubiston katestrepsen, kai tas kathedras ton polounton tas peristeras.

Hebrew/Transliteration
יב. וַיָּבוֹא יֵשׁוּעַ אֶל-מִקְדַּשׁ הָאֱלֹהִים וַיְגָרֶשׁ מִשָּׁם כָּל-הַמּוֹכְרִים וְהַקּוֹנִים בַּמִּקְדָּשׁ וַיַּהֲפֹךְ אֶת-שֻׁלְחֲנוֹת מַחֲלִיפֵי־הַכֶּסֶף וְאֶת-מוֹשְׁבוֹת מֹכְרֵי הַיּוֹנִים

12. Va•ya•vo Yeshua el - mik•dash ha•Elohim va•y`ga•resh mi•sham kol - ha•moch•rim ve•ha•ko•nim ba•mik•dash va•ya•ha•foch et - shool•cha•not ma•cha•li•fey ha•ke•sef ve•et - mosh•vot moch•rey ha•yo•nim.

Rabbinic Jewish Commentary
Jews (s) say, "it is an affirmative command of the law, that every man in Israel should pay the half shekel every year; even though a poor man that is maintained by alms, he is obliged to it, and must beg it of others, or sell his coat upon his back and pay it, as it is said, Exo_30:15. The rich shall not give more, &c.--All are bound to give it, priests, Levites, and Israelites, and strangers, and servants, that are made free; but not women, nor servants, nor children."

This gives us a plain account of these money changers; of their tables, and of their sitting at them in the temple, and on what account. Now these exchangers had a profit in every shekel they changed (y). "When a man went to an exchanger, and changed a shekel for two half shekels, he gave him an addition to the shekel; and the addition is called קלבון, "Kolbon"; wherefore, when two men gave a shekel for them both, they were both obliged to pay the "Kolbon"." (z). "How much is the "Kolbon?" A silver "meah", according to. R. Meir; but the wise men say, half an one."

What these persons bought and sold, whom Yeshua cast out, is not said, but may be collected from Joh_2:14 where besides "doves", of which hereafter, mention is made, of "sheep" and "oxen"; which were brought to be sold, on account of the passover, for it was then near their time of passover as now. The Talmud includes curses on the Sadducean priests for their greed. The restrictions placed on business in the Temple area created monopolistic profits for the merchants and revenue for the authorities.

According to the *Tanakh*, "on that day," that is, in Messianic times, "there shall no longer be a merchant in the house of *Adonai* of Hosts" (Zec_14:21; the word for "merchant," "trafficker" or "trader" is, literally, "Canaanite," as at Job_40:30 (Job_41:6) and Pro_31:24).

(y) Hilch. Shekalim, c, 3. sect. 1. (z) Misn. Shekalim, c. 1. sect. 7.

---

13. And said unto them, It is written, My house shall be called the house of prayer; but ye have made it a den of thieves.

Greek/Transliteration
13. Καὶ λέγει αὐτοῖς, Γέγραπται, Ὁ οἶκός μου οἶκος προσευχῆς κληθήσεται· ὑμεῖς δὲ αὐτὸν ἐποιήσατε σπήλαιον λῃστῶν.

13. Kai legei autois, Gegraptai, 'O oikos mou oikos proseucheis kleitheisetai. 'umeis de auton epoieisate speilaion leiston.

Hebrew/Transliteration
יג. וַיֹּאמֶר אֲלֵיהֶם הֵן כָּתוּב כִּי בֵיתִי בֵּית-תְּפִלָּה יִקָּרֵא וְאַתֶּם עֲשִׂיתֶם אֹתוֹ לִמְעָרַת פָּרִיצִים:

13. Va•yo•mer aley•hem hen ka•toov ki vey•ti beit - te•fi•la yi•ka•re ve•a•tem asi•tem o•to lim•a•rat pa•ri•tzim.

Rabbinic Jewish Commentary
These words are rightly applied by Yeshua to the temple, Isa.56:7; nor can the Jews themselves deny it; for their own Targum paraphrases it thus, בית מקדשי, "the house of my sanctuary shall be called an house of prayer"; or shall be one; for the meaning is not that it should go by such a name, but should be for such use, and not for buying and selling, and merchandise, to which use the Jews now put it.

14. And the blind and the lame came to him in the temple; and he healed them.

Greek/Transliteration
14. Καὶ προσῆλθον αὐτῷ χωλοὶ καὶ τυφλοὶ ἐν τῷ ἱερῷ· καὶ ἐθεράπευσεν αὐτούς.

14. Kai proseilthon auto choloi kai tuphloi en to 'iero. kai etherapeusen autous.

Hebrew/Transliteration
יד. וַיִּגְּשׁוּ אֵלָיו עִוְרִים וּפִסְחִים בְּבֵית הַמִּקְדָּשׁ וַיִּרְפָּאֵם:

14. Va•yig•shoo elav eev•rim oo•fis•chim be•veit ha•mik•dash va•yir•pa•em.

---

15. And when the chief priests and scribes saw the wonderful things that he did, and the children crying in the temple, and saying, Hosanna to the Son of David; they were sore displeased,

Greek/Transliteration
15. Ἰδόντες δὲ οἱ ἀρχιερεῖς καὶ οἱ γραμματεῖς τὰ θαυμάσια ἃ ἐποίησεν, καὶ τοὺς παῖδας κράζοντας ἐν τῷ ἱερῷ, καὶ λέγοντας, Ὡσαννὰ τῷ υἱῷ Δαυίδ, ἠγανάκτησαν,

15. Idontes de 'oi archiereis kai 'oi grammateis ta thaumasya 'a epoieisen, kai tous paidas krazontas en to 'iero, kai legontas, 'Osanna to 'wio Dauid, eiganakteisan,

Hebrew/Transliteration
טו. וַיִּרְאוּ רָאשֵׁי הַכֹּהֲנִים וְהַסּוֹפְרִים אֶת הַנִּפְלָאוֹת אֲשֶׁר עָשָׂה וְאֶת הַיְלָדִים קֹרְאִים וְעֹנִים בַּמִּקְדָּשׁ הוֹשַׁע-נָא:לְבֶן-דָּוִד וַיִּחַר לָהֶם

15. Va•yir•oo ra•shey ha•ko•ha•nim ve•ha•sof•rim et ha•nif•la•ot asher asa ve•et ha•y`la•dim kor•eem ve•o•nim ba•mik•dash ho•sha - na le•Ven - David va•yi•char la•hem.

Rabbinic Jewish Commentary
It was indeed no unusual thing for children to sing the "Hosanna" at the feast of tabernacles; for, according to the Jewish canons (k), "a child that knew how to shake, was obliged to carry the "Lulab"," or bundle of myrtle, and willow boughs, and palm tree branches, at the shaking of which "Hosanna" was said: but that they should cry "Hosanna" to Jesus, as David's son was very extraordinary, and what the high priests, and Scribes, took notice of with great resentment

(k) T. Bab. Succa, fol. 42. 1. Erachin, fol. 2. 2. Maimon. Hilch. Lulab, c. 7. sect. 19.

16. And said unto him, Hearest thou what these say? And Jesus saith unto them, Yea; have ye never read, Out of the mouth of babes and sucklings thou hast perfected praise?

Greek/Transliteration
16. καὶ εἶπον αὐτῷ, Ἀκούεις τί οὗτοι λέγουσιν; Ὁ δὲ Ἰησοῦς λέγει αὐτοῖς, Ναί· οὐδέποτε ἀνέγνωτε ὅτι Ἐκ στόματος νηπίων καὶ θηλαζόντων κατηρτίσω αἶνον;

16. kai eipon auto, Akoueis ti 'outoi legousin? 'O de Yeisous legei autois, Nai. oudepote anegnote 'oti Ek stomatos neipion kai theilazonton kateirtiso ainon?

Hebrew/Transliteration
טז. וַיֹּאמְרוּ אֵלָיו הֲכִי שָׁמַעְתָּ מָה אֵלֶּה אֹמְרִים וַיֹּאמֶר אֲלֵיהֶם יֵשׁוּעַ הֵן הֲלֹא קְרָאתֶם מִפִּי עוֹלְלִים וְיוֹנְקִים: יִסַּדְתָּ עֹז

16. Va•yom•roo elav ha•chi sha•ma•ata ma ele om•rim va•yo•mer aley•hem Yeshua hen ha•lo ke•ra•tem mi•pi o•le•lim ve•yon•kim yi•sa•de•ta oz.

Rabbinic Jewish Commentary
have ye never read; that passage of Scripture in Psa_8:2. The Jews themselves seem to be conscious, that these words relate to the Messiah; for they say (l), that

"babes and sucklings, יהבין תוקפא, shall give strength to the king Messiah" manifestly referring to this passage. (l) Zohar in Exod. fol. 4. 2.

---

17. And he left them, and went out of the city into Bethany; and he lodged there.

Greek/Transliteration
17. Καὶ καταλιπὼν αὐτοὺς ἐξῆλθεν ἔξω τῆς πόλεως εἰς Βηθανίαν, καὶ ηὐλίσθη ἐκεῖ.

17. Kai katalipon autous exeilthen exo teis poleos eis Beithanian, kai eiulisthei ekei.

Hebrew/Transliteration
:יז. וַיַּעַזְבֵם וַיֵּצֵא אֶל-מִחוּץ לָעִיר אֶל-בֵּית-עַנְיָה וַיָּלֶן שָׁם

17. Va•ya•az•vem va•ye•tze el - mi•choo•tz la•eer el - Beit - An•ya va•ya•len sham.

---

18. Now in the morning as he returned into the city, he hungered.

Greek/Transliteration
18. Πρωΐας δὲ ἐπανάγων εἰς τὴν πόλιν, ἐπείνασεν·

18. Proias de epanagon eis tein polin, epeinasen.

Hebrew/Transliteration
יח. וַיָּשָׁב הָעִירָה בַּבֹּקֶר וְהוּא רָעֵב:

18. Va•ya•shov ha•ee•ra ba•bo•ker ve•hoo ra•ev.

---

19. And when he saw a fig tree in the way, he came to it, and found nothing thereon, but leaves only, and said unto it, Let no fruit grow on thee henceforward for ever. And presently the fig tree withered away.

Greek/Transliteration
19. καὶ ἰδὼν συκῆν μίαν ἐπὶ τῆς ὁδοῦ, ἦλθεν ἐπ' αὐτήν, καὶ οὐδὲν εὗρεν ἐν αὐτῇ εἰ μὴ φύλλα μόνον· καὶ λέγει αὐτῇ, Μηκέτι ἐκ σοῦ καρπὸς γένηται εἰς τὸν αἰῶνα. Καὶ ἐξηράνθη παραχρῆμα ἡ συκῆ.

19. kai idon sukein mian epi teis 'odou, eilthen ep autein, kai ouden 'euren en autei ei mei phulla monon. kai legei autei, Meiketi ek sou karpos geneitai eis ton aiona. Kai exeiranthei parachreima 'ei sukei.

Hebrew/Transliteration
יט. וַיַּרְא תְּאֵנָה אַחַת בַּדֶּרֶךְ וַיִּקְרַב אֵלֶיהָ וְלֹא־מָצָא בָהּ מְאוּמָה זוּלָתִי עָלִים לְבַדָּם וַיֹּאמֶר לָהּ לֹא־תַעֲשִׂי עוֹד־פְּרִי מֵעַתָּה וְעַד־עוֹלָם וַתִּיבַשׁ הַתְּאֵנָה פִּתְאֹם

19. Va•yar te•e•na a•chat ba•da•rech va•yik•rav e•le•ha ve•lo - me•tza va me•oo•ma zoo•la•tee alim le•va•dam va•yo•mer la lo - ta•a•si od p`ri me•a•ta ve•ad - o•lam va•ti•vash ha•te•e•na pit•om.

Rabbinic Jewish Commentary
This tree was an emblem of the Jews: Yeshua being hungry, and very desirous of the salvation of men, came first to them, from whom, on account of their large profession of religion, and great pretensions to holiness, and the many advantages they enjoyed, humanly speaking, much fruit of righteousness might have been expected; but, alas! he found nothing but mere words, empty boasts, an outward show of religion, an external profession, and a bare performance of trifling ceremonies, and oral traditions; wherefore Yeshua rejected them, and in a little time after, the kingdom of God, the Gospel, was taken away from them, and their temple, city, and nation, entirely destroyed. See also Luke 13:6-9.

"I found Israel like grapes in the wilderness; I saw your forefathers as the earliest fruit on the fig tree in its first *season. But* they came to Baal-peor and devoted themselves to shame, And they became as detestable as that which they loved." (Hosea 9:10)

20. And when the disciples saw it, they marvelled, saying, How soon is the fig tree withered away!

Greek/Transliteration
20. Καὶ ἰδόντες οἱ μαθηταὶ ἐθαύμασαν, λέγοντες, Πῶς παραχρῆμα ἐξηράνθη ἡ συκῆ;

20. Kai idontes 'oi matheitai ethaumasan, legontes, Pos parachreima exeiranthei 'ei sukei?

Hebrew/Transliteration
:כ. וְהַתַּלְמִידִים רָאוּ וַיִּתְמְהוּ לֵאמֹר אֵיךְ יָבְשָׁה הַתְּאֵנָה פִּתְאֹם

20. Ve•ha•tal•mi•dim ra•oo va•yit•me•hoo le•mor eych yav•sha ha•te•e•na pit•om.

---

21. Jesus answered and said unto them, Verily I say unto you, If ye have faith, and doubt not, ye shall not only do this which is done to the fig tree, but also if ye shall say unto this mountain, Be thou removed, and be thou cast into the sea; it shall be done.

Greek/Transliteration
21. Ἀποκριθεὶς δὲ ὁ Ἰησοῦς εἶπεν αὐτοῖς, Ἀμὴν λέγω ὑμῖν, ἐὰν ἔχητε πίστιν, καὶ μὴ διακριθῆτε, οὐ μόνον τὸ τῆς συκῆς ποιήσετε, ἀλλὰ κἂν τῷ ὄρει τούτῳ εἴπητε, Ἄρθητι καὶ βλήθητι εἰς τὴν θάλασσαν, γενήσεται.

21. Apokritheis de 'o Yeisous eipen autois, Amein lego 'umin, ean echeite pistin, kai mei dyakritheite, ou monon to teis sukeis poieisete, alla kan to orei touto eipeite, Artheiti kai bleitheiti eis tein thalassan, geneisetai.

Hebrew/Transliteration
כא. וַיַּעַן יֵשׁוּעַ וַיֹּאמֶר אֲלֵיהֶם אָמֵן אֲנִי אֹמֵר לָכֶם אִם־יֵשׁ בָּכֶם אֱמוּנָה וְאֵינְכֶם פֹּסְחִים עַל־שְׁתֵּי הַסְּעִפִּים לֹא לְבַד כְּמַעֲשֵׂה הַזֶּה אֲשֶׁר נַעֲשָׂה לַתְּאֵנָה תַּעֲשׂוּ כִּי אִם־גַּם תֹּאמְרוּ לָהָר הַזֶּה הִנָּשֵׂא וְהִתְנַפֵּל אֶל־תּוֹךְ הַיָּם וִיהִי־כֵן

21. Va•ya•an Yeshua va•yo•mer aley•hem Amen ani o•mer la•chem eem - yesh ba•chem e•moo•na ve•eyn•chem pos•chim al - sh`tey ha•se•ee•pim lo le•vad ka•ma•a•se ha•ze asher na•a•sa la•te•e•na ta•a•soo ki eem - gam tom•roo la•har ha•ze hi•na•se ve•hit•na•pel el - toch ha•yam vi•y`hi chen.

---

22. And all things, whatsoever ye shall ask in prayer, believing, ye shall receive.

Greek/Transliteration
22. Καὶ πάντα ὅσα ἐὰν αἰτήσητε ἐν τῇ προσευχῇ, πιστεύοντες, λήψεσθε.
22. Kai panta 'osa ean aiteiseite en tei proseuchei, pisteuontes, leipsesthe.

Hebrew/Transliteration
וְכָל־דָּבָר אֲשֶׁר תִּשְׁאֲלוּ בִתְפִלָּה אִם רַק בֶּאֱמוּנָה שְׁאֶלְתֶּם יֻתַּן לָכֶם׃ כב:

22. Ve•chol - da•var asher tish•a•loo vit•fi•la eem rak be•e•moo•na sh`el•tem yoo•tan la•chem.

---

23. And when he was come into the temple, the chief priests and the elders of the people came unto him as he was teaching, and said, By what authority doest thou these things? And who gave thee this authority?

Greek/Transliteration
23. Καὶ ἐλθόντι αὐτῷ εἰς τὸ ἱερόν, προσῆλθον αὐτῷ διδάσκοντι οἱ ἀρχιερεῖς καὶ οἱ πρεσβύτεροι τοῦ λαοῦ, λέγοντες, Ἐν ποίᾳ ἐξουσίᾳ ταῦτα ποιεῖς; Καὶ τίς σοι ἔδωκεν τὴν ἐξουσίαν ταύτην;

23. Kai elthonti auto eis to 'ieron, proseilthon auto didaskonti 'oi archiereis kai 'oi presbuteroi tou laou, legontes, En poia exousia tauta poieis? Kai tis soi edoken tein exousian tautein?

Hebrew/Transliteration
כג. וַיָּבֹא אֶל־הַמִּקְדָּשׁ וַיִּגְּשׁוּ אֵלָיו רָאשֵׁי הַכֹּהֲנִים וְזִקְנֵי הָעָם בְּעוֹדוֹ מְלַמֵּד לָעָם וַיֹּאמְרוּ בְּאֵיזֶה רִשְׁיוֹן אַתָּה עֹשֶׂה אֵלֶּה וּמִי־נָתַן לְךָ הָרִשְׁיוֹן הַזֶּה׃

23. Va•ya•vo el - ha•mik•dash va•yig•shoo elav ra•shey ha•ko•ha•nim ve•zik•ney ha•am be•o•do me•la•med la•am va•yom•roo be•ey•ze rish•yon ata o•se ele oo•mi - na•tan le•cha ha•rish•yon ha•ze?

Rabbinic Jewish Commentary
Jewish writers interpret the word "elders", in Deu_21:2 "thy elders, and thy judges"; that is, "thy elders, who are thy judges: it is a tradition, R. Eliezer ben Jacob says, זקניך :זה בית דין הגדול, "thine elders; this is the great sanhedrim" (a).

Hebrew *s'mikhah*, rendering Greek *exousia* ("authority"), means "leaning" or "laying" on of hands in the ordination ceremony for a judge, elder or rabbi. Laying on of hands is, in the *Tanakh*, a symbolic act that confers or transfers an office, along with its duties and privileges, by dramatizing God's bestowal of the blessings and giftings needed for the work. In Judaism the practice is traced back to Moses' ordination of Joshua and of the seventy elders (Num_11:16-17, Num_11:24-25; Num_27:18-23; Deu_34:9).

(a) T. Hieros Sota, fol. 23. 3. Jarchi in Deut. xxi. 2.

---

24. And Jesus answered and said unto them, I also will ask you one thing, which if ye tell me, I in like wise will tell you by what authority I do these things.

Greek/Transliteration
24. Ἀποκριθεὶς δὲ ὁ Ἰησοῦς εἶπεν αὐτοῖς, Ἐρωτήσω ὑμᾶς κἀγὼ λόγον ἕνα, ὃν ἐὰν εἴπητέ μοι, κἀγὼ ὑμῖν ἐρῶ ἐν ποίᾳ ἐξουσίᾳ ταῦτα ποιῶ.

24. Apokritheis de 'o Yeisous eipen autois, Eroteiso 'umas kago logon 'ena, 'on ean eipeite moi, kago 'umin ero en poia exousia tauta poio.

Hebrew/Translieration
כד. וַיַּעַן יֵשׁוּעַ וַיֹּאמֶר אֲלֵיהֶם אֶשְׁאַל מִכֶּם גַּם-אָנֹכִי שְׁאֵלָה אַחַת וְאִם-תַּגִּידוּ לִי גַּם-אָנֹכִי אַגִּיד לָכֶם בְּאֵיזֶה:רִשְׁיוֹן אֲנִי עֹשֶׂה אֵלֶּה

24. Va•ya•an Yeshua va•yo•mer aley•hem esh•al mi•kem gam - ano•chi sh`a•la a•chat ve•eem - ta•gi•doo li gam - ano•chi agid la•chem be•ey•ze rish•yon ani o•se ele.

---

25. The baptism of John, whence was it? from heaven, or of men? And they reasoned with themselves, saying, If we shall say, From heaven; he will say unto us, Why did ye not then believe him?

Greek/Transliteration
25. Τὸ βάπτισμα Ἰωάννου πόθεν ἦν; Ἐξ οὐρανοῦ ἢ ἐξ ἀνθρώπων; Οἱ δὲ διελογίζοντο παρ' ἑαυτοῖς, λέγοντες, Ἐὰν εἴπωμεν, Ἐξ οὐρανοῦ, ἐρεῖ ἡμῖν, Διὰ τί οὖν οὐκ ἐπιστεύσατε αὐτῷ;

25. To baptisma Yoannou pothen ein? Ex ouranou ei ex anthropon? 'Oi de dielogizonto par 'eautois, legontes, Ean eipomen, Ex ouranou, erei 'eimin, Dya ti oun ouk episteusate auto?

Hebrew/Transliteration
כה. טְבִילַת יוֹחָנָן מִפִּי - מִי הָיְתָה מִצִּנְוָתָהּ מִן - הַשָּׁמַיִם אוֹ מִבְּנֵי - אָדָם וַיְהִי הֵם שֹׁקְלִים בְּדַעְתָּם לֵאמֹר אִם נֹאמַר:מִן - הַשָּׁמַיִם יֹאמַר לָנוּ וּמַדּוּעַ לֹא הֶאֱמַנְתֶּם לוֹ

25. T`vi•lat Yo•cha•nan mi•pi - mee hai•ta mitz•va•ta min - ha•sha•ma•yim oh mi•b`ney - adam vay•hi hem shok•lim be•da•a•tam le•mor eem no•mar min - ha•sha•ma•yim yo•mar la•noo oo•ma•doo•a lo he•e•man•tem lo.

Rabbinic Jewish Commentary
from heaven, or of men? that is, from God or man? as the opposition requires; and as it was usual for the Jews to call God by the name of "heaven": in this sense it is used by them, when they say (b), that such have no part in the world to come, who affirm, that the law is not מן השמים, "from heaven", that is, from God; which is exactly the phrase here: and when they observe (c), that care should be taken that a man does not pronounce שם שמים, "the name of heaven", that is, God, in vain: and when they tell (d) us of a certain man that built large buildings by the way side, and put food and drink there, so that everyone that came went in and eat, and drank, וברך לשמים, "and blessed heaven"; that is blessed, or gave thanks to God; and when they speak of (e) מיתה לשמים, "death by heaven"; that is, death which is

immediately inflicted by God.

(b) T. Hieros. Sanhedrin, fol. 27. 3. Vid. ib. fol. 19. 3. T. Bab. Sanhedrin, fol. 99. 1. (c) T. Bab. Megilla, fol. 3. 1. (d) Abot. R. Nathan, c. 7. fol. 3. 2. (e) Ib. c. 11. fol. 4. 1. Vid. ib. c. 14. fol. 4. 4. & 5. 1. & c. 27. fol. 7. 1.

---

26. But if we shall say, Of men; we fear the people; for all hold John as a prophet.

Greek/Transliteration

26. Ἐὰν δὲ εἴπωμεν, Ἐξ ἀνθρώπων, φοβούμεθα τὸν ὄχλον· πάντες γὰρ ἔχουσιν τὸν Ἰωάννην ὡς προφήτην.

26. Ean de eipomen, Ex anthropon, phoboumetha ton ochlon. pantes gar echousin ton Yoannein 'os propheitein.

Hebrew/Transliteration

:כו. וְאִם נֹאמַר מִבְּנֵי אָדָם יְרֵאִים אֲנַחְנוּ אֶת-הָמוֹן הָעָם כִּי-כֻלָּם חֹשְׁבוּ אֶת-יוֹחָנָן לְנָבִיא

26. Ve•eem no•mar mi•b`ney adam ye•re•eem a•nach•noo et - ha•mon ha•am ki - choo•lam chish•voo et - Yo•cha•nan le•na•vi.

---

27. And they answered Jesus, and said, We cannot tell. And he said unto them, Neither tell I you by what authority I do these things.

Greek/Transliteration

27. Καὶ ἀποκριθέντες τῷ Ἰησοῦ εἶπον, Οὐκ οἴδαμεν. Ἔφη αὐτοῖς καὶ αὐτός, Οὐδὲ ἐγὼ λέγω ὑμῖν ἐν ποίᾳ ἐξουσίᾳ ταῦτα ποιῶ.

27. Kai apokrithentes to Yeisou eipon, Ouk oidamen. Ephei autois kai autos, Oude ego lego 'umin en poia exousia tauta poio.

Hebrew/Transliteration

כז. וַיַּעֲנוּ אֶת-יֵשׁוּעַ וַיֹּאמְרוּ לֹא יָדַעְנוּ וַיֹּאמֶר אֲלֵיהֶם גַּם-אֲנִי לֹא אַגִּיד לָכֶם בְּאֵיזֶה רִשְׁיוֹן אֲנִי עֹשֶׂה אֵלֶּה:

27. Va•ya•a•noo et - Yeshua va•yom•roo lo ya•da•a•noo va•yo•mer aley•hem gam - ani lo agid la•chem be•ey•ze rish•yon ani o•se ele.

---

28. But what think ye? A certain man had two sons; and he came to the first, and said, Son, go work to day in my vineyard.

Greek/Transliteration

28. Τί δὲ ὑμῖν δοκεῖ; Ἄνθρωπος εἶχεν τέκνα δύο, καὶ προσελθὼν τῷ πρώτῳ εἶπεν, Τέκνον, ὕπαγε, σήμερον ἐργάζου ἐν τῷ ἀμπελῶνί μου.

28. Ti de 'umin dokei? Anthropos eichen tekna duo, kai proselthon to proto eipen, Teknon, 'upage, seimeron ergazou en to ampeloni mou.

Hebrew/Transliteration

כח. אֲבָל מַה-יַּחֲשֹׁב לִבְכֶם אִישׁ הָיָה וְלוֹ שְׁנֵי בָנִים וַיָּבֹא אֶל-הָאֶחָד וַיֹּאמֶר לְכָה-בְּנִי וַעֲבֹד הַיּוֹם אֶת-כַּרְמִי:

28. Aval ma - ya•cha•shov lib•chem eesh ha•ya ve•lo sh`ney va•nim va•ya•vo el - ha•e•chad va•yo•mer le•cha - b`ni va•a•vod ha•yom et - kar•mi.

---

29. He answered and said, I will not: but afterward he repented, and went.

Greek/Transliteration
29. Ὁ δὲ ἀποκριθεὶς εἶπεν, Οὐ θέλω· ὕστερον δὲ μεταμεληθείς, ἀπῆλθεν.

29. 'O de apokritheis eipen, Ou thelo. 'usteron de metameleitheis, apeilthen.

Hebrew/Transliteration
כט. וַיַּעַן וַיֹּאמֶר לֹא חָפַצְתִּי וְאַחֲרֵי-כֵן נֶהְפַּךְ עָלָיו לִבּוֹ וַיֵּלֶךְ:

29. Va•ya•an va•yo•mer lo cha•fatz•ti ve•a•cha•rey - chen ne•he•pach alav li•bo va•ye•lech.

---

30. And he came to the second, and said likewise. And he answered and said, I go, sir: and went not.

Greek/Transliteration
30. Καὶ προσελθὼν τῷ δευτέρῳ εἶπεν ὡσαύτως. Ὁ δὲ ἀποκριθεὶς εἶπεν, Ἐγώ, κύριε· καὶ οὐκ ἀπῆλθεν.

30. Kai proselthon to deutero eipen 'osautos. 'O de apokritheis eipen, Ego, kurie. kai ouk apeilthen.

Hebrew/Transliteration
ל. וַיָּבֹא אֶל-הַשֵּׁנִי וַיְדַבֵּר כַּדָּבָר הַזֶּה וַיַּעַן וַיֹּאמֶר הִנְנִי אֲדֹנִי וְלֹא הָלָךְ:

30. Va•ya•vo el - ha•she•ni va•y`da•ber ka•da•var ha•ze va•ya•an va•yo•mer hi•ne•ni a•do•ni ve•lo ha•lach.

31. Whether of them twain did the will of his father? They say unto him, The first. Jesus saith unto them, Verily I say unto you, That the publicans and the harlots go into the kingdom of God before you.

Greek/Transliteration
31. Τίς ἐκ τῶν δύο ἐποίησεν τὸ θέλημα τοῦ πατρός; Λέγουσιν αὐτῷ, Ὁ πρῶτος. Λέγει αὐτοῖς ὁ Ἰησοῦς, Ἀμὴν λέγω ὑμῖν, ὅτι οἱ τελῶναι καὶ αἱ πόρναι προάγουσιν ὑμᾶς εἰς τὴν βασιλείαν τοῦ θεοῦ.

31. Tis ek ton duo epoieisen to theleima tou patros? Legousin auto, 'O protos. Legei autois 'o Yeisous, Amein lego 'umin, 'oti 'oi telonai kai 'ai pornai proagousin 'umas eis tein basileian tou theou.

Hebrew/Translitration
לא. מִי מִשְׁנֵיהֶם מִלֵּא אַחַר רְצוֹן אָבִיו וַיֹּאמְרוּ הָרִאשׁוֹן וַיֹּאמֶר עֲלֵיהֶם יֵשׁוּעַ אָמֵן אֲנִי אֹמֵר לָכֶם כִּי הַמּוֹכְסִים וְהַזֹּנוֹת יַקְדִּימוּ לָבֹא לְמַלְכוּת הָאֱלֹהִים מִכֶּם

31. Mee mish•ney•hem mi•le achar r`tzon aviv va•yom•roo ha•ri•shon va•yo•mer aley•hem Yeshua Amen ani o•mer la•chem ki ha•moch•sim ve•ha•zo•not yak•di•moo la•vo le•mal•choot ha•Elohim mi•kem.

---

32. For John came unto you in the way of righteousness, and ye believed him not: but the publicans and the harlots believed him: and ye, when ye had seen it, repented not afterward, that ye might believe him.

Greek.Transliteration
32. Ἦλθεν γὰρ πρὸς ὑμᾶς Ἰωάννης ἐν ὁδῷ δικαιοσύνης, καὶ οὐκ ἐπιστεύσατε αὐτῷ· οἱ δὲ τελῶναι καὶ αἱ πόρναι ἐπίστευσαν αὐτῷ· ὑμεῖς δὲ ἰδόντες οὐ μετεμελήθητε ὕστερον τοῦ πιστεῦσαι αὐτῷ.

32. Eilthen gar pros 'umas Yoanneis en 'odo dikaiosuneis, kai ouk episteusate auto. 'oi de telonai kai 'ai pornai episteusan auto. 'umeis de idontes ou metemeleitheite 'usteron tou pisteusai auto.

Hebrew/Transliteration
לב. כִּי יוֹחָנָן בָּא אֲלֵיכֶם בְּדֶרֶךְ צְדָקָה וְלֹא הֶאֱמַנְתֶּם לוֹ וְהַמּוֹכְסִים וְהַזֹּנוֹת הֶאֱמִינוּ לוֹ וְאַתֶּם רְאִיתֶם כָּל-זֹאת:וְלֹא הֲשִׁיבֹתֶם אֶל-לִבְּכֶם לְהַאֲמִין לוֹ

32. Ki Yo•cha•nan ba aley•chem ba•de•rech tze•da•ka ve•lo he•e•man•tem lo ve•ha•moch•sim ve•ha•zo•not he•e•mi•noo lo ve•a•tem r`ee•tem kol - zot ve•lo ha•shi•vo•tem el - lib•chem le•ha•a•min lo.

---

33. Hear another parable: There was a certain householder, which planted a vineyard, and hedged it round about, and digged a winepress in it, and built a tower, and let it out to husbandmen, and went into a far country:

33. Ἄλλην παραβολὴν ἀκούσατε. Ἄνθρωπός τις ἦν οἰκοδεσπότης, ὅστις ἐφύτευσεν ἀμπελῶνα, καὶ φραγμὸν αὐτῷ περιέθηκεν, καὶ ὤρυξεν ἐν αὐτῷ ληνόν, καὶ ᾠκοδόμησεν πύργον, καὶ ἐξέδοτο αὐτὸν γεωργοῖς, καὶ ἀπεδήμησεν.

33. Allein parabolein akousate. Anthropos tis ein oikodespoteis, 'ostis ephuteusen ampelona, kai phragmon auto perietheiken, kai oruxen en auto leinon, kai okodomeisen purgon, kai exedoto auton georgois, ka apedeimeisen.

Hebrew/Transliteration

לג. שִׁמְעוּ מָשָׁל אַחֵר אִישׁ הָיָה בַּעַל־בַּיִת אֲשֶׁר נָטַע כֶּרֶם וַיְעַזְּקֵהוּ מִסָּבִיב וְיֶקֶב חָצֵב בּוֹ וַיִּבֶן מִגְדַּל בְּתוֹכוֹ וְנָתַן אֹתוֹ לַנֹּטְרִים וְהָלַךְ מִחוּץ לָאָרֶץ:

33. Shim•oo ma•shal a•cher eesh ha•ya ba•al - ba•yit asher na•ta ke•rem vay•az•ke•hoo mi•sa•viv ve•ye•kev cha•tzev bo va•yi•ven mig•dal be•to•cho ve•na•tan o•to la•not•rim ve•ha•lach mi•choo•tz la•a•retz.

Rabbinic Jewish Commentary

Which planted a vineyard: of the form of a vineyard, the manner of planting it, and the size of it, the Jews say many things in their Mishna (f), "He that plants a row of five vines, the school of Shammai say, "it is a vineyard"; but the school of Hillell say, it is not a vineyard, unless there are two rows--he that plants two vines over against two, and one at the tail or end, הרי זה כרם, "lo! this is a vineyard"; (it was a little vineyard;) but if two over against two, and one between the two, or two over against two, and one in the midst, it is no vineyard, unless there are two over against two, and one at the tail or end. Again (g), "a vineyard that is planted with less than four cubits (between every row), R. Simeon says, is no vineyard; but the wise men say it is a vineyard. Now by this vineyard is meant, the house of Israel and the men of Judah, the nation of the Jews, as in Isa_5:4-7 from whence our Lord seems to have taken many of the ideas expressed in this parable.

(f) Misna Kilaim, c. 4. sect. 5, 6. Maimon. Hilch. Kilaim, c. 7. sect. 7. (g) Ib. c. 5. sect. 2. Maimon ib. sect. 1.

---

34. And when the time of the fruit drew near, he sent his servants to the husbandmen, that they might receive the fruits of it.

Greek/Transliteration

34. Ὅτε δὲ ἤγγισεν ὁ καιρὸς τῶν καρπῶν, ἀπέστειλεν τοὺς δούλους αὐτοῦ πρὸς τοὺς γεωργούς, λαβεῖν τοὺς καρποὺς αὐτοῦ·

34. 'Ote de eingisen 'o kairos ton karpon, apesteilen tous doulous autou pros tous georgous, labein tous karpous autou.

Hebrew/Transliteration

לד. כְּבֹא עֵת הַבָּצִיר שָׁלַח אֶת־עֲבָדָיו אֶל־הַנֹּטְרִים לְהָבִיא אֶת־פְּרִיוֹ:

34. Ke•vo et ha•ba•tzir sha•lach et - ava•dav el - ha•not•rim le•ha•vee et - pir•yo.

Rabbinic Jewish Commentary
God after a long time, after he had waited a great while for fruit from the Jewish nation, from whom much might have been expected, by reason of the advantages they enjoyed; he sent his servants to the husbandmen: by his servants are meant, the prophets of the Old Testament; who were sent by God from time to time, to the kings, priests, and people of the Jews; to instruct them in their duty, to exhort them to the performance of it, to reprove them for their sins, to stir them up to repentance, and to bring forth fruits meet for it.

---

35. And the husbandmen took his servants, and beat one, and killed another, and stoned another.

Greek/Transliteration
35. καὶ λαβόντες οἱ γεωργοὶ τοὺς δούλους αὐτοῦ, ὃν μὲν ἔδειραν, ὃν δὲ ἀπέκτειναν, ὃν δὲ ἐλιθοβόλησαν.

35. kai labontes 'oi georgoi tous doulous autou, 'on men edeiran, 'on de apekteinan, 'on de elithoboleisan.

Hebrew/Transliteration
לה. וַיִּתְפְּשׂוּ הַנֹּטְרִים בַּעֲבָדָיו וַיַּכּוּ אֶת-אֶחָד מֵהֶם וְאֶת-אַחֵר הָרְגוּ וְאֶת-אַחֵר סָקָלוּ׃

35. Va•yit•pe•soo ha•not•rim ba•a•va•dav va•ya•koo et - e•chad me•hem ve•et - a•cher har•goo ve•et - a•cher si•ke•loo.

Rabbinic Jewish Commentary
There were four kinds of death in the power of the sanhedrim, of which this is one, and what follows is another; and were these, stoning, burning, killing (i.e. beheading with the sword), and strangling: the manner of executing this punishment here expressed, was this:

"They cut off the person's head בסייף, "with a sword", in the manner the government orders it. R. Judah says, this is indecent (i.e. to cut off his head standing, they do not do so), but they put his head upon a block, and cut it off with an axe; they reply to him, there is no death more abominable than this (x). So the prophets, in the time of Elijah, were killed with the sword, 1Ki_19:14.

(x) Misn. Sanhedrin, c. 7. sect. 1, 3.

---

36. Again, he sent other servants more than the first: and they did unto them likewise.

Greek/Transliteration

36. Πάλιν ἀπέστειλεν ἄλλους δούλους πλείονας τῶν πρώτων· καὶ ἐποίησαν αὐτοῖς ὡσαύτως.

36. Palin apesteilen allous doulous pleionas ton proton. kai epoieisan autois 'osautos.

Hebrew/Transliteration

:לו. וַיּוֹסֶף וַיִּשְׁלַח עֲבָדִים אֲחֵרִים רַבִּים מִן-הָרִאשֹׁנִים וְגַם-לָהֶם עָשׂוּ כֵן

36. Va•yo•sef va•yish•lach a•va•dim a•che•rim ra•bim min - ha•ri•sho•nim ve•gam - la•hem a•soo chen.

---

37. But last of all he sent unto them his son, saying, They will reverence my son.

Greek/Transliteration

37. Ὕστερον δὲ ἀπέστειλεν πρὸς αὐτοὺς τὸν υἱὸν αὐτοῦ, λέγων, Ἐντραπήσονται τὸν υἱόν μου.

37. 'Usteron de apesteilen pros autous ton 'wion autou, legon, Entrapeisontai ton 'wion mou.

Hebrew/Transliteration

:לז. וְאַחֲרֵי-כֵן שָׁלַח אֲלֵיהֶם אֶת-בְּנוֹ כִּי אָמַר אֶת-בְּנִי יִירָאוּ

37. Ve•a•cha•rey - chen sha•lach aley•hem et - b`no ki amar et - b`ni yi•ra•oo.

---

38. But when the husbandmen saw the son, they said among themselves, This is the heir; come, let us kill him, and let us seize on his inheritance.

Greek/Transliteration

38. Οἱ δὲ γεωργοὶ ἰδόντες τὸν υἱὸν εἶπον ἐν ἑαυτοῖς, Οὗτός ἐστιν ὁ κληρονόμος· δεῦτε, ἀποκτείνωμεν αὐτόν, καὶ κατάσχωμεν τὴν κληρονομίαν αὐτοῦ.

38. 'Oi de georgoi idontes ton 'wion eipon en 'eautois, 'Outos estin 'o kleironomos. deute, apokteinomen auton, kai kataschomen tein kleironomian autou.

Hebrew/Transliteration

לח. וְהַנֹּטְרִים כִּרְאוֹתָם אֶת-הַבֵּן וַיֹּאמְרוּ אִישׁ אֶל-אָחִיו הִנֵּה הַיּוֹרֵשׁ לְכוּ וְנַהַרְגֵהוּ וְנִירַשׁ לָנוּ אֶת-
:יְרֻשָּׁתוֹ

38. Ve•ha•not•rim kir•o•tam et - ha•ben va•yom•roo eesh el - a•chiv hee•ne ha•yo•resh le•choo ve•na•har•ge•hoo ve•ni•rash la•noo et - ye•roo•sha•to.

Rabbinic Jewish Commentary

this is the heir; Here it seems to denote, his being heir to the throne of Israel, the government of the Jewish nation, as he was the son of David; and the Jews confess (y), that because it was said that Yeshua of Nazareth was קרוב למלכות, "near to the kingdom", therefore they put him to death: (y) T. Bab. Sanhedrin, fol. 43. 1.

---

39. And they caught him, and cast him out of the vineyard, and slew him.

Greek/Transliteration
39. Καὶ λαβόντες αὐτὸν ἐξέβαλον ἔξω τοῦ ἀμπελῶνος καὶ ἀπέκτειναν.

39. Kai labontes auton exebalon exo tou ampelonos kai apekteinan.

Hebrew/Transliteration
לט. וַיִּתְפְּשׂוּ בּוֹ וַיַּשְׁלִיכֻהוּ אֶל-מִחוּץ לַכֶּרֶם וַיַּהַרְגֻהוּ:

39. Va•yit•pe•soo bo va•yash•li•choo•hoo el - mi•choo•tz la•ke•rem va•ya•har•goo•hoo.

---

40. When the lord therefore of the vineyard cometh, what will he do unto those husbandmen?

Greek/Transliteration
40. Ὅταν οὖν ἔλθῃ ὁ κύριος τοῦ ἀμπελῶνος, τί ποιήσει τοῖς γεωργοῖς ἐκείνοις;

40. 'Otan oun elthei 'o kurios tou ampelonos, ti poieisei tois georgois ekeinois?

Hebrew/Transliteration
מ. וְעַתָּה כְּבֹא בַּעַל הַכֶּרֶם מַה-יַּעֲשֶׂה לַנֹּטְרִים הָהֵם:

40. Ve•a•ta ke•vo ba•al ha•ka•rem ma - ya•a•se la•not•rim ha•hem.

TaNaKh-Old Testament/Rabbinic Jewish Commentary

When the Lord therefore of the vineyard cometh,.... In a way of providence, to call these husbandmen to an account; not only for the fruit they were to bring to him; but for their barbarity to his servants, the prophets, time after time; and especially, for the inhuman usage and murder of his own son, what will he do unto those husbandmen? This question is put to the chief priests, elders, and Scribes: and they themselves, who are designed hereby, are made judges in this case, just as the inhabitants of Jerusalem and men of Judah are, in Isa_5:4-7 which passage of Scripture our Lord had greatly in view when he spake this parable.

"What more could have been done to My vineyard that I have not done in it? Why, when I waited for the yielding of grapes, did it yield rotten ones? "So now let Me tell you what I am going to do to My vineyard: I will remove its hedge and it will be consumed; I will break down its wall and it will become trampled ground. "I will lay it waste; It will not be pruned or hoed, But briars and thorns will come up. I will also charge the clouds to rain no rain on it." For the vineyard of the LORD of hosts is the house of Israel And the men of Judah His delightful plant. Thus He looked for justice, but behold, bloodshed; For righteousness, but behold, a cry of distress." Isa_5:4-7

---

41. They say unto him, He will miserably destroy those wicked men, and will let out his vineyard unto other husbandmen, which shall render him the fruits in their seasons.

Greek/Transliteration
41. Λέγουσιν αὐτῷ, Κακοὺς κακῶς ἀπολέσει αὐτούς, καὶ τὸν ἀμπελῶνα ἐκδώσεται ἄλλοις γεωργοῖς, οἵτινες ἀποδώσουσιν αὐτῷ τοὺς καρποὺς ἐν τοῖς καιροῖς αὐτῶν.

41. Legousin auto, Kakous kakos apolesei autous, kai ton ampelona ekdosetai allois georgois, 'oitines apodosousin auto tous karpous en tois kairois auton.

Hebrew/Transliteration
מא. וַיֹּאמְרוּ אֵלָיו הַשְׁמֵד יַשְׁמִיד אֶת־בְּנֵי הַבְּלִיַּעַל הָאֵלֶּה וְנָתַן כַּרְמוֹ לְנֹטְרִים אֲחֵרִים אֲשֶׁר יִתְּנוּ לוֹ אֶת־פִּרְיוֹ בְּעִתּוֹ.

41. Va•yom•roo elav hash•med yash•mid et - b`ney hab•li•ya•al ha•e•le ve•na•tan kar•mo le•not•rim a•che•rim asher yit•noo lo et - pir•yo be•ee•to.

---

42. Jesus saith unto them, Did ye never read in the scriptures, The stone which the builders rejected, the same is become the head of the corner: this is the Lord's doing, and it is marvellous in our eyes?

Greek/Transliteration
42. Λέγει αὐτοῖς ὁ Ἰησοῦς, Οὐδέποτε ἀνέγνωτε ἐν ταῖς γραφαῖς, Λίθον ὃν ἀπεδοκίμασαν οἱ οἰκοδομοῦντες, οὗτος ἐγενήθη εἰς κεφαλὴν γωνίας· παρὰ κυρίου ἐγένετο αὕτη, καὶ ἔστιν θαυμαστὴ ἐν ὀφθαλμοῖς ἡμῶν;

42. Legei autois 'o Yeisous, Oudepote anegnote en tais graphais, Lithon 'on apedokimasan 'oi oikodomountes, 'outos egeneithei eis kephalein gonias. para kuriou egeneto 'autei, kai estin thaumastei en ophthalmois 'eimon?

Hebrew/Transliteration
מב. וַיֹּאמֶר אֲלֵיהֶם יֵשׁוּעַ הֲלֹא קְרָאתֶם בַּכְּתוּבִים אֶבֶן מָאֲסוּ הַבּוֹנִים הָיְתָה לְרֹאשׁ פִּנָּה מֵאֵת יְהֹוָה הָיְתָה זֹּאת:הִיא נִפְלָאת בְּעֵינֵינוּ

42. Va•yo•mer aley•hem Yeshua ha•lo ke•ra•tem ba•k`too•vim even ma•a•soo ha•bo•nim hai•ta le•rosh pi•na me•et Adonai hai•ta zot hee nif•lat be•ey•ney•noo.

Rabbinic Jewish Commentary
Very appropriately is this Scripture cited, and applied to the present case; which expresses the rejection of the Messiah by the Jewish builders, priests, and scribes: the whole Psalm may be understood of the Messiah. R. David Kimchi owns (z), that there is a division among their Rabbins about it: some say that the Psalm is spoken of David, and others, that it is spoken of the days of the Messiah; and these are certainly in the right; and as for this particular passage, it is applied by some of them to the Messiah: so on mentioning Hos_3:5 they (a) say, "David was king in this world, and David shall be king in the time to come: wherefore it is said, the stone which the builders refused. And one of their noted commentators (b) on those words, "though thou be little among the thousands of Judah", has this note:

"It is fit thou shouldest be little among the families of Judah, because of the impurity of Ruth the Moabitess, which is in thee: out of thee shall come forth unto me, Messiah, the son of David; for so he saith, "the stone which the builders refused".

The Jews used to call their Rabbi's and their scholars "builders" (c): says R. Jochanan, "the disciples of the wise men are called בנאין, "builders", because they study in the building of the world all their days, which is the law.

(z) In Psal. cxviii. 1. (a) Zohar in Exod. fol. 93. 3. (b) Jarchi in Mic. v. 2. (c) T. Bab. Subbut, fol. 114. 1. Vid. En Israel, fol. 64. 3. & Juchasin, fol. 80. 2. & 81. 1.

---

43. Therefore say I unto you, The kingdom of God shall be taken from you, and given to a nation bringing forth the fruits thereof.

Greek/Transliteration
43. Διὰ τοῦτο λέγω ὑμῖν ὅτι ἀρθήσεται ἀφ᾽ ὑμῶν ἡ βασιλεία τοῦ θεοῦ, καὶ δοθήσεται ἔθνει ποιοῦντι τοὺς καρποὺς αὐτῆς.

43. Dya touto lego 'umin 'oti artheisetai aph 'umon 'ei basileia tou theou, kai dotheisetai ethnei poiounti tous karpous auteis.

Hebrew/Transliteration
מג: עַל־כֵּן אֲנִי אֹמֵר לָכֶם כִּי תוּסַר מַלְכוּת הָאֱלֹהִים מִכֶּם וְתִנָּתֵן לְגוֹי אֲשֶׁר יִתֵּן אֶת־פִּרְיָהּ.

43. Al - ken ani o•mer la•chem ki too•sar mal•choot ha•Elohim mi•kem ve•ti•na•ten le•goy asher yi•ten et - pir•ya.

Rabbinic Jewish Commentary
One of the Jewish commentators (d) on these words, in Jer_13:17 "my soul shall weep in secret places for your pride", has this note, "because of your grandeur,

which shall cease; because of the excellency of "the kingdom of heaven", שתנתן לפסילים, "which shall be given to the profane"; i.e. the nations of the world, (d) Jarchi in Jer. xiii. 17.

---

44. And whosoever shall fall on this stone shall be broken: but on whomsoever it shall fall, it will grind him to powder.

Greek/Transliteration
44. Καὶ ὁ πεσὼν ἐπὶ τὸν λίθον τοῦτον συνθλασθήσεται· ἐφ᾽ ὃν δ᾽ ἂν πέσῃ, λικμήσει αὐτόν.

44. Kai 'o peson epi ton lithon touton sunthlastheisetai. eph 'on d an pesei, likmeisei auton.

Hebrew/Transliteration
מד. וְהַנֹּפֵל עַל-הָאֶבֶן הַזֹּאת יִתְפּוֹרָר וְכָל-מִי אֲשֶׁר תִּפֹּל עָלָיו תְּדַכְּאֶנּוּ לֶעָפָר:

44. Ve•ha•no•fel al - ha•e•ven ha•zot yit•po•rar ve•chol - mee asher ti•pol alav te•dak•e•noo le•a•far.

Rabbinic Jewish Commentary
As the former part of this verse expresses the sin of unbelievers, and the danger they are exposed unto by it, this sets forth their punishment; and has respect both to the vengeance of Yeshua, on the Jewish nation, at their destruction, which would fall heavy from him in his state of exaltation, for their evil treatment of him in his state of humiliation; and to his severe wrath, which will be executed at the day of judgment on all unbelievers, impenitent Messiahless sinners, who have both offended him, and been offended at him; when their destruction will be inevitable, their salvation irretrievable, and their souls irrecoverably lost, and ruined. Some have thought, that there is an allusion in these words to the manner of stoning among the Jews, which was this (e):

"the place of stoning was two men's heights; one of the witnesses struck him on his loins, to throw him down from thence, to the ground: if he died, it was well; if not, they took a stone, which lay there, and was as much as two men could carry, and cast it, with all their might, upon his breast: if he died, it was well; if not, he was stoned by all Israel.

Maimonides observes (f), that "stoning, or throwing down from the high place, was that he might fall upon the stone, or that the stone might fall upon him; and which of them either it was, the pain was the same.

(e) Misu. Sanhedrin, c. 6. sect. 4. T. Bab. Sanhedrin, fol. 45. 1, 2. Maimon. Hilch. Sanhedrin, c. 15. sect 1. Moses Kotsensis Mitzvot Tora pr. Affirm. 99. (f) In Misn. Sanhedrin, c. 6. sect. 4.

45. And when the chief priests and Pharisees had heard his parables, they perceived that he spake of them.

Greek/Transliteration
45. Καὶ ἀκούσαντες οἱ ἀρχιερεῖς καὶ οἱ Φαρισαῖοι τὰς παραβολὰς αὐτοῦ ἔγνωσαν ὅτι περὶ αὐτῶν λέγει.

45. Kai akousantes 'oi archiereis kai 'oi Pharisaioi tas parabolas autou egnosan 'oti peri auton legei.

Hebrew/Translitreration
מה. וְרָאשֵׁי הַכֹּהֲנִים וְהַפְּרוּשִׁים בְּשָׁמְעָם אֶת-מְשָׁלָיו יָדְעוּ כִּי עֲלֵיהֶם דִּבֵּר:

45. Ve•ra•shey ha•ko•ha•nim ve•haP`roo•shim be•shom•am et - me•sha•lav yad•oo ki aley•hem di•ber.

---

46. But when they sought to lay hands on him, they feared the multitude, because they took him for a prophet.

Greek/Transliteration
46. Καὶ ζητοῦντες αὐτὸν κρατῆσαι, ἐφοβήθησαν τοὺς ὄχλους, ἐπειδὴ ὡς προφήτην αὐτὸν εἶχον.

46. Kai zeitountes auton krateisai, ephobeitheisan tous ochlous, epeidei 'os propheitein auton eichon.

Hebrew/Transliteration
מו. וַיְבַקְשׁוּ לְתָפְשׂוֹ אַךְ יָרְאוּ מִפְּנֵי הֲמוֹן הָעָם כִּי חָשְׁבוּ אֹתוֹ לְנָבִיא:

46. Vay•vak•shoo le•tof•so ach yar•oo mip•ney ha•mon ha•am ki chish•voo o•to le•na•vi.

Matthew, Chapter 22

1. And Jesus answered and spake unto them again by parables, and said,

Greek/Transliteration
1. Καὶ ἀποκριθεὶς ὁ Ἰησοῦς πάλιν εἶπεν αὐτοῖς ἐν παραβολαῖς, λέγων,

1. Kai apokritheis 'o Yeisous palin eipen autois en parabolais, legon,

Hebrew/Transliteration
א. וַיַּעַן יֵשׁוּעַ עוֹד וַיִּשָּׂא לָהֶם מְשָׁלוֹ לֵאמֹר:

1. Va•ya•an Yeshua od va•yi•sa la•hem me•sha•lo le•mor.

---

2. The kingdom of heaven is like unto a certain king, which made a marriage for his son,

Greek/Transliteration
2. Ὡμοιώθη ἡ βασιλεία τῶν οὐρανῶν ἀνθρώπῳ βασιλεῖ, ὅστις ἐποίησεν γάμους τῷ υἱῷ αὐτοῦ·

2. 'Omoiothei 'ei basileia ton ouranon anthropo basilei, 'ostis epoieisen gamous to 'wio autou.

Hebrew/Translieration
ב. דָּמְתָה מַלְכוּת הַשָּׁמַיִם לְמֶלֶךְ אֲשֶׁר הֵכִין חֲתֻנָּה לִבְנוֹ:

2. Dam•ta mal•choot ha•sha•ma•yim le•me•lech asher he•chin cha•too•na liv•no.

Rabbinic Jewish Commentary
The allusion is to the custom of the Jews, and of other nations, in making feasts and grand entertainments at such times. The Jews used to make feasts both at espousals, and at marriage: hence we (g) read of סעודת אירוסין, "a feast of espousals", and of סעודת נישואין, "a marriage feast": the reference here is to the latter; and which used to be made at the charge of the father: for so runs one of their canons (h): "a father marries his son, ועשה לו משתה, "and makes a feast for him", and the expense is the father's."

(g) T. Bab. Yebamot, fol. 43. 1, 2. (h) Maimon. Hilch. Nechalot, c. 9. sect. 13. Vid. Misn. Sheviith, c. 7. sect. 4. & Juchasin, fol. 88. 1.

---

3. And sent forth his servants to call them that were bidden to the wedding: and they would not come.

Greek/Transliteration
3. καὶ ἀπέστειλεν τοὺς δούλους αὐτοῦ καλέσαι τοὺς κεκλημένους εἰς τοὺς γάμους, καὶ οὐκ ἤθελον ἐλθεῖν.

3. kai apesteilen tous doulous autou kalesai tous kekleimenous eis tous gamous, kai ouk eithelon elthein.

Hebrew/Transliteration
ג. וַיִּשְׁלַח אֶת־מְשָׁרְתָיו לִקְרֹא אֶת־הַקְּרֻאִים אֶל־הַמִּשְׁתֶּה וְלֹא אָבוּ לָבֹא:

3. Va•yish•lach et - me•shar•tav lik•ro et - hak•roo•eem el - ha•mish•te ve•lo avoo la•vo.

Rabbinic Jewish Commentary
to call them that were bidden to the wedding; הקרואים, "those that were called", as in 1Sa_9:13 by whom are meant the Jews, who were the "bidden", or "called ones"; called of God, and therefore styled "Israel my called" Isa_48:12 and by the Targum interpreted מזמני, "my bidden". They were called by the name of God, and called the people of God, and the children of God, and were the children of the kingdom.

---

4. Again, he sent forth other servants, saying, Tell them which are bidden, Behold, I have prepared my dinner: my oxen and my fatlings are killed, and all things are ready: come unto the marriage.

Greek/Transliteration
4. Πάλιν ἀπέστειλεν ἄλλους δούλους, λέγων, Εἴπατε τοῖς κεκλημένοις. Ἰδού, τὸ ἄριστόν μου ἡτοίμασα, οἱ ταῦροί μου καὶ τὰ σιτιστὰ τεθυμένα, καὶ πάντα ἕτοιμα· δεῦτε εἰς τοὺς γάμους.

4. Palin apesteilen allous doulous, legon, Eipate tois kekleimenois. Ydou, to ariston mou 'eitoimasa, 'oi tauroi mou kai ta sitista tethumena, kai panta 'etoima. deute eis tous gamous.

Hebrew/Transliteration
ד. וַיֹּסֶף וַיִּשְׁלַח מְשָׁרְתִים אֲחֵרִים לֵאמֹר הַגִּידוּ לַקְּרֻאִים הִנֵּה הֲכִינוֹתִי הַכֵּרָה הַבָּקָר וְהַמְּרִיאִים טְבוּחִים וְהַכֹּל עָרוּךְ בֹּאוּ־נָא אֶל־מִשְׁתֵּה הַחֲתֻנָּה׃

4. Va•yo•sef va•yish•lach me•shar•tim a•che•rim le•mor ha•gi•doo lak•roo•eem hee•ne ha•chi•no•ti ha•ke•ra ha•ba•kar ve•ham•ri•eem te•voo•chim ve•ha•kol a•rooch bo•oo – na el - mish•te ha•cha•too•na.

---

5. But they made light of it, and went their ways, one to his farm, another to his merchandise:

Greek/Transliteration
5. Οἱ δὲ ἀμελήσαντες ἀπῆλθον, ὁ μὲν εἰς τὸν ἴδιον ἀγρόν, ὁ δὲ εἰς τὴν ἐμπορίαν αὐτοῦ·

5. 'Oi de ameleisantes apeilthon, 'o men eis ton idion agron, 'o de eis tein emporian autou.

Hebrew/Transliteration
ה. וְהֵם לֹא-שָׁתוּ לִבָּם גַּם-לָזֹאת וַיֵּלְכוּ לָהֶם אִישׁ אֶל-שָׂדֵהוּ וְאִישׁ אֶל-מִסְחָרוֹ:

5. Ve•hem lo - sha•too li•bam gam - la•zot va•yel•choo la•hem eesh el - sa•de•hoo ve•eesh el - mis•cha•ro.

Rabbinic Jewish Commentary
Such a division of worldly employment is made by the Jews (k); "the way of that host is like to a king, who makes a grand entertainment, and says to the children of his palace, all the rest of the days ye shall be everyone in his house; this shall do his business, ודא אזיל בסחרתיה, "and this shall go about his merchandise", ודא אזיל בחקליה, "and this shall go to his field", except on my day." (k) Zohar in Lev. fol. 40. 2.

---

6. And the remnant took his servants, and entreated them spitefully, and slew them.

Greek/Transliteration
6. οἱ δὲ λοιποὶ κρατήσαντες τοὺς δούλους αὐτοῦ ὕβρισαν καὶ ἀπέκτειναν.

6. 'oi de loipoi krateisantes tous doulous autou 'ubrisan kai apekteinan.

Hebrew/Transliteration
ו. וְהַנִּשְׁאָרִים מֵהֶם תָּפְשׂוּ בִמְשָׁרְתָיו וַיָּזִידוּ עֲלֵיהֶם וַיַּהַרְגוּם:

6. Ve•ha•nish•arim me•hem taf•soo vim•shar•tav va•ya•zi•doo aley•hem va•ya•har•goom.

---

7. But when the king heard thereof, he was wroth: and he sent forth his armies, and destroyed those murderers, and burned up their city.

Greek/Transliteration
7. Καὶ ἀκούσας ὁ βασιλεὺς ἐκεῖνος ὠργίσθη, καὶ πέμψας τὰ στρατεύματα αὐτοῦ ἀπώλεσεν τοὺς φονεῖς ἐκείνους, καὶ τὴν πόλιν αὐτῶν ἐνέπρησεν.

7. Kai akousas 'o basileus ekeinos orgisthei, kai pempsas ta strateumata autou apolesen tous phoneis ekeinous, kai tein polin auton enepreisen.

Hebrew/Transliteration
ז. וַיִּקְצֹף הַמֶּלֶךְ וַיִּשְׁלַח אֶת-צְבָאָיו וַיַּשְׁמֵד אֶת-הַמְרַצְּחִים הָאֵלֶּה וְאֶת-עִירָם שָׁלַח בָּאֵשׁ

7. Va•yik•tzof ha•me•lech va•yish•lach et - tze•va•av va•yash•med et - ha•me•ratz•chim ha•e•le ve•et - ee•ram sha•lach ba•esh.

Rabbinic Jewish Commentary
The Roman armies are here meant; called "his", because they came by the Lord's appointment and permission; and were used by him, for the destruction of these people. *and burnt up their city*; the city of Jerusalem, the metropolis of the Jews, and where the principal of these murderers dwelt; and which was burnt and destroyed by the Roman army, under Titus Vespasian. And a worse punishment than this, even the vengeance of eternal fire, may all the neglecters of the Gospel, and persecutors of the ministers of it expect, from him, whose vengeance is, and who will repay it; for if judgment began at the house of God, the people of the Jews who were so called, what will be the end of them that obey not the Gospel of Yeshua?

---

8. Then saith he to his servants, The wedding is ready, but they which were bidden were not worthy.

Greek/Transliteration
8. Τότε λέγει τοῖς δούλοις αὐτοῦ, Ὁ μὲν γάμος ἕτοιμός ἐστιν, οἱ δὲ κεκλημένοι οὐκ ἦσαν ἄξιοι.

8. Tote legei tois doulois autou, 'O men gamos 'etoimos estin, 'oi de kekleimenoi ouk eisan axioi.

Hebrew/Transliteration
ח. אָז אָמַר אֶל-מְשָׁרְתָיו מִשְׁתֵּה-הַחֲתֻנָּה עָרוּךְ וְהַקְּרֻאִים לֹא-נִמְצְאוּ כֵן:

8. Az amar el - me•shar•tav mish•te - ha•cha•too•na a•rooch ve•hak•roo•eem lo - nim•tze•oo chen.

---

9. Go ye therefore into the highways, and as many as ye shall find, bid to the marriage.

Greek/Transliteration
9. Πορεύεσθε οὖν ἐπὶ τὰς διεξόδους τῶν ὁδῶν, καὶ ὅσους ἂν εὕρητε, καλέσατε εἰς τοὺς γάμους.

9. Poreuesthe oun epi tas diexodous ton 'odon, kai 'osous an 'eureite, kalesate eis tous gamous.

Hebrew/Transliteration
ט. לָכֵן לְכוּ-נָא אֶל-פֶּתַח עֵינַיִם בְּרֹאשׁ נְתִיבוֹת וְכָל-אִישׁ אֲשֶׁר תִּמְצְאוּ קִרְאוּ אֹתוֹ אֶל-הַמִּשְׁתֶּה:

9. La•chen le•choo - na el - pe•tach ey•na•yim be•rosh n`ti•vot ve•chol - eesh asher tim•tze•oo kir•oo o•to el - ha•mish•te.

---

10. So those servants went out into the highways, and gathered together all as many as they found, both bad and good: and the wedding was furnished with guests.

Greek/Transliteration

10. Καὶ ἐξελθόντες οἱ δοῦλοι ἐκεῖνοι εἰς τὰς ὁδοὺς συνήγαγον πάντας ὅσους εὗρον, πονηρούς τε καὶ ἀγαθούς· καὶ ἐπλήσθη ὁ γάμος ἀνακειμένων.

10. Kai exelthontes 'oi douloi ekeinoi eis tas 'odous suneigagon pantas 'osous 'euron, poneirous te kai agathous. kai epleisthei 'o gamos anakeimenon.

Hebrew/Transliteration

י. וַיֵּצְאוּ הַמְשָׁרְתִים הָהֵם אֶל-הַנְּתִיבוֹת וַיַּאַסְפוּ מִכֹּל אֲשֶׁר מָצָאוּ גַם-רָעִים וְגַם-טוֹבִים וַיִּמָּלֵא בֵית-הַחֲתֻנָּה:אֶת-הַקְּרֻאִים

10. Va•yetz•oo ha•me•shar•tim ha•hem el - ha•ne•ti•vot va•ya•as•foo mi•kol asher ma•tza•oo gam - ra•eem ve•gam - to•vim va•yi•ma•le veit - ha•cha•too•na et - hak•roo•eem.

---

11. And when the king came in to see the guests, he saw there a man which had not on a wedding garment:

Greek/Transliteration

11. Εἰσελθὼν δὲ ὁ βασιλεὺς θεάσασθαι τοὺς ἀνακειμένους εἶδεν ἐκεῖ ἄνθρωπον οὐκ ἐνδεδυμένον ἔνδυμα γάμου·

11. Eiselthon de 'o basileus theasasthai tous anakeimenous eiden ekei anthropon ouk endedumenon enduma gamou.

Hebrew/Transliteration

יא. וַיְהִי כְּבוֹא הַמֶּלֶךְ לִרְאוֹת אֶת-הַבָּאִים וַיַּרְא אִישׁ מֵהֶם אֲשֶׁר אֵינֶנּוּ מְלֻבָּשׁ לְבוּשׁ הַחֲתֻנָּה:

11. Vay•hi ke•vo ha•me•lech lir•ot et - ha•ba•eem va•yar eesh me•hem asher ey•ne•noo me•loo•bash le•voosh ha•cha•too•na.

---

12. And he saith unto him, Friend, how camest thou in hither not having a wedding garment? And he was speechless.

Greek/Transliteration

12. καὶ λέγει αὐτῷ, Ἑταῖρε, πῶς εἰσῆλθες ὧδε μὴ ἔχων ἔνδυμα γάμου; Ὁ δὲ ἐφιμώθη.

12. kai legei auto, 'Etaire, pos eiseilthes 'ode mei echon enduma gamou? 'O de ephimothei.

Hebrew/Transliteration
יב. וַיֹּאמֶר אֵלָיו רֵעִי אֵיךְ בָּאתָ הֲלֹם בִּלְתִּי מְלֻבָּשׁ לְבוּשׁ הַחֲתֻנָּה וַיְהִי כְּמַחֲרִישׁ:

12. Va•yo•mer elav re•ee eych ba•ta ha•lom bil•tee me•loo•bash le•voosh ha•cha•too•na vay•hi ke•ma•cha•rish.

Rabbinic Jewish Commentary
The Jews have a tradition (l), that "Esau the wicked, will veil himself with his garment, and sit among the righteous in paradise, in the world to come; and the holy blessed God will draw him, and bring him out from thence, which is the sense of those words, Oba_1:4. "Though thou exalt thyself as the eagle, and though thou set thy nest among the stars, thence will I bring thee down, saith the Lord."" (l) T. Hieros. Nedarim, fol. 38. 1.

---

13. Then said the king to the servants, Bind him hand and foot, and take him away, and cast him into outer darkness; there shall be weeping and gnashing of teeth.

Greek/Transliteration
13. Τότε εἶπεν ὁ βασιλεὺς τοῖς διακόνοις, Δήσαντες αὐτοῦ πόδας καὶ χεῖρας, ἄρατε αὐτὸν καὶ ἐκβάλετε εἰς τὸ σκότος τὸ ἐξώτερον· ἐκεῖ ἔσται ὁ κλαυθμὸς καὶ ὁ βρυγμὸς τῶν ὀδόντων.

13. Tote eipen 'o basileus tois dyakonois, Deisantes autou podas kai cheiras, arate auton kai ekbalete eis to skotos to exoteron. ekei estai 'o klauthmos kai 'o brugmos ton odonton.

Hebrew/Transliteration
יג. וַיְצַו הַמֶּלֶךְ אֶת-מְשָׁרְתָיו לֵאמֹר אִסְרוּ אֹתוֹ יָדָיו וְרַגְלָיו וּנְשָׂאתֶם וְהִשְׁלִיכֻהוּ אֶל-מְקוֹם אֹפֶל וְצַלְמָוֶת שָׁם:יִהְיֶה בְכִי וַחֲרֹק שִׁנָּיִם

13. Vay•tzav ha•me•lech et - me•shar•tav le•mor ees•roo o•to ya•dav ve•rag•lav oon•sa•tem ve•hash•li•choo•hoo el - me•kom o•fel ve•tzal•ma•vet sham yi•hee•ye ve•chi va•cha•rok shi•na•yim.

---

14. For many are called, but few are chosen.

Greek/Transliteration
14. Πολλοὶ γάρ εἰσιν κλητοί, ὀλίγοι δὲ ἐκλεκτοί.

14. Polloi gar eisin kleitoi, oligoi de eklektoi.

Hebrew/Transliteration

יד. כִּי רַבִּים הֵם הַנִּקְרָאִים וְהַנִּבְחָרִים מְעַטִּים:

14. Ki ra•bim hem ha•nik•ra•eem ve•ha•niv•cha•rim me•a•tim.

---

15. Then went the Pharisees, and took counsel how they might entangle him in his talk.

Greek/Transliteration

15. Τότε πορευθέντες οἱ Φαρισαῖοι συμβούλιον ἔλαβον ὅπως αὐτὸν παγιδεύσωσιν ἐν λόγῳ.

15. Tote poreuthentes 'oi Pharisaioi sumboulion elabon 'opos auton pagideusosin en logo.

Hebrew/Transliteration

טו. אָז הָלְכוּ הַפְּרוּשִׁים וַיִּוָּעֲצוּ יַחְדָּו אֵיךְ יְנַקְשֻׁהוּ בִדְבָרָיו:

15. Az hal•choo ha•P`roo•shim va•yi•va•a•tzoo yach•dav eych ye•nak•shoo•hoo vid•va•rav.

---

16. And they sent out unto him their disciples with the Herodians, saying, Master, we know that thou art true, and teachest the way of God in truth, neither carest thou for any man: for thou regardest not the person of men.

Greek/Transliteration

16. Καὶ ἀποστέλλουσιν αὐτῷ τοὺς μαθητὰς αὐτῶν μετὰ τῶν Ἡρῳδιανῶν, λέγοντες, Διδάσκαλε, οἴδαμεν ὅτι ἀληθὴς εἶ, καὶ τὴν ὁδὸν τοῦ θεοῦ ἐν ἀληθείᾳ διδάσκεις, καὶ οὐ μέλει σοι περὶ οὐδενός, οὐ γὰρ βλέπεις εἰς πρόσωπον ἀνθρώπων.

16. Kai apostellousin auto tous matheitas auton meta ton 'Eirodyanon, legontes, Didaskale, oidamen 'oti aleitheis ei, kai tein 'odon tou theou en aleitheia didaskeis, kai ou melei soi peri oudenos, ou gar blepeis eis prosopon anthropon.

Hebrew/Transliteration

טז. וַיִּשְׁלְחוּ אֵלָיו אֶת-תַּלְמִידֵיהֶם עִם-אַנְשֵׁי הוֹרְדוֹס לֵאמֹר רַבִּי יָדַעְנוּ כִּי-אִישׁ נֶאֱמָן אַתָּה וְאֶת-דֶּרֶךְ אֱלֹהִים:תּוֹרֶה בְּמֵישָׁרִים לֹא תָגוּר מִפְּנֵי-אִישׁ כִּי לֹא תִשָּׂא פְנֵי-גָבֶר

16. Va•yish•le•choo elav et - tal•mi•dey•hem eem - an•shey Hordos le•mor Rabbi ya•da•a•noo ki - eesh ne•e•man ata ve•et - de•rech Elohim to•re ve•mey•sha•rim lo ta•goor mip•ney - eesh ki lo ti•sa p`ney - ga•ver.

Rabbinic Jewish Commentary
The Jewish writer referring to a passage in the Misna (m), which speaks of יוֹנֵי חַרְדְּסִיאוֹת, "Herodian doves"; that is, tame ones, such as were brought up in houses: for these are meant, is clear from the Misnic and Talmudic writers, and their commentators (n); and were so called, because that Herod was the first that tamed wild doves, and brought up tame ones in his own palace.

(m) Cholin, c. 12. sect 1. (n) T. Bab. Cholin, fol. 139. 1. & Betza, fol. 24. 1. & 25. 1. Misn. Sabbat. c. 24. 8. & Cholin, c. 12. sect. 1. & Maimon. & Bartenora in ib.

---

17. Tell us therefore, What thinkest thou? Is it lawful to give tribute unto Caesar, or not?

Greek/Transliteration
17. Εἰπὲ οὖν ἡμῖν, τί σοι δοκεῖ; Ἔξεστιν δοῦναι κῆνσον Καίσαρι, ἢ οὔ;

17. Eipe oun 'eimin, ti soi dokei? Exestin dounai keinson Kaisari, ei ou?

Hebrew/Transliteration
יז. לָכֵן הַגֶּד-לָנוּ מַה-יֶּהְגֶּה לִבֶּךָ הֲנָכוֹן הוּא לָתֵת מַס לַקֵּיסָר אִם-אָיִן:

17. La•chen ha•ged - la•noo ma - ye•he•ge li•be•cha ha•na•chon hoo la•tet mas la•Key•sar eem - a•yin.

---

18. But Jesus perceived their wickedness, and said, Why tempt ye me, ye hypocrites?

Greek/Transliteration
18. Γνοὺς δὲ ὁ Ἰησοῦς τὴν πονηρίαν αὐτῶν εἶπεν, Τί με πειράζετε, ὑποκριταί;

18. Gnous de 'o Yeisous tein poneirian auton eipen, Ti me peirazete, 'upokritai?

Hebrew/Transliteration
יח. וְיֵשׁוּעַ יָדַע אֶת-מְזִמָּתָם וַיֹּאמַר חֲנֵפִים לָמָּה-זֶּה תְּנַסּוּנִי:

18. Ve•Yeshua ya•da et - me•zi•ma•tam va•yo•mar cha•ne•fim la•ma - ze te•na•soo•ni.

---

19. Shew me the tribute money. And they brought unto him a penny.

Greek/Transliteration
19. Ἐπιδείξατέ μοι τὸ νόμισμα τοῦ κήνσου. Οἱ δὲ προσήνεγκαν αὐτῷ δηνάριον.

19. Epideixate moi to nomisma tou keinsou. 'Oi de proseinegkan auto deinarion.

Hebrew/Transliteration
:יט. הַרְאוּנִי אֶת־כֶּסֶף הַמַּס וַיָּבִיאוּ אֵלָיו אֶת־הַכָּסֶף

19. Har•oo•ni et - ke•sef ha•mas va•ya•vi•oo elav et - ha•ka•sef.

---

20. And he saith unto them, Whose is this image and superscription?

Greek/Transliteration
20. Καὶ λέγει αὐτοῖς, Τίνος ἡ εἰκὼν αὕτη καὶ ἡ ἐπιγραφή;

20. Kai legei autois, Tinos 'ei eikon 'autei kai 'ei epigraphei?

Hebrew/Transliteration
:כ. וַיֹּאמֶר אֲלֵיהֶם לְמִי הַתְּמוּנָה וְהַכְּתֹבֶת הָהֵנָּה

20. Va•yo•mer aley•hem le•mi ha•t`moo•na ve•ha•k`to•vet ha•he•na.

Rabbinic Jewish Commentary

This is enough to show, that this penny was not a Jewish, but a Roman one; for the Jews, though they put inscriptions, yet no images on their coin; and much less would they put Caesar's thereon, as was on this: it is asked (r),

"What is the coin of Jerusalem? The answer is, David and Solomon on one side, and Jerusalem the holy city off the other side, i.e. as the gloss observes, David and Solomon were "written" on one side, and on the other side were written Jerusalem the holy city."

It follows, "and what was the coin of Abraham our father? an old man and an old woman, (Abraham and Sarah,) on one side, and a young man and a young woman, (Isaac and Rebekah,) on the other side."

The gloss on it is, "not that there was on it the form of an old man and an old woman on one side, and of a young man and a young woman on the other, for it is forbidden to make the form of a man; but so it was written on one side, an old man and an old woman, and on the other side, a young man and a young woman."

(r) T. Bab. Bava Kama, fol. 97. 2. Vid. Bereshit Rabbas sect. 39. fol. 34. 4. & Midrash Kohelet, fol 95. 4.

---

21. They say unto him, Caesar's. Then saith he unto them, Render therefore unto Caesar the things which are Caesar's; and unto God the things that are God's.

Greek/Transliteration
21. Λέγουσιν αὐτῷ, Καίσαρος. Τότε λέγει αὐτοῖς, Ἀπόδοτε οὖν τὰ Καίσαρος Καίσαρι· καὶ τὰ τοῦ θεοῦ τῷ θεῷ.

21. Legousin auto, Kaisaros. Tote legei autois, Apodote oun ta Kaisaros Kaisari. kai ta tou theou to theo.

Hebrew/Transliteration
כא. וַיֹּאמְרוּ אֵלָיו לַקֵּיסָר וַיֹּאמֶר אֲלֵיהֶם עַל-כֵּן הָבוּ לַקֵּיסָר אֶת אֲשֶׁר לַקֵּיסָר וְלֵאלֹהִים אֶת אֲשֶׁר לֵאלֹהִים:

21. Va•yom•roo elav la•Key•sar va•yo•mer aley•hem al - ken ha•voo la•Key•sar et asher la•Key•sar ve•le•Elohim et asher le•Elohim.

Rabbinic Jewish Commentary
(t): "A king whose "coin" is "current" in any country, the inhabitants of that country agree about him, and it is their joint opinion, שהוא אדוניהם והם לו עבדים "that he is their Lord, and they are his servants"."

And the Jews themselves allow, that a king ought to have his dues, whether he be a king of Israel, or of the Gentiles: "a publican, or tax gatherer, (they say (u),) that is appointed by the king, whether a king of Israel, or of the Gentiles, and takes what is fixed by the order of the government; it is forbidden to refuse payment of the tax to him, for דינא דמלכות דינא, "the right of a king is right"."

(t) Maimon. Hilch. Gerala, c. 5. sect. 18. (u) Maimon. & Bartenora in Misn. Nedarim. c. 3. sect. 4. & Maimon. Hilch. Gezala, c. 5. sect. 11.

---

22. When they had heard these words, they marvelled, and left him, and went their way.

Greek/Transliteration
22. Καὶ ἀκούσαντες ἐθαύμασαν· καὶ ἀφέντες αὐτὸν ἀπῆλθον.

22. Kai akousantes ethaumasan. kai aphentes auton apeilthon.

Hebrew/Transliteration
כב. וַיִּשְׁמְעוּ וַיִּשְׁתָּאוּ וַיַּעַזְבוּ אֹתוֹ וַיֵּלְכוּ לָהֶם:

22. Va•yish•me•oo va•yish•ta•oo va•ya•az•voo o•to va•yel•choo la•hem.

---

23. The same day came to him the Sadducees, which say that there is no resurrection, and asked him,

Greek/Transliteration
23. Ἐν ἐκείνῃ τῇ ἡμέρᾳ προσῆλθον αὐτῷ Σαδδουκαῖοι, οἱ λέγοντες μὴ εἶναι ἀνάστασιν, καὶ ἐπηρώτησαν αὐτόν,

23. En ekeinei tei 'eimera proseilthon auto Saddoukaioi, 'oi legontes mei einai anastasin, kai epeiroteisan auton,

Hebrew/Transliteration
כג: בַּיּוֹם הַהוּא נִגְּשׁוּ אֵלָיו צְדוּקִים הָאֹמְרִים כִּי אֵין תְּקוּמָה לַמֵּתִים וַיִּשְׁאָלֻהוּ לֵאמֹר.

23. Ba•yom ha•hoo nig•shoo elav Tza•doo•kim ha•om•rim ki eyn te•koo•ma la•me•tim va•yish•a•loo•hoo le•mor.

Rabbinic Jewish Commentary
They denied that there were angels and spirits, and the immortality of the soul; they affirmed, that the soul died with the body, and that there was no future state: the rise of this sect, and of these notions of their's, was this, as the Jews relate (w).

"...But if our fathers had known that there is another world, and that there is תהיית המתים, "a resurrection of the dead", they would not have said thus: they stood and separated from the law, and of them there were two parties, the Sadducees and Baithusites; the Sadducees on account of Sadoc, and the Baithusites on account of Baithus." (w) Abot R. Nathan, c. 5. fol. 3. 1.

---

24. Saying, Master, Moses said, If a man die, having no children, his brother shall marry his wife, and raise up seed unto his brother.

Greek/Transliteration
24. λέγοντες, Διδάσκαλε, Μωσῆς εἶπεν, Ἐάν τις ἀποθάνῃ μὴ ἔχων τέκνα, ἐπιγαμβρεύσει ὁ ἀδελφὸς αὐτοῦ τὴν γυναῖκα αὐτοῦ, καὶ ἀναστήσει σπέρμα τῷ ἀδελφῷ αὐτοῦ.

24. legontes, Didaskale, Moseis eipen, Ean tis apothanei mei echon tekna, epigambreusei 'o adelphos autou tein gunaika autou, kai anasteisei sperma to adelpho autou.

Hebrew/Transliteration
כד. רַבִּי הִנֵּה מֹשֶׁה אָמַר אִישׁ כִּי-יָמוּת וּבָנִים אֵין-לוֹ וְיִבֵּם אָחִיו אֶת-אִשְׁתּוֹ וְהֵקִים זֶרַע עַל-שֵׁם אָחִיו:

24. Rabbi hee•ne Moshe amar eesh ki - ya•moot oo•va•nim eyn - lo ve•yi•bem a•chiv et - eesh•to ve•he•kim ze•ra al - shem a•chiv.

Rabbinic Jewish Commentary
This law only took place, when a man died without children; for if he left any children, there was no need for his brother to marry his wife; yea, as a Jewish writer observes (x), she was forbidden, it was not lawful for him to marry her, and

was the case if he had children of either sex, or even grandchildren: for as another of their commentators notes (y), his having no child, regards a son or a daughter, or a son's son, or a daughter's son, or a daughter's daughter; and it was the eldest of the brethren, or he that was next in years to the deceased, that was obliged by this law (z), though not if he had a wife of his own; and accordingly in the following case proposed, each of the brethren married the eldest brother's wife in their turn, according to the course of seniority; and by this law, the first child that was born after such marriage, was reckoned the seed of the deceased, and was heir to his inheritance. The Jews in their Misna, or oral law, have a whole tract on this subject, called Yebamot, which contains various rules and directions, for the right observance of this law.

(x) Aben Ezra in Deut. xxv. 5. (y) Jarchi in ib. Vid. Maimon. Hilch. Yebum, c. 1. sect. 3. (z) Jarchi in Deut. xxv. 5. Misn. Yebamot, c. 2. sect. 8. & 4, 5. Maimon. Hilch. Yebum, c. 2. sect. 6.

---

25. Now there were with us seven brethren: and the first, when he had married a wife, deceased, and, having no issue, left his wife unto his brother:

Greek/Transliteration
25. Ἦσαν δὲ παρ᾽ ἡμῖν ἑπτὰ ἀδελφοί· καὶ ὁ πρῶτος γαμήσας ἐτελεύτησεν· καὶ μὴ ἔχων σπέρμα, ἀφῆκεν τὴν γυναῖκα αὐτοῦ τῷ ἀδελφῷ αὐτοῦ.

25. Eisan de par 'eimin 'epta adelphoi. kai 'o protos gameisas eteleuteisen. kai mei echon sperma, apheiken tein gunaika autou to adelpho autou.

Hebrew/Transliteration
כה. וְאִתָּנוּ הָיוּ שִׁבְעָה אַחִים הָרִאשׁוֹן לָקַח לוֹ אִשָּׁה וַיָּמָת וְזֶרַע לֹא הִשְׁאִיר אַחֲרָיו וַיַּעֲזֹב אֶת-אִשְׁתּוֹ לְאָחִיו:

25. Ve•ee•ta•noo ha•yoo shiv•ah a•chim ha•ri•shon la•kach lo ee•sha va•ya•mot ve•ze•ra lo hish•eer a•cha•rav va•ya•a•zov et - eesh•to le•a•chiv.

Rabbinic Jewish Commentary
The eldest of these seven brethren married a wife, and after some time died, having no children, son or daughter, by his wife; and therefore, according to the above law, leaves her to his next brother to marry her, and raise up seed unto him; which, according to the Jewish canons (b), could not be done before ninety days, or three months after the decease of his brother; for so long they were to wait and see, whether she was with child by his brother or not; for if she was, it was not necessary, yea, it was unlawful for him to marry her.

(a) Maimon. Hilch. Yebum, c. 1. sect. 7. (b) T. Bab. Erubin, fol. 47. 1. Maimon. ib. c. 1. sect. 19.

26. Likewise the second also, and the third, unto the seventh.

Greek/Transliteration
26. Ὁμοίως καὶ ὁ δεύτερος, καὶ ὁ τρίτος, ἕως τῶν ἑπτά.

26. 'Omoios kai 'o deuteros, kai 'o tritos, 'eos ton 'epta.

Hebrew/Transliteration
כו. וּכְמוֹ-כֵן גַּם-הַשֵּׁנִי וְגַם-הַשְּׁלִישִׁי עַד הַשְּׁבִיעִי:

26. Ooch•mo - chen gam - ha•she•ni ve•gam - hash•li•shi ad ha•sh`vi•ee.

---

27. And last of all the woman died also.

Greek/Transliteration
27. Ὕστερον δὲ πάντων ἀπέθανεν καὶ ἡ γυνή.

27. 'Usteron de panton apethanen kai 'ei gunei.

Hebrew/Transliteration
כז. וְאַחֲרֵי כֻלָּם מֵתָה הָאִשָּׁה:

27. Ve•a•cha•rey choo•lam me•ta ha•ee•sha.

---

28. Therefore in the resurrection whose wife shall she be of the seven? for they all had her.

Greek/Transliteration
28. Ἐν τῇ οὖν ἀναστάσει, τίνος τῶν ἑπτὰ ἔσται γυνή; Πάντες γὰρ ἔσχον αὐτήν.

28. En tei oun anastasei, tinos ton 'epta estai gunei? Pantes gar eschon autein.

Hebrew/Transliteration
כח. וְעַתָּה לְמִי מִן-הַשִּׁבְעָה תִּהְיֶה לְאִשָּׁה בַּתְּקוּמָה אַחֲרֵי אֲשֶׁר הָיְתָה אֵשֶׁת כֻּלָּם:

28. Ve•a•ta le•mi min - ha•shiv•ah ti•hi•ye le•ee•sha vat•koo•ma a•cha•rey asher hai•ta eshet koo•lam.

---

29. Jesus answered and said unto them, Ye do err, not knowing the scriptures, nor the power of God.

Greek/Transliteration
29. Ἀποκριθεὶς δὲ ὁ Ἰησοῦς εἶπεν αὐτοῖς, Πλανᾶσθε, μὴ εἰδότες τὰς γραφάς, μηδὲ τὴν δύναμιν τοῦ θεοῦ.

29. Apokritheis de 'o Yeisous eipen autois, Planasthe, mei eidotes tas graphas, meide tein dunamin tou theou.

Hebrew/Transliteration
כט. וַיַּעַן יֵשׁוּעַ וַיֹּאמֶר אֲלֵיהֶם שְׁגִיתֶם כִּי לֹא יְדַעְתֶּם אֶת-הַתּוֹרָה וְלֹא אֶת-גְּבוּרַת הָאֱלֹהִים:

29. Va•ya•an Yeshua va•yo•mer aley•hem sh`gi•tem ki lo ye•da•a•tem et - ha•Torah ve•lo et - g`voo•rat ha•Elohim.

---

30. For in the resurrection they neither marry, nor are given in marriage, but are as the angels of God in heaven.

Greek/Transliteration
30. Ἐν γὰρ τῇ ἀναστάσει οὔτε γαμοῦσιν, οὔτε ἐκγαμίζονται, ἀλλ᾽ ὡς ἄγγελοι τοῦ θεοῦ ἐν οὐρανῷ εἰσιν.

30. En gar tei anastasei oute gamousin, oute ekgamizontai, all 'os angeloi tou theou en ourano eisin.

Hebrew/Transliteration
ל. כִּי בַתְּקוּמָה לֹא יִבְעֲלוּ וְלֹא תִבָּעַלְנָה כִּי אִם-יִהְיוּ כְּמַלְאֲכֵי-אֵל בַּשָּׁמָיִם:

30. Ki bat•koo•ma lo yiv•a•loo ve•lo ti•ba•al•na ki eem - yi•hee•yoo ke•mal•a•chey – El ba•sha•ma•yim.

Rabbinic Jewish Commentary
This agrees with the notion of the other Jews, who say (c); that "In "the world to come", there is neither eating nor drinking, ולא פריה ורביה, "nor fructification, nor increase" (of children), no receiving and giving, (no commerce), nor envy, nor hatred, nor contention. The spirits of the saints before the resurrection, during their separate state, are in some sense like the messengers, to which may be applied those words of Maimonides (d),

"In the world to come, there is no body, but the spirit of the righteous only, without a body, כמלאכי השרת "as the ministering messengers"; and seeing there is no body, there is no eating nor drinking in it, nor any of all the things which the bodies of the children of men stand in need of in this world; nor does anything befall which happens to bodies in this world, as sitting or standing, or sleep or "death", or grief, or laughter, or the like. (e), "At the appointed time known by me, to quicken the dead, I will return to thee that body which is holy and renewed, as at the first, to be כמלאכים קדושים, "as the holy angels".

(c) T. Bab. Beracot, fol. 17. 1. (d) Hilch. Teshuba, c. 8. sect. 2. (e) Midrash Hanneelam in Zohar in Gen. fol. 66. 4. (f) Vid. Abot. R. Nathan, c. 1. fol. 1. 3. Caphtor, fol. 18. 2. Philo de Sacrific. Abel & Cain, p. 131.

31. But as touching the resurrection of the dead, have ye not read that which was spoken unto you by God, saying,

Greek/Transliteration
31. Περὶ δὲ τῆς ἀναστάσεως τῶν νεκρῶν, οὐκ ἀνέγνωτε τὸ ῥηθὲν ὑμῖν ὑπὸ τοῦ θεοῦ, λέγοντος,

31. Peri de teis anastaseos ton nekron, ouk anegnote to 'reithen 'umin 'upo tou theou, legontos,

Hebrew/Transliteration
לא. וְעַל-דְּבַר תְּקוּמַת הַמֵּתִים הֲלֹא קְרָאתֶם אֵת אֲשֶׁר-נֶאֱמַר לָכֶם מִפִּי הָאֱלֹהִים לֵאמֹר:

31. Ve•al - de•var te•koo•mat ha•me•tim ha•lo ke•ra•tem et asher - ne•e•mar la•chem mi•pi ha•Elohim le•mor.

---

32. I am the God of Abraham, and the God of Isaac, and the God of Jacob? God is not the God of the dead, but of the living.

Greek/Transliteration
32. Ἐγώ εἰμι ὁ θεὸς Ἀβραάμ, καὶ ὁ θεὸς Ἰσαάκ, καὶ ὁ θεὸς Ἰακώβ; Οὐκ ἔστιν ὁ θεὸς θεὸς νεκρῶν, ἀλλὰ ζώντων.

32. Ego eimi 'o theos Abra'am, kai 'o theos Ysa'ak, kai 'o theos Yakob? Ouk estin 'o theos theos nekron, alla zonton.

Hebrew/Transliteration
לב. אָנֹכִי אֱלֹהֵי אַבְרָהָם וֵאלֹהֵי יִצְחָק וֵאלֹהֵי יַעֲקֹב וַיהוָֹה אֵינֶנּוּ אֱלֹהֵי הַמֵּתִים כִּי אִם-אֱלֹהֵי הַחַיִּים:

32. Ano•chi Elohey Avraham ve•Elohey Yitzchak ve•Elohey Yaakov va•Adonai ey•ne•noo Elohey ha•me•tim ki eem - Elohey ha•cha•yim.

Rabbinic Jewish Commentary
"Says R. Eliezer, with R. Jose (g), I have found the books of the Sadducees to be corrupt; for they say that the resurrection of the dead is not to be proved out of the law: I said unto them, you have corrupted your law, and ye have not caused anything to come up into your hands, for ye say the resurrection of the dead is not to be proved out of the law; lo! he saith, Num_15:31 "That soul shall be utterly cut off, his iniquity shall be upon him; he shall be utterly cut off" in this world; "his iniquity shall be upon him", is not this said with respect to the world to come?.

The other Jews say (h), that "Though a man confesses and believes that the dead will be raised, yet that it is not intimated in the law, he is an heretic; since it is a fundamental point, that the resurrection of the dead is of the law.

(i), "Says R. Simai, from whence is the resurrection of the dead to be proved out of the law? From Exo_6:4 as it is said, "I have also established my covenant with them, to give them the land of Canaan: to you" it is not said, but "to them"; from hence then, the resurrection of the dead may be proved out of the law.

The gloss upon it is, "the sense is, that the holy blessed God, promised to our fathers Abraham, Isaac, and Jacob, that he would give to them the land of Israel; and because he gave it to them, has he not given it to their children? But we learn from hence, that they shall be raised, and that God will hereafter give them the land of Israel. (k): "from whence is it proved, (say they,) that the righteous, even in their death, קרויין חיים, "are called living?"

(g) T. Bab. Sanhedrin, fol. 90. 2. (h) Gloss. in ib. col. 1. (i) T. Bab. Sanhedrin, fol. 90. 2. (k) T. Hieros. Betacot, fol. 4. 4, Midrash Kohelet, fol. 78. 2. Tzeror Hammor, fol. 158. 3.

---

33. And when the multitude heard this, they were astonished at his doctrine.

Greek/Transliteration
33. Καὶ ἀκούσαντες οἱ ὄχλοι ἐξεπλήσσοντο ἐπὶ τῇ διδαχῇ αὐτοῦ.

33. Kai akousantes 'oi ochloi exepleissonto epi tei didachei autou.

Hebrew/Transliteration
לג. וַיִּשְׁמְעוּ הֲמוֹן הָעָם וַיֹּאמְרוּ מַה-נִּפְלָאָה תּוֹרָתוֹ:

33. Va•yish•me•oo ha•mon ha•am va•yom•roo ma - nif•le•ah to•ra•to.

---

34. But when the Pharisees had heard that he had put the Sadducees to silence, they were gathered together.

Greek/Transliteration
34. Οἱ δὲ Φαρισαῖοι, ἀκούσαντες ὅτι ἐφίμωσεν τοὺς Σαδδουκαίους, συνήχθησαν ἐπὶ τὸ αὐτό.

34. 'Oi de Pharisaioi, akousantes 'oti ephimosen tous Saddoukaious, suneichtheisan epi to auto.

Hebrew/Transliteration
לד. וְהַפְּרוּשִׁים שָׁמְעוּ כִּי סָכַר פִּי הַצַּדּוּקִים וַיִּוָּעֲדוּ שָׁם יַחְדָּו:

34. Ve•ha•P`roo•shim sham•oo ki sa•char pi ha•Tza•doo•kim va•yi•va•a•doo sham yach•dav.

---

35. Then one of them, which was a lawyer, asked him a question, tempting him, and saying,

Greek/Transliteration
35. Καὶ ἐπηρώτησεν εἷς ἐξ αὐτῶν νομικός, πειράζων αὐτόν, καὶ λέγων,

35. Kai epeiroteisen 'eis ex auton nomikos, peirazon auton, kai legon,

Hebrew/Transliteration
:לה. וְתַלְמִיד חָכָם אֶחָד מֵהֶם שָׁאַל אֹתוֹ וַיְנַסֵּהוּ לֵאמֹר

35. Ve•tal•mid cha•cham e•chad me•hem sha•al o•to vay•na•se•hoo le•mor.

---

36. Master, which is the great commandment in the law?

Greek/Transliteration
36. Διδάσκαλε, ποία ἐντολὴ μεγάλη ἐν τῷ νόμῳ;

36. Didaskale, poia entolei megalei en to nomo?

Hebrew/Transliteration
:לו. רַבִּי אֵי-זוֹ הִיא הַמִּצְוָה הַגְּדוֹלָה בַּתּוֹרָה

36. Rabbi ey - zoo hee ha•mitz•va ha•g`do•la ba•To•rah.

Rabbinic Jewish Commentary
The question is not which of the laws was the greatest, the oral, or the written law: the Jews give the preference to the law delivered by word of mouth; they prefer the traditions of the elders before the written law of Moses. Some thought the commandment of the sabbath was the greatest: hence they say (n), that he that keeps the sabbath is as if he kept the whole law: yea, they make the observance of the three meals, or feasts, which, according to the traditions of the elders, they were obliged to eat on the sabbath, to be at least one of the greatest of them,

"These three meals (says one of their writers (o)) are a great matter, for it is one מהמצות הגדולות שבתורה, "of the great commandments in the law".

(n) Zohar in Exod. fol. 37. 1. (o) Tzeror Hammor, fol. 3. 3.

---

37. Jesus said unto him, Thou shalt love the Lord thy God with all thy heart, and with all thy soul, and with all thy mind.

Greek/Transliteration
37. ὁ δὲ Ἰησοῦς ἔφη αὐτῷ, Ἀγαπήσεις κύριον τὸν θεόν σου, ἐν ὅλῃ καρδίᾳ σου, καὶ ἐν ὅλῃ ψυχῇ σου, καὶ ἐν ὅλῃ τῇ διανοίᾳ σου.

37. 'o de Yeisous ephei auto, Agapeiseis kurion ton theon sou, en 'olei kardia sou, kai en 'olei psuchei sou, kai en 'olei tei dyanoia sou.

Hebrew/Transliteration
לז. וַיֹּאמֶר יֵשׁוּעַ אֵלָיו וְאָהַבְתָּ אֵת יְהֹוָה אֱלֹהֶיךָ בְּכָל-לְבָבְךָ וּבְכָל-נַפְשְׁךָ וּבְכָל-מְאֹדֶךָ:

37. Va•yo•mer Yeshua elav ve•a•hav•ta et Adonai Elohe•cha be•chol - le•vav•cha oov•chol - naf•she•cha oov•chol - me•o•de•cha.

---

38. This is the first and great commandment.

Greek/Transliteration
38. Αὕτη ἐστὶν πρώτη καὶ μεγάλη ἐντολή.

38. 'Autei estin protei kai megalei entolei.

Hebrew/Transliteration
לח. זוּ הִיא הַמִּצְוָה הַגְּדוֹלָה וְהָרִאשֹׁנָה:

38. Zoo hee ha•mitz•va ha•g`do•la ve•ha•ri•sho•na.

Rabbinic Jewish Commentary

his is the first command in order of nature, time, dignity, and causality; God being the first cause of all things, infinitely above all creatures, and love to him being the source, spring and cause of love to the neighbour; and it is the greatest in its object, nature, manner, and end. That this command, and these words our Lord cites, are so full and comprehensive, the Jews themselves cannot deny. A noted writer of their's (x) says, "the root of "all the commandments" is, when a man loves God with all his soul, and cleaves unto him.

And, says (y) another, "in this verse only, "thou shalt love the Lord thy God"

כלולים עשרת הדברות, "the ten words, or decalogue, are comprehended".

(x) Aben Ezra in Exod. xxxi. 18. (y) Tzeror Hammor, fol. 138. 1.

---

39. And the second is like unto it, Thou shalt love thy neighbour as thyself.

Greek/Transliteration
39. Δευτέρα δὲ ὁμοία αὐτῇ, Ἀγαπήσεις τὸν πλησίον σου ὡς σεαυτόν.

39. Deutera de 'omoia autei, Agapeiseis ton pleision sou 'os seauton.

Hebrew/Transliteration
לט. וְהַשְּׁנִיָּה דָּמְתָה לָּהּ וְאָהַבְתָּ לְרֵעֲךָ כָּמוֹךָ:

39. Ve•hash•ni•ya dam•ta la ve•a•hav•ta le•re•a•cha ka•mo•cha.

Rabbinic Jewish Commentary

"Thy neighbour"; that is, (say they (a),) thy friend in the law; and "this is the great comprehensive rule in the law", to show that it is not fit there should be any division, or separation, between a man and his companion, but one should judge every man in the balance of equity: wherefore, near unto it is, "I am the Lord"

Maimonides agrees, saying (b), that "all the commands, or duties, respecting a man, and his neighbour, נכנסות בגמילות חסידים, "are comprehended in beneficence."

(a) Moses Kotsensis Mitzvot Tora pr. affirm. 9. (b) In Misn. Peah, c. 1. sect. 1.

---

40. On these two commandments hang all the law and the prophets.

Greek/Transliteration
40. Ἐν ταύταις ταῖς δυσὶν ἐντολαῖς ὅλος ὁ νόμος καὶ οἱ προφῆται κρέμανται.

40. En tautais tais dusin entolais 'olos 'o nomos kai 'oi propheitai kremantai.

Hebrew/Transliteration
מ׃ וְעַל-שְׁתֵּי הַמִּצְוֹת הָאֵלֶּה תְּלוּיִים כָּל-הַתּוֹרָה וְהַנְּבִיאִים

40. Ve•al - sh`tey ha•mitz•vot ha•e•le t`loo•yim kol - ha•Torah ve•ha•n`vi•eem.

Rabbinic Jewish Commentary

Jews have a saying (c), that "all the prophets stood on Mount Sinai", and received their prophecies there, because the sum of them, as to the duty part, was then delivered. Maimonides says (d), "the knowledge of this matter is an affirmative precept, as it is said, "I am the Lord thy God"; and he that imagines there is another God besides this, transgresses a negative, as it is said, "thou shalt have no other Gods before me"; and he denies the fundamental point, for this is the great foundation, שהכל תלוי בו, "on which all hang":

(c) Jarchi in Isa. xlviii. 16. & in Mal. i. 1. (d) Hilch. Yesode Hatorah, c. 1. sect. 6.

---

41. While the Pharisees were gathered together, Jesus asked them,

Greek/Transliteration
41. Συνηγμένων δὲ τῶν Φαρισαίων, ἐπηρώτησεν αὐτοὺς ὁ Ἰησοῦς,

41. Suneigmenon de ton Pharisaion, epeiroteisen autous 'o Yeisous,

Hebrew/Transliteration
מא׃ וַיְהִי בְּהִתְאַסֵּף הַפְּרוּשִׁים שָׁאַל אֹתָם יֵשׁוּעַ לֵאמֹר

41. Vay•hi be•hit•a•sef ha•P`roo•shim sha•al o•tam Yeshua le•mor.

42. Saying, What think ye of Christ? whose son is he? They say unto him, The Son of David.

Greek/Transliteration
42. λέγων, Τί ὑμῖν δοκεῖ περὶ τοῦ χριστοῦ; Τίνος υἱός ἐστιν; Λέγουσιν αὐτῷ, Τοῦ Δαυίδ.

42. legon, Ti 'umin dokei peri tou christou? Tinos 'wios estin? Legousin auto, Tou Dauid.

Hebrew/Transliteration
:מב. מַה-תֹּאמְרוּן עַל-הַמָּשִׁיחַ בֶּן-מִי הוּא וַיֹּאמְרוּ אֵלָיו בֶּן-דָּוִד

42. Ma - tom•roon al - ha•Ma•shi•ach ben - mee hoo va•yom•roo elav Ben - David.

---

43. He saith unto them, How then doth David in spirit call him Lord, saying,

Greek/Transliteration
43. Λέγει αὐτοῖς, Πῶς οὖν Δαυὶδ ἐν πνεύματι κύριον αὐτὸν καλεῖ, λέγων,

43. Legei autois, Pos oun Dauid en pneumati kurion auton kalei, legon,

Hebrew/Transliteration
:מג. וַיֹּאמֶר אֲלֵיהֶם אִם-כֵּן אֵפוֹא אֵיךְ קֹרֵא לוֹ דָוִד בָּרוּחַ אָדוֹן בְּאָמְרוֹ

43. Va•yo•mer aley•hem eem - ken e•fo eych ko•re lo David ba•roo•ach Adon be•om•ro,

---

44. The LORD said unto my Lord, Sit thou on my right hand, till I make thine enemies thy footstool?

Greek/Transliteration
44. Εἶπεν ὁ κύριος τῷ κυρίῳ μου, Κάθου ἐκ δεξιῶν μου, ἕως ἂν θῶ τοὺς ἐχθρούς σου ὑποπόδιον τῶν ποδῶν σου;

44. Eipen 'o kurios to kurio mou, Kathou ek dexion mou, 'eos an tho tous echthrous sou 'upopodion ton podon sou?

Hebrew/Transliteration
:מד. נְאֻם יְהוָה לַאדֹנִי שֵׁב לִימִינִי עַד-אָשִׁית אֹיְבֶיךָ הֲדֹם לְרַגְלֶיךָ

44. N`oom Adonai la•Ado•ni shev li•y`mi•ni ad - asheet oy•ve•cha ha•dom le•rag•le•cha?

Rabbinic Jewish Commentary
And the same is owned by some of their Rabbi's, ancient, and modern,

"Says R. Joden, in the name of R. Chijah, in time to come the holy blessed God will cause the king Messiah to sit at his right hand; as it is said, "the Lord said unto my Lord". (f).

And the same says, R. Berachiah, in the name of R. Levi, elsewhere (g). And, says, another of their writers (h),

"we do not find any man, or prophet, whose birth was prophesied of before the birth of his father and mother, but Messiah our righteousness; and of him it is intimated, "from the womb of the morning". i.e. before the womb of her that bore thee was created, thy birth was prophesied of: and this these words respect, "before the sun, his name is Yinnon", Psa_72:17 i, e. before the creation of the sun, the name of our Messiah was strong and firm, and he shall sit at the right hand of God; and this is what is said, "sit at my right hand".

(f) Midrash Tillira in Psal. xviii. 35. apud Galatin. de Cath. ver. arcan. l. 8. c. 24. (g) R. Moses Hadarsan in Gen. xviii. 1. apud ib. (h) R. Isaac Arama in Gen. xlvii. 6. spud ib. l. 3. c. 17.

---

45. If David then call him Lord, how is he his son?

Greek/Transliteration
45. Εἰ οὖν Δαυὶδ καλεῖ αὐτὸν κύριον, πῶς υἱὸς αὐτοῦ ἐστιν;

45. Ei oun Dauid kalei auton kurion, pos 'wios autou estin?

Hebrew/Transliteration
מה. וְאִם-דָּוִד קֹרֵא לוֹ אָדוֹן אֵיךְ הוּא בְנוֹ:

45. Ve•eem - David ko•re lo Adon eych hoo v`no.

Rabbinic Jewish Commentary
The question is to be answered upon true and just notions of the Messiah, but unanswerable upon the principles of the Pharisees; who expected the Messiah only as a mere man, that should be of the seed of David, and so his son. Had they understood and owned the proper divinity of the Messiah, they might have answered, that as he was God, he was David's Lord, his maker, and his king; and, as man, was David's son, and so both his root and offspring; and this our Lord meant to bring them to a confession of, or put them to confusion and silence, which was the consequence, Jer_23:6.

46. And no man was able to answer him a word, neither durst any man from that day forth ask him any more questions.

Greek/Transliteration
46. Καὶ οὐδεὶς ἐδύνατο αὐτῷ ἀποκριθῆναι λόγον· οὐδὲ ἐτόλμησέν τις ἀπ' ἐκείνης τῆς ἡμέρας ἐπερωτῆσαι αὐτὸν οὐκέτι.

46. Kai oudeis edunato auto apokritheinai logon. oude etolmeisen tis ap ekeineis teis 'eimeras eperoteisai auton ouketi.

Hebrew/Transliteration
מו. וְלֹא־יָכֹל אִישׁ לְהָשִׁיב אֹתוֹ דָּבָר גַּם־לֹא הֵעֵז עוֹד אִישׁ לְהִתְוַכַּח אִתּוֹ בִּדְבָרִים מֵהַיּוֹם הַהוּא וָמָעְלָה:

46. Ve•lo - ya•chol eesh le•ha•shiv o•to da•var gam - lo he•ez od eesh le•hit•va•kach ee•to bid•va•rim me•ha•yom ha•hoo va•ma•ala.

Rabbinic Jewish Commentary
They saw the dilemma they were reduced to, either to acknowledge the deity of the Messiah, or confess their ignorance; and neither of them they cared to do, and therefore judged it to be the wisest part to be silent.

Matthew, Chapter 23

1. Then spake Jesus to the multitude, and to his disciples,

Greek/Transliteration
1. Τότε ὁ Ἰησοῦς ἐλάλησεν τοῖς ὄχλοις καὶ τοῖς μαθηταῖς αὐτοῦ,

1. Tote 'o Yeisous elaleisen tois ochlois kai tois matheitais autou,

Hebrew/Transliteration
א: אָז יְדַבֵּר יֵשׁוּעַ אֶל-הֲמוֹן הָעָם וְאֶל-תַּלְמִידָיו לֵאמֹר

1. Az ye•da•ber Yeshua el - ha•mon ha•am ve•el - tal•mi•dav le•mor.

---

2. Saying, The scribes and the Pharisees sit in Moses' seat:

Greek/Transliteration
2. λέγων, Ἐπὶ τῆς Μωσέως καθέδρας ἐκάθισαν οἱ γραμματεῖς καὶ οἱ Φαρισαῖοι·

2. legon, Epi teis Moseos kathedras ekathisan 'oi grammateis kai 'oi Pharisaioi.

Hebrew/Transliteration
ב: הַסּוֹפְרִים וְהַפְּרוּשִׁים יֹשְׁבִים עַל-כִּסֵּא מֹשֶׁה

2. Ha•sof•rim ve•haP`roo•shim yosh•vim al - ki•se Moshe.

Jewish New Testament Commentary
The seat (Greek *kathedra*) *of Moshe.* The Midrash Rabbah says: "They made for him [Moses] a *katedra* like that of the advocates, in which one sits and yet seems to be standing." (Exodus Rabbah 43:4)

Pesikta diRav Kahana 1:7 mentions the seat of Moses, and the editors of the English edition comment: "The particular place in the synagogue where the leaders used to sit was known metaphorically as the seat of Moses or as the throne of Torah, symbolizing the succession of teachers of Torah down through the ages." (William G. Braude and Israel J. Kapstein, *Pesikta diRav Kahana*, Philadelphia: Jewish Publication Society of America, 1975, p. 17)

A third-century C.E. "Chair of Moses" from Korazin (Mat_11:21) is on display at the Israel Museum in Jerusalem; a photograph and description may be found in *Biblical Archeology Review* 13:5 (1987), pp. 32-35. According to the Hebrew University scholarly journal *Tarbitz* I, p. 145, they can also be found in Hamot, Tiberias and Delos (Greece).

3. All therefore whatsoever they bid you observe, that observe and do; but do not ye after their works: for they say, and do not.

Greek/Transliteration
3. πάντα οὖν ὅσα ἐὰν εἴπωσιν ὑμῖν τηρεῖν, τηρεῖτε καὶ ποιεῖτε· κατὰ δὲ τὰ ἔργα αὐτῶν μὴ ποιεῖτε, λέγουσιν γὰρ καὶ οὐ ποιοῦσιν.

3. panta oun 'osa ean eiposin 'umin teirein, teireite kai poieite. kata de ta erga auton mei poieite, legousin gar kai ou poiousin.

Hebrew/Transliteration
ג. לָכֵן כֹּל אֲשֶׁר-יֹאמְרוּ אֲלֵיכֶם לִשְׁמֹר תִּשְׁמְרוּ וַעֲשִׂיתֶם אַךְ כְּמַעֲשֵׂיהֶם אַל-תַּעֲשׂוּ כִּי הֵם אֹמְרִים וְאֵינָם עֹשִׂים:

3. La•chen kol asher - yom•roo aley•chem lish•mor tish•me•roo va•a•si•tem ach ke•ma•a•sey•hem al - ta•a•soo ki hem om•rim ve•ey•nam o•sim.

Rabbinic Jewish Commentary
The word "observe", in this clause, is omitted by the Vulgate Latin, Arabic, and Ethiopic versions, and in Munster's Hebrew Gospel; and Beza says, it is wanting in one ancient copy, but is in others; and is retained in the Syriac and Persic versions.

In the Shem Tov Hebrew Matthew we have a different reading of "...*they* bid you observe...". The Shem Tov version reads "...*he* bid you observe..." referring back to Moses and not to the scribes and Pharisees. The difference is one letter in the Hebrew. The Hebrew word for *they* is *yomroo* while the Hebrew for *he* is *yomar*. The Hebrew letter vav suffix in the word *yomar* makes it a third person plural. It appears that the scribe was translating this gospel from Hebrew to Greek and did not understand the difference in the Hebrew. Yeshua is saying to obey and observe Moses but do not do after their works, the scribes and Pharisees, because they say but do not do what Moses says as in Matthew 15:3.

---

4. For they bind heavy burdens and grievous to be borne, and lay them on men's shoulders; but they themselves will not move them with one of their fingers.

Greek/Transliteration
4. Δεσμεύουσιν γὰρ φορτία βαρέα καὶ δυσβάστακτα, καὶ ἐπιτιθέασιν ἐπὶ τοὺς ὤμους τῶν ἀνθρώπων, τῷ δὲ δακτύλῳ αὐτῶν οὐ θέλουσιν κινῆσαι αὐτά.

4. Desmeuousin gar phortia barea kai dusbastakta, kai epititheasin epi tous omous ton anthropon, to de daktulo auton ou thelousin kineisai auta.

Hebrew/Transliteration
ד. כִּי קֹשְׁרִים מַשָּׂא קָשֶׁה כָּבֵד מִנְּשֹׂא וְעֹמְסִים עַל-שִׁכְמָם אֲנָשִׁים וְאֵין אֶת-נַפְשָׁם לְהָנִיעַ אֹתוֹ גַּם-בְּאֶצְבָּעָם:

4. Ki kosh•rim ma•sa ka•she ka•ved min•so ve•om•sim al - sh`chem a•na•shim ve•eyn et - naf•sham le•ha•nia o•to gam - be•etz•ba•am.

Rabbinic Jewish Commentary

(o)"It is a tradition of R. Ishmael, there are in the words of the law, that, which is bound or forbidden, and that which is loose or free; and there are in them light things, and there are in them heavy things; but the words of the Scribes, כולן חמורין הן, "all of them are heavy"."

And a little after, "the words of the elders, חמורים, "are heavier" than the words of the prophets."

Hence frequent mention is made of "the light things of the school of Shammai, ומחומרי, "and of the heavy things of the school of Hillell" (p)"

In the Misna (r), mention is made of "a crafty wicked man", along with a woman Pharisee, and the blows of the Pharisees before spoken of; and in the Gemara (s), is explained by R. Hona, of one, "that makes things "light" for himself, and makes them "heavy" for others."

Such crafty wicked men were Scribes and Pharisees; though R. Meir pretended that he made things "light" to others and "heavy" to himself (t).

(o) T. Hieros. Peracot, fol. 3. 2. (p) T. Hieros. Sota, fol. 19. 2. Yom Tob. fol. 60. 2. & Berncot, fol. 3. 2. (r) Ubi supra. (Misn. Sota, c. 3. sect. 4.) (s) T. Bab. Sota, fol. 21. 2. (t) T. Hieros. Beracot, fol. 3. 1.

---

5. But all their works they do for to be seen of men: they make broad their phylacteries, and enlarge the borders of their garments,

Greek/Transliteration

5. Πάντα δὲ τὰ ἔργα αὐτῶν ποιοῦσιν πρὸς τὸ θεαθῆναι τοῖς ἀνθρώποις· πλατύνουσιν δὲ τὰ φυλακτήρια αὐτῶν, καὶ μεγαλύνουσιν τὰ κράσπεδα τῶν ἱματίων αὐτῶν·

5. Panta de ta erga auton poiousin pros to theatheinai tois anthropois. platunousin de ta phulakteirya auton, kai megalunousin ta kraspeda ton 'imation auton.

Hebrew/Transliteration

ה. וְכָל-מַעֲשֵׂיהֶם יַעֲשׂוּן לְהֵרָאוֹת בָּם לְעֵינֵי בְנֵי-אָדָם יַרְחִיבוּ לָהֶם הַתְּפִלִּין וְהַצִּיצִית יַגְדִּילוּן:

5. Ve•chol - ma•a•sey•hem ya•a•soon le•he•ra•ot bam le•ei•ney v`ney - adam yar•chi•voo la•hem ha•t`fi•lin ve•ha•tzi•tzit yag•di•loon.

Rabbinic/Jewish New Testament Commentary

T'fillin are small leather boxes containing parchment scrolls on which are written excerpts from the *Tanakh* (specifically, Deu_6:4-9, Deu_11:13-20, Exo_13:1-16). Observant Jewish men past *bar-mitzvah* age (13) strap one on one arm and the other around the head during the morning weekday synagogue service, in literal obedience to Deu_6:8, "You shall bind them [that is, God's *mitzvot*] for a sign on your hand, and they shall be for frontlets between your eyes." Other English versions of the New Testament have here the word "phylacteries"; this transliterates the Greek word used in the text, "*phulakterion*," which means "safeguard, amulet, charm," and thus does not reflect the purpose of *t'fillin*.

Those that were for the head, were written and rolled up separately, and put in four distinct places, in one skin, which was fastened with strings to the crown of the head, towards the face, about the place where the hair ends, and where an infant's brain is tender; and they took care to place them in the middle, that so they might be between the eyes. Those that were for the hand, were written in four columns, on one parchment, which being rolled up, was fastened to the inside of the left arm, where it is fleshy, between the shoulder and the elbow, that so it might be over against the heart (u). They imagined there was a great deal of holiness in, and valued themselves much upon the use of them (w); and the Pharisees, because they would be thought to be more holy and religious, and more observant of the law than others, wore these things broader than the rest of the people.

We (z) read of one Ben Tzitzith Hacceseth, a man of this complexion, who was so called, because his Tzitzith, or fringes, were drawn upon, a pillow; and there are some that say, that the pillow was bore between the great men of Rome: it was drawn after him, not upon the ground, but upon a cloth or tapestry, and the train supported by noblemen, as is pretended. This was one of those, that enlarged the Tzitzith, or fringes, beyond the ordinary size; hence Mark calls it, "long clothing."

(u) Targ. Jon. Jarchi, & Baal Hatturim in Exod. xiii. 16. & Deut. vi. 8. Maimon. Hilch. Tephillin, c. 1. sect. 1. & c. 2. sect. 2. & c. 3. sect. 1, 2, 3, 4, 5, 6. & c. 4. sect. 1, 2. (w) Maimon. ib. c. 4. sect. 25, 26. Moses Kotsensis Mitzvot Tora, pr. affirm. 3. 23. Targ. in Cant. viii. 3. (z) T. Bab. Gittin, fol. 56. 1.

---

6. And love the uppermost rooms at feasts, and the chief seats in the synagogues,

Greek/Transliteration
6. φιλοῦσίν τε τὴν πρωτοκλισίαν ἐν τοῖς δείπνοις, καὶ τὰς πρωτοκαθεδρίας ἐν ταῖς συναγωγαῖς,

6. philousin te tein protoklisian en tois deipnois, kai tas protokathedrias en tais sunagogais,

Hebrew/Transliteration
:ו. וְאֹהֲבִים הֵם אֶת-הַמְּקֹמוֹת הַנִּכְבָּדִים בְּבָתֵּי הַמִּשְׁתֶּה וְאֶת-הַמּוֹשָׁבוֹת הָרִאשֹׁנִים בְּבָתֵּי-הַכְּנֶסֶת

6. Ve•o•ha•vim hem et - ha•m`ko•mot ha•nich•ba•dim be•va•tey ha•mish•te ve•et - ha•mo•sha•vot ha•ri•sho•nim be•va•tey - ha•k`ne•set.

Rabbinic Jewish Commentary

It is said (d) of Simeon ben Shetach, a noted Pharisee, about, or rather before the time of Christ, that having fled upon a certain account from king Jannai, he sent for him, and when he came, "he sat himself between the king and the queen: the king said to him, why dost thou mock me? he replied to him, I do not mock thee, thou hast riches and I have learning, as it is written, "Wisdom is a defence, and money is a defence", Ecc_7:12. He said to him, but why dost thou "sit between the king and queen?" He replied, in the book of Ben Sira, it is written, "Exalt her and she shall promote thee, and cause thee to sit among princes." He ordered to give him a cup, that he might ask a blessing; he took the cup and said, blessed be the food that Jannai and his friends eat."

And so says Maimonides (e), "How do the people sit in the synagogues?" "The elders sit, i.e. first, and their faces are towards the people, and their backs are to the temple, or holy place; and all the people sit in rows, and the faces of one row are to the backs of the row that is before them; so that the faces of all the people are to the holy place, and to the elders, and to the ark."

(d) T. Hieros. Betacot, fol. 11. 2. Beresh. Rabba, sect. 91. fol. 78. 4. (e) Hilchot Tephilla, c. 11. sect. 4.

---

7. And greetings in the markets, and to be called of men, Rabbi, Rabbi.

Greek/Transliteration
7. καὶ τοὺς ἀσπασμοὺς ἐν ταῖς ἀγοραῖς, καὶ καλεῖσθαι ὑπὸ τῶν ἀνθρώπων, ῾Ραββί, ῾Ραββί·

7. kai tous aspasmous en tais agorais, kai kaleisthai 'upo ton anthropon, 'Rabbi, 'Rabbi.

Hebrew/Transliteration
ז. שְׁאֵלַת שָׁלוֹם לָהֶם בַּשְּׁוָקִים וּלְהִקָּרֵא בְּשֵׁם רַבִּי רַבִּי בְּפִי הָאֲנָשִׁים:

7. Sh`e•lat sha•lom la•hem bash•va•kim ool•hi•ka•re be•shem Rabbi Rabbi be•fi ha•a•na•shim.

Rabbinic Jewish Commentary
It is reported (f) of R. Eleazar ben Simeon, of Migdal Gedur, that having reproached a deformed man he met in the road; when he came to the city where the man lived, "the citizens came out to meet him, and said to him, peace be upon thee, רבי רבי מורי מורי, "Rabbi, Rabbi, Master, Master"; he (Eleazar) said to them, who do you call "Rabbi, Rabbi?" They replied to him, he who followed thee: he said unto them, if this be a Rabbi, let there not be many such in Israel."

They say (g), "whenever he saw a disciple of the wise men, he rose from his throne, and embraced and kissed him, and called him, אבי אבי רבי רבי מרי מרי, "Father, Father, Rabbi, Rabbi, Master, Master"."

This title began but to be in use in the time of our Lord, or a very little while before: none of the prophets had it, nor Ezra the Scribe, nor the men of the great synagogue, nor Simeon the Just, the last of them; nor Antigonus, a man of Socho, a disciple of his: and it is observed by the Jews themselves (i), that

"the five couple are never called by the name of Rabban, nor by the name of Rabbi, only by their own name." By whom are meant, Joseph ben Joezer, and Joseph ben Jochanan; Joshua ben Perachia, said to be the master of Jesus of Nazareth, and Nittai the Arbelite; Judah ben Tabai, and Simeon ben Shetach; Shemaiah and Abtalion; Hillell and Shammai. The sons, or disciples of the two last, first took these titles. The Karaite Jews make much the same complaint, and give much the same account of the pride and vanity of the Rabbinical doctors, as Christ here does; for so one of them says (m);

"The Karaites do not use to act according to the custom of the wise men among the Rabbans, to make to themselves gods of silver, and guides of gold, with this view, להקרא רב, "to be called Rab"; and also to gather wealth and food to fulness."

(f) T. Bab. Taanith, fol. 20. 2. (g) T. Bab. Maccot, fol. 24. 1. & Cetubot, fol. 103. 2. (h) T. Bab. Gittin, fol. 62. 1. (i) Ganz. Tzemach David, par. 1. fol. 21. 1. (k) Ganz. Tzemach David, par. 1. fol. 25. 1. (m) Eliahu Adderet, c. 6. apud Trigland. de. Sect. Kar. c. 10. p. 164.

---

8. But be not ye called Rabbi: for one is your Master, even Christ; and all ye are brethren.

Greek/Transliteration

8. ὑμεῖς δὲ μὴ κληθῆτε Ῥαββίꞏ εἷς γάρ ἐστιν ὑμῶν ὁ καθηγητής, ὁ χριστόςꞏ πάντες δὲ ὑμεῖς ἀδελφοί ἐστε.

8. 'umeis de mei kleitheite 'Rabbi. 'eis gar estin 'umon 'o katheigeiteis, 'o christos. pantes de 'umeis adelphoi este.

Hebrew/Transliteration

ח. אָכֵן אַתֶּם אַל-יִקָּרֵא לְאִישׁ מִכֶּם רַבִּי כִּי רַב אֶחָד לָכֶם הַמָּשִׁיחַ וְאַתֶּם כֻּלְּכֶם אַחִים:

8. A•chen atem al - yi•ka•re le•eesh mi•kem Rabbi ki Rav e•chad la•chem ha•Ma•shiach ve•a•tem kool•chem a•chim.

---

9. And call no man your father upon the earth: for one is your Father, which is in heaven.

Greek/Transliteration
9. Καὶ πατέρα μὴ καλέσητε ὑμῶν ἐπὶ τῆς γῆς· εἷς γάρ ἐστιν ὁ πατὴρ ὑμῶν, ὁ ἐν τοῖς οὐρανοῖς.

9. Kai patera mei kaleseite 'umon epi teis geis. 'eis gar estin 'o pateir 'umon, 'o en tois ouranois.

Hebrew/Transliteration
ט. וְאַל-תֹּאמְרוּ לְאִישׁ בָּאָרֶץ אָבִי אַתָּה כִּי אָב אֶחָד לָכֶם הוּא אֲשֶׁר בַּשָּׁמָיִם:

9. Ve•al - tom•roo le•eesh ba•a•retz avi ata ki Av e•chad la•chem hoo asher ba•sha•ma•yim.

Rabbinic Jewish Commentary
The Scribes and Pharisees loved to be called by, did: and who were called not only by the name of Rabbi, but Abba, "Father", also: hence we read of Abba Saul, or "Father" Saul (n); Abba Jose ben Jochanan, a man of Jerusalem (o), Abba Chanan (p), Abba Chelphetha, a man of the village of Hananiah (q); Abba Gorion (r), and others; and this name was לשון כבוד כמו רבי, "a name of honour, even as Rabbi" (s), and of great authority: the wise men are said to be אבות הכל, "the fathers of all" (t), to whom all gave heed, and upon whom all depended, as so many oracles. There is a whole treatise in their Mishna, called Pirke Abot, which contains some of the oracles, and peculiar sayings of these "fathers", the Misnic Rabbi's, and which are preferred to the writings of Moses, and the prophets.

(n) Pirke Abot, c. 2. sect. 8. (o) T. Bab. Yebamot, fol. 53. 2. (p) Ib. fol. 64. 1. (q) T. Bab. Bava Metzia, fol. 94. 1. & Bava Bathra. fol. 56. 2. (r) Massech Sopherim, c. 15. sect. 10. (s) Juchasiu, fol. 31. 2. & 61. 2. (t) Maimon. in Misn. Peah, c. 1. sect. 1.

---

10. Neither be ye called masters: for one is your Master, even Christ.

Greek/Transliteration
10. μηδὲ κληθῆτε καθηγηταί· εἷς γὰρ ὑμῶν ἐστιν ὁ καθηγητής, ὁ χριστός.

10. meide kleitheite katheigeitai. 'eis gar 'umon estin 'o katheigeiteis, 'o christos.

Hebrew/Transliteration
י. וְאַל-יִקָּרֵא לְאִישׁ מִכֶּם מוֹרֶה דֶּרֶךְ כִּי מוֹרֶה אֶחָד לָכֶם הַמָּשִׁיחַ:

10. Ve•al - yi•ka•re le•eesh mi•kem mo•re de•rech ki Mo•re e•chad la•chem ha•Ma•shi•ach.

11. But he that is greatest among you shall be your servant.

Greek/Transliteration
11. Ὁ δὲ μείζων ὑμῶν ἔσται ὑμῶν διάκονος.

11. 'O de meizon 'umon estai 'umon dyakonos.

Hebrew/Transliteration
יא: וְהַגָּדוֹל בֵּינֵיכֶם יִהְיֶה לִמְשָׁרֵת לָכֶם.

11. Ve•ha•ga•dol bey•ney•chem yi•hee•ye lim•sha•ret la•chem.

---

12. And whosoever shall exalt himself shall be abased; and he that shall humble himself shall be exalted.

Greek/Transliteration
12. Ὅστις δὲ ὑψώσει ἑαυτόν, ταπεινωθήσεται· καὶ ὅστις ταπεινώσει ἑαυτόν, ὑψωθήσεται.

12. 'Ostis de 'upsosei 'eauton, tapeinotheisetai. kai 'ostis tapeinosei 'eauton, 'upsotheisetai.

Hebrew/Transliteration
יב: וְהַמִּתְנַשֵּׂא בְגַאֲוָתוֹ יִשָּׁפֵל וּשְׁפַל רוּחַ יִנָּשֵׂא.

12. Ve•ha•mit•na•se ve•ga•a•va•to yi•sha•fel oosh•fal roo•ach yi•na•se.

Rabbinic Jewish Commentary
It seems to be a proverbial expression, and much in use among the Jews: it is said in so many words in the Talmud (u), as here; "whosoever shall humble himself, the holy blessed God shall exalt him; and whosoever shall exalt himself, the holy blessed God shall humble him." (u) T. Bab. Erubin, fol. 13. 2. & 54. 1. & Nedarim, fol. 55. 1.

---

13. But woe unto you, scribes and Pharisees, hypocrites! for ye shut up the kingdom of heaven against men: for ye neither go in yourselves, neither suffer ye them that are entering to go in.

Greek/Transliteration
13. Οὐαὶ δὲ ὑμῖν, γραμματεῖς καὶ Φαρισαῖοι, ὑποκριταί, ὅτι κατεσθίετε τὰς οἰκίας τῶν χηρῶν, καὶ προφάσει μακρὰ προσευχόμενοι· διὰ τοῦτο λήψεσθε περισσότερον κρίμα.

13. Ouai de 'umin, grammateis kai Pharisaioi, 'upokritai, 'oti katesthiete tas oikias ton cheiron, kai prophasei makra proseuchomenoi. dya touto leipsesthe perissoteron krima.

Hebrew/Transliteration
יג. אַךְ-אוֹי לָכֶם סוֹפְרִים וּפְרוּשִׁים חֲנֵפִים כִּי תִסְגְּרוּ מַלְכוּת הַשָּׁמַיִם מִפְּנֵי בְנֵי-הָאָדָם אַתֶּם לֹא תָבֹאוּ שָׁמָּה:וְאֶת-הַבָּאִים לֹא תִתְּנוּ לָבֹא

13. Ach - oy la•chem sof•rim ooF•roo•shim cha•ne•fim ki tis•ge•roo mal•choot ha•sha•ma•yim mip•ney v`ney - ha•a•dam atem lo ta•vo•oo sha•ma ve•et - ha•ba•eem lo tit•noo la•vo.

Jewish New Testament Commentary

The Mishna remarks that the "plagues" (or "hits" or "self-inflicted wounds") "of Pharisees... ruin the world" (Sotah 3:4). The Jerusalem and Babylonian Talmuds both comment on this in famous passages delineating seven kinds of Pharisees (J. B'rakhot 14b, Sotah 20c; B. Sotah 22b). The following is a hybrid combining elements from both Talmuds with rabbinic expositions; it mentions eight kinds.

There are seven kinds of Pharisees: the "shoulder" Pharisee, who ostentatiously carries his good deeds on his shoulder so all can see them; the "wait-a-moment" Pharisee, who wants you to wait while he performs a *mitzvah*; the bruised Pharisee, who runs into a wall while looking at the ground to avoid seeing a woman; the "reckoning" Pharisee, who commits a sin, then does a good deed and balances the one against the other; the "pestle" Pharisee, whose head is bowed in false humility, like a pestle in a mortar; the Pharisee who asks, "What is my duty, so that I may do it?" as if he thought he had fulfilled every obligation already (compare Php_3:5-6); the Pharisee from fear of the consequences if he doesn't perform the commandments; and the Pharisee from love-either love of the rewards God promises for performing the commandments, or love of *Torah* itself [no matter which, he is understood here to be the one good kind of Pharisee].

---

14. Woe unto you, scribes and Pharisees, hypocrites! for ye devour widows' houses, and for a pretence make long prayer: therefore ye shall receive the greater damnation.

Greek/Transliteration
14. Οὐαὶ ὑμῖν, γραμματεῖς καὶ Φαρισαῖοι, ὑποκριταί, ὅτι κλείετε τὴν βασιλείαν τῶν οὐρανῶν ἔμπροσθεν τῶν ἀνθρώπων· ὑμεῖς γὰρ οὐκ εἰσέρχεσθε, οὐδὲ τοὺς εἰσερχομένους ἀφίετε εἰσελθεῖν.

14. Ouai 'umin, grammateis kai Pharisaioi, 'upokritai, 'oti kleiete tein basileian ton ouranon emprosthen ton anthropon. 'umeis gar ouk eiserchesthe, oude tous eiserchomenous aphiete eiselthein.

Hebrew/Transliteration
יד. אוֹי לָכֶם סוֹפְרִים וּפְרוּשִׁים חֲנֵפִים כִּי תֹאכְלוּן אֶת-בָּתֵּי הָאַלְמָנוֹת וּלְמַרְאֵה עַיִן תַּרְבּוּ תְפִלָּה וְלָכֵן גַּם-קַו:הַמִּשְׁפָּט יִנָּטֶה עֲלֵיכֶם פִּי-שְׁנָיִם

14. Oy la•chem sof•rim ooF•roo•shim cha•ne•fim ki toch•loon et - ba•tey ha•al•ma•not ool•mar•eh a•yin tar•boo te•fi•la ve•la•chen gam - kav ha•mish•pat yi•na•te aley•chem pi - sh`na•yim.

Rabbinic Jewish Commentary

Maimonides (x) says, that "the ancient saints, or good men, used to stay an hour before prayer, and an hour after prayer, ומאריכם בתפלה שעה and "prolonged", or "held an hour in prayer":" and this being three times a day, nine hours every day, as is observed in the Talmud (y), were spent in this manner; and on this account they got the character of very devout and religious men, and hereby covered all their avarice, rapine, and oppression of the poor: but God will not be mocked.

In Munster's Hebrew Gospel it is called משפט ארוך, "a long judgment", or "damnation", in allusion to their long prayers: and is the very reverse of what they expect on account of them: they say (z). "three things prolong a man's days and years, המאריך בתפלתו, "he that is long in his prayer"'.

(x) Hilch. Tephillah, c. 4. sect. 16. (y) T. Bab. Beracot, fol. 32. 2. (z) Ib. fol. 54. 2.

---

15. Woe unto you, scribes and Pharisees, hypocrites! for ye compass sea and land to make one proselyte, and when he is made, ye make him twofold more the child of hell than yourselves.

Greek/Transliteration

15. Οὐαὶ ὑμῖν, γραμματεῖς καὶ Φαρισαῖοι, ὑποκριταί, ὅτι περιάγετε τὴν θάλασσαν καὶ τὴν ξηρὰν ποιῆσαι ἕνα προσήλυτον, καὶ ὅταν γένηται, ποιεῖτε αὐτὸν υἱὸν γεέννης διπλότερον ὑμῶν.

15. Ouai 'umin, grammateis kai Pharisaioi, 'upokritai, 'oti peryagete tein thalassan kai tein xeiran poieisai 'ena proseiluton, kai 'otan geneitai, poieite auton 'wion ge'enneis diploteron 'umon.

Hebrew/Translitaration

טו. אוֹי לָכֶם סוֹפְרִים וּפְרוּשִׁים חֲנֵפִים כִּי תָסֹבּוּ יָם וְיַבָּשָׁה לַעֲשׂוֹת גֵּר אֶחָד וְאַחֲרֵי אֲשֶׁר נַעֲשָׂה כֵן - תַּעֲשׂוּהוּ לְבֶן-גֵּיהִנֹּם כִּפְלַיִם יוֹתֵר מִכֶּם.

15. Oy la•chem sof•rim ooF•roo•shim cha•ne•fim ki ta•so•boo yam ve•ya•ba•sha la•a•sot ger e•chad ve•a•cha•rey asher na•a•sa chen ta•a•soo•hoo le•ven - Gey•hi•nom kif•la•yim yo•ter mi•kem.

Rabbinic Jewish Commentary

Our Lord here seems to oppose a common notion and saying of their's (m), that when "one was made a proselyte, he became entirely like a new born babe;" but so far from being like one in innocence and harmlessness, that he became a child of Gehenna, filled with wrath and malice, and fitted for destruction; and so opposes another notion of their's, that hellfire has no power over their disciples, nor even over the transgressors of Israel (n): but they will find it, by experience, that neither their descent from Abraham, nor their learning, nor their religion, will save them from the devouring flames, which their sins have made them so deserving of, and so are בני גיהנם, "children of Gehenna" (o); a Talmudic phrase; the meaning of which they understood well enough, and which was applicable to them, and more so to their proselytes; and that as owing to them, which was an aggravation of their own guilt and condemnation.

(m) T. Bab. Yebamot, fol. 22. 1. & 48. 2. & 62. 1. & 97. 2. Maimon. Hilch. Issure Biah, c. 14. sect. 11. & Eduth, c. 13. sect. 2. (n) T. Bab. Chagiga, fol. 27. 1. (o) T. Bab. Roshhashanah, fol. 17. 1.

---

16. Woe unto you, ye blind guides, which say, Whosoever shall swear by the temple, it is nothing; but whosoever shall swear by the gold of the temple, he is a debtor!

Greek/Transliteration
16. Οὐαὶ ὑμῖν, ὁδηγοὶ τυφλοί, οἱ λέγοντες, Ὃς ἂν ὀμόσῃ ἐν τῷ ναῷ, οὐδέν ἐστιν· ὃς δ᾽ ἂν ὀμόσῃ ἐν τῷ χρυσῷ τοῦ ναοῦ, ὀφείλει.

16. Ouai 'umin, 'odeigoi tuphloi, 'oi legontes, 'Os an omosei en to nao, ouden estin. 'os d an omosei en to chruso tou naou, opheilei.

Hebrew/Transliteration
טז. אוֹי לָכֶם מְנַהֲלִים עִוְרִים הָאֹמְרִים כִּי יִשָּׁבַע אִישׁ בַּהֵיכָל אֵין-דָּבָר וְכִי יִשָּׁבַע בִּזְהַב הַהֵיכָל שְׁבוּעָתוֹ עָלָיו:

16. Oy la•chem me•na•ha•lim eev•rim ha•om•rim ki yi•sha•va eesh ba•hey•chol eyn - da•var ve•chi yi•sha•va biz•hav ha•hey•chal sh`voo•a•to alav.

Rabbinic Jewish Commentary
It was usual with them to swear by the temple: take an instance or two. "Says R. Jochanan (p), היכלא, "by the temple", it is in our hands; but what shall I do?"

The gloss upon it is; "it is an oath by the temple of God, that it is in our power to reveal the illegitimacy of the families of the land of Israel."

"Says R. Zechariah ben Hakatzab (q), המעון הזה, "by this habitation" (meaning the temple), her hand was not removed from my hand from the time the Gentiles entered into Jerusalem, to the time they went out."

Jarchi and Bartenora's note on it is, this is an oath. Again, "says R. Simeon ben Gamaliel (r), המעון הזה, "by this habitation"; I will not rest this night until they (doves) are sold for pence apiece." The gloss on it is, "he swore by the sanctuary."

(p) T. Bab. Kiddushin, fol. 71. 1. (q) Misn. Cetubot, c. 2. sect. 9. Juchasin, fol. 56. 1. (r) T. Bab. Bava Bathra, fol 166. 1. Misn. Ceritot, c. 1. sect. 7. Vid. c. 6. sect. 3.

17. Ye fools and blind: for whether is greater, the gold, or the temple that sanctifieth the gold?

Greek/Transliteration
17. Μωροὶ καὶ τυφλοί· τίς γὰρ μείζων ἐστίν, ὁ χρυσός, ἢ ὁ ναὸς ὁ ἁγιάζων τὸν χρυσόν;

17. Moroi kai tuphloi. tis gar meizon estin, 'o chrusos, ei 'o naos 'o 'agyazon ton chruson?

Hebrew/Transliteration
יז. סְכָלִים וְעִוְרִים מֶה הוּא הַגָּדוֹל הַזָּהָב אוֹ הַהֵיכָל הַמְקַדֵּשׁ אֶת-הַזָּהָב:

17. Se•cha•lim ve•eev•rim ma hoo ha•ga•dol ha•za•hav oh ha•hey•chal ham•ka•desh et - ha•za•hav?

---

18. And, Whosoever shall swear by the altar, it is nothing; but whosoever sweareth by the gift that is upon it, he is guilty.

Greek/Transliteration
18. Καί, Ὃς ἐὰν ὀμόσῃ ἐν τῷ θυσιαστηρίῳ, οὐδέν ἐστιν· ὃς δ' ἂν ὀμόσῃ ἐν τῷ δώρῳ τῷ ἐπάνω αὐτοῦ, ὀφείλει.

18. Kai, 'Os ean omosei en to thusyasteirio, ouden estin. 'os d an omosei en to doro to epano autou, opheilei.

Hebrew/Transliteration
יח. וְכִי-יִשָּׁבַע אִישׁ בַּמִּזְבֵּחַ אֵין-דָּבָר וְכִי-יִשָּׁבַע בַּקָּרְבָּן אֲשֶׁר עַל-גַּבּוֹ שְׁבוּעָתוֹ עָלָיו:

18. Ve•chi - yi•sha•va eesh ba•miz•be•ach eyn - da•var ve•chi - yi•sha•va ba•kor•ban asher al - ga•bo sh`voo•a•to alav.

Rabbinic Jewish Commentary
One said to another (r), "swear to me that thou wilt not discover me, and he swore to him; by what did he swear? says R. Jose bar Chanina, במזבח הפנימי, "by the innermost altar"." Again, it is said of Zedekiah (s), "that he (Nebuchadnezzar) made him to swear; by what did he make him to swear? says R. Jose, by the covenant he made him to swear; Rabbi says במזבח, "by the altar" he made him to swear."

And elsewhere (t) it is said of him, ""and he also rebelled against king Nebuchadnezzar, who made him swear by God", 2Ch_36:13. By what did he make him swear? says R. Jose bar Chanina, "by the horns of the innermost altar" he made him swear."

(r) Echa Rabbati, fol. 54. 1. (s) Midrash Kohelet, fol. 78. 1. (t) Midrash Megillat Esther, fol. 89. 1.

19. Ye fools and blind: for whether is greater, the gift, or the altar that sanctifieth the gift?

Greek/Transliteration
19. Μωροὶ καὶ τυφλοί· τί γὰρ μεῖζον, τὸ δῶρον, ἢ τὸ θυσιαστήριον τὸ ἁγιάζον τὸ δῶρον;

19. Moroi kai tuphloi. ti gar meizon, to doron, ei to thusyasteirion to 'agyazon to doron?

Hebrew/Translitration
:יט. עִוְרִים מָה הוּא הַגָּדוֹל הַקָּרְבָּן אוֹ הַמִּזְבֵּחַ הַמְקַדֵּשׁ אֶת-הַקָּרְבָּן

19. Eev•rim ma hoo ha•ga•dol ha•kor•ban oh ha•miz•be•ach ham•ka•desh et - ha•kor•ban?

Rabbinic Jewish Commentary
Yeshua speaks the sense of the law, and their own traditions, and in their own language, and argues from the same to the confutation of them: המזבח מקדש, "the altar", they say (u), "sanctifies" that which is fit for it; that is, that which is proper to be offered up upon it: "as the altar sanctifies that which is fit for it, so the ascent unto it sanctifies; and as the altar, and the ascent, sanctify what is fit for them, so the vessels sanctify; the vessels for liquids sanctify the liquids, and the dry measures sanctify the dry; the vessels for liquids do not sanctify the dry, nor the dry measures sanctify the liquids; the holy vessels, which are bored, (or broken,) when they do the service they used to do, when whole, sanctify, if not, they do not sanctify; nor does anything sanctify but in the sanctuary."

Korban, was binding; seeing the gift, or offering, received its sanctity from the altar: hence, of the two, an oath made by the altar should be more sacred and obligatory than one made by the gift.

(u) Misn. Zebachim, c. 9. sect. 7.

---

20. Whoso therefore shall swear by the altar, sweareth by it, and by all things thereon.

Greek/Transliteration
20. Ὁ οὖν ὀμόσας ἐν τῷ θυσιαστηρίῳ ὀμνύει ἐν αὐτῷ καὶ ἐν πᾶσιν τοῖς ἐπάνω αὐτοῦ·

20. 'O oun omosas en to thusyasteirio omnuei en auto kai en pasin tois epano autou.

Hebrew/Transliteration
:כ. לָכֵן הַנִּשְׁבָּע בַּמִּזְבֵּחַ נִשְׁבַּע בּוֹ וּבְכָל אֲשֶׁר עַל-גַּבּוֹ

20. La•chen ha•nish•ba ba•miz•be•ach nish•ba bo oov•chol asher al - ga•bo.

---

21. And whoso shall swear by the temple, sweareth by it, and by him that dwelleth therein.

Greek/Transliteration
21. καὶ ὁ ὀμόσας ἐν τῷ ναῷ ὀμνύει ἐν αὐτῷ καὶ ἐν τῷ κατοικήσαντι αὐτόν·

21. kai 'o omosas en to nao omnuei en auto kai en to katoikeisanti auton.

Hebrew/Transliteration
כא. וְהַנִּשְׁבָּע בַּהֵיכָל נִשְׁבַּע בּוֹ וּבְשֹׁכֵן בּוֹ:

21. Ve•ha•nish•ba ba•hey•chol nish•ba bo oo•va•sho•chen bo.

---

22. And he that shall swear by heaven, sweareth by the throne of God, and by him that sitteth thereon.

Greek/Transliteration
22. καὶ ὁ ὀμόσας ἐν τῷ οὐρανῷ ὀμνύει ἐν τῷ θρόνῳ τοῦ θεοῦ καὶ ἐν τῷ καθημένῳ ἐπάνω αὐτοῦ.

22. kai 'o omosas en to ourano omnuei en to throno tou theou kai en to katheimeno epano autou.

Hebrew/Transliteration
כב. וְהַנִּשְׁבָּע בַּשָּׁמַיִם נִשְׁבַּע בְּכִסֵּא אֱלֹהִים וּבְיוֹשֵׁב עָלָיו:

22. Ve•ha•nish•ba ba•sha•ma•yim nish•ba be•chi•se Elohim oo•va•yo•shev alav.

---

23. Woe unto you, scribes and Pharisees, hypocrites! for ye pay tithe of mint and anise and cummin, and have omitted the weightier matters of the law, judgment, mercy, and faith: these ought ye to have done, and not to leave the other undone.

Greek/Transliteration
23. Οὐαὶ ὑμῖν, γραμματεῖς καὶ Φαρισαῖοι, ὑποκριταί, ὅτι ἀποδεκατοῦτε τὸ ἡδύοσμον καὶ τὸ ἄνηθον καὶ τὸ κύμινον, καὶ ἀφήκατε τὰ βαρύτερα τοῦ νόμου, τὴν κρίσιν καὶ τὸν ἔλεον καὶ τὴν πίστιν· ταῦτα ἔδει ποιῆσαι, κἀκεῖνα μὴ ἀφιέναι.

23. Ouai 'umin, grammateis kai Pharisaioi, 'upokritai, 'oti apodekatoute to 'eiduosmon kai to aneithon kai to kuminon, kai apheikate ta barutera tou nomou, tein krisin kai ton eleon kai tein pistin. tauta edei poieisai, kakeina mei aphienai.

Hebrew/Transliteration
כג. אוֹי לָכֶם סוֹפְרִים וּפְרוּשִׁים חֲנֵפִים כִּי תְעַשְׂרוּ אֶת-הַמִּנְתָּא וְאֶת-הַשֶּׁבֶת וְאֶת-הַכַּמֹּן וַתַּעַזְבוּ אֶת-הַנִּכְבָּדוֹת:בַּתּוֹרָה אֶת-הַמִּשְׁפָּט אֶת-הַחֶסֶד וְאֶת-הָאֱמוּנָה אֵלֶּה עֲלֵיכֶם לַעֲשׂוֹת וְאֶת-אֵלֶּה אַל-תַּעַזֹבוּ

23. Oy la•chem sof•rim ooF•roo•shim cha•ne•fim ki te•as•roo et - ha•min•ta ve•et - ha•she•vet ve•et - ha•ka•mon ve•ta•az•voo et - ha•nich•ba•dot ba•To•rah et - ha•mish•pat et - ha•che•sed ve•et - ha•e•moo•na ele aley•chem la•a•sot ve•et - ele al - ta•a•zo•voo.

Rabbinic Jewish Commentary
The distinction of the commandments of the law into lighter and heavier, or weightier, to which Yeshua here refers, is frequent with the Jews. When one comes to be made a proselyte, they acquaint him with some of מצות קלות, "the light commands", and some of מצות חמורות, "the heavy", or "weighty commands" (i). So again, they paraphrase the words in Isa_33:18 "where is the scribe?" he that numbers all the letters in the law. "Where is the receiver?" who weighs the "light" things, וחמורין שבתורה, and "heavy", or "weighty things in the law" (k). Again (l),

"in the words of the law there are some things "light", and some things "heavy", or "weighty":" but those weighty things they omitted, and regarded those that were light; yea, that had no foundation in the law at all: and no wonder, since, in the place last cited, they say (m), that "the words of the Scribes are all of them "weighty" and that the sayings of the elders are more "weighty" than the words of the prophets."

(i) T. Bab. Yebamot, fol. 47. 1. Maimon. Hilch. Issure Bia, c. 14. sect. 2, 6, 9. Moses Kotsensis Mitzvot Tora, pr. neg. 116. (k) T. Bab. Chagiga, fol. 15. 2. & Sanhedrin, fol. 106. 2. (l) T. Hieros Beracot, fol. 3. 2.

---

24. Ye blind guides, which strain at a gnat, and swallow a camel.

Greek/Transliteration
24. Ὁδηγοὶ τυφλοί, οἱ διϋλίζοντες τὸν κώνωπα, τὴν δὲ κάμηλον καταπίνοντες.

24. 'Odeigoi tuphloi, 'oi diulizontes ton konopa, tein de kameilon katapinontes.

Hebrew/Transliteration
כד. מְנַהֲלִים עִוְרִים הַמְסַנְּנִים אֶת-הַיַּתּוּשׁ וּבֹלְעִים אֶת-הַגָּמָל:

24. Me•na•ha•lim eev•rim ha•me•sa•ne•nim et - ha•ya•toosh oo•vol•eem et - ha•ga•mal.

Rabbinic Jewish Commentary

The Jews had a law, which forbid them the eating of any creeping thing, Lev_11:41 and of this they were strictly observant, and would not be guilty of the breach of it for ever so much, "One that eats a flea, or a gnat; they say (p) is מומר, "an apostate";

Maimonides says (s), "He that strains wine, or vinegar, or strong liquor, and eats "Jabchushin" (a sort of small flies found in wine cellars (t), on account of which they strained their wine), or gnats, or worms, which he hath strained off, is to be beaten on account of the creeping things of the water, or on account of the creeping flying things, and the creeping things of the water.

Moreover, it is said (u), "a man might not pour his strong liquors through a strainer, by the light (of a candle or lamp), lest he should separate and leave in the top of the strainer (some creeping thing), and it should fail again into the cup, and he should transgress the law, in Lev_11:41.

(p) T. Bab. Avoda Zara, fol. 26. 2. & Horaiot, fol. 11. 1. (q) Mainon. Hilch. Maacolot Asurot, c. 2. sect. 22. (r) T. Bab. Megilla, fol, 13. 2. Vid. T. Hietos. Sota, fol. 17. 1. (s) Ubi supra, (Mainon. Hilch. Maacolot Asurot, c. 2.) sect. 20. (t) Gloss. in T. Bab. Cholin, fol. 67. 1. (u) Ib.

---

25. Woe unto you, scribes and Pharisees, hypocrites! for ye make clean the outside of the cup and of the platter, but within they are full of extortion and excess.

Greek/Transliteration

25. Οὐαὶ ὑμῖν, γραμματεῖς καὶ Φαρισαῖοι, ὑποκριταί, ὅτι καθαρίζετε τὸ ἔξωθεν τοῦ ποτηρίου καὶ τῆς παροψίδος, ἔσωθεν δὲ γέμουσιν ἐξ ἁρπαγῆς καὶ ἀδικίας.

25. Ouai 'umin, grammateis kai Pharisaioi, 'upokritai, 'oti katharizete to exothen tou poteiriou kai teis paropsidos, esothen de gemousin ex 'arpageis kai adikias.

Hebrew/Transliteration

כה. אוֹי לָכֶם סוֹפְרִים וּפְרוּשִׁים חֲנֵפִים הַמְטַהֲרִים אֶת-הַכּוֹס וְאֶת-הַקְּעָרָה מִחוּץ וּמִבִּפְנִים מְלֵאוֹת הֵן עֹשֶׁק וְעַוְלָה:

25. Oy la•chem sof•rim ooF•roo•shim cha•ne•fim ham•ta•ha•rim et - ha•kos ve•et - hak•a•ra mi•choo•tz oo•mi•bif•nim me•le•ot hen o•shek ve•av•la.

Rabbinic Jewish Commentary

In like manner the Jews themselves say of hypocrites (w), "They make show of a pure and clean soul, but under it lies hid a leprosy: they are like to "vessels full of uncleanness"; they are outwardly washed with the water of fraud and craftiness; but whatsoever is within, in the midst or them, is unclean."

(w) R. Sol Gabirol in Cether Malcuth apud L. Capell in loc.

---

26. Thou blind Pharisee, cleanse first that which is within the cup and platter, that the outside of them may be clean also.

Greek/Transliteration

26. Φαρισαῖε τυφλέ, καθάρισον πρῶτον τὸ ἐντὸς τοῦ ποτηρίου καὶ τῆς παροψίδος, ἵνα γένηται καὶ τὸ ἐκτὸς αὐτῶν καθαρόν.

26. Pharisaie tuphle, katharison proton to entos tou poteiriou kai teis paropsidos, 'ina geneitai kai to ektos auton katharon.

Hebrew/Transliteration

כו. פָּרוּשׁ עִוֵּר טַהֵר רִאשֹׁנָה אֶת-הַכּוֹס וְאֶת-הַקְּעָרָה מִבִּפְנִים וְאָז תִּטְהַרְנָה גַם-מִחוּץ:

26. Pa•roosh ee•ver ta•her ri•sho•na et - ha•kos ve•et - hak•a•ra mi•bif•nim ve•az tit•har•na gam - mi•choo•tz.

---

27. Woe unto you, scribes and Pharisees, hypocrites! for ye are like unto whited sepulchres, which indeed appear beautiful outward, but are within full of dead men's bones, and of all uncleanness.

Greek/Transliteration

27. Οὐαὶ ὑμῖν, γραμματεῖς καὶ Φαρισαῖοι, ὑποκριταί, ὅτι παρομοιάζετε τάφοις κεκονιαμένοις, οἵτινες ἔξωθεν μὲν φαίνονται ὡραῖοι, ἔσωθεν δὲ γέμουσιν ὀστέων νεκρῶν καὶ πάσης ἀκαθαρσίας.

27. Ouai 'umin, grammateis kai Pharisaioi, 'upokritai, 'oti paromoyazete taphois kekonyamenois, 'oitines exothen men phainontai 'oraioi, esothen de gemousin osteon nekron kai paseis akatharsias.

Hebrew/Transliteration

כז. אוֹי לָכֶם סוֹפְרִים וּפְרוּשִׁים חֲנֵפִים הַדֹּמִים לִקְבָרִים מְלֻבָּנִים בַּשִּׂיד הַנִּרְאִים יָפִים מִחוּץ וּמִבִּפְנִים מְלֵאִים:הֵם עַצְמוֹת אָדָם וְכָל-טֻמְאָה

27. Oy la•chem sof•rim ooF•roo•shim cha•ne•fim ha•do•mim lik•va•rim me•loo•ba•nim ba•sid ha•nir•eem ya•fim mi•choo•tz oo•mi•bif•nim me•le•eem hem atz•mot adam ve•chol - toom•ah.

Rabbinic Jewish Commentary

This appears from various passages in their writings: "The vineyard of the fourth year, they marked with clods of earth, and an uncircumcised one with dust, **ושל קברות בסיד**, "and graves with chalk", mixed (with water) and poured (on them (x).

Of this marking of the graves, the reason of it, the time and manner of doing it, Maimonides (y) gives us this account: "Whoever finds a grave, or a dead carcass, or anything for the dead that defiles, by the tent he is obliged to put a mark upon it, that it may not be a stumbling to others."

(x) Misn. Maaser Sheni, c. 5. sect. 1. (y) Hilch. Tumath Meth, c. 8. sect. 9.

---

28. Even so ye also outwardly appear righteous unto men, but within ye are full of hypocrisy and iniquity.

Greek/Transliteration
28. Οὕτως καὶ ὑμεῖς ἔξωθεν μὲν φαίνεσθε τοῖς ἀνθρώποις δίκαιοι, ἔσωθεν δὲ μεστοί ἐστε ὑποκρίσεως καὶ ἀνομίας.

28. 'Outos kai 'umeis exothen men phainesthe tois anthropois dikaioi, esothen de mestoi este 'upokriseos kai anomias.

Hebrew/Transliteration
:כח. כֵּן נִרְאִים גַּם-אַתֶּם מִחוּץ כְּצַדִּיקִים לְעֵינֵי אֲנָשִׁים וּמִבִּפְנִים הִנְּכֶם מְלֵאִים חֹנֶף וָאָוֶן

28. Ken nir•eem gam - atem mi•choo•tz ke•tza•di•kim le•ei•ney a•na•shim oo•mi•bif•nim hin•chem me•le•eem cho•nef va•a•ven.

Rabbinic Jewish Commentary
(e) "every disciple of a wise man, **שאין תוכו כברו**, "whose inside is not as his outside", is no disciple of a wise man.

And it is expressly ascribed by some of their writers to one sort of the Pharisees, of whom they say (f), "they are desirous to appear to men to be holy, but their inside is not as their outside; which is much the same Yeshua here says of them. What our Lord charges these men with, is owned by their own Rabbi's; they say (g), that "the iniquity of those that were under the first temple, was open and manifest, but the iniquity of those that were under the second temple, was not open.

But as the gloss says, "the children of the second temple, **רשעים היו בסתר**, "were secretly wicked".

(e) T. Bab. Yoma, fol. 72. 2. (f) Bartenora in Misn. Sota, c. 3. sect. 4. (g) T. Bab. Yoma, fol. 9. 2.

29. Woe unto you, scribes and Pharisees, hypocrites! because ye build the tombs of the prophets, and garnish the sepulchres of the righteous,

Greek/Transliteration
29. Οὐαὶ ὑμῖν, γραμματεῖς καὶ Φαρισαῖοι, ὑποκριταί, ὅτι οἰκοδομεῖτε τοὺς τάφους τῶν προφητῶν, καὶ κοσμεῖτε τὰ μνημεῖα τῶν δικαίων,

29. Ouai 'umin, grammateis kai Pharisaioi, 'upokritai, 'oti oikodomeite tous taphous ton propheiton, kai kosmeite ta mneimeia ton dikaion,

Hebrew/Transliteration
כט. אוֹי לָכֶם סוֹפְרִים וּפְרוּשִׁים חֲנֵפִים הַבֹּנִים אֶת-קִבְרֵי הַנְּבִיאִים וְאֶת-מַצְּבוֹת קִבְרַת הַצַדִּיקִים תְּפָאֵרוּן:

29. Oy la•chem sof•rim ooF•roo•shim cha•ne•fim ha•bo•nim et - kiv•rey ha•n`vi•eem ve•et - matz•vot ke•voo•rat ha•tza•di•kim te•fa•e•roon.

Rabbinic Jewish Commentary

Rightly is the word "build", used of tombs and sepulchres; the Jews have a canon, which runs thus (h), "they do not dig graves nor sepulchres, on a feast day.

The commentators (i) on it say, that the graves are the holes which they dig in the earth, and the sepulchres are the buildings over the graves. In the Gemara it is asked (k), "what are the graves? and what are the sepulchres? says R. Judah, the graves are made by digging and the sepulchres or tombs בבנין, "by building"

Among the excellent characters given of Benaah, R. Jochanan's master, it is said (l), "that he was a very wise man, and a judge, and understood mysteries and parables; וציין מערת, "and painted the cave" of Adam the first, and the cave of Abraham.

Though perhaps this is to be understood of him in a figurative sense, but yet must allude to a literal one: the sepulchres of the prophets, were especially very sacred:

"all sepulchres (they say (m)) might be removed, but the sepulchres of a king, and the "sepulchres of a prophet"; they say unto him, were not the sepulchres of the sons of David removed? and the sepulchres of the sons of Huldah were in Jerusalem, and a man might not touch them, to remove them for ever. R. Akiba replied to them because of decency it was forgiven (or allowed) there, and from thence the uncleanness being channelled, went out to the brook Kidron.

(h) Misn. Moed Katon, c. 1. sect. 6. (i) Maimon. & Bartenora in ib. (k) T. Bab. Moed Katon, fol. 8. 2. (l) Juchasin, fol. 86. 1. (m) T. Hieros. Nazir, fol. 57. 4. (n) T. Hieros. Shekalim, fol. 47. 1.

30. And say, If we had been in the days of our fathers, we would not have been partakers with them in the blood of the prophets.

Greek/Transliteration
30. καὶ λέγετε, Εἰ ἦμεν ἐν ταῖς ἡμέραις τῶν πατέρων ἡμῶν, οὐκ ἂν ἦμεν κοινωνοὶ αὐτῶν ἐν τῷ αἵματι τῶν προφητῶν.

30. kai legete, Ei eimen en tais 'eimerais ton pateron 'eimon, ouk an eimen koinonoi auton en to 'aimati ton propheiton.

Hebrew/Transliteration
ל: וְתֹאמְרוּן אִם-הָיִינוּ בִימֵי אֲבוֹתֵינוּ לֹא-הָיְתָה יָדֵנוּ עִמָּהֶם לִשְׁפֹּךְ דַּם-הַנְּבִיאִים

30. Ve•tom•roon eem - ha•yi•noo viy•mey avo•tey•noo lo - hai•ta ya•de•noo ee•ma•hem lish•poch dam - ha•n`vi•eem.

---

31. Wherefore ye be witnesses unto yourselves, that ye are the children of them which killed the prophets.

Greek/Translitration
31. Ὥστε μαρτυρεῖτε ἑαυτοῖς ὅτι υἱοί ἐστε τῶν φονευσάντων τοὺς προφήτας·

31. 'Oste martureite 'eautois 'oti 'wioi este ton phoneusanton tous propheitas.

Hebrew/Transliteration
לא: עַל-כֵּן עֵדִים אַתֶּם בָּכֶם כִּי-בָנִים הִנְּכֶם לַאֲשֶׁר הָרְגוּ אֶת-הַנְּבִיאִים

31. Al - ken e•dim atem ba•chem ki - va•nim hin•chem la•a•sher har•goo et - ha•n`vi•eem.

---

32. Fill ye up then the measure of your fathers.

Greek/Transliteration
32. καὶ ὑμεῖς πληρώσατε τὸ μέτρον τῶν πατέρων ὑμῶν.

32. kai 'umeis pleirosate to metron ton pateron 'umon.

Hebrew/Transliteration
לב: וְגַם-אַתֶּם מַלְאוּ כַיּוֹם אֶת-מִדַּת אֲבוֹתֵיכֶם

32. Ve•gam - atem mal•oo ka•yom et - mi•dat avo•tei•chem.

Rabbinic Jewish Commentary
They have a saying (o), that "the holy blessed God does not take vengeance on man, עד שתתמלא סאתו, "until his measure is filled up"; according to Job_20:22.

Which the Chaldee paraphrase renders, "when his measure is filled up, then shall he take vengeance on him; and that this is Yeshua's sense, appears from what follows, (o) T. Bab. Sota, fol. 9. 1.

---

33. Ye serpents, ye generation of vipers, how can ye escape the damnation of hell?

Greek/Transliteration
33. Ὄφεις, γεννήματα ἐχιδνῶν, πῶς φύγητε ἀπὸ τῆς κρίσεως τῆς γεέννης;

33. Opheis, genneimata echidnon, pos phugeite apo teis kriseos teis ge'enneis?

Hebrew/Transliteration
לג. נְחָשִׁים יִלְדֵי צִפְעֹנִים אֵיכָה תִנָּצְלוּ מִדִּין גֵּיהִנֹּם:

33. N`cha•shim yil•dey tzif•o•nim ey•cha ti•natz•loo mi•din Gey•hi•nom?

Rabbinic Jewish Commentary
The phrase, דינה של גיהנם, "the judgment, or damnation of Gehenna", is a phrase often used in the Talmud (p), and Midrashes (q) of the Jews; and intends future judgement, and the everlasting vengeance and wrath of God, the unquenchable fire prepared for the devil and his messengers, and which impenitent unbelieving sinners cannot escape,

(p) T. Bab. Berncot, fol. 61. 1. Erubin, fol. 18. 2. Yebamot, fol. 102. 2. Sota, fol. 4. 2. & 5. 1. & Bava Bathra, fol. 10. 1. (q) Bemidbar Rabba, fol. 203. 1. Shirhashirim Rabba, fol. 14. 2. & Midrash Kohelet, fol. 76. 1.

---

34. Wherefore, behold, I send unto you prophets, and wise men, and scribes: and some of them ye shall kill and crucify; and some of them shall ye scourge in your synagogues, and persecute them from city to city:

Greek/Transliteration
34. Διὰ τοῦτο, ἰδού, ἐγὼ ἀποστέλλω πρὸς ὑμᾶς προφήτας καὶ σοφοὺς καὶ γραμματεῖς· καὶ ἐξ αὐτῶν ἀποκτενεῖτε καὶ σταυρώσετε, καὶ ἐξ αὐτῶν μαστιγώσετε ἐν ταῖς συναγωγαῖς ὑμῶν καὶ διώξετε ἀπὸ πόλεως εἰς πόλιν·

34. Dya touto, idou, ego apostello pros 'umas propheitas kai sophous kai grammateis. kai ex auton apokteneite kai staurosete, kai ex auton mastigosete en tais sunagogais 'umon kai dioxete apo poleos eis polin.

Hebrew/Transliteration
לד. עַל־כֵּן הִנְנִי שֹׁלֵחַ אֲלֵיכֶם נְבִיאִים חֲכָמִים וְסוֹפְרִים וּמֵהֶם תַּהֲרֹגוּ וְתִצְלְבוּ וּמֵהֶם תְּיַסְּרוּ בְּבָתֵּי הַכְּנֵסֶת אֲשֶׁר־לָכֶם וְתִרְדְּפוּם מֵעִיר לָעִיר

34. Al - ken hi•ne•ni sho•le•ach aley•chem n`vi•eem cha•cha•mim ve•sof•rim oo•me•hem ta•har•goo ve•titz•le•voo oo•me•hem te•yas•roo be•va•tey ha•k`ne•set asher la•chem ve•tir•de•foom me•eer la•eer.

Rabbinic Jewish Commentary

and some of them ye shall kill; as Stephen, the first "martyr", who was stoned to death by them; and James, the brother of John, whom Herod, to their good liking, killed with the sword; and the other James they threw headlong from off the pinnacle of the temple, and killed him with a fuller's club (r),

And crucify; so Simeon, the son of Cleophas, was crucified at the instigation of the Jews, as Eusebius relates (s),

And some of them ye shall scourge in your synagogues; as John, Peter, and Paul:

and persecute them from city to city; as they did Paul and Barnabas, as the Acts of the Apostles testify,

(r) Euseb. Eccl. Hist. l. 2. c. 23. (s) Ib. l. 3. c. 32.

---

35. That upon you may come all the righteous blood shed upon the earth, from the blood of righteous Abel unto the blood of Zacharias son of Barachias, whom ye slew between the temple and the altar.

Greek/Transliteration

35. ὅπως ἔλθῃ ἐφ᾽ ὑμᾶς πᾶν αἷμα δίκαιον ἐκχυνόμενον ἐπὶ τῆς γῆς, ἀπὸ τοῦ αἵματος Ἄβελ τοῦ δικαίου, ἕως τοῦ αἵματος Ζαχαρίου υἱοῦ Βαραχίου, ὃν ἐφονεύσατε μεταξὺ τοῦ ναοῦ καὶ τοῦ θυσιαστηρίου.

35. 'opos elthei eph 'umas pan 'aima dikaion ekchunomenon epi teis geis, apo tou 'aimatos Abel tou dikaiou, 'eos tou 'aimatos Zachariou 'wiou Barachiou, 'on ephoneusate metaxu tou naou kai tou thusyasteiriou.

Hebrew/Transliteration

לה. לְבַעֲבוּר יָבֹא עֲלֵיכֶם כָּל-דָּם נָקִי הַשָּׁפוּךְ עַל-הָאָרֶץ מִדַּם-הֶבֶל הַצַּדִּיק עַד-דַּם זְכַרְיָה בֶן-בֶּרֶכְיָה אֲשֶׁר: הֲרַגְתֶּם אֹתוֹ בֵּין הַהֵיכָל וְלַמִּזְבֵּחַ

35. Le•va•a•voor ya•vo aley•chem kol - dam na•ki ha•sha•fooch al - ha•a•retz mi•dam - he•vel ha•tza•dik ad - dam Ze•char•ya ven - B`rech•ya asher ha•rag•tem o•to bein ha•hey•chal ve•la•miz•be•ach.

Rabbinic Jewish Commentary

This epithet of "righteous" seems to be what was commonly given him by the Jews: hence, with a peculiar emphasis, he is called, הבל הצדיק, "Abel the righteous" (t); as he is also said to be ראש לנהרגים, "the head of them that killed" (u); he being the first man that was slain; for which reason he is mentioned here by Yeshua; and also, upon all such persons that should commit the like crime.

The Jerusalem Targum paraphrases the words in this remarkable manner, "the price of the bloods of "the multitude of the righteous", that shall spring from Abel thy brother."

And Targum Onkelos thus, "the voice of the blood of the seed that shall rise from thy brother."

Jewish Targumist speaks of a Zechariah, the son of Iddo, as slain by the Jews in the temple. His words are these (a), "as ye slew Zechariah, the son of Iddo, the high priest, and faithful prophet, in the house of the sanctuary of the Lord, on the day of atonement; because he reproved you, that ye might not do that evil which is before the Lord.

It is often said by the Jewish writer (c), that "R. Joden (sometimes it is R. Jonathan) asked R. Acha, whether they slew Zechariah, in the court of the Israelites, or in the court of the women? he answered him, neither in the court of the Israelites, nor in the court of the women, but in the court of the priests.

And elsewhere they say (d), that they "slew a priest and a prophet in the sanctuary; this is Zechariah the son of Jehoiada. (g)"the Israelites committed seven transgressions on that day: they slew a priest, and a prophet, and a judge; and they shed innocent blood, and they blasphemed God, and defiled the court, and it was a sabbath day, and the day of atonement."

Though this was not done by the individual persons in being in Yehsua's time, yet by the same people; and so they are said to slay him, and his blood is required of them: and their horrible destruction was a punishment for that load of national guilt, which had been for many hundreds of years contracting, and heaping upon them.

(t) Tzeror Hammor, fol. 8. 2. (u) Juchasin, fol. 5. 2. (a) Targum in Lam. ii. 20. (c) T. Hieros. Tannioth, fol. 69. 1. Praefat. ad Echa Rabbati, fol. 36. 4. & Echa Rabbati, fol. 52. 4. & 58. 3. Midrash Kohelet, fol. 68. 3. (d) Echa Rabbati, fol. 55. 1. (g) T. Hieros. Taanioth, fol. 69. 1. Echa Rabbati, fol. 53. 1. & 58. 3. Midrash Kobelet, fol. 68. 4.

---

36. Verily I say unto you, All these things shall come upon this generation.

Greek/Transliteration
36. ᾽Αμὴν λέγω ὑμῖν, ὅτι ἥξει πάντα ταῦτα ἐπὶ τὴν γενεὰν ταύτην.

36. Amein lego 'umin, 'oti 'eixei panta tauta epi tein genean tautein.

Hebrew/Transliteration
לו. אָמֵן אֲנִי אֹמֵר לָכֶם כִּי כָל־אֵלֶּה יָבֹאוּ עַל־הַדּוֹר הַזֶּה:

36. Amen ani o•mer la•chem ki kol - ele ya•vo•oo al - ha•dor ha•ze.

37. O Jerusalem, Jerusalem, thou that killest the prophets, and stonest them which are sent unto thee, how often would I have gathered thy children together, even as a hen gathereth her chickens under her wings, and ye would not!

Greek/Transliteration
37. Ἰερουσαλήμ, Ἰερουσαλήμ, ἡ ἀποκτένουσα τοὺς προφήτας καὶ λιθοβολοῦσα τοὺς ἀπεσταλμένους πρὸς αὐτήν, ποσάκις ἠθέλησα ἐπισυναγαγεῖν τὰ τέκνα σου, ὃν τρόπον ἐπισυνάγει ὄρνις τὰ νοσσία ἑαυτῆς ὑπὸ τὰς πτέρυγας, καὶ οὐκ ἠθελήσατε.

37. 'Yerousaleim, 'Yerousaleim, 'ei apoktenousa tous propheitas kai lithobolousa tous apestalmenous pros autein, posakis eitheleisa episunagagein ta tekna sou, 'on tropon episunagei ornis ta nossia 'eauteis 'upo tas pterugas, kai ouk eitheleisate.

Hebrew/Transliteration
לז. יְרוּשָׁלַיִם יְרוּשָׁלַיִם הַהֹרֶגֶת אֶת-הַנְּבִיאִים וְהַסֹּקֶלֶת אֶת-הַשְּׁלוּחִים אֵלָיִךְ עַד-כַּמָּה פְעָמִים חָפַצְתִּי לְקַבֵּץ-אֶת-בָּנַיִךְ כַּאֲשֶׁר תְּקַבֵּץ תַּרְנְגֹלֶת אֶת-אֶפְרֹחֶיהָ תַּחַת כְּנָפֶיהָ וְלֹא אֲבִיתֶם

37. Ye•ye•roo•sha•la•yim Ye•roo•sha•la•yim ha•ho•re•get et - ha•n`vi•eem ve•ha•so•ke•let et - ha•sh`loo•chim ela•yich ad - ka•me pe•a•mim cha•fatz•ti le•ka•betz et - ba•na•yich ka•a•sher te•ka•betz tar•ne•go•let et - ef•ro•che•ha ta•chat ke•na•fe•ha ve•lo avi•tem.

Rabbinic Jewish Commentary
The Jews themselves are obliged to own, that this character belongs to them: say (k) they, "when the word of God shall come, who is his messenger, we will honour him. Says R. Saul, did not the prophets come, והרגנום, "and we killed them", and shed their blood, and how shall we receive his word? or how shall we believe?

And a celebrated writer of their's, on those words (l), "but now murderers", has this note, "they have killed Uriah, they have killed Zechariah."

An expression much like to this here is used by an apocryphal writer of 2 Esdras: "I gathered you together, as a hen gathereth her chickens under her wings: but now, what shall I do unto you? I will cast you out from my face." (2 Esdras 1:30).

(k) R. Isaac Arama in Gen. xlvii. apud Galatin. Arcan. Cath. ver. l. 3. c. 5. (l) Jarchi in Isa. i. 21. (m) Zohar in Numb. fol. 106. 3. & Imre binah in ib.

---

38. Behold, your house is left unto you desolate.

Greek/Transliteration
38. Ἰδού, ἀφίεται ὑμῖν ὁ οἶκος ὑμῶν ἔρημος.

38. Ydou, aphietai 'umin 'o oikos 'umon ereimos.

Hebrew/Transliteration
:לח. הִנֵּה בֵּיתְכֶם יִשָּׁאֵר לָכֶם חָרְבָה

38. Hee•ne veit•chem yi•sha•er la•chem chor•ba.

Rabbinic Jewish Commentary
Our Lord seems to have in view those passages in Jer_12:7 and which the Jewish (o) writers understood of the temple. (o) Targum & Kimchi in Jer. xii. 7.

The author of the apocryphal the second book of Esdras has much such an expression as this: "Thus saith the Almighty Lord, Your house is desolate, I will cast you out as the wind doth stubble." (2 Esdras 1:33).

---

39. For I say unto you, Ye shall not see me henceforth, till ye shall say, Blessed is he that cometh in the name of the Lord.

Greek/Transliteration
39. Λέγω γὰρ ὑμῖν, οὐ μή με ἴδητε ἀπ' ἄρτι, ἕως ἂν εἴπητε, Εὐλογημένος ὁ ἐρχόμενος ἐν ὀνόματι κυρίου.

39. Lego gar 'umin, ou mei me ideite ap arti, 'eos an eipeite, Eulogeimenos 'o erchomenos en onomati kuriou.

Hebrew/Transliteration
:לט. כִּי אֲנִי אֹמֵר לָכֶם לֹא תִרְאוּנִי עוֹד מִן-הַיּוֹם הַזֶּה עַד כִּי-תֹאמְרוּן בָּרוּךְ הַבָּא בְּשֵׁם יְהֹוָה

39. Ki ani o•mer la•chem lo tir•oo•ni od min - ha•yom ha•ze ad ki - tom•roon ba•rooch ha•ba be•shem Adonai.

Matthew, Chapter 24

1. And Jesus went out, and departed from the temple: and his disciples came to him for to shew him the buildings of the temple.

Greek/Transliteration
1. Καὶ ἐξελθὼν ὁ Ἰησοῦς ἐπορεύετο ἀπὸ τοῦ ἱεροῦ· καὶ προσῆλθον οἱ μαθηταὶ αὐτοῦ ἐπιδεῖξαι αὐτῷ τὰς οἰκοδομὰς τοῦ ἱεροῦ.

1. Kai exelthon 'o Yeisous eporeueto apo tou 'ierou. kai proseilthon 'oi matheitai autou epideixai auto tas oikodomas tou 'ierou.

Hebrew/Transliteration
א. וַיֵּצֵא יֵשׁוּעַ מִן-הַמִּקְדָּשׁ וַיֵּלֶךְ לְדַרְכּוֹ וַיִּגְּשׁוּ אֵלָיו תַּלְמִידָיו לְהַרְאֹתוֹ אֶת-בִּנְיְנֵי הַמִּקְדָּשׁ:

1. Va•ye•tze Yeshua min - ha•mik•dash va•ye•lech le•dar•ko va•yig•shoo elav tal•mi•dav le•har•o•to et - bin•ye•ney ha•mik•dash.

Rabbinic/Jewish Commentary
They say (p), that Herod built the house of the sanctuary, "an exceeding beautiful building"; and that he repaired the temple, in beauty "greatly exceeding" that of Solomon's (q). They moreover observe (r), that "he who has not seen the building of Herod, has never seen, בניין נאה, "a beautiful building." With what is it built? says Rabbah, with stones of green and white marble. And there are others say, that it was built with stones of spotted green and white marble."

(p) Juchasin, fol. 139. 1. (q) Ganz Tzemach David, par. 1. fol. 24. 2. (r) T. Bab. Bava Bathra, fol. 4. 1. & Succa, fol. 51. 2.

---

2. And Jesus said unto them, See ye not all these things? verily I say unto you, There shall not be left here one stone upon another, that shall not be thrown down.

Greek/Transliteration
2. Ὁ δὲ Ἰησοῦς εἶπεν αὐτοῖς, Οὐ βλέπετε πάντα ταῦτα; Ἀμὴν λέγω ὑμῖν, οὐ μὴ ἀφεθῇ ὧδε λίθος ἐπὶ λίθον, ὃς οὐ καταλυθήσεται.

2. 'O de Yeisous eipen autois, Ou blepete panta tauta? Amein lego 'umin, ou mei aphethei 'ode lithos epi lithon, 'os ou katalutheisetai.

Hebrew/Transliteration
ב. וַיַּעַן יֵשׁוּעַ וַיֹּאמֶר אֲלֵיהֶם הֲלֹא רְאִיתֶם כָּל-אֵלֶּה אָמֵן אֲנִי אֹמֵר לָכֶם כִּי כֻלָּם יֵהָרְסוּן וְלֹא-תִשָּׁאֵר אֶבֶן עַל-אָבֶן:

2. Va•ya•an Yeshua va•yo•mer aley•hem ha•lo r`ee•tem kol - ele amen ani o•mer la•chem ki choo•lam ye•har•soon ve•lo - ti•sha•er even al - aven.

Rabbinic/Jewish New Testament Commentary

Josephus (y), who relates, that both the city and temple were dug up, and laid level with the ground; also by other Jewish writers; who tell us (z) that

"on the ninth of Ab, a day prepared for punishments, Turnus Rufus the wicked, **חרש את ההיכל**, "ploughed up the temple", and all round about it, to fulfil what is said, "Zion shall be ploughed as a field"." (y) De Bello Jud. l. 7. c. 7. (z) Maimon. Hilch. Taaniot, c. 5. sect. 3. T. Bab. Taanith, fol. 23. 1. & Gloss. in ib.

It is interesting to compare with this chapter a Talmud passage that predicts events prior to the Messiah's coming: "Rabbi Yitzchak said that Rabbi Yochanan said, 'In the generation when the Son of David is to come, scholars will be few in number. As for others, their eyes will fail from sorrow and grief. There will be much trouble, and evil decrees will be renewed, with each new evil coming quickly, even before the other has ended.'

"Our Rabbis taught that the following would happen during the seven years at the end of which the Son of David is to come. In the first year, 'I will cause it to rain upon one city and cause it not to rain upon another city' (Amo_4:7). In the second, the arrows of hunger will be sent forth [food shortages, with no one being fully satisfied]. In the third, there will be a great famine, during which men, women, children, pious men and saints will die; and [hunger will cause] the *Torah* to be forgotten by its *talmidim*. In the fourth, there will be surpluses of some things but shortages of others. In the fifth there will be great plenty-people will eat, drink and rejoice; and the *Torah* will return to its *talmidim*. In the sixth year, there will be sounds [in the light of what follows, either rumors of wars or heavenly voices or *shofar* blasts announcing the Messiah's coming]. In the seventh year there will be wars. And at the end of the seven years the Son of David will come."
(Sanhedrin 97a)

---

3. And as he sat upon the mount of Olives, the disciples came unto him privately, saying, Tell us, when shall these things be? and what shall be the sign of thy coming, and of the end of the world [age]?

Greek/Transliteration
3. Καθημένου δὲ αὐτοῦ ἐπὶ τοῦ ὄρους τῶν Ἐλαιῶν, προσῆλθον αὐτῷ οἱ μαθηταὶ κατ' ἰδίαν, λέγοντες, Εἰπὲ ἡμῖν, πότε ταῦτα ἔσται; Καὶ τί τὸ σημεῖον τῆς σῆς παρουσίας, καὶ τῆς συντελείας τοῦ αἰῶνος;

3. Katheimenou de autou epi tou orous ton Elaion, proseilthon auto 'oi matheitai kat idian, legontes, Eipe 'eimin, pote tauta estai? Kai ti to seimeion teis seis parousias, kai teis sunteleias tou aionos?

Hebrew/Transliteration
ג. וּבְשִׁבְתּוֹ עַל-הַר הַזֵּיתִים וַיִּגְּשׁוּ אֵלָיו תַּלְמִידָיו לְבַדָּם וַיֹּאמְרוּ הַגֶּד-נָא לָנוּ מָתַי תִּקְרֶאנָה אֵלֶּה וּמָה אוֹת בּוֹאֲךָ וְקֵץ הָעוֹלָם

3. Oov•shiv•to al - Har ha•Zey•tim va•yig•shoo elav tal•mi•dav le•va•dam va•yom•roo ha•ged - na la•noo ma•tai tik•re•na ele oo•ma ot bo•a•cha ve•ketz ha•o•lam?

Rabbinic Jewish Commentary
It is said (b), "all the walls which were there, were very high, except the eastern wall; for the high priest, when he burned the heifer, stood on the top of the mount of Olives, and directed himself, and looked to the gate of the temple, at the time he sprinkled the blood."

saying, tell us, when shall these things be? That this house will be left desolate, these buildings will be destroyed, and not one stone left upon another? This question relates purely to the destruction of the temple, and to this Yeshua answers, from Mat_24:4.

(a) Bartenora in Misn. Middot, c. 1. sect. 3. (b) Misn. lb. c. 2. sect. 4.

---

4. And Jesus answered and said unto them, Take heed that no man deceive you.

Greek/Transliteration
4. Καὶ ἀποκριθεὶς ὁ Ἰησοῦς εἶπεν αὐτοῖς, Βλέπετε, μή τις ὑμᾶς πλανήσῃ.

4. Kai apokritheis 'o Yeisous eipen autois, Blepete, mei tis 'umas planeisei.

Hebrew/Transliteration
‏ד. וַיַּעַן יֵשׁוּעַ וַיֹּאמֶר אֲלֵיהֶם הִשָּׁמְרוּ לָכֶם פֶּן-יַתְעֶה אֶתְכֶם אִישׁ:

4. Va•ya•an Yeshua va•yo•mer aley•hem hi•sham•roo la•chem pen - yat•eh et•chem eesh.

---

5. For many shall come in my name, saying, I am Christ; and shall deceive many.

Greek/Transliteration
5. Πολλοὶ γὰρ ἐλεύσονται ἐπὶ τῷ ὀνόματί μου, λέγοντες, Ἐγώ εἰμι ὁ χριστός· καὶ πολλοὺς πλανήσουσιν.

5. Polloi gar eleusontai epi to onomati mou, legontes, Ego eimi 'o christos. kai pollous planeisousin.

Hebrew/Transliteration
‏ה. כִּי רַבִּים יָבֹאוּ בִשְׁמִי לֵאמֹר אֲנִי הוּא הַמָּשִׁיחַ וְהִתְעוּ אֶת-רַבִּים:

5. Ki ra•bim ya•vo•oo vish•mey le•mor ani hoo ha•Ma•shi•ach ve•hit•oo et - ra•bim.

Rabbinic Jewish Commentary

Theudas, not he that Gamaliel speaks of, Act_5:36 for he was before this time; but one that was in the time of Claudius Caesar, when Cuspius Fadus was governor of Judea; who persuaded a great number to follow him to the river Jordan, which he promised to divide, by a word of command, and give them a passage over; and thereby, as the historian observes (c), πολλους ηπατησην, "he deceived many"; which is the very thing that is here predicted: but he and his company were routed Fadus, and his head cut off.

There was another called the Egyptian, mentioned in Act_21:38 who made an uproar, and led four thousand cut-throats into the wilderness; and this same man persuaded thirty thousand men to follow him to Mount Olivet, promising a free passage into the city; but he being vanquished by Felix, then governor of Judea; fled, and many of his followers were killed and taken (d)

There were others also besides these, that set up for deliverers, who called themselves by the name of the Messiah. Among these, we may reckon Simon Magus, who gave out that he was some great one; yea, expressly, that he was the word of God, and the Son of God (e), which were known names of the Messiah; and Dositheus the Samaritan, asserted himself to be Yeshua (f); and also Menander affirmed, that no man could be saved, unless he was baptized in his name (g); these are instances before the destruction of Jerusalem, and confirm the prophecy here delivered.

(c) Joseph. Antiq. l. 20. c. 2. (d) Joseph. Antiq. l. 20. c. 6. (e) Jerom in loc. Iren. adv. Haeres. l. 1. c. 20. (f) Origen contr. Cels. l. 1. p. 44. (g) Tertull. de prescript. Haeret. c. 46.

---

6. And ye shall hear of wars and rumours of wars: see that ye be not troubled: for all these things must come to pass, but the end is not yet.

Greek/Transliteration

6. Μελλήσετε δὲ ἀκούειν πολέμους καὶ ἀκοὰς πολέμων· ὁρᾶτε, μὴ θροεῖσθε· δεῖ γὰρ πάντα γενέσθαι· ἀλλ᾽ οὔπω ἐστὶν τὸ τέλος.

6. Melleisete de akouein polemous kai akoas polemon. 'orate, mei throeisthe. dei gar panta genesthai. all oupo estin to telos.

Hebrew/Transliteration

ו. וְהָיָה כִּי-תִשְׁמְעוּ מִלְחָמָה אוֹ שְׁמֻעוֹת מִלְחָמָה רְאוּ אַל-תִּבָּהֵלוּ כִּי כָל-אֵלֶּה תִּקְרֶאנָה וְעוֹד לֹא הַקֵּץ:

6. Ve•ha•ya ki - tish•me•oo mil•cha•ma oh sh`moo•ot mil•cha•ma r`oo al - ti•ba•he•loo ki chol - ele tik•re•na ve•od lo ha•ketz.

Rabbinic Jewish Commentary

They suppose the Messiah will come in the seventh year, or the year of rest and release: "On the seventh year (they say (h)) will be מלחמות, "wars": and in the going out, or at the close of the seventh year, the son of David will come." Which wars, the gloss says, will be between the nations of the world, and Israel.

Under Cureanus the Roman governor, a sedition was raised on the day of the passover, in which twenty thousand perished; after that, in another tumult, ten thousand were destroyed by cut-throats: in Ascalon two thousand more, in Ptolemais two thousand, at Alexandria fifty thousand, at Damascus ten thousand, and elsewhere in great numbers (i). The Jews were also put into great consternation, upon hearing the design of the Roman emperor, to put up his image in their temple.

but the end is not yet; meaning not the end of the world, but the end of Jerusalem, and the temple, the end of the Jewish state; which were to continue, and did continue after these disturbances in it.

(h) T. Bab. Sanhedrin, fol. 97. 1. & Megilia, fol. 17. 2. Zohar in Exod. fol. 3. 3, 4.
(i) Vid. Joseph. Antiq. l. 20. c. 6. & de Bello Jud. l. 2, &c.

---

7. For nation shall rise against nation, and kingdom against kingdom: and there shall be famines, and pestilences, and earthquakes, in divers places.

Greek/Transliteration
7. Ἐγερθήσεται γὰρ ἔθνος ἐπὶ ἔθνος, καὶ βασιλεία ἐπὶ βασιλείαν· καὶ ἔσονται λιμοὶ καὶ λοιμοὶ καὶ σεισμοὶ κατὰ τόπους.

7. Egertheisetai gar ethnos epi ethnos, kai basileia epi basileian. kai esontai limoi kai loimoi kai seismoi kata topous.

Hebrew/Transliteration
ז. כִּי יָקוּם גּוֹי עַל-גּוֹי וּמַמְלָכָה עַל-מַמְלָכָה וְהָיָה רָעָב וְדֶבֶר וְרַעַשׁ בִּמְקוֹמוֹת רַבִּים:

7. Ki ya•koom goy al - goy oo•mam•la•cha al - mam•la•cha ve•ha•ya ra•av ve•de•ver ve•ra•ash bim•ko•mot ra•bim.

Rabbinic Jewish Commentary
And this also is made a sign of the Messiah's coming by them, for so they say (k);

"when thou seest, מלכיות מתגרות אלו באלו, "kingdoms stirred up one against another", look for the feet of the Messiah: know thou that so it shall be; for so it was in the days of Abraham: by the means of kingdoms stirred up one against another, redemption came to Abraham."

"And one shall undertake to fight against another, one city against another, one place against another, one people against another, and one realm against another." (2 Esdras 13:31)

"the beginning of sorrows and great mournings; the beginning of famine and great death; the beginning of wars, and the powers shall stand in fear; the beginning of evils! what shall I do when these evils shall come?" (2 Esdras 16:18)

"Therefore when there shall be seen earthquakes and uproars of the people in the world:" (2 Esdras 9:3)

"in the second year (of the week of years) in which the son of David comes, they say (l), there will be "arrows of famine" sent forth; and in the third year, רעב גדול, "a great famine": and men, women, and children, and holy men, and men of business, shall die."

And pestilences: a pestilence is described by the Jews after this manner (m): "a city that produces a thousand and five hundred footmen, as Cephar Aco, and nine dead men are carried out of it in three days, one after another, lo! זה דבר, "this is a pestilence"; but if in one day, or in four days, it is no pestilence; and a city that produces five hundred footmen, as Cephar Amiko, and three dead men are carried out of it in three days, one after another, lo! this is a pestilence."

and earthquakes in divers places of the world; as, at Crete (n), and in divers cities in Asia (o), in the times of Nero: particularly the three cities of Phrygia, Laodicea, Hierapolis, and Colosse; which were near to each other, and are all said to perish this way, in his reign (p); "and Rome itself felt a tremor, in the reign of Galba (q)."

(k) Bereshit Rabba, sect. 42. fol. 37. 1. (l) T. Bab. Sanhedrin, fol. 97. 1. Misn. Sota, c. 9. sect. 15. (m) T. Bab. Taanith, fol. 21. & 19. 1. Maimon. Hilch. Taaniot, c. 2. sect. 5. (n) Philostrat. in vit. Apollon. l. 4. c. 11. (o) Sueton. in vit. Nero, c. 48. (p) Orosius, l. 7. c. 7. (q) Sueton. in vit. Galba, c. 13.

---

8. All these are the beginning of sorrows.

Greek/Transliteration
8. Πάντα δὲ ταῦτα ἀρχὴ ὠδίνων.

8. Panta de tauta archei odinon.

Hebrew/Transliteration
ח. וְכָל-אֵלֶּה רַק רֵאשִׁית הַחֲבָלִים:

8. Ve•chol - ele rak re•sheet ha•cha•va•lim.

Rabbinic Jewish Commentary

These were but light, in comparison of what befell the Jews, in their dreadful destruction. The word here used, signifies the sorrows and pains of a woman in travail. The Jews expect great sorrows and distresses in the times of the Messiah, and use a word to express them by, which answers to this, and call them, חבלי המשיח, "the sorrows of the Messiah"; חבלי, they say (r), signifies the sorrows of a woman in travail; and the Syriac version uses the same word here. These they represent to be very great, and express much concern to be delivered from them. They (s) ask,"what shall a man do, to be delivered from "the sorrows of the Messiah?" He must employ himself in the law, and in liberality."

And again (t), "he that observes the three meals on the sabbath day, shall be delivered from three punishments; from "the sorrows of the Messiah", from the judgment of Gehenna, and from Gog and Magog."

(r) Gloss. in T. Bab. Sabbat, fol. 118. 2. (s) T. Bab. Sanhedrin, fol. 98. 2. (t) T. Bab. Sabbat, fol. 118. 2.

---

9. Then shall they deliver you up to be afflicted, and shall kill you: and ye shall be hated of all nations for my name's sake.

Greek/Transliteration
9. Τότε παραδώσουσιν ὑμᾶς εἰς θλίψιν, καὶ ἀποκτενοῦσιν ὑμᾶς· καὶ ἔσεσθε μισούμενοι ὑπὸ πάντων τῶν ἐθνῶν διὰ τὸ ὄνομά μου.

9. Tote paradosousin 'umas eis thlipsin, kai apoktenousin 'umas. kai esesthe misoumenoi 'upo panton ton ethnon dya to onoma mou.

Hebrew/Transliteration
ט. אָז יַצִּיקוּ לָכֶם מִסָּבִיב וְהָרְגוּ בָכֶם וּשְׂנוּאִים תִּהְיוּ לְכָל-הָעַמִּים בַּעֲבוּר שְׁמִי:

9. Az ya•tzi•koo la•chem mi•sa•viv ve•har•goo va•chem oos•noo•eem ti•hi•yoo le•chol - ha•a•mim ba•a•voor sh`mi.

---

10. And then shall many be offended, and shall betray one another, and shall hate one another.

Greek/Transliteration
10. Καὶ τότε σκανδαλισθήσονται πολλοί, καὶ ἀλλήλους παραδώσουσιν, καὶ μισήσουσιν ἀλλήλους.

10. Kai tote skandalistheisontai polloi, kai alleilous paradosousin, kai miseisousin alleilous.

Hebrew/Transliteration
י. וְרַבִּים יִכָּשְׁלוּ אָז וְהִסְגִּירוּ אִישׁ אֶת-רֵעֵהוּ וְאִישׁ אֶת-אָחִיו יִשְׂנָאוּ:

10. Ve•ra•bim yi•kash•loo az ve•his•gi•roo eesh et - re•e•hoo ve•eesh et - a•chiv yis•na•oo.

---

11. And many false prophets shall rise, and shall deceive many.

Greek/Transliteration
11. Καὶ πολλοὶ ψευδοπροφῆται ἐγερθήσονται, καὶ πλανήσουσιν πολλούς.

11. Kai polloi pseudopropheitai egertheisontai, kai planeisousin pollous.

Hebrew/Transliteration
יא. וְקָמוּ נְבִיאֵי שֶׁקֶר רַבִּים וְהִתְעוּ רַבִּים אַחֲרֵיהֶם:

11. Ve•ka•moo n`vi•ey she•ker ra•bim ve•hit•oo ra•bim a•cha•rey•hem.

---

12. And because iniquity shall abound, the love of many shall wax cold.

Greek/Transliteration
12. Καὶ διὰ τὸ πληθυνθῆναι τὴν ἀνομίαν, ψυγήσεται ἡ ἀγάπη τῶν πολλῶν·

12. Kai dya to pleithuntheinai tein anomian, psugeisetai 'ei agapei ton pollon.

Hebrew/Transliteration
יב. וְאַחֲרֵי אֲשֶׁר יִרְבֶּה הַפֶּשַׁע תָּפוּג אַהֲבַת רַבִּים:

12. Ve•a•cha•rey asher yir•be ha•pa•sha ta•foog a•ha•vat ra•bim.

---

13. But he that shall endure unto the end, the same shall be saved.

Greek/Transliteration
13. ὁ δὲ ὑπομείνας εἰς τέλος, οὗτος σωθήσεται.

13. 'o de 'upomeinas eis telos, 'outos sotheisetai.

Hebrew/Transliteration
יג. אַךְ הַמְחַכֶּה עַד-הַקֵּץ הוּא יִוָּשֵׁעַ:

13. Ach ham•cha•ke ad - ha•ketz hoo yi•va•she•a.

Rabbinic Jewish Commentary
the same shall be saved; with a temporal salvation, when Jerusalem, and the unbelieving inhabitants of it shall be destroyed: for those that believed in Yeshua, many of them, through persecution, were obliged to remove from thence; and others, by a voice from heaven, were bid to go out of it, as they did; and removed

to Pella, a village a little beyond Jordan (u), and so were preserved from the general calamity; and also with an everlasting salvation, which is the case of all that persevere to the end, as all true believers in Yeshua will.

(u) Euseb. Eccl. Hist. l. 3. c. 5.

---

14. And this gospel of the kingdom shall be preached in all the world for a witness unto all nations; and then shall the end come.

Greek/Transliteration
14. Καὶ κηρυχθήσεται τοῦτο τὸ εὐαγγέλιον τῆς βασιλείας ἐν ὅλῃ τῇ οἰκουμένῃ εἰς μαρτύριον πᾶσιν τοῖς ἔθνεσιν· καὶ τότε ἥξει τὸ τέλος.

14. Kai keiruchtheisetai touto to euangelion teis basileias en 'olei tei oikoumenei eis marturion pasin tois ethnesin. kai tote 'eixei to telos.

Hebrew/Transliteration
:יד. וּבְשׂוֹרַת הַמַּלְכוּת הַזֹּאת תִּקָּרֵא בְּכָל-הָאָרֶץ לְעֵדוּת לְכָל-הַגּוֹיִם וְאַחַר יָבֹא הַקֵּץ

14. Oov•so•rat ha•mal•choot ha•zot ti•ka•re ve•chol - ha•a•retz le•e•doot le•chol - ha•go•yim ve•a•char ya•vo ha•ketz.

Rabbinic Jewish Commentary
shall be preached in all the world; not only in Judea, where it was now confined, and that by the express orders of Yeshua himself; but in all the nations of the world, for which the apostles had their commission enlarged, after our Lord's resurrection; The apostle Paul makes this claim in Colossians, "…if indeed you continue in the faith firmly established and steadfast, and not moved away from the hope of the gospel that you have heard, which was proclaimed in *all creation under heaven*, and of which I, Paul, was made a minister."

and then shall the end come; not the end of the world, as the Ethiopic version reads it, and others understand it; but the end of the Jewish state, the end of the city and temple: so that the universal preaching of the Gospel all over the world, was the last criterion and sign, of the destruction of Jerusalem; and the account of that itself next follows, with the dismal circumstances which attended it.

---

15. When ye therefore shall see the abomination of desolation, spoken of by Daniel the prophet, stand in the holy place, (whoso readeth, let him understand:)

Greek/Transliteration
15. Ὅταν οὖν ἴδητε τὸ βδέλυγμα τῆς ἐρημώσεως, τὸ ῥηθὲν διὰ Δανιὴλ τοῦ προφήτου, ἑστὼς ἐν τόπῳ ἁγίῳ- ὁ ἀναγινώσκων νοείτω-

15. 'Otan oun ideite to bdelugma teis ereimoseos, to 'reithen dya Danieil tou propheitou, 'estos en topo 'agio- 'o anaginoskon noeito-

Hebrew/Transliteration

טו. לָכֵן כַּאֲשֶׁר תִּרְאוּ אֶת-הַשִּׁקּוּץ הַמְשֹׁמֵם הָאָמוּר בְּיַד-דָּנִיֵּאל הַנָּבִיא עֹמֵד בִּמְקוֹם קֹדֶשׁ וְהַמַּשְׂכִּיל יָבִין:

15. La•chen ka•a•sher tir•oo et - ha•shi•koo•tz ham•sho•mem ha•a•moor be•yad - Da•ni•yel ha•na•vee o•med bim•kom ko•desh ve•ha•mas•kil ya•vin.

Rabbinic Jewish Transliteration

The Roman army is designed; see Luk_21:20 which was the כנף שקוצים משמם, "the wing", or "army of abominations making desolate", Dan_9:27. Armies are called wings, Isa_8:8 and the Roman armies were desolating ones to the Jews, and to whom they were an abomination; not only because they consisted of Heathen men, and uncircumcised persons, but chiefly because of the images of their gods, which were upon their ensigns: for images and idols were always an abomination to them; so the "filthiness" which Hezekiah ordered to be carried out of the holy place, 2Ch_29:5 is by the Targum called, ריחוקא, "an abomination"; and this, by the Jewish writers (w), is said to be an idol, which Ahaz had placed upon the altar; and such was the abomination of desolation, which Antiochus caused to be set upon the altar.

"Now the fifteenth day of the month Casleu, in the hundred forty and fifth year, they set up the abomination of desolation upon the altar, and builded idol altars throughout the cities of Juda on every side;" (1 Maccabees 1:54)

And so the Talmudic writers, by the abomination that makes desolate, in Dan_12:11 to which Yeshua here refers, understand an image, which they say (x) one Apostomus, a Grecian general, who burnt their law, set up in the temple.

spoken of by Daniel the prophet: not in Dan_11:31 which is spoken of the abomination in the times of Antiochus; but either in Dan_12:11 or rather in Dan_9:27 since this desolating abomination is that, which should follow the cutting off of the Messiah, and the ceasing of the daily sacrifice. It is to be observed, that Daniel is here called a prophet, contrary to what the Jewish writers say (y), who deny him to be one; though one of (z) no inconsiderable note among them affirms, that he attained to the end, הגבול הנבואיי, "of the prophetic border", or the ultimate degree of prophecy: when therefore this that Daniel, under a spirit of prophecy, spoke of should be seen.

standing in the holy place: When Antiochus IV ("Epiphanes") conquered Jerusalem in 167 B.C.E. he erected an altar to Zeus in the Temple. 1Ma_1:54 and1Ma_6:7 refer to this as a fulfillment of Daniel's prophecy.

(w) R. David Kimchi, & R. Sol. ben Melech, in 2 Chron. xxix. 5. (x) T. Bab. Taanith, fol. 28. 2. & Gloss. in ib. (y) T. Bab. Sanhedrin, fol. 94. 1. & Megilla, fol. 3. 1. & Tzeror Ham, mor, fol. 46. 4. Zohar in Num. fol. 61. 1. (z) Jacchiades in Dan. i. 17.

---

16. Then let them which be in Judaea flee into the mountains:

Greek/Transliteration
16. τότε οἱ ἐν τῇ Ἰουδαίᾳ φευγέτωσαν ἐπὶ τὰ ὄρη·

16. tote 'oi en tei Youdaia pheugetosan epi ta orei.

Hebrew/Transliteration
:טז. אָז אֵלֶּה אֲשֶׁר בִּיהוּדָה יָנוּסוּ אֶל-הֶהָרִים

16. Az ele asher bi•Y`hoo•da ya•noo•soo el - he•ha•rim.

Rabbinic Jewish Commentary

Josephus (a) takes notice of with surprise, that Cestius Gallus having advanced with his army to Jerusalem, and besieged it, on a sudden, without any cause, raised the siege, and withdrew his army, when the city might have been easily taken; by which means a signal was made; and an opportunity given to the Christians, to make their escape: which they accordingly did, and went over Jordan, as Eusebius says (b), to a place called Pella; so that when Titus came a few mouths after, there was not a Christian in the city, but they had fled as they are here bidden to

flee into the mountains; or any places of shelter and refuge: these are mentioned particularly, because they are usually such; and design either the mountains in Judea, or in the adjacent countries. The Syriac and Persic versions read in the singular number, "into the mountain"; and it is reported that many of them did fly, particularly to Mount Libanus (c).

(a) De Bello Jud. l. 2. c. 19. sect. 7. (b) Eccl. Hist. l. 3. c. 5. p. 75. (c) Joseph. ib.

---

17. Let him which is on the housetop not come down to take any thing out of his house:

Greek/Transliteration
17. ὁ ἐπὶ τοῦ δώματος μὴ καταβαινέτω ἆραι τὰ ἐκ τῆς οἰκίας αὐτοῦ·

17. 'o epi tou domatos mei katabaineto arai ta ek teis oikias autou.

Hebrew/Transliteration
:יז. וּמִי אֲשֶׁר עַל-הַגָּג לֹא יֵרֵד לָקַחַת דָּבָר מִבֵּיתוֹ

17. Oo•mi asher al - ha•gag lo ye•red la•ka•chat da•var mi•bei•to.

Rabbinic Jewish Commentary

They had two ways of going out of, and into their houses; the one they call (d), דרך פתחים, "the way of the doors"; the other, דרך גגין, "the way of the roof": upon which the gloss is, "to go up on the outside, דרך סולם, "by way" or "means" of a ladder, fixed at the entrance of the door of the upper room, and from thence he goes down into the house by a ladder;" (d) T. Bab. Bava Metzia, fol. 117. 1.

---

18. Neither let him which is in the field return back to take his clothes.

Greek/Transliteration
18. καὶ ὁ ἐν τῷ ἀγρῷ μὴ ἐπιστρεψάτω ὀπίσω ἆραι τὰ ἱμάτια αὐτοῦ.

18. kai 'o en to agro mei epistrepsato opiso arai ta 'imatya autou.

Hebrew/Transliteration
יח. וּמִי אֲשֶׁר בַּשָּׂדֶה לֹא יָשׁוּב לְבֵיתוֹ לָשֵׂאת אֶת-שִׂמְלָתוֹ:

18. Oo•mi asher ba•sa•de lo ya•shoov le•vey•to la•set et - sim•la•to.

---

19. And woe unto them that are with child, and to them that give suck in those days!

Greek/Transliteration
19. Οὐαὶ δὲ ταῖς ἐν γαστρὶ ἐχούσαις καὶ ταῖς θηλαζούσαις ἐν ἐκείναις ταῖς ἡμέραις.

19. Ouai de tais en gastri echousais kai tais theilazousais en ekeinais tais 'eimerais.

Hebrew/Transliteration
יט. אַךְ-אוֹי לֶהָרוֹת וְלַמֵּינִיקוֹת בַּיָּמִים הָהֵמָּה:

19. Ach - oy le•ha•rot ve•la•mey•ni•kot ba•ya•mim ha•he•ma.

Rabbinic Jewish Commentary
So that the case of these is much worse than that of men on the house top, or in the field, who could much more easily leave their goods and clothes, than these their children, as well as had more agility and strength of body to flee. So עוברות ומיניקות, "women with child, and that give suck"; are mentioned together in the Jewish writings, as such as were excused from certain fasts, though obliged to others (g).

(g) T. Hieros. Taanioth, fol. 64. 3. Maimon. Hilch. Taanioth, c. 5. sect. 10.

20. But pray ye that your flight be not in the winter, neither on the sabbath day:

Greek/Transliteration
20. Προσεύχεσθε δὲ ἵνα μὴ γένηται ἡ φυγὴ ὑμῶν χειμῶνος, μηδὲ σαββάτῳ.

20. Proseuchesthe de 'ina mei geneitai 'ei phugei 'umon cheimonos, meide sabbato.

Hebrew/Transliteration
כ. וְאַתֶּם הִתְפַּלְלוּ לְבִלְתִּי תִהְיֶה מְנוּסַתְכֶם בַּחֹרֶף וְלֹא בַּשַׁבָּת:

20. Ve•a•tem hit•pa•le•loo le•vil•ti ti•hi•ye me•noo•sat•chem ba•cho•ref ve•lo ba•Sha•bat.

Rabbinic Jewish Commentary
Observed, from a Jewish writer (h), that it is remarked as a favour of God in the destruction of the first temple, that it happened in the summer, and not in winter; whose words are these:

"God vouchsafed a great favour to Israel, for they ought to have gone out of the land on the tenth day of the month Tebeth; as he saith Eze_24:2 "son of man, write thee the name of the day, even of this same day": what then did the Lord, holy and blessed? If they shall now go out in the winter, (saith he,) they will all die; therefore he prolonged the time to them, and carried them away in summer."

(l) "Our Rabbi's teach, that he that is pursued by Gentiles, or by thieves, may profane the sabbath for the sake of saving his life: and so we find of David, when Saul sought to slay him, he fled from him, and escaped. Our Rabbi's say, that it happened that evil writings (or edicts) came from the government to the great men of Tzippore; and they went, and said to R. Eleazar ben Prata, evil edicts are come to us from the government, what dost thou say? נברח, "shall we flee?" and he was afraid to say to them "flee"; but he said to them with a nod, why do you ask me? go and ask Jacob, and Moses, and David; as it is written, of Jacob, Hos_12:12 "and Jacob fled"; and so of Moses, Exo_2:15 "and Moses fled"; and so of David, 1Sa_19:18 "and David fled, and escaped": and he (God) says, Isa_26:20 "come my people, enter into thy chambers"."

(h) Taachuma, fol. 57. 2. (l) Bemidbar Rabba, sect. 23. fol. 231. 4.

---

21. For then shall be great tribulation, such as was not since the beginning of the world to this time, no, nor ever shall be.

Greek/Transliteration
21. Ἔσται γὰρ τότε θλίψις μεγάλη, οἵα οὐ γέγονεν ἀπ᾽ ἀρχῆς κόσμου ἕως τοῦ νῦν, οὐδ᾽ οὐ μὴ γένηται.

21. Estai gar tote thlipsis megalei, 'oia ou gegonen ap archeis kosmou 'eos tou nun, oud ou mei geneitai.

Hebrew/Transliteration
כא. כִּי אָז תִּהְיֶה צָרָה גְדוֹלָה אֲשֶׁר כָּמוֹהָ לֹא-נִהְיְתָה מֵרֵאשִׁית יְמוֹת עוֹלָם וְעַד-הַיּוֹם הַזֶּה וְכָמוֹהָ לֹא-תֹסִף:

21. Ki az ti•hi•ye tza•ra ge•do•la asher ka•mo•ha lo - ni•hiy•ta me•re•sheet ye•mot o•lam ve•ad - ha•yom ha•ze ve•cha•mo•ha lo - to•sif.

Rabbinic Jewish Commentary
Whoever reads Josephus's account will be fully convinced of this; and readily join with him, who was an eyewitness of it, when he says (m), that "never did any city suffer such things, nor was there ever any generation that more abounded in malice or wickedness."

And indeed, all this came upon them for their impenitence and infidelity, and for their rejection and murdering of the Son of God; for as never any before, or since, committed the sin they did, or ever will, so there never did, or will, the same calamity befall a nation, as did them. (m) De Bello Jud. l. 6. c. 11.

---

22. And except those days should be shortened, there should no flesh be saved: but for the elect's sake those days shall be shortened.

Greek/Transliteration
22. Καὶ εἰ μὴ ἐκολοβώθησαν αἱ ἡμέραι ἐκεῖναι, οὐκ ἂν ἐσώθη πᾶσα σάρξ· διὰ δὲ τοὺς ἐκλεκτοὺς κολοβωθήσονται αἱ ἡμέραι ἐκεῖναι.

22. Kai ei mei ekolobotheisan 'ai 'eimerai ekeinai, ouk an esothei pasa sarx. dya de tous eklektous kolobotheisontai 'ai 'eimerai ekeinai.

Hebrew/Transliteration
כב. וְלוּלֵא יִקָּצְרוּ הַיָּמִים הָאֵלֶּה לֹא יִנָּצֵל כָּל-בָּשָׂר אַךְ לְמַעַן הַבְּחִירִים הַיָּמִים הָאֵלֶּה יִקָּצְרוּ:

22. Ve•loo•le yik•tze•roo ha•ya•mim ha•e•le lo yi•na•tzel kol - ba•sar ach le•ma•an ha•b`chi•rim ha•ya•mim ha•e•le yik•tza•roo.

Rabbinic Jewish Commentary
The shortening of those days is not to be understood literally, as if the natural days, in which this tribulation was, were to be shorter than usual. The Jews indeed often speak of the shortening of days in this sense, as miraculously done by God: so they say (n), that "five miracles were wrought for our father Jacob, when he went from Beersheba to go to Haran. The first miracle was, that אתקצרו ליה שעי דיומא, "the hours of the day were shortened for him", and the sun set before its time, because his word desired to speak with him."

They also say (o), "that the day in which Ahaz died, was shortened ten hours, that they might not mourn for him; and which afterwards rose up, and in the day that Hezekiah was healed, ten hours were added to it."

A like manner of speech is used by the Karaite Jews (p), who say, "if we walk in our law, why is our captivity prolonged, and there is not found balm for our wounds? and why are not נתמעטו ימיהם, "the days" of the golden and silver kingdom "lessened", for the righteousness of the righteous, which were in their days?" (n) Targum Jonathan ben Uzziel, & Targum Hieros. in Gem xxviii. 10. (o) R. Sol. Jarchi in Isa. xxxviii. 8. (p) Chilluk M. S. apud Trigland. de sect Karaeorum, c. 9. p. 147.

---

23. Then if any man shall say unto you, Lo, here is Christ, or there; believe it not.

Greek/Transliteration
23. Τότε ἐάν τις ὑμῖν εἴπῃ, Ἰδού, ὧδε ὁ χριστός, ἢ ὧδε, μὴ πιστεύσητε.

23. Tote ean tis 'umin eipei, Ydou, 'ode 'o christos, ei 'ode, mei pisteuseite.

Hebrew/Transliteration
כג. וְאָז אִם-יֹאמַר אֲלֵיכֶם אִישׁ הִנֵּה הַמָּשִׁיחַ פֹּה אוֹ הִנּוֹ-שָׁם אַל-תַּאֲמִינוּ:

23. Ve•az eem - yo•mar aley•chem eesh hee•ne ha•Ma•shi•ach po oh hi•no - sham al - ta•a•mi•noo.

Rabbinic Jewish Commentary
Very quickly after, one Jonathan, a very wicked man, led many into the desert of Cyrene, promising to show them signs and wonders, and was overthrown by Catullius, the Roman governor (q); and after that, in the times of Adrian, the famous Barcochab set up for the Messiah, and was encouraged by R. Akiba, and a multitude of Jews (r).

"Rabbi Shmu'el taught in the name of Rabbi Y'hudah, 'If someone tells you when the day of redemption is coming, don't believe him, for it is written, "The day of vengeance is in my heart" (Isa_63:4). If the heart does not tell its secrets to the mouth, how can the mouth tell anything?' " (Midrash on Psa_9:2 (Psa_9:1))

(q) Joseph. Antiq. l. 7. c. 12. (r) Ganz. Tzemach David, par. 1. fol. 28. 2.

---

24. For there shall arise false Christs, and false prophets, and shall shew great signs and wonders; insomuch that, if it were possible, they shall deceive the very elect.

Greek/Transliteration
24. Ἐγερθήσονται γὰρ ψευδόχριστοι καὶ ψευδοπροφῆται, καὶ δώσουσιν σημεῖα μεγάλα καὶ τέρατα, ὥστε πλανῆσαι, εἰ δυνατόν, καὶ τοὺς ἐκλεκτούς.

24. Egertheisontai gar pseudochristoi kai pseudopropheitai, kai dosousin seimeia megala kai terata, 'oste planeisai, ei dunaton, kai tous eklektous.

Hebrew/Transliteration
כד. כִּי מְשִׁיחֵי-שֶׁקֶר וּנְבִיאֵי-כָזָב יָקוּמוּ וְנָתְנוּ אֹתוֹת וּמוֹפְתִים גְּדֹלִים לְנַסּוֹת אִם יֵשׁ-לְאֵל יָדָם לְהַתְעוֹת גַּם:אֶת-הַבְּחִירִים -

24. Ki me•shi•chey - she•ker oon•vi•ey - cha•zav ya•koo•moo ve•nat•noo o•tot oo•mof•tim ge•do•lim le•na•sot eem yesh - le•el ya•dam le•hat•ot gam - et - ha•b`chi•rim.

Rabbinic Jewish Commentary
Such as before mentioned: these false Messiah's had their false prophets, who endeavoured to persuade the people to believe them to be the Messiah, as Barcochab had Akiba, who applied many prophecies to him. This man was called Barcochab, which signifies the son of a star, in allusion to Num_24:17 he was crowned by the Jews, and proclaimed the Messiah by Akiba; upon which a Roman army was sent against him, and a place called Bitter was besieged, and taken, and he, and a prodigious number of Jews were destroyed. This deceiver was afterwards, by them, called Barcoziba, the son of a lie:

and shall show great signs and wonders; make an appearance of doing them, though they really did them not: so that Jonathan, before mentioned, pretended to show signs and sights; and Barcochab made as if flame came out of his mouth; and many of the Jewish doctors in these times, and following, gave themselves up to sorcery, and the magic art; and are, many of them, often said (s) to be מלומדים בנסים, "expert in wonders", or miracles:

(s) T. Bab. Meila, fol. 17. 2. Juchasin, fol. 20. 1, 2. & 42. 2. & 56. 2. & 77. 1. & 96. 2.

---

25. Behold, I have told you before.

Greek/Transliteration
25. Ἰδού, προείρηκα ὑμῖν.

25. Ydou, proeireika 'umin.

Hebrew/Transliteration
כה. רְאוּ כִּי מֵרֹאשׁ הִגַּדְתִּי לָכֶם:

25. R`oo ki me•rosh hi•ga•d`ti la•chem.

26. Wherefore if they shall say unto you, Behold, he is in the desert; go not forth: behold, he is in the secret chambers; believe it not.

Greek/Transliteration
26. Ἐὰν οὖν εἴπωσιν ὑμῖν, Ἰδού, ἐν τῇ ἐρήμῳ ἐστίν, μὴ ἐξέλθητε· Ἰδού, ἐν τοῖς ταμείοις, μὴ πιστεύσητε.

26. Ean oun eiposin 'umin, Ydou, en tei ereimo estin, mei exeltheite. Ydou, en tois tameiois, mei pisteuseite.

Hebrew/Transliteration
:כו. לָכֵן כִּי-יֹאמְרוּ לָכֶם הִנּוֹ בַמִּדְבָּר אַל-תֵּצֵאוּ הִנּוֹ בַחֲדָרִים אַל-תַּאֲמִינוּ

26. La•chen ki - yom•roo la•chem hi•no va•mid•bar al - te•tze•oo hi•no va•cha•da•rim al - ta•a•mi•noo.

Rabbinic Jewish Commentary
During the siege, Simon, the son of Giora, collected together many thousands in the mountainous and desert parts of Judea (t); and the above mentioned Jonathan, after the destruction of the city, led great multitudes into the desert.

Some reference may be had to the chamber of secrets, which was in the temple (w); "for in the sanctuary there were two chambers; one was called לשכת חשאים, "the chamber of secrets", and the other chamber of vessels."

(t) Joseph de Bello. Jud. l. 5. c. 7. (w) Misn. Shekalim, c. 5. sect. 6.

---

27. For as the lightning cometh out of the east, and shineth even unto the west; so shall also the coming of the Son of man be.

Greek/Transliteration
27. Ὥσπερ γὰρ ἡ ἀστραπὴ ἐξέρχεται ἀπὸ ἀνατολῶν καὶ φαίνεται ἕως δυσμῶν, οὕτως ἔσται καὶ ἡ παρουσία τοῦ υἱοῦ τοῦ ἀνθρώπου.

27. 'Osper gar 'ei astrapei exerchetai apo anatolon kai phainetai 'eos dusmon, 'outos estai kai 'ei parousia tou 'wiou tou anthropou.

Hebrew/Transliteration
:כז. כִּי כַּבָּרָק יֵצֵא מִמִּזְרָח וְיֵרָאֶה עַד-אַחֲרִית יָם כֵּן תִּהְיֶה בִּיאַת פְּנֵי בֶן-הָאָדָם

27. Ki ka•ba•rak ye•tze mi•miz•rach ve•ye•ra•eh ad - acha•rit yam ken ti•hi•ye bi•at p`ney Ven - ha•adam.

TaNaKh-Old Testament/Rabbinic Commentary
"And the LORD will cause His voice of authority to be heard, And the descending of His arm to be seen in fierce anger, And *in* the flame of a consuming fire In cloudburst, downpour and hailstones." Isa_30:30

"Then the LORD will appear over them, And His arrow will go forth like lightning; And the Lord GOD will blow the trumpet, And will march in the storm winds of the south. " Zech_9:14

For this was to be done before the destruction of Jerusalem: but of his coming in his wrath and vengeance to destroy that people, their nation, city, and temple: so that after this to look for the Messiah in a desert, or secret chamber, must argue great stupidity and blindness; when his coming was as sudden, visible, powerful, and general, to the destruction of that nation, as the lightning that comes from the east, and, in a moment, shines to the west.

---

28. For wheresoever the carcase is, there will the eagles be gathered together.

Greek/Transliteration
28. Ὅπου γὰρ ἐὰν ᾖ τὸ πτῶμα, ἐκεῖ συναχθήσονται οἱ ἀετοί.

28. 'Opou gar ean ei to ptoma, ekei sunachtheisontai 'oi aetoi.

Hebrew/Transliteration
:כח. בַּאֲשֶׁר פְּגָרִים שָׁם יִקָּבְצוּ הַנְּשָׁרִים

28. Ba•a•sher pe•ga•rim sham yi•kav•tzoo han•sha•rim.

Rabbinic Jewish Commentary
"what vulture shall have this carcass?" It has a very sharp sight, and quick smell, and will, by both, discern carcasses at almost incredible distance: it will diligently watch a man that is near death; and will follow armies going to battle, as historians relate (a): and it is the eagle which is of the vulture kind, as Aristotle (b) observes, that takes up dead bodies, and carries them to its nest. And Pliny (c) says, it is that sort of eagles only which does so.

Job_39:30 "her young ones also suck up blood, and where the slain are, there is she": an expression much the same with this in the text, and to which it seems to refer; see also Pro_30:17. Though Chrysostom (d) says, both the passage in Job, and this in Matthew, are to be understood of vultures; he doubtless means the eagles that are of the vulture kind, the Gypaeetos, or vulture eagle. There is one kind of eagles, naturalists say (e), will not feed on flesh, which is called the bird of Jupiter; but, in common, the eagle is represented as a very rapacious creature, seizing, and feeding upon the flesh of hares, fawns, geese, &c. and the rather this creature is designed here; since, of all birds, this is the only one that is not hurt with lightning (f), and so can immediately seize carcasses killed thereby; to which there seems to be an allusion here, by comparing it with the preceding verse: however, the Persic version, though it is literally a proper one, yet from the several things observed, it is not to be overlooked and slighted.

(a) Aelian. de Animal. Natura, l. 2. c. 46. (b) De Hist. Animal. l. 9. c. 32. (c) Hist. Nat l. 10. c. 3. (d) In Matt. Homil. 49. (e) Aelian. de Animal. l. 9. c. 10. (f) Plin. Nat. Hist. l. 2. c. 55.

---

29. Immediately after the tribulation of those days shall the sun be darkened, and the moon shall not give her light, and the stars shall fall from heaven, and the powers of the heavens shall be shaken:

Greek/Transliteration
29. Εὐθέως δὲ μετὰ τὴν θλίψιν τῶν ἡμερῶν ἐκείνων, ὁ ἥλιος σκοτισθήσεται, καὶ ἡ σελήνη οὐ δώσει τὸ φέγγος αὐτῆς, καὶ οἱ ἀστέρες πεσοῦνται ἀπὸ τοῦ οὐρανοῦ, καὶ αἱ δυνάμεις τῶν οὐρανῶν σαλευθήσονται.

29. Eutheos de meta tein thlipsin ton 'eimeron ekeinon, 'o 'eilios skotistheisetai, kai 'ei seleinei ou dosei to phengos auteis, kai 'oi asteres pesountai apo tou ouranou, kai 'ai dunameis ton ouranon saleutheisontai.

Hebrew/Translitetation
כט. וְאַחֲרֵי צוֹק הָעִתִּים הָאֵלֶּה פִּתְאֹם תֶּחְשַׁךְ הַשֶּׁמֶשׁ וְהַיָּרֵחַ לֹא יַגִּיהַּ אוֹרוֹ הַכּוֹכָבִים יִפְּלוּ מִן־הַשָּׁמַיִם וּצְבָא־הַמָּרוֹם יָזֵעוּ

29. Ve•a•cha•rey tzok ha•ee•tim ha•e•le pit•om tech•shach ha•she•mesh ve•ha•ya•re•ach lo ya•gi•ha o•ro ha•ko•cha•vim yip•loo min - ha•sha•ma•yim ootz•va ha•ma•rom ya•zoo•oo.

Rabbinic Jewish Commentary
The images used here are not to be taken literally. They are often employed by the sacred writers to denote "any great calamities." As the darkening of the sun and moon, and the falling of the stars, would be an inexpressible calamity, so any great catastrophe - any overturning of kingdoms or cities, or dethroning of kings and princes is represented by the darkening of the sun and moon, and by some terrible convulsion in the elements. Thus the destruction of Babylon is foretold in similar terms Isa_13:10, and of Tyre Isa_24:23. The slaughter in Bozrah and Idumea is predicted in the same language, Isa_34:4. See also Isa_50:3; Isa_60:19-20; Eze_32:7; Joe_3:15. To the description in Matthew, Luke has added Luk_21:25-26, "And upon the earth distress of nations, with perplexity; the sea and the waves roaring; people's hearts failing them for fear, and for looking after those things which are coming on the earth." All these are figures of great and terrible calamities. The roaring of the waves of the sea denotes great tumult and affliction among the people. "Perplexity" means doubt, anxiety; not knowing what to do to escape. "Men's hearts should fail them for fear," or by reason of fear. Their fears would be so great as to take away their courage and strength.

(g)"from the time that the temple was destroyed, the wise men, and sons of nobles, were put to shame, and they covered their heads; liberal men were reduced to poverty; and men of violence and calumny prevailed; and there were none that expounded, or inquired, or asked. R. Elezer the great, said, from the time the sanctuary were destroyed, the wise men began to be like Scribes, and the Scribes like to the Chazans, (or sextons that looked after the synagogues,) and the Chazans like to the common people, and the common people grew worse and worse, and there were none that inquired and asked; that is, of the wise men there were no scholars, or very few that studied in the law, (g) Misn. Sotah, c. 9. sect. 15.

---

30. And then shall appear the sign of the Son of man in heaven: and then shall all the tribes of the earth mourn, and they shall see the Son of man coming in the clouds of heaven with power and great glory.

Greek/Transliteration
30. Καὶ τότε φανήσεται τὸ σημεῖον τοῦ υἱοῦ τοῦ ἀνθρώπου ἐν τῷ οὐρανῷ· καὶ τότε κόψονται πᾶσαι αἱ φυλαὶ τῆς γῆς, καὶ ὄψονται τὸν υἱὸν τοῦ ἀνθρώπου ἐρχόμενον ἐπὶ τῶν νεφελῶν τοῦ οὐρανοῦ μετὰ δυνάμεως καὶ δόξης πολλῆς.

30. Kai tote phaneisetai to seimeion tou 'wiou tou anthropou en to ourano. kai tote kopsontai pasai 'ai phulai teis geis, kai opsontai ton 'wion tou anthropou erchomenon epi ton nephelon tou ouranou meta dunameos kai doxeis polleis.

Hebrew/Transliteration
ל. אָז יֵרָאֶה אוֹת בֶּן-הָאָדָם בַּשָּׁמַיִם וְסָפְדוּ כָּל-מִשְׁפְּחוֹת הָאֲדָמָה וְרָאוּ אֶת-בֶּן-הָאָדָם בָּא בְעַנְנֵי הַשָּׁמַיִם בְּעֹז וּבְהָדָר גָּדוֹל:

30. Az ye•ra•eh ot Ben - ha•adam ba•sha•ma•yim ve•saf•doo kol - mish•pe•chot ha•a•da•ma ve•ra•oo et - Ben - ha•adam ba be•ane•ney ha•sha•ma•yim be•oz oov•ha•dar ga•dol.

Rabbinic Jewish Commentary
Not the sound of the great trumpet, mentioned in the following verse; nor the clouds of heaven in this; nor the sign of the cross appearing in the air, as it is said to do in the times of Constantine: not the former; for though to blow a trumpet is sometimes to give a sign, and is an alarm; and the feast which the Jews call the day of blowing the trumpets, Num_29:1 is, by the Septuagint, rendered ημερα σημασιας, "the day of signification"

and they shall see the son of man coming in the clouds of heaven, with power and great glory. The Arabic version reads it, "ye shall see", as is expressed by Yeshua, in Mat_26:64. Where the high priest, chief priests, Scribes, and elders, and the whole sanhedrim of the Jews are spoken to: and as the same persons, namely, the Jews, are meant here as there; so the same coming of the son of man is intended; not his coming at the last day to judgment; though that will be in the clouds of heaven, and with great power and glory; but his coming to bring on, and give the finishing stroke to the destruction of that people, which was a dark and cloudy dispensation to them: and when they felt the power of his arm, might, if not blind and stupid to the last degree, see the glory of his person, that he was more than a mere man, and no other than the Son of God, whom they had despised, rejected, and crucified; and who came to set up his kingdom and glory in a more visible and peculiar manner, among the Gentiles.

---

31. And he shall send his angels with a great sound of a trumpet, and they shall gather together his elect from the four winds, from one end of heaven to the other.

Greek/Transliteration
31. Καὶ ἀποστελεῖ τοὺς ἀγγέλους αὐτοῦ μετὰ σάλπιγγος φωνῆς μεγάλης, καὶ ἐπισυνάξουσιν τοὺς ἐκλεκτοὺς αὐτοῦ ἐκ τῶν τεσσάρων ἀνέμων, ἀπ᾽ ἄκρων οὐρανῶν ἕως ἄκρων αὐτῶν.

31. Kai apostelei tous angelous autou meta salpingos phoneis megaleis, kai episunaxousin tous eklektous autou ek ton tessaron anemon, ap akron ouranon 'eos akron auton.

Hebrew/Transliteration
לא. וְהוּא יִשְׁלַח אֶת-מַלְאָכָיו בְּקוֹל שׁוֹפָר חָזָק וְקִבְּצוּ אֶת-בְּחִירָיו מֵאַרְבַּע הָרוּחוֹת מִקְצֵה הַשָּׁמַיִם עַד-קְצֵה:הַשָּׁמָיִם

31. Ve•hoo yish•lach et - mal•a•chav be•kol sho•far cha•zak ve•kib•tzoo et - be•chi•rav me•ar•ba ha•roo•chot mik•tze ha•sha•ma•yim ad - k`tze ha•sha•ma•yim.

Rabbinic Jewish Commentary
Not the angels, i.e. ministering spirits, so called, not from their nature, but their office, as being sent forth by God and Yeshua; but men angels, or messengers, the ministers and preachers of the Gospel, whom Yeshua would call, qualify, and send forth into all the world of the Gentiles, to preach his Gospel, and plant churches there still more, when that at Jerusalem was broken up and dissolved. These are called "angels", because of their mission, and commission from Yeshua, to preach the Gospel.

And in the day against Jerusalem and those who practiced against the Law, "The Son of Adam shall send out His messengers, and they shall gather out of His reign all the stumbling-blocks, and those doing lawlessness," Mat_13:41

The Jews (h) say, that "in the after redemption (i.e. by the Messiah) all Israel shall be gathered together by the sound of a trumpet, from the four parts of the world.

(h) Zohar in Lev. fol. 47. 1.

---

32. Now learn a parable of the fig tree; When his branch is yet tender, and putteth forth leaves, ye know that summer is nigh:

Greek/Transliteration

32. Ἀπὸ δὲ τῆς συκῆς μάθετε τὴν παραβολήν· ὅταν ἤδη ὁ κλάδος αὐτῆς γένηται ἁπαλός, καὶ τὰ φύλλα ἐκφύῃ, γινώσκετε ὅτι ἐγγὺς τὸ θέρος·

32. Apo de teis sukeis mathete tein parabolein. 'otan eidei 'o klados auteis geneitai 'apalos, kai ta phulla ekphuei, ginoskete 'oti engus to theros.

Hebrew/Transliteration

לב. קְחוּ לָכֶם מָשָׁל מִן-הַתְּאֵנָה אִם רָטוֹב עֲנָפָהּ וְעָלֶיהָ צָמָחוּ יֹדְעִים אַתֶּם כִּי קָרוֹב הַקָּיִץ:

32. Ke•choo la•chem ma•shal min - ha•te•e•na eem ra•tov ana•fa ve•a•le•ha tza•ma•choo yod•eem atem ki ka•rov ha•ka•yitz.

Rabbinic Jewish Commentary

"And He spoke this parable, "A certain man had a fig tree planted in his vineyard, and he came seeking fruit on it and found none. "And he said to the gardener, 'Look, for three years I have come seeking fruit on this fig tree and find none. Cut it down, why does it even make the ground useless?' Luke_13:6-7

The Temple leadership's corruption had brought Israel down a corrupt path which lead to a low spiritual state, as the prophet Jeremiah says,"From the prophet even to the priest everyone deals falsely. For they have healed the hurt of the daughter of My people slightly, saying, "Peace, peace; when there is no peace." Were they ashamed when they had done an abomination? No, they were not at all ashamed, nor could they blush. Therefore they shall fall among those who fall, in the time of their visitation they shall be cast down,' says YHWH. 'I will utterly consume them,' says YHWH,'there shall be no grapes on the vine, *nor figs on the fig tree*, and the leaf shall fade, and the things that I have given them, those who pass over them. (Jeremiah 8:10-13)

"I found Israel like grapes in the wilderness. I saw your fathers as the first ripe in the fig tree at its first season . . . Hosea 9:10

---

33. So likewise ye, when ye shall see all these things, know that it is near, even at the doors.

Greek/Transliteration

33. οὕτως καὶ ὑμεῖς, ὅταν ἴδητε ταῦτα πάντα, γινώσκετε ὅτι ἐγγύς ἐστιν ἐπὶ θύραις.

33. 'outos kai 'umeis, 'otan ideite tauta panta, ginoskete 'oti engus estin epi thurais.

Hebrew/Transliteration

לג. וְכֵן גַּם-כַּאֲשֶׁר תִּרְאוּ כָּל-אֵלֶּה יָדוֹעַ תֵּדְעוּ כִּי-קָרוֹב הוּא לַפָּתַח:

33. Ve•chen gam - ka•a•sher tir•oo kol - ele ya•doa ted•oo ki - ka•rov hoo la•pe•tach.

---

34. Verily I say unto you, This generation shall not pass, till all these things be fulfilled.

Greek/Transliteration
34. Ἀμὴν λέγω ὑμῖν, οὐ μὴ παρέλθῃ ἡ γενεὰ αὕτη, ἕως ἂν πάντα ταῦτα γένηται.

34. Amein lego 'umin, ou mei parelthei 'ei genea 'autei, 'eos an panta tauta geneitai.

Hebrew/Transliteration
:לד. אָמֵן אֲנִי אֹמֵר לָכֶם כִּי לֹא יַעֲבֹר הַדּוֹר הַזֶּה עַד אֲשֶׁר-יָקוּמוּ כָּל-אֵלֶּה

34. Amen ani o•mer la•chem ki lo ya•a•vor ha•dor ha•ze ad asher - ya•koo•moo kol - ele.

Rabbininc Jewish Commentary
That present age, or generation of men then living in it; and the sense is, that all the men of that age should not die, but some should live. Many of the Jewish Rabbi's now living, when Yeshua spoke these words, lived until the city was destroyed; as Rabban Simeon, who perished with it, R. Jochanan ben Zaccai, who outlived it, R. Zadoch, R. Ishmael, and others: this is a full and clear proof, that not anything that is said before, relates to the second coming of Christ, the day of judgment, and end of the world; but that all belong to the coming of the son of man, in the destruction of Jerusalem, and to the end of the Jewish state.

---

35. Heaven and earth shall pass away, but my words shall not pass away.

Greek/Transliteration
35. Ὁ οὐρανὸς καὶ ἡ γῆ παρελεύσονται, οἱ δὲ λόγοι μου οὐ μὴ παρέλθωσιν.

35. 'O ouranos kai 'ei gei pareleusontai, 'oi de logoi mou ou mei parelthosin.

Hebrew/Transliteration
:לה. הַשָּׁמַיִם וְהָאָרֶץ יַעֲבֹרוּ וּדְבָרַי לֹא יַעֲבֹרוּן

35. Ha•sha•ma•yim ve•ha•a•retz ya•a•vo•roo ood`va•rai lo ya•a•vo•roon.

TaNaKh-Old Testament/Rabbinic Commentary
According to Moses and the prophet Isaiah Heaven and Earth were used to describe the people of Israel, Judah and Jerusalem. The latter two of which will pass during that generation Yeshua spoke those words.

"Give ear, O heavens, and let me speak; And hear, O earth, The words of my mouth." And "The vision of Isaiah the son of Amoz concerning Judah and Jerusalem, which he saw during the reigns of Uzziah, Jotham, Ahaz *and* Hezekiah, kings of Judah. Listen, O heavens, and hear, O earth; For the LORD speaks, "Sons I have reared and brought up, But they have revolted against Me." (Deut.32:1; Isaiah 1:1-2)

---

36. But of that day and hour knoweth no man, no, not the angels of heaven, but my Father only.

Greek/Transliteration
36. Περὶ δὲ τῆς ἡμέρας ἐκείνης καὶ ὥρας οὐδεὶς οἶδεν, οὐδὲ οἱ ἄγγελοι τῶν οὐρανῶν, εἰ μὴ ὁ πατήρ μου μόνος.

36. Peri de teis 'eimeras ekeineis kai 'oras oudeis oiden, oude 'oi angeloi ton ouranon, ei mei 'o pateir mou monos.

Hebrew/Transliteration
:לוֹ. וְעַל-מוֹעֵד הַיּוֹם הַהוּא וְהַשָּׁעָה הַהִיא אֵין אִישׁ יוֹדֵעַ וְלֹא מַלְאָךְ בַּשָּׁמַיִם בִּלְתִּי הָאָב לְבַדּוֹ

36. Ve•al - mo•ed ha•yom ha•hoo ve•ha•sha•ah ha•hee eyn eesh yo•de•a ve•lo mal•ach ba•sha•ma•yim bil•tee ha•Av le•va•do.

Rabbinic Jewish Commentary
Josephus (k) says, "that the temple perished the "tenth" day of "Lous", a day fatal to the temple, as having been on that day consumed in flames, by the king of Babylon.

And yet Rabbi Jochanan ben Zaccai, who was also at the destruction of it, as well as Josephus, with all the Jewish writers, say it was on the "ninth of Ab"; for of this day they (l) say, five things happened upon it: "On the "ninth of Ab" it was decreed concerning our fathers, that they should not enter into the land (of Canaan), the first and second temple were destroyed, Bither was taken, and the city ploughed up.

Though the words of R. Jochanan, cited by the Rabbi, refer to the first, and not to the second temple, and should have been rendered thus: "If I had been in the generation (which fixed the fast for the destruction of the first temple), I would not have fixed it but on the tenth (of Ab); for, adds he, the greatest part of the temple was burnt on that day; but the Rabbins rather regarded the beginning of the punishment (m).

And so the fasting of Rabbi, and R. Joshua ben Levi, on the "ninth" and "tenth" days, were on account of the first temple; for they were under the same difficulty about the one, as the other:

Isa_63:4 it is asked (n), "what is the meaning of these words, "the day of vengeance is in my heart?" Says R. Jochanan, to my heart I have revealed it, to the members I have not revealed it: says R. Simeon ben Lakish, to my heart I have revealed it, למלאכי השרת לא גליתי, "to the ministering angels I have not revealed it".

(k) De Bello Jud. l. 6. c. 26. (l) Misu. Taanith, c. 4. sect. 7. T. Hieros. Taanioth, fol. 68. 3. & Maimon. Hilch. Taanioth, c. 5. sect. 2. (m) T. Bab, Taanith, fol. 29. 1. (n) T. Bab. Sanhedrin, fol. 99. 1.

---

37. But as the days of Noe were, so shall also the coming of the Son of man be.

Greek/Transliteration
37. Ὥσπερ δὲ αἱ ἡμέραι τοῦ Νῶε, οὕτως ἔσται καὶ ἡ παρουσία τοῦ υἱοῦ τοῦ ἀνθρώπου.

37. 'Osper de 'ai 'eimerai tou Noe, 'outos estai kai 'ei parousia tou 'wiou tou anthropou.

Hebrew/Transliteration
לז. וְכִימֵי נֹחַ כֵּן בִּיאַת בֶּן-הָאָדָם:

37. Ve•chi•mey no•ach ken bi•at Ben - ha•adam.

---

38. For as in the days that were before the flood they were eating and drinking, marrying and giving in marriage, until the day that Noe entered into the ark,

Greek/Transliteration
38. Ὥσπερ γὰρ ἦσαν ἐν ταῖς ἡμέραις ταῖς πρὸ τοῦ κατακλυσμοῦ τρώγοντες καὶ πίνοντες, γαμοῦντες καὶ ἐκγαμίζοντες, ἄχρι ἧς ἡμέρας εἰσῆλθεν Νῶε εἰς τὴν κιβωτόν,

38. 'Osper gar eisan en tais 'eimerais tais pro tou kataklusmou trogontes kai pinontes, gamountes kai ekgamizontes, achri 'eis 'eimeras eiseilthen Noe eis tein kiboton,

Hebrew/Transliteration
לח. כִּי כַּאֲשֶׁר לִפְנֵי יְמֵי הַמַּבּוּל אָכְלוּ וְשָׁתוּ בָּעֲלוּ נָשִׁים וְנָשִׁים נִבְעֲלוּ עַד-הַיּוֹם אֲשֶׁר-בָּא נֹחַ אֶל-הַתֵּבָה:

38. Ki ka•a•sher lif•ney ye•mey ha•ma•bool ach•loo ve•sha•too ba•a•loo na•shim ve•na•shim niv•a•loo ad - ha•yom asher - ba no•ach el - ha•te•va.

39. And knew not until the flood came, and took them all away; so shall also the coming of the Son of man be.

Greek/Transliteration
39. καὶ οὐκ ἔγνωσαν, ἕως ἦλθεν ὁ κατακλυσμὸς καὶ ἦρεν ἅπαντας, οὕτως ἔσται καὶ ἡ παρουσία τοῦ υἱοῦ τοῦ ἀνθρώπου.

39. kai ouk egnosan, 'eos eilthen 'o kataklusmos kai eiren 'apantas, 'outos estai kai 'ei Parousia tou 'wiou tou anthropou.

Hebrew/Transliteration
לט. וְהֵם לֹא יָדְעוּ עַד כִּי-בָא הַמַּבּוּל וַיִּמַח אֶת-כֻּלָּם כֵּן תִּהְיֶה בִּיאַת בֶּן-הָאָדָם:

39. Ve•hem lo yad•oo ad ki - va ha•ma•bool va•yi•mach et - koo•lam ken ti•hi•ye bi•at Ben - ha•adam.

Rabbinic Jewish Commentary
Such shall be, as it was, the case of the Jews, before the destruction of Jerusalem: they gave themselves up to all manner of wickedness and uncleanness; they disregarded the warnings of Yeshua and his apostles; they were careless and secure of danger; they would not believe their ruin was at hand, when it was just upon them; they buoyed themselves up to the very last, that a deliverer would arise, and save them; they cried peace, peace, when sudden destruction was nigh; even of them all, their nation, city, and temple, a few only excepted, as in the days of Noah: and though they were so much like the men of that generation, yet they themselves say of them, that "the generation of the flood have no part in the world to come, nor shall they stand in judgment, according to Gen_6:3 (o). (o) Misn. Sanhedrin, c. 11. sect. 3.

---

40. Then shall two be in the field; the one shall be taken, and the other left.

Greek/Transliteration
40. Τότε δύο ἔσονται ἐν τῷ ἀγρῷ· ὁ εἷς παραλαμβάνεται, καὶ ὁ εἷς ἀφίεται.

40. Tote duo esontai en to agro. 'o 'eis paralambanetai, kai 'o 'eis aphietai.

Hebrew/Transliteration
מ. אָז יִהְיוּ שְׁנַיִם בַּשָּׂדֶה אֶחָד יֵאָסֵף וְאֶחָד יֵעָזֵב:

40. Az yi•hee•yoo sh`na•yim ba•sa•de e•chad ye•a•sef ve•e•chad ye•a•zev.

TaNaKh-Old Testament
"The sword is outside and the plague and the famine are within. He who is *in the field* will die by the sword; famine and the plague will also consume those in the city." Ezek_7:15

41. Two women shall be grinding at the mill; the one shall be taken, and the other left.

Greek/Transliteration
41. Δύο ἀλήθουσαι ἐν τῷ μύλωνι· μία παραλαμβάνεται, καὶ μία ἀφίεται.

41. Duo aleithousai en to muloni. mia paralambanetai, kai mia aphietai.

Hebrew/Transliteration
:מא. שְׁתַּיִם טוֹחֲנוֹת בָּרֵחָיִם אַחַת תֵּאָסֵף וְאַחַת תֵּעָזֵב

41. Sh`ta•yim to•che•not ba•re•cha•yim a•chat te•a•sef ve•a•chat te•a•zev.

Rabbinic Jewish Commentary
Though the word women is not in the Greek text, yet it is rightly supplied by our translators, as it is in the Persic version; for the word rendered grinding, is in the feminine gender, and was the work of women, as appears both from the Scripture, Exo_11:5 and from several passages in the Jewish writings, concerning which their canons run thus (p), "These are the works which a woman is to do for her husband, טוחנת, "she must grind", and bake, and wash, and boil, and make his bed.

And elsewhere it is asked (q), "how does she grind? she sits at the mill, and watches the flour, but she does not grind, or go after a beast, that so the mill may not stop; but if their custom is to grind at a hand mill, she may grind. The sanhedrim order this to poor people; for if she brings one handmaid, or money, or goods, sufficient to purchase, she is not obliged to grind.

Frequent mention is made, of women grinding together at the same mill: a case is put concerning two women grinding at an hand mill (r), and various rules are given about it; as, that (s). "a woman may lend her neighbour that is suspected of eating the fruits of the seventh year after time, a meal sieve, a fan, a mill, or a furnace, but she may not winnow, nor "grind with her".

Which it supposes she might do, if she was not suspected: again (t), "the wife of a plebeian, טוחנת, "may grind" with the wife of a learned man, in the time that she is unclean, but not when she is clean.

Nor was this the custom of the Jews only, for women to grind, but also of other countries, as of the Abyssines (u), and of both Greeks and Barbarians (w):

the one shall be taken, and the other left; as before, one shall be taken by the Romans, and either put to death, or carried captive; and the other shall escape their hands, through the singular providence of God. The Ethiopic version, and Munster's Hebrew Gospel add, "two shall be in one bed, one shall be taken, and the other left"; but these words are not in the copies of Matthew in common, but are taken out of Luk_17:34 though they are in the Cambridge copy of Beza's, and in one of Stephens's, see also Ezekiel_7:14:16 for left in a field to die.

(p) Misn. Cetubot, c. 5. sect. 5. Vid. T. Bab. Bava Kama, fol. 47. 9. & 48. 1. (q) Maimon. Hilch. Ishot. c. 21. sect. 5, 6. (r) T. Bab. Nidda, fol. 60. 2. (s) Misn. Sheviith, c. 5. 9. & Gittin, c. 5. sect. 9. (t) T. Hieros. Teruinot, fol. 46. 3. T. Bab. Gittin, fol. 61. 2. & Cholin, fol. 6. 2. Misn. Taharot, c. 7. sect. 4. (u) Ludolph. Hist. Ethiop. l. 4. c. 4. (w) Plutarch apud Beza. in loc.

---

42. Watch therefore: for ye know not what hour your Lord doth come.

Greek/Transliteration
42. Γρηγορεῖτε οὖν, ὅτι οὐκ οἴδατε ποίᾳ ὥρᾳ ὁ κύριος ὑμῶν ἔρχεται.

42. Greigoreite oun, 'oti ouk oidate poia 'ora 'o kurios 'umon erchetai.

Hebrew/Transliteration
מב. לָכֵן הִתְיַצְּבוּ עַל-מִשְׁמַרְתְּכֶם כִּי אֵינְכֶם יֹדְעִים שָׁעָה בּוֹא אֲדֹנֵיכֶם:

42. La•chen hit•yatz•voo al - mish•mar•te•chem ki eyn•chem yod•eem sha•ah bo adoney•chem.

---

43. But know this, that if the goodman of the house had known in what watch the thief would come, he would have watched, and would not have suffered his house to be broken up.

Greek/Transliteration
43. Ἐκεῖνο δὲ γινώσκετε, ὅτι εἰ ᾔδει ὁ οἰκοδεσπότης ποίᾳ φυλακῇ ὁ κλέπτης ἔρχεται, ἐγρηγόρησεν ἄν, καὶ οὐκ ἂν εἴασεν διορυγῆναι τὴν οἰκίαν αὐτοῦ.

43. Ekeino de ginoskete, 'oti ei eidei 'o oikodespoteis poia phulakei 'o klepteis erchetai, egreigoreisen an, kai ouk an eiasen diorugeinai tein oikian autou.

Hebrew/Transliteration
מג. רַק זֹאת שִׂימוּ עַל-לֵב כִּי לוּ-יָדַע בַּעַל הַבַּיִת אֶת-הָאַשְׁמוּרָה בָּהּ יָבוֹא הַגַּנָּב הָיָה עֹמֵד עַל-מִשְׁמַרְתּוֹ וְלֹא:נָתַן לַחְתֹּר אֶת-בֵּיתוֹ

43. Rak zot si•moo al - lev ki loo - ya•da ba•al ha•ba•yit et - ha•ash•moo•ra ba ya•vo ha•ga•nav ha•ya o•med al - mish•mar•to ve•lo na•tan lach•tor et - bei•to.

Rabbinic Jewish Commentary
The Jewish canonists explain, "He that comes in by digging, whether by day or by night, there is no blood for him (i.e. to be shed for him, if he is killed); but if the master of the house, or any other man kill him, they are free; and every man has power to kill him, whether on a weekday, or on a sabbath day; and with whatsoever death he can put him to, as it is said, there is no blood for him, Exo_22:2. And one that comes in, במחתרת, "by digging", or a thief that is found in the midst of a man's roof, or in his court, or within his hedge, whether in the day or

in the night, (may be killed;) and wherefore is it called digging? because it is the way of most thieves to come in by digging in the night (x).
(x) Mairmon. Hilch. Genibah, c. 9. sect. 7, 8.

---

44. Therefore be ye also ready: for in such an hour as ye think not the Son of man cometh.

Greek/Transliteration
44. Διὰ τοῦτο καὶ ὑμεῖς γίνεσθε ἕτοιμοι· ὅτι ᾗ ὥρᾳ οὐ δοκεῖτε, ὁ υἱὸς τοῦ ἀνθρώπου ἔρχεται.

44. Dya touto kai 'umeis ginesthe 'etoimoi. 'oti 'ora ou dokeite, 'o 'wios tou anthropou erchetai.

Hebrew/Transliteration
מד. לָכֵן גַּם-אַתֶּם הֱיוּ נְכֹנִים כִּי בֶן-הָאָדָם יָבוֹא בְשָׁעָה אֲשֶׁר לֹא תָשִׂימוּ עַל-לֵב:

44. La•chen gam - atem he•yoo n`cho•nim ki Ven - ha•adam ya•vo ve•sha•ah asher lo ta•si•moo al - lev.

Rabbinic Jewish Commentary
A readiness the Jews report Bath Kol, or the voice from heaven, gave out concerning the Israelites, "Bath Kol (say (y) they) went out, and said to them, הבא כולכם מזומנין לחיי העולם, "ye are all of you ready for the life of the world to come".

And elsewhere it is said of Bath Kol, that it went forth and affirmed of some particular Rabbins, that they were ready for eternal life; as of Ketiah bar Shalom, R. Eleazar ben Durdia, and R. Chanina (z)

for in such an hour as ye think not, the son of man cometh: this is true of his coming in power to destroy Jerusalem, and of his second coming to judgment. The Jews say much the same of the coming of the Messiah, whom they expect:

"there are three things, they say (a), which come, בהיסח הדעת, "without knowledge", or unthought of, at an unawares; and they are these, the Messiah, anything that is found, and a scorpion.

(y) T. Bab. Moed Katon, fol. 9. 1. (z) T. Bab Avoda Zara, fol. 10. 2. & 17. 1. & 18. 1. & Callah, fol. 17. 2. & Cetubot, fol. 103. 2. (a) T. Bab. Sanhedrin, fol. 97. 1.

---

45. Who then is a faithful and wise servant, whom his lord hath made ruler over his household, to give them meat in due season?

Greek/Transliteration
45. Τίς ἄρα ἐστὶν ὁ πιστὸς δοῦλος καὶ φρόνιμος, ὃν κατέστησεν ὁ κύριος αὐτοῦ ἐπὶ τῆς θεραπείας αὐτοῦ, τοῦ διδόναι αὐτοῖς τὴν τροφὴν ἐν καιρῷ;

45. Tis ara estin 'o pistos doulos kai phronimos, 'on katesteisen 'o kurios autou epi teis therapeias autou, tou didonai autois tein trophein en kairo?

Hebrew/Transliteration
מה. וּמִי-אֵפוֹא הוּא עֶבֶד נֶאֱמָן וְנָבוֹן אֲשֶׁר אֲדֹנָיו הִפְקִידוֹ עַל-בְּנֵי בֵיתוֹ לָתֵת לָהֶם אָכְלָם בְּעִתּוֹ:

45. Oo•mi - e•fo hoo eved ne•e•man ve•na•von asher a•do•nav hif•ki•do al - b`ney vey•to la•tet la•hem och•lam be•ee•to?

---

46. Blessed is that servant, whom his lord when he cometh shall find so doing.

Greek/Transliteration
46. Μακάριος ὁ δοῦλος ἐκεῖνος, ὃν ἐλθὼν ὁ κύριος αὐτοῦ εὑρήσει ποιοῦντα οὕτως.

46. Makarios 'o doulos ekeinos, 'on elthon 'o kurios autou 'eureisei poiounta 'outos.

Hebrew/Transliteration
מו. אַשְׁרֵי הָעֶבֶד הַהוּא אֲשֶׁר בְּבֹא אֲדֹנָיו יִמְצָאֶנּוּ כִּי כֵן עָשָׂה:

46. Ash•rey ha•e•ved ha•hoo asher be•vo a•do•nav yim•tza•e•noo ki chen asa.

---

47. Verily I say unto you, That he shall make him ruler over all his goods.

Greek/Transliteration
47. Ἀμὴν λέγω ὑμῖν, ὅτι ἐπὶ πᾶσιν τοῖς ὑπάρχουσιν αὐτοῦ καταστήσει αὐτόν.

47. Amein lego 'umin, 'oti epi pasin tois 'uparchousin autou katasteisei auton.

Hebrew/Transliteration
מז. אָמֵן אֲנִי אֹמֵר לָכֶם כִּי יַפְקִדֵהוּ עַל-כָּל-אֲשֶׁר יֶשׁ-לוֹ:

47. Amen ani o•mer la•chem ki yaf•ki•de•hoo al - kol - asher yesh - lo.

---

48. But and if that evil servant shall say in his heart, My lord delayeth his coming;

Greek/Transliteration
48. Ἐὰν δὲ εἴπῃ ὁ κακὸς δοῦλος ἐκεῖνος ἐν τῇ καρδίᾳ αὐτοῦ, Χρονίζει ὁ κύριός μου ἐλθεῖν,

48. Ean de eipei 'o kakos doulos ekeinos en tei kardia autou, Chronizei 'o kurios mou elthein,

Hebrew/Transliteration

מח. וְאִם עֶבֶד רָע יֹאמַר בְּלִבּוֹ בֹּשֵׁשׁ אֲדֹנִי לָבוֹא:

48. Ve•eem eved ra yo•mar be•li•bo bo•shesh a•do•ni la•vo.

---

49. And shall begin to smite his fellowservants, and to eat and drink with the drunken;

Greek/Transliteration

49. καὶ ἄρξηται τύπτειν τοὺς συνδούλους, ἐσθίειν δὲ καὶ πίνειν μετὰ τῶν μεθυόντων,

49. kai arxeitai tuptein tous sundoulous, esthiein de kai pinein meta ton methuonton,

Hebrew/Transliteration

מט. וְהֵחֵל לְהַכּוֹת אֶת-אֶחָיו הָעֲבָדִים וְלֶאֱכֹל וְלִשְׁתּוֹת עִם-הַסֹּבְאִים:

49. Ve•he•chel le•ha•kot et - echav ha•a•va•dim ve•le•e•chol ve•lish•tot eem - ha•sov•eem.

---

50. The lord of that servant shall come in a day when he looketh not for him, and in an hour that he is not aware of,

Greek/Transliteration

50. ἥξει ὁ κύριος τοῦ δούλου ἐκείνου ἐν ἡμέρᾳ ᾗ οὐ προσδοκᾷ, καὶ ἐν ὥρᾳ ᾗ οὐ γινώσκει,

50. 'eixei 'o kurios tou doulou ekeinou en 'eimera ou prosdoka, kai en 'ora ou ginoskei,

Hebrew/Transliteration

נ. בּוֹא יָבוֹא אֲדֹנֵי הָעֶבֶד הַזֶּה בְּיוֹם אֲשֶׁר לֹא יְצַפֶּה לוֹ וּבְשָׁעָה אֲשֶׁר לֹא יֵדָע:

50. Bo ya•vo ado•ney ha•e•ved ha•ze be•yom asher lo ye•tza•pe lo oov•sha•ah asher lo ye•da.

---

51. And shall cut him asunder, and appoint him his portion with the hypocrites: there shall be weeping and gnashing of teeth.

Greek/Transliteration

51. καὶ διχοτομήσει αὐτόν, καὶ τὸ μέρος αὐτοῦ μετὰ τῶν ὑποκριτῶν θήσει· ἐκεῖ ἔσται ὁ κλαυθμὸς καὶ ὁ βρυγμὸς τῶν ὀδόντων.

51. kai dichotomeisei auton, kai to meros autou meta ton 'upokriton theisei. ekei estai 'o klauthmos kai 'o brugmos ton odonton.

Hebrew/Transliteration

נא. וְאָז יְשַׁסֵּף אֹתוֹ וְנָתַן אֶת-חֶלְקוֹ עִם-הַחֲנֵפִים שָׁם יִהְיֶה בְּכִי וַחֲרֹק שִׁנָּיִם:

51. Ve•az ye•sha•sef o•to ve•na•tan et - chel•ko eem - ha•cha•ne•fim sham yi•hee•ye ve•chi va•cha•rok shi•na•yim.

Rabbinic Jewish Commentary

Mention is made of some that were sawn asunder, Heb_11:37 and the Jews say (b), that Isaiah was sawn asunder by Manasseh; and such a kind of death is spoken of in the Targum (c); where it is said, that "the priests went before Mordecai, and proclaimed, saying, whoever does not salute, or wish prosperity to Mordecai, and to the Jews, הדמין יתעביד "he shall be cut into pieces", and his house be made a dunghill.

And elsewhere (d) it is said of a wicked man, that they put him upon a carpenter's block, and מנסרים בו, "sawed him asunder"; and he cried out, woe, woe, woe, that I have provoked my Creator. This was also a punishment used among the Heathens, as Gataker (e), and others out of Heathen writers, have shown. It must not here be understood literally, that this wicked servant should be put to such a corporeal death; but that he should be punished in the severest manner, and should be the object of the fierce wrath and sore displeasure of God.

(b) T. Hieros. Sanhedrin, fol. 28. 3. & T. Bab. Yebamot, fol. 49. 2. (c) Targum in Esth. viii. 15. (d) Bereshit Rabba, sect. 65. fol. 58. 4. (e) Adversaria, p. 455.

Matthew, Chapter 25

1. Then shall the kingdom of heaven be likened unto ten virgins, which took their lamps, and went forth to meet the bridegroom.

Greek/Transliteration
1. Τότε ὁμοιωθήσεται ἡ βασιλεία τῶν οὐρανῶν δέκα παρθένοις, αἵτινες λαβοῦσαι τὰς λαμπάδας αὐτῶν ἐξῆλθον εἰς ἀπάντησιν τοῦ νυμφίου.

1. Tote 'omoiotheisetai 'ei basileia ton ouranon deka parthenois, 'aitines labousai tas lampadas auton exeilthon eis apanteisin tou numphiou.

Hebrew/Transliteration
א. אָז תִּדְמֶה מַלְכוּת הַשָּׁמַיִם לְעֶשֶׂר בְּתוּלוֹת אֲשֶׁר לָקְחוּ אֶת-נֵרֹתֵיהֶן וַתֵּצֶאנָה לִקְרַאת הֶחָתָן:

1. Az tid•me mal•choot ha•sha•ma•yim le•e•ser be•too•lot asher lak•choo et - ne•ro•tey•hen va•te•tze•na lik•rat he•cha•tan.

Rabbinic Jewish Commentary

The number "ten" was greatly taken notice of, and used among the Jews: a congregation, with them, consisted of ten persons, and less than that number did not make one (f): and wherever there were ten persons in a place, they were obliged to build a synagogue (g). Ten elders of the city were witnesses of Boaz's taking Ruth to be his wife, Rth_4:2. Now it may be in reference to the former of these, that this number ten is here expressed, since the parable relates to the congregated churches of Yeshua, or to Yeshua's visible church on earth: moreover, they say, that "with less than ten they did not divide the "shema", (i.e. "hear O Israel", and say any part of the blessings that went before it;) nor did (the messenger of the congregation) go before the ark (to pray); nor did (the priests) lift up their hands (to bless the people); nor did they read in the law (in the congregation); nor did they dismiss (the people) with (a passage out of one of) the prophets; nor did they make a standing, and a sitting (when they carried the dead to the grave, which used to be done seven times, to weep over the dead); nor did they say the blessing of the mourners, nor the comforts of the mourners (when they returned from the grave, and stood in a row to comfort the mourner; and there was no row less than ten); וברכת חתנים, "nor the blessing of the bridegrooms"," which consisted of seven blessings, and this was not said but in the presence of ten persons (h)

The custom here alluded to of meeting the bridegroom, and attending the bride home to his house in the night, with lighted torches, or lamps, and such a number of them as here mentioned, was not only the custom of the Jews, but of other eastern nations (i). Jarchi says (k), it was the custom of the Ishmaelites; his words are these: "it was a custom in the land of Ishmael, to bring the bride from her father's house to her husband's house, בלילה, "in the night", before she entered the nuptial chamber; and to carry before her כעשר קונדסין, "about ten staves"; and upon the top of the staff was the form of a brazen dish, and in the midst of it, pieces of garments, oil, and pitch, which they set fire to, and lighted before her."

(f) Misn. Sanhedrin, c. 1. sect. 6. T. Hieros. Beracot, fol. 11. 3. (g) Maimon. Hilch. Tephillah, c. 11. sect. 1. (h) Misn. Megilia, c. 4. sect. 3. Maimon, Hilch. Tephilla, c. 8. sect. 4, 5. (i) Bartenora in Misn. Megilla, c. 4. sect. 3. T. Bab. Cetubot, fol. 8. 2. (k) In Misn. Celim, c. 2. sect. 8.

---

2. And five of them were wise, and five were foolish.

Greek/Transliteration
2. Πέντε δὲ ἦσαν ἐξ αὐτῶν φρόνιμοι, καὶ αἱ πέντε μωραί.

2. Pente de eisan ex auton phronimoi, kai 'ai pente morai.

Hebrew/Transliteration
ב: חָמֵשׁ מֵהֶן בְּנוֹת-כֶּסֶל וְחָמֵשׁ בְּנוֹת תְּבוּנָה.

2. Cha•mesh me•hen b`not - ke•sel ve•cha•mesh b`not te•voo•na.

Rabbinic Jewish Commentary
There is a parable of R. Jochanan ben Zaccai (m), who lived before, and after the destruction of the second temple, which bears some likeness to this part of the parable, and others in it, and is this; "a certain king invited his servants, but did not fix any time for them; those of them that were פקהים, "wise", adorned themselves, and sat at the gate of the king's house, and said, is there any want at the king's house? but those of them that were טפשים, "fools", went and did their work, and said, is there any feast without trouble? on a sudden, the king inquired after his servants: the wise went in before him, as they were, adorned; but the fools went in before him, as they were, filthy: the king rejoiced at meeting the wise, and was angry at meeting the foolish; and ordered, that those who had adorned themselves for the feast should sit and eat, and those that had not adorned themselves for the feast should stand." (m) T. Bab. Sabbat, fol. 153. 1. Vid. R. David Kimchi in Isa. lxv. 13.

---

3. They that were foolish took their lamps, and took no oil with them:

Greek/Transliteration
3. Αἵτινες μωραί, λαβοῦσαι τὰς λαμπάδας αὐτῶν, οὐκ ἔλαβον μεθ᾽ ἑαυτῶν ἔλαιον·

3. 'Aitines morai, labousai tas lampadas auton, ouk elabon meth 'eauton elaion.

Hebrew/Transliteration
ג: וְהַכְּסִילוֹת לָקְחוּ אֶת-נֵרֹתֵיהֶן וְלֹא-לָקְחוּ עִמָּהֶן שָׁמֶן.

3. Ve•hak•si•lot lak•choo et - ne•ro•tey•hen ve•lo - lak•choo ee•ma•hen sha•men.

4. But the wise took oil in their vessels with their lamps.

Greek/Transliteration
4. αἱ δὲ φρόνιμοι ἔλαβον ἔλαιον ἐν τοῖς ἀγγείοις αὐτῶν μετὰ τῶν λαμπάδων αὐτῶν.

4. 'ai de phronimoi elabon elaion en tois angeiois auton meta ton lampadon auton.

Hebrew/Transliteration
ד. וְהַנְּבוֹנוֹת לָקְחוּ שֶׁמֶן בִּכְלֵיהֶן עִם־הַנֵּרוֹת:

4. Ve•han•vo•not lak•choo she•men bich•ley•hen eem - ha•ne•rot.

---

5. While the bridegroom tarried, they all slumbered and slept.

Greek/Transliteration
5. Χρονίζοντος δὲ τοῦ νυμφίου, ἐνύσταξαν πᾶσαι καὶ ἐκάθευδον.

5. Chronizontos de tou numphiou, enustaxan pasai kai ekatheudon.

Hebrew/Transliteration
ה. וְכַאֲשֶׁר אֵחַר הֶחָתָן לָבֹא נָמוּ יָשְׁנוּ כֻלָּן:

5. Ve•cha•a•sher e•char he•cha•tan la•vo na•moo yash•noo choo•lan.

---

6. And at midnight there was a cry made, Behold, the bridegroom cometh; go ye out to meet him.

Greek/Transliteration
6. Μέσης δὲ νυκτὸς κραυγὴ γέγονεν, Ἰδού, ὁ νυμφίος ἔρχεται, ἐξέρχεσθε εἰς ἀπάντησιν αὐτοῦ.

6. Meseis de nuktos kraugei gegonen, Ydou, 'o numphios erchetai, exerchesthe eis apanteisin autou.

Hebrew/Transliteration
ו. וַיְהִי בַּחֲצִי הַלַּיְלָה וַתַּעֲבֹר הָרִנָּה הִנֵּה הֶחָתָן בָּא צְאֶינָה לִקְרָאתוֹ:

6. Vay•hi ba•cha•tzi ha•lai•la va•ta•a•vor ha•ri•na hee•ne he•cha•tan ba tze•ei•na lik•ra•to.

Rabbinic Jewish Commentary
The Jews expect (q), that at the end of the world Moses and Messiah will come in the night, the one from the wilderness, and the other from Rome: and they make frequent mention of God's going into the garden of Eden, or paradise, at midnight,

and there rejoicing with good men. It is said (r), that R. Eliezer and R. Jose "were sitting one night, and studying in the law, and about midnight, a man cried (or the cock crowed), bless ye the blessing; says R. Eliezer, now is, the time that the holy, blessed God goes into the garden of Eden, to rejoice with the righteous."

(q) Targum Hieros. in Exod xii. 42. (r) Zohar in Exod. fol. 76. 4. & in Lev. fol. 21. 1. & 23. 2.

---

7. Then all those virgins arose, and trimmed their lamps.

Greek/Transliteration
7. Τότε ἠγέρθησαν πᾶσαι αἱ παρθένοι ἐκεῖναι, καὶ ἐκόσμησαν τὰς λαμπάδας αὐτῶν.

7. Tote eigertheisan pasai 'ai parthenoi ekeinai, kai ekosmeisan tas lampadas auton.

Hebrew/Transliteration
:ז. אָז הֵקִיצוּ כָּל-הַבְּתוּלוֹת הָאֵלֶּה וַתֵּיטַבְנָה אֶת-נֵרֹתֵיהֶן

7. Az he•ki•tzoo kol - hab•too•lot ha•e•le va•tey•tav•na et - ne•ro•tey•hen.

---

8. And the foolish said unto the wise, Give us of your oil; for our lamps are gone out.

Greek/Transliteration
8. Αἱ δὲ μωραὶ ταῖς φρονίμοις εἶπον, Δότε ἡμῖν ἐκ τοῦ ἐλαίου ὑμῶν, ὅτι αἱ λαμπάδες ἡμῶν σβέννυνται.

8. 'Ai de morai tais phronimois eipon, Dote 'eimin ek tou elaiou 'umon, 'oti 'ai lampades 'eimon sbennuntai.

Hebrew/Transliteration
:ח. וַתֹּאמַרְנָה הַכְּסִילוֹת אֶל-הַנְּבוֹנוֹת תְּנֶינָה לָּנוּ מִשַּׁמְנְכֶן פֶּן-יִכְבּוּ נֵרֹתֵינוּ

8. Va•to•mar•na hak•si•lot el - ha•ne•vo•not te•nei•na la•noo mi•sham•ne•chen pen - yich•boo ne•ro•tey•noo.

---

9. But the wise answered, saying, Not so; lest there be not enough for us and you: but go ye rather to them that sell, and buy for yourselves.

Greek/Transliteration
9. Ἀπεκρίθησαν δὲ αἱ φρόνιμοι, λέγουσαι, Μήποτε οὐκ ἀρκέσῃ ἡμῖν καὶ ὑμῖν· πορεύεσθε δὲ μᾶλλον πρὸς τοὺς πωλοῦντας καὶ ἀγοράσατε ἑαυταῖς.

9. Apekritheisan de 'ai phronimoi, legousai, Meipote ouk arkesei 'eimin kai 'umin. poreuesthe de mallon pros tous polountas kai agorasate 'eautais.

Hebrew/Transliteration
ט: וְהַנְּבוֹנוֹת עָנוּ לֵאמֹר לֹא כֵן פֶּן-לֹא יִשְׂפֹּק לָנוּ וְלָכֶן לִכְנָה אֶל-מֹכְרֵי שֶׁמֶן וּקְנֶינָה לָכֶן

9. Ve•han•vo•not a•noo le•mor lo chen pen - lo yis•pok la•noo ve•la•chen lech•na el - moch•rey she•men ook•nei•na la•chen.

---

10. And while they went to buy, the bridegroom came; and they that were ready went in with him to the marriage: and the door was shut.

Greek/Transliteration
10. Ἀπερχομένων δὲ αὐτῶν ἀγοράσαι, ἦλθεν ὁ νυμφίος· καὶ αἱ ἕτοιμοι εἰσῆλθον μετ' αὐτοῦ εἰς τοὺς γάμους, καὶ ἐκλείσθη ἡ θύρα.

10. Aperchomenon de auton agorasai, eilthen 'o numphios. kai 'ai 'etoimoi eiseilthon met autou eis tous gamous, kai ekleisthei 'ei thura.

Hebrew/Transliteration
י: וַיְהִי בְּלֶכְתָּן לִקְנוֹת וְהִנֵּה הֶחָתָן בָּא וְאֵלֶּה אֲשֶׁר נָכוֹנוּ בָּאוּ אִתּוֹ אֶל-חֲתֻנָּתוֹ וְהַדֶּלֶת נִסְגָּרָה

10. Vay•hi be•lech•tan lik•not ve•hee•ne he•cha•tan ba ve•e•le asher na•cho•noo ba•oo ee•to el - cha•too•na•to ve•ha•de•let nis•ga•ra.

Rabbinic Jewish Commentary
The Jews say (s), that "the Jerusalem of the world to come, is not as the Jerusalem of this world: the Jerusalem of this world, everyone may go into it that will; but the Jerusalem of the world to come, none may go into it, but המזומנין לה, "those that are prepared for it"."

went in with him to the marriage: the Syriac reads it, "into the wedding house", and the Persic, "the nuptial parlour"; the marriage chamber, where the bridegroom and bride celebrated their marriage; kept their marriage feast; and where were received the bridemaids, and friends of the bridegroom, called in Talmudic language, בני עלייה, "the children of the bridechamber" (t)

(s) T. Bab. Bava Bathra, fol. 75. 2. (t) T. Bab. Succa, fol. 45. 2. & Sanhedrin, fol. 97. 2.

---

11. Afterward came also the other virgins, saying, Lord, Lord, open to us.

Greek/Transliteration
11. Ὕστερον δὲ ἔρχονται καὶ αἱ λοιπαὶ παρθένοι, λέγουσαι, Κύριε, κύριε, ἄνοιξον ἡμῖν.

11. 'Usteron de erchontai kai 'ai loipai parthenoi, legousai, Kurie, kurie, anoixon 'eimin.

Hebrew/Transliteration
יא. וְאַחֲרֵי-כֵן בָּאוּ יֶתֶר הַבְּתוּלוֹת וַתֹּאמַרְנָה אֲדֹנֵינוּ אֲדֹנֵינוּ פְּתַח-נָא לָנוּ:

11. Ve•a•cha•rey - chen ba•oo ye•ter hab•too•lot va•to•mar•na Ado•ney•noo Ado•ney•noo pe•tach - na la•noo.

---

12. But he answered and said, Verily I say unto you, I know you not.

Greek/Transliteration
12. Ὁ δὲ ἀποκριθεὶς εἶπεν, Ἀμὴν λέγω ὑμῖν, οὐκ οἶδα ὑμᾶς.

12. 'O de apokritheis eipen, Amein lego 'umin, ouk oida 'umas.

Hebrew/Transliteration
יב. וְהוּא עָנָה וְאָמַר אָמֵן אֲנִי אֹמֵר לָכֶן כִּי לֹא יָדַעְתִּי אֶתְכֶן:

12. Ve•hoo ana ve•a•mar Amen ani o•mer la•chen ki lo ya•da•a•ti et•chen.

---

13. Watch therefore, for ye know neither the day nor the hour wherein the Son of man cometh.

Greek/Transliteration
13. Γρηγορεῖτε οὖν, ὅτι οὐκ οἴδατε τὴν ἡμέραν οὐδὲ τὴν ὥραν, ἐν ᾗ ὁ υἱὸς τοῦ ἀνθρώπου ἔρχεται.

13. Greigoreite oun, 'oti ouk oidate tein 'eimeran oude tein 'oran, en 'o 'wios tou anthropou erchetai.

Hebrew/Transliteration
יג. עַל-כֵּן עִמְדוּ עַל-מִשְׁמַרְתְּכֶם כִּי אֵינְכֶם יֹדְעִים אֶת-הַיּוֹם וְאֶת-הַשָּׁעָה אֲשֶׁר יָבֹא בָהּ בֶּן-הָאָדָם:

13. Al - ken eem•doo al - mish•mar•te•chem ki eyn•chem yod•eem et - ha•yom ve•et - ha•sha•ah asher ya•vo va Ben - ha•adam.

---

14. For the kingdom of heaven is as a man travelling into a far country, who called his own servants, and delivered unto them his goods.

Greek/Transliteration
14. Ὥσπερ γὰρ ἄνθρωπος ἀποδημῶν ἐκάλεσεν τοὺς ἰδίους δούλους, καὶ παρέδωκεν αὐτοῖς τὰ ὑπάρχοντα αὐτοῦ·

14. 'Osper gar anthropos apodeimon ekalesen tous idious doulous, kai paredoken autois ta 'uparchonta autou.

Hebrew/Transliteration
יד. כִּי כְמוֹ-אִישׁ נֹסֵעַ אֶל-מִחוּץ לָאָרֶץ אֲשֶׁר קָרָא לַעֲבָדָיו וַיַּפְקֵד בְּיָדָם אֶת-הוֹנוֹ:

14. Ki k`mo - eesh no•se•a el - mi•choo•tz la•a•retz asher ka•ra la•a•va•dav va•yaf•ked be•ya•dam et - ho•no.

Rabbinic Jewish Commentary
According to the Jewish (u) canons, "a master that had a mind to go out of the land (of Israel) could not take his servant with him, unless he pleased; and this is a rule at all times, even at this time, that the land is in the hand of the Gentiles."
(u) Maimon. Hilch. Abadim, c. 8. sect. 9.

---

15. And unto one he gave five talents, to another two, and to another one; to every man according to his several ability; and straightway took his journey.

Greek/Transliteration
15. καὶ ᾧ μὲν ἔδωκεν πέντε τάλαντα, ᾧ δὲ δύο, ᾧ δὲ ἕν, ἑκάστῳ κατὰ τὴν ἰδίαν δύναμιν· καὶ ἀπεδήμησεν εὐθέως.

15. kai 'o men edoken pente talanta, 'o de duo, 'o de 'en, 'ekasto kata tein idian dunamin. Kai apedeimeisen eutheos.

Hebrew/Transliteration
טו. לְאֶחָד מֵהֶם נָתַן חָמֵשׁ כִּכָּרִים לְאַחֵר שְׁתַּיִם וּלְאַחֵר אֶחָת לְאִישׁ אִישׁ כְּפִי יְכֹלֶת יָדוֹ וַיְמַהֵר וַיִּסַּע לְדַרְכּוֹ:

15. Le•e•chad me•hem na•tan cha•mesh ki•ka•rim le•a•cher sh`ta•yim ool•a•cher e•chat le•eesh eesh ke•fi ye•cho•let ya•do vay•ma•her va•yi•sa le•dar•ko.

---

16. Then he that had received the five talents went and traded with the same, and made them other five talents.

Greek/Tranliteration
16. Πορευθεὶς δὲ ὁ τὰ πέντε τάλαντα λαβὼν εἰργάσατο ἐν αὐτοῖς, καὶ ἐποίησεν ἄλλα πέντε τάλαντα.

16. Poreutheis de 'o ta pente talanta labon eirgasato en autois, kai epoieisen alla pente talanta.

Hebrew/Transliteration
טז. וְזֶה אֲשֶׁר לָקַח חָמֵשׁ הַכִּכָּרִים הָלַךְ וַיִּסְחַר בָּהֶן וַיַּעַשׂ חָמֵשׁ כִּכָּרִים אֲחֵרוֹת

16. Ve•ze asher la•kach cha•mesh ha•ki•ka•rim ha•lach va•yis•char ba•hen va•ya•as cha•mesh ki•ka•rim a•che•rot.

---

17. And likewise he that had received two, he also gained other two.

Greek/Transliteration
17. Ὡσαύτως καὶ ὁ τὰ δύο ἐκέρδησεν καὶ αὐτὸς ἄλλα δύο.

17. 'Osautos kai 'o ta duo ekerdeisen kai autos alla duo.

Hebrew/Transliteration
יז. וְכֵן זֶה אֲשֶׁר לָקַח שְׁתַּיִם רָכַשׁ שְׁתַּיִם אֲחֵרוֹת:

17. Ve•chen ze asher la•kach sh`ta•yim ra•chash sh`ta•yim a•che•rot.

---

18. But he that had received one went and digged in the earth, and hid his lord's money.

Greek/Transliteration
18. Ὁ δὲ τὸ ἓν λαβὼν ἀπελθὼν ὤρυξεν ἐν τῇ γῇ, καὶ ἀπέκρυψεν τὸ ἀργύριον τοῦ κυρίου αὐτοῦ.

18. 'O de to 'en labon apelthon oruxen en tei gei, kai apekrupsen to argurion tou kuriou autou.

Hebrew/Transliteration
יח. וְזֶה אֲשֶׁר לָקַח אֶת-הַכִּכָּר הָאַחַת אָזַל לוֹ וַיַּחְפֹּר בָּאֲדָמָה וַיִּטְמֹן אֶת-כֶּסֶף אֲדֹנָיו:

18. Ve•ze asher la•kach et - ha•ki•kar ha•e•chat azal lo va•yach•por ba•a•da•ma va•yit•mon et - ke•sef a•do•nav.

---

19. After a long time the lord of those servants cometh, and reckoneth with them.

Greek/Transliteration
19. Μετὰ δὲ χρόνον πολὺν ἔρχεται ὁ κύριος τῶν δούλων ἐκείνων, καὶ συναίρει μετ᾽ αὐτῶν λόγον.

19. Meta de chronon polun erchetai 'o kurios ton doulon ekeinon, kai sunairei met auton logon.

Hebrew/Transliteration
יט. וְאַחֲרֵי יָמִים רַבִּים שָׁב אֲדוֹן הָעֲבָדִים הָאֵלֶּה מִדַּרְכּוֹ וַיְחַשֵּׁב עִמָּהֶם:

19. Ve•a•cha•rey ya•mim ra•bim shav Adon ha•a•va•dim ha•e•le mi•dar•ko vay•cha•shev ee•ma•hem.

---

20. And so he that had received five talents came and brought other five talents, saying, Lord, thou deliveredst unto me five talents: behold, I have gained beside them five talents more.

Greek/Transliteration
20. Καὶ προσελθὼν ὁ τὰ πέντε τάλαντα λαβὼν προσήνεγκεν ἄλλα πέντε τάλαντα, λέγων, Κύριε, πέντε τάλαντά μοι παρέδωκας· ἴδε, ἄλλα πέντε τάλαντα ἐκέρδησα ἐπ' αὐτοῖς.

20. Kai proselthon 'o ta pente talanta labon proseinegken alla pente talanta, legon, Kurie, pente talanta moi paredokas. ide, alla pente talanta ekerdeisa ep autois.

Hebrew/Transliteration
כ. וַיִּגַּשׁ זֶה אֲשֶׁר לָקַח חָמֵשׁ הַכִּכָּרִים וַיָּבֵא חָמֵשׁ כִּכָּרִים אֲחֵרוֹת לֵאמֹר אֲדֹנִי חָמֵשׁ כִּכָּרִים נָתַתָּ בְּיָדִי וְהִנֵּה:רָכַשְׁתִּי עוֹד חָמֵשׁ כִּכָּרִים אֲחֵרוֹת

20. Va•yi•gash ze asher la•kach cha•mesh ha•ki•ka•rim va•ya•ve cha•mesh ki•ka•rim a•che•rot le•mor Adoni cha•mesh ki•ka•rim na•ta•ta be•ya•di ve•hee•ne ra•chash•ti od cha•mesh ki•ka•rim a•che•rot.

---

21. His lord said unto him, Well done, thou good and faithful servant: thou hast been faithful over a few things, I will make thee ruler over many things: enter thou into the joy of thy lord.

Greek/Transliteration
21. Ἔφη δὲ αὐτῷ ὁ κύριος αὐτοῦ, Εὖ, δοῦλε ἀγαθὲ καὶ πιστέ, ἐπὶ ὀλίγα ἦς πιστός, ἐπὶ πολλῶν σε καταστήσω· εἴσελθε εἰς τὴν χαρὰν τοῦ κυρίου σου.

21. Ephei de auto 'o kurios autou, Eu, doule agathe kai piste, epi oliga eis pistos, epi pollon se katasteiso. eiselthe eis tein charan tou kuriou sou.

Hebrew/Transliteration
כא. וַיַּעַן אֹתוֹ אֲדֹנָיו הֵיטַבְתָּ עֶבֶד טוֹב וְנֶאֱמָן נֶאֱמָן הָיִיתָ בִּמְעַט וַאֲנִי אַפְקִידְךָ עַל-הַרְבֵּה בֹּא אֶל-שִׂמְחַת אֲדֹנֶיךָ:

21. Va•ya•an o•to a•do•nav hey•tav•ta eved tov ve•ne•e•man ne•e•man ha•yi•ta vim•at va•a•ni af•kid•cha al - har•be bo el - sim•chat a•do•ne•cha.

Rabbinic Jewish Commentary
In such language as this, the Jews used to praise their servants, הוי איש טוב ונאמן "O man! good and faithful", and from whose labour one had (x) profit.

It was usual with the Jews to express the, happiness of the world to come by "joy"; not only that which is from the Lord, but that with which he himself rejoices with his people: for they say (y), "there is no joy before, or in the presence of the holy blessed God, since the world was created, כאותה שמחה, "like that joy", with which he will rejoice with the righteous, in the world to come.

(x) T. Bab. Beracot, fol. 16. 2. (y) Midrash Haneelam in Zohar in Gen. fol. 69. 4.

---

22. He also that had received two talents came and said, Lord, thou deliveredst unto me two talents: behold, I have gained two other talents beside them.

Greek/Transliteration
22. Προσελθὼν δὲ καὶ ὁ τὰ δύο τάλαντα λαβὼν εἶπεν, Κύριε, δύο τάλαντά μοι παρέδωκας· ἴδε, ἄλλα δύο τάλαντα ἐκέρδησα ἐπ᾽ αὐτοῖς.

22. Proselthon de kai 'o ta duo talanta labon eipen, Kurie, duo talanta moi paredokas. ide, alla duo talanta ekerdeisa ep autois.

Hebrew/Transliteration
כב. וְזֶה אֲשֶׁר לָקַח כִּכָּרַיִם נִגַּשׁ גַּם-הוּא וַיֹּאמַר אֲדֹנִי שְׁתֵּי כִכָּרִים נָתַתָּ לִי וְהִנֵּה רָכַשְׁתִּי עֲלֵיהֶן עוֹד כִּכָּרַיִם:

22. Ve•ze asher la•kach kik•ra•yim ni•gash gam - hoo va•yo•mar Adoni sh`tey chi•ka•rim na•ta•ta li ve•hee•ne ra•chash•ti aley•hen od kik•ra•yim.

---

23. His lord said unto him, Well done, good and faithful servant; thou hast been faithful over a few things, I will make thee ruler over many things: enter thou into the joy of thy lord.

Greek/Transliteration
23. Ἔφη αὐτῷ ὁ κύριος αὐτοῦ, Εὖ, δοῦλε ἀγαθὲ καὶ πιστέ, ἐπὶ ὀλίγα ἦς πιστός, ἐπὶ πολλῶν σε καταστήσω· εἴσελθε εἰς τὴν χαρὰν τοῦ κυρίου σου.

23. Ephei auto 'o kurios autou, Eu, doule agathe kai piste, epi oliga eis pistos, epi pollon se katasteiso. eiselthe eis tein charan tou kuriou sou.

Hebrew/Transliteration
כג. וַיַּעַן אֹתוֹ אֲדֹנָיו הֵיטַבְתָּ עֶבֶד טוֹב וְנֶאֱמָן נֶאֱמָן הָיִיתָ בִּמְעַט וַאֲנִי אַפְקִידְךָ עַל-הַרְבֵּה בֹּא אֶל-שִׂמְחַת אֲדֹנֶיךָ:

23. Va•ya•an o•to a•do•nav hey•tav•ta eved tov ve•ne•e•man ne•e•man ha•yi•ta vim•at va•a•ni af•kid•cha al - har•be bo el - sim•chat a•do•ne•cha.

24. Then he which had received the one talent came and said, Lord, I knew thee that thou art an hard man, reaping where thou hast not sown, and gathering where thou hast not strawed:

Greek/Transliteration
24. Προσελθὼν δὲ καὶ ὁ τὸ ἓν τάλαντον εἰληφὼς εἶπεν, Κύριε, ἔγνων σε ὅτι σκληρὸς εἶ ἄνθρωπος, θερίζων ὅπου οὐκ ἔσπειρας, καὶ συνάγων ὅθεν οὐ διεσκόρπισας·

24. Proselthon de kai 'o to 'en talanton eileiphos eipen, Kurie, egnon se 'oti skleiros ei anthropos, therizon 'opou ouk espeiras, kai sunagon 'othen ou dieskorpisas.

Hebrew/Transliteration
כד. וַיִּגַּשׁ גַּם-זֶה אֲשֶׁר לָקַח כִּכָּר אַחַת וַיֹּאמַר אֲדֹנִי יְדַעְתִּיךָ כִּי-אִישׁ קָשֶׁה אַתָּה קֹצֵר בַּאֲשֶׁר לֹא זָרָעְתָּ וְכֹנֵס:בַּאֲשֶׁר לֹא פִזָּרְתָּ

24. Va•yi•gash gam - ze asher la•kach ki•kar a•chat va•yo•mar Adoni ye•da•a•ti•cha ki - eesh ka•she ata ko•tzer ba•a•sher lo za•ra•ata ve•cho•nes ba•a•sher lo fi•zar•ta.

---

25. And I was afraid, and went and hid thy talent in the earth: lo, there thou hast that is thine.

Greek/Transliteration
25. καὶ φοβηθείς, ἀπελθὼν ἔκρυψα τὸ τάλαντόν σου ἐν τῇ γῇ· ἴδε, ἔχεις τὸ σόν.

25. kai phobeitheis, apelthon ekrupsa to talanton sou en tei gei. ide, echeis to son.

Hebrew/Transliteration
כה. וָאִירָא וָאֵלֵךְ וָאֶטְמֹן כִּכָּרְךָ בָּאֲדָמָה וְעַתָּה הֵא-לְךָ אֵת אֲשֶׁר-לָךְ:

25. Va•ee•ra va•e•lech va•et•mon ki•kar•cha ba•a•da•ma ve•a•ta he - le•cha et asher - lach.

---

26. His lord answered and said unto him, Thou wicked and slothful servant, thou knewest that I reap where I sowed not, and gather where I have not strawed:

Greek/Transliteration
26. Ἀποκριθεὶς δὲ ὁ κύριος αὐτοῦ εἶπεν αὐτῷ, Πονηρὲ δοῦλε καὶ ὀκνηρέ, ᾔδεις ὅτι θερίζω ὅπου οὐκ ἔσπειρα, καὶ συνάγω ὅθεν οὐ διεσκόρπισα·

26. Apokritheis de 'o kurios autou eipen auto, Poneire doule kai okneire, eideis 'oti therizo 'opou ouk espeira, kai sunago 'othen ou dieskorpisa.

Hebrew/Transliteration

כו. וַיַּעַן אֲדֹנָיו וַיֹּאמֶר אֵלָיו עֶבֶד רָע וְעָצֵל יָדַעְתָּ כִּי-קוֹצֵר אֲנִי בַּאֲשֶׁר לֹא זָרַעְתִּי וְכֹנֵס אֲנִי בַּאֲשֶׁר לֹא פִזָּרְתִּי:

26. Va•ya•an a•do•nav va•yo•mer elav eved ra ve•a•tzel ya•da•ata ki - ko•tzer ani ba•a•sher lo za•ra•a•ti ve•cho•nes ani ba•a•sher lo fi•zar•ti.

---

27. Thou oughtest therefore to have put my money to the exchangers, and then at my coming I should have received mine own with usury.

Greek/Transliteration

27. ἔδει οὖν σε βαλεῖν τὸ ἀργύριόν μου τοῖς τραπεζίταις, καὶ ἐλθὼν ἐγὼ ἐκομισάμην ἂν τὸ ἐμὸν σὺν τόκῳ.

27. edei oun se balein to argurion mou tois trapezitais, kai elthon ego ekomisamein an to emon sun toko.

Hebrew/Transliteration

כז. וְעַל-כֵּן הָיָה עָלֶיךָ לָתֵת כַּסְפִּי לַמַּחֲלִיפֵי-כָסֶף וַאֲנִי בְּבֹאִי הָיִיתִי מֹצֵא אֵת אֲשֶׁר-לִי בְּתַרְבִּית:

27. Ve•al - ken ha•ya a•le•cha la•tet kas•pi le•ma•cha•li•fey - cha•sef va•a•ni be•vo•ee ha•yi•ti mo•tze et asher - li be•tar•bit.

---

28. Take therefore the talent from him, and give it unto him which hath ten talents.

Greek/Transliteration

28. Ἄρατε οὖν ἀπ' αὐτοῦ τὸ τάλαντον, καὶ δότε τῷ ἔχοντι τὰ δέκα τάλαντα.

28. Arate oun ap autou to talanton, kai dote to echonti ta deka talanta.

Hebrew/Transliteration

כח. לָכֵן קְחוּ אֶת-הַכִּכָּר מִיָּדוֹ וּתְנוּ לָזֶה אֲשֶׁר-לוֹ כִּכָּרִים עָשֶׂר:

28. La•chen ke•choo et - ha•ki•kar mi•ya•do oot•noo la•ze asher - lo ki•ka•rim aser.

---

29. For unto every one that hath shall be given, and he shall have abundance: but from him that hath not shall be taken away even that which he hath.

Greek/Transliteration
29. Τῷ γὰρ ἔχοντι παντὶ δοθήσεται, καὶ περισσευθήσεται· ἀπὸ δὲ τοῦ μὴ ἔχοντος, καὶ ὃ ἔχει, ἀρθήσεται ἀπ' αὐτοῦ.

29. To gar echonti panti dotheisetai, kai perisseutheisetai. apo de tou mei echontos, kai 'o echei, artheisetai ap autou.

Hebrew/Transliteration
כט. כִּי מִי אֲשֶׁר יֶשׁ-לוֹ יִנָּתֶן-לוֹ וְיַעֲדִיף וּמִי אֲשֶׁר אֵין-לוֹ יֻקַּח מִמֶּנּוּ גַּם אֵת אֲשֶׁר יֶשׁ-לוֹ:

29. Ki mee asher yesh - lo yi•na•ten - lo ve•ya•a•dif oo•mi asher eyn - lo yoo•kach mi•me•noo gam et asher yesh - lo.

Rabbinic Jewish Commentary
This seems to be a frequent saying of Yeshua's, or a common maxim of his, which he made use of on different occasions; and accords with some usual sayings, and proverbial expressions of the Jews; who say (a), that "the blessed God does not give wisdom, but to him that has wisdom"; and of a man, in other respects, they use this is a common proverb (b), "if he adds or increases, they add unto him, and if he lessens, they lessen to him." (a) T. Bab. Beracot, fol. 55. 1. Zohar in Exod. fol. 89. 4. (b) Vajikra Rabba, sect. 30. fol. 170. 2.

---

30. And cast ye the unprofitable servant into outer darkness: there shall be weeping and gnashing of teeth.

Greek/Transliteration
30. Καὶ τὸν ἀχρεῖον δοῦλον ἐκβάλετε εἰς τὸ σκότος τὸ ἐξώτερον. Ἐκεῖ ἔσται ὁ κλαυθμὸς καὶ ὁ βρυγμὸς τῶν ὀδόντων.

30. Kai ton achreion doulon ekbalete eis to skotos to exoteron. Ekei estai 'o klauthmos kai 'o brugmos ton odonton.

Hebrew/Transliteration
ל. וְאֶת הָעֶבֶד הַזֶּה אֲשֶׁר לֹא יִצְלַח לַכֹּל הַשְׁלִיכוּ אֶל-אֹפֶל וְצַלְמָוֶת שָׁם יִהְיֶה בְכִי וַחֲרֹק שִׁנָּיִם:

30. Ve•et ha•e•ved ha•ze asher lo yitz•lach la•kol hash•li•choo el - o•fel ve•tzal•ma•vet sham yi•hee•ye ve•chi va•cha•rok shi•na•yim.

Rabbinic Jewish Commentary
into outer darkness: there shall be weeping and gnashing of teeth: he shall be turned out of doors into outer darkness, to be a companion of other unhappy creatures; who are also without, bewailing their miserable condition, and reflecting on their past conduct; whilst faithful, diligent, and laborious servants will be within, partaking of a rich entertainment, prepared by their Lord, accompanied with joy unspeakable, and full of glory.

31. When the Son of man shall come in his glory, and all the holy angels with him, then shall he sit upon the throne of his glory:

Greek/Transliteration
31. Ὅταν δὲ ἔλθῃ ὁ υἱὸς τοῦ ἀνθρώπου ἐν τῇ δόξῃ αὐτοῦ, καὶ πάντες οἱ ἅγιοι ἄγγελοι μετ᾽ αὐτοῦ, τότε καθίσει ἐπὶ θρόνου δόξης αὐτοῦ,

31. 'Otan de elthei 'o 'wios tou anthropou en tei doxei autou, kai pantes 'oi 'agioi angeloi met autou, tote kathisei epi thronou doxeis autou,

Hebrew/Transliteration
לא. וְהָיָה כִּי יָבוֹא בֶן-הָאָדָם בִּגְדֻלָּתוֹ וְכָל-הַמַּלְאָכִים הַקְּדֹשִׁים עִמּוֹ אָז יֵשֵׁב עַל-כִּסֵּא כְבוֹדוֹ:

31. Ve•ha•ya ki ya•vo Ben - ha•adam big•doo•la•to ve•chol - ha•mal•a•chim ha•k`do•shim ee•mo az ye•shev al - ki•se che•vo•do.

---

32. And before him shall be gathered all nations: and he shall separate them one from another, as a shepherd divideth his sheep from the goats:

Greek/Transliteration
32. καὶ συναχθήσεται ἔμπροσθεν αὐτοῦ πάντα τὰ ἔθνη, καὶ ἀφοριεῖ αὐτοὺς ἀπ᾽ ἀλλήλων, ὥσπερ ὁ ποιμὴν ἀφορίζει τὰ πρόβατα ἀπὸ τῶν ἐρίφων·

32. kai sunachtheisetai emprosthen autou panta ta ethnei, kai aphoriei autous ap alleilon, 'osper 'o poimein aphorizei ta probata apo ton eriphon.

Hebrew/Transliteration
לב. וְנִקְבְּצוּ לְפָנָיו כָּל-הַגּוֹיִם וְהִפְרִיד בֵּינֵיהֶם בֵּין אֶחָד לְאֶחָד כַּאֲשֶׁר יַפְרִיד הָרֹעֶה אֶת-הַכְּשָׂבִים מִבֵּין הָעִזִּים:

32. Ve•nik•be•tzoo le•fa•nav kol - ha•go•yim ve•hif•rid bey•ne•hem bein e•chad la•e•chad ka•a•sher yaf•rid ha•ro•eh et - hak•sa•vim mi•bein ha•ee•zim.

---

33. And he shall set the sheep on his right hand, but the goats on the left.

Greek/Transliteration
33. καὶ στήσει τὰ μὲν πρόβατα ἐκ δεξιῶν αὐτοῦ, τὰ δὲ ἐρίφια ἐξ εὐωνύμων.

33. kai steisei ta men probata ek dexion autou, ta de eriphya ex euonumon.

Hebrew/Transliteration
לג. וְהֶעֱמִיד אֶת-הַכְּשָׂבִים לִימִינוֹ וְאֶת-הָעִזִּים לִשְׂמֹאלוֹ:

33. Ve•he•e•mid et - hak•sa•vim li•mi•no ve•et - ha•ee•zim lis•mo•lo.

Rabbinic Jewish Commentary

These different situations plainly pre-signify how things will go with each, that one will be acquitted, and made happy, the other will be condemned, and become miserable. Agreeable to which the Jews say (c), that there is a right hand and a left hand with the Lord: they that are on the right hand, are such as have done well, and are לזכות, "for absolution"; and they that are on the left hand are criminals, and are לחובה, "for condemnation". Some think the allusion is to the two Scribes in the sanhedrim, who stood before the judges, one on the right hand, and the other on the left, and wrote the sentences; the one of those that were acquitted, and the other of those that were condemned (d),

(c) Jarchi in Gen. i. 26. Kimchi in 1 Kings xxii. 19. Lex. Cabalist. p. 132. Zohar in Numb. fol. 93. 4. (d) Misn. Sanhedrin, c. 4. sect. 3. Maimon. Hilch. Sanhedrin, c. 1. sect. 9. Moses Kotsensis Mitzvot Tora pr. affirm. 97.

---

34. Then shall the King say unto them on his right hand, Come, ye blessed of my Father, inherit the kingdom prepared for you from the foundation of the world:

Greek/Transliteration
34. Τότε ἐρεῖ ὁ βασιλεὺς τοῖς ἐκ δεξιῶν αὐτοῦ, Δεῦτε, οἱ εὐλογημένοι τοῦ πατρός μου, κληρονομήσατε τὴν ἡτοιμασμένην ὑμῖν βασιλείαν ἀπὸ καταβολῆς κόσμου.

34. Tote erei 'o basileus tois ek dexion autou, Deute, 'oi eulogeimenoi tou patros mou, kleironomeisate tein 'eitoimasmenein 'umin basileian apo kataboleis kosmou.

Hebrew/Transliteration
לד. אָז יֹאמַר הַמֶּלֶךְ לַאֲשֶׁר מִימִינוֹ בֹּאוּ בְרוּכֵי אָבִי וּרְשׁוּ אֶת-הַמַּלְכוּת אֲשֶׁר הִתְעַתְּדָה לָכֶם לְמִן-הִוָּסֵד עוֹלָם:

34. Az yo•mar ha•Me•lech la•a•sher miy•mi•no bo•oo be•roo•chey Avi oor•shoo et - ha•mal•choot asher hit•ate•da la•chem le•min - hi•va•sed o•lam.

Rabbinic Jewish Commentary
The Jews speak of the law being an inheritance for all Israel, from the six days of the creation; but a much more glorious one is here spoken of: nearer to this is what they say that Bathsheba was appointed to be David's wife from the day that the world was created; and add, but the mystery of the thing is, מלכותא דלעילא, "the kingdom that is above", which is called by her name. So in 2 Esdras, "the kingdom is already prepared for you": "Go, and ye shall receive: pray for few days unto you, that they may be shortened: the kingdom is already prepared for you: watch." (2 Esdras 2:13)

35. For I was an hungred, and ye gave me meat: I was thirsty, and ye gave me drink: I was a stranger, and ye took me in:

Greek/Transliteration
35. Ἐπείνασα γάρ, καὶ ἐδώκατέ μοι φαγεῖν· ἐδίψησα, καὶ ἐποτίσατέ με· ξένος ἤμην, καὶ συνηγάγετέ με·

35. Epeinasa gar, kai edokate moi phagein. edipseisa, kai epotisate me. xenos eimein, kai suneigagete me.

Hebrew/Transliteration
:לה. כִּי רָעַבְתִּי וַתַּאֲכִילֻנִי צָמֵאתִי וַתַּשְׁקוּנִי אֹרֵחַ הָיִיתִי וַתַּאַסְפוּנִי

35. Ki ra•av•ti va•ta•a•chi•loo•ni tza•me•ti va•tash•koo•ni o•re•ach ha•yi•ti va•ta•as•foo•ni.

Rabbinic Jewish Commentary
The Targumist (g) has a passage which may be compared with this: "Solomon said, by a spirit of prophecy from before the Lord; the Lord of the world shall say to all the righteous in the presence of everyone, go taste, with joy, thy bread which is returned unto thee, for thy bread which thou hast given to the poor and needy, who were hungry; and drink with a good heart the wine which is laid up for thee in paradise, instead of thy wine, which thou hast mingled for the poor and needy, who were thirsty; for, lo! now are thy works accepted before the Lord.
(g) Zohar in Eccl. ix. 7.

---

36. Naked, and ye clothed me: I was sick, and ye visited me: I was in prison, and ye came unto me.

Greek/Transliteration
36. γυμνός, καὶ περιεβάλετέ με· ἠσθένησα, καὶ ἐπεσκέψασθέ με· ἐν φυλακῇ ἤμην, καὶ ἤλθετε πρός με.

36. gumnos, kai periebalete me. eistheneisa, kai epeskepsasthe me. en phulakei eimein, kai eilthete pros me.

Hebrew/Transliteration
:לו. עֵרֹם וַתְּכַסֻּנִי חָלִיתִי וַתְּבַקְּרֻנִי עָצוּר בַּכֶּלֶא הָיִיתִי וַתָּבֹאוּ אֵלָי

36. Erom vat•cha•soo•ni cha•li•ti vat•vak•roo•ni atzoor ba•ke•le ha•yi•ti va•ta•vo•oo e•lai.

Rabbinic Jewish Commentary
Visiting of the sick was reckoned, by the Jews, a very worthy action: they speak great things of it, and as what will be highly rewarded hereafter, "Six things, (they say (h),) a man eats the fruit of them in this world, and there is a stable portion for him in the world to come: and the two first of them are, הכנסת אורחין "the taking in

522

of travellers", or "strangers", which is mentioned in the preceding verse, and ביקור חולים, "visiting the sick". One of their Rabbi's (i) says, "he that does not visit the sick, is as if he shed blood: says another, he that visits the sick is the cause of his living; and he that does not visit the sick, is the cause of his death: and, says a third, whoever visits the sick shall be preserved from the damnation of Gehenna.

---

37. Then shall the righteous answer him, saying, Lord, when saw we thee an hungred, and fed thee? or thirsty, and gave thee drink?

Greek/Transliteration
37. Τότε ἀποκριθήσονται αὐτῷ οἱ δίκαιοι, λέγοντες, Κύριε, πότε σὲ εἴδομεν πεινῶντα, καὶ ἐθρέψαμεν; Ἢ διψῶντα, καὶ ἐποτίσαμεν;

37. Tote apokritheisontai auto 'oi dikaioi, legontes, Kurie, pote se eidomen peinonta, kai ethrepsamen? Ei dipsonta, kai epotisamen?

Hebrew/Transliteration
לז. אָז יַעֲנוּ אֹתוֹ הַצַדִּיקִים לֵאמֹר אֲדֹנֵינוּ מָתַי רְאִינוּךָ רָעֵב וַנַשְׂבִּיעֶךָ אוֹ צָמֵא וַנַשְׁקֶךָ:

37. Az ya•a•noo o•to ha•tza•di•kim le•mor Ado•ney•noo ma•tai r`ee•noo•cha ra•ev va•nas•bi•e•cha oh tza•me va•nash•ke•cha?

---

38. When saw we thee a stranger, and took thee in? or naked, and clothed thee?

Greek/Transliteration
38. Πότε δέ σε εἴδομεν ξένον, καὶ συνηγάγομεν; Ἢ γυμνόν, καὶ περιεβάλομεν;

38. Pote de se eidomen xenon, kai suneigagomen? Ei gumnon, kai periebalomen?

Hebrew/Transliteration
לח. מָתַי רְאִינוּךָ אֹרֵחַ וַנְּאַסְפְךָ אוֹ עֵרֹם וַנְכַסְּךָ:

38. Ma•tai r`ee•noo•cha o•re•ach van•as•fe•cha oh erom van•cha•se•cha?

---

39. Or when saw we thee sick, or in prison, and came unto thee?

Greek/Transliteration
39. Πότε δέ σε εἴδομεν ἀσθενῆ, ἢ ἐν φυλακῇ, καὶ ἤλθομεν πρός σε;

39. Pote de se eidomen asthenei, ei en phulakei, kai eilthomen pros se?

Hebrew/Transliteration
לט. וּמָתַי רְאִינוּךָ חֹלֶה אוֹ עָצוּר בַּכֶּלֶא וַנָּבֹא אֵלֶיךָ:

39. Oo•ma•tai r`ee•noo•cha cho•le oh atzoor ba•ke•le va•na•vo e•le•cha?

---

40. And the King shall answer and say unto them, Verily I say unto you, Inasmuch as ye have done it unto one of the least of these my brethren, ye have done it unto me.

Greek/Transliteration
40. Καὶ ἀποκριθεὶς ὁ βασιλεὺς ἐρεῖ αὐτοῖς, Ἀμὴν λέγω ὑμῖν, ἐφ᾽ ὅσον ἐποιήσατε ἑνὶ τούτων τῶν ἀδελφῶν μου τῶν ἐλαχίστων, ἐμοὶ ἐποιήσατε.

40. Kai apokritheis 'o basileus erei autois, Amein lego 'umin, eph 'oson epoieisate 'eni touton ton adelphon mou ton elachiston, emoi epoieisate.

Hebrew/Transliteration
מ. וְהַמֶּלֶךְ יַעֲנֶה אֹתָם לֵאמֹר אָמֵן אֲנִי אֹמֵר לָכֶם אֶת אֲשֶׁר עֲשִׂיתֶם לְאֶחָד מֵאַחַי הַקְּטַנִּים הָאֵלֶּה לְנַפְשִׁי: עֲשִׂיתֶם.

40. Ve•ha•Me•lech ya•a•ne o•tam le•mor Amen ani o•mer la•chem et asher asi•tem le•e•chad me•a•chai ha•ke•ta•nim ha•e•le le•naf•shi asi•tem.

---

41. Then shall he say also unto them on the left hand, Depart from me, ye cursed, into everlasting fire, prepared for the devil and his angels:

Greek/Transliteration
41. Τότε ἐρεῖ καὶ τοῖς ἐξ εὐωνύμων, Πορεύεσθε ἀπ᾽ ἐμοῦ, οἱ κατηραμένοι, εἰς τὸ πῦρ τὸ αἰώνιον, τὸ ἡτοιμασμένον τῷ διαβόλῳ καὶ τοῖς ἀγγέλοις αὐτοῦ.

41. Tote erei kai tois ex euonumon, Poreuesthe ap emou, 'oi kateiramenoi, eis to pur to aionion, to 'eitoimasmenon to dyabolo kai tois angelois autou.

Hebrew/Transliteration
מא. אָז יֹאמַר גַּם - לַאֲשֶׁר מִשְּׂמֹאלוֹ לְכוּ מֵעָלַי אֲרוּרִים אֶל - אֵשׁ עוֹלָם אֲשֶׁר הִתְעַתְּדָה לְשָׂטָן וּלְמַלְאָכָיו:

41. Az yo•mar gam - la•a•sher mis•mo•lo le•choo me•a•lai a•roo•rim el - esh o•lam asher hit•ate•da le•Satan ool•mal•a•chav.

---

42. For I was an hungred, and ye gave me no meat: I was thirsty, and ye gave me no drink:

Greek/Transliteration
42. Ἐπείνασα γάρ, καὶ οὐκ ἐδώκατέ μοι φαγεῖν· ἐδίψησα, καὶ οὐκ ἐποτίσατέ με·

42. Epeinasa gar, kai ouk edokate moi phagein. edipseisa, kai ouk epotisate me.

Hebrew/Transliteration

מב. כִּי רָעַבְתִּי וְלֹא נְתַתֶּם לִי לֶאֱכֹל צָמֵאתִי וְלֹא נְתַתֶּם לִי לִשְׁתּוֹת:

42. Ki ra•av•ti ve•lo n`ta•tem li le•e•chol tza•me•ti ve•lo n`ta•tem li lish•tot.

---

43. I was a stranger, and ye took me not in: naked, and ye clothed me not: sick, and in prison, and ye visited me not.

Greek/Transliteration

43. ξένος ἤμην, καὶ οὐ συνηγάγετέ με· γυμνός, καὶ οὐ περιεβάλετέ με· ἀσθενής, καὶ ἐν φυλακῇ, καὶ οὐκ ἐπεσκέψασθέ με.

43. xenos eimein, kai ou suneigagete me. gumnos, kai ou periebalete me. astheneis, kai en phulakei, kai ouk epeskepsasthe me.

Hebrew/Transliteration

מג. אֹרֵחַ הָיִיתִי וְלֹא אֲסַפְתּוּנִי עֵרֹם וְלֹא כִסִּיתוּנִי חֹלֶה הָיִיתִי וְעָצוּר בַּכֶּלֶא וְלֹא בִקַּרְתּוּנִי:

43. O•re•ach ha•yi•ti ve•lo asaf•too•ni erom ve•lo chi•si•too•ni cho•le ha•yi•ti ve•a•tzoor ba•ke•le ve•lo vi•Kar•tooni.

---

44. Then shall they also answer him, saying, Lord, when saw we thee an hungred, or athirst, or a stranger, or naked, or sick, or in prison, and did not minister unto thee?

Greek/Transliteration

44. Τότε ἀποκριθήσονται καὶ αὐτοί, λέγοντες, Κύριε, πότε σὲ εἴδομεν πεινῶντα, ἢ διψῶντα, ἢ ξένον, ἢ γυμνόν, ἢ ἀσθενῆ, ἢ ἐν φυλακῇ, καὶ οὐ διηκονήσαμέν σοι;

44. Tote apokritheisontai kai autoi, legontes, Kurie, pote se eidomen peinonta, ei dipsonta, ei xenon, ei gumnon, ei asthenei, ei en phulakei, kai ou dieikoneisamen soi?

Hebrew/Transliteration

מד. וְהֵם גַּם-הֵם יַעֲנוּ אֵלָיו לֵאמֹר אֲדֹנֵינוּ מָתַי רְאִינוּךָ רָעֵב אוֹ צָמֵא אוֹ אֹרֵחַ אוֹ עָרֹם אוֹ חֹלֶה אוֹ עָצוּר בַּכֶּלֶא:וְלֹא בָאנוּ לְעֶזְרֶךָ

44. Ve•hem gam - hem ya•a•noo elav le•mor Ado•ney•noo ma•tai r`ee•noo•cha ra•ev oh tza•me oh o•re•ach oh arom oh cho•le oh atzoor ba•ke•le ve•lo va•noo le•ez•re•cha.

45. Then shall he answer them, saying, Verily I say unto you, Inasmuch as ye did it not to one of the least of these, ye did it not to me.

Greek/Transliteration
45. Τότε ἀποκριθήσεται αὐτοῖς, λέγων, Ἀμὴν λέγω ὑμῖν, ἐφ᾽ ὅσον οὐκ ἐποιήσατε ἑνὶ τούτων τῶν ἐλαχίστων, οὐδὲ ἐμοὶ ἐποιήσατε.

45. Tote apokritheisetai autois, legon, Amein lego 'umin, eph 'oson ouk epoieisate 'eni touton ton elachiston, oude emoi epoieisate.

Hebrew/Transliteration
מה. וְהוּא יַעֲנֶה אֹתָם לֵאמֹר אָמֵן אֲנִי אֹמֵר לָכֶם אֵת אֲשֶׁר לֹא עֲשִׂיתֶם לְאַחַד הַקְּטַנִּים הָאֵלֶּה לְנַפְשִׁי לֹא:עֲשִׂיתֶם

45. Ve•hoo ya•a•ne o•tam le•mor Amen ani o•mer la•chem et asher lo asi•tem le•a•chad ha•ke•ta•nim ha•e•le le•naf•shi lo asi•tem.

---

46. And these shall go away into everlasting punishment: but the righteous into life eternal.

Greek/Transliteration
46. Καὶ ἀπελεύσονται οὗτοι εἰς κόλασιν αἰώνιον· οἱ δὲ δίκαιοι εἰς ζωὴν αἰώνιον.

46. Kai apeleusontai 'outoi eis kolasin aionion. 'oi de dikaioi eis zoein aionion.

Hebrew/Transliteration
מו. וְכֵן יֵלְכוּ אֵלֶּה לְדִרְאוֹן עוֹלָם וְהַצַּדִּיקִים לְחַיֵּי עוֹלָם:

46. Ve•chen yel•choo ele le•dir•on o•lam ve•ha•tza•di•kim le•cha•yey o•lam.

Rabbinic Jewish Commentary
The messengers will be ordered to take and cast them into everlasting burnings; they will be driven by them into hell, the place appointed for them; where they shall endure ענש נצחי "everlasting punishment", as the Jews (p) also express it; and that both in soul and body, as the just desert of sin; which being committed against an infinite God, cannot be satisfied for by a finite creature; who therefore must ever bear the punishment of it, because its pollution and guilt will always remain.

The Jews have a saying (q) which agrees with this last clause, "the world to come is not made but for the righteous",

(p) Caphtor, fol. 113. 1. Shalshelet Hakabala, fol. 71. 1. (q) T. Bab. Yebamot, fol, 47. 1.

Matthew, Chapter 26

1. And it came to pass, when Jesus had finished all these sayings, he said unto his disciples,

Greek/Transliteration
1. Καὶ ἐγένετο ὅτε ἐτέλεσεν ὁ Ἰησοῦς πάντας τοὺς λόγους τούτους, εἶπεν τοῖς μαθηταῖς αὐτοῦ,

1. Kai egeneto 'ote etelesen 'o Yeisous pantas tous logous toutous, eipen tois matheitais autou,

Hebrew/Transliteration
א. וַיְהִי כַּאֲשֶׁר כִּלָּה יֵשׁוּעַ לְדַבֵּר כָּל-הַדְּבָרִים הָאֵלֶּה וַיֹּאמֶר אֶל-תַּלְמִידָיו:

1. Vay•hi ka•a•sher ki•la Yeshua le•da•ber kol - ha•d`va•rim ha•e•le va•yo•mer el - tal•mi•dav.

---

2. Ye know that after two days is the feast of the passover, and the Son of man is betrayed to be crucified.

Greek/Transliteration
2. Οἴδατε ὅτι μετὰ δύο ἡμέρας τὸ Πάσχα γίνεται, καὶ ὁ υἱὸς τοῦ ἀνθρώπου παραδίδοται εἰς τὸ σταυρωθῆναι.

2. Oidate 'oti meta duo 'eimeras to Pascha ginetai, kai 'o 'wios tou anthropou paradidotai eis to staurotheinai.

Hebrew/Transliteration
ב. הֲלֹא יְדַעְתֶּם כִּי אַחֲרֵי יוֹמַיִם יִהְיֶה הַפֶּסַח וְאֶת בֶּן-הָאָדָם יַסְגִּירוּ לְהִצָּלֵב:

2. Ha•lo ye•da•a•tem ki a•cha•rey yo•ma•yim yi•hee•ye ha•Pa•sach ve•et Ben - ha•adam yas•gi•roo le•hi•tza•lev.

Rabbinic Jewish Commentary

This was said on Tuesday, and on the Thursday following, the passover began. Yeshua speaks of this as a thing well known to the disciples, as it must be, since it always began on a certain day, the fourteenth of the month Nisan; which month answered to part of our March, and part of our April; and though there was very frequently an intercalation of a whole month in a year, made by the sanhedrim, to keep their festivals regularly in the proper season of the year; yet previous public notice was always given of this, either by fixing a paper upon the door of the sanhedrim (r), signifying such an intercalation made, which served for the inhabitants of Jerusalem; or by sending messengers with letters into all distant places (s), acquainting them with it.

(r) Targum in Cant. vii. 4. (s) Maimon Hilch. Kiddush Hachodesh, c. 4. sect. 17.

3. Then assembled together the chief priests, and the scribes, and the elders of the people, unto the palace of the high priest, who was called Caiaphas,

Greek/Transliteration
3. Τότε συνήχθησαν οἱ ἀρχιερεῖς καὶ οἱ γραμματεῖς καὶ οἱ πρεσβύτεροι τοῦ λαοῦ εἰς τὴν αὐλὴν τοῦ ἀρχιερέως τοῦ λεγομένου Καϊάφα,

3. Tote suneichtheisan 'oi archiereis kai 'oi grammateis kai 'oi presbuteroi tou laou eis tein aulein tou archiereos tou legomenou Kaiapha,

Hebrew/Transliteration
:ג. וַיִּקָּהֲלוּ רָאשֵׁי הַכֹּהֲנִים וְהַסּוֹפְרִים וְזִקְנֵי הָעָם אֶל-חֲצַר הַכֹּהֵן הַגָּדוֹל וּשְׁמוֹ קַיָּפָא

3. Va•yik•ha•loo ra•shey ha•ko•ha•nim ve•ha•sof•rim ve•zik•ney ha•am el - cha•tzar ha•ko•hen ha•ga•dol oo•sh`mo Ka•ya•fa.

---

4. And consulted that they might take Jesus by subtilty, and kill him.

Greek/Transliteration
4. καὶ συνεβουλεύσαντο ἵνα τὸν Ἰησοῦν δόλῳ κρατήσωσιν καὶ ἀποκτείνωσιν.

4. kai sunebouleusanto 'ina ton Yeisoun dolo krateisosin kai apokteinosin.

Hebrew/Transliteration
:ד. וַיִּוָּעֲצוּ לִתְפֹּשׂ אֶת-יֵשׁוּעַ בְּעָרְמָה וְלַהֲמִיתוֹ

4. Va•yi•va•a•tzoo lit•pos et - Yeshua be•or•ma ve•la•ha•mi•to.

---

5. But they said, Not on the feast day, lest there be an uproar among the people.

Greek/Transliteration
5. Ἔλεγον δέ, Μὴ ἐν τῇ ἑορτῇ, ἵνα μὴ θόρυβος γένηται ἐν τῷ λαῷ.

5. Elegon de, Mei en tei 'eortei, 'ina mei thorubos geneitai en to lao.

Hebrew/Transliteration
:ה. אַךְ אָמְרוּ לֹא בֶחָג פֶּן-תִּתְעוֹרֵר מְהוּמָה בָּעָם

5. Ach am•roo lo ve•chag pen - tit•o•rer me•hoo•ma ba•am.

Rabbinic Jewish Commentary
Upon mature deliberation, it was an agreed point with them, at least it was carried by a majority, that nothing of this kind should be attempted to be done on the feast day, on any of the days of the feast of passover, which was now at hand; though this was contrary to their common rules and usages: for, a person that sinned

presumptuously, and such an one they accounted Yeshua to be, they say,

(a) "they do not put him to death by the order of the sanhedrim of his own city, nor by the sanhedrim of Jabneh; but they bring him up to the great sanhedrim at Jerusalem, and keep him "until the feast", and put him to death, ברגל, "on a feast day"; as it is said, Deu_17:13, "and all the people shall hear and fear".

(a) Misn. Sanhedrin, c. 10. sect. 4. Maimon. Hilch. Memarim, c. 3. sect 8.

---

6. Now when Jesus was in Bethany, in the house of Simon the leper,

Greek/Transliteration
6. Τοῦ δὲ Ἰησοῦ γενομένου ἐν Βηθανίᾳ ἐν οἰκίᾳ Σίμωνος τοῦ λεπροῦ,

6. Tou de Yeisou genomenou en Beithania en oikia Simonos tou leprou,

Hebrew/Transliteration
‏:ו. וַיְהִי בִּהְיוֹת יֵשׁוּעַ בְּבֵית-עַנְיָה בְּבֵית שִׁמְעוֹן הַמְצֹרָע

6. Vay•hi bi•hee•yot Yeshua be•Veit - An•ya be•veit Shimon ham•tzo•ra.

---

7. There came unto him a woman having an alabaster box of very precious ointment, and poured it on his head, as he sat at meat.

Greek/Transliteration
7. προσῆλθεν αὐτῷ γυνὴ ἀλάβαστρον μύρου ἔχουσα βαρυτίμου, καὶ κατέχεεν ἐπὶ τὴν κεφαλὴν αὐτοῦ ἀνακειμένου.

7. proseilthen auto gunei alabastron murou echousa barutimou, kai katecheen epi tein kephalein autou anakeimenou.

Hebrew/Transliteration
‏:ז. וַתָּבֹא אֵלָיו אִשָּׁה וּבְיָדָהּ צְלֹחִית שֶׁמֶן יָקָר-עֵרֶךְ מְאֹד וַתִּצֹק עַל-רֹאשׁוֹ בְּמִסִבּוֹ

7. Va•ta•vo elav ee•sha oov•ya•da tz`lo•chit she•men ye•kar - e•rech me•od va•ti•tzok al - ro•sho bim•si•bo.

Rabbinic Jewish Commentary
and poured it on his head, as he sat at meat: which was usually done at festivals, or at any considerable entertainments, as at weddings.

"Says Rab, they "pour ointment on the heads of the Rabbi's"; (the gloss is, the women put ointment on the heads of the scholars;) says R. Papa to Abai, does the doctor speak of the ointment of the bridechamber? He replies, thou orphan, did not thy mother cause for thee, that "they poured out ointment on the heads of the doctors", at thy wedding? for lo! one of the Rabbi's got a wife for his son, in the

529

house of R. Bar Ula; and they say, that R. Bar Ula got a wife for his son in the house of one of the Rabbins, ודרדיג מישחא ארישא דרבנן, "and poured ointment on the head of the Rabbi's"(g) T. Bab. Cetubot, fol. 17. 2.

---

8. But when his disciples saw it, they had indignation, saying, To what purpose is this waste?

Greek/Transliteration
8. Ἰδόντες δὲ οἱ μαθηταὶ αὐτοῦ ἠγανάκτησαν, λέγοντες, Εἰς τί ἡ ἀπώλεια αὕτη;

8. Idontes de 'oi matheitai autou eiganakteisan, legontes, Eis ti 'ei apoleya 'autei?

Hebrew/Transliteration
ח. וַיִּרְאוּ הַתַּלְמִידִים וַיִּחַר לָהֶם לֵאמֹר עַל-מֶה נִבְלַע הַשֶּׁמֶן הַזֶּה:

8. Va•yir•oo ha•tal•mi•dim va•yi•char la•hem le•mor al - me niv•la ha•she•men ha•ze.

---

9. For this ointment might have been sold for much, and given to the poor.

Greek/Transliteration
9. Ἠδύνατο γὰρ τοῦτο τὸ μύρον πραθῆναι πολλοῦ, καὶ δοθῆναι πτωχοῖς.

9. Eidunato gar touto to muron pratheinai pollou, kai dotheinai ptochois.

Hebrew/Transliteration
ט. הֲלֹא טוֹב הָיָה לְתִתּוֹ בְּכֶסֶף רָב וְלַחֲלֹק מִכְרוֹ לָעֲנִיִּים:

9. Ha•lo tov ha•ya le•ti•to ve•che•sef rav ve•la•cha•lok mich•ro la•a•ni•yim.

---

10. When Jesus understood it, he said unto them, Why trouble ye the woman? for she hath wrought a good work upon me.

Greek/Transliteration
10. Γνοὺς δὲ ὁ Ἰησοῦς εἶπεν αὐτοῖς, Τί κόπους παρέχετε τῇ γυναικί; Ἔργον γὰρ καλὸν εἰργάσατο εἰς ἐμέ.

10. Gnous de 'o Yeisous eipen autois, Ti kopous parechete tei gunaiki? Ergon gar kalon eirgasato eis eme.

Hebrew/Transliteration
י. וַיֵּדַע יֵשׁוּעַ וַיֹּאמֶר אֲלֵיהֶם לָמָּה-זֶּה תַּלְאוּ אֶת-הָאִשָּׁה הֲלֹא טוֹב גְּמָלָתְנִי:

10. Va•ye•da Yeshua va•yo•mer aley•hem la•ma - ze tal•oo et - ha•ee•sha ha•lo tov ge•ma•lat•ni.

---

11. For ye have the poor always with you; but me ye have not always.

Greek/Transliteration
11. Πάντοτε γὰρ τοὺς πτωχοὺς ἔχετε μεθ᾽ ἑαυτῶν, ἐμὲ δὲ οὐ πάντοτε ἔχετε.

11. Pantote gar tous ptochous echete meth 'eauton, eme de ou pantote echete.

Hebrew/Transliteration
יא. כִּי אֶת-הָעֲנִיִּים תִּמְצְאוּ לִפְנֵיכֶם תָּמִיד וְאוֹתִי לֹא תִמְצְאוּ תָּמִיד לִפְנֵיכֶם:

11. Ki et - ha•a•ni•yim tim•tze•oo lif•ney•chem ta•mid ve•o•ti lo tim•tze•oo ta•mid lif•ney•chem.

Rabbinic Jewish Commentary
Yeshua seems to have respect to Deu_15:11, and which, agreeably to the sense of the Jews, refers to the times of the Messiah: for they say (h), "there is no difference between this world (this present time) and the times of the Messiah, but the subduing of kingdoms only; as it is said, Deu_15:11, "for the poor shall never cease out of the land": the gloss on it is, from hence it may be concluded, that therefore, לעולם יש עניות, "for ever there will be poverty, and riches" (h) T. Bab. Sabbat, fol. 63. 1.

---

12. For in that she hath poured this ointment on my body, she did it for my burial.

Greek/Transliteration
12. Βαλοῦσα γὰρ αὕτη τὸ μύρον τοῦτο ἐπὶ τοῦ σώματός μου, πρὸς τὸ ἐνταφιάσαι με ἐποίησεν.

12. Balousa gar 'autei to muron touto epi tou somatos mou, pros to entaphyasai me epoieisen.

Hebrew/Transliteration
יב. כִּי בַּאֲשֶׁר יָצְקָה הַשֶּׁמֶן הַזֶּה עַל-גְּוִיָּתִי הֱכִינָה אֹתִי לִקְבֻרָתִי:

12. Ki ba•a•sher yatz•ka ha•she•men ha•ze al - ge•vi•ya•ti he•chi•na o•ti lik•voo•ra•ti.

Rabbinic Jewish Commentary
The Jews used to embalm their dead, to show their constant respect to the deceased, and their belief of the resurrection; at least not only used to wash them, but anoint them with oil; for so runs one of their canons (i): "they do all things necessary to the dead, (i.e. on the sabbath day,) סכין, "they anoint him": that is, as

Bartenora adds, "with oil"; and they wash him;" (i) Misn. Sabbat, c. 23. sect. 5.

---

13. Verily I say unto you, Wheresoever this gospel shall be preached in the whole world, there shall also this, that this woman hath done, be told for a memorial of her.

Greek/Transliteration
13. Ἀμὴν λέγω ὑμῖν, ὅπου ἐὰν κηρυχθῇ τὸ εὐαγγέλιον τοῦτο ἐν ὅλῳ τῷ κόσμῳ, λαληθήσεται καὶ ὃ ἐποίησεν αὕτη, εἰς μνημόσυνον αὐτῆς.

13. Amein lego 'umin, 'opou ean keiruchthei to euangelion touto en 'olo to kosmo, laleitheisetai kai 'o epoieisen 'autei, eis mneimosunon auteis.

Hebrew/Transliteration
יג. אָמֵן אֲנִי אֹמֵר לָכֶם בְּכָל-מָקוֹם אֲשֶׁר תִּשָּׁמַע הַבְּשׂוֹרָה הַזֹּאת בְּכָל-הָאָרֶץ יְסֻפַּר גַּם אֲשֶׁר עָשְׂתָה הִיא לָהּ לְזִכָּרוֹן:

13. Amen ani o•mer la•chem be•chol - ma•kom asher ti•sha•ma ha•be•so•ra ha•zot be•chol - ha•a•retz ye•soo•par gam asher as•ta hee la le•zi•ka•ron.

---

14. Then one of the twelve, called Judas Iscariot, went unto the chief priests,

Greek/Transliteration
14. Τότε πορευθεὶς εἷς τῶν δώδεκα, ὁ λεγόμενος Ἰούδας Ἰσκαριώτης, πρὸς τοὺς ἀρχιερεῖς,

14. Tote poreutheis 'eis ton dodeka, 'o legomenos Youdas Yskarioteis, pros tous archiereis,

Hebrew/Transliteration
יד. אָז קָם אֶחָד מִשְׁנֵים הֶעָשָׂר וּשְׁמוֹ יְהוּדָה אִישׁ-קְרִיּוֹת וַיֵּלֶךְ אֶל-רָאשֵׁי הַכֹּהֲנִים:

14. Az kam e•chad mi•sh`neim he•a•sar oo•sh`mo Yehooda Eesh - K`ri•yot va•ye•lech el - ra•shey ha•ko•ha•nim.

Rabbinic Jewish Commentary
The Jews, in their blasphemous account of Yeshua (l), say as much: they own, that Judas, or Juda, as they call him, offered to betray him into the hands of the wise men, saying to them, almost in the words expressed in the following verse,

"if you will hearken unto me, אמסור אותו, "I will deliver him into your hands tomorrow"; (l) Toldos Jesu, p. 16.

15. And said unto them, What will ye give me, and I will deliver him unto you? And they covenanted with him for thirty pieces of silver.

Greek/Transliteration
15. εἶπεν, Τί θέλετέ μοι δοῦναι, κἀγὼ ὑμῖν παραδώσω αὐτόν; Οἱ δὲ ἔστησαν αὐτῷ τριάκοντα ἀργύρια.

15. eipen, Ti thelete moi dounai, kago 'umin paradoso auton? 'Oi de esteisan auto tryakonta argurya.

Hebrew/Transliteration
טו. וַיֹּאמֶר מַה-תֹּאמְרוּ לָתֶת-לִי כִּי אַסְגִּיר אֹתוֹ בְּיֶדְכֶם וַיִּשְׁקְלוּ-לוֹ שְׁלֹשִׁים כָּסֶף:

15. Va•yo•mer ma - tom•roo la•tet - li ki as•gir o•to be•yed•chem va•yish•ke•loo – lo sh`lo•shim ka•sef.

Rabbinic Jewish Commentary
The silver shekel had on one side stamped upon it the pot of manna, or, as others think, "a censer", or incense cup, with these words around it, in Samaritan letters, "shekel Israel", "the shekel of Israel"; and, on the other, "Aaron's rod" budding, with this inscription about it, "Jerusalem Hakedushah", "Jerusalem the holy" (o). As for the weight and value of it, R. Gedaliah says (p), we know by tradition that the holy shekel weighs 320 grains of barley of pure silver; and the same writer observes (q), that the "selah", or holy shekel, is four "denarii", or pence; that is, Roman pence, each being of the value of seven pence halfpenny of our money: and to this agrees what Josephus (r) says, that a "shekel" is a coin of the Hebrews, which contains four Attic drachms, or drams; and an Attic dram is of the same value with a Roman penny: so that one of these shekels was worth about "half a crown"; and it usually weighed half an ounce, as not only some Jewish writers affirm, who profess to have seen them, and weighed them themselves, as Jarchi (s), Gerundensis (t), Abarbinel (u), and Gedaliah ben Jechaiah (w); but other writers also, as Masius (x) Arias Montanus (y), Waserus (z) and Bishop Cumberland. Now thirty shekels of silver were the price of a servant, Exo_21:32. So (b) Maimonides observes, that the

"atonement of "servants", whether great or small, whether male or female, the fixed sum in the law is "thirty shekels of good silver", whether "the servant" is worth an hundred pound, or whether he is not worth but a farthing,"

(o) Waser ib. & Ar. Montan. Ephron. sive de Siclo in Jud. Antiq. p. 126. Brerewood de ponder. & pret. vet. num. c. 1. (p) Shaishelet Hakabala, fol. (q) Ib. (r) Antiq. l. 3. c. 8. sect. 2. (s) Perush in Exod. xxi. 32. (t) Ad fin. Expos. in Pentateuch. (u) Comment. in 1 Reg. 7. fol. 221. 2. (w) Shalshelet Hahohala, fol. 72. 2. (x) In Joshua, 7. 21. p. 135. (y) De Siclo, ut supra. (in Jud. Antiq. p. 126) (z) De numis Heb. l. 2. c. 3. (b) Hilch. Niske Mammon. c. 11. sect. 1.

16. And from that time he sought opportunity to betray him.

Greek/Transliteration
16. Καὶ ἀπὸ τότε ἐζήτει εὐκαιρίαν ἵνα αὐτὸν παραδῷ.

16. Kai apo tote ezeitei eukairian 'ina auton parado.

Hebrew/Transliteration
:טז. וּמִן-הָעֵת הַהִיא בִּקֵּשׁ-לוֹ תֹאֲנָה לְהַסְגִּיר אֹתוֹ

16. Oo•min - ha•et ha•hee bi•kesh - lo to•a•na le•has•gir o•to.

---

17. Now the first day of the feast of unleavened bread the disciples came to Jesus, saying unto him, Where wilt thou that we prepare for thee to eat the passover?

Greek/Transliteration
17. Τῇ δὲ πρώτῃ τῶν ἀζύμων προσῆλθον οἱ μαθηταὶ τῷ Ἰησοῦ, λέγοντες αὐτῷ, Ποῦ θέλεις ἑτοιμάσομέν σοι φαγεῖν τὸ Πάσχα;

17. Tei de protei ton azumon proseilthon 'oi matheitai to Yeisou, legontes auto, Pou theleis 'etoimasomen soi phagein to Pascha?

Hebrew/Transliteration
יז. וְלִפְנֵי הָרִאשׁוֹן לְחַג הַמַּצּוֹת בָּאוּ הַתַּלְמִידִים לִפְנֵי יֵשׁוּעַ לֵאמֹר אֵיפֹה תִרְצֶה כִּי-נָכִין לְךָ לֶאֱכֹל
:אֶת-הַפָּסַח

17. Ve•lif•ney ha•ri•shon le•chag ha•ma•tzot ba•oo ha•tal•mi•dim lif•ney Yeshua le•mor ey•fo tir•tze ki - na•chin le•cha le•e•chol et - ha•Pa•sach?

Rabbinic Jewish Comemntary
The time of killing the passover was after the middle of the day; and it is said (e) that "if they killed it before the middle of the day it was not right; and they did not kill it till after the evening sacrifice, and after they had offered the evening incense; and after they had trimmed the lamps, they began to slay the passovers, or paschal lambs, unto the end of the day; and if they slayed after the middle of the day, before the evening sacrifice, it was right."

The reason of this was, because the lamb was to be slain between the two evenings; the first of which began at noon, as soon as ever the day declined: and this was not done privately, but in the temple; for thus it is (f) affirmed,

"they do not kill the passover but in the court, as the rest of the holy things."

The time and manner of killing the lamb, and by whom, of the sprinkling of the blood, and of their flaying it, and taking out the fat, and burning it on the altar, may be seen in the Misna (g).

e) Ib. sect. 4. Moses Kotsensis Mitavot Tora pr. affirm. 39. (f) Maimon. lb. sect. 3. (g) Pesachim, c. 5. sect. 1, 2, 3, 4, 5, 6, 9, 10.

---

18. And he said, Go into the city to such a man, and say unto him, The Master saith, My time is at hand; I will keep the passover at thy house with my disciples.

Greek/Transliteration
18. Ὁ δὲ εἶπεν, Ὑπάγετε εἰς τὴν πόλιν πρὸς τὸν δεῖνα, καὶ εἴπατε αὐτῷ, Ὁ διδάσκαλος λέγει, Ὁ καιρός μου ἐγγύς ἐστιν· πρὸς σὲ ποιῶ τὸ Πάσχα μετὰ τῶν μαθητῶν μου.

18. 'O de eipen, 'Upagete eis tein polin pros ton deina, kai eipate auto, 'O didaskalos legei, 'O kairos mou engus estin. pros se poio to Pascha meta ton matheiton mou.

Hebrew/Transliteration
יח. וַיֹּאמֶר לְכוּ הָעִירָה לִפְלֹנִי אַלְמֹנִי וְהִגַּדְתֶּם לוֹ כֹּה אָמַר רַבֵּנוּ הֵן עִתִּי בָאָה וְהִנְנִי לָחֹג אֶת-חַג - הַפֶּסַח עִם:תַּלְמִידַי בְּבֵיתֶךָ

18. Va•yo•mer le•choo ha•ee•ra lif•lo•ni al•mo•ni ve•hi•ga•de•tem lo ko amar Ra•be•noo hen ee•ti va•ah ve•hi•ne•ni la•chog et - chag ha•Pe•sach eem - tal•mi•dai be•vey•te•cha.

Rabbinic Jewish Commentary
I will keep the passover at thy house with my disciples; not with him and his family, but with his disciples, who were a family, and a society of themselves, and a sufficient number to eat the passover together; for there might be two companies eating their distinct passovers in one house, and even in one room: concerning which is the following rule,

שתי חבורות שהיו אוכלים בבית אחד, "two societies that eat in one house"; the one turn their faces this way and eat, and the other turn their faces that way and eat, and an heating vessel (in which they heat the water to mix with the wine) in the middle; and when the servant stands to mix, he shuts his mouth, and turns his face till he comes to his company, and eats; and the bride turns her face and eats (o)."

(o) Misn. Pesachim, c. 7. sect. 13.

---

19. And the disciples did as Jesus had appointed them; and they made ready the passover.

Greek/Transliteration
19. Καὶ ἐποίησαν οἱ μαθηταὶ ὡς συνέταξεν αὐτοῖς ὁ Ἰησοῦς, καὶ ἡτοίμασαν τὸ Πάσχα.

19. Kai epoieisan 'oi matheitai 'os sunetaxen autois 'o Yeisous, kai 'eitoimasan to Pascha.

Hebrew/Translitration
יט. וַיַּעֲשׂוּ הַתַּלְמִידִים כַּאֲשֶׁר צִוָּה אֹתָם יֵשׁוּעַ וַיָּכִינוּ אֶת-הַפָּסַח

19. Va•ya•a•soo ha•tal•mi•dim ka•a•sher tzi•va o•tam Yeshua va•ya•chi•noo et -ha•Pa•sach.

---

20. Now when the even was come, he sat down with the twelve.

Greek/Transliteration
20. Ὀψίας δὲ γενομένης ἀνέκειτο μετὰ τῶν δώδεκα.

20. Opsias de genomeneis anekeito meta ton dodeka.

Hebrew/Transliteration
כ. וַיְהִי בָּעֶרֶב וַיֵּשֶׁב בִּמְסִבּוֹ עִם-שְׁנֵים עָשָׂר

20. Vay•hi ba•a•rev va•ye•shev bim•si•bo eem - sh`neym asar.

Rabbinic Jewish Commentary
The second evening, when the sun was set, and it was dark, and properly night; for

"on the evenings of the passovers near the Minchah, a man might not eat עד שתחשך, "until it was dark" (p)." This was according to the rule, Exo_12:8.

(q) "they do not kill the passover for a single man, according to the words of R. Judah, though R. Jose permits it: yea, though the society consists of an hundred, if they cannot eat the quantity of an olive, they do not kill for them: nor do they make a society of women, servants, and little ones?"

(u) "it is the way of servants to eat standing; but here (in the passover) to eat, מסובין, "sitting", or "lying along", because they (the Israelites) went out of bondage to liberty. Says R. Simon, in the name of R. Joshua ben Levi, that which a man is obliged to in the passover, though it be but the quantity of an olive, he must eat it, מוסב, "lying along".

This custom was so constantly and uniformly observed at the passover, that it is taken particular notice of in the declaration, or showing forth of the passover by the master of the family, when he says (x), "how different is this night from all other nights". and among the many things he mentions, this is one; "in all other nights we eat either sitting, or lying along; that is, which way we please, but this night all of us מסובין, "lie along".

(p) Ib. c. 10. sect. 1. (q) Ib. c. 8. sect. 7. (u) T. Hieros. Pesach. fol. 37. 2. (x) Maimon ib. c. 8. 2. Haggadah Shel Pesach. p. 5.

21. And as they did eat, he said, Verily I say unto you, that one of you shall betray me.

Greek/Transliteration
21. Καὶ ἐσθιόντων αὐτῶν εἶπεν, Ἀμὴν λέγω ὑμῖν ὅτι εἷς ἐξ ὑμῶν παραδώσει με.

21. Kai esthionton auton eipen, Amein lego 'umin 'oti 'eis ex 'umon paradosei me.

Hebrew/Transliteration
:כא. וּבְעוֹד הֵם אֹכְלִים וַיֹּאמַר אָמֵן אֲנִי אֹמֵר לָכֶם כִּי-אֶחָד מִכֶּם יַסְגִּיר אֹתִי

21. Oov•od hem och•lim va•yo•mar Amen ani o•mer la•chem ki - e•chad mi•kem yas•gir oti.

Rabbinic Jewish Commentary
The passover lamb, the unleavened bread, and bitter herbs: he said it was usual, whilst they were thus engaged, to discourse much about the reason and design of this institution. What they talked of may be learnt from what follows (y):

"it is an affirmative precept of the law, to declare the signs and wonders which were done to our fathers in Egypt, on the night of the fifteenth of Nisan, according to Exo_13:3, "remember this day"

(y) Maimon. ib. c. 7. sect. 1, 2, 3, 4, 5. Vid. c. 8. 2, 3, 4, 5. & Haggadah Shel. Pesach. p. 5, 6, 7, 8.

---

22. And they were exceeding sorrowful, and began every one of them to say unto him, Lord, is it I?

Greek/Transliteration
22. Καὶ λυπούμενοι σφόδρα ἤρξαντο λέγειν αὐτῷ ἕκαστος αὐτῶν, Μήτι ἐγώ εἰμι, κύριε;

22. Kai lupoumenoi sphodra eirxanto legein auto 'ekastos auton, Meiti ego eimi, kurie?

Hebrew/Transliteration
:כב. וַיִּתְעַצְּבוּ אֶל-לִבָּם עַד-מְאֹד וַיָּחֵלּוּ לֵאמֹר לוֹ הַאֲנִי הוּא אֲדֹנִי

22. Va•yit•atz•voo el - li•bam ad - me•od va•ya•che•loo le•mor lo ha•a•ni hoo Adoni?

---

23. And he answered and said, He that dippeth his hand with me in the dish, the same shall betray me.

Greek/Transliteration
23. Ὁ δὲ ἀποκριθεὶς εἶπεν, Ὁ ἐμβάψας μετ' ἐμοῦ ἐν τῷ τρυβλίῳ τὴν χεῖρα, οὗτός με παραδώσει.

23. 'O de apokritheis eipen, 'O embapsas met emou en to trublio tein cheira, 'outos me paradosei.

Hebrew/Transliteration
כג: וַיַּעַן וַיֹּאמֶר הַטֹּבֵל אֶת-יָדוֹ עִמִּי בַּקְּעָרָה הוּא הַמַּסְגִּיר אֹתִי

23. Va•ya•an va•yo•mar ha•to•vel et - ya•do ee•mi ba•k`a•ra hoo ha•mas•gir o•ti.

Rabbinic Jewish Commentary
This seems to refer to the dipping of the unleavened bread, or bitter herbs, both, into the sauce called "Charoseth", which the Jews (z) say,

"was made of figs, nuts, almonds, and other fruits; to which they added apples; all which they bruised in a mortar, and mixed with vinegar; and put spices into it, calamus and cinnamon, in the form of small long threads, in remembrance of the straw; and it was necessary it should be: thick, in memory of the clay."

The account Maimonides (a) gives of it is,

"the "Charoseth" is a precept from the words of the Scribes, in remembrance of the clay in which they served in Egypt; and how did they make it? They took dates, or berries, or raisins, and the like, and stamped them, and put vinegar into them, and seasoned them with spices, as clay in straw, and brought it upon the table, in the night of the passover."

And in this he says, the master of the family dipped both the herbs, and the unleavened bread (b), and that both separately and conjunctly; for he says (c), that

"he rolled up the unleavened bread and bitter herbs together, ומטבל and dipped them in the Charoseth."

"Even my close friend in whom I trusted, Who ate my bread, Has lifted up his heel against me." Psalm_41:9

(z) Bartenora in Misn. Pesach. c. 10. sect. 3. Vid. Maimon. & Yom Tob, in ib. & Piske Tos. Pesach. art. 322. (a) Hilch. Chametz Umetzah, c. 7. sect. 11. (b) Ib. c. 8. sect. 2. 8. (c)

---

24. The Son of man goeth as it is written of him: but woe unto that man by whom the Son of man is betrayed! it had been good for that man if he had not been born.

Greek/Transliteration

24. Ὁ μὲν υἱὸς τοῦ ἀνθρώπου ὑπάγει, καθὼς γέγραπται περὶ αὐτοῦ· οὐαὶ δὲ τῷ ἀνθρώπῳ ἐκείνῳ, δι' οὗ ὁ υἱὸς τοῦ ἀνθρώπου παραδίδοται· καλὸν ἦν αὐτῷ εἰ οὐκ ἐγεννήθη ὁ ἄνθρωπος ἐκεῖνος.

24. 'O men 'wios tou anthropou 'upagei, kathos gegraptai peri autou. ouai de to anthropo ekeino, di 'ou 'o 'wios tou anthropou paradidotai. kalon ein auto ei ouk egenneithei 'o Anthropos ekeinos.

Hebrew/Transliteration

כד. הֵן בֶּן-הָאָדָם הֹלֵךְ כַּכָּתוּב עָלָיו אַךְ אוֹי לָאִישׁ הַהוּא אֲשֶׁר יַסְגִּיר אֶת בֶּן-הָאָדָם בְּיַד מְבַקְשֵׁי נַפְשׁוֹ טוֹב הָיָה:לָאִישׁ הַהוּא אִם-לֹא יָצָא מֵרָחֶם

24. Hen Ben - ha•adam ho•lech ka•ka•toov alav ach oy la•eesh ha•hoo asher yas•gir et Ben - ha•adam be•yad me•vak•shey naf•sho tov ha•ya la•eesh ha•hoo eem - lo ya•tza me•ra•chem.

Rabbinic Jewish Commentary

it had been good for that man if he had not been born. This is a Rabbinical phrase, frequently used in one form or another; sometimes thus; as it is said (f) of such that speak false and lying words, and regard not the glory of their Creator, דלא טב לון ייתון לעלמא, it would have been better for them they had never come into the world; and so of any other, notorious sinner, it is at other times said (g), טב ליה דלא אברי, or (h), נוח לו שלא נברא, "it would have been better for him if he had not been created"; signifying, that it is better to have no being at all, than to be punished with everlasting destruction; and which was the dreadful case of Judas, who fell by his transgression, and went to his own place.

(f) Zohar in Gen. fol. 41. 1. Vid. Misn. Chagiga, c. 2. sect. 1. T. Bab Chagiga, fol. 16. 1. (g) Zohar in Gen. fol, 46. 4. & in Exod. fol. 1. 4. & 36. 3. & 62. 3. & 66. 3. & 105. 4. & 106. 1. (h) T. Hieros. Sabbat, fol. 3. 2. T. Bab. Beracot, fol. 17. 1. & Erubin, fol. 13. 2. Midrash Kobelet, fol. 79. 1.

---

25. Then Judas, which betrayed him, answered and said, Master, is it I? He said unto him, Thou hast said.

Greek/Transliteration

25. Ἀποκριθεὶς δὲ Ἰούδας ὁ παραδιδοὺς αὐτὸν εἶπεν, Μήτι ἐγώ εἰμι, ῥαββί; Λέγει αὐτῷ, Σὺ εἶπας.

25. Apokritheis de Youdas 'o paradidous auton eipen, Meiti ego eimi, 'rabbi? Legei auto, Su eipas.

Hebrew/Transliteration

כה. וִיהוּדָה הַמַּסְגִּיר אֹתוֹ עָנָה וְאָמַר הַאֲנִי הוּא רַבִּי וַיֹּאמֶר אֵלָיו אַתָּה אָמָרְתָּ:

25. Vi•Y`hoo•da ha•mas•gir o•to ana ve•a•mar ha•a•ni hoo Rabbi? Va•yo•mer elav ata amar•ta.

Rabbinic Jewish Commentary
he said unto him, thou hast said: that is, it is as thou hast said; thou hast said right, thou art the man; a way of speaking used, when what is asked is assented to as truth: thus it being

"said to a certain person, is Rabbi dead? He replied to them, אתון אמריתון, "ye have said"; and they rent their clothes (i)." Taking it for granted, by that answer, that so it was. (i) T. Hieros Kilaim, fol. 32. 2.

---

26. And as they were eating, Jesus took bread, and blessed it, and brake it, and gave it to the disciples, and said, Take, eat; this is my body.

Greek/Transliteration
26. Ἐσθιόντων δὲ αὐτῶν, λαβὼν ὁ Ἰησοῦς τὸν ἄρτον, καὶ εὐχαριστήσας, ἔκλασεν καὶ ἐδίδου τοῖς μαθηταῖς, καὶ εἶπεν, Λάβετε, φάγετε· τοῦτό ἐστιν τὸ σῶμά μου.

26. Esthionton de auton, labon 'o Yeisous ton arton, kai eucharisteisas, eklasen kai edidou tois matheitais, kai eipen, Labete, phagete. touto estin to soma mou.

Hebrew/Transliteration
:כו. וּבְאָכְלָם וַיִּקַּח יֵשׁוּעַ אֶת-הַלֶּחֶם וַיְבָרֶךְ וַיִּבְצַע וַיִּתֵּן לַתַּלְמִידִים וַיֹּאמֶר קְחוּ אִכְלוּ זֶה הוּא בְּשָׂרִי

26. Oov•och•lam va•yi•kach Yeshua et - ha•le•chem vay•va•rech va•yiv•tza va•yi•ten la•tal•mi•dim va•yo•mar ke•choo eech•loo ze hoo be•sa•ri.

Rabbinic Jewish Commentary
Though this supper is distinct from the "passover", and different from any ordinary meal, yet there are allusions to both in it, and to the customs of the Jews used in either; as in this first circumstance, of "taking" the bread: for he that asked a blessing upon bread, used to take it into his hands; and it is a rule (l), that "a man does not bless, עד שיתפוס הלחם בידו, "until he takes the bread into his hand", that all may see that he blesses over it. So it was common with the Jews, to ask a blessing on their bread: the form in which they did it was this (m):

"Blessed art thou, O Lord, our God, the king of the world, that produceth bread out of the earth."

(n)"if they sit to eat, everyone blesses for himself, but if they lie along, אחד מברך לכלם, "one blesses for them all".

Moreover, they always blessed, before they brake: "Says Rabba (o), he blesses, and after that he breaks."

540

The Jews in the eating of their passover used to say (r) of the unleavened bread, הא לחמא דעניא, this is "the bread of affliction", which our fathers ate in the land of Egypt.

Again, elsewhere (t) it is said, "they bring a table furnished, and on it the bitter herbs and other greens, and the unleavened bread, and the sauce,

וגופו של כבש הפסח "and the body of the paschal lamb".

And a little further (u), "he recites the blessing, blessed art thou O Lord, &c. for the eating of the passover, and he eats, מגופו של פסח, "of the body of the passover".

(l) Levush hattecheleth Num. 167. sect. 3. & Shlchan Aruch in Buxtorf. Exercit. de Coena Dominic. Thes. 45. (m) Haggadah Shel. Pesach. fol. 249. 2. Ed. Basil. Misn. Beracot, c. 6. sect. 1. (n) Ib. sect. 6. T. Bab. Beracot, fol. 42. 2. & 43. 1. (o) T. Bab. Berncot, fol. 39. 2. (r) Haggadah Shel Pesach, p. 4. Ed. Rittangel. fol. 242. 2. Ed. Basil. (t) Maimon. Chametz Umetzah, c. 8. sect. 1. (u) Ib. sect. 7.

---

27. And he took the cup, and gave thanks, and gave it to them, saying, Drink ye all of it;

Greek/Transliteration
27. Καὶ λαβὼν τὸ ποτήριον, καὶ εὐχαριστήσας, ἔδωκεν αὐτοῖς, λέγων, Πίετε ἐξ αὐτοῦ πάντες·

27. Kai labon to poteirion, kai eucharisteisas, edoken autois, legon, Piete ex autou pantes.

Hebrew/Transliteration
:כז. וַיִּקַּח אֶת-הַכּוֹס וַיְבָרֶךְ וַיִּתֵּן לָהֶם לֵאמֹר שְׁתוּ כֻלְּכֶם מִמֶּנָּה

27. Va•yi•kach et - ha•kos vay•va•rech va•yi•ten la•hem le•mor sh`too chool•chem mi•me•na.

Rabbinic Jewish Commentary
For the Jews blessed, or gave thanks for their wine, as well as for their food, and generally did it in this form (w):

"Blessed art thou, O Lord, our God, the king of the world, who hast created the "fruit of the vine".

(y) "When wine is brought to them after food, if there is but that cup there, the house of Shammai say, מברך על היין, "he blesses", or gives thanks "for the wine", and after that gives thanks for the food: the house of Hillell say, he gives thanks for the food, and after that gives thanks for the wine.

It should be further known, that the wine at the passover, and so what Yeshua used at his supper, was red, "Says R. Jeremiah (z) it is commanded to perform this duty, ביין אדום "with red wine".

And elsewhere it is said (a), "that it is necessary, that there should be in it (the wine) taste and look. The gloss on it is, שיהא אדום, "that it should be red"

(w) Haggadah Shel Pesach. fol. 241. 1. (x) Vid. Misn. Beracot, c. 6. sect. 1. 6. (y) Ib. c. 8. sect. 8. (z) T. Hieros. Pesach. fol. 37. 3. & Sabbat, fol. 11. 1. (a) T. Bab. Pesach. fol. 108. 2. & R. Samuel ben Meir in ib.

---

28. For this is my blood of the new testament, which is shed for many for the remission of sins.

Greek/Transliteration
28. τοῦτο γάρ ἐστιν τὸ αἷμά μου, τὸ τῆς καινῆς διαθήκης, τὸ περὶ πολλῶν ἐκχυνόμενον εἰς ἄφεσιν ἁμαρτιῶν.

28. touto gar estin to 'aima mou, to teis kaineis dyatheikeis, to peri pollon ekchunomenon eis aphesin 'amartion.

Hebrew/Transliteration
‏כח. כִּי זֶה הוּא דָמִי דַם-הַבְּרִית הַחֲדָשָׁה הַשָּׁפוּךְ בְּעַד רַבִּים לִסְלִיחַת חַטֹּאתָם:

28. Ki ze hoo da•mi dam - ha•b`rit ha•cha•da•sha ha•sha•fooch be•ad ra•bim lis•li•chat cha•to•tam.

---

29. But I say unto you, I will not drink henceforth of this fruit of the vine, until that day when I drink it new with you in my Father's kingdom.

Greek/Transliteration
29. Λέγω δὲ ὑμῖν ὅτι οὐ μὴ πίω ἀπ᾽ ἄρτι ἐκ τούτου τοῦ γεννήματος τῆς ἀμπέλου, ἕως τῆς ἡμέρας ἐκείνης ὅταν αὐτὸ πίνω μεθ᾽ ὑμῶν καινὸν ἐν τῇ βασιλείᾳ τοῦ πατρός μου.

29. Lego de 'umin 'oti ou mei pio ap arti ek toutou tou genneimatos teis ampelou, 'eos teis 'eimeras ekeineis 'otan auto pino meth 'umon kainon en tei basileia tou patros mou.

Hebrew/Transliteration
‏כט. וַאֲנִי מַגִּיד לָכֶם כִּי מֵעַתָּה לֹא אֶשְׁתֶּה עוֹד מִפְּרִי הַגֶּפֶן הַזֶּה עַד הַיּוֹם הַהוּא אֲשֶׁר חָדָשׁ אֶשְׁתֵּהוּ עִמָּכֶם:בְּמַלְכוּת אָבִי

29. Va•a•ni ma•gid la•chem ki me•a•ta lo esh•te od mip•ri ha•ge•fen ha•ze ad ha•yom ha•hoo asher cha•dash esh•te•hoo ee•ma•chem be•mal•choot Avi.

Rabbinic Jewish Commentary

The Jews often express the joys of the world to come, by such like figurative phrases: they make mention of, יין דעלמא דאתי, "the wine of the world to come" (g); and of שכר רוחני, "a spiritual drink", in the last days, which is called the world to come (h): and so they explain (i) after this manner, Isa_64:4. "Neither hath the eye seen, O God"., זה יין, "this is the wine", which is kept in the grapes from the six days of the creation; of which they often speak in their writings (k).

(g) Zohar in Lev. fol. 17. 2. (h) Tzeror Hammor, fol. 3. 4. En Israel, fol. 30. 1. (i) T. Bab. Berncot, fol. 34. 2, & Sanhed. fol. 99. 1. (k) Targum in Cant. viii. 2. Zohar in Gen. fol. 81. 4. Tzeror Hammor, fol. 30. 3.

---

30. And when they had sung an hymn, they went out into the mount of Olives.

Greek/Transliteration
30. Καὶ ὑμνήσαντες ἐξῆλθον εἰς τὸ ὄρος τῶν Ἐλαιῶν.

30. Kai 'umneisantes exeilthon eis to oros ton Elaion.

Hebrew/Transliteration
ל. וַיִּקְרְאוּ אֶת-הַהַלֵּל וַיֵּצְאוּ אֶל-הַר הַזֵּיתִים:

30. Va•yik•re•oo et - ha•ha•lel va•yetz•oo el - Har ha•Zey•tim.

Rabbinic Jewish Commentary

And when they had sung an hymn,.... The "Hallell", which the Jews were obliged to sing on the night of the passover; for the passover, they say (l), was טעון הלל, "bound to an hymn". This "Hallell", or song of praise, consisted of six Psalms, the 113th, 114th, 115th, 116th, 117th, and 118th (m): now this they did not sing all at once, but in parts. Just before the drinking of the second cup and eating of the lamb, they sung the first part of it, which contained the 113th and 114th Psalms; and on mixing the fourth and last cup, they completed the "Hallell", by singing the rest of the Psalms, beginning with the 115th Psalm, and ending with the 118th; and said over it, what they call the "blessing of the song", which was Psa_145:10., and they might, if they would, mix a fifth cup, but that they were not obliged to, and say over it the "great Hallell", or "hymn", which was the 136th Psalm (n). Now the last part of the "Hallell", Yeshua deferred to the close of his supper; there being many things in it pertinent to him, and proper on this occasion, particularly Psa_115:1, and the Jews themselves say (o), that חבלי של משיח, "the sorrows of the Messiah" are contained in this part.

(l) Misn. Pesach. c. 9. 3. T. Bab. Pesach. fol. 95. 1, 2. (m) Seder Tephillot, fol. 101, &c. Ed. Amstelod. (n) Maimon. Hilch. Chametz Umetzah, c. 8. sect. 5. 10. (o) T. Bab. Pesachim, fol. 118. 1.

31. Then saith Jesus unto them, All ye shall be offended because of me this night: for it is written, I will smite the shepherd, and the sheep of the flock shall be scattered abroad.

Greek/Transliteration

31. Τότε λέγει αὐτοῖς ὁ Ἰησοῦς, Πάντες ὑμεῖς σκανδαλισθήσεσθε ἐν ἐμοὶ ἐν τῇ νυκτὶ ταύτῃ· γέγραπται γάρ, Πατάξω τὸν ποιμένα, καὶ διασκορπισθήσεται τὰ πρόβατα τῆς ποίμνης.

31. Tote legei autois 'o Yeisous, Pantes 'umeis skandalistheisesthe en emoi en tei nukti tautei. gegraptai gar, Pataxo ton poimena, kai dyaskorpistheisetai ta probata teis poimneis.

Hebrew/Transliteration

לא. אָז אָמַר אֲלֵיהֶם יֵשׁוּעַ הֵן כֻּלְּכֶם תִּכָּשְׁלוּ בִי בַּלַּיְלָה הַזֶּה כִּי כָתוּב אַכֶּה אֶת-הָרֹעֶה וּתְפוּצֶיןָ הַצֹּאן:

31. Az amar aley•hem Yeshua hen kool•chem ti•kash•loo vi ba•lai•la ha•ze ki ka•toov a•ke et - ha•ro•eh oot•foo•tzei•na ha•tzon.

Rabbinic Jewish Commentary

I will smite the shepherd, and the sheep of the flock shall be scattered. This text is miserably perverted by the Jewish writers; though they all agree, that by "the shepherd", is meant some great person, as a king; so the Targum renders it, "kill the king, and the princes shall be scattered": one (u) of them says, that a wicked king of Moab is designed; another (w), a king of the Ishmaelites, or of the Turks; and a third (x), that any, and every king of the Gentiles is meant; a fourth says (y), it is a prophecy of the great wars that shall be in all the earth, in the days of Messiah ben Joseph; and a fifth (z), after having taken notice of other senses, mentions this as the last: that "the words "my shepherd, and the man my fellow", in the former part of the verse, are to be understood of Messiah, the son of Joseph; and because he shall be slain in the wars of the nations, therefore the Lord will whet his glittering sword against the nations, to take vengeance on them; and on this account says, "awake, O sword! for my shepherd, and for the man my fellow".

(u) R. Sol. Jarchi, in Zech. xiii. 7. (w) Isaac Chizzuk Emuna, par. 1. c. 37. p. 310. (x) R. David Kirachi, in Zech. xiii. 7. (y) R. Aben Ezra in ib. (z) Abarbitnel, Mashmia Jeshua, fol. 74. 4.

---

32. But after I am risen again, I will go before you into Galilee.

Greek/Transliteration

32. Μετὰ δὲ τὸ ἐγερθῆναί με, προάξω ὑμᾶς εἰς τὴν Γαλιλαίαν.

32. Meta de to egertheinai me, proaxo 'umas eis tein Galilaian.

Hebrew/Transliteration
לב. וְאַחֲרֵי תְקוּמָתִי מִן-הַמֵּתִים אֵלֵךְ לִפְנֵיכֶם הַגָּלִילָה:

32. Ve•a•cha•rey te•koo•ma•ti min - ha•me•tim e•lech lif•ney•chem ha•Ga•li•la.

---

33. Peter answered and said unto him, Though all men shall be offended because of thee, yet will I never be offended.

Greek/Transliteration
33. Ἀποκριθεὶς δὲ ὁ Πέτρος εἶπεν αὐτῷ, Εἰ πάντες σκανδαλισθήσονται ἐν σοί, ἐγὼ δὲ οὐδέποτε σκανδαλισθήσομαι.

33. Apokritheis de 'o Petros eipen auto, Ei pantes skandalistheisontai en soi, ego de oudepote skandalistheisomai.

Hebrew/Translieration
לג. וַיַּעַן פֶּטְרוֹס וַיֹּאמֶר אֵלָיו אַף אִם-כֻּלָּם יִכָּשְׁלוּ בְךָ אֲנִי לֹא אֶכָּשֵׁל לְעוֹלָם:

33. Va•ya•an Petros va•yo•mer elav af eem - koo•lam yi•kash•loo ve•cha ani lo eka•shel le•o•lam.

---

34. Jesus said unto him, Verily I say unto thee, That this night, before the cock crow, thou shalt deny me thrice.

Greek/Transliteration
34. Ἔφη αὐτῷ ὁ Ἰησοῦς, Ἀμὴν λέγω σοι ὅτι ἐν ταύτῃ τῇ νυκτί, πρὶν ἀλέκτορα φωνῆσαι, τρὶς ἀπαρνήσῃ με.

34. Ephei auto 'o Yeisous, Amein lego soi 'oti en tautei tei nukti, prin alektora phoneisai, tris aparneisei me.

Hebrew/Transliteration
לד. וַיֹּאמֶר אֵלָיו יֵשׁוּעַ אָמֵן אֲנִי אֹמֵר לָךְ כִּי בַּלַּיְלָה הַזֶּה טֶרֶם יִקְרָא הַתַּרְנְגֹל תְּכַחֶשׁ-בִּי שָׁלֹשׁ פְּעָמִים:

34. Va•yo•mer elav Yeshua Amen ani o•mer lach ki ba•lai•la ha•ze te•rem yik•ra ha•tar•ne•gol te•cha•chesh - bi sha•losh pe•a•mim.

Rabbinic Jewish Commentary
So cock crowing and midnight are distinguished by the Jews, who say (b),

"that on all other days they remove the ashes from the altar, בקריאת הגבר, "at cock crowing", or near unto it, whether before or after; but on the day of atonement,

מהצות, "at midnight": and who also speak of the cocks crowing a first and second, and even a third time (c), "Says R. Shila, he that begins his journey before cock crowing, his blood be upon his head. R. Josiah says, he may not proceed עד שישוב, "until he repeats"; that is, until he crows twice: and there are, who say, until he trebles it, or crows a third time: of what do they speak? of a middling one, i.e. which neither crows too soon, nor too late.

(b) Misn. Yoma, c. 1. sect. 8. (c) T. Bab. Yoma, fol. 21. 1.

---

35. Peter said unto him, Though I should die with thee, yet will I not deny thee. Likewise also said all the disciples.

Greek/Transliteration
35. Λέγει αὐτῷ ὁ Πέτρος, Κἂν δέῃ με σὺν σοὶ ἀποθανεῖν, οὐ μή σε ἀπαρνήσωμαι. Ὁμοίως δὲ καὶ πάντες οἱ μαθηταὶ εἶπον.

35. Legei auto 'o Petros, Kan deei me sun soi apothanein, ou mei se aparneisomai. 'Omoios de kai pantes 'oi matheitai eipon.

Hebrew/Transliteration
לה. וַיֹּאמֶר אֵלָיו פֶּטְרוֹס אַף אִם-יִהְיֶה עָלַי לָמוּת אִתְּךָ כַּחַשׁ לֹא אֲכַחֶשׁ-בָּךְ וְכֵן דִּבְּרוּ גַם כָּל-הַתַּלְמִידִים:

35. Va•yo•mer elav Petros af eem - yi•hee•ye a•lai la•moot eet•cha ka•chash lo a•cha•chesh - bach ve•chen dib•roo gam kol - ha•tal•mi•dim.

---

36. Then cometh Jesus with them unto a place called Gethsemane, and saith unto the disciples, Sit ye here, while I go and pray yonder.

Greek/Transliteration
36. Τότε ἔρχεται μετ᾽ αὐτῶν ὁ Ἰησοῦς εἰς χωρίον λεγόμενον Γεθσημανῆ, καὶ λέγει τοῖς μαθηταῖς, Καθίσατε αὐτοῦ, ἕως οὗ ἀπελθὼν προσεύξωμαι ἐκεῖ.

36. Tote erchetai met auton 'o Yeisous eis chorion legomenon Gethseimanei, kai legei tois matheitais, Kathisate autou, 'eos 'ou apelthon proseuxomai ekei.

Hebrew/Transliteration
לו. וְאַחֲרֵי-כֵן בָּא יֵשׁוּעַ עִמָּהֶם אֶל-הַמָּקוֹם הַנִּקְרָא גַּת שְׁמָנִים וַיֹּאמֶר אֶל-תַּלְמִידָיו שְׁבוּ-לָכֶם פֹּה עַד-כִּי אֵלֵךְ:וְהִתְפַּלַּלְתִּי שָׁמָּה

36. Ve•a•cha•rey - chen ba Yeshua ee•ma•hem el - ha•ma•kom ha•nik•ra Gat - Sh`ma•nim va•yo•mer el - tal•mi•dav sh`voo - la•chem po ad - ki e•lech ve•hit•pa•lal•ti sha•ma.

Rabbinic Jewish Commentary

Its etymology is very differently given: some read, and explain it, as if it was גי שמנים, "a valley of fatness", or "of olives", as it is called in Munster's Hebrew Gospel; see Isa_28:1; others as if it was גי דסימני, "a valley of signs", or a very famous valley; so Mount Sinai is called (e), הר סימנאי, "Harsemanai", the mountain of signs:

but, to take notice of no more; the true reading and signification of it is, שמני גת, "an olive press", or a press for olives: so we read (f) of a chamber in the temple which is called "the chamber", בית שמניא, "Beth Semania", or "Bethsemani", where they put their wine and oil for temple service.

(e) T. Bab. Sabbat, fol. 89. 1. (f) T. Bab. Yoma, fol. 16. 1.

---

37. And he took with him Peter and the two sons of Zebedee, and began to be sorrowful and very heavy.

Greek/Transliteration

37. Καὶ παραλαβὼν τὸν Πέτρον καὶ τοὺς δύο υἱοὺς Ζεβεδαίου, ἤρξατο λυπεῖσθαι καὶ ἀδημονεῖν.

37. Kai paralabon ton Petron kai tous duo 'wious Zebedaiou, eirxato lupeisthai kai adeimonein.

Hebrew/Transliteration

לז. וַיִּקַּח אִתּוֹ אֶת-פֶּטְרוֹס וְאֶת-שְׁנֵי בְנֵי זַבְדִּי וַיָּחֶל לְהִתְיַפַּח וּלְהִשּׁוֹמֵם:

37. Va•yi•kach ee•to et - Petros ve•et - sh`ney v`ney Zav•di va•ya•chel le•hit•ya•pe•ach ool•hi•sho•mem.

---

38. Then saith he unto them, My soul is exceeding sorrowful, even unto death: tarry ye here, and watch with me.

Greek/Transliteration

38. Τότε λέγει αὐτοῖς ὁ Ἰησοῦς, Περίλυπός ἐστιν ἡ ψυχή μου ἕως θανάτου· μείνατε ὧδε καὶ γρηγορεῖτε μετ᾽ ἐμοῦ.

38. Tote legei autois 'o Yeisous, Perilupos estin 'ei psuchei mou 'eos thanatou. meinate 'ode kai greigoreite met emou.

Hebrew/Transliteration

לח. וַיֹּאמֶר אֲלֵיהֶם נַפְשִׁי מָרָה-לִּי מְאֹד עַד-מָוֶת עִמְדוּ בָזֶה וְשִׁקְדוּ עִמִּי:

38. Va•yo•mer aley•hem naf•shi ma•ra - li me•od ad - ma•vet eem•doo va•ze ve•shik•doo ee•mi.

39. And he went a little further, and fell on his face, and prayed, saying, O my Father, if it be possible, let this cup pass from me: nevertheless not as I will, but as thou wilt.

Greek/Transliteration
39. Καὶ προσελθὼν μικρόν, ἔπεσεν ἐπὶ πρόσωπον αὐτοῦ προσευχόμενος καὶ λέγων, Πάτερ μου, εἰ δυνατόν ἐστιν, παρελθέτω ἀπ᾽ ἐμοῦ τὸ ποτήριον τοῦτο· πλὴν οὐχ ὡς ἐγὼ θέλω, ἀλλ᾽ ὡς σύ.

39. Kai proselthon mikron, epesen epi prosopon autou proseuchomenos kai legon, Pater mou, ei dunaton estin, pareltheto ap emou to poteirion touto. plein ouch 'os ego thelo, all 'os su.

Hebrew/Transliteration
לט. וַיַּעֲבֹר הָלְאָה מְעַט-מִזְעָר וַיִּפֹּל עַל-פָּנָיו וַיִּתְפַּלֵּל וַיֹּאמַר אָבִי אִם-יִתָּכֵן הַדָּבָר תַּעֲבָר-נָא הַכּוֹס הַזֹּאת מֵעָלָי:אַךְ לֹא כִרְצוֹנִי כִּי אִם-כַּאֲשֶׁר רָצִיתָ אָתָּה

39. Va•ya•a•vor hal•ah me•at - miz•ar va•yi•pol al - pa•nav va•yit•pa•lel va•yo•mar Avi eem - yi•ta•chen ha•da•var ta•a•vor - na ha•kos ha•zot me•a•lai ach lo chir•tzo•ni ki eem - ka•a•sher ra•tzi•ta ata.

Rabbinic Jewish Commentary
This was a prayer gesture used when a person was in the utmost perplexity. The account the Jews give of it, is this (g),

כשנופלין על פניהם, "when they fall upon their faces", they do not stretch out their hands and their feet, but incline on their sides.

This was not to be done by any person, or at any time; the rules are these (h): "no man is accounted fit ליפול על פניו, "to fall upon his face", but he that knows in himself that he is righteous, as Joshua.

(g) Gloss. in T. Bab. Beracot, fol. 34. 2. (h) Maimon. Hilch. Tephilla, c. 5. sect. 14, 15.

---

40. And he cometh unto the disciples, and findeth them asleep, and saith unto Peter, What, could ye not watch with me one hour?

Greek/Transliteration
40. Καὶ ἔρχεται πρὸς τοὺς μαθητάς, καὶ εὑρίσκει αὐτοὺς καθεύδοντας, καὶ λέγει τῷ Πέτρῳ, Οὕτως οὐκ ἰσχύσατε μίαν ὥραν γρηγορῆσαι μετ᾽ ἐμοῦ;

40. Kai erchetai pros tous matheitas, kai 'euriskei autous katheudontas, kai legei to Petro, 'Outos ouk ischusate mian 'oran greigoreisai met emou?

Hebrew/Transliteration
מ. וַיָּבֹא אֶל-הַתַּלְמִידִים וַיִּמְצָאֵם יְשֵׁנִים וַיֹּאמֶר אֶל-פֶּטְרוֹס הֲאִם לֹא-הָיָה לְאֵל יֶדְכֶם לִשְׁקֹד עִמִּי שָׁעָה אֶחָת:

40. Va•ya•vo el - ha•tal•mi•dim va•yim•tza•em ye•she•nim va•yo•mer el - Petros ha•eem lo - ha•ya le•el yed•chem lish•kod ee•mi sha•ah e•chat?

41. Watch and pray, that ye enter not into temptation: the spirit indeed is willing, but the flesh is weak.

Greek/Transliteration
41. Γρηγορεῖτε καὶ προσεύχεσθε, ἵνα μὴ εἰσέλθητε εἰς πειρασμόν· τὸ μὲν πνεῦμα πρόθυμον, ἡ δὲ σὰρξ ἀσθενής.

41. Greigoreite kai proseuchesthe, 'ina mei eiseltheite eis peirasmon. to men pneuma prothumon, 'ei de sarx astheneis.

Hebrew/Transliteration
מא. שִׁקְדוּ וְהִתְפַּלְלוּ פֶּן-תָּבֹאוּ לְמַסָּה הֵן הָרוּחַ חֲפֵצָה אַךְ הַבָּשָׂר רָפֶה:

41. Shik•doo ve•hit•pa•le•loo pen - ta•vo•oo le•ma•sa hen ha•roo•ach cha•fe•tza ach ha•ba•sar ra•fe.

---

42. He went away again the second time, and prayed, saying, O my Father, if this cup may not pass away from me, except I drink it, thy will be done.

Greek/Transliteration
42. Πάλιν ἐκ δευτέρου ἀπελθὼν προσηύξατο, λέγων, Πάτερ μου, εἰ οὐ δύναται τοῦτο τὸ ποτήριον παρελθεῖν ἀπ᾽ ἐμοῦ, ἐὰν μὴ αὐτὸ πίω, γενηθήτω τὸ θέλημά σου.

42. Palin ek deuterou apelthon proseiuxato, legon, Pater mou, ei ou dunatai touto to poteirion parelthein ap emou, ean mei auto pio, geneitheito to theleima sou.

Hebrew/Transliteration
מב. וַיּוֹסֶף וַיֵּלֶךְ-לוֹ שֵׁנִית וַיִּתְפַּלֵּל וַיֹּאמַר אָבִי אִם זֹאת לֹא תִתָּכֵן לַעֲבֹר בִּלְתִּי אִם-שָׁתִיתִי אוֹתָהּ יֵעָשֶׂה רְצוֹנֶךָ:

42. Va•yo•sef va•ye•lech - lo she•nit va•yit•pa•lel va•yo•mar Avi eem zot lo ti•ta•chen la•a•vor bil•tee eem - sha•ti•ti o•ta ye•a•se r`tzo•ne•cha.

---

43. And he came and found them asleep again: for their eyes were heavy.

Greek/Transliteration
43. Καὶ ἐλθὼν εὑρίσκει αὐτοὺς πάλιν καθεύδοντας, ἦσαν γὰρ αὐτῶν οἱ ὀφθαλμοὶ βεβαρημένοι.

43. Kai elthon 'euriskei autous palin katheudontas, eisan gar auton 'oi ophthalmoi bebareimenoi.

Hebrew/Transliteration
מג. וַיּוֹסֶף וַיָּשָׁב וַיִּמְצָאֵם יְשֵׁנִים עוֹד כִּי עֵינֵיהֶם הָיוּ כְבֵדוֹת:

43. Va•yo•sef va•ya•shov va•yim•tza•em ye•she•nim od ki ey•ne•hem ha•yoo ke•ve•dot.

---

44. And he left them, and went away again, and prayed the third time, saying the same words.

Greek/Transliteration
44. Καὶ ἀφεὶς αὐτοὺς ἀπελθὼν πάλιν προσηύξατο ἐκ τρίτου, τὸν αὐτὸν λόγον εἰπών.

44. Kai apheis autous apelthon palin proseiuxato ek tritou, ton auton logon eipon.

Hebrew/Transliteration
מד. וַיַּעֲזֹב אֹתָם וַיֵּלֶךְ עוֹד וַיִּתְפַּלֵּל שְׁלִישִׁית וַיְדַבֵּר כַּדְּבָרִים הָאֵלֶּה:

44. Va•ya•azov o•tam va•ye•lech od va•yit•pa•lel sh`li•sheet va•y`da•ber ka•d`va•rim ha•e•le.

---

45. Then cometh he to his disciples, and saith unto them, Sleep on now, and take your rest: behold, the hour is at hand, and the Son of man is betrayed into the hands of sinners.

Greek/Transliteration
45. Τότε ἔρχεται πρὸς τοὺς μαθητὰς αὐτοῦ, καὶ λέγει αὐτοῖς, Καθεύδετε τὸ λοιπὸν καὶ ἀναπαύεσθε· ἰδού, ἤγγικεν ἡ ὥρα, καὶ ὁ υἱὸς τοῦ ἀνθρώπου παραδίδοται εἰς χεῖρας ἁμαρτωλῶν.

45. Tote erchetai pros tous matheitas autou, kai legei autois, Katheudete to loipon kai anapauesthe. idou, eingiken 'ei 'ora, kai 'o 'wios tou anthropou paradidotai eis cheiras 'amartolon.

Hebrew/Transliteration
מה. אָז שָׁב אֶל-תַּלְמִידָיו וַיֹּאמֶר אֲלֵיהֶם תְּנוּ שֵׁנָה לְעֵינֵיכֶם וּמְנוּחָה הִנֵּה בָאָה הַשָּׁעָה וּבֶן-הָאָדָם נִסְגַּר בִּידֵי:חַטָּאִים

45. Az shav el - tal•mi•dav va•yo•mer aley•hem t`noo she•na le•ey•ne•chem oom•noo•cha hee•ne ba•ah ha•sha•ah oo•Ven - ha•adam nis•gar biy•dey cha•ta•eem.

46. Rise, let us be going: behold, he is at hand that doth betray me.

Greek/Transliteration
46. Ἐγείρεσθε, ἄγωμεν. Ἰδού, ἤγγικεν ὁ παραδιδούς με.

46. Egeiresthe, agomen. Ydou, eingiken 'o paradidous me.

Hebrew/Transliteration
מו. קוּמוּ וְנֵלֵכָה הִנֵּה הַמַּסְגִּיר אֹתִי הֹלֵךְ וְקָרֵב:

46. Koo•moo ve•ne•le•cha hee•ne ha•mas•gir o•ti ho•lech ve•ka•rev.

---

47. And while he yet spake, lo, Judas, one of the twelve, came, and with him a great multitude with swords and staves, from the chief priests and elders of the people.

Greek/Transliteration
47. Καὶ ἔτι αὐτοῦ λαλοῦντος, ἰδού, Ἰούδας εἷς τῶν δώδεκα ἦλθεν, καὶ μετ᾽ αὐτοῦ ὄχλος πολὺς μετὰ μαχαιρῶν καὶ ξύλων, ἀπὸ τῶν ἀρχιερέων καὶ πρεσβυτέρων τοῦ λαοῦ.

47. Kai eti autou lalountos, idou, Youdas 'eis ton dodeka eilthen, kai met autou ochlos polus meta machairon kai xulon, apo ton archiereon kai presbuteron tou laou.

Hebrew/Transliteration
מז. עוֹדֶנּוּ מְדַבֵּר וְהִנֵּה יְהוּדָה אֶחָד מִשְׁנֵים הֶעָשָׂר בָּא וְעִמּוֹ הָמוֹן-רַב בַּחֲרָבוֹת וּבְמַטּוֹת מֵאֵת רָאשֵׁי הַכֹּהֲנִים:וְזִקְנֵי הָעָם

47. O•de•noo me•da•ber ve•hee•ne Yehooda e•chad mi•sh`neim he•a•sar ba ve•ee•mo ha•mon - rav ba•cha•ra•vot oov•ma•tot me•et ra•shey ha•ko•ha•nim ve•zik•ney ha•am.

---

48. Now he that betrayed him gave them a sign, saying, Whomsoever I shall kiss, that same is he: hold him fast.

Greek/Transliteration
48. Ὁ δὲ παραδιδοὺς αὐτὸν ἔδωκεν αὐτοῖς σημεῖον, λέγων, Ὃν ἂν φιλήσω, αὐτός ἐστιν· κρατήσατε αὐτόν.

48. 'O de paradidous auton edoken autois seimeion, legon, 'On an phileiso, autos estin. krateisate auton.

Hebrew/Transliteration
מח. וְהַמַּסְגִּיר אֹתוֹ נָתַן לָהֶם אוֹת לֵאמֹר הָאִישׁ אֲשֶׁר אֲנַשֶּׁק-לוֹ זֶה הוּא תִּפְשׂוּ אֹתוֹ:

48. Ve•ha•mas•gir o•to na•tan la•hem ot le•mor ha•eesh asher ana•shek - lo ze hoo tif•soo o•to.

---

49. And forthwith he came to Jesus, and said, Hail, master; and kissed him.

Greek/Transliteration
49. Καὶ εὐθέως προσελθὼν τῷ Ἰησοῦ εἶπεν, Χαῖρε, ῥαββί· καὶ κατεφίλησεν αὐτόν.

49. Kai eutheos proselthon to Yeisou eipen, Chaire, 'rabbi. kai katephileisen auton.

Hebrew/Transliteration
מט. וַיְמַהֵר וַיִּגַּשׁ אֶל-יֵשׁוּעַ וַיֹּאמֶר הֲשָׁלוֹם לְךָ רַבִּי וַיִּשָּׁקֵהוּ:

49. Vay•ma•her va•yi•gash el - Yeshua va•yo•mer ha•sha•lom le•cha Rabbi va•yi•sha•ke•hoo.

Rabbinic Jewish Commentary
and said, hail, master; and kissed him. Just as Joab asked Amasa of his health, and took him by the beard to kiss him, and smote him under the fifth rib, 2Sa_20:9. The salutation he gave him was wishing him all health, prosperity, and happiness. The Syriac version renders it, "peace, Rabbi"; and the Persic, "peace be upon thee, Rabbi"; which was the very form of salutation the disciples of the wise men gave to their Rabbi's,

"Says (n) Aba bar Hona, in the name of R. Jochanan, in what form is the salutation of a disciple to his master? רבי.

שלום עליך, "peace be upon thee, Rabbi". (n) T. Hieros. Shebuot. fol. 34. 1.

---

50. And Jesus said unto him, Friend, wherefore art thou come? Then came they, and laid hands on Jesus, and took him.

Greek/Transliteration
50. Ὁ δὲ Ἰησοῦς εἶπεν αὐτῷ, Ἑταῖρε, ἐφ' ᾧ πάρει; Τότε προσελθόντες ἐπέβαλον τὰς χεῖρας ἐπὶ τὸν Ἰησοῦν, καὶ ἐκράτησαν αὐτόν.

50. 'O de Yeisous eipen auto, 'Etaire, eph 'o parei? Tote proselthontes epebalon tas cheiras epi ton Yeisoun, kai ekrateisan auton.

Hebrew/Transliteration
נ. וַיֹּאמֶר אֵלָיו יֵשׁוּעַ רֵעִי עַל-מָה בָּאתָ וְהֵם נָפְלוּ עַל-יֵשׁוּעַ וַיִּשְׁלְחוּ בוֹ אֶת-יְדֵיהֶם וַיִּתְפְּשֻׂהוּ:

50. Va•yo•mer elav Yeshua re•ee al - me ba•ta ve•hem naf•loo al - Yeshua va•yish•le•choo bo et - ye•dey•hem va•yit•pe•soo•hoo.

---

51. And, behold, one of them which were with Jesus stretched out his hand, and drew his sword, and struck a servant of the high priest's, and smote off his ear.

Greek/Transliteration
51. Καὶ ἰδού, εἷς τῶν μετὰ Ἰησοῦ, ἐκτείνας τὴν χεῖρα, ἀπέσπασεν τὴν μάχαιραν αὐτοῦ, καὶ πατάξας τὸν δοῦλον τοῦ ἀρχιερέως ἀφεῖλεν αὐτοῦ τὸ ὠτίον.

51. Kai idou, 'eis ton meta Yeisou, ekteinas tein cheira, apespasen tein machairan autou, kai pataxas ton doulon tou archiereos apheilen autou to otion.

Hebrew/Transliteration
נא. וְהִנֵּה אֶחָד מֵאַנְשֵׁי יֵשׁוּעַ שָׁלַח אֶת-יָדוֹ וַיִּשְׁלֹף אֶת-חַרְבּוֹ וַיַּךְ אֶת-עֶבֶד הַכֹּהֵן הַגָּדוֹל וַיְקַצֵּץ אֶת-אָזְנוֹ:

51. Ve•hee•ne e•chad me•an•shey Yeshua sha•lach et - ya•do va•yish•lof et - char•bo va•yach et - eved ha•ko•hen ha•ga•dol vay•ka•tzetz et - oz•no.

---

52. Then said Jesus unto him, Put up again thy sword into his place: for all they that take the sword shall perish with the sword.

Greek/Transliteration
52. Τότε λέγει αὐτῷ ὁ Ἰησοῦς, Ἀπόστρεψόν σου τὴν μάχαιραν εἰς τὸν τόπον αὐτῆς· πάντες γὰρ οἱ λαβόντες μάχαιραν ἐν μαχαίρᾳ ἀποθανοῦνται.

52. Tote legei auto 'o Yeisous, Apostrepson sou tein machairan eis ton topon auteis. pantes gar 'oi labontes machairan en machaira apothanountai.

Hebrew/Transliteration
נב. וַיֹּאמֶר אֵלָיו יֵשׁוּעַ הָשֵׁב חַרְבְּךָ אֶל-מְקוֹמָהּ כִּי כָל-תֹּפְשֵׂי חֶרֶב בַּחֶרֶב יֹאבֵדוּ:

52. Va•yo•mer elav Yeshua ha•shev char•be•cha el - me•ko•ma ki kol - tof•sey che•rev ba•che•rev yo•ve•doo.

---

53. Thinkest thou that I cannot now pray to my Father, and he shall presently give me more than twelve legions of angels?

Greek/Transliteration
53. Ἢ δοκεῖς ὅτι οὐ δύναμαι ἄρτι παρακαλέσαι τὸν πατέρα μου, καὶ παραστήσει μοι πλείους ἢ δώδεκα λεγεῶνας ἀγγέλων;

53. Ei dokeis 'oti ou dunamai arti parakalesai ton patera mou, kai parasteisei moi pleious ei dodeka legeonas angelon?

Hebrew/Transliteration
נג. אוֹ הֲתֹאמַר בְּלִבְּךָ כִּי לֹא אוּכַל לִשְׁאֹל מֵאֵת אָבִי אֲשֶׁר יִשְׁלַח לִי גַּם-עַתָּה רַב מִשְׁנַיִם עָשָׂר גְּדוּדִים מַלְאָכִים:

53. Oh ha•to•mar be•lib•cha ki lo oo•chal lish•ol me•et Avi asher yish•lach li gam – ata rav mi•sh`neim asar g`doo•dim mal•a•chim?

---

54. But how then shall the scriptures be fulfilled, that thus it must be?

Greek/Transliteration
54. Πῶς οὖν πληρωθῶσιν αἱ γραφαί, ὅτι οὕτως δεῖ γενέσθαι;

54. Pos oun pleirothosin 'ai graphai, 'oti 'outos dei genesthai?

Hebrew/Transliteration
נד. אֲבָל אֵיךְ יִכֹּנוּ הַכְּתוּבִים כִּי כָל-אֵלֶּה תִּקְרֶאנָה:

54. Aval eych yi•ko•noo ha•k`too•vim ki chol - ele tik•re•na.

TaNaKh-Old Testament
that thus it must be; that the Messiah must be apprehended, and suffer, and die. The several parts of the sufferings of the Messiah are foretold in the writings of the Old Testament; the spirit of Christ, in the prophets, testified before hand of them; as that he should be reproached and despised of men, Psa_22:6, be spit upon, smote, and buffeted, Isa_1:5, be put to death, Psa_22:15, and that the death of the cross, Psa_22:15, and be buried, Isa_53:9, and also the several circumstances of his sufferings, which led on to them, or attended them; as the selling him for thirty pieces of silver, Zec_11:12, the betraying him by one of his familiar friends,

Psa_41:9, the seizing and apprehending him, and which is particularly referred to here, Isa_53:7, his disciples forsaking him, Zec_13:7, and even his God and Father, Psa_22:1, his suffering between two thieves, Isa_53:12, the parting of his garments, and casting lots on his vesture, Psa_22:18, the giving him gall and vinegar when on the cross, Psa_69:21, and not breaking any of his bones, Psa_34:20, yea, the Scriptures not only declared, that these things should be; but the necessity of them also, that they must be.

---

55. In that same hour said Jesus to the multitudes, Are ye come out as against a thief with swords and staves for to take me? I sat daily with you teaching in the temple, and ye laid no hold on me.

Greek/Transliteration

55. Ἐν ἐκείνῃ τῇ ὥρᾳ εἶπεν ὁ Ἰησοῦς τοῖς ὄχλοις, Ὡς ἐπὶ λῃστὴν ἐξήλθετε μετὰ μαχαιρῶν καὶ ξύλων συλλαβεῖν με; Καθ᾽ ἡμέραν πρὸς ὑμᾶς ἐκαθεζόμην διδάσκων ἐν τῷ ἱερῷ, καὶ οὐκ ἐκρατήσατέ με.

55. En ekeinei tei 'ora eipen 'o Yeisous tois ochlois, 'Os epi leistein exeilthete meta machairon kai xulon sullabein me? Kath 'eimeran pros 'umas ekathezomein didaskon en to 'iero, kai ouk ekrateisate me.

Hebrew/Transliteration

נה. בָּעֵת הַהִיא אָמַר יֵשׁוּעַ אֶל-הֲמוֹן הָעָם הַבַּחֲרָבוֹת וּבְמַטּוֹת בָּאתֶם לִתְפֹּשׂ אֹתִי כְּפָרִיץ וְיוֹם יוֹם יָשַׁבְתִּי:לְהוֹרֹת לָכֶם בַּמִּקְדָּשׁ וְלֹא שְׁלַחְתֶּם בִּי יָד

55. Ba•et ha•hee amar Yeshua el - ha•mon ha•am ha•va•cha•ra•vot oov•ma•tot ba•tem lit•pos o•ti ke•fa•ritz ve•yom yom ya•shav•ti le•ho•rot la•chem ba•mik•dash ve•lo sh`lach•tem bi yad.

Rabbinic Jewish Commentary

The Jews themselves confirm in their account; for they say (o) the elders of Jerusalem took Jesus, and brought him to the city. (o) Toldos Jesu, p. 17.

---

56. But all this was done, that the scriptures of the prophets might be fulfilled. Then all the disciples forsook him, and fled.

Greek/Transliteration

56. Τοῦτο δὲ ὅλον γέγονεν, ἵνα πληρωθῶσιν αἱ γραφαὶ τῶν προφητῶν. Τότε οἱ μαθηταὶ πάντες ἀφέντες αὐτὸν ἔφυγον.

56. Touto de 'olon gegonen, 'ina pleirothosin 'ai graphai ton propheiton. Tote 'oi matheitai pantes aphentes auton ephugon.

Hebrew/Transliteration

נו. אֲבָל כָּל-זֹאת הָיְתָה לְמַלֹּאת אֶת-כִּתְבֵי הַנְּבִיאִים אָז עָזְבוּ אֹתוֹ תַלְמִידָיו כֻּלָּם וַיָּנֻסוּ:

56. Aval kol - zot hai•ta le•ma•lot et - kit•vey ha•n`vi•eem az az•voo o•to tal•mi•dav koo•lam va•ya•noo•soo.

Rabbinic Jewish Commentary

the Jews themselves say of it; for they report (p), that "when his disciples saw that he was taken, and that they could not fight against them, ירוצו ברגליהם," they ran away on foot", and lift up their voice and wept greatly.

Though they also pretend, that the citizens of Jerusalem killed many of them, and that the rest "fled" to the mountain, which is false.

(p) Toldos Jesu, p. 16, 17.

57. And they that had laid hold on Jesus led him away to Caiaphas the high priest, where the scribes and the elders were assembled.

Greek/Transliteration
57. Οἱ δὲ κρατήσαντες τὸν Ἰησοῦν ἀπήγαγον πρὸς Καϊάφαν τὸν ἀρχιερέα, ὅπου οἱ γραμματεῖς καὶ οἱ πρεσβύτεροι συνήχθησαν.

57. 'Oi de krateisantes ton Yeisoun apeigagon pros Kaiaphan ton archierea, 'opou 'oi grammateis kai 'oi presbuteroi suneichtheisan.

Hebrew/Transliteration
נז. וְתֹפְשֵׂי יֵשׁוּעַ הוֹלִיכוּ אֹתוֹ אֶל-קַיָּפָא הַכֹּהֵן הַגָּדוֹל אֲשֶׁר בְּבֵיתוֹ נִקְהֲלוּ הַסּוֹפְרִים וְהַזְּקֵנִים:

57. Ve•tof•sey Yeshua ho•li•choo o•to el - Ka•ya•fa ha•ko•hen ha•ga•dol asher be•vey•to nik•ha•loo ha•sof•rim ve•ha•z`ke•nim.

Rabbinic Jewish Commentary
The year before this, Simeon, or Simon ben Camhith, was high priest; and the year before that, Eleazar, the son of Ananus; and before him, Ishmael ben Phabi, who were all three, successively, made high priests by the Roman governor: as was also this Caiaphas, this year; and who by Josephus (r), and in the Talmud (s) likewise, is called Joseph. From whence he had his name Caiaphas, is not certain: Jerom (t) says, it signifies "a searcher", or "a sagacious person"; but may be better interpreted, he adds, "one that vomits at the mouth"; deriving the word, as I suppose, from קוא, "to vomit", and פי, "the mouth".

(r) Antiq. l. 18. c. 14. (s) T. Bab. Yoma, fol. 47. 1. (t) De Heb. nominibus, fol, 104. col. 4. Tom. 3.

---

58. But Peter followed him afar off unto the high priest's palace, and went in, and sat with the servants, to see the end.

Greek/Transliteration
58. Ὁ δὲ Πέτρος ἠκολούθει αὐτῷ ἀπὸ μακρόθεν, ἕως τῆς αὐλῆς τοῦ ἀρχιερέως, καὶ εἰσελθὼν ἔσω ἐκάθητο μετὰ τῶν ὑπηρετῶν, ἰδεῖν τὸ τέλος.

58. 'O de Petros eikolouthei auto apo makrothen, 'eos teis auleis tou archiereos, kai eiselthon eso ekatheito meta ton 'upeireton, idein to telos.

Hebrew/Transliteration
נח. וּפֶטְרוֹס הָלַךְ אַחֲרָיו מֵרָחוֹק עַד-לַחֲצַר הַכֹּהֵן הַגָּדוֹל וַיָּבוֹא וַיֵּשֶׁב שָׁם עִם-הַמְשָׁרְתִים לִרְאוֹת אֵיךְ יִפֹּל דָּבָר:

58. Oo•Fetros ha•lach a•cha•rav me•ra•chok ad - la•cha•tzar ha•ko•hen ha•ga•dol va•ya•vo va•ye•shev sham eem - ha•me•shar•tim lir•ot eych yi•pol da•var.

59. Now the chief priests, and elders, and all the council, sought false witness against Jesus, to put him to death;

Greek/Transliteration
59. Οἱ δὲ ἀρχιερεῖς καὶ οἱ πρεσβύτεροι καὶ τὸ συνέδριον ὅλον ἐζήτουν ψευδομαρτυρίαν κατὰ τοῦ Ἰησοῦ, ὅπως θανατώσωσιν αὐτόν.

59. 'Oi de archiereis kai 'oi presbuteroi kai to sunedrion 'olon ezeitoun pseudomarturian kata tou Yeisou, 'opos thanatososin auton.

Hebrew/Transliteration
נט. וְרָאשֵׁי הַכֹּהֲנִים וְהַזְּקֵנִים וְכָל-הַסַּנְהֶדְרִין בִּקְשׁוּ עֵדוּת שֶׁקֶר עַל-יֵשׁוּעַ לַהֲמִיתוֹ וְלֹא מָצָאוּ:

59. Ve•ra•shey ha•ko•ha•nim ve•ha•z`ke•nim ve•chol - ha•San•hed•rin bik•shoo e•doot she•ker al - Yeshua la•ha•mi•to ve•lo ma•tza•oo.

TaNaKh-Old Testament/Rabbinic Jewish Commentary
"…then your elders and your judges shall go out and measure to the cities which are around the slain one." Deut_21:2

"The judges shall investigate thoroughly, and if the witness is a false witness *and* he has accused his brother falsely," Deut_19:18

Their Jewish canon runs thus (z): "the judgment of a deceiver, is not as the rest of capital judgments; his witnesses are hid; and he has no need, or ought not to have any premonition, or warning, as the rest of those that are put to death; and if he goes out of the sanhedrim acquitted, and one says I can prove the charge against him, they turn him back; but if he goes out condemned, and one says I can prove him innocent the do not return him.

So in the Misna (a) it is said, "of all that are condemned to death in the law, none have their witnesses hidden but this (the deceiver, or one that entices to idolatry)-- and they hide his witnesses behind a wall, or hedge; and he (whom he endeavoured to seduce) says to him, say what thou hast said to me privately; and if he repeats it to him, he must say, how shall we leave our God that is in heaven, and go and serve stocks and stones! if he repents, it is well; but if he should say, so we are bound to do, and so it becomes us, they that stand behind the wall, or hedge, shall carry him to the sanhedrim and stone him.

In the Gemara it is thus expressed (b), "they light up a lamp in the innermost house, and set the witnesses in the outermost house, so that they can see him and hear his voice, and he cannot see them.

(z) Ib. c. 11. sect. 5. (a) Sanhedrin, c. 7. sect. 10. (b) T. Bab. Sanhedrin, fol. 67. 1.

60. But found none: yea, though many false witnesses came, yet found they none. At the last came two false witnesses,

Greek/Transliteration
60. Καὶ οὐχ εὗρον· καὶ πολλῶν ψευδομαρτύρων προσελθόντων, οὐχ εὗρον.

60. Kai ouch 'euron. kai pollon pseudomarturon proselthonton, ouch 'euron.

Hebrew/Transliteration
ס: וְאַף כִּי עֵדֵי-שֶׁקֶר רַבִּים בָּאוּ שָׁם לֹא מָצָאוּ וְאַחֲרֵי-כֵן נִגְּשׁוּ שְׁנַיִם עֵדֵי-שָׁקֶר:

60. Ve•af ki e•dey - she•ker ra•bim ba•oo sham lo ma•tza•oo ve•a•cha•rey – chen nig•shoo sh`na•yim e•dey - she•ker.

---

61. And said, This fellow said, I am able to destroy the temple of God, and to build it in three days.

Greek/Transliteration
61. Ὕστερον δὲ προσελθόντες δύο ψευδομάρτυρες εἶπον, Οὗτος ἔφη, Δύναμαι καταλῦσαι τὸν ναὸν τοῦ θεοῦ, καὶ διὰ τριῶν ἡμερῶν οἰκοδομῆσαι αὐτόν.

61. 'Usteron de proselthontes duo pseudomartures eipon, 'Outos ephei, Dunamai katalusai ton naon tou theou, kai dya trion 'eimeron oikodomeisai auton.

Hebrew/Transliteration
סא: וַיַּעֲנוּ כִּי זֶה אָמַר יָדִי רַב לִי לַהֲרֹס אֶת-הֵיכַל הָאֱלֹהִים וְלִבְנוֹתוֹ בִּשְׁלֹשֶׁת יָמִים:

61. Va•ya•a•noo ki ze amar ya•di rav li la•ha•ros et - hey•chal ha•Elohim ve•liv•no•to bish•lo•shet ya•mim.

---

62. And the high priest arose, and said unto him, Answerest thou nothing? What is it which these witness against thee?

Greek/Transliteration
62. Καὶ ἀναστὰς ὁ ἀρχιερεὺς εἶπεν αὐτῷ, Οὐδὲν ἀποκρίνῃ; Τί οὗτοί σου καταμαρτυροῦσιν;

62. Kai anastas 'o archiereus eipen auto, Ouden apokrinei? Ti 'outoi sou katamarturousin?

Hebrew/Transliteration
סב: וַיָּקָם הַכֹּהֵן הַגָּדוֹל וַיֹּאמֶר אֵלָיו הַאֵינְךָ מֵשִׁיב דָּבָר עַל-אֲשֶׁר עָנוּ-בְךָ אֵלֶּה:

62. Va•ya•kom ha•ko•hen ha•ga•dol va•yo•mer elav ha•eyn•cha me•shiv da•var al - asher anoo - ve•cha ele?

63. But Jesus held his peace. And the high priest answered and said unto him, I adjure thee by the living God, that thou tell us whether thou be the Christ, the Son of God.

Greek/Transliteration
63. Ὁ δὲ Ἰησοῦς ἐσιώπα. Καὶ ἀποκριθεὶς ὁ ἀρχιερεὺς εἶπεν αὐτῷ, Ἐξορκίζω σε κατὰ τοῦ θεοῦ τοῦ ζῶντος, ἵνα ἡμῖν εἴπῃς εἰ σὺ εἶ ὁ χριστός, ὁ υἱὸς τοῦ θεοῦ.

63. 'O de Yeisous esiopa. Kai apokritheis 'o archiereus eipen auto, Exorkizo se kata tou theou tou zontos, 'ina 'eimin eipeis ei su ei 'o christos, 'o 'wios tou theou.

Hebrew/Transliteration
סג. וַיִּדֹּם יֵשׁוּעַ וַיֹּאמֶר אֵלָיו הַכֹּהֵן הַגָּדוֹל הִנְנִי מַשְׁבִּיעֲךָ בֵּאלֹהִים חַיִּים כִּי תַגִּיד לָנוּ אִם-אַתָּה הוּא הַמָּשִׁיחַ בֶּן-הָאֱלֹהִים׃

63. Va•yi•dom Yeshua va•yo•mer elav ha•ko•hen ha•ga•dol hi•ne•ni mash•bi•a•cha be•Elohim cha•yim ki ta•gid la•noo eem - ata hoo ha•Ma•shi•ach Ben - ha•Elohim.

---

64. Jesus saith unto him, Thou hast said: nevertheless I say unto you, Hereafter shall ye see the Son of man sitting on the right hand of power, and coming in the clouds of heaven.

Greek/Transliteration
64. Λέγει αὐτῷ ὁ Ἰησοῦς, Σὺ εἶπας. Πλὴν λέγω ὑμῖν, ἀπ᾽ ἄρτι ὄψεσθε τὸν υἱὸν τοῦ ἀνθρώπου καθήμενον ἐκ δεξιῶν τῆς δυνάμεως καὶ ἐρχόμενον ἐπὶ τῶν νεφελῶν τοῦ οὐρανοῦ.

64. Legei auto 'o Yeisous, Su eipas. Plein lego 'umin, ap arti opsesthe ton 'wion tou anthropou katheimenon ek dexion teis dunameos kai erchomenon epi ton nephelon tou ouranou.

Hebrew/Transliteration
סד. וַיֹּאמֶר אֵלָיו יֵשׁוּעַ אַתָּה אָמָרְתָּ אָכֵן אֲנִי מַגִּיד לָכֶם כִּי מֵעַתָּה תִרְאוּ אֶת-בֶּן-הָאָדָם יֹשֵׁב לִימִין הַגְּבוּרָה וּבָא בְּעַנְנֵי הַשָּׁמָיִם׃

64. Va•yo•mer elav Yeshua ata amar•ta a•chen ani ma•gid la•chem ki me•a•ta tir•oo et - Ben - ha•adam yo•shev li•y`min ha•g`voo•ra oo•va be•ane•ney ha•sha•ma•yim.

Rabbinic Jewish Commnetary
In the Jewish writings (e), God is frequently called, הגבורה, "the power": such a thing, say they, we have heard, מפי הגבורה, "from the mouth of power", or might; that is, from God himself: and so he is by the Grecians called δυναμις, "power" (f)

and coming in, the clouds of heaven. So Christ's coming to take vengeance on the Jewish nation, as it is often called the coming of the son of man. "from this time"; meaning, that in a very little while, they should begin to see the effects of his being set down at the right hand of God, and which would be full proofs of it, and should see him come in the clouds of heaven, at the last day: reference seems to be had to Dan_7:13, where one like unto the son of man is said to come in the clouds of heaven, and which is understood of the Messiah by many, both of the ancient and modern Jews (g): with whom one of his names is "Anani" (h), which signifies "clouds".

(e) T. Bab. Maccot, fol. 24. 1. & Horayot, fol. 8. 1. Debarim Rabba, fol. 245. 4. Maimon. Hilch. Memarim, c. 5. sect. 15. & Melacim, c. 8. sect. 10. & alibi passim. (f) Sententiae Secundi, p. 21. Ed. Gale. (g) Zohar in Gert. fol. 85. 4. Bemidbar Rabba, sect. 13. fol. 209. 4. R. Jeshuah in Aben Ezra, in Dan. vii. 13. & Jarchi & Saadiah Gaon in loc. (h) Targum in 1 Chron. iii. 24. & Beckius in ib. Midrash Tillim apud Galatin. de arcan. Cathol. ver. l. 10. c. 1.

---

65. Then the high priest rent his clothes, saying, He hath spoken blasphemy; what further need have we of witnesses? behold, now ye have heard his blasphemy.

Greek/Transliteration
65. Τότε ὁ ἀρχιερεὺς διέρρηξεν τὰ ἱμάτια αὐτοῦ, λέγων ὅτι Ἐβλασφήμησεν· τί ἔτι χρείαν ἔχομεν μαρτύρων; Ἴδε, νῦν ἠκούσατε τὴν βλασφημίαν αὐτοῦ.

65. Tote 'o archiereus dierreixen ta 'imatya autou, legon 'oti Eblaspheimeisen. ti eti chreian echomen marturon? Yde, nun eikousate tein blaspheimian autou.

Hebrew/Transliteration
סה. אָז יִקְרַע הַכֹּהֵן הַגָּדוֹל אֶת-בְּגָדָיו לֵאמֹר מְגַדֵּף הוּא מַה-לָּנוּ עוֹד וּלְעֵדִים הִנֵּה זֶה שְׁמַעְתֶּם גִּדּוּפוֹ מִפִּיו:

65. Az yik•ra ha•ko•hen ha•ga•dol et - be•ga•dav le•mor me•ga•def hoo ma - la•noo od ool•e•dim hee•ne ze sh`ma•a•tem gi•doo•fo mi•piv.

Rabbinic Jewish Commentary
In Lev_21:10, where it is said, that "the high priest--shall not uncover his head, nor rend his clothes": and it is one of the Jews' negative precepts (i), that "an high priest is prohibited, לעולם, "ever" to rend his garments: nd so Jonathan ben Uzziel paraphrases the text, "nor rent his clothes": בשעת אניקי "in the time of mourning"; and so the Jewish (k) interpreters, in general, expound it; and besides, this prohibition, according to them, only regards the manner of rending: their rule is this (l)

In case of hearing blasphemy, everyone, be he what he would, was obliged to rend his garments (o): "Whosoever hears the cursing of the name (of God) is obliged to rend, even at the cursing of the surnames he is obliged to rend; and he that hears it from an Israelite, both he that hears, and he that hears from the mouth of him that hears, he is obliged to rend; but he that hears from the mouth of a Gentile, is not obliged to rend; and Eliakim and Shebna would not have rent, but because Rabshakeh was an apostate.

(p) "a blasphemer is not guilty, unless he expresses the name (of God); says R. Joshua ben Korcha, all the day the witnesses are examined by the surnames; but when the cause is finished, they do not put to death because of the surnames, but they bring every man out, and ask the chief among them, and say to him, say expressly what thou hast heard, and he says it: then the judges stand upon their feet, וקורעין, "and rend their garments", and do not sow them up again; and then the second and the third say, I have heard the same as he.

(i) Moses Kotsensis Mitzvot Tora, pr. neg. 302. (k) Jarchi, Aben Ezra, &c. in loc. (l) Misn. Horayot, c. 3. sect. 5. (o) Maimon. Hilch. Obede Cochabim, c. 2. sect. 10. Vid. T. Hieros. Sanhedrin, fol. 25. 1. (p) Misn. Sanhedrin, c. 7. sect. 5.

---

66. What think ye? They answered and said, He is guilty of death.

Greek/Transliteration
66. Τί ὑμῖν δοκεῖ; Οἱ δὲ ἀποκριθέντες εἶπον, Ἔνοχος θανάτου ἐστίν.

66. Ti 'umin dokei? 'Oi de apokrithentes eipon, Enochos thanatou estin.

Hebrew/Transliteration
סו. אָמְרוּ מַה-דַּעְתְּכֶם וַיַּעֲנוּ וַיֹּאמְרוּ מִשְׁפַּט-מָוֶת לוֹ:

66. Eem•roo ma - da•at•chem va•ya•a•noo va•yom•roo mish•pat - ma•vet lo.

Rabbinic Jewish Commentary
Now this was in the night, in which they begun, carried on, and finished this judicial procedure, quite contrary to one of their own canons (w) which runs thus:

"pecuniary causes they try in the day, and finish in the night; capital causes (such was this) they try in the day, and finish in the day; pecuniary causes they finish the same day, whether for absolution, or condemnation; capital causes they finish the same day for absolution, and the day following for condemnation; wherefore they do not try causes neither on the sabbath eve, nor on the eve of a feast day.

But in this case, they begun the trial in the night, examined the witnesses, finished it, and passed the sentence of condemnation, and that in the eve of a grand festival, their Chagigah,

(w) Misn. Sanhedrin, c. 4. sect. 1. Maimom. Hilch. Sanhedrin, c. 11. sect. 1, 2. T. Hieros. Yom Tob, fol. 63. 1.

67. Then did they spit in his face, and buffeted him; and others smote him with the palms of their hands,

Greek/Transliteration
67. Τότε ἐνέπτυσαν εἰς τὸ πρόσωπον αὐτοῦ καὶ ἐκολάφισαν αὐτόν· οἱ δὲ ἐρράπισαν,

67. Tote eneptusan eis to prosopon autou kai ekolaphisan auton. 'oi de errapisan,

Hebrew/Transliteration
סז. אָז יָרְקוּ בְפָנָיו וַיַּכֻּהוּ בְאֶגְרֹף וְיֵשׁ מֵהֶם אֲשֶׁר מַחֲאוּ אֹתוֹ מַכַּת לֶחִי:

67. Az yar•koo be•fa•nav va•ya•koo•hoo be•eg•rof ve•yesh me•hem asher ma•cha•oo o•to ma•kat le•chi.

Rabbinic Jewish Commentary
The Jews (x) say, that he that spits before, or in the presence of his master, is guilty of death, so nauseous and filthy was it accounted; and how much more must it be so, to spit in the face of anyone? hereby a prophecy was fulfilled, Isa_50:6, "I hid not my face from shame and spitting": and hereby, together with his sweat and blood, his visage was more marred than any man's, and his form than the sons of men. In Mic_5:1, "they shall smite the judge of Israel with a rod upon the cheek".

This was very injurious treatment, the Jews themselves being witnesses; who have in their canons enjoined (y), that "if a man strikes his neighbour with his double fist, he must give him a shekel; R. Judah says, on account of R. Jose the Galilean, a pound: if he gives him a slap of the face, he must pay him two hundred zuzims, or pence; and if with the back of his hand (which was accounted (z) the more ignominious) four hundred zuzims: if he plucked him by his ear, or plucked off his hair, or spit, so as that the spittle came upon him, or took away his cloak--he must pay four hundred zuzims, and all according to his honour or dignity.

All these indignities were done to Christ; see Isa_50:6.

(x) T. Bab. Erubin, fol. 99. 1. (y) Misn. Bava Kama, c. 8. sect. 6. (z) Maimon. & Bartenora in ib.

---

68. Saying, Prophesy unto us, thou Christ, Who is he that smote thee?

Greek/Transliteration
68. λέγοντες, Προφήτευσον ἡμῖν, Χριστέ, τίς ἐστιν ὁ παίσας σε;

68. legontes, Propheiteuson 'eimin, Christe, tis estin 'o paisas se?

Hebrew/Transliteration
סח. וַיֹּאמְרוּ הִנָּבֵא לָנוּ מָשִׁיחַ מִי זֶה הַמַּכֶּה אֹתָךְ:

68. Va•yom•roo hi•na•ve la•noo Mashi•ach mee ze ha•ma•ke o•tach?

---

69. Now Peter sat without in the palace: and a damsel came unto him, saying, Thou also wast with Jesus of Galilee.

Greek/Transliteration
69. Ὁ δὲ Πέτρος ἔξω ἐκάθητο ἐν τῇ αὐλῇ· καὶ προσῆλθεν αὐτῷ μία παιδίσκη, λέγουσα, Καὶ σὺ ἦσθα μετὰ Ἰησοῦ τοῦ Γαλιλαίου.

69. 'O de Petros exo ekatheito en tei aulei. kai proseilthen auto mia paidiskei, legousa, Kai su eistha meta Yeisou tou Galilaiou.

Hebrew/Transliteration
סט. וּפֶטְרוֹס יָשַׁב מִחוּץ בְּתוֹךְ הֶחָצֵר וַתִּגַּשׁ אֵלָיו שִׁפְחָה אַחַת לֵאמֹר גַּם-אַתָּה הָיִיתָ עִם-יֵשׁוּעַ הַגְּלִילִי:

69. Oo•Fetros ya•shav mi•choo•tz be•toch he•cha•tzer va•ti•gash elav shif•cha a•chat le•mor gam - ata ha•yi•ta eem - Yeshua ha•Ga•li•li.

---

70. But he denied before them all, saying, I know not what thou sayest.

Greek/Transliteration
70. Ὁ δὲ ἠρνήσατο ἔμπροσθεν αὐτῶν πάντων, λέγων, Οὐκ οἶδα τί λέγεις.

70. 'O de eirneisato emprosthen auton panton, legon, Ouk oida ti legeis.

Hebrew/Transliteration
ע. וַיְכַחֵשׁ לְעֵינֵי כֻלָּם לֵאמֹר לֹא יָדַעְתִּי מָה-אַתְּ אֹמֶרֶת:

70. Vay•cha•chesh le•ei•ney choo•lam le•mor lo ya•da•a•ti ma - at o•me•ret.

---

71. And when he was gone out into the porch, another maid saw him, and said unto them that were there, This fellow was also with Jesus of Nazareth.

Greek/Transliteration
71. Ἐξελθόντα δὲ αὐτὸν εἰς τὸν πυλῶνα, εἶδεν αὐτὸν ἄλλη, καὶ λέγει αὐτοῖς ἐκεῖ, Καὶ οὗτος ἦν μετὰ Ἰησοῦ τοῦ Ναζωραίου.

71. Exelthonta de auton eis ton pulona, eiden auton allei, kai legei autois ekei, Kai 'outos ein meta Yeisou tou Nazoraiou.

Hebrew/Transliteration
עא. וַיֵּצֵא אֶל-הָאוּלָם וַתִּרְאֵהוּ שִׁפְחָה אַחֶרֶת וַתֹּאמֶר אֶל-הָעֹמְדִים שָׁם גַּם-זֶה הָיָה עִם-יֵשׁוּעַ הַנָּצְרִי:

71. Va•ye•tze el - ha•oo•lam va•tir•e•hoo shif•cha a•che•ret va•to•mer el - ha•om•dim sham gam - ze ha•ya eem - Yeshua ha•Notz•ri.

---

72. And again he denied with an oath, I do not know the man.

Greek/Transliteration
72. Καὶ πάλιν ἠρνήσατο μεθ᾿ ὅρκου ὅτι Οὐκ οἶδα τὸν ἄνθρωπον.

72. Kai palin eirneisato meth 'orkou 'oti Ouk oida ton anthropon.

Hebrew/Transliteration
עב. וַיּוֹסֶף לְכַחֵשׁ וַיִּשָּׁבַע לֵאמֹר לֹא יָדַעְתִּי אֶת-הָאִישׁ:

72. Va•yo•sef le•cha•chesh va•yi•sha•va le•mor lo ya•da•a•ti et - ha•eesh.

---

73. And after a while came unto him they that stood by, and said to Peter, Surely thou also art one of them; for thy speech bewrayeth thee.

Greek/Transliteration
73. Μετὰ μικρὸν δὲ προσελθόντες οἱ ἑστῶτες εἶπον τῷ Πέτρῳ, ᾿Αληθῶς καὶ σὺ ἐξ αὐτῶν εἶ· καὶ γὰρ ἡ λαλιά σου δῆλόν σε ποιεῖ.

73. Meta mikron de proselthontes 'oi 'estotes eipon to Petro, Aleithos kai su ex auton ei. kai gar 'ei lalya sou deilon se poiei.

Hebrew/Transliteration
עג. וְעוֹד מְעַט וַיִּגְּשׁוּ הָעֹמְדִים שָׁם וַיֹּאמְרוּ אֶל-פֶּטְרוֹס אוּלָם גַּם-אַתָּה אֶחָד מֵהֶם כִּי גַם-בִּשְׂפָתְךָ תִּתְנַכֵּר:

73. Ve•od me•at va•yig•shoo ha•om•dim sham va•yom•roo el - Petros oo•lam gam – ata e•chad me•hem ki gam - bis•fat•cha tit•na•ker.

Rabbinic/Transliteration
Hence the Talmudists say (b), that "the men of Judah, who were careful of their language, their law was confirmed in their hands; the men of Galilee, who were not careful of their language, their law was not confirmed in their hands--the men of Galilee, who do not attend to language, what is reported of them? a Galilean went and said to them, אמר למאן אמר למאן, they said to him foolish Galilean, חמר, "Chamor" is to ride upon, or "Chamar" is to drink, or "Hamar" is for clothing, or "Immar" is for hiding for slaughter.

By which instances it appears, that a Galilean pronounced "Chamor", an ass, and "Chamar", wine, and "Hamar", wool, and "Immar", a lamb, all one, and the same way, without any distinction; so that it was difficult to know which of these he meant.

(b) T. Bab. Erubin, fol. 53. 1, 2. Vid. Buxtorf. Lex. Talmud. in rad,

74. Then began he to curse and to swear, saying, I know not the man. And immediately the cock crew.

Greek/Transliteration
74. Τότε ἤρξατο καταθεματίζειν καὶ ὀμνύειν ὅτι Οὐκ οἶδα τὸν ἄνθρωπον. Καὶ εὐθέως ἀλέκτωρ ἐφώνησεν.

74. Tote eirxato katathematizein kai omnuein 'oti Ouk oida ton anthropon. Kai eutheos alektor ephoneisen.

Hebrew/Transliteration
עד. וַיָּחֶל לָעֲנוֹת בְּאָלָה וּבִשְׁבֻעָה לֵאמֹר לֹא יָדַעְתִּי אֶת-הָאִישׁ וּבְרֶגַע זֶה קָרָא הַתַּרְנְגֹל:

74. Va•ya•chel la•a•not be•a•la oo•vish•voo•ah le•mor lo ya•da•a•ti et - ha•eesh oov•re•ga ze ka•ra ha•tar•ne•gol.

Rabbinic Jewish Commentary
It is forbid, by a Jewish canon, to keep cocks at Jerusalem; it runs thus (c):

"they do not bring up cocks in Jerusalem, because of the holy things, neither do the priests in all the land of Israel, because of the purifications.

Whether this canon was then in being, or how it was dispensed with, or whether there was any particular providence in the cock being here now, and so nigh the high priest's palace, is not certain; but one there was: nor can the Jews deny that there were cocks at Jerusalem; for they themselves speak of a cock, שנסקל בירושלים (d), "that was stoned at Jerusalem",

(c) Misn. Bava Kama, c. 7. sect. 7. T. Bab. Bava Kama, fol. 82. 2. Abot R. Nathan, c. 35. Maimon. Hilch. Beth Habechirah, c. 7. sect. 14. Shalshelet Hakabala, fol. 9. 2. (d) T. Hieros Erubin, fol. 26. 1. Caphtor, fol. 42. 1.

---

75. And Peter remembered the word of Jesus, which said unto him, Before the cock crow, thou shalt deny me thrice. And he went out, and wept bitterly.

Greek/Transliteration
75. Καὶ ἐμνήσθη ὁ Πέτρος τοῦ ῥήματος τοῦ Ἰησοῦ εἰρηκότος αὐτῷ ὅτι Πρὶν ἀλέκτορα φωνῆσαι, τρὶς ἀπαρνήσῃ με. Καὶ ἐξελθὼν ἔξω ἔκλαυσεν πικρῶς.

75. Kai emneisthei 'o Petros tou 'reimatos tou Yeisou eirekotos auto 'oti Prin alektora phoneisai, tris aparneisei me. Kai exelthon exo eklausen pikros.

Hebrew/Transliteration
עה. וַיִּזְכֹּר פֶּטְרוֹס אֶת-דְּבַר יֵשׁוּעַ אֲשֶׁר אָמַר כִּי-טֶרֶם יִקְרָא הַתַּרְנְגֹל תְּכַחֶשׁ-בִּי שָׁלֹשׁ פְּעָמִים וַיֵּצֵא הַחוּצָה:וַיְמָרֵר בִּבְכִי

75. Va•yiz•kor Petros et - de•var Yeshua asher amar ki - te•rem yik•ra ha•tar•ne•gol te•cha•chesh - bi sha•losh pe•a•mim va•ye•tze ha•choo•tza vay•ma•rer ba•be•chi.

Matthew, Chapter 27

1. When the morning was come, all the chief priests and elders of the people took counsel against Jesus to put him to death:

Greek/Transliteration
1. Πρωΐας δὲ γενομένης, συμβούλιον ἔλαβον πάντες οἱ ἀρχιερεῖς καὶ οἱ πρεσβύτεροι τοῦ λαοῦ κατὰ τοῦ Ἰησοῦ, ὥστε θανατῶσαι αὐτόν·

1. Proias de genomeneis, sumboulion elabon pantes 'oi archiereis kai 'oi presbuteroi tou laou kata tou Yeisou, 'oste thanatosai auton.

Hebrew/Transliteration
א. הַבֹּקֶר אוֹר וְכָל-רָאשֵׁי הַכֹּהֲנִים וְזִקְנֵי הָעָם נוֹסְדוּ יַחַד עַל-יֵשׁוּעַ לַהֲמִיתוֹ:

1. Ha•bo•ker or ve•chol - ra•shey ha•ko•ha•nim ve•zik•ney ha•am nos•doo ya•chad al - Yeshua la•ha•mi•to.

Rabbinic Jewish Commentary
This was the time of their morning prayers, of their saying their phylacteries, and reciting the "shema", "hear, O Israel! the Lord our God is one Lord", according to their canon, which is this (e):

"from what time do they read the "shema" in the morning? from such time that a man can distinguish between blue and white: says R. Eliezer, between blue and green; and he finishes it before the sun shines out. R. Joshua says, before three hours had elapsed:"

Their rule was this (f); "the sanhedrim, consisting of seventy and one (as this was), are obliged to sit all of them as one, (or all, and everyone of them,) in their place in the temple; but at what time there is a necessity of their being gathered together, מתקבצין כולן, "they are all of them assembled"; but, at other times, he who has any business may go, and do his pleasure, and return: yet so it is, that there may not be less than twenty three sitting continually all the time of their sitting; (their usual time of sitting was from the morning daily sacrifice, to the evening daily sacrifice (g);) one that is under a necessity of going out; this looks upon his companions that remain, and if twenty three remain, he may go out; but if not, he may not, until the other returns."

(e) Misn. Beracot, c. 1. sect. 2. (f) Maimon. Hilch. Sanhedrin, c. 3. sect. 2. (g) Ib. c. 3. sect. 1. Bernidbar Rabba, sect. 1. fol. 177. 3.

---

2. And when they had bound him, they led him away, and delivered him to Pontius Pilate the governor.

Greek/Transliteration
2. καὶ δήσαντες αὐτὸν ἀπήγαγον καὶ παρέδωκαν αὐτὸν Ποντίῳ Πιλάτῳ τῷ ἡγεμόνι.

2. kai deisantes auton apeigagon kai paredokan auton Pontio Pilato to 'eigemoni.

Hebrew/Transliteration
ב. וַיַּאַסְרוּ אֹתוֹ וַיּוֹלִיכֻהוּ וַיַּסְגִּירֻהוּ בִּידֵי פּוֹנְטִיוֹס פִּילָטוֹס הַהֶגְמוֹן:

2. Va•ya•as•roo o•to va•yo•li•choo•hoo va•yas•gi•roo•hoo vi•dey Pon•tiyos Filatos ha•heg•mon.

Rabbinic Jewish Commentary
Philo the Jew (h) makes mention of him: "Pilate, says he, was επιτροπος της Ιουδαιας, "procurator of Judea"; who not so much in honour of Tiberius, as to grieve the people, put the golden shields within the holy city in the palace of Herod."

And so Tacitus (i) calls him the procurator of Tiberius, and Josephus also (k). It is said (l) of him, that falling into many calamities, he slew himself with his own hand, in the times of Caligula, and whilst Publicola and Nerva were consuls; which was a righteous judgment of God upon him for condemning Yeshua, contrary to his own conscience.

(h) De Legat. ad Caium, p. 1033, 1034. (i) Hist. l. 15. (k) De Bello Jud. l. 2. e. 9. sect. 2. (l) M. Aurel-Cassiodor. Chronicon in Caligula, Joseph. Antiq. l. 18. c. 11. Euseb. Eccl. Hist. l. 2. c. 7.

---

3. Then Judas, which had betrayed him, when he saw that he was condemned, repented himself, and brought again the thirty pieces of silver to the chief priests and elders,

Greek/Transliteration
3. Τότε ἰδὼν Ἰούδας ὁ παραδιδοὺς αὐτὸν ὅτι κατεκρίθη, μεταμεληθεὶς ἀπέστρεψεν τὰ τριάκοντα ἀργύρια τοῖς ἀρχιερεῦσιν καὶ τοῖς πρεσβυτέροις,

3. Tote idon Youdas 'o paradidous auton 'oti katekrithei, metameleitheis apestrepsen ta tryakonta argurya tois archiereusin kai tois presbuterois,

Hebrew/Transliteration
ג. וַיַּרְא יְהוּדָה הַמַּסְגִּיר אֹתוֹ כִּי הִרְשִׁיעֻהוּ וַיִּנָּחֶם וַיָּשֶׁב אֶת-שְׁלֹשִׁים הַכֶּסֶף אֶל-רָאשֵׁי הַכֹּהֲנִים וְאֶל-הַזְּקֵנִים:

3. Va•yar Yehooda ha•mas•gir o•to ki hir•shi•oo•hoo va•yi•na•chem va•ya•shev et - sh`lo•shim ha•ke•sef el - ra•shey ha•ko•ha•nim ve•el - haz`ke•nim.

4. Saying, I have sinned in that I have betrayed the innocent blood. And they said, What is that to us? see thou to that.

Greek/Transliteration
4. λέγων, Ἥμαρτον παραδοὺς αἷμα ἀθῷον. Οἱ δὲ εἶπον, Τί πρὸς ἡμᾶς; Σὺ ὄψει.

4. legon, 'Eimarton paradous 'aima athoon. 'Oi de eipon, Ti pros 'eimas? Su opsei.

Hebrew/Transliteration
ד: וַיֹּאמֶר חָטָאתִי בַּאֲשֶׁר הִסְגַּרְתִּי דָם נָקִי וְהֵם אָמְרוּ מַה-לָּנוּ וְלָזֹאת רְאֵה אָתָּה

4. Va•yo•mar cha•ta•ti ba•a•sher his•gar•ti dam na•ki ve•hem am•roo ma - la•noo ve•la•zot r`•eh ata.

---

5. And he cast down the pieces of silver in the temple, and departed, and went and hanged himself.

Greek/Transliteration
5. Καὶ ῥίψας τὰ ἀργύρια ἐν τῷ ναῷ, ἀνεχώρησεν· καὶ ἀπελθὼν ἀπήγξατο.

5. Kai 'ripsas ta argurya en to nao, anechoreisen. kai apelthon apeigxato.

Hebrew/Transliteration
ה: וַיַּשְׁלֵךְ אֶת-הַכֶּסֶף בַּהֵיכָל וַיֵּצֵא וַיֵּלֶךְ וַיֵּחָנַק

5. Va•yash•lech et - ha•ke•sef ba•hey•chol va•ye•tze va•ye•lech va•ye•cha•nak.

Rabbinic Jewish Comemntary
There they were sitting; in their council chamber, לשכת הגזית, "the paved chamber", where the sanhedrim used to meet (m): for it seems they would not take the money of him; and he was determined not to carry it back with him, and therefore threw it down before them, left it.

A disease called the squinancy, or quinsy, a suffocation brought upon him by excessive grief, deep melancholy, and utter despair; when being choked by it, he fell flat upon his face, and the rim of his belly burst, and his entrails came out. This disease the Jews call אסכרא, "Iscara"; and if it was what he was subject to from his infancy, his parents might call him Iscariot from hence; and might be designed in providence to be what should bring him to his wretched end: and what is said of this suffocating disorder, seems to agree very well with the death of Judas. They say (n), that "it is a disease that begins in the bowels, and ends in the throat:" they call death by it, מיתה רעה, "an evil death" (o);

And say (p), that "there are nine hundred and three kinds of deaths in the world, but that קשה שבכלן אסכרא, "the hardest of them all is Iscara"; which the Gloss calls "strangulament", and says, is in the midst of the body.

Moreover, they affirm (s), that "whoever tastes anything before he separates (i.e. lights up the lamp on the eve of the sabbath, to distinguish the night from the day), shall die by "Iscara", or suffocation."

Upon which the Gloss says, this is "measure for measure: he that satisfies his throat, or appetite, shall be choked: as it is said (t) he that is condemned to be strangled, either he shall be drowned in a river, or he shall die of a quinsy, this is "Iscara"."

(m) T. Bab. Sanhedrin, fol. 88. 2. (n) Gloss. in T. Bab. Sabbat, fol 33. 1. (o) T. Bab. Yebamot, fol. 62. 9. (p) Beracot, fol. 3. 1. (q) Gloss. in T. Bab. Taanith, fol. 19. 2. (r) T. Bab. Sota, fol. 35. 1. (s) T. Bab. Pesachim, fol. 105. 1. (t) T. Bab. Cetubot, fol. 30. 2.

---

6. And the chief priests took the silver pieces, and said, It is not lawful for to put them into the treasury, because it is the price of blood.

Greek/Transliteration
6. Οἱ δὲ ἀρχιερεῖς λαβόντες τὰ ἀργύρια εἶπον, Οὐκ ἔξεστιν βαλεῖν αὐτὰ εἰς τὸν κορβανᾶν, ἐπεὶ τιμὴ αἵματός ἐστιν.

6. 'Oi de archiereis labontes ta argurya eipon, Ouk exestin balein auta eis ton korbanan, epei timei 'aimatos estin.

Hebrew/Transliteration
ו׃ וַיִּקְחוּ רָאשֵׁי הַכֹּהֲנִים אֶת-הַכֶּסֶף וַיֹּאמְרוּ לֹא-כַתּוֹרָה הוּא לְתִתּוֹ אֶל-הָאוֹצָר כִּי-שְׂכַר דָּמִים הוּא׃

6. Va•yik•choo ra•shey ha•ko•ha•nim et - ha•ke•sef va•yom•roo lo - cha•Torah hoo le•ti•to el - ha•o•tzar ki - s`char da•mim hoo.

Rabbinic Jewish Commentary
Josephus (u) observes, that "there was, with the Jews, an holy treasure, which is called "Corbonas;"" and this is the לשכת הקרבן, "the chamber of the Korban", of which the Jews make mention (w): the reason the high priests give why it was not lawful to put this money into the treasury, or into any of the chests in the "Corban" chamber, because it was the price of blood.

(u) De Bello Jud. l. 2. c. 9. sect. 3. (w) Misn. Middot, c. 1. sect, 1.

7. And they took counsel, and bought with them the potter's field, to bury strangers in.

Greek/Transliteration
7. Συμβούλιον δὲ λαβόντες ἠγόρασαν ἐξ αὐτῶν τὸν ἀγρὸν τοῦ κεραμέως, εἰς ταφὴν τοῖς ξένοις.

7. Sumboulion de labontes eigorasan ex auton ton agron tou kerameos, eis taphein tois xenois.

Hebrew/Transliteration
ז. וַיִּוָּעֲצוּ וַיִּקְנוּ בָּהֶם אֶת-שְׂדֵה הַיּוֹצֵר לִקְבוּרַת גֵּרִים:

7. Va•yi•va•a•tzoo va•yik•noo va•ke•sef ha•ze et - s`de ha•yo•tzer lik•voo•rat ge•rim.

---

8. Wherefore that field was called, The field of blood, unto this day.

Greek/Transliteration
8. Διὸ ἐκλήθη ὁ ἀγρὸς ἐκεῖνος Ἀγρὸς Αἵματος, ἕως τῆς σήμερον.

8. Dio ekleithei 'o agros ekeinos Agros 'Aimatos, 'eos teis seimeron.

Hebrew/Transliteration
ח. עַל-כֵּן יִקָּרֵא לַשָּׂדֶה הַהוּא שְׂדֵה דָמִים עַד הַיּוֹם הַזֶּה:

8. Al - ken yi•ka•re la•sa•de ha•hoo S`de Da•mim ad ha•yom ha•ze.

---

9. Then was fulfilled that which was spoken by Jeremy the prophet, saying, And they took the thirty pieces of silver, the price of him that was valued, whom they of the children of Israel did value;

Greek/Transliteration
9. Τότε ἐπληρώθη τὸ ῥηθὲν διὰ Ἰερεμίου τοῦ προφήτου, λέγοντος, Καὶ ἔλαβον τὰ τριάκοντα ἀργύρια, τὴν τιμὴν τοῦ τετιμημένου, ὃν ἐτιμήσαντο ἀπὸ υἱῶν Ἰσραήλ·

9. Tote epleirothei to 'reithen dya Yeremiou tou propheitou, legontos, Kai elabon ta tryakonta argurya, tein timein tou tetimeimenou, 'on etimeisanto apo 'wion Ysraeil.

Hebrew/Transliteration
ט. אָז הוּקַם הַדָּבָר אֲשֶׁר נֶאֱמַר בְּיַד-הַנָּבִיא לֵאמֹר וַיִּקְחוּ אֶת-הַשְּׁלֹשִׁים הַכֶּסֶף אֶדֶר הַיְקָר אֲשֶׁר יָקַר מֵעַל-בְּנֵי יִשְׂרָאֵל:

9. Az hoo•kam ha•da•var asher ne•e•mar be•yad - ha•na•vee le•mor va•yik•choo et - sh`lo•shim ha•ke•sef eder hay•kar asher ya•kar me•al - b`ney Israel.

Rabbinic Jewish Commentary

The Syriac and Persic versions make no mention of any prophet's name, only read, "which was spoken by the prophet"; and so may as well be ascribed to Zechariah, as to Jeremy, Zech_11:12

The Jews (d) themselves own, that this prophecy belongs to the Messiah, though they interpret it of him in another manner.

"Says R. Chanun, the Israelites will have no need of the doctrine of the king Messiah in the time to come; as it is said, Isa_11:10, "to him shall the Gentiles seek", and not the Israelites: if so, for what does the king Messiah come? and what does he come to do? to gather the captives of Israel, and to give them the thirty precepts, as it is said, Zec_11:12, "and I said unto them, if ye think good". Rab says, these are the thirty mighty men; and Jochanan says, these are the thirty commands." (d) Bereshit Rabba, sect. 98. fol. 85. 3, 4.

---

10. And gave them for the potter's field, as the Lord appointed me.

Greek/Transliteration

10. καὶ ἔδωκαν αὐτὰ εἰς τὸν ἀγρὸν τοῦ κεραμέως, καθὰ συνέταξέν μοι κύριος.

10. kai edokan auta eis ton agron tou kerameos, katha sunetaxen moi kurios.

Hebrew/Transliteration

י. וַיִּתְּנוּם בְּעַד-שְׂדֵה הַיּוֹצֵר כַּאֲשֶׁר צִוָּה אֹתִי אֲדֹנָי:

10. Va•yit•noom be•ad - s`de ha•yo•tzer ka•a•sher tzi•va o•ti Adonai.

---

11. And Jesus stood before the governor: and the governor asked him, saying, Art thou the King of the Jews? And Jesus said unto him, Thou sayest.

Greek/Transliteration

11. Ὁ δὲ Ἰησοῦς ἔστη ἔμπροσθεν τοῦ ἡγεμόνος· καὶ ἐπηρώτησεν αὐτὸν ὁ ἡγεμών, λέγων, Σὺ εἶ ὁ βασιλεὺς τῶν Ἰουδαίων; Ὁ δὲ Ἰησοῦς ἔφη αὐτῷ, Σὺ λέγεις.

11. 'O de Yeisous estei emprosthen tou 'eigemonos. kai epeiroteisen auton 'o 'eigemon, legon, Su ei 'o basileus ton Youdaion? 'O de Yeisous ephei auto, Su legeis.

Hebrew/Transliteration
יא. וְיֵשׁוּעַ עָמַד לִפְנֵי הַהֶגְמוֹן וַיִּשְׁאַל אֹתוֹ הַהֶגְמוֹן לֵאמֹר הַאַתָּה הוּא מֶלֶךְ הַיְּהוּדִים וַיֹּאמֶר אֵלָיו יֵשׁוּעַ אַתָּה:אָמָרְתָּ

11. Ve•Yeshua o•med lif•ney ha•heg•mon va•yish•al o•to ha•heg•mon le•mor ha•a•ta hoo Me•lech ha•Ye•hoo•dim va•yo•mer elav Yeshua ata amar•ta.

Rabbinic Jewish Commentary

Pilate who sat; for so was the custom for the judge to sit, and those that were judged, to stand, especially whilst witness was bore against them (f).

"Says R. Bo, in the name of Rab Hona, the witnesses ought to stand whilst they bear witness. Says R. Jeremiah, in the name of R. Abhu, also הנידונין צריכן להיות עומדין, "those that are judged ought to stand", whilst they receive their witness."

And again (g), "how do they judge? the judges sit, והנידונין עומדין, and "they that are judged stand"."

(f) T. Hieros. Yoma, fol. 43. 2, 3. (g) Ib. Sanhedrin, fol. 21. 2.

---

12. And when he was accused of the chief priests and elders, he answered nothing.

Greek/Transliteration
12. Καὶ ἐν τῷ κατηγορεῖσθαι αὐτὸν ὑπὸ τῶν ἀρχιερέων καὶ τῶν πρεσβυτέρων, οὐδὲν ἀπεκρίνατο.

12. Kai en to kateigoreisthai auton 'upo ton archiereon kai ton presbuteron, ouden apekrinato.

Hebrew/Transliteration
יב. וְרָאשֵׁי הַכֹּהֲנִים וְהַזְּקֵנִים הֵבִיאוּ עָלָיו שִׂטְנָתָם וְלֹא עָנָה אֹתָם דָּבָר:

12. Ve•ra•shey ha•ko•hanim ve•ha•z`ke•nim he•vi•oo alav sit•na•tam ve•lo ana otam davar.

---

13. Then said Pilate unto him, Hearest thou not how many things they witness against thee?

Greek/Transliteration
13. Τότε λέγει αὐτῷ ὁ Πιλάτος, Οὐκ ἀκούεις πόσα σοῦ καταμαρτυροῦσιν;

13. Tote legei auto 'o Pilatos, Ouk akoueis posa sou katamarturousin?

Hebrew/Transliteration
יג. וַיֹּאמֶר אֵלָיו פִּילָטוֹס הֲלֹא שֹׁמֵעַ אַתָּה עַד-כַּמָּה הִכְבִּירוּ לַעֲנוֹת בָּךְ:

13. Va•yo•mer elav Pilatos ha•lo sho•me•a ata ad - ka•ma hich•bi•roo la•a•not bach?

---

14. And he answered him to never a word; insomuch that the governor marvelled greatly.

Greek/Transliteration
14. Καὶ οὐκ ἀπεκρίθη αὐτῷ πρὸς οὐδὲ ἓν ῥῆμα, ὥστε θαυμάζειν τὸν ἡγεμόνα λίαν.

14. Kai ouk apekrithei auto pros oude 'en 'reima, 'oste thaumazein ton 'eigemona lian.

Hebrew/Transliteration
יד. וְלֹא נָתַן לוֹ מַעֲנֶה אַף לֹא דָבָר אֶחָד עַד אֲשֶׁר-הָיָה לְפֶלֶא בְּעֵינֵי הַהֶגְמוֹן:

14. Ve•lo na•tan lo ma•a•ne af lo da•var e•chad ad asher - ha•ya le•fe•le be•ei•ney ha•heg•mon.

---

15. Now at that feast the governor was wont to release unto the people a prisoner, whom they would.

Greek/Transliteration
15. Κατὰ δὲ ἑορτὴν εἰώθει ὁ ἡγεμὼν ἀπολύειν ἕνα τῷ ὄχλῳ δέσμιον, ὃν ἤθελον.

15. Kata de 'eortein eiothei 'o 'eigemon apoluein 'ena to ochlo desmion, 'on eithelon.

Hebrew/Transliteration
טו. וּבֶחַג הַזֶּה הַסְכֵּן הִסְכִּין הַהֶגְמוֹן לְשַׁלַּח אֶחָד מֵהָאֲסִירִים אֲשֶׁר יִבְחֲרוּ בוֹ הָעָם לַחָפְשִׁי:

15. Oo•ve•chag ha•ze has•ken his•kin ha•heg•mon le•sha•lach e•chad me•ha•a•si•rim asher yiv•cha•roo vo ha•am la•chof•shi.

Rabbinic/Jewish Commentary
It was but once a year that this was done; at every returning passover; and so the Persic version renders it, "every year on the day of the feast"; that is, of the passover, and which was frequently called by way of emphasis, חג, "the feast".

---

16. And they had then a notable prisoner, called Barabbas.

Greek/Transliteration
16. Εἶχον δὲ τότε δέσμιον ἐπίσημον, λεγόμενον Βαραββᾶν.

16. Eichon de tote desmion episeimon, legomenon Barabban.

Hebrew/Transliteration
טז. וּבָעֵת הַהִיא הָיָה לָהֶם אִישׁ אָסִיר נוֹדָע לָעָם וּשְׁמוֹ בַּר-אַבָּא:

16. Oo•va•et ha•hee ha•ya la•hem eesh asir no•da la•am oo•sh`mo Bar - Aba.

Rabbinic Jewish Commentary

called Barabbas; that is, as the Syriac version reads it, בר אבא, which signifies "the son of a father": a father's child that was spoiled and ruined, and a child of his father the devil. This was a name common among the Jews. Frequent mention is made of R. Abba (h), and Bar Abba is the son of Abba: hence we read of Abba Bar Abba (i), and of R. Samuel Bar Abba (k) and of R. Simeon Bar Abba (l), and of R. Chijah Bar Abba (m). In Munster's Hebrew Gospel it is read בר רבה, "Bar Rabbah, the son of a master"; and so Jerom says, that in the Gospel according to the Hebrews it is interpreted, "the son of their master"; but the former is the right name, and the true sense of the word. The Ethiopic version adds, "the prince", or "chief of robbers, and all knew him"; and the Arabic, instead of a "prisoner", reads, a "thief", as he was.

(h) Juchasin, fol. 70. 1, &c. (i) T. Bab. Beracot, fol. 18. 2. & Hieros Pesachim, fol. 32. 1. & Juchasin, fol. 104. 1. (k) T. Hieros. Pesachim, fol. 32. 1. (l) T. Hieros. Succa, fol. 53. 3. Juchasin, fol. 105. 1. (m) T. Hieros. Succa, fol, 55. 3. Juchasin, fol. 91. 2.

---

17. Therefore when they were gathered together, Pilate said unto them, Whom will ye that I release unto you? Barabbas, or Jesus which is called Christ?

Greek/Transliteration
17. Συνηγμένων οὖν αὐτῶν, εἶπεν αὐτοῖς ὁ Πιλάτος, Τίνα θέλετε ἀπολύσω ὑμῖν; Βαραββᾶν, ἢ Ἰησοῦν τὸν λεγόμενον χριστόν;

17. Suneigmenon oun auton, eipen autois 'o Pilatos, Tina thelete apoluso 'umin? Barabban, ei Yeisoun ton legomenon christon?

Hebrew/Transliteration
יז. וַיְהִי בְּהִקָּהֲלָם וַיֹּאמֶר אֲלֵיהֶם פִּילָטוֹס בְּמִי תִבְחֲרוּ וַאֲשַׁלְּחֵהוּ לָכֶם בְּבַר-אַבָּא אוֹ בְיֵשׁוּעַ הַנִּקְרָא מָשִׁיחַ:

17. Vay•hi be•hi•ka•ha•lam va•yo•mer aley•hem Pilatos be•mi tiv•cha•roo va•a•shal•che•hoo la•chem be•Var - Aba oh ve•Yeshua ha•nik•ra Mashi•ach?

18. For he knew that for envy they had delivered him.

Greek/Transliteration
18. ῎δει γὰρ ὅτι διὰ φθόνον παρέδωκαν αὐτόν.

18. dei gar 'oti dya phthonon paredokan auton.

Hebrew/Transliteration
:יח. כִּי יָדַע אֲשֶׁר מִקִּנְאָתָם בּוֹ הִסְגִּירֻהוּ

18. Ki ya•da asher mi•kin•a•tam bo his•gi•roo•hoo.

---

19. When he was set down on the judgment seat, his wife sent unto him, saying, Have thou nothing to do with that just man: for I have suffered many things this day in a dream because of him.

Greek/Transliteration
19. Καθημένου δὲ αὐτοῦ ἐπὶ τοῦ βήματος, ἀπέστειλεν πρὸς αὐτὸν ἡ γυνὴ αὐτοῦ, λέγουσα, Μηδέν σοι καὶ τῷ δικαίῳ ἐκείνῳ· πολλὰ γὰρ ἔπαθον σήμερον κατ᾽ ὄναρ δι᾽ αὐτόν.

19. Katheimenou de autou epi tou beimatos, apesteilen pros auton 'ei gunei autou, legousa, Meiden soi kai to dikaio ekeino. polla gar epathon seimeron kat onar di auton.

Hebrew/Transliteration
יט. וְגַם-בְּשִׁבְתּוֹ בִּמְקוֹם הַמִּשְׁפָּט שָׁלְחָה לּוֹ אִשְׁתּוֹ לֵאמֹר אַל-תִּתְעָרֶב בִּדְבַר הַצַּדִּיק הַזֶּה כִּי זֶה הַיּוֹם עֻנֵּיתִי:בַחֲלוֹם עַד-מְאֹד עַל-אֹדוֹתָיו

19. Ve•gam - be•shiv•to bim•kom ha•mish•pat shal•cha lo eesh•to le•mor al - tit•a•rav bid•var ha•tza•dik ha•ze ki ze ha•yom oo•ney•ti va•cha•lom ad - me•od al - o•do•tav.

---

20. But the chief priests and elders persuaded the multitude that they should ask Barabbas, and destroy Jesus.

Greek/Transliteration
20. Οἱ δὲ ἀρχιερεῖς καὶ οἱ πρεσβύτεροι ἔπεισαν τοὺς ὄχλους ἵνα αἰτήσωνται τὸν Βαραββᾶν, τὸν δὲ Ἰησοῦν ἀπολέσωσιν.

20. 'Oi de archiereis kai 'oi presbuteroi epeisan tous ochlous 'ina aiteisontai ton Barabban, ton de Yeisoun apolesosin.

Hebrew/Transliteration
:כ. וְרָאשֵׁי הַכֹּהֲנִים וְהַזְּקֵנִים הֵסִיתוּ אֶת-הֲמוֹן הָעָם לִשְׁאֹל לָהֶם אֶת בַּר-אַבָּא וּלְהַשְׁמִיד אֶת-יֵשׁוּעַ

20. Ve•ra•shey ha•ko•ha•nim ve•ha•z`ke•nim he•si•too et - ha•mon ha•am lish•ol la•hem et Bar - Aba ool•hash•mid et - Yeshua.

21. The governor answered and said unto them, Whether of the twain will ye that I release unto you? They said, Barabbas.

Greek/Transliteration
21. Ἀποκριθεὶς δὲ ὁ ἡγεμὼν εἶπεν αὐτοῖς, Τίνα θέλετε ἀπὸ τῶν δύο ἀπολύσω ὑμῖν; Οἱ δὲ εἶπον, Βαραββᾶν.

21. Apokritheis de 'o 'eigemon eipen autois, Tina thelete apo ton duo apoluso 'umin? 'Oi de eipon, Barabban.

Hebrew/Transliteration
:כא. וַיַּעַן הַהֶגְמוֹן וַיֹּאמֶר אֲלֵיהֶם אֶת-מִי מִן-הַשְּׁנַיִם תַּחְפְּצוּ וַאֲשַׁלְּחֵהוּ לָכֶם וַיֹּאמְרוּ אֶת בַּר-אַבָּא

21. Va•ya•an ha•heg•mon va•yo•mer aley•hem et - mee min - hash•na•yim tach•pe•tzoo va•a•shal•che•hoo la•chem va•yom•roo et Bar - Aba.

22. Pilate saith unto them, What shall I do then with Jesus which is called Christ? They all say unto him, Let him be crucified.

Greek/Transliteration
22. Λέγει αὐτοῖς ὁ Πιλάτος, Τί οὖν ποιήσω Ἰησοῦν τὸν λεγόμενον χριστόν; Λέγουσιν αὐτῷ πάντες, Σταυρωθήτω.

22. Legei autois 'o Pilatos, Ti oun poieiso Yeisoun ton legomenon christon? Legousin auto pantes, Staurotheito.

Hebrew/Transliteration
:כב. וַיֹּאמֶר אֲלֵיהֶם פִּילָטוֹס וּמַה-אֶעֱשֶׂה לְיֵשׁוּעַ הַנִּקְרָא מָשִׁיחַ וַיֹּאמְרוּ כֻלָּם יִצָּלֵב

22. Va•yo•mer aley•hem Pilatos oo•ma - e•e•se le•Yeshua ha•nik•ra Mashi•ach va•yom•roo choo•lam yi•tza•lev.

23. And the governor said, Why, what evil hath he done? But they cried out the more, saying, Let him be crucified.

Greek/Transliteration
23. Ὁ δὲ ἡγεμὼν ἔφη, Τί γὰρ κακὸν ἐποίησεν; Οἱ δὲ περισσῶς ἔκραζον, λέγοντες, Σταυρωθήτω.

23. 'O de 'eigemon ephei, Ti gar kakon epoieisen? 'Oi de perissos ekrazon, legontes, Staurotheito.

Hebrew/Transliteration
:כג. וַיֹּאמֶר וְלָמָּה מֶה-רָעָה עָשָׂה וְהֵם הוֹסִיפוּ לִצְעֹק וְלֵאמֹר יִצָּלֵב

23. Va•yo•mer ve•la•ma me - ra•ah asa ve•hem ho•si•foo litz•ok ve•le•mor yi•tza•lev.

---

24. When Pilate saw that he could prevail nothing, but that rather a tumult was made, he took water, and washed his hands before the multitude, saying, I am innocent of the blood of this just person: see ye to it.

Greek/Transliteration
24. Ἰδὼν δὲ ὁ Πιλάτος ὅτι οὐδὲν ὠφελεῖ, ἀλλὰ μᾶλλον θόρυβος γίνεται, λαβὼν ὕδωρ, ἀπενίψατο τὰς χεῖρας ἀπέναντι τοῦ ὄχλου, λέγων, Ἀθῷός εἰμι ἀπὸ τοῦ αἵματος τοῦ δικαίου τούτου· ὑμεῖς ὄψεσθε.

24. Idon de 'o Pilatos 'oti ouden ophelei, alla mallon thorubos ginetai, labon 'udor, apenipsato tas cheiras apenanti tou ochlou, legon, Athoos eimi apo tou 'aimatos tou dikaiou toutou. 'umeis opsesthe.

Hebrew/Transliteration
כד. וַיַּרְא פִּילָטוֹס כִּי לֹא-יָכֹל לָהֶם אַךְ עוֹד תּוֹסִיף הַמְּהוּמָה וַיִּקַּח מַיִם וַיִּרְחַץ אֶת-יָדָיו לְעֵינֵי הָעָם וַיֹּאמֶר נָקִי אָנֹכִי מִדַּם הַצַּדִּיק הַזֶּה רְאוּ אַתֶּם

24. Va•yar Pilatos ki lo - ya•chol la•hem ach od to•sif ham•hoo•ma va•yi•kach ma•yim va•yir•chatz et - ya•dav le•ei•ney ha•am va•yo•mar na•ki ano•chi mi•dam ha•tza•dik ha•ze r`oo atem.

Rabbinic Jeweish Commentary
but that rather a tumult was made; there was an uproar among the people, and he might fear the consequences of it, should he not grant their request; otherwise, as Philo the (p) Jew says of him, he was, την φυσιν ακαμπης και μετα του ανθαδους αμειλικτος, "naturally inflexible, rigid, and self-willed"

He took water, and washed his hands before the multitude; either in conformity to a custom among the Jews, whereby they testified their innocence as to the commission of murder; see Deu_21:6, or to a Gentile one, used when murder was committed, for the lustration or expiation of it (q)

(p) De Legat. ad Caium, p. 1034. (q) Vid. Ovid. Fast. l. 2. Anticlidis Redit. l. 74. Triclinius in Ajac. Sophocl. 3. 1.

---

25. Then answered all the people, and said, His blood be on us, and on our children.

Greek/Translitration
25. Καὶ ἀποκριθεὶς πᾶς ὁ λαὸς εἶπεν, Τὸ αἷμα αὐτοῦ ἐφ᾽ ἡμᾶς καὶ ἐπὶ τὰ τέκνα ἡμῶν.

25. Kai apokritheis pas 'o laos eipen, To 'aima autou eph 'eimas kai epi ta tekna 'eimon.

Hebrew/Transliteration
:כה. וַיַּעֲנוּ כָל-הָעָם לֵאמֹר דָּמוֹ עָלֵינוּ וְעַל-בָּנֵינוּ

25. Va•ya•a•noo chol - ha•am le•mor da•mo aley•noo ve•al - ba•ney•noo.

TaNaKh-Old Testament/Rabbinic Jewish Commentary

"It shall come about that anyone who goes out of the doors of your house into the street, his blood *shall be* on his own head, and we *shall be* free; but anyone who is with you in the house, his blood *shall be* on our head if a hand is *laid* on him."
(Joshua_2:19)

The Talmud (s): and it is a notion of the Jews, that the guilt of innocent blood, and the blood of that innocent man's children, lie not only upon the persons immediately concerned, but upon their children to the end of the world: and so the judges used to address the witnesses upon a trial, after this manner (t);

"know ye, that capital causes, are not as pecuniary ones: in pecuniary causes, a man gives his money, and it atones for him; but in capital causes, דמו ודם זרעו תלויין בו, "his blood, and the blood of his seed, hang upon him", to the end of the whole world: for lo! of Cain it is said, "the voice of the blood of thy brother cryeth", his blood, and the blood of his seed."

Five hundred of the Jews and more, were sometimes crucified in a day, whilst Titus was besieging the city; till at length there wanted "room for crosses", και σταυροι τοις σωμασι "and crosses for bodies", as Josephus (u) says, who was an eyewitness of it: and to this day, this dreadful wish of the blood of Yeshua upon them, is to be seen in their miserable, abject, and captive state; and will be, until such time that they look to him whom they have pierced, and mourn in repentance.

(s) T. Bab. Pesachim, fol. 110. 1. Yoma, fol. 21. 1. & Avoda Zara, fol. 12. 2. (t) Maimon. Hilch. Sanhedrin, c. 12. sect. 3. (u) De Bello Jud. l. 6. c. 12.

---

26. Then released he Barabbas unto them: and when he had scourged Jesus, he delivered him to be crucified.

Greek/Transliteration
26. Τότε ἀπέλυσεν αὐτοῖς τὸν Βαραββᾶν· τὸν δὲ Ἰησοῦν φραγελλώσας παρέδωκεν ἵνα σταυρωθῇ.

26. Tote apelusen autois ton Barabban. ton de Yeisoun phragellosas paredoken 'ina staurothei.

Hebrew/Transliteration
:כו. אָז שִׁלַּח לָהֶם אֶת בַּר-אַבָּא וְאֶת יֵשׁוּעַ יִסַּר בַּשּׁוֹטִים וַיִּתְּנֵהוּ לְהִצָּלֵב

26. Az shi•lach la•hem et Bar - Aba ve•et Yeshua yi•sar ba•sho•tim va•yit•ne•hoo le•hi•tza•lev.

Rabbinic Jewish Commentary
The Jews themselves own this scourging of Jesus, only they ascribe it to the elders of Jerusalem, and relate it thus (y): "the elders of Jerusalem took Yeshua, and brought him to the city, and bound him to a marble pillar in the city, ויכוהו בשוטים, "and smote him with whips", or "whipped him"; and said unto him, where are all thy miracles which thou hast done?"
(y) Toldos Jesu, p. 17.

---

27. Then the soldiers of the governor took Jesus into the common hall, and gathered unto him the whole band of soldiers.

Greek/Transliteration
27. Τότε οἱ στρατιῶται τοῦ ἡγεμόνος, παραλαβόντες τὸν Ἰησοῦν εἰς τὸ πραιτώριον, συνήγαγον ἐπ' αὐτὸν ὅλην τὴν σπεῖραν·

27. Tote 'oi stratiotai tou 'eigemonos, paralabontes ton Yeisoun eis to praitorion, suneigagon ep auton 'olein tein speiran.

Hebrew/Transliteration
:כז. וַיִּקְחוּ אַנְשֵׁי צְבָא הַהֶגְמוֹן אֶת-יֵשׁוּעַ אֶל-בֵּית-הַמִּשְׁפָּט וַיַּזְעִיקוּ עָלָיו אֶת כָּל-הַגְּדוּד

27. Va•yik•choo an•shey tz`va ha•heg•mon et - Yeshua el - beit -ha•mish•pat hoo Pe•ra•to•rin va•yaz•ee•koo alav et kol - ha•g`dood.

---

28. And they stripped him, and put on him a scarlet robe.

Greek/Transliteration
28. καὶ ἐκδύσαντες αὐτόν, περιέθηκαν αὐτῷ χλαμύδα κοκκίνην.

28. kai ekdusantes auton, perietheikan auto chlamuda kokkinein.

Hebrew/Transliteration
:כח. וַיַּפְשִׁיטוּ אֹתוֹ וַיַּלְבִּישֻׁהוּ מְעִיל אַרְגָּמָן

28. Va•yaf•shi•too o•to va•yal•bi•shoo•hoo me•eel ar•ga•man.

29. And when they had platted a crown of thorns, they put it upon his head, and a reed in his right hand: and they bowed the knee before him, and mocked him, saying, Hail, King of the Jews!

Greek/Transliteration
29. Καὶ πλέξαντες στέφανον ἐξ ἀκανθῶν, ἐπέθηκαν ἐπὶ τὴν κεφαλὴν αὐτοῦ, καὶ κάλαμον ἐπὶ τὴν δεξιὰν αὐτοῦ· καὶ γονυπετήσαντες ἔμπροσθεν αὐτοῦ ἐνέπαιζον αὐτῷ, λέγοντες, Χαῖρε, ὁ βασιλεὺς τῶν Ἰουδαίων·

29. Kai plexantes stephanon ex akanthon, epetheikan epi tein kephalein autou, kai kalamon epi tein dexyan autou. kai gonupeteisantes emprosthen autou enepaizon auto, legontes, Chaire, 'o basileus ton Youdaion.

Hebrew/Transliteration
כט. וַיְשָׂרְגוּ כֶתֶר קוֹצִים וַיָּשִׂימוּ עַל-רֹאשׁוֹ וְקָנֶה בִימִינוֹ וַיִּכְרְעוּ לְפָנָיו עַל-בִּרְכֵיהֶם וַיְהַתֵּלּוּ בוֹ לֵאמֹר יְחִי מֶלֶךְ הַיְּהוּדִים:

29. Vay•sar•goo ke•ter ko•tzim va•ya•si•moo al - ro•sho ve•ka•ne viy•mi•no va•yich•re•oo le•fa•nav al - bir•chey•hem vay•hat•loo vo le•mor Ye•chi Me•lech ha•Ye•hoo•dim.

Rabbinic Jewish Commentary
The Jews acknowledge this circumstance of the sufferings of Jesus, though they ascribe it to the elders of Jerusalem; who, they say (d),

"took thorns and made a crown of them, and put it upon his head."
(d) Toldos Jesu, p. 17.

---

30. And they spit upon him, and took the reed, and smote him on the head.

Greek/Transliteration
30. καὶ ἐμπτύσαντες εἰς αὐτόν, ἔλαβον τὸν κάλαμον, καὶ ἔτυπτον εἰς τὴν κεφαλὴν αὐτοῦ.

30. kai emptusantes eis auton, elabon ton kalamon, kai etupton eis tein kephalein autou.

Hebrew/Transliteration
ל: וַיָּרֹקּוּ בְּפָנָיו וַיִּקְחוּ אֶת-הַקָּנֶה וַיַּכֵּהוּ עַל-רֹאשׁוֹ

30. Va•ya•ro•koo be•fa•nav va•yik•choo et - ha•ka•ne va•ya•koo•hoo al - ro•sho.

---

31. And after that they had mocked him, they took the robe off from him, and put his own raiment on him, and led him away to crucify him.

Greek/Transliteration
31. Καὶ ὅτε ἐνέπαιξαν αὐτῷ, ἐξέδυσαν αὐτὸν τὴν χλαμύδα, καὶ ἐνέδυσαν αὐτὸν τὰ ἱμάτια αὐτοῦ, καὶ ἀπήγαγον αὐτὸν εἰς τὸ σταυρῶσαι.

31. Kai 'ote enepaixan auto, exedusan auton tein chlamuda, kai enedusan auton ta 'imatya autou, kai apeigagon auton eis to staurosai.

Hebrew/Transliteration
לא. וְאַחֲרֵי אֲשֶׁר הֵתֵלּוּ בוֹ הִפְשִׁיטוּ אֹתוֹ אֶת-הַמְּעִיל וַיַּלְבִּישֻׁהוּ אֶת-בְּגָדָיו וַיּוֹלִיכֻהוּ לִצְלֹב אֹתוֹ:

31. Ve•a•cha•rey asher he•te•loo vo hif•shi•too o•to et - ham•eel va•yal•bi•shoo•hoo et - be•ga•dav va•yo•li•choo•hoo litz•lov o•to.

Rabbinic Jewish Commentary
and led him away to crucify him; for a condemned person was always executed the same day: their canon is (e),

"after that his judgment, or sentence is finished, they do not tarry with him, but slay him, ביומו, "that very day".

And their custom was this, "he whose sentence for death is finished, they bring him out from the house of judgment; and one stands at the door of it, and linen clothes in his hand, and a horse at some distance from him; and a crier goes out before him, "saying", such an one is going to be executed with such a death, because he has committed such a sin, in such a place, at such a time, such and such being witnesses; whoever knows him to be innocent, let him come, and speak in his favour: if one says, I have something to say in his favour: this waves with the linen clothes, and the other rides upon the horse, and runs and brings back him that is judged, to the sanhedrim; and if he is found innocent, they dismiss him: but if not, he returns, and goes to execution (f). The Jews pretend (g), that a crier went out before Jesus of Nazareth, forty days before his execution, and made such a proclamation, but found none that had any thing to say in his favour, and therefore hanged him on the evening of the passover. But this is false; Yeshua had no such length of time, or his friends any liberty granted them to speak for him.

(e) Maimon. Hilch. Sanhedrin, c. 12. sect. 4. Misn. Sanhed. c. 6. sect. 1. (f) Maimon. Hilch. Sanhedrin, c. 13. sect. 1. (g) T. Bab. Sanhedrin, fol. 43. 1.

---

32. And as they came out, they found a man of Cyrene, Simon by name: him they compelled to bear his cross.

Greek/Transliteration
32. Ἐξερχόμενοι δὲ εὗρον ἄνθρωπον Κυρηναῖον, ὀνόματι Σίμωνα· τοῦτον ἠγγάρευσαν ἵνα ἄρῃ τὸν σταυρὸν αὐτοῦ.

32. Exerchomenoi de 'euron anthropon Kureinaion, onomati Simona. touton eingareusan 'ina arei ton stauron autou.

Hebrew/Transliteration

לב: וְכַאֲשֶׁר יָצְאוּ פָּגְעוּ בְּאִישׁ קוּרִינִי וּשְׁמוֹ שִׁמְעוֹן אֹתוֹ אִלְּצוּ לָהֲלֹךְ אִתָּם וְלָשֵׂאת לוֹ אֶת-צְלָבוֹ

32. Ve•cha•a•sher yatz•oo pag•oo be•eesh Koo•ri•ni oo•sh`mo Shimon o•to eel•tzoo la•ha•loch ee•tam ve•la•set lo et - tze•la•vo.

Rabbinic Jewish Commentary

Of the city; for no execution was made, neither in the court of judicature, nor in the city, but at some distance; as it was at stoning, so at crucifixion (h):

"when judgment was finished, they brought him out to be stoned; the place of stoning was without the sanhedrim, as it is said, Lev_24:14, "bring forth him that hath cursed without the camp".

Upon which the gloss and Gemara say (i), without the three camps; which were these, the court which was the camp of the Shekinah; or the divine presence; and the mountain of the house, the camp of the Levites; and the city, the camp of Israel; so that he that was executed, was had without the city.

Maimonides (k) says, "the place in which the sanhedrim executed, was without it, and at a distance from it, as it is said, Lev_24:14, and it appears to me, that it was about six miles distant; for so far it was between the sanhedrim of Moses our master, which was before the door of the tabernacle of the congregation, and the camp of Israel.

(h) Misn. Sanhedrin, c. 6. sect. 1. (i) T. Bab. Sanhedrin, fol. 42. 2. (k) Hilch. Sanhedrin, c. 12. sect. 3.

---

33. And when they were come unto a place called Golgotha, that is to say, a place of a skull,

Greek/Transliteration

33. Καὶ ἐλθόντες εἰς τόπον λεγόμενον Γολγοθᾶ, ὅ ἐστιν λεγόμενος Κρανίου Τόπος,

33. Kai elthontes eis topon legomenon Golgotha, 'o estin legomenos Kraniou Topos,

Hebrew/Transliteration

לג: וַיָּבֹאוּ אֶל-הַמָּקוֹם הַנִּקְרָא גָּלְגָּלְתָּא אֲשֶׁר יֵאָמֵר מְקוֹם הַגֻּלְגֹּלֶת

33. Va•ya•vo•oo el - ha•ma•kom ha•nik•ra Gol•gal•ta asher ye•a•mer me•kom ha•gool•go•let.

Rabbinic Jewish Commentary

Some say Adam's skull was found here, and from thence the place had its name; this is an ancient tradition, but without foundation (m): it seems to be so called, because it was the place where malefactors were executed, and afterwards buried; whose bones and skulls in process of time might be dug up, and some of them might lie scattered about in this place: for, one that was executed as a malefactor,

(n)"they did not bury him in the sepulchres of his ancestors; but there were two places of burial appointed by the sanhedrim; one for those that were stoned, and for those that were burnt; and another for those that were killed with the sword, and for those that were strangled; and when their flesh was consumed, they gathered the bones, and buried them in their place"; i.e. in the sepulchres of their ancestors.

(m) Misn. Sanhedrin, c. 6. sect. 4. 5. (n) T. Bab. Sanhedrin, fol. 43. 1. Maimon. Hilch. Sauhedrin, c. 13. sect. 2, 3.

---

34. They gave him vinegar to drink mingled with gall: and when he had tasted thereof, he would not drink.

Greek/Transliteration
34. ἔδωκαν αὐτῷ πιεῖν ὄξος μετὰ χολῆς μεμιγμένον· καὶ γευσάμενος οὐκ ἤθελεν πιεῖν.

34. edokan auto piein oxos meta choleis memigmenon. kai geusamenos ouk eithelen piein.

Hebrew/Transliteration
:לד. וַיִּתְּנוּ-לוֹ יַיִן מָהוּל בְּרֹאשׁ לִשְׁתּוֹת וַיִּטְעַם וְלֹא אָבָה לִשְׁתּוֹתוֹ

34. Va•yit•noo - lo ya•yin ma•hool be•rosh lish•tot va•yit•am ve•lo ava lish•to•to.

Rabbinic Jewish Commentary
It was a custom with the Jews (o) when "a man went out to be executed, to give him to drink a grain of frankincense in a cup of wine, that his understanding might be disturbed, as it is said, Pro_31:6. "Give strong drink to him that is ready to perish, and wine to those that be of heavy hearts"; and the tradition is, that the honourable women in Jerusalem gave this freely; but if they did not, it was provided at the charge of the congregation.

the Jews had a notion of vinegar's being expressive of the chastisements of the Messiah; the words in Rth_2:14, they say (q), "speak of the king Messiah; "come thou hither", draw nigh to the kingdom; "and eat of the bread", this is the bread of the kingdom, "and dip thy morsel in the vinegar",

אלו הייסורין, "these are the chastisements", as it is said in Isa_53:5, "he was wounded for our transgressions".

By this offer was fulfilled the prophecy in Psa_69:21, and which he did not altogether refuse; for it follows,

(o) T. Bab. Avoda Zara, fol. 12. 2. (p) Midrash Ruth, fol. 33. 2.

---

35. And they crucified him, and parted his garments, casting lots: that it might be fulfilled which was spoken by the prophet, They parted my garments among them, and upon my vesture did they cast lots.

Greek/Transliteration
35. Σταυρώσαντες δὲ αὐτόν, διεμερίσαντο τὰ ἱμάτια αὐτοῦ, βάλλοντες κλῆρον.

35. Staurosantes de auton, diemerisanto ta 'imatya autou, ballontes kleiron.

Hebrew/Transliteration
לה. וַיִּצְלְבוּ אֹתוֹ שָׁם וַיְחַלְּקוּ אֶת-בְּגָדָיו וַיַּפִּילוּ עֲלֵיהֶם גּוֹרָל לְמַלֹּאת אֶת אֲשֶׁר-נֶאֱמַר בְּפִי הַנָּבִיא יְחַלְּקוּ בְגָדַי:לָהֶם וְעַל-לְבוּשִׁי יַפִּילוּ גוֹרָל

35. Va•yitz•le•voo o•to sham va•ye•chal•koo et - be•ga•dav va•ya•pi•loo aley•hem go•ral le•ma•lot et asher - ne•e•mar be•fi ha•na•vee ye•chal•koo ve•ga•dai la•hem ve•al - le•voo•shi ya•pi•loo go•ral.

Rabbinic Jewish Commentary
and parted his garments, casting lots: for they stripped him of his clothes before they fixed him to the cross, and crucified him naked, as was the custom of the Romans (s); as it was of the Jews to stone and hang persons naked: their canons say this (t), "when he is four cubits off of the place of stoning, they strip off his garments; a man they cover before, a woman both behind and before; the words of Judah: but the wise men say, a man is stoned naked, and a woman is not stoned naked: a man, they hang him with his face to the people; a woman, with her face to the tree. R. Eliezer, and the wise men say, a man is hanged, but a woman is not hanged.

On which the Gemara (u) says, "what is the sense of the Rabbins? the Scripture says, "thou shalt hang him"; him, and not her: and, says R. Eliezer, him, בלא כסותו, "without his clothes".

(s) Lipsius de Cruce, l. 2. c. 7. (t) Misn. Sanhedrin, c. 6. sect. 3, 4. (u) T. Bab. Sanhedrin, fol. 46. 1.

---

36. And sitting down they watched him there;

Greek/Transliteration
36. Καὶ καθήμενοι ἐτήρουν αὐτὸν ἐκεῖ.

36. Kai katheimenoi eteiroun auton ekei.

Hebrew/Transliteration
לו. וַיֵּשְׁבוּ וַיִּשְׁמְרוּ אֹתוֹ שָׁמָּה:

36. Va•yesh•voo va•yish•me•roo o•to sha•ma.

---

37. And set up over his head his accusation written, THIS IS JESUS THE KING OF THE JEWS.

Greek/Transliteration
37. Καὶ ἐπέθηκαν ἐπάνω τῆς κεφαλῆς αὐτοῦ τὴν αἰτίαν αὐτοῦ γεγραμμένην, Οὗτός ἐστιν Ἰησοῦς ὁ βασιλεὺς τῶν Ἰουδαίων.

37. Kai epetheikan epano teis kephaleis autou tein aitian autou gegrammenein, 'Outos estin Yeisous 'o basileus ton Youdaion.

Hebrew/Transliteration
לז. וַיָּשִׂימוּ דְבַר אַשְׁמָתוֹ בִּכְתֹבֶת מֵעַל לְרֹאשׁוֹ זֶה הוּא יֵשׁוּעַ מֶלֶךְ הַיְּהוּדִים:

37. Va•ya•si•moo de•var ash•ma•to bich•to•vet me•al le•ro•sho ze hoo Yeshua Me•lech ha•Ye•hoo•dim.

---

38. Then were there two thieves crucified with him, one on the right hand, and another on the left.

Greek/Transliteration
38. Τότε σταυροῦνται σὺν αὐτῷ δύο λῃσταί, εἷς ἐκ δεξιῶν καὶ εἷς ἐξ εὐωνύμων.

38. Tote staurountai sun auto duo leistai, 'eis ek dexion kai 'eis ex euonumon.

Hebrew/Transliteration
לח. וְאַחֲרֵי-כֵן נִצְלְבוּ עִמּוֹ שְׁנֵי אַנְשֵׁי-חָמָס אֶחָד מִימִינוֹ וְאֶחָד מִשְּׂמֹאלוֹ:

38. Ve•a•cha•rey - chen nitz•le•voo ee•mo sh`ney an•shey - cha•mas e•chad miy•mi•no ve•e•chad mis•mo•lo.

Rabbinic Jewish Commentary
Then were there two thieves crucified with him,.... Which seems contrary to one of their canons, which runs thus; ביום אחד.

אין דנין שנים, "they do not judge two in one day" (y), unless they were both in the same crime, and died the same death: but here were three persons, Yeshua, and these two malefactors, condemned and executed in one, and the same day.

(y) T. Bab. Sanhedrin, fol. 35. 1. & 46. 1. Bemidbar Rabba, sect. 8. fol. 190. 1.

---

39. And they that passed by reviled him, wagging their heads,

Greek/Transliteration
39. Οἱ δὲ παραπορευόμενοι ἐβλασφήμουν αὐτόν, κινοῦντες τὰς κεφαλὰς αὐτῶν,

39. 'Oi de paraporeuomenoi eblaspheimoun auton, kinountes tas kephalas auton,

Hebrew/Transliteration
לט׃ וְהָעֹבְרִים שָׁם גִּדְפוּ אֹתוֹ וַיָּנִיעוּ אַחֲרָיו אֶת-רֹאשָׁם

39. Ve•ha•ov•rim sham gid•foo o•to va•ya•ni•oo a•cha•rav et - ro•sham.

TaNaKh-Old Testament/Rabbinic Jewish Commentary
"With which Your enemies have reproached, O LORD, With which they have reproached the footsteps of Your Anointed.(Messiah)" (Psa_89:51)

Jarchi explains by סופי, "the ends of the king Messiah"; his last times, towards the close of his days; and cites that passage in the Misna (z),

"in the heels, or, as Buxtorf renders it, in the end of the days of the Messiah impudence shall be multiplied, as it now was exceedingly:
(z) Sota, c. 9. sect. 15.

---

40. And saying, Thou that destroyest the temple, and buildest it in three days, save thyself. If thou be the Son of God, come down from the cross.

Greek/Transliteration
40. καὶ λέγοντες, Ὁ καταλύων τὸν ναὸν καὶ ἐν τρισὶν ἡμέραις οἰκοδομῶν, σῶσον σεαυτόν· εἰ υἱὸς εἶ τοῦ θεοῦ, κατάβηθι ἀπὸ τοῦ σταυροῦ.

40. kai legontes, 'O kataluon ton naon kai en trisin 'eimerais oikodomon, soson seauton. ei 'wios ei tou theou, katabeithi apo tou staurou.

Hebrew/Transliteration
מ. וַיֹּאמְרוּ אַתָּה הוּא הַהֹרֵס אֶת - הַהֵיכָל וְהַבּוֹנֶה אֹתוֹ בִּשְׁלֹשֶׁת יָמִים הוֹשִׁיעָה אֶת-נַפְשְׁךָ אִם בֶּן-אֱלֹהִים אַתָּה:רְדָה מִן-הָעֵץ

40. Va•yom•roo ata hoo ha•ho•res et - ha•hey•chal ve•ha•bo•ne o•to bish•lo•shet ya•mim ho•shi•ah et - naf•she•cha eem Ben - Elohim ata r`da min - ha•etz.

Rabbinic Jewish Commentary
The Jews themselves say (a) that the following words were said to Jesus on the cross, "if thou be the Son of God, why dost thou not deliver thyself out of our hands?" (a) Toldos Jesu, p. 17.

---

41. Likewise also the chief priests mocking him, with the scribes and elders, said,

Greek/Transliteration
41. Ὁμοίως δὲ καὶ οἱ ἀρχιερεῖς ἐμπαίζοντες μετὰ τῶν γραμματέων καὶ πρεσβυτέρων καὶ Φαρισαίων ἔλεγον,

41. 'Omoios de kai 'oi archiereis empaizontes meta ton grammateon kai presbuteron kai Pharisaion elegon,

Hebrew/Transliteration
מא. וְכֵן גַּם-שָׂחֲקוּ עָלָיו רָאשֵׁי הַכֹּהֲנִים עִם-הַסּוֹפְרִים וְהַזְּקֵנִים לֵאמֹר:

41. Ve•chen gam - sa•cha•koo alav ra•shey ha•ko•hanim eem - ha•sofrim ve•ha•z`ke•nim le•mor.

---

42. He saved others; himself he cannot save. If he be the King of Israel, let him now come down from the cross, and we will believe him.

Greek/Transliteration
42. Ἄλλους ἔσωσεν, ἑαυτὸν οὐ δύναται σῶσαι. Εἰ βασιλεὺς Ἰσραήλ ἐστιν, καταβάτω νῦν ἀπὸ τοῦ σταυροῦ, καὶ πιστεύσομεν ἐπ᾽ αὐτῷ.

42. Allous esosen, 'eauton ou dunatai sosai. Ei basileus Ysraeil estin, katabato nun apo tou staurou, kai pisteusomen ep auto.

Hebrew/Transliteration
מב. אֶת-אֲחֵרִים הוֹשִׁיעַ וְאֶת-נַפְשׁוֹ לֹא יוּכַל לְהוֹשִׁיעַ אִם-מֶלֶךְ יִשְׂרָאֵל הוּא יֵרֶד-נָא עַתָּה מִן-הָעֵץ וְנַאֲמִין בּוֹ:

42. Et - a•che•rim ho•shia ve•et - naf•sho lo yoo•chal le•ho•shi•a eem - Me•lech Israel hoo ye•red - na ata min - ha•etz ve•na•a•min bo.

---

43. He trusted in God; let him deliver him now, if he will have him: for he said, I am the Son of God.

Greek/Transliteration
43. Πέποιθεν ἐπὶ τὸν θεόν· ῥυσάσθω νῦν αὐτόν, εἰ θέλει αὐτόν. Εἶπεν γὰρ ὅτι θεοῦ εἰμι υἱός.

43. Pepoithen epi ton theon. 'rusastho nun auton, ei thelei auton. Eipen gar 'oti theou eimi 'wios.

Hebrew/Transliteration
מג. בָּטַח בֵּאלֹהִים יַצִּילֵהוּ כִּי חָפֵץ בּוֹ כִּי הֲלֹא אָמַר בֶּן־הָאֱלֹהִים אָנִי:

43. Bo•te•ach be•Elohim ya•tzi•le•hoo ki cha•fetz bo ki ha•lo amar Ben - ha•Elohim ani.

TaNaKh-Old Testament/Rabbinc Jewish Commentary
if he will have him; or if he is well pleased with him as his own Son, or delights in him as such, and will show him any favour and good will; see Psa_22:8, where are these very words, and which are predicted should be said by these men to Christ; and are a wonderful confirmation of the truth of that Psalm and prophecy belonging to him.

"Commit *yourself* to the LORD; let Him deliver him; Let Him rescue him, because He delights in him." Psa_22:8

---

44. The thieves also, which were crucified with him, cast the same in his teeth.

Greek/Transliteration
44. Τὸ δ᾽ αὐτὸ καὶ οἱ λῃσταὶ οἱ συσταυρωθέντες αὐτῷ ὠνείδιζον αὐτόν.

44. To d auto kai 'oi leistai 'oi sustaurothentes auto oneidizon auton.

Hebrew/Tranliteration
מד. וְגַם־אַנְשֵׁי־הֶחָמָס אֲשֶׁר נִצְלְבוּ עִמּוֹ חֵרְפֻהוּ כְּמוֹ־כֵן:

44. Ve•gam - an•shey - he•cha•mas asher nitz•le•voo ee•mo cher•foo•hoo k`mo - chen.

---

45. Now from the sixth hour there was darkness over all the land unto the ninth hour.

Greek/Transliteration
45. Ἀπὸ δὲ ἕκτης ὥρας σκότος ἐγένετο ἐπὶ πᾶσαν τὴν γῆν ἕως ὥρας ἐνάτης·

45. Apo de 'ekteis 'oras skotos egeneto epi pasan tein gein 'eos 'oras enateis.

Hebrew/Transliteration
מה. וְחֹשֶׁךְ כִּסָּה אֶת־פְּנֵי כָל־הָאָרֶץ מִן־הַשָּׁעָה הַשִּׁשִׁית עַד הַשָּׁעָה הַתְּשִׁיעִית:

45. Ve•cho•shech ki•sa et - p`ney chol - ha•a•retz min - ha•sha•ah ha•shi•sheet ad ha•sha•ah hat•shi•eet.

Rabbinic Jewish Commentary
there was darkness over all the land unto the ninth hour; till three o'clock in the afternoon, the time the Jews call "between the two evenings"; and which they say (c) is "from the sixth hour, and onwards"

Amo_8:9. The Jews (g) have a notion, that in the times of the Messiah

"the sun shall be darkened, בפלגות יומא, "in the middle of the day", (as this was,) as that day was darkened when the sanctuary was destroyed.

Yea, they speak (h) of a darkness that shall continue a long time: their words are these:

"the king Messiah shall be made known in all the world, and all the kings shall be stirred up to join together to make war with him; and many of the profligate Jews shall be turned to them, and shall go with them, to make war against the king Messiah; so יתחשך כל עלמא, "all the world shall be darkened" fifteen days, and many of the people of Israel shall die in that darkness.

(c) T. Hieros Pesachim, fol. 31. 3. (g) Zohar in Exod. fol. 4. 1. (h) Ib. fol. 3, 4.

---

46. And about the ninth hour Jesus cried with a loud voice, saying, Eli, Eli, lama sabachthani? that is to say, My God, my God, why hast thou forsaken me?

Greek/Transliteration
46. περὶ δὲ τὴν ἐνάτην ὥραν ἀνεβόησεν ὁ Ἰησοῦς φωνῇ μεγάλῃ, λέγων, Ἠλί, Ἠλί, λιμὰ σαβαχθανί; Τοῦτ᾽ ἔστιν, Θεέ μου, Θεέ μου, ἵνα τί με ἐγκατέλιπες;

46. peri de tein enatein 'oran aneboeisen 'o Yeisous phonei megalei, legon, Eili, Eili, lima sabachthani? Tout estin, The'e mou, The'e mou, 'ina ti me egkatelipes?

Hebrew/Transliteration
מו. וּבַשָּׁעָה הַתְּשִׁיעִית צָעַק יֵשׁוּעַ בְּקוֹל גָּדוֹל לֵאמֹר אֱלֹהִי אֱלֹהִי לְמָה שְׁבַקְתָּנִי אֲשֶׁר יֵאָמֵר אֵלִי אֵלִי לָמָה עֲזַבְתָּנִי:

46. Oo•va•sha•ah hat•shi•eet tza•ak Yeshua be•kol ga•dol le•mor Elo•hi Elo•hi le•ma sh`vak•ta•ni asher ye•a•mer Eli Eli la•ma azav•ta•ni.

Rabbinic Jewish Commentary
Or three o'clock in the afternoon, which was about the time of the slaying and offering of the daily sacrifice, which was an eminent type of Christ. The Jews say (i), that "every day the daily sacrifice was slain at eight and a half, and was offered up at nine and a half: about which time also the passover was killed, which was another type of Christ; and as they say (k), "was offered first, and then the daily sacrifice." Though the account they elsewhere (l) give of these things, is this,

"the daily sacrifice was slain at eight and a half, and was offered up at nine and a half; (that is, on all the common days of the year;) on the evenings of the passover, it was slain at seven and a half, and offered at eight and a half, whether on a common day, or on a sabbath day: the passover eve, that happened to be on the sabbath eve, it was slain at six and a half, and offered at seven and a half, and the passover after it.

The Jews themselves own (n), that these words were said by Jesus when he was in their hands. They indeed apply the passage to Esther; and say (o), that "she stood in the innermost court of the king's house; and when she came to the house of the images, the Shekinah departed from her, and she said, "Eli, Eli, lama Azabthani?" my God, my God, why hast thou forsaken me?

Though others apply the "Psalm" to David, and others to the people of Israel in captivity (p): but certain it is, that it belongs to the Messiah; and many things in it were fulfilled with respect to Jesus, most clearly show him to be the Messiah, and the person pointed at.

(i) T. Hieros. Pesachim, fol. 31. 3, 4. (k) lb. (l) Misn. Pesachim, c. 5. sect. 1 (n) Toldos Jesu, p. 17. (o) Bab. Megilia, fol. 15. 2. & Gloss. in T. Bab. Yoma, fol. 29. 1. (p) Vid. Jarchi & Kimchi in Psal. xxii. 1.

---

47. Some of them that stood there, when they heard that, said, This man calleth for Elias.

Greek/Transliteration
47. Τινὲς δὲ τῶν ἐκεῖ ἑστώτων ἀκούσαντες ἔλεγον ὅτι Ἠλίαν φωνεῖ οὗτος.

47. Tines de ton ekei 'estoton akousantes elegon 'oti Eilian phonei 'outos.

Hebrew/Transliteration
:מז. וּמִן־הָעֹמְדִים שָׁם כַּאֲשֶׁר שָׁמְעוּ אָמְרוּ הוּא קֹרֵא אֶל־אֵלִיָּהוּ

47. Oo•min - ha•om•dim sham ka•a•sher sham•oo am•roo hoo ko•re el - Eli•ya•hoo.

---

48. And straightway one of them ran, and took a spunge, and filled it with vinegar, and put it on a reed, and gave him to drink.

Greek/Transliteration
48. Καὶ εὐθέως δραμὼν εἷς ἐξ αὐτῶν, καὶ λαβὼν σπόγγον, πλήσας τε ὄξους, καὶ περιθεὶς καλάμῳ, ἐπότιζεν αὐτόν.

48. Kai eutheos dramon 'eis ex auton, kai labon spongon, pleisas te oxous, kai peritheis kalamo, epotizen auton.

Hebrew/Transliteration
מח. וַיְמַהֵר אֶחָד מֵהֶם וַיָּרָץ וַיִּקַּח סְפוֹג וַיְמַלְאֵהוּ חֹמֶץ וַיְשִׂימֵהוּ עַל־קָנֶה וַיַּשְׁקֵהוּ:

48. Vay•ma•her e•chad me•hem va•ya•rotz va•yi•kach se•fog asher mil•oh cho•metz va•ye•si•me•hoo al - ka•ne va•yash•ke•hoo.

---

49. The rest said, Let be, let us see whether Elias will come to save him.

Greek/Transliteration
49. Οἱ δὲ λοιποὶ ἔλεγον, Ἄφες, ἴδωμεν εἰ ἔρχεται Ἠλίας σώσων αὐτόν.

49. 'Oi de loipoi elegon, Aphes, idomen ei erchetai Eilias soson auton.

Hebrew/Transliteration
מט. וְיֶתֶר הָאֲנָשִׁים אָמְרוּ הֶרֶף וְנִרְאֶה אִם־יָבֹא אֵלִיָּהוּ לְהוֹשִׁיעַ לוֹ:

49. Ve•ye•ter ha•a•na•shim am•roo he•ref ve•nir•eh eem - ya•vo Eli•ya•hoo le•ho•shi•a lo.

---

50. Jesus, when he had cried again with a loud voice, yielded up the ghost.

Greek/Transliteration
50. Ὁ δὲ Ἰησοῦς πάλιν κράξας φωνῇ μεγάλῃ ἀφῆκεν τὸ πνεῦμα.

50. 'O de Yeisous palin kraxas phonei megalei apheiken to pneuma.

Hebrew/Transliteration
נ. וְיֵשׁוּעַ הוֹסִיף וַיִּקְרָא בְּקוֹל גָּדוֹל וַיַּפְקֵד אֶת־רוּחוֹ:

50. Ve•Yeshua ho•sif va•yik•ra ve•kol ga•dol va•yaf•ked et - roo•cho.

---

51. And, behold, the veil of the temple was rent in twain from the top to the bottom; and the earth did quake, and the rocks rent;

Greek/Transliteration
51. Καὶ ἰδού, τὸ καταπέτασμα τοῦ ναοῦ ἐσχίσθη εἰς δύο ἀπὸ ἄνωθεν ἕως κάτω· καὶ ἡ γῆ ἐσείσθη· καὶ αἱ πέτραι ἐσχίσθησαν·

51. Kai idou, to katapetasma tou naou eschisthei eis duo apo anothen 'eos kato. kai 'ei gei eseisthei. kai 'ai petrai eschistheisan.

Hebrew/Transliteration
נא. וְהִנֵּה פָּרֹכֶת הַהֵיכָל נִקְרְעָה לִשְׁנַיִם קְרָעִים מִלְמַעְלָה לְמָטָּה רָעֲשָׁה אָרֶץ וְצוּרִים הִתְבַּקֵּעוּ

51. Ve•hee•ne pa•ro•chet ha•hey•chal nik•re•ah lish•na•yim ke•ra•eem mil•ma•a•la le•ma•ta e•retz ra•a•sha ve•tzoo•rim hit•ba•ka•oo.

Rabbinic Jewish Commentary
The account the Jews give of the vail, is this (w): "R. Simeon ben Gamaliel said, on account of R. Simeon, the son of the Sagan, the thickness of the vail is an hand's breadth, and it is woven of seventy two threads, and every thread has twenty four threads in it: it is forty cubits long, and twenty broad, and is made of eighty two myriads; (which is either the number of the threads in it, or the sum of the golden pence it cost. Some copies read, is made by eighty two virgins (x);) two are made every year; and three hundred priests wash it. R. Jochanan ben Zaccai reproved them, saying, O temple! temple! wherefore dost thou fright thyself? I know thy end is to be destroyed; for so prophesied of thee Zechariah, the son of, Iddo, "open thy gates, O Lebanon", Zec_11:1.

"Our Rabbis taught that throughout the forty years that Shim'on the *Tzaddik* served,... the scarlet cloth would become white. From then on it would sometimes become white and sometimes not .... Throughout the last forty years before the Temple was destroyed ... the scarlet cloth never turned white." (Yoma 39a-39b)

(w) Misn. Shekalim, c. 8. sect. 5. Shernot Rabba, sect. 50. fol. 144. 2. Bernidbar Rabba, sect. 4. fol. 183. 2. (x) Vid. Bartenora & Yom. Tob. in ib.

---

52. And the graves were opened; and many bodies of the saints which slept arose,

Greek/Transliteration
52. καὶ τὰ μνημεῖα ἀνεῴχθησαν· καὶ πολλὰ σώματα τῶν κεκοιμημένων ἁγίων ἠγέρθη·

52. kai ta mneimeia aneochtheisan. kai polla somata ton kekoimeimenon 'agion eigerthei.

Hebrew/Transliteration
נב. וּקְבָרִים נִפְתָּחוּ וַיָּקִיצוּ רַבִּים מֵעַצְמוֹת הַקְּדוֹשִׁים אֲשֶׁר בָּאָרֶץ יְשֵׁנִים הֵמָּה:

52. Ook•va•rim nif•ta•choo va•ya•ki•tzoo ra•bim me•atz•mot ha•k`do•shim asher ba•a•retz ye•she•nim he•ma.

Rabbinic Jewish Commentary
In the Septuagint on Job_42:17, Job is said to be one of them, and a tradition is there recorded, which runs thus: "it is written, that he rose with whom the Lord rose.

53. And came out of the graves after his resurrection, and went into the holy city, anappeared unto many.

Greek/Transliteration
53. καὶ ἐξελθόντες ἐκ τῶν μνημείων μετὰ τὴν ἔγερσιν αὐτοῦ εἰσῆλθον εἰς τὴν ἁγίαν πόλιν, καὶ ἐνεφανίσθησαν πολλοῖς.

53. kai exelthontes ek ton mneimeion meta tein egersin autou eiseilthon eis tein 'agian polin, kai enephanistheisan pollois.

Hebrew/Transliteration
נג: וַיֵּצְאוּ מִקִּבְרֵיהֶם אַחֲרֵי תְקוּמָתוֹ וַיָּבֹאוּ אֶל-עִיר הַקֹּדֶשׁ וַיֵּרָאוּ לָרַבִּים

53. Va•yetz•oo mi•kiv•rey•hem a•cha•rey te•koo•ma•to va•ya•vo•oo el - eer ha•ko•desh va•ye•ra•oo la•ra•bim.

---

54. Now when the centurion, and they that were with him, watching Jesus, saw the earthquake, and those things that were done, they feared greatly, saying, Truly this was the Son of God.

Greek/Transliteration
54. Ὁ δὲ ἑκατόνταρχος καὶ οἱ μετ' αὐτοῦ τηροῦντες τὸν Ἰησοῦν, ἰδόντες τὸν σεισμὸν καὶ τὰ γενόμενα, ἐφοβήθησαν σφόδρα, λέγοντες, Ἀληθῶς θεοῦ υἱὸς ἦν οὗτος.

54. 'O de 'ekatontarchos kai 'oi met autou teirountes ton Yeisoun, idontes ton seismon kai ta genomena, ephobeitheisan sphodra, legontes, Aleithos theou 'wios ein 'outos.

Hebrew/Transliteration
נד. וְשַׂר-הַמֵּאָה וְהָאֲנָשִׁים אֲשֶׁר אִתּוֹ הַשֹּׁמְרִים אֶת-יֵשׁוּעַ בִּרְאוֹתָם אֶת-הָרַעַשׁ וְאֶת-כָּל-אֲשֶׁר קָרָה - חָרְדוּ עַד-מְאֹד וַיֹּאמְרוּ אָכֵן זֶה הָיָה בֶן-אֱלֹהִים

54. Ve•sar - ha•me•ah ve•ha•ana•shim asher ee•to ha•shom•rim et - Yeshua bir•o•tam et - ha•ra•ash ve•et - kol - asher ka•ra char•doo ad - me•od va•yom•roo a•chen ze ha•ya Ben - Elohim.

---

55. And many women were there beholding afar off, which followed Jesus from Galilee, ministering unto him:

Greek/Transliteration
55. Ἦσαν δὲ ἐκεῖ γυναῖκες πολλαὶ ἀπὸ μακρόθεν θεωροῦσαι, αἵτινες ἠκολούθησαν τῷ Ἰησοῦ ἀπὸ τῆς Γαλιλαίας, διακονοῦσαι αὐτῷ·

55. Eisan de ekei gunaikes pollai apo makrothen theorousai, 'aitines eikoloutheisan to Yeisou apo teis Galilaias, dyakonousai auto.

Hebrew/Transliteration
נה: וְנָשִׁים רַבּוֹת אֲשֶׁר הָלְכוּ אַחֲרֵי יֵשׁוּעַ מִן-הַגָּלִיל לְשָׁרְתוֹ הָיוּ רֹאוֹת אֶת-הַנַּעֲשָׂה שָׁם מֵרָחוֹק

55. Ve•na•shim ra•bot asher hal•choo a•cha•rey Yeshua min - ha•Galil le•shar•to ha•yoo ro•ot et - ha•na•a•sa sham me•ra•chok.

---

56. Among which was Mary Magdalene, and Mary the mother of James and Joses, and the mother of Zebedee's children.

Greek/Transliteration
56. ἐν αἷς ἦν Μαρία ἡ Μαγδαληνή, καὶ Μαρία ἡ τοῦ Ἰακώβου καὶ Ἰωσῆ μήτηρ, καὶ ἡ μήτηρ τῶν υἱῶν Ζεβεδαίου.

56. en 'ais ein Maria 'ei Magdaleinei, kai Maria 'ei tou Yakobou kai Yosei meiteir, kai 'ei meiteir ton 'wion Zebedaiou.

Hebrew/Transliteration
נו: וּבֵינֵהֶן הָיְתָה מִרְיָם הַמַּגְדָּלִית וּמִרְיָם אֵם-יַעֲקֹב וְיוֹסֵי וְאֵם בְּנֵי זַבְדִּי

56. Oo•vey•ne•hen hai•ta Mir•yam ha•Mag•da•lit oo•Miryam em - Yaakov ve`Yo•sey ve•em b`ney Zav•di.

Rabbinic Jewish Commentary
Out of whom Yeshua had cast out seven devils; and who having received much from him, loved much, which she showed by her zealous and constant attachment to him. She was called Magdalene, either because she was an inhabitant of Magdala, Mat_15:39, so we read (e) of R. Isaac, מגדלאה, of "Magdala", or "Magdalene"; and the rather, because that Magdala was famous, or rather infamous, for whoredom; for which reason the Jews (f) say, it was destroyed: or else she was so called, because she was גדלת, a "tonstrix", or plaiter of women's hair, as the word signifies (g); and so we often read of Mary, מגדלא שיער נשייא, "the plaiter of women's hair" (h); by whom the Jews seem to design Mary, the mother of Jesus, whom they confound with this Mary Magdalene. Jerom says (i), her name signifies "towered", or "fortified", because of her care and diligence, and the ardour of her faith; and "Migdal", in Hebrew, does signify a tower.

(e) Juchasin, fol. 96. 2. (f) T. Hieros. Taaniot, fol. 69. 1. Echa Rabbati, fol. 52. 4. (g) Maimon. & Bartenora in Misn. Kiddushin, c. 2. sect. 3. (h) T. Bab. Sabbat, fol. 104. 2. Chagiga, fol. 4. 2. & Sanhedrin, fol. 67. 1. (i) Ad Principiam, Tom. l. fol. 41.

---

57. When the even was come, there came a rich man of Arimathaea, named Joseph, who also himself was Jesus' disciple:

Greek/Transliteration
57. Ὀψίας δὲ γενομένης, ἦλθεν ἄνθρωπος πλούσιος ἀπὸ Ἀριμαθαίας, τοὔνομα Ἰωσήφ, ὃς καὶ αὐτὸς ἐμαθήτευσεν τῷ Ἰησοῦ·

57. Opsias de genomeneis, eilthen anthropos plousios apo Arimathaias, tounoma Yoseiph, 'os kai autos ematheiteusen to Yeisou.

Hebrew/Transliteration
נז: וַיְהִי בָּעֶרֶב וַיָּבֹא אִישׁ עָשִׁיר מִן-הָרָמָתַיִם וּשְׁמוֹ יוֹסֵף וְגַם-הוּא הָיָה אֶחָד מִתַּלְמִידֵי יֵשׁוּעַ

57. Vay•hi va•e•rev va•ya•vo eesh ashir min - ha•Ra•ma•ta•yim oo•sh`mo Yo•sef ve•gam - hoo ha•ya e•chad mi•tal•mi•dey Yeshua.

---

58. He went to Pilate, and begged the body of Jesus. Then Pilate commanded the body to be delivered.

Greek/Transliteration
58. οὗτος προσελθὼν τῷ Πιλάτῳ, ᾐτήσατο τὸ σῶμα τοῦ Ἰησοῦ. Τότε ὁ Πιλάτος ἐκέλευσεν ἀποδοθῆναι τὸ σῶμα.

58. 'outos proselthon to Pilato, eiteisato to soma tou Yeisou. Tote 'o Pilatos ekeleusen apodotheinai to soma.

Hebrew/Transliteration
נח: הוּא בָא אֶל-פִּילָטוֹס וַיִּשְׁאַל מִמֶּנּוּ אֶת-גּוּף יֵשׁוּעַ וַיְצַו פִּילָטוֹס כִּי-יִנָּתֶן לוֹ

58. Hoo va el - Pilatos va•yish•al mi•me•noo et - goof Yeshua vay•tzav Pilatos ki - yi•na•ten lo.

Rabbinic Jewish Commentary
and begged the body of Jesus; which could not be taken down and interred, without the leave of the Roman governor; and which was generally granted to the friends of the deceased, when asked; otherwise they were buried in places (l) appointed for such persons. (l) See Misn. Sanhedrin, c. 6. sect. 5, 6. Maimon. Hilch. Sanhedrin, c. 14. sect. 9.

---

59. And when Joseph had taken the body, he wrapped it in a clean linen cloth,

Greek/Transliteration
59. Καὶ λαβὼν τὸ σῶμα ὁ Ἰωσὴφ ἐνετύλιξεν αὐτὸ σινδόνι καθαρᾷ,

59. Kai labon to soma 'o Yoseiph enetulixen auto sindoni kathara,

Hebrew/Transliteration
נט: וַיִּקַּח יוֹסֵף אֶת-הַגּוּף וַיַּעֲטֵהוּ בְּתַכְרִיךְ-בַּד טָהוֹר

59. Va•yi•kach Yo•sef et - ha•goof va•ya•a•te•hoo be•tach•ri•ch - bad ta•hor.

Rabbinic Jewish Commentary
he wrapped it in a clean linen cloth: that is, he wound up the body in it round and round, as was the custom of the Jews; see Act_5:6.

Joh_11:44. Nor was it usual to bury in any thing but linen: so it is said (m),

"let the wrappings, or grave clothes, be של פשתן לבנים, "of white linen"; and let not the price of them be dear, for it is forbidden to bury in wrappings of silk, or broidered garments, even to a prince of Israel: for this is pride and destruction, and the work of the Gentiles.

(m) Juchasin, fol. 54. 2. Vid. Maimon. Hilchot Ebel, c. 4. sect. 2.

---

60. And laid it in his own new tomb, which he had hewn out in the rock: and he rolled a great stone to the door of the sepulchre, and departed.

Greek/Transliteration
60. καὶ ἔθηκεν αὐτὸ ἐν τῷ καινῷ αὐτοῦ μνημείῳ, ὃ ἐλατόμησεν ἐν τῇ πέτρᾳ· καὶ προσκυλίσας λίθον μέγαν τῇ θύρᾳ τοῦ μνημείου, ἀπῆλθεν.

60. kai etheiken auto en to kaino autou mneimeio, 'o elatomeisen en tei petra. kai proskulisas lithon megan tei thura tou mneimeiou, apeilthen.

Hebrew/Transliteration
ס. וַיְשִׂימֵהוּ בְּקֶבֶר חָדָשׁ אֲשֶׁר חָצַב-לוֹ בַּצּוּר וַיָּגֶל אֶבֶן גְּדוֹלָה עַל-פִּי הַקֶּבֶר וַיֵּלֶךְ:

60. Va•ye•si•me•hoo be•ke•ver cha•dash asher cha•tzav - lo ba•tzoor va•ya•gel even ge•do•la al - pi ha•ke•ver va•ye•lech.

Rabbinic Jewish Commentary
The Jews distinguish between a new grave, and an old grave (n): "a new grave may be measured, and sold, and divided; an old one may not be measured, nor sold, nor divided: there is a new grave, which is as an old one; and an old one, which is as a new one; an old grave, in which are ten dead bodies, which is not in the power of the owners, lo! this is as a new grave.

Which he had hewn out in the rock; it was usual with the Jews to make their sepulchres in rocks: "in the midst (of the court of the sepulchre, they say (o)) two caves are opened, one on one side, and the other on the other; R. Simeon says, four on the four sides; Rabban Simeon ben Gamaliel says, all are לפי הסלע, "according to the rock"; i.e. according to the nature of the rock, out of which the sepulchre is hewn; see Isa_22:16.

It may be observed, that all this was done on a feast day; on one of the days of the feast of the passover, when no servile work was to be done; and yet this was agreeably to the Jewish canons, which say (u), "they do all things needful for the dead on a feast day; they shave his head, and wash his clothes, and make him a coffin; and if they have no boards, they bring timber and saw boards of it, silently within doors; and if the person is a man of note, they do it even in the street; but they do not cut wood out of the forest, to saw planks of it for the coffin; nor do they hew stones, to build a tomb with them.

(n) Massech. Semachto, c. 14. fol. 16. 2. (o) Misn. Bava Bathra, c. 6. sect. 8. (u) Maimon. Hilchot Yom. Tob. c. 7. sect. 15.

---

61. And there was Mary Magdalene, and the other Mary, sitting over against the sepulchre.

Greek/Transliteration
61. Ἦν δὲ ἐκεῖ Μαρία ἡ Μαγδαληνή, καὶ ἡ ἄλλη Μαρία, καθήμεναι ἀπέναντι τοῦ τάφου.

61. Ein de ekei Maria 'ei Magdaleinei, kai 'ei allei Maria, katheimenai apenanti tou taphou.

Hebrew/Transliteration
סא. וּמִרְיָם הַמַּגְדָּלִית וּמִרְיָם הָאַחֶרֶת הָיוּ יֹשְׁבוֹת שָׁם מִמּוּל הַקָּבֶר:

61. Oo•Miryam ha•Mag•dalit oo•Miryam ha•a•che•ret ha•yoo yosh•vot sham mi•mool ha•ka•ver.

Rabbinic Jewish Commentary
Sitting was a mourning posture, which now they were allowed, the body being taken down from the cross, and interred by leave of the governor; for, for one that died as a malefactor, they might not use the outward signs of mourning: the canon is this (w); for such

"they do not mourn, but they grieve; and there is no grieving but in the heart" (w) Misn. Sarhedrin, c. 6. sect. 4.

---

62. Now the next day, that followed the day of the preparation, the chief priests and Pharisees came together unto Pilate,

Greek/Transliteration
62. Τῇ δὲ ἐπαύριον, ἥτις ἐστὶν μετὰ τὴν Παρασκευήν, συνήχθησαν οἱ ἀρχιερεῖς καὶ οἱ Φαρισαῖοι πρὸς Πιλάτον,

62. Tei de epaurion, 'eitis estin meta tein Paraskeuein, suneichtheisan 'oi archiereis kai 'oi Pharisaioi pros Pilaton,

Hebrew/Transliteration
סב: וַיְהִי מִמָּחֳרַת אַחֲרֵי עֶרֶב הַשַּׁבָּת וַיִּקָּהֲלוּ רָאשֵׁי הַכֹּהֲנִים וְהַפְּרוּשִׁים אֶל-פִּילָטוֹס.

62. Vay•hi mi•mo•cho•rat a•cha•rey erev ha•Sha•bat va•yi•ka•ha•loo ra•shey ha•ko•ha•nim ve•haP`roo•shim el - Pilatos.

---

63. Saying, Sir, we remember that that deceiver said, while he was yet alive, After three days I will rise again.

Greek/Transliteration
63. λέγοντες, Κύριε, ἐμνήσθημεν ὅτι ἐκεῖνος ὁ πλάνος εἶπεν ἔτι ζῶν, Μετὰ τρεῖς ἡμέρας ἐγείρομαι.

63. legontes, Kurie, emneistheimen 'oti ekeinos 'o planos eipen eti zon, Meta treis 'eimeras egeiromai.

Hebrew/Transliteration
סג: וַיֹּאמְרוּ אֲדֹנֵינוּ זָכַרְנוּ כִּי בְעוֹדֶנּוּ חַי אָמַר הַמַּתְעֶה הַהוּא מִקְצֵה שְׁלֹשֶׁת יָמִים אָקוּם.

63. Va•yom•roo ado•ney•noo za•char•noo ki be•o•de•noo chai amar ha•mat•eh ha•hoo mik•tze sh`lo•shet ya•mim a•koom.

Rabbinic Jewish Commentary
Meaning Jesus; for no better name could they give him alive or dead, and they chose to continue it; and the rather to use it before Pilate, who had a good opinion of his innocence; and to let him see, that they still retained the same sentiments of him: מסית, "a deceiver", is with the Jews (x),

"a private person, that deceives a private person; saying to him there is a God in such a place, so it eats, and so it drinks; so it does well, and so it does ill.
(x) Misn. Sanhedrin, c. 7. sect. 10.

---

64. Command therefore that the sepulchre be made sure until the third day, lest his disciples come by night, and steal him away, and say unto the people, He is risen from the dead: so the last error shall be worse than the first.

Greek/Transliteration
64. Κέλευσον οὖν ἀσφαλισθῆναι τὸν τάφον ἕως τῆς τρίτης ἡμέρας· μήποτε ἐλθόντες οἱ μαθηταὶ αὐτοῦ νυκτὸς κλέψωσιν αὐτόν, καὶ εἴπωσιν τῷ λαῷ, Ἠγέρθη ἀπὸ τῶν νεκρῶν· καὶ ἔσται ἡ ἐσχάτη πλάνη χείρων τῆς πρώτης.

64. Keleuson oun asphalistheinai ton taphon 'eos teis triteis 'eimeras. meipote elthontes 'oi matheitai autou nuktos klepsosin auton, kai eiposin to lao, Eigerthei apo ton nekron. kai estai 'ei eschatei planei cheiron teis proteis.

Hebrew/Tranliteration

סד. לָכֵן צַוֵּה-נָא לִנְצֹר אֶת-הַקֶּבֶר עַד-יוֹם הַשְּׁלִישִׁי פֶּן-יָבֹאוּ תַלְמִידָיו בַּלַּיְלָה וּגְנָבֻהוּ וְאָמְרוּ אֶל-הָעָם הִנֵּה:קָם מִן-הַמֵּתִים וְרָעָה הַמִּרְמָה הָאַחֲרֹנָה מִן-הָרִאשֹׁנָה -

64. La•chen tza•ve - na lin•tzor et - ha•ke•ver ad - yom hash•li•shi pen - ya•vo•oo tal•mi•dav ba•lai•la oog•na•voo•hoo ve•am•roo el - ha•am hee•ne - kam min - ha•me•tim ve•ra•ah ha•mir•ma ha•a•cha•ro•na min - ha•ri•sho•na.

---

65. Pilate said unto them, Ye have a watch: go your way, make it as sure as ye can.

Greek/Transliteration

65. Ἔφη δὲ αὐτοῖς ὁ Πιλάτος, Ἔχετε κουστωδίαν· ὑπάγετε, ἀσφαλίσασθε ὡς οἴδατε.

65. Ephei de autois 'o Pilatos, Echete koustodian. 'upagete, asphalisasthe 'os oidate.

Hebrew/Transliteration

:סה. וַיֹּאמֶר אֲלֵיהֶם פִּילָטוֹס הֵא-לָכֶם אַנְשֵׁי מִשְׁמָר לְכוּ וְנִצְרוּ כַּאֲשֶׁר תֵּדָעוּן

65. Va•yo•mer aley•hem Pilatos he - la•chem an•shey mish•mar le•choo ve•nitz•roo ka•a•sher te•da•oon.

---

66. So they went, and made the sepulchre sure, sealing the stone, and setting a watch.

Greek/Transliteration

66. Οἱ δὲ πορευθέντες ἠσφαλίσαντο τὸν τάφον, σφραγίσαντες τὸν λίθον, μετὰ τῆς κουστωδίας.

66. 'Oi de poreuthentes eisphalisanto ton taphon, sphragisantes ton lithon, meta teis koustodias.

Hebrew/Transliteration

:סו. וַיֵּלְכוּ וַיִּצְרוּ אֶת-הַקֶּבֶר וַיַּחְתְּמוּ אֶת-הָאֶבֶן וַיַּעֲמִידוּ עָלָיו אֶת-הַמִּשְׁמָר

66. Va•yel•choo va•yitz•roo et - ha•ke•ver va•yach•te•moo et - ha•a•ven va•ya•a•mi•doo alav et - ha•mish•mar.

Matthew, Chapter 28

1. In the end of the sabbath, as it began to dawn toward the first day of the week, came Mary Magdalene and the other Mary to see the sepulchre.

Greek/Transliteration
1. Ὀψὲ δὲ σαββάτων, τῇ ἐπιφωσκούσῃ εἰς μίαν σαββάτων, ἦλθεν Μαρία ἡ Μαγδαληνή, καὶ ἡ ἄλλη Μαρία, θεωρῆσαι τὸν τάφον.

1. Opse de sabbaton, tei epiphoskousei eis mian sabbaton, eilthen Maria 'ei Magdaleinei, kai 'ei allei Maria, theoreisai ton taphon.

Hebrew/Transliteration
א. וַיְהִי אַחַר הַשַׁבָּת לִפְנוֹת-בֹּקֶר בְּאֶחָד-בַּשַׁבָּת וַתָּבֹא מִרְיָם הַמַּגְדָּלִית וּמִרְיָם הָאַחֶרֶת לִרְאוֹת אֶת-הַקָּבֶר:

1. Vay•hi achar ha•Sha•bat lif•not - bo•ker be•e•chad - ba•Sha•bat va•ta•vo Mir•yam ha•Mag•da•lit oo•Miryam ha•a•che•ret lir•ot et - ha•ka•ver.

Rabbinic Jewish Commentary
The Vulgate Latin, Arabic, and Ethiopic versions, and Munster's Hebrew Gospel render it, "the evening of the sabbath"; and the Persic version, "the night of the sabbath"; but must mean, not the evening and night, which preceded the sabbath, and was a part of it, but what followed it, and belonged to the first day.

towards the first day of the week, or "sabbaths"; so the Jews used to call the days of the week, the first day of the sabbath, the second day of the sabbath, take an instance or two (z). "The stationary men fast four days in the week, from the second day to the fifth day; and they do not fast on the sabbath eve (so they sometimes call the sixth day), because of the glory of the sabbath; nor באחד בשבת, "on the first day of the sabbath", or week, that they may not go from rest and delight, to labour and fasting, and die."

On which the Gemara has these words (a); "the stationary men go into the synagogue, and sit four fastings; בשני בשבת, "on the second of the sabbath", or "week": on the third, and on the fourth, and on the fifth."

(z) Misn. Taanilh, c. 4. sect. 3. (a) T. Bab. Taanith, fol. 27. 2. Vid. T. Bab. Nidda, fol. 4. 2. & 11. 1. & 67. 2.

---

2. And, behold, there was a great earthquake: for the angel of the Lord descended from heaven, and came and rolled back the stone from the door, and sat upon it.

Greek/Transliteration
2. Καὶ ἰδού, σεισμὸς ἐγένετο μέγας· ἄγγελος γὰρ κυρίου καταβὰς ἐξ οὐρανοῦ, προσελθὼν ἀπεκύλισεν τὸν λίθον ἀπὸ τῆς θύρας, καὶ ἐκάθητο ἐπάνω αὐτοῦ.

2. Kai idou, seismos egeneto megas. angelos gar kuriou katabas ex ouranou, proselthon apekulisen ton lithon apo teis thuras, kai ekatheito epano autou.

Hebrew/Transliteration
:ב. וַיְהִי רַעַשׁ גָּדוֹל כִּי-מַלְאַךְ יְהֹוָה יָרַד מִן-הַשָּׁמַיִם וַיָּבֹא וַיָּגֶל אֶת-הָאֶבֶן מִן-הַפֶּתַח וַיֵּשֶׁב עָלֶיהָ

2. Vay•hi ra•ash ga•dol ki - mal•ach Adonai ya•rad min - ha•sha•ma•yim va•ya•vo va•ya•gel et - ha•e•ven min - ha•pe•tach va•ye•shev a•le•ha.

---

3. His countenance was like lightning, and his raiment white as snow:

Greek/Transliteration
3. Ἦν δὲ ἡ ἰδέα αὐτοῦ ὡς ἀστραπή, καὶ τὸ ἔνδυμα αὐτοῦ λευκὸν ὡσεὶ χιών.

3. Ein de 'ei idea autou 'os astrapei, kai to enduma autou leukon 'osei chion.

Hebrew/Transliteration
:ג. וּמַרְאֵהוּ כַּבָּרָק וּלְבוּשׁוֹ לָבָן כַּשָּׁלֶג

3. Oo•mar•e•hoo ka•ba•rak ool•voo•sho la•van ka•sha•leg.

Rabbinic Jewish Commentary
It being a commonly received notion of the Jews, that ministering messengers were clothed in white (b). "Said R. Ame to R. Levi, show me the Persians; he said to him, they are like to the mighty men of the house of David: show me the Chaberin, (another nation near the Persians,) they are like to destroying messengers: show me the Ishmaelites, they are like to devils of the house of Hacsa: show me the disciples of the wise men in Babylon, they are like to the ministering messengers."

Upon which the gloss says, "to the devils", because they are clothed in black, and are like to devils; to "the ministering messengers", לבושי לבנים, "they are clothed in white", and veiled like the ministering messengers; as it is written in Eze_9:2, "and the man was clothed with linen": and it is said (c) of R. Judah, that he was veiled, and sat in fine linen fringed, and was like to an messenger of the Lord of hosts: and elsewhere (d) it is said, who are the ministering messengers? the Rabbi's: and why are they called ministering messengers? because they are fringed, as the ministering messengers, in beautiful garments."

(b) T. Bab. Kiddushin, fol. 72. 1. (c) T. Bab. Sabbat, fol. 25. 2. (d) T. Bab. Nedarim, fol. 20. 2.

4. And for fear of him the keepers did shake, and became as dead men.

Greek/Transliteration
4. Ἀπὸ δὲ τοῦ φόβου αὐτοῦ ἐσείσθησαν οἱ τηροῦντες καὶ ἐγένοντο ὡσεὶ νεκροί.

4. Apo de tou phobou autou eseistheisan 'oi teirountes kai egenonto 'osei nekroi.

Hebrew/Transliteration
ד. וּמֵאֵימָתוֹ אַנְשֵׁי הַמִּשְׁמָר נִבְהָלוּ וַיִּהְיוּ כַּמֵּתִים:

4. Oo•me•ey•ma•to an•shey ha•mish•mar niv•ha•loo va•yi•hi•oo ka•me•tim.

---

5. And the angel answered and said unto the women, Fear not ye: for I know that ye seek Jesus, which was crucified.

Greek/Transliteration
5. Ἀποκριθεὶς δὲ ὁ ἄγγελος εἶπεν ταῖς γυναιξίν, Μὴ φοβεῖσθε ὑμεῖς· οἶδα γὰρ ὅτι Ἰησοῦν τὸν ἐσταυρωμένον ζητεῖτε.

5. Apokritheis de 'o angelos eipen tais gunaixin, Mei phobeisthe 'umeis. oida gar 'oti Yeisoun ton estauromenon zeiteite.

Hebrew/Transliteration
ה. וַיַּעַן הַמַּלְאָךְ וַיֹּאמֶר אֶל־הַנָּשִׁים אַל־תִּירֶאןָ הֵן יָדַעְתִּי כִּי אֶת־יֵשׁוּעַ הַנִּצְלָב תְּבַקֵּשְׁנָה:

5. Va•ya•an ha•mal•ach va•yo•mer el - ha•na•shim al - ti•re•na hen ya•da•a•ti ki et - Yeshua ha•nitz•lav te•va•kesh•na.

---

6. He is not here: for he is risen, as he said. Come, see the place where the Lord lay.

Greek/Transliteration
6. Οὐκ ἔστιν ὧδε· ἠγέρθη γάρ, καθὼς εἶπεν. Δεῦτε, ἴδετε τὸν τόπον ὅπου ἔκειτο ὁ κύριος.

6. Ouk estin 'ode. eigerthei gar, kathos eipen. Deute, idete ton topon 'opou ekeito 'o kurios.

Hebrew/Tranliteration
ו. אֵינֶנּוּ פֹה כִּי הוּא קָם כַּאֲשֶׁר אָמָר בֹּאנָה וּרְאֶינָה אֶת־הַמָּקוֹם אֲשֶׁר שָׁכַב־שָׁם הָאָדוֹן:

6. Ey•ne•noo fo ki hoo kam ka•a•sher amar bo•na oor•ei•na et - ha•ma•kom asher sha•chav - sham ha•Adon.

7. And go quickly, and tell his disciples that he is risen from the dead; and, behold, he goeth before you into Galilee; there shall ye see him: lo, I have told you.

Greek/Transliteration
7. Καὶ ταχὺ πορευθεῖσαι εἴπατε τοῖς μαθηταῖς αὐτοῦ ὅτι Ἠγέρθη ἀπὸ τῶν νεκρῶν· καὶ ἰδού, προάγει ὑμᾶς εἰς τὴν Γαλιλαίαν· ἐκεῖ αὐτὸν ὄψεσθε· ἰδού, εἶπον ὑμῖν.

7. Kai tachu poreutheisai eipate tois matheitais autou 'oti Eigerthei apo ton nekron. kai idou, proagei 'umas eis tein Galilaian. ekei auton opsesthe. idou, eipon 'umin.

Hebrew/Transliteration
ז. וּמִהַרְתֶּן אֶל-תַּלְמִידָיו וַאֲמַרְתֶּן כִּי הוּא קָם מִן-הַמֵּתִים וְהִנֵּה הוּא הוֹלֵךְ לִפְנֵיכֶם הַגָּלִילָה וְשָׁם תִּרְאוּ אֹתוֹ:הִנֵּה אָמַרְתִּי לָכֶן

7. Oo•mi•har•ten el - tal•mi•dav va•a•mar•ten ki hoo kam min - ha•me•tim ve•hee•ne hoo ho•lech lif•ney•chem ha•Ga•li•la ve•sham tir•oo o•to hee•ne amar•ti la•chen.

---

8. And they departed quickly from the sepulchre with fear and great joy; and did run to bring his disciples word.

Greek/Transliteration
8. Καὶ ἐξελθοῦσαι ταχὺ ἀπὸ τοῦ μνημείου μετὰ φόβου καὶ χαρᾶς μεγάλης, ἔδραμον ἀπαγγεῖλαι τοῖς μαθηταῖς αὐτοῦ.

8. Kai exelthousai tachu apo tou mneimeiou meta phobou kai charas megaleis, edramon apangeilai tois matheitais autou.

Hebrew/Transliteration
ח. וַתֵּצֶאנָה כְרֶגַע מִן-הַקֶּבֶר בְּיִרְאָה וּבְשָׂשׂוֹן רָב וַתָּרֹצְנָה לְהַגִּיד לְתַלְמִידָיו:

8. Va•te•tze•na ke•re•ga min - ha•ke•ver be•yir•ah oov•sa•son rav va•ta•rotz•na le•ha•gid le•tal•mi•dav.

---

9. And as they went to tell his disciples, behold, Jesus met them, saying, All hail. And they came and held him by the feet, and worshipped him.

Greek/Transliteration
9. Ὡς δὲ ἐπορεύοντο ἀπαγγεῖλαι τοῖς μαθηταῖς αὐτοῦ, καὶ ἰδού, Ἰησοῦς ἀπήντησεν αὐταῖς, λέγων, Χαίρετε. Αἱ δὲ προσελθοῦσαι ἐκράτησαν αὐτοῦ τοὺς πόδας, καὶ προσεκύνησαν αὐτῷ.

9. 'Os de eporeuonto apangeilai tois matheitais autou, kai idou, Yeisous apeinteisen autais, legon, Chairete. 'Ai de proselthousai ekrateisan autou tous podas, kai prosekuneisan auto.

Hebrew/Transliteration
ט. הִנֵּה הֹלְכוֹת לְסַפֵּר אֶל-תַּלְמִידָיו וַיֵּרָא אֲלֵיהֶן יֵשׁוּעַ וַיֹּאמֶר שָׁלוֹם וַתִּגַּשְׁנָה וַתֹּאחַזְנָה בְרַגְלָיו וַתִּשְׁתַּחֲוֶיןָ לוֹ:

9. He•na hol•chot le•sa•per el - tal•mi•dav va•ye•ra aley•hen Yeshua va•yo•mer sha•lom va•ti•gash•na va•to•chaz•na ve•rag•lav va•tish•ta•cha•vey•na lo.

---

10. Then said Jesus unto them, Be not afraid: go tell my brethren that they go into Galilee, and there shall they see me.

Greek/Tranliteration
10. Τότε λέγει αὐταῖς ὁ Ἰησοῦς· Μὴ φοβεῖσθε· ὑπάγετε, ἀπαγγείλατε τοῖς ἀδελφοῖς μου ἵνα ἀπέλθωσιν εἰς τὴν Γαλιλαίαν, καὶ ἐκεῖ με ὄψονται.

10. Tote legei autais 'o Yeisous. Mei phobeisthe. 'upagete, apangeilate tois adelphois mou 'ina apelthosin eis tein Galilaian, kai ekei me opsontai.

Hebrew/Transliteration
י. וַיֹּאמֶר אֲלֵיהֶן יֵשׁוּעַ אַל-תִּירֶאנָה לֵכְנָה הַגֵּדְנָה לְאַחַי כִּי יֵלְכוּ הַגָּלִילָה וְשָׁם יִרְאוּנִי:

10. Va•yo•mer aley•hen Yeshua al - ti•re•na lech•na ha•ged•na le•a•chai ki yel•choo ha•Ga•li•la ve•sham yir•oo•ni.

---

11. Now when they were going, behold, some of the watch came into the city, and shewed unto the chief priests all the things that were done.

Greek/Transliteration
11. Πορευομένων δὲ αὐτῶν, ἰδού, τινὲς τῆς κουστωδίας ἐλθόντες εἰς τὴν πόλιν ἀπήγγειλαν τοῖς ἀρχιερεῦσιν ἅπαντα τὰ γενόμενα.

11. Poreuomenon de auton, idou, tines teis koustodias elthontes eis tein polin apeingeilan tois archiereusin 'apanta ta genomena.

Hebrew/Transliteration
יא. וַיְהִי בְּלֶכְתָּן וְהִנֵּה אֲנָשִׁים מֵאַנְשֵׁי הַמִּשְׁמָר בָּאוּ הָעִירָה וַיַּגִּידוּ לְרָאשֵׁי הַכֹּהֲנִים אֵת-כֹּל אֲשֶׁר קָרָה:

11. Vay•hi be•lech•tan ve•hee•ne a•na•shim me•an•shey ha•mish•mar ba•oo ha•ee•ra va•ya•gi•doo le•ra•shey ha•ko•ha•nim et - kol asher ka•ra.

12. And when they were assembled with the elders, and had taken counsel, they gave large money unto the soldiers,

Greek/Transliteration

12. Καὶ συναχθέντες μετὰ τῶν πρεσβυτέρων, συμβούλιόν τε λαβόντες, ἀργύρια ἱκανὰ ἔδωκαν τοῖς στρατιώταις,

12. Kai sunachthentes meta ton presbuteron, sumboulion te labontes, argurya 'ikana edokan tois stratiotais,

Hebrew/Transliteration

יב. וַיִּקָּהֲלוּ עִם־הַזְּקֵנִים וַיִּוָּעֲצוּ וַיִּתְּנוּ־כֶסֶף רַב אֶל־אַנְשֵׁי הַצָּבָא לֵאמֹר:

12. Va•yi•ka•ha•loo eem - haz`ke•nim va•yi•va•a•tzoo va•yit•noo - che•sef rav el - an•shey ha•tza•va le•mor.

---

13. Saying, Say ye, His disciples came by night, and stole him away while we slept.

Greek/Transliteration

13. λέγοντες, Εἴπατε ὅτι Οἱ μαθηταὶ αὐτοῦ νυκτὸς ἐλθόντες ἔκλεψαν αὐτὸν ἡμῶν κοιμωμένων.

13. legontes, Eipate 'oti 'Oi matheitai autou nuktos elthontes eklepsan auton 'eimon koimomenon.

Hebrew/Transliteration

יג. אִמְרוּ כִּי־בָאוּ תַלְמִידָיו לַיְלָה וַיִּגְנְבֻהוּ בְּעוֹד אֲנַחְנוּ יְשֵׁנִים:

13. Eem•roo ki - va•oo tal•mi•dav lai•la va•yig•ne•voo•hoo be•od a•nach•noo ye•she•nim.

---

14. And if this come to the governor's ears, we will persuade him, and secure you.

Greek/Transliteration

14. Καὶ ἐὰν ἀκουσθῇ τοῦτο ἐπὶ τοῦ ἡγεμόνος, ἡμεῖς πείσομεν αὐτόν, καὶ ὑμᾶς ἀμερίμνους ποιήσομεν.

14. Kai ean akousthei touto epi tou 'eigemonos, 'eimeis peisomen auton, kai 'umas amerimnous poieisomen.

Hebrew/Transliteration

יד. וְכִי־יִשָּׁמַע הַדָּבָר לְאָזְנֵי הַהֶגְמוֹן אֲנַחְנוּ נְדַבֵּר עַל־לִבּוֹ וְהָיִינוּ לְמָגֵן לָכֶם מִכָּל־רָע:

14. Ve•chi - yi•sha•ma ha•da•var le•oz•ney ha•heg•mon a•nach•noo n`da•ber al - li•bo ve•ha•yi•noo le•ma•gen la•chem mi•kol - ra.

---

15. So they took the money, and did as they were taught: and this saying is commonly reported among the Jews until this day.

Greek/Transliteration
15. Οἱ δὲ λαβόντες τὰ ἀργύρια ἐποίησαν ὡς ἐδιδάχθησαν. Καὶ διεφημίσθη ὁ λόγος οὗτος παρὰ Ἰουδαίοις μέχρι τῆς σήμερον.

15. 'Oi de labontes ta argurya epoieisan 'os edidachtheisan. Kai diepheimisthei 'o logos 'outos para Youdaiois mechri teis seimeron.

Hebrew/Transliteration
טו: וַיִּקְחוּ אֶת-הַכֶּסֶף וַיַּעֲשׂוּ כַּאֲשֶׁר שָׂמוּ בְּפִיהֶם וְהַשְּׁמוּעָה הַזֹּאת יָצְאָה בֵּין הַיְּהוּדִים עַד הַיּוֹם הַזֶּה

15. Va•yik•choo et - ha•ke•sef va•ya•a•soo ka•a•sher sa•moo be•fi•hem ve•hash•moo•ah ha•zot yatz•ah bein ha•Ye•hoo•dim ad ha•yom ha•ze.

Rabbinic Jewish Commentary
They say (e), that Judas, seeing where the body was laid, and the disciples sitting upon the tomb, and mourning over it, in the middle of the night, took his opportunity to take away the body, and buried it in his own garden, under a current of water; having first turned the water another way, and then put it in the same course as before; and which he afterwards discovered to the Jews; and the body was taken up and exposed, and insulted in the most ignominious manner: but alas! Judas had hanged himself some days before; and had he been living, would not have been capable of doing what they ascribe unto him.

(e) Toldos Jesu, p. 18, 19, 21.

---

16. Then the eleven disciples went away into Galilee, into a mountain where Jesus had appointed them.

Greek/Transliteration
16. Οἱ δὲ ἕνδεκα μαθηταὶ ἐπορεύθησαν εἰς τὴν Γαλιλαίαν, εἰς τὸ ὄρος οὗ ἐτάξατο αὐτοῖς ὁ Ἰησοῦς.

16. 'Oi de 'endeka matheitai eporeutheisan eis tein Galilaian, eis to oros 'ou etaxato autois 'o Yeisous.

Hebrew/Transliteration
טז: וְאַחַד עָשָׂר הַתַּלְמִידִים הָלְכוּ הַגָּלִילָה אֶל-הָהָר הַהוּא אֲשֶׁר יָעַד לָהֶם יֵשׁוּעַ

16. Ve•a•chad asar ha•tal•mi•dim hal•choo ha•Ga•li•la el - ha•har ha•hoo asher ya•ad la•hem Yeshua.

17. And when they saw him, they worshipped him: but some doubted.

Greek/Translitration
17. Καὶ ἰδόντες αὐτὸν προσεκύνησαν αὐτῷ· οἱ δὲ ἐδίστασαν.

17. Kai idontes auton prosekuneisan auto. 'oi de edistasan.

Hebrew/Transliteration
יז. וַיְהִי כִּרְאוֹתָם אֹתוֹ וַיִּשְׁתַּחֲווּ-לוֹ וְיֵשׁ מֵהֶם פָּסְחוּ עַל-שְׁתֵּי סְעִפִּים:

17. Vay•hi kir•o•tam o•to va•yish•ta•cha•voo - lo ve•yesh me•hem pas•choo al - sh`tey s`ee•pim.

---

18. And Jesus came and spake unto them, saying, All power is given unto me in heaven and in earth.

Greek/Transliteration
18. Καὶ προσελθὼν ὁ Ἰησοῦς ἐλάλησεν αὐτοῖς, λέγων, Ἐδόθη μοι πᾶσα ἐξουσία ἐν οὐρανῷ καὶ ἐπὶ γῆς.

18. Kai proselthon 'o Yeisous elaleisen autois, legon, Edothei moi pasa exousia en ourano kai epi geis.

Hebrew/Transliteration
יח. וַיִּגַּשׁ יֵשׁוּעַ וַיְדַבֵּר אֲלֵיהֶם לֵאמֹר נִתַּן-לִי כָּל-מִמְשָׁל בַּשָּׁמַיִם וּבָאָרֶץ:

18. Va•yi•gash Yeshua va•y`da•ber aley•hem le•mor ni•tan - li kol - mim•shal ba•sha•ma•yim oo•va•a•retz.

---

19. Go ye therefore, and teach all nations, baptizing them in the name of the Father, and of the Son, and of the Holy Ghost:

Greek/Transliteration
19. Πορευθέντες μαθητεύσατε πάντα τὰ ἔθνη, βαπτίζοντες αὐτοὺς εἰς τὸ ὄνομα τοῦ Πατρὸς καὶ τοῦ Υἱοῦ καὶ τοῦ Ἁγίου Πνεύματος·

19. Poreuthentes matheiteusate panta ta ethnei, baptizontes autous eis to onoma tou Patros kai tou 'Wiou kai tou 'Agiou Pneumatos.

Hebrew/Transliteration
יט. לְכוּ אֶל-כָּל-הָעַמִּים לְהוֹרֹתָם וְלַעֲשֹוֹתָם לִי לְתַלְמִידִים וּטְבַלְתֶּם אֹתָם בְּשֵׁם הָאָב וְהַבֵּן וְרוּחַ הַקֹּדֶשׁ:

19. Le•choo el - kol - ha•a•mim le•ho•ro•tam ve•la•a•so•tam li le•tal•mi•dim oot•val•tem o•tam be•shem ha•Av ve•ha•Ben ve•Roo•ach ha•Ko•desh.

Rabbinic Jewisn Commentary

This is the first, and indeed the only, place in which the Trinity of persons is expressed in this order, and in the selfsame words. Galatinus (f) pretends, that the ancient Jews used the same way of speaking. It would be well if proof could be made of it: he asserts it to be in Zohar on Deu_6:4, and in the Targum of Jonathan ben Uzziel on Isa_6:3. In the former he says, it is expressed thus, "hear, O Israel; the Lord", he is called "the Father; our God", he is called the Son; "is one Lord", this is "the Holy Ghost", who proceeds from both; and again, by the same R. Simeon, it is said, "holy", this is אב, "the Father"; "holy", this is בן, "the Son"; "holy", this is רוח הקדש, "the Holy Ghost": and in the latter after this manner, "Holy Father, Holy Son, and Holy Holy Ghost"; but no such words are now to be found in either of these places. He affirms, that he himself saw a copy of Jonathan's Targum that had these words. The Jews often speak of the Tetragrammaton, or name of four letters, the name YHWH, which they say is not lawful to be pronounced; and also of the name of twelve letters, which the above writer (g) makes to be "Father, Son, and Holy Ghost"; and of forty two letters, which from a book called Gale Razia, he says is,

"Father God, Son God, Holy Ghost God, three in one, and one in three;"

which in the Hebrew language make up so many letters; but this wants better authority.

(f) L. 2. c. 1. (g) Ib. c. 11, 12. Vid. Buxtorf. Lex. Heb. in voce הוה.

---

20. Teaching them to observe all things whatsoever I have commanded you: and, lo, I am with you always, even unto the end of the world. Amen.

Greek/Transliteration
20. διδάσκοντες αὐτοὺς τηρεῖν πάντα ὅσα ἐνετειλάμην ὑμῖν· καὶ ἰδού, ἐγὼ μεθ᾽ ὑμῶν εἰμι πάσας τὰς ἡμέρας ἕως τῆς συντελείας τοῦ αἰῶνος. ᾽Αμήν.

20. didaskontes autous teirein panta 'osa eneteilamein 'umin. kai idou, ego meth 'umon eimi pasas tas 'eimeras 'eos teis sunteleias tou aionos. Amein.

Hebrew/Transliteration
כ. וְלִמַּדְתֶּם אֹתָם לִשְׁמֹר אֶת-כָּל-אֲשֶׁר צִוִּיתִי אֶתְכֶם וְהִנֵּה אָנֹכִי אֶהְיֶה עִמָּכֶם עַד-אַחֲרִית הַשָּׁנִים לְעֵת קֵץ:הָעוֹלָם אָמֵן

20. Ve•li•ma•de•tem o•tam lish•mor et - kol - asher tzi•vi•ti et•chem ve•hee•ne ano•chi e•he•ye ee•ma•chem ad - acha•rit ha•sha•nim le•et ketz ha•o•lam Amen.

^end^

JEWISH INTERTESTAMENTAL AND EARLY RABBINIC LITERATURE: BIBLIOGRAPHY

Berenbaum, Michael and Fred Skolnik. *Encyclopaedia Judaica.* 2d ed.; 22 vols.; Detroit: Macmillan Reference USA and Keter, 2007. Also available elec-
* David Chapman is associate professor of New Testament and Archaeology at Covenant Theological
Seminary, 12330 Conway Road, St. Louis, MO 63141. Andreas Köstenberger is research professor of
New Testament and Biblical Theology at Southeastern Baptist Theological Seminary, 120 S. Wingate St.,
Wake Forest, NC 27587.
1 *JETS* 43 (2000): 577–618. Appreciation is again expressed to friends at Tyndale House and to the
university and seminary libraries in Cambridge, Tübingen, and St. Louis.
236 JOURNAL OF THE EVANGELICAL THEOLOGICAL SOCIETY
tronically from Gale Virtual Reference Library. A fine substantial update of the original and still useful 16 volume *Encyclopaedia Judaica* (Jerusalem: Keter, 1972), which originally received several annual yearbooks and two update volumes (1982, 1994) and was issued on CD-ROM in 1997. Both editions were preceded by an incomplete 10-volume German set entitled *Encyclopaedia Judaica: das Judentum in Geschichte und Gegenwart* (Berlin: Eschkol, 1928–34), which only covered articles beginning with the letters A–L but often contained longer treatments than the 1972 version. [*EncJud*]

Collins, John J. and Daniel C. Harlow, eds. *The Eerdmans Dictionary of Early Judaism.* Grand Rapids/Cambridge: Eerdmans, 2010. Brief survey articles introduce "Early Judaism" (pp. 1–290) followed by dictionary entries on more specific matters (pp. 291–1360). Quite helpful. [*EDEJ*]

Evans, Craig A. and Stanley E. Porter, eds. *Dictionary of New Testament Background.* Downers Grove/Leicester: InterVarsity, 2000. Helpful articles with good bibliography. [*DNTB*]

Freedman, David Noel, ed. *The Anchor Bible Dictionary.* 6 vols. New York: Doubleday, 1992. Includes useful introductory articles on much intertestamental literature. Also on CD-ROM. [*ABD*]

Neusner, Jacob and Alan J. Avery-Peck, eds. *Encyclopaedia of Midrash: Biblical Interpretation in Formative Judaism.* 2 vols. Leiden: Brill, 2005.

Neusner, Jacob, Alan J. Avery-Peck, and William Scott Green, eds. *The Encyclopedia of Judaism.* 5 vols. New York: Continuum/Leiden: Brill, 1999–2003. 3 initial volumes plus 2 supplement volumes. Some articles with bibliography.

Neusner, Jacob and William Scott Green, eds. *Dictionary of Judaism in the Biblical Period: 450 B.C.E. to 600 C.E.* 2 vols. New York: Macmillan, 1996; repr.

Peabody, MA: Hendrickson, 1999. Relatively short articles with no bibliography.
Singer, Isidore et al., eds. *The Jewish Encyclopedia.* 12 vols. New York/London: Funk & Wagnalls, 1901–1906. Older than *EncJud* but often has fuller articles. Available online at http://www.jewishencyclopedia.com and scanned images at http://archive.org. [*JE*]
Werblowsky, R. J. Zwi and Geoffrey Wigoder, eds. *The Oxford Dictionary of the Jewish Religion.* Oxford: OUP, 1997. Competent (but very concise) articles with limited bibliography. [*ODJR*]

1.2 Works Containing Surveys of Jewish Literature

Davies, W. D., Louis Finkelstein, John Sturdy, William Horbury, and Steven T. Katz, eds. *Cambridge History of Judaism.* 4 vols. Cambridge: CUP, 1984–2006. [*CHJ*]
Evans, Craig A. *Ancient Texts for New Testament Studies: A Guide to the Background Literature.* Peabody, MA: Hendrickson, 2005. Update of his *Noncanonical Writings and New Testament Interpretation* (1992).
Grabbe, Lester L. *A History of the Jews and Judaism in the Second Temple Period.* 4 vols. London/New York: T & T Clark, 2004–. Emphasis on discussing sources, with a tendency toward some skepticism and late dating.
Haase, Wolfgang, ed. *Aufstieg und Niedergang der Römischen Welt* II.19.1–2, II.20.1–2, and II.21.1–2. Berlin: de Gruyter, 1979–1987. [*ANRW*]
Helyer, Larry R. *Exploring Jewish Literature of the Second Temple Period: A Guide for New Testament Students.* Downers Grove: InterVarsity, 2002.
Kraft, Robert A. and George W. E. Nickelsburg, eds. *Early Judaism and Its Modern Interpreters.* Philadelphia: Fortress/Atlanta: Scholars, 1986.
McNamara, Martin. *Intertestamental Literature.* Wilmington, DE: Michael Glazier, 1983.
Mulder, Martin Jan, ed. *Mikra: Text, Translation, Reading and Interpretation of the Hebrew Bible in Ancient Judaism and Early Christianity.* CRINT 2.1. Assen/Maastricht: Van Gorcum, 1988; Philadelphia: Fortress, 1988. Very helpful, especially on LXX, Targums, and other versions of the OT. [*Mikra*]
Neusner, Jacob, ed. *Judaism in Late Antiquity, Vol. 1: The Literary and Archaeological Sources.* Handbuch der Orientalistik 1.16; Leiden: Brill, 1995. [*JLA*]
Nickelsburg, George W. E. *Jewish Literature Between the Bible and the Mishnah.* 2d ed. Philadelphia: Fortress, 2005. Principally discusses DSS, Apocrypha, and Pseudepigrapha. With CD-ROM of entire book, plus images and a study guide. [Nickelsburg, *Jewish Literature*]

Sæbø, Magne, ed. *Hebrew Bible, Old Testament: The History of its Interpretation: Vol. 1 From the beginnings to the Middle Ages (until 1300). Part 1: Antiquity.* Göttingen:
Vandenhoeck & Ruprecht, 1996.
Schürer, Emil. *The History of the Jewish People in the Age of Jesus Christ (175 B.C.–
A.D. 135).* Ed. Geza Vermes et al. Rev. English ed. 3 vols. in 4. Edinburgh:
T & T Clark, 1973–1987. For decades the standard work in the
field (not to be confused with Hendrickson's reprinted translation of the
original German edition, which is now out of date). [*HJPAJC*]
Stemberger, Günter. *Introduction to the Talmud and Midrash.* Fine work; see full
bibliography under Rabbinic Literature. [Stemberger, *Introduction*]
Stone, Michael E., ed. *Jewish Writings of the Second Temple Period.* CRINT 2.2.
Assen: Van Gorcum; Philadelphia: Fortress, 1984. See further CRINT
volumes under Rabbinic Literature below. [*JWSTP*]
VanderKam, James C. *An Introduction to Early Judaism.* Grand Rapids:
Eerdmans,
2001. Esp. pp. 53–173.

1.3 Sourcebooks

Barrett, C. K. *The New Testament Background: Writings from Ancient Greece and the
Roman Empire that Illuminate Christian Origins.* San Francisco: Harper,
1987. A more recent edition (with different subtitle) of this classic
sourcebook.
Chilton, Bruce D., gen. ed. *A Comparative Handbook to the Gospel of Mark: Comparisons
with Pseudepigrapha, the Qumran Scrolls, and Rabbinic Literature.* The
New Testament Gospels in their Judaic Contexts 1. Leiden: Brill, 2009.
After each pericope in Mark, an extensive array of comparable Jewish
sources are quoted and followed by a very brief commentary on those
sources.
De Lange, Nicholas. *Apocrypha: Jewish Literature of the Hellenistic Age.* New York:
Viking, 1978. Excerpts Apocrypha and Pseudepigrapha writings in thematic
categories.
Elwell, Walter A. and Robert W. Yarbrough, eds. *Readings from the First-Century World: Primary Sources for New Testament Study.* Encountering Biblical
Studies. Grand Rapids: Baker, 1998. Intended for college students. First
part topical, second part quotes illuminating Jewish and Graeco-Roman
sources in NT canonical order.
Feldman, Louis H. and Meyer Reinhold. *Jewish Life and Thought among Greeks and Romans: Primary Readings.* Minneapolis: Augsburg Fortress, 1996;
Edinburgh:
T & T Clark, 1996. A fine collection covering a broad array of
key topics.
Fitzmyer, Joseph A. and Daniel J. Harrington. *A Manual of Palestinian Aramaic Texts (second century B.C.–second century A.D.).* BibOr 34. Rome: Biblical

Institute Press, 1978. Highly significant collection of texts with translations and introduction (includes many Qumran documents).

Ginzberg, Louis. *The Legends of the Jews.* 7 vols. Jewish Publication Society of America, 1909–1938; repr. Baltimore: Johns Hopkins, 1998. Puts in narrative form the various rabbinic and apocryphal stories about OT heroes. Vols. 5–6 notes; vol. 7 index. Currently available online at several sites, though often without the vital endnotes and index volumes (see http://archive.org).

Hayward, C. T. R. *The Jewish Temple: A non-biblical sourcebook.* London/New York: Routledge, 1996.

Instone-Brewer, David. *Traditions of the Rabbis from the Era of the New Testament.*
Grand Rapid: Eerdmans, 2004–. Following the order of Mishnah, excerpts selections from the Mishnah and the Tosefta that likely predate the year 70; provides text, translation, and brief commentary. [*TRENT*]

Nadich, Judah. *The Legends of the Rabbis.* 2 vols. London: Jason Aronson, 1994. Puts in narrative form the various rabbinic stories about early rabbis (Neusner's *Rabbinic Traditions about the Pharisees* is to be preferred for academic use).

Neusner, Jacob. *The Rabbinic Traditions about the Pharisees before 70.* 3 vols. Leiden:
Brill, 1971. An enormously helpful source book with commentary and summary analysis (reprints from University of South Florida and Wipf & Stock).

Runesson, Anders, Donald D. Binder, and Birger Olsson. *The Ancient Synagogue from its Origin to 200 C.E.: A Source Book.* Leiden: Brill, 2008; paperback Brill, 2010. Ancient literary sources, inscriptions and archaeological remains for both the land of Israel and the diaspora. Also includes a chapter on Jewish temples outside Jerusalem (e.g. Leontopolis).

Schiffman, Lawrence H. *Texts and Traditions: A Source Reader for the Study of Second Temple and Rabbinic Judaism.* Hoboken: Ktav, 1998. Complements his history of early Judaism.

Williams, Margaret H, ed. *The Jews among the Greeks and Romans: A Diasporan Sourcebook.* Baltimore: Johns Hopkins, 1998; London: Duckworth, 1998.

1.4 Bibliography

Anderson, Norman Elliott. *Tools for Bibliographical and Backgrounds Research on the New Testament.* 2d ed. South Hamilton, MA: Gordon-Conwell Theological Seminary, 1987.

Delling, Gerhard. *Bibliographie zur Jüdisch-Hellenistischen und Intertestamentarischen Literatur 1900–1965.* TU 106. Berlin: Akademie, 1969.

Noll, Stephen F. *The Intertestamental Period: A Study Guide.* Inter-Varsity

Christian Fellowship of the United States of America, 1985.

1.5 General Computer Programs and English-based Websites (current at time of writing)

Dinur Center for Research in Jewish History of the Hebrew University in Jerusalem (useful web links under "Second Temple and Talmudic Era"): http://jewishhistory.huji.ac.il/links/texts.htm.

Early Jewish Writings by Peter Kirby (links to older translations and introductions to Apocrypha, Pseudepigrapha, Philo and Josephus; currently many broken links but still useful): http://www.earlyjewishwritings.com.

4 Enoch: The Online Encyclopedia of Second Temple Judaism and Christian Origins by the Enoch Seminar (edited wiki that is still in process): http://www.4enoch.org.

HebrewBooks.org (classical Hebrew books for free download; website in Hebrew): http://www.hebrewbooks.org.

Internet Sacred Text Archive (older English translations of Jewish literature; primarily rabbinic works): http://www.sacred-texts.com/jud/index.htm.

The Judaic Classics Deluxe Edition: CD-ROM from Davka Software available for Windows or Mac (see below under Rabbinic Literature).

New Testament Gateway (Judaica page): http://www.ntgateway.com/tools-andresources/judaica.

Paleojudaica by James R. Davila: http://paleojudaica.blogspot.com.

Princeton University Library Jewish Studies Resources: http://www.princeton.edu/~pressman/jewsub.htm.

Resource Pages for Biblical Studies by Torrey Seland: http://torreys.org/bible.

Second Temple Synagogues by Donald Binder (includes links to introductions, texts, and photos of early Jewish literature): http://www.pohick.org/sts.

Thesaurus Linguae Graecae (searchable database of ancient Greek literature available on CD-ROM or via internet subscription; includes Philo, Josephus, Greek Apocrypha and Pseudepigrapha). Website at http://www.tlg.uci.edu.

Tyndale House (helpful links for Biblical Studies): http://www.tyndale.cam.ac.uk/index.php?page=weblinks.

Virtual Religion Index: http://virtualreligion.net/vri/judaic.html (note links to Biblical Studies and to Jewish Studies).

2. Old Testament Versions

2.1 Greek Versions

2.1.1 Septuagint

The term "Septuagint" is properly attributed only to the Old Greek Pentateuch (translated c. 3d cent. BC), but common parlance labels the whole Old Greek OT and Apocrypha as Septuagint (LXX). It represents the earliest extant Jewish Greek translation of the OT. However, since the major LXX manuscripts are Christian, the possibility exists of Christian tampering with the text at some junctures. While earlier studies frequently focused on the LXX as a textual witness to its Hebrew *Vorlage*, a significant trend now also views its renderings of the OT as representing traditional Jewish interpretation. The individual biblical books vary in their translation style, indicating a plurality of translators and dates of translation. Some biblical books differ significantly from the MT (e.g. Jeremiah, Samuel), and others exist in double recensions (e.g. Judges, Esther, Tobit, Daniel). The LXX also provides a major witness to all the Apocrypha except 4 Ezra [= 2 Esdras] (including also 3–4 Maccabees and Odes, which are not in the traditional English Apocrypha).

Bibliographies:

Dogniez, Cécile. *Bibliography of the Septuagint (1970–1993)*. VTSup 60. Leiden: Brill, 1995.

Brock, Sebastian P., Charles T. Fritsch, and Sidney Jellicoe. *A Classified Bibliography of the Septuagint*. ALGHJ 6. Leiden: Brill, 1973.

See also: bibliographic updates in *The Bulletin of the International Organization for Septuagint and Cognate Studies* (webpage at http://ccat.sas.upenn.edu /ioscs); also note the Septuagint Online webpage at http:// www.kalvesmaki.com/LXX and the bibliography to the Septuaginta Deutsch at http://www.septuagintaforschung.de/files/WUNT-219-Bibilographie.pdf.

Critical and Diplomatic Texts:

Septuaginta: Vetus Testamentum Graecum Auctoritate Academiae Scientiarum Gottingensis editum. 16 vols. Göttingen: Vandenhoeck & Ruprecht, 1931–. The standard scholarly critical edition, but incomplete. Known as the "Göttingen edition." Some volumes are divided into separate "parts."

Barthélemy, Dominique. *Les Devanciers D'Aquila: Première Publication Intégrale du Texte des Fragments du Dodécaprophéton*. VTSup 10. Leiden: Brill, 1963. Greek Minor Prophets scroll from Na☐al ☐ever (8HevXIIgr). Also see DJD 8, and Lifshitz in *IEJ* 12 (1962) 201–207 and in *Yedio☐ t* 26 (1962) 183–90.

Brooke, Alan England, Norman McLean, and Henry St. John Thackeray, eds. *The Old Testament in Greek*. London: Cambridge University Press, 1906–1940. Text of Codex Vaticanus with extensive apparatus. Since the Göttingen edition is incomplete, this still provides the best critical apparatus for the Former Prophets and Chronicles. Available online at http://archive.org.

Handbook Text:

Rahlfs, Alfred and Robert Hanhart, eds. *Septuaginta*. Rev. ed. 2 vols. in 1. Stuttgart: Deutsche Bibelgesellschaft, 2006. An eclectic text, but without adequate critical apparatus to evaluate editorial decisions (with a "moderate revision" from Rahlfs's 1935 edition). Rahlfs's original text is frequently found in Bible software (e.g. Accordance, BibleWorks, etc.) and online.

Text and Translation:

Brenton, Lancelot C. L. *The Septuagint with Apocrypha: Greek and English.* London: Samuel Bagster & Sons, 1851; repr. Peabody, MA: Hendrickson, 1992. Now dated in comparison to the NETS translation (see below), but has the advantage of a facing Greek text. Digitized pages available free online at http://www.archive.org and at http://www.ccel.org /ccel/brenton/lxx.html and English text of Brenton at http://www.ecclesia.org/truth/septuagint-hyperlinked.html.

Translation:

Pietersma, Albert and Benjamin G. Wright, eds. *A New English Translation of the Septuagint.* Oxford/New York: Oxford University Press, 2007. Fine translation by a team of Septuagint scholars. Abbreviated NETS. Available for some Bible software, and free online access at http://ccat.sas.upenn.edu /nets/edition.

Concordance:

Hatch, Edwin and Henry A. Redpath. *A Concordance to the Septuagint and the Other Greek Versions of the Old Testament.* 3 vols. Oxford: Clarendon, 1897–1906. Available online at http://archive.org. "Second edition" (Grand Rapids: Baker, 1998) contains a Hebrew-Greek reverse index by Muraoka.

A number of volumes have been released in the Computer Bible Series (series editors J. Arthur Baird, David Noel Freedman, and Watson E. Mills) published by Biblical Research Associates or by Edwin Mellen Press. These have been produced by J. David Thompson and are entitled similar to *A Critical Concordance to the Septuagint Genesis* or to *A Critical Concordance to the Apocrypha: 1 Maccabees*. Each provides book-by-book concordances of the LXX with a number of statistical aides.

Many computer programs also contain tagged Septuagint texts (e.g. BibleWorks, Accordance).

Lexicons:

Chamberlain, Gary Alan. *The Greek of the Septuagint: A Supplemental Lexicon.* Peabody, MA: Hendrickson, 2011. Includes all words not in BDAG, and otherwise only supplements BDAG on words when Septuagintal Greek meanings differ from standard NT definitions (thus this book by itself does not include all LXX vocabulary).

Lust, Johan, Erik Eynikel, and Katrin Hauspie. *A Greek-English Lexicon of the Septuagint.* Rev. ed. Stuttgart: Deutsche Bibelgesellschaft, 2003. First edition issued in two volumes (1992, 1996). Helpful glosses of all LXX vocabulary.

Muraoka, T. *A Greek-English Lexicon of the Septuagint.* Louvain: Peeters, 2009. Now complete, whereas previous iterations just focused on the Twelve Prophets (1993) or the Twelve Prophets and the Pentateuch (2002). A fine work by a careful lexicographer; should be consulted regularly.

Muraoka, T. *A Greek-Hebrew-Aramaic Two-way Index to the Septuagint.* Louvain:

Peeters, 2010. Allows one to see what Greek words are used to translate the Hebrew/Aramaic OT, and vice versa. Previous parts of this tool were published in his earlier LXX lexicons (1993 and 2002) and in the Baker edition of Hatch's LXX concordance; but with the publication of his 2009 lexicon, this is now a stand-alone document.

Rehkopf, Friedrich. *Septuaginta-Vokabular.* Göttingen: Vandenhoeck & Ruprecht, 1989. Provides a single German gloss for each Greek word. For each entry he lists some LXX texts and compares with word count usage in the NT.

Taylor, Bernard A. *Analytical Lexicon to the Septuagint: Expanded edition.* Peabody, MA: Hendrickson; Stuttgart: Deutsche Bibelgesellschaft, 2009. Revision of his 1994 Zondervan edition, listing every word form found in Rahlfs's edition and employing glosses from the Lust/Eynikel/Hauspie lexicon; especially helpful for difficult parsings.

Grammars:

Conybeare, F. C. and St. George Stock. *Grammar of Septuagint Greek.* Boston: Ginn & Co., 1905; repr. Peabody, MA: Hendrickson, 1995. Introductory, but with section on syntax not in Thackeray (or in the German grammar by Helbing). Available online at http://archive.org and at http://www.ccel.org/c/conybeare /greekgrammar.

Thackeray, Henry St. John. *A Grammar of the Old Testament in Greek*, Vol. 1: Introduction, Orthography and Accidence. Cambridge: CUP, 1909; repr. Hildesheim: Olms, 1987. Available online at http://archive.org.

Introductions:

Dines, Jennifer M. *The Septuagint.* Understanding the Bible and its World. London: T & T Clark, 2004. Good short survey, especially helpful for first exposure to LXX studies.

Fernández Marcos, Natalio. *The Septuagint in Context: Introduction to the Greek Versions of the Bible.* Trans. Wilfred G. E. Watson from 2d Spanish ed. Atlanta: Society of Biblical Literature, 2009. Useful introduction from standpoint of Spanish scholarship (previous English edition published by Leiden: Brill, 2000).

Harl, Marguerite, Gilles Dorival, and Olivier Munnich. *La Bible Grecque des Septante: Du judaïsme hellénistique au christianisme ancient.* Initiations au christianisme ancien; Paris: Cerf, 1988. Introduction by important French scholars.

Jellicoe, Sidney. *The Septuagint and Modern Study.* Oxford: Clarendon, 1968; repr. Winona Lake: Eisenbrauns, 1993. Assumes the earlier *Introduction* by Swete.

Jobes, Karen H. and Moisés Silva. *Invitation to the Septuagint.* Grand Rapids: Baker, 2000. Fine volume providing overall orientation to Septuagint study.

Siegert, Folker. *Zwischen Hebräischer Bibel und Altem Testament: Eine Einführung in die Septuaginta.* Münsteraner Judaistische Studien 9. Münster: LIT, 2001. Additional volume provides index and "Wirkungsgeschichte" of the LXX in antiquity (see *Register zur "Einführung in die Septuaginta"*; Münster: LIT, 2003).

Swete, Henry Barclay. *An Introduction to the Old Testament in Greek.* Rev. Richard Rusden Ottley. Cambridge: CUP, 1914; repr. Peabody, MA: Hendrickson, 1989. Classic textbook available online at http://archive.org and at http://www.ccel.org/s/ swete/greekot.

Also see *HJPAJC* 3.1:474–493; *Mikra* 161–88; *CHJ* 2:534–562; *ABD* 5:1093–1104.

Commentaries:

Harl, Marguerite, et al. *La Bible d'Alexandrie.* 17+ vols. Paris: Cerf, 1986–. Focuses on how the LXX would have been read by Greek speakers in Jewish and Christian antiquity.

Septuagint Commentary Series. Leiden: Brill, 2005–. Edited by S. E. Porter, R. Hess, and J. Jarick.

Wevers, John William. *Notes on the Greek Text of Genesis.* SBLSCS 35. Atlanta: Scholars, 1993. Discusses textual and philological issues. Wevers has produced similar volumes for the rest of the Pentateuch.

The International Organization for Septuagint and Cognate Studies (IOSCS) announced plans in 2005 to publish the SBL Commentary on the Septuagint (though no volumes have appeared at time of writing).

2.1.2 Aquila, Symmachus, Theodotion

Known primarily from the fragmentary sources of Origen's Hexapla, "the Three" represent Jewish Greek translations from the early Common Era (though there are some early traditions that Symmachus and even Theodotion were Ebionite Christians). Extensive Syro-Hexaplaric fragments and remnants of the Three exist in other languages (notably Armenian). Bibliographies, concordances, and introductions on the Three are also listed in works on the LXX above (see also *HJPAJC* 3.1:493–504).

Text:

Field, Fridericus. *Origenis Hexaplorum quae supersunt.* 2 vols. Oxford: Clarendon, 1875. Available online at http://archive.org. Other fragments have surfaced since Field, thus see the bibliographies and introductions noted under LXX. Also note that Göttingen LXX volumes list Hexaplaric traditions in the bottom apparatus. An English translation of Field's own Latin prolegomena to this work has been produced by Gérard J. Norton (Paris: Gabalda, 2005). The "Hexapla Institute" has announced plans to publish a new critical edition of Hexapla fragments (see http://www.hexapla.org).

Concordance:

Reider, Joseph and Nigel Turner. *An Index to Aquila.* VTSup 12. Leiden: Brill, 1966. Use in addition to the listing in Hatch and Redpath, Vol. 3 (see under LXX).

Commentary:

Salvesen, Alison. *Symmachus in the Pentateuch.* JSS Monograph 15. Manchester: University of Manchester, 1991.

2.2 Targumim

Aramaic translations and paraphrases of the OT are known from as early as the Qumran community. The targumim appear to originate from liturgical use in the synagogue, when a *meturgeman* would compose an (occasionally paraphrastic or expansive) Aramaic rendering of the biblical text to be read in the service. Such targumim can testify to how the biblical text was interpreted in Judaism. "Official" targumim on the Pentateuch (*Tg. Onqelos*) and the Prophets (*Tg. Jonathan*) have been passed down from Babylonian rabbinic circles, while parallel traditions are also known from Palestine. There are additional targumic traditions for each of the non-Aramaic books of the Writings. Besides MSS and printed editions devoted to targumim, the official targumim are printed with the MT in Rabbinic Bibles alongside traditional rabbinic commentaries. Targumic texts also occur in Polyglot editions (e.g. those printed in Antwerp, Paris, and London [=Walton's]) in parallel with the MT and other translations. The issues of dating and transmission history of the various targumim are often quite complex.

2.2.1 General Bibliography

Bibliography:

Grossfeld, Bernard. *A Bibliography of Targum Literature.* Vols. 1 and 2: Bibliographica Judaica 3 and 8. New York: Ktav, 1972, 1977. Vol. 3: New York: Sepher-Hermon, 1990.

Forestell, J. T. *Targumic Traditions and the New Testament: An Annotated Bibliography with a New Testament Index.* SBL Aramaic Studies 4. Chico, CA: Scholars, 1979.

Nickels, Peter. *Targum and New Testament: A Bibliography together with a New Testament Index.* Scripta Pontificii Instituti Biblici 117. Rome: Pontifical Biblical Institute, 1967. Updated in Forestell.

Ongoing listing of publications in the *Newsletter for Targumic and Cognate Studies* (now with its own website, including some targum translations at http://targum.info). Note also the bibliographic articles by Díez Macho in Vols. 4 and 5 of *Neophyti 1* (listed below).

Critical Texts:

Sperber, Alexander. *The Bible in Aramaic: Based on Old Manuscripts and Printed Texts.* 4 vols. in 5. Leiden: Brill, 1959–1973. Vol. 4b presents a series of helpful studies on the preceding volumes. Major critical text of *Targums Onqelos* and *Jonathan*; less reliable on the Writings.

Translations:

McNamara, Martin, gen. ed. *The Aramaic Bible.* 22 vols. Edinburgh: T & T Clark, 1987–2007. Standard contemporary translation series, with typically good introductions and notes.

Also see: Etheridge under Pentateuch. Some translations are also being made available online (see http://targum.info/targumic-texts). Eldon Clem is producing English translations for Accordance Bible Software of Targums Onkelos, Jonathan, Neofiti, and Pseudo-Jonathan; see http://www.accordancebible.com and note the review in *Aramaic Studies* 5 (2007) 151–58.

Concordances:

Searchable morphologically tagged Aramaic texts are currently available for Accordance, BibleWorks, and Logos software packages. These are based on texts from the Comprehensive Aramaic Lexicon Project (sometimes drawing on older editions, such as those by Lagarde).

Lexicons:

Cook, Edward M. *A Glossary of Targum Onkelos: According to Alexander Sperber's Edition.* Studies in the Aramaic Interpretation of Scripture. Leiden: Brill, 2008.

Dalman, Gustav. *Aramäisch-neuhebräisches Wörterbuch zu Targum, Talmud, und Midrasch.* Göttingen, 1938. Available online at http://archive.org.

Jastrow, Marcus. *A Dictionary of the Targumim, the Talmud Babli and Yerushalmi, and the Midrashic Literature.* 2 vols. New York: Pardes, 1950; singlevolume repr. New York: Judaica, 1971 and Peabody, MA: Hendrickson, 2005. Convenient resource for translating all targumic and early rabbinic literature. Available online at http://www.tyndalearchive.com/tabs/jastrow.

Levy, J. *Chaldäisches Wörterbuch über die Targumim und einen grossen Theil des rabbinischen Schrifttums.* 2 vols. Leipzig: Baumgärtner, 1867–1868; repr. Köln: Joseph Melzer, 1959. Available online at http://archive.org.

Sokoloff, Michael. *A Dictionary of Jewish Babylonian Aramaic of the Talmudic and Geonic Periods.* Dictionaries of Talmud, Midrash and Targum 3. Ramat-Gan, Israel: Bar Ilan University Press; Baltimore: Johns Hopkins, 2002. Sokoloff's dictionaries generally employ better informed lexicography than Jastrow.

Sokoloff, Michael. *A Dictionary of Jewish Palestinian Aramaic of the Byzantine Period.* 2d ed. Dictionaries of Talmud, Midrash and Targum 2; Ramat-Gan, Israel: Bar Ilan University Press; Baltimore: Johns Hopkins, 2002. Also contains a marvelous set of indexes to the passages cited.

Also see: Comprehensive Aramaic Lexicon Project of Hebrew Union College at http://cal1.cn.huc.edu. This website includes a searchable database of Aramaic lexical information and of Aramaic texts through the 13th century. It also houses a bibliographic database, and lists "Addenda et Corrigenda" to the two Sokoloff dictionaries above.

Grammars:

Dalman, Gustaf. *Grammatik des Jüdisch-Palästinischen Aramäisch: Nach den Idiomen des Palästinischen Talmud des Onkelostargum und Prophetentargum und der Jerusalemischen Targume.* 2d ed. Leipzig: Hinrichs, 1905; repr. Darmstadt: Wissenschaftliche Buchgesellschaft, 1960. Available online at http://archive.org.

Fassberg, Steven E. *A Grammar of the Palestinian Targum Fragments from the Cairo Genizah.* HSS 38. Atlanta: Scholars, 1991. Focuses primarily on phonology and morphology.

Golomb, David M. *A Grammar of Targum Neofiti.* HSM 34. Chico, CA: Scholars, 1985. Attends primarily to morphology, but contains a final chapter reviewing matters of verbal and nominal syntax.

Kuty, Renaud J. *Studies in the Syntax of Targum Jonathan to Samuel.* Ancient Near Eastern Studies Supplements 30. Leuven: Peeters, 2010. Whereas other studies focus on morphology, this highlights key syntactical matters.

Stevenson, William B. *Grammar of Palestinian Jewish Aramaic.* 2d ed. Oxford: Clarendon, 1962. Beginning grammar (though without exercises) introducing the language of both Palestinian and Babylonian post-biblical Jewish Aramaic. Includes syntactical notes missing in Dalman. Secondedition reprint of 1924 with a new "Appendix on Numerals" by J. A. Emerton.

Some beginning grammars of Biblical Aramaic also touch on Targumic Aramaic (and other works of rabbinic origin); e.g. F. E. Greenspahn, *An Introduction to Aramaic.* 2d ed. Atlanta: SBL, 2003. Also see Y. Frank, *Grammar for Gemara* (below under Babylonian Talmud).

Introductions:

Bowker, John. *The Targums and Rabbinic Literature.* Cambridge: CUP, 1969. An introduction to the targumim in relation to other rabbinic literature. Also contains a translation of a substantial portion of *Tg. Ps.-J.* to Genesis.

Díez Macho, Alejandro. *El Targum: Introducción a las traducciones aramaicas de la Biblia.* Textos y Estudios 21. Madrid: Consejo Superior de Investigaciones Científicas, 1982. The classic introduction by the foremost member of the "Spanish school."

Flesher, Paul V. M., and Bruce Chilton. *The Targums: A Critical Introduction.* Studies in the Aramaic Interpretation of Scripture 12; Leiden: Brill, 2011; Waco, TX: Baylor University Press, 2011. Significant recent introduction that covers a wide array of academic topics.

Gleßmer, Uwe. *Einleitung in die Targume zum Pentateuch.* TSAJ 48. Tübingen: J. C. B. Mohr [Paul Siebeck], 1995.

Grelot, Pierre. *What Are the Targums? Selected Texts.* Trans. Salvator Attanasio; Old Testament Studies 7; Collegeville, MN: Liturgical, 1992. Selections of expansive targumic passages with introduction. Caution is required since Grelot combines different targumic traditions.

Le Déaut, Roger. *Introduction à la Littérature Targumique*. Rome: Institut Biblique Pontifical, 1966. "Premiere partie" and thus incomplete, but quite helpful. Also see his brief article in *CHJ* 2:563–90; and his more substantial treatment of "Targum" in L. Pirot and A. Robert, *Supplément au Dictionnaire de la Bible*. Paris: Letouzey, 2005, 13:1*–344*.

Levine, Etan. *The Aramaic Version of the Bible: Contents and Context*. BZAW 174. Berlin: de Gruyter, 1988. Addresses the targumim as a whole, focusing on targumic themes.

McNamara, Martin. *Targum and Testament Revisited: Aramaic Paraphrases of the Hebrew Bible*. 2d ed. Grand Rapids: Eerdmans, 2010. Also contains a helpful appendix that introduces all extant targums.

See also: the useful articles by P. S. Alexander in *Mikra* 217–53 and in *ABD* 6:320–331; also note *HJPAJC* 1:99–114; *CHJ* 2:563–590.

2.2.2 Targumim on the Pentateuch

Divided into the following categories:

(1) Official Targum of Babylonia = Onqelos (text in Sperber above).

(2) "Palestinian Targumim" (editions noted below)

(a) Neofiti 1
(b) Pseudo-Jonathan
(c) Fragment Targum
(d) Cairo Genizah Fragments
(e) Toseftot
(f) Festival Collections
(g) Targumic Poems

For texts and bibliography on the last three categories see: Sperber, *Bible in Aramaic* 1:354–57 (above); *Mikra* 251; and Klein, *Genizah Manuscripts* Vol. 1: xxviii–xxxix (below).

Texts:

Diez Macho, Alexander, L. Diez Merino, E. Martinez Borobio, and Teresa Martinez Saiz, eds. *Biblia Polyglotta Matritensia IV: Targum Palaestinense in Pentateuchum*. 5 vols. Madrid: Consejo Superior de Investigaciones Científicas, 1977–88. Contains Palestinian Targumim in parallel columns (Neofiti, Pseudo-Jonathan, Fragment Targum, Cairo Genizah fragments) along with a Spanish translation of Pseudo-Jonathan. Very helpful.

Díez Macho, Alejandro, ed. *Neophyti 1: Targum Palestinense MS de la Biblioteca Vaticana*. 6 vols. Textos y Estudios 7–11 and 20; Madrid-Barcelona: Consejo Superior de Investigaciones Científicas, 1968–1979. Text of *Tg. Neof.* with facing Spanish translation and appended French and English translations. Each volume is prefaced with extensive introductory essays by Díez Macho. Volumes 2–5 also include verse-by-verse listings of (mostly rabbinic, but also pseudepigraphic and Christian) parallels to the interpretive elements in *Tg. Ps.-J.* and *Tg. Neof.* Volume 6 contains addenda, corrigenda, and indexes. A photocopy edition of the manuscript also exists (Jerusalem: Makor, 1970).

Ginsburger, M. *Pseudo-Jonathan (Thargum Jonathan ben Usiël zum Pentateuch). Nach der Londoner Handschrift (Brit. Mus. add. 27031).* Berlin: S. Calvary, 1903; repr. New York: Hildesheim, 1971. Editor's name can also be spelled Ginsberger in catalogs. There is another edition of this manuscript by D. Rieder (Jerusalem, 1974), reprinted with Modern Hebrew translation in 2 vols. in 1984–85. Also note the edition by Clarke (below under Concordances).

Klein, Michael L. *Genizah Manuscripts of Palestinian Targum to the Pentateuch.* 2 vols. Cincinnati: Hebrew Union College, 1986. Vol. 1 contains introduction, text, and translation of Genizah MSS of Pentateuchal targumim, also of festival collections, toseftot and targumic poems (additionally listing helpful bibliography for locating other toseftot, festival collections and targumic poems). Vol. 2 includes notes, glossary of vocabulary, and plates.

Klein, Michael L. *The Fragment-Targums of the Pentateuch: According to their Extant Sources.* 2 vols. AnBib 76. Rome: Biblical Institute Press, 1980. Vol. 1 introduction, text and indexes; Vol. 2 translation. Strongly preferred over Ginsburger's 1899 edition.

For Onqelos see Sperber (§2.2.1 above). Note also Masorah in Michael L. Klein, *The Masorah to Targum Onqelos: as preserved in MSS Vatican Ebreo 448, Rome Angelica Or. 7, Fragments from the Cairo Genizah and in Earlier Editions by A. Berliner and S. Landauer.* Targum Studies 1. Academic Studies in the History of Judaism; Binghamton, NY: Global Publications, SUNY Binghamton, 2000.

Translation:

Etheridge, J. W. *The Targums of Onkelos and Jonathan ben Uzziel on the Pentateuch with the Fragments of the Jerusalem Targum.* 1862; repr. New York: Ktav, 1968. Available online at http://targum.info/targumic-texts/pentateuchal-targumim and at http://archive.org. Also available for BibleWorks and Logos software. The McNamara *Aramaic Bible* series above is now generally preferred.

Le Déaut, Roger, with collaboration by Jacques Robert. *Targum du Pentateuque.* 5 vols. SC; Paris: Cerf, 1978–1981. French translation of Targum Neofiti and Targum Pseudo-Jonathan in parallel pages, with brief translational notes. The fifth volume serves as a topical index.

Also see: The Aramaic Bible series (above under 2.2.1 Targumim General Bibliography).

Concordances:

Brederek, Emil. *Konkordanz zum Targum Onkelos.* BZAW 9. Giessen: Alfred Töpelmann, 1906. Available online at http://archive.org.

Clarke, E. G., W. E. Aufrecht, J. C. Hurd, and F. Spitzer. *Targum Pseudo-Jonathan of the Pentateuch: Text and Concordance.* Hoboken: Ktav, 1984.

Contains the same manuscript as Ginsberger and Rieder with KWIC concordance; on the concordance see M. Bernstein's cautious review in *JQR* 79 (1988) 227–30.

Kassovsky,. 5 vols. in 1. Jerusalem:
Kiriath Moshe, 1933–40. For Onqelos.

Kaufman, Stephen A., Michael Sokoloff, and with the assistance of Edward M. Cook. *A Key-Word-in-Context Concordance to Targum Neofiti.* Publications of the Comprehensive Aramaic Lexicon Project 2. Baltimore: John Hopkins University Press, 1993. Also presents English glosses of the Aramaic words.

Note also some rabbinic search software contain searchable targumic texts (see under Rabbinic Literature).

Commentaries:

Aberbach, Moses and Bernard Grossfeld. *Targum Onkelos to Genesis: A Critical Analysis together with an English Translation of the Text.* New York: Ktav, 1982. Text of A. Berliner with English translation and comments (based on Sperber's edition).

Drazin, Israel. *Targum Onkelos to Exodus: An English Translation of the Text With Analysis and Commentary.* New York: Ktav, 1990. Text of A. Berliner with English translation and comments (based on Sperber's edition). Drazin has produced similar commentaries for *Tg. Onq.* to Leviticus (1994), Numbers (1998), and Deuteronomy (1982). Drazin emphasizes the literal translational elements of the Targum rather than seeing it as a full rabbinic interpretation. Note the cautious reviews by Emerton in *VT* 43 (1993) 280–81 and by Levine in *CBQ* 57 (1995) 766–67.

Grossfeld, Bernard. *Targum Neofiti 1: An Exegetical Commentary to Genesis, Including Full Rabbinic Parallels.* New York: Sepher-Hermon, 2000. Includes transcription of text and commentary with emphasis on rabbinic texts that parallel the Targum.

2.2.3 Targumim on the Prophets

Targum Jonathan forms the "official" targum to the Former and Latter Prophets (text in Sperber, *Bible in Aramaic*, Vols. 2 and 3). There are also Palestinian Toseftot (marginal comments of other targumic traditions alongside Targum Jonathan in the MSS). On the Toseftot: see pp. vi–xlii of De Lagarde, *Prophetae Chaldaice* (below); see also Sperber, *Bible in Aramaic*, descriptions on pp. ix–x of Vol. 2 and p. xi of Vol. 3; further bibliography in *Mikra* 252. Translation (with notes) in McNamara, *The Aramaic Bible* (see above).

Text:

De Lagarde, Paul. *Prophetae Chaldaice.* Leipzig: Teubner, 1872. Standard edition before Sperber (on which see §2.2.1 above). Available online at http://archive.org.

Stenning, J. F. *The Targum of Isaiah.* Oxford: Clarendon, 1949. A pointed critical text of Targum Jonathan to Isaiah with translation; Palestinian

Toseftot to the Targum on pp. 224–28.

Concordances:

Moor, Johannes C. de, et al., eds. *A Bilingual Concordance to the Targum of the Prophets.* 21 vols. Leiden: Brill, 1995–2005. A concordance of the individual books of *Tg. Jon.* to the Former and Latter Prophets. Also lists Hebrew equivalents to the Aramaic vocabulary (providing English glosses to both the Aramaic and Hebrew terms).

Van Zijl, J. B. *A Concordance to the Targum of Isaiah: Based on the Brit. Mus. Or. MS. 2211.* SBLAS 3. Missoula, MT: Scholars, 1979.

Commentaries:

Levine, Etan. *The Aramaic Version of Jonah.* New York: Sepher-Hermon, 1975. Introduction, text, translation, and commentary of *Tg. Jon.* to Jonah.

Smelik, Willem F. *The Targum of Judges.* OTS 36. Leiden: Brill, 1995. Extensive introduction and commentary.

Van Staalduine-Sulman, Eveline. *The Targum of Samuel.* Studies in the Aramaic Interpretation of Scripture 1. Leiden: Brill, 2002. Commentary, translation, and study.

2.2.4 Targumim on the Writings

No known rabbinic targumic traditions exist for Daniel or for Ezra-Nehemiah (note these books already employ Aramaic). The study of the targumim to the Writings necessitates caution since frequently several targumic recensions exist for any one OT book (for overview see *ABD* 6:320–331). Note that Targum Job is different than the Qumran Job Targum (=11QtgJob =11Q10; see DJD 23 and further bibliography below under "Dead Sea Scrolls"). Two targumic traditions to Esther are recognized (Targum Rishon and Targum Sheni = *Tg. Esth I and II*). A so-called "Third Targum to Esther" exists in the Antwerp Polyglot, but it is disputed whether this Third Targum is essentially a condensation of Targum Rishon, the predecessor of Rishon, or properly a targum at all.

General Texts:

Sperber, Alexander. *The Bible in Aramaic: Based on Old Manuscripts and Printed Texts.* Vol. 4a. Leiden: Brill, 1968. Contains *Tg. Chron* (MS Berlin 125) and *Tg. Ruth* as in the De Lagarde edition, and includes from Brit. Mus. Or. 2375: *Tg. Cant, Tg. Lam, Tg. Eccl, and Tg. Esth* (mixed text type of Esther, due to the manuscript used).

De Lagarde, Paul. *Hagiographa Chaldaice.* Leipzig: Teubner, 1873. Text of targumim to the Writings, including those not in Sperber (Psalms, Job, Proverbs, and both Esther Rishon and Esther Sheni). Available online at http://books.google.com.

Individual Texts:

Díez Merino, Luis. *Targum de Salmos: Edición Príncipe del Ms. Villa-Amil n. 5 de Alfonso de Zamora.* Bibliotheca Hispana Biblica 6. Madrid: Consejo Superior de Investigaciones Científicas, 1982. Introduction, text, Latin translation (by Alfonso de Zamora) and studies on this manuscript of *Tg. Psalms*.

Stec, David M. *The Text of the Targum of Job: An Introduction and Critical Edition.* AGJU 20. Leiden: Brill, 1994. A fine edition.

Díez Merino, Luis. *Targum de Job: Edición Principe del Ms. Villa-Amil n° 5 de Alfonso de Zamora.* Bibliotheca Hispana Biblica 8. Madrid: Consejo Superior de Investigaciones Científicas, 1984.

Díez Merino, Luis. *Targum de Proverbios. Edición Principe del Ms. Villa-Amil n° 5 de Alfonso de Zamora.* Madrid: Consejo Superior de Investigaciones Científicas, 1984. The next major edition of *Tg. Proverbs* since De Lagarde, *Hagiographa Chaldaice* (above).

Levine, Etan. *The Aramaic Version of Ruth.* AnBib 58. Rome: Biblical Institute Press, 1973. Introduction, text, translation, and commentary.

Jerusalmi, Isaac. *The Song of Songs in the Targumic Tradition: Vocalized Aramaic Text with Facing English Translation and Ladino Versions.* Cincinnati: Ladino, 1993.

Alonso Fontela, Carlos. *El Targum al Cantar de los Cantares (Edición Critica).* Collección Tesis Doctorales. Madrid: Editorial de la Universidad Complutense de Madrid, 1987.

Melamed, R. H. *The Targum to Canticles according to Six Yemenite MSS.* PhiladelJEWISH phia: Dropsie College, 1921. Covers the Yemenite recension, which differs from the Western texts at points. Reprinted from a series of articles in *JQR* n.s. 10–12 (1919–1921). Available online at http://archive.org.

Díez Merino, Luis. *Targum de Qohelet: Edición Principe del Ms. Villa-Amil n° 5 de Alfonso de Zamora.* Bibliotheca Hispana Biblica 13. Madrid: Consejo Superior de Investigaciones Científicas, 1987. An important edition of a manuscript otherwise unavailable.

Levine, Etan. *The Aramaic Version of Qohelet.* New York: Sepher-Hermon, 1978. Photocopy of MS Urb. 1 with translation and "conceptual analysis."

Levy, A. *Das Targum zu Qohelet nach sudarabischen Handschriften herausgegeben.* Breslau, 1905. Critical edition of *Tg. Eccl.*

Brady, Christian M. M. *The Rabbinic Targum of Lamentations: Vindicating God.* Studies in the Aramaic Interpretation of Scripture 3. Leiden: Brill, 2003. Study of this targum that includes a transcription of Codex Urbinas Hebr. 1 and translation.

Heide, Albert van der. *The Yemenite Tradition of the Targum of Lamentations: Critical Text and Analysis of the Variant Readings.* Leiden: Brill, 1981. The Yemenite tradition is significantly different from the Western text tradition.

Levine, Etan. *The Aramaic Version of Lamentations.* New York: Hermon, 1976. Introduction, text, translation, and commentary.

Ego, Beate. *Targum Scheni zu Ester: Übersetzung, Kommentar und theologische*

Deutung. TSAJ 54. Tübingen: Mohr Siebeck, 1996.
Grossfeld, Bernard. *The Targum Sheni to the Book of Esther: A Critical Edition based on MS. Sassoon 282 with Critical Apparatus.* New York: Sepher-Hermon, 1994. Includes a full-length concordance and a photocopy of this manuscript.
Grossfeld, Bernard. *The First Targum to Esther: According to the MS Paris Hebrew 110 of the Bibliotheque Nationale.* New York: Sepher-Hermon, 1983. Critical text, translation, and commentary with introduction to Targum Rishon to Esther. Includes plates.
Le Déaut, R., and J. Robert. *Targum des Chroniques (Cod. Vat. Urb. Ebr. 1).* 2 vols. AnBib 51. Rome: Biblical Institute Press, 1971. Vol. 1 introduction and (French) translation; Vol. 2 text, indexes, and a glossary of vocabulary in Aramaic, French, and English.

Concordance:
Grossfeld, Bernard. *Concordance of the First Targum to the Book of Esther.* SBLAS 5. Chico, CA: Scholars, 1984. For the Second Targum (Targum Sheni) see the KWIC concordance in Grossfeld's edition noted above.

2.3 Other (Latin and Syriac)

Whereas the Vulgate is clearly Christian (translated by Jerome), the lineage of the Old Latin is more obscure. A frequent dependence on the LXX, and occasional portions that agree with Jewish tradition over the LXX, make it possible that the Old Latin contains some certifiable Jewish passages. The Peshi□ta, though ultimately a Christian Bible, may originally have been allied with Jewish tradition, especially when it agrees with the targumim. For sake of space, standard Latin and Syriac grammars and lexicons are not listed below. Other early translations that appear largely dependent on the Septuagint, such as Bohairic Coptic or Christian Palestinian Aramaic, are not represented below. For introductions see *Mikra* 255–97, 299–313; *ABD* 6:794–803.

Old Latin Texts:
Vetus Latina: Die Reste der altlateinischen Bibel. Freiburg: Herder, 1951–. Critical edition currently covering Genesis, Canticles, Wisdom, Ecclesiasticus, and Isaiah from the OT and Apocrypha. Projected 26 volumes (with multiple parts).
Sabatier, Petri, ed. *Bibliorum Sacrorum Latinae Versiones Antiquae.* 3 vols. Rheims: Reginald Florentain, 1743–1749. Vulgate and Old Latin in parallel columns. Some volumes available on http://archive.org.

Peshi□ta Bibliography:
Dirksen, P. B. *An Annotated Bibliography of the Peshi□ta of the Old Testament.* Monographs of the Peshi□ta Institute 5. Leiden: Brill, 1989.

Syriac Peshi□ta Text:
Vetus Testamentum Syriace Iuxta Simplicem Syrorum Versionem [= *The Old Testament*

in Syriac According to the Peshita Version]. Leiden: Brill, 1973–. In four parts, with multiple fascicles.

Peshita Translation:

Lamsa, George M. *The Holy Bible from Ancient Eastern Manuscripts: Containing the Old and New Testaments, translated from the Peshitta, the authorized Bible of the church of the East.* Philadelphia: Holman, 1957; repr. San Francisco: Harper & Row, 1985. Not fully reliable. Available online at http://www.aramaicpeshitta.com/OTtools/LamsaOT.htm.

Gorgias Press has inaugurated its Surath Ktobh series (overseen by George A. Kiraz, projected to be 30 volumes), featuring facing pages of the Peshiṭta (without textual apparatus) and a literal English translation.

Peshita Concordances:

Borbone, P. G. and K. D. Jenner, eds. *The Old Testament in Syriac According to the Peshitta Version: Part 5 Concordance.* Vetus Testamentum Syriace. Leiden: Brill, 1997–.

Strothmann, Werner, Kurt Johannes, and Manfred Zumpe. *Konkordanz zur Syrischen Bibel: Die Propheten.* 4 vols. GOF Reihe 1, Syriaca 25. Wiesbaden: Otto Harrassowitz, 1984. They also produced a four volume 1986 concordance for *Der Pentateuch* (GOF Reihe 1, Syriaca 26).

Peshiṭta texts are increasingly coming available for Bible software (e.g. Accordance and BibleWorks).

Peshita Introduction:

Weitzman, M. P. *The Syriac Version of the Old Testament: An Introduction.* University of Cambridge Oriental Publications 56. Cambridge: CUP, 1999.

See also: Pp. 1057–59 in *EDEJ*.

3. Apocrypha

Various Christian OT manuscripts (Greek, Latin, Syriac, etc.) contain books not found in the Masoretic tradition. Translations may be found in some English Bibles (e.g. RSV, NRSV, NEB, REB) of the Greek (LXX) apocrypha as well as Latin "2 Esdras." Other translations may be found in the editions edited by Charles, by Charlesworth (for 4 Ezra), and by Kümmel listed under General Pseudepigrapha Bibliography below (cf. esp. Charlesworth, *OTP* 2:609–24 for apocryphal Psalms). English "2 Esdras" is listed in the Vulgate as 4 Ezra and should not be confused with LXX 2 Esdras (which is the Greek version of OT Ezra and Nehemiah). Most modern scholars believe 4 Ezra is a compilation, often designating (the probably Christian) chapters 1–2 and chapters 15–16 as 5 Ezra and 6 Ezra respectively. Thus the name "4 Ezra" in much modern scholarship has been reserved for Vulgate 4 Ezra 3–14.

The above listed LXX editions and concordances serve for the Greek Apocrypha. Greek fragments of 4 Ezra have been discovered (see Denis, *Fragmenta pseudepigraphorum* below under Pseudepigrapha). Latin versions of these books as well as the whole of 4 Ezra are also known in the Old Latin (see above) and Vulgate (for concordances to Latin 4 Ezra, see Denis or Lechner-Schmidt under General Pseudepigrapha Bibliography below). For Syriac editions, see the Peshi☐ta bibliography above. Many books of the Apocrypha are thought to stem from Semitic originals. Prior to the DSS, fragments in Hebrew were known of Ben Sira (= Sirach = Ecclesiasticus). Hebrew and Aramaic texts have been found in the DSS for Tobit (4Q196–200 in DJD XIX), Sirach (2Q18 in DJD III; 11QPsa [=11Q5] xxi–xxii in DJD IV; some Masada texts) and some of the apocryphal Psalms (11QPsa in DJD IV; for 4Q380–381 see Schuller, *Non-Canonical Psalms from Qumran* below under "Dead Sea Scrolls"); for a list see Peter W. Flint "Appendix II," in Flint & Vanderkam, eds., *The Dead Sea Scrolls After Fifty Years*, pp. 666–68 (see "Introductions" under Dead Sea Scrolls below).

Other Bibliography:

Reiterer, Friedrich Vinzenz, ed. *Bibliographie zu Ben Sira.* BZAW 266. Berlin: de Gruyter, 1998. Not well indexed or annotated.

See also: Bibelwissenschaft by Franz Böhmisch (http://www.animabit.de/bibel/sir.htm).

Other Texts (Ordered by apocryphal book):

Beentjes, Pancratius C. *The Book of Ben Sira in Hebrew: A Text Edition of all Extant Hebrew Manuscripts and a Synopsis.* VTSup 68. Leiden: Brill, 1997. Paperback repr. Society of Biblical Literature (2006).

The Book of Ben Sira: Text, Concordance and an Analysis of the Vocabulary. The Historical Dictionary of the Hebrew Language. Jerusalem: Academy of the Hebrew Language and Shrine of the Book, 1973. Synoptic edition of Hebrew MSS with concordance.

Yadin, Yigael. *The Ben Sira Scroll from Masada.* Jerusalem: Israel Exploration Society, 1965. Repr. from *Eretz-Israel* vol. 8.

Schechter, S. and C. Taylor. *The Wisdom of Ben Sira: Portions of the Book of Ecclesiasticus from Hebrew Manuscripts in the Cairo Genizah Collection Presented to the University of Cambridge by the Editors.* Cambridge: CUP, 1899.

Klijn, Albertus Frederik J. *Die Esra-Apokalypse (IV. Esra): Nach dem lateinischen Text unter Benutzung der anderen Versionen übersetzt.* GCS. Berlin: de Gruyter, 1992.

Stone, Michael E. *The Armenian Version of IV Ezra.* University of Pennsylvania Armenian Texts and Studies. Missoula, MT: Scholars Press, 1979.

Sievers, Joseph. *Synopsis of the Greek Sources for the Hasmonean Period: 1–2 Maccabees and Josephus War 1 and Antiquities 12–14.* Rome: Editrice Pontificio Istituto Biblico, 2001. Useful for comparative and historical studies.

Texts are only presented in Greek.

Weeks, S. D. E., S. J. Gathercole, L. T. Stuckenbruck. *The Book of Tobit: Texts from the Principal Ancient and Medieval Traditions. With Synopsis, Concordances, and Annotated Texts in Aramaic, Hebrew, Greek, Latin, and Syriac.* Fontes et subsidia ad Bibliam pertinentes 3. Berlin: de Gruyter, 2004.

Wagner, Christian J. *Polyglotte Tobit-Synopse: Griechisch, Lateinisch, Syrisch, Hebräisch, Aramäisch: mit einem Index zu den Tobit-Fragmenten vom Toten Meer.* Mitteilungen des Septuaginta-Unternehmens 28. Göttingen: Vandenhoeck & Ruprecht, 2003. Greek, Latin, and Syriac in parallel columns, with separate section on Hebrew and Aramaic fragments.

See also: Berger synopsis of 4 Ezra with 2 Baruch (below under Pseudepigrapha: 2 Baruch).

Other Concordances:

Barthélemy, D. and O. Rickenbacher. *Konkordanz zum hebräischen Sirach mit syrisch-hebräischem Index.* Göttingen: Vandenhoeck & Ruprecht, 1973. Also see concordance in *The Book of Ben Sira* (above).

Muraoka, T. *A Greek-Hebrew/Aramaic Index to 1 Esdras.* SBLSCS 11. Chico, CA: Scholars Press, 1984.

Strothmann, Werner, ed. *Wörterverzeichnis der apokryphen-deuterokanonischen Schriften des Alten Testaments in der Peshitta.* Göttinger Orientforschungen Reihe 1, Syriaca 27. Wiesbaden: Otto Harrassowitz, 1988. Also provides a Latin gloss for each Syriac word.

Winter, Michael M. *A Concordance to the Peshi☐ta Version of Ben Sira.* Monographs of the Peshitta Institute 2. Leiden: Brill, 1976.

Lexicon:

For Greek see above under Septuagint and below under General Pseudepigrapha Bibliography. For Hebrew text of Ben Sira see Clines, ed., *Dictionary of Classical Hebrew* (below under Dead Sea Scrolls).

Introductions:

Brockington, L. H. *A Critical Introduction to the Apocrypha.* London: Gerald Duckworth, 1961.

DeSilva, David A. *Introducing the Apocrypha: Message, Context, and Significance.* Grand Rapids: Baker, 2002.

Harrington, Daniel J. *Invitation to the Apocrypha.* Grand Rapids: Eerdmans, 1999.

Kaiser, Otto. *The Old Testament Apocrypha: An Introduction.* Peabody, MA: Hendrickson, 2004. Translation of his 2000 German edition.

Longenecker, Bruce W. *2 Esdras.* Guides to the Apocrypha and Pseudepigrapha; Sheffield: Sheffield Academic Press, 1995. Other helpful introductions have also appeared in this series, including Bartlett on *1 Maccabees*, DeSilva on *4 Maccabees*, Coggins on *Sirach*, Grabbe on *Wisdom of Solomon*, Otzen on *Tobit and Judith*.

Metzger, Bruce M. *An Introduction to the Apocrypha.* Oxford: OUP, 1957.

Oesterley, W. O. E. *An Introduction to the Books of the Apocrypha.* New York: Macmillan, 1935.
Torrey, Charles Cutler. *The Apocryphal Literature: A Brief Introduction.* New Haven:
Yale University Press, 1945. Also introduces many books of the Pseudepigrapha.
See also: Nickelsburg, *Jewish Literature*; *JWSTP*; *HJPAJC* Vol. 3; *CHJ* 2:409–503; *ABD* 1:292–94 and s.v. by book; *EDEJ* 143–62 and s.v. by book.
Commentaries:
Abel, P. F.-M. *Les Livres des Maccabées.* Études Bibliques. Paris: J. Gabalda, 1949.
Larcher, C. *Le Livre de la Sagesse ou La Sagesse de Salomon.* Études Bibliques n.s.
1; 3 vols. Paris: J. Gabalda, 1983–1985.
Scarpat, Giuseppe. *Libro della Sapienza: Testo, traduzione, introduzione e comment.* 3
vols. Biblica Testi e studi 1, 3, 6. Brescia: Paideia, 1989–1999.
Talshir, Zipora. *I Esdras: A Text Critical Commentary.* SBLSCS 50. Atlanta: Society
of Biblical Literature, 2001.
Commentaries exist on each book in some biblical commentary series. In English note especially Septuagint Commentary Series (Brill), Commentaries on Early Jewish Literature series (de Gruyter), Anchor Bible series (Doubleday), Jewish
Apocryphal Literature series from Dropsie University (Harper), and Stone on *Fourth Ezra* in the Hermeneia series (Fortress). Shorter but still helpful are the volumes in the Cambridge Bible Commentary series (CUP) and the OT Message series (Michael Glazier). Also see the UBS Handbook Series (United Bible Societies)
for translation comments. In German note the Herders Theologischer Kommentar zum Alten Testament series (Herder), Das Alte Testament Deutsch: Apokryphen, Neuer Stuttgarter Kommentar Altes Testament (Katholisches Bibelwerk), and Die Neue Echter Bibel (Echter). Some one-volume commentaries also include the Apocrypha; e.g. *Eerdmans Commentary on the Bible* (Eerdmans, 2003).

4. Pseudepigrapha (Jewish)

The term "pseudepigrapha" properly refers to literature written under an assumed name (generally of some famous OT person). However, "the Pseudepigrapha" has become almost a catch-all category for intertestamental works
which do not fit elsewhere. The translation volume edited by Charlesworth, while focusing on works of primarily Jewish origin, also includes some Christian works. Below are listed the most important pseudepigraphal works for the study of Judaism. Since some Christian pseudepigrapha may include original Jewish material,
a few of these are also noted. For bibliography of other Christian pseudepigrapha and some lesser known works see Haelewyck, *Clavis Apocryphorum* (noted below).

Pseudo-Philo and named Jewish authors are listed later in this bibliography.
4.1 General Pseudepigrapha Bibliography
Bibliography:
Orlov, Andrei A. *Selected Studies in the Slavonic Pseudepigrapha.* SVTP 23. Leiden/
Boston: Brill, 2009. Note the "Selected Bibliography on the Transmission of the Jewish Pseudepigrapha in the Slavic Milieux" on pp. 201–434.
DiTommaso, Lorenzo. *A Bibliography of Pseudepigrapha Research 1850–1999.* JSPSup 39. Sheffield: Sheffield Academic Press, 2001. 1067 very helpful pages.
Lehnardt, Andreas. *Bibliographie zu den jüdischen Schriften aus hellenistisch-römischer Zeit. JSHRZ* VI/2. Gütersloh: Gütersloher Verlagshaus, 1999. Very useful.
Haelewyck, J.-C. *Clavis Apocryphorum Veteris Testamenti.* CChr. Turnhout: Brepols, 1998. Valuable list of texts, translations, and concordances for each pseudepigraphal book.
Charlesworth, James H. *The Pseudepigrapha and Modern Research with a Supplement.* New ed. SBLSCS. Chico, CA: Scholars, 1981. Dated, but also contains competent brief introductions.
See also: Arbeitshilfen für das Studium der Pseudepigraphen (http://www.unileipzig. de/~nt/asp/index.htm).
Texts (general):
Stone, Michael E. *Armenian Apocrypha Relating to Adam and Eve.* SVTP 14. Leiden:
Brill, 1996. Not all of this material is early. Also see W. Lowndes Lipscomb, *The Armenian Apocryphal Adam Literature.* University of Pennsylvania
Armenian Texts and Studies 8. Scholars Press, 1990.
Stone, Michael E. *Armenian Apocrypha Relating to the Patriarchs and Prophets.* Jerusalem:
Israel Academy of Sciences and Humanities, 1982.
Denis, Albert-Marie. *Fragmenta pseudepigraphorum quae supersunt graeca.* PVTG 3.
Leiden: Brill, 1970. The standard edition of Greek fragments. Bound with Black's edition of Greek 1 Enoch.
See also: Online Critical Pseudepigrapha (http://ocp.tyndale.ca), which provides introductions (with bibliography on modern editions of texts) and original language texts for many works.
Translations:
Charles, R. H., ed. *The Apocrypha and Pseudepigrapha of the Old Testament in English.*
2 vols. Oxford: Clarendon, 1913. Still quite useful, though supplanted by Charlesworth and Sparks. Available online at http://archive.org or at http://www.ccel.org/c/charles/otpseudepig.
Charlesworth, James H., ed. *The Old Testament Pseudepigrapha.* 2 vols. New

York: Doubleday, 1983–1985; paperback repr. Peabody, MA: Hendrickson, 2009. The current most common English translation; includes helpful introductions and notes (see also Scripture Index listed below). Many contributions are excellent, but some have been critiqued for poor textual basis or for inadequacies in the notes and introductions; cf. the detailed reviews by S. P. Brock in *JJS* 35 (1984) 200–209 and *JJS* 38 (1987) 107–14. [=*OTP*]

Kümmel, Werner Georg, et al., gen. eds. *Jüdische Schriften aus hellenistischrömischer Zeit.* Gütersloh: G. Mohn/Gütersloher Verlagshaus, 1973–2005. A highly respected multi-volume German translation series with fine introductions and commentary. [= JSHRZ]

Lichtenberger, Hermann and Gerbern S. Oegema, gen. eds. *Jüdische Schriften aus hellenistisch-römischer Zeit Neue Folge.* Gütersloh: Gütersloher Verlagshaus, 2005–. Multi-volume continuation of *JSHRZ*. [=*JSHRZNF*]

Sparks, H. F. D., ed. *The Apocryphal Old Testament.* Oxford: Clarendon, 1984. A useful one-volume edition with succinct introductions of a subset of works also found in Charlesworth's *OTP*; for comparison with *OTP* see review by G. W. E. Nickelsburg in *CBQ* 50 (1988) 288–91 and those by M. E. Stone and R. A. Kraft in *Religious Studies Review* 14 (1988) 111–17. [= AOT]

Further important translations appear in Spanish (Alejandro Díez Macho, et al., eds., *Apocrifos del Antiguo Testamento.* 5 vols. Madrid: Ediciones Cristiandad, 1982–1987) and in Italian (Paulo Sacchi, et al., eds., *Apocrifi Dell'Antico Testamento.* 5 vols. Turin: Unione Tipografico-Editrice Torinese/ Brescia: Paideia, 1981–1997).

A new two-volume collection of lesser known pseudepigrapha is due out soon, published by Eerdmans and edited by Richard Bauckham and James R. Davila under the auspices of the More Old Testament Pseudepigrapha Project (see http://www.st-andrews.ac.uk/divinity/rt/moreoldtestamentpseudepigrapha).

Also see: Translations of varying qualities available online at http://sacredtexts.com/chr/apo/index.htm and at http://www.piney.com/ ApocalypticIndex.html and at http://jewishchristianlit.com/Texts.

Concordances:

Bauer, Johannes B. *Clavis Apocryphorum supplementum: complectens voces versionis Germanicae Libri Henoch Slavici, Libri Jubilaeorum, Odarum Salomonis.* Grazer theologische Studien 4. Graz: Institut für Ökumenische Theologie und Patrologie an der Universität Graz, 1980. Not a concordance to the original languages but to German translations. For his book-by-book concordance of Greek pseudepigrapha, see below under "Lexicon."

Denis, Albert-Marie. *Concordance grecque des Pseudépigraphes d'Ancien Testament: Concordance, Corpus des textes, Indices.* Louvain-la-Neuve: Institut Orientaliste, 1987. Very useful. Denis produced an earlier concordance of the Greek version of Baruch (Leuven: Peeters, 1970).

Denis, Albert-Marie. *Concordance latine des Pseudépigraphes d'Ancien Testament:*
Concordance, Corpus des textes, Indices. Turnhout: Brepols, 1993. A fine work. Denis released an earlier concordance of the Latin version of Jubilees (Université catholique de Louvain, 1973; repr. Turnhout: Brepols, 2002).
Lechner-Schmidt, Wilfried. *Wortindex der lateinisch erhaltenen Pseudepigraphen zum Alten Testament.* TANZ 3. Tübingen: Francke, 1990. Also contains some texts.
See also: the *Thesaurus Linguae Graecae* database for searchable Greek texts, as well as tagged Greek modules available for Accordance, BibleWorks, and Logos software.

Scripture Index:
Delamarter, Steve. *A Scripure Index to Charlesworth's The Old Testament Pseudepigrapha.* London/New York: Sheffield Academic Press, 2002. Indexes all references to OT and NT books in the introductions, notes and margins of *OTP*; necessarily dependent on the work of the original translators (which varies "in terms of quantity and focus" from book to book).

Lexicon:
Wahl, Christian Abraham. *Clavis Librorum Veteris Testamenti Apocryphorum Philologica.* Leipzig: Johannes Ambrosius Barth, 1853; repr. Graz: Akademische Druck, 1972. Repr. contains Wahl's lexicon of the Greek Apocrypha and Pseudepigrapha, and J. B. Bauer's book-by-book concordance of the Greek Pseudepigrapha.

Introductions:
De Jonge, M., ed. *Outside the Old Testament.* Cambridge: CUP, 1985. Selected Jewish Pseudepigrapha excerpts with commentary.
Denis, Albert-Marie, et al. *Introduction à la littérature religieuse judéo-hellénistique.* 2 vols. Turnhout: Brepols, 2000. Also note his previous *Introduction aux Pseudépigraphes grecs d'Ancien Testament.* SVTP 1. Leiden: Brill, 1970.
Díez Macho, Alejandro. *Apocrifos del Antiguo Testamento.* Vol. 1: Introduccion General a Los Apocrifos del Antiguo Testamento. Madrid: Ediciones Cristiandad, 1984.
Turdeanu, Emile. *Apocryphes slaves et roumains de l'Ancien Testament.* SVTP 5. Leiden: Brill, 1981.
See also: Nickelsburg, *Jewish Literature*; Helyer, *Exploring Jewish Literature*; *JWSTP*; *HJPAJC* Vol. 3; *CHJ* 2:409–503; *EDEJ* 143–62 and s.v. by book. Older introduction by Torrey (see under Apocrypha). Individual introductions are appearing in the "Guides to the Apocrypha and Pseudepigrapha" series from Sheffield Academic Press (some are noted below).

4.2 Special Pseudepigrapha Bibliography (alphabetical by book)
This list contains the best-known books with likely Jewish lineage in collections of "Old Testament Pseudepigrapha." The principal languages of extant

MSS for each book are noted below. Dates largely concur with those in Charlesworth *OTP*. If the texts available are clearly Christian (with an assumed Jewish substratum), this is indicated. Not included are some highly fragmented texts and those unlikely to be of Jewish provenance. Pseudo-Philo and other individual writers are found later in this bibliography. Consult also the General Pseudepigrapha Bibliography above (especially Lehnardt's *Bibliographie* and the introductions and translations in *OTP* and *JSHRZ*). More detailed bibliography of texts (including fragments and later versions) in Haelewyck, *Clavis Apocryphorum* and
DiTommaso, *Bibliography*.

AHIQAR (Aramaic; 7th–6th cent. BC).
In the Elephantine papyri, with later recensions in many languages; thought to be related to the (Greek) Life of Aesop and so listed in Denis, *Fragmenta pseudepigraphorum*
(see above).

Text and Translation:
Porten, Bezalel, and Ada Yardeni. *Textbook of Aramaic Documents from Ancient Egypt.* Vol. 3: Literature, Accounts, Lists. Winona Lake: Eisenbrauns, 1986–1993, 23–53.

Cowley, A. *Aramaic Papyri of the Fifth Century B.C.* Oxford: Clarendon, 1923, 204–48. Widely known edition with translation and extensive notes. Available online at http://archive.org.

Conybeare, F. C., J. Rendel Harris, and Agnes Smith Lewis. *The Story of A☐i☐ar from the Syriac, Arabic, Armenian, Ethiopic, Greek and Slavonic Versions.* London:
C. J. Clay & Sons, 1898. Extensive introduction with translations of versions listed in the title plus texts of Greek (Life of Aesop), Armenian, Syriac, and Arabic. Available online at http://archive.org.

Commentary:
Lindenberger, James M. *The Aramaic Proverbs of Ahiqar.* JHNES. Baltimore: Johns Hopkins University Press, 1983.

Grammar:
Muraoka, Takamitsu and Bezalel Porten. *A Grammar of Egyptian Aramaic.* 2d rev. ed. Leiden: Brill, 2003.

Concordance:
Porten, Bezalel and Jerome A. Lund. *Aramaic Documents from Egypt: A Key-Word-in-Context Concordance.* Winona Lake: Eisenbrauns, 2002.

APOCALYPSE OF ABRAHAM (Old Slavonic; 1st–2d cent. AD)
Text, Translation, and Commentary:
Rubinkiewicz, Ryszard. *L'Apocalypse d' Abraham en vieux slave: Introduction, texte*
critique, traduction et commentaire. Lublin: Société des Lettres et des Sciences de l'Université Catholique de Lublin, 1987. Apparently edited without reference to the Philonenko edition.

Philonenko-Sayar, Belkis and Marc Philonenko. "L'Apocalypse d'Abraham: Introduction, texte slave, traduction et notes." *Sem* 31 (1981) 1–119.

APOCALYPSE OF ADAM (Coptic; 1st–4th cent. AD)

Found among Nag Hammadi gnostic texts, yet considered to be Jewish in origin. Consult Nag Hammadi scholarship for further translations (e.g. J. M. Robinson, ed., *Nag Hammadi Library in English*) and concordances (e.g. Folker Siegert, *Nag-Hammadi-Register*). Another possible Jewish gnostic text is *Poimandres*
in the *Corpus Hermeticum* (see further *JWSTP* 443–81).
Text and Translation:
Parrott, Douglas M., ed. *Nag Hammadi Codices V,2–5 and VI with Papyrus Berolinensis 8502, 1 and 4.* NHS 11. Leiden: Brill, 1979, 151–95. Text edited by G. W. MacRae.
Text, Translation, and Commentary:
Morard, Françoise. *L'Apocalypse d' Adam (NH V, 5).* Bibliothèque copte de Nag Hammadi: Section textes 15. Québec: Les Presses de l'Université Laval, 1985.

APOCALYPSE OF ELIJAH (Coptic, Greek; 1st–4th cent. AD)
Christian text with likely Jewish substratum.
Text and Translation:
Pietersma, Albert, Susan Turner Comstock, and Harold W. Attridge. *The Apocalypse of Elijah based on P. Chester Beatty 2018.* SBLTT 19. Chico, CA, Scholars, 1981. Coptic text and translation, includes appendix on Greek fragment. Also in Denis, *Fragmenta pseudepigraphorum* (above). *See also* material
in *HJPAJC* 3.2:799–803.

APOCALYPSE OF MOSES (*see* Life of Adam and Eve)
APOCALYPSE OF SEDRACH (*see note below* under 4 Ezra)
APOCALYPSE OF ZEPHANIAH (Coptic and Greek fragments; 1st cent. BC–1st cent. AD)
Christian with possible Jewish substratum.
Text and Discussion:
Steindorff, Georg. *Die Apokalypse des Elias, eine unbekannte Apokalypse und Bruchstücke der Sophonias Apokalypse.* TU 17.3. Leipzig: Hinrichs, 1899. Available online at http://archive.org. Also see Denis, *Fragmenta pseudepigraphorum.*

APOCRYPHON OF EZEKIEL (Greek and Hebrew fragments; 1st cent. BC–1st cent. AD)
Probable Jewish work with possible Christian influence in extant fragments.
Text, Translation and Discussion:
Stone, Michael E., Benjamin G. Wright, and David Satran, eds. *The Apocryphal Ezekiel.* SBLEJL 18. Atlanta: Society of Biblical Literature, 2000. Includes the five fragments previously published by Mueller plus other possible contenders. Also studies later Christian traditions about Ezekiel.
Mueller, James R. *The Five Fragments of the Apocryphon of Ezekiel: A Critical Study.*
Journal for the Study of the Pseudepigrapha Supplement Series 5. Sheffield: Sheffield Academic Press, 1994. Also see Denis, *Fragmenta pseudepigraphorum.*

(PSEUDO-) ARISTEAS, [LETTER OF] (Greek; 2nd cent. BC, possibly later)

Critical Text, Translation, Notes, and Concordance:
Pelletier, André. *Lettre D'Aristée à Philocrate: Introduction, texte critique, traduction et notes, index complet des mots grecs.* SC 89. Paris: Cerf, 1962. Best current critical text. A text can also be found appended to Swete's *Introduction to the Old Testament in Greek.*

Critical Text:
Wendland, Paul. *Aristeae ad Philocratem Epistula cum Ceteris de Origine Versionis LXX Interpretum Testimoniis.* Leipzig: Teubner, 1900. Available online at http://archive.org.

Text and Notes:
Hadas, Moses. *Aristeas to Philocrates (Letter of Aristeas).* New York: Harper & Brothers, 1951. Includes text, lengthy introduction, and brief notes.

Meecham, Henry G. *The Letter of Aristeas: A Linguistic Study with Special Reference to the Greek Bible.* Manchester: Manchester University Press, 1935. Notes focus on use of Greek language.

Online see http://www.voskrese.info/spl/miller-arist.pdf (Greek text and translation) and http://www.ccel.org/c/charles/otpseudepig/aristeas.htm (Charles, ed., translation).

Introduction:
See Jellicoe, *Septuagint and Modern Study* 29–58 (under Septuagint); Bartlett, *Jews in the Hellenistic World* 11–34 (under Josephus).

ASCENSION OF ISAIAH (Ethiopic, Latin, Greek fragments, etc.; 2d cent. BC–4th cent. AD)
Christian with a probable Jewish section known as "Martyrdom of Isaiah" in 1:1–3:12 [omit 1:2b–6a] and 5:1b–14.

Texts:
Bettiolo, Paolo, et al. *Ascensio Isaiae: Textus.* CChr.SA 7. Turnhout: Brepols, 1995. Contains Ethiopic, Greek, Coptic, Latin, and Slavonic texts (with Italian translation). Earlier edition of Ethiopic and Latin texts by Dillmann (*Ascencio Isaiae: Aethiopice et Latine*, Leipzig: Brockhaus, 1877) available free at http://books.google.com. Greek text also in Denis, *Fragmenta pseudepigraphorum.*

Translation and Commentary:
Charles, R. H. *The Ascension of Isaiah.* London: Adam & Charles Black, 1900. Also includes Ethiopic, Latin, and Slavonic (transcribed) texts in parallel columns. Available online at http://archive.org.

Tisserant, Eugène. *Ascension d'Isaie.* Paris: Letouzey et Ané, 1909. Available online at http://archive.org.

Introduction:
Knight, Jonathan. *The Ascension of Isaiah.* Sheffield: Sheffield Academic Press, 1995.

Commentary:
Norelli, Enrico. *Ascensio Isaiae: Commentarius.* CChr.SA 8. Turnhout: Brepols,

1995. In Italian.
Assumption (Testament) of Moses (Latin; 1st cent. AD)
Text, Translation, and Commentary:
Tromp, Johannes. *The Assumption of Moses: A Critical Edition with Commentary.* SVTP 10. Leiden: Brill, 1993. Supplants R. H. Charles, *Assumption of Moses.* London: Black, 1897. Abraham Schalit also began a commentary on chapter one before his death which was later published as *Untersuchungen zur Assumptio Moses* (Leiden: Brill, 1989).

2 BARUCH (=Syriac Apocalypse of Baruch; also Greek fragments and Arabic version; 2nd cent. AD)
Text:
Gurtner, Daniel M. *Second Baruch: A Critical Edition of the Syriac Text With Greek and Latin Fragments, English Translation, Introduction, and Concordances.* Jewish and Christian Texts in Contexts and Related Studies 5. London: T & T Clark, 2009.
Leemhuis, F., A. F. J. Klijn, and G. J. H. Van Gelder. *The Arabic Text of the Apocalypse of Baruch: Edited and Translated with a Parallel Translation of the Syriac Text.* Leiden: Brill, 1986.
Dedering, S., ed. *Apocalypse of Baruch.* Vetus Testamentum Syriace IV, 3. Leiden: Brill, 1973. For the final *Epistle* the Leiden edition remains forthcoming, use M. Kmoskó, *Epistola Baruch filii Neriae*, in R. Graffin, *Patrologia Syriaca* 1,2 (Paris: Firmin-Didot, 1907) col. 1208–1237. For Greek fragments see Denis, *Fragmenta pseudepigraphorum* in general bibliography.
Translation and Commentary:
Bogaert, Pierre. *Apocalypse de Baruch: Introduction, traduction du syriaque et commentaire.* 2 vols. SC 144–45. Paris: Cerf, 1969.
Also see: Berger, Klaus, Gabriele Fassbeck, and Heiner Reinhard. *Synopse des Vierten Buches Esra und der Syrischen Baruch-Apokalypse.* TANZ 8. Tübingen: Francke, 1992. Based on German translation.

3 BARUCH (= Greek Apocalypse of Baruch; Slavonic version in two recensions; 1st–3rd cent. AD)
Christian with Jewish substratum.
Text:
Picard, J.-C. *Apocalypsis Baruchi Graece.* PVTG 2. Leiden: Brill, 1967.
Commentary:
Kulik, Alexander. *3 Baruch: Greek-Slavonic Apocalypse of Baruch.* CEJL. Berlin: de Gruyter, 2010.

4 BARUCH (*see* Paraleipomena Jeremiou)

1 ENOCH (Ethiopic Enoch; also in Greek, Aramaic fragments, and other versional fragments; 2d cent. BC–1st cent. AD)
Texts (and Translations):
Knibb, Michael A., in consultation with Edward Ullendorff. *The Ethiopic Book of Enoch: A New Edition in the Light of the Aramaic Dead Sea Fragments.* 2

vols. Oxford: Clarendon, 1978. Vol. 1: Text and Apparatus; Vol. 2: Introduction, Translation, and Commentary. Supplants previous editions by R. H. Charles (1906) and A. Dillmann (1851).

Milik, J. T. and Matthew Black. *The Books of Enoch: Aramaic Fragments of Qumrân Cave 4.* Oxford: Clarendon, 1976. Texts, translations, plates, and extensive comments.

Black, M. *Apocalypsis Henochi Graece.* PVTG 3. Leiden: Brill, 1970. Edition of Greek text; bound with Denis, *Fragmenta pseudepigraphorum.* For addenda and corrigenda see Black and Vanderkam, *The Book of Enoch or I Enoch* (below).

Commentaries:

Black, Matthew, in consultation with James C. Vanderkam. *The Book of Enoch or I Enoch: A New English Edition with Commentary and Textual Notes.* SVTP 7. Leiden: Brill, 1985. Extensive commentary, consciously revising Charles's 1912 commentary. With Otto Neugebauer on chaps. 72–82.

Charles, R. H. *The Book of Enoch or 1 Enoch.* Oxford: Clarendon, 1912. Translation with extensive commentary. The author prefers this (what amounts to a 2d edition) over his earlier *The Book of Enoch* (1893). Available online at http://archive.org.

Nickelsburg, George W. E. *1 Enoch 1: A Commentary on the Book of 1 Enoch, Chapters 1–36; 81–108.* Hermeneia; Minneapolis: Fortress, 2001.

Nickelsburg, George W. E. and James C. Vanderkam. *1 Enoch 2: A Commentary on the Book of 1 Enoch, Chapters 37–82.* Hermeneia. Minneapolis: Fortress, 2012. Nickelsburg and Vanderkam have also produced *1 Enoch: A New Translation.* Philadelphia: Fortress, 2004.

Stuckenbruck, Loren T. *1 Enoch 91–108.* CEJL. Berlin: de Gruyter, 2007.

Tiller, Patrick A. *A Commentary on the Animal Apocalypse of I Enoch.* SBL Early Judaism and Its Literature 4. Atlanta: Scholars, 1993.

Earlier important commentaries by A. Dillmann (Vogel, 1853) and François Martin (Letouzey, 1906). Short commentary article by Daniel C. Olson in J. D. G. Dunn, gen. ed., *Eerdmans Commentary to the Bible.* Grand Rapids: Eerdmans, 2003.

2 ENOCH (Slavonic Enoch, in two recensions; 1st cent. AD)

Text and Translation:

Vaillant, A. *Le Livre des secrets d'Hénoch.* Paris: Institut d'Etudes Slaves, 1952.

Translation and Commentary:

Morfill, W. R. and R. H. Charles. *The Book of the Secrets of Enoch.* Oxford: Clarendon, 1896.

Concordance to German Translation:

See above Bauer, *Clavis Apocryphorum Supplementum.*

3 ENOCH (Hebrew Enoch; 5th – 6th cent. AD): *See below* under Hekhalot literature.

4 EZRA (*see above* under Apocrypha)

Several Christian pseudepigraphic works also draw on Ezra as a central figure and may be indebted to Jewish sources (e.g. Greek Apocalypse of Ezra, Vision of Ezra, and Apocalypse of Sedrach); *see* Charlesworth *OTP* 1:561–613; text of some in Otto Wahl, ed. *Apocalypsis Esdrae—Apocalypsis Sedrach—Visio beati Esdrae.* PVTG 4. Leiden: Brill, 1977.

HISTORY OF JOSEPH (*see* Charlesworth, ed., *OTP* 2:467–75)

HISTORY OF THE RECHABITES (Greek, Syriac, and many versions; 1st–4th cent. AD)

Substantially Christian, possible Jewish substratum.

Text and Translation:

Charlesworth, James H. *The History of the Rechabites. Volume I: The Greek Recension.*
SBLTT 17. Chico, CA: Scholars, 1982. Critical Greek text; an edition
of the Syriac text is still desired. Brief commentary by Chris H.
Knights in *JSJ* 28 (1997) 413–36.

JANNES AND JAMBRES (Greek and Latin fragments)

Text, Translation, and Commentary:

Pietersma, Albert. *The Apocryphon of Jannes and Jambres the Magicians.*
Religions
in the Graeco-Roman World 119. Leiden: Brill, 1994. Includes facsimile plates.

JOSEPH AND ASENETH (Greek and Latin versions in two recensions, also Armenian, and other versions; 1st cent. BC–2d cent. AD)

Text and Translation:

Burchard, Christoph. *A Minor Edition of the Armenian Version of Joseph and Aseneth.*
Hebrew University Armenian Studies 10. Leuven: Peeters, 2010.
Diplomatic text supplemented with 12 other important manuscripts.

Fink, Uta Barbara. *Joseph und Aseneth: Revision des griechischen Textes und Edition
der zweiten lateinischen Übersetzung.* Fontes et subsidia ad Bibliam pertinentes
5. Berlin/New York: de Gruyter, 2008. Important revision of Burchard's
provisional Greek text of the long recension (though without a
full textual apparatus), with a synoptic edition of Latin "L2" manuscripts.
Includes study of manuscript stemma. See review in *BBR* 20 (2010) 110–12.

Burchard, Christoph with Carsten Burfeind and Uta Barbara Fink. *Joseph und Aseneth: Kritisch Herausgegeben.* PVTG 5. Leiden/Boston: Brill, 2003. Critical
edition focusing on the longer Greek recension (which Burchard believes
is earlier than the short recension). While the apparatus is excellent,
the text itself remains the same as Burchard's "provisional" Greek
text. Burchard himself translated this longer recension into English in
Charlesworth, *OTP.*

Philonenko, Marc. *Joseph et Aséneth: Introduction, texte critique, traduction et notes.*
SPB 13. Leiden: Brill, 1968. Standard edition of the shorter Greek reJEWISH cension plus word index. ET of this shorter recension in H. F. D.
Sparks, *Apocryphal Old Testament.*

Introduction:
Humphrey, Edith M. *Joseph and Aseneth.* Guides to the Apocrypha and Pseudepigrapha 8. Sheffield: Sheffield Academic Press, 2000.

Other:
Burchard, Christoph. *Gesammelte Studien zu Joseph und Aseneth.* SVTP 13. Leiden: Brill, 1996. Collection of significant articles on the text, importance, and state of study (including bibliography). Includes a reprint of Burchard's Vorläufiger Text ("provisional text") of the long recension (pp. 161–209).

Reinmuth, Eckart, ed. *Joseph und Aseneth: Eingeleitet, ediert, übersetzt und mit interpretierenden Essays.* Scripta Antiquitatis Posterioris ad Ethicam Religionemque pertinentia 15. Tübingen: Mohr-Siebeck, 2009).

Note also "The Aseneth Home Page" at http://markgoodacre.org/aseneth/index.htm.

JUBILEES (Hebrew fragments; Ethiopic Versions; Latin, Greek, and Syriac fragments; 2d cent. BC)

Hebrew Texts:
For extensive Qumran cave 4 fragments (4Q216–228) see DJD 13; other fragments in DJD 1, 3, and 7. Also cf. *RevQ* 12.4 [= 48] (1987) 529–36; *RevQ* 14.1 [= 53] (1989) 129–30. For possible Masada fragments see *Er-Isr* 20 (1989) 278–86.

Texts:
Vanderkam, James C., ed. *The Book of Jubilees: A Critical Text.* CSCO 510. Leuven: Peeters, 1989. A critical text of the Ethiopic, supplanting the older edition by R. H. Charles (Oxford, 1895); also with Greek, Syriac, Latin, and some Hebrew fragments (though not the bulk of 4Q216–228). Not all Greek and Syriac fragments are included (cf. Denis, *Fragmenta pseudepigraphorum* above).

Translation and Textual Notes:
Vanderkam, James C. *The Book of Jubilees.* CSCO 511. Leuven: Peeters, 1989. Translates his critical text (including the fragments), with extensive notes on text and translation.

Translation and Commentary:
Charles, R. H. *The Book of Jubilees or The Little Genesis.* London: Adam & Charles Black, 1902. Available online at http://archive.org.

Concordance to German Translation:
See above Bauer, *Clavis Apocryphorum Supplementum.*

Introduction:
Vanderkam, James C. *The Book of Jubilees.* Guides to Apocrypha and Pseudepigrapha. Sheffield: Sheffield Academic Press, 2001.

LADDER OF JACOB (Slavonic)
Only known from Slavonic Christian excerpts, H. G. Lunt (in *OTP* 2:401–411)

suggests a possible 1st-cent. date and potential Jewish Greek substratum. Cf. *HJPAJC* 3.2:805.

LIFE OF ADAM AND EVE

The subject of Adam and Eve appears in different manuscript traditions: Greek (= Apocalypse of Moses; also Armenian and other versions; 1st cent. AD), Latin, two Slavonic recensions, the Armenian "Penitence of Adam," and other recensions.

Textual Synopsis:

Anderson, Gary A., and Michael E. Stone, eds. *A Synopsis of the Books of Adam and Eve.* 2d rev. ed. SBL Early Judaism and Its Literature 5. Atlanta: Scholars, 1999. Armenian, Georgian, Greek, Latin, and Slavonic texts. Also see their website with translations (http://jefferson.village.virginia.edu/anderson, which links to http://www2.iath.virginia.edu/anderson).

Text:

Tromp, Johannes. *The Life of Adam and Eve in Greek: A Critical Edition.* PVTG 6. Leiden: Brill, 2005.

Stone, Michael E. *Texts and Concordances of the Armenian Adam Literature.* Volume 1. SBLEJL 12. Atlanta: Scholars Press, 1996. Volume 1 includes the Penitence of Adam, the Book of Adam, and Genesis 1–4 in Armenian (with concordances to each and a non-critical text of each). Volume 2 has been published as *A Concordance of the Armenian Apocryphal Adam Books* (Leuven: Peeters, 2001). For a critical edition of the Armenian texts see above works by Stone and by Lipscomb under General Pseudepigrapha Bibliography; also M. E. Stone, *The Penitence of Adam.* 2 vols. CSCO 429–430. Leuven: Peeters, 1981.

Text, Translation, and Commentary:

Dochhorn, Jan. *Die Apokalypse des Mose: Text, Übersetzung, Kommentar.* TSAJ 106. Tübingen: Mohr-Siebeck, 2005.

Bertrand, Daniel A. *La vie grecque d'Adam et Eve: Introduction, texte, traduction et commentaire.* Recherches intertestamentaires 1. Paris: Maisonneuve, 1987.

Introductions:

De Jonge, Marinus and Johannes Tromp. *The Life of Adam and Eve and Related Literature.* Guides to the Apocrypha and Pseudepigrapha 4. Sheffield: Sheffield Academic Press, 1997.

Stone, Michael E. *A History of the Literature of Adam and Eve.* SBL Early Judaism and Its Literature 3. Atlanta: Scholars, 1992.

LIVES OF THE PROPHETS (Greek, Latin, Syriac, Armenian, Ethiopic, and other versions; 1st cent. AD). Christian with Jewish substratum.

Text, Translation, and Commentary:

Schwemer, Anna Maria. *Studien zu den frühjüdischen Prophetenlegenden* Vitae Prophetarum*: Einleitung, Übersetzung und Kommentar.* 2 vols. TSAJ 49–50; Tübingen: Mohr-Siebeck, 1995–1996. Based on the Greek text, which is edited in a synoptic edition at the end of Vol. 2 (this edition has also been published separately as *Synopse zu den Vitae Prophetarum*). Previous

edition by C. C. Torrey (SBLMS 1; Philadelphia: Scholars Press, 1946).
For other versions see listing in Schwemer's Vol. 1, pp. 18–22 (cf.
Haelewyck, *Clavis Apocryphorum* 167–73).
3–4 Maccabees (Greek, Syriac, and other versions)
3 Maccabees (1st cent. BC) is edited in the Göttingen LXX, and 4 Maccabees
(1st cent. AD) is found in Rahlfs's LXX; both appear in the LXX concordances;
translations in *OTP* 2:509–64. See also LXX bibliography above.

Introduction:
DeSilva, David A. *4 Maccabees*. Guides to the Apocrypha and Pseudepigrapha
7. Sheffield: Sheffield Academic Press, 1998.

Commentaries:
Commentaries can be found in the Jewish Apocryphal Literature series
(Dropsie/Harper) by Hadas, and in the Septuagint Commentary Series
(Brill) on 3 Maccabees (by N. Clayton Croy) and 4 Maccabees (by David
A. deSilva).

MARTYRDOM OF ISAIAH (*see* Ascension of Isaiah)
(PSEUDO-) MENANDER (Syriac; 3d cent. AD)
Traditionally included with Jewish corpus, though actual provenance is unsure.
See discussion and translation in *OTP* 2:583–606; also *HJPAJC* 3.1:692–94.

ODES (*see* Septuagint)
ODES OF SOLOMON (Syriac, also portions in Greek and Coptic; 1st–2d
cent. AD)
Christian, though some propose a Jewish origin.

Texts, Translations, Concordance, and Bibliography:
Lattke, Michael. *Die Oden Salomos in ihrer Bedeutung für Neues Testament und
Gnosis*.
4 vols. OBO 25. Fribourg Suisse: Editions Universitaires/Göttingen:
Vandenhoeck & Ruprecht, 1979–1986. Band I contains texts (with a
separate part Ia printing a Syriac facsimile with plates). Band II includes
a concordance of each language. Band III is an extensive annotated bibliography
of studies on Odes (from 1799 to 1984). Band IV is a collection
of articles by Lattke (note he extends his bibliography list to 1997
on pp. 233–51).

Text and Translation:
Charlesworth, James Hamilton. *The Odes of Solomon: The Syriac Texts.* SBLTT
13. Missoula, MT: Scholars Press, 1977. Corrected repr. of 1973 OUP
edition. See also facsimile edition *Papyri and Leather Manuscripts of the Odes
of Solomon* (Duke University, 1981). Charlesworth also released a translation
under the title *The Earliest Christian Hymnbook* (Eugene, OR: Cascade,
2009).
Also see the Rendell Harris items listed under the Psalms of Solomon. An
older text with German translation by Walter Bauer. *Die Oden Salomos.*
Berlin: de Gruyter, 1933.

Translation and Commentary:
Lattke, Michael. *Odes of Solomon.* Trans. Marianne Ehrhardt. Hermeneia.
Minneapolis:
Fortress, 2009. Translates his 3 volume German commentary

originally in NTOA 41. Göttingen: Vandenhoeck & Ruprecht, 1999–
2005. Lattke produced a German translation with shorter notes for Fontes
Christiani. FC 19. Freiburg: Herder, 1995.
Pierre, Marie-Joseph, with the collaboration of Jean-Marie Martin. *Les Odes de
Salomon.* Apocryphes 4. Turnhout: Brepols, 1994.
Concordance to German Translation:
See above Bauer, *Clavis Apocryphorum Supplementum.*
PARALEIPOMENA JEREMIOU (also called 4 Baruch; Greek in two recensions,
Ethiopic and other versions; 1st–3d cent. AD)
Text, Translation and Commentary:
Herzer, Jens. *4 Baruch (Paraleipomena Jeremiou).* SBLWAW 22. Atlanta:
Society
of Biblical Literature, 2005. Fine critical text.
Riaud, Jean. *Les Paralipomènes du Prophète Jérémie: Présentation, texte original,
traduction
et commentaries.* Université Catholique de l'Ouest, 1994.
Text and Translation:
Kraft, Robert A. and Ann-Elizabeth Purintun. *Paraleipomena Jeremiou.* SBLTT
1. Missoula, MT: Society of Biblical Literature, 1972.
PRAYER OF JACOB and PRAYER OF JOSEPH (*see* Charlesworth, ed.,
OTP 2:699–723; cf. *HJPAJC* 3.2:798–99)
PRAYER OF MANASSEH (*see* Septuagint; also in Charlesworth, ed., *OTP*
2:625–37)
PSALMS OF SOLOMON (Greek and Syriac; 1st cent. BC)
Greek Text:
Wright, Robert B. *The Psalms of Solomon: A Critical Edition of the Greek Text.*
Jewish and Christian Texts in Contexts and Related Studies 1. London:
T & T Clark, 2007. Wright also offers a CD-ROM with color images of
extant Greek and Syriac manuscripts (see p. 224).
Gebhardt, Oscar von. *Die Psalmen Salomos.* TU 13/2. Leipzig: Hinrichs, 1895.
Earlier critical text of Greek that only collates 8 of the 12 available MSS.
Available online at http://archive.org. A handy Greek text can be found
in Rahlfs's LXX edition (based on Gebhardt).
Syriac Critical Text:
See above "Syriac Peshi☐ta Text" (Vol. IV, 6).
Greek and Syriac texts:
Trafton, Joseph L. *The Syriac Version of the Psalms of Solomon: A Critical
Evaluation.*
SBLSCS 11. Atlanta: Scholars, 1985. Comes with a separate fascicle
of facing Greek and Syriac texts (with apparatus). See review in *JSS* 32
(1987) 204–207.
Translation:
Also translated in the NETS LXX translation (see above under Septuagint
and http://ccat.sas.upenn.edu/nets/edition/31-pssal-nets.pdf).
Commentaries:
Atkinson, Kenneth. *An Intertextual Study of the Psalms of Solomon.* Studies in the
Bible and Early Christianity 49. Lewiston, NY: Edwin Mellen, 2001. Includes
Greek text, translation, parallel passages in other Jewish literature

(esp. OT and Apocrypha), and commentary.
Rendell Harris, J. and A. Mingana. *The Odes and Psalms of Solomon Re-edited.* 2 vols. Manchester: John Rylands University Library, 1916–1920. Also note Rendell Harris's earlier *The Odes and Psalms of Solomon: Now First Published from the Syriac Version.* Cambridge: CUP, 1909. Both are available online at http://archive.org.
Ryle, Herbert Edward, and Montague Rhodes James. *Psalms of the Pharisees Commonly Called The Psalms of Solomon.* Cambridge: CUP, 1891. Classic edition with text, translation, introduction, and extensive notes. The Pharisaic identification is not accepted by all. Available at http://archive.org.
Viteau, J. *Les Psaumes de Salomon: Introduction, texte grec et traduction.* Paris: Letouzey et Ané, 1911. With extensive notes. Available online at http://archive.org.

SENTENCES OF (PSEUDO-) PHOCYLIDES (Greek; 1st cent. BC–1st cent. AD)

Wisdom poetry of Jewish origin, but with muted OT references and written under a pagan Greek pseudonym.

Text:
Young, D. *Theognis, Ps-Pythagoras, Ps-Phocylides, Chares, Anonymi Aulodia, fragmentum teleiambicum.* 2 vols.; Leipzig, 1961, 1971. Volume 2 includes the critical text of Ps.-Phocylides.

Text, Translation, and Commentary:
Horst, P. W. van der. *The Sentences of Pseudo-Phocylides: With Introduction and Commentary.* SVTP 4. Leiden: Brill, 1978. Also includes a concordance.
Wilson, Walter T. *The Sentences of Pseudo-Phocylides.* CEJL. Berlin: de Gruyter, 2005.

SIBYLLINE ORACLES (Greek with Latin fragments; 2d cent. BC–7th cent. AD)

Large portions of Books 3 and 5 are considered Jewish; book 4 may have been ultimately redacted by a Jewish editor, and books 11–14 may have a later Jewish origin (this is disputed).

Greek Text:
Geffcken, Johannes. *Die Oracula Sibyllina.* GCS. Leipzig: Hinrichs, 1902. Available online at http://archive.org.

Introductions and Studies on Jewish Sections:
Buitenwerf, Rieuwerd. *Book III of the Sibylline Oracles and its Social Setting: with an Introduction, Translation, and Commentary.* SVTP 17. Leiden: Brill, 2003.
Collins, John J. *The Sibylline Oracles of Egyptian Judaism.* SBLDS 13. Missoula, MT: Society of Biblical Literature, 1974.
Nikiprowetzky, Valentin. *La troisième Sibylle.* Ecole pratique des hautes Etudes270 JOURNAL OF THE EVANGELICAL THEOLOGICAL SOCIETY Sorbonne; Etudes juives 9; Paris: Mouton, 1970. Includes text, translation, notes, and extensive introduction.
Parke, H. W. *Sibyls and Sibylline Prophecy in Classical Antiquity.* Ed. B. C.

McGing. London/New York: Routledge, 1988.
See also: Bartlett, *Jews in the Hellenistic World* 35–55 (under Josephus); older translation of Books 3–5 by H. N. Bate (SPCK, 1918).
TESTAMENT OF ABRAHAM (Greek, also Coptic and other versions; 1st–2nd cent. AD)
Exists in both a long and short recension, with likely common ancestry.

Critical Text:

Roddy, Nicolae. *The Romanian Version of the Testament of Abraham: Text, Translation, and Cultural Context.* SBLEJL 19. Atlanta: SBL, 2001.

Schmidt, Francis. *Le Testament grec d'Abraham: Introduction, édition critique des deux recensions grecques, traduction.* TSAJ 11. Tübingen: Mohr-Siebeck, 1986.

Text and Translation:

Stone, Michael E. *The Testament of Abraham: The Greek Recensions.* SBLTT 2. Missoula, MT: Society of Biblical Literature, 1972. Based on M. R. James's (1892) edition of Greek texts. An older translation by G. H. Box (London: SPCK, 1927) exists of both recensions along with Gaselee's translation of the Testaments of Isaac and Jacob.

Commentary:

Allison, Dale C. Jr. *Testament of Abraham.* CEJL. Berlin: de Gruyter, 2003.

Delcor, Mathias. *Le Testament d'Abraham: Introduction, Traduction du texte grec, et Commentaire de la recension grecque longue.* SVTP 2. Leiden: Brill, 1973.

Bibliography:

Nickelsburg, George W. E. Jr. "Review of the Literature." In *Studies on the Testament of Abraham*, ed. George W. E. Nickelsburg Jr. SBLSCS 6. Missoula, MT: Scholars Press, 1976, 9–22. The same volume also contains translations of the Church Slavonic and Coptic versions.

TESTAMENT OF ADAM (Several recensions in Syriac, Greek, Armenian, and other versions; 2d–5th cent. AD). Christian, with possible Jewish substratum.

Texts and Translations:

Robinson, Stephen Edward. *The Testament of Adam: An Examination of the Syriac and Greek Traditions.* SBLDS 52. Chico, CA: Scholars, 1982. For Armenian editions, see Stone volumes in General bibliography of Pseudepigrapha. See further Haelewyck, *Clavis Apocryphorum* 8–12.

TESTAMENT OF ISAAC and TESTAMENT OF JACOB (both Coptic, Arabic, Ethiopic; 2d–3d cent. AD). Christian, with some possible Jewish elements; see both Delcor and Box under *Testament of Abraham*, and note *OTP* 1:903–18; *JTS* n.s. 8 (1957) 225–39.

TESTAMENT OF JOB (Greek, also Coptic and Slavonic; 1st cent. BC–1st cent. AD)

Bibliography:

Spittler, Russell P. "The Testament of Job: a history of research and interpretation."
In *Studies on the Testament of Job*, ed. Michael A. Knibb and Pieter

W. Van Der Horst. SNTSMS 66. Cambridge: CUP, 1989, 7–32. The same volume also has an edition of the Coptic text.
Text:
Brock, S. P., ed. *Testamentum Iobi.* PVTG 2. Leiden: Brill, 1967.
Text and Translation:
Kraft, Robert A., et al., eds. *The Testament of Job: According to the SV Text.* SBLTT 5. Missoula, MT: SBL, 1974.
TESTAMENT OF MOSES (*see* Assumption of Moses)
TESTAMENT OF SOLOMON (Greek; 1st–3d cent. AD) Christian, with possible Jewish substratum.
Text:
McCown, Chester Charlton. *The Testament of Solomon.* Leipzig: Hinrichs, 1922. Available online at http://archive.org. For translation and introduction see *OTP* 1:935–87.
Commentary:
Busch, Peter. *Das Testament Salomos: Die älteste christliche Dämonologie, kommentiert*
und in deutscher Erstübersetzung. TU 153. Berlin/New York: de Gruyter, 2006.
TESTAMENTS OF THE TWELVE PATRIARCHS (Aramaic and Hebrew fragments; two Greek recensions; Syriac, Armenian, and other versions; 2d cent. BC with later interpolations [disputed]). Christian, with Jewish substratum. Cf. with 1Q21 (in DJD 1), 3Q7 (in DJD 3), 4Q213–215 (in DJD 22); 4Q484, and 4Q537–541.
Bibliography:
Slingerland, H. Dixon. *The Testaments of the Twelve Patriarchs: A Critical History of*
Research. SBLMS 21. Missoula, MT: Scholars Press, 1977.
Text:
Stone, Michael E. *An Editio Minor of the Armenian Version of the Testaments of the*
Twelve Patriarchs. Hebrew University Armenian Studies 11. Leuven: Peeters, 2012. Text (based on 11 selected extant MSS), translation and commentary.
De Jonge, M., et al. *The Testaments of the Twelve Patriarchs: A Critical Edition of the*
Greek Text. PVTG I,2. Leiden: Brill, 1978. Updates Charles's 1908 edition and De Jonge's own shorter Brill edition of a single Cambridge UL manuscript from 1964 (entitled *Testamenta XII Patriarcharum*). Includes word index and partial listing of Armenian variants (note bibliography on p. 193).
Stone, Michael E. *The Armenian Version of the Testament of Joseph: Introduction, Critical Edition, and Translation.* SBLTT 6. Missoula, MT: Scholars Press, 1975.
Stone, Michael E. *The Testament of Levi: A First Study of the Armenian MSS of the*

Testaments of the XII Patriarchs in the Convent of St. James, Jerusalem: with Text,
Critical Apparatus, Notes and Translation. Jerusalem: St. James, 1969.
Charles, Robert Henry. *The Greek Versions of the Testaments of the Twelve Patriarchs:*
Edited from nine MSS together with the Variants of the Armenian and Slavonic versions and some Hebrew Fragments. Oxford: Clarendon, 1908; repr. Darmstadt: Wissenschaftliche Buchgesellschaft, 1966. Available online at http://archive.org. Versional materials are unfortunately only in retroverted Greek. Aramaic fragments from Cairo Genizah.
Commentary:
Charles, R. H. *The Testaments of the Twelve Patriarchs: Translated from the Editor's*
Greek Text and Edited, with Introduction, Notes, and Indices. London: Adam & Charles Black, 1908. Available online at http://archive.org.
Hollander, H. W., and M. de Jonge. *The Testaments of the Twelve Patriarchs: A Commentary.* SVTP 8. Leiden: Brill, 1985.
Introduction:
Kugler, Robert A. *The Testaments of the Twelve Patriarchs.* Guides to Apocrypha and Pseudepigrapha. Sheffield: Sheffield Academic Press, 2001.
TREATISE OF SHEM (Syriac; 1st cent. BC [disputed])
Text and Translation:
Charlesworth, James H. "Die 'Schrift des Sem': Einführung, Text und Übersetzung," in *ANRW* II.20.2. Berlin: de Gruyter, 1987, 951–87.

END

www.ingramcontent.com/pod-product-compliance
Lightning Source LLC
Chambersburg PA
CBHW070721020526
44116CB00031B/978